Ablution, Initiation, and Baptism
Waschungen, Initiation und Taufe

I

Beihefte zur Zeitschrift für die neutestamentliche Wissenschaft

und die Kunde der älteren Kirche

Herausgegeben von
James D. G. Dunn · Carl R. Holladay
Hermann Lichtenberger · Jens Schröter
Gregory E. Sterling · Michael Wolter

Band 176/I

De Gruyter

Ablution, Initiation, and Baptism
Waschungen, Initiation und Taufe

Late Antiquity, Early Judaism, and Early Christianity
Spätantike, Frühes Judentum und Frühes Christentum

Edited by
David Hellholm, Tor Vegge, Øyvind Norderval,
Christer Hellholm

I

De Gruyter

ISBN 978-3-11-024751-0
e-ISBN 978-3-11-024753-4
ISSN 0171-6441

Library of Congress Cataloging-in-Publication Data

Ablution, initiation, and baptism : late antiquity, early Judaism, and early Christianity = Waschungen, Initiation und Taufe : Spätantike, frühes Judentum und frühes Christentum / [edited by] David Hellholm ... [et al.].
   p. cm. – (Beihefte zur zeitschrift für die neutestamentliche wissenschaft und die kunde der älteren kirche, ISSN 0171-6441 ; Bd. 176)
   English and German.
   Includes bibliographical references and indexes.
   ISBN 978-3-11-024751-0 (hardcover 23 × 15,5 : alk. paper)
   1. Baptism – History – Early church, ca. 30–600 – Congresses.   2. Baptism – Judaism – History – Congresses.   3. Lustrations – History – Congresses.   4. Rome – Religion – Congresses.   I. Hellholm, David.   II. Title: Waschungen, Initiation und Taufe.
   BV803.A25   2010
   234'.1610901–dc22

2010027619

Bibliographic information published by the Deutsche Nationalbibliothek

The Deutsche Nationalbibliothek lists this publication in the Deutsche Nationalbibliografie; detailed bibliographic data are available in the Internet at http://dnb.d-nb.de.

© 2011 Walter de Gruyter GmbH & Co. KG, Berlin/Boston

Printing: Hubert & Co. GmbH & Co. KG, Göttingen

∞ Printed on acid-free paper

Printed in Germany

www.degruyter.com

In memoriam

Wiard Popkes

30 Jun 1936 – 2 Jan 2007

Table of Contents

Volume / Teilband I

Introduction
Einführung

Preface .... *xlv*

Einführung
Christoph Markschies xlix

    1. Was wir wissen xlix

    2. Was wir noch nicht wissen lx

I. Methodological Considerations
Methodische Überlegungen

Rituals of Purification, Rituals of Initiation
Phenomenological, Taxonomical and Culturally Evolutionary Reflections
Anders Klostergaard Petersen 3

    1. The Relationship between Rituals of Purification and Initiation 3

    2. The Prevalence of Water as a Ritual Means in the Ancient Mediterranean World 6

    3. Accounting for Water as a Ritual Means 11

    4. An Evolutionary Framework for the Discussion 15

    5. The Need for a Revision of Terminology 17

    6. Rites of Passage 20

    7. The Individual Phases of the Ritual 21

8. Problems Regarding the Classification of van Gennep 24
9. Rituals of Initiation 25
10. Rituals of Initiation and Other Rituals: Criteriological Basis 28
   10.1. External Description of a Ritual of Initiation 30
   10.2. Internal Description of Rituals of Initiation 31
   10.3. Definition of a Ritual of Initiation 31
11. Rituals of Purification 32
12. The Two Types of Rituals during the Antiquity of the
    Mediterranean World. A Brief Conclusion 34

II. Religions of Late Antiquity – Outside of Judaism and Christianity
Religionen in der Spätantike – Außerhalb von Judentum und Christentum

Wasserriten im Alten Ägypten
JAN ASSMANN UND ANDREA KUCHAREK 43

1. Das Wasser im kulturellen Blick der Alten Ägypter 43
2. Die ägyptische Theorie der Nilflut 46
3. Wasserspende und Reinigung im Toten- und Osiriskult 50
4. Das thebanische Dekadenfest und der Totenkult der Spätzeit 53
5. Der „Baptism of Pharaoh" 54

The Mandean Water Ritual in Late Antiquity
ANDERS HULTGÅRD 69

1. Introduction 69
   1.1. Aim of the Contribution 69
   1.2. Terminological Questions 69
   1.3. Problems of Reconstruction 70
   1.4. Mandaean World-View and Doctrine 71
2. Mandaean Water Rituals 72

  2.1. Description of the Early 20th Century Rituals 73

3. The *maṣbūtā* as a Late Antiquity Ritual 76
  3.1. Manuscripts and Colophons.. 76
  3.2. Main View-Points... 76
  3.3. Arguments for a Continuity from Late Antiquity............................. 79

4. Iranian Elements in the *maṣbūtā* Ritual... 87
  4.1. Bihrām and the Cultic Banner... 87
  4.2. The *kuštā*: The Concept and the Act... 89

5. The *maṣbūtā* and the Problem of Mandaean Origins 92

6. Concluding Remarks 94

Baptism and Graeco-Roman Mystery Cults
Fritz Graf 101

1. Justin on Pagan Baptismal Rituals 102

2. Tertullian's Testimonies 105

3. Baptismal Cleansing and Pagan Purification Rituals 110

4. Summary 114

Baptism in Sethian Gnostic Texts
Birger A. Pearson 119

1. Sethian Gnosticism 119
  1.1. Defining Sethian Gnosticism.. 119
  1.2. Essential Features of Sethian Gnosticism... 121

2. Sethian Gnostic Baptism.. 123
  2.1. Previous Scholarship.. 123
  2.2. Primary Evidence for Sethian Baptism 124
  2.3. Baptism in the Apocryphon of John.. 124
  2.4. Baptism in Trimorphic Protennoia.. 126
  2.5. Baptism in the Apocalypse of Adam 129
  2.6. Baptism in the Gospel of the Egyptians 131
  2.7. Baptism in Zostrianos.. 134
  2.8. Baptism in Melchizedek 135
  2.9. Baptism in the Untitled Text from the Bruce Codex..................... 137
  2.10. Baptism in the Gospel of Judas.. 138

3. Summary and Conclusions.. 139

Initiationsriten im Manichäismus
GREGOR WURST 145

    1. Manis Ablehnung der Taufe in seiner Auseinandersetzung mit den Elchesaiten 145
    2. Verwerfung und Spiritualisierung der Taufe in (anti-) manichäischen Quellen 147
    3. Initiationsriten im Manichäismus 148

III. Early Judaism
Frühjudentum

Aus dem Wasser kommt das Leben
Waschungen und Reinigungsriten in frühjüdischen Texten
ANTJE LABAHN 157

    1. Einleitung 157
    2. Waschungen und rituelle Reinigung im Judentum – ein kurzer Überblick 158
    3. Frühjüdische Texte außerhalb von Qumran 159
        3.1. Testamentum Levi 160
        3.2. Jubiläenbuch 163
        3.3. Aristeasbrief 164
        3.4. Frühjüdische Reinigungsaussagen außerhalb von Qumran 168
    4. Reinigungsriten in den Schriften vom Toten Meer 168
        4.1. Tempelrolle (11Q19 / 11Q20) 169
        4.2. Halachisches Material 176
        4.3. Gemeinschaftsregel (1QS / 4QS) 195
        4.4. Damaskusschrift 203
        4.5. Zusammenfassung zu den Belegen aus den Schriften vom Toten Meer 207
    5. Waschen bringt Lebensqualität zurück 208

Jewish Immersion and Christian Baptism
Continuity on the Margins?
SEÁN FREYNE 221

1. Introduction 221
2. Jewish Ritual Washing: Theory and Practice 225
   2.1. Literary Evidence 226
   2.2. The Evidence of Archaeology: Miqva'oth 230
3. The In-Between World of Jewish Christian Baptism and Immersion 237
4. Concluding Reflection 246

"Echo of a Whisper"
The Uncertain Authenticity of Josephus' Witness to John the Baptist
CLARE K. ROTHSCHILD 255

1. Introduction 255
2. Literary Analysis: Text and Context 258
   2.1. Text of *A.J.* 18.116–119 258
   2.2. External Context within the Narrative 269
   2.3. Summation 271
3. Reception History 273
   3.1. Manuscript Evidence 273
   3.2. Origen 274
   3.3. Eusebius 278
   3.4. Summation: Origen and Eusebius as Witnesses to Josephus 283
4. Conclusion 283

„Ist er heraufgestiegen, gilt er in jeder Hinsicht als ein Israelit" (bYev 47b)
Das Proselytentauchbad im frühen Judentum
DIETER SÄNGER 291

1. Hinführung zum Thema 291
2. Problemstellung 294
3. Zur Terminologie 298
4. Proselytentauchbad – Johannestaufe – christliche Taufe 298
5. Die Quellen 303

    5.1. TestLev 14,6 305
    5.2. Sib 4,162–169 307
    5.3. Epiktet, Diss II 9,19–21 309
    5.4. Rabbinische Texte 311
    5.5. Ertrag 322
6. Das Proselytentauchbad – ein Initiationsritus? 323
7. Rückblick und Ausblick 325

IV. Earliest Christianity
Urchristentum

Kreative Erinnerung als nachösterliche Nachschöpfung
Der Ursprung der christlichen Taufe
MICHAEL LABAHN 337

1. Methodische Vorüberlegungen 337
2. Die historische Ausgangslage 339
    2.1. Zwei historische Eckpunkte zum Ursprung der christlichen
        Taufe in der frühchristlichen Literatur 339
    2.2. Erklärungsmodelle zum Ursprung der christlichen Taufe in
        der exegetischen Literatur 341
3. Die Suche nach Verbindungslinien und Ausgangspunkten 344
    3.1. Jesus, der Getaufte, aber nicht der Taufende 344
    3.2. Die christliche Taufe am Anfang der Urgemeinde 347
    3.3. Jesus als Täufer und der Täufer. Johanneische
        Akzentverschiebungen 350
4. Lösungsmodell: Nachösterliche Nachschöpfung als
    Eingangsritual in die neue Gemeinschaft 355
    4.1. Der nachösterliche Ursprung der christlichen Taufe 355
    4.2. Überlegungen zu Kontinuität und Diskontinuität von der
        Johannestaufe zur christlichen Taufe: Die Johannestaufe als
        Modell in gewandelter Zeit 362
    4.3. Die frühchristliche Taufe als Eingang in die neue Gemeinschaft 364
5. Zusammenfassung: Nachösterliche Nachschöpfung in
    Kontinuität zur Johannestaufe 366

Jesus' Baptism and the Origins of the Christian Ritual
HANS DIETER BETZ 377

1. Preliminary Historical Questions 378
   1.1. Issues of Historiography 378
   1.2. Issues of Comparative Religion 381
2. The Earliest Account (Mark 1:9–11) 385
3. The Interpretation in Other Gospels 387
   3.1. Matthew 3:13–17 387
   3.2. Luke 3:21–22 389
   3.3. John 1:19–34 390
4. Conclusion 391

Usages — Some Notes on the Baptismal Name-Formulae
LARS HARTMAN 397

1. The Formulae 397
2. Different Communication Situations 399
   2.1. The Enigmatic Beginning 399
   2.2. Outside the New Testament 403
   2.3. Some Christian Greek Texts after the New Testament 407
3. Conclusion 411

Vorgeformte Tauftraditionen und deren Benutzung in den Paulusbriefen
DAVID HELLHOLM 415

1. Vorgeformte Tauftraditionen bei Paulus – Die inter-textuellen Ko-texte 416
   1.1. Der Taufspruch bei der Taufe – Die „Namensformel" 417
   1.2. Die Taufaffirmation der Neugetauften – Die „Eingliederungsformel" 422
   1.3. Die Bestätigung an die Neugetauften – Die „Rechtfertigungsformel" 430
   1.4. Der Heilszuspruch an die Neugetauften – Die „Bekleidungsformel" 436
   1.5. Die Taufaffirmation der Neugetauften – Die „Identifikationsformel" 439
   1.6. Vorläufige Reflexion hinsichtlich der Textanalyse 452
2. Die Situationskontexte der drei Paulusbriefe – Die pragmatischen Präsuppositionen 453

    2.1. Die Situation in der korinthischen Gemeinde 454
    2.2. Die Situation in den galatischen Gemeinden 458
    2.3. Die Situation in den Romgemeinden 459
3. Der Gebrauch von Tauftraditionen in der Argumentation –
   Die intra-textuellen Ko-Texte 462
    3.1. Die Argumentation des Paulus im 1. Korintherbrief 462
    3.2. Die Argumentation des Paulus im Galaterbrief 467
    3.3. Die Argumentation des Paulus im Römerbrief 468
    3.4. Die Argumentationsstrategie des Paulus 470
4. Abschluss – Ertrag 471

Baptismal Phrases in the Deuteropauline Epistles
Tor Vegge 497

1. Introduction 497
    1.1. Theory – Baptism and the Texts Referring to Baptism 497
    1.2. The Deuteropauline Letters within the History of Early
        Christian Literature 499
    1.3. Which Texts Contain References to Baptism? 500
2. Baptismal Language in Colossians 501
    2.1. Structure and Genre 501
    2.2. The Function of the Writing 503
    2.3. Line of Reasoning in Colossians 2 504
    2.4. The Attitude of the Implied Author 507
    2.5. Baptismal References in Colossians 2 507
    2.6. Concluding Remarks 516
3. Baptismal Language in Ephesians 517
    3.1. Structure and Genre 518
    3.2. The Function of the Writing 519
    3.3. Ephesians 2:1–10 522
    3.4. Ephesians 4:5 528
4. Baptismal Language in the Pastoral Epistles 536
    4.1. Setting, Genre and Key Issue 536
    4.2. Baptismal Language in Second Timothy 538
    4.3. Baptismal Language in the Epistle to Titus 544

Die Taufe in der Apostelgeschichte
JENS SCHRÖTER 557

1. Die Taufe im Rahmen der lukanischen Geschichtstheologie 557
2. Aspekte der Tauferzählungen in der Apostelgeschichte 559
   2.1. Taufe als Befähigung zur Zeugenschaft: Die Ankündigung
        der Geistausgießung in Act 1,4–8 als Taufgeschehen.................... 559
   2.2. Taufe als Eintritt in die Gemeinschaft der Glaubenden:
        Die Grundlegung des Taufverständnisses in Act 2,37–41 562
   2.3. Taufe auf den Namen Jesu, Johannestaufe und
        Geistverleihung:
        Act 8,4–25 und 19,1–7.. 567
   2.4. Taufe als Öffnung des Gottesvolkes für die Heiden: Act
        10,1–11,18 570
3. Die Taufe des Äthiopiers und des Saulus als individuelle
   „Sonderfälle"... 572
   3.1. Taufe ohne Geist: Der äthiopische Eunuch.................................... 572
   3.2. Die Taufe des Saulus.. 576
4. Die Traditionsgrundlage der Tauferzählungen 578
5. Fazit: Die Tauferzählungen als Bestandteil der
   Geschichtstheologie der Act.. 581

Baptism in the Letter to the Hebrews
SAMUEL BYRSKOG..587

1. Introduction.. 587
2. The Texts 589
   2.1. Hebrews 6:1–6 589
   2.2. Hebrews 9:9–10 594
   2.3. Hebrews 10:21–23 595
3. Thematic Implications... 597
   3.1. Baptism as Initiation.. 597
   3.2. Baptism as a Christological Event... 598
   3.3. Baptism as an Eschatological Event 599
   3.4. Baptism as a Non-Repeatable Event 600

Because of "The Name of Christ"
Baptism and the Location of Identity in 1 Peter
HALVOR MOXNES 605

    1. Baptism in 1 Peter: The Central Text 3:18–22 605

    2. Baptism and the Structure and Composition of 1 Peter 608

    3. Placed "in Christ" as a Spatial Metaphor in 1 Peter 609

    4. Conflict with the World as Dislocation of Identity 612

    5. Displacement as Stigmatization and Shame 616

    6. From Displacement to Place "in Christ" 618

    7. Conclusion 621
        7.1. "In Christ" as a New Place 621
        7.2. "In Christ" – An Ethnic Identity? 623

Salbung, Geist und Taufe im 1. Johannesbrief
UDO SCHNELLE 629

    1. Die historische Situation des 1. Johannesbriefes 629

    2. Die Auseinandersetzung mit der Falschlehre 630

    3. Das Chrisma im kulturgeschichtlichen Vor- und Umfeld des
       1. Johannesbriefes 638

    4. Das Chrisma im 1. Johannesbrief 641

    5. Chrisma und Geist im 1. Johannesbrief 644

    6. Fazit 649

Matthew 28:9–20 and Mark 16:9–20
Different Ways of Relating Baptism to the Joint Mission of God, John the Baptist, Jesus, and their Adherents
KIRSTEN MARIE HARTVIGSEN 655

    1. Introduction 655

    2. The Authenticity and Genre of Matthew 28:16–20 656

2.1. Did the Reference to Baptism and the Triadic Phrase Belong
        to the Original Version of Matthew 28:16–20? 657
   2.2. The Historicity of the Commission to Baptize 659
   2.3. The Genre of Matthew 28:16–20 661
   2.4. Implications – Baptism in Relation to Christology,
        Ecclesiology, and Eschatology 662

3. The Authenticity of Mark 16:9–20 663

4. Comparison of Matthew 28:8–20 and Mark 16:8–20 666
   4.1. Comparison of Matthew 28:8–15 and Mark 16:8–13..................... 666
   4.2. Synopsis of Matthew 28:16–20 and Mark 16:14–20 668
   4.3. Hermeneutical Implications 673

5. Oral Performance of Gospels 674

6. Baptism in the Gospel of Matthew and Mark 676
   6.1. Baptism in the Gospel of Matthew Prior to 28:16–20 676
   6.2. Baptism in the Context of Matthew 28:16–20 685
   6.3. Baptism in the Gospel of Mark Prior to the Longer Ending 694
   6.4. Baptism in the Context of Mark 16:14–20 701

7. When the End is Not the End 707
   7.1. Baptism as a Link between the Gospel Worlds and the Real
        World of Audience Members.. 707
   7.2. Comparison of Baptism in Matthew 28:16–20 and Mark
        16:14–20 708

Baptismal Reflections in the Fourth Gospel
Turid Karlsen Seim 717

1. Introductory Remarks on Methodology... 717

2. The Baptismal Practices of John and Jesus 719

3. Generation from Above (3:1–21)... 722

4. Life-Giving Spirit 727

5. Concluding Intimations 730

Hermeneutische Aspekte der Taufe im Neuen Testament
ODA WISCHMEYER 735

   1. Methodische Vorüberlegungen 735

   2. Taufe bei Paulus 738
       2.1. Rituelle Handlung 738
       2.2. Semantik 739
       2.3. Deutungsmöglichkeiten 739
       2.4. Literarische Zusammenhänge 744

   3. Taufe im Markusevangelium 745
       3.1. Rituelle Handlung 746
       3.2. Semantik 746
       3.3. Deutungsmöglichkeiten 747
       3.4. Literarische Zusammenhänge 749

   4. Taufe im Matthäusevangelium 750

   5. Taufe in der Apostelgeschichte 751
       5.1. Rituelle Handlung 751
       5.2. Deutungsmöglichkeiten 752
       5.3. Literarische Zusammenhänge 755

   6. Taufe im Johannesevangelium 755

   7. Späte neutestamentliche Texte 757

   8. Fazit 758

Volume / Teilband II

V. The Patristic Period
Die patristische Periode

Zur frühchristlichen Taufpraxis
Die Taufe in der Didache, bei Justin und in der Didaskalia
Andreas Lindemann 767

1. Die Didache 767
   1.1. Einleitung 767
   1.2. Zur Textüberlieferung, Datierung und Gliederung der Didache 768
   1.3. Zwei-Wege-Lehre und Taufe 772
   1.4. Der Vollzug der Taufe nach der Didache 774
   1.5. Fasten als Vorbereitung auf die Taufe 781
   1.6. Die Taufe in der Didache 784
2. Justin 785
   2.1. Einleitung 785
   2.2. Die *Apologie* 786
   2.3. Die Taufe in Justins *Dialog mit dem Juden Trypho* 794
   2.4. Die Taufpraxis nach Justin 796
3. Die *Didaskalia Apostolorum* 797
   3.1. Einleitung 797
   3.2. Die Taufe in der Didaskalia 798
   3.3. Anweisungen der Didaskalia zum Taufvollzug 803
   3.4. Zum Ablauf der Taufhandlung 805
   3.5. Taufe und Sündenvergebung 805
   3.6. Die Taufe nach der Didaskalia 806

Taufinterpretationen bei Ignatius und im Barnabasbrief
Christologische und soteriologische Deutungen
DIETRICH-ALEX KOCH 817

1. Die Taufe bei Ignatius... 817
   1.1. Einführung... 817
   1.2. Die Taufe Jesu bei Ignatius.. 818
   1.3. Die Taufe der Christen bei Ignatius..................................... 827
   1.4. Ergebnis.. 830

2. Die Taufe im Barnabasbrief... 832
   2.1. Einführung... 832
   2.2. „Das Land, das von Milch und Honig fließt" (Barn 6,8–18)........ 833
   2.3. Die Taufe als Gabe des „Lebenswassers" (Barn 11).................. 837
   2.4. Taufe und Kultmetaphorik.. 843
   2.5. Ergebnis.. 844

The Teaching on Baptism in the Shepherd of Hermas
VEMUND BLOMKVIST 849

1. Introduction... 849
2. The Composition of the *Shepherd*... 850
3. The Themes of Baptism and Metanoia in the *Shepherd*................... 853
4. Baptism in the Allegory of the Tower... 856
   4.1. Baptism in *Visio* III.. 857
   4.2. Baptism in *Similitudo* IX... 861
5. Conclusion.. 865

Taufe bei Marcion – eine Spurensuche
EVE-MARIE BECKER 871

1. Zur Fragestellung... 871
2. ‚Taufe' bei *Marcion* und *Tertullian*... 875
   2.1. ‚Taufe' bei *Marcion* nach *adversus Marcionem*.................. 877
   2.2. ‚Taufe' bei *Tertullian* nach *de baptismo*........................... 883
3. Zur Bedeutung des ‚Apostolikon' und des Evangeliums bei *Marcion* . 886
4. Grundzüge des marcionitischen Taufverständnisses........................ 888

Baptism among the Valentinians
EINAR THOMASSEN 895

1. Introduction 895
2. Sources 895
3. The Performance of Baptism 897
   3.1. The Similarity with "Orthodox" Practice 897
   3.2. The "Bridal Chamber" 899
4. The Value of Baptism and Its Components 899
   4.1. The Value of Ritual in General 899
   4.2. The Relative Value of Water Baptism and Anointing 901
5. The Meaning of Baptism 902
   5.1. "Redemption" 902
   5.2. Jesus' Baptism as a Model 903
   5.3. The "Name" 903
   5.4. The Bridal Chamber and the Union with Angels 905
   5.5. Other Ideas Associated with Baptism 908
6. Conclusion 912

Initiation/Baptism in the Montanist Movement
WILLIAM TABBERNEE 917

1. The New Prophecy ("Montanism") 919
2. An Heretical Baptismal Formula? 920
   2.1. Basil of Caesarea's Research 920
3. The Synod of Iconium 923
4. Cyprian of Carthage and Montanism in North Africa 923
5. North-African Inscriptions 925
6. The Cult of the *Martyr* Montanus 927
7. Montanist Initiation/Baptism in Phrygia 928

	7.1.	"Polluted Sacraments"	929
	7.2.	"Passing Over" or "Passing On"?	931
	7.3.	Bread and Cheese	932
	7.4.	Predisposed to Believe the Worst	934
	7.5.	Drunken Orgies	935
	7.6.	Copper Needles and Initiation	935
	7.7.	From Easter Sunday to Maundy Thursday	936
	7.8.	Augustine's Special Source	937
	7.9.	Martyr or Priest?	938
8.	Rebaptism		939
9.	Baptism of or on Behalf of the Dead?		941
10.	Conclusion		942

Simplicity and Power
Tertullian's *De Baptismo*
ØYVIND NORDERVAL 947

1. *De Baptismo* – Its Historical Context 947
2. Tertullian's Theology of Baptism 949
3. The Baptismal Rite 956
4. Other Baptismal Regulations 961
5. Concluding Remarks 966

Baptism in Clement of Alexandria
HENNY FISKÅ HÄGG 973

1. Introduction 973
2. Aspects of Baptismal Practice in Clement 974
   - 2.1. The Baptismal Season and the Catechumenate 974
   - 2.2. Jesus' Own Baptism as Paradigm 976
3. Clement's Theology of Baptism 977
   - 3.1. Baptism as Purification of Sins and the Question of Hereditary Guilt 978
   - 3.2. Baptism as Restoration and New Birth 980
   - 3.3. Baptism as Perfection 982
   - 3.4. Baptism as Enlightenment 983

More Than Initiation? Baptism According to Origen of Alexandria
GUNNAR AF HÄLLSTRÖM..989

1. Introduction.. 989
2. Terminology 990
3. The Background 992
4. The Baptism of Jesus 995
5. The Purpose of Baptism 996
6. Infant Baptism 1000
7. Post-Baptismal Life 1004
8. Baptism and Platonism 1006
9. Concluding Remarks... 1007

Initiation in the *Apostolic Tradition*
ANDERS EKENBERG...1011

1. Textual Problems... 1012
   1.1. The Textual Witnesses 1012
   1.2. The Interrelations Between the Textual Witnesses 1015
   1.3. Reconstruction Principles.. 1017
2. The Initiation Process.. 1018
   2.1. Post-Third-Century Traits... 1018
   2.2. A Western Order of Initiation 1025
   2.3. Easter Baptism? 1028
3. The Meaning Attributed to Initiation/Baptism....................... 1028
   3.1. "Baptism"... 1028
   3.2. Baptism and Conversion 1029
   3.3. Escaping the Evil Forces 1030
   3.4. Initiation and Community... 1032
   3.5. Forgiveness of Sins and New Birth 1033
4. Conclusion... 1034
5. Appendix: The *Apostolic Tradition*, Chapters 15–21 1034

- 5.1. On Newcomers 1035
- 5.2. On Crafts and Professions 1035
- 5.3. On the Time During which They are to Hear the Word 1037
- 5.4. On the Prayer of the Catechumens 1037
- 5.5. On a Catechumen who Is Arrested 1038
- 5.6. Of those who Will Receive Baptism 1038
- 5.7. On the Handing over of Holy Baptism 1040
- 5.8. Conclusion 1044

Die Tauftheologie Cyprians
Beobachtungen zu ihrer Entwicklungsgeschichte und schrifthermeneutischen Begründung
Enno Edzard Popkes 1051

1. Thematische Hinführung 1051
2. Das facettenreiche Spektrum tauftheologischer Aussagen in den Schriften Cyprians 1053
3. Das Verhältnis von Wassertaufe und Bluttaufe 1056
4. Cyprians Position im Ketzertaufstreit 1059
   - 4.1. Historische Rahmenbedingung der tauftheologischen Ausführungen Cyprians im Kontext des Ketzertaufstreits 1059
   - 4.2. Der 73. Brief als die wichtigste tauftheologische Schrift Cyprians 1060
   - 4.3. Das offene Ende des Ketzertaufstreits 1067

Taufvorstellungen in den Pseudoklementinen
Jürgen Wehnert 1071

1. Der pseudoklementinische Roman und seine Entstehungsgeschichte 1072
   - 1.1. Der Plot des Romans 1072
   - 1.2. Die Entstehungsgeschichte der Pseudoklementinen 1073
2. Die Taufvorstellungen in den pseudoklementinischen Literarschichten 1077

Table of Contents   XXV

    2.1. Zur Taufe in der vorpseudoklementinischen Petrus/Simon-Novelle 1078
    2.2. Die Taufe im pseudoklementinischen Roman 1084
    2.3. Der Redaktor Ad Jacobum.. 1093
    2.4. Die Taufe in den Homilien... 1094
    2.5. Die Taufe in den Rekognitionen 1095
  3. Johannes der Täufer in den Pseudoklementinen................................. 1103
  4. Die Taufvorstellungen in den Pseudoklementinen – ein Resümee.... 1108

„Taufe" und „untertauchen" in Aphrahats ܬܚܘܝܬܐ (taḥwyāṯā)
MICHAEL LATTKE 1115

  1. Kurze Einführung in das syrische Christentum bis zum Konzil von Chalkedon 1115
    1.1. Abgrenzung.. 1115
    1.2. Zentren, Autoren und Werke... 1117
  2. Aphrahat, sein Werk und seine Quellen 1119
    2.1. Aphrahat, der persische Weise 1119
    2.2. Aphrahats ܬܚܘܝܬܐ (taḥwyāṯā) 1120
    2.3. Aphrahats Quellen 1121
  3. Anspielungen auf und Zitate von Stellen des Neuen Testaments....... 1122
    3.1. Anspielungen 1122
    3.2. Zitate 1122
  4. Terminologie... 1123
  5. Definitionen von Beschneidung und Taufe... 1124
    5.1. Definitionen von Beschneidung... 1124
    5.2. Definitionen von Taufe.. 1125
  6. Taufe Jesu durch Johannes den Täufer 1125
  7. Einsetzung der christlichen Taufe durch den Erlöser 1126
  8. Glaube an die Taufe, Glaube und Taufe 1127
    8.1. Glaube an die Taufe.. 1127
    8.2. Glaube und Taufe 1127
  9. Taufe als zweite Beschneidung 1127
  10. Taufe als zweite Geburt (Wiedergeburt)... 1128
  11. Taufe als Waschung und Sündenvergebung 1129
  12. Taufe und Ehe(losigkeit).. 1130

13. Heiliger Geist und Taufe 1130

14. Taufe und das Leiden Jesu Christi 1131

15. Appendix I – Titelübersicht 1132

16. Appendix II – Textauswahl 1133

Baptismal Mystery in St. Ephrem the Syrian and *Hymnen de Epiphania*
Serafim Seppälä 1139

1. *Hymnen de Epiphania* and the Baptismal Event 1141

2. The Baptism of Christ as Cosmic Mystery 1145

3. Mysticism of Immersion 1150

4. Mysticism of Oil 1151

5. Dimensions of Baptism 1155
   5.1. Pneumatic Dimension of Baptism 1155
   5.2. Trinitarian Dimension of Baptism 1157
   5.3. Paschal Dimension of Baptism 1158
   5.4. Personal Dimension of Baptism 1160

6. Baptism as a Call for Struggle 1165

7. Hermeneutic Context of Baptism: Biblical Imagery 1169
   7.1. Paradise 1169
   7.2. Other Imagery of the Old Covenant 1171

The Catechetical Lectures of Cyril of Jerusalem
A Source for the Baptismal Liturgy of Mid-Fourth Century Jerusalem
Juliette Day 1179

1. Introduction 1179

2. *Cats* and the *Letter of Macarius* (*Ep. Mac.*) 1180

3. The Jordan Event as Theological Framework 1183

4. The Liturgy of Baptism in *Cats* 1186

- 4.1. Ritual Sequence 1187
- 4.2. The Ministers 1189
- 4.3. Pre-Immersion Rituals 1190
- 4.4. The Seal 1192
- 4.5. Immersion 1195
- 4.6. Anointing 1197
- 4.7. Imposition of Hands 1198
- 4.8. Transitional Rituals 1198
- 4.9. Summary Conclusion 1199
5. The Baptismal Liturgy of *MC* 1200
6. From *Cats* to *MC* 1201
7. Conclusion 1203

Baptism in Gregory of Nyssa's Theology and Its Orientation to Eschatology
Ilaria L. E. Ramelli 1205

1. Introduction and Methodological Guidelines 1205
2. Baptism and the Restoration of the Image of God 1206
3. The Relation of Baptism to the Resurrection and Restoration 1208
    - 3.1. Baptism and Christ's Victory over Evil, between Christ's Resurrection and the End 1209
    - 3.2. Baptism and Christ's Divinity and Humanity 1210
    - 3.3. Baptism and Death 1212
    - 3.4. Baptism and Human Free Will 1214
    - 3.5. Baptism Preludes the Mystery of ἀποκατάστασις. Necessity and Grace 1214
    - 3.6. Purification of the "Unbaptised"/"Non-Purified" and Universal ἀποκατάστασις 1216
    - 3.7. A Parallel in Nazianzen: Purification by Fire for the "Unbaptised"/"Non-Purified" 1219
4. Further Proofs of the Eschatological Orientation of Baptism for Nyssen 1221
    - 4.1. Baptism as Illumination and Purification: The "First Way" 1222
    - 4.2. Baptism in *De Vita Moysis*: Liberation from the Skin Tunics and Restoration to Paradise 1223
    - 4.3. Baptism, a μυστήριον: Its Relation to the Mysteries of Universal Salvation and of Christ 1224
5. Conclusion 1227

Johannes Chrysostomus: Die zehn Gaben (τιμαί oder δωρεαί) der Taufe
RUDOLF BRÄNDLE...1233

1. Hinführung zum Thema..1233
   1.1. Forschungsgeschichtlicher Abriss...1233
   1.2. Besonderheiten der antiochenischen Tauftheologie....................1234
   1.3. Ausserordentliche Ereignisse...1235
   1.4. Einige für das Taufverständnis von Johannes Chrysostomus bezeichnende Aspekte 1239

2. Die zehn Gaben (τιμαί oder δωρεαί) der Taufe 1240
   2.1. Sermo ad neophytos...1240
   2.2. Gewährt die Taufe nur den Nachlass der Sünden?......................1242
   2.3. Kleine Kinder haben keine Sünden 1244
   2.4. Johannes Chrysostomus und die spätere Lehre von der Erbsünde..1245
   2.5. Johannes Chrysostomus in den pelagianischen Diskussionen ..1246

Ambrose and Augustine
Two Bishops on Baptism and Christian Identity
REIDAR AASGAARD..1253

1. *Introitus* in Milan 1253

2. Baptism and Identity in Ambrose and Augustine 1255

3. Identity and Identity Construction..1257

4. Ambrose's *The Sacraments* and *The Mysteries*......................................1258

5. Ambrose on Baptism and Christian Identity 1259
   5.1. Theology of Baptism 1260
   5.2. Use of the Bible 1263
   5.3. The Social Dimension..1264

6. Augustine's Easter *Sermones*..1268

7. Augustine on Baptism and Christian Identity 1269
   7.1. Theology of Baptism 1270
   7.2. Use of the Bible 1272
   7.3. The Social Dimension..1273

8. Baptism and Christian Identity in Ambrose and Augustine: Final Reflections...1277

The Efficacy of Baptism in Augustine's Theology
J. Patout Burns...1283

   1. The African Conflicts over Baptism 1283
      1.1. Tertullian 1283
      1.2. Cyprian 1284
      1.3. The *Treatise on Rebaptism* 1287
      1.4. The Donatist Conflict 1288
      1.5. Optatus of Milevis 1289

   2. Augustine's Theology of Baptism 1290
      2.1. Baptism in Unity and in Schism 1290
      2.2. Baptismal Consecration 1292
      2.3. Baptismal Sanctification 1293
      2.4. The Minister of Baptism 1295
      2.5. Baptism in Special Circumstances 1298
      2.6. Baptism in the Pelagian Controversy 1299

   3. Conclusion 1300

Der Streit über die Wirkung der Taufe im frühen Mönchtum
Die Taufe bei Makarios/Symeon, Markos Eremites und den Messalianern
Otmar Hesse 1305

   1. Die Taufe bei Makarios 1306
      1.1. Die „unpolemischen" Aussagen 1307
      1.2. Die „polemischen" Aussagen 1309
      1.3. „Symeons endgültige Stellungnahme" (Dörries) 1312
      1.4. Typologische Aussagen zur Taufe 1312
      1.5. Die Gegner des Makarios 1314

   2. Das Taufverständnis des Markos Eremites 1315
      2.1. Die Taufauseinandersetzung in den Schriften des Markos......... 1316
      2.2. Die gegnerische Tauflehre 1317
      2.3. Die Tauflehre des Markos 1320
      2.4. Die Tauflehre der Gegner des Markos und das
          Taufverständnis des Makarios 1330
      2.5. Anhang: „Ein neuer Zeuge für das altkirchliche
          Taufbekenntnis" (Kunze) 1331

   3. Die Taufe bei den Messalianern 1332

Table of Contents

    3.1. Theodoret von Kyros.. 1333
    3.2. Timotheos von Konstantinopel 1334
    3.3. Johannes von Damaskus 1335
    3.4. Das Taufverständnis der Messalianer im Vergleich zu
         Makarios und Markos bzw. zu ihren Gegnern 1337
4. Zusammenfassung 1338

Baptism in the Monasteries of Upper Egypt
The Pachomian Corpus and the Writings of Shenoute
Hugo Lundhaug 1347

1. Introduction 1347
2. The Pachomian Sources 1348
    2.1. Baptism from a Pachomian Perspective 1349
    2.2. Summary 1357
3. The Writings of Shenoute 1358
    3.1. Baptism from Shenoute's Perspective 1359
    3.2. Summary 1373
4. Conclusion: The Pachomian and Shenoutean Sources Compared 1373

VI. Thematic Surveys
Thematische Darstellungen

Taufrituale im frühen Christentum und in der Alten Kirche
Historische und ritualwissenschaftliche Perspektiven
Christian Strecker 1383

1. Problematisierungen 1385
2. Taufrituale in den ersten vier Jahrhunderten: ein historischer
    Querschnitt 1388
    2.1. Neutestamentlicher Befund 1388
    2.2. Taufrituale in vornizänischer Zeit (2.–3. Jh.) 1391
    2.3. Taufrituale im 4. Jh. 1396
3. Ritualwissenschaftliche Annäherungen 1404

3.1. Transformation – Liminalität 1406
  3.2. Embodiment – Habitus 1416
  3.3. Kulturelle Performanz 1429

Seal and Baptism in Early Christianity
KARL OLAV SANDNES 1441

  1. Introductory Comments 1441
  2. A Non-Religious Idea 1442
     2.1. A Mark of Branding: Belonging, Authority, Protection and
          Obligation 1443
  3. "… Putting His Seal on Us" (2 Cor 1:21–22) 1446
     3.1. Baptism in 2 Cor 1:21–22? 1447
  4. Hermas' *The Shepherd*: "The Seal is the Water" 1450
     4.1. *Visio 3* 1450
     4.2. *Similitudo 8* 1452
     4.3. *Similitudo 9* 1453
     4.4. Sealing: Repentance – Exorcism – Postponement 1455
  5. Melito of Sardis *On Pascha*: The Seal and Exod 12 1457
     5.1. *On Pascha* 14–17 1457
  6. *2 Clement*: "Preserve the Seal" 1460
  7. *Thecla*: "Give me the Seal" 1463
  8. The Seal in *Acts of Thomas* 1466
     8.1. Mygdonia Asks for the Seal 1467
     8.2. Gundaphorus Asks for the Seal 1468
  9. Summary 1474

Taufe und Taufeucharistie
Die postbaptismale Mahlgemeinschaft in Quellen des 2. und 3. Jahrhunderts
HANS-ULRICH WEIDEMANN 1483

  1. Die Taufeucharistie bei Justin dem Märtyrer 1485
     1.1. Taufeucharistie und Sonntagseucharistie 1485
     1.2. Die Taufeucharistie 1486
     1.3. Mimesis und Erinnerung 1488
     1.4. Die Sonntagseucharistie (Apol I 67) 1490
  2. Eine Zwischenüberlegung 1491
  3. Die Initiation von Heiden zur Eucharistie: Die Didache 1492

3.1. Gliederung und Abfassungszweck der Didache.................................... 1493
3.2. Separation und Limination von Heiden 1495
3.3. Aggregation: Die Eucharistie als Abschluss der Initiation.......... 1498

4. Initiation zur asketischen Tischgemeinschaft...................................... 1499
   4.1. Die Taufe der Artemilla (*Acta Pauli*: PHam 2ff.) 1500
   4.2. Die Taufe Theons (*Acta Petri*: Actus Vercellenses) 1500
   4.3. Die Taufeucharistien der *Thomasakten* 1502
   4.4. Initiation in die jüdische Tischgemeinschaft:
        Die Pseudoclementinen... 1508

5. Milch und Honig: Die Traditio Apostolica... 1513
   5.1. Die Suche nach dem „core-document".................................... 1513
   5.2. Die Zulassung zur Taufeucharistie... 1515
   5.3. Der Taufgottesdienst... 1516
   5.4. Milch und Honig... 1518
   5.5. Taufeucharistie und Gemeindemähler...................................... 1521

6. Schlussbemerkungen... 1522

Kindertaufe im frühen Christentum
Beobachtungen an den neutestamentlichen Apokryphen
HERMUT LÖHR...1531

1. Einführung... 1531
2. Methodische Reflexion: Die „neutestamentlichen Apokryphen"
   als Quellen für das entstehende Christentum 1534
3. Indizien für Kindertaufe in den
   Neutestamentlichen Apokryphen? 1535
   3.1. Direkte Erwähnung von Kindertaufen..................................... 1536
   3.2. Die sogenannte οἶκος-Formel... 1536
   3.3. Massentaufen 1538
   3.4. Taufpraxis... 1539
   3.5. Taufverständnis – Tauftheologie 1543
   3.6. Kindertaufe in den Pseudo-Clementinen 1546
4. Ergebnisse 1547

Das Taufbekenntnis in der frühen Kirche
REINHART STAATS...1553

1. Bekenntnis, Glaube, Symbol als Leitbegriffe... 1553
2. Das öffentliche Bekenntnis und das Bekenntnis in der Taufliturgie.. 1556
3. Das Credo als Bekenntnis der Kirche... 1559
4. Die Taufe des einzelnen Menschen... 1562
5. Absage an das Böse und Zusage an Christus 1564
6. In frühen Credo-Texten werden Taufe und Eucharistie nicht genannt.. 1566
7. Die „eine Taufe" im dritten Glaubensartikel... 1567
8. Frühkirchliche Apologetik und Bekenntnis im Vergleich................... 1570
   8.1. Die Weltgerichtsklausel
   Et iterum venturus est iudicare vivos et mortuos........................... 1570
   8.2. Die Klausel *crucifixus sub Pontio Pilato*.................................... 1571
   8.3. Das Bekenntnis Jesu „vor vielen Zeugen" 1571
9. Sonderformen im Orient 1573
10. Taufbekenntnis und kirchliche Arkandisziplin..................................... 1575
11. Das Nizänum (325) als kanonischer Text und die Folgen für die Ökumene... 1576

VII. Archaeology and Art History
Archäologie und Kunstgeschichte

Understanding the Structures of Early Christian Baptisteries
OLOF BRANDT 1587

1. Introduction.. 1587
2. Terminology: a Particular Kind of Bath Building................................. 1588
3. Origin: from Rivers to Private Baths 1589
4. History of Research: From Badly Illustrated Catalogues to New Methods... 1590
5. A Survey of Forms and Decoration 1592

	5.1. Forms	1592
	5.2. Decoration	1594
6.	Understanding Structure	1595
	6.1. Understanding Structure: Typology	1595
	6.2. Understanding Structure: Topography	1597
	6.3. Understanding Structure: Symbolism	1599
	6.4. Understanding Structure: Space	1602

Neues zu den alt- und neutestamentlichen Darstellungen im Baptisterium von Dura-Europos
Dieter Korol in Verbindung mit Jannike Rieckesmann 1611

1. Zum Baubefund 1611
2. Die Malereiausstattung 1616
    - 2.1. Das Lünettenbild 1617
    - 2.2. Die Heilung des Paralytikers und der Wasserwandel Petri und Christi 1621
    - 2.3. Die so genannte Garten-Szene 1645
    - 2.4. Die Samariterin am Brunnen und der Sieg Davids über Goliath 1645
    - 2.5. Darstellungen im unteren Bildregister an der Nord- und an der Ostwand 1649
    - 2.6. Zu den „Parallelen" mit dem figürlichen Dekor von San Giovanni in fonte in Neapel 1659
3. Schlussbemerkung 1662

Baptismal Practices at North African Martyrs' Shrines
Robin M. Jensen 1673

1. Introduction 1673
2. The Case of Bir Ftouha 1673
    - 2.1. Discovery and First Excavations 1673
    - 2.2. Recent Excavations 1675
    - 2.3. North African Architectural Parallels 1676
3. Possible Identity and Function of the Bir Ftouha Complex 1678
4. Comparable Evidence for Pilgrimage Baptism outside North Africa 1680
5. Parallel Installations in North African Pilgrimage Churches 1681

6. The Association of Martyrdom with Baptism 1685
     6.1. Martyrs and the Forgiveness of Post-Baptismal Sins 1687
     6.2. The Cult of the Martyrs and Penitential Pilgrimages 1690
     6.3. Ablution Pools at Saints' Shrines 1692
  7. Conclusion 1693

Die Entwicklung der Taufbecken in der Spätantike
Hannah Schneider 1697

  1. Von der Erwachsenen- zur Kindertaufe 1698
  2. Einordnung der hispano-portugiesischen und nordafrikanischen
     Taufbecken 1701
     2.1. Datierung 1702
     2.2. Topographie 1704
  3. Charakteristika der Taufbecken 1707
     3.1. Formenspektrum 1707
     3.2. Piscinatiefe 1710
  4. Umwandlung der Taufbecken 1711
     4.1. Verkleinerung 1712
     4.2. Konstruktion von Nebenpiscinen 1713
  5. Schlusswort 1714

'I understand the mystery, and I recognize the sacrament.'
On the Iconology of Ablution, Baptism, and Initiation
Diane Apostolos-Cappadona 1721

  1. Prolegomenon 1721
  2. The Beginnings of Christian Art and the "Image" of Ablution,
     Initiation, and Baptism 1723
  3. Baptism in Early Christian Art 1726
  4. New Questions, Methodologies, and Early Christian Art 1728
     4.1. On the Questions of "The Body," Virginity and
          Gender in the Iconography of Baptism 1730
     4.2. Horizontal and Vertical Water in the Iconography of Baptism .. 1732
  5. Preliminary Conclusions 1733

The Poetics and Politics of Christian Baptism in the
Abercius Monument
Margaret M. Mitchell 1743
 1. Introduction to the Source, Questions and Methodological
   Assumptions 1743
   1.1. The "Abercius Inscription" 1743
   1.2. The Modern Framing of the Inscription and of the Inquiry 1744
   1.3. Toward the Text and Translation 1747

 2. "The Much Disputed Passage" (lines 7–9) 1750
   2.1. The Hermeneutics of Decoding 1750
   2.2. Interpretive Options 1752
   2.3. Conclusion: An Epigram Read Oppositionally 1760

 3. A Proposal: Abercius' "Dual Identity" 1761
   3.1. Proposition: Ambiguity does not Require Antinomy 1761
   3.2. Reading Abercius with the Apologists and Roman Encomiasts 1762
   3.3. What Abercius the Citizen "saw" at Rome 1763
   3.4. What Abercius the Disciple "saw" at Rome 1770

 4. What an Ancient Viewer "saw" 1775
   4.1. The "Framing of the Inscription" in the Full Monument 1775
   4.2. In the *vita Abercii* 1776

 5. A Sustainable Ambiguity? 1777

Volume / Teilband III

VIII. Appendix

Images and Illustrations/Abbildungen und Illustrationen

Fig. 1.	Seth in der Sonnenbarke	1786
Fig. 2.	Die personifizierte Nilquelle	1787
Fig. 3.	Das Nilmosaik von Praeneste, Gesamtansicht. 120–110 v.Chr.	1788
Fig. 4.	Das Nilmosaik von Praeneste, Detail: Tempel des Osiris-Kanopus	1789
Fig. 5.	Die Höhle des Claudian. Vincenzo Cartari, 1571	1790
Fig. 6.	"Baptism of Pharaoh". Medinet Habu, Totentempel Ramses' III. 20. Dynastie	1791
Fig. 7.	"Baptism of Pharaoh"	1791
Fig. 8.	Reinigung beim Vollzug des Mundöffnungsrituals	1792
Fig. 9.	Reinigung des Verstorbenen	1793
Fig. 10.	"Baptism of Pharaoh" in einem Privatgrab	1794
Fig. 11.	Die vierfache Reinigung des Verstorbenen	1795
Fig. 12.	Verstorbene wird nach bestandenem Totengericht von Horus bei Osiris eingeführt	1796
Fig. 13.	"Baptism of Pharaoh" auf einem Sarg	1797
Fig. 14.	"Baptism of Pharaoh" auf dem Sarg der Tjentmutengebtiu	1798
Fig. 15.	Mithra-Apollo	1799
Fig. 16.	Artagnes-Heracles and Antiochos I *Dexiosis* Relief from Arsameia on Nymphaios	1800
Fig. 17.	Miqveh in the Palace Compound of Herod in Jericho	1801
Fig. 18.	Two-Stairs Pool in the third Winter Palace Compound of Herod in Jericho	1801
Fig. 19.	Miqveh from Private House	1802

Fig. 20. Sepphoris miqveh 1803

Fig. 21. Roofed Courtyard Miqveh 1804

Fig. 22. Miqveh with Divider 1805

Fig. 23. Miqveh without Divider 1806

Fig. 24. Miqveh from Qumran 1807

Fig. 25. Planzeichnung des Baptisteriums in Kourion 1808

Fig. 26. Taufbecken-Nische in Kourion 1809

Fig. 27. The Lateran Baptistery 1810

Fig. 28. Baptistery plans 1811

Fig. 29. The baptistery of Albenga 1812

Fig. 30. Baptistery of Qal'at Sem'an, Syria 1813

Fig. 31. Baptistery of Albenga, Italy 1814

Fig. 32. Baptistery of Aquileia, Italy 1815

Fig. 33. Baptistery of Abu Mina, Eqypt 1816

Fig. 34. Baptistery of Naples, Italy 1817

Fig. 35. Baptistery of Albenga, Italy 1818

Fig. 36. Baths of Constantine, Rome 1819

Fig. 37. Lateran Baptistery, Rome 1820

Fig. 38. Baptistery of Aquileia, Italy 1821

Fig. 39. Baptistery of Poreč, Croatia 1822

Fig. 40. Grundriss der Hauskirche von Dura-Europos 1823

Fig. 41. Rekonstruktion des Baptisteriums von Dura-Europos 1824

Fig. 42. Dura-Europos, Baptisterium, Aufrisse 1825

Fig. 43. Dura-Europos, Baptisterium, Taufbecken 1826

Fig. 44. Dura-Europos, Baptisterium, Süd- und Westseite 1827

Fig. 45. Dura-Europos, Baptisterium, Lünettenbild 1828

Fig. 46. Dura-Europos, Baptisterium, Lünettenbild 1829

Fig. 47. Vergleichsdenkmäler zum Lünettenbild in Dura-Europos 1830

Fig. 48. Spätantike Darstellungen der Heilung des Paralytikers 1831

Fig. 49. Dura-Europos/New Haven, Baptisterium (Nordwand) 1832

Fig. 50. Dura-Europos, Baptisterium (Nordwand) 1833

Fig. 51. Dura-Europos, Baptisterium, Wasserwandel 1834

Fig. 52. Dura-Europos, Baptisterium, Wasserwandel- und Lünettenbild 1835

Fig. 53. Dura-Europos, Baptisterium, Wasserwandel 1836

Fig. 54. Vergleichsdenkmäler aus Rom 1837

Fig. 55. Vergleichsdenkmäler zum Wasserwandel (Rom, Neapel, Bobbio) 1838

Fig. 56. Vergleichsdenkmäler zum Wasserwandel (Chersonnes, Rom) .1839

Fig. 57. Vergleichsdenkmäler zum Wasserwandel (Paris, Rom) 1840

Fig. 58. Dura-Europos, Baptisterium, ‚Gartenszene' 1841

Fig. 59. Dura-Europos, Baptisterium, Samariterin am Brunnen 1842

Fig. 60. Samariterin am Brunnen (Rom, Catania) 1843

Fig. 61. Dura-Europos, Baptisterium (David- und Goliath-Bild) 1844

Fig. 62. Dura-Europos, Baptisterium (David- und Goliath-Bild) – Münzvergleiche 1845

Fig. 63. Dura-Europos, Baptisterium, Nordwestseite 1846

Fig. 64. Dura-Europos, Baptisterium, Frauen am Grabe 1847

Fig. 65. Dura-Europos, Baptisterium. – Rom, Coemeterium Maius 1848

Fig. 66. Dura-Europos/New Haven, Baptisterium, Grab Christi. – Jerusalem, „Tomb of the Grapes" 1849

Fig. 67. Dura-Europos/New Haven, Baptisterium (Ostwand). – Gefäßvergleiche 1850

Fig. 68. Neapel, Baptisterium San Giovanni in fonte 1851

Fig. 69. Neapel, Baptisterium San Giovanni in fonte 1852

Fig. 70. Neapel, Baptisterium San Giovanni in fonte 1853

Fig. 71. Dura-Europos (Baptisterium) und Neapel (San Giovanni in fonte) 1854

Fig. 72. Mosaic from Bir Ftouha basilica 1855

Fig. 73. Plan of Bir Ftouha basilica 1855

Table of Contents

Fig. 74. Baptistery of Qal'at Sem'an 1856

Fig. 75. Ciborium at Djemila 1857

Fig. 76. Tigzert Baptismal font 1858

Fig. 77. Timgad Baptismal font 1859

Fig. 78. Cresconius mosaic from Tabarka 1860

Fig. 79. Uppenna Baptismal font 1861

Fig. 80. Jucundus baptismal font at Sbeitla 1862

Fig. 81. Sidi Jdidi II 1863

Fig. 82. Taufschale 1864

Fig. 83. Barcelona 1865

Fig. 84. San Pédro de Alcantara 1866

Fig. 85. Las Vegas de Padraza 1867

Fig. 86. Casa Herrera 1868

Fig. 87. Sbeitla 1869

Fig. 88. Henchir el-Faouar 1870

Fig. 89. Bulla Regia 1871

Fig. 90. Nativity and Baptism of Christ, and Raising of the Dead 1872

Fig. 91. Baptism of Pharaoh (Philip Arrhiados) 1873

Fig. 92. Jonah, Orans, Philosopher/Teacher, Good Shepherd and Baptism of Christ 1874

Fig. 93. Baptism of Christ – Ravenna 1875

Fig. 94. Baptism of Christ – Ravenna 1876

Fig. 95. Baptism of Christ with water flowing vertically 1877

Fig. 96. Detail from Fig. 90 1878

Fig. 97. Abercius Monument 1879

Fig. 98. Abercius Monument 1880

Fig. 99. Abercius Monument 1881

Fig. 100. Faustina Augusta (Iunior) 1882

Fig. 101. Iunoni Reginae 1882

Fig. 102. Faustina Augusta (Iunior) 1883

Fig. 103. Matri Magnae 1883

Fig. 104. Abercius Monument fragments 1884

Fig. 105. Group photo from the Norwegian Institute in Rome, Italy,
September 2008 1885

Fig. 106. Group photo from Metochi on Lesbos, Greece,
September 2009 1886

Abbreviations *1887*

1. Abbreviations of Biblical Books et cetera 1887

2. Abbreviations of Periodicals and Series 1887

3. Abbreviations not available in JBL or TRE 1887

List of Technical Terms *1889*

Indexes *1893*

Index of Modern Authors 1893

Index of Subjects 1921

Index of Passages 1961

Editors and Contributors *2019*

Introduction
Einführung

Preface

The aim of this preface is merely to inform the readers about the circumstances leading to the launching of the project "Ablution, Initiation and Baptism in Antiquity", to give an account of the development of the work, and to express the editors' gratitude to everyone involved in the process of bringing it to a fruitful end. An introduction to the volumes is provided by Christoph Markschies.

In connection with a lecture on baptism in the Pauline letters by David Hellholm at the University of Kiel in 2002 the late Professor Wiard Popkes asked Hellholm for the paper with the intent of including it in a planned anthology on baptism. In a telephone conversation right before Christmas 2006 Popkes told Hellholm that due to severe illness he was not able to carry out his plans, and he asked Hellholm to take on the responsibility for the project, without, however, disclosing in detail what kind of preparations had been made. To our deep regret and sorrow Wiard Popkes passed away only a few weeks later.

Hellholm promised to take over the project, not knowing the consequences of his commitment. In order to be able to realize the plan, he invited first a former doctoral student of his, Tor Vegge at the University of Agder (Kristiansand), and then a colleague from the University of Tromsø (later at the University of Oslo), Øyvind Norderval, to be partners in an Organizing Committee. In order to broaden the committee, two more colleagues were invited, Lars Hartman from the University of Uppsala and Gunnar af Hällström from Åbo Akademi University (Åbo/Turku).

The committee decided first that the project should in scope be *international* with participants from Australia, the USA, and several European countries; it should also be *interdisciplinary* with Historians of Religion, Classicists, Egyptologists, Biblical and Patristic scholars as well as Art Historians and Archaeologists; it should further be *interdenominational* with among others Orthodox, Catholic and Protestant scholars.

Due to the kind invitations of the Directors of the Norwegian Institute in Rome, Turid Karlsen Seim, and of the Finnish Institute also in Rome, Kai Sandberg, ca. 35 participants met at the beginning of September 2008 in a first symposium at which each participant presented a synopsis indicating what she/he was going to work on until the second and final symposium in September 2009 at the Study Center of the University of Agder, Metochi (Lesbos), under the hospitality of the local office manager Kari Grødum.

Prior to the meeting at Metochi the participants had been asked to send out their papers in advance. These were then discussed in four groups during five days, and each day the discussions were summarized in plenary reports. At the end of the conference the contributors were asked to rework their papers in light of the critical discussions, assessments and suggestions at Metochi. During that meeting suggestions were made to include still more texts and topics and invite further scholars to be involved in the process by writing additional contributions to be incorporated in the final proceedings of the symposium. We are much obliged to these colleagues for their willingness to take on these tasks at a very late stage of the project.

When this project was conceived, the organizers were unaware of the imminent publication of the important volume on baptism authored by Everett Ferguson, *Baptism in the Early Church: History, Theology, and Liturgy in the First Five Centuries*, Grand Rapids, Mich.: Eerdmans 2009. This magisterial work of more than 900 pp. written by a single author is a remarkable achievement, though not to be regarded as a competitive but rather as a complementary opus to our three volume work written by 58 specialists from different countries, disciplines and denominations. A work of this kind is to our knowledge not to be found anywhere in the scholarly world.

During both conferences, excursions were organized: In Rome to the Baptistery of San Giovanni in Laterano under the guidance of Olof Brandt (Rome) and to the Museo Pio Cristiano at the Vatican arranged by Diane Apostolos-Cappadona and under the guidance of the Director Dr. Umberto Utro. Dr. Antonio Paolucci of the Direzione dei musei has graciously given permission to publish photographs taken by Diane Apostolos-Cappadona, Margaret M. Mitchell and Christer Hellholm in the museum on that occasion. During the meeting at Metochi, excursions took place to the local Orthodox Church in Agiassos, where we witnessed a baptismal service, to the monastery Limónos, where Abbot Nikodemos provided the opportunity to see the recently discovered manuscript Μονὴ Λείμωνος ed. by among others Rudolf Brändle, and finally to Pergamon (Turkey), an excursion arranged by Dietrich-Alex Koch, where a visit was paid to the Red Hall under the guidance of Dr. Martin Bachmann of the Deutsches Archäologisches Institut in Istanbul. The participants were also given the opportunity to visit the Asclepieion on site. To all these gracious persons we express our sincere gratitude.

In addition to thanking committee members and participants for their suggestions we want to express our gratitude to the following colleagues, who recommended scholars to be invited to take part in this undertaking: Professors Amy-Jill Levine (Vanderbilt), Friedrich Avemarie (Marburg), Joseph Verheyden (Leuven), and Stig Frøyshov (Oslo).

In spite of the generous support by our sponsors, most expenses were to a large extent self-financed by the participants. This fact, in addition to the enthusiasm shown at the conferences and in the production and finalizing of the contributions, has been a source of encouragement and satisfaction for the Organizing Committee as well as for the editors of these volumes.

In connection with the publishing process we have experienced great help and support from among others Vemund Blomkvist, Otmar Hesse, Dietrich-Alex Koch, Berit Hellholm and above all from Michael Lattke, who has read all articles with his sharp eye for formal details and saved us from numerous inadvertencies and errors.

Thanks are also due to the institutions which by means of substantial financial support made the two symposia possible: the Faculty of Theology at the University of Oslo (Norway), the Faculty of Humanities and Education at the University of Agder (Kristiansand, Norway), and to the Diocese of Karlstad (The Church of Sweden).

Furthermore, we want to express our heartfelt gratitude to the Norwegian Research Council, the Faculty of Theology at the University of Oslo and the Faculty of Humanities and Education at the University of Agder for making the publication possible by covering most of the cost for layout and typesetting of the entire work, and compilation of the indices, all of which was done by Christer Hellholm. Thanks are also due to the publishing company Walter de Gruyter and its representatives, initially Carsten Burfeind and presently Dr. Albrecht Döhnert, as well as to the editorial board of the series BZNW for accepting the volumes for publication in this prestigious series.

The volumes are dedicated to the memory of the late Wiard Popkes.

Hammarö • Kristiansand • Oslo • Karlstad 2011-05-02

David Hellholm • Tor Vegge • Øyvind Norderval • Christer Hellholm

Einführung

Christoph Markschies

Die hier vorgelegten einführenden Bemerkungen gehen auf das abschließende Votum zur ersten Autorentagung in Rom zurück. Sie sind in zwei Abschnitte geteilt und stellen zunächst in einem *ersten Abschnitt* zusammen, was wir – nicht zuletzt dank der beiden Autorentagungen und der Arbeit an der hier vorgelegten Publikation – über die Geschichte der christlichen Taufe samt ihrer Vorgeschichte und deren unmittelbarer Wirkung wissen. Daran schließt sich ein *zweiter Abschnitt* an, der die offenen Fragen und Probleme sowie Anregungen für die künftige Weiterarbeit markiert. Eine solche Zweiteilung folgt einem in der französischen Geschichtswissenschaft des zwanzigsten Jahrhunderts etablierten Verfahren, Kenntnisse und Probleme methodisch möglichst streng voneinander zu unterscheiden[1].

1. Was wir wissen

1.1. Eine Darstellung der Geschichte der christlichen Taufe in Kaiserzeit und Spätantike, ihrer (möglichen) jüdischen Vorgeschichte und ihrer paganen Kontexte (bzw. Vorbilder) erfordert zunächst eine präzise Methodik wie Terminologie des religionsgeschichtlichen Vergleichs. Außerdem sind religionswissenschaftliche Vorfragen zu klären, die (*möglichst allen gemeinsame*) Definitionen zentraler Begriffe wie beispielsweise ‚Ritus' bzw. ‚Initiationsritus', ‚Magie' oder ‚Mythos' voraussetzen. Erst dann lassen sich solche wichtigen Vorfragen beantworten: Was verbindet Taufe mit bzw. was unterscheidet Taufe von anderen Initiationsriten? Welche Rolle spielt der Einzelne, der getauft wird, welche Rolle die konkrete Gemeinde, in die er hineingetauft wird? Was grenzt die Taufe als rituelle Handlung genau von Magie ab, wenn Taufe eine Versiegelung des Lebens vor lebensbedrohlichen Gefahren impliziert, welchen Stellenwert hat Mythos in dieser rituellen Handlung, wie wirkt sie auf Individuen, Gruppen, eine Kultur, wie kann man die Mehrdeutigkeit ihrer Symbolwelten, wie die symbolische Reserve (den jeweils nicht ausgeschöpften symbolischen Mehrwert) beschreiben? Deswegen wird die vorliegende Publikation mit einem entsprechenden Beitrag von

---

1 Seitenangaben im Haupttext, die durch „S." eingeleitet werden, und Hinweise auf Aufsätze in den Fußnoten, die nicht im Literaturverzeichnis aufgelöst sind, beziehen sich auf die vorliegende Publikation.

Anders Klostergaard Petersen unter dem Titel „Rituals of Purification, Rituals of Initiation. Phenomenological, Taxonomical and Culturally Evolutionary Reflections" eröffnet (S. 3–40). Ein vorzügliches Beispiel der verschiedenen Deutungsebenen ist die sogenannte „Abercius-Inschrift", die von *Margaret M. Mitchell* behandelte früheste datierbare antike christliche Inschrift (s.u. S. 1741–1780) mit ihrer Formulierung: λαὸν δ'εῖδον ἐκεῖ (sc. in Rom) λαμπρὰν σφραγεῖδαν ἔχοντα (Z. 9; s.u. S. 1746), die in der Antike wie Moderne auf die Taufe bezogen werden konnte, aber nicht musste: Es lässt sich eine tabellarische Zusammenstellung möglicher Bedeutungen geben (S. 1750–1757) und damit über die „doppelte Identität" des Abercius spekulieren (S. 1759). Am nämlichen Begriff σφραγίς kann man sich zudem klarmachen (wie *Karl Olav Sandnes* zeigt: S. 1439–1479), dass ein und dieselbe Metapher in unterschiedlichen Texten sehr unterschiedlich verwendet wird und damit höchst unterschiedliche Sinnwelten erschließt: Schlichte Identifikationen in der Art des Satzes „Das Siegel ist das Wasser" (Hermas, *Sim* IX 16,4 = 93,4: S. 1448[2]) und die in Quellen aus Syrien belegte „Versiegelung" in Gestalt einer Salbung mit Öl (*const. App.* III 16[3]) sind nur über den gemeinsamen Begriff „Siegel" verbunden; im liturgischen Vollzug dagegen werden seit der Spätantike diverse Rituale in paulinischer Tradition als „Versiegelung" angesprochen und ausdifferenziert (vgl. II Kor 1,21f.)[4]. Blickt man zudem auf den paganen Kontext, so verlängert sich die Liste möglicher Bedeutungen der antiken Begrifflichkeit, dazu kommen noch, wie beispielsweise *Gregor Wurst* an manichäischen Texten zeigt, die Gnostiker (oder, wenn man den Manichäismus davon noch einmal abheben will, neben den christlichen Gnostikern diese spätantike synkretistische Religion)[5]. Daneben tritt gegenwärtige Sprachpraxis wissenschaftlicher Beschäftigung mit der christlichen Taufe wie mit ihren potentiellen Vor- und Nebengeschichten, in der das Begriffsfeld ebenfalls verwendet wird: So wird im Blick auf die sogenannte „Proselytentaufe" des Judentums, die mit *Dieter Sänger* besser als „Proselytentauchbad" bezeichnet wird (S. 291–334), trotz aller Unklarheiten über das Alter des Rituals und aller Debatten über die Interpretation rabbinischer Texte auf der Ebene der neuzeitlichen Beschreibung der Vorgänge von „Versiegelung" gesprochen (S. 324). „Siegel" ist ein klassischer „Umbrella-Term" (*Sandnes*).

---

2   Vgl. auch V. BLOMKVIST, "The Teaching on Baptism in the Shepherd of Hermas", 849–870.

3   Zu dieser Hypothese von Erik Peterson vgl. allerdings kritisch A. LINDEMANN, "Zur frühchristlichen Taufpraxis", 776.

4   Zur Taufe als „Siegel" vgl. K. O. SANDNES, "Seal and Baptism in Early Christianity", 1439–1479; zu den späteren Entwicklungen vgl. CHR. STRECKER, "Taufrituale im frühen Christentum und in der Alten Kirche", 1386–1402.

5   G. WURST, "Initiationsriten im Manichäismus", 148 mit Berufung auf *Bema-Psalm* 227, 11,1–4 (Wurst) = *Psb.* II 22,11–15; vgl. auch ebd. 151.

1.2. Für die seit den Zeiten der Religionsgeschichtlichen Schule beliebte Methode religionswissenschaftlicher Komparatistik (beispielsweise im Rahmen einer methodologisch nicht unproblematischen, aber mindestens anregenden religionsphänomenologischen Typisierung) müssen mögliche antike Vergleichsphänomene zunächst präzise beschrieben werden (beispielsweise in Form der berühmten „dichten Beschreibung"). In vorliegender Publikation wird (von *Anders Klostergaard Petersen*) vorgeschlagen, die Taufe als Ritual der Reinigung und Initiation im Zusammenhang des von *Jonathan Z. Smith* so bezeichneten „utopian type of religion" (S. 19 u. 35) zu beschreiben; andere Optionen im Rahmen älterer und neuerer Disziplinen und Paradigmen nennt *Oda Wischmeyer* (S. 735). *Fritz Graf* behandelt Verbindungen zwischen antiken Mysterienkulten und der christlichen Taufe, die keineswegs nur von neuzeitlichen Religionswissenschaftlern, sondern bereits von antiken Kritikern des Christentums und den Apologeten, die sie zu widerlegen suchten, beobachtet wurden (S. 101–118; zu Justin vgl. S. 103–105, aber auch S. 783–794). Freilich gibt es keine der Wassertaufe wirklich vergleichbare Initiations- und Purifikationshandlung in diesen paganen antiken Kulten (S. 101f. u. 110–114). Die Wasserriten der ägyptischen Religion, die im vorliegenden Werk von *Jan Assmann* und *Andrea Kucharek* behandelt werden (S. 43–68), eignen sich, wenn sie so präzise analysiert werden, nur bedingt für einen Vergleich, weil hier zwar Reinigung mit einem Lebenswasser erfolgt und Lebenskraft restituiert wird (beziehungsweise Verjüngung ausgelöst wird), aber ein zyklisches Zeitmodell vorausgesetzt und damit gerade keine Einheitlichkeit intendiert ist. Der von *Alan Gardiner* geprägte Ausdruck „Baptism of Pharaoh" (S. 54–64) ist daher ebenso missverständlich wie die Rede von einer „mandäischen Taufzeremonie" im Blick auf das *maṣbūtā*[6]. Neben den bekannten paganen Vergleichsphänomenen, in denen ein Eid oder sonstige Verpflichtung den Wandel von Lebensformen, sittlichen Maßstäben und einen Wechsel der sozialen Gruppe bzw. Gemeinschaft zur Folge hat – beispielsweise die Eingliederung in die römische Armee durch den Fahneneid (*sacramentum*; vgl. Tert., cor. 11[7]) oder die verschiedenen *symbola* –, ist auch an die Veränderungen zu denken, die die verschiedenen Formen des Unterrichts in der Antike auslösen. Die wiederholten Waschungen im Judentum, bes. in den Qumranschriften sowie den archäologischen Befunden sind von *Antje Labahn* (S. 157–219) und *Seán Freyne* (S. 221–253) behandelt worden.

1.3. Neben Antworten auf die religionsgeschichtlichen und religionswissenschaftlichen Fragen ist eine möglichst präzise Rekonstruktion der Geschichte der christlichen Taufe notwendig: Zwei Grunddaten stehen zu Beginn einer solchen Geschichte der Taufe unverrückbar fest: Jesus wurde selbst getauft und

---

6   Vgl. A. HULTGÅRD, "The Mandean Water Ritual in Late Antiquity", 69f.
7   Dazu vgl. E.-M. BECKER, "Taufe bei Marcion – eine Spurensuche", 883 und SANDNES, "Seal and Baptism in Early Christianity", 1443.

wurde durch Johannes den Täufer am Jordan getauft, wie *Hans Dieter Betz* ungeachtet aller sorgfältigen Bemerkungen zu den historiographischen Problemen noch einmal klar hervorhebt (S. 377–396). Irgendwann im ersten Jahrhundert wurde diese Form eines Wasserritus (übrigens durchaus mit der Johannes eigenen Sinndeutung der Sündenvergebung) in vielen Gemeinden so selbstverständlich als Initiationsritus in das Christentum hinein angesehen, dass der Apostel Paulus diese Tatsache ohne Diskussion voraussetzt. Er argumentiert nicht für die Notwendigkeit der Taufe, sondern setzt gegen Mißbräuche und Mißdeutungen autoritativ seine eigene Interpretation. Man kann mit *Hans Dieter Betz* zwischen der vollkommen unstrittigen, ja selbstverständlichen „performance" des Rituals und umstrittener „meaning" unterscheiden[8]. Wie freilich dieser Prozess der Verselbständigung (und Ritualisierung) der Taufe in so erstaunlich kurzer Zeit genau ablief und wieso er so stattfand, bleibt wohl auch mangels Quellen im Dunkel und ist ein Zeichen der ungeheuer beschleunigten hochdynamischen Entwicklung des frühen Christentums, auf die mein verstorbener neutestamentlicher Lehrer Martin Hengel gern aufmerksam gemacht hat. Die von *David Hellholm* behandelten vorgeformten Tauftraditionen, die in den Paulusbriefen benutzt werden (S. 415–?), sind ebenso wie die von *Jens Schröter* untersuchte Apostelgeschichte (S. 557–586) lediglich ein sprechendes Zeichen dieser Entwicklung, aber erklären sie kaum.

1.4. Die Geschichte der christlichen Taufe beginnt bei der Taufe des Juden Jesus durch den jüdischen Frommen Johannes, genannt „der Täufer" (ὁ βαπτιστής). Allerdings ist diese Figur von zentraler Bedeutung für die Geschichte der christlichen Taufe. Selbstverständlich muss – wie *Clare K. Rothschild* zeigt (S. 255–290) – die christliche wie jüdische Präsentation des Täufers und seiner Botschaft vom „historischen Täufer" unterschieden werden, womit sich freilich all' die methodischen und inhaltlichen Probleme der Debatten um den historischen Jesus erneut einstellen. Sorgfältige Exegese der neutestamentlichen Perikopen erklärt beispielsweise, warum in kaiserzeitlichen Darstellungen der Taufe Jesu auf den Reliefs von Sarkophagen und in den Katakomben gelegentlich die Taube fehlt, es müssen nur ὡσεὶ περιστεράν (Mt 3,16)[9] und σωματικῷ εἴδει ὡς περιστεράν (Lk 3,22) und die (alt-)lateinischen Versionen verglichen werden. Wieso Josephus zwar vom taufenden Handeln des Täufers berichtet, aber das Wortfeld βαπτίζειν κτλ. gar nicht erklärt, so, als ob es sich um einen Eigennamen (in der Art von: „Jesus, der [frisch] Gestrichene"[10]) handelt, wissen wir nicht. Ähnlich schwierig

---

8   O. Wischmeyer, „Hermeneutische Aspekte der Taufe im Neuen Testament", 736f.
9   Vgl. in der Rezension von A. Jülicher zu Mt 3,16 *sicut columbam*, 14.
10 G. Zuntz, „Ein Heide las das Markusevangelium. Ein Vortrag", 205–222, insbesondere 205: Zuntz versucht Übersetzungen von Mk 1,1 durch einen unkundigen kaiserzeitlichen Heiden nachzuempfinden „Die gute Botschaft von Jesus-Salbe" „Jesus, dem Bemalten oder Geschminkten".

ist die Suche nach der Traditionsgrundlage der Episode über Apollos und die Johannesjünger in Ephesus[11].

1.5. Auch die Frage einer weiteren jüdischen Parallele zur Johannestaufe ist nicht einfach zu beantworten: Dass es zur Zeit Jesu eine regelrechte „Proselytentaufe" gab (wie beispielsweise Joachim Jeremias behauptete[12]), bleibt aufgrund der spärlichen Textzeugnisse unsicher. Um die einschlägigen paulinischen Texte zu verstehen, müssen die (unter Umständen nur schwer abgrenzbaren) vorpaulinischen Traditionen separat interpretiert, dann aber auch in ihren spezifischen paulinischen Kontexten gelesen werden – dies geschieht hier, wie gesagt, bei *David Hellholm* (S. 415–?). Es geht dabei um die sogenannte Namensformel (εἰς τὸ ὄνομα), die Bekleidungsformel (Χριστὸν ἐνεδύσασθε) und die Identifikationsformel (εἰς τὸν θάνατον αὐτοῦ ἐβαπτίσθημεν); *Lars Hartman* hat diese unterschiedlichen Formeln übersichtlich geordnet (S. 397–413). Man kann sich diese Formeln als Teil eines Taufgottesdienstes vorstellen; ob sie das wirklich waren, bleibt freilich offen. Das Verhältnis von Geist- und Wassertaufe wird in den verschiedenen neutestamentlichen Texten sehr unterschiedlich bestimmt; die klassischen Alternativen einer sakramentalen oder nichtsakramentalen Deutung des Johannesevangeliums sind überwunden zugunsten einer präzisen Nachzeichnung der diversen Anspielungen auf Taufe und Eucharistie und literaturwissenschaftlich fundierten Überlegungen zur antiken Leserschaft und ihren Erfahrungen mit Lustration und ähnlichen Spenderiten (so *Turid Karlsen Seim*, S. 717–734). Wie bei der sogenannten Abercius-Inschrift in der Interpretation von *Margaret M. Mitchell* (s.o. u. unten S. 1775f.) muss mit bewusster Polyvalenz der Texte gerechnet werden, die durch unterschiedlichste Leserschaften eher noch verstärkt wird. In den Deuteropaulinen wird die Taufe im Rahmen anamnetischer und exhortativer Passagen eingesetzt, die auch an damalige moralphilosophische Unterrichtssituationen und entsprechende Texte (z.B. Arrians Werke über Epiktet) erinnert (so *Tor Vegge*, S. 516f.).

1.6. Schon sehr früh, spätestens aber am Anfang des zweiten Jahrhunderts, zeigen erste Kirchenordnungstexte wie die *Didache*, dass Taufe vor aller theologischen Reflexion gebildete *liturgische Praxis* konkreter christlicher Gemeinden ist, die in einer sich zur Reichsreligion globalisierenden Lokalreligion mit Anspruch auf Geltung geordnet werden muss, wie *Andreas Lindemann* in seinen Beobachtungen zur Taufpraxis dokumentiert (S. 767–816). Dabei spielt mindestens im zweiten Jahrhundert „lebendiges", d.i. fließendes Wasser (*Did* 7,1–3; vgl. aaO.

---

11 M. Wolter, „Apollos und die ephesinischen Johannesjünger", 49–73 [≈ "Apollos und die Johannesjünger von Ephesus (Apg 18,24–19,7)", 402–426].

12 Nachweise und Diskussion bei D. Sänger, „Ist er heraufgestiegen, gilt er in jeder Hinsicht als ein Israelit (bYev 47b)", 294ff.

S. 776f. und die sogenannte *Traditio Apostolica* 21,2)[13] eine zentrale Rolle, ist aber nicht unabdingbare Voraussetzung. Der Täufling bereitet sich durch Akte der Reinigung wie beispielsweise das Fasten vor; die allgemeinen Entwicklungen des christlichen Amtes in der Antike spiegeln sich selbstverständlich auch in den Bestimmungen über Taufvorbereitung und Taufakt (beispielsweise durch die Zuweisung bestimmter liturgischer Funktionen an Frauen in der sogenannten „Syrischen Didaskalie", aber deren Ausgrenzung aus dem taufenden Akt selbst, der männlichen Bischöfen vorbehalten ist). Die exakte Reihenfolge von vorbereitenden Katechesen, Exorzismen, Salbungen und postbaptismaler Anwendung dieser Akte differiert lokal erheblich und entwickelt sich nach den allgemeinen liturgiewissenschaftlichen Gesetzen der Ausdifferenzierung „from freedom to formula" (dazu *Christian Strecker*, S. 1383–1402). Ein besonderes Problem in der Gruppe dieser Kirchenordnungen ist die sogenannte *Traditio Apostolica* (= *TA*; einschlägige Texte in englischer Übersetzung unten bei *Anders Ekenberg* S. 1035–1044), weil derzeit sehr umstritten ist, welche Teile des umfangreichen Materials auf welche Zeit und welche liturgische Landschaft zurückgehen. *Anders Ekenberg* votiert dafür, zwar den Archetyp der Schrift in das römische Syrien zu lozieren (S. 1018), aber den in den meisten Versionen beschriebenen Initiationsakt als eine Widerspiegelung von liturgischer Realität der ersten Hälfte des dritten Jahrhunderts „irgendwo im Westen" zu verstehen (gegen Bradshaw und andere: S. 1022 mit Anm. 40 sowie S. 1025–1027); Voraussetzungen (z.B. im Blick auf den Beruf der Taufbewerber) und Ablauf der Taufe mit Exorzismen und Ölungen werden in einer zu rekonstruierenden Grundform beschrieben (*TA* §§ 15–21 Botte), die entsteht, wenn man bestimmte Passagen als spätere Ergänzungen ausscheidet (wie z.B. das dreijährige Katechumenat: § 17,1f.). Ob die sogenannten *Interrogationes de fide* zu solchen Ergänzungen gehören oder nicht, wäre noch einmal zu diskutieren[14].

1.7. Die einzelnen Erwähnungen der Taufe bei den christlichen Theologen des zweiten und dritten Jahrhunderts differieren sehr nach Gattung und Zielrichtung der unterschiedlichen Schriften. Dadurch entsteht eine reiche Fülle von „Tauftheologien" oder Ansätzen von Tauftheologien, die jeweils auch sehr unterschiedliche Elemente aus den neutestamentlichen Schriften aufgreifen. Im „*Hirt des Hermas*", den *Vemund Blomkvist* behandelt (S. 849–870), ist erkennbar, wie

---

13 Vgl. zu dieser komplizierten Schrift hier A. Ekenberg, „Initiation in the *Apostolic Tradition*", 1011–1050. Wenn man ungeachtet der Abbildungen aufgrund der Abmessungen des sogenannten „Taufbeckens" den Raum in Dura Europos nicht als Baptisterium deutet, sondern mit einer Taufe im nahegelegenen *fließenden Wasser* des Euphrat rechnet, der bis auf den heutigen Tag majestätisch an der (Ruine der) Stadt vorbeifließt, würde sich dies auch zu anderen Nachrichten über die Taufpraxis fügen (vgl. aber D. Korol in Verbindung mit J. Rieckesmann, „Neues zu den Darstellungen im Baptisterium von Dura-Europos", 1609–1670).

14 Vgl. dazu W. Kinzig, „'… natum et passum etc.' Zur Geschichte der Tauffragen in der lateinischen Kirche bis Luther", 75–184.

zentral Taufe als Fundament der Kirche (*Vis* III 3,3–5) bereits ist, „absolut notwendig für das Heil", aber als die *„eine* Taufe zur Vergebung der Sünden" (wie es später im Bekenntnis des Reichskonzils von Konstantinopel 381 n.Chr. heißt) nicht wiederholbar. *Ignatius von Antiochien* dagegen greift, wie *Dietrich-Alex Koch* zeigt (S. 817–848), auf neutestamentliche Texte zurück (*IgnSm* 1,1 z.B. auf Mt 3,15, aber auch auf vorpaulinische Überlieferung: S. 819) und thematisiert Taufe im Rahmen seiner spezifischen theologischen Akzente (*IgnSm* 8,2: Taufe ist ein Symbol der Einheit, daher soll der Bischof taufen). Es bleiben viele Unklarheiten, beispielsweise die offene Frage, warum nach *IgnEph* 18,2 Jesu Leiden das Wasser (des Jordans? alle Wasser?: dazu *Koch*, aaO. S. 824f.) reinigt. Der Mitte des zweiten Jahrhunderts in Rom als öffentlicher Lehrer des Christentums auf dem Viminal wirkende Apologet *Justin der Märtyrer* differiert insofern von den meisten anderen sogenannten Apologeten, als er ausführlich den Ablauf der Taufe erklärt und – angesichts bekannter Vorwürfe gegen christliche Versammlungen – für deren Harmlosigkeit argumentiert. Er verwendet den auch paganen Lesern verständlichen Terminus φωτισμός (*1 Apol.* 61,12). Taufe vermittelt nach Justin nicht nur (in strenger Aufnahme von biblischen, vor allem neutestamentlichen Theologumena) Sündenvergebung und Wiedergeburt, sondern macht aus den Getauften auch (ganz im Sinne einer griechischen philosophischen Erziehung) „Kinder der freien Entscheidung und Einsicht" (τέκνα ... προαιρέσεως καὶ ἐπιστήμης). Wieder liegt Polysemie vor. Doppelt kodiert sind auch die Passagen über die Taufe bei *Clemens Alexandrinus*, dessen von *Henny Fiskå Hägg* behandelte Texte deutlich vor neutestamentlichem Hintergrund formuliert sind (Adoption als Söhne Gottes, Erleuchtung, Unsterblichmachung: S. 973–987), zugleich aber auch die pagane, näher platonisierend zugespitzte Mysterienterminologie aufgreifen (so schon Christoph Riedweg[15]): Der Begriff φωτισμός erinnert an den Hebräerbrief (vgl. Hebr 6,4; dazu *Samuel Byrskog*, S. 587–604), aber zugleich auch an die Mysterienkulte (S. 983–985). Selbstverständlich finden sich aber natürlich auch allerlei Spuren der praktischen Arbeit des Autors in der Vorbereitung von Taufbewerbern in den Werken des Alexandriners (S. 974–976). Der zeitweilig ebenfalls in Alexandria lehrende *Origenes* („Horusspross") bietet in seiner „Grundlagenschrift" (Περὶ ἀρχῶν/*De principiis*) kein Taufkapitel, obwohl er laut Eusebius im katechetischen Unterricht der Metropole tätig war – vielleicht gibt es deswegen keine eigenen Schriften über Taufe (im Unterschied etwa zu Tertullianus), weil Origenes (ebenfalls laut Eusebius) erst in Caesarea, d.h. ab den vierziger Jahren des dritten Jahrhunderts, seine Predigten und Vorlesungen mitzustenographieren erlaubte[16]. Vielleicht hielt er die Taufe aber auch für theologisch nicht problematisch; jedenfalls muss bedacht werden, dass sie auch in

---

15 CHR. RIEDWEG, *Mysterienterminologie bei Platon, Philon und Klemens von Alexandrien*.
16 CHR. MARKSCHIES, „"... für die Gemeinde im Grossen und Ganzen nicht geeignet ..."? Erwägungen zu Absicht und Wirkung der Predigten des Origenes", 39–68 [= IDEM., *Origenes und sein Erbe. Gesammelte Studien*, 35–62].

den ältesten *regula fidei*-Formulierungen nicht erwähnt wird. Die Taufe wird im Rahmen seiner platonisierenden Bibeltheologie in ein platonisches Zweiwelten-Schema eingefügt, es gibt eine unsichtbare, nur noetische Taufe Christi und die Wassertaufe; allerdings bemüht sich Origenes mit durchaus antignostischer Spitze, beides nicht auseinanderfallen zu lassen (vgl. dazu den Beitrag von *Gunnar af Hällström*, S. 989–1009, besonders S. 991f.). Der kirchliche Bibeltheologe Origenes orientiert sich bei seiner biblisch grundierten Tauftheologie selbstverständlich auch an alttestamentlichen Texten, vor allem an der Perikope vom Durchzug des Gottesvolkes durch das Schilfmeer (Ex 14: S. 992f.) und durch den Fluss Jordan (Jos 3: S. 994f.). Im langen dritten Jahrhundert ist auch *Caecilius Cyprianus, qui et Thascius* wie Tertullianus ein Beispiel für die lokale Kontextualisierung der mehrheitskirchlichen Tauftheologie und für die Rekonstruktion lokaler liturgischer Praxis, aber auch für eine eigenständige theologische Tradition von lokalen Christentümern wie dem nordafrikanischen (zu Tertullian vgl. *Øyvind Norderval*: S. 947–972; zu Cyprian vgl. *Enno Edzard Popkes*: S. 1051–1070). Das wird an seiner Position im sogenannten „Ketzertaufstreit" deutlich, aber auch in anderen tauftheologischen Passagen seiner Schriften: Das Lebenswasser der Taufe wäscht die Sünde ab, es vermittelt himmlischen Geist und ist so die notwendige Lebenswende, eine „zweite Geburt" (*Don.* 5. 14f.), sie wird durch den Bischof oder von ihm legitimierte Presbyter vollzogen (*Ep.* 72,1). Im Kontext der großen reichsweiten Verfolgungen in der Jahrhundertmitte aktualisiert der Bischof von Karthago die neutestamentliche Bezeichnung der Passion Jesu als Taufe (Mk 10,38f./Lk 12,49f.); wer durch die irdische (Wasser-)Taufe nicht getauft werden konnte, wird durch die zweite, himmlische (Blut-)Taufe trotzdem (oder besser: gerade besonders) gerettet. Es ist mindestens wieder ein Zeichen der Polysemie von Formulierungen, wenn Clemens Alexandrinus unter der „zweiten Taufe" in seiner Predigt *Quis dives salvetur* etwas gänzlich anderes versteht und den Ausdruck rein metaphorisch für die Konversion eines Räubers und Mörders verwendet (*Hägg*, S. 980–982). Ein besonders spannendes Beispiel der Entwicklung christlicher Tauftheologie sind, wie *Jürgen Wehnert* nachzeichnet (S. 1071–1114), die Pseudoklementinen: Hier kann anhand des literarischen Wachstums einer Schriftengruppe nachvollzogen werden, wie sich aus wiederholbaren Reinigungsriten und einem einmaligen „Initiationsritus für bußfertige Heiden" (S. 1108) eine sakramental gedeutete Sündenvergebungstaufe entwickelt und sich eine geordnete Reihenfolge von Riten für diese Taufe etabliert. Umgekehrt kann man an den Nachrichten über die Taufe der sogenannten „Neuen Prophetie", also der in der reichskirchlichen Polemik „Montanismus" genannten, ursprünglich phrygischen prophetischen Bewegung sehen, dass geringfügige Abweichungen devianter Gruppen im Taufritual (nämlich Tätowierungen) im häresiologischen Diskurs zu grotesken Anwürfen führen (nämlich, Kannibalismus zu üben), so jedenfalls *William Tabbernee* (S. 917–945). Stark umstritten ist die Frage, ob die bei sethianischen Gnostikern geübte Taufe Berührungspunkte zur christlichen Taufe verrät; wer wie *Birger A. Pearson* in der Verlängerung einschlägiger Tendenzen des zwanzigsten Jahrhunderts den sogenannten Sethianismus für eine ursprünglich nichtchristliche Gnosis hält, wird diese Frage verneinen (S. 119–143)[17]; mindestens für das Ritual könnte dann auch gelten, was *Einar Thomassen* im Blick auf die valentinianische Gnosis formuliert: „the similarity with 'Orthodox' practise" (S. 897). Das schließt Polemik gegen die mehrheitskirchliche Sakramententheologie und -praxis in einzelnen gnostischen Texten wie dem jüngst partiell publizierten Judasevangelium aus dem Codex Tchacos nicht aus (*Birger A. Pearson*, S. 138f.).

1.8. Die unterschiedlichen Schriften aus christlichen und entchristlichten Sonder-Gruppen scheinen also nur auf den ersten Blick streng getrennt neben den mehrheitskirchlichen Texten aus diversen Gattungen zu stehen. Wie wenig dieses durch die antiken christlichen Häresiologen vermittelte und durch die Gnosisforschung des zwanzigsten Jahrhunderts teilweise kanonisierte Bild zutrifft, zeigt beispielsweise *Einar Thomassen* in seinem Beitrag. Er behandelt die einschlägigen mehrheitskirchlichen Referate über die sogenannte „valentinianische Gnosis" und ihre eigene Überlieferung von Traktaten (S. 895–915). Die in diesen Texten bezeugten liturgischen Formulare und Inschriften dokumentieren einen Ritus (oder mehrere Riten) und theologische Deutungen dieser Riten; das berühmte, stellenweise (z.B. dank Irenaeus, *haer*. I 21,3) berüchtigte „Brautgemach" ist kein eigener Ritus und schon gar kein eigenes Sakrament, sondern eine Bezeichnung für die ganze rituelle Handlung (ebenso die „Erlösung" [ἀπολύτρωσις]: S. 899). Wie in den mehrheitskirchlichen Tauftheologien werden Elemente biblischer Texte mit eigenen Akzentsetzungen verbunden, beispielsweise der Figur der Rückkehr des Geistes aus seiner verderblichen Verbindung mit der Materie in die himmlische Fülle. Wenn immer wieder betont wird, dass die Taufe Jesu den Charakter eines Modells für die übrigen Getauften hat, dann liegt eine ältere, eher adoptianistische Christologie dem zugrunde. Wenn die Taufe als „Brautgemach", d.h. als Akt der Verbindung mit einem persönlichen Schutzengel, gedeutet wird, dann bedient die valentinianische Tauftheologie (wie auch die Magie) populäre Erwartungen an einen numinosen Helfer im Alltag des Lebens. Möglicherweise gehört zu den mehrheitskirchlichen Nachwirkungen des valentinianischen Taufverständnisses auch die stark antidämonische Ausrichtung der Taufe, die die sogenannte *Traditio Apostolica* mit ihren mehrfachen Exorzismen für den Entstehungsort ihrer Grundschrift bzw. der Überarbeitung bezeugt, in der die Passagen über die Taufliturgie ein-

---

17 Eine gänzliche abweichende Sicht des Sethianismus hat der Verf. vorgelegt: MARKSCHIES, *Die Gnosis*, 95–101. Je stärker die unter dem Label „sethianische Gnosis" zusammengefassten Richtungen als Teil des antiken Christentums begriffen werden, desto deutlicher lässt sich unter den Schichten von mehrheitskirchlicher Polemik wie gnostischer Abgrenzung die Verwandtschaft basaler Rituale und gleichfalls grundlegender biblischer Theologumena thematisieren.

gefügt worden sind (Rom? Ägypten?). Haben die Valentinianer diese Details der Taufliturgie erfunden? Marcion und seine Anhänger haben, wie *Eve-Marie Becker* zeigt (S. 871–894), offenbar die Wassertaufe wie auch die übrige Mehrheitskirche praktiziert (so auch schon *Barbara Aland*: S. 872), aber man muss natürlich fragen, ob die spezifischen Akzente der Theologie Marcions diese gleiche Handlung nicht ganz anders kontextualisiert haben. Am Manichäismus kann man studieren, wie selbst unter den Bedingungen strikter Abgrenzung (nämlich der rationalistischen Argumentation gegen die Taufe im Kölner Mani-Codex [*CMC* p. 80–85)]und entsprechenden Ersatzritualen in den „Kephalaia des Lehrers") Elemente der mehrheitskirchlichen christlichen Tauftheologie verwendet werden können (p. 232,3–233,1), ein spiritualisiertes Taufverständnis rezipiert wird[18] und sogar eine (freilich in Gestalt und Zweck unklare) Ölsalbung in einigen christlichen Quellen bezeugt ist. Besonders rätselhaft sind die mandäischen Wasserrituale, weil gegenwärtig vollkommen unsicher geworden ist, wann sie in die Religion eingeführt worden sind, und die alte Vermutung Hans Lietzmanns, dass die mandäischen Ursprünge im Kreis von jüdischen Täufergruppen des Ostjordanlandes ein (sehr?) spätes Konstrukt darstellen, immer mehr Anhänger findet (so auch *Anders Hultgård*: S. 92–94[19]). Der ganze Komplex bedarf weiterer Forschung, vor allem aber sind zuverlässige Quelleneditionen und eine belastbare Chronologie wie Traditionsgeschichte nötig.

1.9. Man muss sich klarmachen, dass die mehrheitschristliche Initiation im Kontext eines „religiösen Marktplatzes", also im Kontext der Religionskonkurrenz in der globalisierten antiken Welt, stattfindet, in der beispielsweise durch reisende Kaufleute (Dura Europos, eventuell die sogenannte „Chronik von Arbela") der Aktionsradius bestimmter gesellschaftlicher Gruppen sehr hoch ist und es auch erhebliche soziale Mobilität gibt[20]. Wenn Johannes Chrysostomus bestreitet, dass die Taufe nur zur Sündenvergebung dient, und „zehn Gaben" – zehn gratis gewährte Geschenke – der Taufe aufzählt (*catech. bapt.* 2/4: vgl. dazu *Rudolf Brändle*, S. 1231–1250), dann ist dies Propaganda in der Konkurrenz einer Gesellschaft, in der es auch zu anderen Festen Gratisgeschenke gibt, zum Beispiel vom Kaiser, vom Magistrat usf. Die großen Taufliturgien, die seit dem vierten Jahrhundert bezeugt und einigermaßen rekonstruierbar sind, konkurrierten mit ihrem Einsatz von stimulierenden Transformationserfahrungen (Licht/Dunkelheit, Nacktheit/Bekleidung) mit den großen mystagogischen Zeremonien der Antike (Eleusis, aber auch die Mysterienreligionen), überboten sie aber, wenn in Konstantinopel tatsächlich dreitausend Menschen in einer Osternacht getauft

---

18 *Bema-Psalm* 227, 11,1–4 (Wurst) = *Psb.* II 22,11–15.

19 In der seinerzeit stark diskutierten Originalveröffentlichung: H. LIETZMANN, „Ein Beitrag zur Mandäerfrage", 596–608 [= IDEM., *Kleine Schriften Bd. I Schriften zur spätantiken Religionsgeschichte*, 124–140.

20 MARKSCHIES, *Das antike Christentum*, 23–31.

worden sein sollten (zur Massentaufe des Jahres 404 n.Chr.: S. 1234f. mit Anm. 32; vgl. für die Zahl Act 2,41), und machten das Heilige zunehmend für die Massen zugänglich.

1.10. Noch einmal stark verändert sich der Befund seit dem vierten Jahrhundert, also in reichskirchlicher Zeit. Eine zentrale Quelle für Palästina sind die (im Einzelnen sehr unterschiedlichen) „Katechetischen Homilien" des Bischofs *Cyrill von Jerusalem* und die „Mystagogischen Katechesen" eines *Pseudo-Cyrill* (Johannes von Jerusalem? um 380 n.Chr.?), die Parallelen zur *Traditio Apostolica* aufweisen; sie werden in dieser Publikation von *Juliette Day* behandelt (S. 1179–1204). Ein Vergleich der Informationen über Taufvorbereitung und Taufvollzug, die sich in den beiden Textcorpora befinden, zeigt, dass innerhalb weniger Jahre bzw. Jahrzehnte sich die Liturgie außerordentlich anreicherte. Die syrische Tradition spielt – schon aufgrund der besonderen literarischen Form der Hymnen *De Epiphania* des Ephraem – eine besondere Rolle, verwendet sehr eigenartige Bilder und Metaphern, die aber nicht in der Tradition Herders und anderer als „semitisch" hypostasiert und einem „hellenisierten" Denken gegenübergestellt werden dürfen. Das auffälligste Zeichen der Veränderung in der sogenannten „konstantinischen Wende" ist die Einfügung von deklaratorischen Taufbekenntnissen; ihr behaupteter vornizänischer Ursprung in Rom beruht auf einem Zirkelschluss mit der *Traditio Apostolica*, alle Belege stammen aus dem vierten Jahrhundert – freilich muss erklärt werden, warum vergleichsweise plötzlich dieser Brauch aufkommt und warum er sich so schnell verbreitet (so *Reinhart Staats*, S. 1551–?): *Augustinus* referiert in seinem Bericht über die spektakuläre Bekehrung und Taufe des Philosophen Marius Victorinus die stadtrömische Ansicht, es handle sich um einen alten Brauch (S. 1576); möglicherweise spielt auch die gestiegene rechtliche Bedeutung der Taufe in einer Zeit eine Rolle, in der die Kirche wie ihre Mitglieder immer mehr dezidierte Aufgaben im politischen und Rechts-System des spätantiken Reiches übernehmen. Es bleibt freilich bei der Polysemie, bei der Ambiguität von Formeln, Riten und theologischen Reflexionen: Der kluge Theologe Augustinus weiß nicht, ob Getaufte nach der Taufe noch Sünde im eigentlichen Sinne begehen können – er schwankt in seinen Texten und man kann das Schwanken auch nicht chronologisch als Entwicklung erklären (s. dazu *Reidar Aasgaard*, S. 1251–1253). Vereindeutigt worden ist seine Position erst in der frühen Neuzeit, als das Konzil von Trient für die eine Variante und die lutherischen Bekenntnisse für die andere votierten[21].

---

21 MARKSCHIES, „Taufe und Concupiscentia bei Augustinus", 92–108.

2. Was wir noch nicht wissen

2.1. Wir sahen, dass die ungeheuer rasche Entwicklung hin zu einer – mit Betz gesprochen – performativen Selbstverständlichkeit der Taufe ungeachtet aller interpretatorischen Varianzen, Differenzen und Dispute leichter zu konstatieren als zu erklären ist – es sei denn, man wolle die Tatsache, dass Jesus von Nazareth getauft wurde (obwohl er selbst gar nicht taufte), als den zentralen Grund dafür in Anschlag bringen, dass auch die Menschen, die ihm nachfolgen wollten, dieses für seinen Lebensweg charakteristische Ritual in nachösterlicher Zeit nachformten und dadurch neu schufen (*Michael Labahn*)[22]. Um hier weiterzukommen, empfiehlt sich wieder die mehrfach erwähnte Methode der dichten Beschreibung. Das meint in unserem Fall eine Aufmerksamkeit auf die leisen Textsignale, beispielsweise auf den sekundären Markusschluss und die Frage, ob in solchen in unseren Zusammenhängen eher übersehenen Texten etwas über die Rolle der Taufe in der christlichen Mission und Propaganda erkennbar ist (so *Kirsten Marie Hartvigsen* in ihrem Beitrag „Matthew 28:9–20 and Mark 16:9–20", unten S. 663–674).

2.2. Die Erforschung der Taufe in der hohen Kaiserzeit und der christlichen Spätantike ist als ein Teil der Erforschung des antiken Christentums charakterisiert durch die in langen Jahrzehnten nur ansatzweise überwundenen Einseitigkeiten und blinden Flecken in der Forschungsgeschichte. Während in vorliegender Publikation die oft zu konstatierende Vernachlässigung des sogenannten christlichen Orients vorbildlich vermieden wird (beispielsweise allein durch die terminologischen Beobachtungen zur Taufe in der syrischen Sprache und zu Texten Aphrahats von *Michael Lattke*: S. 1115–1138 oder durch den Beitrag zu Ephraem von *Serafim Seppälä*: S. 1139–1177), besteht noch Forschungsbedarf auf dem Gebiet des Kirchenrechts und der Liturgiegeschichte, die insbesondere im Bereich der protestantisch geprägten Erforschung des antiken Christentums, von großen Ausnahmen wie dem Berliner Kirchenhistoriker Hans Lietzmann einmal abgesehen, oft vernachlässigt wurde. So sind die wichtigen kirchenrechtlichen Fragen für die spätere Zeit der Spätantike, also beispielsweise die notorische Frage der Anerkennung von Häretiker- bzw. Schismatikertaufe im Westen bzw. Osten, bislang noch nicht genügend diskutiert worden und vor allem für das dritte und vierte Jahrhundert aufgearbeitet worden[23]. Auf den ersten Blick scheint die Geschichte des Taufgottesdienstes in der christlichen Antike

---

22 Weitere Modelle aus der Forschungsgeschichte bei M. Labahn, „Kreative Erinnerung als nachösterliche Nachschöpfung", 341–344.

23 Vgl. dazu hier E. E. Popkes, „Die Tauftheologie Cyprians. Beobachtungen zu ihrer Entwicklungsgeschichte und schrifthermeneutischen Begründung", 1059–1068, insbesondere 1067f. zum „offenen Ende" der Auseinandersetzungen und entsprechend knapp J. P. Burns, „The Efficacy of Baptism in Augustine's Theology", 1286f.

wie Spätantike nach langer Vernachlässigung im protestantischen Bereich durch Georg Kretschmar im Jahre 1970 in seiner großen Monographie mustergültig und daher auch abschließend aufgearbeitet[24]; die ausführlichen Beiträge von *Christian Strecker* zur allgemeinen Entwicklung (S. 1381–1438), aber auch von *Juliette Day* zur Tauflitugie, die Cyrill (bzw. Pseudo-Cyrill) von Jerusalem in den unterschiedlichen Serien von Katechesen voraussetzt (S. 1200–1203), dokumentieren, wie vielfältig die liturgische Praxis war, wie stark Normierungen (in den Kirchenordnungen und liturgischen Büchern) und faktischer Vollzug in den Gemeinden differierte. Angesichts solcher Vielfalt, die nur noch mühsam im bewährten klassischen Modell geographisch konzentrierter „liturgischer Familien" gebändigt werden kann, legt sich der theologiegeschichtlich grundierte Zugang zu den Tauftheologien einzelner klar abgrenzbarer Individuen nahe, die als „Kirchenväter" ebenfalls eine wie auch immer zu bestimmende Autorität von den antiken Christen zugeschrieben bekommen haben. Der Beitrag von *Christian Strecker* zeigt zudem, dass die Anwendung ritualtheoretischer und sonstiger kulturwissenschaftlicher Fragestellungen auf die aus den einschlägigen Quellen rekonstruierten Abläufe von Taufvorbereitung, Taufhandlung und Taufnachbereitung durch die Liturgiewissenschaft erst in den Anfängen steckt, aber reichen Gewinn verspricht. Dagegen sind, wie der Beitrag von *Hermut Löhr* zeigt (S. 1529–1550), die einstigen heftigen Auseinandersetzungen über das Verhältnis von Kindertaufe, Erwachsenentaufe und Klinikertaufe pazifiziert; spannend bleiben die Zusammenhänge natürlich: So ist bislang die Frage nach dem Verhältnis von Taufe und – anachronistisch gesprochen – Kirchenmitgliedschaft auf dem Weg zur konstantinischen bzw. theodosianischen Reichskirche noch kaum thematisiert worden und vor allem auch nicht ihre weitere Entwicklung nach dem vierten Jahrhundert[25].

2.3. Eine letzte Bemerkung: Die drei hier vorgelegten Bände sind schlechterdings umfassend, integrieren neben den Texten die Bilder, untersuchen die einschlägigen jüdischen, christlichen, aber auch paganen Schriften in wünschenswerter Tiefe wie Gründlichkeit. Und doch müssten diese beiden im wahrsten Sinne des Wortes gewichtigen Bände irgendwann einmal durch einen dritten ergänzt werden, denn wenn es um „Waschungen, Initiation und Taufe" in „Spätantike, frühem Judentum und frühem Christentum" geht, dann muss auch noch einmal auf der Basis des hier Vorgelegten die Spätantike in ihrer *ganzen Ausdehnung* bis ins achte Jahrhundert in den Blick genommen werden. Schon relativ lange impliziert das im Bereich patristischer Forschung, dass als letzter Autor der Spätantike im Osten der 754 im Kloster Mar Saba in der judäischen Wüste südlich von

---

24 Vgl. die Nachweise bei CHR. STRECKER, „Taufrituale im frühen Christentum und in der Alten Kirche", 1382f.

25 Vgl. einstweilen MARKSCHIES, „Kirchenmitgliedschaft in der Geschichte der Kirche – drei Erkundungsgänge in einem weiten Feld", 7–18.

Jerusalem gestorbene Johannes von Damaskus berücksichtigt wird. Inzwischen ist auch deutlicher geworden, dass der Islam, mit dem sich Johannes von Damaskus auseinandersetzt, ebenfalls in die Spätantike gehört und im Kontext der spätantiken Religionsgeschichte interpretiert werden muss und nicht einfach als Beginn des Mittelalters und als frühmittelalterliche Religion aus der Zahl der Untersuchungsgegenstände der Altertumswissenschaften ausgegrenzt werden darf[26]. Da im Band bereits die archäologische Überlieferung der Taufbecken (*Robin Jensen*, S. 1671–1693) bzw. frühchristlichen Baptisterien (*Olof Brandt*, S. 1585–1608) bis ins siebente Jahrhundert behandelt wurde (im Beitrag von *Hannah Schneider*, S. 1695–1718), müssen auch die Texte von christlichen wie nichtchristlichen Autoren des fünften bis siebenten Jahrhunderts irgendwann einmal ausführlicher berücksichtigt werden[27].

Bibliographie

FERGUSON, E., *Baptism in the Early Church. History, Theology, and Liturgy in the First Five Centuries*, Grand Rapids, Mich./Cambridge, U.K.: Eerdmans 2009.

JÜLICHER, A., *Itala. Das neue Testament in altlateinischer Überlieferung*, im Auftrage der Kirchenväterkommission der preussischen Akademie der Wissenschaften zum Druck besorgt von W. Matzkow, Bd. I Matthäus-Evangelium, Berlin: Walter de Gruyter 1938.

KINZIG, W., „‚… natum et passum etc.' Zur Geschichte der Tauffragen in der lateinischen Kirche bis Luther", in: W. Kinzig, Chr. Markschies und M. Vinzent, *Tauffragen und Bekenntnis. Studien zur sogenannten Traditio Apostolica, zu den Interrogationes de fide und zum Römischen Glaubensbekenntnis* (AKG 74), Berlin: Walter de Gruyter 1999, 75–184.

LIETZMANN, H., „Ein Beitrag zur Mandäerfrage", in: *SPAW.PH*, Berlin: Walter de Gruyter 1930, 596–608 [= IDEM, *Kleine Schriften Bd. I Schriften zur spätantiken Religionsgeschichte*, hg. v. K. Aland (TU 67), Berlin: Akademie-Verlag 1958, 124–140].

MARKSCHIES, CHR., „Taufe und Concupiscentia bei Augustinus", in: Th. Schneider und G. Wenz (Hgg.), *Gerecht und Sünder zugleich? Ökumenische Klärungen* (Dialog der Kirchen. Veröffentlichungen des Ökumenischen Arbeits-

---

26 Programmatisch zeigt das: A. NEUWIRTH, *Der Koran als Text der Spätantike. Ein europäischer Zugang*.
27 Dies gilt insbesondere, da auch in dem voluminösen Werk von E. FERGUSON, *Baptism in the Early Church. History, Theology, and Liturgy in the First Five Centuries*, nur Autoren bis in die Mitte des fünften Jahrhunderts behandelt werden, aber die archäologische Überlieferung wesentlich weiter verfolgt wird (aaO. 819–860). Vor allem die Texte des christlichen Orients würden sowohl im Blick auf Theologie wie Liturgie eine Neuverhandlung lohnen!

kreises evangelischer und katholischer Theologen 11), Freiburg: Herder 2001, 92–108.

— *Das antike Christentum. Frömmigkeit, Lebensformen, Institutionen* (Beck'sche Reihe 1692), München: C. H. Beck 2006, 23–31.

— „'... für die Gemeinde im Grossen und Ganzen nicht geeignet ...'? Erwägungen zu Absicht und Wirkung der Predigten des Origenes", in: *ZThK* 94 (1997), 39–68 [= IDEM, *Origenes und sein Erbe. Gesammelte Studien* (TU 160), Berlin/New York: Walter de Gruyter 2007, 35–62.

— „Kirchenmitgliedschaft in der Geschichte der Kirche – drei Erkundungsgänge in einem weiten Feld", in: *Zwischen Taufschein und Reich Gottes. Kirchenmitgliedschaft im Spannungsfeld von Freiheit und Verbindlichkeit. Referate einer Tagung vom 28. bis zum 30. September [2007] in der Evangelischen Akademie zu Berlin* (epd-Dokumentation 46), Berlin: Evangelischer Pressedienst 2007, 7–18.

— *Die Gnosis* (C. H. Beck Wissen in der Beck'schen Reihe 2173), München: C. H. Beck ³2010.

NEUWIRTH, A., *Der Koran als Text der Spätantike. Ein europäischer Zugang*, Berlin: Verlag der Weltreligionen 2010.

RIEDWEG, CHR., *Mysterienterminologie bei Platon, Philon und Klemens von Alexandrien* (UALG 26), Berlin/New York: Walter de Gruyter 1987.

WOLTER, M., „Apollos und die ephesinischen Johannesjünger", in: *ZNW* 78 (1987) 49–73 [≈ „Apollos und die Johannesjünger von Ephesus (Apg 18,24–19,7)", in: IDEM, *Theologie und Ethos im frühen Christentum* (WUNT 236), Tübingen: Mohr Siebeck 2009, 402–426].

ZUNTZ, G., „Ein Heide las das Markusevangelium. Ein Vortrag", in: H. Cancik (Hg.), *Markus-Philologie* (WUNT 33), Tübingen: J. C. B. Mohr (Paul Siebeck) 1984, 205–222.

Part/Teil I

Methodological Considerations
Methodische Überlegungen

Rituals of Purification, Rituals of Initiation
Phenomenological, Taxonomical and Culturally Evolutionary Reflections

ANDERS KLOSTERGAARD PETERSEN

1. The Relationship between Rituals of Purification and Initiation

When Paul in 1 Corinthians 6:1–11 discusses that some members of the Corinthian community were having law suits against one another, he condemns their practice by emphatically stating that: "And such were some of you. But you were washed (ἀλλὰ ἀπελούσασθε), but you were sanctified (ἀλλὰ ἡγιάσθητε), but you were justified (ἀλλὰ ἐδικαιώθητε) in the name of the Lord Jesus and by the Spirit of our God" (6:11).[1]

Although the translation is not wrong, the New Jerusalem Bible renders the translation of ἀπελούσασθε in a more precise manner than the New King James version by explicating Paul's use of the cleansing metaphor: "But you have been washed clean." The ritual is said to have cleansed the ritual participants from the state of being that existed prior to the ritual. By means of the ritual they have acquired a state of purity categorically different from the one that characterised their previous state of being, i.e. they have been transferred from a state of impurity to a state of purity. It is certainly not coincidental that the cleansing metaphor precedes the next two metaphors which serve to make it clear to the recipients that the Corinthian Christ-believers have been initiated into a new form of being. They have not only been set apart from the world which is ultimately what the metaphor of sanctification implies but due to their justification in the name of the Lord Jesus and by means of the spirit of God they have also entered into a new legal state before God, i.e. they have been justified or acquitted of their previous guilt. In order to obtain justification, however, it is essential that the ritual participants have been transferred to a state in which they have been made ritually prepared for the acquisition of the justification.

---

[1] The translations used in this article from New Testament texts are if nothing else is stated based on the New King James version. Translations of the Church fathers are unless otherwise stated taken from A. ROBERTS AND J. DONALDSON (eds.), *The Writings of the Fathers down to A.D. 325. Ante-Nicene Fathers*, Peabody, Mass., Hendrickson Publishers 1995. Translations from classical Greek and Latin literature are if nothing else is stated taken from the Loeb Classical Library.

That part of the ritual which pertains to the preparation of the ritual participants for their subsequent justification is expressed by the two metaphors ἀλλὰ ἀπελούσασθε and ἀλλὰ ἡγιάσθητε.

It is the final metaphor of the verse, however, denoting justification which makes it clear that we are dealing with a religio-historical context that places emphasis on what for lack of better terminology I will term moral purity at the expense of a focus on ontological purity.[2] In the context of Paul, the purity of Christ-believers is first and foremost a matter of a moral state; but it is also noticeable that in order to express the moral purity of the Christ-believers Paul perpetually has recourse to terms that are closely linked with basic notions of ontological purity: "Do all things without complaining and disputing, that you may become blameless (ἄμεμπτος) and harmless (ἀκέραιος, literally 'without mixture', i.e. pure), children of God without fault (ἄμωμος, literally 'without blemish' or 'stain') in the midst of a crooked and perverse generation, among whom you shine as lights in the world" (Phil 2:14–15, cf. 1 Thess 2:10; 3:13; Rom 16:19; 1 Cor 7:14; 8:7).[3]

We do not need to enter into the discussion whether Paul in 1 Cor 6:11 is quoting from a pre-Pauline tradition or not. It suffices to note that in one of the earliest strands of what later became known as Christianity we find an amalgamation of elements pertaining to rituals of purification as well as rituals of initiation. Apparently, the two do not exclude each other. The fusion of motifs belonging to what in modern scholarship has frequently been conceived of as two essentially different rituals points to an intricate relationship between them.[4] Needless to say, one may discuss the extent to which Paul's metaphorical circumlocution of baptism as a cleansing should lead to a categorisation of

---

2   By the category 'ontological purity' I am thinking in terms of the emphasis placed in priestly theology on different forms of impurity stemming from the natural or biological constitution of being human such as, for instance, different skin diseases, menstruation blood, semen, dead bodies, physical deformity, etc. For the discussion of the terminology, see J. KLAWANS, *Impurity and Sin in Ancient Judaism*, 21–36, who prefers to speak about 'ritual' and moral purity. Since purity in Paul and other comparable representatives of Second Temple Judaism also has much to do with ritual, I find it infelicitous to term this form of purity ritual. See also the discussion in T. KAZEN, *Jesus and Purity* Halakhah, 200–222, who rightly emphasises that in most forms of Judaism during the Second Temple period we are talking about a sliding scale of emphasis and not a watertight alternative between what I term ontological and moral purity and what Kazen calls inner and outer purity (214).

3   It is, of course, hardly coincidental that Paul in Phil 2:14–15 takes up this metaphor of purity originating in the Jewish Bible in the context of priestly theology with respect to the status of the sacrificial animals, since Paul in the subsequent passage metaphorically expresses his own role with regard to the Philippian community that he has founded as that of a priest offering sacrifice to God: "Yes, and if I am being poured out as a drink offering on the sacrifice and service (σπένδομαι ἐπὶ τῇ θυσίᾳ λειτουργίᾳ) of your faith, I am glad and rejoice with you all" (Phil 2:17).

4   For an overview of previous scholarship's understanding of rituals of initiation, see J. A. M. SNOEK, *Initiations*, 90–147.

the ritual as a ritual of purification, but that is to anticipate the course of the argument. What we cannot do, however, is to neglect the occurrence of motifs common to rituals of purification and rituals of initiation within the same context. In fact I will argue that a ritual of initiation cannot be separated from the element of cleansing irrespective of whether that element is merely present in the form of a metaphorical formulation or as an independent, preparatory rite of purification.[5]

Although a rite of purification may not be part of the ritual of initiation *per se*, it does play a prominent role in the preparatory rites that precede Lucius' initiation into the mysteries of Isis as recounted in the eleventh book of the *Metamorphoses* or *The Golden Ass* by Apuleius. To what extent the narrative is a parodical charade on an actual ritual need not concern us here.[6] It suffices to note that the ritual process recounted must have been rhetorically and narratively persuasive to the intended audience, precisely because it resembled a genuine ritual of initiation. At the signal of the goddess, Lucius understands that he has finally received the favour of being allowed to become initiated into the mysteries of Isis (22:1–2), which in the case of Lucius eventually (by two additional initiations into the mysteries of Osiris) will lead to his transformation from the form of a donkey back into that of a human being. After the old priest has led Lucius to the gate of the great temple in order to introduce him to "the pious mysteries of the sacred things" (*piisima sacrorum arcana*, 22:6), he is shown the mysterious temple books written in unknown characters and painted with figures of beasts, i.e. presumably hieroglyphs. The priest interprets to Lucius "such things as were necessary to the use and preparation of mine order (*ad usum teletae necessario praeparanda*)" (22:7). Thereupon Lucius is taken to the bath. After he has taken a habitual bath (*sueto lavacro*), the priest prays for the favour (*venia*) of the god and cleanses Lucius most purely (*purissime abluit*) by sprinkling him with water all around (*circumrorans*) (23:2). After a period of ten days of fasting, Lucius is finally ready to become initiated into the mysteries of Isis. Even though the rite of cleansing represents a pre-stage to the actual ritual of initiation, it is indispensable for transferring Lucius into the state in which he is ritually pure and, thereby, fit to undergo the subsequent initiation into the mysteries of the goddess.

The two examples document, on the one hand, the difference between rituals of initiation and rituals of purification but, on the other hand, they also point to their commonality. To undergo initiation, one has to be in a ritually

---

5 I will throughout the article make a distinction between 'ritual' and 'rite'. Whereas I use ritual to denote a whole ritual complex consisting of different rites, I will use rite to designate the individual ritual sequences within a given ritual. It is the assemblage of rites that together make up a whole ritual.

6 For the satirical elements in *The Golden Ass*, see N. SHUMATE, *Crisis and Conversion in Apuleius* Metamorphoses, 7. 32.

pure state, i.e. purity is apparently a prerequisite for the subsequent encounter or even merging with powers of the trans-mundane and trans-human realms. Even in cases with no actual encounter conveyed by the ritual, there is still the idea that in order to undergo a decisive transformation – as in rituals of initiation – one has to be cleansed of one's previous dirt, regardless of whether that is understood in ontological or moral terms. It is a prevalent phenomenon frequently found in connection with rituals of initiation that a rite of cleansing or purification is somehow related to it.[7] In fact Walter Burkert contests that: "Purification rituals are therefore involved in all intercourse with the sacred and in all forms of initiation; but they are also employed in crisis situations of madness, illness, and guilt."[8] In the same context – and important for our topic – Burkert also adds that: "The most widespread means of purification is water, and in Greek purification rituals contact with water is fundamental."[9] Burkert's observation is confirmed from a number of other religio-historical contexts, where water also features prominently in connection with both rituals of purification and rituals of initiation.

2. The Prevalence of Water as a Ritual Means in the Ancient Mediterranean World

The prevalent use of water in the context of purification and cleansing may also be seen from archaeological evidence from all around the ancient Mediterranean world. Fountains and extravagant water systems with cisterns and immersion pools are often found as part of temple complexes.[10] In Delphi, for instance,

---

7   Cf. A. F. SEGAL, "Paul and the Beginning of Christian Conversion", 85.
8   W. BURKERT, *Greek Religion*, 76.
9   BURKERT, *Greek Religion*, 76.
10 See, for instance, the discussion of the Red Hall of Pergamum in which according to one author "... ganz offensichtlich wurde in diesem Kult viel Wasser benutzt", see W. RADT, *Pergamon. Geschichte und Bauten einer antiken Metropole*, 205. One may also think of the widespread use of water in the context of the Asclepius cult. P. GOOCH, *Dangerous Food*, 18, mentions that "many Asklepeia were founded around springs or sacred wells, and water was an important element of cure. All of the major centres of the cult that have been excavated—Epidauros, Pergamon and Kos—have facilities for springs and/or baths. Smaller sanctuaries show the same feature: that in Troizen contained a monumental fountain, and in Athens the Asklepeion included a cave and its sacred springs." It is also well-known how water was used in the cult of Isis (cf. my previous reference to the initiation of Lucius as depicted in Apuleius' *Metamorphoses*). In the ritual the myth of Osiris dying and later being resuscitated was closely related to the seasonal changes of the Nile. The living Osiris was identified with the life-giving water of the Nile that dwindles away as Osiris is dying, and yet comes back as flood with the resuscitated Osiris during the summer season. Similarly, the initiates had, in principle, to bathe themselves in water that had been brought specially from the Nile, see R. MERKELBACH, *Isis regina — Zeus Serapis*, 152. For the architecture of the Isis temple of Pompeii, see M. BEARD, *Pompeii*, 304–308. Needless to say, the same widespread use of water in cultic contexts also applies to ancient Judaism.

Pythia is recounted to have said: "Come, stranger, pure in mind to the precinct of the pure god, after dipping thy hand in the water of the Nymphs (νυμφαίου νάματος ἀψάμενος). For a little drop suffices for the righteous, but not the whole ocean shall cleanse (νίψαι) a wicked man with its streams (νάμασιν)."[11] There is ample textual evidence that the Castalian spring played an important role for ritual purity deemed to be a prerequisite for priests and pilgrims approaching the religious precinct of the temple of Apollo at Delphi. In Euripides' Ion it is not only said that the priests and pilgrims had to purify themselves with the water from the Castalian spring but also that the temple itself was sometime sprinkled with the water (*Ion* 94–108). From all we know about the Eleusinian mysteries, water also played a prominent role in this cultic context.[12] Both at the occasion of the Lesser Mysteries taking place in February/March and at the occasion of the Greater Mysteries performed in September lustration rites were involved. As part of the Lesser Mysteries the ritual participants bathed themselves in the river of Illisos outside the city walls of Athens. As part of the Greater Mysteries the ritual participants on the third day took a bath in the sea on the way between Athens and Eleusis. In a discussion in Epictetus' *Arrian's Discourses* on people who have only acquired introductory philosophical learning and yet think themselves capable of lecturing to others, Epictetus compares these light-hearted people to men who vulgarise the Mysteries of Eleusis. The true philosopher, however, "ought to come also with a sacrifice (μετὰ θυσίας), and with prayers, and after a preliminary purification (προηγνευκότα), and with his mind predisposed to the idea that he will be approaching holy rites (ἱεροῖς), and holy rites of great antiquity (ἱεροῖς παλαιοῖς)" (III xxi. 14).

Similar widespread uses of water as ritual means are also attested in the context of Roman religion. In the *Aeneid* Aeneas urges his father, Anchises, to collect the sacred things, since Aeneas after warfare has become impure: "Father, do thou take in thy hand the sacred things and our country's household gods; for me, fresh from such a conflict and recent carnage, it were sin to handle them, until I have washed me (*abluero*) in a running stream (*flumine vivo*)" (II 717–720). The underlying raison d'être is, of course, that one cannot approach the sacred things unless one is in a pure state of being.

Although the water system with its advanced aqueducts and basins at Qumran originally may have had other purposes, I believe it is beyond doubt that sometime during the so-called period 2 of the settlement – beginning around the turn of the common era and lasting to approx. the outbreak of the First Jewish War in 66 – the water system to a large extent functioned as an integral part of the community's cultic practices. For a recent assessment of archaeological questions pertaining to Qumran, see K. GALOR AND J. ZANGENBERG, "Introduction", 1–9, and Y. HIRSCHFELD, "Qumran in the Second Temple Period: A Reassessment", 223–239.

11 *The Greek Anthology*, XIV 71; cf. also XIV 74 likewise from Delphi. This as well as some of the examples below I have taken from A. D. NOCK, "Early Gentile Christianity and Its Hellenistic Background", 97–104, and E. FERGUSON, *Baptism in the Early Church*, 25–37.

12 For a discussion of the Eleusinian mysteries, see BURKERT, *Greek Religion*, 285–290.

In the famous festival of the Parilia whose enigmatic origin is lost in the past, water also played a prominent role.[13] The myth pertaining to the Parilia is at the same time one of the myths related to the foundation of Rome. The festival refers to the fabled founding of the city and the creation of its – non-less-famous – sacred boundary, the *pomerium*, although the Parilia by Ovid is said to even predate the founding of the city. In his *Fasti*, which poetically recounts the mythical background of the *Parilia* (IV 721–862), Ovid twice refers to water used for purification. Ultimately the Parilia is a festival which seeks to purify the sheep and the cattle by calling on the god, Pales. The poet evokes the god/goddess Pales (the sex of the deity was uncertain) and asks for a favour (*faveas*), since he by his singing will pay his respect to the god and his/her festival (723–724). As a way of legitimising his endeavour, the poet recalls how he has previously honoured the festal requirements: "Sure it is that I have often brought with full hands the ashes of the calf and the beanstraws, chaste means of expiation (*februa casta*). Sure it is that I have leaped over the flames ranged three in a row, and the moist laurel-bough has sprinkled water (*misit aquas roratas*) on me" (725–728). Whereas the ashes of the calf and the beanstraws seem to represent preliminary sacrificial means of purification, the subsequent leaping over the fires indicates 'serious' personal commitment to the extent that one symbolically risks one's life by engaging with fire. The function of the final sprinkling with water from a laurel-bough is ambiguous. From the context it is impossible to see whether it represents an additional purification in the sense of removal of impurity or rather is to be understood as a ritual act of essence transfer, i.e. water functioning as a channel for transferring magical agency to the ritual participant. Be that as it may, there is no doubt about the central role of the sprinkling with water as the preliminary completion of a sequence of purificatory rites.[14]

In a subsequent part of the text, Ovid proceeds to discuss the rural festival of purification of sheep and cattle (735–782). Here once again he mentions the use of water as ritual means: "Shepherd, do thou purify (*lustra*) thy well-fed sheep at fall of twilight; first sprinkle (*spargat*) the ground with water and sweep it with a broom…" (736). The time of the day when this rite has to take place has been set apart, i.e. a temporal demarcation of ritual space. It must take place at

---

13   For a discussion of the Parilia, see M. Beard, J. North and S. R. F. Price, *Religions of Rome*, 174–176.

14   Ovid's own explanation of the function of the water is threefold. First, Ovid argues that fire and water is used together because everything is composed out of opposite elements (787–790). Second, he contests that fire and water are used because they contain the source of life and as such their use reflects the symbolism of exile and marriage (791–792). Third, he claims that some argue that the use of these two elements has to do with Phaeton's and Deucalion's flood (793–794). In the section 783–806, Ovid gives altogether seven interpretations of the origin of the Parilia, but I have concentrated on the three that have to do with the use of water as ritual means.

twilight. Secondly, the ritual space is also spatially demarcated. The shepherd shall sprinkle the ground with water and subsequently sweep it with a broom, i.e. a special spatial context has been set apart for the ritual. In order to conduct the subsequent ritual actions the ground must be purified so that the ritual action can take place, i.e. the space must be decontaminated in order for a merger between human beings and the gods to occur. In the Durkheimian tradition, of course, that is precisely what we customarily understand by sanctification.[15]

Water rituals are, of course, also referred to in the context of late Second Temple Judaism. Three examples will suffice. In the Community Scroll of Qumran in the context of the famous teaching of the Two Spirits it is said about God that:

> God will refine (יברר), with his truth, all man's deeds, and will purify (יזקק) for himself the structure of man, ripping out all spirit of injustice from the innermost part of his flesh, and cleansing (ולטהרו) him with the spirit of holiness (ברוח קודש) from every wicked deeds. He will sprinkle (ויז) over him the spirit of truth (רוח אמת) like lustral water (כמי נדה) (in order to cleanse him) from all the abhorrences of deceit (תועבות שקר) and (from) the defilement of the unclean spirit (והתגולל ברוח נדה), in order to instruct the upright ones with knowledge of the Most High, and to make understand the wisdom of the sons of heaven to those of perfect behaviour. For those God has chosen for an everlasting covenant and to them shall belong all the glory of Adam (כול כבוד אדם) (1QS IV 20–23).[16]

Similar to the previously addressed Pauline texts we find in this passage of 1QS an emphasis on moral purity. The focus on moral purity here is not generally characteristic of the Qumran texts which – depending upon the individual text – appear to vacillate between emphasis on ontological and moral purity.[17] In this essay we do not need to enter into that discussion. Even though the passage refers to both 'sprinkling' and 'lustral water' it is not altogether clear whether the text is referring to an actual ritual practised among its intended audience or is simply using a metaphor. But even in the case of a metaphor one will have to acknowledge that the persuasiveness of the metaphor depends upon knowledge among the recipients of the text of actual purification rituals with water. The

---

15 See my essay "Ritualet og det hellige", 118–120. See also F. A. ISAMBERT, "L'Elaboration de la Notion de Sacré dans l'École' Durkheimienne", 35–56, as well as W. E. PADEN, "Before the "Sacred " Became Theological", 10–23.

16 The translation is from F. G. MARTÍNEZ and E. J. C. TIGCHELAAR, *The Dead Sea Scrolls*.

17 Cf. the two unfortunately rather fragmentarily transmitted texts 4Q414 and 4Q512 which appear to be two different recensions of the same composition. 4Q414 was previously given the infelicitous sobriquet Baptismal Liturgy, but that is under all circumstances a misnomen, since the text deals with various forms of ontological impurity stemming from contamination by corpses and menstrual blood. The text contains liturgies of blessing that had to be recited at situations of impurity. It mentions how the impure person had to immerse himself at the first, third and seventh days to purify himself, and thereby also contributing to the purification of his people (4Q414 2 ii 3, 4, 2).

text also seems to indicate a blending between two ritual capacities. On the one hand, the ritual transfers a super-natural essence to the ritual participants, when they are being sprinkled with the spirit of truth. On the other, the ritual also has a purifying capacity, since it is said to function as lustral water that will cleanse the ritual participants from all the abhorrences of deceit and the defilement of the unclean spirit, i.e. the ritual will remove a correspondingly negative essence from the ritual participants to the one that by means of the ritual has been conferred upon them. Finally, we see how the ritual is thought to effectuate a transfer of the ritual participants to a state of being and doing in which they are reckoned to be able to act in accordance with God by adhering to the wisdom of God. Ultimately, the upright ones are said to obtain the state of being that existed prior to the fall of Adam by being conferred upon the glory of Adam. The reference to water rituals in this passage is not unique for 1QS. In 1QS III 4–5 we also find an important reference to purification rituals with water. The man who belongs to the lot of Belial "will not be purified (יטהר) by the cleansing waters (במי נדה), nor will he be made holy by seas or rivers, nor will he be purified by all the water of ablution (בכול מי רחץ)."

In Josephus' biography, *Vita*, he tells how in his youth he went to the ascetic and prophet-like figure Bannus. Apart from the fact that Bannus lived on the borders of civilisation by dwelling in the wilderness, wearing clothing made of leaves, and eating only such things as grew of themselves, Josehus recounts how Bannus used "frequent ablutions (λουόμενος) of cold water, by day and night, for purity's sake (πρὸς ἁγνείαν)" (*Vita* 11). Unfortunately we do hardly know anything about this enigmatic figure, but we can see from Josephus' report that John the Baptist was not the only one practising water rituals on the fringe of civilisation. Bannus' ritual, however, seems to be an ordinary one of purity.

The last example comes from Philo's tractate *De Cherubim*. Here Philo argues with respect to feasts celebrated by human beings in contrast to the feast celebrated by God that:

> Such are the feasts of those whom men call happy. And so long as they confine their unseemly doings to houses or unconsecrated places, their sin seems less to me. But when their wickedness like a rushing torrent spreads over every place and invades and violates the most sacred temples, it straightway overturns all that is venerable in them, and as a result come sacrifices unholy, offerings unmeet, vows unfulfilled, their rites and mysteries a mockery, their piety but a bastard growth, their holiness debased, their purity impure, their truth falsehood, their worship a sacrilege. Furthermore they cleanse (ἀπορρύπτονται) their bodies with lustrations (λουτροῖς) and purifications (καθαρσίοις), but they neither wish nor practise to wash off (ἐκνίψασθαι) from their souls the passions by which life is defiled. They are zealous to go to the temples white-robed, attired in spotless raiment, but with a spotted heart they pass into the inmost sanctuary and are not ashamed (94–95).

Similar to our previous findings in Paul, we see in Philo how his focus in this passage is exclusively on moral forms of impurity. We also observe how he makes a distinction between ritual and cognitive cleansing. The persons castigated by Philo willingly partake in ritual cleansing practices, but according to Philo they do not supplement this by a corresponding cognitive inclination for cleansing.[18] They are not willing to purify the desires from their thinking.

Be this as it may. These are just a few instances that serve to document the pervasiveness of water as a ritual medium used in the context of rituals of purification and initiation in the ancient Mediterranean world.

3. Accounting for Water as a Ritual Means

I believe that the reason for the prevalence of water as ritual medium in the context of rituals of both purification and initiation can be cognitively accounted for. First, water has the great advantage that by being sprinkled upon either human beings, animals or artefacts can trigger mental representations about agency transference, i.e. the water can somehow be attributed the role of conveying substances from one element to another. To the extent that the water is accorded the role of conveying magical agency it may be used in a ritual context to transfer the magical substance upon the ritual participants.[19] When I lived in Southern Germany some years ago, it was still common at one monastery in the Roman-Catholic parts of Würtemberg in the week before Easter to offer to the members

---

[18] A similar distinction is found in Josephus' portrayal of the baptism of John the Baptist in Ant. XVIII 117.

[19] In order to clarify my use of the traditionally contested term 'magic', I want to emphasise that I am using it at an *etic* level as a second-order concept to neutrally signify 'ritual efficacy'. Despite the fact that magic is and often has been used as a social-relational concept to denigrate those forms of religiosity which one particular religious party, group or, for that matter, guild of scholars cannot accept as legitimate forms of religion, i.e. 'superstition' or a 'primitive form of religiosity', I do not side with those prevalent currents in modern scholarship promoting the view that the term should be altogether abandoned by scholars, see, for instance, J. Z. SMITH, "Trading Places", 16. See also T. E. KLUTZ, "Reinterpreting 'Magic' in the World of Jewish and Christian Scripture", 4–8; and D. B. MARTIN, *Inventing Superstition*. Contrary to this line of thinking, I believe that we should not throw the baby out with the bath water, but retain the concept as an apt and time-honoured category to denote ritual efficacy. In order to avoid common misunderstandings, however, it is crucial that the concept is analytically defined and embedded in a lucid theory of both ritual and religion that avoids the traditional pitfalls of scholarship. I think that such a definition and a concomitant theory of religion can now be found in J. SØRENSEN, *A Cognitive Theory of Magic*, 32, who defines magic as being about "changing the state or essence of persons, objects, acts and events through certain special and non-trivial kinds of actions with opaque causal mediation." Sørensen emphasises how the "ascription of magical agency is a fundamental prerequisite for representations of efficacy in ritual, when these are not only understood as purely symbolic expressions, but are believed to change or uphold a state of affairs either by ritual means alone or in combination with technological action." See also I. PYYSIÄINEN, *Magic, Miracles, and Religion*, 96.

of the church the opportunity of taking their cars to one gate of the monastery on Palm Sunday and having them sprinkled with holy water. The underlying idea is, of course, that the car by being sprinkled with holy water is less prone to enter into car accidents and, perhaps, may be an even better vehicle than before. Comparable uses of holy water to transfer magical agency to artefacts were being recounted during the Balkan wars in the 1990s, when priests of the belligerent Serbs and Croatians were reported to sprinkle the canons of their respective armies with holy water.[20]

Second, water as ritual medium also has a correspondingly negative function of removing essences from persons, animals or artefacts. This function is, of course, fully compliant with the correspondingly positive function of transferring magical agency to the same subjects or things. If water can be ascribed the role of transferring essence, it can by the same logic also be accorded the role of removing essences as is seen in rituals of purification, where the water is understood to remove impurity or dirt. Comparable to simple representations of water as being capable of taking away dirt as in a customary bath, water can in the ritual context be attributed the function of removing (metaphorical) dirt. One may think of Romans 6, where Paul makes it blatantly clear to his recipients that by their ritual ordeal they have once and for all left sin behind: "What shall we say then? Shall we continue in sin that grace may abound? Certainly not! How shall we who died to sin live any longer in it? Or do you not know that as many of us as were baptized into Christ Jesus were baptized into His death?" (Rom 6:1–3). Paul obviously does not exclude the possibility that Christ-believers – subsequent to their baptism – continue to have the capability of sinning, but his argument presupposes that he considers Christ-believers to be in a state, where they – helped by the Spirit – will in fact fulfil the righteous requirement of the law (cf. Romans 6:12–23; 8:4).[21]

An even more conspicuous example of the connection between water as ritual medium and the idea of its cleansing function is found in the later liturgical development of the Christian ritual of baptism as recounted by Justin Martyr in his *First Apology*:

> I will also relate the manner in which we dedicated (ἀνεθήκαμεν) ourselves to God when we had been made new (καινοποιηθέντες) through Christ; lest, if we omit this, we seem to be unfair in the explanation we are making. As many as are persuaded and believe that what we teach and say is true, and undertake to be able to live accordingly, are instructed to pray and to entreat God with fasting for the remission of their sins that are past, we (are, sic) praying and fasting with them. Then they are brought by us where there is water, and are regener-

---

20 For an analysis of how water may be attributed the special qualities of transferring magical agency, see the analysis in E. T. LAWSON AND R. N. MCCAULEY, *Rethinking Religion*, 95–113.

21 For a discussion of this aspect, see my essay "Paraenesis in Pauline Scholarship and in Paul – an Intricate Relationship", 284–293.

ated (ἀναγενῶνται) in the same manner[22] in which we were ourselves regenerated (ἀνεγεννήθημεν). For, in the name of God, the Father and Lord of the universe, and of our saviour Jesus Christ, and of the Holy Spirit, they then receive the washing with water (τὸ ἐν τῷ ὕδατι τότε λουτρὸν ποιοῦνται). For Christ also said, "Except ye be born again, ye shall not enter into the kingdom of heaven." Now, that it is impossible for those who have once been born to enter into their mothers' wombs, is manifest to all. And how those who have sinned and repent shall escape their sins, is declared by Esaias the prophet, as I wrote above; he thus speaks: "Wash you (λούσασθε), make you clean (καθαροὶ γένεσθε), put away the evil of your doings from your souls; learn to do well; judge the fatherless, and plead for the widow: and come and let us reason together, saith the Lord. And though your sins be as scarlet, I will make them white like wool; and though they be as crimson, I will make them white as snow. But if ye refuse and rebel, the sword shall devour you: for the mouth of the Lord hath spoken it" (*First Apology* 61).

Apart from the fact that we compared to the evidence of earlier Christian texts referring to baptism in Justin see an increasing growth of the individual rites pertaining to baptism – not least with regard to the preparatory rites such as fasting and praying – the text also makes it clear that the baptismal water effectuates a cleansing of the Christ-believers. The ritual and its water is said to invest the former sinners with garments as white as wool. To the extent that their sins have been as crimson they have by means of the ritual been transformed into beings as white as snow. Birth and cleansing are metaphorically blended with each other in Justin's interpretation of baptism.

Needless to say, neither here nor in the majority of texts that have survived from antiquity do we have access to the actual ritual practice. Unlike what some scholars seem to think, texts like Romans 6 and the passages discussing baptism in Justin's *First Apology* cannot be taken at face value as direct representations of the actual baptismal practice. The depiction is deeply embedded in theological interpretations of what baptism is about. That, of course, as I already indicated in my comments on the ritual of initiation depicted in Apuleius' *Metamorphoses* does not exclude there being a connection between the theological interpretations and the actual ritual practice, but it is important to keep the difference in mind as well. Ultimately, it is the lack of acknowledgement of this difference which has often led scholars to endorse the view that ritual is a re-enactment of myth, and that the doctrinarian content of the myth is present in the representations of the ritual participants.[23] In this manner, ritual is fre-

---

22 The Greek text has καὶ τρόπον ἀναγεννήσεως which literally means "and in the manner of regeneration", whereby Justin thrice emphasises baptism as a ritual that effectuates regeneration.

23 Whereas the classical discussion of this topic in the history of scholarship was debated in terms of the dualism between myth and ritual, it is nowadays more often formulated in terms of dualisms between language and action, meaning and practice, or content and form of the particular ritual. For the history of scholarship, see C. Bell, *Ritual: Perspectives and Dimensions*, 3–8. 64–68.

quently understood as a means by which one exerts political control or power.[24] Edmund Leach was a profound exponent of the view that a close relationship exists between myth and ritual, when he argued that:

> ... myth, in my terminology, is the counterpart of ritual; myth implies ritual, ritual implies myth, they are one and the same... Myth regarded as a statement in words 'says' the same thing as ritual regarded as a statement in action. To ask questions about the content of belief which are not contained in the content of ritual is nonsense.[25]

Few scholars nowadays will argue for such an intrinsic relationship between myth and ritual without thereby necessarily giving up the idea that a connection between the two exists. Firstly, the relationship between myth and ritual is of a manifold nature. Secondly, myth and ritual may frequently occur in contexts, where they are independent of each other.[26] Thirdly, the understanding is not capable of explaining why in some situations ritual is the preferred means and in other contexts myth if the two are more or less identical with each other. Fourthly, on the basis of such a view it is difficult to understand why rituals exist in the first place if that which is expressed by means of rituals just as well could have been expressed by means of myth. It is under all circumstances important to keep in mind that we only to a limited extent have direct access to ancient ritual. The predominant number of sources provides us with mythological and theological interpretations of ritual, which we then have to analyse in terms of a possible ritual practice.

To sum up the discussion, we have seen how ritual water may function either to effectuate a transfer of magical agency to the ritual participants or to remove negative essences from their bodies. Needless to say, all kinds of theological or symbolic interpretations (as, for example, in the cases of Paul and Justin) may, of course, at a later stage be ascribed to these more basic cogni-

---

[24] C. BELL, *Ritual Theory*, 171–181, has fervently criticised this line of thinking by pointing among other things to the fact that rituals may often have the opposite effect, that is, that rituals can cause as much social erosion as they can contribute to creating social coherence. Additionally, Bell argues that ritual *per se* does not control, but that it may constitute "a particular dynamic of social empowerment" (181). Bell also strongly underlines "... that symbols and symbolic action not only fail to communicate clear and shared understandings, but the obvious ambiguity or overdetermination of much religious symbolism may even be integral to its efficacy" (184). Although I agree with Bell on many points I think that her argument (fully parallel with the now herostratically famous argument of FRITS STAAL, "The Meaninglessness of Ritual", 2–22, on which Bell draws heavily, that ultimately rituals are meaningless) suffers from a basic conflation of meaning with what can be expressed in symbolic propositional language. There are other and more basic forms of meaning which are not only integral to ritual but also basic to their purported efficacy. This has not least been persuasively documented by R. A. RAPPAPORT, most comprehensively in *Ritual and Religion in the Making of Humanity*, 69–138.

[25] E. R. LEACH, *Political Systems of Highland Burma*, 13. Cf. J. S. LA FONTAINE, "Introduction", xvii.

[26] G. S. KIRK, *Myth. Its meaning & Functions in Ancient and Other Cultures*, 23–25.

tive representations of either essence transfer or removal, but underlying every form of doctrinarian exegesis of the meaning of the rituals are the more basic cognitive representations. There is now firm empirical evidence from a variety of psychological experiments conducted by neuropsychologists and cognitive scholars that support this observation.[27] Be that as it may, as preparatory rites to rituals of initiation rites of purification may be found in a plethora of forms. They vary from sexual abstinence to chastisement, fasting, baptising with various means, different forms of ablution, the drinking of different fluids, etc. In this essay, however, I will concentrate on those forms that involve the use of water whether in the form of baptism or ablution.

4. An Evolutionary Framework for the Discussion

The primary aim in the remaining part of this essay is to explore the relationship between the two types of rituals with a special focus on what traditionally has been called religions of salvation, *Erlösungsreligionen*, in contrast to religions of blessing or *Segensreligionen*. I will concentrate on the two types of rituals during the period in the history of religions in which so-called religions of salvation came to the fore. This focus will enable us to take up the problem covered by the overall topic of this book, which is the examination of one particularly prominent ritual of initiation, i.e. baptism found in a variety of forms. The book's concentration on baptism in this publication motivates my paying more heed to the discussion of rituals of initiation and focusing less on rituals of purification. By analysing the topic in connection with one set of transitions in the history of religion I intend to include what I consider to be an important evolutionary perspective in the general discussion.

Whereas religions of salvation traditionally are understood to be oriented towards salvation from this world, religions of blessing are directed towards maintaining the proper balance between gods and humans in order that the blessings of the god or the gods in the form of, for instance, fat oil, abundant wine, fertile women and old age (see, for example, 1 Macc 14:4–15) may flow incessantly to the human beings. The emphasis on the ontological difference between human beings and gods is the dominant element of religions of blessing. Breaches of this structure threaten to bring the flow of blessings to a halt. Religions of salvation, on the other hand, represent a blatant attack on this structure and its underlying *raison d'être*. Needless to say I am talking about the two religions as ideal types – in reality the individual religions will often embody more muddled forms of the two, but that does not detract from the analytical value of making a distinction between them as we will see below. In

---

27 See J. SØRENSEN, *A Cognitive Theory of Magic*, 95–96. 164. 177 with reference to the experiments conducted by Subbotsky and, secondarily, by Rozin and Nemeroff.

contrast to religions of blessing, religions of salvation purport not only to bring an elect group of human beings into direct contact with the godhead or the gods, but even to transfer them to a world conceived to be located outside the empirically accessible world. To enable this transposition, human beings have to be transformed into the image of the god. To a certain extent one could, of course, argue that the structure of ontological difference is thereby retained within religions of salvation, since the premise for human beings to achieve transfer to the 'other' world is that they undergo a categorical transformation which changes them into the nature of the godhead:

> The first man was of the earth, made of dust; the second Man is the Lord from heaven. As was the man of dust, so also are those who are made of dust; and as is the heavenly Man, so also are those who are heavenly. And as we have borne the image of the man of dust, we shall also bear the image of the heavenly Man. Now this I say, brethren, that flesh and blood cannot inherit the kingdom of God; nor does corruption inherit incorruption. Behold, I tell you a mystery: We shall not all sleep, but we shall all be changed – in a moment, in the twinkling of an eye, at the last trumpet. For the trumpet will sound, and the dead will be raised incorruptible, and we shall be changed (1 Cor 15:47–52).

In addition to these observations, we may note that religions of blessing lack eschatology *sensu stricto*.[28] It is, of course, true that we find, for instance, in the Hebrew Bible depictions of a golden era that will succeed what is perceived to be the present miserable one (see, for example, Isa. 11; 51; 61). In much traditional scholarship there has been no reluctance to designate these texts as eschatological; but the idea of the golden era echoed by these passages implies the return of a previous glorious epoch that once again will be manifested on earth rather than the concept of a truly different aeon that once and for all brings history to an end. That is certainly the case in Isaiah, where eschatology is a meaningful concept only to the extent that it can be used to designate a new situation subsequent to a catastrophe in which the broken relationship between Yahweh and his adherents has been restored and the world once again has been set right.[29] The situation is different within the context of religions of salvation, where eschatology traditionally designates the existence of a new era that has radically replaced the present one and brought history to an end.

Be that as it may, my contention is that in order to shed light on the difference between rituals of purification and rituals of initiation, it is incumbent upon us that we pay heed to the type of religion in which the ritual category in question is embedded. It makes a difference whether one is examining a ritual of initiation belonging to the context of a religion of salvation or one originating

---

28 This is an observation that I owe to my colleague Hans Jørgen Lundager Jensen, who in several publications has argued in favour of giving up the notion of eschatology with respect to the Hebrew Bible. See, for instance, H. J. L. JENSEN, *Gammeltestamentlig religion*, 257–260.

29 So JENSEN, *Gammeltestamentlig religion*, 257.

in the context of a religion of blessing. In both types of religion, of course, we find rituals of initiation and rituals of purification as already indicated by our previous discussion; but the rituals vary considerably with respect to semantic content depending on the underlying form of religiosity. Additionally, it may well be that one type of ritual is prevailing depending on the type of religion in question. Although I cannot entirely prove it in this essay, I will suggest that rituals of purification prevail in religions of blessing, whereas rituals of initiation are accorded a more prominent position in religions of salvation — or to be more exact, I will argue that one particular type of ritual of initiation prevail in religions of salvation, i.e. initiations into associations and special cults.

5. The Need for a Revision of Terminology

Due to the strongly Christian-flavoured and anachronistic terminology, I will abstain from using the distinction between religions of blessing and religions of salvation. Instead of this dualism, I will use the slightly revised vocabulary of Jonathan Z. Smith and throughout the article refer respectively to locative forms of religion and utopian ones.

Smith's argument is that the distinction between locative and utopian types of religion can be heuristically used to shed light on all of the Mediterranean religions in late Antiquity, and that it constitutes a basis for conceiving an analogical relationship between these religions and early forms of Christianity. Smith's focus is directed towards what traditionally has been called mystery religions and emerging Christianity.[30] However, I think that Smith's distinction can advantageously be extended to include not only the longer period from say the fifth century BCE (with the rise of Platonic philosophy) to the seventh century CE (the emergence of Islam included, but at the same time signifying the end of late Antiquity) but also to cover a wider geographical area that would include religions in the periphery of the Mediterranean basin such as, for instance, Indian ones.[31] One reason for moving Smith's concept of utopian

---

30   It has during the last couple of decades of scholarship become increasingly clear that the time-honoured category 'mystery religions' has several problems pertaining to it. It is a religio-historical construal that has often served as apologetic foil for emphasising the genuineness of nascent Christianity. In addition, Walter Burkert among others has convincingly documented that the mysteries should be seen as a special form of worship offered in the larger context of polytheistic religion. They never constituted a closed system. See BURKERT, *Ancient Mystery Cults*, 10. Finally, one may add that the so-called mystery religions were mutually as different from each other as some of the religions (notably Christianity), which they have traditionally been contrasted with.

31   I realise and acknowledge the convergence between my view and Karl Jasper's often problematised talk of an 'Axial Age'. Although Jaspers has been met with severe criticism for his concept, I think it is worthwhile to revitalise it but without the apologetic tenor implied by Jasper's ideas. See the essays by J. P. ARNASON, "The Axial Age and its Interpreters", 19–49; S. N. EISENSTADT,

religions backwards in time is to include different strands of Greek philosophy in the concept. Plato's philosophy, for instance, is from my perspective an exemplary case of what Smith has termed a utopian world-view by its strong emphasis on the sovereignty of the soul over the body, the need for cognition to detach itself from the boundaries of the mundane world, and the importance attributed to the element of 'becoming like god' (cf. *Theaetetus* 176b).[32] Some may, of course, object to the inclusion of philosophical currents into the category, but I see no reason not to include them, given the fact that the philosophy of Graeco-Roman antiquity represented a subset of what we nowadays etically term religion. Additionally, the inclusion of philosophical strands may also help us to a greater appreciation of the resemblances that exist between what we are accustomed to think of in terms of two categorically different discourse formations, i.e. philosophy and religion.

Smith argues that the locative world-view "is concerned primarily with the cosmic and social issues of keeping one's place and reinforcing boundaries. The vision is one of stability and confidence with respect to an essentially fragile cosmos, one that has been reorganised, with effort out of previous modes of order, and whose 'appropiate order' must be maintained through acts of conscious labour."[33] Smith, therefore, also terms this type of religion a religion of sanctification. With respect to its soteriology, this type of religion celebrates emplacement as the norm. Rectification, cleansing or healing is undertaken if the norm is breached. Israelite religion as witnessed by the Hebrew Bible is an obvious example of such a religion of sanctification, just as any traditional religion is, be it Vedic, Greek or Roman. One may, as we have already noted, add that a basic structure of this type of religion is the idea of an essential ontological difference between god and human beings that need to be kept in balance and which cannot be transcended. According to this world-view human beings can never acquire the status of a god-like existence, and hence, cannot undergo processes of divinisation. To the extent that a direct merger between human beings and the god/gods occur problems arise. The utopian world-view, on the other hand, is characteristic of religions that rebel against the clearly defined boundaries of the locative types of religion. Smith contends that:

> in such a world-view, the structures of order are perceived to have been reversed. Rather than the positive limits they were meant to be, they have become oppressive. Man is no longer defined by the degree to which he harmonizes himself and his society to the cosmic patterns of order; but rather by the degree to which he

---

"Axial Civilizations and the Axial Age Reconsidered", 531–564, and R. N. BELLAH, "What is Axial about the Axial Age?", 69–87. See also EISENSTADT, *Comparative Civilizations and Multiple Modernities*.

32 The importance of the motif of godlikeness in Plato's philosophy is elegantly dealt with by D. SEDLEY, "Becoming Like God", 327–339; idem, "The Ideal of Godlikeness", 309–328.

33 SMITH, *Drudgery Divine*, 121.

can escape the patterns. Rather than the hero-that-failed of the locative worldview, the paradigm here is the hero-that-succeeded, succeeded in escaping the tyrannical order. Every man is called to be such a hero. The man of wisdom is no longer the sage but the savior–he who knows the escape routes.[34]

On the basis of such a world-view, imitation of God and the continuous process of divinisation become intrinsic to religion, since one can only acquire happiness, *eudaimonia* or salvation through a breach with one's ontological situation. In that sense, similitude with god is a central tenet of all manifestations of a utopian type of religion. It does not necessarily imply the identification with the god/gods, but it points to the fact that human beings must somehow transcend their present boundaries by undergoing processes of imitation or increasing likeness with god or the gods in order to be released from the evils of the present era and space. By the distinction between locative and utopian forms of religion, Smith emphasises the transition that occurred at different velocity throughout the Mediterranean basin during the Hellenistic period from locative forms of religion to utopian ones. Smith has sometimes been misunderstood to say that utopian manifestations of religion are not directed towards a place, i.e. that they are without a spatial dimension, but that is a misunderstanding of Smith's argument. Utopian religions are as indicated by the Greek loanword not without space, i.e. *atopos*, but they are directed towards a space conceived to lie outside this world, i.e. utopian. But what has this to do with the discussion about different types of rituals?

Although I am not entirely happy with the terminology of Smith – as indicated also by my wish to extend his distinction to a wider geographical area and a longer period – I believe that his distinction may help us to shed light not only on the difference between rituals of purification and rituals of initiation but also on the fact that their nature depends upon whether they occur in the context of locative or utopian forms of religion. We will leave this discussion for the time being and proceed to the question of what characterises a ritual of initiation. Since in this essay I focus on matters predominantly pertaining to the classificatory differences between different types of rituals, I will mainly concentrate on that older trajectory of scholarship in ritual studies that was concerned with developing a typological basis for distinguishing between different types of rituals. Needless to say and as also indicated by some of my previous references, during the past decade ritual studies have undergone rapid development, particularly with respect to cognitively informed studies about ritual and ritualised behaviour. Although I consider this development to be of an epoch-making nature for the field, I feel justified in this article in concen-

---

34 SMITH, *Map Is not Territory*, 139.

trating on older works, since my concern here is about developing a classificatory basis for distinguishing between different ritual types.[35]

6. Rites of Passage

From the perspective of the history of scholarship within ritual studies, anthropology and the study of religion, it is obvious to take one's point of departure in Arnold van Gennep's groundbreaking work *Les Rites de Passage*. The book was published in 1909, but it was not until the English translation of 1960 that the book gained wide scholarly attention.[36] It is the merit of van Gennep to have coined the concept 'rites of passage' as central to anthropology and to the study of religion, and to have used this neology by documenting how it constitutes a common pattern to all so-called life crisis rituals. By life crisis one understands a decisive turning point in the physical and/or social development of human beings (for instance in connection with pregnancy, birth, wedding or death) and in the structural foundation of society (for instance related to the change of seasons, the change of leadership, or the turn of the year). The life crises, however, of human beings are not confined to the individual only. They also pertain to the society of which the individual is a member. When the being and status of the individual is changed by a life crisis, his or her relationship to society is also changed. In situations of life crises, rites of passage establish, accentuate and interpret all transitions from one state to another, whether it is physical or social, individual or societal. Every transition is necessarily experienced as a crisis, because the transition implies an irreversible change in the being of the individual.

Through the study of different social and religious rites of passage, van Gennep was able to document how different rituals in the structuring of the individual sequences of the ritual and in the existential situation of the ritual participant not only emphasise but also accomplish a radical change in the being of the ritual participant.

Secondly, he demonstrated how such rituals follow the same structural pattern comprising three stages: 1) the preliminal phase characterised by separation; 2) the liminal phase characterised by transition; 3) and the postliminal phase which is characterised by incorporation.

Van Gennep was predominantly using the terms 'separation', 'transition' or 'margin', and 'aggregation' or 'incorporation' with respect to the ritual, while he was primarily applying 'preliminal', 'liminal' and 'postliminal' to designate

---

[35] In the next sections I am drawing on arguments which I developed for the first time in my essay "Begravet og oprejst", 119–146.

[36] A. VAN GENNEP, *The Rites of Passage*.

spatial transitions.[37] The temporal dimension is included in both sets of concepts. Thirdly, as a consequence of these observations van Gennep isolated one distinct ritual category, whereby he became pioneer of the subsequent discussion on ritual classification, i.e. rites of passage.

7. The Individual Phases of the Ritual

Victor Turner elaborated on van Gennep's work by highlighting not only the importance of the transitional or liminal phase but also by showing how the different phases of the ritual each have their particular substructures. The substructures of the individual phases separate them from the other phases, but at the same time enable them to be incorporated in the entire symbolic-ritual pattern. The distinct ritual classes are different from each other by their different emphasis on one of these aspects. Although they contain all three elements, rituals of birth, for example, frequently attribute the moment of incorporation the greatest role, while rituals pertaining to betrothal particularly emphasise the moment of transition. They are representative of a situation in which the ritual participants have already left the phase of pre-marriage behind, but have not yet entered into the phase of post-marriage.

The preliminal phase is understood to represent a radical break with one's previous being. This is symbolically accentuated and ritually staged in such a manner that the ritual participant is according to the ritual *raison d'être* located in a new sphere beyond that of the mundane world.[38] Already in the break with the pre-ritual being, the ritual participant is understood to have irreversibly left it behind and to have been incorporated into a new state of being. The radical nature of the break may be spatially staged as, for instance, the passage through a gate, but frequently the separation is iconically and indexically expressed as a death. From the semantic perspective of the ritual, death is the decisive end to and departure from one mode of being to which the ritual participant subsequent to the completion of the ritual does not any longer have access to. Through the ritual death the ritual participant has been incorporated into an existential process of change that inevitably is oriented towards a new life perceived to be qualitatively different from the one completed.

Unlike the pre- and postliminal phases, the liminal phase is characterised by ambivalence. It is ambiguous by its tension between an 'already' completed mode of being, i.e. the termination of the pre-ritual initiatory state during the

---

37   SNOEK, *Initiations*, 149, correctly criticises van Gennep for using the first conceptual set, since it causes confusion. Separation and incorporation are not intrinsic to the preliminal and postliminal phases, but may also occur in connection with the transitions from one ritual stage to another. The postliminal phase, for instance, may, at least in principle, include both rites of separation, transition and incorporation.

38   Cf. V. W. TURNER, *The Ritual Process*, 94.

preliminal phase, and a 'not yet', i.e. the integration during the postliminal phase into a new state of being. In the liminal phase, the values that structure and define normal society have been abolished in order to emphasise that the ritual participant has irreversibly left that society and the values pertaining to it behind. In compliance with this observation, Turner has pointed out that profane society does not allow definitions such as "not-boy-not-man, which is what a novice in a male puberty rite is (if he can be said to be anything)";[39] but precisely such unstructured classifications characterise the state of being of the liminal phase: "Liminality may perhaps be regarded as the Nay to all positive structural assertions, but as in some sense the source of them all, and, more than that, as a realm of pure possibility whence novel configurations of ideas and relations may arise."[40]

A person situated in the liminal phase is inevitably embedded in a dialectic and paradoxical existence as one who is no longer what he used to be, although he/she has not yet acquired the state of what he/she is going to become in a time characterised by not-past, but not yet future, and in a space defined by neither here, nor there. During this limbo or state of 'betwixt and between' the ritual participant shirks cognitive classification, because he/she is neither this nor that, neither here nor there, and neither the one nor the other.[41] According to Turner, normal society has during the liminal phase been replaced by a *communitas*, where the ordinary, differentiated, well-structured and hierarchical society – divided into political, judicial and economic positions "with many types of evaluation, separating men in terms of "more" or "less" – has been substituted by an unstructured or rudimentarily structured society.[42] This state may be expressed in manifold ways, but the common characteristic is the emphasis on the absolute equality of the ritual participants: "They have no status, property, insignia, secular clothing, rank, kinship, position, nothing to demarcate them structurally from their fellows."[43]

In the liminal state the ordinary societal structures have been abolished or even replaced by inverse structures frequently formulated in terms of *coincidentia oppositorum*: "So the last will be first, and the first last" (Matt 20:16a).[44] Therefore all liminal beings are equal, because they have all died the same ritual death and have left the structures and differentiations of their previous life behind. It is this common, undifferentiated state that enables their

---

39 TURNER, *The Forest of Symbols*, 95.
40 TURNER, *The Forest of Symbols*, 97.
41 TURNER, "Variations on a Theme of Liminality", 37. The neologism 'betwixt and between' as epitome of the liminal phase stems from one of the essays in Turner 1967.
42 TURNER *The Ritual Process*, 96.
43 TURNER *The Forest of Symbols*, 98–99.
44 See in particular TURNER, "Metaphors of Anti-Structure in Religious Culture", 272–299.

incorporation into a new life as 'new creatures'. According to Turner, they embody with the words of King Lear "naked unaccommodated man".[45]

Despite this field of vexation between life and death, between already and not yet, characteristic of the liminal phase, the liminal existence stretched 'betwixt and between' is not understood to be less real, or less complete.[46] The orientation of the liminal phase towards the future, towards what has not yet come into existence, but which will – from the ritual point of view – by necessity come about, neither reduces the degree of completion nor the authenticity of what takes place. This is an important point with respect to understanding the earnestness and gravity implied by metaphors encircling the liminal phase. And we may add that the same holds true for those groups which conceive of post-ritual life as a perpetual state of liminality. In light of this observation, the often celebrated so-called eschatological tension detected by New Testament scholarship to be an epitome of early Christian world-views in general and the Pauline in particular does not imply a perpetual uncertainty about future salvation. On the contrary, the tension is – at least in Paul – an indication of how far Christ-believers have already progressed toward the final goal of their orientation.

In the third and last ritual phase, the transition or process of change is completed. Thereby the state of being towards which the preliminal phase was oriented and which the liminal phase anticipatory and partly realised is completed and perfected. Through the incorporation, the ritual participant is reintegrated as a 'new creature' different from the pre-ritual into the structured society. He/she is no longer the same as before. The new status achieved by the ritual participant places him or her in a new contractual relationship. He/she is obliged to comply with the claims and demands required by the new mode of being. The young boy who through his participation in a puberty ritual has been transformed into a male is not only expected to behave accordingly but he cannot – i.e. from the perspective of the ritual semantics – return to his previous state as a boy and behave accordingly. Correspondingly, the person who has been ritually reborn cannot at his/her return to society behave in the same manner as he or she used to, because a 'real death' separates the two states from each other. It is not coincidental that early Christian texts often use the metaphor of sealing in connection with baptism to emphasise the irreversibility of the ritually completed change (cf. the extensive discussion of the metaphor in Karl

---

45 TURNER *The Forest of Symbols*, 99. Cf. TURNER *The Ritual Process*, 103. 143–144.
46 Turner is not entirely clear in his use of the term 'liminality'. Generally, he uses it to designate the middle phase of so-called rites of passage, but he may also use it as a characteristic of groups which have turned the entire life into a perpetual state of liminality or what Turner at other places designates *communitas*, see, for instance, *The Ritual Process*, 143–147. In order to make a differentiation, I have in several of my publications pertaining to this subject proposed to distinguish between what I call 'ritual' and 'ideological' liminality. See, for instance, my article "Shedding New Light on Paul's Understanding of Baptism", 16. 27.

Olav Sandnes' essay in this publication). Sealing is a strong way of expressing the completed transfer of ownership, since the metaphor implies a strong sense of inculcation, i.e. something has been imposed or even inscribed on the ritual participant to the extent that he/she has become an indexical representation of the one whose seal he/she is carrying. In this manner, the metaphor expresses a sense of completeness that is fully congruent with the irreversibility implied by the last phase of the ritual. In principle, there is no return to the pre-ritual state of being.

8. Problems Regarding the Classification of van Gennep

Eliot Chapple and Carleton Coon have rightly contested that the so-called calendrical rites represent a category *sui generis*. Therefore they cannot – as in the classification of van Gennep – be assigned to rites of passage. They do not create any existential transition of the individual, nor can they be said to establish a radical difference between two modes of being.[47] Chapple's and Coon's discussion of van Gennep's tripartite classificatory structure as unique to all rites of passage raises an important question: To what extent can the tripartite structure be said to be unique to this type of ritual, and how do they differ from other types?[48]

The tripartite structure as the central criterion for the classification of rites of passage was further challenged when scholarship began to appreciate the important work by Henri Hubert and Marcel Mauss, *Essai sur la Nature et la Fonction sociale du Sacrifice*.[49] They documented how sacrifice as a ritual was also structured according to a tripartite sequence ('consecration', 'sacrifice', and 'purification').[50] Based on this and other works, one is forced to conclude that it

---

47   E. D. CHAPPLE AND C. S. COON, *Principles of Anthropology*, 485. 507–508. They assign calendrical rites to a category which they entitle 'rites of intensification' understood to restore equilibrium for the group after a disturbance affecting all or most of its members, whereas they claim that rites of passage restore equilibrium in a system after a crisis that has involved an individual (507).

48   J. P. SCHJØDT has for analytical purposes in several publications proposed to extend the tripartite sequence into a quinpartite structure which would enable us to better differentiate the preliminal phase from the initial state to which the ritual is a reaction, and, secondarily, to better distinguish the postliminal phase from the final state into which the ritual participant is incorporated subsequent to the completion of the ritual. See, for example, SCHJØDT, "Ritualstruktur og ritualklassifikation", 2–23, and SCHJØDT, "Initiation and the Classification of Rituals", 93–108. Cf. also SNOEK, *Initiations*, 149.

49   H. HUBERT AND M. MAUSS, *Essai sur la Nature et la Fonction sociale du Sacrifice*.

50   Cf. W. E. H. STANNER, *On Aboriginal Religion*, 4, who with respect to the initiation ritual *Karwadi* or *Punj* among the Murinbata people argues that "the *Karwadi* ceremony conforms generically to the operational character of sacrifice as I have sketched it. I do not maintain that there is an exact congruence, but a likeness which cannot be dismissed out of hand and can in fact be shown to be homologous". See also J. VAN BAAL AND W. E. A. BEEK, *Symbols for Communication*, 131, who also point to the resemblances between sacrifice and rituals of initiation.

is rather limited what the term rite of passage as a designation of a particular structural ritual category may amount to. I concur with van Baal and van Beek when they endorse the view that: "… the tripartite structure is not a characteristic of a ceremony connected with a change of status but of ritual performance in general."[51] And we may add to this observation, that the tripartite nature of ritual is congruent with a corresponding basic structure of narratives.[52]

9. Rituals of Initiation

Let us now turn to another and for our purposes especially important category: rituals of initiation. It is not least the merit of Mircea Eliade to have focused on rituals of initiation as a special class of rituals. Although van Gennep spoke of rituals of initiation as a subcategory within the class of rites of passage, he did not seem to have made it the subject of any systematic examination, but Eliade has examined the class of rituals rubricated by van Gennep as rituals of initiation.[53] They are categorised into three distinct groups: 1) age rituals; 2) initiations into associations and mystery cults; 3) and shaman initiations.

According to Eliade, the first group is constituted by collective rituals related to the function of ensuring the transfer from one age group to another. Unlike the first category, the two other categories are confined to the individual or to a smaller group. They are not of a collective nature. Whereas the age group rituals are unavoidable, because nobody within a given society can evade them, the rituals in the other two groups are inevitable to a lesser extent, since they are confined to either the individual or the smaller group. It is a further merit of Eliade that he has elaborated on the connection between rituals of initiation and the symbolism of death and rebirth often used in the metaphorical language of the ritual.

Even though Eliade to some extent has nuanced the differences that exist between different groups of rituals within the subcategory of rituals of initiation in the classification of van Gennep, he has not come closer to answering the question how this class of rituals differs from other types. The birth and

---

51   Van Baal and Beek *Symbols for Communication*, 131. Cf. Schjødt, *Initiation*, 98–99.
52   Due to constraints of space, I am not able to elaborate on this point in this essay, but there is a conspicuous relationship between ritual and narrative structure, which may have to do with the fact that rituals are narratively staged processes that create different forms of transformation for the subjects of being undergoing the ritual. Even in cases, where human beings are not the objects of ritual performance, the ritual continues to show close resemblances to fundamental narrative structures, since ritual is ultimately about "changing the state or essence of persons, objects, acts, and events through certain special and non-trivial kinds of actions with opaque causal mediation," see Sørensen, *A Cognitive Theory of Magic*, 32. The only way such transformations can be linguistically represented is by means of narrative.
53   See, in particular, M. Eliade, *Birth and Rebirth*, later published as *Rites and Symbols of Initiation. The Mysteries of Birth and Rebirth*, New York, Harper and Row 1975, "Initiation", 224–229.

death symbolism frequently related to rituals of initiation and examined by Eliade does not serve as a classificatory criterion either, since other types of ritual may exploit the same metaphors. Hence, we are facing two questions. First, is it possible that an elaborated version of Eliade's distinction between three different groups of rituals of initiation may serve as criterion for distinguishing between different groups of initiation rituals? Second, how can we distinguish between rituals of initiation and other types of ritual, if neither the tripartite structural sequence, nor the birth and death metaphors can be used as criteria for demarcation?

If we nuance Eliade's distinction by taking into consideration the subject of being of the ritual participant and the form of being into which the ritual participant is integrated subsequent to the ritual, I believe that such a refined understanding can function as a heuristic basis for an internal classification of initiation rituals.[54] Unlike Eliade's categorisation, I do not think that the important difference should be placed between what Eliade termed type one, on the one hand, and types two and three, on the other hand. I would rather argue that initiations into associations or mystery cults, such as found in the previous examples from Paul and Apuleius, constitute one group, because the ritual has an intransitive or reflexive nature, whereas the characteristic of the two other groups is that the rituals are transitive by nature. In rituals pertaining to the initiation into associations or mystery cults, it is characteristic that the subject of doing of the ritual is submitting him/herself as the object of the ritual. In this sense, the ritual is of a reflexive nature. In the two other types of initiation ritual, the ritual participant is the object of other peoples' doing.

Although I do not in this essay have the opportunity to elaborate the argument, I believe that this is exactly the point which accounts for the close resemblances that exist between sacrifice and this particular group of initiation rituals.[55] This group of initiation rituals may be seen as an excessive form of sacrifice, since the ritual participant is not only surrendering some of his/her goods such as the first-born of the cattle, parts of the first harvest etc; but also, in principle, immolating him/herself by handing over his/her life – whether it is in the symbolic form of castration as in circumcision rituals or as a ritual drowning as in baptism – to the god/gods in question. It is certainly not coincidental that in the previously discussed text by Justin (*First Apology* 61), Justin is making the argument that in baptism Christians have dedicated themselves (ἀνεθήκαμεν) to God, which, of course, amounts to saying that they have surrendered themselves as in a sacrifice. The connection between sacrifice and this particular type of initiation ritual may also partly explain the use of purity metaphors or cleansing rituals as preparatory rites preceding the initiation

---

54 I gratefully acknowledge my debt to my colleague Hans Jørgen Lundager Jensen, with whom I have discussed these matters.

55 Cf. SNOEK, *Initiations*, 132–135.

ritual proper. For the ritual participants to be able to encounter the god/gods, they must present themselves as "a living sacrifice, holy, acceptable to God" (cf. Paul Romans 12:1). Additionally, we may note that with respect to sacrifices we also find the element of purification. For the sacrificial animal to be able to be sacrificed it first has to undergo a process of cleansing to acquire the status of being unblemished and without stain. From the semantics of the ritual, the animal can obviously not as a potential conveyor of contamination be given over to the god/gods, unless it has been made ritually clean. Therefore there is always in the consecration of the sacrificial animal an element of cleansing involved, whether that is staged as a separate rite of purification or as an element immediately preceding the actual consecration.

In Eliade's two other groups of rituals, the ritual participant is – admittedly – also the object, but he or she is the object of being for other peoples' actions. In age rituals of initiation it is the group or the community/society at large which is the acting part, while in shaman initiations it is often the priesthood that is the acting part.[56] These distinctions may be further elaborated by taking into consideration the form of being, into which the ritual participant is incorporated. By initiations into a priesthood or appointment as a king, i.e. rituals of type three, the ritual has a non-integrative nature. The ritual participant is subsequent to the completion of the ritual incorporated into a being isolated from ordinary society/community. Age rituals of initiation of type one, on the other hand, have an integrative character. Through the ritual by his/her community/society, the ritual participant is transferred to a higher form of being, but he/she is reintegrated into the community/society, albeit in a new relationship. It is important to acknowledge the ambivalence or doubleness that pertains to the being into which the ritual participants of type two, i.e. initiations into associations and mystery cults, are incorporated. The ritual is simultaneously integrative and non-integrative. It is integrative to the extent that the ritual participant is reintegrated into 'normal' life, i.e. a life as a being situated in the profane world. It is non-integrative to the extent that the state into which the ritual participant is incorporated is said to be located beyond the 'realms of this world'.

On the basis of these clarifications of Eliade's ritual taxonomy, I believe we have come to a more appropriate understanding of the criteria for distinguishing internally between different types of initiation rituals. The second important question we are facing concerns the criteria for distinguishing externally between rituals of initiation and other types of rituals.

---

56 Obviously, community/society as the acting part in the ritual may be expressed in different manners with more or less emphasis, but even in cases with less emphasis on the community/society as the acting ritual agent the community/society is somehow metonymically present as the subject of doing in the ritual.

10. Rituals of Initiation and Other Rituals: Criteriological Basis

In an important contribution to the modern study of classification of rituals, Lauri Honko has developed a model for classifying different types of ritual. Although they are all included in van Gennep's concept of rites of passage, his model is well suited for ritual classification. Honko distinguishes between (1) rites of passage; (2) calendrical rites; and (3) crisis rites. He further differentiates between category and model and uses category to constitute a 'practical taxonomy', whereas model serves to solve structural problems.[57] Honko is well aware of the fact that a model may serve more categories, whereby he acknowledges that van Gennep's category 'rites of passage' encompasses all the categories discussed by Honko.[58]

As an example, Honko discusses a model of a calendrical ritual where the succession of a liminal phase after a non-liminal phase not only corresponds to the structure of a calendrical ritual but also to the structure of that type of ritual which he entitles rites of passage.[59] He is further advocating a number of characteristics such as individual vs. collective,[60] predictable vs. unpredictable, recurrent vs. unique as important for the ritual classification. According to Honko, it is the application of these different criteria to a particular ritual and the combination of such criteria, which enables us to classify particular rituals.

Properties	Rites of Passage	Calendrical Rites	Crisis Rites
Individual	x		x
Collective		x	x
Predictable	x	x	
Unpredictable			x
Recurrent		x	
Unique	x		x

---

57 L. Honko, "Theories Concerning the Ritual Process: An Orientation", 372.
58 Honko, "Theories Concerning the Ritual Process: An Orientation", 380.
59 Honko, "Theories Concerning the Ritual Process: An Orientation", 387–388.
60 Although Honko does not specify it, it is of course important to underline that the distinction between 'individual' and 'collective' pertains to the subject of being in the ritual. Any ritual of initiation, for example, may have a collective impact to the extent that a whole group or society may be involved in the celebration of the ritual, but that does not make it individual in the sense referred to by Honko. It is individual to the extent that the subjects of being in the ritual are individual persons who by means of the ritual are being transferred from one form of being to another.

While Honko's ritual classification is partly impeded by his reliance on a strong functional view-point and a lack of analytical clarity pertaining to the level at which the different criteria are located, Jens Peter Schjødt has elaborated the adequacy and usefulness of this taxonomic model. Schjødt has extended the distinction between the three ritual types at the level of category to include also differentiations at the level of model.[61]

Schjødt has persuasively argued for this distinction as a decisive taxonomic criterion for differentiating between the ritual types evoked by Honko. The crucial criterion pertains to the value differences ascribed to the states prior and subsequent to the ritual, i.e. the relationship between the initial state and the final state. In light of such considerations, a crisis ritual may be defined as a protection from an initial state characterised by negative value, i.e. minus, to a final state accorded the value zero.[62] The ritual restores the state of being that existed prior to the crisis. Only superficially can a crisis rite be said to exemplify progression. From the wider perspective, it embodies the narrative genre of protection, since it restores the state that preceded the realised crisis of the initial state.

A calendrical ritual, on the other hand, may be defined as the transition from an initial state assigned the neutral value zero to a final state also accorded the neutral value of zero. Such rituals – as is well known from, for instance, the Babylonian New Years ritual – first and foremost serve the safeguarding and maintenance of the established order of being. In this manner, calendrical rituals similar to crisis rituals exemplify the narrative genre of protection; but the protection is of another nature than in crisis rituals. In order to explicate the difference, it is crucial also to reflect on the modality in question.[63] There is a great difference whether a ritual is meant as a reaction to a state that is either of a virtual, actualised, or realised nature. Unlike the crisis ritual, the calendrical ritual is meant as a reaction to a virtual crisis in the form of a threat occurring in the initial state immediately prior to the ritual: "If we do not perform this ritual, the crisis is bound to occur." The performance of the ritual prevents the crisis from being realised. Unlike the genuine crisis rituals, where the crisis in the initial state preceding the ritual performance is either actualised or realised,

---

61   Schjødt, "Initiation and the Classification of Rituals" and "Ritualstruktur og Ritualklassifikation". See also A. Jackson, "Commentaries", 416–418.

62   Schjødt does not speak about 'protection', but it is obvious to elaborate his reflections in the light of semiotic considerations about the four basic narrative genres: (1) progression; (2) degression; (3) repression; and (4) protection. See O. Davidsen, *The Narrative Jesus*, 61–62.

63   These considerations are indebted to the great importance Greimas attributes to the role of modalities for conceiving narrative processes. As already indicated by note 52, I believe there is good reason to make use of semiotic theorising on narrative in the context of ritual studies. For the importance of modalities, see A. J. Greimas, "Pour une Théorie des Modalités", and "De la modalisation de l'être". Additionally, see the relevant entries in A. J. Greimas and J. Courtès, *Sémiotique. Dictionnaire raisonné de la théorie du langage*, Paris: Hachette 1979.

the crisis of calendrical rituals pertaining to the initial state which the calendrical rituals are meant to counteract, are of a virtual nature only.

Finally, rites of passage, which Honko uses as a designation for one of his three groups of rituals under scrutiny, may be defined as the progressive transition from the neutral value zero of the initial state to a positive value pertaining to the final state into which the ritual participant is incorporated at the completion of the ritual. In this manner, the ritual participant has acquired a higher state of being than the one he/she had in the initial state. Needless to say, we may develop this taxonomy far more by taking other rituals into consideration, but these will suffice for the time being. We have now come to the point where we may tentatively define the ritual of initiation. In order to avoid misunderstandings about the nature of this definition, I want to make it clear from my previous argument that the definition through a continuous and reciprocal process of paying heed to both theory and empirical matter has been abductively (in the Peircian sense) developed.

10.1. External Description of a Ritual of Initiation

1. The ritual participants in the ritual of initiation consist of one or, at the very maximum, a few individuals. It never includes an entire community or society.
2. Through the ritual performance the ritual participants acquire a higher form of being radically different from the one conceived as characterising the initial state.
3. The qualitative changes acquired by the ritual participant through the completion of the ritual are of an irreversible nature, i.e. they cannot be lost unless, and very seldom, a new narratively staged ritual process is initiated.[64]
4. The qualitative changes obtained by the ritual participant through the completion of the ritual may be defined as the acquisition of one or more new modalities:[65]

---

64 One may think, for instance, of rituals of degression, whereby a priest for various reasons is deprived of his priesthood. This may as in former days be ritually staged as a public performance before the altar, where the priest is being defrocked or decollared, i.e. his collar – the indexical token of his priesthood – is torn away from him.

65 The fact that certain modalities pertain to distinctive phases of the ritual does not exclude that modalities pertaining to other phases may occur in the context of phases, where they do not properly belong. In that case, it is still the modalities belonging to that distinctive phase that overdetermine the occurrence of the other modalities. Being and doing often occur in the middle phase, but in that case they are overdetermined by 'knowledge' and 'being able to' such as in 'being able to be', 'being able to do', 'knowing to be', and 'knowing to do'.

Modalities Pertaining to Virtuality	Modalities Pertaining to Actualisation	Modalities Pertaining to Realisation
Wanting	Being able to	Being
Having to	Knowing	Doing

5. The structure of the ritual is tripartite and its performance is non-recurrent with respect to the individual ritual participant.

6. The tripartite ritual structure frequently contains symbolic elements expressing the parting from the initial state (often metaphorically conveyed as a death); symbolic elements suggesting transition (for instance, pregnancy, gestation etc.); and, finally, symbolic elements expressing incorporation in the final state (frequently metaphorically conveyed in birth symbolism).

7. The relationship between the two non-liminal phases and the liminal one is expressed through the use of analogical, binary contrasts.

10.2. Internal Description of Rituals of Initiation

1. Transitive ritual with an integrative final state as in age rituals.
2. Intransitive/reflexive ritual with an ambivalent final state as in initiations into associations or and special cults.
3. Transitive ritual with a non-integrative final state as in initiations into shaman- or priesthood.

10.3. Definition of a Ritual of Initiation

On the basis of these two descriptions of external and internal characteristics of rituals of initiation, we may, perhaps, sharpen the argument by developing an even more concise definition *per genus proximum et per differentiam specificam* of rituals of initiation:

> A ritual of initiation represents a sub-class of the category ritual. The class covers three different types of rituals that mutually differ from each other by the subject of doing of the ritual, as well as the state into which the ritual participant through the ritual is incorporated. Rituals of initiation effectuate an irreversible transfer of individual persons into a higher state of being than the one they had prior to the ritual act.

11. Rituals of Purification

With these considerations in mind, let us now proceed to discussing the other ritual type under examination, i.e. rituals of purification. We may take our point of departure in the previous reflections. Similar to rituals of initiation, rituals of cleansing also concern "the changing of the state or essence of persons, objects, acts, and events through certain special and non-trivial kinds of actions with opaque causal mediation" (cf. note 19). Correspondingly, rituals of purification also imply a double temporal orientation. They are both of a retrospective and a prospective nature. In order to reduce or remove the danger of contamination, the ritual object, whether it is a person, an animal or an object, must first be cleansed. At the same time, it is prospective with regard to the future transfer into the realm of the sacred. In order to prepare the ritual participant, animal or object to encounter the sacred, they have to undergo a process of decontamination or deprofanisation for the transfer to succeed. The idea of the ontological difference characteristic of religions of blessing in particular permeates all rituals of cleansing. There can be no ritual approach towards or even encounter with the god/gods, unless the ritual object has been transformed into a state in which it poses no contaminating danger to the god/gods.

As is evident from use of the terms decontamination and deprofanisation, rituals of purification are representative of basically two different reactions towards dirt and impurity. Essentially, both types embody a ritually staged version of the foundational narrative genre, protection. In the case of decontamination, the ritual is a reaction towards an actualised or realised crisis of impurity, i.e. impurity is either present in the form of actualisation or realisation in the stage preceding the ritual action: ultimately the state which the ritual is meant to overcome. In that sense, a ritual of purification is conceived of as a ritual of rectification, i.e. it restores a negative state ascribed the value minus to a neutral state assigned the value zero. It is a protection to the extent that it restores the person, animal, object or even the world to the state that prevailed prior to the occurrence of the crisis of impurity.

The situation is different with rituals of purity pertaining to deprofanisation. In this case, the ritual is also representative of rectification or restoration, but unlike the previous category it is a reaction towards a virtual source of contamination. Often this is not acknowledged, when scholars in ritual theory prefer to speak about this ritual category as some sort of progression to a higher state of being. That may, of course, well be, but it is important to acknowledge that it is a higher state of being that closely resembles the one that preceded the ritual performance except for the fact that the virtual threat of contamination somehow adhering to profanity has been removed. When, for instance, in the context of a ritual of initiation or sacrifice, the ritual participant or animal is undergoing ritual actions that remove him/her/it from the realm of profanity in order to prepare him/her/it for the transfer into the realm of sacredness, the preparatory rite is meant to remove the risk of potential contamination from the subsequent encounter between beings that – from the perspective of the ritual – belong to ontologically, categorically different domains.

What we find is a ritual type that is meant as a reaction towards an initial state ascribed the neutral value of zero, but with the potential risk of losing this value and declining into a negative state. Through the ritual performance, the neutral value of the initial state is secured by removing the danger of contamination. On this basis, it may, perhaps, be argued that this type of ritual is closely related to the prospective dimension of purification rituals, whereas the first type of cleansing ritual may be intrinsically connected to the retrospective aspect. Needless to say, in reality we often find amalgamations of the two types in the very same ritual, but that does not detract from the value of making the analytical distinction. If rituals of purification are, ultimately, about protection and world maintenance it is understandable that they inevitably occur in the context of rituals of initiation, whether in the form of a separate, preparatory rite or as an element embedded in the preliminal and liminal phases. This has to do with the central element of transfer inherent in all ritual activity.

Due to constraints of space, I will not dwell on the different forms of transfer in connection with purification rituals, but I will briefly note that they display a plethora of ordeals which in different iconic and indexical ways signify removal. They may take the form of ejection such as in blood-letting or vomiting conceived to have purgative effects, or they may be expressed as transmission such as it is found in different forms of scapegoating perceived to transfer the impurities onto other beings. For transfer to take place there must be some sort of cleansing that iconically or indexically prepares the way for the cognitive appreciation of the symbolism involved. To move from profanity to the sacred, one must take leave with the elements pertaining to profanity. That transition is among other things facilitated by rituals of cleansing which cognitively even more fundamentally than the symbolic communication conveyed by the ritual is obtained through the use of basic iconic and indexical image schemes.[66]

As already indicated, sacredness and impurity are mutually exclusive categories: one cannot at the same time be holy and impure. For holiness to exist impurity must be extinguished, i.e. sacredness and impurity are contrarily related to each other. Sacredness and profanity, on the other hand, are contradictorily related, since they do not exclude each other. Here we find a different scenario, where the one category overdetermines, but does not exclude the other.[67] One may be holy and profane at the same time. My basic contention is that rituals of purification enable the transitions between the different states

---

66   See SØRENSEN *A Cognitive Theory of Magic*, 95–139.

67   See my criticism of Durkheim for not specifying the logical relationship between the categories 'sacred', 'profane', 'pure', and 'impure' in "Ritualet og det hellige", 119–120.

of these four categories (sacredness, purity, profanity, impurity), and that this type of ritual essentially embodies the ritually staged narrative genre of protection, i.e. it removes by restoring, whether that restoration takes the form of rectification with respect to a virtual crisis of contamination or an actualised or realised crisis of impurity.

12. The Two Types of Rituals during the Antiquity of the Mediterranean World. A Brief Conclusion

In conclusion, I will briefly return to the topic of cultural evolution. Already in the Hebrew Bible there is a certain competition between two different forms of theology that perceive impurity in conspicuously different manners. The one is the priestly theology found in a particular literary layer of the Torah and in other parts of the Hebrew Bible (notably Ezekiel). Its focus is on cultic purity pertaining to the Temple. Unlike the Priestly theology, the Deuteronomist theology – found in Deuteronomy and echoed in the works of history of the Deuteronomian tradition – is mostly preoccupied with moral categories of purity/impurity. The capital sin of Deuteronomy, as it has been acutely observed by Jan Assmann in several publications, is oblivion of Yahwe.[68] The Israelites are incessantly enjoined to remember the benefits which they owe to Yahweh and to turn away from the gods of the foreign peoples. Although the one category can hardly be thought of without the existence of the other, there is a difference in religious type whether one is conceiving purity in predominantly ontological, cultic categories or in moral terms. The tension – verging on vexation – between these two different theologies of the Torah (whereby I do not mean to say that these are the only distinct theologies found in the Hebrew Bible) may well be a pre-stage – at the level of ideas – to the later development characterised by Jonathan Z. Smith as the transition from a locative form of religion to a utopian type. The Qumran texts are another astonishing corpus exemplifying a parallel tension pertaining to the difference between these two distinct theologies — this may partly explain the ritual variety of different types of rituals witnessed by the Qumran texts as well as conflicts in the writings between different ways of perceiving purity/impurity.

I do not contend that utopian types of religion are without ontological categories of impurity/purity. I do not think this is the case. On the other hand, I do think that the transition from formulating concepts of purity/impurity in notably ontological, cultic categories to expressing them in predominantly moral terms, which is a token of utopian manifestations of religion, also has an impact on the ritual outlook of the groups in question. Manifestations of religion preoccupied with the perpetual flow of the god's or the gods' favours to mankind

---

68 See for example J. Assmann, *Religion and Cultural Memory*, 98–100.

have a strong interest in rituals of rectification and restoration, which is ultimately what rituals of purification and cleansing are about. Religious communities, on the other hand, which strive to find a way to detach themselves from the fetters of this world place more emphasis on rituals of initiation, so that their members can be transferred to a state that will enable them to leave this world behind. Since rituals of initiation are found cross-culturally and, presumably, played a prominent role in the construction of culture/religion from a very early period in the history of homo sapiens, it would be presumptuous to argue that rituals of initiation are intrinsically bound to utopian types of religion. There is, however, one type of initiation ritual that appears to be closely connected to the emergence of utopian types of religion, i.e. the one which Mircea Eliade designated rituals of initiation into associations and mystery cults, and which I have specified as reflexive rituals of initiation with an ambivalent final state into which the rituals incorporate the ritual participants.

In order not to be misunderstood, I want to emphasise once again that I do not suggest that particular ritual categories are exclusive to certain forms of religion. Rituals of purification and initiation are found cross-culturally, and have presumably been known throughout the entire history of homo sapiens. However, I do maintain that different ritual classes prevail according to the type of religion in question. My concomitant claim is that the ritual of baptism studied in this publication on the basis of a variety of different texts, groups, ideologies, theologies, etc. is closely related to the emergence of the utopian type of religion. To substantiate this claim, it is, of course, incumbent upon us to engage in a 'thick description' of the various periods, the different geographical areas, the different groups etc. – but that is a task I leave to the other contributors to pursue.

Bibliography

Arnason, Johann P., "The Axial Age and Its Interpreters: Reopening a Debate," in: J. P. Arnason, S. N. Eisenstadt and B. Wittrock (eds.), *Axial Civilizations and World History*, JSRC 4, Leiden and Boston: Brill 2005, 19–49.

Assmann, Jan, *Religion and Cultural Memory. Ten Studies*, transl. by R. Livingstone, Stanford: Stanford University Press 2006.

van Baal, J. and Beek, W. E. A., *Symbols for Communication. An Introduction to the Anthropological Study of Religion*, Assen: Van Gorcum 1985.

Beard, Mary, *Pompeii. The Life of a Roman Town*, London: Profile Books 2008.

Beard, Mary, North, John, and Price, Simon R. F., *Religions of Rome. Volume I. A History*, Cambridge: Cambridge University Press 1998.

BELL, CATHERINE, *Ritual Theory. Ritual Practice*, New York and Oxford: Oxford University Press 1992.

— *Ritual: Perspectives and Dimensions*, New York and Oxford: Oxford University Press 1997.

BELLAH, ROBERT N., "What is Axial about the Axial Age?", in: *Arch.europ.sociol.* XLVI (2005) 69–87.

BURKERT, WALTER, *Greek Religion*, transl. by J. Raffan, Cambridge, Mass.: Harvard University Press 1985.

— *Ancient Mystery Cults*, Carl Newell Jackson Lectures, Cambridge, Mass., and London: Harvard University Press 1987.

CHAPPLE, ELIOT D., AND COON, CARLETON S., *Principles of Anthropology*, New York: Henry Holt and Company 1942.

DAVIDSEN, OLE, *The Narrative Jesus. A Semiotic Reading of Mark's Gospel*, Århus, Aarhus University Press 1993.

EISENSTADT, S. N., *Comparative Civilizations and Multiple Modernities*, Leiden and Boston: Brill 2003.

— "Axial Civilizations and the Axial Age Reconsidered", in: J. P. Arnason, S. N. Eisenstadt and B. Wittrock (eds.), *Axial Civilizations and World History*, JSRC 4, Leiden and Boston: Brill 2005, 531–564.

ELIADE, MIRCEA, *Birth and Rebirth: The Religious Meanings of Initiation in Human Culture*, London, Harvill Press 1958.

— "Initiation", in: *The Encyclopedia of Religion*, vol. 13, New York: Macmillan 1987, 224–229.

FERGUSON, EVERETT, *Baptism in the Early Church. History, Theology, and Liturgy in the First Five Centuries*, Grand Rapids, Mich. and Cambridge: Eerdmans 2009.

LA FONTAINE, JEAN S., "Introduction", in: J. S. La Fontaine (ed.), *The Interpretation of Ritual*, London: Tavistock 1972, ix-xviii.

GALOR, KATHARINA AND ZANGENBERG, JÜRGEN, "Introduction", in: K. Galor, J.-B. Humbert and J. Zangenberg (eds.), *The Site of the Dead Sea Scrolls: Archaeological Interpretations and Debates* (STDJ 57), Leiden and Boston: Brill 2006, 1–9.

GARCÍA MARTÍNEZ, FLORENTINO AND TIGCHELAAR, EIBERT J. C., *The Dead Sea Scrolls. Study Edition*, Leiden/New York/Köln: Brill 1997.

van Gennep, Arnold, *The Rites of Passage*, transl. by M. B. Vizedom and G. L. Caffee, Chicago: Chicago UP 1960.

Gooch, Peter, *Dangerous Food. 1 Corinthians 8–10 in Its Context* (Studies in Early Christianity and Judaism 5), Waterloo: Wilfred Laurier 1993.

Greimas, Algirdas Julien, "Pour une Théorie des Modalités", in: idem, *Du sens II. Essais sémiotique*, Paris: Seuil 1983, 67–91.

— "De la modalisation de l'être", in: idem *Du sens II. Essais sémiotique*, Paris: Seuil 1983, 93–102.

Greimas, Algirdas Julien and Courtès, Joseph, *Sémiotique. Dictionnaire raisonné de la théorie du langage*, Paris: Hachette 1979.

Hirschfeld, Yizhar, "Qumran in the Second Temple Period: A Reassessment", in: K. Galor, J.-B. Humbert and J. Zangenberg (eds.), *The Site of the Dead Sea Scrolls: Archaeological Interpretations and Debates* (STDJ 57), Leiden and Boston: Brill 2006, 223–239.

Honko, Lauri, "Theories Concerning the Ritual Process: An Orientation", in: L. Honko (ed.), *Science of Religion: Studies in Methodology* (Religion and Reason 13), The Hague/Paris/New York: Mouton 1979, 369–390.

Hubert, Henri and Mauss, Marcel, *Essai sur la Nature et la Fonction sociale du Sacrifice* (L'Année Sociologiques II), Paris 1899 (Paris: Librairie Félix Alcan ²1929).

Isambaert, Francois A., "L'Elaboration de la Notion de Sacré dans l'École' Durkheimienne", in: *Archives de Sciences Sociales des Religions* 43 (1976) 35–56.

Jackson, Andrew, "Commentaries", in: L. Honko (ed.), *Science of Religion: Studies in Methodology* (Religion and Reason 13), The Hague/Paris/New York: Mouton 1979, 414–420.

Jensen, Hans Jørgen Lundager, *Gammeltestamentlig Religion*, Copenhagen: Anis 1998.

Kazen, Thomas, *Jesus and Purity Halakhah. Was Jesus Indifferent to Impurity?* (CB. NT 38), Stockholm: Almqvist & Wiksell 2002.

Kirk, G. S., *Myth. Its meaning & Functions in Ancient and Other Cultures* (Sather Classical Lectures 40), Cambridge and Berkeley: Cambridge University Press and University of California Press 1973.

Klawans, Jonathan, *Impurity and Sin in Ancient Judaism*, Oxford: Oxford University Press 2000.

Klutz, Todd, "Reinterpreting 'Magic' in the World of Jewish and Christian Scripture: An Introduction", in: T. Klutz (ed.), *Magic in the Biblical World. From the Rod of Aaron to the Ring of Solomon* (JSNT SS 245), London/New York: T & T Clark 2003, 1-9.

Lawson, E. Thomas and McCauley, Robert N., *Rethinking Religion. Connecting Cognition and Culture*, Cambridge: Cambridge University Press 1990.

Leach, Edmund R., *Political Systems of Highland Burma. A Study of Kachin Social Structure*, London/Cambridge, Mass.: Harvard University Press 1954.

Martin, Dale B., *Inventing Superstition. From the Hippocratics to the Christians*, Cambridge, Mass., and London, Harvard University Press 2004.

Merkelbach, Reinhold: *Isis Regina — Zeus Serapis. Die griechisch-ägyptische Religion nach den Quellen dargestellt*, Stuttgart and Leipzig: Teubner 1995.

Nock, Arthur Darby, "Early Gentile Christianity and Its Hellenistic Background", in: Z. Stewart (ed.), *Arthur Darby Nock: Essays on Religion and the Ancient World*, Oxford: Oxford University Press 1972, 97-104.

Paden, William E., "Before the 'Sacred' Became Theological: Rereading the Durkheimian Legacy", in: *MThSR* 3/1 (1991) 10-23.

Petersen, A. K., "Begravet og oprejst: Dåben som initiationsrite belyst ud fra Rom 6,1-14" [Buried and Raised: Baptism as a Ritual of Initiation in Light of Rom 6:1-14], in: *RvT* 27 (1995) 119-146.

— "Shedding New Light on Paul's Understanding of Baptism: a Ritual-Theoretical Approach to Romans 6", in: *STh* 52/1 (1998) 3-28.

— "Ritualet og det Hellige" [Ritual and the Sacred], in: *DTT* 2 (1999) 106-128.

— "Paraenesis in Pauline Scholarship and in Paul – an Intricate Relationship", in: J. Starr and T. Engberg-Pedersen (eds.), *Early Christian Paraenesis in Context* (BZNW 125), Berlin and New York: de Gruyter 2004, 267-295.

Pyysiäinen, Ilkka, *Magic, Miracles, and Religion. A Scientist's Perspective* (Cognitive Science of Religion Series), Watnut Creek/Lanham/New York/Toronto/Oxford: AltaMira 2004.

Radt, Wolfgang, *Geschichte und Bauten einer antiken Metropole*, Darmstadt: Wissenschaftliche Buchgesellschaft 1999.

Rappaport, Roy A., *Ritual and Religion in the Making of Humanity* (Cambridge Studies in Social and Cultural Anthropology 110), Cambridge: Cambridge University Press 1999.

SCHJØDT, JENS PETER, "Initiation and the Classification of Rituals", in: *Temenos* 22 (1986) 93–108.

— "Ritualstruktur og ritualklassifikation" [Ritual Structure and Ritual Classification], in: *RvT* 20 (1992) 2–23.

SEDLEY, DAVID, "'Becoming Like God' in the *Timaeus* and Aristotle", in: T. Calvo and L. Brisson (eds.), *Interpreting the 'Timaeus' – 'Critias': Proceedings of the IV Symposium Platonicum. Selected Papers* (International Plato Studies 9), Sankt Augustin: Academia 1997, 327–339.

— "The Ideal of Godlikeness", in: G. Fine (ed.), *Plato. Volume 2. Ethics, Politics, Religion, and the Soul* (Oxford Readings in Philosophy), Oxford: Oxford University Press 1999, 309–328.

SEGAL, ALLAN F., "Paul and the Beginning of Christian Conversion", in: P. Borgen and D. Gowler (eds.), *Recruitment, Conquest, and Conflict: Strategies in Judaism, Early Christianity, and the Greco-Roman World* (Emory Studies in Early Christianity 6), Atlanta, Ga.: Scholars Press 1998.

SHUMATE, NANCY, *Crisis and Conversion in Apuleius* Metamorphoses, Ann Arbor, Mich.: University of Michigan Press 1996.

SMITH, JONATHAN Z., *Map Is Not Territory. Studies in the History of Religions* (SJLA 23), Leiden: Brill 1978.

— *Drudgery Divine. On the Comparison of Early Christianities and the Religions of Late Antiquity* (Jordan Lectures in Comparative Religion 14 1988), Chicago: Chicago University Press 1990.

— "Trading Places", in: M. Meyer and P. Mirecki (eds.), *Ancient Magic & Ritual Power* (RGRW 129), Leiden/New York/Köln: Brill 1995, 13–27.

SNOEK, JOANNES A. M., *Initiations. A Methodological Approach to the Application of Classification and Definition Theory in the Study of Rituals*, The Hague: Pijnacker 1987.

STAAL, FRITS, "The Meaninglessness of Ritual", in: *Numen* 26/1 (1975) 2–22.

STANNER, W. H. E., *On Aboriginal Religion* (Oceania Monograph 11, 1959–63, republished as Oceania Monograph 36), Sydney: Oceania Publications 1989.

SØRENSEN, JESPER, *A Cognitive Theory of Magic*, Lanham, Md.: Alta Mira 2007.

TURNER, VICTOR W., *The Forest of Symbols. Aspects of Ndembu Ritual*, Ithaca, N.Y. and London: Cornell University Press 1967.

— *The Ritual Process. Structure and Anti-Structure*, Ithaca, N.Y.: Cornell University Press 1969.

- *Drama, Fields, and Metaphors. Symbolic Action in Human Society* (Symbol, Myth and Ritual 5), Ithaca and London: Cornell University Press 1974.
- "Variations on a Theme of Liminality," in: S. F. Moore and B. G. Myerhoff (eds.), *Secular Ritual*, Assen/Amsterdam: Van Gorcum 1977, 36–52.

Part/Teil II

Religions of Late Antiquity – Outside of Judaism and Christianity

Religionen in der Spätantike – Außerhalb von Judentum und Christentum

Wasserriten im Alten Ägypten

Jan Assmann und Andrea Kucharek

1. Das Wasser im kulturellen Blick der Alten Ägypter

„Das Beste aber ist das Wasser" heißt es bei Pindar.[1] Diese Wertschätzung des Wassers als der wichtigsten Lebensgrundlage ist allen alten Kulturen des Mittelmeerraums und des Orients gemein. Doch gibt es so gut wie überall auch Überlieferungen, in denen die vernichtende, lebensbedrohende, zerstörerische Seite des Wassers zum Ausdruck kommt, Sagen von vernichtenden Flutkatastrophen, Mythen von Kämpfen zwischen den Göttern des Meeres und des Landes, von Meeresungeheuern, die das Land verwüsten und zu ihrer Versöhnung Menschenopfer fordern, Ausgeburten der See, die das Unheimliche, Drohende und Todbringende des Wassers verkörpern. Das Alte Ägypten bildet hier die einzige Ausnahme. Seine kulturelle Grundeinstellung zum Wasser war einseitig positiv. Das lässt sich an zwei Beispielen illustrieren.

Auch die Ägypter kannten ein aquatisches Ungeheuer: den Apopisdrachen, der im Himmelsozean lebt und den Sonnengott bei seiner Barkenfahrt durch den oberen Himmel und durch die Kanäle der Unterwelt bedroht. Apopis ist der Götterfeind schlechthin, die Verkörperung des Chaos, gegen die sich der Sonnengott unablässig durchzusetzen hat. Was Apopis aber *nicht* verkörpert, ist die gefährliche Macht des Wassers. Im Gegenteil: er ist kein Geschöpf, sondern der geschworene Feind des Wassers. Die Gefahr, die von ihm ausgeht, besteht darin, den Himmelsozean auszusaufen, so daß die Sonnenbarke auf Grund läuft. Dagegen können die Götter nur die stärkste Gegengewalt aufbieten, die es gibt, nämlich den Gott Seth, christlich gesprochen den Teufel selbst, der in fast allen sonstigen Bezügen die Rolle des Götterfeindes, des Osiris-Mörders, des geschworenen Feindes von Recht und Ordnung spielt, aber in diesem einen Fall von den Göttern für die Sache von Recht, Ordnung und Leben in den Dienst genommen und gegen den noch viel radikaleren Feind, den Apopisdrachen, in Dienst genommen wird. Seth steht am Bug der Sonnenbarke und stößt seinen Speer in Apopis, so dass dieser das Wasser wieder ausspeien muss, das er verschluckt hat (Fig. 1).

Das zweite Beispiel besteht in einer signifikanten Fehlanzeige. Alle Nachbarkulturen des Alten Ägypten, Mesopotamien, Anatolien, Griechenland, Ka-

---

1   *Olympische Oden*, I, 1.

naan, die Bibel, kennen die Überlieferung einer globalen Flutkatastrophe, die fast alles Leben auf Erden ausgelöscht hat. Solche Sagen, wie sie uns vor allem durch die biblische Sintflut vertraut sind, finden sich über die ganze Welt verbreitet. Schon im Jahre 1906 konnte J. Riem 300 sintflutähnliche Sagen aus allen Weltteilen zusammentragen.[2] Daher hat man immer wieder versucht, darin Erinnerungsspuren an ein Ereignis, eine kosmische Kollision, einen Meteoriteneinschlag ungeheuren Ausmaßes zu erblicken, das die ganze damalige Menschheit in Mitleidenschaft gezogen hätte. Auch die Ägypter kennen den Mythos einer Urkatastrophe mit der fast vollständigen Vernichtung des Menschengeschlechts. Die Flut spielt darin aber keine Rolle. Im Gegenteil, es ist die Göttin Sachmet, die flammenspeiende, löwengestaltige Verkörperung der Sonnenglut, die hier als Agent der Vernichtung auftritt.[3]

Dabei grenzt Ägypten ebenso ans Mittelmeer wie Griechenland, Anatolien, die Ägäis, die Levante, und wie Babylonien an den Persischen Golf. Auch die Ägypter sind zur See gefahren und hatten Gelegenheit genug, der lebensbedrohenden Macht des Meeres zu begegnen. In ihrem Pantheon gibt es aber, wie schon Herodot feststellte, keinen Poseidon, und auch der kanaanäische Gott Yam, der Gott des Meeres, hat in der ägyptischen Mythologie keine Entsprechung. Die Ägypter haben das Meer gekannt, aber sie haben damit mythologisch nichts angefangen. Ebenso hatten die Ägypter genau wie die Mesopotamier, bei denen die Sintflutsage zuhause ist, reichliche Anschauungen und durchaus auch schmerzliche Erfahrungen mit Flussüberschwemmungen. Einmal im Jahr trat der Nil über seine Ufer und setzte das ganze Land unter Wasser. Das war für Ägypten zwar lebensnotwendig; ohne diese Überschwemmungen würde der Nil nicht durch eine Oase, sondern eine unbewohnbare Wüste fließen, aber es war ein durchaus ambivalentes Phänomen. Überstieg die Überschwemmung ein bestimmtes Maß, dann überflutete sie die Siedlungen, richtete an Tempeln und Wohnhäusern schwerste Zerstörungen an und riß in ihrem Strom Menschen und Tiere in den Tod. Nichts hätte näher gelegen, als den Nil mythologisch als eine ambivalente, Leben und Tod spendende Macht zu gestalten. Das ist aber nicht der Fall. Die lebenspendende Funktion der Nilüberschwemmung stand für die Ägypter derart einseitig im Vordergrund, dass sie alle negativen Aspekte ausblendete. Für sie konnte die Überschwemmung gar nicht hoch genug sein. Fiel sie zu niedrig aus, bedeutete das Hungersnot. Das ägyptische Wort für Hungersnot bedeutet wörtlich „Sandbank" und bezog sich auf die Sandbänke, die sich bei allzu niedrigem Nilstand im Flusslauf bildeten. Man sprach auch von der „Sandbank des Apopis" und setzte das himmlische und das irdische Niedrigwasser zueinander in Beziehung. Der Nilstand wurde an verschiedenen Stellen des Landes unablässig gemessen. Solche Messungen

---

2 J. RIEM, *Sintflut in Sage und Wissenschaft*.
3 E. HORNUNG, *Buch von der Himmelskuh*.

gehen bis in die Gründung des pharaonischen Staates um 3000 v.Chr. zurück.[4] Die Ägypter wussten genau, dass die Zone segensreicher Pegelstände nicht nur nach unten unter-, sondern auch nach oben überschritten werden konnte. Aus der Antike sind eine Reihe von Pegelständen überliefert, die nach den Erfahrungen ähnlich hoher Überschwemmungen aus dem 19. Jh. schwerste Verwüstungen angerichtet haben müssen und als Naturkatastrophen einzustufen sind.[5] Das Erstaunliche ist aber, dass sie aller ihrer zerstörenden Auswirkungen zum Trotz in den Quellen als Wunder und Gnade gepriesen werden. Der kulturelle Blick der Ägypter war so einseitig auf den Segen des Wassers und seine lebensspendende Kraft gerichtet, dass er die Opfer der Überschwemmung nicht wahrnam, jedenfalls nicht der Erwähnung wert hielt. Über eine solche allem Anschein nach katastrophale Nilüberschwemmung berichtet z.B. König Taharqa aus dem 6. Jahr seiner Regierungszeit und deutet sie als Zeichen des besonderen Segens, mit dem die Götter seine Regierungszeit bedachten. Hierzu schreibt Stephan Seidlmayer: „Über die Nilflut aus dem sechsten Regierungsjahr des Königs Taharka gibt es weitere Informationen. So steht auf der Tribünenfront des großen Tempels von Karnak eine Serie von Flutmarken aus der Zeit zwischen 950 und 650 vor Christus. Hier ist auch der Maximalpegel des sechsten Jahres des Taharka notiert. Wir wissen daher exakt, dass diese Flut die höchste war, die unter diesen Inschriften verzeichnet ist und eine wahre Naturkatastrophe gewesen sein muss. Dennoch preisen fast alle Texte im Alten Ägypten die gewaltige Flut in lyrischen Tönen. Der Befund ist so auffallend, dass einige Forscher daraus schlossen, die hohe Flut sei in alter Zeit nicht zerstörerisch gewesen; obgleich der Nil die Dörfer, Städte, die Kanal- und Deichsysteme, das Vieh und die Menschen bedrohte".[6] Die hohe Flut war in alter Zeit genauso zerstörerisch wie in neuer, aber der Blick auf diese Ereignisse war im Alten Ägypten ein anderer. Eine Gesellschaft, die von Jahr zu Jahr ängstlich auf die Nilüberschwemmung wartet, ihre Höhe mißt, um den zu erwartenden Ernteertrag zu berechnen, und mit jeder zusätzlichen Elle jubelt und feiert, auch wenn diese übergroßen Überschwemmungen durchaus auch Schaden anrichten, kann daher auch mit dem Motiv der Flutkatastrophe schlechterdings nichts anfangen. Diese kulturelle Grundeinstellung zum Wasser gilt es in Rechnung zu stellen, wenn wir uns im Folgenden der kultischen Bedeutung des Wassers im Alten Ägypten zuwenden wollen.

---

4   S. hierzu S. SEIDLMAYER, „Die Vermessung des Nils".
5   SEIDLMAYER verweist a.a.O. auf Überschwemmungen der Jahre 1874 und 1878.
6   SEIDLMAYER, a.a.O.

2. Die ägyptische Theorie der Nilflut

Unter Ptolemäus V. wurde auf der Insel Sehel im ersten Katarakt eine Inschrift angebracht, die vorgibt, von König Djoser (um 2750 v.Chr.) errichtet worden zu sein. Der König berichtet, daß für sieben Jahre die Nilüberschwemmung ausgeblieben und infolgedessen eine katastrophale Hungersnot ausgebrochen sei. „Da beschloß ich, mich zur Vergangenheit zurückzuwenden, und ich fragte einen Angehörigen der Priesterschaft des Ibis, den obersten Vorlesepriester Imhotep, den Sohn des Ptah südlich seiner Mauer: Wo entspringt der Nil? Wer ist der Gott dort?" Imhotep rüstet keine Forschungsexpedition ins Innere Afrikas aus, sondern konsultiert die heiligen Schriften (die „Machterweise des Re") im „Lebenshaus" von Hermopolis(?). Aus ihnen geht in aller Klarheit hervor, daß der Nil (entgegen allem Augenschein) in Elephantine entspringt und daß Chnum, der Herr dieser Stadt, der für die Nilquellen zuständige Gott sei.

„Es ist eine Stadt inmitten des Wassers, aus der der Nil entspringt, mit Namen Elephantine. Sie ist der Anfang des Anfangs, der uranfängliche Gau gegenüber Wawat (Unternubien). Sie ist die Vereinigung des Landes, der Urhügel, der Thron des Re ... ‚Angenehm zu leben' ist der Name seiner Wohnung, ‚Die beiden Höhlen' ist der Name des Wassers; sie sind die beiden Brüste, die alle guten Dinge ausströmen. Hier ist das Bett des Nils, darin er sich verjüngt ... Chnum ist dort als Gott". Als der König dies erfährt, weiß er, an welchen Gott er sich zu wenden hat, um die Katastrophe in den Griff zu bekommen. Befriedigt schläft er ein, und Chnum, der zuständige Gott, erscheint ihm im Traum:

> Ich bin Chnum, der dich geformt hat ...
> Ich kenne den Nil. Wenn er eingeführt wird auf die Felder, dann gibt seine Einführung Leben an jede Nase, so wie die Zuführung von Leben auf die Felder ...
> Der Nil wird Wasser für dich ausströmen, ohne ein Jahr des Aussetzens oder der Abschwächung für irgendein Land. Pflanzen werden wachsen und sich unter der Last der Früchte niederbeugen. Die Erntegöttin wird an der Spitze von allem sein.
> ... Die Abhängigen werden ihren Herzenswunsch erfüllen ebenso wie die Herren. Das Jahr der Hungersnot wird vergehen ... und Zufriedenheit wird einkehren in die Herzen mehr als zuvor.[7]

Die Motive der sieben Jahre lang ausbleibenden Nilflut und eines darauf bezüglichen Traums des Königs finden sich auch in dem nur fragmentarisch erhaltenen „Buch vom Tempel", dessen Edition wir von seinem Entdecker, J. Quack, erwarten[8], sowie in der biblischen Josephgeschichte. Pharao träumt von sieben

---

7 Hungersnotstele (P. BARGUET, *Stèle de la famine*).
8 S. dazu J. F. QUACK, „Der historische Abschnitt des Buches vom Tempel". Der entsprechende Passus steht in einem Berliner Papyrus aus der Römerzeit, den G. Burkard („Frühgeschichte und Römerzeit") veröffentlicht hat. In diesem Text ist ebenfalls von sieben Jahren ausbleibender Nilüberschwemmung die Rede. Auch dort hat Pharao einen Traum, worin er die Weisung empfängt: „[fahre du in jede Stadt von] Oberägypten und fahre du in jede Stadt von Unter-

fetten und sieben mageren Kühen, sieben starken und sieben dürren Ähren, und Joseph ist der einzige, der diesen Traum auf die Nilschwelle deuten kann, die sieben hohe und sieben niedrige Überschwemmungen bringen wird.

Nach ägyptischer Vorstellung entspringt der Nil also nicht etwa im äthiopischen Hochland und in Zentralafrika, sondern in Elephantine. Gemeint ist aber nicht der Fluss, sondern die Nilüberschwemmung. Sie quillt dort aus der Unterwelt, aus einer Höhle, in der der Gott der Nilüberschwemmung sie aus seinen Krügen ausgießt (Fig. 2). Kultisch zugänglich ist aber nicht dieser verborgene kosmische Gott selbst, sondern der Stadtgott von Elephantine, der Gott Chnum als Herr des Kataraktengebiets.

In der Zeit des Hellenismus verbreitet sich diese Vorstellung der Nilüberschwemmung als des Inbegriffs elysischer Fülle zusammen mit der Isis-Religion in der gesamten Alten Welt und findet seinen typischen Ausdruck im ikonographischen Motiv der Nillandschaft, einem der beliebtesten Themen für die Ausstattung vornehmer Villen mit Wandbildern und Mosaikfußböden. Allein in Pompei führt Schefold in seinem Buch über die pompeianische Wandmalerei 27 Beispiele an.[9] Nillandschaften gibt es sogar in Form dreidimensionaler Installationen. Am bekanntesten ist der „Kanopus" in der Villa Hadriana bei Tivoli. Im Garten beim Haus des Octavius Quarto in Pompeji gab es ein T-förmiges Wasserbecken mit einem „oberen Nil" von 10m Länge und einem „Nil", der 25m lang war. Hier ist die religiöse Bedeutung eindeutig; der Garten wird beherrscht von einem kleinen Isis-Heiligtum.[10] Das Religiöse und das Dekorative verbinden sich auch in der schönsten und berühmtesten der erhaltenen Nillandschaften, in dem Fußbodenmosaik aus Präneste (Fig. 3 und 4).

Auf den ersten Blick scheint nichts näher zu liegen als eine religiöse Interpretation. Dieses Mosaik stammt nicht aus einem Privathaus, sondern aus dem Tempel der Fortuna-Tyche, die mit Isis gleichgesetzt wurde. Es gehörte jedoch nicht zum eigentlichen Tempel, sondern zu einem öffentlichen Gebäude auf der unteren Terrasse.[11] Es war in einem Nympheum in der Apsis einer langen Halle angebracht und mit Wasser bedeckt. Auf der linken Seite der unteren Terrasse gab es eine entsprechende Halle mit einem entsprechenden Nympheum in der Apsis. Hier stellte das Mosaik schwimmende Fische dar. Daher muß man wohl auch die Bedeutung der Nillandschaft nicht im Zusammenhang mit Isis und ihrem Kult suchen, sondern im Zusammenhang des Wassers und seiner

---

ägypten und begründe fest den Tempel […] ihrer Götter. Du sollst das Verfallene erneuern und du sollst das verloren Gefundene ausfüllen und du sollst das Ritual vollziehen …". Auch dort geht es im weiteren Verlauf um eine Konsultation der Schriften: „[…] um zu veranlassen, daß er sieht im Bücherhaus des Tempels (?) des Königs von Ober- und Unterägypten, Cheops …".

9   K. Schefold, Die Wände Pompejis.
10 R. Merkelbach, Isis-Regina, Zeus-Sarapis, Abb. 33–50.
11 P. G. P. Meyboom, The Nile Mosaic of Palestrina.

Symbolik. Der leitende Gedanke der Nilikonographie scheint eine Allegorie des Wassers und seiner Gaben zu sein: Fülle, Glück, Segen und Fest.

In seinem gegenwärtigen Zustand ist das Mosaik ein patchwork aus 21 originalen Szenen in einem nachträglich restaurierten Gesamtzusammenhang. Die originale Komposition wurde um 1625 zerstört, als das Mosaik in Einzelstücke zerschnitten und nach Rom verbracht wurde. Etwas später fertigte Cassiano da Pozzo Aquarell-Kopien dieser Einzelstücke an. Von der Gesamtkomposition aber existiert keine Aufzeichnung. 1640 wurden die Stücke nach Palestrina zurückgebracht, wobei sie noch mehr beschädigt wurden, und dort von Giovanni Battista Calandra restauriert. Die gegenwärtige Zusammenstellung der Szenen verdient daher nicht allzuviel Vertrauen, und auch bei einigen Details kann es sich um Zusätze des 17. Jahrhunderts handeln.

Im oberen Teil des Mosaiks sehen wir Aethiopien als eine bergige Landschaft, belebt von Tieren und Jägern. Der untere Teil stellt Ägypten dar in verschiedenen Szenen zivilisierten Lebens. Die meisten Szenen haben einen kultischen und festlichen Charakter. Ägypten ist in der Jahreszeit der Nilüberschwemmung dargestellt, wenn das Land überflutet ist und die Tempel, Siedlungen und Straßen auf Inseln und Deichen aus dem Wasser aufragen.

Eine der auffallendsten Szenen zeigt einen großen Tempel im ägyptischen Stil. Vor dem Pylon stehen vier Osirisstatuen mit Lotusblüten auf dem Kopf. Über dem Eingang sieht man einen Adler. Es handelt sich um den Tempel des Osiris-Kanopus. Bei Osiris-Kanopus handelt es sich um einen Wasserkult, der eng mit dem Nil und seiner Überschwemmung verbunden ist. Das Kultbild ist ein mit Nilwasser gefülltes Gefäß mit einem Deckel in Gestalt des Osiriskopfes. Das Mosaik verbindet auf eine ganz besondere Weise das Spezifische mit dem Allgemeinen. Während die äthiopischen Szenen rein generisch und mit keinem spezifischen Ort oder Datum verbunden sind, spielen die ägyptischen Szenen in der Jahreszeit der Überschwemmung (von Mitte Juli bis Mitte November). Das umfassende Thema ist der Nil. Wir dürfen nicht vergessen, daß das Mosaik ein Nymphaeum schmückte und daß es von Wasser bedeckt war. Die Botschaft des Mosaiks von Praeneste muß etwas zu tun haben mit dem Wasser als der all-erschaffenden und all-erhaltenden Macht, mit Isis und Osiris, in denen sich diese Macht personifiziert, und mit Ägypten als dem Ort auf Erden, an dem sich sie sich am unmittelbarsten manifestieren.

Ebenso wie auf den Ort kommt es aber auch auf die Zeit an. Ägypten wird in seinen paradiesischen Zügen nicht nur räumlich sondern auch zeitlich determiniert. Ägypten erscheint als heilige Landschaft, bewohnt von Göttern und Priestern, und gesehen in einer heiligen Zeit, der Zeit der Überschwemmung. Die Nilüberschwemmung bedeutet die Wiederkehr der Urflut, die Erneuerung der Schöpfung, die Regeneration allen Lebens, die Rückkehr der Menschheit und der Welt im Ganzen in einen Urzustand von Unschuld, Reinheit, Frieden und Glückseligkeit, eine Wiederherstellung von Sinn, Ordnung, Fülle, Tugend und Gerechtigkeit.

Es gibt einen spätantiken Text, der etwas von der Vorstellungswelt andeutet, die man in der Antike inner- und außerhalb Ägyptens mit dem Nil und seiner jährlichen Überschwemmung verbundet hat und die auch der ikonographischen Tradition bis zu einem gewissen Grade zugrundeliegen mag. Das ist eine Passage in dem Gedicht des Claudian auf das Konsulat des Stilicho, die sich auf die unterirdische Höhle beim ersten Katarakt bezieht, aus der, wie schon die Ägypter glaubten, die Nilüberschwemmung hervorbricht (Fig. 5). In diesem Gedicht tritt auch der Zeit-Aspekt der Nilüberschwemmung sehr klar hervor. Die Regelmäßigkeit dieses jährlichen Ereignisses setzt die Nilüberschwemmung nicht nur zu Fruchtbarkeit und Erneuerung in Beziehung, sondern auch zur Zeit. Sie ist ein Symbol für Zeit, Ewigkeit und die Wiederkehr des Goldenen Zeitalters, in der Fülle, Frieden und Gerechtigkeit auf Erden herrschten.

Est ignota procul, nostraeque impervia genti	Weit entfernt, unbekannt, unzugänglich unserem Geschlecht,
Vix adeunda Deis, annorum squalida mater,	und fast auch den Göttern verboten gibt es die dunkle Mutter der Jahre,
Immensi speluncum aevi, quae tempora vasto	Die Höhle der unermeßlichen Zeit, die in ihrem ungeheuren Inneren die Zeitalter
Suppeditat revocatque sinu: complectitur antrum,	hervorbringt und zurückruft. Eine Schlange umringt die Grotte
Omnia qui placido consumit numine, serpens,	die friedlichen Sinnes alles verschlingt
Perpetuumque viret squamis, caudamque reducto	und sich mit ihren Schuppen ewig verjüngt, ihren Schwanz aber
Ore vorat, tacito relegens exordia lapsu.	rückwärts gewandten Hauptes verschlingt und lautlos gleitend zum Anfang zurückkehrt.[12]

Diese Idee einer paradiesischen Erneuerung verband sich in der Spätantike mit apokalyptischen, messianischen oder chiliastischen Ideen, mit der Hoffnung auf die bevorstehende Heraufkunft oder Wiederkehr einer besseren Welt, die gelegentlich auch eine revolutionäre Wendung nehmen konnte.[13] Daraus mag

---

12 Claudianus, *De Consulatu Stilichonis* (PH. DERCHAIN, „À propos de Claudien").
13 Für Rom s. A. ALFÖLDI, „Die alexandrinischen Götter".

sich das Fortleben der Nillandschaften und Nilmotive in den Kirchen der frühen Christenheit erklären.

Entscheidend ist jedenfalls die Verbindung von Landschaft, Wasser und Zeit, die es so nur in Ägypten gibt. Einmal im Jahr verwandelt sich Ägypten in ein Land, das im Himmel zu schweben scheint. Der ungeheure, lichterfüllte Himmel, der es überwölbt, spiegelt sich in der stillen Wasserfläche des alles bedeckenden Nils wider und zwischen dem oberen Himmel und dem unteren Himmel schweben ebenfalls verdoppelt die Tempel, Dörfer, Deiche und Bäume in festlicher Schwerelosigkeit.

3. Wasserspende und Reinigung im Toten- und Osiriskult

Jede Studie ägyptischer Wasserriten hat auszugehen von der sakramentalen Grundbedeutung des Wassers als kosmogonischer Substanz. Für die Ägypter ist die Welt aus dem Wasser entstanden, und dieser Urozean, ägyptisch „Nun", trägt und umgibt auch die geschaffene Welt; der Nil entspringt aus dem Urozean in der Unterwelt. Als kosmogonische Substanz besitzt das Wasser die Kraft der Erneuerung. Diese Kraft ist grundlegender als die Wirkungen der Reinigung, Tränkung und Konsekration, für die es im Kult eingesetzt wird. Sie ist dem Wasser als natürlichem Element inhärent, kommt ihm also nicht erst durch einen rituellen Akt sakramentaler „Aufladung" zu (wie im Christentum dem Weih- und dem Taufwasser). Die Unterscheidung zwischen elementarem und konsekriertem Wasser, die Ambrosius macht, trifft also auf Ägypten gerade nicht zu:

> Du hast das Wasser gesehen; aber nicht jedes Wasser heilt, sondern nur dasjenige Wasser heilt, das die Gnade Christi besitzt. Eines ist das Element, ein anderes die Konsekration. Eines ist die Sache, ein anderes die Wirksamkeit. Die Sache ist des Wassers, die Wirksamkeit aber des heiligen Geistes. Kein Wasser heilt, wenn nicht der Heilige Geist herabsteigen und jenes Wasser weihen würde.[14]

Solche in der Opfergabe wirkenden Kräfte kann man „sakramentale Potenzen" nennen. Der begleitende Spruch hat die Aufgabe, diese sakramentalen Potenzen zu aktivieren. Wir nennen das „sakramentale Ausdeutung" im Sinne eines Kommentars, der dem Wasser durch den Libationsspruch zuteil wird.[15]

Die meisten wenn nicht alle Riten des ägyptischen Götter- und Totenkults wurzeln im „Pyramidenkult", d.h. dem königlichen Totenkult des Alten Reichs. Daher haben alle Riten etwas mit Belebung, Rückerstattung von Lebenskraft, Heilung von Todesbefallenheit zu tun. Das gilt insbesondere für alle Wasseran-

---

14 *Vidisti aquam; sed non aqua omnis sanat, sed aqua sanat, quae habet gratiam Christi. Aliud est elementum, aliud consecratio: aliud opus, aliud operatio. Aquae opus est, operatio spiritu sancti est. Non sanat aqua, nisi spiritus sanctus descenderit et aquam illam consecraverit* (Ambr. sacr. I 5, 15 nach B. POSTL, *Bedeutung des Nils*, 199).

15 Zum Prinzip der „sakramentalen Ausdeutung" s. J. ASSMANN, *Tod und Jenseits*, 453–476.

wendungen. Dieser „göttliche Totenkult" setzt sich nach dem Zusammenbruch des Alten Reichs im Osiriskult fort. Osiris ist der „gestorbene Gott", dem im Medium des Kults Leben zugeführt wird. Daher spielt gerade im Osiriskult das Wasser als Opfersubstanz eine so zentrale Rolle.

Die wichtigsten Wasserriten im „Pyramidenkult" sind die Libation, ägyptisch *stj mw* „Wasser spenden", und *rdj.t mw* „Wasser darbringen", und die Ablution, ägyptisch „Reinigung mit vier *nemset*-Krügen". Die klassische sakramentale Ausdeutung des Libationswassers identifiziert dieses mit dem Leichensekret des Osiris. Das stellt auch Plutarch im 36. Kapitel seines Traktats „Über Isis und Osiris" fest: „Die Ägypter nennen nicht nur den Nil, sondern ganz allgemein jedes Wasser ‚den Ausfluß des Osiris (Osiridos aporrhoe)'".[16]

Der klassische, hundertfach zu belegende Spruch zur Wasserspende lautet:

> Dies dein Libationswasser, Osiris,
> dies dein Libationswasser, o Unas,
> ist *hervorgekommen von deinem Sohn*,
> ist hervorgekommen von Horus.
>
> Ich bin gekommen, dir das *Horusauge* zu bringen,
> damit dein Herz dadurch glänze.
> Ich habe es dir unter dich, unter deine Sohlen gebracht.
>
> *Nimm dir den Ausfluß, der aus dir hervorgekommen ist*,
> möge dein Herz nicht müde werden davon.[17]

Hier geht es weder darum, den Verstorbenen zu reinigen, noch ihn zu tränken. Die Wasserspende soll ihm das Wasser als belebende Substanz zuführen. Der Spruch ist dreigeteilt. Im ersten Teil wird betont, daß das Wasser von Horus ausgeht. Worum es dabei geht, ist die *Verbindung von Vater und Sohn*. Das Wasser wirkt hier als eine Art Kitt, der die durch den Tod zerrissene Verbindung zwischen Osiris und Horus, Vater und Sohn, wiederherstellen soll. Der zweite Teil nennt das Wasser „Horusauge" und gibt den Zweck der Wasserspende an. Das Wasser soll das Herz des Toten glänzend machen, d.h. erfrischen, beleben. Horusauge ist der kultische Ausdruck für jede Opfergabe, nicht nur für das Wasser. Damit wird jede Opfergabe als eine *Substanz* dargestellt, *die etwas Verlorenes restituiert*, etwas Geraubtes zurückerstattet, etwas Verbrauchtes erneuert, etwas Verringertes auffüllt, etwas Zerfallenes zusammenfügt, kurz: das Symbol einer Reversibilität, die alles, auch den Tod, zu heilen vermag. Der dritte Teil deutet dann das Wasser als Ausfluß, der aus dem Toten selbst herausgekommen ist.

---

16 J. Gw. Griffiths, *Plutarch's De Iside and Osiride*, 172ff., 436ff. Zu den verschiedenen Ausdeutungen des Wassers und der „Ausflüsse" bei Mumifizierung s. vor allem J. Kettel, „Canopes", 315–330 mit reichen bibliographischen Hinweisen. Zum Wasserkult der Isis-Serapis-Religion s. R. A. Wild, *Water*.

17 Spruch 32 der Pyramidentexte (K. Sethe, *Pyramidentexte*).

Dabei ist der Tote allerdings in seiner mythischen Rolle als Osiris gemeint. Der Verstorbene wird im ägyptischen Totenkult mit Osiris gleichgesetzt. Das gilt zunächst nur für den König, wird aber nach dem Untergang des Alten Reichs zu Ende des 3. Jt. auf alle Toten ausgedehnt. Wenn der Tote Osiris ist, dann ist das Wasser, das ihm gespendet wird, aus ihm selbst als Osiris ausgeflossen.

Der Osiris-Mythos, auf den hier angespielt wird, erklärt das Phänomen der jährlichen Nilüberschwemmung als Lebens- und Leichensaft, der aus dem von Seth ermordeten und ins Wasser geworfenen Osiris ausfloß. In Form der Wasserspende mit Nilwasser wird dem zu Osiris gemachten Toten daher sein eigener Ausfluß restituiert. Noch einmal wird die restituierende, erneuernde Kraft des Wassers mobilisiert. Das Wasser symbolisiert die *Lebenskraft als Lebenssaft*, der aus dem Toten ausgeflossen ist und der ihm mit der Libation zurückgegeben wird.

Die „Reinigung mit vier *nemset*-Krügen" wird in ähnlicher Weise ausgedeutet, vgl. z.B. Spruch 676 der Pyramidentexte, in dem sogar von acht *nemset*- und acht *aabet*-Krügen die Rede ist:

Dein Wasser werde dir zuteil,
deine Überschwemmung werde dir zuteil,
deine Ausflüsse werden dir zuteil,
die aus Osiris hervorgegangen sind!

Versammle dir deine Knochen,
rüste dir deine Glieder,
schüttle dir deinen Staub ab,
löse dir deine Fesseln!

Das Grab ist dir geöffnet,
die Türen der Sargkammer sind für dich zurückgeschoben,
aufgetan sind dir die Türflügel des Himmels!

„Zu mir, zu mir!" sagt Isis,
„in Frieden!" sagt Nephthys,
wenn sie ihren Bruder erblicken am Fest des Atum.
Diese deine Libation, Osiris, ist es,
die dein Fleisch beschützt in Geregu-baef.
Dein Ba ist in dir,
deine Macht ist hinter dir/um dich,
bleibend an der Spitze deiner Mächte.

Erhebe dich, N hier,
mögest du die südlichen Stätten durchfahren,
mögst du die nördlichen Stätten durchfahren,
indem deine Macht die Mächte in dir sind.
Deine Verklärten wurden dir gegeben,
die Schakale, die Horus von Hierakonpolis dir gegeben hat.

Erhebe dich, N hier,

um dich auf deinen ehernen Thron zu setzen!
Anubis an der Spitze des Gotteszelts hat befohlen,
daß du gereinigt werdest mit deinen acht *nemset*-Krügen
und mit deinen acht *aabet*-Krügen, die aus dem Gottespalast kommen,
auf daß du göttlich werdest.

(…)

Auch hier geht es um die Restitution von Lebenskraft im Sinne körperlicher Unversehrtheit, Bewegungsfreiheit und sozialer (d.h. götterweltlicher) Integration.

4. Das thebanische Dekadenfest und der Totenkult der Spätzeit

Amun von Luxor setzte alle zehn Tage auf die Westseite über, um im Tempel der 18. Dynastie in Medinet Habu seinen Vorfahren eine Wasserspende darzubringen.[18] Es handelt sich also um einen Totenkult auf der Ebene der Götter. Die Choachyten[19] hatten diese zehntägige Wasserspende in den Gräbern der Toten darzubringen.[20] Dadurch waren alle in Theben-West begrabenen Toten an diese Wasserspende des Amun von Luxor angeschlossen: „Empfangen mögest du die Wasserspende durch Amun von Luxor in Djeme an allen ersten Dekaden" heißt es in einem demotischen Papyrus aus spätptolemäischer Zeit[21] und ähnlich in zahlreichen Totensprüchen der griechisch-römischen Zeit.[22] Der Papyrus BM 10209 des Nesmin stellt Sprüche zusammen, die zu solcher Wasserspende der Choachyten rezitiert wurden, um sie zum Medium einer umfassenden Opferdarbringung auszugestalten. Man kann sich daher gut vorstellen, daß dieser Papyrus auf das Handbuch eines Choachyten zurückgeht.[23]

Der letzte dieser zehn Sprüche im Papyrus Nesmin bezieht sich nun gleich zu Anfang auf jene eigentümliche Gleichsetzung des Wassers mit den Leichenausflüssen des Osiris, die Plutarch hervorhob:

Sokar-Osiris, nimm dir diese Libation,
deine Libation von Horus

---

18 Diese Überfahrt ist seit der 18. Dynastie bis in die römische Zeit belegt.
19 „Wasserspender", die griechische Bezeichnung für die Totenpriester der Spätzeit.
20 Vgl. dazu S. P. Vleeming/P. W. Pestman, *Hundred-Gated Thebes*.
21 Papyrus Berlin 3115. Zur Kultgenossenschaft der Choachyten und zum thebanischen Dekadenfest s. F. de Cenival, *Les associations religieuses*, 103 ff.; K. Parlasca, „Bemerkungen".
22 J. F. Herbin, *Livre*, 142–145.
23 Für Übersetzung und Kommentar dieses Papyrus s. J. Assmann, *Totenliturgien* III, 499–544; M. Smith, *Traversing Eternity*, 178–192. Im *Buch vom Durchwandeln der Ewigkeit* wird überdies Osiris in Djeme mit dem Talfest in Verbindung gebracht. Herbin meint, daß diese Verbindung bis auf die 25. Dynastie zurückgeht (Herbin, *Livre*, 139 zu A II, 26 und II, 27).

in jenem deinem Namen „Kataraktengebiet".
Nimm dir die Ausflüsse, die aus dir herausgekommen sind,
die Horus dir gibt bis hin zu jedem Ort, an dem du im Wasser getrieben bist.[24]

Das spielt an auf jene Episode des Osirismythos, derzufolge Seth den erschlagenen Osiris ins Wasser geworfen hat. Aus den Leichensekreten des erschlagenen Osiris läßt der Mythos die Nilüberschwemmung entstehen.

Entscheidend für diesen Gedankenzusammenhang ist die Idee des Kreislaufs. Mit dem Wasser wird dem Toten der Lebenssaft zurückgegeben, der aus ihm, aus Osiris, ausgetreten ist. Das Wasser ist ein Ausfluß, der im Opfer rückerstattet wird. Aus dieser Zyklusidee ergibt sich die Vorstellung der „Verjüngung". Der Begriff der „Verjüngung" verweist auf das Mysterium der zyklischen Zeit, die in sich selbst zurückläuft. In der Tat gibt es im ägyptischen Denken einen engen Zusammenhang zwischen dem Wasser und der Zeit. Dieser Zusammenhang ergibt sich aus der jährlichen Nilüberschwemmung. Das ägyptische Jahr beginnt (wenigstens theoretisch) mit dem Einsetzen der Nilflut im Sommer.[25] Daher hängen im ägyptischen Denken die Begriffe „Jahr", „Nil" und „Verjüngung" im Sinne von Reversibilität, Rückläufigkeit und Regeneration ganz eng zusammen. Das ägyptische Wort für „Jahr" ist „das Verjüngte" (oder „sich verjüngende"), genau wie der Ausdruck „verjüngtes (oder: sich verjüngendes) Wasser" für die Nilüberschwemmung. Man stellt sich vor, daß in der jährlich ansteigenden Flut der Nil sowohl sich selbst als auch die Ackerfluren verjüngt. Die Nilüberschwemmung ist das Zentralsymbol der zyklischen Zeit, die nicht irreversibel auf ein Ziel zustrebt sondern kreisförmig in sich selbst zurückläuft und auf diese Weise Erneuerung, Wiederholung, Regeneration ermöglicht. Deshalb ist das Wasser die zentrale Totenspende. Im Wasser liegt die Kraft der Umkehr.

5. Der „Baptism of Pharaoh"

Im Jahr 1950 prägte der eminente britische Ägyptologe Sir Alan Gardiner den Begriff des „Baptism of Pharaoh" für einen sehr häufig bezeugten Ritus.[26] Seiner Ansicht nach war der Terminus „Taufe" aufgrund der engen Analogie dieses Ri-

---

24 ASSMANN, *Totenliturgien* III, 532f.
25 Neben dem Mondkalender, der auf Beobachtung beruhte und alle 2–3 Jahre die Einschaltung eines Schaltmonats erforderte (das Mondjahr hat 354 Tage) und dem Sonnenkalender, der auf Berechnung basierte, 12 Monate zu 360 Tagen + 5 Zusatztage umfasste, also hinter dem Sonnenjahr um einen Vierteltag zurückblieb, kannten die Ägypter einen ebenfalls auf Beobachtung beruhenden Sothiskalender, der den Neujahrstag auf den heliakischen Frühaufgang des Sirius (Sothis) festsetzte. Dieser Tag (Mitte Juli) markierte zugleich den Beginn der Nilüberschwemmung.
26 A. GARDINER, „Baptism"; GARDINER, „Addendum".

tus zur christlichen Taufe gerechtfertigt. Gardiner zufolge diente sowohl beim „Baptism of Pharaoh" wie auch bei der christlichen Taufe „a symbolic cleansing by means of water … as initiation into a properly legitimated religious life".[27] Ägyptologischerseits ist die Gültigkeit dieser Begriffsprägung unseres Wissens nie wirklich diskutiert worden; vielmehr wird der Begriff des "Baptism" in der einschlägigen Literatur eher selten und dann meist als konventioneller Terminus verwendet. Stattdessen wird schlicht, dem ägyptischen Text entsprechend, von "Reinigung" gesprochen, auch von "Lustration"[28] oder von „Krönungsbad".[29] Nur ganz vereinzelt wird einer Analogie des ägyptischen „Baptism of Pharaoh" zur christlichen Taufe ausdrücklich zugestimmt.[30]

Mit „Baptism of Pharaoh" bezeichnete Gardiner einen in spezifischer Weise abgebildeten symbolischen Akt, bei dem der König von zwei Gottheiten mit Wasser übergossen wird (Fig. 6). Dieser Bildtyp ist über zweieinhalbtausend Jahre hinweg belegt.[31] Die Identität der agierenden Gottheiten ist im Grunde variabel, seit dem Neuen Reich überwiegen aber Horus und Thot bei weitem.[32] Die begleitenden Texte nehmen im Laufe der Zeit immer mehr an Umfang zu. Abgesehen von Namensbeischriften ist hier als ältestes Element die stets recht kurze Reinigungsformel zu nennen sowie die eigentlichen Reden der göttlichen Offizianten.[33]

Die ältesten Belege sind so fragmentarisch, daß eine gesicherte Kontextualisierung nicht möglich ist.[34] Erst aus der späteren 12. Dynastie ist eine Szene *in situ* an der Wand eines Tempels erhalten.[35] Es scheint, daß bereits in dieser Epoche der „Baptism of Pharaoh" mit dem Eintritt des Königs in den Tempel einherging[36], aber offenbar nicht mit einem Akt der Krönung bzw. Krönungsbestätigung verbunden war, wie dies dann seit der 18. Dynastie regelmäßig der

---

27 GARDINER, „Baptism", 6.
28 So L. CORCORAN, *Portrait Mummies*, 59–60.
29 So S. SCHOTT, „Reinigung Pharaos", 87–90.
30 SCHOTT, „Reinigung Pharaos", 89; CORCORAN, *Portrait Mummies*, 59; A. I. SADEK, „Rites baptismaux", sowie, aus religionswissenschaftlicher Sicht, S. G. F. BRANDON, „Lustration".
31 24. Jh. v.Chr. – 2. Jh. n.Chr.: erstmals in der 5. Dynastie, verstärkt seit dem Neuen Reich (16. Jh. ff.).
32 Auswahl und ideelle Anzahl der Gottheiten diskutieren GARDINER, „Baptism", 8–11; A. SMITH, „Kingship, Water and Ritual", 332–336.
33 Die Reinigungsformel ist in einer vertikalen Zeile vor dem jeweiligen Offizianten angebracht, die Götterrede über und hinter ihm.
34 Nach R. LANDGRÁFOVÁ, *Faience Inlays*, 20–22 wurden im Totentempel des Königs Raneferef (5. Dynastie) Fragmente einer „Baptism"-Szene gefunden, aber auch solche, die sich zu einer Krönungsszene und einer Sedfestszene ergänzen lassen. Ob hier aber einst eine Sequenz vorlag, ist nicht mehr zu klären; da die Fragmente in verschiedenen Räumen gefunden wurden, erscheint dies eher unwahrscheinlich. S. auch A. OPPENHEIM, *Aspects*, 563.
35 A. VOGLIANO, *Secondo Rapporto*, 24; Abbildung bei OPPENHEIM, *Aspects*, Tf. 406.
36 OPPENHEIM, *Aspects*, 567.

Fall war.[37] Von dieser Zeit an ist der „Baptism of Pharaoh" gewöhnlich in eine Sequenz eingebunden, die in ihrer vollständigen Form fünf Elemente umfaßt (Fig. 7):[38]

- Der König verläßt seinen Palast
- Reinigung des Königs („Baptism of Pharaoh")
- Krönung des Königs
- Einführung des Königs
- Bestätigung der Krönung durch die Hauptgottheit des jeweiligen Tempels

Bleibt diese Abfolge ikonographisch im Rahmen einer gewissen Variabilität von nun an konstant, so gilt dies nicht für die begleitenden Texte.[39]

Daß der „Baptism" eine Reinigung des Herrschers intendiert, bestätigt bereits die älteste erhaltene Beischrift aus der 12. Dynastie: *„Rezitation: Gereinigt seist du, gereinigt sei dein Ka mit diesem Wasser des Lebens."* Die Substanz, die aus zwei Krügen über den König ausgegossen wird, wird zwar bereits hier als Wasser bezeichnet, als solches dargestellt – nämlich in Gestalt gezackter Wasserlinien – wird es jedoch insgesamt sehr selten. Häufig wird der Wasserstrom als eine Kette von *anch*-Zeichen, dem Symbol des Lebens, visualisiert (*„Wasser des Lebens"*), später tritt als alternierendes Element das *was*-Szepter hinzu, ein Sinnbild für Macht, Heil, Herrschaft. Entsprechende Beischriften bezeichnen das Wasser daher auch konkret als ‚*dieses Wasser aus anch und was*'.

Der Aspekt der Reinigung wird von der Mitte der 18. Dynastie an ausführlicher thematisiert und mit den ausführenden Gottheiten verknüpft. Erstmals erscheint nun die knappe, von der Gottheit gesprochene Reinigungsformel ‚*Deine Reinheit ist meine Reinheit*'.[40] Über diese Formel kann eine Verbindung zu zwei einleitenden Szenen (2 und 3) des sogenannten Mundöffnungsrituals hergestellt werden. Dieses Ritual ist als Sequenz einzelner Riten vor allem seit dem Neuen Reich und im Kontext der Bestattung von Privatpersonen faßbar; es wurde jedoch beispielsweise auch an sakralen Bauwerken und für verstorbene Könige vollzogen. Eine Sammlung sämtlicher bekannter Einzelriten des

---

37 Der Szenentyp kommt auch auf einer Reihe ägyptisierender syro-palästinensischer Rollsiegel der Zweiten Zwischenzeit vor (B. TEISSIER, *Egyptian Iconography*, Nrn. 4, 43, 88), muß also bereits in dieser Epoche einen Verbreitungs- bzw. Bekanntheitsgrad erreicht haben, der anhand der innerägyptischen Funde nicht mehr nachzuvollziehen ist.

38 W. WAITKUS, *Untersuchungen*, 10–11; GARDINER, „Baptism", 8. B. ALTENMÜLLER-KESTING, *Reinigungsriten*, 90 unterscheidet vier Elemente, da sie die abschließende Krönungsbestätigung nicht mit aufnimmt. Sehr häufig ist die Sequenz in reduzierter Form wiedergegeben und dann auf die Schlußelemente Einführung und Krönungsbestätigung konzentriert.

39 Vgl. ASSMANN, „Semiosis and Interpretation", 98–99.

40 Im Tempel Amenophis' II. im nubischen Amada: H. GAUTHIER, *Amada* I, 114–116, Tf. XXIIIA; II, Tf. XXIX.

Mundöffnungsrituals umfaßt 75 Szenen.[41] Die ersten Szenen behandeln die Reinigung des Verstorbenen, wobei eine Reinigung aus zuerst vier *nemset*-Krügen und dann aus vier *descheret*-Krügen den Anfang macht (Fig. 8).[42] Die jeweiligen Rezitationen sind fast identisch und lauten:

> Deine Reinheit ist die Reinheit des Horus – und umgekehrt.
> Deine Reinheit ist die Reinheit des Seth – und umgekehrt.
> Deine Reinheit ist die Reinheit des Thot – und umgekehrt.
> Deine Reinheit ist die Reinheit des Dewen-anui – und umgekehrt.

Daß die knappe Formel des Tempeltextes tatsächlich auf den Text zur Mundöffnung Bezug nimmt, erweist sich in zahlreichen Götterreden des „Baptism of Pharaoh" seit Beginn der 19. Dynastie, in die die vollständige Mundöffnungsformel aufgenommen wurde. Die Mundöffnungsformel wiederum verweist zurück auf zwei Sprüche aus dem ältesten Ritualtextbestand Ägyptens, den Pyramidentexten. Die beiden Reinigungssprüche PT 35 und PT 36 enthalten Formulierungen, die sie als Vorläufer der Sprüche des Mundöffnungsrituals ausweisen:

> Dein Natron ist das Natron des Horus,
> Dein Natron ist das Natron des Seth,
> Dein Natron ist das Natron des Thot,
> Dein Natron ist das Natron des Dewen-anui.

In diesen Pyramidensprüchen wurde die Reinigung nicht mit Wasser, sondern mit (in Wasser gelöstem) Natron vollzogen. Anders als beim Mundöffnungsritual wird der „Baptism of Pharaoh" jedoch nie mit *nemset*-Krügen vollzogen, sondern ausschließlich mit *hes*- bzw. *qebeh*-Vasen.[43]

Diejenigen Bestandteile der Götterreden, die über die Mundöffnungsformel hinausgehen, betreffen im Neuen Reich wie in der Griechisch-Römischen Zeit die Regeneration des Herrschers. Im Neuen Reich war der „Baptism" des Königs regelmäßig mit der Verleihung langer Lebenszeit und zahlloser Regierungsjubiläen (Sedfeste) seitens der göttlichen Offizianten einhergegangen.[44] In der Griechisch-Römischen Zeit ist die Mundöffnungsformel weiterhin regelhafter Bestandteil der Götterreden; aus den Erweiterungen geht hervor, daß nunmehr die Ausdeutung des Reinigungswassers in den Vordergrund tritt,

---

41   E. Otto, *Mundöffnungsritual*; Assmann, *Tod und Jenseits*, 408–417.
42   Vorläufer zu diesen Szenen sind bereits im Mittleren Reich belegt (A. M. Blackman, „Washing the Dead").
43   Eine Reinigung aus vier *nemset*-Krügen ist in anderem Kontext in den Pyramidentexten ebenfalls belegt. Während *nemset*- und *descheret*-Krüge einzig zur Reinigung verwendet werden, ist die *hes*- oder *qebeh*-Vase im wesentlichen ein Libationsgefäß. Nach A. Smith, „Kingship, Water and Ritual", 331–332 ist dies ein Indiz dafür, daß beim „Baptism" die Götter den König nicht nur mit „Leben" und „Herrschaft" in Gestalt von Wasser reinigen, sondern ihm diese Eigenschaften gleichsam als Opfer darbringen.
44   Beispiele bei Altenmüller-Kesting, *Reinigungsriten*, 95–111.

wobei besonderer Wert auf dessen Herkunft – meist aus den osirianisch gedeuteten Nilquellen am Ersten Katarakt – gelegt wird.[45] Die Reinigung betrifft nun ganz unmittelbar den Leib des Herrschers, der durch das Reinigungswasser neu vereint und von allem „Bösen", das ihm anhaftet, gereinigt wird.[46] Wurde in früherer Zeit das Ergebnis der gesamten Ritualsequenz, die Krönungs- und damit Herrschaftsbestätigung, bereits in den Reden zum „Baptism" vorweggenommen und damit die Szene der Gesamtfunktion untergeordnet, so scheint sie nun an Eigenständigkeit gewonnen zu haben, da nun die unmittelbaren Auswirkungen der Reinigung auf den König im Zentrum stehen. Obwohl er in die identische Szenenabfolge eingebunden ist wie im Neuen Reich, weist der „Baptism" als Einheit nicht mehr über sich selbst hinaus. Dazu paßt der Befund eines etwa in die Zeitenwende zu datierenden Papyrus, der ausschließlich Rezitationen zur Reinigung des Königs enthält.[47] Daß es sich hierbei um Riten handelt, die denen des „Baptism of Pharaoh" zumindest eng verwandt sind, geht aus zahlreichen Parallelen zwischen den Sprüchen des Papyrus und den Götterreden zum „Baptism of Pharaoh" in Tempeln der Griechisch-Römischen Zeit hervor.

Welche Funktion erfüllt der „Baptism of Pharaoh", die Reinigung des Königs, innerhalb der eingangs skizzierten Ritensequenz? Seine vermittelnde Position ist allein schon aus der Situierung innerhalb der Sequenz zu ersehen: die Reinigung steht zwischen dem Verlassen des Palastes und der Krönung durch die Götter und ist damit vor dem Eintritt in den eigentlichen Tempel anzusiedeln:[48] die Reinigung, wie es die Formeln ‚*Deine Reinheit ist meine Reinheit*' und ‚*Deine Reinheit ist die Reinheit des Horus*' etc. andeuten, versetzt den König in einen gottgleichen Zustand der Reinheit, der es ihm erst ermöglicht, den Göttern handelnd gegenüberzutreten und von diesen als ihresgleichen anerkannt zu werden.[49] Im dreigliedrigen Schema eines „rite de passage" nähme die Reinigung also die vermittelnde Phase der Umwandlung ein. Die erste Phase der Ablösung wird durch das Verlassen des Palastes markiert, die dritte Phase der Wiedereingliederung durch Krönung, Einführung und Krö-

---

45 Vgl. ALTENMÜLLER-KESTING, *Reinigungsriten*, 113–130.
46 Beispiele bei ALTENMÜLLER-KESTING, *Reinigungsriten*, 131–142. Schon der oben zitierten viergliedrigen Rezitation aus Szene 2 des Mundöffnungsrituals folgt abschließend der Passus: ‚Empfange dir deinen Kopf! Vereinige dir deine Knochen, sagt Geb! Thot, vereinige ihn, so daß vergehe, was (Schlechtes) an ihm ist!' (nach OTTO, *Mundöffnungsritual*, 38).
47 SCHOTT, *Reinigung Pharaos* (Papyrus Berlin 13242).
48 Archäologisch schlägt sich der liminale Charakter der Reinigung durch die Plazierung der Reinigungskapelle im Tempeleingangsbereich nieder, s. die Belege bei ALTENMÜLLER-KESTING, *Reinigungsriten*, 167–171.
49 Vgl. U. RUMMEL, *Pfeiler seiner Mutter*, 192, 224.

nungsbestätigung.[50] Diese rituell wiederholte Krönung wurde offenbar als eine Verjüngung oder gar Wiedergeburt des Herrschers interpretiert.[51] Eine Reinigung als Voraussetzung für die Einführung bei der Gottheit war auch beim Eintritt ins Jenseits erforderlich. Sie vollzog sich durch das Bestehen der Prüfung des Herzens im Totengericht.[52] So heißt es im Titel des einschlägigen Totenbuchspruches 125: „Den NN von allem Bösen befreien, das er begangen hat; das Angesicht der Götter schauen".[53] Genau dies war die Funktion der Reinigung auch beim Eintritt des Königs in den Tempel.[54] Eine Reinigung des Verstorbenen durch die Götter Horus und Thot im Kontext der Rechtfertigung ist mindestens seit dem Mittleren Reich belegt: „Wasche dich mit diesen vier *nemset*-Krügen und *aabet*-Krügen, mit denen sich die Götterneunheit reinigt ... Horus hat dich gereinigt, Thot hat dich verklärt, deine beiden Söhne, die Herren der *wereret*-Krone. Abgelöst wird die Beleidigung, verhütet wird das Böse an deinem Fleisch".[55] Aus derselben Epoche stammt auch die älteste Darstellung der Reinigung eines Verstorbenen aus *hes*-Vasen, deren Ikonographie Ähnlichkeiten mit der des „Baptism of Pharaoh" aufweist (Fig. 9). Freilich wird die Reinigung hier von Priestern bzw. Angehörigen vollzogen.[56] Wenn also das ursprünglich allein dem König und der Sphäre des Götterkults vorbehaltene Bild der Reinigung durch Gottheiten von der frühen 19. Dynastie an ganz ver-

---

50 ASSMANN, Maʿat, 147–148 subsumiert im selben Zusammenhang Reinigung und Einführung unter dem Begriff der Initiation, die sich in den Akt der „Qualifikation" (Reinigung) und den Akt der „Aufnahme" (Einführung, Bestätigung) aufgliedert.

51 Im Rahmen des sogenannten „Geburtsmythos" von der göttlichen Geburt des Herrschers wird der „Baptism" an einem kindlichen König vollzogen (s. ASSMANN, „Zeugung des Sohnes", 69–71; ASSMANN, „Tod und Initiation", 141–143). Die Krönungsbestätigung kann mit der Säugung des nunmehr kindlich dargestellten Königs durch eine Göttin einhergehen, etwa auf dem Granitsanktuar des Philipp Arrhidaeus in Karnak (R. LEPSIUS, Denkmäler, Tafelband 9 Abt. IV, Blatt 2; GARDINER, „Baptism", Tf. II), einer genauen Kopie eines Vorgängerbaus der 18. Dynastie.

52 In wenigen Fällen ist die Gerichtsszene sogar mit einer expliziten Reinigungsszene des Verstorbenen verbunden, so z.B. im Papyrus Kairo JE 95880 (3. Zwischenzeit; unpubl.); Papyrus Hildesheim 2128 (Griechisch-Römische Zeit; unpubl.). Im Totenbuch des Ani (19. Dyn.) sind dem Bild des nach bestandenem Totengericht den Osiris verehrenden Verstorbenen je zwei *nemset*- und zwei *descheret*-Reinigungsgefäße beigefügt (Fig. 12).

53 E. HORNUNG, Totenbuch, 233. Am Schluß des sogenannten „Negativen Sündenbekenntnisses" von Spruch 125 verkündet der Verstorbene: „Ich bin rein, ich bin rein, ich bin rein, ich bin rein! Meine Reinheit ist die Reinheit jenes großen Benu-Vogels, der in Herakleopolis ist." (HORNUNG, Totenbuch, 235). Zur Reinigung des Verstorbenen vor dem Totengericht der Sargtexte s. R. GRIESHAMMER, Das Jenseitsgericht in den Sargtexten, 63. Zum Reinigungsgedanken bei der seit dem Neuen Reich vorherrschenden Form des Totengerichts s. CH. SEEBER, Untersuchungen zur Darstellung des Totengerichts, 66–67; ASSMANN, Tod und Jenseits, 106–107.

54 Zur Parallelität von kultischer Reinheit und Totengericht vgl. ASSMANN, Maʿat, 140–149; A. KUCHAREK, „Reinheit für alle".

55 Sargtextspruch 74 (nach ASSMANN, Totenliturgien I, 419–420).

56 BLACKMAN, „Washing the Dead", Tf. XVIII.

einzelt seinen Weg in das Dekorationsprogramm von Privatgräbern findet (Fig. 10),[57] so besteht die Neuerung im wesentlichen in der Übernahme der königlichen Ikonographie bzw. in der Substitution realweltlicher Akteure (Priester) durch götterweltliche (Horus und Thot). Die Ikonographie macht anfangs noch Anleihen bei hergebrachten privaten Reinigungsszenen, die ihrerseits wiederum auf das Mundöffnungsritual zurückgehen, aber häufig separat abgebildet wurden (Fig. 11).[58] In den folgenden Epochen und gehäuft in römischer Zeit erscheint das Motiv des „Baptism of Pharaoh" – in Ermangelung dekorierter Grabstätten – dann vor allem auf Särgen (Fig. 13).[59] Die wenigen Beischriften der privaten „Baptism"-Bilder enthalten fast nie – im Unterschied zu den zeitgenössischen königlichen Szenen – die Reinigungsformel aus dem Mundöffnungsritual, die in Privatgräbern ansonsten häufig vorkommt. Vielmehr handelt es sich um kurze Formeln, die, ähnlich wie die späten königlichen Beischriften, die Herkunft des Wassers thematisieren: „Ich reinige dich mit dem kühlen Wasser, das aus der Höhle des Osiris hervorkommt".[60] Die nunmehr funeräre Konnotation schlägt sich in ikonographischen Details nieder, die darauf verweisen, daß der „Baptism" im privaten Kontext auf die Rechtfertigung im Totengericht Bezug nimmt:[61] so etwa die gelösten Mumienbinden, die die wiedergewonnene Bewegungsfreiheit des verklärten Toten andeuten (Fig. 14);[62]

---

57 Aus der Ramessidenzeit sind drei Belege bekannt: zwei aus der 19. Dynastie (Zeit Ramses' II., um 1250 v.Chr.), die beide etwa zeitgleich in Gräbern des Dorfes Deir el-Medine bei Theben angebracht wurden, dessen Bewohner durch ihre Arbeit an den Königsgräbern einen privilegierten Zugang zur königlichen Ikonographie besaßen, der sich auch sonst in der Dekoration ihrer Gräber niederschlägt (TT 5 und TT 335, in letzterem ist die Szene weitestgehend zerstört): J. VANDIER, *Nefer-abou*, Tf. XIX; B. BRUYÈRE, *Deir el Médineh (1924–1925)*, 97 Abb. 65, 126–127 Abb. 87). Ein dritter Beleg aus der 20. Dynastie befindet sich im Grab des Pennut im nubischen Aniba nördlich von Abu Simbel (LEPSIUS, *Denkmäler*, Tafelband 7 Abt. III, Blatt 231b).

58 Beispielsweise im Grab des Sennefer in Theben (*Sen-nefer*, 55); weitere Belege bei E. BUZOV, „Role of the Heart". Hierbei wird der Verstorbene nicht von zwei Gottheiten, sondern von vier Priestern gereinigt, und zwar, wie beim Mundöffnungsritual, aus *nemset*-Krügen. In die Ikonographie der frühesten privaten Darstellungen des „Baptism of Pharaoh" wurde hiervon das Alabasterbecken, in dem der Verstorbene steht, sowie das Herz, das er bei sich trägt, übernommen.

59 Beispiele aus römischer Zeit bei CORCORAN, *Portrait Mummies*, 138, 149, 197, Tf. 14, 15, 22, 30, 31.

60 Rede des Thot im Grab des Pennut in Aniba. In TT 5: „Ich (Thot) gebe dir Wasser an der Schöpfstelle" sowie „Wasser, die aus Elephantine hervorkommen", vielleicht zu verbinden zu: „Ich (Thot) gebe dir Wasser an der Schöpfstelle (von den) Wassern, die aus Elephantine hervorkommen". Das „Wasser von der Schöpfstelle" paßt nicht in einen Reinigungskontext, da es sonst stets mit dem Wunsch verbunden ist, davon zu trinken, so auch unmittelbar unterhalb der besprochenen Szene.

61 Vgl. M. FITZENREITER, „Konzepte vom Tod", 54–55.

62 Sarg BM 22939: C. ANDREWS, *Egyptian Mummies*, 46 Abb. 50. Auf dem römerzeitlichen Sargbrett Boston MFA 1989.75 (unpubliziert) geht der Verstorbene als nacktes, von losen Mumien-

und das Herz des Verstorbenen, das beim Totengericht gewogen und ihm zugesprochen wird (Fig. 10).[63] Das Totengericht als Reinigung von allen Vergehen verweist wiederum auf die Mumifizierung in der Balsamierungshalle (ägyptisch oft als „Reinigungshalle" bezeichnet).[64] Der mittels der physischen Reinigung durch Einbalsamierung und der moralischen Reinheit durch das Totengericht gewonnene gottgleiche Zustand versetzt den Verstorbenen in die Lage, den Göttern gegenüberzutreten[65], so wie er es dem König – und in seiner Stellvertretung einem Teil der Priesterschaft – bereits auf Erden im Tempel erlaubt. Die Reinigung bereitet also vor und ist Voraussetzung, bewirkt aber nicht selbst die Einführung bei und Anerkennung durch die Gottheit.[66]

Dies wie auch die Konsequenzen gehen deutlich aus einem der raren ausführlichen Texte zu einem „Baptism of Pharaoh" an einer Privatperson hervor, der in einem Totenpapyrus der Zeitenwende überliefert ist.[67] Der erste Abschnitt entspricht inhaltlich weitgehend den Götterreden der zeitgenössischen

---

binden umhangenes Kind aus dem Totengericht hervor. Vgl. auch Pyramidentextspruch 536: „Erhebe dich, löse dir deine Fesseln, schüttele dir deinen Staub ab! Setze dich doch auf deinen ehernen Thron, indem du gereinigt bist mit deinen vier *nemset*-Krügen und deinen vier *aabet*-Krügen, die für dich aus dem Gottespalast hervorgekommen sind, damit du göttlich wirst, die für dich aus dem göttlichen Kanal geschöpft wurden und die Horus von Hierakonpolis dir gegeben hat" (nach J. ASSMANN/A. KUCHAREK, *Totenliteratur*, 14). Zur Befreiung aus dem Mumienzustand s. HORNUNG, „Vom Sinn der Mumifizierung".

63 TT 5 (s. Fußnote 57); Sarg Louvre E. 3864 (BOREUX, *Guide-Catalogue*, 302). Das Herz als Sitz nicht nur der Gedanken und Gefühle, sondern auch des Gedächtnisses ist beim Totengericht dasjenige Organ, das über die Lebensführung des Verstorbenen Auskunft geben soll. Zur Bedeutung des Herzens im ägyptischen Totenkult s. ASSMANN, *Tod und Jenseits*, 139–143.

64 ASSMANN, *Tod und Jenseits*, 102–105 und M. SMITH, *Traversing Eternity*, 6 weisen auf den engen Zusammenhang von Totengericht und Rechtfertigung mit der Balsamierung hin, die ägyptisch als „Reinigung" bezeichnet wurde. Auf einigen Särgen der Ptolemäerzeit ist die Reinigung der Mumie bei der Balsamierung ikonographisch offenbar dem „Baptism of Pharaoh" nachempfunden (Hildesheim Inv. 1954: A. EGGEBRECHT, *Suche nach Unsterblichkeit*, 31; Hildesheim Inv. 1953: R. GERMER, *Das Geheimnis der Mumien*, 16).

65 Dies wird besonders deutlich an zwei privaten Szenen, die nicht nur das Ikon des „Baptism", sondern auch die darauf folgende Einführung bei der Gottheit aus der königlichen Sequenz übernommen haben: verkürzt im Grab des Pennut in Aniba (s. Fußnote 57), ausführlich im Grab der Gottesgemahlin Mutirdis in Theben, wo die Reinigung zwar nur von Horus vollzogen wird, die Grabherrin aber im folgenden von Horus und Thot vor Osiris geleitet wird (26. Dynastie; ASSMANN, *Mutirdis*, 56–58, Tf. 20, 20a). In beiden Gräbern der 19. Dynastie, die eine „Baptism"-Szene enthalten (s. Fußnote 57), ist diese jeweils eng mit einer weiteren Vignette vergesellschaftet, die den Grabherrn beim Öffnen der Türen zum Totenreich zeigt (VANDIER, *Nefer-abou*, Tf. XIX; BRUYÈRE, *Deir el Médineh (1924–1925)*, 142, 143 Abb. 94), womit ebenfalls der Eintritt in die göttliche Sphäre angedeutet wird.

66 Zur Liminalität der Reinigungssituation vgl. FITZENREITER, „Konzepte vom Tod", 54–55; RUMMEL, *Pfeiler seiner Mutter*, 192.

67 Papyrus Rhind I, VI,1–3 (G. MÖLLER, *Totenpapyrus*, 30–33; neuere Gesamtübersetzungen: ASSMAN/KUCHAREK, *Totenliteratur*, 597–613 (hieratische Version); M. SMITH, *Traversing Eternity*, 318–332 (demotische Version).

königlichen „Baptism of Pharaoh"-Szenen: Die Reinigung bereitet hier aber nicht den König auf den Eintritt in den Tempel vor, sondern den Toten auf den Eintritt ins Totenreich, und sie entfernt nicht allein Schmutz und Verfehlungen, sondern auch „Fäulnis". In den folgenden Passagen geht es um die durch die einleitende Reinigung (d.h. Balsamierung) ermöglichte Einführung bei Osiris („den Großen Gott schauen") und die hierdurch erwirkten Existenzformen des Verstorbenen, dessen Ba-Seele in den Himmel aufsteigt, während sein Leib im Totenreich bei Osiris weilt; auch der Mumie im Grab ist Leben eigen. Der verklärte Verstorbene ist aber nicht nur in die Lage versetzt, in Gegenwart der Götter zu dauern, er kann genauso an den religiösen Festen auf Erden teilnehmen, insbesondere am Dekadenfest im Westen von Theben.[68] Die Preisung des Verstorbenen durch seine Familie weist auf seinen nunmehr göttlichen Status hin, und zuletzt werden der Vollzug der Reinigung und ihr Resultat bestätigt:

> Spruch von der Reinigung durch Horus und Thot.
> Rezitation:
> Horus reinigt dich,
> wenn du eintrittst in das Totenreich; andere Lesart: die abgesonderte Duat[69],
> um den Großen Gott zu schauen im Totenreich,
> indem nichts Böses an dir ist.
> Thot reinigt dich,
> indem du in deine Gewänder gekleidet bist,
> indem alle deine Glieder gesalbt sind,
> indem kein Gottesmakel an dir ist
> und indem keinerlei Fäulnis in deinem Leib ist.
>
> Wir reinigen dich mit Wasser, das aus Elephantine hervorgekommen ist,
> mit Horus-Materie[70], die aus Elkab hervorgekommen ist,
> und mit Milch aus Athribis.
>
> Möge dein Ba leben beim Herrn der Luft,
> möge dein Leib sich mit dem Ba im Himmel vereinigen.
> Möge es deinen Gliedern gutgehen bei Wennefer, er möge leben,
> möge deine Mumie dauern bei Schu.
> Mögest du empfangen werden unter den Gerechten,
> möge dein Ba aufsteigen zum Himmel zusammen mit Orion[71]
> und den Sternen im Gefolge der Sothis.[72]
>
> Möge dir Atemluft gegeben werden im Inneren deines Grabes,
> mögen deine Nüstern den Hauch des Lebens atmen.
> Möge dir deine Zunge gegeben werden,

---

68 S. hierzu Abschnitt 4.
69 Das unterweltlich gedachte Totenreich.
70 Natron.
71 Das Sternbild galt als eine Erscheinungsform des Osiris.
72 Der Sirius, eine Erscheinungsform der Isis.

indem sie beweglich ist in deinem (Hirn-)Kasten
wie der Skarabäus, der aus dem Kopf des „Dessen Nase lebt" hervorgekommen ist.
Möge dir dein Grab gegeben werden wie ein blühender Garten,
mögest du darin das Leben wiederholen für immerdar.
Mögest du gehen und kommen vor den Müdherzigen,
mögest du eine Libation empfangen aus den Händen von Isis und Nephthys,
mögest du dauern in deiner Schetit in (der Nekropole) „Die gegenüber ihrem Herrn",
möge Nut ihre Arme ausstrecken, um dich zu empfangen
in ihrer Gestalt als Hathor, Gebieterin des Westens.

Mögest du am Beginn jeder Dekade herauskommen,
möge dein Ba von den Ausflüssen leben,
die aus Osiris herauskommen,
aus den Händen des Amenemope.
Mögest du das Totenreich täglich durchschreiten und (dabei) Opferkuchen empfangen
aus den Händen dessen, der mit Opfergaben hervorkommt aus Djeme
in seinem Namen Chons-Schu in Theben.

Möge man sagen: Du bist gepriesen
bei deinem Vater und bei deiner Mutter,
dir wird Lobpreis vollzogen bei deinen Geschwistern.
Du bist rein, dein Herz ist rein,
alle deine Glieder sind rein!

Der „Baptism of Pharaoh" war im Verlauf der ägyptischen Geschichte einem zweifachen Wandel unterworfen: Zwar blieb er bis in späteste Zeit Bestandteil der königlichen Kultikonographie, fand jedoch bereits im Neuen Reich den Weg in die Privatikonographie. Bei dieser Übernahme vollzog sich gleichzeitig ein Wechsel des situativen Rahmens vom Tempelkult zum Funerären. Konstant blieb dabei die Situierung in einem Bereich des Übergangs in einen gottähnlichen Zustand, dem nicht nur belebende bzw. verjüngende, sondern vor allem legitimierende Wirkung zukam. Beim „Baptism of Pharaoh" gewann dabei, den Beischriften zufolge, im Laufe der Zeit der Akt der Reinigung an sich, durch den der König den Göttern gleich wurde, immer mehr an Bedeutung, während die ursprüngliche Gewährung der langen Regierungszeit noch im Verlauf des Neuen Reiches zurücktrat. Was gleichblieb, war der sowohl dem Sedfest als auch den späten Beischriften inhärente Gedanke der zyklischen Verjüngung: Im Sedfest sollte der alternde König sich jeweils im Abstand mehrerer Jahre verjüngen,[73] und dem Wasser, das beim „Baptism" über dem König ausgegossen wurde, wurde explizit verjüngende und heilende Wirkung zugeschrieben. Beim nichtköniglichen Verstorbenen stand die Reinigung hingegen symbolhaft

---

[73] E. Hornung/E. Staehelin, Neue Studien zum Sedfest, 91, 97.

für die Einbalsamierung, für das Abstreifen der Verwesungsstoffe, die die Herstellung des unverweslichen, vollständigen und unzerstörbaren Mumienleibes gefährdeten, der Voraussetzung war für die Aufnahme ins Totenreich und in die Gemeinschaft der Götter. Untrennbar damit verbunden war die Vorstellung von der moralischen Reinigung im Totengericht: „Rechtfertigung ist moralische Mumifizierung"[74] und Reinigung ist rituelle Rechtfertigung.

Bibliographie

ALFÖLDI, ANDREAS, „Die alexandrinischen Götter und die Vota Publica am Jahresbeginn", in: *Jahrbuch für Antike und Christentum* 8/9 (1965/66) 58–87.

ALTENMÜLLER-KESTING, BRIGITTE, *Reinigungsriten im ägyptischen Kult*, Hamburg: (ohne Verlag) 1968.

ANDREWS, CAROL, *Egyptian Mummies*, London: British Museum Publications 1984.

ASSMANN, JAN, *Altägyptische Totenliturgien I. Totenliturgien in den Sargtexten des Mittleren Reiches*, Heidelberg: Winter 2002.

— *Altägyptische Totenliturgien III. Osirisliturgien in Papyri der Spätzeit*, Heidelberg: Winter 2008.

— *Ma'at. Gerechtigkeit und Unsterblichkeit im Alten Ägypten*, München: C. H. Beck 1990.

— *Das Grab der Mutirdis, Grabung im Asasif 1963–1970, Band VI*, Archäologische Veröffentlichungen 13, Mainz: Ph. v. Zabern 1977.

— „Semiosis and Interpretation in Ancient Egyptian Ritual", in: S. Biderman/B.-A. Scharfstein (Hg.), *Interpretation in Religion* (Philosophy and Religion 2), Leiden: Brill 1992, 87–109.

— „Tod und Initiation im altägyptischen Totenglauben", in: J. Assmann (Hg.), *Ägyptische Geheimnisse*, München: Fink 2004, 135–156.

— *Tod und Jenseits im Alten Ägypten*, München: C. H. Beck 2001.

— „Die Zeugung des Sohnes. Ikonizität, Narrativität und Ritualität im ägyptischen Mythos", in: J. Assmann (Hg.), *Ägyptische Geheimnisse*, München: Fink 2004, 59–98.

ASSMANN, JAN/KUCHAREK, ANDREA, *Ägyptische Religion. Totenliteratur*, Frankfurt am Main: Verlag der Weltreligionen 2008.

---

[74] ASSMANN, *Tod und Jenseits*, 103. Dem fügt M. SMITH, *Traversing Eternity*, 6 hinzu, man könne umgekehrt ebenso von der Mumifizierung als „corporeal justification" sprechen.

BARGUET, PAUL, *La stèle de la famine, à Séhel* (Bibliothèque d'Étude 34), Kairo: Institut Français d'Archéologie Orientale 1953.

BLACKMAN, AYLWARD M., „Some Notes on the Ancient Egyptian Practice of Washing the Dead", in: *Journal of Egyptian Archaeology* 5 (1918) 117–124.

BOREUX, CHARLES, *Musée national du Louvre. Département des antiquités égyptiennes. Guide-catalogue sommaire* II, Paris: Musée national du Louvre 1932.

BRANDON, SAMUEL G. F., „The Life-Giving Significance of Lustration in the Osirian Mortuary Ritual and in Primitive Christian Baptism", in: C. J. Bleeker (ed.), *Guilt or Pollution and Rites of Purification*. Proceedings of the XIth International Congress of the International Association for the History of Religions Vol. II, Leiden: Brill 1968, 52–53.

BRUYÈRE, BERNARD, *Rapport sur les fouilles de Deir el Médineh (1924–1925)*, (Fouilles de l'Institut Français d'Archéologie Orientale du Caire III/3), Kairo: Institut Français d'Archéologie Orientale 1926.

BURKARD, GÜNTER, „Frühgeschichte und Römerzeit: P. Berlin 23071 vso.", in: *Studien zur Altägyptischen Kultur* 17 (1990) 107–133.

BUZOV, EMIL, „The Role of the Heart in the Purification", in: A. Amenta/M. M. Luiselli/M. N. Sordi (Hg.), *L'acqua nell'antico Egitto: vita, regenerazione, incantesimo, medicamento*, Rom: «L'Erma» di Bretschneider 2005, 273–281.

DE CENIVAL, FRANÇOISE, *Les associations religieuses en Egypte d'après les documents démotiques* (Bibliothèque d'Étude 46), Kairo: Institut Français d'Archéologie Orientale 1972.

CORCORAN, LORELEI H., *Portrait Mummies from Roman Egypt (I-IV Centuries A.D.)* (Studies in Ancient Oriental Civilization 56), Chicago: Oriental Institute 1995.

DERCHAIN, PHILIPPE, „À propos de Claudien. Éloge de Stilichon 2,424–436", in: *Zeitschrift für Ägyptische Sprache und Altertumskunde* 81 (1956) 4–6.

EGGEBRECHT, ARNE (Hg.), *Suche nach Unsterblichkeit. Totenkult und Unsterblichkeitsglaube im Alten Ägypten*. Ausstellungskatalog Hildesheim, Mainz: Ph. v. Zabern 1990.

FITZENREITER, MARTIN, „Konzepte vom Tod und den Toten im pharaonischen Ägypten – Notizen zum Grab des Pennut/2", in: M. Fitzenreiter (Hg.), *Die ägyptische Mumie: Ein Phänomen der Kulturgeschichte* (Internet-Beiträge zur Ägyptologie und Sudanarchäologie 1), Berlin: Humboldt-Universität 2004 (http://www2.hu-berlin.de/nilus/net-publications/ibaes1/publikation.html), 27–71.

GARDINER, ALAN, „The Baptism of Pharaoh", in: *Journal of Egyptian Archaeology* 36 (1950) 3-12.

— „Addendum to 'The Baptism of Pharaoh'", in: *Journal of Egyptian Archaeology* 37 (1951) 111.

GAUTHIER, HENRI, *Le temple d'Amada* I, *Les temples immergés de la Nubie*, Kairo: Institut Français d'Archéologie Orientale 1913; II, 1926.

GERMER, RENATE, *Das Geheimnis der Mumien. Ewiges Leben am Nil*. Ausstellungskatalog Hamburg, München: Prestel 1997.

GRIESHAMMER, REINHARD, *Das Jenseitsgericht in den Sargtexten* (Ägyptologische Abhandlungen 20), Wiesbaden: Harrassowitz 1970.

GRIFFITHS, JOHN GWYN, *Plutarch's De Iside et Osiride, with Introduction, Translation, and Commentary*, Cardiff: University of Wales Press 1970.

HERBIN, FRANÇOIS RENÉ, *Le Livre de parcourir l'éternité* (Orientalia Lovaniensia Analecta 58), Leuven: Peeters 1994.

HORNUNG, ERIK, *Der ägyptische Mythos von der Himmelskuh. Eine Ätiologie des Unvollkommenen* (Orbis Biblicus et Orientalis 46), Fribourg/Göttingen: Vandenhoeck & Ruprecht 1982.

— „Vom Sinn der Mumifizierung", in: *Die Welt des Orients. Wissenschaftliche Beiträge zur Kunde des Morgenlandes* XIV (1983) 167-175.

— *Das Totenbuch der Ägypter*, Zürich/München: Artemis 1979.

HORNUNG, ERIK/STAEHELIN, ELISABETH, *Neue Studien zum Sedfest* (Aegyptiaca Helvetica 20), Basel: Schwabe 2006.

KETTEL, JEANNOT, „Canopes, $r\underline{d}w.w$ d'Osiris et Osiris-Canope", in: C. Berger-el Naggar (Hg.), *Hommages à Jean Leclant* 3, *Etudes Isiaques* (Bibliothèque d'Étude 106/3), Kairo: Institut Français d'Archéologie Orientale 1994, 315-330.

KUCHAREK, ANDREA, „Reinheit für alle. Priesterliche Reinheitsvorschriften und das ‚Negative Sündenbekenntnis' in Totenbuch 125", in: C. Ambos/St. Hotz/G. Schwedler/St. Weinfurter (Hg.), *Die Welt der Rituale. Von der Antike bis heute*, Darmstadt: Wissenschaftliche Buchgesellschaft 2005, 71-78.

LANDGRÁFOVÁ, RENATA, *Faience Inlays from the Funerary Temple of King Raneferef. Raneferef's Substitute Decoration Programme* (Abusir XIV), Prague: Czech Institute of Egyptology 2006.

LEPSIUS, RICHARD, *Denkmäler aus Ägypten und Äthiopien*, 12 Tafelbände, Leipzig: Nicolaische Buchhandlung 1849-1858.

MERKELBACH, REINHOLD, *Isis-Regina, Zeus-Sarapis*, Stuttgart: Teubner 1995.

MEYBOOM, PAUL G. P., *The Nile Mosaic of Palestrina. Early Evidence of Egyptian religion in Italy*, Leiden: Brill 1995.

MÖLLER, GEORG, *Die beiden Totenpapyrus Rhind des Museums zu Edinburg*, Leipzig: Hinrichs 1913.

OPPENHEIM, ADELA, *Aspects of the Pyramid Temple of Senwosret III at Dahshur. The Pharaoh and Deities*, Ann Arbor, Mich.: UMI 2008.

OTTO, EBERHARD, *Das ägyptische Mundöffnungsritual* (Ägyptologische Abhandlungen 3), Wiesbaden: Harrassowitz 1960.

PARLASCA, KLAUS, „Bemerkungen zum ägyptischen Gräberwesen der griechisch-römischen Zeit", in: *Ägypten, Dauer und Wandel* (Sonderschriften des Deutschen Archäologischen Instituts Kairo 18), Mainz: Ph. v. Zabern 1987, 97–103.

POSTL, BRIGITTE, *Die Bedeutung des Nils in der römischen Literatur*, Wien: Notring 1970.

QUACK, JOACHIM F., „Der historische Abschnitt des Buches vom Tempel", in: J. Assmann/E. Blumenthal (Hg.), *Literatur und Politik im pharaonischen und ptolemäischen Ägypten* (Bibliothèque d'Étude 127), Kairo: Institut Français d'Archéologie Orientale 1999, 267–278.

RIEM, JOHANNES, *Die Sintflut in Sage und Wissenschaft*, Hamburg: Agentur des Rauhen Hauses 1925.

RUMMEL, UTE, *Pfeiler seiner Mutter – Beistand seines Vaters. Untersuchungen zum Gott Iunmutef vom Alten Reich bis zum Ende des Neuen Reiches*, Dissertation Hamburg 2007 (http://www.sub.uni-hamburg.de/opus/volltexte/2007/3444/index.html).

SADEK, ASHRAF I., „Les rites baptismaux dans l'Égypte ancienne: Préfiguration du Baptême chrétien?", in: *Le monde copte* 13 (1988) 4–11.

SCHEFOLD, KARL, *Die Wände Pompejis, Topographisches Verzeichnis der Bildmotive*, Berlin: de Gruyter 1957.

SCHOTT, SIEGFRIED, „Die Reinigung Pharaos in einem memphitischen Tempel (Berlin P 13 242)", in: *Nachrichten der Akademie der Wissenschaften in Göttingen. I. Philologisch-Historische Klasse*, Göttingen: Vandenhoeck & Ruprecht 1957, 45–92.

SEEBER, CHRISTINE, *Untersuchungen zur Darstellung des Totengerichts im Alten Ägypten* (Münchner Ägyptologische Studien 35), München/Berlin: Deutscher Kunstverlag 1976.

SEIDLMAYER, STEPHAN, „Die Vermessung des Nils im Alten Ägypten", in: *Fundiert* 2/2004 (http://www.fuberlin.de/presse/publikationen/fundiert/2004_02/04_02_seidlmayer/index.html), Berlin: Freie Universität 2004.

Sen-nefer. Die Grabkammer des Bürgermeisters von Theben. Ausstellungskatalog Köln; Mainz: Ph. v. Zabern 1986.

SETHE, KURT, *Die altägyptischen Pyramidentexte*, Leipzig: Hinrichs 1908–1922.

SMITH, AARON, „Kingship, Water and Ritual: The Ablution Rite in the Coronation Ritual of the Pharaoh", in: A. Amenta/M. M. Luiselli/M. N. Sordi (Hg.), *L'acqua nell'antico Egitto: vita, regenerazione, incantesimo, medicamento*, Rom: «L'Erma» di Bretschneider 2005, 329–336.

SMITH, MARK, *Traversing Eternity. Texts for the Afterlife from Ptolemaic and Roman Egypt*, Oxford: Oxford University Press 2009.

TEISSIER, BEATRICE, *Egyptian Iconography on Syro-Palestinian Cylinder Seals of the Middle Bronze Age* (Orbis Biblicus et Orientalis 11), Fribourg/Göttingen: Vandenhoeck & Ruprecht 1996.

VANDIER, JACQUES, *La Tombe de Nefer-abou* (Mémoires publiés par les membres de l'Institut Français d'Archéologie Orientale 69), Kairo: Institut Français d'Archéologie Orientale 1935.

VLEEMING, SVEN P./PESTMAN, PIETER W. (Hg.), *Hundred-Gated Thebes. Acts of a Colloquium on Thebes in the Graeco-Roman Period*, Leiden: Brill 1995.

VOGLIANO, ACHILLE, *Secondo Rapporto degli Scavi Condotti dalla Missione Archeologica d'Egitto della R. Università di Milano nella Zona di Madinet Madi* (Campagna Inverno e Primavera 1936-XIV), Milano: Pubblicazioni della Regia Università di Milano 1937.

WAITKUS, WOLFGANG, *Untersuchungen zu Kult und Funktion des Luxortempels* (Aegyptiaca Hamburgensia 2), Gladbeck: PeWe 2008.

WILD, ROBERT A., *Water in the cultic worship of Isis and Sarapis* (Études préliminaires aux religions orientales dans l'Empire romain 87), Leiden: Brill 1981.

The Mandean Water Ritual in Late Antiquity

ANDERS HULTGÅRD

1. Introduction

1.1. Aim of the Contribution

The Mandaeans are the representatives of the only ancient 'gnostic' religion that still survives but their origins and early history is one of the most intriguing problems in the field of the history of religions. Mark Lidzbarski who with his translations and commentaries of Mandaean texts provided a scholarly basis for the study of Mandaeism stated: "Die mandäische Religion bietet eines der schwierigsten Probleme auf religionsgeschichtlichem Gebiete".[1] His statement is corroborated by most scholars who have studied Mandaeism.[2]

The aim of my contribution is to investigate aspects of the Mandaean water ceremonies in the form they had in Late Antiquity. Focus will be on the main water ritual, the *maṣbūtā* (from the root *ṣby* or *ṣbʿ* ,"dip, immerse"). The question pertaining to their origin will also be addressed. Particular attention will be given to the Iranian background. Besides the *masiqtā*, the funeral ceremony, the *maṣbūtā* stands out as the most fundamental ritual in Mandaeism.

1.2. Terminological Questions

Conventionally the term "baptism" is used for the main Mandaean water ritual but a more appropriate term would be immersion or ablution ritual. The word "baptism" may produce connotations of the Christian ritual where baptism in general is administered to a person only once in a lifetime. Although the act of immersion is at the centre of the Mandaean ritual the *maṣbūtā* could be taken repeatedly by the believers and was also part of other ceremonies like the wedding ritual and the consecration of priests. It formed the central element in the weekly community ritual on "the first day of the week" (*habšabbā*).[3] Thus, the Mandae-

---

1   Mandäische Liturgien (= *ML*), p. xv.
2   See for example E. SEGELBERG, *Maṣbūtā*, 13; K. RUDOLPH, *Die Mandäer I*, 11; G. WIDENGREN, "Einleitung" in *Der Mandäismus*, 11–13; C. MÜLLER-KESSLER, "The Mandaeans and the Question of Their Origin", 47.
3   In citations of Mandaean texts I have for stylistic reasons retained the word 'baptism' as a translation of *maṣbūtā*. Mandaean words and expressions are cited in a simplified transcription of

an *maṣbūtā* corresponds phenomenologically more to the Christian mass, the Jewish sabbath prayer and the *ṣalāt* of the Muslims than to the Christian baptism and the Jewish circumcision, these being initiation rituals performed once in a lifetime. In this article, the general term 'water ritual' will be used and for the various rituals the Mandaic terms are given.

1.3. Problems of Reconstruction

There are great difficulties in attempting to reconstruct Mandaean water rituals as they were practised in Late Antiquity. The main reason is that the dating of the traditions preserved in the Mandaean scriptures can only be approximative, at best. We have also to reckon with changes in a ritual over time. Add to this the complexity of Mandaean doctrine and mythology where different and sometimes contradictory views can be found within the same text corpus. The earliest extant manuscript was written in the year 1529 (a collection of prayers) but most manuscripts are of later date. The manuscript tradition is of a later date compared to that of other religions of Late Antiquity. However, the study of manuscript colophons can help to elucidate the history of Mandaean texts before the 16th century back to Late Antiquity.[4]

The principal textual source for the main water ritual is found in the *Qolastā*, "selections", a collection of prayers.[5] It is to be noted, however, that the *Qolastā* is not a liturgical manual in the strict sense prescribing the exact sequence and performance of the various rites.[6] The ritual instructions usually found after one or more prayers are mainly there to inform the priests of the right moments to recite the prayers. The *Qolastā* opens with prayers for the *maṣbūtā* (CP 1–31), then follow the *masiqtā* prayers (CP 32–72) and a large block of various prayer categories of which many are connected with the *maṣbūtā*. Thus the first part of

---

their 'classical' forms. The precise pronunciation of early Mandaic, in particular the vowels, is not fully known (cf. M. LIDZBARSKI, *ML* pp. xi-xii: "Von der Aussprache des Mandäischen wissen wir wenig.") but the transcriptions may give the reader the possibility to make a comparison with related terms in Hebrew, Aramaic and Syriac. For inscribed texts on lead rolls and bowls from Late Antiquity transliteration is used in most cases (cf. E. S. DROWER & R. MACUCH, *A Mandaic Dictionary*, R. MACUCH, *Handbook* and MÜLLER-KESSLER, "A Mandaic Gold Amulet" and other publications which she has written (see Bibliography).

4   Cf. MACUCH, *Anfänge der Mandäer*, 158–165 and J. BUCKLEY, *The Great Stem of Souls*, 275–295.

5   The first scholarly edition by M. LIDZBARSKI, *Mandäische Liturgien* in 1920 is based on the oldest Mandaean manuscript known, Oxford Marsh, 691, written in 1529. Lidzbarski's edition contained all *maṣbūtā* and *masiqtā* prayers. The full version of the liturgical book possessed by the priests was published by Drower in 1959 under the title *The Canonical Prayerbook of the Mandaeans*. She based her edition on a manuscript in her own collection, D.C. No. 53 which she acquired in 1954 from a Mandaean *ganzibra*. For a detailed study of particular passages, both editions have to be consulted.

6   "Rite" is here used to denote the separate components that together make up a ritual.

the Responses, *Aniānē* (*CP* 78–90) are explicitly connected with the *maṣbūtā*,[7] as are the Banner (*drabša*) hymns (*CP* 330–347).[8] Complementary information can be found in the *Ginzā* and other writings.[9] What has been transmitted in the prayer collections and other texts does not suffice to explain the present ritual. We have to assume a stable oral transmission among the priests over a long time instructing them of how to perform the ritual in all its detail.

1.4. Mandaean World-View and Doctrine

The complexity of Mandaean theology and mythology makes it difficult to sort out 'normative' beliefs.[10] Yet some basic ideas and recurrent topics emerge that keep Mandaean myths and theologies together. The *Ginzā* and the *Qolastā* include for the most part traditions of the pre-Islamic period and combined with what the Late Antiquity 'magical' texts tell about mythology and world-view these sources make it possible to draw a picture of early Mandaeism. The following is but a short outline in order to provide a background for the enquiry into Mandaean water rituals.

The Mandaeans believe in a supreme deity called 'Life' (*Hayyē*; also 'First Life') who is addressed with other names too such as 'Lord of Greatness', 'the Father', and the 'King of light'.[11] Sometimes the 'Great *Mānā*' stands for 'Life' as the supreme being.[12] His image *Demūthā*, like the *Niṭuftā* of 'Life' appears as a kind of female supreme beings. 'Life' dwells in a heavenly world of light and is surrounded by a number of light beings (sing. *uthrā*) who are created by him or emanate from him, usually in different stages. These stages are denoted with the terms 'Second Life', 'Third Life' and 'Fourth Life' and are personified as *Yōšamin*, *Abathur* and *Ptahil* respectively. They have their own abodes of light (sing. *škīnā*). Some of these light beings play a more prominent role than others. Among them is *Yāwar* who appears in the role of a divine helper and messenger. The highest being is *Mandā d-Hayyē* ("Knowledge of Life") created by 'Life' himself in a first stage. *Hibil*, mostly called *Hibil Zīwā* ('the radiant Hibil'), *Šitil* and *Anōš* belong to the second stage of emanations or creations and

---

7   Stated in the ritual instruction after hymn 90, see *CP* p. 95: "Up to this point are the hymns and chants of baptism".

8   For example *CP* p. 237: "Chant these hymns before you convey the banner to the jordan"; *CP* p. 239: "Recite these two hymns after you have performed the baptism, and take the banner to the cult-hut".

9   *The Book of John* and some priestly commentaries.

10 Cf. also K. Rudolph, "Mandaean Sources", 134.

11 Exceptionally it is thought that 'Life' emanates from a still higher entity, the Great Mānā (see *GR* III, 66,14–21).

12 The term *mānā* denotes on the cosmic level a spiritual being but refers also to the spiritual element in man.

are in Mandaean mythology often mentioned as a group.[13] There is also a world of darkness and evil that was formed and emerged from a primordial element, 'the black waters'. It is ruled by the Lord of darkness together with his mother the fallen spirit *Rūhā*. The planets, the 'Seven', and the signs of the the Zodiac, the 'Twelve', are her servants.

Creation of the present world (*tibil*) is attributed to *Ptahil* who collaborates in good faith with the evil powers but cannot resist when they take over his creation. The anthropogony plays a central part in Mandaeism since it is exemplary of the salvation of man. The body of the first man, *Adam*, was formed by Ptahil and the Planets, but the soul came from the World of Light. *Mandā d̲-Hayyē* descends to Adam and reveals to him the mystery of life and of cosmos. He teaches him the way of redemption. *Adam* was given a wife *Hawwā* so that they might bring forth a stem (*šurbā*) of 'Life'. Essential is the idea of sending out a messenger from the World of Light to the world and the realm of evil with the task to enlighten man of his spiritual origin and to combat the evil forces when they threaten to become too powerful. *Mandā d̲-Hayyē* is the foremost messenger but in some traditions *Hibil Zīwā* takes that role. At death the soul returns to the World of Light but the journey is beset with dangers. The funeral liturgy, the *masiqtā*, helps the soul to achieve the ascension.

The concept of *kuštā* is central in Mandaean thought and ritual (see further § 4.2.) as is also the notion of *laufā* which refers to the communion between the Light World and the human world. To establish this communion is the essential meaning of the *maṣbūtā* ritual.

2. Mandaean Water Rituals

The starting point must be the Mandaean water rituals as they were practiced in the 20th century when they first were accurately described by Western scholars and also explained to them by celebrants. These descriptions have then to be compared with the textual sources, in the first place with the parts of the *Qolastā* that concern the *maṣbūtā*-ritual where also remarks on ritual performance are found.[14] The descriptions provided by Lady Drower are used here since they date from the first decades of the 20th century.[15] Jorunn Buckley's description of the *maṣbūtā* as performed by Iranian Mandaeans in the late 20th century is also valu-

---

13 They are commonly identified with the biblical figures of Abel (Hebrew: *Hæbæl*), Seth and Enosh. Seth and Enosh are well known as revealers in Jewish, Christian and Gnostic circles. The form of the name Seth appears in the *Mani Codex* (50,8) as Σηθηλ which recalls the Mandaean form *Šitil*. More difficult to explain is the question why Abel was promoted to a high rank figure among the Mandaeans.

14 Translation and text in DROWER, *The Canonical Prayerbook of the Mandaeans*, 1–32, Mandaic text columns 1–46, and in LIDZBARSKI, *Mandäische Liturgien*, 3–61.

15 The descriptions are found in DROWER, *The Mandaeans of Iraq and Iran*, 100–123.

able.[16] The ritual observed at that time is essentially the same as that described by Lady Drower.

2.1. Description of the Early 20th Century Rituals

2.1.1. Minor Water Rituals

Besides the main water ritual two minor rituals were in use, which did not require the assistance of priests. The first is called *rišama* which should be performed daily at the river and can be characterized as an ablution of the body but without immersion.[17] The second called *ṭamaša* (meaning "immersion") consisted of a triple immersion in the river and was required after certain acts considered to imply a defilement.[18] These two minor rituals seem to reach as far back in time as the major water ritual.

2.1.2. The *maṣbūtā*

The main Mandaean water ritual, the *maṣbūtā*, was celebrated on *habšabbā*, "first day of the week" (Sunday), at particular feasts mainly the Panja and as a part of other ceremonies (cf. 1.1.).[19] The ritual included several aspects and was rich in detail. The following description is based on Lady Drower's observations which I have supplemented with some citations from the liturgical prayers.[20] Only the main aspects and features are retained here.[21]

The *maṣbūtā* required priestly guidance and was performed at a river or at a cult hut (*mandi*) where a pool connected to running water had been dug out. Myrtle twigs were collected to be used for the wreath (*klila*) of the priest and of those who participated in the ritual. A clay table (*ṭoriana*) was used, but in the case of many celebrants being present, a larger clay box (*qintha*) was used, on which the ritual objects were placed: the drinking bowls (*keptha*) for the sacred water (*mambuha*), the incense cube (*qauqa* or *bit riha*) and a fire-saucer (*brihi*).

---

16 Buckley, *The Mandaeans*, chapter 7.

17 Described with accompanying formulas in Drower, *The Mandaeans of Iraq and Iran*, 102–104.

18 See Drower, *The Mandaeans of Iraq and Iran*, 105.

19 The Panja (from Middle-Iranian *panǰ* ('five') is a religious festival celebrated in springtime. Each of the five days is dedicated to a light figure and it is believed that "the doors of the world of light are open during Panja by night as well as by day", Drower, *The Mandaeans of Iraq and Iran*, 90.

20 This is a legitimate procedure since Lady Drower states herself: "The baptism ritual, translated by Lidzbarski (Q.) was the same as that which I have described in the above notes" (Drower, *The Mandaeans of Iraq and Iran*, 113).

21 Except for *maṣbūtā*, the transcription of Mandaean terms taken from the descriptions by Lady Drower are hers.

Flour and salt were at hand and the sacred banner (*drabša*) was usually erected.[22] The banner consisted of a strip of white silk about three meters long and with a width of about one meter; this was attached to a wooden pole. The white ritual dress (*rasta*) should be carried by priests as well as by laymen at every religious ceremony.[23] It included a headdress resembling a turban which is called *burzinqa* (or *ṭarṭabuna*).[24] In addition to the parts of the *rasta* common to all Mandaeans, priests had two other insignia, the crown (*taga*) and the gold ring (*šum*) which was carried on the little finger of the right hand. One end of the headdress (*burzinqa*) was left hanging over the shoulder and the priests used it to form a mouth-covering (*pandama*) to prevent the breath or spittle from polluting the sacred objects. When officiating the priest must always carry a staff (*margna*) of olive wood. The water (rivers and cult pools) used for the immersion ritual is called "living water" or "jordan" (*yardna*).

After the priests had consecrated themselves and the cult objects, the Mandaeans who during the ritual are called 'souls' (*nšimta*) came in small groups, all provided with their myrtle wreaths, and they grasped the banner while repeating a formula pronounced by the officiating priest. Before going into the water they placed an offering for partaking in the ritual and splashed it three times with water. The priest recited an invitation to come and go down to the jordan and be baptized and receive the pure sign.[25] Then they descended one by one into the water, waded out to the priest who had placed his staff firmly in the water, and they immersed themselves completely three times. The priest seized them and dipped their forehead three times beneath the water and then passed his forefinger three times across the forehead while reciting the formula of signing which occurs at the same central moment of the ritual as the trinity formula of Christian baptism:[26]

> You have been signed with the sign of 'Life'. The name of 'Life' and the name of Mandā ḏ-Hayyē were pronounced upon you. You have been baptized with the baptism of the great Bihrām, son of the Mighty ('Life'). May your baptism protect you and may it be successful. The name of the 'Life' and the name of Mandā ḏ-Hayyē have been pronounced upon you.

---

22 According to Lady Drower, the banner was not present in every *maṣbūta*, but it was always used at the days of the Panja feast, *The Mandaeans of Iraq and Iran*, 108–109. The *drabša* was never carried in procession, which is important to note for the comparison with Christian rituals.

23 For reasons of modesty women wore a black mantle (*aba*) over the *rasta*, DROWER, *The Mandaeans of Iraq and Iran*, 112.

24 DROWER, *The Mandaeans of Iraq and Iran*, 30 mentions only *burzinqa*. The word *ṭarṭabuna* that occurs in ritual prayers is interpreted by LIDZBARSKI, *Mandäische Liturgien*, 136, 164, 226 as a turban; cf. also SEGELBERG, *Maṣbūtā*, 117. DROWER, *The Canonical Prayerbook*, 81 is inclined to think that it is not a headdress.

25 *CP* 18; *ML* 18; cf. also SEGELBERG, *Maṣbūtā*, 50.

26 *CP* p. 14 (English trans.), Mandaic text col. 24; *ML* 18.

Thereafter he invested them with the myrtle wreath pronouncing the prayer for the wreath.[27] Each celebrant drank three times from the hollow of the priest's hand while taking his right hand in their own and repeating the *kuštā* formula after him: "May *kuštā* heal you and raise you up".[28]

On emerging from the water, each 'soul' walked clockwise around the fire and the *drabšā* before joining the group of wet 'souls' waiting for the next main moment of the ritual. The priest first anointed the forehead of the immersed person with a threefold application, followed by another hand-grasp. Every participant in the group now extended his or her right arm pronouncing the formula "ask and find, speak and listen" and went down to the water to wash their bared arm.[29] They returned and crouched to receive the sacred bread (*pihta*) and the sacred water (*mambuha*) that were administered to the whole group together. The priest then went behind the crouching group and touched their heads with his fingertips several times. The participants extended their right hands towards the *yardna* and pointed to it as a witness of their ablution. A third and final *kuštā* was then performed during which all were standing.[30]

The moment when the participants rose from a crouching to a standing position is presupposed in the description of Lady Drower, but received no further attention from her. The ritual text states, however: "Then make them stand and recite 'You are set up and raised up'" which is immediately followed by the hymn "What did your Father do for you, O Soul".[31]

To judge from the contents of the two prayers, the ritual raising had an important symbolic meaning. The ceremony proper came to an end when each participant threw his or her wreath (*klila*) in the immersion water.

The whole ritual was accompanied by prayers, blessings and formulas, which were recited by the priest both by heart and by reading from a book.[32] Some short formulas were repeated by the lay people. The living ritual as observed by

---

27 *CP* p. 15 (English trans.), Mandaic text col. 25–26.

28 Transcribed into classical Mandaic, it would run as follows: *kuštā assiak uqayymak*. For this formula, see Drower, *The Mandaeans*, 112 and Segelberg, *Maṣbūtā*, 65. As noted by Segelberg *ibid.*, the formula is not given in the texts of the baptismal liturgy proper, *ML* 3–61 and *CP* 1–32, but it is undoubtedly of ancient origin.

29 *B'i weška amar waštemma* as it is also found in the performance instructions of *CP* p. 27.

30 Segelberg, *Maṣbūtā*, 102 refers to this as the fourth *kuštā*, but it is not clear how he arrives to that number.

31 *CP* p. 24.

32 The relationship between orality and literacy is complicated. A candidate for priesthood must recite from memory the whole liturgies of *maṣbūtā* and *masiqtā* and Lady Drower noted that the priests followed "with their copies open before them to see that no mistake is made", *The Mandaeans of Iraq and Iran*, 152. As to the ritual observed by Lady Drower for a woman after childbirth, she states that at a given moment of the consecration prayers the priest "stops praying, and opens a book from which he reads rapidly in the same chanting voice employed in praying", Drower, *The Mandaeans of Iraq and Iran*, 110.

Lady Drower corresponds in general with the instructions for the *maṣbūtā* as inserted between the prayers in the texts used by the priests.[33]

3. The *maṣbūtā* as a Late Antiquity Ritual

The problem that confronts us here is to know whether the chief water ritual as it was performed in the early 20th century agrees in its essentials with the form it had in Late Antiquity. Since the time and place for the beginnings of Mandaean religion cannot be determined with certainty, there is not much sense in trying to trace its early history in any detail. My concern is to argue for a Late Antiquity origin of the *maṣbūtā* irrespective of possible transformations up to the 6th century AD.

3.1. Manuscripts and Colophons

A first step brings us back to the early 16th century with the oldest *Qolastā* manuscript that has survived.[34] It may safely be assumed that this manuscript is a copy of copies which is also indicated by the colophons found in manuscripts of the *Qolastā*.[35] The prayers and performance instructions in the *Qolastā* correspond in general with the modern ritual. References to the *maṣbūtā* in the *Ginzā* and other texts show that at the time of the final redaction of the book, in the early Islamic period, the *maṣbūtā* was an important ritual. However, the details of its performance and the order of the ritual moments cannot be ascertained from the *Ginzā*. A brief presentation of the scholarly discussion will be useful for introducing the problems posed by the *maṣbūtā* as a Late Antiquity ritual.[36]

3.2. Main View-Points

In theory, the *maṣbūtā* may be interpreted as the result of a development from a short and more simple ritual to the extensive and complex ceremony of the early 20th century. Some scholars state that the single sections and prayers of the

---

33 Cf. the remark in note 20.

34 Dated by a colophon to 936 after Hidjra, that is 1529; see LIDZBARSKI, *Mandäische Liturgien*, p. VI.

35 The colophons refer back to a certain Zāzai d-Gawāzta as the first scribe of the *Qolastā*, see CP pp. 67, 71. A later copyist Ramuia son of Qaimat stated that 368 years had passed since Zāzai wrote his collection of liturgies and that he wrote this "in the years when the Arabs advanced" (*CP* p. 71). If we can trust the colophons, this brings us back to the latter half of the 3rd century AD. Cf. also MACUCH, *Anfänge der Mandäer*, 159 and BUCKLEY, *The Great Stem of Souls*, 192, 278–280.

36 An overview of the research on the *maṣbūtā* before the 1950s is given by SEGELBERG, *Maṣbūtā*, 14–18.

ritual certainly originated from very different periods, which cannot be further specified.[37] Others emphasize the transformations that the *maṣbūtā* underwent over time. The main studies of the *maṣbūtā* were made by Eric Segelberg and Kurt Rudolph, who carefully analysed the ritual and its details. Their approach is criticised by Jorunn Jacobsen Buckley for bypassing the contents of the baptismal prayers and engaging in "surface comparisons", in particular with various Christian (including Gnostic) rituals.[38]

Segelberg considered the Mandaean immersion ritual in its present form to be "comparatively recent", by which he meant "not before early Arabic times".[39] Analysing the ritual texts, he came to the conclusion that the unction with oil and the sacred meal were later accretions, although he admitted that the sacred meal (distribution of the *pihtā* and the *mambūhā*) had a longer history.[40] According to Segelberg, elements of the primitive ritual could also be suppressed. The original ritual differed from the present one by adding an act of investiture which was preceded by a divestment.[41] The order of the ritual actions at this juncture was also different as is shown by the following table (for comparison I add the corresponding actions in the description of Lady Drower):

Original form	Modern form
Divestment	—
Descending into the water	Descending into the water
Immersion	Immersion
Signing of the forehead	Signing of the forehead
Drinking water from the hand of the priest	Drinking water from the hand of the priest
Ascending from the water	—
Investiture	—
Coronation	Coronation
Laying on of the hand	Laying on of the hand
Giving the *kuštā*	Giving the *kuštā*
—	Ascending from the water

---

37 Cf. LIDZBARSKI, *Mandäische Liturgien*, p. VI: "Die einzelnen Stücke der Rituale sind sicherlich zu sehr verschiedenen Zeiten entstanden, aber bei unserer Unkenntnis der Geschichte der Mandäer ist es nicht möglich, sie irgendwie zeitlich zu fixieren".
38 BUCKLEY, "Polemics and Exorcism …", 157.
39 SEGELBERG, *Maṣbūtā*, 183.
40 SEGELBERG, *Maṣbūtā*, 145–150.
41 SEGELBERG, *Maṣbūtā*, 122–129.

This ritual was according to Segelberg also the primitive form of the *maṣbūtā*, which was expanded to include firstly the sealing prayers, secondly the sacred meal and thirdly the unction, when also the investiture was removed.[42]

Kurt Rudolph's comprehensive analysis of the *maṣbūtā* comes to a different conclusion.[43] For him, the immersion rite and the sacred meal are the two main components that cannot be separated. Geo Widengren came to the same conclusion independently of Rudolph.[44] The primitive elements ("Grundbestandteile") of the ritual were according to Rudolph the following (the table is adapted from the German version):

Baptism	Meal
Triple immersion	Sacred meal, bread and water
Triple signation	Giving the *kuštā*
Triple drinking of water	
Coronation	
Laying on of the hand Giving the *kuštā*	

The formula used by the priest when he passed his finger in the front of the forehead was according to Rudolph originally twofold ("zweigliedrig"), the reference to the "baptism of the great Bihrām" being secondary.[45] Moreover the juxtaposition of two immersions is suspicious, one performed by the celebrant himself, the other by the priest (although not complete, see § 2.1.2.). Rudolph states that both cannot be original and sees in the self-immersion an ancient element in accordance with the origin of the *maṣbūtā* in purification rites. Probably, this rite was prior to the requirement of having a priest or baptizer.[46]

Christa Müller-Kessler has a radical viewpoint, in that she doubts that the *maṣbūtā* belonged to the "original doctrine of the Mandaeans at all".[47] The reasons for this are the alleged absence of any allusions to the *maṣbūtā* in the Mandaic incantations on lead rolls and bowls from Late Antiquity in which the root *ṣby* does not occur, nor is there any mention of the river Jordan. Furthermore, the Mandaean hymns, which served as a model for the Coptic Thomas Psalms

---

42   SEGELBERG, *Maṣbūtā*, 154, where he sums up his results. The changes mentioned were according to Segelberg most probably introduced before the Islamic period, *ibid.* p. 154.
43   See RUDOLPH, *Die Mandäer II. Der Kult*, 340–348.
44   WIDENGREN, "Die Mandäer", 88: "In der mandäischen Taufe ist das wichtigste vor allem, dass Taufhandlung und Kommunion nur eine Haupthandlung bilden".
45   RUDOLPH, *Die Mandäer II. Der Kult*, 345–346.
46   RUDOLPH, *Die Mandäer II. Der Kult*, 347–348.
47   MÜLLER-KESSLER, "The Mandaeans and the Question of Their Origin", 57–58.

of the Manichees, lack any reference to the *maṣbūtā* and the *yardnā*. The emergence of the *maṣbūtā* could be attributed to the rising power of Christianity.[48] I interpret her statement as follows: she does not deny the presence of some minor water lustrations in early Mandaeism but that the full *maṣbūtā* and the central role it played was the result of a later development.

3.3. Arguments for a Continuity from Late Antiquity

The following are some arguments for the main water ritual as a constituent of primitive Mandaeism:

- The *maṣbūtā* is well integrated in the mythology
- The conservative character of the Mandaean priesthood
- References to ritual in the lead scrolls and 'magical' bowls
- Ablutions and baptisms as a Late Antiquity phenomenon

3.3.1. *Maṣbūtā* in Mandaean Mythology

We may first note that the main water ritual is well integrated in the fabric of Mandaean thought and mythology. The following examples will illustrate this fact.

The first part of the Ginza is made up by two variants of the same text (*GR* I and *GR* II,1).[49] They include the teaching given by a heavenly messenger to the first man, Adam. It has the form of a long paraenesis (*GR* I, §§ 89–180; II, §§ 24–116) and one passage exhorts the faithful to perform the *maṣbūtā* (*GR* I, §§ 123–124 and II, § 48). Here the distribution of the *pihtā* and the *mambūhā* is presented as an essential element in the *maṣbūtā* and *GR* II, § 48 also adds the signing with oil. The tradition common to the two variants of this paraenesis ('Moralkodex') seems to belong to an early period of Mandaean religion.[50]

The coming of the apostle of Light (*šlīhā ḏ-nhūrā*) in this world is described in *GR* II,3.[51] He brings with him light, praise and splendour but also other things:

> a call and a proclamation is on me, the sign (*rušūmā*) is on me and the baptism (*maṣbūtā*).

---

48 As stated by Müller-Kessler, "The Mandaeans and the Question of Their Origin", 57: "It is conceivable that the cultural importance (of the *maṣbūtā*) came up as competition for the rising Christianity in the East".
49 The two versions are thought to go back to a common source, see Lidzbarski, *Ginzā*, 3–4.
50 Cf. Lidzbarski, *Ginzā*, 4; Schou Pedersen, *Bidrag til en Analyse*, 146–182.
51 Mandaic text in H. Petermann, *Thesaurus*, 64,10–65,11.

The word *rušūmā* refers most probably to the signing with oil of the water ritual (see § 2.1.2.)

The *maṣbūtā* has its own foundation myth which is told in GR XV,3. In the beginning when heaven and earth were put in place and the bodily Adam was formed, a plan was devised to draw out living water (*māyyē hayyē*) from the abode of light and pour it into the turbid water of this world. Two guardians, Šilmai and Nidbai, were appointed and they dragged the living water down to earth. The living water complained of its miserable state being cut off from its heavenly origin and exposed to the impurity and evil of the dark waters in this world. Their guardians reply that living water was sent to the world (*tibil*) in order to serve as ablution water for the souls so that they shall not perish in the dark and unclean waters. The living water shall call them with the call of life and be a helper (*adyaura*) for the souls who are persecuted for the sake of Yāwar:

> in you they shall receive the living baptism
> and in you they shall be signed with the pure sign
> (GR XV,3)[52]

In the same myth it is also said of Ptahil that he did not receive the sign of jordan and was not immersed in living water nor did he get the precious *kuštā*. When the great judgement day arrives and the world is destroyed, Ptahil together with Jošamin and Abathur will be taken from the world of decay by Hibil-Ziwa and immersed and purified "in the jordan of the mighty 'First Life'".

Another primordial myth tells how 'Life', the supreme god, performed his own *maṣbūtā*. He gave himself the *kuštā* and took it from his own hand, he kissed his right hand and said:

> 'I am the first baptizer who believed in the *kuštā* and this *maṣbūtā*. Anyone who adheres to me and believes in my *kuštā* and my *maṣbūtā* shall be in communion (*laufā*) with me and find a place in my abode (*škīnā*)'.[53]

Thereupon, the first heavenly mansion *škīnā* appeared, which is above the water and the living fire, and the splendour of Life spread its light. 'Life' created a son to be his companion and placed him in the jordan of living water, gave him the *kuštā* and invested him with part of his splendour and light. 'Life' let him dwell in his own *škīnā* beyond the living fire.

Summing up myths and paraenesis thus points to the centrality of the *maṣbūtā* in Mandaean beliefs and ethics.

---

52   LIDZBARSKI, *Ginzā*, 310; PETERMANN, *Thesaurus*, 309.
53   GR X; LIDZBARSKI, *Ginzā*, 239–241; PETERMANN, *Thesaurus*, 238–240.

3.3.2. Conservatism of Mandaean Priesthood

Secondly, general considerations as to the reliability of Mandaean transmission also point to an ancient origin of the *maṣbūtā*. We have first the character of the Mandaean priesthood which in many respects recalls that of the Zoroastrians.[54] Both are hereditary and show many similarities. Several parts of the white ritual dress of the Mandaean priests (and of the lay people) correspond to the dress of the magi and carry also names of Iranian origin: *šarwala* "trousers", *himyānā* "the girdle", *burzenqā* "the turban" and for the priests also the *pandāmā* "the mouth cover", *tāgā* "the crown" and the staff, *margnā*. Most of these words are probably derived from the Parthian dialect.[55] The white dress of the Iranian priests was recorded already by Plutarch.[56] To be especially noted is the preponderant role of the myrtle twigs in the Mandaean rituals that clearly reflects the *barsom* twigs in the Iranian sacrificial cult, and the *pandāmā*, which corresponds strikingly with the mouth cover of the Zoroastrian magi. This feature of the ritual appearance of the magi is depicted already on Late Achaemenian monuments from Asia Minor and described by Greek authors.[57]

The Iranian priests of the pre-Islamic period are known for having preserved ritual traditions through oral transmission over long periods, for some texts more than a thousand years.[58] This is astonishing and must be explained by the fact that we have to do with central ritual texts and above all with a competent priesthood well versed in the techniques of oral transmission. For the Mandaean priests written transmission was equally important, however. They copied themselves the scrolls with the texts they needed and combined ritual and scribal functions. The emergence of the Mandaean priesthood is most probably explained as coming from a double background, the models being some of the specialized Mesopotamian priest classes and the Iranian magi.[59] The Mesopotamian temples to which the priests and the scribes were attached relied on accurate written transmission to perform the rituals. Given the influ-

---

54 Noted also by A. DE JONG, "Vexillologia sacra", 196–197.

55 See WIDENGREN, "Die Mandäer", 92 and IDEM, "Heavenly Enthronement", 552–555.

56 *Questiones Romanae*, 26. Plutarch remarks that the Magi wore the white ritual dress in order to protect them from the powers of darkness and to resemble light and radiance: Πότερον ὡς τοὺς μάγους φασὶν πρὸς τὸν Ἅιδην καὶ τὸ σκότος ἀντιταττομένους, τῷ δὲ φωτεινῷ καὶ λαμπρῷ συνεξομοιοῦντας ἑαυτοὺς τοῦτο ποιεῖν; cf. also M. STAUSBERG, *Die Religion Zarathustras III*, 93.

57 In the first place Strabo, *Geography*, XV,15.

58 The oldest parts of the Avesta, the Gāthā and the Yasna haptaŋhāiti are by modern research dated approximately to 1000 BCE and were not committed to writing until the late Sasanian and early Islamic periods.

59 There was no clear hierarchy in Mesopotamian priesthood but a variety of priestly classes specializing in different ritual areas, cf. L. OPPENHEIM, *Ancient Mesopotamia*, 106–107; H. RINGGREN, *Die Religionen des Alten Orients*, 151.

ence that the Mesopotamian and Iranian religions exerted on the formation of Mandaean priesthood, we may assume that the Mandaean priests knew how to faithfully pass on their ritual traditions over the centuries.

The Mandaean priesthood included a group of 'elite' priests (*ganzibrē*, sing. *ganzibrā*) that had a comprehensive education. They, as well as the ordinary priests (*tarmidē*), were subject to extensive ritual restrictions and as Lady Drower remarked "faults in ritual are not easily expiated".[60] The same goes for the ritual dress and insignia of the priest which must be in perfect order otherwise the ritual becomes invalid and the priest has to undergo repeated purifications.[61] The emphasis on knowledge and ritual perfection that characterizes the Mandaean *ganzibrē* may also be taken as a warrant for the ability to preserve inherited traditions over a long time.

3.3.3. References to ritual in Mandaean Lead Scrolls and 'Magical' Bowls

The objects with their inscriptions belong in the time span from the 4th to the 7th centuries. The inscriptions have been copied from earlier models[62] and there are clear indications that the oldest material must be dated to the first half of the 3rd century.[63] In general, the lead scrolls predate the bowls with some centuries.[64] It should be emphasized that the texts preserved on these objects represent private worship and deal with specific matters in which a public ritual like the *maṣbūtā* need not be evoked.

The prayers and incantations of the lead scrolls and 'magical' bowls are not entirely devoid of references to public ritual, however. A lead roll amulet states: "secured (or 'disseminated', *zʿyrʾ*) are the words of Light and armed (*mzrzʾ*)".[65] This recalls clearly a passage in the *Qolastā* 47 to be recited in the *masiqtā* ceremony:[66]

---

60   These ritual restrictions and the way they could be expiated are described in DROWER, *The Mandaeans of Iraq and Iran*, 146–147 and 174–176.

61   Lady Drower gives the following example: "If, for instance, the *pandama* slips aside during a baptism, his (i.e. the priest's) ministrations are invalid", DROWER, *The Mandaeans of Iraq and Iran*, 32.

62   Cf. MÜLLER-KESSLER, "The Mandaeans and the Question of Their Origin", 52.

63   Cf. MÜLLER-KESSLER, "The Mandaeans and the Question of Their Origin", 54.

64   Cf. LIDZBARSKI, "Ein mandäisches Amulett", 350. For the present paper the following publications of Mandaean amulets and lead scrolls have been investigated: A. CAQUOT, "Un phylactère mandéen"; LIDZBARSKI, "Ein mandäisches Amulett"; MACUCH, "Altmandäische Bleirollen"; MÜLLER-KESSLER, "A Mandaic Gold Amulet"; EADEM, "Interrelations between Mandaic lead scrolls", and the other articles of hers listed in the bibliography; E. YAMAUCHI, *Mandaic Incantation Texts*.

65   For the amulet, see MACUCH, "Altmandäische Bleirollen (Fortsetzung)", 34–35.

66   As pointed out by MACUCH, "Altmandäische Bleirollen (Fortsetzung)", 51–53 where he also discusses the signification of *zʿyrʾ* for the *zhyrʾ* of the prayer book.

Secured (*zhyr'*) and well secured (*mz'h'r'*) are the words of Light for the souls of this ascent, secured and well secured (are they), armed (*zryz'*) and well armed (*mz'rz'*).[67]

Another lead roll amulet written in order to guarantee divine protection for the family of Pīr Nukhrāyā includes a passage where 'Life', the supreme deity, authorizes a higher light being to be the guardian of the family:[68]

> He ('Life') called upon the outer Yāwar and the inner Yāwar from the water, the abundant blessing of the jordan (*yardnā*). He then clothed him (Yāwar) with a garment of radiance (*uṣṭlā d-zīwā*) and covered him with a good and pure turban of light (*ṭarṭbūnā ṭābā dakyā d-nhūrā*). He armed him (*zarzē*), raised him up (*qayymē*) and crowned him with the wreath of aether (*klīlā d-āyar*).

In my opinion, the whole passage can be read as a symbolic reference to the *maṣbūtā* and some of its ritual actions. Yāwar, who figures prominently in *maṣbūtā* contexts, is summoned to ascend from the water of immersion, the *yardnā*. Life acting as priest and baptizer invests him with a radiant garment and a turban of light and sets a wreath on his head. This corresponds to the coronation of the celebrant in the water with the myrtle-wreath. The investiture with garment and turban is to be taken symbolically as expressing the new status conferred by the immersion rite to the person who ascends from the water. The expressions of the amulet "armed him" and "raised him up" occur frequently in baptismal prayers and hymns. To raise somebody up refers to the point of the ritual, when the celebrants change from a crouching position to a standing one (see § 2.1.2.) but also to the benefit obtained by the whole ritual. Often the verb *qwm* (in pael and afel "to raise") is used more or less synonymously with *ṣby* "immerse, baptize".[69]

Some texts from the *Qolastā* and the *Ginzā* may here be cited to elucidate the connection of the Mandaean amulet passage with the *maṣbūtā*. The consecration prayer for the wreath (CP 6, ML 6) emphasizes its heavenly origin and promises the celebrants a place in the World of Light:

> The wreath of aether light (*klīl nhūr āyar*) shone forth from the House of 'Life',
> Uthras brought it from the House of 'Life'
> and the mighty 'First Life' set it up in his abode (*škīnā*).
> He who sets it up shall be set up (*tarṣī nitrīṣ*)
> and he who raises it up shall be raised up (*mqayymanē nitqayyam*),
> he who set it up into the World of light, he who raised it up into the shining Abode.
> You are set up (*etreṣtūn*) and raised up (*etqayyamtūn*) in the place where the Good are raised up.

---

67 *CP* p. 42, and col. 62; *ML* p. 78.
68 Lidzbarski, "Ein mandäisches Amulett", 55–61.
69 Cf. Lidzbarski, *ML* p. xxiii and Segelberg, *Maṣbūtā*, 91.

When the wreath is set upon the head of the baptized in the water a prayer is recited that begins:

> Mandā called me,[70] Uthras raised me up,
> they clothed me with radiance (*zīwā*), covered me with light (*nhūrā*),
> Hazazban[71] set the wreath (*klīlā*) on my head ...   (*CP* 19; *ML* p. 19)

The prayer to be recited before daybreak (*CP* 114, *ML* p. 177) alludes most probably to the *maṣbūtā* with the wording:

> I was clothed with garments of radiance (*uṣṭlē ḏ-zīwā*) and light fell on my shoulders, a wreath of aether (*klīl āyar*) was set on my head.

According to the *Ginzā*, Yōhānā (John) is clothed in a robe of light and covered with a good and pure turban of light (*ṭarṭbūnā tābā dakyā ḏ-nhūrā*) in the jordan.[72] Another passage of the *Ginzā* describes how a higher light being baptizes the son of the great Nbaṭ (another light being):

> He baptized me (*ṣban*) with his baptism (*maṣbūtā*) and raised me up (*qayyman*) with his word.
> With his word he raised me up and signed me with the pure sign.
> He clothed me in a robe of radiance, wonderful and without end.
> He set on me a pure wreath whose leaves are shining.
> He covered me with a turban which was made of the earth of Light.
>   *GR* XVI,1; Petermann p. 364

This passage which alludes to some essential aspects of the water ritual,[73] shows the importance attributed to the symbolism of clothing and light to convey the meaning of the ritual. The same symbolic language of investiture appears in the context of the *masiqtā* when the heavenly companion comes to take the soul to the Light world as for example in *ML* p. 226:

> I shall bring you garments of splendor (*uṣṭlē ḏ-zīwā*) ... I shall bring you a good and pure turban of light (*ṭarṭbūnā tābā dakyā ḏ-nhūrā*).

and in *CP* 98 (*ML* p. 98):

> The man (*gabrā*) who brought me hither,
> brought me a beautiful robe.
> He clothed me in a robe of radiance (*uṣṭlā ḏ-zīwā*)
> and covered me with a turban of light.
> He put on me a wreath of aether (*klīl āyar*)

---

70 With Segelberg, *Maṣbūtā*, 51 I take the root QRA here in the sense "call" which gives a better meaning in the context. Lidzbarski, *ML* p. 29 and Drower, *CP* p. 15 translate it as "create".
71 Hazazban is here a higher light being, cf. Lidzbarski, *ML*, 29 n. 2.
72 *GR* V,4 (Lidzbarski, *Ginzā*, 193).
73 Cf. Segelberg, *Maṣbūtā*, 124.

The ascent from the water of the jordan in the *maṣbūtā* is clearly paralleled with the ascent after death to the Light world. In both cases a new status is conferred upon the individual which makes the use of a similar symbolism adequate.

3.3.4. Ablutions and Baptisms as a Late Antiquity Phenomena

Another consideration speaking in favour of an ancient origin of the Mandaean *maṣbūtā* is the emergence of religious groups that practiced different types of water ablutions in the centuries around the beginning of our era.[74] The Essenes apparently had their water lustrations and John and his adherents in the Jordan valley represented another Jewish group which attached a particular significance to purification and immersion rituals. Sethian Gnostics and Valentinians had their own water rituals. Early Christianity developed soon its own forms of baptism,[75] as is well known. Thanks to the Mani Codex we are now better informed of the Elchesaites, who are listed among various baptizing movements by the heresiologists. Among these movements were the Hemerobaptists and the Masbothei. The latter are mentioned by Hegesippus and it is tempting to link them with the Mandaeans but the evidence is not conclusive.[76]

3.3.5. Form and Meaning of the Late Antiquity Ritual

Faced with a comprehensive water ritual we do not have to explain it as a result of a gradual development from a short and simple ritual.[77] Some details may have changed, such as the introduction of additional *kuštā*'s, and some actions present in the early ritual might have been suppressed, e.g. a rite of investiture.[78] However, the main elements of the present *maṣbūtā* were certainly part of the Mandaean water ritual in Late Antiquity. To account for changes within that period of Mandaean history which probably covers almost five hundred years, is a matter of speculation. The available evidence for tracing ritual changes is simply not conclusive.

The performance of the *maṣbūtā* ritual followed basically the same structure as is found in the 20th century ritual. According to my interpretation, the main elements and their order were the following:

1° the officiating priests consecrated themselves and the cult objects;

---

74 An overview of early Jewish and Christian Baptist groups is given in RUDOLPH, "Antike Baptisten", in: IDEM, *Gnosis and spätantike Religionsgeschichte*, 569–603 (English version in the *Cambridge history of Judaism* vol. 3, 471–500).
75 All these groups and their water rituals are treated in detail in the present publication.
76 Cf. B. A. PEARSON, *Ancient Gnosticism*, 329.
77 Cf. BUCKLEY, "Polemics and Exorcism in Mandaean Baptism", 157.
78 As argued by SEGELBERG, *Maṣbūtā*, 121–130.

2° the celebrants arrived and grasped the *drabšā*;
3° the priest recited the invitation prayer;
4° the offering for the priest was bestowed on the river bank;
5° the celebrants descended one by one into the water;
6° they waded out to the priest and immersed themselves three times;
7° the priest dipped their forehead three times in the water and signed them with his finger three times and pronounced the formula of signing;
8° the priest invested the celebrant with the wreath (and with the sacred dress) and he or she drank three times from the water of the river;
9° then followed the ritual hand clasp, the *kušṭā*;
10° ascending from the water the priest anointed each celebrant with a threefold application on the forehead;
11° the sacred meal took place on the river bank: the priest administered the *pihtā* and the *mambūhā* to the whole group of celebrants together;
12° the celebrants rose from a crouching to a standing position whilst pointing to the *yardnā* as a witness of their *maṣbūtā*.

There is no reason to doubt the ancient origin of the meanings that are attributed to the *maṣbūtā* in the *Qolastā* and the *Ginzā*. It is stated in the *Ginzā* that the water ritual has a twofold effect, on the one hand it gives remission from sins and transgressions, and on the other, when combined with good deeds, it offers a straight way to the world of 'Life' (GR I, 123–124). The prayer recited at the moment when the participants in the *maṣbūtā* rise from a crouching to a standing position indicate that the immersion in the water is seen as an anticipation of their coming salvation:

> In the name of the 'Life'! You are set up and raised up into the Place of the Good. Established among *mānās* of light are these souls who went down to the jordan and were baptised (and those) of our fathers and teachers and of our brothers and sisters who have departed the body and those who are still in the body. There, in the light shall you be raised up. And 'Life' is victorious".[79]

The formula of signing after the immersion in the water (cited in § 2.1.) emphasizes the protection that the *maṣbūtā* gives the individual. More important is the idea of a communion (*laufā*) with the Light world that runs through the prayers. Its splendour and force are present in "the living water", the *yardnā*, as well as in the sacred banner, the *drabšā* (see further § 4.1.). Otherworldly radiance shines forth from both the water and the banner. The life giving flow of light is thus transferred to the celebrants in a double way: through immersion and drinking living water on the one hand, and through touching the banner on the other.

---

79 CP p. 24.

4. Iranian Elements in the *maṣbūtā* Ritual

The Mandaean water ritual in Late Antiquity is a complex one in which the various parts are nevertheless well integrated and form a functional unity. It bears the stamp of an innovation where the one (or the ones) who shaped the ritual seem to have been inspired by different traditions. Here I want to draw attention to the Iranian elements of the *maṣbūtā*.

4.1. Bihrām and the Cultic Banner

After the immersion and signing the Mandaean priests recited the confirmation formula (see § 2.1.2.) which includes a reference to an Iranian deity:

> You have been baptized with the baptism of the great Bihrām, son of the mighty ('Life').

A similar formula is used in the *ṭamaša* ritual (see § 2.1.1.) where the person who himself or herself performs the ceremony declares:

> I am baptized with the baptism of Bahram the Great, son of the mighty, and my baptism shall guard me and ascends to the summit.[80]

A closer investigation reveals that Bihrām or Bahrām is in fact particularly associated with the water rituals. He is seldom mentioned in the *Ginzā*[81] and only a couple of times in the *Book of John*.[82] Conversely, there are a number of passages in the *Qolastā* that refer to Bihrām in connection with the *maṣbūtā* ritual.[83] Of special interest are the banner hymns (*CP* 330–347, *ML* pp. 264–277) that reveal a particular relation of Bihrām with the cultic banner, the *drabšā*, which in its turn is closely linked to the main water ritual. The ritual instructions given after the hymns explicitly connect the banner with different aspects of the *maṣbūtā*.[84]

---

80 Cited after DROWER, *The Mandaeans*, 105. She gives the formula also in Mandaic. Note the pronunciation *Bahram*.

81 *GR* XV,7 (p. 323): "the House of Bihrām, the son of Life"; XVII,1 (p. 403): Prayers of Bihrām have been left on earth for the faithful; XVII, 2 (p. 406): the soul leaving the earth will have a robe like the robe of Bihrām-Uthra.

82 LIDZBARSKI, *Das Johannesbuch*, 15,12; 23,17; 111,11; 212,9. Only the last mentioned passage gives some information on Bihrām. He is regarded as the one who in primordial times spread the light over the sky and illuminated the uthra's in their abodes. In 111,11 Bihrām is said to be one of the sons of Yahyā (John) in Jerusalem.

83 *CP* 10, 22, 24, 25, 26 which belong to the *maṣbūtā* part of the *Qolastā*; further *CP* 77 (a hymn of praise); *CP* 80 in the Responses connected with the *maṣbūtā*; 104 the *rušma* prayer which is recited during the minor ablutions and before each stage of a ritual, see *CP* p. 102 n. 3; *CP* 166 a daily devotional prayer; *CP* 171 a hymn of praise.

84 *CP* 330 to 336 are recited when the banner is unfolded; *CP* 338 to 341 are chanted when the banner is brought to the jordan and planted on the bank; *CP* 342 and 343 when the priest

Besides Šišlam the Great, the mythic prototype of the priest, it is Bihrām the Great who is the lord of the banner. The first one to unfurl the *drabšā* was however another light being, Arspan, whose name seems to be of Iranian origin (*CP* 330, *ML* p. 264). The radiance (*zīwā*) of the banner and its capacity of illuminating the whole world is repeatedly emphasized. Numerous worlds of light assemble around the banner and pronounce a blessing over the banner of the Great Bihrām (*CP* 334, *ML* p. 266). The radiance of the banner shines out on the jordan which gets strength and flow from it (*CP* 334). On the day when Bihrām unfurled the banner Šišlamēl, its radiance shone out over the waters, from the waters it flooded upwards and spread over the world (*CP* 335, *ML* p. 267). Another hymn says that Great Bihrām's banner shone forth like the great mirror which rests in the jordan (*CP* 336, *ML* pp. 267–68).[85] It is also Bihrām who performs the prototypic rite of furling the banner (*CP* 346, *ML* p. 273).

Bihrām or Bahrām is the Iranian god *Wahrām* (Middle Iranian form, known in the Avesta as *Vərəθragna*). In Seleucid and Parthian times, the god enjoyed a great popularity in Iran, Armenia and Mesopotamia. His identification with Heracles and with the name of the fire temples called *ātaxš ī Wahrām* contributed a good deal to his popularity.[86] In Iranian tradition Wahrām receives epithets emphasizing his power, *warzāwand*, which has also connotations of "miraculous" and "radiant" and *amāwand*, which refers to his strength.[87] His role in the Pahlavi texts is predominantly eschatological.[88]

For the Armenians, *Vahagn* (< *Varθragna*) was one of the most prominent deities of the pre-Christian period.[89] In Mesopotamia too, Wahrām seems to have been worshipped particularly in the Parthian period. An inscription in Greek and Parthian from the mid-second century AD states that the Parthian king Vologeses conquered Mesene in southern Babylonia from his rival Mithridates and took the cult image of the god Heracles with him.[90] To the Greek expression Ἡρακλέους θεοῦ corresponds in the Parthian text *Wartragan bag*. Farther north in the Hellenistic kingdom of Commagene which borders to

---

grasps the banner, and 344 and 345 after the performance of the *maṣbūtā*. *CP* 346 is recited when the banner is folded up.

85   *CP* 345, *ML* p. 273 speaks of the "banner Bihrām".
86   Probably *wahrām* in the name of the fire temple is originally the adjective "victorious" as suggested by Mary Boyce in M. BOYCE & F. GRENET, *A History of Zoroastrianism III*, 65. For the spread of the cult of Wahrām, see also M. CARTER, "Aspects of the imagery of Verethragna".
87   For the meaning of *warzāwand* and *amāwand*, see H. S. NYBERG, *A Manual of Pahlavi* II, 203 and 15.
88   In the first place Bahman Yašt and Jāmasp Nāmag.
89   MOVSES KHORENATSI, *History of the Armenians* I,31 even quotes some stanzas from a popular song about Vahagn describing his birth and appearance. The god is associated with fire and radiance.
90   For the inscription, see E. MORANO, "Contributi all'interpretazione …".

Mesopotamia, the rulers worshipped the Greco-Iranian deities Zeus–Oromazdes, Apollon-Mithras and Artagnes–Heracles (Artagnes <*Varthragna*). The last deity's name bears witness of the importance both of the Greek Heracles and the Iranian Varthragna in the 2nd century BC in an area close to Mesoptamia. The Mandaeans were certainly acquainted with this Iranian deity and he became an important divine being for them too and connected especially with the *maṣbūtā*.[91]

The close relationship of Bihrām with the cultic banner, and the water ritual, suggests that the figure of Bihrām and the banner formed a unity and was taken over as such from Iranian tradition already in Parthian times.[92] The Mandaic name of the banner, *drabšā*, is Iranian (Avestan *drafša-*, Middle Iranian *drafš* "banner") and refers clearly to a corresponding object in Iranian culture.[93] The evidence points to the fact that in ancient Iran the banner had primarily religious connotations.[94]

4.2. The *kuštā*: The Concept and the Act

4.2.1. The Concept of *kuštā*

The term *kuštā* "truth, justice" is a key concept in Mandaean thought and life. To grasp all its connotations in a single term is impossible.[95] For our purpose the most interesting thing is that the notion of *kuštā* corresponds strikingly in its function and meaning with the Iranian concept of *arta-* (Avestan *aša-*, Middle Iranian adj. *ardā*) which plays an equally prominent role in Iranian religion. I suggest that the significance of the concept *kuštā* in Mandaeism arose in contact with the Iranian tradition and its central notion of *arta-*.

---

91 E. Lupieri, *The Mandaeans*, 163 states that the Hyspaosinnidic dynasty which ruled Charakene/Mesene in southern Babylonia in the Parthian period had Wahrām depicted on their coins. References to the sources are not given, however.

92 Segelberg, *Maṣbūtā*, 58–59 argues that the mention of Bihrām in the baptismal liturgy is secondary. He suggests that Bihrām was introduced in the Sasanian period when the Mandaeans settled in the East "in order to legitimize the new religion to the rulers of the country".

93 The banner in Iranian traditions is investigated by A. de Jong, "Vexillogica sacra" who also includes the Mandaean and Georgian evidence. De Jong suggests that both Mandaeans and the Georgian community religions of the Caucasus derived their religious use of the banner from Iranian culture.

94 For a detailed discussion, see A. de Jong, "Vexillologica sacra".

95 Cf. Lidzbarski, *Das Johannesbuch*, xvii: "Das religiöse Ideal für die Mandäer ist כושטא. Dies ist über die ursprüngliche Bedeutung „Wahrheit, Richtigkeit" weit hinausgegangen. Es ist für die Mandäer der Inbegriff ihrer Religion …". Drower, *The Canonical Prayer Book*, 2 states: "*Kuštā* = Right, Troth, Truth, Sincerity, 'a pact', an 'oath' etc." W. Sundberg, *Kushṭa I-II* provides the basis for a detailed study of the concept in collecting and interpreting the passages where the word *kuštā* occurs.

4.2.2. The Act of Giving the *kušṭā*

As we have seen the term *kušṭā* also denotes the ritual hand grasp. I know of no other ritual in which the hand grasp plays such a prominent role as in the Mandaean water ceremony. The reasons for the importance of the ritual *kušṭā* may be diverse. One possible source of inspiration is to be found in rites of trust and loyalty where the hand grasp, the δεξίωσις, and similar gestures have a particular significance. The evidence is both textual and iconographic.

There is evidence for linking the ritual hand grasp particularly with Iranian tradition. In his *Anabasis* Xenophon connects the δεξίωσις with Achaemenid rulers and members of the Persian elite.[96] It can be seen as an official act of loyalty between the king and his Persian noblemen.[97] Diodorus Siculus says that the custom of offering the right hand means for the Persians a sign of "the most firm fidelity" (ἔστι δ' ἡ πίστις αὕτη βεβαιοτάτη παρὰ τοῖς Πέρσαις).[98] Another testimony to the Iranian background of performing the hand grasp comes from Josephus. In describing the dealings of the Parthian king Artaban with the Jewish brothers Asinaeus and Anilaeus,[99] Josephus reports that Artaban swore by his ancestral gods not to harm the brothers whereupon he offered his right hand to Asinaeus (τὴν δεξιὰν ἐδίδου). This is followed by the remark that the hand grasp is the highest expression of assurance (μέγιστον ... παράδειγμα τοῦ θαρσεῖν) among the "barbarians" of the Parthian realm when making visits.[100]

The Iranian hand grasp is ritualized and performed as a sign of fidelity and agreement and is usually accompanied by oath taking and invocation of deities. The ritual hand grasp seems to have been taken over from the Persians by the Seleucids as is indicated by the iconography of the rulers of Commagene.[101]

---

96 *Anabasis* I,6,6: Cyrus says to Orontas that they confirmed their peace agreement by taking and offering the right hand, καὶ δεξιὰν ἔλαβον καὶ ἔδωκα. In II,5,3 Klearkhos addresses Tissaphernes with the words: "I know that we swore oaths and offered the right hand in order not to harm each other". Xenophon seems to be the first one to attest this Persian custom as he is also the first to introduce the Persian concept παράδεισος in Greek literature.

97 Cf. P. Briant, *Histoire de l'empire perse*, 336–337.

98 Diodorus Siculus XVI, 43,4.

99 *Antiquitates* XVIII, 310–371. According to Josephus the brothers succeeded in establishing themselves as a powerful force in Mesopotamia during a short period.

100 *Antiquitates* XVIII, 328–329.

101 In Greek the act of offering the right hand δεξιὰν or δεξιὰς διδόναι seems to have developed into a simple figurative expression for "conclude an agreement", "make terms". It is so used in several passages of *1* and *2 Maccabees*. In *1 Macc* 6:58 Lysias appeals to the Seleucid king: "Let us offer these men (the Jews) terms (δῶμεν δεξιὰς τοῖς ἀνθρώποις τούτοις) and make peace with them and their whole nation". Further 11;50, 62 and 66; 13:46 and 50. In *2 Macc* 12:12 we are told that Judas agreed to make peace with the defeated nomads "and after receiving assurances (λαβόντες δεξιὰς) from him, they went back to their tents". *2 Macc.* 14:19 reports that Nicanor sent representatives "to negotiate a settlement" (δοῦναι καὶ λαβεῖν δεξιὰς) with

The Iranian type of a ritual δεξίωσις is to be distinguished from the type of a pure metaphorical expression in which a deity takes or holds the hand of somebody to give him or her strength and protection. Jahve, the god of Israel, holds his people by the right hand (Isa 41:13), he takes his servant by the hand to protect him (Isa 42:6), and he grasps the right hand of Cyrus, his anointed prince, to give him strength to beat down the nations (Isa 45:1). The Hebrew expression uses the hifʿil of the verb *ḥāzaq* in the sense of "take" or "hold", which the Septuagint renders with various forms of κρατεῖν.[102] In Greek the two types of hand grasp are denoted by different wordings, τὴν δεξιὰν διδόναι καὶ λαμβάνειν for the Persian rite and τῆς δεξιᾶς κρατεῖν for the Hebrew metaphor.

A number of reliefs from Commagene display scenes of a δεξίωσις.[103] The most common motif represents a deity who takes the hand of the king as a sign of divine consent. The early stage of Antiocus' royal cult show him in a δεξίωσις with Apollo represented as Helios.[104] The reliefs of the second and main stage of the cult show the king taking the hand of one of the Greco-Persian deities mentioned in the cult inscriptions. The δεξίωσις scenes with the god Mithras (identified with Apollo-Helios-Hermes) and king Antiochus I depict the god in a Persian tiara surrounded by a solar halo (Fig. 15).[105] The reliefs representing the hand grasp between Zeus-Oromasdes and the king show the god both with Greek and Persian features.[106] Conversely the reliefs that represent the king and Artagnes-Heracles show the god in his Greek image (Fig. 16).[107]

---

the Maccabees. In all the above cases there is little to indicate that a hand grasp ceremony was actually performed.

102 It has been suggested that there might have been a ritual background to the Hebrew expression of taking somebody's right hand. See F. Hesse, חזק in: *ThWAT*, II, 851.

103 The δεξίωσις stelae in Commagene include two types of scenes: 1° the farewell δεξίωσις found at Karakuş showing king Mithradates II and his sister Laodice (J. Wagner, "Die Könige von Kommagene", 21), and more importantly 2° the investiture of the ruler by a deity.

104 For the two stages of the cult, see Wagner, "Die Könige von Kommagene", 16–17. The fragmentary stela of Adiyaman (original locality unknown) and the relief from Sofraz Köy show the king grasping the hand of a naked deity with a solar disc. The inscription on the stela from Sofraz Köy identifies the deity with Apollo Epekoos. For the stela of Adiyaman, see also H. Waldmann, "Die kommagenischen Kultreformen", 8–9.

105 Arsameia on Nymphaios: 1. fragment of a relief from an unknown base (J. Young in F. Dörner & Th. Goell, *Arsameia*, 208–209), 2. fragment of a relief belonging to base II (Young in Dörner & Goell, *Arsameia*, 199–203). Nemrud Dağ: Two fragmentary reliefs (K. Humann & O. Puchstein, *Reisen in Kleinasien*, 320–321).

106 Nemrud Dağ, see Humann & Puchstein, *Reisen in Kleinasien*, 324–326.

107 Arsameia on Nymphaios (Young in Dörner & Goell, *Arsameia*, 203–208); Seleukeia on Euphrat/Zeugma (Wagner, "Die Könige von Kommagene", 15); Nemrud Dağ (Humann & Puchstein, *Reisen in Kleinasien*, 327). See also D.-A. Koch, *Bilder aus der Welt des Urchristentums*, 256 with Fig. 416,

The δεξίωσις scenes with the king and a deity have been differently interpreted.[108] In my opinion they intended to convey the idea of consent and divine protection. The δεξίωσις reliefs were at display in the royal cult places (ἱεροθέσια) all over Commagene.[109] The impressive monuments attracted the attention of many visitors and came certainly to be known over vast areas of northern Mesopotamia and eastern Anatolia.

The Iranian type of ritual hand grasp seems to me to offer the most probable background for the Mandaean *kušṭā*. When the Mandaeans emerged in Mesopotamia in the Parthian period, they would have been well acquainted with the Iranian δεξίωσις as it was practiced in life and depicted in iconographical monuments. It could be applied in other religious rituals as the Mandaean *maṣbūtā*.[110] Here it was 'Life', the supreme god, who gave his consent and protection through the priest to the celebrants of the water ritual.

5. The *maṣbūtā* and the Problem of Mandaean Origins

The origins of the Mandaean community is a much debated issue. The traditional view locates them first in Palestine and the Jordan valley among Jewish non-mainstream groups of the 1st and 2nd cent. A.D. who practiced various water rituals.[111] From this area they are thought to have migrated to northern Mesopotamia, sojourning in the Median hills and then, in a final stage, they settled in central and southern Babylonia. The *maṣbūtā* ritual would consequently have its roots in the practices of Jewish or early Christian baptismal groups. This opinion on the 'Mandäerfrage' (coming close to a scholarly consensus) has recently been challenged and it is suggested that the Mandaeans had always been in the

---

108 HUMANN & PUCHSTEIN, *Reisen in Kleinasien*, 340 saw them as scenes of apotheosis. J. H. YOUNG, "Skulpturen aus Arsameia", 224 emphasised the connection of the δεξίωσις scenes with the horoscope representations: "Sie stellen daher Empfangsszenen dar, in denen der Gott den König empfängt und mit Handschlag bekräftigt, daß er in der Tat die schützende Gottheit ist und in seiner Hut das Schicksal des Königs in Übereinstimmung mit den Planeten und Konstellationen steht". By contrast WALDMANN, "Die kommagenischen Kultreformen", 197–202 suggested that it is the king who welcomes a group of new gods in his kingdom. For H. DÖRRIE, *Der Königskult*, 205 the constellation of stars in the summer 62 BC produced the image of a celestial *dexiosis* where the planets approached and greeted Regulus.

109 The historical map in WAGNER, "Die Könige von Kommagene", 12 gives a good idea of the distribution of the royal cult places.

110 The Manichaeans seem to have practised the handgrasp as part of the initiation ritual, but without any connection with water ablutions and baptisms; for further details, see the contribution by G. WURST in this publication, § 3.: "Initiationsriten im Manichäismus", 145–154.

111 Chief proponents of this line of interpretation are: LIDZBARSKI, *Ginzā*, Einleitung I-XII; BULTMANN, "Die Bedeutung…"; W. BOUSSET, "Die Religion der Mandäer" (with some modifications); RUDOLPH, *Die Mandäer I*, 252–255; SEGELBERG, *Maṣbūtā*, 182–184; WIDENGREN, "Die Mandäer"; MACUCH, "Anfänge der Mandäer"; Ṣ. GÜNDÜZ, *The Knowledge of Life*, 119 and 233, and more tentatively also BUCKLEY, *The Great Stem of Souls*, 315–341.

Mesopotamian area.[112] There is much in favour of this view-point and the linguistic arguments put forward by Müller-Kessler seem to me convincing. Methodologically it seems plausible to assume an origin for a community where they are first historically attested. Only if clear evidence points in another direction we should abandon the assumption of the Mesopotamian origin (Mesopotamia should here be taken in a wide sense). The cultural milieu of that region is well reflected in the Mandaean incantation texts, as well as in the early literature, the *Ginzā* and the *Qolastā*. On the other hand, one has to explain why the concept *yardnā* as an appellative "jordan", plays such a prominent role for the Mandaeans. This fact has been used as a decisive argument for a western origin of Mandaeism among Jewish baptist movements in the Jordan valley.[113] The question why John the Baptist came to be adopted by the Mandaeans has likewise to be answered but this is also coupled with the discussion of the age of the Mandaean traditions about John and their independence of the Christian tradition.

The basic components of Mandaeism are usually interpreted as 'layers' that also are seen as indications of its 'syncretistic' history. To follow the presentation of Geo Widengren[114] which is representative of a number of scholars, we have first the Jewish and West Semitic layer, then the Mesopotamian one, and finally the Iranian layer. Polemics against Christian ideas and figures are usually considered to belong to a later stage though still pre-Islamic.[115] When it comes to the *maṣbūtā*, however, an early Christian influence is considered by several scholars to be apparent.[116]

However, all the three main components of Mandaeism can be derived from the cultural milieu of Mesopotamia, where large Jewish communities were present and where Babylonian temples were still in use in the first two centuries AD.[117] In the Parthian and early Sasanian periods Iranian influence was strong and Iranian population groups had settled in the area. The prosopography of the Mandaean incantation texts from the Late Antiquity shows a considerable

---

112 So Lupieri, *The Mandaeans*, esp. 162–165; Müller-Kessler, "The Mandaeans and the Question of Their Origin". It should be noted that W. Brandt, *Die Mandäer*, 34–37 suggested a "homeland" for the Mandaeans in the mountainous regions of northern Mesopotamia.

113 Lidzbarski, *Ginzā* p. VI; Bultmann, "Die Bedeutung …"; Drower, *The Mandaeans*, p. xxiv; Segelberg, *Maṣbūtā*, 38–39; Widengren, "Die Mandäer".

114 Widengren, "Die Mandäer".

115 Lupieri, *The Mandaeans*.

116 For H. Lietzmann, "Ein Beitrag zur Mandäerfrage" in a decisive way. For Segelberg, *Maṣbūtā*, and *Gnostica-Mandaica-Liturgica*, 135–144 only in part. By contrast R. Reitzenstein, *Vorgeschichte* regarded the Mandaean water ritual to have influenced the Christian baptism.

117 For the survival of Babylonian cults and deities, see C. Müller-Kessler, "Aramäische Beschwörungen" und C. Müller-Kessler & K. Kessler, "Spätbabylonische Gottheiten".

number of Iranian personal names.[118] The Iranian component becomes less understandable if Mandaeism originated in a Palestinian context.

If we opt for an homeland of the Mandaeans in Mesopotamia (in its wide sense) the water ritual has most probably a local origin. It could be useful to search for a late Babylonian origin of the Mandaean immersion ritual.[119] The various water purifications attested in the *bīt rimki* series and other comparable series provide a possible background, and a reminiscence may be found in the terms *pihtā* and *mambūhā*.[120]

The Zoroastrian purification rituals, in Middle Iranian called *pādyāb* and *barašnūm*, included in pre-Islamic time also elements of water ablutions, but these never implied immersion in rivers or sacred pools.[121] In my opinion the immersion rite of the Mandaeans must derive from elsewhere and here Mesopotamia is the most probable alternative.

6. Concluding Remarks

It seems reasonable to assume that water ceremonies were a characteristic feature of the Mandaean religion from the very beginning and that the basic structure of these ceremonies has been preserved both in the ritual texts and in the 20th century performance of the *maṣbūtā*.

Instead of assuming a gradual growth of Mandaean doctrine and ritual reflected in the different layers of constitutive elements (Jewish, Mesopotamian, Iranian and Christian) one should seriously consider the possibility of a founder figure (or group of founders) who shaped the basic character of Mandaeism and its main ritual, the *maṣbūtā*, uniting elements of different traditions into a coherent whole. A parallel would be Roman Mithraism with its blend of Greco-Roman and Iranian traditions for which such a founder (or founder group) has been suggested. Personalities such as Elchesai, Valentinus and Mani who founded new religious groups show the importance of founder figures.

---

118 Iranian personal names prevail in the texts referred to above (note 63); cf. also YAMAUCHI, *Mandaic Incantation Texts*, 12. The client's name is given with reference to his or her mother's name. Iranian names are Abandukht, Adurdukht, Guntai, Newandukht (women) and Anušag, Dukhtanube, Mahdur (< Mah-Adur), Šabur (men).

119 This would require a study of its own and the competence of an assyriologist.

120 A Babylonian background for the *pihtā* and the *mambūhā* was pointed out by H. ZIMMERN, "Das vermutliche Babylonische Vorbild". WIDENGREN, "Heavenly Enthronement and Baptism", 573–587 adduced further material pertaining to Mesopotamian water lustrations.

121 Best treatment in STAUSBERG, *Die Religion Zarathustras III*, 275–296.

Bibliography

BOUSSET, WILHELM, "Die Religion der Mandäer", in: *ThR* 17 (1920) 185–205.

BOYCE, MARY & GRENT, FRANTZ, *A History of Zoroastrianism, Vol. III*, Leiden: Brill 1991.

BRANDT, WILHELM, *Die Mandäer, ihre Religion und ihre Geschichte*, Amsterdam: J. Müller 1915 (= Leipzig 1889).

BRIANT, PIERRE, *Histoire de l'empire perse*, Paris: Fayard 1996.

BUCKLEY, JORUNN JACOBSEN, *The Mandaeans: Ancient Texts and Modern People*, Oxford: Oxford University Press 2002.

— *The Great Stem of Souls. Reconstructing Mandaean History*, Piscataway, N.J.: Gorgias Press 2005.

— "Polemics and Exorcism in the Mandaean Baptism", in: *HR* 47 (2008) 156–170.

BULTMANN, RUDOLF, "Die Bedeutung der neuerschlossenen mandäischen und manichäischen Quellen für das Verständnis des Johannesevangeliums", in: *ZNW* 24 (1925) 100–146 (= in: idem, *Exegetica. Aufsätze zur Erforschung des Neuen Testaments*, ausgewählt, eingeleitet und herausgegeben von E. Dinkler, Tübingen: J. C. B. Mohr [Paul Siebeck] 1967, 55–104).

CAQUOT, ANDRÉ, "Un phylactère mandéen en plomb", in: *Semitica* 22 (1972) 67–87.

CARTER, MARTHA L., "Aspects of the imagery of Verethragna: The Kushan empire and Buddhist Central Asia", in: B. Fragner et al. (eds), *Proceedings of the Second European Conference of Iranian Studies*, Roma: Istituto italiano per il Medio ed Estremo oriente 1995, 119–140.

DÖRNER, KARL & GOELL, THERESA, *Arsameia am Nymphaios*, Berlin: Gebr. Mann 1963.

DÖRRIE, H., *Der Königskult des Antiochos von Kommagene im Lichte neuer Inschriften-Funde* (AAWG.PH), Göttingen: Vandenhoeck & Ruprecht 1964.

DROWER, ETHEL STEFANA, *The Mandaeans of Iraq and Iran*, Oxford: Clarendon Press 1937.

— *The Canonical Prayerbook of the Mandaeans*, Leiden: Brill 1959.

DROWER, E. S. & MACUCH, R., *A Mandaic Dictionary*, Berlin: De Gruyter 1963.

GÜNDÜZ, ŞINASI, *The Knowledge of Life*, Oxford: Oxford University Press 1994.

HESSE, F., . חזק in: *Theologisches Wörterbuch zum Alten Testament*, Bd. II, Stuttgart: Kohlhammer 1977, 846–857.

HUMANN, KARL & PUCHSTEIN, OTTO, *Reisen in Kleinasien und Nordsyrien*, Berlin: Reimer 1890.

DE JONG, ALBERT, "Vexillologica sacra: searching the cultic banner", in: C. Cereti, M. Maggi & E. Provasi (eds.), *Religious themes and texts of pre-Islamic Iran and Central Asia*, Wiesbaden: Ludvig Reichert Verlag 2003, 191–202.

KHORENATSI, MOVSES, *History of the Armenians*, Cambridge, Mass.: Harvard University Press 1978.

LIDZBARSKI, MARK, "Ein mandäisches Amulett", in: *Florilegium ou recueil de travaux d'érudition dédies à Monsieur le Marquis Melchior de Vogüé*, Paris: Impr. nationale 1909, 349–373.

— *Das Johannesbuch der Mandäer I-II*, Giessen: Alfred Töpelmann 1915.

— *Mandäische Liturgien, mitgeteilt, übersetzt und erklärt*, Berlin: Weidmann 1920.

— *Ginzā. Der Schatz oder das grosse Buch der Mandäer*, Göttingen: Vandenhoeck & Ruprecht 1925.

LIETZMANN, HANS, "Ein Beitrag zur Mandäerfrage", in: *SPAW.PH*, Berlin: Springer 1930, 596–608.

LUPIERI, EDMONDO, *The Mandaeans. The Last Gnostics*. Grand Rapids, Mich.: Eerdman 2002 (Italian original 1993).

MACUCH, RUDOLPH, *Handbook of Classical and Modern Mandaic*, Berlin: de Gruyter 1965.

— "Anfänge der Mandäer", in: F. Altheim & R. Stiehl (eds), *Die Araber in der alten Welt*, vol. 2, Berlin: de Gruyter 1965, 76–190.

— "Altmandäische Bleirolle (Erster Teil)", in: F. Altheim & R. Stiehl (eds), *Die Araber in der alten Welt. IV. Neue Funde*, Berlin: de Gruyter 1967, 91–203.

— "Altmandäische Bleirollen (Fortsetzung)" in: F. Altheim & R. Stiehl (eds), *Die Araber in der alten Welt. V. Weitere Neufunde*, Berlin: de Gruyter 1968, 34–71.

MORANO, ENRICO, "Contributi all'interpretazione della bilingue greco-partica dell'Eracle di Seleucia", in: Gh. Gnoli & A. Panaino (eds), *Proceedings of the First European Conference of Iranian Studies, Part 1 Old and Middle Iranian Studies*, Roma: Istituto italiano per il Medio ed Estremo oriente 1990, 229–238.

MÜLLER-KESSLER, CHRISTA, "A Mandaic Gold Amulet in the British Museum", in: *BASOR* 311 (1998) 83–88.

— "Interrelations between Mandaic Lead Scrolls and Incantation Bowls", in: Tzvi Abusch & Karel van der Toorn (eds.), *Mesopotamian Magic*, Groningen: Styx 1999, 197–209.

— "Aramäische Beschwörungen und astronomische Omina in nachbabylonischer Zeit. Das Fortleben mesopotamischer Kultur im Vorderen Orient", in: J. Renger (ed.), *Babylon. Focus mesopotamischer Geschichte, Wiege früher Geschichte, Mythos in der Moderne*, Saarbrücker Druckerei und Verlag 1999, 427–443.

— "A Charm Against Demons of Time", in: Cornelia Wunsch (ed.), *Mining the Archives: Festschrift for Christopher Walker*, Dresden: ISLET 2002, 183–189.

— "The Mandaeans and the Question of Their Origin", in: *Aram* 16 (2004) 47–60.

MÜLLER-KESSLER, CHRISTA & KESSLER, KARLHEINZ, "Spätbabylonische Gottheiten in spätantiken mandäischen Texten", in: *ZA* 89 (1999) 65–87.

NYBERG, H. S., *A Manual of Pahlavi. Part II: Glossary*, Wiesbaden: Harrassowitz 1974.

OPPENHEIM, LEO A., *Ancient Mesopotamia. Portrait of a Dead Civilization*, revised edition completed by Erica Reiner, Chicago, Ill.: University of Chicago Press 1977.

PEARSON, BIRGER A., *Ancient Gnosticism. Traditions and Literature*, Minneapolis, Minn.: Fortress Press 2007.

PEDERSEN, V. SCHOU, *Bidrag til en Analyse af de Mandaeiske skrifter, med hinblik paa bestimmelsen af mandaernes forhold til Jødedom og Kristendom*, Aarhus: Universitetsforlaget 1940.

PETERMANN, HEINRICH, *Thesaurus sive Liber magnus vulgo "Liber Adami" appellatus opus mandaeorum summi pondens*, Lipsiae: P. O. Weigel 1867.

REITZENSTEIN, RICHARD, *Die Vorgeschichte der christlichen Taufe*, Leipzig – Berlin: B. G. Teubner 1929 (Reprint: Darmstadt: Wissenschaftliche Buchgesellschaft 1967).

RINGGREN, HELMER, *Die Religionen des Alten Orients*, Göttingen: Vandenhoeck & Ruprecht 1979.

RUDOLPH, KURT, *Die Mandäer I. Prolegomena: Das Mandäerproblem*, Göttingen: Vandenhoeck & Ruprecht 1960.

— *Die Mandäer II. Der Kult.* Göttingen: Vandenhoeck & Ruprecht 1961.

— "Mandaean Sources", in: *Gnosis*, Oxford: Oxford University Press 1974, 123–147.

— "Antike Baptisten", in: *Gnosis und spätantike Religionsgeschichte. Gesammelte Aufsätze*, Leiden: Brill 1996,

— "The Baptist Sects", in: *The Cambridge History of Judaism Vol. 3*. Cambridge: Cambridge University Press 1999, 471–500.

— "The relevance of Mandaean literature for the study of Near Eastern religions", in: *Aram* 16 (2004) 1–12.

SEGELBERG, ERIC, *Maṣbūtā. Studies in the Ritual of Mandaean Baptism*, Uppsala: Almqvist & Wiksell 1958.

— *Gnostica-Mandaica-Liturgica*, Uppsala: Almqvist & Wiksell International 1990.

STAUSBERG, MICHAEL, *Die Religion Zarathustras. Geschichte – Gegenwart – Rituale*, Band 3, Stuttgart: Kohlhammer 2004.

SUNDBERG, WALDEMAR, *Kushṭa. A Monograph on a principal Word in Mandaean Texts. I. The Descending Knowledge, II. The Ascending Soul*, Lund: Gleerup 1953 and Lund Univeristy Press 1994.

WAGNER, JÖRG, "Die Könige von Kommagene und ihr Herrscherkult", in: Jörg Wagner (ed.), *Gottkönige am Euphrat. Neue Ausgrabungen und Forschungen in Kommagene*, Mainz am Rhein: Philipp von Zabern 2000, 11–25.

WALDMANN, HELMUT, *Die kommagenischen Kultreformen unter König Mithradates I. Kallinikos und seinem Sohne Antiochos I.*, Leiden: Brill 1973.

WIDENGREN, GEO, "Die Mandäer", in: B. Spuler (ed.), *Religionsgeschichte des Orients in der Zeit der Weltreligionen* (HO Abt. 1, VIII, 2), Leiden: Brill 1961, 83–101.

— "Heavenly Enthronement and Baptism. Studies in Mandaean Baptism", in: J. Neusner (ed.), *Religions in Antiquity*, Leiden: Brill 1968, 551–582.

— (ed.) *Der Mandäismus* (WdF 167), Darmstadt: Wissenschaftliche Buchgesellschaft 1982.

YAMAUCHI, EDWIN M., *Mandaic Incantation Texts*, New Haven, Conn.: American Oriental Society 1967.

YOUNG, JOHN H., "Skulpturen aus Arsameia am Nymphaios", in: Karl Dörner & Theresa Goell, *Arsameia am Nymphaios*, 197–227.

ZIMMERN, HEINRICH, "Das vermutliche Babylonische Vorbild des pehtā und mambūhā der Mandäer", in: C. Bezold (ed.), *Orientalische Studien. Theodor Nöldeke zum siebzigsten Geburtstag*, Giessen: Alfred Töpelmann 1906, 959–967.

Baptism and Graeco-Roman Mystery Cults

Fritz Graf

Whether and how Christian baptism was related to pagan mystery cults is an old question; it intrigued already Christian apologists and early modern antiquarians.[1] In the late nineteenth century, it entered the world of ideological disputes, driven by the political secularization of the new European nation states of Germany, France and Italy; at this time, the *Religionswissenschaftliche Schule* explored the affinities between Christian liturgy and theology on the one side and Graeco-Roman mystery cults on the other.[2] Alfred Loisy's *Les mystères païens et le mystère chrétien* (1919) carried the dispute from the secularization debate in Europe's nascent national states before the First World War into the post-war years, inspiring, among others, Vittorio Macchioro's long-living *From Orpheus to Paul* (1930).[3] In 1957, the learned Jesuit Father, Hugo Rahner, summarized the state of the debate in a scathing sentence: "Unfortunately the most recent scholarship is quite remarkably firm in rejecting the whole notion of any such influences".[4] On Pauls' doctrine of baptism, a well-trodden battle-ground, Günter Wagner reached a similar conclusion in his densely-knit monograph of 1962: "The religio-historical documents are of no help to us in the interpretation of Romans vi".[5] Rahner's "rather sweeping assertion perhaps outruns the facts of the case," as Devon Wiens remarked, and it did not mark the end of the larger debate, despite Walter Burkert's assertion in 1987 "that there is hardly any evidence for baptism in pagan mysteries".[6] Nowadays, however, much less seems at

---

1 For the apologists see below; for the antiquarians see Casaubon, *De rebus sacris et ecclesiasticis exercitationes XVI: Exercitatio 16*, chapter 43, pp. 388–407 in the edition Frankfurt: Ruland 1615.
2 E. g. H. Gunkel, *Zum religionsgeschichtlichen Verständnis des Neuen Testaments* or P. Wendland, *Die hellenistisch-römische Kultur und ihr Verhältnis zu Judentum und Christentum*; for an overview over the relevant research see D. H. Wiens, "Mystery Concepts in Primitive Christianity and in its Environment", and as to baptism G. Wagner, *Das religionsgeschichtliche Problem von Römer 6,1–11*.
3 On Vittorio Macchioro, see F. Graf, "A history of scholarship on the tablets," in: F. Graf and S. I. Johnston, *Ritual Texts for the Afterlife*, 50–65, esp. 59–61.
4 H. Rahner, "Das Mysterium der Taufe," 70.
5 Wagner, *Das religionsgeschichtliche Problem von Römer 6,1–11*, 268.
6 W. Burkert, *Ancient Mystery Cults*, 101.

stake, and the discussion should not carry much ideological baggage anymore.[7] In what follows, I will look at the problems very consciously through the eyes of a historian of the religions of the Roman Imperial Epoch.[8] I will not start with the most problematical question as to how baptism and mystery cults were related to each other, nor even with the wider question of how the widely attested ritual use of water for purification in ancient cults related to baptism; instead, I will first have a look at the apologists and their way of dealing with such relationships; the other two questions will then follow from this one.

1. Justin on Pagan Baptismal Rituals

As soon as we hear the voices of the Apologists, we discern a (somewhat one-sided) discourse that connects Christian baptism with rituals outside the young Christian tradition that appeared to be comparable. In his (First) Apology, Justin Martyr talks extensively about the Christian rituals, especially baptism, albeit in a seemingly rambling way.[9] After having described its performance and expounded its theological meaning, he adds a chapter in which he talks about the imitation of the rite by the δαίμονες:

Καὶ τὸ λουτρὸν δὴ τοῦτο ἀκούσαντες οἱ δαίμονες διὰ τοῦ προφήτου κεκηρυγμένον ἐνήργησαν καὶ ῥαντίζειν ἑαυτοὺς τοὺς εἰς τὰ ἱερὰ αὐτῶν ἐπιβαίνοντας καὶ προσιέναι αὐτοῖς μέλλοντας, λοιβὰς καὶ κνίσας ἀποτελοῦντας· τέλεον δὲ καὶ λούεσθαι ἀπιόντας πρὶν ἐλθεῖν ἐπὶ τὰ ἱερά, ἔνθα ἵδρυνται, ἐνεργοῦσι.

And after having heard this washing announced by the prophet, the demons induced also those to rinse themselves who are entering their temples and are about to worship them with libations and burnt-offerings; and they caused them also to bathe themselves entirely when they are setting out, before they enter the shrines in which they were set [*Apologia* 1.62.1; my translation].

Although in what follows Justin talks about the Jewish custom of entering the Temple without shoes, here he must refer to polytheist cult, with libations (λοιβαί), animal sacrifice (κνίση) and cult images (ἵδρυνται[10]). The link between the two seemingly incongruous details is the ritual of baptism that uses water and in which the baptized did not wear shoes; as to the underlying symbolic

---

7 See the reasonable, although superficial remarks of H. Bowden, *Mystery Cults of the Ancient World*, 209–211.

8 The still most rewarding contribution from this side is the long paper by A. D. Nock, "Hellenistic Mysteries and Christian Sacraments;" see also his "Religious Developments from the Close of the Republic to the Reign of Nero".

9 Justin, *Apologia* 1.61–63; see the contribution by A. Lindemann, "Zur frühchristlichen Taufpraxis", in the present publication.

10 ἱδρύω, "to seat", is the standard term for setting up a cult image, e.g. Eur. *IT* 1453; Aristophanes, *Plutus* 1153 etc.; the image itself is usually τὸ ἕδος, "the seat".

structure, Justin compares baptism to entering a (Greek, Roman or Jewish) sanctuary and thus coming into close contact with a divinity: baptism performs the permanent and life-changing transition into the space of the true God.

Justin describes two forms of lustration rituals that were common in Greek and Roman cult, the routine aspersion (ῥαντίζειν ἑαυτούς) from the wash-basin, περιρραντήριον, at the entrance of a sanctuary, and the more extensive washing or even bathing (λούεσθαι) that certain categories of defilement demanded before one could enter a sanctuary. This second purification was more often not performed at the sanctuary, but at home or in a public bath; sanctuaries usually lacked the installations for bathing.

Both types of rites are well attested in the ancient world, the latter somewhat better than the former: the former was routine, the latter needed more explanation and instruction.[11] Despite a somewhat spotty archaeological record, we can assume that lustral basins belonged to the standard items that marked the entrance into a sanctuary. Most of the evidence comes from the Greek East. Lucian remarks that "the inscription at the entrance forbids to enter a sanctuary further than the wash-basins, if someone has no clean hands": this presupposes hand washing as a routine act.[12] At least one epigraphical purity ordinance seems to confirm this, a second century CE text from Lindos that prescribes that one should enter the shrine with clean hands and a clean mind;[13] a somewhat later Lindian text specifies that purity begins "inside of where the wash-basins and the gates of the shrine are".[14] An inscription from Western Anatolia makes the use of an "ever-flowing spring" in the sanctuary conditional of one's purity: only those who had not incurred pollution could get away with simply washing.[15] In Rome, the ordinary formula spoken before a ritual excluded "who

---

11 M. NINCK, *Die Bedeutung des Wassers im Kult und Leben der Alten*; R. GINOUVÈS, *Balaneutiké*, 375–404; S. G. COLE, "The uses of water in Greek sanctuaries".

12 LUCIAN, *De sacrificiis* 13: τὸ μὲν πρόγραμμά φησι μὴ παριέναι ἐς τὸ εἴσω τῶν περιρραντηρίων, ὅστις μὴ καθαρὸς τὰς χεῖρας.

13 Introduction to a law in Lindos, 2ⁿᵈ cent CE, *Inscriptiones Graecae* 12:1.798 (= F. SOKOLOWSKI, *Lois sacrées des cités grecques,* no. 139) ἀφ' ὧν χρ[ὴ] πα[ρ]ῖν[α]ι αἰσίως εἰς τὸ ἱε[ρ]όν· πρῶτον μὲν καὶ τὸ μέγιστον· χεῖρας καὶ γνώμην καθαροὺς καὶ ὑγιε[ῖς] ὑπάρχοντας – "What one needs to avoid to enter the shrine lawfully: First and foremost to have the hands and the mind clean and healthy".

14 [π]εριραντηρίων εἴσω καὶ τῶν τοῦ ναοῦ [πυλῶν], C. BLINKENBERG and K. F. KINCH, *Lindos,* vol. 2, no. 487 (= F. SOKOLOWSKI, *Lois sacrés des cités grecques. Supplément,* no. 91), ca. 225 CE; see also L. VIDMAN, *Sylloge Inscriptionum Religionis Isiacae et Sarapicae,* no. 313 (early Imperial epoch), a dedication of wash-basins "in front of the gate", πρὸ τοῦ πυλῶνος, of the Sarapeum in Pergamum.

15 H. MALAY, *Greek and Latin Inscriptions in the Manisa Museum* 31, no. 24 (origin unknown, Imperial epoch).

had no clean hands," to the extent that a grammarian could derive *delubrum* "shrine" from (*de*)*luere* "to wash".[16]

There was no uniform way as to deal with cases of pollution that needed more than a simple rinsing of one's hands or face; Greek inscriptions give a bewildering variety of cases, tied to specific places, times and cults.[17] But the overall impression is clear: it was possible to enter a sanctuary after some minor pollution only after "washing/bathing", λουσάμενος;[18] often this was combined with a waiting time of one to several days. An inscription from a small Hellenistic temple in Miletus gives the principle:

..... εἰσιέναι]ι εἰς τὸν νε|ὼ τῆς Ἀρτέμιδ|ος τῆς Κιθώνης· | ἀπὸ μὲν κήδεος | καὶ γυναικὸς λε|χοῦς καὶ κυνὸς | τετοκυίας τρι|ταίους λουσα|μένους, ἀπὸ δὲ | τῶν λοιπῶν αὐ|θημερὸν λουσα|μένους.

To enter pure the temple of Artemis Kithone: from a death, a birthing woman and a birthing bitch after three days and a wash/bath, from the rest on the same day after washing/bathing.[19]

The Greek term λούεσθαι, "to wash one's body", is ambivalent and can refer either to a thorough wash or a full-body bath. Only a few texts give clearer details, such as λουσάμενος κατακέφαλα, "washing starting with the head" in a purity law of the early Imperial Age that concerns the cult of the Anatolian god Men,[20] or, in a fifth century BCE funerary law from Keos, τοὺς μιαι[νομένους] λουσαμένο[υ]ς π[--- ὕδατ]ος [χ]ύσι κα[θαρ]οὺς εἶναι, "the polluted will be pure after washing themselves [...] with showers of water".[21] Similar customs were in use in Rome, once again not in a uniform way; again, sexuality and death were the main causes that necessitated additional purification.[22] In what must be a late systematization with uncertain reality in cult, Macrobius informs us that

---

16 Formula LIVY 45.5.4; *delubrum* CINCIUS in SERVIUS, *Ad Vg. Aen.* 2.225.

17 See TH. WÄCHTER, *Die Reinheitsvorschriften im griechischen Kult*; L. MOULINIER, *Le pur et l'impur dans la pensée des Grecs, d' Homère à Aristote*; R. PARKER, *Miasma. Pollution and Purification in Early Greek Religion*; F. HOESSLY, *Katharsis. Reinigung als Heilverfahren. Studien zum Ritual der archaischen und klassischen Zeit sowie zum Corpus Hippocraticum*; O. PAOLETTI, G. CAMPOREALE, V. SALADINO, "Purificazione," in: *ThesCRA* 2, 3–87.

18 Λουσάμενος after intercourse e.g. F. SOKOLOWSKI, *Lois sacrées de l'Asie Mineure*, nos. 12.6 (Pergamon, after 133 BCE) and 18.9 (Maeonia, 147/146 BCE); SOKOLOWSKI, *Lois sacrées des cités grecques, Supplément*, nos. 91.17 (Lindos, 3rd cent. CE); washing only when intercourse takes place during the day, no. 115 A 12 (Kyrene, 4th cent. BCE); pork, no. 54.3 (Delos, ca. 100 BCE; Syrian Gods, i.e. an Eastern custom); other defilement SOKOLOWSKI, *Lois sacrées de l'Asie Mineure*, no. 52 (Miletus, end of the 1st cent. BCE).

19 SOKOLOWSKI, *Lois sacrées de l'Asie Mineure*, 51; the missing Greek word at the very beginning is one of the two words for pure, καθαροὺς or ἁγνοὺς.

20 *Inscriptiones Graecae* II² 1365 and 1366 (Athens, 1st cent. CE), after intercourse.

21 *Inscriptiones Graecae* XII 5.593 = SOKOLOWSKI, *Lois sacrées des cités grecques*, no. 97 A 29f.

22 See the material collected in *ThesCRA* 2 (2004), 71–72 (death); COLUMELLA 12.4.3 (intercourse).

after pollution by death sacrifices to the Olympian gods needed a preliminary washing of the entire body, those to underworld gods only a sprinkling.[23] He buttresses this observation with two passages from Vergil, but it remains unclear whether he thinks these rites of purification routinely preceded every sacrifice or were performed only after a specific case of pollution.

However one decides this last question, it is obvious that, according to Justin, the non-Christian parallels to baptism are standard pagan purification rites that preceded and conditioned the access to a sanctuary and the participation in its cult, in the same way in which baptism allowed Christians to participate in Christian cult. Surprisingly to us, Justin disregards the fact that baptism is unique whereas ritual washings recur every time one enters a sanctuary. More surprisingly still, nothing in these pagan rituals resonated with the theological meaning of the rite Justin had just exposed, total rebirth and spiritual illumination.[24] I thus doubt that this rather superficial parallelism is the result of Justin's observation: it is something that polytheist observers had noticed and were pointing out, to comfortably insert Christianity, Pliny's *prava superstitio*, into the framework of known ritual activity, instead of accepting its self-defined uniqueness and the following urge to conversion. Justin's argument – that the demons imitated Christian rituals – makes sense especially, if not uniquely in a situation where the Christian apologist had to refute pagan arguments levelled against the revealed uniqueness of Christian ritual.

2. Tertullian's Testimonies

In Justin's list, initiation rituals of mystery cults are irrelevant for baptism. Not that he is unaware of mystery cults that must have been prominent in his Roman environment, but he mentions them only in connection with the eucharist: in the initiation rituals of those who are introduced to the Mithraic cult (ἐν ταῖς τοῦ μυομένου τελεταῖς, *Apol.* 1.66.4), he says, they offer bread and water to the neophyte, with some ritual formulae.[25] We have to wait for Tertullian to connect baptism with mystery cults. But he too draws his parallels from a much wider range of pagan ritual activity (*De baptismo* 5.1):

> Sed enim nationes extraneae ab omni intellectu spiritualium potestatem eadem efficacia idolis suis subministrant. sed viduis aquis sibi mentiuntur. nam et sacris quibusdam per lavacrum initiantur, Isidis alicuius aut Mithrae; ipsos etiam deos suos lavationibus efferunt. ceterum villas, domos, templa totasque urbes aspergine

---

23 MACROB. *Sat.* 3.1.6 *constat dis superis sacra facturum corporis ablutione purgari, cum vero inferis litandum esset, satis actum videtur si aspersio sola contingat.*
24 *Apol.* 1.61.4–13.
25 The pagan side of this discussion in KELSOS, ap. ORIGEN. *Adv. Cels.* 6.24.

circumlatae aquae expiant passim. certe ludis Apollinaribus et Pelusiis[26] *tinguntur idque se in regenerationem et impunitatem periurorum suorum agere praesumunt. item penes veteres quisque se homicidio infecerat, purgatrices aquas explorabat.*

Well, but the nations, who are strangers to all understanding of spiritual things, apply a power of the self-same efficacy to their idols. But they cheat themselves with waters which are powerless. For they are initiated through a bath into some sacred rites – of some Isis or Mithras. Likewise, they carry out their gods themselves to some washings. Moreover, by carrying water around, and sprinkling it, they everywhere purify country-seats, houses, temples, and whole cities. And certainly at the Apollinarian Games and the Pelusia they are sprinkled, and they presume that they do so for their regeneration and remission of the penalties due to their perjuries. Among the ancients, again, whoever had defiled himself with murder, was wont to go in quest of purifying waters. [Translation after S. Thelwall]

Again, as in Justin, there are ample parallels in Greek and Roman culture that confirm Tertullian's observation. But unlike Justin, Tertullian does not even try to explain why there should be parallels: the pagans perform similar rituals, but since they have not been inspired by the Holy Spirit and lack deeper insight, their rituals remain without effect and are unable to wash away the sins and change the person. The most famous and often discussed case of an initiatory bath is Lucius' initiation into the mysteries of Isis in Kenchreai as described by Apuleius in book 11 of his *Metamorphoses*.[27] As soon as Lucius is admitted to initiation and has bought all the necessary things, the priest "led me with an escort of the faithful to the baths next door, first submitted me to the customary bath and, praying for the forgiveness of the gods and besprinkling me cleansed me most purely".[28] This is far from being the initiation proper: it is a preliminary cleansing performed outside the sanctuary in a public bath, visible to all other users of the facility; the initiation (*dies divino destinatus vadimonio*) follows only after another preliminary phase of secret teaching and ten days of fasting; Christian baptism is comparable only as to the use of water for a ritual washing, not as to

---

26 Instead of *Pelusiis* that is in the one ms. T and the two early editions (Paris 1545 and Basel 1554), Fulvio Ursino offered *Eleusiniis*, presumably as his own idea; whereas *CSEL* (ed. REIFFERSCHEID and WISSOWA, 1890, before T was known) follow Orsini, later editions (J. G. P. BORLEFFS, *Mnemosyne* 59 [1931] 1–102 and R. F. REFOULÉ, 1952, in the *Sources Chrétiennes*) have *Pelusiis*. Almost at the same time, A. D. NOCK, "Pagan Baptism in Tertullian" and F. J. DÖLGER, "Die Apollinarischen Spiele und das Fest Pelusia. Zu Tertullian De Baptismo 5," convincingly showed that *Pelusiis* is the correct reading.

27 APUL. *Met.* 11.23–24; see especially the commentary of J. G. GRIFFITHS, *Apuleius of Madaura. The Isis-Book*.

28 APUL. *Met.* 11.23 *stipatum me religiosa cohorte deducit ad proximas balneas et prius sueto lavacro traditum prefatus deum veniam purissime circumrorans abluit.* The text is somewhat ambivalent as to whether Lucius underwent two washings, first the regular bath (*suetum lavacrum*), then a ritual ablution (*circumrorans abluit*), or whether it is only one step, performed in the "usual bathing space".

the function of the ritual. And unlike baptism, these baths can be repeated: ritual bathing remained part of the duties that a person initiated to Isis performed.[29] Mithraic "baptism", on the other hand, has mainly to rely on Tertullian.[30] We lack other literary attestations; the closest ancient testimony is a scene depicted in the mithraeum of Capua in which the Mithraic *pater* holds an unidentifiable object, perhaps a crown or a cup, over a bound naked initiate: this is far from certain as baptism and would not even have suggested a baptismal ablution to the modern interpreter without Tertullian's text.[31]

These are the only mystery cults that Tertullian mentions in connection with baptism. The prominent case of the Eleusinian mysteries with their preliminary bath in the the sea is as absent as ritual washings that must have been part of minor mystery cults.[32] This selection is no coincidence: Tertullian's pagan interlocutors to whom he reacts used rituals they knew in their own world, the Latin West, not the least in North Africa, and that they could observe there: the ritual washing of an Isiac initiate in a public bath was visible to all and might well have entertained idle on-lookers. Demeter's mystery cult was confined to Eleusis and non-initiates outside of Athens might not have known about the bath in the sea; Bacchic mysteries on the other hand, mobile and well known even in later times, must not have contained any ritual that reminded contemporaries of Christian baptism.

The occasional washing of divine images is known in East and West; it usually belongs to a New Year's ritual in which the removal, washing and new instauration of the image marked a major temporal caesura. At the Plynteria, the Greek "Washing Festival", several Greek cities washed an image of their city goddess; we know the ritual best from Athens, where at the end of Thargelion

---

29 Tibull, 1.3.25; Juvenal, *Sat.* 6.522 etc. – See especially R. A. Wild, *Water in the Cultic Worship of Isis and Sarapis,* who finds no evidence for a baptism proper.

30 In a more general sense, he repeats the assertion in *De praescriptione haereticorum* 40.3–4: *tingit et ipse* [sc. *diabolus*] *quosdam utique credentes et fideles suos; expositionem delictorum de lauacro repromittit, et si adhuc memini Mithrae, signat illic in frontibus milites suos. celebrat et panis oblationem et imaginem resurrectionis inducit et sub gladio redimit coronam.* Although the only mystery cult named in this passage, not all the rituals do necessarily belong to the Mithraic mysteries.

31 Tentatively R. Merkelbach, *Mithras*, 136.

32 On the Eleusinian bath in the sea *Inscriptiones Greacae* II² 847.20; Polyaen. 3.11.2; Plut. *Phocion* 28.6. – On a possible bath in the Samothracian mysteries S. G. Cole, *Theoi Megaloi. The Cult of the Great Gods at Samothrace*, n. 267; on the use of a local stream for the *"thiasoi"*, i.e. presumably the Bacchic mysteries Hesych., s.v. Ρειτοί; on bathing in the initiation of the Erythraen Kyrbantes/Korybantes see F. Graf, *Nordionische Kulte*, 320. – The bathing mentioned in the ordinance for the mysteries of Andania, Sokolowski, *Lois sacrées des cités grecques,* no. 65.106–111 seems to be recreational rather than ritual, see N. Deshours, *Les mystères d'Andania. Étude d'épigraphie et d'histoire religieuse*, 91, see also Ginouvès, *Balaneutiké*, 375–404.

the old wooden image of Athena Polias was cleansed in the sea at Phaleron.[33] In Rome, at the festival named *Lavatio* on March 27, the venerable image (or rather sacred stone) of Magna Mater was carried out to a bath in the river Almo;[34] at the Saturnalia, another New Year's festival, the image of Saturnus was freed of its fetters and washed.[35]

The occasional sprinkling of buildings or entire cities with water again is known both in the Greek East and the Latin West, although more elaborate rituals are more often described than the simple use of water. To give just two examples: in an oracle from Klaros given to the Lydian town Caesarea Troketta in order to stop a plague at some point in the later second century CE, Apollo prescribes the purification ritual: "Seek to prepare a drink from seven fountains that one has to cleanse with sulphur from afar and then quickly to draw and then to sprinkle the houses with the waters".[36] And Juvenal describes how a rich Roman lady travels to Egypt to provide Nile water with which she then sprinkles the Roman sanctuary of her goddess.[37]

A similar purification was intended by the rites at the *ludi Apollinares* and the *Pelusia*. Their aim, according to Tertullian, was regeneration and remission from the punishment for perjury. This is somewhat puzzling, not just because of our lack of detailed knowledge on these festivals. *Regeneratio* is a typical Christian word, not just in Tertullian, mostly associated with baptism. We can suspect that it could be used for the healing from a severe illness, but we lack attestations for this use; the sematically related verb *recreare*, however, often means "to recover from illness", as does the rare noun *recreatio*.[38] Perjury is too serious a transgression both in religious and in social terms to be dealt with ritually in a city festival; the fear of divine punishment for the perjurer or his descendants was what guaranteed its efficiency, after all.[39] Only Ovid tells us that in a private purification ritual to Mercurius at a fountain near the Roman porta Capena, a merchant might pray to the god that the ablution from the spring would remove the dangers of his perjuries, and hope for Mercurius's forgiveness; but this prayer might well be the poet's idea.[40]

---

33   See especially W. Burkert, "Buzyge und Palladion. Gewalt und Gericht in altgriechischem Ritual"; on a similar ritual on Samos, Graf, *Nordionische Kulte*, 95.

34   Ovid, *Fasti* 4.337–340; see G. Wissowa, *Religion und Kultus der Römer*, 319.

35   At least according to Arnob. *Adv. Nat.* 4.24.

36   R. Merkelbach and J. Stauber, "Die Orakel des Apollon von Klaros", no. 8. – See also Theocr., *Ecl.* 24.96–98.

37   Juvenal, *Satire* 6.526–529.

38   *recreatio ab aegritudine* Plin. *Nat.* 22.102.

39   Parker, *Miasma*, 10: "There is no question of formal purification from the consequences of perjury, but nor is there from temple-robbing".

40   Ovid, *Fasti* 5.673–692, on May 15, the Traders' Festival (Festus, s.v. *Mais idibus*, p. 135.4 Lindsay).

Tertullian's remark is not easy to connect with the scanty other evidence for the two festivals. The urban *ludi Apollinares* (provided it is these Tertullian means) were instituted in 212 BCE to heal a plague, in a belief that our main witness, Livy, contradicts: this belief might explain the otherwise unattested purification of all participants by sprinkling them with water, and this ritual in turn will have kept the belief alive, against Livy's protests.[41] The Pelusia in turn were an Egyptian style festival in the city of Rome introduced presumably under Marcus Aurelius, of which not much is known otherwise.[42] Its aetiological story connects it with the temporary absence and return of the waters of the Nile.[43] This is crucial: Nile water was always important in Egyptian festivals,[44] and ritual sprinkling with it is attested for the Iseum Campestre in Rome, although confined to the space, not to persons.[45] Insofar as the Nile floods were seen as instrumental for the annual regeneration of the country, *regeneratio* could make some sense in the ideology of this festival; the equation of Osiris with the (god of the) Nile gives it additional force, but presupposes not necessarily a connection with any mystery cult.[46] Neither festival has any connection with perjury even in the playful way Ovid's Merchants Festival has.

Murder, finally, can be washed off with water in both Greek and Roman cultures, although other, more powerful liquids such as blood and more complex rituals than simple ablutions are attested as well, and the Roman material is again rarer than the Greek one.[47]

---

41 Wissowa, *Religion und Kultus*, 295, see Livy 25.12.8–15 who insists that the ludi were instuted *victoriae non valetudinis ergo ut plerique rentur* (Macrobius, *Saturnalia* 1.17.27–30 follows Livy): Livy is arguing against an interpretation that was common when he wrote.

42 Main information John Lydus, *De mensibus* 4.57; date *Hist. Aug. Marc. Aur.* 23.8; the festival was still celebrated in the mid-4th century, according to the calendar of 354, M. R. Salzman, *On Roman Time*, 174.

43 The story is not only recent but Greek: it hinges on the (wrong) derivation of the festival name from Greek πηλός, "clay, mud".

44 See hereto the article by J. Assmann/A. Kucharek, "Wasserriten im Alten Ägypten", in the present publication.

45 On the use of Nile water in Egyptian cults F. J. Dölger, "**Nilwasser und Taufwasser**". – Aspersion with Nile water in the Roman Iseum Juvenal, *Satire* 6.526–529; much more common are water libations, e.g. Apul. *Met.* 11.20, with the notes of J. G. Griffiths, *Apuleius of Madauros. The Isis-Book*, 274f.

46 On the equation Plut. *De Iside* 32, 363B with the comments of J. G. Griffiths, *Plutarch's De Iside et Osiride*, 420f. who points out that the concept is late; thus, the creators of the new festival might well have been inclined to use it.

47 The Greek evidence in *ThesCRA* 2.13–17; water e.g. FGrH 356 F 1 (fragment of an Athenian sacred law regarding supplicants) or the purification law of Kyrene, Sokolowski, *Lois sacrées des cités grecques. Supplément*, no.115 B 50–55. Evidence from Rome is less common, but see Vergil, *Aeneid* 2.717–719 (Aeneas, just returned from battle, has to wash himself in running water before he can touch the Penates) or Ovid, *Fasti* 2.39–40 (Greek myths).

Thus, an analysis of Tertullian's large catalogue of pagan rituals arrives at a similar conclusion as the analysis of Justin's shorter list. Tertullian, like Justin, focusses on purification, not just of the transition into sacred space as Justin did, but in a much wider sense. He is interested in any purificatory use of water that parallels the purificatory use of the baptismal bath (*eadem efficacia*), and he is far from confining himself to mystery rituals, nor does he in any way privilege the initiation rituals in the cults of Isis and Mithras over other rites. Pagan beliefs were fractionally more radical, however, than the Christian ones: whereas Christian baptism washed away sins as heavy as idolatry, sexual transgression, and fraud (*idolatria, stuprum et fraus*, 4.5), some of the pagan rites could wash off even the results of perjury and murder.

3. Baptismal Cleansing and Pagan Purification Rituals

Thus, neither Justin nor Tertullian justify the modern focus on mystery initiations as crucial antecedents of Christian baptism in its ritual form or its theological content. In their own indigenous readings, the pagan rituals that imitated baptism were purificatory rituals, and mystery cults could be associated simply because they contained rituals that cleansed human beings to make them fit for their encounter with the divine, as do the rituals listed by Justin that precede the entrance into a shrine. Justin reflects a contemporary discussion between Christians and pagans who noticed the similarities between pagan and Christian rituals and agreed on their existence but could not agree on their explanation. Pagans used the similarities to contest the uniqueness of Christianity on which the Christian refusal to participate in pagan cult was based, whereas Christians underlined the revelatory character of their rites and thus argued with imitations by the demons; this argument makes sense only if it is used to refute pagan observations on the similarities of rituals. Tertullian follows in the wake of this discussion; without entering into it in detail, he simply rejects the efficacy of the pagan rituals that have been compared to baptism.

Thus, this discussion and its underlying perception of contemporary ritual practice is irrelevant for the modern discussion about the origins of baptism or of any other Christian ritual. The fact that contemporary observers understood Christian baptism as yet another ritual ablution of the sort they knew from their regular ritual practice or from some mystery cult that they had observed does not necessarily argue against the modern view that baptism has been influenced by pagan mystery cults, but neither does it confirm it; the modern theory has to be evaluated on its own merits. The same is true for the conciliatory and less radical view that baptism and ancient iniatory rites share a common structure which would explain the similarities pointed out by modern historians.

The radical view, attributed to the *Religionsgeschichtliche Schule*, has been discussed and refuted so often that little remains to say. The main argument against it is the simple fact that the ritual baths or ablutions that are attested in some but by no means all mystery cults usually have a very different function from that of the baptismal bath.[48] As in the case of the Isis mysteries discussed above, the washing, ablution or bath is a preliminary rite that serves to prepare the novice for the main rite whose core was the encounter with the divine. The fact that the purification ritual could be witnessed by any visitors of a Roman bath in Apuleius' case or any bystander in the case of the mass bath of the Eleusinian initiates in the sea at Phaleron is enough to show that it was not part of any secret mystery rite. It was not this preliminary purificatory bath but the ritualized encounter with the divinity that procured the "extraordinary experience" at the core of a mystery initiation.[49] In baptism, however, the very bath and its accompanying verbal rites performed the radical change of personality that turned a pagan into a Christian; the bath and prayer thus was the core rite. None of the major mystery rituals – of Eleusis, of Isis, or of Dionysos, on which the *Religionsgeschichtliche Schule* relied – contained a ritual bath in such a position and function; none could have served as model and antecedent of Christian baptism.

But what about the structural parallels? There are, after all, a few instances of mystery rituals whose initiatory trajectory from purification to communal meal comes close to the Christian sequence of baptism and eucharist that marks the initiatory transformation into a member of the Christian congregation according to Justin's description.[50] In the mysteries of the Kyrbantes in Ionian Erythrai that are attested in a fourth century BCE inscription, a bath (λοῦτρον) is followed by a κρατηρισμός, a ritual that uses a mixing bowl and is accompanied by a sheep sacrifice: this must have been a drinking ritual that lead to a common meal, according to regular Greek sacrificial practice.[51] In some private mysteries in Athens that were performed by the mother of Aeschines and thus are almost contemporaneous to the Erythraean rites, the purification – not with water, but with mud and corn husks – was followed by the exclamation "I escaped evil, I acquired something better" (ἔφυγον κακὸν εὗρον ἄμεινον), and like the Erythraen cult, these mysteries contained a κρατηρισμός, whose position in the sequence is uncertain but presumably later than the purification.[52]

---

48 For example F. J. DÖLGER, "Die ‚Taufe' an den Apollinarischen und Pelusischen Spielen", 157.
49 I borrow the term "extraordinary experience" from BURKERT, *Ancient Mystery Cults*, 89–114.
50 See BOWDEN, *Mystery Cults of the Ancient World*, 209. – JOHN CHRYSTOSTOM, *Homilia* 4.364 neatly summarizes the trajectory (μετὰ τὴν κοινωνίαν τῶν μυστηρίων, μετὰ τὴν ἀπόλαυσιν τοῦ λουτροῦ, μετὰ τὸ συντάξασθαι τῶι Χριστῶι).
51 H. ENGELMANN and R. MERKELBACH, *Die Inschriften von Erythrai*, no. 206.
52 DEMOSTHENES, *De corona* 259–260.

But these cults are either local or altogether private, and it would be pushing the evidence much too far if one would posit any direct influence on Christian baptism; rather, in the wake of Macchioro, one would have to reconstruct some utterly hypothetical Bacchic or Orphic rituals in order to argue for a direct influence, and there is no compelling reason to do so. Still, the correspondance is noteworthy: in both pagan rites, as in Christian baptism, the purificatory ritual is not just a preliminary act that lies outside the secrecy of the central ritual; it is the main ritual. It has been charged with a more fundamental transformatory meaning, from bad to better in the Athenian rite, from sinfulness to a new form of existence in baptism. Details are less clear in the Erythraean rite, especially since the ritual record is deficient and it must remain uncertain whether other rites were part of the trajectory that are hiding under the term τελεῖν, "to initiate": our text is a public ordinance that regulates the offices of a priest and might well be silent about many details.[53] In the light of the Christian discussion about women baptizing women, it should be noticed that in Erythrai both genders underwent bathing: the priest bathes the men, the priestess the women; despite its focus on what are basically male entities, the dancing Korybantes, the local cult was open to both genders.[54] But at any rate, the Erythraean rites led to a changed status as well: at the end (and for the rest of his life), the initiate is κεκορυβαντισμένος, "one who has become an initiate of the Korybantes".[55] Thus, on the backdrop of the general ritual structure of a rite of passage, several specific instantiations arrived at a comparable solution in which the purification ritual is used to express not just the purity necessary for any encounter with the divine, but a change of personality.

The Erythraen ritual deserves some consideration also because it is the only unequivocal text on the bath of women: "the buyers of the priesthoods initiate and offer to them from the mixing bowl and bathe the initiates, the man the men, the woman the women" – the buyers are a priest and a priestess.[56] Given the strict separation of genders in public baths,[57] one would have assumed a

---

53   Plato describes a more complex ritual scenario, see I. LINFORTH, "The Corybantic Rites in Plato".

54   See the contribution of Andreas Lindemann in this publication. – There might have been female entities connected in some form with this cult, to judge from the "orgion of Herse, -ore and Phanis" attested in the same inscription no. 206; but the text is broken at this point, and the connection is unclear, see F. GRAF, *Nordionische Kulte*, 332–334.

55   The expression in an inscription on Samos that presumably comes from Erythrae as well, *Inscriptiones Graecae* 12:6:2 no. 119. – Similarly, in Bacchic mysteries the iniatiate has become βεβακχευμένος, a state that expresses itself in a separate burial, see the ordinance from Italian Cumae, SOKOLOWSKI, *Lois sacrées des cités grecques. Supplément*, no. 120.

56   ENGELMANN and MERKELBACH, *Die Inschriften von Erythrai*, no. 206. 6–10 οἱ δὲ π[ριάμενοι] τὰς ἱερητείας τελεῦσι κ[αὶ κρητηρ]ιεῦσι καὶ λούσουσι τοὺς [τελευμέν]ους, ὁ μὲν ἀνὴρ ἄνδρας, ἡ δ[ὲ γυνὴ γυνα]ῖκας.

57   GINOUVÈS, *Balaneutiké*, 220–224, see e.g. PLATO, *Critias* 117B.

separation in ritual bathing even without such a prescription, at least in the context of individual bathing. The Eleusinian crowds walking into the sea at Phaleron could not have been separated by gender, but this was a washing without priestly assistance, and presumably even in some clothing. The intimacy of an individual ritual bath with the concomitant nudity is something different; the Erythraean text is a welcome confirmation that this created the necessity for female priesthoods as well; we know from the Roman Bacchanalia how much the ritual community of both genders in secret rituals stimulated sexual phantasies even without the presence of ritual bathing.[58]

One can highlight this resemantization of purification when comparing it with two instances of a similar trajectory which, however, did not lead to a communal meal but to a result that is pictorially expressed as close contact with the main divinity of the ritual. Several monuments from the early Imperial Epoch, the best known being a marble vase in Rome, the so-called "Urna Lovatelli," represent an initiation in three pictorial steps: first a priest performs the sacrifice of a piglet or a libation; then an attendant purifies the initiate (or Herakles) with a winnowing fan (air) or a torch (fire) while the initiate, with his head veiled, sits on a stool; finally, in a scene that is missing in some monuments, the initiate encounters Demeter and her snake.[59] The sequence must derive from a Hellenistic original; the exact identification of the underlying cult is somewhat debated, but Eleusinian associations seem obvious.[60] Again, purification is more than just a preliminary act; again, it constitutes the main transformatory act, although the images offer a choice between two forms, by air and by fire.[61] Already Albrecht Dieterich compared the central image in this sequence to the famous scene in Aristophanes' *Clouds* in which Socrates initiates the philistine Strepsiades into his secret philosophical society, with the aim of superior knowledge (εἰδέναι σαφῶς, v. 250) and a direct meeting with the ruling divinities, the Clouds (ξυγγενέσθαι ταῖς Νεφέλαις εἰς λόγους, ταῖς ἡμετέραισι δαίμοσι).[62] The ritual, however, is far from exactly parallel: Strepsia-

---

58 See LIVY 39.8.5–7; similar accusations were levelled against Christians.

59 For a catalog of the monuments see W. BURKERT, "Initiation", 96–97 nos. 34–40.

60 See BURKERT, "Initiation", 93.

61 One can imagine that water is the least impressive and therefore most common and ordinary means of purification, whereas the mystery experience calls for something more unusual and thus memorable; the association with the elements (earth with Aeschines' mother, fire or air on these images) might be a coincidence, although philosophical speculation insists on purification of the soul through the elements, VERGIL, *Aeneid* 6.740–742 (air, water and fire), with AUGUSTINE, *CD* 21.13 and E. NORDEN, *P. Vergilius Maro. Aeneis Buch VI*, 28.

62 ARISTOPHANES, *Clouds* 250–475. – The connection between the images and Aristophanes first in A. DIETERICH, "Über eine Szene der Aristophanischen Wolken", who understood it as "Orphic mysteries," which has become highly problematical; a parody of Eleusis e.g. according to BURKERT, "Initiation", 94 no. 1 and R. EDMONDS, "To Sit in Solemn Silence? Thronosis in Ritual, Myth, and Iconography", 347f.; P. BONNECHÈRE, "La scène d'initiation des *Nuées* d'Aristophane

des is first crowned, then powdered with flour, and hides his head in his coat to avoid being rained on by the clouds; only the ritual of Aeschines' mother together with the image suggests that this has to be understood as purification, Strepsiades rather fears to be sacrificed (v. 258). Still, both in Aristophanes and in the images, the cleansing ritual (since cleansing is implied in Aristophanes, behind all the parodistic distortions) allows the initiate to meet his divinity. This is different from Christian baptism, however: it does not lead to permanent membership in a new group, but remains a one-time personal experience.[63]

4. Summary

All in all then, neither an evolutionary derivation of Christian baptism from specific rituals in the world of early Christiniaty nor the rejection of any connection between the two worlds are feasible assumptions. Already the first apologists and their pagan adversaries noticed the connection between baptism and purificatory rituals that either marked the transition from daily life to a ritually pure space or that aimed at the removal of extraordinary pollution: given the metaphor of pollution and cleaning common to most religious systems, this is not surprising. Our reading, however, stressed the fact that in baptism, the full-body bath is the single ritual that performs the radical change of existence that is meant by becoming a Christian; ablutions in the polytheist world of early Christianity were mostly a preliminary rite that even in mystery cults such as the cult of Isis or of Demeter at Eleusis could be viewed by everyone. Only in a small number of initiation rites, purification is the central transformative rite that can precede a common meal to mark adherence to a new group of changed people. These rites, however, are not close to early Christian communities neither in space nor in time, and not all make use of water as the main agent of purification; mud (earth), fire or air were other and more impressive means to create this memorable experience. These rites then share with baptism only the common structure and the fact that one item of the van Gennepian sequence, the separational cleansing, was singled out and transformed into a comparable role as a marker of a lasting change of personality; but everything suggests that these were independent developments in the common ritual language.

---

et Trophonios: nouvelles lumières sur le culte lébadéen," argued for the oracular cult of Trophonios at Lebadeia.

63 I am aware that the borderline between one-time experience and permanent group membership is less sharp than I represent it for heuristic reasons, see the remark on the camaraderie (ἑταιρία) created by the Eleusian mysteries in PLATO, *Epistula* 7.333E; but these feelings do not translate into creating a group apart from any other group, as with Christians.

Bibliography

BLINKENBERG, C. and K. F. KINCH (eds.), *Lindos. Fouilles et recherches 1902–1914*, Vol. 2: *Les inscriptions*, Berlin: de Gruyter 1941.

BONNECHÈRE, P., "La scène d'initiation des *Nuées* d'Aristophane et Trophonios: nouvelles lumières sur le culte lébadéen," in: *Revue des Études Grecques* 111 (1998) 436–480.

BOWDEN, H., *Mystery Cults of the Ancient World*, Princeton, N.J.: Princeton University Press 2010.

BURKERT, W., *Ancient Mystery Cults*, Cambridge, Mass.: Harvard University Press 1987.

— "Buzyge und Palladion. Gewalt und Gericht in altgriechischem Ritual," in: *ZRGG* 22 (1970) 356–336 [= *Wilder Ursprung. Opferritual und Mythos bei den Griechen*, Berlin: Wagenbach 1990, 77–85].

— "Initiation." in *Thesaurus Cultus et Rituum Antiquorum* (*ThesCRA*), vol. II. Los Angeles: The J. Paul Getty Museum, 2005, 91–124.

CASAUBON, I., *De rebus sacris et ecclesiasticis exercitationes XVI*, Geneva: Sumptibus Ioannis Antonij & Samuelis de Tournes 1654.

COLE, S. G., *Theoi Megaloi. The Cult of the Great Gods at Samothrace* (EPRO 96), Leiden: Brill 1983.

— "The Uses of Water in Greek Sanctuaries," in: R. Hägg, N. Marinatos, and G. C. Nordquist (eds.), *Early Greek Cult Practice. Proceedings of the Fifth International Symposium at the Swedish Institute at Athens (26–29 June 1986)*, Stockholm: Paul Åströms 1988, 161–165.

DESHOURS, N., *Les mystères d'Andania. Étude d'épigraphie et d'histoire religieuse*, Pessac: Ausonius 2006.

DIETERICH, A., "Über eine Szene der Aristophanischen Wolken", in: *Rheinisches Museum* 48 (1893) 275–283 [= *Kleine Schriften*, Leipzig and Berlin: Teubner 1911, 117–124].

DÖLGER, F. J., "Die Apollinarischen Spiele und das Fest Pelusia. Zu Tertullian De baptismo 5," in: *Antike und Christentum* 1, Münster: Aschendorff 1929, 150–155.

— "Die ‚Taufe' an den Apollinarischen und Pelusischen Spielen. Zu Tertullian De baptismo 5," in: *Antike und Christentum* 1, Münster: Aschendorff 1929, 156–159.

— "Nilwasser und Taufwasser. Eine religonsgeschichtliche Auseinandersetzung," in: *Antike und Christentum* 5, Münster: Aschendorff 1936, 153-187.

EDMONDS, R., "To Sit in Solemn Silence? Thronosis in Ritual, Myth, and Iconography," in: *AJP* 127 (2006) 347-366.

ENGELMANN, H. and R. MERKELBACH, *Die Inschriften von Erythrai* (IKS 1/2), Bonn: Habelt 1971/1972.

GINOUVÈS, R., *Balaneutiké. Recherches sur le bain dans l'antiquité grecque* (BEFAR 200), Paris: E. de Boccard 1962.

GRAF, F., *Nordionische Kulte. Religionsgeschichtliche und epigraphische Untersuchungen zu den Kulten von Chios, Erythrai, Klazomenai und Phokaia*, Rome: Istituto Svizzero 1985.

GRAF, F., and S. I. JOHNSTON, *Ritual Texts for the Afterlife*, London: Routledge 2007.

GRIFFITHS, J. G., *Plutarch's De Iside et Osiride*, Bangor: University of Wales Press 1970.

GRIFFITHS, J. G. (ed.), *Apuleius of Madauros. The Isis-Book (Metamorphoses XI)* (EPRO 39), Brill: Leiden 1975.

GUNKEL, H., *Zum religionsgeschichtlichen Verständnis des Neuen Testaments*, Göttingen: Vandenhoeck & Ruprecht 1930 [1st ed. 1903].

HOESSLY, F., *Katharsis. Reinigung als Heilverfahren. Studien zum Ritual der archaischen und klassischen Zeit sowie zum Corpus Hippocraticum*, Göttingen: Vandenhoeck & Ruprecht 2001.

LINFORTH, I., "The Corybantic Rites in Plato," in: *University of California Publications in Classical Philology* 13 (1946) 121-162.

MALAY, H., *Greek and Latin Inscriptions in the Manisa Museum*, Wien: Verlag der Österreichischen Akademie der Wissenschaften 1994.

MERKELBACH, R., *Mithras*, Meisenheim: Hain 1984.

MERKELBACH, R. and J. STAUBER (eds.), "Die Orakel des Apollon von Klaros," *Epigraphica Anatolica* 27 (1996) 1-53 [= R. Merkelbach, *Philologica. Ausgewählte Kleine Schriften*, Stuttgart and Leipzig: Teubner 1997, 155-218].

MOULINIER, L., *Le pur et l'impur dans la pensée des Grecs, d' Homère à Aristote*, Paris: Klincksieck 1952.

NINCK, N., *Die Bedeutung des Wassers im Kult und Leben der Alten. Eine symbolgeschichtliche Untersuchung*, Leipzig: Teubner 1921.

Nock, A. D., "Hellenistic Mysteries and Christian Sacraments," in: *Mnemosyne* 5 (1952) 177–213 [= Z. Stewart (ed.), *Arthur Darby Nock: Essays on Religion and the Ancient World*, Oxford: Clarendon Press 1970, 791–820].

— "Religious Developments from the Close of the Republic to the Reign of Nero," in: *The Cambridge Ancient History* 10, Cambridge: Cambridge University Press 1963, 465–511.

— "Pagan Baptism in Tertullian," in: *JThS* 28 (1927) 289–290.

Norden, E., *P. Vergilius Maro. Aeneis Buch VI*, 4th ed., Darmstadt: Wissenschaftliche Buchgesellschaft 1957.

Parker, R., *Miasma. Pollution and Purification in Early Greek Religion*, Oxford: Clarendon Press 1983.

Rahner, H., "Das Mysterium der Taufe", in: *Griechische Mythen in christlicher Deutung*, Zürich: Rhein-Verlag 1957 [citations from the English translation, New York: Harper & Row 1963].

Salzman, M. R., *On Roman Time. The Codex-Calendar of 354 and the Rhythms of Urban Life in Late Antiquity*, Berkeley, Calif.: University of California Press 1991.

Sokolowski, F., *Lois sacrées de l'Asie Mineure*, Paris: de Boccard 1955.

— *Lois sacrées des cités greques. Supplément*, Paris: de Boccard 1962.

— *Lois sacrées des cités grecques*, Paris: de Boccard 1969.

Thesaurus Cultus et Rituum Antiquorum (ThesCRA), 7 vols., Los Angeles, Calif.: Getty 2004–2006.

Vidman, L., *Sylloge Inscriptionum Religionis Isiacae et Sarapicae*, Berlin: de Gruyter 1969.

Wagner, G., *Das religionsgeschichtliche Problem von Römer 6,1–11* (AThANT 39), Zürich: Zwingli-Verlag 1962 [citations from the English translation, Edinburgh: Oliver & Boyd 1967].

Wächter, Th., *Die Reinheitsvorschriften im griechischen Kult*, Giessen: Töpelmann 1910.

Wendland, P., *Die hellenistisch-römische Kultur und ihr Verhältnis zu Judentum und Christentum* (HNT 2), Tübingen: J. C. B. Mohr (Paul Siebeck) 1912.

Wiens, D. H., "Mystery Concepts in Primitive Christianity and in Its Environment," in: W. Hasse (ed.), *Aufstieg und Niedergang der Römischen Welt* 2:23:2, Berlin and New York: de Gruyter 1980, 1252–1267.

WILD, R. A., *Water in the Cultic Worship of Isis and Sarapis* (EPRO 87), Leiden: Brill 1981.

WISSOWA, G., *Religion und Kultus der Römer*, München: Beck 1912.

Baptism in Sethian Gnostic Texts

Birger A. Pearson

This essay consists of two main parts. In the first part I discuss the phenomenon of Sethian Gnosticism, how it is to be delimited, and the sources in which it is attested. In the second part I discuss the most important passages in eight of the Sethian Gnostic tractates preserved in Coptic that feature Sethian baptismal practices. A brief summary and final conclusions are included at the end of the essay.

1. Sethian Gnosticism

1.1. Defining Sethian Gnosticism

In an important article published in 1974, Hans-Martin Schenke noted that several of the Gnostic texts included in the thirteen Coptic codices discovered near Nag Hammadi in 1945 share certain common features that reflect a special Gnostic system that he labelled as "Sethian."[1] As is well known, the term "Sethian" was used by some church fathers for certain Gnostic groups whose teachings they described, and combatted as dangerous heresies. Schenke adopted this term because of the prominent role played in the Gnostic texts by the biblical figure of Seth, son of Adam. In the Sethian "system" defined by Schenke Seth plays an important role in salvation history. Those who have received gnosis (knowledge) are referred to in the texts as Seth's "seed" or "race." Schenke finds this system reflected in the following Coptic texts: the *Apocryphon of John* (NHC II,1; III,1; IV,1; BG, 2); the *Hypostasis of the Archons* (NHC II,4); the *Gospel of the Egyptians* (NHC III,2; IV,2); the *Apocalypse of Adam* (NHC V,5), the *Three Steles of Seth* (NHC VII,5); *Zostrianos* (NHC VIII,1); *Melchizedek* (NHC IX,1), the *Thought of Norea* (NHC IX,2); and *Trimorphic Protennoia* (NHC XIII,1).[2]

---

1   H.-M. Schenke, "Das sethianische System nach Nag-Hammadi-Schriften."
2   In this article I use the tractate titles and abbreviations found in J. M. Robinson, ed., *The Nag Hammadi Library in English*. Different titles are used in the more recent collection of texts: M. Meyer, ed., *The Nag Hammadi Scriptures*. For the tractates named above the following titles are used in that volume: the *Secret Book of John*, the *Nature of the Rulers*, the *Holy Book of the Great Invisible Spirit*, the *Revelation of Adam*, the *Three Steles of Seth*, *Zostrianos*, *Melchizedek*, the *Thought of Norea*, and *Three Forms of First Thought*.

The Sethian system defined by Schenke includes a divine trio of Father (Invisible Spirit), Mother (First Thought, Barbelo), and Son (Autogenes, "Self-Begotten"). Associated with the Son Autogenes are four luminaries named Harmozel, Oroiael, Daveithe, and Eleleth. Included in the Sethian system is the world-creator Yaldabaoth, who has shackled humanity's divine spirit in material bodies. Humans can escape from his creation by receiving gnosis. The Sethian system also includes speculation on world history and the salvation of Seth's seed. Schenke argues that this system has a pre-Christian origin.

In 1978 an important international conference was held at Yale University in New Haven, Connecticut, organized by Bentley Layton. The theme of the conference was "The Rediscovery of Gnosticism." Two large volumes containing the conference papers were published in 1981, one on Valentinian Gnosticism and the other on Sethian Gnosticism.[3] One of the most important papers in the second volume is by Hans-Martin Schenke, "The Phenomenon and Significance of Gnostic Sethianism."[4] Included in his new list of Sethian writings from Nag Hammadi are *Marsanes* (NHC X,1) and *Allogenes* (NHC XI,3). He also includes the *Untitled Text* in the Codex Brucianus, a late Coptic manuscript discovered in the 18th century and first published in the late 19th century. From the writings of the church fathers he includes Irenaeus' discussion of a system used by certain "Gnostics" (*Haer.* 1.29; Irenaeus does not use the term "Sethian"), and the doctrines of the "Gnostics, "Sethians, and "Archontics" discussed by Epiphanius (*Haer.* 26.29.40).[5]

Of special interest is his discussion of the ritual practices of the Sethian Gnostics. Two sacraments are attested in the Sethian Nag Hammadi texts of various genres: baptism and a ritual of cultic ascent. Baptism involves five "seals" and the ascent ritual leads to a vision of the invisible Father. The *Gospel of the Egyptians* is centered on baptism and its liturgy. The *Three Steles of Seth* is devoted to cultic ascent, and consists of prayers used by the participants in the ritual.[6]

Since Schenke's articles two new texts have been published which can now be included in the list of Sethian writings, both of them from the recently published Codex Tchakos: the *Book of Allogenes* (CTchakos 3, a tractate preserved only in a few fragments), and the now famous *Gospel of Judas* (CTchakos 4).[7]

Scholarship has gone on apace, and much has been published on Sethian Gnosticism since Schenke's pioneering papers. Of the numerous works that

---

3   B. Layton, ed., *The Rediscovery of Gnosticism*.
4   In Layton, ed., *Rediscovery* 2:588–616. See also my paper, "The Figure of Seth in Gnosticism," in *Rediscovery* 2:472–504.
5   Schenke, "Gnostic Sethianism," 588–589.
6   Ibid., 598–607. See discussion below.
7   R. Kasser et al., *The Gospel of Judas, Together with the Letter of Peter to Philip, James, and a Book of Allogenes from Codex Tchakos*.

might be cited in this connection, by far the most important is the recent monograph by John Turner on Sethian Gnosticism.[8] I should also mention Bentley Layton's anthology of Gnostic texts, the first and most extensive part of which is devoted to what he calls "Classic Gnostic Scripture."[9] The texts so designated are essentially the same as those designated by Schenke as Sethian. While Schenke's starting point for his discussion of the Sethian system was the Nag Hammadi collection of Coptic texts, Layton's starting point is Irenaeus' discussion of the "Gnostics" so designated by St. Irenaeus (Haer. 1.29–31). Layton includes in his list of "Classic Gnostic" texts those preserved in Coptic which seem to reflect the mythic and ritual features identified as "Gnostic" by Irenaeus. One could easily conclude from this that "Sethian" Gnosticism is the same as Layton's "Classic" Gnosticism.

Tuomas Rasimus has meanwhile proposed that we enlarge the list of texts to be included in "Classic" Gnosticism by including those that feature what he calls an "Ophite" mythology. The most important of these are Celsus and Origen's description of an "Ophite diagram" (Origen, *Contra Celsum* 6.24–38), plus what he considers to be Ophite mythology found in Irenaeus (*Adv. Haer.* 1.30).[10] The diagram described by Celsus and Origen features an anointing ritual designed to guarantee the soul's asscent through the archontic spheres. But there is no reference to baptism in the Ophite texts; Ophite material can safely be ignored for our purposes here.

1.2. Essential Features of Sethian Gnosticism

1.2.1. Common Doctrines and Mythologoumena

Turner lists the following "common Sethian doctrines and mythologoumena" reflected in the Sethian tractates:

1. The self-understanding of the Gnostics that they are the spiritual seed of Seth (*Apoc. Adam*; *Gos. Eg.*; *Ap. John*, *Steles Seth*; *Melch.*; *Zost.*).
2. Seth as the heavenly-earthly savior of his seed (*Gos. Eg.*), perhaps under different names (*Allogenes*; *Marsanes*; *Zost.*; *Apoc. Adam*).
3. The heavenly triad of Father (Invisible Spirit), Mother (Ennoia, Barbelo), and the Son Autogenes (*Ap. John*; *Trim. Prot.*; *Gos. Eg.*; *Allogenes*; *Steles Seth*; *Zost.*; *Norea*; perhaps *Marsanes*).

---

8   J. Turner, *Sethian Gnosticism and the Platonic Tradition*, 2001.
9   B. Layton, *The Gnostic Scriptures*, 5–201. The other parts of the anthology are devoted to Valentinus and the Valentinians, the "School of St. Thomas," and "other early currents," including fragments of Basilides and two Hermetic treatises.
10 T. Rasimus, *Paradise Reconsidered in Gnostic Mythmaking*, esp. 9–62.

4. A division of the aeon of Mother Barbelo into the triad of Kalyptos, Protophanes, Autogenes (in the late "Platonizing" treatises *Steles Seth*; *Zost.*; *Allogenes*; *Marsanes*).
5. The four Luminaries of the Son Autogenes (Harmozel, Oroiael, Daveithai, and Eleleth) who constitute the dwelling places of the heavenly Adam, Seth, and the seed of Seth (*Ap. John*; *Hyp. Arch.*; *Gos. Eg.*; *Zost.*; *Melchizedek*; *Trim. Prot.*).
6. The evil Demiurge Yaldabaoth who tries to destroy the seed of Seth (*Ap. John*; *Trim. Prot.*; *Hyp. Arch.*).
7. A division of history into three ages and the appearance of the savior in each (*Ap. John*; *Apoc. Adam*; *Gos. Eg.*; *Trim. Prot.*).
8. A special prayer (*Steles Seth* 125,24–126,17; *Allogenes* 54,11–37; *Zost.* 51,24–52,8. 86,13–24. 88,9–25).
9. A specific instance of negative theology (*Ap. John* and *Allogenes*).
10. A specific philosopical terminology (*Steles Seth*; *Zost.*; *Allogenes*; *Marsanes*).
11. Secondary Christianization (*Ap. John*; *Hyp. Arch.*; *Melchizedek*).
12. Presupposition of a triad or tetrad of ministers of the four Luminaries (*Gos. Eg.*; *Apoc. Adam*; *Zost.*; *Melchizedek*; *Marsanes*; *Trim. Prot.*; perhaps *Norea*).
13. The designation "Pigeradamas" for Adamas (*Ap. John*; *Steles Seth*; *Zost.*; *Melchizedek*).
14. A baptismal rite of "Five Seals" (longer version of *Ap. John*; *Gos. Eg.*; *Trim. Prot.*; perhaps *Melchizedek*), related to an ascent ritual in the late "Platonizing" treatises (*Zost.*; *Allogenes*; *Steles Seth*; *Marsanes*).[11]

Sethian Gnosticism features a basic myth in four parts, consisting of theogony, cosmogony, anthropogony, and soteriology. Soteriology also includes an eschatology. The best example of this myth is found in the *Apocryphon of John*.

An important mythologoumenon absent from Turner's list is the Sophia myth. Sophia ("Wisdom") plays an essential role in Sethian Gnosticism. Perhaps this myth is lacking in Turner's list just because Sophia plays a key role in all forms of the Gnostic religion, including the earliest attested in our ancient sources (Simon Magus).

Two Sethian tractates feature Seth's sister-consort, Norea (*Hyp. Arch.* and *Norea*). Norea functions as a feminine counterpart to Seth in these tractates, and can also be seen as a Sophia-type figure in Sethian mythology.

The basic Sethian Gnostic myth involves a radical reinterpretation of the Bible, especially Genesis, and Jewish interpretations of biblical texts. It can be concluded from this that the earliest form of Sethian Gnosticism was of Jewish

---

11 TURNER, *Sethian Gnosticism*, 63–64.

origin.¹² Christian forms of Sethian Gnosticism are secondary developments in the history of Sethianism.

1.2.2. Literary Genres Used in Sethian Gnosticism

Several literary genres are reflected in the extant Sethian literature. John Turner has identified the following: apocalypse, testament, didactic treatise, revelation discourse (monologue), revelation dialogue, self-predicatory aretalogy, liturgical manual, and ritual etiology. The most characteristic genres of Gnostic literature are the revelation discourse and the revelation dialogue. Some Sethian tractates reflect more than one genre. For example, the *Apocryphon of John* consists of a revelation monologue plus a revelation dialogue, with an (obviously secondary) apocalyptic frame at the beginning and end.¹³

The Gnostic revelation dialogue and revelation monologue probably originated among Gnostics who based the new genres on the forms taken by Jewish apocalypses of the Second Temple period. Several Gnostic tractates have the term "apocalypse" in their titles. Indeed, the Sethian tractates *Zostrianos* and *Allogenes* are referred to as "apocalypses" by Porphyry in his *Life of Plotinus* (*Vit. Plot.* 16).

2. Sethian Gnostic Baptism

2.1. Previous Scholarship

Several important treatments of Sethian baptism have been published since Schenke's article in the Yale congress volume.¹⁴ Jean-Marie Sevrin published in 1986 a full-scale monograph on Gnostic baptism as reflected in some Sethian texts preserved in Coptic.¹⁵ He presents detailed analyses of the baptismal passages in the following tractates: *Apocryphon of John, Trimorphic Protennoia, Gospel of the Egyptians, Apocalypse of Adam, Zostrianos,* the *Untitled Text* in the Codex Brucianus, and *Melchizedek*.

John Turner published in 2006 a lengthy article in which he provides new analyses of the baptismal passages in the same tractates as treated by Sevrin.¹⁶ And Augusto Cosentino published in 2007 a full-scale monograph on initia-

---

12   See chapter 4, "Gnostic Biblical Interpretation: the Gnostic Genesis," pp. 101–133 in my book, *Ancient Gnosticism*.
13   See § 2.3., below.
14   Cit. n. 5.
15   J.-M. SEVRIN, *Le dossier baptismal séthien: Études sur la sacramentaire gnostique*.
16   J. TURNER, "The Sethian Baptismal Rite," in L. PAINCHAUD and P.-H. POIRIER, eds., *Coptica—Gnostica—Manichaica: Mélanges offerts à Wolf-Peter Funk*, pp. 941–992.

tory rites reflected in a wide range of Gnostic (and some non-Gnostic) texts. He devotes a full chapter to Sethian baptism.[17]

In what follows I am especially indebted to the work of Sevrin and Turner.

2.2. Primary Evidence for Sethian Baptism

In discussing the evidence for Sethian baptism we are confronted with a number of problems. The first problem is its paucity. We have comparatively little evidence for the Sethian rite of baptism. There are no liturgical handbooks, no actual descriptions of how the baptismal rite was performed, or even how often it was performed. Gnostic authors seem to have been quite reticent in discussing the ritual actions performed in their communities. For the most part, references to baptism in our extant texts are more allusive than descriptive. But I would tentatively suggest that Sethian baptism was, at least originally, a rite of initiation, involving the use of real water, and performed only once. In this respect Sethian baptism differs from Mandaean baptism, which was (and is) a repeatable rite.

Another problem with the evidence is its ambiguity. Our available texts differ remarkably in their treatments of baptism. Indeed, there seems to have been little uniformity in the ritual actions performed in Sethian communities. We should also note that there seems to have been a development over time in Sethian communities as to how baptisms were performed and how the ritual actions were interpreted. Indeed, it seems likely that, at least in some later Sethian communities, baptism was interpreted metaphorically rather than actually administered with real water.

In what follows I shall treat the baptismal passages in the following Sethian texts: the *Apocryphon of John*, *Trimorphic Protennoia*, the *Apocalypse of Adam*, the *Gospel of the Egyptians*, *Zostrianos*, *Melchizedek*, the *Untitled Text* in the Bruce Codex, and the *Gospel of Judas*. Then some conclusions can be drawn on Sethian baptismal praxis and its history.

2.3. Baptism in the Apocryphon of John

The *Apocryphon of John* is extant in four copies, three from the Nag Hammadi corpus and one from the Berlin Gnostic Codex. Two different recensions are reflected in these, a longer one (NHC II,1; IV,1) and a shorter one (NHC III,1; BG,2).[18] The versions in Codices III and IV are very fragmentary, and can be ignored for our purposes here. In terms of literary genre *Ap. John* is an apoca-

---

17   A. Cosentino, *Il battesimo gnostico*, pp. 107–128.
18   M. Waldstein and F. Wisse, The Apocryphon of John: *Synopsis of Nag Hammadi Codices II,1; III,1; and IV,1 with BG 8502,2*. I use the translation in that edition here (with modifications). For my own previous studies on *Ap. John* see B. Pearson, "Apocryphon Johannis Revisited," in: P. Bilde et al., eds., *Apocryphon Severini, presented to Søren Giversen*, pp. 155–165; "The

lypse, containing secrets revealed by the risen Christ to his disciple John, son of Zebedee. Within the apocalypse frame at the beginning and end of the tractate there are two main sections, a revelation discourse and a Gnostic commentary on Genesis 1–7. The commentary has been modified into a revelation dialogue between Jesus and John. A number of sources seem to be reflected in the document as a whole, and there is some internal confusion. But its basic structure is clear enough, and can be seen in the following brief outline. I cite the Coptic text of the longer version (Codex II), and the shorter one (BG) in parentheses:

Preamble and apocalyptic frame	1,1–2,26 (19,6–22,17)
I. Revelation discourse	2,26–13,13 (22,17–44,18)
A. Theogony	2,26–9,24 (22,17–36,15)
B. Cosmogony	9,25–13,13 (36,15–44,18)
II Revelation dialogue: soteriology	13,13–31,25 (44,19–75,15)
Apocalyptic frame and title	31,25–32,9 (75,14–77,5)

The theogony begins with a treatment of the unknown invisible Father, the Invisible Spirit, from whom is emanated his First Thought Barbelo. Barbelo conceives from the Father Autogenes ("self-begotten," also called "Christ"), who is the Son in a primal divine triad of Father, Mother, and Son. A whole host of other heavenly beings are emanated, including heavenly projections of Adam and Seth and the Seed of Seth. Among the last of the aeons emanated is Sophia ("wisdom").

The cosmogony begins with the fall of Sophia, who wished to produce beings from herself without the aid of her consort. She produces the demiurge Yaldabaoth, creator of the cosmic world of darkness. The cosmogony concludes with the blasphemy of the demiurge, in which Yaldabaoth claims to be the highest god.

The dialogue in the second main part consists essentially of a commentary on Genesis 1–7, including an anthropogony. In the larger version the dialogue concludes with a hymn in which Pronoia ("Providence," probably = Barbelo) recounts her triple descent to the lower world. This hymn is absent from the shorter version.

Two passages in *Ap. John* can be seen as reflecting aspects of Sethian baptism. The first one occurs in the theogony, in a passage treating the invisible Father. I quote here from the version in Codex II:

> For it is he who contemplates him[self] in his light which surrounds [him], namely the spring [of] living water. And it is he who provides [all] the [aeons.] And in every direction he [perceives] his image by seeing it in the spring of the [Spirit]. It is he who puts his desire in his [water]-light [which is in the] spring of the [pure light]-water [which] surrounds him. (4,19–26)

Problem of 'Jewish Gnostic' Literature," in: PEARSON, *The Emergence of the Christian Religion*, 122–146, esp. 126–134; and PEARSON, *Ancient Gnosticism*, 61–74.

This passage is immediately followed by the emanation of Barbelo, who appears before the Father in brilliant light.

To be sure, there is no explicit reference to baptism in this passage. What is of interest to us in this passage are the references to "living water," "water-light," and "light-water," which surrounds the transcendent Father. One can readily surmise that this transcendent light is connected in some fashion with the water of baptism in Sethian myth and ritual.

The second baptismal passage in *Ap. John* is found in the Pronoia hymn, which is absent from the shorter version. Pronoia recounts her third descent from the "pure light" above to the chaotic world, where she is able to raise up the soul imprisoned in the chaotic lower world. She tells him that she has raised him up and counsels him to guard himself against the evil angels and demons (II 31,11–22). Referring to him now in the third person she continues, "And I raised him up and sealed him in the light of the water with five seals in order that death might not have power over him from this time on (31,22–25). She then announces that she will now ascend to the perfect aeon (31,26–27).

We note again the prominence of luminous water, and now we see that this luminous water is administered in a series of five "seals." This passage can undoubtedly be seen as reflecting an actual initiation rite used in Sethian ritual. The "five seals" can presumably be taken as a reference to a quintuple immersion or lustration using real water.[19] This action, presumably accompanied by invocations of celestial beings, brings the initiate into contact with the luminous water that surrounds the Invisible Father. The goal of the initiate is to ascend to the spiritual realm of the Father. Baptism is the guarantee that the initiate's spirit will be released from the body upon its physical death.

2.4. Baptism in Trimorphic Protennoia

It is likely that the Pronoia hymn in the longer version of the *Ap. John* was used in the composition of *Trimorphic Protennoia* (NHC XIII,1), a hymnic text in which Barbelo as "First Thought" reveals herself in a series of "I am" statements.[20] Protennoia tells of her three descents into "chaos," that is, the lower world. The text itself is divided into three subtractates, each of them telling of a descent of Protennoia, first as "Voice" (35,1–42,3), then as "Sound" (42,4–46,4), and finally as articulated "Word" (Logos, 46,5–50,21). The text as it now stands has a complicated structure, with alternating sections of poetic material and prose. It clearly reflects editorial development in stages over time.

---

19 So SEVRIN, *Le dossier baptismal séthien*, 31–37.

20 The critical edition used here is that of John Turner in CHARLES HEDRICK, ed., *Nag Hammadi Codices XI, XII, XIII*, pp. 371–454. In quotations from *Trim. Prot.* in what follows, I use Turner's translation (with modifications).

Trim. Prot. contains several references to the Gnostic myth in *Ap. John*. These include the divine triad of Father, Mother, and Son (37,22); the four luminaries Harmozel, Oroiael, Daveithai, and Eleleth (38,33–39,5); and the demonic creator and ruler over this chaotic world with the three names Saklas, Samael, and Yaldabaoth (39,21–28), who arrogantly claims that there is no god above him (43,33–44,2).

Protennoia in her final descent "puts on Jesus" (50,12), and Christian elements are present throughout the text. The descent of Protennoia as "Logos" reminds us of the prologue to the Gospel of John. It is possible that the Johannnine prologue and *Trim. Prot.* share a common sapiential background. Of course, it is also possible that the author of *Trim. Prot.* was familiar with the Gospel of John and adapted its prologue.[21]

Protennoia begins her account of her third descent as Logos in the following way:

> I [descended to the] midst of the underworld and I shone [down upon the] darkness. It is I who poured forth the [water]. It is I who am hidden within [radiant] waters. I am the one who gradually put forth the All by my Thought. It is I who am laden with the Voice. It is through me that Gnosis comes forth. (36,4–10)

The water that Protennoia pours forth is, of course, to be understood as the luminous water that surrounds the ineffable Father, referred to in *Ap. John*.[22] This water is available in the water used in Sethian initiation, for which gnosis is a prerequisite. Several references to this water follow: "Water of Life" (37,3); the "Living [Water]" that surrounds the Father "in glorious Light" (37,35–38,3); the "Water of Life" from which the human spirit originated (41,22–23); the "Living Water" and the "immeasurable Light" that is "the source of the All" (46,17–25). Baptism as such, however, is not mentioned in these passages, but in other passages there are what can be taken as references to ritual actions presumably performed in the Sethian baptismal rite. These occur in the following two passages:

> And I am inviting you into the exalted, perfect Light. Moreover, (as for) this (Light), when you enter it, you will be glorified by those [who] give glory, those who enthrone will enthrone you. You will be invested by those who invest, and the Baptists will baptize you and you will become gloriously glorious, the way you first were when you were (Light). (45,12–20)

> [And I gave to him] from the Water [of Life, which strips] him of the Chaos [that is in the] uttermost [darkness] that exists [inside] the entire [abyss], that is, the thought of [the corporeal] and the psychic. All these I put on. And I stripped him of it and I put upon him a shining Light, that is, the knowledge of the Thought of the Fatherhood. And I delivered him to those who invest – Yammon, Elasso,

---

21 For discussion of the relationships between *Trim. Prot.* and the Gospel of John see Turner's introduction to *Trim. Prot.* in his critical edition.

22 See discussion above.

> Amenai – and they [covered] him with a robe from the robes of the Light, and I delivered him to the Baptists and they baptized him – Micheus, Michar, Mn[e]sinous – and they immersed him in the spring of the [Water] of Life. And I delivered him to those who enthrone – Bariel, Nouthan, Sabenai – and they enthroned him from the throne of glory. And I delivered him to those who glorify – Ariom, Elien, Phariel – and they glorified him with the glory of the Fatherhood. And those who rapture raptured – Gamaliel, [...]anen, Samblo, the servants of <the> great holy Luminaries – and they took him into the light-[place] of his Fatherhood. And he received the Five Seals from [the Light] of the Mother, Protennoia, and it was [granted] him [to] partake of the mystery of knowledge and [he became a light] in Light. (48,6–35)

These two passages would appear to refer to a series of ritual actions actually performed in the Sethian baptismal rite. But note the difference between them: Four actions are referred to in the first passage in the following order: glorification, enthronement, investiture, baptism. Five actions are referred to in the second passage in the following order: investiture, baptismal immersion, enthronement, glorification, and rapture. In this passage each action is performed symbolically by three mythological beings. In both passages the order of the actions is problematic. A more logical sequence would be 1) baptismal immersion (for which the reception of gnosis in some sort of catechesis would be a prerequisite), 2) investiture, 3) enthronement, 4) glorification, and 5) rapture, performed symbolically by heavenly "receivers" who bring the saved spirits into the Light. Notably absent from the list is another ritual action we would expect in a baptismal context, namely anointing with oil.

Turner has pointed out that the sequence of five ritual actions in *Trim. Prot.* is close to that of the Mandaean *maṣbuta*: investiture, entrance into the "Jordan," triple self-immersion, triple immersion by the priest, triple signation with water, ritual *kushta* handshake, triple drink, receipt of the myrtle wreath, anointing with apotropaic sesame paste, another *kushta*, invocation of divine names, ritual *kushta* handshake, ascent from the Jordan, and eating of *pihta* and drinking of *mambuha*, and another *kushta*.[23] While this comparison may be apposite, the problem with it is that we have insufficient evidence for how the ritual actions specified in *Trim. Prot.* were actually performed.

Another reference to the Five Seals is found in a passage at the end of the tractate, in which Protennoia summarizes her saving actions:

> And I taught them about the ineffable ordinances, and (about) the brethren, but they are inexpressible to every sovereignty and every ruling power except to the Sons of the Light alone, that is, the ordinances of the Father. These are the glories that are higher than every glory, that is, [the Five] Seals complete by virtue of Intellect. He who posseses the Five Seals of these particular names has stripped

---

23 Turner, "The Sethian Baptismal Rite" (cit. n. 15), 952–953, citing K. Rudolph, *Die Mandäer: II. Der Kult*, 88–89.

off (the) garments of ignorance and put on a shining Light.... [...].[24] until I reveal myself [to all my fellow brethren] and until I gather [together] all [my fellow] brethren within my [eternal] kingdom. And I proclaimed to them the ineffable [Five Seals in order that I might] abide in them and they also might abide in me. (49,22–50,12)

Protennoia then announces that she "put on Jesus" and "bore him from the cursed wood, and established him in the dwelling places of his Father" (50,12–14). She concludes her discourse by promising to bring her "Seed" into the "holy Light within an incomprehensible Silence" and utters a final "Amen" (50,14–20).

We can assume that the "Five Seals" referred to in the third passage quoted above involve the same ritual actions specified in the previous two passages. But questions still remain: Do the "Five Seals" refer to a quintuple immersion such as we posited in our discussion of the Pronoia hymn in *Ap. John*? Or do the "Five Seals" refer to the five ritual actions specified in the second passage, of which only one involves baptismal immersion? I would tentatively suggest that the "Five Seals" refer to a quintuple baptismal immersion. This would seem to be corroborated by a reference to the "Five Seals in the spring-baptism" in the *Gospel of the Egyptians* (III 66,3–4).[25]

2.5. Baptism in the Apocalypse of Adam

The *Apocalypse of Adam* is one of four "apocalypses" contained in Nag Hammadi Codex V (V,5).[26] It is a testamentary revelation given to Adam by three heavenly visitors and mediated by Adam to his son Seth. Adam tells of the subsequent history of the world and the salvation of the Gnostic elect. At the end of the tractate it is said that the revelations contained in it will be inscribed in stone on a high mountain (85,9–11). This detail reflects a first-century Jewish tradition recorded by the historian Josephus, according to which the progeny of Seth recorded their astrological and other lore on two steles, one of brick to survive fire and one of stone to survive the Flood.[27]

Following upon an introduction the tractate is made up of two main parts. The first part consists of Adam's testamentary speech to Seth (64,5–67,21), in

---

24 Considerable material is lost from the first six lines of p. 50 of the ms.
25 See discussion below, § 2.6..
26 The edition used here is that of George MacRae, in: D. Parrott, ed., *Nag Hammadi Codices V,2–5 and VI with Papyrus Berolinensis 8502, 1 and 4*, 154–195. Quotations from the text in what follows are from MacRae's translation. For my own previous studies on *Apoc. Adam* see B. Pearson, "The Problem of 'Jewish Gnostic' Literature," in: Pearson, *The Emergence of the Christian Religion*, 122–146, esp. 135–144; and Pearson, *Ancient Gnosticism*, 69–74.
27 Josephus, *Ant.* 1.69–71. References to such inscriptions associated with Seth are found in a number of Sethian Gnostic texts. See B. Pearson, "The Figure of Seth in Gnostic Literature," in: Pearson, *Gnosticism, Judaism, and Egyptian Christianity*, 52–83, esp. 72–74.

which he narrates his and Eve's experiences with their Creator. Adam reports a dream vision featuring an appearance of three heavenly beings and declares his intention to transmit revelations received to Seth. The second main part consists of the revelation proper (67,22–85,18), followed by two conclusions (85,19–22; 85,22–32). The tractate reflects considerable redactional activity over time.

The main revelation consists essentially of Adam's predictions concerning the end of his generation; the Flood and a first deliverance of the elect; Destruction by fire and a second deliverance of the elect; and an end-time threat and final deliverance involving the coming of the Illuminator (the heavenly Seth). The Illuminator brings salvation to the seed of Seth.

References to baptism occur at the end of the tractate in what may very well be secondary additions to an earlier version of *Apoc. Adam*. The Illuminator comes to enlighten the chosen generation "without a king over it," providing gnosis to his elect (82,19–83,4). The text continues, "then the seed, those who will receive his name upon the water and (that) of them all, will fight against the power. And a cloud of darkness will come upon them" (83,4–8). "The seed" is obviously the seed of Seth, whose name is received "upon the water," i.e. presumably the water of baptism.

This passage is followed by a cry from "the peoples" who repentantly acknowledge the superiority of those with gnosis. They acknowledge their sin, for which their "souls will die the death" (83,8–84,3). There follows this problematic passage:

> Then a voice came to them saying: "Micheu and Michar and Mnesinous, who are over the holy baptism and the living water, why were you crying out against the living God with lawless voices, and tongues without law over them, and souls full of blood and foul [deeds]? You are full of works that are not of the truth, but your ways are full of joy and rejoicing. Having defiled the water of life, you have drawn it within the will of the powers to whom you have been given to serve them. And your thought is not like that of those men whom you persecute. (84,3–26)

This passage is especially problematic because of what is said here of Micheu and Michar and Mnesinous, beings we already encountered in our discussion of *Trim. Prot.*[28] Early interpreters of the text assumed that these beings were here treated negatively as part of an over-all polemic against water baptism.[29] But this interpretation certainly cannot be upheld. One can only conclude that the Coptic text here is corrupt. Certainly, these beings associated with "living water" cannot be included among the "lawless" people here excoriated.[30] Those who have "defiled the water of life" are presumably people without gnosis who

---

28 See discussion above.
29 See, e.g., Ch. Hedrick, *The Apocalypse of Adam*, 192–194.
30 See Sevrin's discussion of this passage in *Le dossier baptismal séthien*, 159–169.

practice a water baptism without taking into account the "living water" that is bestowed in true, i.e. Sethian baptism.

Another reference to baptism is found in the second conclusion:

> This is the hidden knowledge of Adam, which he gave to Seth, which is the holy baptism of those who know the eternal knowledge through those born of the word and the imperishable illuminators, who came from the holy seed: Yesseus, Mazareus, [Yesse]dekeus, [the Living] Water. (85,22–31)

Here "holy baptism" appears to be spiritualized by being equated with "hidden knowledge." I don't think, however, that this should be seen as a rejection of baptism in water. As for the names Yesseus, Mazareus, and Yessedekeus, they are also associated with Sethian baptism in the *Gospel of the Egyptians*, to which we now turn.

2.6. Baptism in the Gospel of the Egyptians

The *Gospel of the Egyptians* is partially preserved in two versions, one in Nag Hammadi Codex III (III,2) and one in Codex IV (IV,2).[31] It is a highly complex tractate, reflecting editorial development over time. The two extant versions differ somewhat from one another and represent Coptic translations of two different Greek versions. The text is not complete in either of the versions we have, owing to damage to the manuscripts; so modern translations utilize the best preserved passages from one or the other of the two versions.

The correct title of the tractate is found at the very end of the version in Codex III: "The Holy Book of the Great Invisible Spirit" (68,18–19; the end of the version in Codex IV is lost). In a preceding colophon another title is given: "The Egyptian Gospel" (III 69,6, missing from the codex IV version). The editors of the first edition emended the text to read "The Gospel of the Egyptians." Since that title for the tractate has been in use for many years, it is retained here. But this work should not be confused with an apocryphal New Testament gospel called *Gospel of the Egyptians*, extant in fragments quoted by Clement of Alexandria.

In two conclusions to *Gos. Eg.* It is said that the book was written by "the great Seth" (III 68,1–2.10). He is said to have placed it on a mountain called Charaxio for the benefit of the "holy race of the great savior" (i.e. Seth).[32]

The tractate has three main parts. The first deals with the origin of the heavenly world and the divine beings that populate it (III 40,12–44,28; IV 55,20–60,30; III 49,1–55,16). The second main part is a history of the seed of Seth (III

---

[31] The edition used here is the first edition published by A. BÖHLIG and F. WISSE, *Nag Hammadi Codices III,2 and IV,2: The Gospel of the Egyptians*.

[32] On this motif see n. 26, above. The mountain's name in *Gos. Eg.*, Charaxio, is probably related to the Greek verb "inscribe" (*charatto*).

55,16–64,9). The third is a baptismal liturgy that includes a series of hymns and prayers (III 64,9–68,1).

The first part features the same divine beings as are found in *Ap. John*, beginning with the Invisible Spirit, the unnameable Father. But the heavenly world of *Gos. Eg.* has a much heavier population than that of *Ap. John*, featuring additional divine beings and triads, and a series of ogdoads. The climax of the series of emanations comes with the appearance of Seth, the father of those who would constitute the "seed of the Great Seth," the Gnostic elect.

The second main section of *Gos. Eg.* is dominated by the work of Seth. He appears in three "advents" (Greek *parousia*). In the third he "puts on" Jesus and through Pronoia (= Barbelo) establishes baptism (III 63,4–64,9). This section concludes as follows:

> (He) established through her the holy baptism that surpasses the heaven, through the incorruptible Logos-begotten one, even Jesus the living one, even he whom the great Seth has put on. And through him he nailed the powers of the thirteen aeons, and established those who are brought forth and taken away. He armed them with an armor of knowledge of this truth, with an unconquerable power of incorruptibility. (III 63,23–64,9)

The third section begins with a list of heavenly beings who are said to have appeared to the saved, beginning with those particularly associated with baptism:

> There appeared to them the great attendant Yesseus Mazareus Yessedekeus, the living water, and the great commanders (Greek *strategos*) Yakobos the great and Theopemptos and Isavel, and they who preside over the spring of truth, Micheus and Michar and Mnesinous, and he who presides over the baptism of the living,[33] and the purifiers, and Sesengenpharanges, and they who preside over the gates of the waters, Micheus and Michar.... (III 64,9–19)

We have already encountered Yesseus Mazareus Yessedekeus in our discussion of *Apoc. Adam*; and Micheus, Michar, and Mnesinous in our discussions of *Apoc. Adam* and *Trim. Prot*. The role of the "commanders" is obscure; who the "purifiers" are is not stated, but Sesengenbarpharanges is given the role of a "purifier" in the codex IV version (IV 76,6). Such names are typical of the mystifications found in Gnostic mythology, comparable to those found in magical texts.

The list of heavenly beings who appeared continues with others of various functions, and concludes with mention of four illuminators Harmozel, Oroiael, Daveithe, and Eleleth (III 64,19–65,26). The Codex III version adds an anomolous fifth, Ioel, who is absent in the Codex IV version.

This section concludes with an assurance of present salvation for the children of Seth:

---

33 In the Codex IV version his name is given in a damaged part of the page: Mep[. .]el (IV 76,2). I have no idea who this might be.

From now on through the incorruptible man Poimael, and they who are worthy of (the) invocation, the renunciations of the five seals in the spring-baptism, these will know their receivers as they are instructed about them, and they will be known by them. These will by no means taste death. (III 65,26–66,8)

The name of the mediator of salvation, Poimael, is anomalous. A connection with the revealer in the Hermetic tracatate *Poimandres* has been suggested.[34] Invocations, renunciations, and quintuple immersions (the Five Seals), are features of the Sethian baptismal ritual. The "receivers" are the heavenly beings who bring the Gnostic's spirit up to the Light after death.

There follows in the text a series of hymnic invocations and prayers, the first part of which begins with an invocation of Yesseus Mazareus Yessedekeus. Included in these invocations are *nomina barbara*, sometimes referred to as "glossolalia." The letters are rendered with superlinear strokes, as is common in Greek and Coptic manuscripts to render "sacred names." The first editors render these in their translation with Greek letters, and I follow them here:

IH IEYZ HΩ OY HΩ ΩYA. Really truly, O Yesseus Mazareus Yessedekeus, O living water, O child of the child, O glorious name, really truly, the one who is, IIII HHHH EEEE OOOO YYYY ΩΩΩΩAAAA, really truly, HI AAAA ΩΩΩΩ O, existing one who sees the aeons! Really truly. AEE HHHH IIII YYYYY ΩΩΩΩΩΩΩΩ, who is eternally eternal, really truly, IHA AIΩ in the heart, who exists, Y forever and ever, you who exist, you who exist. (III 66,8–22)

These invocations are followed by others, interspersed with references to the experience of the initiate and some ritual actions performed by him/her. Here are some examples of possible ritual actions, interspersed with glorifications of the invisible Father: "I have stretched out my hands while they were folded. I was shaped in the circle of the riches of the light … " (III 67,7–9). "Therefore the incense of life is in me. I mixed it with water after the model of all archons" (III 67,22–24). In the conclusion to this section the initiate indicates that he/she has done all this "in order that I may live with you in the peace of the saints, you who exist really truly for ever" (67,24–68,1).

It is obvious that the obscurities that are part and parcel of *Gos. Eg.* prevent us from saying much about how the baptismal ritual was performed. Sevrin and Turner have suggested that the essential parts include 1) a prebaptismal profession of the various beings associated with the rite, 2) an invocation of the principle powers at work in baptism, 3) a purificatory renuciation of the lower world, 4) baptismal immersions in actual water understood symbolically as the "living water" of gnosis, 5) a raising up of the initiate, 6) the utterance of a post-baptismal hymn of thanksgiving, and 7) and such ritual actions as the

---

[34] *Corpus Hermeticum* I. This connection is suggested by Böhlig and Wisse in their edition (p. 197).

extension of ones arms in the form of a circle, 8) investiture, 9) enthronement, and 10) coronation. The rite was probably administered by a mystagogue.[35]

Sevrin and Turner conclude that the obvious Christian elements found in the *Gospel of the Egyptians* are secondary. The baptismal rite itself is a Gnostic one, and did not originate in Christianity. The rite may very well have originated in a heterodox Jewish baptismal sect.[36]

2.7. Baptism in Zostrianos

Zostrianos (NHC VIII,1) is one of the Gnostic tractates reported by the philosopher Porphyry to have been circulating in Plotinus' school in Rome during the third quarter of the third century (*Vit. Plot.* 16).[37] It is the longest tractate in the Nag Hammadi Corpus, comprising 132 pages.[38] Unfortunately, the manuscript is badly damaged, especially in its middle portion. In terms of genre, *Zostrianos* is an apocalypse, presenting a series of revelations consisting of visions and auditions given to Zostrianos[39] by heavenly beings. It is composed of three parts: Zostrianos' autobiographical prologue (1,1–4,20), a lengthy first-person account of his ascent through the heavens (4,20–129,2), and Zostrianos' descent and mission (129,2–132,5).

In the first part of the tractate, Zostrianos recounts how, while meditating, he is visited by "the angel of knowledge," who invites Zostrianos to accompany him on an ascent through the heavens. At each level of his visionary ascent Zostrianos is baptized in the names of the beings at that level, and is given a revelation by the guide for that particular aeon. The content of the various revelations include names of various heavenly beings, many of them found in other Sethian texts but many more besides.

Zostrianos' first baptism occurs as he is traversing the "atmospheric" realm, where he is immersed seven times in "living water." He then ascends to the "self-generated Aeons" where he is baptized in the name of the divine Autogenes:

> I was baptized in the [name of] the divine Autogenes [by] those powers that preside [over the] living water, Michar and Mi[cheus]. I was purified by [the great Barpharanges]. I was [glorified] and inscribed in glory. I was sealed by those who preside over these powers, [Michar], Micheus, Seldao, Ele[nos] and Zogenethlos. I [became] a [contemplative] angel and stood upon the first – that is the fourth

---

35 See TURNER, "Sethian Baptismal Rite," 947–948.
36 Ibid., 948; SEVRIN, *Le dossier baptismal séthien*, 143–144.
37 See § 1.2.2., above.
38 The critical edition used here is that of C. BARRY, W.-P. FUNK, P.-H. POIRIER, and J. TURNER, *Zostrien (NH VIII,1)*. John Turner includes a complete English translation in his lengthy commentary (pp. 483–662). I use his translation in quotations of the text here.
39 Zostrianos is the name given in a late tradition to the grandfather of Zoroaster (Zarathustra), the Iranian prophet.

– aeon together with the souls. I blessed the divine Autogenes and the forefather Pigeradamas, [an eye of] the Autogenes, the first perfect [human being]; and Seth Emm[acha Seth], the son of [A]damas, the [father of] the [immovable race]; and the [Four] Lights, [Armozel], and [Oroiael, Daveithe and Eleleth]; and Mirothea – she is the mother [of Adamas] – and Prophania – [she is the mother] of the Lights – and Ple[sithea] the [mother of the angels].

(6,7–7,1)

Zostrianos is subsequently baptized in the name of Autogenes another four times, for a total of five. When he is baptized a fifth time in the name of Autogenes he becomes divine. This fifth baptism involves a quintuple immersion presided over by various divine beings, including Yesseus Mazareus Yessedekeus and others (53,26–54,25). Other baptisms follow. After the final baptism by a revealer figure named Youel Zostrianos is said to have become perfected and in the Aeon of Barbelo he receives a "perfect crown" (129,15–16).

It is clear that all of the baptisms experienced by Zostrianos are part of an ecstatic ascent, and are completely transcendent. No real water is involved. Moreover, Zostrianos' baptisms are completely individual, and do not involve ritual actions performed by a community.

At the end of the tractate Zostrianos descends back to earth and begins a mission to "an errant multitude," inviting them to release themselves and escape from bondage. His appeal includes the following admonition:

> Do not baptize yourselves with death nor entrust yourselves to things inferior to you as if to superior things. Flee the madness and the bondage of femininity, and choose for yourselves the salvation of masculinity. (131,2–8)

It is not at all clear what is involved in the baptism here referred to. This admonition may function as a critique of those who have a rite of baptism with water without any connection to the transcendent "living water" that surrounds the invisible Father. We saw something like this at the conclusion of the *Apocalypse of Adam*.[40]

2.8. Baptism in Melchizedek

The tractate Melchizedek (NHC IX,1) is only partially extant, owing to serious damage to the manuscript.[41] Less than half of its content remains. It is pseudonymously attributed to the ancient "priest of God Most High" named in Genesis 14:18. In terms of genre it is an apocalypse in which Melchizedek conveys to those who are worthy secret revelations received from heavenly emissaries. The

---

40 See discussion above, § 2.5.
41 The critical edition used here is that of B. PEARSON and S. GIVERSEN in: B. Pearson, ed., *Nag Hammadi Codices IX and X*. 19–85. Quotations of the text are given in my most recent translation, published in: MEYER, ed., *The Nag Hammadi Scriptures* (cit. n. 2), 599–605.

tractate is made up of three main parts: a revelation mediated by the angel Gamaliel (1,1–14,15); a liturgy performed by the priest Melchizedek in behalf of his community (14,15–18,23+); and a revelatory vision mediated to Melchizedek by unnamed heavenly brethren, probably including Gamaliel (18,bottom–27,10).

The first revelation contains a prophecy of the earthly work of Jesus Christ and the rise of false teachings after his resurrection, and includes invocations of heavenly beings who inhabit the heavenly world. In the second part Melchizedek undertakes a series of ritual actions, including baptism and a series of invocations addressed to the same heavenly beings invoked earlier. These beings include the Sethian primal triad of Father, Mother, and Son, and others. In the third part Melchizedek experiences a vision of the sufferings and resurrection of Christ. The Sethian Gnostic features of the text appear to be secondary additions to an earlier non-Gnostic Christian apocalypse.[42]

The first reference to baptism is found in the first part of the tractate, as part of Gamaliel's revelation to Melchizedek. Unfortunately, the manuscript at this point is severely damaged. Here is what can be read at this point:

> ... [world] ... world ... to be [baptized ... in the] waters .... For the waters that are [above] ... who is baptized ... but [baptize yourself] in the waters that are [below] ... as he is coming to ... great ... [baptism] as they ... upon ...[43] ... by ... of the .... Pray for [the offspring of the] archons and [all] the angels, together with [the] seed <that> emanated [from the Father] of the All. ... the entire seed from the .... (7,25–9,4)

Possible indicators of a Sethian context for this passage are the reference to the waters above, and to the "seed" that emanated from the Father of the All. The "seed" may (or may not) be that of Seth.

The other mention of baptism in this tractate is found in the second part, in which Melchizedek undergoes a baptism as part of what I take to be some sort of priestly installation. He offers up the following prayer to God the Father:

> I have presented myself to you as an offering, together with those who are mine, to you yourself, O God, Father of the All, with those whom you love, who came forth from you who are holy and [living.] And <according> to the [perfect] laws I shall pronounce my name as I receive baptism, [now] and forever, among the living and holy [names] and in the [waters]. Amen. (16,7–16)

He then pronounces a series of trishagia, addressed to heavenly beings that we recognize as part of the Sethian theogony, beginning with the divine triad:

> [Holy], holy, holy are you, O [Father of those] who truly exist, [with those who] do [not] exist, Ab[el Bar]u[ch], for [ever] and ever. Amen. Holy, holy, holy [are

---

42 See the discussion in my Introduction to the tractate in the critical edition.
43 About 14 lines are missing here.

you, who exist before] … az,[44] [for ever and] ever. Amen. Holy, holy, [holy are you, Mother of the] aeons, Ba[r]belo, for ever and ever. Amen. [Holy], holy, holy are you, [first]born of the aeons, [Doxo]medon … [for ever] and ever. Amen. (16,16–17,1).

Other trishagia follow, addressed to other divine beings, including the four luminaries of the Sethian theogony. The final one is addressed to Jesus Christ: "[Holy], holy, holy are you, chief [commander of the All], Jesus Christ, [for ever and ever]. Amen" (18,4–7).

We note, however, the absence of any divine beings usually associated with Sethian baptism, and we are entitled to doubt whether the baptism undergone by Melchizedek has any connection at all with Sethian baptism as attested in the texts we have already treated. Melchizedek's baptism is probably to be understood as paradigmatic of the baptism that is to be undergone by members of his community, "those who are his." But who they are is completely uncertain.

2.9. Baptism in the Untitled Text from the Bruce Codex

The beginning and end portions of this tractate are missing; so we don't know what title, if any, was applied to it.[45] It is exceedingly prolix and confusing; so it is no wonder that it has not attracted much attention since its original publication in 1892. It seems to be a compilation of various Gnostic traditions and sources put together sometime in the early fourth century for purposes that are obscure. Perhaps the compiler used his work for his own personal meditations.

The tractate contains an elaborate cosmology involving beings known from Sethian and other Gnostic texts, including the heavenly Seth himself, who is invariably referred to as Setheus. Jesus and Christ are also included in it, and there are some quotations from the New Testament.

The only reference to baptism in this tractate is found toward the end of the tractate. In chapter 20 of Violet MacDermot's arrangement of the translation, we read about certain inhabitants of "the land of air," who participate in some sort of baptism:

> In that place they are immersed in the name of the self-begotten one who is God over them. And in that place over the source of living water were put powers which were brought forth as they came. These are the names of the powers which are over the living water: Michar and Micheu. And they are purified through Barpharanges. And within these <are> the aeons of the Sophia. Within these <is> truth in verihood. The Pistis Sophia is there, and the pre-existent living Jesus, and the aerodioi and the twelve aeons. In that place were put Sella, Eleinos, Zogeneth-

---

44 An unreadable mystical name, of which there are many in Gnostic texts that end in –az. This page of the manuscript is very fragmentary.

45 The critical edition used here is that of Carl Schmidt (ed.) and Violet MacDermot (trans.), *The Books of Jeu and the Untitled Text in the Bruce Codex*, 214–317.

les, Selmelche, and the self-begotten one of the aeons. And within it were placed four lights Eleleth, Daveide, Oroiael .... (ch 20, p. 263 of Schmidt's edition, lines 22 – p. 264, line 6)

The text breaks off at that point, owing to damage to the manuscript. This passage is a hodge-podge of various Gnostic mythological figures, including several associated with Sethian baptism. But we learn nothing about Sethian baptismal practice in this passage.

2.10. Baptism in the Gospel of Judas

The *Gospel of Judas* was first published in English translation in 2006 by the National Geograpic Society, and immediately caused quite a stir both among scholars and among the general public.[46] The critical edition of the Codex Tchacos, in which the *Gospel of Judas* is the third tractate, was published in 2007.[47] Considerable controversy has arisen over the interpretation of the figure of Judas Iscariot in the *Gospel of Judas*. Whereas the National Geographic team of scholars treated him as a hero, other scholars, including myself, treat him as a demonic being.[48] That controversy need not detain us here. I shall treat here an obscure passage in the tractate that I think refers to Sethian baptism.

The *Gospel of Judas* is full of ambiguities, some of them owing to damage to the manuscript in which it is contained.[49] In the *Gospel of Judas* Jesus makes several appearances to his disciples, and especially to Judas, who alone receives extensive revelation from Jesus. In a part of the text in which Jesus speaks to all of the disciples the following material occurs at the top of p. 43 of the codex:[50]

> in [...] who has not come [... spring] for the tree [...] of this aeon [...] after a time [...] but he has come to water God's paradise, and the race that will last, because [he] will not defile the [walk of life of] that generation, but [...] for all eternity. (43,1–11)

I am convinced that the unnamed "he" who has come to water God's paradise is the Sethian Gnostic savior, Seth.[51] Reflected in this passage is a Hellenistic Jewish tradition about Seth and his "seed." In his comment on "another seed" in Genesis

---

46   R. Kasser, G. Wurst, and M. Meyer, *The Gospel of Judas*. A second, much improved, edition was published in 2008.

47   R. Kasser, M. Meyer, G. Wurst, and F. Gaudard, *The Gospel of Judas, together with the Letter of Peter to Philip, James, and a Book of Allogenes from Codex Tchacos*. I use that edition here.

48   For my interpretation of Judas see B. Pearson, "Judas Iscariot in the *Gospel of Judas*".

49   No more than 85% of the text has been restored.

50   The bottom half of p. 42 is totally lost. Considerable material from the first 10 lines of p. 43 is also lost.

51   I have treated this passage, and others related to Seth, in an article entitled "Some Aporiae in the *Gospel of Judas*," forthcoming in a Festschrift for Bentley Layton.

4:25 Philo of Alexandria writes, "This seed is a male offspring, Seth or "Watering" (ποτισμός), raised up to the soul whose fall did not originate in itself" (*On the Posterity and Exile of Cain* 10).[52] In the same treatise, commenting on Seth as "watering," Philo writes, "As, then, the seeds and plants in the earth, when watered, grow and sprout and are prolific in producing fruit, but, if no water be poured on them, whither away, so the soul, as is evident, when it is fostered with a fresh sweet stream of wisdom shoots up and improves" (*Ibid*, 124–126).

Philo's interpretation is probably related to a traditional interpretation of Seth's name (*Shet* in Hebrew) as etymologically related to the Hebrew word *shatah*, "to drink."

In this passage in the *Gospel of Judas* I find a probable allusion to Sethian baptism. This baptism, in contrast to that of the catholic church, is symbolically related to the "spring of living water" that surrounds the ineffable Father in Gnostic theology.[53] Seth comes to "water" the "generation that will last," i.e. the "generation of Seth,"[54] with the heavenly water given in Sethian baptism.

3. Summary and Conclusions

In the foregoing discussion we have treated the work of Schenke and others who have defined a "Sethian" Gnostic system of myth and ritual reflected in a large number of Gnostic texts preserved in Coptic. We set forth the essential features of Sethian Gnosticism, which include a basic Sethian Gnostic myth involving theogony, cosmogony, anthropogony, and soteriology. The best example of this myth is found in the *Apocryphon of John*. We noted that that myth is preserved in *Ap. John* within a "Christianizing" framework, with Christianizing interpolations in the text. The building blocks of the basic Sethian Gnostic myth involve a radical reinterpretation of the Bible, especially Genesis, and Jewish interpretations of biblical texts. We concluded that the earliest form of Sethian Gnostic mythology is of Jewish origin. Christian forms of Sethian Gnosticism are secondary developments in the history of Sethianism.[55]

We then turned to the issue of baptism as reflected in Sethian Gnostic texts. We noted that baptism is not referred to in all Sethian texts. The primary evidence preserved in Gnostic tractates is limited, and the texts reveal that differences existed among Sethian Gnostic groups as to their interpretations of baptism and baptismal praxis. We posited that Sethian baptism originated as a rite of initiation, involving the use of real water, and performed only once.

---

52 Translated by Colson and Whitaker in the LCL edition.
53 See esp. *Ap. John* II 4,19–26, treated above, § 2.3..
54 Cf. 49,6, the "seed of Seth" in Sethian Gnosticism.
55 See esp. § 1.2.1., above.

In our discussion of the relevant texts we noted the close relationship between myth and ritual in Sethian baptism. In our discussion of the *Apocryphon of John* we noted that the "living water" in Sethian baptism is construed as the transcendent water that surrounds the invisible Father. In the longer version of *Ap. John* we noted that this living water is administered in a ritual of "five seals," involving a quintuple immersion in water. In our discussion of *Trimorphic Protennoia*, we noted references to other ritual actions involving investiture, enthronement, glorification, and rapture, as well as the "five seals".

In our discussion of the *Apocalypse of Adam*, *Melchizedek*, and the *Untitled Text* in the Bruce Codex we did not find much information as to how Sethian baptism was administered. In some of the texts we noted the important mythological roles played by certain divine figures, especially Micheus, Michar, and Mnesinous (*Trim Prot.*, *Apoc. Adam*, *Gos. Eg.*, Bruce *Untitled*, *Zostrianos*), and Yesseus, Mazareus, and Yessedekeus (*Apoc. Adam*, *Gos. Eg.*, *Zostrianos*). In our discussion of Zostrianos we noted that in that text baptism is entirely transcendent, part of an ecstatic ascent experience.

The best evidence for how Sethian baptism was administered is supplied by the *Gospel of the Egyptians*, wherein ritual references can be found in hymnic invocations and prayers used in the ritual. We found evidence for the following ritual elements: 1) a prebaptismal profession beings associated with the rite, 2) an invocation of the principle powers at work in baptism, 3) a purificatory renunciation of the lower world, 4) baptismal immersions in real water understood symbolically as the "living water" of gnosis, 5) raising up of the initiate, 6) the utterance of a post-baptismal hymn of thanksgiving, 7) certain physical gestures, 8) investiture, 9 enthronement, and 10) coronation. Especially noteworthy is the absence of anointing with oil, which was so prominent in early Christian baptism. The baptismal immersions are again referred to as the "five seals."

Can we at this point suggest an answer to an obvious question posed by the texts: What is the significance of the number five in the references to the "five seals"? Tuomas Rasimus has recently called attention to the "pentadic concept of divinity" found in the theogony of the *Apocryphon of John*, and has proposed a connection with the "five seals."[56] In *Ap. John* we read that the Father contemplates himself in the light which is the spring of living water that surrounds him, and the result is the actualization of his thought (*ennoia* = Barbelo, II 4,19–27). Barbelo requests of the Father that he grant her Foreknowledge, Indestructibility, Eternal Life, and Truth. These, together with Providence, which is Barbelo, constitute "the pentad of aeons of the Father" (II 5,11–6,3). This "Pentad of aeons" resulting from the Father's contemplation of himself in living water, may account for the pentad of immersions in Sethian baptism.

---

56   RASIMUS, *Paradise Reconsidered*, 257–258.

While Rasimus sees a correspondence with the Christian trinitarian formula in Christian baptism which he thinks influenced Sethian baptismal practice,[57] I see no connection at all between Christian baptism and Sethian Gnostic baptism. As for the use of the term "seal" (*sphragis*), no Christian influence need be posited. For example, the term is used metaphorically for circumcision in Judaism, and in connection with baptism in Mandaeism.[58]

It is difficult to reconstruct an actual history of the development of Sethian baptism, but I would suggest that we can draw the same conclusions regarding Sethian baptismal practice as we did regarding Sethian mythology. Sethian baptism, and Sethian Gnosticism itself, arose in a Jewish environment, probably as early as the first century. The Christian elements found in some of the texts are secondary. As for the place where Sethian baptism originated, a Syro-Palestinian locus is likely.

Bibliography

BARRY, C., W.-P. FUNK, P.-H. POIRIER, J. TURNER, *Zostrien (NH VIII,1)*, Bibliothèque copte de Nag Hammadi ("Textes" 24), Québec: Université Laval, Louvain: Peeters 2000.

BÖHLIG, A., and F. WISSE (eds.), *Nag Hammadi Codices III,2 and IV,2: The Gospel of the Egyptians (The Holy Book of the Great Invisible Spirit)* (NHS 4), Leiden: Brill 1975.

COSENTINO, A. *Il battesimo gnostico: Dottrine, simboli e riti iniziatici nello gnosticismo*, Cosenza: Lionello Giordano 2007.

FITZER, G., σφραγίς, in: *TDNT* 7: 939–953.

HEDRICK, CH., *The Apocalypse of Adam: A Literary and Source Analysis* (SBLDS 46), Chico, Calif.: Scholars Press 1980.

KASSER, R., M. MEYER, G. WURST: *The Gospel of Judas*, Washington DC: National Geographic Society 2006, 2nd ed. 2008.

KASSER, R., M. MEYER, G. WURST, and F. GAUDARD (eds.), *The Gospel of Judas together with the Letter of Peter to Philip, James, and a Book of Allogenes from Codex Tchacos: Critical Edition*, Washington DC: National Geographic Society 2007.

LAYTON, B. (ed.), *The Rediscovery of Gnosticism*, Volume 2: *Sethian Gnosticism* (SHR 41), Leiden: Brill 1981.

---

57   *Ibid*, 258.
58   See G. FITZER, σφραγίς, in: *TDNT* 7:939–953, esp. 947, 953.

LAYTON, B., *The Gnostic Scriptures: A New Translation with Annotations and Introductions*, Garden City, N.Y.: Doubleday 1987.

MEYER, M. *The Nag Hammadi Scriptures: The International Edition*, New York: HarperOne 2007.

MACRAE, G., "NHC V,5: The Apocalypse of Adam," in: D. Parrott (ed.), *Nag Hammadi Codices V,2-5 and VI with Papyrus Berolinensis 8502, 1 and 4* (NHS 11), Leiden: Brill 1979, 151-195.

PEARSON, B., "The Figure of Seth in Gnostic Literature," in: B. Layton (ed.), *The Rediscovery of Gnosticism*, vol. 2: *Sethian Gnosticism*, (SHR 41), Leiden: Brill 1981, 472-504.

— *Gnosticism, Judaism, and Egyptian Christianity*, Minneapolis, Minn.: Fortress Press 1990.

— "*Apocryphon Johannis* Revisited," in: P. Bilde et al. (eds.), *Apocryphon Severini presented to Sören Giversen*, Aarhus: Aarhus University Press 1993, 155-165.

— *The Emergence of the Christian Religion: Essays on Early Christianity*, Harrisburg, Pa.: Trinity Press International 1993.

— *Ancient Gnosticism: Traditions and Literature*, Minneapolis, Minn.: Fortress Press 2007.

— "Melchizedek" (Introduction and Translation), in: M. Meyer (ed.), *The Nag Hammadi Scriptures*, New York: HarperOne 2007, 595-605.

— "Judas Iscariot in the *Gospel of Judas*," in: A. DeConick (ed.), *Codex Judas Papers: Proceedings of the International Congress on the Tchacos Codex held at Rice University, Houston, Texas, March 13-16, 2008* (NHMS 71), Leiden and Boston: Brill 2009, 137-152.

RASIMUS, T., *Paradise Reconsidered in Gnostic Mythmaking: Rethinking Sethianism in Light of the Ophite Evidence* (NHMS 68), Leiden and Boston, Mass.: Brill 2009.

ROBINSON, J. M., *The Nag Hammadi Library in English*, 3rd ed., San Francisco, Calif.: Harper & Row 1988.

SCHENKE, H.-M., "Das sethianische System nach Nag-Hammadi-Handschriften," in: P. Nagel (ed.), *Studia Coptica*, Berlin: Akademie-Verlag 1974, 731-746.

— "The Phenomenon and Significance of Gnostic Sethianism," in: B. Layton (ed.), *The Rediscovery of Gnosticism*, vol. 2: *Sethian Gnosticism* (SHR 41), Leiden: Brill 1981, 588-616.

SCHMIDT, C. and V. MACDERMOT, *The Books of Jeu and the Untitled Text in the Bruce Codex* (NHS 13), Leiden: Brill 1978.

SEVRIN, J.-M., *Le dossier baptismal séthien, Bibliothèque copte de Nag Hammadi*, ("Études 2), Québec: Université Laval/Louvain: Peeters 1986.

TURNER, J., "XIII,1: *Trimorphic Protennoia*," in: Ch. Hedrick (ed.), *Nag Hammadi Codices XI, XII, XIII* (NHS 28), Leiden: Brill 1990, 371–454.

— *Sethian Gnosticism and the Platonic Tradition*, Bibliothèque copte de Nag Hammadi ("Études" 6), Québec: Université Laval, Louvain: Peeters 2001.

— "The Sethian Baptismal Rite," in: L. Painchaud and P.-H. Poirier (eds.), *Coptica-Gnostica-Manichaica: Mélanges offerts à Wolf-Peter Funk*, Bibliothèque copte de Nag Hammadi ("Études" 7), Québec: Université Laval/Louvain: Peeters 2005, 399–433.

WALDSTEIN, M., and F. WISSE (eds.), *The Apocryphon of John: Synopsis of Nag Hammadi Codices II,1; III,1 and IV,1 with BG 8502,2* (NHMS 33), Leiden: Brill 1995.

Initiationsriten im Manichäismus

GREGOR WURST

1. Manis Ablehnung der Taufe in seiner Auseinandersetzung mit den Elchesaiten

Im Vergleich mit den jüdischen, christlichen und gnostischen religiösen Traditionen der ersten christlichen Jahrhunderte und ihren unterschiedlichen Taufverständnissen nimmt der Manichäismus insofern eine Sonderstellung ein, als die Religion des Lichts jegliche Praxis einer einmaligen Initiationstaufe oder wiederholbarer Reinigungs- und Tauchbäder kategorisch verworfen hat. Wie wir seit der Publikation des *Codex Manichaicus Coloniensis* (*CMC*) wissen, wuchs Mani selbst (*14. April 214; †276/277) zwar im Kreis der judenchristlichen Täufersekte der Elchesaiten auf, der sich sein Vater Pattikios angeschlossen hatte, als der Sohn etwa vier Jahre alt war.[1] Nach Darstellung der Tradenten des *CMC*, insbesondere nach dem Zeugnis des Lehrers Baraies, geriet er jedoch, kurz nachdem er im Alter von 24 Jahren die zweite Offenbarung seines Syzygos erhalten hatte, in einen ernsthaften Konflikt mit den Täufern u. a. „über die Taufe" sowie „über die von ihnen praktizierte Gemüsetaufe".[2] In diesem Kontext heißt es:

> Die Taufe, mit der ihr eure Speisen tauft, hat [keinen] Wert; denn dieser Leib ist unrein und wurde in einer unreinen Schöpfung geformt. Seht (den Beweis): Wenn jemand seine Nahrung gereinigt und zu sich genommen hat, nachdem sie bereits im Zustand der (rituellen) Reinheit war, dann entstehen, wie uns klar ist, aus ihr Blut, Galle, Winde, schändlicher Kot und die Unreinheit des Leibes. Aber wenn sich jemand einige Tage lang dieser Nahrung enthält, so zeigt sich auf der Stelle, daß alle [diese] schändlichen und ekelhaften Ausscheidungen im Körper ausbleiben und weniger werden; wenn [er aber dann] Nahrung zu sich nimmt, dann werden sie entsprechend wieder zahlreicher im Leib. Das beweist, daß sie aufgrund eben der Nahrung an Zahl zunehmen. Wenn aber jemand getaufte und gereinigte Speise und (hinwieder) jene ungetaufte zu sich nimmt, dann erkennt man offensichtlich, daß die Schönheit und die Kraft des Körpers dieselbe ist; entsprechend zeigt sich auch, daß sich die Ekelhaftigkeit und der Bodensatz in beiden Fällen nicht voneinander unterscheiden.[3]

---

1   Vgl. A. HENRICHS, „Mani and the Babylonian Baptists".
2   *CMC* p. 79,21–80,3: „... πε]ρὶ τοῦ βαπτίσματος καὶ περὶ ὧν βαπτίζουσιν λαχάνων ..."; vgl. L. KOENEN, „From Baptism to the Gnosis of Manichaeism", 734–738.
3   *CMC* p. 80,22–82,18.

Die Elchesaiten praktizierten also einerseits eine „Gemüsetaufe", einen Ritus zur Reinigung ihrer Nahrung. Mani weist diese Praxis mit der quasi-rationalen Argumentation zurück, daß die Ausscheidungen des Körpers in jedem Fall „ekelhaft" seien, unabhängig davon, ob die Nahrung nun getauft sei oder nicht. „Folglich ist jene getaufte Speise, welche er (*scil.* der Körper) abgestoßen und ausgeschieden hat, nicht besser als jene [andere] ungetaufte."[4]

Mit ähnlichen Argumenten kritisiert Mani andrerseits die häufigen Lustrationen der Elchesaiten:

> Auch das aber hat keinen Wert, daß ihr euch jeden Tag im Wasser tauft. Warum tauft ihr euch denn erneut jeden Tag, nachdem ihr einmal getauft und gereinigt seid? Gerade dadurch wird ja deutlich, daß ihr euch jeden Tag vor euch ekelt und euch wegen des Ekels tauft, ohne je rein werden zu können. Gerade dadurch zeigt sich ja aufs deutlichste, daß die Ekelhaftigkeit vom Leib kommt. Siehe, auch ihr seid damit bekleidet. Daher betrachtet an euch selbst, [was es] mit eurer Reinheit [auf sich hat]. Es ist nämlich unmöglich, euren Leib ganz rein zu machen; denn jeden Tag gerät der Leib in Bewegung und kommt (wieder) zur Ruhe, weil die Nahrungsrückstände ausgeschieden sind. Folglich handelt ihr in dieser Sache ohne das Gebot des Heilands.[5]

Auch hier lautet das quasi-rationale Argument Manis nach der Darstellung des *CMC*, daß die Praxis häufig wiederholter Tauchbäder nicht zu einem Zustand wirklicher Reinheit führe, also letztlich ineffektiv sei. In beiden Fällen, sowohl bei der Taufe der Speisen als auch bei der Taufe des Körpers, bleibe es bei demselben Befund, daß der menschliche Körper ekelhafte und schmutzige Ausscheidungen, einen, wie es wörtlich heißt, „Bodensatz" (ὑποστάθμη),[6] produziere. Entsprechend werfen die Elchesaiten Mani vor: „Er tauft sich nicht wie wir, und er tauft auch sein Essen nicht, wie wir es tun".[7]

Auffällig an dieser Argumentation ist, daß sie sich ausschließlich gegen die ständig zu wiederholenden Lustrationen richtet, die die Elchesaiten geübt haben. Die christliche Praxis einer einmaligen Taufe wird in der Kritik Manis im *CMC* nicht in den Blick genommen, und eine vergleichbare Auseinandersetzung damit ist in manichäischen Originalquellen auch nicht überliefert. Man kann nur festhalten, daß diese Kritik Manis an der Taufpraxis der Elchesaiten in der manichäischen Tradition offenbar auf jede Form einer Taufe übertragen worden ist. So heißt es im sechsten Kapitel der *Kephalaia*:

---

4 *CMC* p. 82,18–23.
5 *CMC* p. 82,23–84,9.
6 *CMC* p. 84,6.
7 *CMC* p. 88,12–15.

Der Geist des Königs der Archonten des Wassers ist derjenige, der heutzutage in den Sekten des Irrtums herrscht, welche mit der Wassertaufe taufen und ihre Hoffnung und ihr Vertrauen auf die Wassertaufe setzen.[8]

2. Verwerfung und Spiritualisierung der Taufe in (anti-)manichäischen Quellen

Diese Ablehnung einer jeden Form einer Wassertaufe ist für den Manichäismus charakteristisch, obgleich die Mehrzahl der Belege aus antimanichäischen Quellen stammt. So schreibt Augustinus im Kontext der Kontroverse mit den Pelagianern, die eine Kindertaufe ablehnten: „Die Manichäer nennen das Bad der Wiedergeburt, das heißt das Wasser selbst, überflüssig und bestehen mit unheiligem Herzen darauf, daß es nichts nütze";[9] ähnlich äußern sich in der Mitte des 5. Jh. Papst Leo I. über Manichäer in Rom[10] oder zu Beginn des 7. Jh. Timotheus von Konstantinopel: „Die Taufe nimmt er (scil. Manichaeus) nicht an".[11] Vereinzelte Belege, die *prima facie* für den gegenteiligen Befund sprechen – so etwa die Nennung der Manichäer in einer Reihe von Häresien, deren Taufe zu verwerfen sei, bei Basilius von Caesarea[12] oder auch die rhetorisch geschickt gestellte Frage des Manichäers Felix in seiner öffentlichen Disputation mit Augustinus „wozu sind wir getauft?"[13] – erweisen sich bei näherer Untersuchung als nicht überzeugend.

Demgegenüber ist im Manichäismus eine spiritualisierte Form einer Waschung bzw. Wassertaufe im Kontext des individuellen Seelenaufstiegs belegt, die die Seele im sog. „Vollkommenen Menschen" bzw. in der „Säule der Herrlichkeit" – d. h. jene, ganz materiell gedachte ‚Säule' (*scil.* die Milchstraße), auf der die Lichtpartikel zurück in das Königreich des Lichtes gelangen – empfan-

---

8   *Keph.* 33,29–32; das 130. Kapitel der *Kephalaia*, das offenbar ein Streitgespräch Manis mit einem Anhänger einer christlichen Gruppierung behandelt und wo es u. a. um die Wirksamkeit von „Taufe" und „Eucharistie" geht (*Keph.* 307,21–310), ist leider nur sehr schlecht erhalten.

9   Aug., *c. ep. Pel.* II, 3 (Urba/Zycha): „*Manichei 'lauacrum regenerationis, id est aquam ipsam dicunt esse superfluam nec prodesse aliquid profano corde contendunt'*"; vgl. auch *c. ep. Pel.* IV, 5: „*Quid eis* [scil. *Pelagianis*] *prodest 'baptismum omnibus aetatibus necessarium confiteri', quod Manichei dicunt omni aetati superfluum ....*"; *haer.* 46,17 (Vander Plaetse/Beukers): „*baptismum in aqua nihil cuiquam perhibent salutis affere: nec quemquam eorum, quos decipiunt, baptizandum putant.*"

10 Leo M., *serm.* 9,4 (Schipper/Van Oort): „*baptismum regenerationis totius gratiae virtute dispoliant* (scil. *Manichaei*)".

11 Tim. CP, *haer.* PG 86, 21C: „τὸ βάπτισμα οὐ παραδέχεται".

12 Bas., *epist.* 188,1 (Courtonne): „αἱρέσεις δὲ οἷον ἡ τῶν Μανιχαίων, καὶ Οὐαλεντινῶν, καὶ Μαρκιωνιστῶν, καὶ αὐτῶν τούτων τῶν Πεπουζηνῶν. ... ἔδοξε τοίνυν τοῖς ἐξ ἀρχῆς τὸ μὲν τῶν αἱρετικῶν (scil. βάπτισμα) παντελῶς ἀθετῆσαι ...".

13 Aug., *c. Fel.* I 19 (Zycha): „*si adversarius nullus contra deum est, ut quid baptizati sumus?*"

gen wird.¹⁴ In einem der Psalmen für das Bemafest, dessen jährliche Feier dem Gedächtnis des Todes Manis gewidmet war und an welchem der Gemeinde als Antizipation des Endgerichts die Sünden des jeweils vergangenen Jahres vergeben wurden, heißt es:

> Empfange das heilige Siegel (σφραγίς) vom Nous der Kir[che] |
> und erfülle die Gebote;
> der Richter selbst, d[er in] | der Luft ist,
> er wird dir seine drei Geschenke überreichen;
> die Taufe (βάπτισμα) | der Götter,
> im [Vollkommenen] Menschen wirst du sie empfangen;
> (und) [die] | (Himmels-) Erleuchter werden dich vollenden
> und in dein [König]reich geleiten.¹⁵

Weitere Belege für diese Vorstellung finden sich in Psalmen bzw. Hymnen, die zum größten Teil in den Kontext einer manichäischen Seelen- oder Totenmesse zu gehören scheinen: *Psb.* II 58,27: „[Das (?) . . .] einer heiligen Taufe, das die Bekränzten empfangen werden"; *Psb.* II 59,26–27: „… und wasche mich mit deinen heiligen Wassern / und mache mich rein gemäß der Art, wie ich bin"; *Herakleides-Psalm* Nr. 282, 7 (Richter) = *Psb.* II 103,34–35: „O Erlöser, du Sohn Gottes, [nimm] mich rasch bei dir auf, / wasche mich mit den Tauwassern der Säule der Herrlichkeit […]"; *Psb.* II 139,19–23: „Die geehrte Säule, / die der vollkommene Mensch ist, / … die Taufe des Lebens, / der Reinigungsort für die Seelen"; *T. Kell. Copt.* 2, Text A 5 (Gardner): „Ich wusch mich in der Säule, und ich wurde vollendet im Vollkommenen Menschen"; vgl. auch das mittelpersische Fragment M 564 /R/5–6, das zu einem Hymnus der lebendigen Seele gehört:

> Und abwaschen wird er mir den Schmutz und die sehr große Sündigkeit,
> und baden wird er mich und hell (licht) wird er mich machen.¹⁶

Die Manichäer haben dieser spiritualisierten eschatologischen Taufe also eine umfassende sündenvergebende Wirkung zugeschrieben, was als (juden-) christliches Erbe zu charakterisieren ist.

3. Initiationsriten im Manichäismus

Es sind zwar nur sehr wenige Quellen überliefert, in denen die Initiation im Manichäismus thematisiert wird,¹⁷ doch erlauben sie es uns durchaus, die we-

---

14 Vgl. G. Wurst, *Bemafest*, 134; P. A. Mirecki, „Coptic Manichaean Psalm 278", 247–248.
15 *Bema-Psalm* 227, 11,1–4 (Wurst) = *Psb.* II 22,11–15; zum Bemafest vgl. Wurst, *Bemafest*; zum postmortalen Seelenaufstieg, S. G. Richter, *Aufstiegspsalmen*.
16 F. C. Andreas/W. B. Henning, „Mitteliranische Manichaica II", 30.
17 Die Literatur zum Thema der manichäischen Initiationsriten stammt ausschließlich von H.-Ch. Puech: „Liturgie et pratiques rituelles", 319–389; „Manichéisme", 620–625; *Le manichéisme*.

sentlichen Vorstellungen und Riten zu rekonstruieren. Zunächst ist darauf hinzuweisen, daß der Übertritt zur Religion des Lichts als ein intellektueller Akt, als Akt der Annahme der Gnosis des Apostels des Lichts, in der manichäischen Kirche verstanden worden ist. Der ehemalige Manichäer Augustinus spielt darauf an, wenn er bemerkt, er und seine Freunde seien „Erleuchtete" genannt worden, nachdem man ihnen den *Grundlagenbrief* Manis vorgelesen hätte.[18] Die Hoffung und den Glauben anzunehmen bedeutet nach Kapitel 91 der *Kephalaia*, das Licht von der Finsternis zu trennen und die Mysterien der Lebendigen Seele zu erkennen.[19] Durch die Annahme des manichäischen Glaubens wird man ein Katechumen bzw. *auditor*.[20] L. Koenen hat dies treffend mit folgenden Worten zum Ausdruck gebracht: „*Gnosis* as separation (*scil.* of Light from Darkness) is ... the center of the Manichaean religion. It is by this *gnosis* that ... Mani wanted to replace the baptismal rites of the baptists ...".[21]

Diese ‚Annahme des Glaubens' hat darüber hinaus, wie Mani in Kapitel 91 der *Kephalaia* lehrt, ebenso wie die spiritualisierte eschatologische Taufe die Wirkung einer vollständigen Sündenvergebung: „Wisset so: Seine ersten Sünden alle, in denen er (*scil.* der Mensch, der zum manichäischen Glauben gefunden hat) gesündigt hat vom Tage, da er geboren wurde, bis zum Tage, da er die Hoffnung Gottes annahm und sein Herz wegnahm von allen Sekten und Götzenbildern des Irrtums, sie werden ihm alle vergeben. Nicht wird er nach ihnen gefragt von dieser Stunde an, noch empfängt er Vergeltung für sie".[22]

Beides, die Annahme des manichäischen Glaubens wie der Empfang der Sündenvergebung, vollziehen sich dabei sinnfällig im Rahmen eines Initiationsritus, der nur in einer einzigen Originalquelle dargestellt wird, und zwar im neunten Kapitel der *Kephalaia*, das den Titel trägt: „Die Deutung des Friedens(-grußes), was er bedeutet, die Rechte, der Kuß, die Verehrung". Abweichend von der Überschrift ist im Text dieses Kapitels dann aber mit der „Handauflegung" noch von einer fünften rituellen Handlung die Rede. Sie gelten dabei als Geheimnisse und Zeichen, die in der göttlichen Welt entstanden und von einem Apostel in der Welt verkündigt worden seien:

Son fondateur – sa doctrine, 87. 180–183 (Anm. 363–366).

18 Aug., *c. ep. Man.* 5 (Zycha): „*ipsa* (scil. *epistula fundamenti*) *enim nobis illo tempore miseris quando lecta est, illuminati dicebamur a uobis*".
19 *Keph.* 232,3–5: „Jeder Mensch, der die Hoffnung und den Glauben angenommen hat, hat das Licht von der Finsternis getrennt, er hat erkannt (αἰσθάνεσθαι) die Mysterien der Lebendigen Seele ...".
20 *Keph.* 224,21–24: „Denn viele Katechumenen stehen in der Welt, indem sie wandeln in Irrlehre und Verirrung, bevor sie den Glauben Gottes annehmen"; vgl. Aug., *c. lit. Pet.* III 17,20 (Petschenig).
21 KOENEN, „From Baptism to the Gnosis of Manichaeism", 745; vgl. *CMC* p. 84,9–17.
22 *Keph.* 232,8–13.

> Diese fünf Mysterien, diese fünf Zeichen (*scil.* der Friedensgruß, die Rechte, der Kuß, die Verehrung, die Handauflegung) sind zuerst entstanden in der Gottheit; sie wurden in dieser Welt verkündigt durch einen Apostel; die Menschen lernten sie und setzten sie in ihrer Mitte ein. [Es bestanden aber] nicht von Urbeginn diese Mysterien inmitten der Kräfte der Finsternis.[23]

Es folgt der entscheidende Abschnitt, der es gestattet, einen aus diesen „fünf Zeichen" bestehenden Initiationsritus zu rekonstruieren, dessen genauer Ablauf freilich unsicher bleibt:

> Der Licht-Nous, der in die Welt kommt, kommt in diesen verschiedenen τύποι. *Mit diesen fünf Dingen wählt er seine Kirche aus.* Zuerst (und) vor allen Dingen wählt er seine Kirche aus vermittels eines Frieden(sgrußes) und gibt den Frieden(sgruß) zuerst den Menschen. Wenn der Mensch den Frieden(sgruß) empfängt und ein Sohn des Friedens wird, wird er darnach ausgewählt zum Glauben. Wann er nun den Frieden(sgruß) empfängt, empfängt er [die] Rechte und wird zugehörig zur Rechten. *Wenn er nun [empfängt] die Rechte, zieht der Licht-Nous ihn zu sich und stellt [ihn hinein in die] Kirche.* — Durch die Rechte empfängt er den Kuß [der Liebe] und *wird ein Sohn der [Kirche]* . . . . . . durch den Kuß. Er empfängt Ehrenbezeugung und erweist Ehrenbezeugung dem Gott der Wahrheit und erweist auch Ehrenbezeugung der heiligen Kirche . . . die Hoffnung des Glaubens der (?) guten Dinge. — Wenn er empfängt den Frieden(sgruß) und die Rechte, den Kuß und die Ehrenbezeugung, dann wird zum Schluß von alledem ihnen die Rechte der Gnade aufgelegt (und) sie selbst [empfangen] die Handauflegung, die ihnen aufgelegt werden wird, *und sie werden geordnet und gebaut in der Wahrheit und befestigt in ihr auf ewig.* Sie gehen ein zum Licht-Nous vermittels dieser guten Zeichen und werden vollkommene Menschen und erweisen Ehrenbezeugung und preisen den Gott der Wahrheit.[24]

Die „Auswahl der Kirche" wird also als Werk des Licht-Nous, des archetypischen „Vaters aller Apostel" des Lichts (z.B. Buddhas, Zarathustras und Jesu) und somit auch Manis selbst, verstanden; und wenn ein einzelner Mensch diese Zeichen empfängt, „wird er zu einem Sohn der [Kirche]". Die Reichung der „Rechten (*scil.* Hand)" scheint dabei eine so entscheidende Rolle zu spielen, daß eine Aufnahme in die manichäische Kirche an anderer Stelle auch nur durch dieses eine ‚Zeichen' angedeutet werden kann. Dies ist in Kapitel 90 der *Kephalaia* der Fall, wo es heißt: „Vom ersten Tage an, da er (*scil.* der Katechumen) die erste Irrlehre verlassen hat, in der er sich befand, *und die Friedensrechte ergriffen hat*, sich überzeugt und hingestellt hat auf der Stufe des wahren Katechumenentums . . .".[25] Dies erklärt sich vor dem Hintergrund, daß die Reichung der Rechten im Kontext der Errettung des Urmenschen durch den lebendigen Geist – und somit an einer ganz zentralen Stelle des manichäischen Mythos – eine wichtige Rolle

---

23 *Keph.* 40,19–24.
24 *Keph.* 40,24–41,10.
25 *Keph.* 226,7–10.

spielt: „Die zweite Rechte ist diejenige, die der Lebendige Geist dem Urmenschen gegeben hat, als er ihn aus dem Kampf heraufgeführt hat".[26] Zwar führt das neunte Kapitel der *Kephalaia* alle fünf Zeichen auf diese Episode des Mythos zurück,[27] doch kann der Lebendige Geist auch einfach nur als „unsere erste Rechte" tituliert werden.[28] Die Handauflegung wird dabei schon von Mani selbst als ihm vom Vater durch seinen Syzygos offenbart bezeichnet, wenn er in einem Fragment des *Lebendigen Evangeliums* sagt:

> Er (*scil.* der Syzygos) ist zu mir gekommen und hat mir die beste Hoffnung, die Erlösung zum ewigen Leben, die Lehren der Wahrheit und *die von meinem Vater herabkommende Handauflegung* (ἡ χειροτησία ἡ ἐκ τοῦ π(ατ)ρ(ὸ)ς τοῦ ἐμοῦ) gebracht. Durch sein Kommen wählte er mich vor den anderen aus und, mich zu sich ziehend, trennte er mich von den Anhängern jenes Gesetzes, in dem ich aufgewachsen war.[29]

Der Initiationsritus, wie ihn das neunte Kapitel der *Kephalaia* voraussetzt, scheint also zumindest teilweise auf Mani selbst zurückzugehen.

Während in dem oben zitierten *Bema-Psalm* 227, 11,1 vom „Empfang des heiligen Siegels (σφραγίς) durch den Nous der Kirche" im Kontext der Feier des Bemafestes die Rede ist, so daß darunter der jährliche Empfang der Sündenvergebung, wohl ebenfalls unter der Form einer Handauflegung, zu verstehen ist,[30] wird man, unter Vergleich von *Keph.* 225,17–19 („... der Katechumene ..., der mit dem Siegel des Glaubens und dem Siegel (σφραγίς) der Wahrheit gesiegelt ist"), die die Initiation abschließende „Handauflegung" des neunten Kapitels eventuell mit einer an zwei Stellen bezeugten Ölzeichnung in Verbindung bringen können: Laut Turribius von Astorga unterscheiden sich spanische Priscillianisten von Manichäern u. a. dadurch, daß letztere die Taufe in Form einer Ölzeichnung vollzögen, erstere hingegen der orthodoxen Praxis der Wassertaufe folgten, wie der Herr sie verkündet habe.[31] In dieselbe Richtung weist die achte antimanichäische These des *Codex vaticanus graecus 1838*, wonach byzantinische Manichäer wohl des 6. Jh.[32] eine solche Ölzeichnung als Ersatz für die Wassertaufe praktizierten.[33] Beide Belege sind jedoch singulär, so daß

---

26   *Keph.* 39,19–21.

27   *Keph.* 38,8–40,19; vgl. H.-Ch. Puech, „Manichéisme", 622–623.

28   *Bema-Psalm* 219, 10,2 (Wurst) = *Psb.*I 2,5.

29   *CMC* p. 69,20–70,10.

30   Vgl. Wurst, *Bemafest*, 133–137.

31   Turrib., *epist.* 5 (Schipper/Van Oort): „*Illud autem specialiter in illis actibus qui sancti Thomae dicuntur, prae caeteris notandum atque exsecrandum est, quod dicit eum non baptizare per aquam, sicut habet dominica praedicatio, sed per oleum solum: quod quidem isti nostri* (sc. Priscillianistae) *non recipiunt, sed Manichaei sequuntur*".

32   Vgl. Puech, „Liturgie et pratiques rituelles", 346.

33   PG 88, 572C: „Εἰ γνώσει καὶ πίστει διασῴζονται οἱ Μανιχαῖοι, τί χρῄζουσι τῆς διὰ τοῦ ἐλαίου σφραγίδος; καὶ εἰ δυνατὸν σωθῆναι τοὺς μετὰ γνώσεως καὶ πίστεως χρῄζοντας τῆς διὰ τοῦ

es fraglich ist, ob die Existenz einer Ölzeichnung als Ersatz für die Wassertaufe für den gesamten Manichäismus angenommen werden darf.

Bibliographie

QUELLEN

Aug. *c. ep. Man.* Zycha, Joseph, *Sancti Aureli Augustini De utilitate credendi, De duabus animabus, Contra Fortunatum, Contra Adimantum, Contra epistulam fundamenti, Contra Faustum* (CSEL 25,1), Wien: F. Tempsky 1891.

Aug., *c. Fel.* Zycha, Joseph, *Sancti Aureli Augustini Contra Felicem, De natura boni, Epistula Secundini, Contra Secundinum, accedunt Euodii De fide contra Manichaeos* (CSEL 25,2), Prag, Wien und Leipzig: G. Freytag 1892.

Aug., *c. ep. Pel.* Urba, Karl F./Zycha, Joseph, *Sancti Aureli Augustini Contra duas epistulas Pelagianorum libri quattuor* (CSEL 60), Wien und Leipzig: G. Freytag 1913.

Aug., *c. lit. Pet.* Petschenig, Michael. *Sancti Aureli Augustini scripta contra Donatistas.* Pars II: *Contra litteras Petiliani libri tres* (CSEL 52), Wien und Leipzig: G. Freytag 1909.

Aug., *haer.* Vander Plaetse, Rol/Beukers, Clemens, *Sancti Aurelii Augustini De haeresibus ad Quodvultdeum,* in: CCL 46, Turnhout: Brepols 1969, 263–345.

Bas., *epist.* Courtonne, Yves, *Saint Basile. Lettres, Tome II* (Collection des Universités de France), Paris: Les Belles Lettres 1961.

CMC Koenen, Ludwig/Römer, Cornelia, *Der Kölner Mani-Kodex. Über das Werden seines Leibes. Kritische Edition* (ARWAW. Sonderreihe Papyrologica Coloniensia 14), Opladen: Westdeutscher Verlag 1988.

Keph. Polotsky, Hans Jakob/Böhlig, Alexander. *Kephalaia I. 1. Hälfte (Lieferung 1–10)* (Manichäische Handschriften der staatlichen Museen Berlin, Bd. 1). Stuttgart: Kohlhammer 1940.

Funk, Wolf-Peter, *Kephalaia I. Zweite Hälfte (Lieferung 13/14)* (Manichäische Handschriften der staatlichen Museen zu Berlin), Stuttgart: Kohlhammer 1999.

Leo M., *serm.* Schipper, Hendrik G./Van Oort, Johannes, *St. Leo the Great. Sermons and Letters Against the Manichaeans. Selected Fragments* (Corpus Fontium Manichaeorum, Series Latina 1), Turnhout: Brepols 2000.

ἐλαίου σφραγίδος, πῶς ἀδύνατον σωθῆναι τοὺς ἐν γνώσει καὶ πίστει προσιόντας τῷ διὰ τοῦ ὕδατος βαπτίσματι;"

Psb. II Allberry, Charles R.C., *A Manichaean Psalm-Book. Part II* (Manichaean Manuscripts in the Chester Beatty Collection, Bd. 2), Stuttgart: Kohlhammer 1938.

Wurst, Gregor. *Die Bema-Psalmen* (Corpus Fontium Manichaeorum, Series Coptica I: Liber Psalmorum Pars II, Fasc. 1. The Manichaean Coptic Papyri in the Chester Beatty Library), Turnhout: Brepols 1996.

Richter, Siegfried G., *Die Herakleides-Psalmen* (Corpus Fontium Manichaeorum, Series Coptica I: Liber Psalmorum, Pars II, Fasc. 2. The Manichaean Coptic Papyri in the Chester Beatty Library), Turnhout: Brepols 1998.

T. Kell. Copt. Gardner, Iain, *Kellis Literary Texts* I (Dakhleh Oasis Project: Monograph 4), Oxford: Oxford University Press 1996.

Turrib., *epist.* Schipper, Hendrik G./Van Oort, Johannes, *St. Leo the Great. Sermons and Letters Against the Manichaeans. Selected Fragments* (Corpus Fontium Manichaeorum, Series Latina I), Turnhout: Brepols 2000, 78–85.

Literatur

Andreas, Friedrich C./Henning, Walter B., „Mitteliranische Manichaica aus Chinesisch-Turkestan II," in: SPAW (1933) 3–72. [= Duchesne-Guillemin, Jacques (Hg.), *W. B. Henning. Selected Papers* I (Acta Iranica 14), Leiden: Brill 1977, 191–260].

Henrichs, Albert, „Mani and the Babylonian Baptists. A Historical Confrontation", in: *Harvard Studies in Classical Philology* 77 (1973) 23–59.

Koenen, Ludwig, „From Baptism to the Gnosis of Manichaeism", in: Bentley Layton (Hrsg.), *The Rediscovery of Gnosticism. Proceedings of the International Conference on Gnosticism at Yale New Haven, Connecticut, March 28–31, 1978*, Bd. 2: *Sethian Gnosticism* (Studies in the History of Religions, Supplements to Numen 41), Leiden: Brill 1981, 735–756.

Mirecki, Paul A., „Coptic Manichaean Psalm 278 and Gospel of Thomas 37", in: A. van Tongerloo, S. Giversen (Hgg.), *Manichaica Selecta. Studies presented to Professor J. Ries* (Manichaean Studies 1), Louvain, Lund: Departement Orientalistiek 1991, 243–262.

Puech, Henri-Charles, *Le manichéisme. Son fondateur – sa doctrine* (Musée Guimet. Bibliothèque de diffusion 56), Paris: Civilisations du sud 1949.

— „Le manichéisme", in: ders. (Hg.), *Histoire des Religions* Bd. 2 (Encyclopédie de la Pléiade), Paris: Gallimard, 1972, 523–645.

— „Liturgie et pratiques rituelles dans la manichéisme (Collège de France, 1952–1972)", in: ders., *Sur le manichéisme et autres essais*, Paris: Flamarion 1979, 235–394.

RICHTER, SIEGFRIED G., *Die Aufstiegspsalmen des Herakleides. Untersuchungen zum Seelenaufstieg und zur Seelenmesse bei den Manichäern* (Sprachen und Kulturen des christlichen Orients Bd. 1), Wiesbaden: Reichert Verlag 1997.

WURST, GREGOR, *Das Bemafest der ägyptischen Manichäer* (Arbeiten zum spätantiken und koptischen Ägypten 8), Altenberge: Oros-Verlag 1995.

Part/Teil III

Early Judaism

Frühjudentum

Aus dem Wasser kommt das Leben
Waschungen und Reinigungsriten in frühjüdischen Texten

Antje Labahn

1. Einleitung

Die gestellte Aufgabe besteht darin, frühjüdische Belege über Waschungen und Reinigungsriten vorzustellen. Das Feld ist weit und kann in einem Aufsatz naturgemäß nur in Auswahl bearbeitet werden.[1] Diese beruht auf einer Grunddefinition, die als Leitfaden für die Vorstellung der Texte dient. Ein wesentliches Kriterium für die Auswahl der Belege stellen das Element Wasser und seine Bedeutung dar. Es ist das Wasser, in dem und mit dem etwas getan wird und das bei Personen und Gegenständen, die damit in Berührung kommen, etwas bewirkt. Es geht also um eine *Handlung mit Wasser, die lebensverändernde Qualität bei dem Menschen hat*, an dem sie vollzogen wird.[2] Der Mensch geht aus der Handlung als ein Veränderter hervor. Nach der Handlung ist er in der Regel in die Lage versetzt, Gott begegnen zu können bzw. der Begegnung mit Gott standzuhalten. Bevor der Mensch mit Gott in Kontakt treten kann, muss er dazu die Voraussetzung schaffen, d.h. er muss sich einer Reinigung unterziehen.

Von diesen Grundgedanken ausgehend wird nach Lebensbezügen gefragt, wie sie im Zusammenhang mit Waschungen und Reinigungen im Frühjudentum abgebildet sind.[3] Ihre Funktionen und deren Bedeutung werden vorgestellt. Die untersuchten Texte beziehen sich auf religiöse Waschungen – im Folgenden rituelle Waschung bzw. Reinigung genannt –, womit eine Unterscheidung ge-

---

1 Eine umfangreichere Studie hat jüngst 2006 J. D. Lawrence, *Washing in Water*, vorgelegt, die sich genau mit der Fragestellung befasst und untersucht: „Christian baptism and Jewish ritual immersion were somehow related, but have claimed an inability to be certain as to the nature and origins of these practices." (Zitat 1) Diesen geht Lawrence nach, indem er sich um solche Belege mit „intersection of ritual washing and ritual purity" (a.a.O. 2) kümmert, wobei er neben Texten auch archäologische Funde untersucht.
Des Weiteren ist auf die Studie von I. C. Werrett, *Ritual Purity*, aus dem Jahr 2007 zu verweisen, die für sich beansprucht, erstmals alle Belege über rituelle Reinigungen zu analysieren. Zur Forschungsgeschichte vgl. dessen Einleitung a.a.O., 4–17.

2 Hierin liegt ein wesentlicher Unterschied zu den atl. Belegen, über die Lawrence, *Washing* 7, urteilt: „bathing in the Hebrew Bible … never mentions water as a source of life and death".

3 Ich beschränke mich dabei auf Belege aus der Zeit des Zweiten Tempels, vorzugsweise der zweiten Hälfte dieser Periode, die naturgemäß mit der Zerstörung des Tempels 70 n.Chr. endet.

genüber profanen Waschungen vollzogen wird. Ob und inwiefern aus dem facettenreichen Bild der Texte kultisch-liturgische Abläufe rekonstruiert werden können, ist eine Frage, auf die hier allenfalls am Rande eingegangen werden kann.[4] Der Fokus meines Beitrags wird sich auf die Funktion und Bedeutung von Waschungen im Zusammenhang mit Reinigungsriten im Frühjudentum konzentrieren,[5] wobei auch damit verbundene theologische, ethische und soteriologische Aspekte zur Sprache kommen werden.

2. Waschungen und rituelle Reinigung im Judentum – ein kurzer Überblick

Frühjüdische Wasserriten knüpfen im Allgemeinen an Aussagen aus dem Alten Testament an, wo verschiedentlich – vor allem in Gesetzestexten des Pentateuch – vom Waschen oder Eintauchen (in Wasser) die Rede ist, und zwar so, dass das Wasser der Reinigung von Körper und Kleidung dient. Die Reinigung wird nach einer vorhergehenden Verunreinigung notwendig. Diese Reinigung ist eine rituelle Reinigung, die die Reinheit oder Vollkommenheit des Menschen vor Gott herstellt, so dass der Mensch für die Begegnung mit Gott im Tempel gerüstet ist.

Die Septuaginta übernimmt weitgehend die Reinigungsvorschriften der Hebräischen Bibel mit gelegentlichen Veränderungen im Detail.[6] Sie werden damit zur Grundlage des Verständnisses von Waschungen im Frühjudentum. An die rituellen Reinigungsriten wird verschiedentlich angeknüpft, wie zu zeigen sein wird, wobei auch Veränderungen zu erkennen sind.

---

4   Zur methodischen Trennung zwischen den Aussagen der Texte und der Auswertung des archäologischen Materials vgl. auch den Ansatz von WERRETT, *Ritual Purity* 17f. Als methodisch gegensätzlichen Weg führt er die „Qumran/Essene hypothesis" an, worunter er eine (vorschnelle) Applizierung der Aussagen der Schriften vom Toten Meer auf eine in der Siedlung Qumran lebende jüdische Gruppe versteht. Die methodische Trennung zwischen den Texten und den (vor allem aus dem archäologischen Material rekonstruierbaren) Lebensverhältnissen der Gruppe bedeutet umgekehrt nicht automatisch, dass es keine Gemeinsamkeit zwischen beiden gäbe. Der methodischen Trennung geht es jedoch darum, zunächst die Texte mit ihren eigenen Aussagen zur Geltung zu bringen, bevor (ggf. in einem zweiten Schritt) nach Gemeinsamkeiten und Differenzen gegenüber der Qumrangemeinschaft gefragt wird. In diesem Sinn beschränke ich meinen Beitrag auf eine Sichtung des literarischen Materials aus den Schriften vom Toten Meer, wie es bis *dato* in Editionen erschlossen ist. – Zu einem neuen methodischen Ansatz, aus literarkritisch diskutierten Texten zu historischen Aussagen zu kommen, vgl. M. L. GROSSMAN, *Reading for History*.

5   Dass es durchaus Reinigungen gibt, bei denen kein Wasser verwendet wird, sei vermerkt, doch kann auf diese Belege nicht weiter eingegangen werden. Vgl. z.B. das bei LAWRENCE, *Washing*, 119–134, präsentierte Material, dessen prominentes Beispiel etwa die Hodayot (1QII) sind.

6   Z.B. Num 19,12, wo LXX ergänzend zur HB von Reinigungswasser, ὕδωρ ῥαντισμοῦ, spricht (zum Beleg s.u. in Abschnitt 4.1.2.).

Von der ntl. Semantik her wäre zu erwarten, dass die Waschungen mit dem Begriff βάπτω bezeichnet sind. In der Tat erscheint das Verb βάπτω auch im Kontext der Belege für Waschungen. Die Statistik gibt 16 Belege in der Grundbedeutung „eintauchen, untertauchen" an, wobei βάπτω 12 mal für טבל (in der transitiven Bedeutung „eintauchen", intransitiv „untertauchen")[7] verwendet wird und 11 mal ein rituelles Eintauchen meint. Subjekt zu βάπτω ist jedoch nicht der zu reinigende Mensch oder seine Kleidung. βάπτω wird stattdessen mehrheitlich mit dem Subjekt „Ysop" benutzt, das eingetaucht wird, zumeist in Blut, um dieses zu versprengen, zumeist an die Hörner des Altars.[8] Die Waschung selbst wird demgegenüber mit anderen Termini ausgedrückt: entweder mit πλύνω oder λούω oder mit νίπτω (jeweils in der Bedeutung „waschen").

Folglich ist auf breiterer semantischer Basis nach Waschungen zu schauen, in denen durch das Element Wasser Wesentliches passiert; es geht also um rituelle Reinigung, die mittels eines bestimmten Ablaufs unter Verwendung von Wasser hergestellt wird.[9] Dabei wird sich zeigen, dass die Abläufe Leerstellen bieten und nicht alle Details ausgeführt sind. Die Leerstellen werden bewusst als Leerstellen wahrgenommen, ist es doch die Aufgabe anderer aus diesem Kreis, die Leerstellen anhand anderer literarischer oder materieller Belege zu füllen.[10]

Die Mehrzahl der frühjüdischen Belege stammt aus den Schriften vom Toten Meer.[11] Bevor diese behandelt werden (4.), kommen frühjüdische Belege vor oder außerhalb von Qumran zur Sprache (3.).

3. Frühjüdische Texte außerhalb von Qumran

Es gibt nur wenige Belege für Waschungen außerhalb von Qumran.[12] Es handelt sich dabei um Stellen, die an atl. Passagen anknüpfen, diese partiell aufnehmen und zugleich interpretieren. Betrachtet man die sparsame Verwendung von Motiven aus dem Feld der Reinigungsthematik, so ist auf den ersten Blick zu

---

7   Vgl. HAH[17] 271; HAL 353. Die Bedeutung „baden" wird in den frühjüdischen Schriften vom Toten Meer stark gemacht, indem sie unter טבל zumeist ein Baden als Waschung des ganzen Körpers verstehen.
8   Die Belege sind in Abschnitt 3.1. genannt.
9   Zum Thema Reinheit und Unreinheit in frühjüdischen Texten, das über den hier interessierenden Bereich hinaus reicht, da nicht in allen Belegen Wasser verwendet wird, vgl. z.B. J. NEUSNER, *Idea of Purity*, 32–71, sowie WERRETT, *Ritual Purity*, passim.
10 Vgl. dazu die Beiträge von SEÁN FREYNE und DIETER SÄNGER in dieser Publikation. S.a. LAWRENCE, *Washing*, 155–184, der Miqwaoth aus Palästina und Jordanien untersucht, sowie B. ZISSU/D. AMIT, "Common Judaism", *passim*.
11 S.a. den eher generellen Hinweis von TH. KAZEN, *Jesus and Purity* Halakhah, 51 mit Anm. 50, auf diesen Textbereich.
12 Eine vergleichbare Bilanz zieht auch LAWRENCE, *Washing*, 77f.

erkennen, dass den Reinigungsriten in diesem Umfeld keine große Bedeutung zukommt.

3.1. Testamentum Levi

Innerhalb der Testamente der Zwölf Patriarchen (TestXII) gibt es nur einen Beleg für Waschungen im Testament Levi. In 9,11 ist von rituellen Waschungen im Zusammenhang mit Opfern die Rede. Die Waschungen begegnen innerhalb eines Traumes, den Jakob über seinen Sohn Levi träumt. Levi berichtet von diesem Traum, dass er Priester vor Gott werden wird (ἔσομαι αὐτοῖς εἰς ἱερέα πρὸς τὸν θεόν, 9,3). Der Textfluss in TestLev 9 ist nicht ganz durchsichtig, da der Erzählstrang des Traumes mit dem Bericht von einer Reise, die Jakob und Levi zu ihrem Großvater Isaak nach Bethel unternehmen, und dem Thema des Priestertums Levi, in das Levi von seinem Großvater Isaak eingeführt wird, verwoben ist; zusätzlich sind ethische Appelle eingestreut.[13]

Im Zusammenhang des Priestertums Levis ist von Waschungen die Rede, die aufgrund des Priestergesetzes (νόμος ἱεροσύνης, 9,7) anfallen.[14] V. 11 spricht von drei Waschungen:

> 1. Levi soll sich waschen, bevor er den Tempel betritt (καὶ πρὸ τοῦ εἰσελθεῖν εἰς τὰ ἅγια, λούου).
> 2. Er soll sich waschen, wenn er das Opfer durchführt (καὶ ἐν τῷ θύειν, νίπτου).
> 3. Er soll eine erneute Waschung vornehmen, wenn er das Opfer vollendet hat (καὶ ἀπαρτίζων πάλιν τὴν θυσίαν, νίπτου).

Die Waschungen werden mit zwei Verben bezeichnet: λύω und νίπτω. Der Zusammenhang gibt nicht zu erkennen, ob die Verben eine sachliche Differenz widerspiegeln. Möglich wäre es, dass λύω einen Vorgang weiter außerhalb im Vorhof des Tempels bezeichnet, während die mit νίπτω bezeichnete Handlung in räumlicher Nähe zum Opferaltar stattfindet. Das würde bedeuten, dass verschiedene Becken vorausgesetzt wären, die für unterschiedliche Waschungen verwendet worden wären. Doch sollte man den Text nicht überbeanspruchen und mit einer zu weit reichenden Interpretation eher zurückhaltend sein.

Nähere Auskünfte zu den Reinigungsriten werden in TestLev 9 weiter nicht gegeben. Es bleibt offen, welche Körperteile im Einzelnen gewaschen werden sollen (Hände, Hände und Füße, der ganze Körper), worin die Waschung geschieht und welche Qualität das Wasser hat. Die Intention in TestLev ist nicht,

---

13   Zu TestLev bzw. den TestXII vgl. die monographischen Untersuchungen von J. BECKER, *Untersuchungen*; J. H. ULRICHSEN, *Grundschrift der Testamente*; M. SEGAL, *Book of Jubilees*, die auch das redaktionsgeschichtliche Wachstum der Schrift (mit je eigenen Entwicklungsmodellen) verfolgen.

14   Das Priestergesetz über die Darbringung der Opfer befindet sich in 9,7f.11–14, unterbrochen von V. 9f. durch ethische Mahnungen; zu TestLev 9 und Levis Priestertum vgl. A. LABAHN, *Licht und Heil*, 64ff.

eine Auskunft über Reinigungsriten zu geben, sondern Levi als Priester in den Vordergrund zu stellen. Die Waschung dient dabei lediglich der Vorbereitung des Opfernden für die Durchführung der Opfer im Heiligtum.

Die Waschungen knüpfen an verschiedene Aussagen des Pentateuchs an, die hier verbunden werden:

Erstens: Über die Priesterinvestitur ist in Ex 29,4 und 40,12 zu erfahren, dass zunächst eine Waschung in Wasser erfolgt (λούσεις αὐτοὺς [ἐν] ὕδατι/ רחצת אתם במים)[15], bevor die Gewänder angelegt werden.

Eine Variante dazu bietet Num 8,7, wo über die Einsetzung der Leviten gesagt wird, dass über sie Wasser der Sünde (הזה עליהם מי חטאת) bzw. Wasser der Reinigung (περιρρανεῖς αὐτοὺς ὕδωρ ἁγνισμοῦ) gesprengt wird und sie ihre Kleider waschen (πλυνοῦσιν τὰ ἱμάτια αὐτῶν/כבסו בגדיהם); danach sind sie rein (καθαροὶ ἔσονται/והטהרו).

Zweitens: In Lev 11–20 begegnen Vorschriften zur rituellen Reinigung, die nach einer Verunreinigung von Menschen etwa durch Fälle von Krankheit oder Kontakt mit Blut notwendig wird. Der rituellen Reinigung geht eine Veränderung der Lebenssituation voraus, d.h. z.B. ein Ende der Krankheit oder ein Ende der Wartezeit nach dem Kontakt mit Blut (im Todesfall oder bei Menstruation). Der Vorgang der rituellen Reinigung ist jeweils der gleiche, da er vom Gesetz vorgegeben ist und vom Priester durchgeführt wird. Die Reinigung kann nur im Zusammenhang mit einem Opfer, das der zu Reinigende aufbringt, wieder erlangt werden. Die Reinigung erfolgt dabei als Waschung mit Wasser, so dass der Zustand ritueller Reinheit wieder hergestellt wird (z.B. Lev 15,21f.: λούσεται ὕδατι καὶ ἀκάθαρτος ἔσται). Der Mensch wird damit ins Leben zurückgebracht. Die Reinigung vollzieht sich wie folgt: Der Priester taucht (βάπτει) Ysop in das Blut des Opfertieres und sprengt es an den Altar. Der zu Reinigende wäscht seine Kleider (πλύνει) sowie seinen Körper in Wasser (λούσηται τὸ σῶμα αὐτοῦ ὕδατι, 14,8; 15,13 u.ö.). Dadurch kommt rituelle Reinigung zustande (καθαρισμός). Diese Reinigung wird weiterhin als Sühne interpretiert, die der Priester durch das Sündopfer oder das Brandopfer erwirkt (ἐξιλάσεται;[16] vgl. Lev 14,19.21; 15,15.30).[17]

An die Terminologie des Waschens knüpft die Anweisung für Aaron in Lev 16,24.26 an, dass er beim Betreten des Tempels am Versöhnungstag zunächst seinen Körper (λούσεται τὸ σῶμα αὐτοῦ ὕδατι) und danach seine Kleider (πλύνει τὰ

---

15 In Ex 29,4 ist die Wendung mit ἐν, in Ex 40,12 ohne die Präposition überliefert. Anders als LXX gibt HB den gleichen Wortlaut an. S.a. Lev 8,6 über Aaron und die Aaroniden: Ααρων καὶ τοὺς υἱοὺς αὐτοῦ καὶ ἔλουσεν αὐτοὺς ὕδατι.

16 Zur atl. Vorstellung von Sühne vgl. grundlegend B. Janowski, *Sühne*.

17 Hier ist nicht der Ort, von einer atl. Entwicklung der Opfer zu handeln. Das ursprüngliche selbstständige Sündopfer ist später mit anderen Opferarten verbunden worden, oft mit dem Brandopfer (vgl. dazu A. Labahn, *Levitischer Herrschaftsanspruch*, Kapitel 2.3.5.2). Für den im 2. Jh. von TestXII rezipierten Nomos lagen die Opfervorschriften jedoch schon in ihrer schriftlichen Form des Pentateuchs vor und hatten normative Autorität.

ἱμάτια) in Wasser waschen soll, bevor er Brandopfer darbringt.[18] Die Waschungen sind terminologisch unterschieden, indem das Waschen von Körperteilen mit dem Begriff λούω bezeichnet wird und für das Waschen von Kleidern πλύνω verwendet wird.

Drittens: Ein andere Art von Waschung benennt Ex 30,17–21, wo ein Waschbecken[19] zwischen Stiftshütte und Altar vorgestellt wird, das zur Reinigung von Händen und Füßen vor dem Betreten des Zeltes und dem Darbringen von Opfern Verwendung findet. Das Waschbecken ist aus Kupfer (V.18: λουτῆρα χαλκοῦν) und enthält Wasser (ὕδωρ). Aaron und die Aaroniden sollen ihre Hände und Füße darin eintauchen (νίψεται … τὰς χεῖρας καὶ τοὺς πόδας ὕδατι, V. 19.21; vgl. V. 18.20). Mit dem Terminus νίπτω wird hier ein anderer Begriff verwendet. Die Abweichung könnte schlicht eine sprachliche Varianz darstellen oder aber auf einen abweichenden Ritus hindeuten, der eine Reinigung vor dem Betreten des heiligen Raumes bezeichnet.

Aufgenommen wird diese Waschung bei Josephus und Philo. In Jos Ant 3,114 wird dem Bronzebecken die Funktion zugewiesen, dass die Priester darin ihre Hände waschen und mit dem Wasser ihre Füße besprengen (χεῖρας ἀπολύνει καὶ τῶν ποδῶν καταχεῖν). In SpecLeg 1,198 legt Philo in Auslegung von Lev 1,3 jedem, der ein Opfer in den Tempel bringt, nahe, zunächst die Hände zu waschen und sie dann dem Opfertier aufzulegen. Nach Mos 2,138 wird den Priestern aufgetragen, beim Betreten des Tempels zur Vorbereitung der Opfer, ihre Füße und Hände zu waschen (οἱ μέλλοντες εἰς τὸν νεὼν εἰσιέναι ἱερεῖς … πόδας μάλιστα καὶ χεῖρας ἀπονιπτόμενοι).

Diese drei Kategorien von Waschungen werden in TestLev 9 miteinander verbunden, so dass sie sich gegenseitig interpretieren und dabei Neues entsteht. Dies geht bereits aus der Terminologie hervor. Während die LXX-Begriffe πλύνει und βάπτει aus dem Themenbereich der Opferdarbringung nicht mehr erscheinen, erhält der Begriff νίπτω in TestLev 9 eine größere Bedeutung, die aus dem Themenfeld des Betretens der Stiftshütte stammt. Die Waschungen in Lev 9, das Darbringen der Opfer einleiten, sind hier zugleich mit der Investitur Levis als Priester verknüpft. Möglich ist die Verknüpfung der atl. Waschungen in TestLev 9 dadurch, dass in der frühjüdischen Schrift keine detaillierten Angaben über die Waschungen zu finden sind. Auch geben die Reminiszenzen an das atl. Material keine eindeutigen Aufschlüsse, um die Leerstellen in TestLev 9 zu füllen.

---

18 Diesen Text sieht L. H. Schiffman, "Halakhah", 181–183.187f., im Hintergrund von TestLev 9,11 stehen.

19 Aufgenommen ist dieser Zusammenhang noch einmal in II Chr 4,6, wo allerdings von zehn Kesseln (λουτῆρας δέκα) die Rede ist, in denen das, was zum Brandopfer gehört, gewaschen wird. Hier liegt eine Traditionsmischung vor. Die Becken werden aus I Kön 8 aufgenommen, während die funktionale Zuordnung des Waschens (τοῦ πλύνειν) aus Ex 30 stammt, in II Chr 4,6 jedoch dem Brandopfer zugeordnet wird (τὰ ἔργα τῶν ὁλοκαυτωμάτων). Von Reinigungsriten im klassischen Fall ist hier also keine Rede mehr.

TestLev 9 interpretiert die atl. Reinigungsriten, in denen Wasser zur Reinigung und Wiederherstellung ritueller Reinheit dient, und bezieht diese auf Levi als Durchführenden. Levi wird zu der entscheidenden Figur, die Reinheit für sich und die Opfer herstellt, ohne dass allerdings explizit von Reinheit gesprochen wird. Bezieht man das Schweigen von Reinheit in TestLev 9 in die Interpretation des Textes mit ein, so muss man nach anderen Deutungssignalen für die Relevanz der Figur in der Schrift suchen. Die Bedeutung Levis für TextLev liegt m.E. eher in seiner Nähe zu Gott, die er in seinen Himmelsreisen erlebt und auch in Gottes Segen und Erwählung erfährt. Das Priestertum hat Funktionen im Kult, bedeutet aber auch Macht, die zudem militärische und ansatzweise königliche Implikationen hat; des Weiteren erscheint Levi als zukünftige Heilsgestalt.[20] Durch diese Heilsgestalt garantiert Gott Leben für die Zukunft in seiner Vielfältigkeit. In diesem Rahmen von Levi als zukünftiger Heilsgestalt ist die priesterliche Rolle ein Aspekt neben anderen.

3.2. Jubiläenbuch

Im Jubiläenbuch gibt es nur einen Beleg für Reinigungsriten, der recht isoliert im Kontext steht. Nach Jub 21,16 erteilt Abraham an Isaak die Weisung, auf Reinheit zu achten. Danach soll er sich vor dem Darbringen von Opfern am Altar im Tempel seine Hände und Füße waschen. Der gleiche Vorgang wird nach Abschluss des Opfers wiederholt. Weitere Hinweise sind der Passage nicht zu entnehmen. So werden keine näheren Auskünfte über das Waschen gegeben. Auch wird nichts über die Art des Wassers gesagt, ob es fließendes oder stehendes Wasser ist und wo es sich befindet. Es geht in Jub 21,16 lediglich um die Präparation des Opfernden zum Opferdarbringen. Wichtig ist dabei, dass rituelle Reinheit hergestellt wird, doch nicht, wie dies im Einzelnen geschieht.

Jub 21,16 nimmt verschiedene Gesetzesanweisungen aus dem AT auf und gestaltet daraus eine neue Anweisung. Vor allem ist Ex 30,18–21 aufgenommen, wo es heißt, dass Aaron und seine Söhne vor dem Betreten der Stiftshütte oder dem Altar ihre Hände und Füße im Wasser der Kupferbecken waschen sollen.[21] V. 21 fügt eine Warnung hinzu: die Regel ist zu beachten, damit sie nicht sterben. Von einer Handlung nach dem Opfer ist in Ex 30 nichts erwähnt. Aus Ex 30 ist in Jub 21,16 das Waschen von Händen und Füßen aufgenommen und gedoppelt, indem es nach dem Opfern wiederholt wird. – Möglicherweise liegt auch ein Einfluss aus TestLev 9,11 vor, wo allerdings drei Waschungen begegnen. – Die Waschgefäße aus Ex 30 tauchen in Jub 21 nicht mehr auf, auch geht es in Jub lediglich um den Altar, ohne dass darüber Auskunft erteilt wird, wo der Altar steht (ob er wie in Ex 30 vor der Stiftshütte vorgestellt ist oder ob ein

---

20 Vgl. TestLev 4,3f.; TestSim 7,1; TestNaph 8,1–3; s.a. TestGad 8,1.
21 Zu Ex 30,18–21 s.o. Abschnitt 3.1., wo die atl. Reinigungsriten näher beschrieben sind.

anderer Platz anzunehmen ist, etwa vor oder im Tempel, wie es für die kontemporäre Praxis im 2. Jh. v. Chr. zu erwarten wäre).

Die Todesfolge, die Ex 30,21 im Fall eines Fehlers ankündigt, fehlt in Jub. Stattdessen ist der Kontext von einer ähnlichen Thematik geprägt: dem „Interesse am Blut".[22] So erfolgt mehrmals eine Warnung vor dem Blutgenuss von Opfertieren (21,6f.17f.). Das Blut muss ordnungsgemäß an den Altar gegossen werden und darf keine anderweitige Verwendung finden, da das Blut das Leben enthält.[23] V. 19f. schließen an diesen Gedanken an, indem sie davor warnen, dass das Blut eines Menschen nicht vergossen werden darf (V. 19), und anschließend die Talioformel zitieren: Blut für Blut, d.h. Leben für Leben (V. 20). Diesem Kontext entspricht es, wenn die Waschung von Händen und Füßen nach dem Opfervorgang nunmehr in Jub wiederholt wird. Das Blut darf auf keinen Fall woanders als an den Altar hin gelangen.

Der rituellen Waschung in Jub geht es also einerseits um eine adäquate Vorbereitung auf den Dienst am Altar, für den Reinheit grundlegend ist, sowie andererseits um die Vermeidung von Kontakt mit Blut. Hierin liegt ein Spezifikum dieses Textes. Das Thema Reinheit und Unreinheit ist mit dem Aspekt von Leben und Tod verbunden.[24] Rituelle Reinheit beim Umgang mit dem Altar bedeutet Leben, während ein fehlerhafter Umgang mit Blut den Tod bedeutet. Reinheit und Leben stehen also im Vordergrund.

Dieser Zusammenhang findet sich bei dem Bild Isaaks wieder, insofern er das Leben der Menschen fördern soll.[25] Isaak soll zum Segen für die Menschen werden und das Leben an seine Nachkommen weitergeben (21,25). Dies wird möglich, wenn er sich von Unreinheit fernhält und „das zu Bewahrende des höchsten Gottes" bewahrt (21,23).[26] Das von Gott gewollte Leben lebt in Isaak und seinen Nachkommen also weiter, wenn Unreinheit und Vergießen von Blut vermieden werden. Die Funktion der rituellen Waschung in Jub zeigt damit meines Erachtens eine Ausrichtung auf das Leben. Reinheit und Waschung dienen dazu, das Todbringende zu entfernen und das Leben zu fördern.

3.3. Aristeasbrief

Von Waschungen ist in einem kurzen thematischen Zwischenspiel gegen Ende der Schrift die Rede. In Arist 305f. wird berichtet, wie die Übersetzer des hebräischen Alten Testament ins Griechische jeden Tag vorgehen. Nachdem sie mor-

---

22 K. BERGER, in: *Buch der Jubiläen*, 429, für das Kapitel Jub 21.
23 BERGER, *Buch der Jubiläen*, 432, übersetzt: „denn Blut ist die Seele".
24 Einen Zusammenhang zwischen Unreinheit und Tod stellt auch H. K. HARRINGTON, "Outsiders", 202, her.
25 Zu Jub als Interpretation der Genesis vgl. J. T. A. G. M. VAN RUITEN, *Primaeval History*; J. VANDERKAM, „Origins and Purposes".
26 So die Übersetzung von BERGER, *Buch der Jubiläen*, 434.

gens dem König ihre Aufwartung machten, wuschen sie ihre Hände im Meer, wie wenn sie beteten (Arist 305). Danach gingen sie an ihr Werk, die Schriften zu lesen, zu interpretieren und zu übersetzen. In Anschluss wird in Arist 306 eine Frage gestellt, wie man sie von Nicht-Juden, denen jüdische Bräuche fremd sind, erwarten würde. Die Frage lautet, warum das Waschen von Händen vor dem Beten überhaupt notwendig sei. Die Antwort lautet: damit sie bezeugen, nichts Schlechtes zu tun, denn jede Tätigkeit geschieht durch Hände.[27] Der Text erläutert weiter, dass es einem frommen Juden um ein Leben in Gerechtigkeit und Wahrheit gehe.

In diesen zwei Versen ist zweimal vom dem Brauch, vor dem Beten die Hände zu waschen, die Rede. Dies wird mittels der Vergleichspartikel ὡς auf den Übersetzungsvorgang übertragen. Arist 305 bildet dabei die detailliertere Angabe: Das Waschen soll *im Meer* erfolgen (ἀνανιψάμενοι τῇ θαλάσσῃ τὰς χεῖρας). Arist 306 nimmt das Waschen auf und fügt eine erläuternde Begründung hinzu, die eine Deutung zu den Händen gibt. Vom spezifischen Vorgang von Beten und Übersetzen wird nunmehr auf das Leben von Juden überhaupt eingegangen und der Brauch auf eine generelle Ethik der Alltagswelt bezogen. Wer als frommer (ὅσιος) Jude lebt, handelt nach den Maßstäben von Gerechtigkeit (δικαιοσύνη) und Wahrheit (ἀλήθεια). Damit wird das Waschen der Hände zugleich mit der im Aristeasbrief häufig begegnenden Deutung von „Geboten als Mahnung zur Gerechtigkeit und Warnung vor Machtmißbrauch" verbunden[28]. Es geht am Ende von Arist 306 nicht mehr nur um die Personengruppe der Übersetzer selbst, sondern die Deutung wird auf eine ethnisch und zugleich religiös qualifizierte Gruppe ausgeweitet.

Arist 305f. führt einen jüdischen Brauch (ἔθος ἐστίν) an. Woher der Brauch stammt und inwieweit er tatsächlich verbreitet war, geht aus dem Schreiben nicht hervor.[29] Sucht man nach Vorbildern für das Waschen von Händen im Meer vor dem Beten im AT, so fallen unterschiedliche Anknüpfungen an atl. Aussagen auf, ohne dass der Brauch aus Arist 305f. ein exaktes Vorbild hätte.

> Am nächsten kommt ihm Dtn 21,6, wo es um das Waschen der Hände (νίψονται τὰς χεῖρας) geht. Der Zusammenhang ist jedoch recht speziell, da es sich um eine kasuistische Anweisung als Sühne für Blutschuld (ἐξιλασθήσεται αὐτοῖς τὸ αἷμα, 21,8) in einem anonymen Mordfall außerhalb einer Stadt handelt. Es soll einer jungen Kuh das Genick gebrochen werden. Danach sollen sich die Ältesten der Stadt (als Gremium ἡ γερουσία τῆς πόλεως in LXX und als Gruppe von leitenden

---

27 Vgl. die Übersetzung von N. MEISER, *Aristeasbrief*, 83: „dass sie damit bezeugten, nichts Schlechtes getan zu haben – denn jede Tätigkeit geschieht vermittels der Hände".
28 Vgl. MEISER, *Aristeasbrief*, 40.
29 Nach MEISER, *Aristeasbrief*, 39f., stammt Arist 305f. wie aus 128–171 „aus einem breiten Strom ... des hellenistischen Judentums" (ebd., 40), der Gemeinsamkeiten mit Philo habe. Außer einem Verweis auf Mos 2,138 (a.a.O., 83; dazu s.o.) gibt Meiser leider keine nähere Auskünfte, worauf er sich bezieht.

Verantwortlichen זקני העיר in HB) über dem Kopf der Kuh die Hände waschen, was als Ausdruck ihrer Unschuld interpretiert wird. Der geschilderte Fall ist also ein gänzlich anderer als die Szene in Arist.

Eine gewisse Nähe ergibt sich des Weiteren zu Ex 19,10.14, wo gesagt wird, dass das Volk Israel vor dem Verlesen des Dekalogs durch Mose die Kleider gewaschen hat (19,14: πλυνάτωσαν τὰ ἱμάτια). Dieser Vorgang dient der Heiligung des Volkes (ἅγνισον αὐτοῦ, V. 14). Gemeinsamkeit mit Arist 305 besteht darin, dass eine Waschung vor dem Kontakt mit den Worten Gottes bzw. der Schrift geschieht. Ein weiterer Anknüpfungspunkt liegt darin, dass das Waschen eine zusätzliche Deutung erhält, die über den rituellen Vorgang hinausgeht. Ist dies hier mit dem Begriff der Heiligung umschrieben, so setzt Arist dafür die im alexandrinischen Frühjudentum verbreiteten Stichworte Gerechtigkeit (δικαιοσύνη) und Wahrheit (ἀλήθεια) ein.[30] Als Differenz zwischen beiden Belegen ist festzuhalten, dass in Arist die Hände gewaschen werden, während es in Ex 19 um Kleidung geht.

Eine weitere Nähe könnte zu Judit 12,7f. bestehen. Hier geht es um eine Vorbereitung zum Festmahl. Drei Tage lang badet sich Judit in einer Quelle (ἐβαπτίζετο ἐπὶ τῆς πηγῆς τοῦ ὕδατος) und betet anschließend zu Gott (καὶ ὡς ἀνέβη ἐδέετο τοῦ κυρίου θεοῦ Ισραηλ), dass er ihren Weg gelingen lassen möge. Übereinstimmung mit Arist besteht in der Abfolge von Waschen und Beten. Ferner ist das Wasser vergleichbar, insofern jeweils fließendes Wasser verwendet wird, einmal als Quellwasser und einmal als Meerwasser. Ferner könnte man darin eine Gemeinsamkeit sehen, dass die Waschung als eine Vorbereitung auf eine folgende Handlung dient. Eine Differenz besteht allerdings in der Terminologie (βαπτίζω gegenüber ἀνανίψω). Auch ist nicht eindeutig zu entscheiden, ob die Reinigung als Vorbereitung auf das Gebet oder das anschließende Essen dient.[31]

Schließlich könnte man auch noch auf Jes 1,16 verweisen, wo es um eine innere Reinigung geht. Dort ergeht die Aufforderung an das Volk, sich zu waschen, um sich vom Blut zu reinigen, bevor Gott die Gebete wieder hören will: „Wascht euch, damit ihr rein werdet ...entfernt das Böse" (λούσασθε καθαροὶ γένεσθε ἀφέλετε τὰς πονηρίας ἀπὸ τῶν ψυχῶν ὑμῶν). Die Gemeinsamkeit mit Arist besteht in der Verbindung von Waschen und dem Entfernen des Bösen. Ferner ist die Verbindung von Beten und Waschen zu beachten. Dabei ist interessant, dass in Jes 1 das Beten nicht nur durch die Wendung πληθύνητε τὴν δέησιν bezeichnet ist, sondern auch anhand seiner charakteristischen Geste dem Ausbreiten der Hände (τὰς χεῖρας ἐκτείνητε πρός με) genannt ist, wodurch die Nähe zu Arist 305f. größer wird, weil beide Male die Hände ins Spiel gebracht werden. Es sind aber auch Differenzen auszumachen. So geht es in Jes 1 nicht um eine rituelle Reinigung, sondern um ein Ablegen von Schuld und eine ethische Veränderung des Lebenswandels. Die Reinheit zielt auf eine innere Haltung, die erfüllt sein soll, bevor das Volk wieder vor Gott treten kann.

---

30 S.a. Philo Fug 1,41; Mut 1,49; SpecLeg 1,259f.
31 Vgl. die Überlegungen bei LAWRENCE, Washing, 59f.

Die atl. Belege sprechen allesamt nicht von einem Brauch, wie er in Arist 305f. im Blick ist. Sie illustrieren Einzelsituationen, die eine größere oder kleinere Schnittmenge mit dem in Arist 305f. begegnenden Vorgang haben. Einen allgemein gültigen jüdischen Brauch (ἔθος ἐστὶν πᾶσι τοῖς Ἰουδαίοις, Arist 305) kann man aus ihnen aber nicht ableiten.[32]

Ähnliches findet sich allenfalls noch bei Josephus, der aber seinerseits von Arist abhängig sein mag.[33] In Ant 12,106 gibt Josephus als Vorgehen der Übersetzer an, dass sie ihre Hände im Meer waschen und sich reinigen, damit sie für das Übersetzen des Gesetzes gerüstet sind (τῇ θαλάσσῃ τὰς χεῖρας ἀπονιπτόμενοι καὶ καθαίροντες αὑτοὺς οὕτως ἐπὶ τὴν τῶν νόμων ἑρμηνείαν ἐτρέποντο). Von einem allgemein gängigen Brauch schreibt Josephus – anders als Arist – allerdings nichts.

Wenn es tatsächlich einen solchen Brauch gegeben hat, so stellt dieser eine Neuerung im 2. Jh. v. Chr. dar,[34] der in Arist womöglich Autorität verliehen werden sollte.[35] Nimmt man die Textaussagen ernst und fragt nach einer möglichen Praxis eines Hände-Waschen-Rituals, so könnte es sich um einen lediglich lokalen Brauch handeln[36] oder eine Praxis schildern, die aufgrund der spezifischen Aufgabe der Übersetzung in Geltung kam.[37] Angesichts der sparsamen Bezeugung eines solchen Brauchs kommt man hier über Mutmaßungen jedoch nicht hinaus.

Was in Arist 305f. zu erkennen ist, ist eine Deutung des Ritus im Zusammenhang der Aufgabe, die dadurch eine Bewertung erfährt. Das Waschen der

---

32 So auch das Urteil von Lawrence, Washing, 56f.61; s.a.106f.
33 Vgl. Lawrence, Washing, 57.
34 Möglich wäre es, dass hier eine Übertragung aus der griechisch-römischen Literatur vorliegt, wo der Brauch begegnet, nach einer Schlacht die Hände zu waschen. Diesen Hinweis verdanke ich Hans Dieter Betz, den er in der Diskussion auf Lesbos über diesen Beitrag äußerte.
35 So eine Vermutung von Lawrence, Washing, 78.109. Als Parallele verweist er (ebd., 109f.) zudem auf einen Abschnitt aus dem Aramäischen Testamentum Levi (ATL), 4Q213 Kol. I Z.7–10, wo die Abfolge von Waschen und Beten begegnet, wobei Lawrence die Lakunen im Text durch Waschen der Kleidung, Reinigung mit Wasser und Baden ergänzt. Textlich gesichert ist lediglich eine Waschung. Dieses Waschen Levis ist allerdings nicht spezifisch und bildet nach dem (fragmentarischen, doch gesicherten) Wortlaut auch keinen Teil eines Reinigungsritus; Levi dankt im Folgenden für die Gaben, die Gott ihm verliehen hat. Ein Anlass für einen Reinigungsritus liegt nicht vor und ist vom Textbestand weder in ATL noch in TestLev nahegelegt.
36 Als Argument dafür könnte man auf das Waschen *im Meer* hinweisen, das nur an einem Küstenort mit Meerzugang – wie etwa Alexandria – möglich ist.
37 Als Nachwirkung des Brauchs könnte man auf die Annahme von S. Haber, "Judaism", 65, verweisen, die davon ausgeht, dass es im Diasporajudentum rituelle Waschungen in Form von „sprinkling, splashing, or hand washing" gegeben hat, wofür sie wesentlich auch auf Arist 305f, verweist. Nahe dazu steht auch ihre weitere Aussage, a.a.O. 71, dass in Synagogen der Diaspora, die oftmals in Wassernähe errichtet wurden, seit dem 2. Jh. v. Chr. „water was used for ritual ablutions prior to prayer or the handling of the Torah". Des Weiteren (a.a.O. 71ff.) verweist sie auf Miqwaoth in Synagogen, denen hier jedoch nicht weiter nachgegangen werden kann; s. dazu den Beitrag von Seán Freyne in dieser Publikation.

Hände im Meer stellt einen solchen Reinigungsritus dar, der die Übersetzer in die Lage versetzt, Gott in Form seines Wortes begegnen zu können. Wesentlich für Arist ist dabei, dass die Waschung die Übersetzer dem Zustand von Gerechtigkeit (δικαιοσύνη) und Wahrheit (ἀλήθεια) näher bringt. Das Wasser beseitigt das Trennende zwischen Mensch und Gott und lässt den Menschen als Reinen vor Gott treten.

3.4. Frühjüdische Reinigungsaussagen außerhalb von Qumran

Zusammenfassend ist festzuhalten, dass es eine Inhomogenität bezüglich der Reinigungsaussagen in frühjüdischen Texten gibt. Es lässt sich aus ihnen kein fester Ritus ermitteln. Reinigungen sind mit verschiedenen Situationen verbunden und in einen Deutungshorizont einer Schrift integriert worden. Reinigungsaussagen haben dabei nicht so sehr einen Wert an sich, sondern unterstützen in ihrem jeweiligen Kontext die Themen des Gesamtkorpus. So fällt nicht nur der Ritus, sondern auch die thematische Einbindung von Reinigungen indifferent aus.

Trotz des schmalen Befundes zieht Jonathan Lawrence dennoch eine mutige Schlussfolgerung hinsichtlich möglicher Anwendungsbereiche von Reinigungsriten im Frühjudentum:

> The very diversity of practices described in these texts suggests that this period saw a great deal of innovation in the practice of ritual washing and its significance. We cannot say unequivocally how a certain practice was performed, but we can be confident that these practices were being performed in some way and were considered quite important.[38]

Die Schlussfolgerung ist möglich, doch möchte ich etwas zurückhaltender von den Reinigungen sprechen, wie sie im jeweiligen literarischen Textkorpus entfaltet sind. Es ist durchaus möglich, dass hinter den Texten reale Abläufe durchscheinen oder umgekehrt Reinigungsvorgänge der Wirklichkeit von den Texten aufgenommen und gedeutet werden. Allerdings gibt es keine klaren Aussagen über die tatsächlichen Abläufe zu einer bestimmten Zeit und an einem Ort. Es muss m.E. bei Deutungen von Reinigungsaussagen in literarischen Zeugnissen bleiben, in denen das Wasser einen Beitrag zu Themen vom Leben des Menschen vor Gott leistet.

4. Reinigungsriten in den Schriften vom Toten Meer

Der Großteil der frühjüdischen Belege für Reinigungsriten ist in den Schriften vom Toten Meer zu finden. Unter ihnen kommt das besondere Schwergewicht

---

[38] So LAWRENCE, Washing 78.

solchen Schriften oder Schriftteilen zu, die eine Auslegung atl. Gesetzespartien bieten. Unter ihnen wiederum sind drei Gruppen von Schriften zu unterscheiden: die Tempelrolle (4.1.), das halachische Material aus Qumran (4.2.) sowie Schriften, die das Leben der Gemeinschaft regeln (4.3. und 4.4.). Diesen Texten ist nunmehr nachzugehen.

4.1. Tempelrolle (11Q19 / 11Q20)

Die Tempelrolle 11Q19, die eine frühe (vor-qumranische) Schrift vom Toten Meer darstellt,[39] enthält zwei Abschnitte über Reinheitsgesetze, einen in 45,15–46,13 und den anderen in 48–51,10.[40] Sie werden unterbrochen durch Angaben zum Bau des Heiligtums und der Stadt, was wiederum den bis 45,14 reichenden Abschnitt fortsetzt. Die Abfolgen sind strukturell nicht ganz geradlinig, doch lassen sich thematische Blöcke erkennen, in denen die beiden genannten Themen vorherrschen.

Beide Abschnitte über Reinigungsriten bieten Rezeption und Interpretation der Schrift, wie sie auch in anderen Bereichen der Tempelrolle zu finden ist. Entsprechend dem Charakter der Tempelrolle als *rewritten document* oder *rewritten bible* werden atl. Gebote aufgegriffen und neu interpretiert.[41] Wesentlich geht es in den hier vorzustellenden Abschnitten des Dokuments um Fragen der Reinheit, von denen zunächst das Heiligtum und ihm unmittelbar nachfolgend die gesamte Stadt, in der der Tempel steht, betroffen ist (vgl. 46,21–24; 47,11–19). Das Heiligtum strahlt nach dem Entwurf der Tempelrolle – in konzentrischen Kreisen ansteigender Heiligkeit in Richtung auf den Tempel, begründet durch Gottes Präsenz darin – auf sein näheres Umfeld, d.h. die Stadt Jerusalem aus. Die atl. Reinheitsvorschriften werden in dem Entwurf der Tempelrolle damit auf die gesamte Stadt ausgeweitet,[42] so dass sie letztlich als

---

39 Die Entstehungszeit der Tempelrolle im 2. Jh. v.Chr. anzunehmen (vgl. J. MAIER, *Tempelrolle*, 47–51: zwischen 175 und 150 v.Chr.; A. STEUDEL, *Texte*, 3: erste Hälfte des 2. Jh.; Y. YADIN, *Tempelrolle* 238–242, und G. W. E. NICKELSBURG, *Literature*, 158: drittes Viertel des 2. Jh.). Allerdings ist älteres Quellenmaterial aus dem 4. Jh. oder 3. Jh. verarbeitet worden; vgl. S. WHITE CRAWFORD, *Temple Scroll*, 24–26.29.

40 Wenn man dem Modell von A. M. WILSON/L. WILLS, "Literary Sources", 275–288, folgt, an das WERRETT, *Ritual Purity*, 108.111, anschließt, bildet der Abschnitt 48–51,10 eine eigenständige Quelle der Tempelrolle. Gegenüber dieser Abgrenzung ist jedoch auffällig, dass das Thema ritueller Reinheit bereits ab 45,15 beginnt.

41 Vgl. die literarische Kennzeichnung als „nomographic" bei B. A. LEVINE, „Temple Scroll", 17–21, die aus Verschmelzungen, Harmonisierungen und zusätzlichen Anweisungen entsteht, einer dem Pescher oder Midrasch ähnlichen literarischen Technik. SCHIFFMAN, „Deuteronomic Paraphrase", 546, nennt sieben Kategorien von Variationen zur literarischen Stilisierung des *rewritten document*.

42 Vgl. J. KLAWANS, *Impurity*, 49: „We could describe 11QT's approach to ritual impurity as 'expansive.'" S.a. WERRETT, *Ritual Purity*, 171, der „the tendency … to elevate both the city Jerusalem and the laity to a suspicious high level of purity" in der Tempelrolle ausmacht.

der heilige und rituell rein zu haltenden Raum besondere Beachtung findet (vgl. z.B. 47,26f.: ולוא תטמאו את מקדשי ועירי).[43]

4.1.1. 11Q19 45,15–46,13

Die erste Stelle bildet einen Übergang und ist sowohl mit dem vorhergehenden Gedankengang als auch mit dem folgenden Abschnitt thematisch verknüpft.[44] 45,15 beschließt den Teil der Tempelrolle, in dem Dienstabteilungen der Leviten eingeteilt werden. An dessen Ende in 45,13f. ist eine Anweisung zu lesen, dass jede Dienstabteilung nach ihrem Dienstende die Zellen im Tempel reinigen (טהר) soll. Diese Reinigung sieht einerseits wie ein profaner Vorgang einer wöchentlichen Säuberung aus; nach sieben Arbeitstagen entsteht praktischer Bedarf zur Reinigung.[45] Zugleich bildet dieser Vorgang aber die Reinheit des Heiligtums ab (vgl. 45,18; 46,18f.), wofür auch der verwendete Terminus טהר[46] spricht.[47] Dieser Gedankengang ist eine ureigene Neuschöpfung der Tempelrolle mit der ihr eigenen Fokussierung auf die Leviten und deren Rolle in der Sorge für den Tempel.[48]

Die Bedeutung der Reinheit des Tempels und der Stadt geht deutlich aus der Fortsetzung hervor, wobei jetzt atl. Gesetze interpretiert werden. In 45,15–20 ergeht die Anweisung, dass ein Mann nach einem nächtlichen Samenerguss am ersten und am dritten Tag seine Kleider waschen (כבס)[49] und sich baden

---

43 Ist gegen diese Interpretation die Realitätsferne der Angaben in der Tempelrolle eingewendet worden (WHITE CRAWFORD, Tempel Scroll, 49, löst dies durch die Annahme von ausschließlich temporären Bewohnern der Stadt; eine Interpretation, die aber nicht auf Signale im Text zurückgreifen kann), so ist dagegen wiederum einzuwenden, dass die Tempelrolle eine eigenständige Konstruktion bietet, mittels derer eine eigene und neue Sinnzuschreibung erfolgt, die in mehreren Aspekten abweichende Setzungen als die in der Realität gegebenen Voraussetzungen enthält; vgl. A. LABAHN, Licht und Heil, 39–41.

44 Zu den Problemen der Abgrenzung, zum Teil in der Forschung verbunden mit Thesen zur Quellenscheidung, vgl. WHITE CRAWFORD, Tempel Scroll, 42f.

45 Mit dieser Möglichkeit rechnet auch WERRETT, Ritual Purity, 8.

46 Die Grundbedeutung von טהר ist nach HAH[17] 271f. im Qal „rein s., w." und im Piel „reinigen", „f. rein erklären"; s.a. Hitpael: „sich reinigen"; HAL 354 gibt für qal „rein sein" und für piel „f. rein erklären" an. Die Reinheit, die der Terminus bezeichnet, ist also in erster Linie rituelle Reinheit. Zum Gebrauch von טהר in den Schriften vom Toten Meer vgl. auch B. JANOWSKI, H. LICHTENBERGER, „Enderwartung" 32–35.

47 Vgl. WHITE CRAWFORD, Tempel Scroll, 42, die darauf verweist, dass die Themen Heiligkeit und Reinheit von Tempel und Stadt in der Tempelrolle miteinander korreliert sind. S.a. F. GARCÍA MARTÍNEZ, „Problem of Purity", 143–146; JANOWSKI/LICHTENBERGER, „Enderwartung", 37–41.

48 Vgl. A. LABAHN, Licht und Heil, 18ff.

49 Als Bedeutung für כבס gibt HAH[17] 334 im Piel „waschen" an, was oft für Kleidung gebraucht wird. Eine weitere Spezifikation wird nicht genannt. HAL 438 gibt für piel „walken, reinigen" an.

soll (רחץ)[50]. Erst nach Ablauf von drei Tagen und nach Durchführung dieser Reinigungsriten darf er das Heiligtum nach dem Sonnenuntergang (wieder) betreten.[51] Ohne Einhaltung dieser Riten gilt er als ein Unreiner und darf als solcher das Heiligtum nicht betreten. Denn, so die Begründung: das Heiligtum muss rein bleiben (45,18). Die Tempelrolle legt hier Lev 15,16–18 aus. In Lev 15 beträgt die rituelle Unreinheit, die dort naturgemäß lediglich auf den Tempel bezogen ist, nur einen Tag und wird durch eine gründliche Waschung des gesamten Körpers beendet. Demgegenüber gelten in der Tempelrolle strengere Regeln mit weit reicherenden Konsequenzen.[52]

Der Argumentationsgang wird in den folgenden Versen fortgesetzt, indem er auf weitere Fälle körperlicher Unreinheit bezogen wird. In 45,23–25 wird gesagt, dass jemand, der von Ausfluss rein geworden ist, am siebten Tag seine Kleider waschen und seinen ganzen Körper in fließendem Wasser baden soll (רחץ את כול בשרו במים חיים). Erst danach darf er die Stadt und das Heiligtum wieder betreten. Die Tempelrolle legt die Gesetze über Aussätzige aus Lev 14 aus. Während Lev 14 komplizierte verschiedenartige Opfervorgänge nach der Heilung vorsieht, reicht für die Tempelrolle das Baden (רחץ). Allerdings fügt sie hinzu, dass dies in lebendigem Wasser (מים חיים), also fließendem natürlichem Gewässer,[53] geschehen soll. Der Reinigungsvorgang wird damit konzentriert auf den Akt der Waschung. Auch werden keine präzisen Angaben gemacht, wie das Ganzkörperbad zu erfolgen hat. Bei der Reinigung sind keine weiteren Personen als die Betroffenen selbst genannt. Im Fall einer Verunreinigung trägt jeder selbst dafür Verantwortung, die angemessenen Maßnahmen einzuleiten

---

50 Die Grundbedeutung von רחץ ist nach HAH[17] 756 (1) „waschen" und (2) „sich waschen, baden"; HAL 1138 gibt für den qal an: „1. Mit Wasser begießen, abspülen, waschen ... 2. sich waschen ... 3. baden ... 4. abspülen ... sich waschen, baden, ...5. abspülen, waschen". Die Bedeutung „baden" wird in den frühjüdischen Schriften vom Toten Meer zum hauptsächlichen Bedeutungsspektrum dieses Begriffs, indem ein Baden als Waschung des ganzen Körpers zentral wird.

51 Die Frist bis Sonnenuntergang sehen KAZEN, Jesus and Purity Halakhah, 75f.; J. MAGNESS, Archaeology of Qumran, 135, als entscheidende Zeitspanne in der Zeit des Zweiten Tempels an; diese Zeit muss vergehen, bevor ein Unreiner wieder rein wird. Nach KLAWANS, Impurity, 49, stellt dies eine Neuerung der Tempelrolle dar (mit Verweis auf 49,19–21; 51,2–5), die es in Qumran aber auch sonst gibt (mit Verweis auf 1QM 7,4f.; 14,2f.; 1QS 2,4–11; CD 12,1f.). Doch auch das AT kennt schon die Bestimmung, dass Reinheit erst nach Sonnenuntergang wirksam wird.

52 KLAWANS, Impurity, 49, unterscheidet hinsichtlich der Frage nach Reinheit zwischen den Schriften aus Qumran und der Tempelrolle. Während in den Qumran-Schriften rituelle und moralische Unreinheit identifiziert werden, gelte hier, dass die Quelle für rituelle Unreinheit Sünde ist. In der Tempelrolle sei dies anders. Klawans zieht daraus die Schlussfolgerung, dass die Tempelrolle hinsichtlich der rituellen Reinheit mit Qumran übereingeht, hinsichtlich der moralischen Reinheit allerdings mit dem AT.

53 Die Wendung מים חיים wird zur gängigen Bezeichnung für fließendes Wasser, d.h. Flusswasser oder Wasser in einem See ist gemeint.

und diese selbst durchzuführen, ohne dass etwa Priester oder andere Personen dabei beteiligt wären.

Wichtiger als die Festlegung der exakten Durchführung von Reinigungsriten scheint der Tempelrolle die Interpretation der Reinigung zu sein. Wenn lebendiges Wasser benutzt wird, lässt dies die Lebensqualität des Menschen zu ihm zurückkommen. Durch den Vorgang der rituellen Reinigung wird die Unreinheit von ihm abgewaschen, so dass er wieder lebens- und kontaktfähig wird. Die rituelle Veränderung schafft die Grundlage dafür, dass er wieder in die soziale Gruppe der Menschen, die in der Stadt leben und im Heiligtum ihren Glauben praktizieren, aufgenommen wird.[54] Durch die rituelle Reinigung kehrt die Lebendigkeit zum Menschen zurück.

Weitere Vorgaben im Umfeld von Unreinheit schließen sich in der Tempelrolle an diese Aussagen an. Ein analoges Verbot, die Stadt und das Heiligtum zu betreten, gilt nach 45,25f. auch für die Menschen, die entweder Kontakt mit Toten hatten oder von Aussatz betroffen sind oder an einer Hautkrankheit leiden. Sie müssen zuerst rein werden (טהר). Welche Reinigungsriten dabei im Einzelnen vorzunehmen sind, wird jetzt nicht weiter ausgeführt. Wahrscheinlich ist an die zuvor genannten Abläufe oder ganz ähnliche Vorgänge zu denken.[55]

4.1.2. 11Q19 48–51,10

An dieses Themenfeld knüpfen die Angaben über Reinigungen in 49,18–28 an. Dort geht es um Häuser, in denen es einen Sterbefall gab. Nachdem der Tote aus dem Haus gebracht worden ist, soll man das Haus einer gründlichen Reinigung unterziehen und alles im Haus mit Wasser abwaschen (ויכבסו במים, 49,20) sowie die Wände und Türen des Hauses abschaben. Diese Reinigung meint einerseits tatsächlich einen intensiven Hausputz, schließt aber auch eine rituelle Reinigung ein. Dies geht vor allem aus der Anweisung hervor, die Geräte, die rituell rein sein müssen, zu waschen (יתכבסו ... וכול כלים אשר יש להמה טהרה, 49,22f.).

Von der Reinigung sind auch alle Menschen betroffen, die sich dauerhaft oder zwischenzeitig in dem Haus aufgehalten haben (49,23–28). Ihnen sind folgende Reinigungsriten vorgeschrieben: Am ersten und am siebten Tag sollen sie sich im Wasser baden (ירחץ במים, 49,24) und ihre Kleider waschen (ויכבס בגדיו, 49,24). Vom Abend des siebten Tages an gelten sie dann wieder als rein. Außer dem Hinweis auf die Notwendigkeit der Waschung folgen keine konkreten Angaben. So wird nicht gesagt, welche Art Wasser Verwendung finden soll oder in welchem Becken dies geschehen kann.

---

54 Die Reinigungsvorschriften hat García Martínez, "Problem of Purity", 146, als Ausweitung priesterlicher (atl. und rabbinischer) Vorschriften auf alle Menschen interpretiert.

55 Werrett, Ritual Purification, 145f., nimmt daher ein Sprengen von Reinigungswasser (מי נדה) am ersten und siebten Tag an.

Der Abschnitt 49,23–28 ist Schriftauslegung von Num 19,11f., wo festgelegt ist, dass man sich nach der Berührung eines Toten am dritten und am siebten Tag reinigen muss (טמא / ἁγνισθήσεται, V.11), und zwar mit Reinigungswasser (so allerdings nur in LXX: ὕδωρ ῥαντισμοῦ, V.12; vgl. V.13.20, wo es auch in HB steht: מי נדה[56]). Diese Anweisung ist hier generell auf Sterbefälle in den Häusern ausgeweitet. Betroffen von den Reinigungsvorschriften sind nicht mehr nur die Personen, die den Toten berührt haben, sondern alle, die sich mit ihm in einem Haus aufgehalten haben. An der aus Num 19 bekannten zweimaligen Waschung ist festgehalten, allerdings ist aus dem dritten und siebten Tag in Num nunmehr der erste[57] und siebte Tag in der Tempelrolle geworden.

> In Num 19,16–22 ist darüber hinaus noch ein umfangreicherer Vorgang zur Wiedererlangung der Reinheit vorgeschrieben. Wer einen Toten berührt hat,[58] soll einen reinen Mann bitten, ihn mit einer Mischung aus der Asche eines Sündopfers und fließendem Wasser (מים חיים / ὕδωρ ζῶν) zu besprengen, wobei dieses Gemisch mit einem Ysop aufgetragen wird, das ins Wasser getaucht wird (זוב וטבל במים / ὕσσωπον καὶ βάψει εἰς τὸ ὕδωρ, 19,17f.). Der reine Mann, der die Handlung durchführt (איש טהור / ἀνὴρ καθαρός), soll anschließend seine Kleider waschen und sich im Wasser baden (וכבס בגדיו ורחץ במים) und bis zum Abend warten, bis er selbst wieder rein ist (19,19). Dieser Vorgang wird in der Tempelrolle nicht rezipiert. Auch ist nicht davon die Rede, dass eine andere Person als der Unreine an dem Prozess beteiligt sei.

Aus dem Umstand, dass bereits ein Sich-Aufhalten in dem Sterbehaus ausreicht, um Reinheit zu verlieren, ist deutlich zu ersehen, dass es sich hierbei um rituelle Reinheit handelt. Die Ausweitung der Reinheitsvorschriften entspricht einer Intensivierung der Reinheit, wie sie der Tempelrolle eigen ist.[59] Der reine Bezirk

---

56 Die Wendung מי נדה begegnet in HB nicht sehr oft; HAH[17] 487 übersetzt sie mit „Wasser als Reinigungsmittel gegen Unreinheit". Oftmals wird schlicht von „Reinigungswasser" gesprochen, was aber verkürzend ist und dem hebräischen Ausdruck seinen Anstoß nimmt; vgl. als Grundbedeutung von נדה laut HAII[17] 487 „Abscheuliches, Unreines", nach HAL 636 „1. Blutgang, Menstruation ... 2. Ausscheidung, Abscheuliches, Befleckung". Hinsichtlich des Begriffs scheint es im Frühjudentum eine Umorientierung gegeben zu haben. Eine illustrative Deutung bietet WERRETT, *Ritual Purity*, 262, der eine Entwicklung von נדה zu מי נדה beobachtet, indem er feststellt: „The similarity between the word נדה and the phrase מי נדה may well go a long way towards explaining why it is that the מי נדה (…), seems to have evolved into a ritual that was capable of cleansing any sort of contamination that fell under the category of נדה".

57 Zur Diskussion um den ersten Tag der Reinigung vgl. WERRETT, *Ritual Purity*, 139f., der diesen Vorgang als Ermöglichung von „non-sacred contact with persons, objects, and food" (ebd. 139) interpretiert.

58 S.a. die Rezeption dieser Vorschrift in Sir 31,25(34,30): wer einen Toten anrührt und wäscht sich danach und rührt ihn wieder an, was nützt es ihm (βαπτιζόμενος ἀπὸ νεκροῦ καὶ πάλιν ἁπτόμενος αὐτοῦ τί ὠφέλησεν ἐν τῷ λουτρῷ αὐτοῦ). Hier ist zur Waschung jetzt allerdings der Begriff βαπτιζόμενος verwendet. Ist hier ein erstes Anzeichen für eine terminologische Veränderung zu erkennen oder liegt poetische Sprache vor, die nicht zu sehr gepresst werden sollte?

59 Ähnlich urteilt WHITE CRAWFORD, *Tempel Scroll*, 44.

und die darin lebenden reinen Menschen werden streng von allem kultisch Unreinen getrennt.

An diesen Gedankengang knüpft der Fortgang des Textes in der Tempelrolle an. In 50,9ff. folgen noch einmal Angaben zur Reinigung, und zwar für den Fall, wenn jemand einen Toten berührt hat. Diese Angaben sind näher an den Vorgaben aus Num 19,16ff. – darauf weist vielleicht auch der Rekurs auf die Gesetzesvorschrift in 50,13: כחוק המשפט (vgl. Z. 14: כמשפט התורה) hin. Da der Anfang des Textes in Spalte 50,1–8 nicht gut überliefert ist, ist der Bezug im Kontext nicht ganz klar. Deutlich ist aber, dass von einer zweiten Waschung am siebten Tag die Rede ist, die mit Reinigungswasser (מי טהרה) durchgeführt werden soll. Weiter heißt es, dass jemand, der einen Toten berührt hat, sein Kleid waschen und sich baden soll, damit er wieder rein wird (יכבס בגדיו ורחץ וטהר, 50,15). Eine Veränderung des Zustandes tritt dann nach Sonnenuntergang ein (Z. 16), wenn die rituelle Reinheit wieder vollständig hergestellt ist.

Ein weiterer Fall von Kontakt mit einem Toten schließt sich an. In 50,17–23 geht es um eine Totgeburt, für die es kein Äquivalent im AT gibt.[60] Bei einer Totgeburt werden sowohl die Mutter als auch jeder und alles, wer und was mit ihr in Kontakt gekommen ist, unrein.[61] Als Reinigungsvorschrift wird angegeben, dass am ersten Tag eine Waschung der Kleider und ein Baden im Wasser erfolgen soll (וכבס בגדיו ורחץ במים, Z. 19.20), wie es zuvor bei den andern Fällen auch schon genannt war. Etwas anders geht es danach weiter. Am dritten Tag soll dies wiederholt werden und zudem soll gesprengt werden (יזה)[62]. Das Objekt des Sprengens wird nicht explizit erwähnt, doch ist wohl an Reinigungswasser zu denken.[63] Am siebten Tag ist der gesamte Vorgang des dritten Tages zu wiederholen, bevor die rituelle Reinheit wieder hergestellt ist. Die Vorschrift ist hier in zweierlei Weise ausgeweitet, indem einerseits ein dritter Tag mit Reinigungsriten verbracht werden muss und andererseits eine dritte Reinigungsart genannt wird: das Besprengen. Wie das Besprengen erfolgen soll, wird leider nicht weiter entfaltet. Weder sind Angaben zum Wasser noch zu den verwendeten Gegenständen zu finden.

Überraschend ist, wie intensiv die Reinigung ausfällt, die hier gefordert ist. Eine Totgeburt stellt offensichtlich einen schweren Fall von Unreinheit dar. Dies liegt wohl daran, dass der unmittelbare und enge körperliche Kontakt von

---

60 Vgl. WHITE CRAWFORD, *Tempel Scroll*, 45, die zudem auf Parallelen bei den Rabbinen verweist, wo ein Dissens darüber besteht, ob der tote Fötus erst beim Verlassen des Uterus für rituelle Unreinheit sorgt oder schon vorher.

61 Diese Angaben betrachtet GARCÍA MARTÍNEZ, "Problem of Purity", 146f., als Verschärfung gegenüber rabbinischen Vorschriften.

62 Als Bedeutung für נזה gibt HAH[17] 494 im Qal „spritzen an etw." und für Hifil „sprengen, spritzen" an; nach HAL 645 bedeutet qal „spritzen" und hifil „1. sprengen ... 2. c. acc. etw. besprengen mit". Im Hifil begegnet זה im Pentateuch.

63 So interpretiert es auch die Übersetzung von STEUDEL, *Texte*, 107.

Totem und Lebendigem, bzw. vom Toten im Lebendigen, Gefährdung für das Leben birgt. Die Tempelrolle sieht in dieser engen Verbindung von Tod und Leben offensichtlich eine große Gefahr derart, dass das Leben vom Tod bedroht ist. Damit das Leben weitergehen kann, müssen intensive Maßnahmen ergriffen werden.

Weitere Fälle von Kontakt mit Toten schließen sich an. Auch in Spalte 51 ist der Anfang nicht erhalten, doch geht es jetzt wohl um den Kontakt mit toten Tieren (vgl. 51,11, wo von Haut, Knochen und Klauen die Rede ist). Auch hierbei gilt, dass ein Waschen der Kleider und ein Baden im Wasser notwendig werden, um Reinheit zurück zu erhalten.

Zum Abschluss dieses Abschnitts folgt noch die allgemeine Aufforderung, sich nicht zu verunreinigen, sondern auf Reinheit zu achten (51,13f.). Die Anweisung zur Beachtung von Reinheit ist autoritativ, spricht hier doch die Stimme Gottes vom Horeb zu den Israeliten. Das mosaische Gesetz wird mit solchen Wendungen in der Tempelrolle zur Stimme Gottes erhoben, der als ein Ich sein Volk anredet.[64] Indem Gott selbst die Reinheit fordert, liegt Nachdruck auf dem Thema der Reinheit. Als Begründung wird das Wohnen Gottes im Tempel und daran anschießend in der Stadt angegeben. Reinheit ist also nicht um ihrer selbst willen einzuhalten, sondern um Gott gegenüber Respekt zu erweisen. Aus der für den Umgang mit ihm notwendigen Reinheit wird die Reinheit für alle weiteren Bezüge im Tempel und in der Stadt abgeleitet. Alle Vorgänge, die das Leben der Menschen in der Stadt ausmachen, sollen daher mit Beachtung von Reinheit erfolgen.

Die rituelle Reinheit, die die Tempelrolle fordert, erstreckt sich damit nicht nur auf Handlungen im Tempel, sondern betrifft das gesamte Leben der Menschen, die in der Stadt leben.[65] Liest man die Reinheitsvorschriften auf diesem Hintergrund, so verwundert es nicht, dass in der Tempelrolle nicht von Sühne die Rede ist. Das Ziel ihrer Reinheitsvorschriften betrifft nicht das Thema von Schuld und Beseitigung der Schuld, sondern es geht ihr um das Leben der Menschen in grundsätzlicher Weise. Daher ist auch öfter vom Wasser des Lebens die Rede. Die durch das Wasser hervorgebrachte Reinheit schafft Lebensbedingungen für die Menschen und umgekehrt bringt das lebendige Wasser das Leben zu den Menschen zurück, wenn Unreinheit entstanden war.

---

64 Die Tempelrolle wird damit zur Stimme Gottes. Vgl. SCHIFFMAN, „Gifts", 495f.; M. WEINFELD, „God", *passim*; R. T. BECKWITH, „Temple Scroll", 4; H.-J. FABRY, „Begriff", 70. Zu einem differenzierten Urteil kommt H. NAJMAN, *Seconding Sinai*, 16f.40–45, die einen Anspruch auf Gleichartigkeit mit der mosaischen Sinaioffenbarung herausarbeitet, der in Interpretation, Aktualisierung und Demonstration von Autorität besteht; die Tempelrolle zielt nicht darauf, die biblischen Schriften zu ersetzen, sondern zu begleiten, um dadurch „to honor the past, while re-presenting it to their distinctive audiences" (ebd. 44). Ähnlich nimmt NICKELSBURG, *Literature*, 158, an, dass die Tempelrolle den Pentateuch interpretieren wolle.

65 S.a. KLAWANS, *Impurity*, 50f. u.ö., der eine Nähe zwischen ritueller und moralischer Reinheit in der Tempelrolle ausmacht.

4.2. Halachisches Material

Eine andere Gruppe von Texten, die sich ebenfalls mit dem Thema Reinheit, beschäftigt, ist das halachische Material aus den Schriften vom Toten Meer, das in der Reihenfolge der vermeintlichen paleographischen Entstehungszeit der Handschriften dargestellt wird (nach Emmanuel Tov).[66] Dadurch kann eine etwaige Entwicklung in den partiell durchaus heterogenen[67] Reinheitsvorschriften vom Toten Meer aufgezeigt werden.[68]

4.2.1. 4QpapRitPur = 4Q512

Die Schrift 4Q Ritual of Purification (B) ist paleographisch von Tov auf ca. 85. v.Chr., von Maier auf den Anfang des 1. Jh. datiert worden.[69] 4Q512 ist in vielen (ca. 200) Fragmenten erhalten, die sich auf etwa 13 Kolumnen Text aufteilen lassen, bietet jedoch nur wenig Textbestand.[70] 4Q512 enthält rituelle und kultische Vorschriften oder Gesetze sowie Gebete, die liturgische Fragmente oder Tagesgebete aufweisen.[71]

Das Thema in der Schrift sind Reinheit[72] und Heiligkeit[73]. Beide Stichworte kommen oft vor, wobei inhaltliche Bezüge aufgrund des fragmentarischen Erhaltungszustandes der Schrift häufig nicht mehr nachvollziehbar sind. Verbunden mit den Stichworten ist allerdings das Thema „Schuld" und „Vergebung von Schuld".

4Q512 Kol. 2 Frg. 39: Hier fällt zunächst das Stichwort „Sühnung" (ggf. sogar im Plural: כפור[ים]), die Gott für den Beter erwirkt hat. Gott empfängt den

---

66 E. Tov, *Texts*, 390ff.

67 Vgl. dazu Werrett, *Ritual Purity*, 293f., der abschließend zu seiner Untersuchung urteilt, dass „the evidence ... fails to support the notion that the scrolls contain a cohesive purity system" (ebd., 293). Einen anderen Ansatz vertritt z.B. Harrington, "Outsiders", 187.

68 Einen ähnlichen Ansatz bietet Klawans, *Impurity*, 90f., der zwischen drei Entstehungsetappen von Texten unterscheidet: zunächst „protosectarian", wozu er 11Q19 und 4QMMT rechnet; danach als Zwischenstufe „composite texts", zu denen die Damaskusschrift gehört; als letzte Stufe „sectarian texts", unter denen er z.B. 1QS, 4Q512, 4Q414, 4Q274 und 4Q277 ansiedelt. Daran schließen sich die Ergebnisse der Studie von Werrett, *Ritual Purity*, 302f., an.

69 Vgl. Tov, *Texts* 390; J. Maier, *Qumran-Essener II*, 661; J. Baumgarten, „Purification Liturgies", 201.

70 Vgl. die Textedition in DJD 7, 262–286, sowie den Text in deutscher Übersetzung bei Maier, *Qumran-Essener II*, 661–673.

71 Vgl. Maier, *Qumran-Essener II*, 661; s.a. J. M. Baumgarten, „Purification Rituals", 200f.

72 Vgl. 4Q512 Kol. 4 Frg. 33 Z. 10; Frg. 16 Z. 4; Kol. 12 Frg. 2 Z. 3; Kol. 13 Frg. 41 Z. 5; s.a. Kol. 7 Frg. 30 Z. 5.7.8 (Reinigung); Frg. 64 (Heiligkeit und Reinigung); Kol.7 Frg. 32 Z. 2 (reinigen); sowie die nachfolgend besprochenen Fragmente.

73 Vgl. 4Q512 Kol. 7 Frg. 29 Z. 2; Kol. 12 Frg. 1 Z. 3; Frg. 48 Z. 3.

Lobpreis dafür, dass er Sühne geschaffen hat.[74] Sühne entstand durch Reinigung.

4Q512 Kol. 5 Frg. 34 führt in diesem Sinn fort, dass Reinigung eine Begnadigung von Schuld bedeutet, die durch „Sexualbefleckung"[75] entstanden war. Gott beseitigt die Unreinheit, indem er durch seine Gnade wieder Reinheit entstehen lässt.

Weitere Klärung bringt 4Q512 Kol. 7 Frg. 30, wo es ebenfalls um Sexualbefleckung geht.

(2) [-- in] Wasser und[--] (3) [--]und er benedeit dort/den Namen[--] (4)[--] vor Dir am Festterm[in --] (5) [--].. mich zur Reinigung[--] (6) [--]und sein Brandopfer, und er benedeit und heb[t an] und spricht: Gepriesen (bist) Du[--] (7) [--]. meine Vergehen und Du reinigst mich von Sexualbefleckungs-Schändlichkeit {und entsühnst}, zum Eintreten [in --] (8) [--]. Reinheit und das Blut vom Brandopfer Deines Wohlgefallens und das Gedächtnis der Beschwichtig[ung --] (9) [--]Räucherwerk Dein[er] Heiligkeit [und Besch]wich[ti]gung Deines Wohlgefallens[--].[76]

Auch in 4Q512 Kol. 7 Frg. 30 ist von Reinigung (טהר, Z. 5.7.8) von seinen Vergehen (ועולתו, Z. 7) die Rede. Als Mittel der Beseitigung der Schuld wird hier – vom Grundsatz her klassisch atl. – das Darbringen von Opfern eingesetzt (Z. 6.7f); und zwar Brandopfer (Z. 6.8, vor allem verbunden mit dem Stichwort Blut, דם עולת) und Räucheropfer (קטר, Z. 9).

Letzteres entspricht so allerdings nicht mehr ganz dem AT, da dort die Vergebung von Schuld durch den Blutritus[77] erwirkt wird. Der Blutritus gehört ursprünglich zum Sündopfer[78] (gelegentlich verbunden mit dem Ritus der Handaufstemmung,

---

74   Den Terminus חטאתי betrachtet BAUMGARTEN, „Purification Rituals", 201, als „confessional expression" in 4Q512.
75   So der Begriff bei MAIER, Qumran-Essener II, 663.
76   Übersetzung bei MAIER, Qumran-Essener II, 663.
77   So programmatisch in Lev 4,6.17; 17,11. Das Blut des Opfertieres wird dabei versprengt, und zwar wird gemäß dem großen Blutritus ein Teil an den Vorhang des Allerheiligsten gesprengt, ein anderer Teil an die Hörner des Brandopferaltars gestrichen und der Rest des Blutes an den Fuß des Altars weggegossen. Zum Blutritus vgl. JANOWSKI, Sühne. 235; I. WILLI-PLEIN, Opfer, 97f.
78   Vgl. Lev 5,11f.; s.a. Lev 12,6.8; 14,21f. Das Sündopfer findet bei zahlreichen Anlässen Verwendung und ist bisweilen auch mit anderen Opfern bzw. Reinigungsriten verbunden. Zum Ritus des Sündopfers vgl. B. JÜRGENS, Heiligkeit 304–339.

der die eigentliche Sühne bedeutet)[79] und wird erst später mit dem Brandopfer verbunden,[80] wie es sich etwa in der Chronik[81] findet.

Inspiriert ist 4Q512 Kol. 7 Frg. 30 Z. 8f., wo es um „das Brandopfer Deines Wohlgefallens und das Gedächtnis der Beschwichtigung" (Z. 8)[82] geht, vielleicht von Anweisungen für Brandopfer in Ex 29,38–42; Lev 6,1–6; Num 28,3–6, bei denen für das ständige bzw. tägliche Brandopfer zugleich Vorschriften für das Feueropfer bzw. Altarfeuer, das einen lieblichen Geruch vor Jahwe erzeugen und seinen Wohlgefallen finden soll, hinzutreten.

Die Beseitigung der Schuld wird in 4Q512 in einem Nachtrag, der über die Zeile hinausreicht,[83] schließlich als Sühne interpretiert (Z. 7). Welcher Teil des Opfers die Sühne erwirkt, wird dabei allerdings nicht ausdrücklich vermerkt. Die Notiz scheint eine Interpretation des Vorgangs darzustellen, die festlegt, dass Opfer zur Vergebung von Schuld dienen.

Zu Beginn des Fragments fällt auch das Stichwort Wasser (Z. 2), doch ist nicht klar, welche Funktion das Wasser hier hat, zumal im weiteren Abschnitt kein Wasser mehr erwähnt wird. Mit der Thematik von Opfer und Schuld lässt es sich nicht einfach verbinden. Ob es mit dem Vorgang von Reinigung und Sühne zu verbinden ist, wie es etwa in 4QTohorot oder 4QMMT begegnet, wo es Reinigungswasser, das gesprengt wird, meint,[84] ist ebenso fraglich.[85] Eher scheint sich die Vorstellung anzubieten, dass der zu Reinigende im Wasser steht und dabei einen Lobpreis auf Gott anstimmt.[86]

Ein interessanter Beleg ist Frg. 15 Kol. i, der von Maier zur Kol 8 gerechnet wird. Dort heißt es:

---

79 Vgl. dazu H. GESE, "Sühne" 95ff. Der Ritus erfüllt die Funktion einer Identifizierung des Opfernden mit dem für seine individuelle Schuld sterbenden Tier; vgl. JANOWSKI, Sühne, 41. Da dieser Ritus in einigen Belegen fehlt, könnte man vermuten, dass die Handaufstemmung nicht fest mit dem Ritus des Sündopfers verbunden ist; vgl. R. RENDTORFF, Studien 214–216.

80 Vgl. RENDTORFF, Studien, 97f; JANOWSKI, Sühne, 217f.; I. WILLI-PLEIN, Opfer, 90; A. LABAHN, Levitischer Herrschaftsanspruch (Kapitel 2.3.5.2. und 2.3.5.3.).

81 Vgl. II Chr 29,22.24; 30,16; 35,11; s. dazu A. LABAHN, Levitischer Herrschaftsanspruch (Kapitel 2.3.5.3.).

82 So mit der Übersetzung von MAIER, Qumran-Essener II, 663.

83 So die Angabe bei MAIER, Qumran-Essener II, 663 Anm. 626; vgl. auch die Edition bei M. BAILLET, DJD 7, 265, wo ותכפר über die eigentliche Textzeile geschrieben ist; eingefügt folgend auf die Worte פשעי ותמהרני מערות נדה und vor לבוא.

84 S.u. Abschnitte 4.2.3. und 4.2.4.

85 Dennoch interpretiert LAWRENCE, Washing, 117, den Abschnitt als Hinweis auf „a concern for purity in connection with the Sabbath and festivals".

86 Vgl. BAUMGARTEN, „Purification Rituals", 201, s.a. 208; DERS., „Purification Liturgies", 205f. Daraus schließt MAGNESS, Archaeology of Qumran, 139: „This passage indicates that the sectarians recited a blessing after immersion, while still standing in the water." Sie macht darin eine Differenz zu den Rabbinen aus, bei denen ein Ablauf in umgekehrter Reihenfolge begegnet; diese Schlussfolgerung findet sich bei BAUMGARTEN, „Purification Rituals", 202, auch.

„(1)... Verschuldung von Schuld (2) ... durch Wasser von (3) ... und er wäscht (4) ... für ihn in drei (5)...."[87].

Leider ist der Text so fragmentarisch erhalten, dass der Zusammenhang keine weiteren Bezüge erkennen lässt.

Eine Parallele[88] bietet jedoch 4Q414 Frg. 2 Kol. ii, wo die gleiche Vorstellung vorliegt.[89] Am ersten, dritten und siebten Tag erfolgt eine Reinigung von Unreinheit. Danach, so heißt es, „komme er ins Wasser" (יבוא במים, Z. 5);[90] „er hebt an und spricht: ‚Gepriesen bist du'..." (fortgesetzt möglicherweise mit einer Anrede des Gottes Israels, וענה ואמר ברוך א[תאה אל ישראל, Z. 6).[91] Im Frg. 7 Kol. ii ist zudem davon die Rede, dass die Kleider mit Wasser gewaschen werden. Der Text 4Q414 bietet damit eine ergänzende Aussage zu Waschungen und Reinigungsriten, wobei hier aufgrund des „danach" im Ablauf zwischen Reinigung und Wasser noch einmal unterschieden zu sein scheint, was sich in dieser Weise in 4Q512 nicht findet.

Doch zurück zu 4Q512 Frg. 15 Kol. i. Anders als im vorherigen Fragment Kol. 7 Frg. 30 scheint das Wasser zum Abwaschen der Schuld Verwendung zu finden – jedenfalls wenn man die identifizierbaren Reste von עוון und במימי so miteinander in einen Zusammenhang stellt, dass sie einen gemeinsamen Ablauf schildern. Für diese Interpretation spricht auch der weiter unten vorzustellende Beleg Kol. 12 Frg. 1–3. Aufgrund des Erhaltungszustandes von Frg. 15 Kol. i ist allerdings Vorsicht gegenüber zu weitreichenden Schlussfolgerungen geboten.

Ein weiteres Mal begegnet Wasser in Frg. 19, das Maier ebenso unter den Fragmenten von Kol. 8 aufführt. Hier findet sich jedoch nur ein einzelner Wortrest, der keine nähere Zuordnung im Kontext hat.

Interessant ist dann wieder Kol. 10 Frg. 11. Hier ist von Reinigung und einer Waschung im Wasser die Rede:

(2) [und haben sich erfül]lt für ihn die sieben Tage [seiner] Reini[gung --] (3) [..... dann] wäscht er seine Kleider mit Wass[er --] (4) und deckt seine Kleider über und benedeit für [--] (5) Gott Isra[els --].[92]

---

87 Übersetzung bei MAIER, Qumran-Essener II, 664; hebräischer Text in DJD 7, 269.

88 4Q414 ist mit WERRETT, Ritual Purity, 216, wohl eine andere Rezension derselben Textkomposition wie 4Q512, so dass beide als Ritual of Purification A (4Q414) und B (4Q512) bezeichnet werden.

89 Vgl. BAUMGARTEN, „Purification Liturgies", 200f.; s.a. LAWRENCE, Washing, 10.145.

90 In der Wendung יבוא במים sieht LAWRENCE, Washing, 145, eine Anspielung an Wasserbecken, wie sie in Qumran gefunden wurden; s. dazu a.a.O. 155–184 sowie den Beitrag von Seán Freyne in dieser Publikation.

91 Übersetzung bei MAIER, Qumran-Essener II, 425, der diesen Text als „Baptismal Liturgie" kennzeichnet (a.a.O. 424), während er in der Edition von Eshel als „4QRitual of Purification A" gekennzeichnet ist; Text in DJD 35, 135–154.

92 Übersetzung bei MAIER, Qumran-Essener II, 666.

Die Reinigung mit Wasser bezieht sich auf die Kleidung (כבס את בגדיו, Z. 3, vgl. Z. 4) und nicht die Person dessen, der die Reinigung vornimmt.[93] Der Beleg schließt an bekannte Motive an, wie sie bereits in der Tempelrolle begegnet sind. Nach sieben Tagen wird eine Reinigung notwendig, wenn jemand vom Aussatz rein geworden ist oder mit Toten Kontakt hatte. So legen 11Q19 45,23–25 und 49,23–28 fest, dass am siebten Tag die Kleider gewaschen werden sollen. Zudem soll nach der Tempelrolle der ganze Körper des Betreffenden in fließendem Wasser gebadet werden.[94] Dieser letzte Teil der Waschung ist in 4Q512 Kol. 10 Frg. 11 nicht zu finden. Ob eine entsprechende Angabe in dem nicht mehr erhaltenen Teil noch gefolgt ist, kann nicht mit Sicherheit gesagt werden. Vom Aufbau des Stückes wäre es nahe liegend, wenn sie etwa in Z. 2 oder Z. 3 erwähnt wäre, doch scheint dafür der Platz in der Lakune eher zu schmal bemessen. Da Z. 4.5 im Anschluss anders weitergehen, ist die Wahrscheinlichkeit, dass in diesem Zusammenhang oder danach noch von Waschungen des Körpers die Rede war, eher gering.

Offen bleibt in dem Stück aus 4Q512 auch, welchen Anlass das Waschen der Kleidung hat. Es könnte sein, dass es ein ähnlicher Anlass für die Reinigung wie in der Tempelrolle ist, doch ist dies nicht zwangsläufig vorauszusetzen. Nicht eindeutig ist auch, ob es sich um eine rituelle oder tatsächliche Reinigung handelt. Für eine rituelle Reinigung sprechen der Aufbau und ihre Analogie in der Tempelrolle. Da aber in Z. 4 weitere Maßnahmen der Kleidung erwähnt werden, ist nicht auszuschließen, dass die Reinigung auch tatsächlicher Säuberung dient. Gleichwohl scheint mir der rituelle Aspekt im Vordergrund zu stehen, da ein Lobpreis Gottes folgt. Die Intention der Reinigung besteht also darin, vor Gott als rein dazustehen.

Der Lobpreiss erinnert an ein früheres Fragment aus 4Q512: Kol. 7 Frg. 30. Dort geht der Lobpreis aber wohl den Opfern voraus. Ob er auch der Reinigung vorausgeht oder umgekehrt an diese anschließt, wird dort nicht deutlich. Mög-

---

93 Ausgehend von der Rekonstruktion des Textes in Z. 3 mit וכבס את בגדיו וברך, wie sie auch in der Textedition in DJD 7, 270, zu finden ist, interpretiert LAWRENCE, Washing, 143, die nachfolgende Lakune allerdings anders: „... and he shall cover his nakedness with his clothes and kneel up[on his knees ... And he shall say in response, 'Blessed are You,] O God of Isr[ael] ...'." Lawrence zieht daraus die Schlussfolgerung, dass die Waschung nackt erfolgt ist, da die Bekleidung danach wieder angelegt werde.

Eine nochmals andere Ergänzung und Deutung des Textes schlägt GARCÍA MARTÍNEZ, Dead Sea Scrolls, 441, vor: „5 [And when] the seven days of his pur[ification have been completed ...] 6 [...] he will purify his clothes with water [and wash his body ...] 7 And he will cover himself with his clothes and bless on [...] 5 God of Israel [...]."

Entscheidendes für die Interpretation hängt von der Füllung der Lakune ab, die Rückwirkungen auf das Verständnis der Aussage über die Kleidung hat. Dass sich eine Ergänzung durch einfachen Hinweis auf ein Stehen im Wasser (על עומדו) nahelegt, schlägt auch BAUMGARTEN, „Purification Rituals", 201f., vor.

94 S.o. Abschnitt 4.1.1.

licherweise liegt die Reinigung davor und der Lobpreis berichtet im Nachhinein lediglich noch einmal davon. Wenn diese Interpretation zutrifft, dann würde sowohl in Kol. 7 Frg. 30 als auch in Kol. 10 Frg. 11 ein Lobpreis unmittelbar auf den Reinigungsritus folgen bzw. diesen abschließen.
Von Reinigung nach Ausfluss ist in Kol. 11 Frg. 9 Z. 2 die Rede.

> ... (2) bei seiner Reinigung von dem Aus[fluß --] (3) zu essen und zu trin[ken -- r]einigtest Du Is[rael --] (4) zu sein ein Volk[-- in den Stä]dten [ihrer] Wohnsitz[e --] (5) ...[95]

Hier wird von einer Reinigung gesprochen, ohne dass nähere Angaben über die Art der Reinigung, die Mittel oder zeitlichen Abläufe gegeben werden. Es wäre möglich, auch diesen Beleg analog zu den Reinigungsvorschriften der Tempelrolle zu verstehen und an eine rituelle Waschung zu denken, doch bleibt dies letztlich Spekulation.

Eine Differenz zwischen 4Q512 und der Tempelrolle liegt insofern vor, als hier im Anschluss ein sonst nicht anzutreffendes „Du" genannt wird, das als Subjekt einer Reinigung des Volkes erscheint. Gemeint ist damit wahrscheinlich Gott, der als der eigentlich Reinigende als aktiv Handelnder gedacht wird. Dafür spricht, dass Z. 4 einen Anklang an die (eingliedrige) Bundesformel[96] bietet,[97] indem Israel als das Volk Gottes angesprochen wird. Hier wird eine theologische Begründung für die Reinigung geliefert, insofern die rituelle Reinheit eine Qualität darstellt, mit der Israel als Gottes Volk vor seinem Gott und von seinem Gott in einen anderen Zustand versetzt wird. Die Reinigung betrifft also das religiöse Gottesverhältnis im Leben Israels.

Eine weitere Textstelle aus 4Q512, in der es um Reinigung geht, findet sich in Kol. 12 Frg. 1–3. In diesem Abschnitt begegnen Aspekte vorhergehender Passagen, die hier allerdings stärker auf einander bezogen sind. Eingebunden in einen Lobpreis Gottes ist von Reinigung, Wasser und Sühne die Rede:

> (2)... [der Du befohlen hast den Unreinen auf Fri]sten, sich zu reinigen von[...] (3) [......]Seele durch Süh[nungen --]Asche von Heiligkeit [.....] (4) ..[...].. durch Wasser der Rein[heit --]. [au]f ew[igen] Tafeln[98] (5) und Ba[de]wasser zur

---

95 Übersetzung bei MAIER, Qumran-Essener II 666.
96 Vgl. z.B. Dtn 4,20; 7,6; 14,2.21; 26,18f. Zur sog. Bundesformel, „Jahwe – Israels Gott; Israel – Jahwes Volk" vgl. O. KAISER, Theologie I, 157.159.189 u.ö. (mit weiteren Belegen).
97 So jedenfalls in der Rekonstruktion von M. BAILLET, DJD 7, durch ולהיות עם וקדש], die auch der Übersetzung bei MAIER, Qumran-Essener II, 666, zugrunde liegt. Einen anderen Vorschlag unterbreitet BAUMGARTEN, „Purification Rituals", 204, der die Lakune durch ולהיות עם אשתו] ergänzt, so dass er zu der Wortfolge „and to be with his wife" kommt.
98 Die Textedition in DJD 7, 272, sieht die Wendung בליחות עולם vor, die auch der Übersetzung von Maier zugrunde liegt. Da dies eine ungewöhnliche lectio difficilior sei, schlägt BAUMGARTEN, „Purification Rituals" 207, abweichend eine Textrekonstruktion durch עולם בליחות vor, was er aus einer Analogie zu 11Q19 49,12 (לחת מים) und 4QMMT (המצוקים לחת, ohne Angabe der Textstelle) gewinnt und als „permanent streams" identifiziert.

Reinigung auf Fristen[--]seine [K]leider und danach[sprenge er auf ihn] (6) das Wasser {der Bespregnung}[99], um ihn zu reinigen und all[--] (7){ }und na[ch] seinem [Aus]sprengen des Wass[ers der Besprengung -- ..[100]

Der Textfluss ist nicht klar zu bestimmen. Es scheint sich um eine Angabe für eine rituelle Waschung zu handeln, die in einer gewissen Frist abläuft. Das Wasser findet einmal zum Waschen der Kleidung Verwendung (Z. 5), aber auch zur Reinigung des betreffenden Menschen (Z. 5.6f.). Die Waschung des Menschen scheint hier einerseits als ein Eintauch-Vorgang gemeint zu sein, wofür das Sich-Reinigen im Wasser der Reinheit (מי רחץ לטהרת, Z. 5; vgl. Z. 2.6) spricht. Andererseits ist aber auch vom Besprengen durch Wasser die Rede (vgl. in Z. 5–7 die Wendungen von נזה[101])[102]. Der Durchführende dieser Reinigung ist dabei nicht der zu Reinigende selbst, was daraus hervorgeht, dass eine Person einen andern besprengt und damit zwei Personen notwendig werden. Damit ist wohl an einen Priester zu denken, der die Reinigungszeremonie durchführt. Der Begriff Asche lässt überlegen, ob diese Reinigung in Zusammenhang mit Opfern oder anderen Räucherriten steht, aus denen Asche als Produkt hervorgeht. Da aber keine weiteren Angaben zur Asche gemacht werden, muss dies hier offen bleiben.

Zwei verschiedene Wasserarten werden genannt: Wasser der Reinigung bzw. Badewasser (מי רחץ)[103] und Wasser der Besprengung (מימי היזה)[104]. Worin der Unterschied liegt, geht aus dem Dokument nicht hervor. Wenn man aus der terminologischen Differenz einen sachlichen Unterschied ableiten darf, dann könnte man beide Wasserarten so unterscheiden, dass das Reinigungswasser dem Untertauchen dient; d.h. dafür wäre entweder ein großes Becken notwendig oder an einen Fluss oder See bzw. Teich zu denken. Demgegenüber könnte das Wasser der Besprengung auch in einem kleinen Becken Platz haben, in das der Priester einen Gegenstand eintaucht, um das Wasser an seinen Bestimmungsort zu spritzen.[105] Der Vorgang des Besprengens wäre dann ein ähnlicher,

---

99 Die Wendung ist unsicher. Der editierte Text in DJD 7, 272, bietet in Z. 6 את מימי למהרו und nach מימי oberhalb der Zeile dazwischen geschrieben ה[ז]יה. Gesichert ist die Wortfolge ואח[ר ה]חזותו את מימ[י allerdings in Z. 7, so dass die Rekonstruktion auch in Z. 6 sinngemäß erscheint. In diesem Sinn ist die Besprengung auch am Ende von Z. 5 ergänzt worden: ואחר [ויזה עליו].

100 Übersetzung bei MAIER, Qumran-Essener II, 666f.

101 Zur Bedeutung von נזה s.o. Anm. 62.

102 Zur Rekonstruktion vgl. Anm. 99. S.a. BAUMGARTEN, „Purification Rituals", 206f, der von מימי היזה spricht, auch wenn diese Wendung nicht direkt im Text von 4Q512 steht.

103 Zum Bedeutungsspektrum von רחץ bzw. מי רחץ s.o. Anm. 50.

104 Dieser Terminus ist so nicht die Lesart von 4Q512 Kol. 12 Frg. 1–3, sondern stammt von BAUMGARTEN, „Purification Rituals", 207, in Interpretation dieser Textstelle.

105 Aus den beiden Vorgängen leitet BAUMGARTEN, „Purification Rituals", 207, ab, dass „sprinkling was preceded by an immersion", was in der rabbinischen Tradition nachgewirkt habe. Allerdings unterscheidet er dieses Eintauchen bzw. Bad von der vorbereitenden מבילה, wie sie z.B. in der TR genannt ist.

wie er im AT das Besprengen des Altars mit Blut durch ein Ysoprohr darstellt (vgl. Lev 14–15; Ps 50,9; s.a. Num 19) – ein Vorgang, der hier möglicherweise übertragen ist.

Interessant ist, dass hier eine Deutung der Reinigung mitgeliefert wird. Die Reinigung dient der Sühne (בכפו[ר], Z. 3) und bewirkt Heiligkeit vor Gott (קודש, Z. 3). Auch diese Deutung spricht dafür, dass hier weniger eine Selbstreinigung im Blick ist als vielmehr eine vom Priester durchgeführte Zeremonie, die vor Gott etwas bewirkt.

Von Schuld und Sünde ist auch in einem weiteren Fragment die Rede, das Maier ebenso Kol 12 zuweist. In Frg. 4 heißt es, dass ein „Du" (gemeint ist wohl Gott) jemanden heiligt, indem seine Herrlichkeit Schuld und Sünde bedeckt. Im Zusammenhang ist erneut von Sexualbefleckung die Rede. Darüber hinaus ist weder über die Situation noch über den Weg, wie Sühne bewirkt wird, etwas Genaueres dem Fragment zu entnehmen. Es geht jedenfalls um die Bereinigung einer Situation, in der es zu Absonderung aufgrund von Verunreinigung kam. Diesen Zusammenhang stellt auch Frg. 40 her, das von Maier Kol 13 zugewiesen worden ist. Wer rituell unrein ist, wird aus der Gruppe der Gott dienenden Menschen ausgeschlossen. Es bedarf eines Vorgangs und Gottes Akzeptanz über den erfolgreichen Abschluss des Vorgangs, damit eine Veränderung der Lebenssituation möglich wird.

Die Deutung von Sühne fügt sich in den Zusammenhang des Dokuments ein. Das Ritual of Purification dient demnach dazu, die Menschen vor Gott in einen anderen Zustand zu versetzen. Nach Unreinheit muss ein bestimmter Vorgang eine Veränderung bringen, an dem der betreffende Mensch wie auch ein Priester und Gott selbst beteiligt sind. Rituelle Reinigung bedeutet damit einen Neuanfang im Leben, nachdem die Zeremonie ordnungsgemäß vollzogen worden ist und Gott dem Menschen daraufhin vergeben hat.[106]

Weitere Fragmente von 4Q512 bieten noch Hinweise auf Wasser oder Waschen (vgl. Frg. 42: Wasser für Waschung; Frg. 54: Kleider im Wasser waschen; Frg. 56 sich im Wasser waschen; Frg. 74: waschen). Sie sind jedoch so fragmentarisch, dass diesen Hinweisen nichts Näheres über Waschungen zu entnehmen ist.

Eine gewisse Nähe von 4Q512 besteht auch zu 4Q284,[107] wo zweimal von Reinigungswasser die Rede ist (Frg. 1 Z. 8 und Frg. 3 Z. 3), hier jedoch mit dem Terminus מי נדה (vgl. Frg. 2 Kol. i Z. 4: er soll seinen Körper im Wasser waschen,

---

106 Vgl. BAUMGARTEN, „Purification Rituals", 201, der in die Reinigung in 4Q512 als „purification from any defilement as a gift of divine grace and a restoration of one's spiritual and social integrity" deutet. S.a. KLAWANS, Impurity, 87, der herausstellt, dass „purification and atonement were conceptually intertwined" in 4Q512.

107 4Q284 = 4QPurification Liturgy besteht aus zehn Fragmenten, von denen lediglich die Frg. 1 bis 5 mit sechs Zeilen einen zusammenhängenden und halbwegs identifizierbaren Text bieten; Text in: DJD 35, 123–129.

ורחץ את בש]רו במים). In 4Q284 geht es um das auf die Reinigung antwortende Verhalten des Gereinigten am „siebten Tag", an dem er eine Segensbitte bzw. ein Gebet als Lobpreis aussprechen soll.

Der Vorgang des Waschens oder die Vorgänge des Waschens gehören in 4Q512 zu Reinigungsritualen, mit denen rituelle Reinheit vor Gott hergestellt wird. Dadurch wird eine Veränderung der Lebenssituation der betreffenden Menschen erwirkt, insofern sie nicht länger ausgesondert sind, sondern wieder in die Lebensgemeinschaft (im Jachat?)[108] integriert werden. Lobpreise, die dies vor Gott bringen und ihn für Reinigung und Sühne loben, drücken dies im Munde derer, die Reinigung erfahren haben, aus.[109]

4.2.2. 4QOrdinances (4Q159; 4Q513; 4Q514)

Das Dokument 4QOrdinances ist mit gleichem oder ähnlichem Inhalt in drei Schriften überliefert: 4Q159; 4Q513; 4Q514.[110] Sie sind vermutlich nacheinander entstanden. Die älteste Fassung ist 4Q513 = 4QOrdinances[b]; ihre paleographischen Angaben lassen sie als hasmonäisch erscheinen; Tov datiert um 55 v.Chr., Maier auf eine Zeit vor 50 v.Chr.[111] Das zweite Dokument ist 4Q514 = 4QOrdinances[c]; nach Tov entstand es kurze Zeit später um 50 v.Chr.; Maier gibt lediglich Mitte des 1.Jh. an.[112] Die letzte bekannte Fassung ist unter dem Signum 4Q159 = 4QOrdinances[a] zu finden; sie datiert nach Tov zwischen 30 v.Chr. und 0, während Maier für sie die Angabe „herodianisch" macht.[113]

4.2.2.1. 4Q159

In 4QOrdinances sind „Torah- und Rechtssammlungen, teilweise in nichtgesetzliche Mose-Stoffe eingearbeitet", enthalten.[114] Dies geht deutlich aus 4Q159 hervor, wo Fälle von Rechtsbruch behandelt werden. Unter ihnen ist allerdings kein Fall, in dem Wasser oder Reinigungsriten zur Anwendung kommen.[115] In den beiden anderen Dokumenten (4Q513 und 514) ist die Zuordnung zu be-

---

108 Zum Stichwort *Jachat*, vgl. die Ausführungen in Anm. 163.

109 Ähnlich interpretiert auch BAUMGARTEN, „Purification Rituals", 207f., den Vorgang: „The liturgy accompanying the purification indicates a definite awareness of the spiritual overtones of lustration. Confession for sin and thanksgiving for the renewal of access to sacred things is a prominent theme in a number of the fragments."

110 Textausgaben: 4Q513: DJD 7,287–295; 4Q514: DJD 7,295–298; 4Q159: DJD 5,6–9.

111 Vgl. Tov, *Texts*, 397; MAIER, *Qumran-Essener II*, 673.

112 Vgl. Tov, *Texts*, 400; MAIER, *Qumran-Essener II*, 678.

113 Vgl. Tov, *Texts*, 414; MAIER, *Qumran-Essener II*, 63.

114 So MAIER, *Qumran-Essener II*, 63. Den Inhalt beschreibt WERRETT, *Ritual Purity*, 211 (vgl. 258), als „a wide range of legal material with no discernable organizational structure".

115 Ebenso verhält es sich auch in den Reinheitsgesetzen 4Q284 und 4Q284a, wo es stattdessen um Reinheit (טהר) in Verbindung mit אמת geht. Vgl. dazu WERRETT, *Ritual Purity*, 261.

stimmten Gesetzestexten gleichwohl komplizierter, da der Erhaltungszustand eine Identifikation oftmals schwierig werden lässt.

4.2.2.2. 4Q513

4Q513 ist so stark fragmentarisch überliefert, dass aus ihm kaum ein zusammenhängender Text zu gewinnen ist. Die verschiedenen Fragmente von 4Q513 bieten einzelne Begriffe oder Wendungen, die aber kaum eine sinnvolle Abfolge aufweisen, dass ihnen spezifische Reinigungsriten zu entnehmen sind. In einigen Fragmenten begegnet das Stichwort Reinheit (Frg. 2 Kol. ii Z. 1; Frg. 10 Kol. ii Z. 6) oder Heiligkeit (Frg. 2 Kol. ii Z. 1), in anderen ist komplementär von Unreinheit (Frg. 13 Z. 4) oder dem Unreinen (Frg. 2 Kol. ii Z. 2) die Rede. Erwähnt werden auch Sühne (Frg. 6; Frg. 13 Z. 2) und Schuld (Frg. 2 Kol. ii Z. 5; Frg. 11 Z. 3; Frg. 22 Z. 3), wie auch Wasser (Frg. 15 Z. 1, als unsicher gekennzeichnet) vorkommt.

Die lesbaren Fragmente bieten Aussagen über Abgaben (Frgg. 2; 4) und Opfer (Frgg. 12; 24), Sabbate (Frg. 3) und Unzucht (Frgg. 2; 13; 30). Aus Frg. 10 geht als Anliegen hervor, die Israeliten nicht mit anderen zu vermischen, sondern auf Reinheit zu achten. Frg. 22 redet von Schuld und Verunreinigung.[116] Nimmt man die Themen zusammen, so scheint es um Fragen der Ethik zu gehen, wobei rituelle Reinheit als besondere Lebensweise Israels angegeben wird.

Die Aussagen zum Wasser sind in diesem Kontext zu sehen, geben jedoch keine Hinweise auf Reinigungsriten. In Frg. 15 ist von Wasser für das Land und das Heiligtum die Rede, ohne dass Näheres über das Wasser oder seinen Gebrauch zu sehen ist. Aufgrund der spärlichen Angaben ist eine Interpretation des Materials fast unmöglich.

4.2.2.3. 4Q514

Deutlichere Angaben sind 4Q514 zu entnehmen. Das Dokument besteht aus zwei Fragmenten, wobei Frg. 1 in Z. 3–10 einen zusammenhängenden Text bietet, während in Frg. 2 nur wenige Worte überliefert sind.

4Q514 nennt dreimal Reinigungsriten, die nach Fällen von Verunreinigung auszuführen sind. Als ein zweigliedriger Vorgang wird angegeben, dass der Betreffende zunächst sich baden und sodann seine Kleider im Wasser waschen soll (Z. 3.5f.8f.). Erst danach ist es dem Betreffenden gestattet, wieder zu essen und an den Mahlzeiten teilzunehmen. Diese Bestimmung wird als Gesetz der Reinheit angeführt.

Von sieben Tagen der Waschung ist in Z. 3 die Rede, bevor der Reinigungsvorgang nachfolgend beschrieben wird. Man könnte die Angabe so lesen, dass an jedem der sieben Tage der Vorgang zu wiederholen ist. Man könnte es aber

---

116 Neben diesen beiden Wörtern ist nur noch „und" erhalten.

auch so lesen, dass an Tag eins bis sechs eine andere Waschung stattfindet und der eigentliche Reinigungsritus, wie er hier beschrieben ist, erst am siebten Tag erfolgt.[117]

Verständnisschwierigkeiten bereitet die Passage des Textes, die von einer „ersten Unreinheit" spricht (בטמאתו הרישנה, Z. 8, vgl. Z. 7). Dies ist insofern problematisch, als keine zweite Unreinheit genannt wird (wenn man nicht annimmt, dass diese im Dokument später noch gefolgt, nun aber nicht mehr erhalten ist) und man im Text auch sonst keinen Anhaltspunkt weiter für diese Zählung hat.

Unklar ist auch die Rede davon, dass der Betreffende rein werden soll „von seiner Quelle her" (ממקרו, Z. 4.7). Die Quelle hat im Text keinen weiteren Bezugspunkt, außer dass sie auf den Sich-Reinigenden geht. Es wird kaum gemeint sein, dass jemand seine eigene Quelle hat. Eher könnte man daran denken, dass jemand in seinem Inneren rein werden soll, so dass der Ausdruck eine anthropologische Erneuerung bezeichnet. Ferner scheint es mir, dass die Quelle eine Bezeichnung für einen Ort lebendigen Wassers angibt, wie es in der Tempelrolle ein Vorbild hat (vgl. 11Q19 45,23–25; 49,23–28, wo davon die Rede ist, dass am siebten Tag die Kleider gewaschen und der ganze Körper des Betreffenden in fließendem Wasser gebadet werden soll).[118] Eine analoge Reinigung scheint mir auch in 4Q514 im Blick zu sein, auch wenn dies nicht explizit entfaltet wird.[119]

Die Waschungen von Körper und Kleidung sind also notwendig, damit der Unreine zum Reinen wird und wieder am Leben der Gemeinschaft teilhaben kann. Das Leben der Quelle überträgt ihm die Lebendigkeit, die ihn rituell vor Gott rein und gegenüber den Israeliten gemeinschaftsfähig macht.

Ob die Waschungen von 4Q514 als Ausdruck von Sühne zu verstehen sind, wie die mehrfache Verwendung der Begriffe in 4Q513 nahelegen könnte (Sühne in Frg. 6; Frg. 13 Z. 2; Schuld in Frg. 2 Kol. ii Z. 5; Frg. 11 Z. 3; Frg. 22 Z. 3), ist Spekulation, da die Begriffe in 4Q514 nicht fallen und die Textfragmente auch ansonsten zu wenig Überschneidungen bieten, als dass man daraus diese Schlussfolgerung mit einiger Sicherheit ziehen könnte.

---

117 Vgl. BAUMGARTEN, „Purification Rituals" 203, der von einer abschließenden Reinigung am siebten Tag ausgeht.
118 S.o. Abschnitt 4.1.1.
119 Eine Parallele zwischen den beiden Texten nimmt auch LAWRENCE, Washing, 87–89, an. 4Q514 interpretiert, ebenso wie die Tempelrolle, Lev 15, lässt allerdings die dort angeordneten Opfer aus und überträgt die Waschung der Priester jetzt auf die Mitglieder der Gemeinschaft.

4.2.3. 4QTohorot (4Q274–279)

Der Text 4QTohorot ist in mehreren Fragmenten überliefert, die auf sechs Schriften mit unterschiedlichem Bestand eingeteilt worden sind: 4Q274–279[120]. Nach Tov stammt die Schrift 4QTohorot gemäß ihrer paleographischen Zuordnung von 30 v.Chr. bis zur Zeitenwende.[121]

4Q274 nennt rituelle Reinigungsriten, die nach Sexualbefleckung durch Menstruationsblut oder Samenerguss notwendig werden.[122] Die Belege knüpfen weitgehend an die bereits aus anderen halachischen Texten bekannten Wendungen an.

In einem längeren Abschnitt über Reinigungsriten gibt 4Q274 Frg. 1 Kol i Z. 3 und Z. 9 Anweisungen an den Unreinen, dass er sich am siebten Tag in Wasser baden (רחץ במים) und seine Kleider waschen (יכבס בגדו) soll. Während der Zeit seiner Unreinheit darf nichts Reines mit ihm in Berührung kommen. Die generelle Anweisung wird im Folgenden in Einzelanweisungen für Menstruierende, für Menschen mit Ausfluss, für Männer mit Samenerguss und für Menschen, die Kontakt mit Toten hatten, wiederholt.

Die hier genannten Reinigungsriten knüpfen an Vorstellungen an, wie sie ähnlich bereits in der Tempelrolle[123] und in kürzerer Form auch in 4Q512[124] begegnet sind. Es handelt sich dabei offenbar um Waschungen, die jemand an sich selbst durchführt.[125] Welches Wasser dafür verwendet werden soll, wird nicht gesagt, eben so wenig wird darüber Auskunft erteilt, wo dieses Wasser zu erhalten ist.

4Q274 Frg. 2 Kol i bietet weitere Varianten von rituellen Waschungen, bei denen eine erstaunliche terminologische Vielfalt begegnet.[126]

(Oberer Kolumnenrand)

(1) [--]. sprengen auf ihn [das] erste Mal und er badet und wäscht (seine Kleider), bevor (2) [--].. auf ihn das siebte Mal am siebten Tag. Nicht sprenge er an einem Sabbat dabei, (3) [--]am Sabbat, nur berühre er nicht die Reinheit, bis

---

120 Allerdings ist 4Q275 (ehemals 4QTohorot B^a genannt) neuerdings als 4QCommunal Ceremony bezeichnet und der Gemeinschaftsregel zugerechnet worden; vgl. WERRETT, *Ritual Purity*, 214.
121 Vgl. Tov, *Texts* 414. Text in DJD 35, 79–122.
122 Text in DJD 35, 103f.; Übersetzung bei MAIER, *Qumran-Essener II*, 235; s.a. WERRETT, *Ritual Purity*, 245f.
123 Vgl. 11Q19 45,23–25; 49,23–28; s.o. Abschnitt 4.1.1.
124 Vgl. 4Q512 Kol. 10 Frg. 11; s.o. Abschnitt 4.2.2.
125 S.a. KLAWANS, *Impurity*, 87f., der auf den Zusammenhang von Sühne und Reinheit auch für 4Q274 hinweist, obwohl hier von Sühne nicht ausdrücklich die Rede ist.
126 Text in DJD 25, 103f.; Übersetzung bei MAIER, *Qumran-Essener II*, 236; s.a. WERRETT, *Ritual Purity*, 248f.

er (ge)wechselt (hat) (4) [--]was den Sperma-Erguß berührt, vom Menschen bis zum Gerät, soll untertauchen (5) [--].[127] und das Kleid, das an ihm ist, und das Gerät, das ihn trägt, tauche unter (6) [--]. und wenn im Lager ein Mann ist, der es nicht vermoch[te], (7) [--]. das Kleid, welches er nicht berührt hat, nur berühre es nicht sein Brot, und wer (es) berü[hrt,] (8) [--]sie sitzen, wenn er es nicht berührt hat, wäscht er es mit Wasser, und wenn (9) [--]wasche er (sein Kleid). Und für alle heiligen Dinge wasch einer das

(Unterer Kolumnenrand)

In diesem Fragment werden Waschungen beim ersten Mal und beim siebten Mal am siebten Tag genannt – dies impliziert wohl, dass das Procedere ebenso an Tag drei bis sechs, also an sieben nacheinander folgenden Tagen ausgeführt werden soll. Auf den Unreinen wird gesprengt – gemeint ist wohl, dass der Priester Wasser auf ihn sprengt. Danach badet er sich und wäscht seine Kleider (Z. 1). Interessant ist, dass in Z. 1 alle Termini für Waschungen, wie sie aus den Schriften vom Toten Meer bekannt sind, hier anzutreffen sind: כאשר יזו עליו את [ה]רי[א]שונה ורחץ ויכבס טרם.

Z. 2f. bietet hier zusätzlich die Anweisung, dass Reinigungswasser an einem Sabbath nicht versprengt werden darf. Diese Forderung, die sich analog auch in 4Q251 Frg. 1–2 Z. 6 und 4Q265 Frg. 7 Z. 3 findet, ist eine Neuerung gegenüber den Vorschriften über das Reinigungswasser (מי נדה) in der Hebräischen Bibel[128] und als Spezifikum des halachischen Materials vom Toten Meer zu beurteilen.

4Q274 Frg. 2 Kol i Z. 4 setzt noch einmal neu an und führt eine weitere terminologische Variante ein. Über Kontakt mit Sperma heißt es, dass alles, was damit in Berührung gekommen ist, d.h. sowohl Menschen als auch Kleidungsstücke, untertauchen soll. Interessant ist hierbei, dass in Z. 4f. dreimal[129] das Verb טבל verwendet wird; mit dieser Terminologie bildet der Beleg eine Ausnahme.[130] Wie der Tauchvorgang, den das Verb טבל ausdrückt, zu den übrigen Ausführungen von Waschungen steht, ist nicht näher entfaltet. Allerdings kann vermutet werden, dass die terminologische Differenz auf einen abweichenden Reinigungsvorgang hinweist. Das würde bedeuten, dass hier ein strengerer Untertauchvorgang als in den übrigen Schriften vom Toten Meer im Blick ist.[131]

In Z. 8f. ist noch einmal vom Waschen die Rede, wobei zunächst für die Kleidung gilt, dass sie mit Wasser gewaschen werden soll (ב]גדיו רחץ במים, Z. 8).

---

127 Die Textedition von Baumgarten in DJD 35, 104, ergänzt die Lakune zu Beginn von Z. 5 mit יטב]ול].
128 Vgl. WERRETT, Ritual Purity, 259f.272f.
129 Die Ergänzung der Lakune in Z. 5 (vgl. Anm. 127) bietet die dritte Verwendung von טבל.
130 An diesem – gemessen am sonstigen sprachlichen Befund – eher seltenen Beleg hängt Entscheidendes für die weitere spätere Entwicklung des Ritus des Untertauchens, wie es bei den Rabbinen und im Christentum später Verbreitung findet; vgl. LAWRENCE, Washing, 142f.
131 Vgl. dazu WERRETT, Ritual Purity, 251.

Vom Waschen im Wasser spricht auch Z. 9 (במים ... וכבס). Allerdings ist aus dem fragmentarischen Text nicht mehr klar zu erschließen, welchem Objekt dies gilt. Zunächst ist die Reinigung wohl auf alle heiligen Geräte und Speisen[132] zu beziehen und dann wohl auch auf die Person selbst.[133] Damit wären Z. 8f. eine adäquate Fortsetzung von Z. 1–3.

Einen neuen Aspekt bringt der Text 4Q276, der eine Auslegung von Num 19 bietet, zur Sprache.

> In Num 19,1–9 ging es um einen Opfervorgang einer roten Kuh, deren Blut als ein Sündopfer dient (19,9). Sieben Mal sprengt der Priester ihr Blut mit Ysop in Richtung der Stiftshütte, bevor er sie verbrennt. Der Priester soll anschließend sich und seine Kleider waschen und bis Sonnenuntergang warten, bis er wieder rein ist. Nach dem Verbrennen soll ein Reiner die Asche der Kuh sammeln und sie verwahren, damit sie für das Reinigungswasser (מי נדה) verwendet werden kann.

An diese Anweisung knüpft 4Q276 unmittelbar an. Der Text ist nur fragmentarisch erhalten, doch lässt er sich eindeutig als Aufnahme von Num 19,1–9 identifizieren,[134] wobei eine Erweiterung auf weitere Fälle von Sexualbefleckung erfolgt.[135] 4Q276 schließt mit der Angabe, dass es sich um ein Sündopfer handelt und der Priester sich (wieder) bekleidet. Danach bricht der Text ab. Das Sündopfer ist hier allerdings eher mit dem Blut der geopferten Kuh verbunden als mit einem Wasserritus.

Wozu das Reinigungswasser (מי נדה) dient,[136] wird hier genauso wenig deutlich wie in Num 19. Allerdings setzt 4Q277 die Thematik fort, indem nunmehr Interpretationen für die Leerstellen von Num 19 gegeben werden. Die Schlussnotiz aus Num 19,9, dass es sich um ein Sündopfer handle, wird dahingehend ausgezogen, dass nunmehr gesagt wird, worin die Sühne besteht.[137] Wesentlich

---

132 Dafür spricht auch der Fortgang des Textes in Frg. 3, wo noch Speisegesetze folgen.

133 Im Anschluss an die Textedition in DJD 35, 104: "וכבס ולכול הקודשים יכבס א[יש] במים את []" übersetzt WERRETT, Ritual Purity, 248f, „he must launder it. And for all sacred (food), a m[an] is to wash in water …". MAIER, Qumran-Essener II, 236, übersetzt stattdessen etwas offener: „wasche er (sein Kleid). Und für alle heiligen Dinge wasche einer das" (Ende des Textes).

134 Wie gesehen, gibt es im halachishen Material unterschiedliche Anknüpfungen an Num 19, die LAWRENCE, Washing, 105, so versteht, dass sie „reflect ongoing debates over the halakah for purification of corpse impurity", im Anschluss an Baumgarten (vgl. z.B. seinen Beitrag „Red Cow"; s.a. DJD 35,118 u.ö.).

135 Vgl. WERRETT, Ritual Purity, 260; s.a. 261, wo er generell festhält, dass „the Red Heifer rite has been expanded far beyond its presentation in Num 19 in order to include certain liturgical elements and additional forms of impurity that are not included in the biblical description in the מי נדה".

136 Allerdings nur als Ergänzung der Lakune, nicht als gesicherter Text.

137 In der Ausweitung auf Sühne sieht WERRETT, Ritual Purity, 60f., eine Ausdehnung der Reinigung auf „ritual and moral transgressions"; die nachfolgende Sühne mache die Einbeziehung eines Priesters als einzig reiner Person in den Vorgang notwendig.

für die Sühne sind allerdings das Blut der Kuh sowie ihre Fettstücke.[138] Nähere Auskünfte werden auch für das Reinigungswasser gegeben: es befindet sich in Kesseln.[139] Für den Priester und die Träger des Kessels mit dem Reinigungswasser wird festgeschrieben, dass sie rein sein sollen.

Der weitere Textfluss von 4Q277 ist sehr fragmentarisch, so dass die Worte nur schwer miteinander zu verbinden sind. Genannt werden Aspekte von Unreinheit, die auch in anderen Dokumenten begegnen und für die rituelle Reinigung notwendig ist, z.B. Menschen mit Ausfluss und Tote. In diesem Zusammenhang erfolgt die Anweisung, dass der Priester Reinigungswasser sprengen soll (בז]רוק ... מי נדה], Z. 9). Gemeint ist in dieser Auslegung von Num 19 und der Interpretation der Reinigungsriten, dass der Priester von dem im Kessel befindlichen Reinigungswasser etwas versprengen soll, um damit Reinigung zu erreichen (לטהר). Obwohl in 4Q277 geregelt wird, wann der Priester welche Personen und in welchen Fällen mit Reinigungswasser besprengen soll, ist angesichts des Erhaltungszustands des Dokuments heute dennoch nicht mehr klar nachzuvollziehen, wie die Reinigungsriten im Einzelnen aussehen.[140]

Abschließend ist zu 4QTohorot festzustellen, dass sich in den Dokumenten eine Entwicklung abzeichnet. War zunächst vom Baden im Wasser und Reinigen der Kleider die Rede, das ein Unreiner an sich selbst an zwei Tagen durchführt, so wird jetzt die Frequenz erhöht und zudem ein zusätzlicher Ritus mit einem Priester als zweiter beteiligter Person eingeführt. Dies wurde nötig, da es jetzt konkret um Sühne geht, die zu erwirken ein Priester notwendig ist. Neben die rituelle Reinigung, die schon aus anderen Schriften vom Toten Meer bekannt ist, tritt mit der Sühne also ein weiterer Aspekt hinzu.[141] Theologische Interpretation und Ausweitung des Ritus unterstützen sich gegenseitig und führen zu einer Neubewertung der Reinigung.

Der Aspekt des Lebens und der Gemeinschaft tritt damit in den Hintergrund und wird zugunsten einer Aussage über Gottes Wirken abgeschwächt. Der Gedanke der Sühne ergänzt nunmehr die rituelle Waschung, indem ihr eine wirkmächtige Bedeutung vor Gott zugeschrieben wird.

---

138 Eine starke Deutung nimmt WERRETT, Ritual Purity, 235, vor, wenn er aus 4Q277 schließt: „the sprinkling of the blood and the sprinkling of the מי נדה were, in addition to being rites of purification, also believed to be rituals of atonement similar to that of Yom Kippur".

139 Nach LAWRENCE, Washing, 106, sind bei dieser Vorstellung möglicherweise die in II Chr 4,6–10 erwähnten zehn Reinigungsbecken aufgenommen.

140 Dennoch schließt WERRETT, Ritual Purity, 231, daraus auf einen zweigliedrigen Ablauf von Baden („preliminary lustration") und Besprengung („sprinkling of the מי נדה"); er leitet dies aus einer Analogie zu 4Q414 und 4Q512 ab (dazu s.o. Abschnitt 4.2.1.). Zu dem Ritus s.a. den Beitrag von BAUMGARTEN, „Red Cow" passim.

141 Vgl. die Bewertung bei WERRETT, Ritual Purity, 232, der festhält, dass „the waters of sprinkling were capable of cleansing individuals from both corpse contamination and bodily discharges".

4.2.4. 4QMMT (4Q394–399)

Als letzten der halachischen Texte ist auf den viel diskutierten Text 4QMMT einzugehen.[142] Der Text liegt in mehreren Fragmenten vor, aufgeteilt auf 6 Handschriften, die unterschiedlich viel Text bieten.[143] Sie sind nach Tov aus paleographischen Gründen zwischen 30 v. – 20 n.Chr. entstanden; nach Maier ist der Text herodianisch; Charlesworth und Rietz bestimmen ihn als „late Hasmonean or early Herodian".[144] 4QMMT ist damit das paleographisch späteste Dokument in dieser Reihe von halachischen Schriften. Das lässt erwarten, dass die hier genannten Reinigungsvorschriften nochmals ausgefeilter sind.

4Q394 Frg. 3 Kol. i (sowie in etwas kürzerer Form 4Q395) schließen an das Thema von 4Q276 und 277 an. In 4Q394 Frg. 3 Kol. i Z. 16ff. werden Regelungen „bezüglich der Reinheit der Kuh des Sühneritus"[145] getroffen. Nachdem von Schlachtopfern und Speisopfern gehandelt worden ist,[146] kommen Z. 16ff. auf das Sündopfer zu sprechen. Vier Personen werden hierbei in ihren Funktionen während des Opfervorgangs genannt, ohne dass über ihren Status nähere Angaben gemacht werden: *erstens einer*, der die Kuh schächtet, *zweitens einer*, der sie verbrennt, *drittens einer*, der ihre Asche einsammelt, und *viertens einer*, der das [Wasser] des Sühneritus' aussprengt. Für diese vier Personen wird festgelegt:

---

142 4QMMT kann hier allerdings nur im Blick auf die Waschungen und Reinigungsriten vorgestellt werden. Zu 4QMMT vgl. ansonsten weiterhin: J. KAMPEN/M. J. BERNSTEIN, *Reading, 4QMMT*; H. VON WEISSENBERG, *4QMMT Reevaluating*; sowie Beiträge in dem Sammelband F. GARCÍA MARTÍNEZ/A. STEUDEL/E. TIGCHELAAR (eds.), *From 4QMMT to Resurrection*.

143 4Q394 ist mit einem Bestand von 9 Fragmenten der längste zusammenhängende Text; 4Q395 ist lediglich ein Fragment mit 12 Zeilen Text; 4Q396 besteht aus zwei Fragmenten mit 39 Zeilen Text; 4Q397 besteht aus insgesamt 23, zum Teil sehr kleinen Fragmenten mit 52 Zeilen Textbestand; 4Q398 besteht aus 34 Textzeilen, die zum Teil nur einzelne Wörter umfassen; 4Q399 enthält 8 sehr fragmentarische Zeilen. Zum Text vgl. die Composite-Textedition in DJD 10 sowie J. H. CHARLESWORTH/H. W. M. RIETZ, *Dead Sea Scrolls III*, 196ff. – Zur Diskussion um die Textrekonstruktion vgl. auch VON WEISSENBERG, *4QMMT Reevaluating*, 40–104 (mit eigener Textrekonstruktion von 4Q397 und 4Q398 im so genannten Epilog). – Einen möglichen Anfang könnte 4Q448 gebildet haben; vgl. STEUDEL, *4Q448 – The Lost*, die Gemeinsamkeiten auflistet und mit der Möglichkeit rechnet, dass beide Dokumente entweder eine gemeinsame Sprache und Gattung repräsentieren (ebd., 258) oder dass 4QMMT mit einer Variante von Ps 154, wie sie 4Q448 bietet, begann, indem „4Q448 might well be a *captatio benevolentiae* in the incipit of the letter MMT – acknowledging Jonathan as political ruler over Israel" (ebd. 262).

144 Vgl. Tov, *Texts*, 420; MAIER, *Qumran-Essener II*, 362; CHARLESWORTH/RIETZ, *Dead Sea Scrolls II,1* 187. Früher datiert WHITE CRAWFORD, *Tempel Scroll*, 78, das älteste Manuskript auf 75 v.Chr., wobei sie weiter annimmt, dass „its date of composition lies in the first half of the second century BCE". Üblicherweise wird für 4QMMT eine Entstehungszeit um 150 v.Chr. angenommen; vgl. die Übersicht bei VON WEISSENBERG, *4QMMT Reevaluating*, 15–17.

145 Übersetzung mit MAIER, *Qumran-Essener II*, 364.

146 Die rituellen Vorgänge der Opfer sind aufgrund des Erhaltungszustandes des Textes und seiner Lakunen nicht klar zu identifizieren. Es folgt jedoch ein Einschnitt, nach dem auf das nächste Thema übergegangen wird.

(16) ... Und auch bezüglich der Reinheit der Kuh des Sühneritus: (17) Der sie schächtet und der sie verbrennt und der [ih]re Asche einsammelt und der da aussprengt das [Wasser] (18) des Sühneritus, für diese gilt, daß man [d]ie Sonne unterge[h]en lassen muß, um rein zu sein, (19) damit der Reine den Unreinen besprenge, denn den Söhnen[147]

(Der Text bricht hier am unteren Kolumnenrand ab.)

Interessant an diesem Reinigungsritus ist einerseits, dass er als Sündopfer (החטאת, Z. 16.18) bzw. Sühneritus (so die Übersetzung von Maier) bezeichnet wird. Das Opfer erfährt also eine Deutung, die den Vorgang wie eine Klammer umrahmt. Es dient der Sühnung von Schuld[148], als deren Ergebnis kultische Reinheit entsteht.

Bemerkenswert sind andererseits auch die Mittel, die eingesetzt werden. Zunächst geht es um einen Opfervorgang, der dann aber durch einen Besprengungsritus begleitet wird. Das Objekt des Versprengens ist im Wortbestand von 4Q394 leider nicht mehr erhalten (4Q395 enthält diesen Abschnitt nicht). Während Charlesworth eine Lakune lässt und in der Anmerkung vorschlägt, „water of" zu ergänzen,[149] füllen sowohl Maier als auch García Martínez den Text mit dem Begriff „Wasser" auf.[150] Diese Ergänzung knüpft an andere halachische Texte vom Toten Meer an, wo ebenfalls Wasser in einem Besprengungsritus zur Erzeugung ritueller Reinheit Verwendung findet:[151] in der Tempelrolle 11Q19 50,17–23; 4Q512 Kol. 12 Frg. 1–3 (dort auch verbunden mit dem Thema Sühne); 4Q274 Frg. 2 Kol i; sowie 4Q276, wo ebenso von Sühne die Rede ist, und damit verbunden 4Q277, wo das Wasser in Kesseln bereit steht. Von Kesseln ist in 4Q394 keine Rede. Doch lässt sich annehmen, dass an Wasser in Kesseln oder großen Gefäßen (womöglich Steingefäßen)[152] gedacht ist, wenn man 4Q394 Frg. 8 Kol. iv sowie 4Q396 Frg. 1 Kol. ii mit in die Interpretation einbezieht. Dort heißt es in Z. 5–8 bzw. Z. 5–9, dass ausgegossene Flüssigkeiten keine Unter-

---

147 Übersetzung mit MAIER, Qumran-Essener II, 364.
148 S.a. 4Q394 Frg. 5–7 Z. 14, wo von der Schuld des Volkes (העם עוון) die Rede ist, wofür Opfer dargebracht werden; mit sachlicher und terminologischer Nähe zu 4Q394 Frg. 3 Kol. i.
149 CHARLESWORTH/RIETZ, Dead Sea Scrolls III, 198/199; Ergänzungsvorschlag ebd., 199 Anm. 18.
150 MAIER, Qumran-Essener II, 364; GARCÍA MARTÍNEZ, Dead Sea Scrolls, 80.
151 In der Mischung bzw. Addition der Vorgänge sieht WERRETT, Ritual Purity, 195, eine Rezeption des gesamten Kapitels Num 19, wobei alle dort genannten Vorschriften durch 4QMMT verbunden werden. Zu Num 19 s.o. die Abschnitte 4.1.2. und 4.2.3.
152 Für dieses Verständnis plädiert KAZEN, Jesus and Purity Halakhah, 83–85, aufgrund der zahlreichen archäologischen Funde von Steingefäßen im 1. Jh. Auf die vielfältigen Steingefäße, Brunnen und Miqwa'ot, die in Qumran entdeckt wurden, macht auch MAGNESS, Archaeology of Qumran, 135–137, aufmerksam; sie sieht diese in 4QMMT angespielt. Die in die Erde eingelassenen Brunnen enthielten ca. 250–1000 Liter Wasser und wurden durch Naturwasser wie Regen oder Quellwasser angefüllt; s.a. ZISSU/AMIT, „Common Judaism", 47. 4QMMT selbst enthält jedoch keine näheren Angaben zu den Gefäßen.

scheidung von rein und unrein mehr zulassen, weil sich das eine mit dem andren vermischt,[153] d.h. aber umgekehrt, dass die Reinheit von Wasser nur dann gewährleistet ist, wenn das Wasser sich in einem dafür vorgesehenen Behälter befindet. Auch der Umstand, dass in 4Q394 Frg. 3 Kol. i keine Auskunft über die Qualität des Wassers gegeben wird (von fließendem Wasser ist keine Rede), legt nahe, an Kessel zu denken, aus denen das Wasser gesprengt wird.

Darüber, wer oder was besprengt wird, wird ebenso keine Auskunft erteilt. Wenn man annehmen darf, dass ein ähnlicher Vorgang wie in 4Q274 Frg. 2 Kol i dahinter steht, so könnte man auch hier daran denken, dass ein Priester denjenigen mit Wasser besprengt, der um Sühne ersucht.

Der Sühneritus wird in 4Q394 nunmehr eindeutig von einem anderen als dem betreffenden zu Reinigenden durchgeführt. Dies geht deutlich aus Z. 19 hervor, wo gesagt wird, dass der Reine für einen Unreinen den Vorgang durchführt. Die Opfervorgänge lassen vermuten, dass der Durchführende ein Priester ist. Dafür spricht auch die Fortsetzung in 4Q395, wo die Söhne Aarons als die Opfernden genannt werden.[154] Durch den Vollzug des Ritus ist auch der Priester zunächst unrein geworden und muss bis zum Abend warten, bevor er wieder den Status ritueller Reinheit erlangt hat.[155]

Ein Sündopfer (החטא) fällt nach 4Q397 Frg. 6–13 Z. 8f. an, wenn sich jemand versehentlich verfehlt hat, d.h. wenn er das Gebot nicht gehalten hat. Welcher Ritus notwendig wird, wird in 4Q397 nicht berichtet, doch ist an den in 4Q394 beschriebenen Vorgang zu denken. Das Sündopfer und damit das rituelle Besprengen mit Wasser kann demnach mehrmals wiederholt werden. Da kein bestimmter Termin angegeben ist, kann man vermuten, dass der Text die Möglichkeit einräumt, dass es je nach Bedarf durchzuführen ist.

Für die Gemeinschaft, die nach der Tora lebt, wird am Ende gelten, dass sie den Segen Gottes empfangen; vgl. 4Q398 Frg. 11–13; 4Q398 Frg. 14 Kol. i und 4Q398 Frg. 15–17.[156] Die Beachtung der Gesetze wie auch die Zurückführung in den Stand ritueller Reinheit wird also mit dem Segen Gottes[157] am Ende der

---

153 In dieser Anordnung sieht García Martínez, „Problem of Purity", 149, einen Vorläufer der Position der Sadduzäer im Gegensatz zu der der Pharisäer.

154 Zur Identität von Priestern und Aaroniden vgl. 4Q396 Frg. 2 Kol. ii Z. 8f. Während das Volk als die Heiligen gilt, werden die Aaroniden als Hochheilige bezeichnet; vgl. 4Q397 Frg. 6–13 Z. 14.

155 In dieser Vorschrift sieht White Crawford, Tempel Scroll, 79, eine Nachwirkung aus der Tempelrolle vorliegen. S. aber oben Anm. 51.

156 Zu den textlichen Unsicherheiten vgl. die Darstellung bei R. G. Kratz, „Mose", 162–166; sie seien hier nur notiert – hinsichtlich der Reinigungsriten berühren diese jedoch nicht die hier vorgelegte Interpretation.

157 Nach Kratz, „Mose", 161, sind damit geschichtstheologische Reminiszenzen verbunden, indem das Stichwort Halten der Tora „seinerseits an Tora und Propheten orientiert ist" und damit einen übergeordneten Bezug zu atl. Geschichtskonzeptionen herstellt. A.a.O., 167 interpretiert Kratz den Segen bzw. die Segnungen korrespondierend zu Fluch bzw. Flüchen als Reflex der

Zeit (באחרית העת) belohnt. 4Q399 Kol. i Z. 9 bezeichnet dies schließlich als Rettung (מצול). Damit steht am Ende von 4QMMT eine deutliche Heilszusage mit eschatologischer Ausrichtung.[158] In diese zukünftige Heilsperspektive ist der Reinigungsvorgang eingebunden. Die Reinigung wird nötig, wenn die Taten nicht entsprechend der Tora erfolgten. Das Ziel der Reinigung ist es demnach, den Menschen wieder in einen Zustand zu versetzen, wo er der Tora entspricht und sich Gerechtigkeit vor Gott und bei sich selbst erwirbt (vgl. 4Q398 Frg. 14 Kol. ii Z. 7).[159] Die rituelle Reinigung bedeutet also, dass der zu Reinigende wieder als rein vor Gott dasteht und Zugang zu den Heilsgaben hat. Das gesprengte Reinigungswasser bringt damit das Heil Gottes zurück und versetzt den Menschen in die Lage, an Gottes endzeitlichen Heilsgütern zu partizipieren.

Gemessen an 4QTohorot geht 4QMMT noch einen Schritt weiter.[160] An die in 4QTohorot vollzogene theologische Interpretation der Reinigung als Sühne knüpft 4QMMT an, indem das Reinigungsritual in das Sündopfer eingebunden wird. 4QMMT eröffnet darüber hinaus aber noch eine weitere Perspektive als 4QTohorot. Das Ziel des Ritus wird in 4QMMT nicht auf die Erlangung der Reinheit beschränkt. Vielmehr wird es auf einen neuen Bereich ausgeweitet, indem es auf Gottes Heil, Gerechtigkeit und Segen ausgerichtet ist. Zugleich wird es um eine zeitliche Komponente ergänzt, insofern der Segen aus der Tora am Ende der Zeit wirksam werden wird. Hier ist deutlich ein eschatologischer Aspekt impliziert, der in den anderen halachischen Schriften nicht zu finden ist. 4QMMT beschreibt damit eine neue Lebensqualität, die zu erlangen, die Reinigung einen wesentlichen Anteil hat.

Die Überlegung nach einer möglichen Entwicklung im halachischen Material findet hier ihren Endpunkt in einer eschatologischen Ausweitung des göttlichen Heilsbereichs.

Geschichtsdeutung der atl. Chronik – „Segen und Fluch werden in historische Einzelakte zerlegt". Allerdings sind auch die endzeitlichen Perspektiven von Dtn 30,1–3; 31,29 eingeholt (a.a.O. 168; VON WEISSENBERG, *4QMMT Reevaluating*, 20–212, nimmt darüber hinaus noch Dtn 4,29f. hinzu). Insgesamt ist damit am Ende von 4QMMT eine „Bewegung von der Vergangenheit zur Zukunft" zu erkennen (ebd.).

158 Andres VON WEISSENBERG, *4QMMT Reevaluating*, 189f., die in der Wendung אחרית הימים lediglich die nahe Zukunft angespielt sieht und dies mit dem Gesamtduktus von 4QMMT verbindet, insofern das Dokument auf „repentance and reformulation of the Jerusalem cult" (a.a.O., 235) ziele.

159 Vgl. KRATZ, "Mose", 171, der den Zusammenhang so interpretiert, dass „die Einsicht in den Ablauf der auf das ‚Ende der Tage' zugehenden Geschichte" zu „Umkehr und Toragehorsam" motivieren soll.

160 S.a. LAWRENCE, *Washing*, 93 Anm. 30: „While the Scrolls are generally stricter than either the Hebrew Bible or the rabbis, this text (sc. 4QMMT) is even stricter than most other texts in the Scrolls".

4.3. Gemeinschaftsregel (1QS / 4QS)

Die sog. Gemeinschaftsregel von Qumran enthält drei Belege, die von Waschungen handeln (3,4–9; 4,21; 5,13f.). Alle drei Belege stehen im Anfangsteil der Schrift, der Regelungen über den Eintritt neuer Mitglieder bietet sowie Auskünfte über die Jahresfeier der Gemeinschaft erteilt. Allerdings gehören die Belege womöglich verschiedenen Entwicklungsstufen der Schrift an. Demnach würde 5,13f. eine frühe Form darstellen, während die anderen beiden Belege erst später in die Schrift integriert wurden. Diese entstehungsgeschichtliche Annahme stützt sich auf Versionen der Gemeinschaftsregel aus Höhle 4; in der Textrezension 4Q258 (= 4QS[d]) fehlen Kap. 1–4, während die ansonsten nahestehende Rezension 4Q256 (= 4QS[b]) diese enthält.[161] In 4QS und 1QS scheinen unterschiedliche Texttraditionen bewahrt zu sein, wobei davon auszugehen ist, dass ein ursprünglich kürzerer Text, wie er von 4QS repräsentiert wird, später gewachsen ist.[162]

Die relevanten Belege geben auf die hier interessierende Frage nach Reinigungsriten allesamt lediglich eine indirekte Auskunft, da sie nicht direkt angeben, wie die Waschungen im Fall des Eintritts erfolgen. Vielmehr werden im Umfeld dieses Themenfeldes Auskünfte zu Menschen außerhalb der Gemeinschaft gegeben. Es können daher nur über den Weg eines negativen Beweisverfahrens Aussagen über Waschungen und Reinigungsriten gegeben werden.

4.3.1. 1QS 3,4–9

Innerhalb des Themenfeldes neue Mitglieder der Gemeinschaft betreffend setzt in 1QS 2,25 ein neuer Abschnitt ein. Es geht jetzt um diejenigen, die nicht der Gemeinschaft beitreten wollen. Hierbei kommt der Abschnitt 3,4–9 auf Waschungen zu sprechen, die denen außerhalb der Gemeinschaft verwehrt werden.

Dazu wird folgende Ausschlussregelung getroffen: Wer sich weigert, in den Bund einzutreten (2,25f.: כול המואס לבוא בבריתם), d.h. wer nicht zur Gemeinschaft des *Jachat*[163] gehören will und weder Unterweisung noch Gesetz

---

161 Vgl. A. SCHOFIELD, *From Qumran*, 76–88.125–130, mit paleographischen Angaben, d.h. für 1QS legt sie eine Datierung zwischen 100 und 75 v.Chr. zugrunde, für 4QS rechnet sie mit einem Zeitraum zwischen 30–0. Beide Textrezensionen sind nach ihrem Entstehungsmodell nebeneinander tradiert worden, wobei 4QS eine frühe Tradition in später Textbezeugung widerspiegelt.

162 Vgl. SCHOFIELD, *From Qumran*, 89–92.104f., mit Beispielen, die eine strengere spätere Auslegung zeigen.

163 Der Begriff Jachat wird hier in der herkömmlichen Weise benutzt, insofern er die Gemeinschaft bezeichnet, die der Siedlung Qumran zugewiesen wird. Demgegenüber wird der Begriff bei J. J. COLLINS, „Yaḥad", 85, und SCHOFIELD, *From Qumran*, 66f., weiter gefasst, wenn sie unter Jachat eine essenische Bewegung verstehen und darin zwischen einem Zentrum in Qumran und weiteren Gemeinschaften in der Peripherie unterscheiden.

annimmt und sich daher auch nicht unter den Vollkommenen (תמימים, d.h. den Mitgliedern der Gemeinschaft, 3,3) befindet, dieser darf nicht gereinigt (יטהר) und nicht geheiligt werden (יתקדש) weder mit Reinigungswasser (מי נדה) noch im Wasser (Lohse: Meereswasser) oder in Flüssen noch durch Wasser der Reinigung / des Badens (מי רחץ) (Z. 4f.). Er soll stattdessen vollständig unrein bleiben (so der starke Ausdruck in 3,5: טמא טמא יהיה).[164]

Die Gemeinschaft legt damit fest, dass die Reinigungsriten den Mitgliedern allein vorbehalten sind. Menschen, die außerhalb der Gemeinschaft leben, wird die Teilnahme daran verweigert. Die Funktion der Reinigung, die hier noch nicht direkt angegeben wird, wird ihnen nicht zuteil. Die Reinigung, um die es hier geht, ist eine rituelle Reinigung,[165] für die mehrere mögliche Abläufe stichwortartig angegeben werden.

Der Fortsetzung des Textes ist zu entnehmen, dass diese Reinigung auch mit dem Aspekt von Sühne verbunden ist (כפר *pual*, als Subjekt ist Gott zu denken[166], 3,6).[167] Sühne wäre für einen Eintretenden durchaus möglich. Anders als in den halachischen Schriften[168] wird sie hier allerdings so angegeben, dass sie durch den wahren Rat Gottes (עצת אמת אל), d.h. durch die von der Qumran-Gemeinschaft vorgegebene Gesetzesinterpretation, erwirkt wird.[169] Das Stichwort Sühne ist hier weniger kultisch geprägt, als vielmehr eingebunden in gemeindebildende Strategien der Eingliederung der Mitglieder in die Regeln der Gemeinschaft des *Jachat*. Käme Sühne zustande, so hätte dies zur Folge, dass das Licht der Lebendigen (אור חיים, Z. 7) erblickt werden könnte. Nur so könnte ein Eintretender gereinigt werden, und zwar durch den heiligen Geist, der der Gemeinschaft in ihrer Wahrheit gegeben ist (ברוח קדושה ליחד באמתו יטהר מכול,

---

164 Nach García Martínez, „Problem of Purity", 155f., zeigt sich in dem Abschnitt ein negatives Menschenbild, das alle Menschen außerhalb der Gemeinschaft als Sünder beurteilt; demgegenüber sind die Menschen innerhalb der Gemeinschaft in Bezug auf die Reinheit den Engeln gleichgestellt.

165 Vgl. Klawans, Impurity, 79–82, der aufzeigt, dass für 1QS alle Menschen außerhalb der Gemeinschaft als potentielle Quelle für rituelle Unreinheit gelten.

166 Vgl. Janowski/Lichtenberger, „Enderwartung", 44f.47.

167 So urteilt Klawans, Impurity, 85, für diesen Abschnitt: „the identification of moral and ritual impurity is manifested at Qumran: repentance from sin and purification from defilement have become mutually dependent".

168 Vgl. vor allem 4Q512, wo auf das Reinigungsritual der Waschung Sühne folgt; s.a. 4Q276; 4Q277; 4Q394 und 4Q397, wo Sühne als Sündopfer erfolgt.

169 S.a. Janowski/Lichtenberger, „Enderwartung", 49–51, die herausstellen, dass „nach 1QS3:6–12 *präsentisch* Sühne gewirkt [wird]: der vollkommene Wandel und das Halten der Gebote – die ihrerseits zur geistbestimmten Entsühnung des einzelnen führen – sind Voraussetzung für die Wirksamkeit der Sühne, die die Gemeinde in ihrer *gegenwärtigen Existenz* für Israel bzw. für sich selbst vollzieht." (Zitat ebd., 50)

Z. 7).[170] Die durch den Geist gewirkte Sühne steht also vor dem möglichen Eintritt in die Gemeinschaft und den Bereich des Lebens. Die danach folgende Reinigung setzt damit zugleich voraus, dass der Eintretende sich unter den Rat demütigt (ענוה „Niedrigkeit", Z. 8)[171]. Wenn das geschehen ist, dann könnte er mit Reinigungswasser besprengt werden (להזות מי נדה, Z.9), dass er sich heiligte durch das Wasser der Reinheit (במי דוכי, Z. 9). Danach wird er vollkommen wandeln auf Gottes Wegen (Z. 10ff.), d.h. zur Gemeinschaft als vollgültiges Mitglied hinzu gehören.[172]

In 3,4f. werden verschiedene Arten von Wasser zur Reinigung genannt: Reinigungswasser (מי נדה), Wasser bzw. Meerwasser[173] (בימים), Wasser in Flüssen (נהרות) oder Wasser für ein Reinigungsbad (מי רחץ). Obwohl die Wasserarten detailliert unterschieden sind, geht doch aus dem Abschnitt nichts Näheres über die Reinigungsriten und deren praktizierte Abläufe hervor. Es könnte sein, dass wenigstens einige der Reinigungsriten in unterschiedlichen Wasserarten durchführbar wären. Es könnte aber auch sein, dass die verschiedenen Wasserarten für divergierende Reinigungsvorgänge stehen. So ist vorgeschlagen worden, dass מי רחץ Wasser zum Baden angibt,[174] während מי נדה Wasser bezeichnet, das gesprengt wird.[175] Letztere Interpretation kann sich immerhin innerhalb des Kontextes auf 1QS 4,21 stützen, wo מי נדה gesprengt wird.[176] Diese spezifische Interpretation stützt sich weitgehend auf die Wortbedeutungen der Verben, stammt aber (abgesehen von 4,21) nicht aus dem Kontext von 1QS. Da immerhin eine Differenzierung des Wassers erfolgt, scheint mir in der Tat nahe zu liegen, an unterschiedliche Reinigungsriten zu denken, auch wenn diese hier nicht ausdifferenziert sind und sie im Folgenden in der Argumentation auch wieder zusammen genommen werden. Dennoch, wenn nur ein Ritus gemeint wäre, hätte zur Argumentation ein genereller Hinweis auf ein Verbot ausgereicht, um den Außenstehenden den Zugang zur Gemeinschaft zu verwehren.

Dass dennoch unterschiedliche Reinigungsarten genannt werden, spricht für eine differenzierte Praxis von Reinigungsriten, die hinter den verschiede-

---

170 Dieser Geist ist nach García Martínez, „Problem of Purity", 156, in der Gemeinschaft aktiv und „makes the sect a place of purification and justification".

171 Vgl. Baumgarten, „Purification Liturgies", 207. ענוה begegnet als ethisches Ideal für die in Qumran lebende „Gemeinschaft des ewigen Bundes" (יחד ברית עולם, 5,5f.) weiter unten in der Gemeinderegel in 4,3; 5,3. Dahinter könnte ein Lebensmotto aus den Psalmen nachwirken, das für ein einfaches und bescheidenes Leben plädiert und darin die Haltung des Frommen ausmacht.

172 Vgl. Baumgarten, „Purification Liturgies", 207f., sowie auch den Beitrag von Sänger, „‚Ist er heraufgestiegen, gilt er in jeder Hinsicht als ein Israelit' (bYev 47b)" in dieser Publikation, 291–334.

173 So E. Lohse, Texte, 9; vgl. Lawrence, Washing, 144, der es als „oceans" wiedergibt.

174 Zum Bedeutungsspektrum von רחץ bzw. מי רחץ s.o. Anm. 50.

175 Vgl. Magness, Archaeology of Qumran, 137.

176 S.u. Abschnitt 4.3.2.

nen Reinigungs- und Wasserarten durchscheinen könnte,[177] hier allerdings nicht näher entfaltet werden. Neben eine anzunehmende unterschiedliche Praxis zwischen Eintauchen und Sprengen mit verschiedenen Wasserarten treten unterschiedliche Bräuche in stehendem und fließendem Wasser, die für verschiedene Reinigungen in Frage kommen.

Wichtiger als die Frage nach unterschiedlichen Reinigungsriten ist in 1QS 3 die Funktion der Reinigungen. Die Reinigungen, von denen in 1QS 3 die Rede ist, stellen eine Art Eintrittsbedingung in die Gemeinschaft dar. Den Vollzug des Rituals oder der Rituale könnte man so verstehen, dass dadurch gleichsam ein Generalerlass rituell erwirkt werde.[178] Dann wäre die rituelle Reinigung so verstanden, dass die bewirkte Sühne (3,6) nicht nur vor dem Rat der Gemeinschaft, sondern auch vor Gott gilt, indem sie Befreiung von Schuld bringt. Dieser Gedanke der Aufhebung von Schuld ist allerdings nicht ausdrücklich ausgesprochen. Wohl aber ist davon die Rede, dass die Wirkung der Reinigung von der Bereitschaft des Eintretenden abhängt.[179] Dieser Gedanke ist neu gegenüber der in 4Q512, 4QTohorot und 4QMMT angesprochenen Sühnewirkung. Die Sühne erfolgt nicht automatisch durch den Vollzug des Ritus, sondern nur, wenn der sich Reinigende sich in die Bestimmungen der Gemeinschaft einfügt.[180] Deren Autorität ist genauso anzuerkennen wie die Gesetze Gottes, und zwar in der Auslegung durch die Gemeinschaft des *Jachat*.[181]

Eintreten kann offensichtlich jeder, unabhängig von Alter, Herkunft oder Geschlecht. Fundamental ist die Eingliederung in die Gemeinschaft, der gegenüber andere Unterscheidungsmerkmale zweitrangig sind. Dies ist jedenfalls daraus zu schließen, dass keine näheren Angaben über die Eintretenden gemacht werden – jedenfalls sofern man nicht annimmt, dass der nicht mehr erhaltene Eingangsteil der Schrift diese enthalten hätte, was aber unwahrscheinlich ist. Zielpunkt ist die Gemeinschaft als eine soziale Größe, in der religiöse Regeln

---

177 Vgl. LAWRENCE, *Washing*, 144: „several different forms of washing were known and recognized as suitable".

178 Ähnlich interpretiert z.B. T. M. FINN, *From Death to Rebirth*, 103–106, der einen vierteiligen Eingliederungsprozess in die Qumran-Gemeinschaft ausmacht, wobei er die in 1QS 3 genannten Rituale dem zweiten Stadium zuweist, an deren Ende ein „preliminary full membership" (ebs., 104) stehe. Er beurteilt den Prozess so, dass „ritual immersion was at the heart of Qumran's rite of entry, the necessary condition for advancing to full membership" (ebd. 106).

179 Vgl. BAUMGARTEN, „Purification Rituals", 199, der von „spiritual transformation demanded of adherents of the sect", die „truly repented inwardly", spricht.

180 S.a. die Interpretation von MAGNESS, *Archaeology of Qumran*, 137: "the Qumran community associated external cleansing with the spiritual transformation demanded of its members."

181 MAGNESS, *Archaeology of Qumran*, 137, zieht daraus die Schlussfolgerung, dass Ethik und rituelle Reinheit in 1QS zusammenfallen.

gelten.¹⁸² Diese Regeln zielen jedoch über den gelebten Raum hinaus, indem durch ihre Einhaltung ein göttlicher Bereich geöffnet wird.

Dem Abschnitt in 1QS 3 ist die Perspektive des Lichts und des Lebens elementar wichtig. Das Licht der Lebendigen (אור חיים, Z. 7) ist als zu erreichendes Ziel der Reinigung genannt. Lohse übersetzt in seiner Textausgabe mit „Licht des Lebens".¹⁸³ Dahinter wird eine Heilsvorstellung stehen, die eine Perspektive für das Leben angibt. Ist in den Texten der Gemeinschaft der Gegensatz von Licht und Finsternis zu finden,¹⁸⁴ so könnte an eine entsprechende Alternative auch hier zu denken sein. Wer zur Gemeinschaft gehört, lebt im Licht; umgekehrt befinden sich die Außenstehenden im Bereich der Finsternis. Der Ausdruck „Licht des Lebens" geht aber noch einen Schritt weiter, da einerseits das Licht näher qualifiziert wird und andererseits der Komplementärbegriff der Finsternis fehlt. Die Wendung „Licht der Lebendigen" (אור חיים) verweist auf einen Bereich, in dem Leben möglich ist. Wenn man diesen Bereich in den Zusammenhang anderer theologischer Aussagen von Qumran stellt, steht er komplementär zu dem Tod als dem Bereich, in dem das Leben unmöglich ist.¹⁸⁵

Da in 3,7 allerdings nur von der Seite des Lebens die Rede ist und dies ausgesprochen qualifiziert geschieht, scheint mir der Beleg eine größere Tragweite zu haben. Das Leben wird durch das Befolgen der Regeln der Gemeinschaft ermöglicht.¹⁸⁶ Dadurch entsteht ein Bereich, in dem das Heil Gottes herrscht und so Leben möglich ist. Wenn dadurch der Raum der Gruppe als Heilsbereich qualifiziert wird, werden mit der Heilskategorie zugleich Gruppengrenzen markiert. Der Eintritt in diesen Bereich bringt damit Leben im doppelten Sinn. Einerseits entsteht eine Teilhabe an der Gemeinschaft als soziale Größe und andererseits bedeutet die Zugehörigkeit zur Gruppe zugleich, dass ihre Mitglieder unter dem göttlichen Segen leben und damit an Gottes Lebensbereich partizipieren. 1QS 3 schafft damit eine qualifizierte Aussage, die der Gemeinschaft des *Jachat* nach Innen eine Identität vermittelt und nach Außen eine Abgrenzung gegenüber Außenstehenden vornimmt.

War zu sehen, dass die Aussagen über die Waschungen in einem Textabschnitt stehen, in dem es um den Zugang neuer Mitglieder zur Gemeinschaft geht, so stellt sich die Frage, ob die Regelungen nur für einen einmaligen Akt

---

182 Dieses spiegelt sich auch bei der Schilderung der Eintrittsbedingungen der Essener von Josephus, Bell 2,137–142, wo allerdings interessanterweise keine Waschungen genannt werden.
183 So Lohse, *Texte*, 11.
184 S.a. die Bezeichnung „Söhne des Lichts" (בני אור) für die Mitglieder der Gemeinschaft des Jachat, wie sie z.B. in 1QS 3,24f begegnet.
185 Vgl. Harrington, „Outsiders", 202.
186 Aufgrund dieser inhaltlichen Füllung macht Werrett, *Ritual Purity*, 303f., eine Übertragung der halachischen Reinheitsvorschriften für den Umgang mit dem Tempel auf die Gemeinschaft des *Jachat* aus: „a structure of stone has been replaced by one of flesh and blood".

gelten[187] oder ob dieser gegebenenfalls auch wiederholt werden kann, etwa dann, wenn sich jemand von der Gemeinschaft abgewandt hat? Der Text ist m.E. offen für beide Interpretationen. Wahrscheinlich ist gemeindeintern der Fall des Verlassens des Weges nicht vorgesehen (vgl. 3,10–12: der beschrittene Weg wird zum Bund ewiger Gemeinschaft werden, והיתה לו לברית יחד עולמים, Z. 11f.). – Wenn in 5,1.8.14; 6,15 von Umkehr gesprochen wird (5,1: שוב מכול רע), so meint dies eine Umkehr vor dem Eintritt in die Gemeinschaft bzw. eine Umkehr, die in die Gemeinschaft hineinführt. – Blickt man jedoch auf die Bestimmungen zur Durchführung des Rituals und seines Zwecks, dann lässt das Reinigungsritual immerhin die Möglichkeit einer Rückkehr nach einem zwischenzeitlichen Ausschluss aus der Gemeinschaft erwägen.[188] Als negativer Beweis mag für diese Interpretation angeführt werden, dass in Kap 6–7 weder unter den Aufnahmeregeln noch unter den Wiedereingliederungsregeln nach Verfehlung ein Reinigungsritual erwähnt ist. Dies lässt immerhin Spielraum für beide Möglichkeiten. Dann wäre das Reinigungsritual ein Vorläufer des Bußrituals und nicht auf ein Aufnahmeritual in die Gemeinschaft zu begrenzen.

4.3.2. 1QS 4,21

Der nächste Beleg führt den Heilsaspekt fort, indem nunmehr eine teleologische Perspektive eröffnet wird.[189] 1QS 4,21 steht in einer Szene über das Endgericht (4,18–26): Gott wird dort die Menschen durch seinen heiligen Geist reinigen (טהר), indem er das Verunreinigende aus dem Inneren der Menschen entfernt, und wird über sie den wahren Geist sprengen (ויז עליו רוח אמת, Z. 21), wie Reinigungswasser (כמי נדה) gesprengt wird. Danach wird es in der neuen Schöpfung[190] nur noch Herrlichkeit geben, da der Frevel für immer vernichtet sein wird (Z. 18f.23).[191] In der vorhergehenden Zeit, d.h. der gegenwärtigen Weltzeit, kämpfen der Geist der Wahrheit und der Geist des Frevels seit dem Anfang der Zeit im-

---

187 Ein solches Verständnis legt die Schilderung der Essener bei Josephus nahe, wenn er von einer Waschung beim Eintritt in die Gemeinschaft spricht (vgl. Bell 2,128f.; 2,137–142; 2,150.161). Die Schriften vom Toten Meer selbst bieten dafür jedoch kein Material, da sie zwar einen Aufnahmeprozess schildern, doch dabei keine Waschung erwähnen, jedenfalls abgesehen von 1QS 3. S.a. LAWRENCE, *Washing*, 135–141.

188 Ähnlich interpretiert KLAWANS, *Impurity*, 85f., wenn er auf eine analoge Behandlung und Bewertung von Außenstehenden und Mitgliedern, die sich verfehlt haben, verweist. S.a. BAUMGARTEN, „Purification Liturgies", 210f.

189 Vgl. dazu JANOWSKI/LICHTENBERGER, „Enderwartung", 52.56–59, die in dem vollkommenen Wandel des *Jachat* jedoch eine „Vorwegnahme des eschatologischen Gottesdienstes" sehen (ebd., 57) und darin eine Umdeutung des Eschatons ausmachen.

190 An dem Motiv sind Anklänge an die neue Schöpfung, die Paulus für die Endzeit als in Christus gegeben erwartet (vgl. II Kor 5,17), erkennbar.

191 Hier sind Anklänge an (oder Rezeption von) Endaussagen in Jes 25,8 zu hören; in Jes 25,8 wird der Tod vernichtet (vgl. A. LABAHN, „Deine Toten werden leben …"', 68–71), hier der Frevel.

mer noch gegen einander. In der darauf folgenden Zeit, d.h. der Endzeit, wird es nur noch den Geist der Wahrheit geben.

In diesem Zusammenhang steht die Reinigung eher am Rande des Interesses. Nähere Auskünfte über Durchführung oder Funktion der Reinigung werden nicht gegeben. Auch ist dem Kontext nicht zu entnehmen, ob es sich bei dieser Reinigung um einen bestimmten rituellen Vorgang mit Wasser handelt. Die Reinigung steht in einem Vergleich, der darauf zielt, dass der Mensch im Inneren gereinigt wird. Gedacht ist hierbei an eine anthropologische Veränderung des menschlichen Wesens. Der Durchführende der Reinigung ist der heilige Geist (רוח קודש), der den Menschen in seinem Inneren anrührt. Offen bleibt, wie sich dieser die Endzeit einleitende Geist zu den beiden im Kontext genannten urzeitlichen[192] Geistern der Wahrheit bzw. des Lichtes und des Frevels bzw. der Finsternis (3,18f.) verhält. Die adjektivische Kennzeichnung als „heilig" weist ihn jedenfalls dem Bereich Gottes zu, aus dem er kommt und die Reinigung durchführt. Aus der Reinigung gehen die Menschen als Vollkommene hervor, wie Gott selbst vollkommen ist, so dass sie danach in seinen Bereich hinüber wechseln können.

Die Reinigung verändert also das Leben des Menschen, insofern sie ihn dazu in die Lage versetzt, dass er von einer Welt in eine andere hinüber gelangt. Die Funktion der Reinigung besteht hier darin, den Übergang von einer Welt in die andere vorzubereiten. Auch diese Reinigung hat demnach lebensverändernde Qualität, auch wenn hier eigentlich kein Wasser zum Einsatz kommt.

Unklar ist, wie im Einzelnen die Abgrenzung der Gruppe aussieht, wer also nach der Reinigung dazu gehören wird. In 4,20 fällt die Wendung, dass „einige der Menschenkinder" (וזקק לו מבני איש) von Gott gereinigt werden. Der Kontext gibt jedoch nicht zu erkennen, ob diese Gruppe aus den Mitgliedern der Gemeinschaft besteht[193] oder ob auch oder vorwiegend andere zu den Geläuterten gerechnet werden. Letzteres scheint mir wahrscheinlicher zu sein, da von den Menschen in der Gemeinschaft erwartet wird, dass sie entsprechend dem Geist des Lichtes und der Wahrheit leben (vgl. 1QS 3,18f.) und sich daher von Frevel fernhalten (vgl. die ethischen Aussagen in 4,2–14). Wenn diese ethische Forderung von den Mitgliedern der Gemeinschaft eingehalten wird, ist unter dieser Gruppe das Potential an Menschen, die für eine Reinigung in Frage kommen, nicht so groß, wie es die Wendung „einige der Menschenkinder" nahelegt. Diese Interpretation des Textes ergibt sich jedenfalls aus der Argumentation in 1QS.

Die Gemeinschaft versteht sich als Gruppe der Reinheit und damit als eine Größe von Vollkommenheit, die im Einklang mit dem Geist der Wahrheit lebt. Eine umfangreiche Läuterung im Gericht wird demgegenüber für solche Men-

---

192 Der Begriff תולדות, der in 3,13 und 4,15 wie eine Klammer um den Abschnitt der zwei Geister gelegt ist, hat deutlich protologische Qualität.
193 So die Interpretation von LAWRENCE, Washing, 120.

schen notwendig, die nicht entsprechend dem Identitätsprogramm der Gemeinschaft leben.

4.3.3. 1QS 5,13f.

Der dritte Beleg für Reinigung steht in 1QS 5,13f. Klarer als in 1QS 3 wird in 1QS 5 eine scharfe Trennlinie zwischen den Mitgliedern der Gemeinschaft und denen außerhalb gezogen, für die das Stichwort „Absonderung" (בדל, 5,10.18) leitend ist. Jegliche Gemeinsamkeit oder Berührung mit anderen ist strikt untersagt. Menschen, die sich nicht der Gemeinschaft anschließen und die auch nicht die Umkehr vollziehen oder das Einführungsritual durchlaufen, müssen unbedingt gemieden werden. Unter dieses Einführungsritual fällt neben der Hinwendung zu den Gesetzen und Regeln der Gemeinschaft auch die Reinigung von Frevel. 5,13f. legt fest, dass jemandem, der außerhalb der Gemeinschaft steht, kein Zugang zu dem reinigenden Wasser gewährt wird. Solche Menschen können nicht gereinigt werden (כיא לוא יטהרו, Z. 13). Mit dieser Aussage geht 5,13f. einen Schritt weiter, als es noch in Kap. 3 zu lesen war.[194] Gab es dort wenigstens theoretisch noch eine Offenheit, so schließt 5,13f. diese Tür.[195]

Versucht man, dem Verbot eine inhaltliche Aussage zu Reinigungsriten in Qumran zu entnehmen, so steht hinter der Verweigerung der Reinigung für bestimmte Kreise eine Voraussetzung, die für eine erfolgreiche Durchführung des Rituals erfüllt sein muss. Reinigung kann nur erfolgen, wenn jemand die Bereitschaft mitbringt, sich der Gemeinschaft anzuschließen und vollständig nach deren Regeln zu leben. Neben der äußeren Bereitschaft zum Eintritt in den *Jachat* verbindet sich damit eine innere Bereitschaft zur Übernahme der Lebens- und Gehorsamsregeln (vgl. 5,8–10).

Wie die hier genannte Reinigung geschieht, welche Abläufe dazu gehören, ob Wasser dabei eine Rolle spielt und, wenn ja, welche Art von Wasser Verwendung findet, wird nicht ausgeführt.[196] In 5,13f. kommt es auf die Funktion der Reinigung an. Sie dient der Eingliederung in die Gemeinschaft und hat damit eine soziale Funktion in der Abgrenzung der Gruppe. Was für 3,4–9 galt, kann auch in 5,13f. gesehen werden. Die Grenzziehung hat eine doppelte Ausrichtung für die Gruppe. Einerseits werden klare Grenzen markiert, die den

---

194 GARCÍA MARTÍNEZ, „Problem of Purity", 152, beurteilt diesen Teil der Schrift als „it exhibits an advanced and structured phase of the sect's existence". Dass sich hierein eine veränderte Sichtweise in späterer Zeit zeigt, nimmt auch SCHOFIELD, *From Qumran*, 91f.101, an. Zudem weist sie, a.a.O., 130, die Fassung 1QS der im Qumran lebenden Gemeinschaft zu, für die partiell strengere Regeln als für andere Gemeinschaften im Jachat (s. Anm. 163) gelten, deren maßgebliche Dokumente mit Gemeinschaftsbestimmungen in 4QS vorliegen.

195 Vgl. HARRINGTON, „Outsiders", 188–190.

196 Allerdings sieht SCHOFIELD, *From Qumran*, 101, darin eine Anspielung auf die in der Siedlung Qumran gefundenen Miqwaoth.

Jachat von anderen sozialen Gruppen und Menschen trennen.[197] Andererseits schafft die Eingliederung in die Gemeinschaft eine Identität nach Innen. Die Gemeinschaft wird theologisch als eine Gruppe von Vollkommenen bestimmt, die durch ein Reinigungsritual zu neuen Menschen verändert worden sind. Dadurch entsteht ein Gruppenprofil mit hohem ethischen Anspruch.

4.4. Damaskusschrift

In der Damaskusschrift ist dreimal von Waschungen die Rede (CD 10,10–13; 11,1.21f.). Alle Belege befinden sich im zweiten Teil des Dokuments (CD 9–16, Handschrift A2), in dem Einzelbestimmungen in Geboten und Verboten notiert sind. Dem Charakter des Abschnitts entsprechend, sind die Bestimmungen äußerst kurz gehalten. Es gibt weder bestimmte Fallschilderungen noch genauere Angaben über die Anwendungsbereiche der Rechtsbestimmungen. Der Kontext in CD 10–11 signalisiert jedoch, dass es sich um Sabbatvorschriften handelt, auch wenn dies nicht bei allen Bestimmungen der Kapitel jedes Mal eigens erwähnt wird. Auch die Passagen betreffend die Waschungen reden nicht explizit vom Sabbat; d.h. wenn man die Anweisungen als Sabbatvorschriften liest, ist dies dem Kontext geschuldet.[198]

Ein weiterer Fall von Wasserriten begegnet im Zusammenhang der Reinigung von Sexualbefleckung in den Fragmenten 4Q272 und 4Q266, die Berührungen mit dem halachischen Material vom Toten Meer haben (s.u. Abschnitt 4.4.4.).

4.4.1. CD 10,10–13

In CD 10,10–13 ist eine Bestimmung über die Reinigung im Wasser (על הטהר במים) zu finden, die regelt, wie eine Waschung oder ein Baden (רחץ) im Wasser vollzogen werden muss. Dabei gilt grundsätzlich, dass eine Waschung in schmutzigem Wasser untersagt ist (Z. 11). An welche Art von Verunreinigung gedacht ist, ob sie rituell oder real zu verstehen ist, wird nicht gesagt. Lässt die Rede vom „Wasser, das schmutzig ist"[199] (במים צואים), an eine tatsächliche Verunreinigung denken, so spricht der folgende Kontext in Z. 13 eher für ein Verständnis als rituelle Verunreinigung (s.u.). Da aber die in Z. 10–12 und Z. 13

---

197 Vgl. dazu zwei Deutungen, die in ähnliche Richtung gehen: Einerseits JANOWSKI/LICHTENBERGER, „Enderwartung", 31: „Die Furcht vor ‚Unreinheit' …, die zum Leitmotiv einer ganzen Gemeinschaft werden konnte, läßt sich … als Ausweis eines zum Schutz der sozialen Ordnung geschaffenen Symbolsystems verstehen, das sich in rituellen Geboten und Verboten konkretisierte". Und andererseits mit etwas anderer Terminologie HARRINGTON, „Outsiders", 197: „impurity labels enforce social boundaries". Weiter schreibt sie: „Preserving group identity then becomes the overall reason for labeling outsiders."
198 Vgl. BAUMGARTEN, „Purification Liturgies", 205.
199 So die Übersetzung von LOHSE, *Texte*, 87.

genannten Verunreinigungen nicht aufeinander bezogen werden, bleibt letztlich offen, wie sich dieses „schmutzige Wasser" zu dem von Unreinen berührtem Wasser aus Z. 13 verhält.

In der Folge werden zwei Bestimmungen für die Reinigung gegeben. Zunächst wird gesagt, dass die Reinigung in einer so großen Menge an Wasser erfolgen soll, dass der zu reinigende Gegenstand vollständig bedeckt wird. Dies gilt sowohl für die Reinigung von Menschen als auch von Gefäßen. Diese Bestimmung richtet sich offensichtlich auf fließendes Wasser, auch wenn dies explizit nicht gesagt wird. Der Kontext macht es jedoch deutlich, da anderenfalls die Fortführung in Z. 13 keinen Sinn ergeben würde.

Die zweite Bestimmung in Z. 13 legt nämlich fest, dass das für die Reinigung zu verwendende Wasser nicht von einem Unreinen berührt worden sein darf, da es im Fall einer solchen Berührung unrein werden würde und damit dem Wasser in einem Gefäß gleichwertig werden würde. Das besagt also, dass für nicht verunreinigtes Wasser vorausgesetzt ist, dass es fließendes, unberührtes Wasser ist.

CD 10 gibt keine Auskunft, wofür das Wasser verwendet wird, ob für eine rituelle Reinigung im Zusammenhang des Tempels oder ob es für die Zubereitung von (bestimmten) Speisen gedacht ist. Möglicherweise sind die Alternativen auch nicht gegen einander auszuspielen, da sowohl Personen als auch Gefäße als zu Reinigende angegeben werden. CD 10 scheint allgemeine Hinweise zu bieten, wie im Fall von Reinigungen mit dem Wasser vorgegangen werden soll. Nachdruck liegt darauf, dass fließendes, lebendiges Wasser Verwendung finden soll. In diesem Wasser sprudelt das Leben, dessen Lebendigkeit und Reinheit auf den Gereinigten übergeht.

4.4.2. CD 11,1

Eine Ergänzung zu dieser Bestimmung bietet ein paar Zeilen später im selben Kontext CD 11,1, wo es erneut um Waschen oder Baden (רחץ) im Wasser geht. Hier öffnet sich ein Nebenkrater, der festlegt: wenn jemand in das Wasser steigt zum Baden oder Waschen, so darf er von dem Wasser trinken, aber es nicht in ein Gefäß schöpfen. Auch diese kurze Bemerkung steht recht isoliert im Zusammenhang, so dass kaum nähere Auskünfte über den Anlass des Waschens zu erhalten sind.

Der in das Wasser Steigende ist ein Mensch – ob Mann oder Frau ist nicht gesagt. Unklar bleibt auch, ob es dabei um einen einmaligen Akt oder um eine mehrmals vollzogene Handlung geht. Ein mögliches Verständnis wäre, den Kontext mit seinen Bestimmungen über den Sabbat (CD 10–11) mit in die Interpretation einzubeziehen, obwohl nicht explizit gesagt wird, dass es sich in 11,1 um Anordnungen für den Sabbat handelt. Doch wäre es immerhin möglich, den Kontakt mit Wasser an einem Sabbat anzunehmen. Dann wäre in der

Regelung eine Anweisung für einen Menschen zu sehen, der aus Absicht einer wahrscheinlich rituellen Reinigung am Sabbat das Wasser betritt.[200]

Möglich wäre es aber auch, den Vers grundsätzlicher zu lesen, wofür auch der nächste Beleg in 11,21f. spricht. Immerhin ist das Verbot, das Wasser zu schöpfen, allgemein formuliert. Dahinter mögen hygienische Gründe zu sehen sein, die für Speisen und Körperpflege unterschiedliche Wasserquellen nahe legen.

4.4.3. CD 11,21–22

In CD 11,21f. ist die Anordnung zu finden, dass jeder (וכל הבא אל) beim Betreten des „Bethauses" (בית השתחות) nicht unrein kommen soll (אל יבא טמא), d.h. dass er sich vorher waschen soll (כבוס). Näheres ist über die Vorgänge nicht gesagt. Es gibt keine genaue Anweisung, für welchen Fall oder welche Personengruppe oder welches Körperteil dies zutrifft. Es wird nicht näher spezifiziert, welcher Ritus einer Waschung notwendig wird. Da hier eine generelle Aussage steht, ist der Stelle wohl lediglich das Verbot zu entnehmen, unrein den Tempel zu betreten. Wenn jemand sich als Unreiner in dieser Situation vorfindet, so muss er entsprechende Maßnahmen einleiten, die jedoch an anderer Stelle genannt sind.

Zu erwägen ist, den Kontext mit seiner Zentrierung auf den Sabbat bei der Interpretation zu berücksichtigen, auch wenn in 11,1 eben so wenig vom Sabbat die Rede ist wie bei den beiden anderen Waschungsbelegen. Das würde dann bedeuten, dass diese Notiz nur auf das Betreten des Tempels am Sabbat zu beziehen ist. Dieses Verständnis ist nicht auszuschließen. Da in 11,1 jedoch generell formuliert wird, ist zu erwägen, ob die Waschung nicht auch für Besuche des Tempels an anderen Tagen gilt. Für diese Interpretation spricht der Sinn des Verbotes, da kaum anzunehmen ist, dass an anderen Wochentagen die Reinigungsriten nicht gelten sollten.

Möglicherweise steht im Hintergrund die Notiz in Jub 21,16; dort war die Bestimmung zu lesen, dass vor dem Opfern im Tempel Hände und Füße gewaschen werden sollen.[201] Wenn der Beleg rezipiert ist, könnte die Angabe vom Betreten des Tempels zu Opferzwecken hier ausgeweitet sein auf jegliches Betreten des Tempels. Wenn dies zutrifft, spricht um so mehr dafür, in CD 11,1 eine allgemeine Bestimmung zu sehen und diese nicht auf den Sabbat zu begrenzen.

4.4.4. 4Q272 // 4Q266

Ein anderer Fall der Verwendung mit Wasser begegnet in zwei Fragmenten aus der Damaskusschrift, die Reinigungsvorschriften ähneln, wie sie bereits in ha-

---

200 Vgl. auch die Diskussion um Reinigungsriten am Sabbath, die LAWRENCE, Washing, 110f., aufgrund der Angaben in CD sich allmählich entwickeln sieht.
201 S.o. Abschnitt 3.2.

lachischen Texten vom Toten Meer begegnet sind,[202] in der Damaskusschrift jedoch eher am Rande vorkommen.[203] Der Text 4Q272 und 4Q266 ist nur sehr fragmentarisch überliefert.[204]

In 4Q272 Frg. 1 Kol. ii 3–7a par 4Q266 Frg. 6 Kol. i Z. 14–16 wird eine rituelle Reinigung für einen Mann nach nächtlichem Samenerguss beschrieben – ein Fall von זב, wobei der Begriff hier wohl auch als Oberbegriff für andere Fälle verwendet wird.[205] Dort heißt es in Z. 6, dass der Mann zur Erlangung ritueller Reinheit seine Kleider waschen (וכבס בג[ד]יו) und sich im Wasser baden soll (ורחץ במים). Erinnern diese Angaben etwa an 11Q19 45,15–20, 4Q512 und 4Q274 Frg. 1 Kol i,[206] so fallen die Angaben hier aufgrund des Erhaltungszustandes des Textes knapper aus, da weder Angaben über die Dauer des Zustandes der rituellen Unreinheit noch über die Anzahl der Waschungen und der dafür vorgesehenen Tage zu finden sind.

Ergänzend zu anderen Texten fügt die nächste Zeile hinzu, dass auch diejenigen, die den Mann berührt haben, sich waschen sollen (בו הנוגע בו ר[חץ). Die Vorschriften, die im Kern auf Opferbestimmungen in Lev 15 zurückgehen, scheinen hier strenger ausgelegt zu sein, insofern weitere Personen unter denen, für die ein Reinigungsvorgang vorgesehen ist, inbegriffen sind. Mit dieser Ausweitung füllt das Fragment zugleich eine Lücke aus Lev 15, die die Frage beantwortet, wie es sich mit den Menschen verhält, die den Unreinen berühren.[207]

---

202 In den Fragmenten 4Q266–273 ist ansonsten von Reinigungen, nicht jedoch von Waschungen die Rede. Dabei gibt es durchaus Überschneidungen mit dem Ritus des Blutes der roten Kuh (in Aufnahme vom Num 19), wie es bereits im halachischen Material begegnet ist. So finden sich Waschungen z.B. in den (nicht unbestritten) ergänzten Passagen in den Fragmenten von 4Q269 Frg. 8 Kol. ii. Z. 3–6 und 4Q271 Frg. 2 Z. 10–13 (u.a. ist von מי הנדה die Rede). Zur Interpretation der Reinigungsriten vgl. z.B. WERRETT, *Ritual Purity*, 24–106, zu 4Q269 Frg. 8 Kol. ii. Z. 3–6; 4Q271 Frg. 2 Z. 10–13 bes. ebd., 41–46. Dass es im halachischen Material Parallelen zu 4QMMT gibt, hat C. HEMPEL, *Laws*, gezeigt; diese schließen jedoch die Reinigungsriten nicht in gleicher Weise mit ein.

203 So auch das Urteil von WERRETT, *Ritual Purity*, 95f. Daher hat HEMPEL, *Laws*, 25–72.187–189; DIES., „Laws", *passim*, vorgeschlagen, die Abschnitte einer generellen Halacha zuzuweisen, die sie als erste Schicht von CD versteht, die später durch eine zweite Redaktionsschicht einer Gemeindegesetzgebung erweitert worden sei. Ob man diese Schlussfolgerung ziehen kann, bedarf einer näheren Prüfung, die hier nicht geschehen kann, doch sind die Belege zu Waschungen immerhin auffällig gemessen an den übrigen Aussagen über die Verwendung von Wasser und ihrem Verhältnis zur gesamten Schrift.

204 Text in DJD 18, 23–94 (hier: 52f.) und 18, 185–192 (hier: 188f.); vgl. die Textdiskussion bei WERRETT, *Ritual Purity*, 48. An welcher Stelle des Dokuments diese Fragmente einzuordnen sind, steht in der Diskussion. Eine mögliche Stelle könnte der Übergang von der Paränese zum Gesetzesteil sein; vgl. WERRETT, *Ritual Purity*, 104f.

205 So die These von WERRETT, *Ritual Purity*, 50f., der darin die verschiedenen Gesetze von Lev 15 zusammengefasst sieht.

206 S.o. Abschnitt 4.1.1., 4.2.2. und 4.2.3.

207 Vgl. WERRETT, *Ritual Purity*, 49f., der in diesem „gap-filling" eine methodische Arbeitsweise des Verfassers des Damakus Dokuments ausmacht.

Im weiteren Verlauf des Textes 4Q272 Frg. 1 Kol. ii Z. 7b–17 folgt ein entsprechendes Gesetz für menstruierende Frauen, dessen Erhaltungszustand allerdings noch fragmentarischer ist. In Z.13.15.16 ist vom Wasser (המים) die Rede, wobei Z.15 Reinigungswasser (ובמי הנדה) und Z.16 lebendiges [Wasser] bietet. Leider ist dem Abschnitt nicht zu entnehmen, welche Reinigungsvorschriften mit dem Wasser vorgesehen waren.

4.5. Zusammenfassung zu den Belegen aus den Schriften vom Toten Meer

Die Belege zu Waschungen in den Schriften von Qumran sind inhomogen. Konkrete Abläufe sind selten geschildert, da zumeist die Waschung bzw. Reinigung lediglich durch eine Verbform bezeichnet ist. Während das nur ganz selten benutzte טבל das Eintauchen bzw. Untertauchen bezeichnet (vgl. 4Q274 Frg. 2 Kol i Z. 4f.), gibt כבס das Waschen (von Menschen und Kleidung) und רחץ schließlich das Besprengen (zumeist durch einen Priester) an. Es scheint, dass es keine festen Riten und Formen gegeben hat; oder wenigstens lassen diese sich nicht aus den Texten erheben. Vielmehr spiegeln die Texte verschiedene Arten von Waschungen, die mit unterschiedlichen Abläufen im Frühjudentum und/oder an verschiedenen Punkten der Lebensgemeinschaft des *Jachat* als zu praktizieren vorgestellt werden. Mit dem Aufkommen ihrer aktuellen Relevanz werden Regelungen geschaffen, die partiell aus dem Traditionsgut der Hebräischen Bibel stammen und partiell kreative und aktuelle Neugestaltungen für die Gemeinschaft sind.

Im halachischen Material, für das die Tempelrolle eine gewisse Vorform bietet, zeichnet sich eine Entwicklung ab, die auf den Lebens- und Heilsaspekt gerichtet ist. Rituelle Waschungen, die mehrmals wiederholt werden können, schaffen auch Sühne und lassen den Menschen rituell rein werden. Damit bringen sie ihn Gott nahe. Das Wasser, welches oft als „lebendiges Wasser" (מים חיים) bezeichnet wird, stellt dabei das wesentliche Mittel dar, das Reinheit und damit eine Veränderung des rituellen Zustandes im Leben des Menschen bringt. Dadurch kommt das Leben rituell zu dem Menschen zurück und macht ihn in seinem sozialen Geflecht lebensfähig.

In 1QS geht es vor allem um die Funktion der Reinigung. Sie wirkt lebensverändernd. Die Reinigung ermöglicht einen neuen Lebensbereich, in den der Gereinigte eintritt. Neben die äußere rituelle Reinheit tritt die innere Reinheit, d.h. eine Bereitschaft zur Übernahme der Lebensregeln der Gemeinschaft des *Jachat* und zur Eingliederung in die Gemeinschaft mit der sie prägenden Gruppenidentität. Wer die Reinigung durchlaufen hat, tritt zugleich in den Bereich Gottes ein, in dem das Licht des Lebens (3,7) herrscht.

CD bringt demgegenüber konkrete Bestimmungen zum Umgang mit Wasser, ohne dass klar daraus hervorgeht, um welche Waschung es sich im Einzelnen handelt. Wichtig ist auch hier dabei, dass es um fließendes Wasser geht. Der Aspekt des Lebens wird also erneut mit dem Thema Wasser verbunden. Die literarischen Belege zeigen beim Thema der Reinigung einen Bezug von Wasser und Leben. Sie deuten Abläufe von Waschungen als rituelle Reinigungen, mit denen Aussagen zum Verhältnis von Gott und Mensch gemacht werden. Ist dabei in Qumran auch der Bereich der Lebensgemeinschaft des *Jachat* mit tangiert, so zeigt sich an den Aussagen der Belege, welche Auswirkungen auf die sozialen Lebensbezüge die rituellen Waschungen haben. Florentino García Martínez sieht in ihnen sogar einen wesentlichen Aspekt der Identitätsbildung der Gemeinschaft des *Jachat*.[208]

Angesichts dessen ist es um so überraschender, dass in den (mehrheitlich durchaus paränetischen und damit präskriptiven) Texten nicht deutlicher und breiter von Reinigungen die Rede ist. Die Beobachtung der Quantität erstaunt um so mehr, wenn man demgegenüber die große Zahl von Reinigungsgefäßen und Becken der materiellen Kultur betrachtet.[209] Diese lassen auf eine frequente und vielfältige Nutzung schließen, wie sie gerade für die Gemeinschaft von Qumran auch immer wieder als ausgeübte Religionspraxis angeführt wird.[210] Die Schriften geben dies nicht in gleicher Weise und Intensität wieder – hier ist eine Differenz festzuhalten.

5. Waschen bringt Lebensqualität zurück

Die Auswertung zu Funktionen und Abläufen von Waschungen wird in sechs Punkten geschehen. Zunächst ist als Ergebnis aus der Sichtung der frühjüdischen Belege ein Negativbefund festzuhalten. Die Zahl an Referenzen auf Reinigungsriten, bei denen Wasser eine Rolle spielt oder im Ablauf vorkommt, fällt eher gering aus. Zudem sind die Belege im Wesentlichen auf solche Texte konzentriert, die eine Interpretation von Gesetzestexten darstellen, wie sie vorzugsweise in den Schriften vom Toten Meer anzutreffen sind. Gegenüber einer gelegentlich anzutreffenden Überschätzung der Rolle der frühjüdischen Waschungen rät diese Beobachtung zur Vorsicht vor allzu globalen Schlussfolgerungen.

Waschungen treten als begleitende Riten bei Reinigungen auf, haben dabei jedoch unterschiedliche Funktionen und sind in verschiedenen Abläufen zu finden. Die nachfolgenden Punkte konzentrieren sich auf die Verwendung und Funktion von Wasser.

---

208 Vgl. García Martínez, „Problem of Purity", 156.
209 Vgl. z.B. Magness, *Archaeology*; Lawrence, *Washing*, 155–184; Zissu/Amit, „Common Judaism", *passim*.
210 Vgl. z.B. W. Brandt, *Baptismen*, 65f.; J. Neusner, *Idea of Purity*, 50–55; Baumgarten, „Purification Rituals", 199f.; H. Stegemann, *Essener*, 265–267; García Martínez, „Problem of Purity", *passim*.

(1.) *Waschen oder Baden im Wasser* begegnet *in verschiedenen Vorgängen*. Es kann sich entweder um ein Waschen oder um ein Tauchen bzw. Untertauchen[211] handeln. Eine weitere Variante ist das Besprengen mit Wasser. Welcher Vorgang jeweils gemeint ist, wird nicht immer deutlich ausgeführt. Es ist zumeist nur von einer Waschung die Rede, wobei offen bleibt, wie sie erfolgt.

Man ist geneigt, nähere Informationen dem jeweils benutzten Verb zu entnehmen, wobei in der Regel כבס ein nicht näher spezifiziertes Waschen bezeichnet und das selten benutzte טבל für ein Eintauchen bzw. Untertauchen verwendet wird, während רחץ ein Besprengen anführt. Allerdings sind die Begriffe nicht zu pressen, da vor allem der oft benutzte Terminus כבס recht unspezifisch ist und wenig Auskunft über den Vorgang gibt.[212] Dies wäre dem Kontext zu entnehmen, der aber leider in dieser Hinsicht oft auch schweigsam ist. In griechischen Texten begegnen die Begriffe λύο, νίπτω und πλύνω einschließlich deren Komposita, die miteinander austauschbar und ebenfalls recht allgemein sind. Gelegentlich wird auch βάπτω verwendet, oftmals dann jedoch in anderer Bedeutung.[213] Auch aus den griechischen Termini lassen sich keine Hinweise auf etwaige Abläufe nehmen. Die Beachtung der Terminologie, aus der leicht zu weitreichende Schlüsse gezogen werden, führt also nicht wirklich zu einem tragfähigen Ergebnis.

Eine offene Frage in diesem Feld ist zunächst einmal die nach dem *Objekt des Waschens*. Einerseits werden *Kleidungsstücke* gewaschen, andererseits sind es *Menschen*, die sich waschen oder baden. Auch kann von dem Waschen bestimmter Körperteile, wie etwa Händen und Füßen, gehandelt werden. Unklar bleibt dabei oftmals, wie die Waschung im Wasser erfolgt, ob ein vollständiges oder partielles Untertauchen geschieht oder ob man eher an ein Eintauchen zu denken hat. Eine weitere Variante bietet das Besprengen einer Person oder eines Objektes mit Wasser.

Unklar bleibt in den Texten oft auch, *welches Wasser* verwendet werden soll. So ist es möglich, dass entweder fließendes Wasser aus einem Bach, einem See und einer Quelle benutzt wird oder dass das Wasser aus einer Zisterne oder Wasserleitung stammt. Es könnte aber auch sein, dass Wasser in Becken bereit steht, wobei dann erneut die Frage nach der Herkunft des Wassers zu stellen ist, d.h. es könnte Quellwasser, Regenwasser oder anders Wasser sein. Wird in den Texten oft darauf Wert gelegt, dass es sich um „lebendiges Wasser" handelt, so ist hierbei an fließendes Wasser zu denken.

(2.) Die meisten rituellen Reinigungen sind *Selbstwaschungen*. Wenn davon die Rede ist, dass jemand baden oder sich waschen soll, so herrscht in der Regel

---

211 G. Barth, „Verständnis", 143, nennt dies „Tauchbad". Der Begriff scheint mir etwas zu groß gewählt, da er einen festen, eindeutigen und unveränderlichen Ablauf suggeriert, was aber für die hier vorgestellten frühjüdischen Belege nicht in dieser Eindeutigkeit nachzuvollziehen ist.

212 Vgl. dazu die Belege in Abschnitt 4.

213 Vgl. dazu die Belege in Abschnitt 3.

die Vorstellung vor, dass der die Reinigung Durchführende diese an sich selbst vollzieht. Zu solchen Waschungen ist also weder Priester noch eine andere Person notwendig.[214]

Die rituelle Reinigung erfolgt, so ist zu erwarten, nach einem festgelegten *Ablauf*. Allerdings weist die Schilderung des Ablaufs auch Leerstellen auf, da oftmals bei den Selbst-Waschungen nicht gesagt wird, ob der ganze Körper oder lediglich Körperteile zu waschen sind. Wenn von Baden die Rede ist, liegt allerdings die Vorstellung nahe, dass der ganze Körper betroffen ist, wie es auch beim Untertauchen gemeint sein dürfte.

Die Waschung bildet einen Teil des *Reinigungsritus*. Dazu gehören weitere Elemente wie z.B. das Darbringen von *Opfern* und das Sprechen von *Gebeten* oder Lobpreisen.

Überlegungen wurden angestellt, ob die Waschung nackt oder bekleidet erfolgt.[215] Die Texte vom Toten Meer geben darüber keine Auskunft. Und inwiefern die Notiz von Josephus in Bell 2,129, dass die Essener in weißen Kleidern gebadet hätten, zutreffend ist, ist fraglich, da sie nicht von Aussagen in den Schriften vom Toten Meer selbst gedeckt ist.

Nur gelegentlich ist neben der sich waschenden Person ein Priester beteiligt. Dies ist vor allem dann der Fall, wenn das Wasser gesprengt wird. In diesem Fall ist das Wasser in der Regel als Reinigungswasser bezeichnet und dient der Sühne. Sühne und Priesterdienste scheinen dabei einander zu bedingen. Insofern kann in diesem Wasserritus eine besondere Form gesehen werden, die dann aber eben nicht als Waschung im eigentlichen Sinn zu verstehen ist.

(3.) Fast alle Waschungen können *wiederholt* werden. Sie fallen immer dann an, wenn Fälle kultischer Verunreinigung vorliegen, z.B. Sexualbefleckung, Aussatz, Berührung mit Blut oder Kontakt mit Toten. Nach solchen Verunreinigungen muss die rituelle Reinheit wieder gestellt werden, wozu Wasserriten nach andern Reinigungsriten notwendig sind. Die Waschungen sind also kein einmaliger Akt, sondern auf Wiederholung angelegt.

Ein einziger Fall von einer Waschung als Initiationsritus könnte in 1QS 3,4–9 gesehen werden.[216] Bei diesem Beleg kann das Baden als ein Teil eines Eintrittsrituals zu begreifen sein. Dann allerdings wäre diese Waschung wohl als eine einmalige vorgestellt.

(4.) Die Waschung vermittelt *kultische Reinheit* und ist daher als eine *rituelle Reinigung* zu verstehen. Dies zeigen vor allem die Fälle, in denen Reinigungsriten nach kultischer Verunreinigung notwendig werden (s.o.). Dafür spricht auch, dass Sühne und Opfer in ihrem Umfeld begegnen, die eindeutig in den Bereich des Tempelkultes gehören.

---

214 Ausnahmen sind 4Q512 Kol. 12 Frg. 1–3 und 4Q277 Z. 9, wo ein Priester (zusätzlich) einen Besprengungsritus durchführt (zu den Belegen s.o.).

215 S.o. Anm. 93.

216 S.o. Abschnitt 4.3.1.

Nur gelegentlich war zu überlegen, ob neben der rituellen Reinigung eine tatsächliche Reinigung gegeben ist. Dies war etwa in der Tempelrolle, 11Q19 45,13–15, zu sehen, wo eine wöchentliche Reinigung der Kammern des Tempels eingefordert wurde.[217]

(5.) Bei den Waschungen geht es zumeist nicht um das Thema von Sühne, um Sünden oder Aufhebung von Schuld. So war es im Jubiläenbuch, dem Testament Levi, im Aristeasbrief und in der Tempelrolle zu finden, wo Waschungen rituelle Reinheit bedeuten. Auch schweigen die Gemeinschaftsregel[218] und die Damaskusschrift von Sühne.

Anders sieht es im halachischen Material der Schriften vom Toten Meer aus. Nicht in allen Schriften,[219] aber doch in vielen Belegen sind Reinigungsriten mit dem Aspekt von Sühne interpretiert. In diesem Zusammenhang ist dann auch von Opfern die Rede, die Heiligkeit bringen. Ist klassisch alttestamentlich die Sühne eine Wirkung der Opfer, wie es in 4Q276 und 4Q277 sowie in 4Q394 und 4Q397 in Elementen des Sündopfers noch nachwirkt, so ist der Aspekt der Sühne über die Verbindung mit dem Opferthema nunmehr auch mit den Waschungen verknüpft. Vor allem in 4Q512 begegnet eine halachische Interpretation, die zu der rituellen Reinheit den Gedanken von Schuldaufhebung (vgl. 4Q394 Frg. 5–7 Z. 14: העם עון) ergänzt. Im Ablauf der Waschungen sind die Vorgänge oft nacheinander genannt, insofern die vom Priester gewirkte Sühne durch Besprengung nach der Selbst-Waschung und der Reinigung folgt. Gelegentlich scheint aber auch der Gedanke vorgetragen zu werden, dass das Wasser die Schuld abwäscht.[220] Bei dieser Vorstellung liegt eine theologische Interpretation für den Waschvorgang vor, die ein Objekt, das abgewaschen wird, ergänzt. Jetzt ist nicht nur der Gegenstand der Waschung genannt, sondern auch das angegeben, was bei der rituellen Waschung entfernt wird. Damit wird der rituellen Waschung eine wirkmächtige Bedeutung vor Gott zugeschrieben. Diese Interpretation scheint innerhalb der halachischen Texte allerdings erst am Ende einer Entwicklung formuliert worden zu sein.

(6.) Wie in vielen Einzelbelegen herausgestellt wurde, ordnen die frühjüdischen Texte die Waschungen in ein Themenfeld ein, in dem es um Aspekte des Lebens geht. Sie nehmen damit eine neue Interpretation der Waschungen vor. Rituelle Reinheit gehört einerseits in das Umfeld des Tempels, betrifft aber andererseits auch das Leben des Menschen. Dies zeigt sich in drei Punkten.

---

217 S.a. den Beleg 4Q512 Kol. 10 Frg. 11 und mit Einschränkung CD 10,10–13.
218 Wenn in 1QS 3,6 das Stichwort „Sühne" begegnet, so ist dies von gemeinschaftsbildenden Aspekten geprägt; s.o. Abschnitt 4.3.1.
219 Aus den Texten 4QOrdinances bietet nur 4Q513 das Stichwort Sühne. Bei 4QTohorot begegnet Sühne in 4Q277 (hier allerdings als Sündopfer bzw. Sühne, die durch das Blut der roten Kuh erwirkt wird); s.a. 4Q276. Bei 4QMMT begegnet das Sündopfer in 4Q394 und 4Q397.
220 Vgl. 4Q512 Kol. 2 Frg. 39 Z. 7 ; 4Q512 Frg. 15 Kol i; 4Q512 Kol 12 Frg. 1–3 und Frg. 4; s.a. 4Q414.

Erstens: Wer rituell unrein ist, kann nicht wie andere Menschen am üblichen Leben und den Wegen im Tempel partizipieren. Er ist ausgeschlossen von der Praxis des Kultes wie des Glaubens und damit abgetrennt von seinem sozialen Gefüge. Um wieder in einen Zustand sozialer Gemeinschaftsfähigkeit zu gelangen, muss er Reinigungsriten durchführen, bei denen Wasser ein entscheidendes Element darstellt.

Zweitens: Der Lebensaspekt der Waschungen findet sich auch in der häufig gestellten Forderung, dass lebendiges Wasser (מים חיים) zu verwenden ist. Auf dieses Qualitätsmerkmal wird oft Wert gelegt, auch wenn die Quelle des Wassers nur selten angegeben ist. Wasser, das selbst Leben in sich trägt, kann Lebensqualität zum Menschen, der sich im Wasser wäscht, zurückbringen.

Drittens: Es finden sich Interpretationen, die die Waschung ebenso in diese Richtung deuten. So war z.B. im Jubiläenbuch zu sehen, dass Reinheit und Waschung dazu dienen, das Todbringende zu entfernen und das Leben zu fördern. Einen ähnlichen Gedanken bietet auch die Tempelrolle, die die Reinheit des Tempels auf die Stadt, in der der Tempel steht, und die Menschen, die darin leben, ausweitet. Auch die Schrift Ritual of Purification (4Q512) stellt heraus, dass die Menschen erst wieder lebensfähig im eigentlichen Sinn sind, wenn Gott das Trennende entfernt und neue Lebensbedingungen hergestellt hat. Gegen Unreinheit, die das Leben der Menschen gefährdet, müssen Waschungen die Reinheit bringen und damit den Menschen wieder lebensfähig und kontaktfähig machen. Die Waschung beseitigt also das, was Gott und Mensch voneinander trennt, und führt damit den Menschen dem von Gott gewollten und geförderten Lebensbereich zu.

Damit zusammenhängen kann dann auch eine weitergehende Interpretation. So stellt 1QS 3,7 das Licht der Lebendigen (אור חיים) als zu erreichendes Ziel des Lebens heraus, was durch immer wieder neue Reinigungen erreicht werden kann. Im 4QMMT folgen schließlich Zukunftsperspektiven, die Gottes Heil und Rettung am Ende der Zeit in Aussicht stellen, wenn Menschen in Reinheit vor Gott leben. Rituelle Reinheit ist demnach nicht um ihrer selbst willen da, sondern gibt dem Leben des Menschen vor Gott eine Perspektive, die zwar in einem Lebensrahmen mit seinen täglichen Abläufen stattfindet, aber dennoch eine Bedeutung über diesen Rahmen hinaus hat.

Den frühjüdischen Belegen, wie sie in diesem Beitrag vorgestellt wurden, geht es – so meine These – um den Zusammenhang von ritueller Reinheit und Leben. Durch Waschungen wird rituelle Reinheit wieder hergestellt und der Mensch zurück ins Leben gebracht.

Bibliographie

Quellen

Allegro, John M., *Qumrân Grotte 4 I (4Q158–4Q186)*, with the Collaboration of Arnold A. Anderson (DJD 5), Oxford: Claredon Press 1968.

Baillet, Maurice, *Qumrân Grotte 4 III (4Q482–4Q520)* (DJD 7), Oxford: Claredon Press 1982.

Baumgarten, Joseph, *Qumran Cave 4. XIII. The Damascus Document (4Q266–273)*. On the Basis of Transcriptions by József T. Milik, with Contributions by Stephen Pfann and Ada Yardeni (DJD 18), Oxford: Claredon Press 1996.

Baumgarten, Joseph/Torleif Elgvin/Esther Eshel/Erik Larson/Manfred R. Lehmann/Stephen Pfann/Lawrence H. Schiffman, *Qumran Cave 4 XXV Halakhic Texts*, Based on Earlier Transcriptions by Jósef T. Milik (DJD 35), Oxford: Claredon Press 1999.

Becker, Jürgen, *Die Testamente der zwölf Patriarchen* (JSHRZ III.1), Gütersloh: Gütersloher Verlagshaus 1974.

Berger, Klaus, *Das Buch der Jubiläen* (JSHRZ II.3), Gütersloh: Gütersloher Verlagshaus, 1981.

Charlesworth, James H./Henry W. M. Rietz (eds.), *The Dead Sea Scrolls. Hebrew, Aramaic, and Greek Texts with English Translations*, Volume 3, *Damascus Document, Some Works of the Torah, and Related Documents*, Tübingen: Mohr Siebeck/Louisville: Westminster John Knox Press 2006.

García Martínez, Florentino, *The Dead Sea Scrolls Translated. The Qumran Texts in English*, Wilfred G. E. Watson, Translator, Leiden/New York: Brill ²1996.

Lohse, Eduard, *Die Texte vom aus Qumran. Hebräisch und Deutsch. Mit Masoretischer Punktation, Übersetzung, Einführung und Anmerkungen*, Darmstadt: Wissenschaftliche Buchgesellschaft ²1971.

Maier, Johann, *Die Qumran-Essener: Die Texte vom Toten Meer*, Band I–III (UTB 1862, 1863, 1916), München/Basel: Ernst Reinhardt Verlag 1995, 1995, 1996.

Meiser, Norbert, *Aristeasbrief* (JSHRZ II.1), Gütersloh: Gütersloher Verlagshaus 1973.

Qimron, Elisha, *The Temple Scroll. A Critical Edition with Extensive Reconstructions*, Beer Sheva/Jerusalem: Ben-Gurion University of the Negev Press 1996.

QIMRON, ELISHA/JOHN STRUGNELL, *Qumran Cave 4 V. Miqsat Ma'aśe Ha-Torah*, in Consultation with Y. Sussmann and A. Yardeni (DJD 10), Oxford: Claredon Press 1994.

PUECH, ÉMILE, *Qumrân Grotte 4 XVIII: Textes Hébreux (4Q521–4Q528, 4Q576–4Q579)* (DJD 25), Oxford: Claredon Press 1998.

STEUDEL, ANNETTE, *Die Texte aus Qumran II. Hebräisch/Aramäisch und Deutsch. Mit Masoretischer Punktation, Übersetzung, Einführung und Anmerkungen*. Unter Mitarbeit von HANS-ULRICH BOESCHE, BIRGIT BREDEREKE, CHRISTOPH A. GASSER, ROMAN VIELHAUER, Darmstadt: Wissenschaftliche Buchgesellschaft 2001.

VANDERKAM, JAMES C., *The Book of Jubilees. A Critical Text* (CSCO 510. Scriptiones Aethiopici 87), Leuven: Peeters Press 1989.

— „Jubilees", in: HAROLD W. ATTRIDGE/TORLEIF ELGVIN/JOZEF MILIK/SAUL OLYAN/JOHN STRUGNELL/EMANUEL TOV/JAMES VANDERKAM/SIDNIE WHITE (eds.), *Qumran Cave 4 VIII Parabiblical Texts*, Part 1 (DJD 13), Oxford: Claredon Press 1994, 1–185.

MONOGRAPHIEN, AUFSÄTZE, ARTIKEL ETC.

BARTH, GERHARD, „Zum Verständnis der Taufe im Neuen Testament", in: *ZThK* 70 (1973) 135–161.

BAUMGARTEN, JOSEPH M., „The Purification Rituals in DJD 7", in: DEVORAH DIMANT/URIEL RAPPAPORT (eds.), *The Dead Sea Scrolls. Forty Years of Research* (STDJ 10), Leiden etc.: Brill 1992, 199–209.

— „The Red Cow Purification Rites in Qumran Textes", in: *JJS* 46 (1995) 112–119.

— „Purification Liturgies", in: PETER W. FLINT/JAMES VANDERKAM (eds.), *The Dead Sea Scrolls After Fifty Years. A Comprehensive Assessment*, Leiden: Brill 1999, 200–212.

BECKER, JÜRGEN, *Untersuchungen zur Entstehungsgeschichte der Testamente der zwölf Patriarchen* (AGAJU 8), Leiden: Brill 1970.

BECKWITH, ROGER T., „The Temple Scroll and Its Calendar: Their Character and Purpose", in: *RdQ* 18 (1997) 3–19.

BRANDT, WILHELM, *Die jüdischen Baptismen oder das religiöse Waschen und Baden im Judentum mit Einschluß des Judenchristentums* (BZAW 18), Gießen: Töpelmann 1910.

COLLINS, JOHN J., „The Yaḥad and 'The Qumran Community'", in: CHARLOTTE HEMPEL/JUDITH LIEU (eds.), *Biblical Traditions in Transmission. Essays in Honour of Michael A. Knibb*, Leiden: Brill 2006, 81–96.

FABRY, HEINZ-JOSEF, „Der Begriff ‚Tora' in der Tempelrolle", in: *RdQ* 18 (1997) 63–72.

FINN, THOMAS M., *From Death to Rebirth. Ritual and Conversion in Antiquity*, Mahwah, N.J.: Paulist Press 1997.

GARCÍA MARTÍNEZ, FLORENTINO, „The Problem of Purity: The Qumran Solution", in: DERS./JULIO TREBOLLE BARRERA, *The People of the Dead Sea Scrolls. Their Writings, Beliefs and Practices*, translated by Wilfred G. E. Watson, Leiden – New York – Cologne: Brill 1995, 139–157.

GESENIUS, WILHELM, *Hebräisches und Aramäisches Handwörterbuch über das Alte Testament*, in Verbindung mit H. ZIMMERN/W. MAX MÜLLER/O. WEBER, bearbeitet von FRANTS BUHL, Neudruck der 17. Auflage (1915), Berlin – Göttingen – Heidelberg: Springer 1962. (zitiert als HAH[17])

GROSSMAN, MAXINE L., *Reading for History in the Damascus Document. A Methodoligcal Method* (STDJ 45), Leiden – Boston – Cologne: Brill 2002.

HABER, SUSAN, „Common Judaism, Common Synagogue? Purity, Holiness, and Sacred Space at the Turn of the Common Era", in: WAYNE O. MCCREADY/ADELE REINHARTZ (eds.), *Common Judaism. Explorations in Second-Temple Judaism*, Minneapolis, Minn.: Fortress Press 2008, 63–80.242–248.

HARRINGTON, HANNAH, *The Impurity System of Qumran and the Rabbis: Biblical Foundations*, Atlanta, Ga.: Scholars Press 1993.

— *The Purity Texts*, London: T & T Clark 2004.

— „Keeping Outsiders out: Impurity at Qumran", in: FLORENTINO GARCÍA MARTÍNEZ/MLADEN POPOVIĆ (eds.), *Defining Identities: We, You, and the Other in the Dead Sea Scrolls. Proceedings of the Fifth Meeting of the IOQS in Groningen* (STJD 70), Leiden – Boston: Brill 2008, 187–203.

HEMPEL, CHARLOTTE, *The Laws of the Damascus Document. Sources, Tradition and Redaction* (STDJ 29), Leiden et al.: Brill, 1998

— „The Laws of the Damascus Document and 4QMMT", in: JOSEPH M. BAUMGARTEN/ESTHER G. CHAZON/AVITAL PINNICK (eds.), *The Damascus Document: A Centennial of Discovery. Proceedings of the Third International Symposium of the Orion Center for the Study of the Dead Sea Scrolls and Associated Literature, 4–8 February, 1998* (STDJ 34), Leiden et cet.: Brill 2000, 69–84.

JANOWSKI, BERND, *Sühne als Heilsgeschehen. Studien zur Sühnetheologie der Priesterschrift und zur Wurzel KPR im Alten Orient und im Alten Testament* (WMANT 55), Neukirchen-Vluyn: Neukirchener Verlag 1982 (^{2}2000).

JANOWSKI, BERND/HERMANN LICHTENBERGER, „Enderwartung und Reinheitsidee. Zur eschatologischen Deutung von Reinheit und Sühne in der Qumrangemeinde", in: *JJS 34* (1983) 31–62.

JÜRGENS, BENEDIKT, *Heiligkeit und Versöhnung. Levitikus 16 in seinem literarischen Kontext* (HBS 28), Freiburg i.Br. et al.: Herder 2001.

KAISER, OTTO, *Der Gott des Alten Testaments. Theologie des Alten Testaments 1: Grundlegung* (UTB 1747), Göttingen: Vandenhoeck & Ruprecht 1993.

KAMPEN, JOHN/MOSHE J. BERNSTEIN (eds.), *Reading 4QMMT. New Perspectives on Qumran Law and History* (SBL Symposium Series 2), Atlanta, Ga.: Scholars Press 1996.

KAZEN, THOMAS, *Jesus and Purity* Halakhah. *Was Jesus Indifferent to Impurity?* (CB.NT 38), Stockholm: Almquist & Wiksell International 2002.

KLAWANS, JONATHAN, *Impurity and Sin in Ancient Judaism*, Oxford: Oxford University Press 2000.

KOEHLER, LUDWIG/WALTER BAUMGARTNER, *Hebräisches und Aramäisches Lexikon zum Alten Testament*, bearbeitet von JOHANN JAKOB STAMM, Leiden: Brill, ^{3}1990ff. (zitiert als HAL)

KRATZ, REINHARD G., „Mose und die Propheten. Zur Interpretation von 4QMMT C", in: FLORENTINO GARCÍA MARTÍNEZ/ANNETTE STEUDEL/EIBERT TIGCHELAAR (eds.), *From 4QMMT to Resurrection. Mélanges qumraniens en hommage à Émile Puech* (STDJ 61), Leiden – Boston: Brill 2006, 151–176.

KRETSCHMAR, GEORG, „Die Geschichte des Taufgottesdienstes in der alten Kirche", in: *Leiturgia. Handbuch des Evangelischen Gottesdienstes Band V*, Kassel: Stauda 1970, 1–348.

LABAHN, ANTJE, „„Deine Toten werden leben ...' (Jes 26,19). Sinngebung mittels der Vorstellung individueller Revifikation als Grenzerweiterung im Jesajabuch", in: Michael Labahn/Manfred Lang (Hg.), *Lebendige Hoffnung – ewiger Tod?! Jenseitsvorstellungen im Hellenismus, Judentum und Christentum* (ABG 24), Leipzig: Evangelische Verlangsanstalt 2007, 53–86.

— *Licht und Heil. Levitischer Herrschaftsanspruch in der frühjüdischen Literatur aus der Zeit des Zweiten Tempels* (BThSt 212), Neukirchen-Vluyn: Neukirchener Verlag 2010.

— *Levitischer Herrschaftsanspruch zwischen Ausübung und Konstruktion. Studien zum multi-funktionalen Levitenbild der Chronik und seiner Identitätsbildung in der Zeit des Zweiten Tempels* (WMANT), Neukirchen-Vlyun: Neukirchener Verlag (erscheint 2011).

LAWRENCE, JONATHAN D., *Washing in Water. Trajectories of Ritual Bathing in the Hebrew Bible and Second Temple Literature* (SBL Academia Biblia 23), Atlanta, Ga.: Scholars Press 2006.

LEVINE, B.A., „The Temple Scroll. Aspects of Its Historical Provenance and Literary Character", in: *BASOR 232* (1979) 5–23.

MAGNESS, JODI, *The Archaeology of Qumran and the Dead Sea Scrolls*, Grand Rapids, Mich.: Eerdmans/Cambridge: Cambridge University Press 2002.

MILGROM, JACOB, „Studies in the Temple Scroll", in: *JBL 97* (1978) 501–523.

NAJMAN, HINDY, *Seconding Sinai: The Development of Mosaic Discourse in Second Temple Judaism* (JSJ.S 77), Leiden – Boston: Brill 2003.

NEUSNER, JACOB, *The Idea of Purity in Ancient Judaism. The Haskell Lectures, 1972–1973. With a Critique and a Commentary by Mary Douglas* (Studies in Ancient Judaism in Late Antiquity from the First to the Seventh Century 1), Leiden: Brill 1973.

NICKELSBURG, GEORGE W. E., *Jewish Literature Between the Bible and the Mishnah. A Historical and Literary Introduction*, Second Edition with CD-Rom, Minneapolis, Minn.: Fortress 2005.

RENDTORFF, ROLF, *Studien zur Geschichte des Opfers im Alten Israel* (WMANT 24), Neukirchen-Vluyn: Neukirchener Verlag 1967.

VAN RUITEN, JACQUES T. A. G. M., *Primaeval History Interpreted. The Rewriting of Genesis 1–11 in the Book of Jubilees* (SJSJ 66), Leiden – Boston – Köln: Brill 2000.

SCHIFFMAN, LAURENCE H., *The Halakhah at Qumran* (Studies in Ancient Judaism in Late Antiquity from the First to the Seventh Century 16), ed. JACOB NEUSNER, Leiden: Brill 1975.

— „The Deuteronomic Paraphrase of the Temple Scroll", in: *RdQ 15* (1992) 543–567.

— „The Temple Scroll and the Systems of Jewish Law of the Second Temple Period", in: GEORGE J. BROOKE (ed.), *Temple Scroll Studies, Papers Presented at the International Symposium on the Temple Scroll 1987* (JSP.S 7), Sheffield: Sheffield Academic Press 1989, 239–255.

— „Priestly and Levitical Gifts in the Temple Scroll", in: DONALD W. PARRY/ EUGENE ULRICH (eds.), *The Provo International Conference on the Dead Sea Scrolls. Technological Innovations, New Texts, and Reformulated Issues* (STDJ 30), Leiden – Boston – Köln: Brill 1999, 480–496.

— „Sacrificial Halakhah in the Fragments of the Aramaic Levi Document from Qumran, the Cairo Genizah, and Mt. Athos Monastery", in: ESTHER G. CHAZON/DEVORAH DIMANT/RUTH A. CLEMENTS (eds.), *Reworking the Bible: Apocryphal and Related Texts at Qumran. Proceedings of a Joint Symposium by the Dead Sea Orion Center for the Study of the Dead Sea Scrolls and Associated Literature and the Hebrew University Institute for Advanced Studies Research Group on Qumran, 15–17 January, 2002* (STDJ 57), Leiden – Boston: Brill 2005, 177–202.

SCHOFIELD, ALISON, *From Qumran to the Yaḥad. A New Paradigm of Textual Development for the Community Rule* (STDJ 77), Leiden/Boston: Brill 2009.

SEGAL, MICHAEL, *The Book of Jubilees. Rewritten Bible, Redaction, Ideology and Theology* (JSJ.S 117), Leiden – Boston: Brill 2007.

STEGEMANN, HARTMUT, „Is the Temple Scroll a Sixth Book of the Torah, Lost for 2500 Years?", in: HERSHEL SHANKS (ed.), *Understanding the Dead Sea Scrolls. A Reader from the Biblical Archaeology Review*, New York: Random House 1992, 126–136.

— *Die Essener, Qumran, Johannes der Täufer und Jesus. Ein Sachbuch* (Herder Spektrum 4128), Freiburg i.Br. etc.: Herder [2]1993.

STEUDEL, ANNETTE, „4Q448 – The Lost Beginning of MMT?", in: FLORENTINO GARCÍA MARTÍNEZ/ANNETTE STEUDEL/EIBERT TIGCHELAAR (eds.), *From 4QMMT to Resurrection. Mélanges qumraniens en hommage à Émile Puech* (STDJ 61), Leiden – Boston: Brill 2006, 247–263.

TOV, EMMANUEL, *The Texts from the Judean Desert. Indices and An Introduction to the Discoveries in the Judean Desert Series* (DJD 39), Oxford: Claredon 2002.

ULRICHSEN, JARL HENNING, *Die Grundschrift der Testamente der Zwölf Patriarchen. Eine Untersuchung zu Umfang, Inhalt und Eigenart der ursprünglichen Schrift* (AUU 10), Uppsala 1991.

VANDERKAM, JAMES C., *Textual and Historical Studies in the Book of Jubilees* (Harvard Semitic Monographs 14), Missoula, Mont., Scholars Press 1977.

— „The Origins and Purposes of the *Book of Jubilees*", in: MATTHIAS ALBANI/ JÖRG FREY/ARMIN LANGE (Hg.), *Studies in the Book of Jubilees* (TSAJ 65), Tübingen: Mohr Siebeck 1997, 1–24.

WEINFELD, MOSHE, „God Versus Moses in the Temple Scroll: 'I do not Speak on my Own but on God's Authority' (Sifrei Deut. Sec 5; John 12,48f.)", in: *RdQ* 15 (1991) 175–180.

VON WEISSENBERG, HANNE, *4QMMT. Reevaluating the Text, the Function, and the Meaning of the Epilogue* (STDJ 82), Leiden – Boston: Brill 2009.

WERRETT, IAN C., *Ritual Purity and the Dead Sea Scrolls* (STDJ 72), Leiden – Boston: Brill 2007.

WHITE CRAWFORD, SIDNIE, *The Temple Scroll and Related Texts* (CQSS 2), Sheffield: Sheffield Academic Press 2000.

WILLI-PLEIN, INA, *Opfer und Kult im alttestamentlichen Israel. Textbefragungen und Zwischenergebnisse* (SBS 153), Stuttgart: Deutsche Bibelgesellschaft 1993.

WILSON, ANDREW M./LAWRENCE WILLS, „Literary Sources of the *Temple Scroll*", in: *HThR* 75 (1982) 275–288.

YADIN, YIGAL, *Die Tempelrolle. Die verborgene Thora vom Toten Meer*. Aus dem Englischen übertragen von Eva Eggebrecht, München – Hamburg: Knaus 1985.

ZISSU, BOAZ/DAVID AMIT, „Common Judaism, Common Purity, and the Second Temple Period *Miqwa'ot* (Ritual Immersion Baths)", in: WAYNE O. MCCREADY/ADELE REINHARTZ (eds.), *Common Judaism. Explorations in Second-Temple Judaism*, Minneapolis, Minn.: Fortress 2008, 47–62.237–242.

Jewish Immersion and Christian Baptism
Continuity on the Margins?

Seán Freyne

1. Introduction

In his informative reflections on the Rome meeting of this group, which unfortunately I could not attend, Professor Christoph Markschies comments on, among other desiderata for our discussions, the need to explore more thoroughly the *Religionsgeschichte* context for Christian baptism. While Professor Markschies mentions specifically the important Greco-Roman and Egyptian contexts, in this paper I would like to contribute to a discussion of the Jewish background by focusing on the rituals of washing that were central to purity maintenance within Second Temple Jewish life and practice. My concern is not to establish genetic links between these practices and the origins of Christian baptism, but rather to highlight the fact that despite the alleged 'parting of the ways' continuity of practice persisted in certain circles of early Christianity for several centuries.

Jewish scholar Jacob Neusner has repeatedly suggested that, as developing symbolic systems from the second century CE onwards, Rabbinic Judaism and emerging Catholic Christianity had very different orientations – the former being concerned with sanctification and the latter with salvation. As generalisations go, this contrast would seem to have considerable merit, even though, as we shall see, there was quite an amount of contact and crossover between them. The foundational Mishnaic system, as least as interpreted by Neusner, was concerned with outlining a comprehensive system for everyday living that would serve Jewish identity maintenance in the wake of the loss of temple and land after the two unsuccessful revolts against Rome in 66–70 and 132–135 CE. According to Neusner this system was the work of scribes, addressed to Jewish householders, but based on the idea of purity as prescribed for the priests in the period of the temple.[1] As will be discussed later, this vision for the ideal Israel had already begun to take shape while the temple still stood. Various sectarian groups such as the Essenes and the Pharisees, but some early Jesus followers also, were interested in purity maintenance based on the priestly and holiness codes of the Pentateuch in the first century already. However, it was the Tannaim of the second century who extended the idea of holiness to all Israel, lead-

---

[1] J. Neusner, *Judaism. The Evidence of the Mishnah*, especially 230–256.

ing to the publication of the Mishnah c. 200 CE. While their efforts to redefine Jewish identity were initially more utopian than practical, it was nevertheless on this foundation, rather than on any of the other 'ways not taken,' that Judaism of late antiquity was built, both in the land of Israel and in Babylonia.

Emerging Catholic Christianity on the other hand had become an increasingly Hellenised movement, building on the missionary success of the law-free gospel of Paul and his followers among the gentiles. Already we can see in Paul's writings the beginnings of the adaptation of the Jesus movement to the categories of Hellenistic religious thinking and practice, despite Paul's own strong assertion of his Jewish identity in his letters, especially in *Romans*. Thus the apocalyptic hopes for a new age, were combined with, or even replaced by the idea of salvation now through the mystical union with the dying and rising saviour, Jesus Christ.

These two highly generalised pictures immediately become blurred, once they are exposed to serious historical scrutiny, however. It is increasingly recognised today that 'the parting of the ways' was by no means as rapid or complete as previous scholarship had maintained on the basis of the *birkat ha-minim* being directed specifically at the Jesus-followers by the end of the first century CE. As late as the fourth century c.e., John Chrysostom felt the need to rail against those of his own flock in Antioch who continued to frequent the synagogue.[2] This should alert us to the fact that in practice, if not in theory, separation was slow, ambivalent and often highly acrimonious. Thus, Daniel Boyarin, perhaps the most insistent of modern scholars to challenge the received paradigm, writes as follows in regard to the emergence in the second century of the notion of *hairesia/minut* in both traditions:

> I do not wish to claim that the rabbinic orthodoxy acted in imitation of the Church, but rather that a structural problem had been produced for both "brothers" the problem of figuring out who was who. The anxieties about boundaries between the newly defined groups – anxieties that were obvious from both sides of the boundary – were the immediate catalyst that produced the invention of the category of heresy as a means of policing borders that were hitherto not problematic *because the categories that they defined did not yet exist*. Christian groups also had no need to define "heresy" as long as their own self-definition did not fundamentally challenge the notion of Jewish peoplehood, that is, as long as they understood themselves as Jews and not as a "new Israel" (Italics added).[3]

An essential aspect of the policing of borders that Boyarin speaks about is the establishment of clear differences of understanding with regard to the rituals of entry and identity maintenance that different groups developed. Inevitably, the rituals of baptism, circumcision and immersion take on a social as well as

---

2   R. L. Wilken, *John Chrysostom and the Jews*, 95–127.
3   D. Boyarin, *Border Lines. The Partition of Judaeo-Christianity*, 66.

an ideological function when viewed in this light. While Boyarin seeks to date the beginning of this process to the mid-second century CE, with Justin Martyr speaking of the Christians as a third race (γένος) in the *Dialogue with Trypho*, it must be said that the process can be dated much earlier. In Paul's letters to the Corinthians, Galatians and Romans, there are indications already that the apostle sees believers in Jesus Christ as constituting an alternative 'Israel of God,' as distinct from the Israel according to the flesh (Gal 6:16; 1 Cor 10:18; Rom 9:1–6). His ambivalence on the matter emerges clearly in *Romans* where on the one hand he identifies himself as an Israelite (but only κατὰ σάρκα, Rom 8:3f.), yet later declares that 'not all who are of Israel are Israel,' just as not all that are of the seed of Abraham are his children, alluding to Gen 21:12 (v. 6f.).

The idea of a 'new Israel' suggests a contrast with the old one, thus implying replacement and superiority, ultimately giving rise to a rhetoric of denigration. Thus e.g., the author of 1 Peter, a document which is often seen as containing early Christian baptismal instruction, can write as follow: 'And baptism which this (i.e. Noah's ark) prefigured, now saves you, not as a *removal of dirt from the body*, but as an appeal to God for a good conscience through the resurrection of Jesus, who has gone into heaven and is at the right hand of God, with angels and powers and principalities subject to him." (1 Pet 3:21f.). In a similar disparaging vein the author of the Epistle to the Hebrews could develop an elaborate contrasting typology of Christ as a high priest whose once-for-all action makes obsolete the rites of Yom Kippur. In line with this perspective he can denigrate Jewish practices generally as follows: 'This (the annual entry of the high-priest into the holy of holies) is a symbol of the present time according to which gifts and sacrifices are offered that cannot perfect the conscience of the worshiper, but deal only with food and drink and various washings (διαφόροις βαπτισμοῖς), regulations for the body imposed until the time comes to set things right' (Heb 9:9–10). For this author βαπτισμοῖ has a negative connotation in view of an earlier usage (βαπτισμῶν διδαχῆς) where it refers to practices that the author describes as dead works to which he does not wish his audience to return (Heb 6:2). This admonition must be read in the light of the work addressing an audience, some of whom may be about to return to Jewish practices, something the author greatly disapproves of (Heb 10:19–25). In both cases the contrast is between the external washing of the body, which had no genuine power to bring about spiritual transformation, and sanctification that comes from identification through baptism with the true high priest who has made direct access to the heavenly realm.

It is interesting to note that the argument deals with the contrasting effects of the water rites, not circumcision, which on the basis of its once-for-all aspect would be the more obvious point of comparison. For this author repetition is a sign of the ineffectual nature of the Jewish system, but it may well also be an indication that the Jesus-followers being addressed, at least in the case of the audience of *Hebrews*, were continuing to practice Jewish purificatory rites, and saw value in the Jewish way of life based on the Pentatuecchal narratives, while still believing in Jesus. In other words, the audience might well reflect a Jewish Christian group of proto-Ebionite persuasion, since according to Epiphanius, at a much later date to be sure, the Ebionites, practiced daily baths as well as baptism, but also glory in circumcision, since 'they boast that it is a seal and mark of the patriarchs' (*Pan.* 30.16,1; 30.26,1).[4]

In contrast to these negative views of Jewish ritual practices based on the Pauline perspective, it is worth mentioning at this point an alternative view as expressed in the Ps-Clementine literature, which though datable in its final form to the 4/5th centuries c.e., is generally believed to have used 2nd century CE Jewish Christian sources that were decidedly anti-Pauline. The author of one of the underlying sources describes the effects of Christian baptism in theological rather than Christological terms, claiming that the regeneration that takes place restores the baptised to their original status as being like God, and therefore enabled to act like God in doing good works. He then goes on to explain the importance of the ritual washing of the body also by establishing the intimate links there are between internal purity of the heart and external purity of the body:

> Moreover, it is good, and tends to purity, also to wash the body with water. I call it good, not as if it were that prime good of the purifying of the mind, but because of this the washing of the body is the sequel of that good. ... For truly, if the mind be purified by the light of knowledge, when once it is clean and clear, then it necessarily takes care of that which is without a man, that is, his flesh, that it also may he purified. But when that which is without, the cleansing of the flesh, is neglected, it is certain that there is no care taken of the purity of the mind and the cleanness of the heart. Thus therefore it comes to pass, that he who is clean inwardly is without doubt cleansed outwardly also, but not always that he who is clean outwardly is also cleansed inwardly-to wit, when he does these things that he may please men (*Rec.* vi, 11; *Hom.* xi, 28).

In short, Christian baptism and Jewish ritual purity support and complement each other according to this early Christian author.

We shall return to discuss the Ps-Clementine material in more detail in the final part of this paper. However, citing it at this point underlines the need for a more detailed examination of the ritual practices in question and the significance attached to them, giving rise to a number of interesting questions and perspectives on the early Jesus-followers also. Responsible Christian scholarship can no longer accept uncritically the Paulinist denigration of such practices as being merely external and outmoded. Already in the fourth century, Jerome declared that the Hebrews 'want to be both Jews and Christians. But they are neither Jews nor Christians' (*Ep.* 113). By and large, this position has

---

[4] M. GOULDER, "Hebrews and the Ebionites," 393–406.

been the received one ever since. Thankfully, there has been a renewal of interest in these in-between movements in recent times, as Christian scholarship belatedly seeks to shed the anti-Jewish biases of much previous discussion of Christianity's relationship with Judaism. What emerges from this critical retrieval is the awareness that both Judaism and Christianity are modern abstractions, the legacy of two developing orthodoxies guarding their boundaries and sedulously avoiding any crossovers. Acknowledgment of the grey areas between them had to be avoided and the categories of orthodoxy and heresy were put to work in order to ensure that the projected 'other', the Jewish Christians had no place at the table of either establishment.

2. Jewish Ritual Washing: Theory and Practice

The fifth order of the Mishnah, *Tohoroth*/Purities deals with three related topics, namely, Sources of Uncleanness, Loci of Uncleanness and Modes of Purification. Two tractates are devoted to this latter topic, namely, *Parah*/Ashes of the Red Heifer and *Miqvaoth*/Ritual Pools. According to Neusner's structural analysis of the Division, these two tractates 'complete and complement each other' representing, as they do, two contrasting aspects of the purificatory process. *Miqvaoth* deals with an aspect from which humans are excluded, namely, the provision of the water for purification. *Parah* on the other hand deals with an aspect for which humans are totally responsible, namely, the collection of the ashes of the red heifer which was used in the rites of Yom Kippur in particular, and which when mixed with water was sprinkled on the individual for the atonement of certain impurities and grave sins. While both have the proper conduct of the cult in view, the actions in fact take place outside the cultic site, the temple. In both cases 'the generative principle' which guides the legal discussion deals with the proper provision of the materials of purification, to the almost total exclusion of the ways in which these materials are to be used.[5]

Rather than assisting us to visualize the actual practice of purification, but in keeping with the Mishnah's mode of discourse, both tractates engage in an exercise of legal imagination, which explores all the doubtful areas where transgressions could occur, and seeks to remove these uncertainties in advance. Strange as this might seem, when one pursues the point of origin of each tractate in the Hebrew Scriptures one can begin to understand the directions that each has taken. *Miqvaoth* takes its point of departure from Lev 15:13 with the injunction for the polluted person (זב) to wash in 'living waters' (מים חיים), a reference that in all probability referred to moving water such as a spring or the sea. Consequently, the tractate develops this idea by declaring that drawn water, i.e. water introduced by a human with a vessel renders the pool unclean. It is for

---

[5] NEUSNER, *Method and meaning in Ancient Judaism*, 101–132, especially 110–112 and 114–115.

this reason that ideally, (though as we shall see more honoured in the breach than the observance), a storage pool with an *otzar* or feeding pipe should be provided also for replenishing the *miqveh* when the water had evaporated or needed to be replaced for other reasons. *Parah's* scriptural base is Num 19:1–10, which already shows a concern with the maintenance of purity in the performance of the rite and the collection of the ashes, an aspect that the Mishnah tractate develops further.

Most scholars recognize the idealized form of these discussions in their attempts to trace the history and development of the rites associated with both tractates. Undoubtedly, some elements do date back to Second Temple times, but as several scholars recognize, it is virtually impossible to separate out the various layers, and Neusner's efforts to date them in relations to pre- and post-Jamnia, and post the Bar Cochba war on the basis of the logical development of the laws, are deemed to be somewhat subjective from the point of view of historical criteria. It is for this reason that the archaeological evidence for *miqvehs* has become so important in determining the nature and practice of purification rites in the Second Temple period. However, even here, as we shall presently see, there is a danger of circularity in deciding when is a stepped pool a *miqveh*, and archaeologists are not always the most critical in their use of literary sources when it comes to interpreting and identifying their discoveries.[6] In this respect, the Qumran site is particularly significant, since it is generally, though of late, not universally, accepted that the texts in the caves and some at least of the cisterns at Khirbet Qumran belong together and can therefore assist in tracing the history of purity.

2.1. Literary Evidence

Unlike the pre-exilic times, the literature of the Second Temple does give clear indications of ritual practices by pious Jews, both in the homeland and the Diaspora. Even though the P strand of the Pentateuch is deemed to be pre-exilic by J. Milgrom, it nevertheless was deeply influential in the work of the Chronicler e.g.[7] The fact that the Persian province of *Yehud* was a temple state, under a hierocracy, meant that the temple and its demands were central to Judean life. This situation continued even when in the late second century BCE the Hasmoneans adopted the title king, but insisted on retaining the role of priest as well (JA 13,288–292). Nor did Herod's appointment as 'king of the Jews' by the Roman senate in 40 BCE change significantly the central role of priesthood and temple, as can be gleaned from such writers of the period as Josephus and Philo. Both combine various different aspects of the Pentateuchal purity regulations in their

---

6   B. G. WRIGHT III, "Jewish Ritual Baths – Interpreting the Digs and the Texts: Some Issues in the Social History of Second Temple Judaism," 190–215, here 204.

7   J. MILGROM, "Priestly ('P') Source," 454–461.

summaries of the Jewish constitution (JA 3,262–265; Spec. Leg. 1,262–262), but also testify to the practice of the observance of ritual purity in their own day.[8]

Not surprisingly, perhaps, the earliest written witness to such observance comes from the Diaspora, where the threat to a separate Jewish identity was likely to be greater than in the homeland. *The Letter of Aristeas*, which is usually dated to the second century BCE, and with an Egyptian provenance, mentions that Jews in Jerusalem 'who are involved in purification rites' avoided traveling on the main thoroughfares for fear of contacts with forbidden objects, as they approached the temple (*Aristeas* 105). Similarly, the Book of Judith also speaks of the pilgrims purifying themselves in Jerusalem before offering their sacrifices (Jdt 16:18). However, *Aristeas*, describing the practice of the translators of the LXX, also testifies to a custom of the Jews to 'wash their hands in the sea in the course of their prayers to God' as an indication that they had done no evil, 'since,' the author declares, 'all activity takes place by means of the hands.' (304–306). Hand-washing was not prescribed in the Pentateuch, but it seems to have become a practice in both the homeland and the Diaspora by the first century, as can be gleaned from the debates attributed to the schools of Hillel and Shammai regarding the handling of food. According to Philo raising the hands in prayer was a feature of the Therapeutae in Alexandria. He explains that this gesture meant that 'they are clean from gain-taking, and not defiled through any form of the profit-making kind' (*De Vita Contemplativa* 66). On the basis of Jdt 9:1 and 12:7–9, it can be assumed that for the Diaspora Jew prayer replaced the temple sacrifices, prompted presumably by the *Tamid* or daily offering. Thus the observant Jew would wish to replicate the conditions that were demanded for temple worship, as prescribed in Exod 30:18–21. According to Mark 7:2,6 hand washing before meals was a practice of the Pharisees, suggesting that according to the evangelist, they regarded the eating of ordinary food as a sacred action, subject to the purity regulations (Cf. Luke 11:38).[9] Josephus is our best witness to the practice in the homeland, especially in his accounts of the Essenes. He himself declares later that his long description of the group in JW 2,119–158 is his definitive treatment (JA 13,1773; 18,11; Life 110). In the JW account Josephus distinguishes between an initial rite of purification for the novices and a further daily one for the initiates before partaking of the common meal. Thus after a probationary period of one year in which the aspirant is expected to observe independently the way of life of the group, he is brought closer to the rule, and 'is allowed to partake in the waters that are more powerful with respect to purity (πρὸς ἁγνείαν) but is not yet received into the common meals (συμβιώσεις) (JW 2,138). Earlier in the account access to these community meals for the fully initiated is described as follows:

---

8   J. D. Lawrence, *Washing in Water. Trajectories of Ritual Bathing in the Hebrew Bible and Second Temple Literature*, 46–52.

9   E. P. Sanders, *Jewish Law from Jesus to the Mishnah*, 228–231 and 259–271.

They are then (i.e. after praying to the sun) dismissed by their superiors to the various crafts in which they are each proficient and are strenuously employed until the fifth hour. They again assemble in one place, and with their loins girded with linen cloths they bathe (ἀπολούονται) the body in cold water and after this purification (ἁγνείαν) they gather in a private room (οἴκημα), entrance to which is not permitted to any of the uninitiated. Pure (καθαροί), themselves, they enter the refectory, as to a holy shrine (ἅγιόν τι τέμενος). (JW 2,129).

Final admission for the aspirant to this fellowship only took place after two further years of noviceship, on the completion of which the aspirant had to pronounce a number of oaths, all to do with strict moral conduct in terms of piety (εὐσεβήσειν) to the Deity and justice (δίκαια) to all men, while also surrendering all his goods to the community (JW 2,122.139–142). Even then, Josephus suggests that there were different degrees of purity, and therefore different ranks within the community, four in all, so that if a member of the superior grade were as much as touched by someone from the lower grade, he would have to undergo rites of purification similar to those required were he to touch a defiled person (JW 2,150).

When this account of Essene practice is compared with what we learn from the scrolls, especially the Community Rule and other documents relating to the *yahad's* rules of admission and its concerns with purity, it seems obvious that we are talking about the same group, despite the differences of insider and outsider views.[10] Thus, terms of admission to and exclusion from the group which Josephus describes are highly developed in the Rule of the Community: 'He who rejects the covenant shall not be reckoned among the perfect; he shall neither be purified by atonement (כפורים), nor cleansed by purifying waters (מי נדה) nor sanctified by seas and rivers, *nor washed clean by any bathing waters*. Unclean, unclean, he shall be. For as long as he despises the precepts of God, he shall receive no instruction in the community of his counsel' (1QS 3,4–6). A more positive statement follows immediately: 'For it is through the spirit of true counsel concerning the ways of man that all his sins shall be expiated. And when his flesh is sprinkled with purifying waters and sanctified by cleansing water, it shall be made clean by the humble submission of his soul to all the precepts of God' (1QS 3,7–9). Just as in Josephus' account of the oaths to be taken by the initiate, there is no distinction made between moral and ritual purity, or to put the matter differently, the cleaning ritual that the members were expected to undergo by '*entering* the water' demanded moral as well as ritual probity in order to partake of 'the pure meal of the men of holiness.' (1QS 5,13–14).

Somewhat later in the same document the process of entry of a new candidate, touched on in Josephus' account, is covered in detail in a four-stage process: (i) *Application for Admission*: 'To any in Israel who freely volunteers

---

10 For a detailed discussion of the notion and practice of washing in the Qumran texts, cf. the article by A. LABAHN in this publication.

to enroll … the instructor who is at the head of the many shall test him with regard to his insight and his deeds; … and depending on the outcome of the lots of the Many he shall be included or excluded.' (ii) *First Probationary Year*: 'If he is included in the Community council he must not touch the pure food of the Many while they test him concerning his insights and his deeds for a full year. Neither should he share in the possessions of the Many.' (iii) *Second Probationary Year*: 'When he has completed a year within the Community, the Many will be questioned about his duties, concerning his insights and his deeds in connection with the law. And if the lot results in him joining the foundation of the Community. … His wealth and his belongings will also be included at the hands of the Inspector of the belongings of the Many. He must not touch the drink of the Many until he completes the second year.' (iv) *Acceptance into Full Membership:* 'And when his second year is complete he will be examined by command of the Many, and if the lot results in him joining the Community, they shall enter him in the Rule according to his rank among the brothers of the law, for the judgment and the purity and the placing of his possessions in common' (1QS 6,13–23).[11]

These details reveal a highly organized community life structured around degrees of purity, but also based on proper knowledge and observance of all the community's regulations and teachings. 4QMMT/396, the letter to the temple authorities in Jerusalem, shows just how concerned the people of the scrolls were about the proper observance of purity in the temple, claiming that they, not the temple authorities, observed the correct *halakah* in several different areas (4QMMT B, 55–58, rejection of the *otzar* solution regarding the supply of water to a *miqveh*, e.g.). The Temple Scroll (11Q *Miqdash*) is closely related to the 4QMMT letter, envisaging as it does, an ideal temple of the future and setting out the detailed observances that would be followed there (11Q Miq col. 29).[12] The overall tendency is to insist on a stringent interpretation of the biblical regulations, in sharp contrast to the later Rabbis who adopted a more lenient approach whenever possible.[13] Thus, the notion of holiness is extended to all the priests, not just to the high priest. (4Q 396,3,2–4; 1QS, 8,5–6). Likewise, in spatial terms holiness is extended beyond the temple to the whole city of Jerusalem, and therefore all bearers of impurity are banned (4Q 394 3.10–12; 11Q Miq. 19, xlv.11–12). Corresponding to the various grades of membership in the community there were different grades of purity to be observed, a detail reflected in the distinction between the 'pure food of the many' (1QS 6,16–17.25) and the 'pure food of the holy men.' (1QS 5,13). Likewise, the process of purification is more demanding. In addition to immersion in sufficient water to cover the body (CD

---

11 S. Pfann, "The Essene Renewal Ceremony and the Baptism of Repentance," 336–352.

12 B. Wood, "To Dip or to Sprinkle. The Qumran Cisterns in Perspective," 46f.

13 H. K. Harrington, *The Purity Texts, Companion to the Qumran Scrolls*, especially Appendix B, 134–138, "A Comparison of the Impurity Laws of the Bible, Qumran and the Rabbis."

10,10–13), members of the community were expected to launder their clothes, don white robes, and engage in a purification liturgy (4Q 512, fr 10–11, col x; cf. 4Q 277). Immersion alone was insufficient to render a person pure, and without genuine repentance of the heart washing alone was meaningless (1QS 3,3–9 and 13–15).[14] Both John the Baptiser (Matt 3:6–11; JA 18,117–18), and Philo (*De Leg. Spec.* 1,191), shared this view,

2.2. The Evidence of Archaeology: Miqva'oth

The work of E. P. Sanders on Jewish practice and belief brought the important archaeological discoveries of stepped pools/*miqva'oth* to the attention of NT scholars in a new and challenging way. For Sanders the variety and frequency of *miqvehs* in all strands of the population, pointing to a general practice of immersion for reasons of purity, is 'quite unexpected' he writes, especially in view of the fact 'that immersion pools are not required by the Bible.'[15] This conclusion fits well with his earlier proposal of a 'common Judaism' in terms of a set of practices and beliefs that were generally shared, independently of the various sectarian regulations. However, Sanders himself recognizes that not all will agree with his interpretation of the archaeological evidence, which involves the claim that those *miqva'oth* which are lacking an *otzar* or storage pool, are non-Pharisaic. Aristocratic priests and Herod did not follow the Pharisaic stringent regulations concerning the need for running water, yet, according to Sanders, they too practiced immersion on the basis of the number of pools found in private houses in the Herodian Quarter and in the palaces at Jericho (Fig. 17; 18).[16]

One might also want to quibble with the claim that stepped pools were distributed consistently throughout the land, even allowing for a concentration in Jerusalem. At Sepphoris, the discovery of up to 20 such pools that have been identified in domestic settings on the Acropolis, raises several questions.[17] (Fig. 19) If these are all in private locations, what is the significance of the fact that they are to be found in some, but not in other houses nearby? In the Sepphoris context, some, but not all of the houses with *miqvehs*, have storage tanks also, again raising the issue as to whether, following Sanders' hypothesis, we are to suppose that Jews both of pharisaic and of non-pharisaic, aristocratic persuasion, as well as non-Jews, or at least Jews for whom immersion was not impor-

---

14   Harrington, *The Purity Texts*, 27–30.
15   Sanders, *Jewish Law from Jesus to the Mishnah*, 223–224.
16   Ibid. 224–227. For the Herodian Quarter cf. N. Avigad, *Discovering Jerusalem*, 139–142. For the Herodian palaces, E. Netzer, *The Architecture of Herod the Great Builder*, 179–202.
17   E. Meyers, "Aspects of Everyday Life in Roman Palestine with special reference to private domiciles and ritual baths," 193–220, especially 211–215; K. Galor, "The Stepped Water Installations of the Sepphoris Akropolis," 201–214.

tant, lived side by side?[18] (Fig. 20). Apart from Sepphoris, however, *miqvehs* are by no means ubiquitous at other first century CE sites in Galilee, sites that for other reasons are presumed to be Jewish (Fig. 21).

Of course this does not necessarily mean that the residents of such places ignored the purity regulations. Immersion could take place in any pool where the water collected naturally, either from a spring or from rain, thereby satisfying the rather vague stipulation of Lev 15:13, which referred to מים חיים, literally 'living water.' Gamla provides an interesting exception because of the presence of a *miqveh* close to the synagogue, which suggests a communal practice. Ronny Reich, who is the most knowledgeable of Israeli archaeologists on the subject of *miqva'oth*, believes that the Gamla one, as well as those found at Masada and Herodion, point to Zealot influences in the immediate pre-revolt period, when strict religious practice was combined with strong nationalistic feelings.[19] However, the fact that *miqva'oth* are now being discovered at some other sites in conjunction with early synagogues and cemeteries suggests that they may indeed reflect general Jewish practice, and not a sectarian intensification, and that their emergence generally should be dated to at least the Hasmonean expansion in the late second and early first centuries BCE.[20] Furthermore, the discovery of *miqva'oth* at some agricultural sites, especially where the grape and the olive were harvested, does smack of Pharisaic concern about liquids as carriers of impurity, based on Lev 11:33–38, and the consequent need for them to be harvested in a state of ritual purity, especially those that were destined for the priests.[21]

Reich estimated that over 150 of the almost 300 examples of stepped pools that had been unearthed at the time of his study, are to be found in Jerusalem

---

18 S. Miller, "Stepped Pools and the Non-existent Monolithic 'Miqveh,'" 215–234.

19 R. Reich, "The Synagogue and the *miqveh* in Eretz-Israel in the Second Temple, Mishnaic, and Talmudic Periods," 289–297.

20 Y. Magen/Y. Tzionit/O. Sirkis, "Khirbet Badd 'Isa – Qiriat Sefer,'" 179–242, especially 185 and 190 on the *miqva'oth* and 200–205 on the synagogue at a village site in Judea dating from the 2nd century BCE; B. Zissu/A. Ganor, "Horvat 'Ethri – a Jewish Village from the Second Temple Period and the Bar Kokhba Revolt in the Judean Foothills," 90–135; M. Aviam, "The Hellenistic and Hasmonean Fortress and Herodian Siege Complex at Qeren Naftali," in: idem, *Jews, Pagans and Christians in the Galilee*, 59–80.

21 Cf. J. M. Baumgarten, "Liquids and Susceptibility to Defilement in New 4Q Texts," 91–101. For a recent, general discussion of the issue cf. Y. Adler, "Second Temple Ritual baths Adjacent to Agricultural Installations: The Archaeological Evidence in Light of Halakhic Sources," 62–72, with a heavy reliance, however, on later Rabbinic evidence. Among recent discoveries of *miqva'oth* at agricultural sites cf. B. Zissu/Y. Tepper/D. Amit, "*Miqva'ot* at Kefar 'Othnai near Legio," 59–66, (Olive Press); S. Gutman, "Gamla," in: *NEAEHL* 2, 459–463, (Olive Press); Y. Hirschfeld/R. Birger-Calderon, "Ramat Ha-Nadiv," (Wine Press), in: *NEAEHL* 4, 12576–60; D. Amit, "A *Miqveh* Complex Near Alon Shevut," 75–84. (Vineyards). For *miqva'oth* close to cemeteries, cf. Y. Adler, "Ritual Baths adjacent to Tombs: An Analysis of the Archaeological Evidence in Light of the Halakhic Sources," 55–73.

and its environs. This fact is surely indicative of the holiness associated with the temple itself, and the need for purificatory facilities for pilgrims and for the priests and Levites serving in the temple. As discussed above, the Qumran Essenes extended the notion of the sanctity of the temple to the whole city. Purification before entry into a temple was a common feature of the Greco-Roman world, as illustrated by an inscription from the temple of Athene at Pergamum.[22] Excavations to the south and west of the temple mount in Jerusalem have uncovered as many as 10 ritual pools, all pre-dating the destruction of 70 CE some of which are to be dated to Hasmonean times. They do not all conform to the same pattern, and only one has a divider on the steps, separating the clean from the unclean as they exit and enter the pool (Fig. 22; 23). Scholarly discussion has been mainly concerned with the precise halachic requirements that these pools may have been intended to serve. Do they represent some extra purification that pious Israelites undertook before entering the sacred precincts beyond the women's court? In this view it is assumed that they would have previously taken care of purity regulations at various points within the city, even if they were unaccustomed to observing the purity regulations in their everyday lives.[23] Or, alternatively, it has been argued, they were based on *halacha*, at least as this was expounded later by the Rabbis.[24] In general it can be assumed that the facilities for purification before entering the temple would have been an important element in the temple complex. The arrangements at the Hulda Gate for entrance and exit by separate routes (M. Hag 2,6; M. Mid 2,2) is indicative of the need for attention to detail and the dangers of defilement through contact, the closer one came to the holy place.

As noted already, the Qumran Essenes saw themselves as constituting a temple community in the wilderness, and this explains the focus on purity in the various surviving documents and in Josephus' account of their lifestyle. The archaeology of Khirbet Qumran would seem to confirm this concern. Despite some recent attempts to detach the scrolls from the settlement, which, it was claimed, should be identified as a fortress or a rural villa, most scholars still

---

22 D. FIENSY, *Jesus the Galilean. Soundings in a First Century Life*, 165–167.

23 A. OPPENHEIMER, *The 'Am ha-Aretz, A Study of the Social History of the Jewish People in the Hellenistic-Roman Period*, 92–94 and 164–166, on the trust with regard to purity maintenance between observant members of the *havuroth* and the *'am ha-aretz*, especially during the festivals. The identification of the Pool of Siloam (John 9:7) in the Tyropoeon Valley, with features similar to a *miqveh* (plastered steps and platforms at various intervals) points to the possibility of large communal pools to cater for the pilgrim crowds coming from different directions (Cf. R. REICH/E. SHUKRON, "The Pool of Siloam," in: *NEAEHL*, vol 5, Supplementary Volume, 1807 and plate XVII). The Pool of Bethesda (John 5:2) is another example of such communal pools according to S. GIBSON, "The Pool of Bethesda in Jerusalem and Jewish Purification Practices of the Second Temple Period," 270–293.

24 E. REGEV, "The Ritual Baths near the Temple Mount and Extra-Purification before Entering the Temple Courts," 194–204; ADLER, "The Ritual Baths near the Temple Mount and Extra-Purification before Entering the Temple Courts: A Reply to Eyal Regev," 208–215.

accept the original identification made by Roland de Vaux, namely, that the ruins were those of an Essene foundation, and that the scrolls in the nearby caves belonged to this group also.[25] Allowance must of course be made for the fact that both the literary and archaeological evidence spans a period of almost 200 years, and changes undoubtedly occurred over that time-span both to the make-up of the community and the physical layout of the settlement. The earthquake of 31 BCE which lead to the abandonment of the site for a short period, is the most visible sign of such changes.

While there are significant differences among scholars with regard to the precise number of *miqvehs* within the settlement complex, there is a general agreement that some at least of the cisterns were for ritual purposes, while others were by necessity storage pools for domestic and industrial use in such a barren location (Fig. 24). Despite these differences of opinion, our knowledge of Qumran ritual practices is much more detailed than is the case with the overall situation in Judea in the same period.[26] It is generally recognised that many of the stepped pools/*miqva'oth* throughout the land do indeed date to the Second Temple period. Yet, as noted previously, the literary evidence, mainly tractate *Miqva'oth* in the Mishnah, is to be dated to a much later time (2/3rd century CE), and in many cases it may reflect the legal imagination of the Rabbis rather than the earlier historical situation, as previously mentioned. A key question that the Qumran evidence raises, therefore, is whether it can be used to document a more general attitude to purity, or whether it reflects a particular focus of the inhabitants of the settlement because of their close ties with and desire to replicate the temple in their community life. Can a consideration of the water installations at the site assist?

The archaeologist of Khirbet Qumran, Roland de Vaux, was originally of the opinion that all the water installations were functional in terms of the daily living condition of the inhabitants, even though he did allow later for the possibility that some may have been for ritual purposes. Further investigation of the water system as a whole, including the aqueduct and the internal channels connecting various pools, especially those with steps convinced scholars that

---

25 Cf. R. DE VAUX, *Archaeology and the Dead Sea Scrolls*, HIRSCHFELD, *Qumran in Context*, Peabody, Mass: Hendrickson, 2004 is the main spokesman for the revisionist position; for a critical review cf. H. ESHEL, "Qumran Archaeology," 389–394.

26 DE VAUX, *Archaeology*, 8–10 and 131–132 thought that the majority of the pools were cisterns and only loci 61 and 138 were ritual baths. However, more recent discussion puts the figure of ritual baths higher: J. MAGNESS, *The Archaeology of Qumran and the Dead Sea Scrolls*,134–162, especially 147–150, follows REICH in identifying 10 of the 16 pools/cisterns as ritual baths, whereas Y. MAGEN/Y. PELEG, "Back to Qumran: Ten Years of Excavation and Research 1993–2004," 55–116, especially 86–94, conclude that only three of Reich's 10 stepped pools qualify as ritual baths on the basis of the ways in which water was collected. These are loci 68, 118 and 138. According to them, a number of larger cisterns with steps do not qualify as ritual baths because of non-compliance with the halachic regulations.

the majority of the pools were indeed intended for ritual practices, as the scrolls had indicated. An important study by Benjamin Wood came to the conclusion that the large cisterns without steps could supply the domestic needs of the community at the different phases of its occupation from the late 2nd century BCE to the abandonment of the site after the first revolt in 73 CE. The proportion of stepped pools to those without steps was in the ratio of 2/1 throughout the different phases of the settlement's existence convinced Wood that ritual washing was a very important aspect of the community's daily life. Thus, e.g. when two pools from period 1b were seriously damaged by the earthquake of 31 BCE, the subsequent inhabitants made up for the loss of these two pools by dividing a large one into two separate pools, even though now one must have functioned as a storage pool, since there are no steps, but also no sign of a connecting pipe.[27]

Building on the analysis of Reich, who claims that there were 10 immersion pools in all at the site, Magness seeks to relate their location to different aspects of the Community's life.[28] Thus, e.g. locus 138 at the entrance replicates the pools at the entrance to the temple in Jerusalem, and might serve the purpose for novices who were precluded from bathing with the 'holy men of the pure congregation.' L 117 and L 118 are two rectangular pools lying adjacent to a large round cistern that predates the sectarians' arrival and which served as the main storage cistern for the residents' domestic use, it would seem. The two rectangular pools are very similar in layout, except that L 117 has two dividers on the steps and L 118 has a small landing step at the bottom. This is the largest pair of pools of a number of such adjacent pairs within the complex (loci 48/49; 56/58; 85/91), a feature, which according to Reich, was also prominent in Jerusalem. Other pools, such as L 56, L 71 and L 49, are, according to Magness, each strategically located close by the refectory, the pottery-making studio and the latrine, respectively.

While the arrangement of separate pools could be necessary in a mixed domestic setting in the city, where males and females might use separate pools, almost certainly this did not apply at Qumran. Thus, Magness offers the alternative solution of one pool acting as back-up to the other when the need arose for cleaning or some other emergency. Furthermore, she notes, that the sectarian *halakah* as expressed in 4QMMT did not allow for pure and impure liquids to be mixed as a way of rendering unclean water clean.[29] Consequently, there are no examples of *otzars*, or connecting pipes in Qumran, such as occurred in the Hasmonean palace at Jericho. Yet only two of the ten *miqvehs* identified by Reich lack one or other feature associated generally with ritual pools – divid-

---

27 Wood, "To Dip or to Sprinkle." 45–60.
28 Magness, *The Archaeology of Qumran*, 147–150.
29 C. Selkin Wise, "*Miqvaot* and Second Temple Sectarianism," 181–200.

ers, platforms between rows of steps which extend the full width of the pool, e.g. Comparisons with other excavated settlements of indigenous cultures of the region such as the Phoenicians and the Nabateans convinces Magness that Qumran is a unique location and that indeed the water installations confirm that this place was settled by a group who practiced ritual purity to a unique degree demanding a high attention to the purity regulations of those fully initiated into the group.

Clearly, when one approaches a site such as Kh. Qumran with the profile of the scrolls in view, it is possible and plausible to explain the archaeological features as reflecting the ethos and beliefs of the group described in the literature. Not all archaeologists agree with Reich, Netzer, Wood, Magness and others who support this interpretation, however. In a recent article Y. Magen and Y. Peleg pose the most serious challenge from an archaeological point of view to those who argue for a ritual interpretation of the pools.[30] They are critical of the assumption that steps in some of the larger pools indicate that they should be identified as *miqvehs*. Instead they claim that there are good structural reasons for the use of steps and internal dividing walls in order to support the walls of the pools, since the ground at Qumran consists of 'unstable marl which swells when wet' thus rendering the walls liable to collapse. The steps and the lateral walls were intended by the masons to take the pressure off the external walls of the pools, it is suggested. Furthermore, they argue that since the main supply of water to the settlement came through the large sedimentation pool in L 132 near the north western corner, it would not be deemed suitable for ritual immersion according to M. Miq 1,4, but would rather be deemed 'drawn water.' In the authors' view L 68, L 138 and L 117 are the only sites that qualify as potential ritual baths in accordance with the *halakah*, since they were not fed from the sedimentation pool and the channel leading from it, and in the case of L117 it was probably fed by rainwater. In general the authors are sceptical of the presuppositions of the 'ritualists', claiming that many of the pools had to do with the pottery industry. Following de Vaux's original observations, they suggest that this industry was highly developed at Qumran because of the manner in which the clay was gathered naturally by the floodwaters from the stream beds where it had been deposited.

This is not the place to discuss these opposing views in any detail. Indeed, Magen and Peleg could also be accused of allowing their original presuppositions about the site to determine their views of the pools. Neither position is absolutely definitive, though it must be said that once the scrolls are linked with the inhabitants of the site, it seem very difficult to ignore the views of Reich and Magness, even if they too can be accused of over-interpreting in some instances. It should be recalled that according to the Rabbinic writings pottery produc-

---

30   Magen/Peleg, "Back to Qumran," especially 86–92.

tion in Israel demanded strict observance of the purity laws and was strictly supervised, as indeed Magen and Peleg stress.[31] The way forward, therefore, might be to attempt to determine how extensively the Qumran pottery was distributed, and to identify the contexts outside the site in which it was found. To the best of my knowledge no such investigation of the Qumran pottery, similar to that of David Adan-Bayewitz in regard to the Kefar Hanania ware, has so far been conducted.[32] This would focus on provenience and distribution, employing such scientific methods as neutron activation analysis. The results of such a study would, perhaps, tell us more about the labours of the inhabitants of the site, which up to now have perhaps been overly influenced by the agricultural model of later monastic settlements. It would also confirm the extent to which purity concerns determined the operations of the production centre, and what that in turn could tell us about the general observance of purity in the population at large.

Our lengthy trawl through the literary and archaeological evidence to do with ritual washings in Second Temple Judaism has raised as many questions as it has provided answers to the meaning and practice of the purity regulations. Yet several interesting points did surface:

(1) The discussion of *miqvehs* and their significance as tracers of Jewish ethnic and religious identity outside Jerusalem and away from the temple is somewhat inconclusive, mainly due to lack of definitive evidence. Nevertheless, it seems important to stress the likelihood that all pilgrims to Jerusalem were expected to, and in fact did undergo immersion before entering the temple precinct. The silence of the gospels with regard to Jesus' and his disciples' practice in this regard can be readily explained either because of later Christian polemic and practice in the circles that produced the canonical gospels, or possibly because the practice was so common, not just in regard to the Jerusalem temple, but in the Greco-Roman world generally, that is was taken for granted.

(2) In view of the cost of installing and maintaining a private *miqveh*, and the possibility of using alternate locations for immersion, such as rivers, springs and even the Sea of Galilee, it would be wrong to draw any negative conclusions regarding Galilean indifference to ritual matters, simply because the distribution of these installations is thus far so patchy, at least for the first century CE. If we are looking for positive links with Jerusalem and its ritual practices in the archaeological evidence the widespread distribution of domestic stone ware in terms of mugs, cooking pots, jugs and lamps, is undoubtedly more compelling.

---

31 MAGEN/PELEG, "Back to Qumran," 92–94.

32 Ware from this Galilean centre was highly regarded by the Rabbis, since the local clay was of a superior quality and ensured that the vessels did not crack easily, thereby endangering liquid contents incurring impurity. Cf. D. ADAN-BAYEWITZ, *Common Pottery in Roman Galilee. A Study of Local Trade.*

(3) The linking of ritual and moral purity, especially in the Dead Sea Scrolls, but also in Philo and Josephus, is highly instructive in terms of understanding the stance of the Jesus-movement. The profile of John the Baptist, however much his actual historical role has been subordinated to that of Jesus in other respects in the early Christian writings, is in conformity with contemporary Jewish thought with regard to the relationship between moral and ritual purity. Contextual plausibility would strongly suggest that Jesus' view was no different in this regard. Significantly, Josephus in describing John's preaching as 'justice towards the fellow man and piety towards God' uses exactly the same terminology as that of the oath that the Essene initiate was expected to take (JA 18,117; JW 2,139). It is only when such practice was in place that John called for undergoing his baptismal rite.

(4) Though some scholars have suggested that the practice of purity had already begun to take on a life of its own, independently of the temple, thereby indicating a more individualistic approach to the deity, it is difficult to document this with specific examples.[33] Perhaps the suggested dichotomy is inappropriate. Disaffection with or distance from the existing temple did not obliterate the desire for what the temple stood for, namely, the divine *Shekinah* whose protective presence was available for all Israel, a presence that was at once, mysterious, consoling and awesome. According to 1QS 5,11f., those who exclude themselves from joining the covenant (i.e. the community) are described as follows: 'They are not included in his covenant since they have neither sought nor examined his decrees in order to learn the hidden matters in which they err by their own fault, and because they treated revealed matters with disrespect.'[34] Entering the covenant means engaging with the mystery that has been revealed and this demands 'both a whole heart and a dedicated soul' (1QS 5,9). Against this background, the external practice of purity is the tangible recognition of being in the divine presence, experiencing the mystery and accepting the ethical demands of what has been revealed.

3. The In-Between World of Jewish Christian Baptism and Immersion

The early Christian criticism of the repetition and ineffectiveness of Jewish washings stands in stark contrast to the attention to detail that is reflected in the attitudes of at least some Jews in the first century. Furthermore, at least among the Essenes and the followers of the Baptist, repentance and a change of heart was required in order for the washing to be effective. Denigration of these practices as external and meaningless can be dismissed as either anti-Jewish bias stem-

---

33 REGEV, "Pure Individualism: The Idea of Non-Priestly Purity in Ancient Judaism," 176–201.
34 PFANN, "The Essene Yearly Renewal," 340f.

ming from more general pagan views about Jewish practices, or gentile Christian theological rhetoric that consciously distorts the reality. The loss of the temple did not mean that the observance of the purity laws should now be abandoned. Instead, the development of the Mishnah, with its focus on purity, and its eventual acceptance as the foundation document of post-Biblical Judaism, strongly suggests that already in the first century the observance of the purity regulations had begun to be relevant, independently of the temple, however much this institution may have dominated the religious, and indeed the social and economic landscape of Judea and Judeans everywhere up to 70 CE.

This process may have been hastened by what historian Martin Goodman has suggested had been occurring in Judea ever since Herod had come to rule as king of the Jews. His replacement, indeed his obliteration of the Hasmonean priestly aristocracy meant that the emotional attachment to the central institutions as these had functioned previously, had been greatly weakened.[35] The new Herodian elite failed to placate the unrest of the populace, much less win their affection, throughout the turbulent decades leading up to the first revolt. It is interesting to note that archaeologist Andrea Berlin has been able to detect the emergence of a strong anti-Roman attitude in her analysis of the pottery and cooking habits at several of the more nationalistic centres in Galilee.[36] Issues of purity maintenance had political as well as religious traction in a situation in which national identity and the institutions that were meant to maintain it were being eroded by outside influences, political and cultural.

The Jesus-movement, at least in its Palestinian setting could not, and did not remain immune from these issues. The fate of the two James, is perhaps the most obvious sign of hostility to the new movement. Apart from the arrest, trial and crucifixion of Jesus, James the son of Zebedee in 40, CE and James the brother of Jesus in 62 CE both fell victim to the Jewish aristocratic rule, the one under Herod Agrippa I and the latter under the high priest Ananus, during an interregnum in the procuratorship of Judea. Indeed the wonder was how James, the brother of Jesus had managed to survive for so long, given the public execution of his brother by the Romans and the inevitable suspicion that this must have aroused for his followers among an aristocratic Jewish elite who did not want to become embroiled in anti-Roman activities of any kind. In my opinion, James and others from the Jesus-movement felt the need to maintain a presence in Jerusalem as a public symbol of their belief that Jesus was Israel's messiah and that they were forming the nucleus of a restored Israel based on

---

35 M. Goodman, *The Ruling Class of Judea. The Origins of the Jewish Revolt against Rome, A.D. 66–70*, especially 109–135.

36 A. Berlin, "Romanisation and anti-Romanisation in pre-Revolt Galilee," 57–73; Berlin, *Gamla I, The Pottery of the Second Temple Period*, especially 133–156.

the memory of Jesus, thereby realising the promises made to Zion, as these were expressed in the literature of the Second Temple period.[37]

Unfortunately, we do not have adequate sources for understanding the historical James' role more fully. It is all the more remarkable, therefore, that Luke in his *Acts of the Apostles* is prepared to give James precedence over both Peter and Paul at certain crucial points in his narrative account from a Paulinist perspective of the development of the early Christian movement: Acts 12:17 (Peter message to James as he departs Jerusalem); Acts 15:13–21 (Formulation of the apostolic decree with regard to admission of the gentiles); Acts 21:17–26 (James as advisor to Paul with regard to placating hostility from the Jewish authorities towards his acceptance of gentiles). However, the legend of James the Just was to develop further not only in Jewish Christian circles, but also among both gnosticising and catholic Christians as well. All of which indicates the importance of this foundational link with Jerusalem and its Jewish roots for the various branches of emerging Christianity over several centuries.[38]

We may well ask how did these developments play themselves out in terms of both Christian Baptism and Jewish immersion rites, both rites acting as markers of developing separate identities. Justin Martyr's *Dialogue with Trypho* from the mid-second century provides a good sounding board as to how the situation reflected in the New Testament had developed in the interim. Justin was clearly interested in establishing clear boundaries and a distinct identity for Christians as another race (ἄλλο γένος, *Dial.* 138,2), over against the Jewish matrix.[39] Baptism, described as an initiation (τελεῖος γενόμενος), as in the mystery religions, is the gateway to salvation for Trypho and his companions (*Dial.* 8,2f.). Trypho, however, sees circumcision as the door that leads to the practices enjoined in Torah: e.g. Sabbath observance, new moons and ritual washing. After a lengthy discussion in which Justin argues that the blood of circumcision has been replaced by the blood of Christ, he makes and impassioned plea: 'To you, Trypho and to those who wish to become proselytes, I proclaim the divine message' (*Dial.* 23,3). Despite some claims that the term 'proselyte' here refers to gentile converts to Christianity, I agree with Stanton that it is much more likely to refer to gentiles who were converting to Judaism. This judgement is based on the immediate sequel, consisting of a very strong statement that circumcision has been rendered useless by the blood of Christ (*Dial.* 23,4). Would-be converts to Judaism are, like Trypho himself, pursuing a dead end.[40]

Later in the Dialogue the position of Jewish converts to Christianity comes up for closer examination. Clearly, Jewish practices, including ritual washing,

---

37 S. Freyne, "Jesus and the 'Servant' Community in Zion: Continuity in Context," 109–124.

38 Freyne, *Retrieving James/Yakov, the Brother of Jesus.*

39 D. K. Buell, *Why This New Race*, especially 94–115 on Justin's *Dialogue.*

40 G. Stanton, "Justin Martyr's Dialogue with Trypho," 267–271.

were attractive to gentiles. Justin presents himself as being more tolerant towards their continuance with these than were some fellow gentile Christians. These latter had refused to share table-fellowship with such Jewish-Christian converts, because of their refusal to make a clean break with their Jewish past. Trypho wants to know which Jewish observances are permissible for the new convert:

> But if some, even now, wish to live in the observance of the institutions given by Moses, and yet believe in this Jesus who was crucified, recognising Him to be the Christ of God, and that it is given to Him to be absolute Judge of all, and that His is the everlasting kingdom, can they also be saved?" he (Trypho) inquired of me. And I replied, "Let us consider that also together, whether one may now observe all the Mosaic institutions." And he answered, "No. For we know that, as you said, it is not possible either anywhere to sacrifice the lamb of the Passover, or to offer the goats ordered for the fast; or, in short, [to present] all the other offerings." And I said, "Tell then yourself, I pray, some things which can be observed; for you will be persuaded that, though a man does not keep or has not performed the eternal decrees, he may assuredly be saved." Then he replied, "To keep the Sabbath, to be circumcised, to observe months, and *to be washed if you touch anything prohibited by Moses, or after sexual intercourse (Dial. 46).*

Trypho accepts that it is not possible to follow all aspects of the Mosaic law, such as animal sacrifices, and at the same time believe in Jesus as the Christ of God, but does claim that Sabbath observance, circumcision, and the practice of ritual purity could continue without compromising one's belief in Christ. This admission now raises a further question as to whether the person who adopts this latter course, namely, observes those aspects of the Jewish way of life which would not necessarily compromise faith in Christ, would such a person be saved? Justin is careful in his answer, declaring himself to be more tolerant than other Gentile converts who refuse to have any contact with Jewish Christians. However, those who continue to practice Jewish observances must not seek to persuade other gentile converts to imitate them, as though these practices were necessary. In Justin's view such Jewish Christians will indeed be able to participate in future salvation. However, the fact that he feels the need to reiterate his rejection of any proselytizing of gentile converts to Jewish ways more than once, suggests that this was a live issue. Clearly, some gentile converts to Christianity would seem to have accepted the whole Mosaic dispensation without any distinction, but in Justin's view they were thereby not only abandoning Christ, but in fact joining those other Jews who did not believe in Jesus and who anathematized Christian believers in their synagogues (*Dial.* 47). The lines are beginning to be drawn, it would seem.

Justin is witness to the fact that by the mid-second century Jewish Jesus-believers, who still wished to continue aspects of their ancestral practices, including ritual washing were becoming a problem for both the emerging main-line gentile Christian group and the Jewish synagogue. In fact he mentions the anathematizing of Christians in the synagogues three times in the *Dialogue* (16,4; 47,4; 96,2). By pointing to the late and legendary nature of the Rabbinic reports of such an enactment, Boyarin seeks to minimize the significance of these references in terms of a clear separation between Judaism and Christianity, dating back to a putative enactment of the *birkath ha-minim* at a putative council of Jamnia.[41] While his point regarding a process of separation rather than a punctiliar expulsion of Christians is well taken, he nevertheless minimises the relevance of the references to the anathematization of Christians in the *Dialogue*. Denise Buell's categories of fixity and fluidity in both traditions seem to capture the situation more accurately, at least as Justin represents it.[42] According to her reading of the *Dialogue*, peoplehood, both Jewish and Christian, was a flexible concept, and should not be understood in terms of ethnoracial categories or clearly defined social formations. Rather, in both traditions the concept is 'concurrent and overlapping' even though Justin tends to present Jewishness as more fixed and Christianness as more fluid because of its universalist outlook. Yet, as we have seen, he is prepared, however grudgingly, to tolerate those who continue to practice certain Jewish rituals. Furthermore, the representation of Trypho as a Jew who is willing to debate alternative views regarding salvation, on the one hand, and Justin's own views on the absolute necessity of knowing Christ and being baptized, on the other (*Dial.* 44,4), introduce respectively a note of fluidity into ideas of Jewishness, and a non-negotiable fixity into the boundaries of Christian identity.

Behind the Pseudo-Clementine writings, which are dated to the 4th/5th centuries, scholars have long recognized Jewish Christian sources that could be dated to the 2nd century.[43] These would provide an insider view on the issues that Justin as an outsider to the Jewish Christian circles had been debating, especially regarding Baptism and Jewish ritual practices. The passage cited at the outset shows that there was no contradiction between the requirement of baptism and the practice of Jewish ritual washings, even when the essential importance of baptism is clearly stated. In order to appreciate the perspective of these writings with regard to baptism and Jewish ritual practices it is important to recognize the strong anti-Pauline bias that runs through them. James and Peter, not Paul are the central figures.

The 'Letter of Peter to James' and the related *Contestatio* of James, which have been appended to the Greek ms. of the *Homilies*, set the tone. Peter requests that, just as Moses had done, the books containing his preaching which he was sending to James should be entrusted only to someone who was found to

---

41 Boyarin, *Border Lines*, 67–73.
42 Buell, *Why this New Race*, 96 and 112f.
43 Stanton, "Jewish Christian Elements in the Pseudo-Clementine Writings," 307–324.

be worthy, so that the teaching would not be distorted as 'some among the gentiles' had done, preferring a lawless and absurd doctrine of the man who is my enemy' (*Ep. Petri*, 2,1–4). In response, James takes an oath that the books would only be handed over to an approved candidate, a man who is circumcised and was a believing Christian, and had gone through a probationary period of six years. At the end of this period the prospective candidate was to be brought 'to a river or a fountain where there is living water (ὕδωρ ζῶν), and the regeneration (ἀναγένεσις) of the righteous takes place.' (*Contestatio* 1,1–2).[44] The terminology is clearly baptismal, yet since the candidate was already a Christian, this water rite, which resembles that of the Essene initiation ceremony, involves purification before the books of Peter's preaching can be handed over. Water rites continue to play an important role even after baptism, therefore.

In the light of this observation we may well enquire what the specific understanding of baptism was in the circles where the original novel, which probably bore the title *Periodoi Petrou* (dealing with Peter's missionary journeys), circulated.[45] According to F. S. Jones, 'the purpose of the novel is to illustrate how Christian rebirth (baptism) can overcome astrological determination,' while its 'framework is the distinctive doctrine that the history of the present world is dominated by ten pairs of figures (called *syzygies* in Greek), one of which was wicked and the other good. This pattern is followed through biblical history, ending up with Simon Magus and Peter (8th pair) and the false and true gospel (9th pair), referring to the 'false gospel of a certain deceiver' (i.e. Paul) and the true gospel of conversion (i.e. the message of the work based on Peter's preaching to gentile Christians).[46] Within this framework, Baptism as rebirth, plays an absolutely essential role, using the first created element water and thereby conforming to the Father's will:

> But when you have come to the Father you will learn that this is His will that you be born anew by means of waters, which were first created. For he who is regener-

---

44 G. STRECKER, "The *Kerygmata Petrou*", 111–113.

45 STRECKER, *Das Judenchristentum*, building on earlier efforts to discover the Grundschrift that served as the Source for both the *Homilies* and the *Recognitions*, speaks of the *Kerygmata Petrou*, based on Peter's preaching and teaching. On the other hand, F. S. JONES, "The Pseudo-Clementines," 285–304 and 331–333 (notes), speaks of the Clementine novel as a 'self-conscious, independent production' rather than a compilation of different and heterogeneous material. This work is entitled *The Circuits of Peter (Periodoi tou Petrou)*, building on the fiction of Peter's missionary journeys after the Resurrection. The original of this novel is now lost but Jones bases his reconstruction by working from the parallels in both the *Homilies* and the *Recognitions*, in a manner not dissimilar to Strecker. The difference between them seems to be more a question of what was the correct framework for the novel, and how this is now to be retrieved.

46 JONES, "Jewish Christianity in the Pseudo-Clementines," 314–319; STRECKER, *Das Judenchristentum*, 190–196.

ated by water, having filled up the measure of good works is made heir of Him by whom he has been regenerated in incorruption (*Rec.* vi, 8.9–10).[47]

The rebirth of baptism contrasts with the first birth, which was the result of human desire (ἐπιθυμία).[48] According to the author this desire arises from the sexual urge, so that humans were born 'from disgusting drop' ('impure stock'/ἐκ μυσαρᾶς σταγόνος, *Hom.* iii, 20,1), whereas the true nature is to be child of God, which is achieved through baptism:

> When you are regenerated and born again of water and of God, *the frailty of your former birth, which you have through men*, is cut off, and so at length you shall be able to attain salvation; but otherwise it is impossible (*Rec.* vi, 9. 9–10).

Undergoing the rite of Baptism demonstrated that one recognized that one's sins were the result of ignorance, based on the faulty nature of human birth. The practice of chastity is one of its direct effects, an essential requirement for future blessedness (*Rec.* vii, 38.3–4; *Hom.* xiii, 13,2). On the other hand failure to be baptized meant that 'the idol of unbelief' is present (*Rec.* vi, 9,11). Therefore, no amount of good works could spare one from judgment. Good works are indeed essential, but only if they are in conformity with God's command:

> Now God has ordered every one who worships Him to be sealed by baptism; but if you refuse, and obey your own will rather than God's, you are doubtless contrary and hostile to His will (*Rec.* vi, 8,12).

Why the insistence on water baptism, especially in view of the strong emphasis on good works also? The first answer is simply because God has ordered it. However, the author, basing himself on the account of creation in Genesis 1, has explored the significance of water 'which was the first-made,' immediately preceding the treatment of baptism in both of the later redactions of the *Periodoi*:

> In the beginning God made the heaven and the earth. But the earth was invisible, and unarranged; and darkness was over the deep: *and the Spirit of God was upon the waters*. Which Spirit, *like the Creator's hand*, by command of God separated light from darkness; and after that invisible heaven produced this visible one, that He might make the higher places a habitation for angels, and the lower for men. For your sake, therefore, by command of God, the water which was upon the face of the earth withdrew, that the earth might produce fruits for you; and into the earth also he inserted veins of moisture, *that fountains and rivers might flow forth from it for you* (*Hom.* xi, 23; *Rec.* vi, 7).

---

47 Anti-Nicene Fathers, English Translations, 10 vols. www.searchgodsword.org: vol. 8: The Pseudo-Clementine Literature.

48 Strecker, *Das Judenchristentum*, 145–147 and 199f., points out that the understanding of human birth as deeply flawed has its roots in Gnostic ideas. The creation of the first man, Adam, was by the hand of God and he was thereby gifted with the Holy Spirit, unlike others who are from 'the impure stock' and are, therefore, the result of human desire.

Because the waters of Baptism partake in this power of the Spirit that was linked with the water from the beginning, those who are baptised under the name of the 'thrice blessed invocation' are rescued from future punishments, as the true prophet had declared, according to John 3:5 (*Rec.* vi, 9, 11).[49]

In the original account of creation in Genesis the water over which God's spirit hovered was first divided into the waters above and below the vault of heaven, and these latter were then gathered together to separate the seas from the dry land. However, the Clementine adaptation speaks of the water below being channeled through fountains and rivers flowing for the benefit of humans. One could see this as a reference to the plentiful supply of natural water that was one of the blessings of the Promised Land according to the Deuteronomist (Deut 8:11-13; 11:10-12). Yet, in the context of the discussion on baptismal water it is difficult not to detect a reference to the metaphorical significance of water as a bearer of the spirit and therefore as life-giving at a deeper level. This appreciation of the symbolic power of water appears at various points throughout both recensions of the original in such expressions as ὕδωρ ζῶν or ὕδωρ σωζῶν, as is the case in *Contestatio* 1, 2 already cited. This usage links the *Periodoi* with the Johannine statements regarding the salvific role of water and spirit (John 3:5; 4:14; 7:38). However, it also reflects the stipulation of מים חיים or '*living water*' in certain purificatory rites (Lev 14:5,50-52; 15:13), a usage found in Qumran texts also (11Q, 19, xlv 15-17, e.g.).[50]

The intimate connection between baptismal and ritual washing has already been noted in both the *Homilies* and the *Recognitions*. This combination is carried further in the context of the works that the baptized are expected to perform. One shows one's likeness to the Father who has begotten the baptized by honouring him in keeping his will, as expressed in various commands of the Decalogue (*Rec.* vi, 10,1-4; *Hom.* xi, 27,3). Somewhat surprisingly in the context of moral exhortation, the case of avoiding intercourse with a menstruating wife is introduced 'as a case of purity, of which there are many' as 'the law of God commands this' (*Hom.* xi, 28,1), or, 'For the law of God considers this accursed' (*Rec.* vi, 10,5). As was the case in the Essene ordinances there is no distinction between moral and ritual stipulations, thus explaining the relationship between the two types of washing, baptismal and ritual, already highlighted.

In a study of the source that he has identified as the *Kerygmata Petrou*, Strecker suggests that there is a certain tension between a sacramental and a moralistic understanding of baptism in the work. According to him, the idea that the baptized is in the likeness of God is given a strong moral emphasis in

---

[49] JONES, "The Pseudo-Clementines," 292, remarks that this formula, though found regularly in the *Periodoi* is slightly unusual. However, it surely reflects the Matthean injunction to use the Trinitarian formula (Matt 28:19) in view of the popularity of Matthew's gospel in the Jewish Christian circles.

[50] LAWRENCE, *Washing in Water*, 132-134.

the immediate context of the discussion about the effects of baptism, whereas elsewhere this *homoiotes* with God is seen as a gift rather than a demand.[51] However, Strecker's repeated suggestion that the background to the Baptismal theology of the work has a Gnostic colouring would seem to lie behind his observations about possible tensions. While not denying certain affinities, especially, it would seem with Sethian Gnostic conceptions, the parallels with the Qumran writings need to be explored further in my opinion.[52] This suggestion underlines the strong ethical understanding of what it means to be a righteous person in terms of stricter Jewish observance of both moral and ritual stipulations. What is clear is that the teaching on baptism is very different from the Pauline idea of dying and rising of the baptized in sacramental union with the Saviour, as this is developed in Rom 6, and as it was expressed by Justin also in the *Dialogue*.

The emphasis of the *Periodoi Petrou* is theological and cosmological rather than Christological, it would seem. Christ is the true prophet like Moses who explains the importance of baptism, rather than fulfilling the role of Redeemer/Saviour in accordance with the Pauline tradition. That this was a well-received viewpoint in the circles behind the collection emerges from another putative source identified in *Rec.* 1,27–71. Although this source may not be identical with the Ebionite work alluded to by Epiphanius, his summary of their teaching is not dissimilar to what is to be found in this other Ps. Clementine *Acts*.[53] Epiphanius declares: 'They say that he (Jesus) came and announced the abolition of sacrifices, as is contained in their so-called gospel, namely: "I have come to abrogate the sacrifices, and if you do not cease to sacrifice, the wrath upon you will not cease."' (*Pan.* 30,16.5). James, the brother of Jesus, after whom the Ebionite *Acts* is named, is also said by Epiphanius to have spoken against the temple and the altar (*Pan.* 30,16,6). This anti-sacrificial stance of James is also strongly suggested by Hegesippus in his account of the martyrdom of James, who is said to have entered the temple dressed in high priestly garb as prescribed for *Yom Kippur*, and prayed, not sacrificed, for the sins of the people (Eusebius *H.E.* 2, 23. 4–18). There are several possible explanations for this anti-sacrificial stance, not least the fact that Jesus had prophesied the destruction of the temple, a prophecy that figured prominently in early Christian polemic. However, another suggestion is prompted by Justin's Trypho recognizing that it would not be possible to believe in Jesus and continue to offer sacrifices, in the

---

51 STRECKER, *Das Judenchristentum*, 205f.

52 Cf. B. A. PEARSON, *Gnosticism, Judaism and Egyptian Christianity*, especially 131f., where he discusses the notion of the Sethians as 'the seed of the Father' in some of their writings. JONES, "The Pseudo-Clementines," 297–300, also suggests possible links with the Book of Elchasai.

53 For the most recent delineation of the source and a discussion of its contents cf. JONES, *An Ancient Jewish Christian Source on the History of Christianity* (1995).

context of a discussion as to what Jewish practices could still be continued by believers in Jesus (*Dial.* 47).

That this strong stance against sacrifices continued to be a problem for the circles behind the Clementine *Acts* is clear from the following passage, in which Peter seems to be responding to an anxiety of some of his audience regarding the forgiveness of sins, now that sacrificing had ceased:

> Then as there was this need for the required reformation, the time came when it was fitting for the prophet to appear who was proclaimed earlier by Moses. At his coming by the mercy of God he would admonish them first to stop and cease with the sacrificing. In order that they not think that they were deprived of the forgiveness of sins that accrued through sacrifices and in order that this might be a hindrance with the result that they would not believe, baptism through water for the forgiveness of sins was instituted. What in truth gives forgiveness of sins was manifested to them. It is able to preserve in eternal life those who are perfect so that they will not die (*Rec.* i, 39,1- 2, Latin text).

Jones notes that this work does not give much information of Jewish-Christian observances, pointing, however, to Peter's declaration that the only difference between 'non-believers among our people' is whether or not Jesus is the prophet declared by Moses (*Rec.* i, 43,1–2).[54] Yet, the underlying understanding of Baptism seems to be in continuity with what we have discovered in the *Periodoi Petrou*. Baptism is both necessary and sufficient for eternal life, but significantly, the Syriac version of the final statement changes the overly optimistic rendering of the Latin version, cited above, by accenting the need for the baptized to continue to live the new life: 'and henceforth *following a perfect life* they might remain in immortality, purified not through the blood of animals but through the *purification of God's wisdom*.' Later in the work James repeats the importance of baptism, instructing the people 'to wash in the name of the glorious Trinity in the waters *whose flow is living*, as the Prophet of truth showed' (*Rec.* i, 69.5).

4. Concluding Reflection

This paper sought to recover the Jewish Christians' practice of ritual washing, despite their 'borderline' existence in relation to the two developing orthodoxies of Rabbinic Judaism and Catholic Christianity. The search for a *Religionsgeschichte* context for the practice of Christian baptism brought us in particular to the Essenes and their practices, as these can be re-imagined from the remains of Kh. Qumran. A water rite as an initiation ceremony into the community, combined with a strong emphasis on continued practice of ritual immersion in order to maintain the sense of ritual and moral holiness that was the foundation for the group's existence, were readily discernible from both the scrolls and the archi-

---

54   JONES, "The Pseudo Clementines," 302.

tectural remains of the Qumran settlement. We have no similar data for reconstructing Jewish Christian practices, and must rely for the most part on comments and innuendo from opponents in our attempts to reconstruct their rituals. In particular specific archaeological evidence is virtually non-existent, unless we can draw on contemporary Jewish data, such as the stepped pools, as well as later Christian baptisteries. Yet from what can be discerned there are definite similarities with the Essenes. The renewed interest in Jewish Christianity in general and in the Ps. Clementine literature in particular is to be greatly welcomed therefore, if students of early Christianity are not to continue the denigration of this ostracized, but important branch of the early Christian movement, in which their canonical texts engage.

In light of this situation, one final piece of information concerning Jewish Christian washing practices is worth considering briefly, namely, P. Oxyrhynchus 840. While this relatively modern (1905) discovery cannot match the range and significance of the discovery of the Nag Hammadi codices, it still provides a fascinating, if largely ignored window on the issues this paper has sought to address. Instead of taking this short account of an exchange between Jesus (designated as the Saviour) and the Jewish high priest within the sacred precincts (τὸ ἱερόν) as a possible historical memory, Francois Bovon suggests reading it within the context of inner Christian disputes about baptism and purity in the 2nd century CE.[55]

This suggestion is based on the terminology of washing and purity, which dominates the piece, as well as on the semantic fields of movement and vision, all of which points Bovon in the direction of an early Christian liturgical experience. Thus, the high priest, who has meticulously observed the proper ritual washing by entering and exiting 'the pool of David' by different staircases and donning the white robe of purity, is upbraided by the Saviour, who declares:

> Woe to you, O blind ones, who do not see. You have washed yourselves in these running waters (χεόμενοις ὕδασιν) where dogs and pigs wallow night and day, and you have cleansed and wiped the outside skin, which the prostitutes and flute girls anoint, which they wash and wipe and make beautiful for human desire, but inwardly these women are full of scorpions and every wickedness. But I and my disciples who you say have not bathed, we have bathed in the waters of eternal life, which comes down from the God of heaven. But woe unto you ….

This criticism of external washing and its effects is in stark contrast to the Jewish Christian lauding of washings as reflected in both Epiphanius' accounts and in the *Periodoi Petrou*, as we have seen. However, as Bovon shows, it is typical of various other groups of a Gnostic leaning, such as the Naasenes and Valentinians. He points in particular to the anti-baptist tendencies of the *Paraphrase of Shem* and *Testimony of Truth* among the Nag Hammadi texts, the former in

---

55   F. BOVON, "Fragment of Oxyrhynchus 840," 705–728.

particular speaking of the 'impure practice' of baptism in water.[56] It would seem that the shared marginality experienced by both Jewish Christians and gnosticising Christians in relation to Catholic Christianity, did not mean that their views were any more amenable to each other. It was not just a matter of differing sectarian attitudes, but rather a radical difference of ideological grounding, the one firmly based in the Jewish priestly system, and the other in a Middle-Platonist anthropology.

Bibliography

ADAN-BAYEWITZ, DAVID, *Common Pottery in Roman Galilee. A Study of Local Trade*, Ramat Gan: Bar Ilan University Press 1993.

ADLER, YONATAN, "The Ritual Baths near the Temple Mount and Extra-Purification before Entering the Temple Courts: A Reply to Eyal Regev," in: *IEJ* 56 (2006) 208–215.

— "Ritual Baths adjacent to Tombs: An Analysis of the Archaeological Evidence in Light of the Halakhic Sources," in: *JSJ* 40 (2009) 55–73.

— "Second Temple Period Ritual Baths Adjacent to Agricultural Installations: The Archaeological Evidence in Light of the Halakhic Sources," in: *JJS* 59 (2009) 62–72.

AMIT, DAVID, "A *Miqveh* Complex Near Alon Shevut," in: *'Atiqot* 38 (1990) 75–84.

AVIAM, MORDECHAI, *Jews, Pagans and Christians in the Galilee*, Institute of Galilean Archaeology, Rochester, N.Y.: University of Rochester Press 2004.

AVIGAD, N., *Discovering Jerusalem*, Oxford: Blackwell 1980.

BARTLETT, JOHN R. (ed.), *Jews in the Hellenistic and Roman Cities*, London and New York: Routledge 2002.

BAUMGARTEN, JOSEPH M., "Liquids and Susceptibility to Defilement in New 4Q Texts," in: *JQR* 85 (1994) 91–101.

---

56   BOVON, "Fragment Oxyrhynchus 840," 723–726. A. STEWART-SYKES, "Bathed in Living Waters," has recently challenged Bovon's reading of the Papyrus in relation to anti-Baptist tendencies in the second century, proposing instead to see the fragment in the context of disputes reflected in the *Didascalia Apostolorum*. These are concerned with the implications of continued ritual washing for a correct understanding of Baptism, to which the Saviour's mention of 'living water' refers, according to Stewart-Sykes. However, apart from the problem of precise dating, which applies to Stewart Sykes' reading also, a problem of which Bovon is quite aware, the vitriolic manner in which the Saviour denigrates the water of the Pool of David, and the mention of the living water coming down from heaven, suggests a more hostile attitude to any earthly ritual than Stewart Sykes' suggestions seems to allow for.

BERLIN, ANDREA, "Romanisation and anti-Romanisation in pre-Revolt Galilee," in: Andrea Berlin and Andrew Overman (eds.), *The First Jewish Revolt. Archaeology, History and Ideology*, London: Routledge 2002, 57–73.

— *Gamla I, The Pottery of the Second Temple Period* (IAA Reports 29), Jerusalem: Israel Antiquities Authority 2006.

BOVON, FRANÇOIS. "Fragment of Oxyrhynchus 840," in: *JBL* 119 (2000) 705–728.

BOYARIN, DANIEL, *Border Lines. The Partition of Judaeo-Christianity*, Philadelphia, Penn.: University of Pennsylvania Press 2007.

BUELL, DENISE K., *Why this New Race. Ethnic Reasoning in Early Christianity*, New York: Columbia University Press 2005.

DE VAUX, ROLAND, *Archaeology and the Dead Sea Scrolls*, Rev. ed., Oxford: Oxford University Press 1973.

EDWARDS, DOUGLAS AND MCCOLLOUGH, C. THOMAS (eds.), *The Archaeology of Difference: Gender, Ethnicity, Class and the "Other" in Antiquity. Studies in Honor of Eric M. Meyers* (AASOR 60/61), Boston, Mass.: ASOR 2007.

ESHEL, HANAN, "Qumran Archaeology," in: *JAOS* 125 (2005) 389–394.

FIENSY, DAVID, *Jesus the Galilean. Soundings in a First Century Life*, Philadelphia, Penn.: Gorgias Press 2007.

FREEDMAN, DAVID NOEL (ed.), *Anchor Bible Dictionary*, 6 vols., New York: Doubleday 1992.

FREYNE, SEÁN, "Jesus and the 'Servant' Community in Zion: Continuity in Context," in: TOM HOLMEN (ed.), *Jesus from Judaism to Christianity. Continuum Approaches to the Historical Jesus*, London and New York: T & T Clark International (Continuum) 2007, 109–124.

— *Retrieving James/Yakov, the Brother of Jesus. From Legend to History*, Annadale on Hudson: Bard College. Center for the Study of James the Brother 2008.

GALOR, KATHARINA, HUMBERT, JEAN-BAPTISTE and ZANGENBERG, JÜRGEN (eds.), *The Site of the Scrolls. Archaeological Interpretations and Debates*, Leiden and Boston, Mass.: Brill 2006.

— "The Stepped Water Installations of the Sepphoris Akropolis," in: EDWARDS and MCCOLLOUGH (eds.), *The Archaeology of Difference: Gender, Ethnicity, Class and the "Other" in Antiquity*, 201–214.

GOODMAN, MARTIN, *The Ruling Class of Judea. The Origins of the Jewish Revolt against Rome, A.D. 66-70*, Cambridge: Cambridge University Press 1987.

GOULDER, MICHAEL, "Hebrews and the Ebionites," in: *NTS* 48 (2003) 393–406.

GIBSON, SHIMON, "The Pool of Bethesda in Jerusalem and Jewish Purification Practices of the Second Temple Period," in: *Proche Orient Chrétien* 55 (2005) 270–293.

GUTMAN, SHAMARYAHU, "Gamala," in: E. STERN (ed.), *New Encyclopedia of Archaeological Explorations in the Holy Land (NEAEHL)*, vol. 2, 459–463.

HARRINGTON, HANNAH. K., *The Purity Texts. Companion to the Qumran Scrolls*, London: T & T Clark International (Continuum) 2004.

HENNECKE, ERNST and SCHNEEMELCHER. WILHELM (eds.), *New Testament Apocrypha*, 2 vols. English trans. R. Mc. L. Wilson, London: Lutterworth Press 1965.

HIRSCHFELD, YIZHAR, *Qumran in Context, Reassessing the Archaeological Evidence*, Peabody, Mass.: Hendrickson 2004.

HIRSCHFELD, YITZAR and BIRGER-CALDERON, RIVKA, "Ramat Ha-Nadiv," in: EPHRAIM STERN (ed.), *New Encyclopedia of Archaeological Explorations in the Holy Land (NEAEHL)*, 1993, vol. 4, 1257–1260.

JACKSON-MCCABE, MATT (ed.), *Jewish Christianity Reconsidered. Rethinking Ancient Groups and Texts*, Minneapolis, Minn.: Fortress Press 2007.

JONES, F. STANLEY *An Ancient Jewish Christian Source on the History of Christianity, Pseudo-Clementine Recognitions* 1, 27–71 (SBL.TT 37), Atlanta Ga.: Scholars Press 1995.

— "The Pseudo-Clementines", in: M. JACKSON-MCCABE (ed.), *Jewish Christianity Reconsidered, Rethinking Groups and Texts*, 285–304 and 331–333.

— "Jewish Christianity in the Pseudo-Clementines," in: ANTTI MARJANEN and PETRI LUOMANEN (eds.), *A Companion to Second-Century Christian 'Heretics,'* Leiden and Boston, Mass.: Brill 315–334.

LAWRENCE, JONATHAN D., *Washing in Water. Trajectories of Ritual Bathing in the Hebrew Bible and Second Temple Literature* (SBL Academia Biblica 23), Atlanta: Society of Biblical Literature Publications 2006.

MAGEN, YIZHAK, ARIEL DONALD, BIJOVSKY GABRIELA, TZIONIT YOAV, and SIRKIS ORNA (eds.), *The Land of Benjamin* (Judea and Samaria Publications 3), Jerusalem: IAA Publications 2004.

MAGEN YIZHAK and PELEG YUVAL, "Back to Qumran: Ten Years of Excavation and Research 1993–2004," in: GALOR, HUMBERT and ZANGENBERG (eds.), *The Site of the Scrolls. Archaeological Interpretations and Debates*, 55–116.

MAGNESS, JODI, *The Archaeology of Qumran and the Dead Sea Scrolls*, Grand Rapids, Mich.: Eerdmans 2002.

MARJANEN, ANTTI and LUOMANEN, PETRI, *A Companion to Second-Century Christian 'Heretics,'* Leiden and Boston, Mass.: Brill 2008.

MEYERS, ERIC M., "Aspects of Everyday Life in Roman Palestine with special reference to private domiciles and ritual baths," in: BARTLETT (ed.), *Jews in the Hellenistic and Roman Cities*, London and New York: Routledge 2002, 193–220.

MILGROM, JACOB, "Priestly ('P') Source," in: FREEDMAN (ed.), *Anchor Bible Dictionary*, vol. 5, 454–461.

MILLER, STUART, "Stepped Pools and the Non-Existent Monolithic 'Miqveh'", in: EDWARDS and McCOLLOUGH (eds.), *The Archaeology of Difference: Gender, Ethnicity, Class and the "Other" in Antiquity*, 215–234.

NETZER, EHUD, *The Architecture of Herod the Great Builder*, Grand Rapids, Mich.: Baker 2006.

NEUSNER, JACOB, *Method and Meaning in Ancient Judaism* (BJSt 10), Missoula, Mo.: Scholars Press 1979.

— *Judaism. The Evidence of the Mishnah*, Chicago, Ill.: University of Chicago Press 1981.

OPPENHEIMER, AARON, *The 'Am ha-Aretz, A Study of the Social History of the Jewish People in the Hellenistic-Roman Period*, Leiden: Brill 1977.

PEARSON, BIRGER, A., *Gnosticism, Judaism and Egyptian Christianity*, Minneapolis, Mich.: Fortress Press 1990.

PFANN, STEPHEN, "The Essene Renewal Ceremony and the Baptism of Repentance," in: DAVID PARRY and EUGENE ULRICH (eds.), *The Provo International Conference on the Dead Sea Scrolls: Technological Innovations, New Texts and Reformulated Issues*, Leiden: Brill 1999, 336–352.

REGEV, EYAL, "Pure Individualism: The Idea of Non-Priestly Purity in Ancient Judaism," in: *JSJ* 31 (2000) 176–201.

— "The Ritual Baths near the Temple Mount and Extra-Purification before Entering the Temple Courts," in: *IEJ* 55 (2005) 194–204.

REICH, RONNY, "The Synagogue and the *miqveh* in Eretz-Israel in the Second Temple, Mishnaic, and Talmudic Periods," in: URMAN and FLESHER (eds.), *Ancient Synagogues, Historical Analysis and Archaeological Discovery*, vol 1, 289–297.

REICH, RONNY, and SHUKRON, ELI, "The Pool of Siloam," in: *New Encyclopedia of Archaeological Explorations in the Holy Land (NEAEHL)*, vol. 5 (Supplementary Volume), 1807 and plate XVII.

SANDERS, ED PARIS, *Jewish Law from Jesus to the Mishnah. Five Studies*, London: SCM Press 1990.

SELKIN WISE, CAROL, "*Miqvaot* and Second Temple Sectarianism," in: EDWARDS and MCCOLLOUGH (eds.), *The Archaeology of Difference: Gender, Ethnicity, Class and the "Other" in Antiquity*, 181–200.

SILBERMAN, NEIL A. and SMALL, DAVID (eds.), *The Archaeology of Israel. Constructing the Past, Interpreting the Present* (JSOT Supplement Series 237), Sheffield: Sheffield Academic Press 1997.

SKARSAUNE, OSKAR and HVALIK, REIDAR (eds.), *Jewish Believers in Jesus. The Early Centuries*, Peabody, Mass.: Hendrickson 2007, 307–324.

STANTON, GRAHAM and STROUMSA, GUY (eds.), *Tolerance and Intolerance in Early Judaism and Christianity*, Cambridge: Cambridge University Press 1998.

STANTON, GRAHAM, "Justin Martyr's Dialogue with Trypho," in: STANTON and STROUMSA (eds.), *Tolerance and Intolerance in Early Judaism and Christianity*, Cambridge: Cambridge University Press 1998, 267–271.

— "Jewish Elements in the Pseudo-Clementine Writings," in: SKARSAUNE and HVALIK (eds.), *Jewish Believers in Jesus. The Early Centuries*, 307–324.

STERN, EPHRAIM (ed.), *New Encylopedia of Archaeological Explorations in the Holy Land*, *(NEAEHL)*, 5 vols., Jerusalem: Israel Exploration Society/Carta 1993–2008.

STEWART-SYKES, ALISTAIR, "Bathed in living waters. Papyrus Oxyrhynchus 840 and Christian Baptism reconsidered," in: *ZNW* 100 (2009) 278–286.

STRECKER, GEORG, *Das Judenchristentum in den Pseudoklementinen*, Berlin: Akademie-Verlag ²1981.

— "The *Kerygmata Petrou*", in: HENNECKE and SCHNEEMELCHER (eds.), *New Testament Apocrypha*, vol. 2, 102–127.

— *Die Pseudoklementinen I, Homilien*, (Die Griechischen Christlichen Schriftsteller), 3., verbesserte Auflage, Berlin: Akademi Verlag, 1992.

— *Die Pseudoklementinen, Zweiter Band, Rekognitionen in Rufins Übersetzung*, (Die Griechischen Christlichen Schriftsteller), 2., verbesserte Auflage, Berlin: Walter de Gruyter, 2009.

URMAN, DAN and FLESHER, PAUL V. M. (eds.), *Ancient Synagogues. Historical Analysis and Archaeological Discovery*, 2 vols., Leiden: Brill 1995.

WILKEN, ROBERT, L., *John Chrysostom and the Jews. Rhetoric and Reality in the Fourth Century*, Berkley, Calif.: University of California Press 1983.

WOOD, BENJAMIN, "To Dip or to Sprinkle. The Qumran Cisterns in Perspective," in: *BASOR* 256 (1984) 45–60.

WRIGHT, BENJAMIN G. III, "Jewish Ritual Baths – Interpreting the Digs and the Texts: Some Issues in the Social History of Second Temple Judaism," in: SILBERMAN and SMALL (eds.), *The Archaeology of Israel. Constructing the Past, Interpreting the Present*, 190–215.

ZISSU, BOAZ, TEPPER, YOTAM, and AMIT, DAVID, '*Miqwa'ot* at Kefar 'Othnai near Legio,' in: *IEJ* 56 (2006) 59–66.

ZISSU, BOAZ and GANOR, AMIR, "Horvat 'Ethri' – A Jewish Village from the Second Temple Period and the Bar Kokhba Revolt in the Judean Foothills," in: *JJS* 60 (2009) 90–135.

"Echo of a Whisper"
The Uncertain Authenticity of Josephus' Witness to John the Baptist[1]

CLARE K. ROTHSCHILD

1. Introduction

According to the oldest remaining manuscripts of the *Antiquitates judaicae*,[2] the first-century Jewish historian Josephus reports the life and work of John the Baptist (*A.J.* 18.116–19).[3] This narrative excerpt is crucial to any study of John. It offers the only corroboration outside of early Christian literature to his life. Unlike the study of its Christian counterparts about Jesus (*A.J.* 18.63–64, the so-called *Testimonium Flavianum*)[4] and James (*A.J.* 20.197–203), the authenticity of Josephus' excerpt about John is hardly debated.[5] Without demur, theologians

---

[1] Citation from: R. H. LIGHTFOOT, *History and Interpretation in the Gospels*, 225). My thanks to Robert Matthew Calhoun, Richard I. Pervo, and James A. Kelhoffer for very helpful comments on earlier drafts of this essay. I also wish to thank those at Linguistic Software who helped convert my Greek to Unicode.

[2] The earliest is eleventh century (see discussion below). See L. H. FELDMAN, "The *Testimonium Flavianum*: The State of the Question," 179–199, here: 181–185.

[3] Throughout this essay, Greek text is that of LOUIS H. FELDMAN, *Josephus, Jewish Antiquities Books XVIII–XIX, 80–84*. Feldman relies substantially on Niese's *editio maior* but with emendations based on the work of other scholars (see "Prefatory Note," ix).

[4] Literature on the *Testimonium Flavianum* or Josephus in general consulted for this essay includes: R. EISLER, *Iesous Basileus on Basileusas*, 2 vols.; in ET: abridged and corrected by A. H. KRAPPE, *The Messiah Jesus and John the Baptist According to Flavius Josephus' Recently Discovered "Capture of Jerusalem" and the Other Jewish and Christian Sources*; FELDMAN, "The *Testimonium Flavianum*: The State of the Question," 179–199; IDEM, *Josephus and Modern Scholarship 1937–1980*; IDEM, *Josephus' Interpretation of the Bible*; IDEM, *Studies in Josephus' Rewritten Bible*; IDEM, "Josephus," in: *ABD* 3:981–98; L. H. FELDMAN/G. HATA, *Josephus, Judaism and Christianity*; I. HEINEMANN, "Josephus' Method in the Presentation of Jewish Antiquities," 180–203; S. MASON, *Josephus and the New Testament*; J. P. MEIER, "John the Baptist in Josephus: Philology and Exegesis," 225–237; É. NODET, "Jésus et Jean-Baptiste selon Josephe," 321–348; K. OLSEN, "Eusebius and the *Testimonium Flavianum*," 305–322.

[5] L. HERRMANN (*Chrestos. Témoignages paiens et juifs sur le christianisme du premier siècle*, 99–104) rejects the authenticity of the Baptist passage, whereas PER BILDE (*Flavius Josephus between Jerusalem and Rome. His Life, His Works, and their Importance*, 223) accepts its authenticity.

and historians alike rely on this passage for reconstructions of John's life.[6] For example, Joan Taylor, in an excellent study of John the Baptist, cites the passage with only this footnote: "For the authenticity of the passage see Meier, *Marginal Jew*, vol. 2, 19-20."[7] As one of the only scholars treating the problem at length, Meier's influential study is worth citing in full:

> Unlike the *Testimonium Flavianum* (Ant. 18.3.3 §63–64) explored in Chapter 3, Josephus' account of John the Baptist in Ant. 18.5.2 §116–119 does not require a lengthy defense of its authenticity. The basic text is witnessed in all relevant manuscripts of the *Jewish Antiquities*, and the vocabulary and style are plainly those of Josephus, especially as evidenced in books 17–19 of the *Antiquities*. Unlike the *Testimonium*, Josephus' treatment of the Baptist is clearly referred to by Origen in his *Contra Celsum* (1.47) as he seeks to prove the existence of the Baptist .... The whole text of Josephus' passage on the Baptist is given, with slight variations, by Eusebius in his *Ecclesiastical History* (1.11.4–6). The content of the Baptist passage also argues for its authenticity. The account Josephus gives of the Baptist is literarily and theologically unconnected with the account of Jesus, which occurs earlier in Book 18 and correspondingly lacks any reference to the Baptist. The passage about the Baptist, which is more than twice as long as the passage about Jesus, is also more laudatory. It also differs from (but does not formally contradict) the Four Gospels in this presentation both of John's ministry and of his death. Hence it is hard to imagine a Christian scribe inserting into Book 18 of the *Antiquities* two passages about Jesus and the Baptist in which the Baptist appears on the scene after Jesus dies, has no connection with Jesus, receives more extensive treatment than Jesus, and is praised more highly than Jesus. It is not

---

6   Standard works on this topic include E. Bammel, "The Baptist in Early Christian Tradition," 95–128; J. Becker, *Johannes der Täufer und Jesus von Nazareth*; M. Dibelius, *Die urchristliche Überlieferung von Johannes dem Täufer*; J. Ernst, *Johannes der Täufer: Interpretation, Geschichte, Wirkungsgeschichte*; A. S. Geyser, "The Youth of John the Baptist: A Deduction from the Break in the Parallel Account of the Lucan Infancy Story," 70–75; M. Goguel, *Au seuil de l'évangile: Jean-Baptiste*; P. W. Hollenbach, "Social Aspects of John the Baptist's Preaching Mission in the Contexts of Palestinian Judaism," 850–875; C. H. Kraeling, *John the Baptist*; H. Lichtenberger, "Reflections on the History of John the Baptist's Communities," 45–49; E. Lohmeyer, *Das Urchristentum 1: Johannes der Täufer*; E. Lupieri, *Giovanni Battista fra Storia e Leggenda*; J. P. Meier, *A Marginal Jew: Rethinking the Historical Jesus. Volume Two: Mentor, Message, and Miracles*, 199–223; idem, "John the Baptist in Matthew's Gospel," 383–405; J. Murphy-O'Connor, "John the Baptist and Jesus: History and Hypothesis," 359–374; J. Reumann, "The Quest for the Historical Baptist," 181–199; J. Schütz, *Johannes der Täufer*; C. H. H. Scobie, *John the Baptist*; J. Steinmann, *Saint John the Baptist and the Desert Tradition*; W. B. Tatum, *John the Baptist and Jesus: A Report of the Jesus Seminar*; J. E. Taylor, *The Immerser: John the Baptist in Second Temple Judaism*; W. Trilling, "Die Täufertradition bei Matthäus," 271–289; W. Wink, *John the Baptist in the Gospel Tradition*; idem, "Jesus' Reply to John: Matt. 11:2–6/Luke: 7:18–23," 121–128; R. L. Webb, *John the Baptizer and Prophet: A Socio-Historical Study*; idem, "John the Baptist and his Relationship to Jesus," 214–299; idem, "The Activity of John the Baptist's Expected Figure at the Threshing Floor (Matthew 3.12–Luke 3.17)," 103–111; A. Yarbro Collins, "The Origin of Christian Baptism," 28–46.

7   Meier, *The Immerser*, 6 n. 14.

surprising, therefore, that few contemporary critics question the authenticity of the Baptist passage.⁸

Nearly every one of Meier's claims elicits questions. For example, his reference to "all relevant manuscripts" demands serious qualification. Today we have only three Greek manuscripts of this portion of the *Antiquitates*, the earliest of which dates to the eleventh century. Meier claims that both the "vocabulary and style" of this passage "are plainly those of Josephus." Yet many scholars, most famously H. St. J. Thackeray, argue that Josephus uses one or more assistants (συνεργοί), or if not assistants then sources, for this section of the *Antiquitates*.⁹ Meier himself

---

8   MEIER, *Marginal Jew*, 2.19. Cf. also corroborating comments on p. 56.

9   *C. Ap.* 1.50: "I kept a careful record of all that went on under my eyes in the Roman camp, and was alone in a position to understand the information brought by deserters. Then, in the leisure which Rome afforded me, with all my materials, in readiness, and with the aid of some assistants for the sake of the Greek (χρησάμενός τισι πρὸς τὴν Ἑλληνίδα φωνὴν συνεργοῖς), at last I committed to writing my narrative of the events" (ET: H. J. St. Thackeray). H. St. J. Thackeray even refers to this secretary as "hack!" See *Josephus The Man and The Historian*, 132. This statement refers to *B.J.*, but *B.J.* became a source for *A.J.* Cf. also *Ant.* 1.7 where Josephus expresses hesitation over "rendering so vast a subject into a foreign and unfamiliar tongue" (ET: Thackeray). This thesis is old, but not, as many assume, debunked. MASON, with Rajak, rejects Thackeray's 'secretaries' theory (referring to it as "rightly rejected") at *Josephus, Judea and Christian Origins*, 233–234. However, earlier in this essay collection (with specific but not exclusive reference to *B.J.*) MASON simply prefers a modified version of the Thackeray's "literary assistants" as "co-workers and literary friends" (συνεργοί, *C. Ap.* 1.50) at *Josephus, Judea and Christian Origins*, 56 incl. n. 43. Concerning *B.J.*, Mason writes: "In Josephus's enlistment of co-workers (συνεργοί) or literary friends in the capital for this massive project, we again witness a social affair and *not the work of an isolated author*. Another point raised by this notice concerns Josephus's ability in Greek, since the collaborators helped particularly with the Greek sound (or possibly "language": φωνή)" (56). Horst R. Moehring too assumes some intervention by assistants. In defense of and as a means of defining Josephus' authorship, MOEHRING writes: "Josephus can justly be called the author, in the true sense of this term, of the works ascribed to him: even when he borrows and even when he uses assistants, he impresses his own personality upon his work" (*"Novelistic Elements in the Writings of Flavius Josephus"*), 145. See also IDEM, "Joseph Ben Matthia and Flavius Josephus". CH. BEGG, *Josephus' Account of the Early Divided Monarchy (AJ 8, 212–420): Rewriting the Bible*; MASON, *Josephus, Judea, and Christian Origins: Methods and Categories*, esp. 105–107; NODET, *La Bible de Josèphe*. The discussion is likewise older than Thackeray: J. VON DESTINON, *Die Quellen des Flavius Josephus in der Jüd. Arch. Buch XII–XVII – Jüd. Krieg. Buch I*, 19–39; G. HÖLSCHER, "Josephus," 1934–2000. In contrast, D. R. Schwartz argues for the presence of sources (and likewise absence of authorial or other editing) in the final volumes of *A.J.*; see SCHWARTZ, *Agrippa I: The Last King of Judaea*, 2; IDEM, "Josephus and Nicolaus on the Pharisees," 157–171. In a brief critical review of Schwartz's project MASON (¹2003) counters Schwartz by echoing Thackeray: "Finally, Schwartz does not explain why the very section of *Antiquities* he would like to assign to incompatible sources, books 17 to 19, exhibits an impressive, if bizarre (mock-Thucydidean), stylistic conformity" (*Josephus, Judea, and Christian Origins*, 112; Thackeray is acknowledged in n. 58). Mason, however, also points out that it is dangerous to assume that Josephus himself was always consistent: "It is an uncomfortable fact for the more ambitious varieties of source criticism that Josephus has the authorial habit of repeating and contradicting himself, and of varying his terminology. These oddities call for analysis, but they may result from a variety of causes (e.g., sloppiness, rhetorical artifice, multiple editions, copyist's interventions, and yes, sources); they do not *ohne weiteres*

has written a very helpful excursus treating difficulties of this passage's Greek.[10] Origen's reference to the passage in *Contra Celsum* 1.47 is far from straightforward. It shares verbatim agreement with Eusebius' citation, but, on the argument of scholars such as Ken Olsen, Eusebius' "verbatim agreement" with Josephus indicates Eusebius' original composition![11] The laudatory content of the passage is certainly no proof that the passage is genuine: absence of Christian tampering does not constitute positive proof of authenticity. Meier's claims thus generate at least as many questions as they answer. This essay attempts to address the questions involved, arguing that (1) methods for establishing this text's historical reliability lack cogency[12] and (2) arguments both for and against authenticity of the passage have advantages and flaws of equal weight making a clear decision either way impossible.

2. Literary Analysis: Text and Context

2.1. Text of *A.J.* 18.116–119

The literary analysis begins with a preliminary overview of the narrative. The English translation is that of Louis H. Feldman (LCL) with emendations where noted.[13] Issues of the Greek text are taken up below.

The piece reflects chiastic structure. The topic of the narrative – continuing from previous paragraphs (beginning in *A.J.* 101) – is Herod Antipas. The segment overall begins and ends with a literary *inclusio* both distinguishing it from the ongoing narrative and serving to link it at each end with the Herodian saga in which it is embedded (cf. *A.J.* 115 and 120).[14] Statements (labeled 'A' below) concerning Herod's army constitute the *inclusio*: some Jews interpret the army's destruction in the battle with Aretas as just repayment for the execution

---

imply incompatible sources" (112). See also Shutt, *Studies in Josephus*, 68–75; Rajak, *Josephus: The Historian and His Society*, 235. This essay's question of the authenticity of the Baptist passage is related, but not identical to the question of the historicity of Josephus' writings in general. The latter topic is of intense interest to the scholars named in this note as well as others; see Mason, *Josephus, Judea, and Christian Origins*, 105–113.

10   Meier, *Marginal Jew*, 2.56–62.
11   Olsen, "Eusebius and the *Testimonium Flavianum*," 305–322.
12   S. Mason offers an excellent discussion of methodological problems inherent to the entire Josephan project in *Josephus, Judea, and Christian Origins*, 103–140. This essay is dedicated to the narrow set of problems arising with respect to Josephus' Baptist passage. Mason is in turn reliant on J. McLaren, *Turbulent Times? Josephus and Scholarship on Judaea in the First Century*.
13   Josephus, *Jewish Antiquities*, Feldman, trans. (LCL).
14   Meier too notes the inclusion (*Marginal Jew*, 2:56–57). The *inclusio* suggests views of the passage as beginning in *A.J.* 117 are incorrect (J. Ernst, *Johannes der Täufer*, 253).

of a "baptizer" named John. Just inside of the 'A' section, additional statements (labeled 'B') that Herod brought John in chains to prison in Machaerus and put him to death also begin and end the account. 'C²' represents the narrative climax. The following diagram depicts the passage schematically.

A. But to some of the **Jews** the **destruction of Herod's army** seemed to be divine vengeance, and certainly a just **vengeance,** for his treatment of John, surnamed the Baptist (τισὶ δὲ τῶν Ἰουδαίων ἐδόκει ὀλωλέναι τὸν Ἡρώδου στρατὸν ὑπὸ τοῦ θεοῦ καὶ μάλα δικαίως τιννυμένου κατὰ τοινὴν Ἰωάννου τοῦ ἐπικαλουμένου βαπτιστοῦ).[15]

B. For Herod had *put him to death*,

C¹. though he was a good man and had **exhorted the Jews** to lead righteous lives, to practice justice towards their fellows and piety toward God, and so doing to join in *baptism*.

[Definition of *baptism*:]

1. In his view this was a necessary preliminary if baptism was to be acceptable [to God].[16]

2. They must not employ it to gain pardon of whatever sins they committed, but as a consecration of the body implying that the soul was already thoroughly cleansed by right behavior.

C². When **others too joined** the crowds about him, because they were aroused to the highest degree by his **sermons,** *Herod became alarmed.*

[Explanation for *Herod's alarm*:]

1. Eloquence that had so great an effect on humankind might lead to some form of sedition, for it looked as if they would be guided by John in everything that he did.

2. Herod decided therefore that it would be much better to strike first and be rid of him before his work led to an uprising, than to wait for an upheaval, get involved in a difficult situation and see his mistakes.

B. Though John, because of Herod's suspicions, was brought in chains to Machaerus, the stronghold that we have previously mentioned, and there *put to death,*

A. yet the verdict of the **Jews** was that *the destruction visited upon Herod's army* was a **vindication** of John, since God saw fit to inflict such a blow on Herod (τοῖς δὲ Ἰουδαίοις δόξα ἐπὶ τιμωρίᾳ τῇ ἐκείνου τὸν ὄλεθρον ἐπὶ τῷ στρατεύματι γενέσθαι τοῦ θεοῦ κακῶσαι Ἡρώδην θέλοντος).

---

15 A possible analogy, already in the NT, is the Christian topos of divine vengeance against those who killed Jesus. See Origen and Eusebius below.

16 "To God" is absent in Greek, but supported by context. See MEIER, *Marginal Jew*, 2.97 n. 178. Also, ἀπόδεκτος ("acceptable, welcome") – represents only occurrence in Josephus' corpus. The word does not occur in the LXX.

This textual unit represents a balanced composition, both connected to, yet also distinct from, the rest of the narrative. The passage's climax conveys that John's articulate public speeches eventually attracted crowds forcing Antipas to intervene. Meier's hypothesis is persuasive: if John's crowds were comprised of tax collectors and soldiers (as Luke 3:10–14 qualifies them), then it is no wonder John's attracting "the rest" (καὶ τῶν ἄλλων) compelled Antipas to take action.[17] However, such observations neither validate nor invalidate the passage's authenticity. Josephus, a secretary, a later editor, or the author of a source, would be equally capable of composing or inserting a distinct compositional unit.

The Greek of this passage, however, favors a hand other than that of Josephus.[18] H. St. J. Thackeray observes:

> The phraseology of this passage betrays the unmistakable marks of the hack employed for this portion of the *Antiquities*. His love of periphrasis is illustrated by the phrase "come to" or "consort with" baptism, for "be baptized"; his avoidance of the commonplace vocabulary by the strange words which he uses for "punish," "kill," and "sin";[19] and there are other words found only in this portion of the work.[20] The hand is the hand of the secretary; the voice that prompts it is that of Josephus.[21]

Furthermore, in the introduction to his LCL translation Thackeray expounds on the participation by secretaries:

> Reference has been made elsewhere to the aid which the historian received from Greek assistants (συνεργοί). His indebtedness to them in the *Jewish War* is acknowledged and apparent in the uniformly excellent style of that earlier work. In the *Antiquities* there is no similar acknowledgement, and the style is much more uneven; but there too the collaborators have left their own impress. Two of these – the principal assistants – betray themselves in the later books where the author, wearying of his *magnum opus*, seems to have entrusted the composition in the main to other hands. Books xv–xvi are the work of one of the able assistants

---

17 The thesis also finds support in Pervo's argument that Luke relies on a written copy of the *Antiquitates*. MEIER, *Marginal Jew*, 2.61–62. PERVO, *Dating Acts: Between the Evangelists and the Apologists*, 149–199. A possible example is Luke's omission of Mark's reference to Philip as Herodias' husband. If Luke corrected Mark on the basis of Josephus, recognizing that Antipas must have fallen in love with his brother Herod II's, not Philip's, wife, then Luke is by far our earliest witness to Josephus' account.

18 See THACKERAY, *Josephus: The Man and the Historian*, 132.

19 Thackeray spells out some of the difficulties: "τινυμένου, else only xvii.60 (similarly of divine vengeance); κτίννυται, + xv.118, xvii.182, xviii.99; ἁμαρτάς (Ionic for ἁμαρτία), + *Ant*. xviii.350, and in *Ant*. 3.204, &c. (the same phrase ἐπὶ παραιτήσει ἁμαρτάδων iii.238, cf. 221) doubtless from the same hand" (THACKERAY, *Josephus: The Man and the Historian*, 132 n. 18).

20 Thackeray notes: "ἀκρόασις, φέρειν ἐπί τινι, "lead to something," *Ant*. xvii.354, xviii.128, 169, xix.61, 242; τοσόσδε is characteristic of this assistant" (THACKERAY, *Josephus: The Man and the Historian*, 132 n. 19).

21 THACKERAY, *Josephus: The Man and the Historian*, 132.

already employed in the *War*, a cultured writer with a love of the Greek poets and of Sophocles, in particular (I call him the "Sophoclean" assistant); xvii–xix show the marked mannerisms of a hack, a slavish imitator of Thucydides (I call him the "Thucydidean"). In these five books (xv–xix) these two assistants have, it seems, practically taken over the entire task. In the earlier books (i–xiv) they have lent occasional aid – the Thucydidean rarely, the poet-lover more frequently.[22]

Although R. J. H. Shutt, Tessa Rajak and Steve Mason all dismiss Thackeray's thesis as too simplistic, only Shutt and Rajak completely reject participation by assistants in the composition of the *Antiquitates*. Rajak prefers to infer that, where for example imitation of Thucydides, Sophocles or another ancient writer is obvious, Josephus himself relies on and/or imitates sources.[23] For establishing authenticity, assistants and sources elicit the same difficulty, to be explored below.

Meier, too, despite his conviction in the passage's authenticity, notes the following difficulties with the Greek: τιννυμένου κατὰ ποινήν in §116; ἐπασκοῦσιν and χρωμένοις in §117; and καὶ τῶν ἄλλων in §118.[24] The following analysis builds on these observations, identifying eight specific questions related to authenticity.

---

22 *Josephus: Jewish Antiquities Books 1–3*, THACKERAY, trans. (LCL), xiv–xv. Thackeray develops these claims with examples from the text on pp. xv–xvi. For the Baptist passage's editor ("the Thucydidean") Thackeray notes plagiarisms from Thucydides and a few tell-tale mannerisms. Of the author himself, Thackeray writes: "After elimination of the work of these two assistants, whose large aid in the later books enables us in some measure to identify their style elsewhere, it is difficult to say how much of the composition is left to the author himself. But there are cruder passages in A. i–xiv, xx and the *Life*, which it is not unreasonable to refer to him; and it may even be possible to detect an occasional trace of the influence of his native Aramaic speech as in the colloquial use of ἄρχεσθαι with infinitive, familiar in the New Testament" (xvi–xvii).

23 RAJAK, *Josephus: The Historian and His Society*, 233–236; cf. SHUTT, *Studies in Josephus*, 59–75; MASON, *Josephus, Judea, and Christian Origins*, 56–57.

24 Although MEIER's treatment of this passage is thorough and reliable, some of his major conclusions (*Marginal Jew*, 60–61) contradict each other. For example, Meier holds that "stark juxtaposition of *kteinei* and *agathon*" suggests an "apologetic intention" (*Marginal Jew*, 2.60). He also argues that the relationship between John's immersion (Meier understands John's "baptism" unproblematically as: "once-and-for-all") and his message: "twin virtues seen in Philo and other Jewish Diaspora authors: justice toward one another and piety toward God" is unclear in the *Antiquitates* (*Marginal Jew*, 2.61). According to Meier, this relationship begs an explanation provided by the canonical gospels' record of "John's fiery eschatological proclamation of a day of judgment that will make irrelevant all ethnic ties, a judgment to be administered by a mysterious figure to come, a judgment that can be avoided only by submitting to John's baptism of repentance, in short, all these strange, disruptive, or disturbing ideas" (*Marginal Jew*, 2.60). Yet at the same time, Meier finds no reason to doubt Josephus' position that John's "religious" program was apolitical. Meier also finds no necessary contradiction between *Ant*. 18.116–119 and the NT Gospels, bypassing that the latter give John's accusation of Herod for adultery as the "political" (?) basis for his arrest.

First, the extant account characterizes John as an ἀνὴρ ἀγαθός. In contrast, Slavonic Josephus refers to John as ἄγριος ("a wild man.")[25] Eusebius records "good man." The difference between Slavonic Josephus and Eusebius elicits the question of whether Eusebius improved John's image with a switch from ἄγριος to ἀγαθός. Although Eusebius was hardly reluctant to rewrite Josephus wherever necessary,[26] it is not inconsistent with Josephus' presentation that John be considered "good." Four times Josephus' oeuvre uses ἀνὴρ ἀγαθός to refer to righteous men whose lives are unjustly threatened and/or taken:

(1) *B.J.* 1.361: innocent men whose lives are taken;
(2) *B.J.* 7.341: men determined to live with honor or die;
(3) *A.J.* 9.100: righteous men slain; and,
(4) *A.J.* 10.204: good men unjustly ordered to be put to death.

In *B.J.* 5.413, Josephus even uses the expression with reference to himself in defense of his treachery:

> Nay, an honorable man (ἀλλ᾽ ἀνὴρ μὲν ἀγαθὸς) will fly from a wanton house and abhor its inmates, and can you persuade yourselves that God still remains with his household in their iniquity – God who sees every secret thing and hears what is buried in silence?[27]

These passages demonstrate that reference to John as ἀνὴρ ἀγαθός fits not only his overall positive treatment in the immediate context, but an oeuvre-wide inclination to designate as ἀγαθοί men who suffer wrongful deaths. Furthermore, it is clear from *Vita* 11 that Josephus not only believes that teachers of piety may dwell in the wilderness (κατὰ τὴν ἐρημίαν διατρίβειν), but considers a certain such man worth three years of his life. In other words, no *a priori* reason exists to rule out favorable treatment of John. Moreover, in Mark 1:6 and Matt 3:4 the honey of John's diet is described as ἄγριος.[28] It is possible, therefore, that Slavonic Josephus emends ἀγαθός to ἄγριος to harmonize John's portrait in Josephus with the Gospel accounts. Hence, in the history of research, ἀγαθός is both refuted as Christian tampering *and* more coherent with the immediate and larger con-

---

25 ET: EISLER; likewise, FOAKES-JACKSON/LAKE. In *Marginal Jew*, 2.64–65, MEIER helpfully provides the ET of this text from F. J. FOAKES-JACKSON/KIRSOPP LAKE, *The Beginnings of Christianity: Part I: The Acts of the Apostles*, 1.433–435. Contrast the version by JOHN MARTIN CREED, "The Slavonic Version of Josephus' History of the Jewish War," *HTR* 25 (1932): 277–319. Although these Old Russian insertions in to *B.J.* are entertaining, attempts to identify their sources have been unsuccessful. These readings likely emerged only in the Middle Ages. One item of possible interest, as MEIER points out, is that John the Baptist is never named only described (*Marginal Jew*, 64 n. 3).

26 See OLSEN, "Eusebius and the *Testimonium Flavianum*," 319.

27 In his account of the Essenes, Josephus refers to the group's trusted money and produce collectors (ἀποδέκτας δὲ τῶν προσόδων καὶ ὁπόσα ἡ γῆ) as ἄνδρας ἀγαθούς ("good men") (*A.J.* 18.2). Cf. Luke 3:10–14.

28 See J. A. KELHOFFER, *The Diet of John the Baptist*, esp., 121–128.

text. Moreover, ἄγριος is equally suspicious as Christian tampering. The extant reading and proposed variant are equally weighted in terms of authenticity and, more importantly, the criterion of Christian tampering is exposed as shifting sand. This conclusion offers little to the debate about the passage's authenticity. If the original account (ἀγαθός) was coherent within the immediate and larger context, it is as likely the construction of an author as an editor.

Second, βαπτισμῷ συνιέναι may suggest group baptism. If it does, questions arise in scholarship as to coherence with NT accounts. The idea is thought to be foreign to NT accounts about John. Yet, Mark 1:5 reports: "And people from the whole Judean countryside and all the people of Jerusalem were going out to him, and [they] were baptized (ἐβαπτίζοντο) by him in the river Jordan, confessing their [pl.] sins" (καὶ ἐξεπορεύετο πρὸς αὐτὸν πᾶσα ἡ Ἰουδαία χώρα καὶ οἱ Ἱεροσολυμῖται πάντες, καὶ ἐβαπτίζοντο ὑπ' αὐτοῦ ἐν τῷ Ἰορδάνῃ ποταμῷ ἐξομολογούμενοι τὰς ἁμαρτίας αὐτῶν).[29] The verb ἐβαπτίζοντο is ambiguous as to whether those who flocked to John were individually or corporately immersed. Group immersion is neither certain nor ruled out in either Mark or Josephus. The force of the passage containing the phrase in Josephus is, however, clear: a small group followed John's teachings on righteousness, justice and piety, symbolizing purity (individual and/or corporate purity) by means of the outward act of immersion. When the number of those assembling grew, Herod acted.[30] In a note to his translation of Eusebius, *Hist. eccl.* 1.11, Kirsopp Lake explains the question of group baptism in Josephus, noting *modern* tampering with the critical text:

> Eusebius has slightly altered the text of Josephus. This ran: "For Herod killed him, a good man and one who commanded the *Jews training themselves in virtue and practicing righteousness towards one another and piety towards God to come together* for baptism." It would seem to mean that John was preaching to ascetics and suggested baptism as a final act of perfection. This explains the reference to "when the rest collected." So long as John preached to ascetics Herod did not mind but was disturbed when the rest of the public manifested interest. *Whiston's translation of Josephus and an unnecessary emendation in the text of Niese's edition of Josephus have conspired to obscure these facts.*[31]

In the final sentence Lake refers to Whiston's English translation: "for Herod slew him, who was a good man, and commanded the Jews to exercise virtue, both as to righteousness towards one another, and piety towards God, and so to

---

29 Cf. Matt 3:5. Although it acknowledges presence of crowds (v. 7), Luke 3:3 suggests John is preacher rather than 'baptizer.' John 3:23 is unclear as to whether crowd is baptized as group or individually.

30 Cf. esp. MEIER's careful ET which clarifies this force of the passage: *Marginal Jew*, 2.58–59.

31 *Eusebius, Ecclesiastical History Books I–V*, K. LAKE, trans. (LCL), 80–81, n. 1, emphasis added.

come to baptism."³² According to Lake, Whiston errs by translating the circumstantial participles ἐπασκοῦσιν and χρωμένοις modifying John's followers (τοῖς Ἰουδαίοις), as parataxis with κελεύοντα – John's command to the Jews *to practice justice and piety*.³³ In so doing, Whiston obscures that only a narrow group of Jews training in a specific form of piety joined in John's baptism, viz., John directed [only] the Jews practicing justice and piety to join in baptism. While it does seem to be the central legate of John's ministry, baptism not only describes the activity of only a small group of followers, it is *for these followers* conditional³⁴ on a specialized and demanding standard of ethical behavior. Baptism is thus the rite of a small sect of Baptists and Herod's act, while unjust, is not irrational. Χράομαι in the next line likewise describes the activity of the baptized alone.³⁵ The passage does not broaden John's effect to include Jews at large until §118 when τοῖς ἀνθρώποις emphasizes the power of John's persuasion *potentially* (φέροι "might lead") to include all people.³⁶ These observations may make the text less favorable toward Christians, but from this disfavor it would be wrong to deduce that the text is authentic. The text, in this case, is simply coherent – again, the product of either a primary or secondary hand.

Third, as Lake notes above, καὶ τῶν ἄλλων συστρεφομένων probably suggests a shift in circumstances. Initially attracting only a small group, the expansion of John's audience compels a preemptive attack. Robert I. Eisler argues that the sense of οἱ ἄλλοι is best captured by the Latin phrase *perplurima multitudo*.³⁷ Eisler seeks to avoid, with his English translation "the masses," deliberate Christian mitigation of John's seditious preaching. Whether masses were involved or not, the text still suggests that a change in circumstances compelled Herod's intervention. Eisler's dispute is one of magnitude. Regardless of how great or small the crowd was, the passage still asserts that a shift of some kind threatens Herod's jurisdiction. The Latin version may exaggerate the number to clarify Herod's impetus. With or without crowds, the text is coherent, offering nothing to the debate over authorship.

Fourth, concerning the explanatory clause following provocation of a larger group: ἤρθησαν ἐπὶ πλεῖστον τῇ ἀκροάσει τῶν λόγων, Eisler argues to main-

---

32 W. Whiston, *The Works of Josephus: Complete and Unabridged*, 484. B. Niese, *Flavii Josephi Opera*, 7 vols. 4–5: 161–162. Nodet's text-critical examination applies only to *Ant.* 1–3: É. Nodet, *Flavius Josèphe. Les antiquités juives. Volume I: Livres I à III. A. Introduction et texte.* For a treatment of manuscripts relevant to *A.J.* 11–20, see Niese, *Flavii Josephi Opera*, 3. III–LVII.

33 Meier, *Marginal Jew*, 2.57.

34 Emphasizing this point, Meier writes: "A proper appreciation of the circumstantial participles, employed in a conditional sense in both sentences, is therefore of great importance for grasping the thrust of the whole passage" (*Marginal Jew*, 2.58).

35 So Meier, *Marginal Jew*, 2.58.

36 So Meier, *Marginal Jew*, 2.59.

37 See Meier, *Marginal Jew*, 2.97 n. 180.

tain the reading ἤρθησαν ("they were aroused") over the variant in Eusebius' ἥσθησαν on the grounds that Eusebius' "they were overjoyed," also found in the Slavonic Josephus, represents fourth-century Christian preference for John as a religious reformer (exhorting joy) rather than as a revolutionary (arousing/fomenting insurrection).[38] Because Schürer[39] and Niese found Josephus' text sympathetic to John (literary coherency argument) and did not think that Josephus would view a revolutionary with sympathy, they adopted "overjoyed." Once again, replacement of the more positively valued ἥσθησαν for the more negatively valued ἤρθησαν, as with ἀγαθός/ἄγριος, (discussed above), compromises narrative coherence.[40] Here again, modifications based on purported Christian editing disrupt the text's logic. It is difficult to argue for an alteration that compromises a text's unity no matter what type or level of Christianization is perceived. That said, logic, coherence and unity do not prove authenticity.

Eisler also argues that στάσις ("sedition") has a clearer sense of revolution than Eusebius' ἀπόστασις and that Christians corrupted the manuscripts to avoid John's connection with political insurrection. As above, lessening John's effect as seditious has the first effect of obscuring an otherwise clear account. The report needs sedition, not to unduly tarnish an otherwise honorable Baptist, but to reflect Herod's perception. The extant text uses the logical equation: "good" (ἀγαθός) + "overjoyed" (ἥσθησαν) = "sedition" (ἀπόστασις). The alternate equation "wild" (ἄγριος) + "aroused" (ἤρθησαν) = "apostasy" (στάσις) is illogical. Neither logic nor its absence implies authenticity, but they do demonstrate weaknesses in the hypotheses of Christian editing. Not only are they too trivial to affect the account's overall positive impact but the emendations are often illogical in the context and unclear in terms of what 'Christian' position they represent. Returning to the question of ἀπόστασις, Louis H. Feldman points out that this word means not only a turning away from established traditions but also actual defection or revolt, that is, it is *not* necessarily more seditious than στάσις.[41] Feldman retains ἤρθησαν + στάσει.

Other arguments against authenticity include that Josephus would not have referred to John as "baptist" (ὁ βαπτιστής) without explaining the nature of his baptism[42] and that Josephus would not have used different forms of the word

---

38 ἥσθησαν is not universally attested in the mss of Eusebius; see MEIER, *Marginal Jew*, 2.96 n. 169.

39 *The History of the Jewish People in the Age of Jesus Christ*, 4 vols., ed. GEZA VERMES/FERGUS MILLAR, 1.438 n. 2.

40 That said, Eusebius certainly would have seen that the replacement of a single word disrupts an otherwise lucid narrative. He would recognize that a single more positive word is incapable of shifting the tide of an otherwise approving narrative.

41 Josephus, *Jewish Antiquities*, 83.

42 FELDMAN reports this debate in *Josephus, Jewish Antiquities*, 81. The title/surname is unusual. Both the gospels and Josephus preserve it (*Ant.* 18.5.2). See discussion in MEIER, *Marginal Jew*,

"baptism," ὁ βαπτισμός and τὸ βάπτισμα, in the same sentence. These objections have limited merit. In his *TDNT* article, "βάπτω, βαπτίζω, βαπτισμός, βάπτισμα, βαπτιστής," Albrecht Oepke concludes about βάπτω, βαπτίζω that "this usage shows that baptism is felt to be something new and strange."[43] If usage of the βαπτ- stem as related to purifying immersion is generally "new and strange," then it is legitimate to expect Josephus to explain the practice. According to all sources, immersion was a central component of John's ministry. Yet his appellation "baptizer," has no precedents in Second Temple Judaism.[44] If "Baptist" functioned or was perceived as John's surname in the same way as Jesus' "Christ" for Christians, then the epithet alone might indicate a Christian hand. Such an argument is, however, unsusceptible to proof.[45] Joan Taylor points out that in both the *Bellum* and the *Antiquitates*, Josephus uses the verb βαπτίζειν in the sense of drowning or becoming overwhelmed or overtaken as if by drowning (i.e., drowning as metaphor).[46] Although most occurrences feature ships sinking, the best known example is the "baptizing" by Herod's agents of the last Hasmonean priest Aristobulus III (*Ant.* 15.55):[47]

σκότους ἐπέχοντος, βαροῦντες ἀεὶ καὶ βαπτίζοντες ὡς ἐν παιδιᾷ νηχόμενον οὐκ ἀνῆκαν ἕως καὶ παντάσιν ἀποπνῖξαι.[48]

That said, Joseph Thomas' well-known study demonstrates that any alleged baptizing by John can and should be viewed in the context of a trend of baptizing movements in and around the region of the Jordan during the 1st century BCE and 1st century CE.[49] If different communities reflect individual adaptations of the practice, immersion itself, according to Thomas, merits no special explana-

---

    2.67 n. 10.

43   *TDNT* 1.529–46, here 530.

44   Taylor, *The Immerser*, 49–50: "The title, 'the Immerser' may refer to someone who immerses himself often, but it is generally understood to mean that he immersed others. Mark quotes John as saying: 'I immerse you with [or 'in'] water...' (Mark 1:8a) which suggests that John was understood to be the agent of immersion. He is active, and those whom he immerses are to some extent passive" (*The Immerser*, 50). On John as the "one baptizing" vs. the "Baptist," see also C. R. Bowen, "Prolegomena to a New Study of John the Baptist" and "John the Baptist in the New Testament," 30–76, esp. 33–48.

45   Contrast: ἀδελφὸς Ἰησοῦ τοῦ λεγομένου Χριστοῦ and εἰς αὐτὸ τὸν ἀδελφὸν Ἰησοῦ, τοῦ Χριστοῦ λεγομένου (*Hist. eccl.* 2.23) and κατὰ ποινὴν Ἰωάννου τοῦ καλουμένου Βαπτιστοῦ (*Hist. eccl.* 1.11, citing *Ant.* 18.116).

46   Eighteen occurrences: *A.J.* 18.117 (3x); 4.81; 9.212; 10.169; 15.55; *Vita* 15.1; *B.J.* 1.437; 1.490; 2.476; 2.556 (2x); 3.368; 3.424; 3.525; 3.527; 4.137.

47   Taylor, *The Immerser*, 49–50.

48   ET: "But with darkness coming on while he swam, some of the friends who had been given orders to do so, kept pressing him down and holding him under water as if in sport, and they did not let up until they had quite suffocated him" (Feldman). Cf. *B.J.* 1.437.

49   J. Thomas, *Le mouvement baptiste en Palestine et Syrie (150 av. J.C. – 300 ap. J.C.)*. Some scholars think that the popularity of ablutions increased during the late Hellenistic and early Roman

tion. In all likelihood the location (environs of the Jordan River) bore more significance (i.e., re-crossing Jordan into land as a symbol of renewal) than the rite performed in this environs. In any event, Josephus, his secretaries, or Christian interpolators could each potentially have used the epithet "Baptist" without explaining the nature of the baptism. The question of authenticity gains little from this line of reasoning.

John's epithet notwithstanding, it is, however, possible that the passage *does* in fact explain baptism's meaning. Josephus mentions purification rites earlier in Book 18 with reference to the Essenes (§19), using ἁγνεία ("purification") to describe the rite. In *Vita* 11, also with reference to his teacher of three years, Bannus, he uses ἁγνεία for this teacher's practice of wilderness ablutions: ψυχρῷ δὲ ὕδατι τὴν ἡμέραν καὶ τὴν νύκτα πολλάκις λουόμενον πρὸς ἁγνείαν ("using frequent ablutions of cold water, by day and night, for purity's sake" [ET: Feldman]).[50] Also, in *A.J.* 18.117, after references to John as Baptist and his βαπτισμός and βάπτισμα, ἁγνεία defines John's practice as one of ablutions able to consecrate body, not soul: "they must not employ it to gain pardon for whatever sins they committed, but as a consecration of the body implying that the soul was already thoroughly cleansed by right behavior" (ET: Feldman). If the baptism had eschatological implications, the *Antiquitates* is silent on them.[51] Hence, collaborators in *A.J.* might presume that the meaning of John's baptism is comprehensible in terms of prior references to ablutions for the sake of ἁγνεία in Book 18 and elsewhere in Josephus' corpus. In sum, references to baptism in Josephus' passage fit relatively comfortably within *A.J.* – as likely the work of Josephus himself as a co-worker or scribe.

Finally, contrary to the popular opinion that assumes a non-Christian contradiction of Mark 1:4 par., the notion reflected in *A.J.* 18.117.5 that people must *not* enjoin John's baptism for pardon of sin (μὴ ἐπί τινων ἁμαρτάδων παραιτήσει χρωμένων) raises (even in the absence of variants) the suspicion of Christian editorial work. We know from Matt 3:14–15 of discomfort with the concept of Jesus' baptism by John for remission of sins.[52] Needless to say, Matt 3:14–15 arises in response to the more famous proclamation about John in Mark 1:4 par.: that he announces a βάπτισμα μετανοίας εἰς ἄφεσιν ἁμαρτιῶν ("baptism

---

period and were used in place of sacrifice. See, for example, C. Scobie, *John the Baptist*, 107 and A. Y. Collins, "The Origin of Christian Baptism," 36.

50 Cf. *C. Ap.* 2.203.

51 Scobie does not see eschatology in Josephus' presentation of John (*John the Baptist*, 18–19). Some have argued Josephus is reliant on the gospels; others argue borrowing in the other direction. Meier prefers Josephus' independence of the gospels: see *Marginal Jew* 2.66 n. 5. Meier points out that E. P. Sanders equivocates on the issue (*Jesus and Judaism*, 92). Becker argues that Josephus deemphasizes eschatology in general (*Johannes der Täufer*, 19).

52 Matt 3:14–15: "John would have prevented him, saying, 'I need to be baptized by you, and do you come to me?' But Jesus answered him, 'Let it be so now; for it is proper for us in this way to fulfill all righteousness.' Then he consented." (NRSV)

of repentance for the forgiveness of sins)."[53] Most scholars think that Christian redaction cannot account for the claim in *A.J.* because it contradicts the celebrated Markan proclamation – contradicting Christian claims being equated with authenticity. It is possible, however, that in not just removing but denying "baptism of repentance for the forgiveness of sins" (Mark 1:4 par.) a Christian editor sought to settle once and for all the question that surfaces in Matthew. One may, therefore, view this line as a Christian contradiction of Mark 1:4 par., as a Christian insertion favoring Matt 3:14–15 over Mark 1:4 par., or as bypassing – even unaware of – the Christian debate altogether. Here we see for the first time how the criterion of Christian tampering may be self-contradictory. Christian tampering may be thought to both endorse and counter a position in Josephus' Baptist passage. These shifting sands cripple the criterion's cogency as an authenticity index.

In conclusion, the first (18.116) and last (18.119) statements in Josephus' Baptist passage assess the demise of Herod's army against Aretas as divine vengeance for Herod's murder of the "good" man John. These statements separate this unit from the rest of the text, breaking the continuity of the ongoing narrative. This sub-section is a well-balanced composition – coherent in its themes and aim. Substituting pejorative terms for words in the passage arguably more favorable to John on the assumption that the former signal Christian interpolation creates from a consistent an inconsistent report. Although it might be more logical for Herod to murder a savage revolutionary, the passage's narrative brackets (question of authorship notwithstanding) dictate that some believe *God exacted vengeance* against Herod, implying that Herod murdered a good, virtuous and pious immerser – even if the nature of that immerser's rite is somewhat ambiguously presumed. Of chief importance for the thesis under discussion is, however, the recognition that *neither* the report's impression as self-contained *nor* its effect as logical, unified, and coherent constitutes a positive argument for its authenticity.[54] A well-balanced consistent literary unit is as likely the product of Josephus as posited assistants, sources, or Christian tinkers.

---

53 Meier sees a "poignant ... unintended irony in the use of *metanoeo* for the deliberation of Herod that led to John's execution" (MEIER, *Marginal Jew*, 2.97 n. 182). Naturally, Meier adds, that Josephus does not include *metanoia* as an aspect of John's message (98 n. 182).

54 In his largely skeptical evaluation of SCHWARTZ's *Agrippa I*, MASON suggests the effectiveness of this criterion of authenticity against source-critical theories as follows: "It seems that attention to the larger literary themes of Josephus's works has direct implications for the postulation of sources" (*Josephus, Judea, and Christian Origins*, 110).

2.2. External Context within the Narrative

The segment's placement within the greater narrative is also frequently assumed to inform the question of its authenticity. Three themes feature in this dispute: (1) messianism; (2) divine vengeance; and (3) Christianity. Each is explored in turn.

2.2.1. Theme: Messianism

Concerning the *Testimonium Flavianum*, Olsen argues that any reference to messianism in the Josephan corpus is suspect:

> Josephus, writing for a Roman audience in the aftermath of the Jewish War, avoids discussing Jewish messianism, and he is not likely to have dropped the word "Messiah" casually into his text as a means of identifying a minor character.[55]

However, Olsen is not quite correct. Albeit negatively, Josephus discusses messianism at length, simply avoiding its label. Numerous messianic pretenders appear in *A.J.* 17–20. J. C. O'Neill enumerates no fewer than ten leaders in Josephus' oeuvre that may be considered messiahs – six in *A.J.*: Judas son of Ezekias (*A.J.* 17.271–272), Simon, the ex-slave of Herod (*A.J.* 17.273–276), Athronges the shepherd (*A.J.* 17.278–284), Theudas (*A.J.* 20.47ff.), the Egyptian who led thirty thousand to the Mount of Olives (*A.J.* 20. 167–171; cf. *B.J.* 2.261–263), and the Samaritan who promised to show the sacred vessels of Moses (*A.J.* 18.85–89); and four in *B.J.*: Menahem the Galilean (*B.J.* 2.433ff.), Simon bar Giora (*B.J.* 4.503), Jonathan of Cyrene (*B.J.* 7.437–438) and Jesus son of Ananas (*B.J.* 6.400–309). Neither *A.J.* nor *B.J.* keeps silent regarding the role of messianism in the War. It is possible that direct references are avoided as a means of superficially concealing the subversive quality of Jewish hostility to the Romans.[56] What is important for the present argument is only that John's association with messianism is by itself not a strike against the passage's authenticity.

Furthermore, different from Jesus in the *Testimonium*, John is not directly associated with messianism in the *Antiquitates*. According to *A.J.* 18, John's ablution is an outward symbol of inner purification obtained through righteous, just and pious behavior. References to John as Messiah in Luke 3:15, John 1:20 and Acts 13:25 are absent from Josephus' account. What is more, Josephus reserves discussion of messianic movements for later in the *Antiquitates*. In *A.J.* 20 such movements are featured as the rebellious and disloyal catalysts of the Jewish War with Rome. In such unflattering descriptions of movements led by Judas (described in Book 18, but referred to and placed chronologically in Book 20) and Theudas, Josephus reveals his view of their role in antagonizing Rome

---

55 OLSEN, "Eusebius and the *Testimonium Flavianum*," 315.
56 FELDMAN, "The *Testimonium Flavianum*: The State of the Question," 190–194.

and provoking military intervention. The report about John the Baptist depicts him some thirty years before the War. It is at home in the final books of *A.J.* in terms of messianism, but this fit does not make the passage genuine.

2.2.2. Theme: Divine Vindication

Moreover, the passage's central theme of vindication is at home within the Josephan corpus. In the text on John the Baptist, two different words are used to express God's vengeance against Herod: τινυμένου and τιμωρία.[57] The former occurs only as far back as *A.J.* 17.60.3 in precisely the same way as it is used in 18.116.2, namely to describe God's vengeance on a person, in this case Antipater, for acts of hubris.[58] A TLG search for τιμωρία (advanced lemma search) retrieves 157 instances. Sometimes referring to punishment only, the word frequently denotes punishment as revenge by human beings in the *A.J.*, sometimes by God (e.g., *A.J.* 1.49, 1.199, 3.311, 4.57, 5.340, 10.61, 10.262, 11.268, 14.28; *B.J.* 7.33–34 [2x], *et al.*). Admittedly also a NT idea, this theme of the Baptist passage is again at home in the Josephan oeuvre, implying nothing about its authenticity.

2.2.3. Theme: Christianity

With regard to the presence of John the Baptist in Josephus' corpus overall, Feldman observes that all Christian passages (about Jesus, John and James) are absent from parallel passages in the *Bellum judaicum*.[59]

> It is significant, but seldom noted, that none of the passages relevant to early Christianity –about Jesus, John, and James – is to be found in the parallel passages in the *Jewish War*. This may be explained by noting that the *Antiquities* covers this period often at considerably greater length, though the events in Pilate's procuratorship that are narrated in *Antiquities* 18.55–62 (37 lines in Niese's Greek text) are told at almost the same length (35 lines in Niese's Greek text) in *War* 2.169–177.

Feldman proposes that perhaps Christians had risen in importance since the composition of the *Bellum* or that the passages were inserted in *Antiquitates* for specific purposes, admitting that this case is not strong.[60] *Ex silencio* arguments for later Christian redaction, tempting as they may be, are inconclusive. Authen-

---

57 τινυμένου: codd. E Eus.: τινυμένου NIESE.
58 A TLG search for τίνω turns up 73 instances in the Josephan corpus.
59 For a comparison between *A.J.* 18–20 and *B.J.*, see also S. COHEN, *Josephus in Galilee and Rome*, 58–65.
60 FELDMAN, "The Testimonium Flavianum: The State of the Question," 187.

ticity of a passage in *A.J.* cannot be debunked on the basis of its absence in *B.J.* The two accounts vary in many regards.[61]

2.3. Summation

Method hampers attempts to ascertain the authenticity of Josephus' Baptist passage. The above analysis exposes significant flaws of the two chief criteria for establishing authenticity of Josephus' Baptist passage: (1) absence of Christian interference and (2) coherence within the greater narrative. First, the *Christian Interference Index* falls short for at least four reasons: (A) proposed emendations to rid text of Christian redaction often violate the overall text's logic multiplying arguments (while implying that writers such as Eusebius overlooked this problem); (B) so-called 'Christian' participation is ambiguous, calling upon NT accounts and ideals unsystematically and in an *ad hoc* manner; (C) the approach assumes Christian tampering sought to improve John's portrait when NT redaction of Baptist traditions is typically disapproving *and* John's portrait in Josephus' narrative is already positive (making positive traits *fit* not differ from the text); and (D) Christian improvements focus on minor discrepancies, ignoring major disagreements between the text and early Christian accounts about John, such as that John is not portrayed as forerunner, the clear contention of all four canonical Gospels, that he was imprisoned, not for political insurrection of which the gospels admit nothing, but for questioning Herod's right to marry his sister-in-law, and that he must have died earlier than the last year of Pilate's reign (36 CE) as Josephus' text implies.[62]

More importantly, however, absence of Christian involvement does not guarantee authenticity. Without warrant, such a strategy elevates Christianity to a decisive role in the evaluative process when, ironically, if the Baptist passage is authentic, an important implication of its message is that Jesus and his followers held little importance for Josephus and his audience.[63] Such a recognition exposes argumentative circularity on the part of later Christian interpreters: if Christians can identify and extricate their influence and/or involvement in Josephus' Baptist passage, they can recover it to corroborate their own highly apologetic corpus.

---

61 Cohen writes: "The extraordinarily small number of verbal reminiscences of BJ indicate that AJ is not a simple paraphrase of the earlier work. Only two parallels of note can be cited …. But Josephus may have remembered these even without direct consultation of BJ" (*Josephus in Galilee and Rome*, 59).

62 Not to mention: Christian texts famously subjugate John (if not, perhaps, always to the extent thought; see C. K. ROTHSCHILD, *Baptist Traditions and Q*, 36–45, by characterizing him as "forerunner" to Jesus.

63 E.g., "Under Tiberias all was quiet!" (Tacitus, *Hist.* 5.9.15). See M. GOODMAN, *The Ruling Class of Judaea: The Origins of the Jewish Revolt against Rome A.D. 66–70*, 72–73.

A second chief strategy used to establish the Baptist passage's authenticity is evaluation of the text in its narrative context. This *Textual Coherence Index* uses continuity of the passage's stylistic, thematic, and logical integration in the *A.J.* to establish authenticity. Yet some level of reliance on assistants, if not Thackeray's "Sophoclean" and "Thucydidean" secretaries, and sources, if not Schwartz's hypothetical *Life of Agrippa*,[64] in the composition of this section of *A.J.*, imply that literary coherence was *not* a feature of the original composition, undermining not only the index but any possibility of establishing authenticity on the basis of inner-textual evidence. That during the seventeenth century Thomas Gale of Cambridge claimed to possess large fragments of Josephus omitted from the *textus receptus*[65] compounds the problem.

Unsurprisingly, results of evaluations based on defective indices are likewise defective. That is, they offer nothing to the question of authenticity. Generally speaking, we find that the passage provides a coherent, positive, and logical portrayal of John the Baptist with both similarities and differences from the disparate data in the canonical gospels. Such a brief composition may be the product of Josephus, secretaries, Christians, Baptists, or unknown others. As a favorable depiction, it is, after all, possible that the Baptist fragment represents a Baptist interpolation.[66] Evidence of John's followers is available into the late first century in Asia Minor (Ephesus).[67] That they possessed a rival body of lit-

---

64 See n. 8 above.

65 J. S. KENNARD, JR., "Gleanings from the Slavonic Josephus Controversy," *Jewish Quarterly Review*, 161–170.

66 A version of this thesis is proposed by H. LICHTENBERGER, "Täufergemeinden und frühchristliche Täuferpolemik im letzten Drittel des 1. Jahrhunderts," 36–57 who argues that the Baptist passage is Josephus' polemic against Baptist disciples in Rome.

67 Outside the NT Gospels, evidence of disciples of the Baptist persisting in the period of early Christianity includes Acts 18–19, Justin Martyr, *Dial.* 80; *Ps.-Clem.* Rec. 1.54, 60; Hom. 2.23–24. Cf. also references to "Hemerobaptists," appearing in *Ps.-Clem.* Hom. 2.23–24; Hegesippus (Eusebius, *Hist. eccl.* 4.22.7); and Epiphanius, *Pan.* 17; *Apos. Con.* 6.6.5. Ephrem of Syria too possesses a parallel report to *Ps.-Clem.* Rec. 1.60 possibly based on a common source (so THOMAS, *Le mouvement baptiste*, 116). Käsemann presents a cogent assimilation of the evidence. Characterizing past scholarship on the topic rather brutally as a "barely conceivable variety of naïveté, defeatism and fertile imagination … from the extremely ingenuous on the one hand to the extremely arbitrary on the other," Käsemann concludes that, despite Luke's depiction of these twelve Ephesian disciples as "immature Christians … it is disciples of the Baptist who are the subject of the passage; *the Gospels themselves presuppose the existence of a Baptist community in competition with the young Church*. These disciples have naturally no contact with the Christian fellowship, know nothing of the Spirit which has been bestowed on Christendom and therefore have to be enlightened about the place of the Baptist as the forerunner of Jesus and be subjected to re baptism, which incorporates them into the Church and imparts to them the Spirit. This gives us a consistent and historically intelligible situation at which, on any other hypothesis, we cannot arrive" (E. KÄSEMANN "The Disciples of John the Baptist in Ephesus," 136–148, here 140–142, emphasis added). See ROTHSCHILD, *Baptist Traditions and Q*, 3–5 n. 8.

erature to Christians is widely assumed.[68] Such a thesis would explain tensions between the passage and canonical portrayals of John and might account for Origen's reference to Josephus' identification of Zechariah (cf. Matt 23:35) as the father of John the Baptist (treated below).[69] The claim in *Ant.* 18 that John's baptism is a symbol backed by a comprehensive philosophy featuring positions on the essentials: righteousness (ethics), justice (politics) and piety (religion, esp. purity [ἁγνεία]), makes excellent sense as apologetic propaganda of the Baptist sect. Evidence is too limited to make this case, although expanding the scope of speculation successfully emphasizes again the complexity of the problem.

3. Reception History

If inner-textual evidence cannot establish the authenticity of Josephus' Baptist passage, three groups of external evidence offer hope: (1) manuscript evidence, (2) Origen's testimony (*Cels.* 1.47), and (3) Eusebius' testimonies. Each is addressed in turn.

3.1. Manuscript Evidence

In the article, "The *Testimonium Flavianum*: The State of the Question," Feldman lays out manuscript evidence for the *Testimonium Flavianum*, as well as citations in the church fathers.[70] This evidence applies to the Baptist passage. Only three manuscripts of the *Antiquitates judaicae* 18–20 survive.[71] The earliest, Ambrosianus 370 (F 128), contains *Ant.* 11–20 and dates to the eleventh century. Vaticanus Graecus 148 (also eleventh century) does not omit the Baptist passage, but only contains the *Bellum* and the *Testimonium Flavianum*. Yale 275 and Bononiensis Graecus 3568 contain the Baptist passage and date to the fourteenth century. All three manuscripts represent the same textual family. Manuscripts containing the sixth-century Cassiodorus Latin translation, some earlier than the earliest Greek witnesses (i.e., ninth century) also contain the Baptist passage. Feldman argues concerning the authenticity of the *Testimonium Flavianum* that

---

68   Mostly based on assumption of Baptist source behind Luke 1–2, 3; see e.g., J. A. Fitzmyer, *The Gospel According to Luke I–IX*, 316–317.

69   Katenen Fragment 457.2: Ἐν ταῖς βασιλείαις φησὶν ἱερέα φονευθέντα ἐγγὺς τοῦ ναοῦ καὶ τοῦ θυσιαστηρίου ὑπὸ Ἰωὰς βασιλέως Ἰούδα. Ἰώσηππος δὲ ἱστορεῖ τὸν υἱὸν Βαρὰχ Ζαχαρίαν εἶναι πατέρα Ἰωάννου τοῦ βαπτιστοῦ in: E. Klostermann, ed., *Origenes Werke. Zwölfter Band. Origenes Matthäuserklärung. III. Fragmente und Indices, 1. Hälfte*, 190. Such a fragment again begs the question of the relationship between the extant versus Origen's version of *A.J.* Josephus mentions the death of Ζαχαρίαν υἱὸν Βάρεις in *B.J.* 4.335.

70   Pp. 181–185. Feldman relies in part on H. Schreckenberg, *Die Flavius-Josephus-Tradition in Antike und Mittelalter*.

71   *Josephus 6: Jewish Antiquities, Books IX–XI*, ed. R. Marcus (LCL), vii–ix.

as in modern courts of law the passage must be assumed innocent until proven guilty.[72] Against Feldman, we must consider that three manuscripts of the same text type, the earliest of which dates to the eleventh century, each exhibiting variants, are – to continue the metaphor – at least partially guilty. The question is only the measure of guilt. On one hand, no manuscript witness drops the Baptist passage, eliciting the question of whether it was more likely added or taken away. On the other hand, rarity, late dating,[73] and uniformity of text-type constitute an unstable witness base. Manuscript witnesses alone are thus too frail to bear the burden of authentication.

3.2. Origen

Louis H. Feldman notes that twelve Christian authors cite Josephus prior to Eusebius (ca. 265–339/40 C.E.) but *none* shows knowledge of the passage about Jesus, the so-called *Testimonium Flavianum*.[74] Furthermore, the earliest post-Eusebian citation of the *Testimonium* is by Jerome (*ca.* 347–419 C.E.), nearly a century later.[75] In terms of later witnesses, the Baptist passage is only moderately different from the *Testimonium*. Of sixteen citations of Josephus in the surviving ante-Nicene Christian literature, four are Origen's. No single writer cites Josephus more than Origen, making Origen the author best acquainted with Josephus that we know. Moreover, he is the only known author to cite *A.J.* 11–20[76] and, likewise, the only person to mention the fragment on the Baptist (*A.J.* 18.116–119) until Eusebius. After Eusebius, John Chrysostom (who refers to Josephus frequently) cites the passage about John the Baptist four times.[77] Thus, Origen's witness is of enormous value to the question of authenticity because it is the earliest. Yet as we will see the record concerning the Baptist is not straightforward. Among other difficulties, it does not match the extant version of the text.

Origen notes that Josephus writes about John.[78] The context of the passage is Origen's dispute with Celsus over the baptism of Jesus, in particular the descent of the dove:

> I would like to have told Celsus, when he represented the Jew as in some way accepting John as a Baptist in baptizing Jesus, that a man who lived not long after John and Jesus recorded that John was a Baptist who baptized for the remission of

---

72 FELDMAN, "The *Testimonium Flavianum*: The State of the Question," 181.
73 Josephus completed *A.J.* in 93 CE.
74 FELDMAN, "The *Testimonium Flavianum*: The State of the Question," 181–185.
75 FELDMAN, "The *Testimonium Flavianum*: The State of the Question," 184.
76 M. E. HARWICK, *Josephus as a Historical Source in Patristic literature through Eusebius*; A. WHEALEY, *Josephus on Jesus*.
77 FELDMAN, "The *Testimonium Flavianum*: The State of the Question," 184.
78 H. CHADWICK dates Origen's *Contra Celsum* to ca. 247–248 (*Origen: Contra Celsum*, xv).

sins. For Josephus in the eighteenth book of the *Jewish Antiquities* bears witness that John was a Baptist and promised purification (καθάρσιον) to people who were baptized (*Cels.* 1.47).[79]

This passage testifies to the presence of a Josephan segment on John the Baptist in Origen's version of *A.J.* 18 with at least superficial resemblance to the extant version. The extant account in Book 18 neither qualifies John's baptism as "for the remission of sins" nor distinguishes John's baptism as "purification" for those baptized. On the contrary, it specifies that John's baptism should *not* be employed to gain pardon for sin, but only as consecration of the body subsequent to soul cleansing through lives exhibiting righteousness, justice and piety. Yet Origen's reference is suspiciously accurate with regard to the chapter in which the reference is found.

In subsequent lines, however, Origen criticizes Josephus for incorrectly (and irrationally) reporting that Jerusalem's destruction resulted from James' rather than Jesus' death, particularly given the Jewish historian's chronological proximity to the events:

> The same author, although he did not believe in Jesus as Christ, sought for the cause of the fall of Jerusalem and the destruction of the temple. *He ought to have said* (δέον αὐτὸν εἰπεῖν) that the plot against Jesus was the reason why these catastrophes came upon the people, because they had killed the prophesied Christ; however, although unconscious of it (καὶ ὥσπερ ἄκων οὐ μακράν τῆς ἀληθείας γενόμενος), he is not far from the truth when he says that these disasters befell the Jews to avenge James the Just, who was a brother of 'Jesus the so-called Christ,' since they had killed him who was a very righteous man. This is the James whom Paul, the true disciple of Jesus, says that he saw, describing him as the Lord's brother, not referring so much to their blood-relationship or common upbringing as to his moral life and understanding. If therefore he says that the destruction of Jerusalem happened because of James, *would it not be more reasonable* (εὐλογώτερον) to say this happened on account of Jesus the Christ? His divinity is testified by great numbers of churches, which consist of men converted from the flood of sins and who are dependent on the Creator and refer every decision to His pleasure.[80]

The criticisms of this excerpt, undermining Josephus' credibility, may recommend a reinterpretation of the passage's first half. Apparently, Celsus claimed that certain Jews know and receive John the Baptist – perhaps as over and against Jesus. Origen refutes this argument by attacking the source. Note that Origen accuses Josephus of deliberately obfuscating the truth. Whereas Chadwick translates: "although *unconscious* of it, he is not far from the truth," the Greek ἄκων connotes a witting, willful act. According to Origen, Josephus is not *willing*, in this case, to acknowledge and report the facts. Even though Josephus lived close

---

79 M. Borret, ed., *Origène. Contre Celse (Livres I et II)*, 1:198.
80 Chadwick, *Origen: Contra Celsum*, 43.

in time to the events he describes and, therefore, undoubtedly should know what took place, he intentionally distorts the truth which is that disasters came upon the Jews as a result of Jesus' execution.[81] A second reference to incident in *Cels.* 2.13 is similar:

> His son, Titus, captured Jerusalem, so Josephus says, on account of James the Just, the brother of Jesus the so-called Christ, *though in reality* (ὡς δὲ ἡ ἀλήθεια παρίστησι) it was on account of Jesus the Christ of God. (ET: H. CHADWICK, emphasis added)

Origen also refers to it in *Comm. in Matt.* 10.17 without citation, although in this case he does not indict Josephus' for falsifying facts. Rather, he supports Josephus for correctly assessing the importance of James:

> And James is he whom Paul says in the Epistle to the Galatians that he saw, "But other of the Apostles saw I none, save James the Lord's brother." [5267] And to so great a reputation among the people for righteousness did this James rise, that Flavius Josephus, who wrote the "Antiquities of the Jews" in twenty books, when wishing to exhibit the cause why the people suffered so great misfortunes that even the temple was razed to the ground, said, that these things happened to them in accordance with the wrath of God in consequence of the things which they had dared to do against James the brother of Jesus who is called Christ. [5268] *And the wonderful thing is, that, though he did not accept Jesus as Christ, he yet gave testimony that the righteousness of James was so great*; and he says that the people thought that they had suffered these things because of James. (ET: John Patrick)[82]

Returning to *Cels.* 1.47, allegation of the unreliability of Josephus is startling. Although employing the Baptist passage polemically, the passage is not cited and his point for the fleeting allusion is neither spelled out nor developed. What is more, either Origen does not check or does not know the work (or at least not the extant version): his facts bear only superficial resemblance to the extant text, borrowing rather from John's portrayal in Mark and Matthew.[83] It thus seems that Origen's reference to the Baptist purely provides the occasion to dispute Josephus' reliability. Elsewhere in *Contra Celsum,* Origen references Josephus to corroborate a point. In two such cases, he cites *Contra Apionem,* naming it "two books on the antiquities of the Jews" (1.16; 4.11).[84] In *Cels.* 5.50 he reports the legend recorded in *Ant.* 11.317–339 that Alexander the Great once bowed before the Jewish high priest, but without noting Josephus. In all such references

---

81 Eusebius later reports the same information in *Hist. eccl.* 2.23.

82 *Origen's Commentary on the Gospel of Matthew*, ed. A. ROBERTS/J. DONALDSON.

83 According to Eusebius, the library in Caesarea held a copy of the *Antiquitates* (*Hist. eccl.* 4.3). Citations from one part of *A.J.* does not necessarily imply knowledge of its entirety. Such a large opus was frequently passed down in part rather than in whole.

84 CHADWICK notes: "Commonly called *contra Apionem*" (18).

Celsus is portrayed as *not* having read Josephus' writings. Celsus was evidently erudite, well read, and informed about not just philosophy, but gnostic sects and Egyptian lore.[85] If Celsus, long since dead when Origen so forcefully addresses him (*Praef.* 4), had not read Josephus and/or was suspicious of his writings, this might explain why Origen, when addressing him, neither relies on nor extols Josephus' reliability. General scorn for historicity during Origen's Caesarean period (during which time he wrote *Cels.*) may likewise account for the position.[86]

The implication of *Cels.* 1.47 is, nevertheless, clear: Josephus' *A.J.* offers outside corroboration of certain Christian tenets, but not more. Clearly, Origen's agenda is to refute Celsus, not bear witness to Josephus. Nevertheless, in view of the present thesis concerning the authenticity of the Baptist passage, on the one hand, it is difficult to see why Origen would have fabricated the notion of a pericope about John in *A.J.* 18. On the other hand, the shift from John to a discussion of James' death taints the witness's usefulness to the question of authenticity. Did Origen have a copy of Josephus' *A.J.* or did he simply have access to a list of the contents? If he had a copy, did it possess the Baptist passage in Book 18? If his copy had the passage, did his version of the passage match the extant version? Currently these questions cannot be answered. The extant version of *A.J.* possesses no report that James' death represents divine vengeance for the Jewish war with Rome;[87] it merely states that James' execution may have instigated Albinus to take revenge on Ananus (*Ant.* 20.199–203).[88] Feldman posits that, in writing about James, Origen may have been thinking of Josephus' report about the death of John the Baptist as divine vengeance for the destruction of Herod's army *ca.* 36 CE. To be sure, a non sequitur in the account would be avoided if references to 'James the Just' were switched to 'John the Baptist.'

---

85   See Chadwick, Origen: Contra Celsum, xxiv–xxix.

86   The historicizing quality of the prose in *A.J.* 18 which Thackeray attributes to Josephus' hack 'Thucydidean' secretary may have further put Origen off.

87   "The sufferings that the Jews endured during the war against the Romans are said by Origen (*Cels.* 1.47) and Eusebius (*Hist. eccl.* 2.23) to have been ascribed by Josephus to God's vengeance for the death of James, but there is no such passage extant in Josephus. Origen and Eusebius may be thinking of Josephus' statement about the divine vengeance for the murder of John the Baptist by Herod (*Ant.* 18.116)" (Lake, *Eusebius, Ecclesiastical History*, 109 n. "e")

88   "The younger Ananus thought that he had a favorable opportunity because Festus was dead and Albinus was still on the way. And so he convened the judges of the Sanhedrin and brought before them a man named James, the brother of Jesus who was called the Christ, and certain others. He accused them of having transgressed the law and delivered them up to be stoned. Those of the inhabitants of the city who were considered the most fair-minded and who were strict in the observance of the law were offended at this. They therefore secretly sent to king Agrippa urging him, for Ananus had not even been correct in his first step, to order him to desist from any further such actions … Convinced by these words, Albinus angrily wrote to Ananus threatening to take vengeance (λήψεσθαι παρ' αὐτοῦ δίκας) upon him. King Agrippa, because of Ananus' action, deposed him from the high priesthood he has held for three months and replaced him with Jesus the son of Damnaueus."

Yet, reference to destruction of Jerusalem (rather than the slaying of Herod's army), "the brother of Jesus" (according to Luke, John was cousin not brother of Jesus) as well as Origen's comment that Paul refers to James (Gal 1:19; cf. also *Comm. in Matt.* 10.17) would create new inconsistencies.[89] Other possibilities include that Origen's text of *A.J.* 18 originally featured either the extant or another account about James immediately after that of John the Baptist or that Origen's account of John was about James, but both possibilities are remote.[90] Thackeray argues that Origen confuses Josephus with Hegesippus (*ca.* 165–175 CE), whose extant fragments offer a Christian account of the death of James, (*apud* Eusebius, *Hist. eccl.* 2.23), including that just after James' martyrdom, Vespasian besieged Judea taking the city captive.[91]

Whether accidental or deliberate, it remains that to refute Celsus, Origen undermines Josephus, misrepresenting the extant *Antiquitates* in the process. Even if the mistake was unintentional, one must nevertheless conclude that the best witness to Josephus' passage on John the Baptist prior to Eusebius cannot be directly associated with the extant text, placing modern examinations of the passage's authenticity in the identical circumstance as for the *Testimonium Flavianum*: namely lacking Origen's or any other witness prior to Eusebius.

3.3. Eusebius

In *Hist. eccl.* 1.11.1–4 (cf. *Dem. ev.* 3.5), Eusebius too mentions John the Baptist:[92]

> The divine scripture of the Gospels relates that not long afterwards John the Baptist was beheaded by Herod the younger, and Josephus confirms the narrative, mentioning Herodias by name, and telling how, though she was his brother's wife, Herod took her in marriage, by putting aside her who had formerly been legally married to him (and she was the daughter of Aretas the king of the Petraeans)

---

89 It is unclear as to how many different persons in the NT bear the name James. It occurs 42 times, most in the Gospel of Mark, never in the Gospel of John. Half of all occurrences refer to James the son of Zebedee, one of the twelve disciples chosen by Jesus. One quarter of all occurrences refer to James the brother of Jesus, who was to assume leadership of the early Jerusalem church. A second disciple named James is mentioned in all four lists of the Twelve specified as son of Alphaeus. James is the name of a son of a certain Mary, unless this is the brother of Jesus (e.g., Mark 16:1). James is the father of Judas in the Lukan disciple lists (e.g., Luke 6:16). James is the author of the book of James (probably refers pseudonymously to the brother of Jesus). James is the brother of the author of the book of Jude (probably refers pseudonymously to brother of Jesus). See D. A. HAGNER, "James," 616–618.

90 This solution however posits the death of Jesus' brother James in 36 CE too early for the assumption that he held leadership in the early church, (cf. Herod kills "James, the brother of John" by the sword, Acts 12:2), thus creating more problems than *A.J.*'s problematically late date of John's death.

91 *Josephus: The Man and The Historian*, 134.

92 See G. BARDY, *Eusèbe de Césarée. Histoire Ecclésiastique. Livres I–IV*, 36–38.

and separating Herodias from her husband who was alive. For her sake, too, after killing John, he waged war with Aretas for the dishonor done his daughter; and Josephus says that in a battle in this war the whole army of Herod was destroyed, and that he suffered this because of the plot against John (καὶ ταῦτα πεπονθέναι τῆς ἐπιβουλῆς ἕνεκεν τῆς κατὰ τοῦ Ἰωάννου γεγενημένης). The same Josephus admits that John was peculiarly righteous, and a Baptist, confirming the testimony recorded in the text of the Gospels concerning him. He also relates that Herod was deprived of his kingdom for the sake of the same Herodias, and was exiled with her, being condemned to live in Vienne, a city of Gaul. The account of these things is given in the eighteenth book of the *Antiquities*, where he writes concerning John exactly as follows ....[93]

The above excerpt amalgamates information about Herod in *A.J.* 18.115 with information about John in *A.J.* 116–119. The extant version of *A.J.* makes no explicit connection between the information about Herod and that about John other than that the former explains why Herod's army went to battle, eventually suffering devastating loss. Eusebius also mistakes the fate of Herod Antipas, banished to Lyons, for that of Archelaus, banished to Vienne (*A.J.* 18.7.2). Nevertheless, in what follows, Eusebius cites the extant text of the *Antiquitates* nearly verbatim (1.11.4–6):

> Now to some of the Jews it seemed that the army of Herod had been destroyed by God and that he was paying a very just penalty for John who was called the Baptist. For Herod killed him, a good man and one who commanded the Jews, training themselves in virtue, to practice righteousness towards one another and piety towards God, and to come together for baptism. For he said that baptism would prove acceptable to him only in those who used it not to escape from any sins but for bodily purity, on condition that the soul also had been previously cleansed thoroughly by righteousness. And when the rest collected, for they were greatly excited at hearing his words, Herod feared his great persuasiveness with men lest it should lead to some rising, for they appeared ready to do everything under his advice. He therefore considered it much better, before a revolt should spring from John, to put him to death in anticipation, rather than be involved in difficulties through the actual revolution and then regret it. And John, through Herod' suspicion, was sent a prisoner to Macherus, the prison mentioned already, and was there put to death.[94]

---

93 See n. 85 next.

94 ET: KIRSOPP LAKE. Cf. also *Dem. ev.* 9.5: "Josephus, too, records his story in the Eighteenth Book of the *Jewish Archeology*, writing as follows: 'Now some of the Jews thought that the destruction of Herod's army came from God, and that very justly as a punishment of what he did against John, that was called the Baptist; for Herod slew him, who was a good man, and commanded the Jews to exercise righteousness towards one another, and piety towards God, and so to come to baptism. For so the washing would be acceptable to Him'" (ET: W. J. FERRAR). See also Eusebius, *Dem. ev.* 9.5.15 in: *Eusebius Werke, Sechster Band. Die Demonstratio Evangelica*, 416.

Four minor differences between the extant text of Josephus and the above passage by Eusebius can be identified. First, in section 5, δή is omitted after γάρ and before τοῦτον: i.e., κτείνει γὰρ τοῦτον Ἡρῴδης. Second, in section 6, (as noted above) Josephus' ἐπὶ στάσει is replaced by ἐπὶ ἀποστάσει, perhaps connoting a less seditious act (see above). Third, also in section 6, Eusebius replaces ἐξ with ὑπ' in the phrase πρίν τι νεώτερον ἐξ αὐτοῦ γενέσθαι. And, fourth, Eusebius records in section 6:

προλαβὼν ἀναιρεῖν, ἢ μεταβολῆς γενομένης εἰς πράγματα ἐμπεσὼν μετανοεῖν;

whereas Josephus (in 18.118) reports:

προλαβὼν ἀνελεῖν τοῦ μεταβολῆς γενομένης μὴ εἰς πράγματα ἐμπεσὼν μετανοεῖν.

These adaptations are inconsequential.[95] One additional Eusebian adaptation, noted by Lake (see above), implies that originally John preached to a closed group of ascetics, inciting Herod, only when a greater public manifested interest. In other words, the original text implies that Herod did not mind John's baptizing when it was confined to a narrow group. Lake blames an unnecessary emendation in the text of Niese's edition of Josephus in addition to William Whiston's English translation for obscuring what was originally Herod's essentially rational approach to John.[96]

What is unusual about Eusebius' text is that, although he cites Josephus' Baptist passage nearly verbatim, his explication of that text inaccurately reflects its message. Four problems are crucial. First, Eusebius writes that Josephus confirms the gospels' claim (Mark, Matthew) that Antipas beheaded John, when in fact Josephus' report omits this allegation. Second, as noted above, Eusebius reproduces Josephus' juxtaposition of two narrative accounts about Herod Antipas (*A.J.* 18.109–115; 18.116–119) as reports about John the Baptist. Third, Eusebius infers from his version of *A.J.*, claiming its corroboration in the canonical gospels, that Herod killed John for accusing him of immoral behavior (i.e., marrying his brother's wife) when, according to the extant version, Herod imprisons John for fomenting crowds and threatening sedition. Fourth, a permutation of the third problem, in place of the extant text's claim that Herod lost his army in a war with Aretas as divine retribution for arresting John for insurrection, Eusebius claims that Herod lost his army as divine retribution for arresting John for condemnation of Herod's marriage to Herodias. That is to say, both Eusebius' cause (Herod kills John) and posited effect (divine retribution) for John's alternate action disagree with the extant text.

---

95   "The μή is omitted by Eusebius and is placed in brackets by both Niese and Feldman. It may come from the lingering idea of the object of Herod's fear (*deisas*). In any case, it does not affect the sense of the passage or its translation" (MEIER, *Marginal Jew*, 2.96 n. 170).

96   LAKE's note in *Eusebius, Ecclesiastical History* (LCL), 81.

The subsequent section of Eusebius' account is also different from the extant account. Although the *Testimonium Flavianum* appears before the segment on John the Baptist in the extant *Antiquitates*, Eusebius refers to it as coming *after* the piece about John:

> After narrating these things about John in the same historical work he speaks as follows concerning our Saviour.

Next, Eusebius cites the *Testimonium Flavianum* with virtually no changes from Josephus' extant version.[97] Although a setting after the segment about John makes more sense, in the extant *Antiquitates* the *Testimonium* appears first (*A.J.* 18.63–64). Such a placement is unexpected if Eusebius composed the *Testimonium Flavianum*. It would not have been in Eusebius' best interest either to place his forged fragment about Jesus prior to the narrative about John the Baptist, or to refer to it in this way, or to dissemble about its placement. Nevertheless, if John's section precedes the *Testimonium* in Eusebius' version of the *Antiquitates* (irrespective of who composed it), then Eusebius' version differs from extant copies of *Antiquitates* in at least one additional significant way.

Eusebius closes the section on John by referencing Josephus' reliability. Different from Origen, Eusebius expresses confidence in the Jewish historian's testimony:

> When a writer sprung from the Hebrews themselves handed on in his own writing these details concerning John the Baptist and our Savior, what alternative is there but to convict of shamelessness those who have concocted the reports about them? But let this suffice.[98]

As a point of comparison, Eusebius also cites Josephus in *Hist. eccl.* 2.23.20–25. In this passage, he quotes the *Antiquitates* passage on James at length (20.197, 199–203). The report resembles the extant *Antiquitates* with the exception of this initial phrase:

> Of course Josephus did not shrink from giving written testimony to this, as follows: "And these things happened to the Jews to avenge James the Just, who was the brother of Jesus the so-called Christ, for the Jews killed him in spite of his great righteousness."

---

97 "At this time arose Jesus, a wise man, if indeed he must be called a man, for he was a doer of marvelous deeds, a teacher of men who received the truth with pleasure, and he led after him many of the Jews and many also of the Gentile population. This was the Christ; and when Pilate had condemned him to the cross at the instigation of the leading men among us, those who had first loved him did not cease to do so, for he appeared to them when three days dead restored to life, and the divine prophets had told these and ten thousand other wonders concerning him. And up till now the tribe of Christians which are named after him has not died out" (Eusebius, *Hist. eccl.* 1.11.7–8; ET: Lake [LCL]).

98 "Concocted reports" refers to the Acts of Pilate, a text Eusebius attempts to discredit by citing Josephus.

As noted above, Origen also cites this exceptional passage as belonging to the *Antiquitates* in *Cels.* 1.47 (cf. *Comm. in Matt.* 10.17). The passage does not occur in any extant witness of Josephus in the *A.J.* or elsewhere. Eusebius' passage shares verbatim agreement with Origen's, merely modifying *oratio obliqua* to *oratio recta*. Lawlor and Oulton find Eusebius to be independent of Origen here,[99] but Henry Chadwick argues persuasively that Eusebius' overall debt to Origen is enormous and that this passage's verbatim agreement suggests literary reliance.[100]

The next part of this passage by Eusebius cites *A.J.* 20.197, 199–203. As elsewhere, although the interpretative comment *about* the purported citation does *not* reflect the extant text, the verifiable citation veers in only insignificant ways from it:

> The same writer also narrates his death in the twentieth book of the *Antiquities* as follows: "Now when Caesar heard of the death of Festus he sent Albinus as governor to Judaea, but the younger Ananus, who, as we said, had received the High Priesthood, was bold in temperament and remarkably daring. He followed the sect of the Sadducees, who are cruel in their judgments beyond all the Jews, as we have already explained. Thus his character led Ananus to think that he had a suitable opportunity through the fact that Festus was dead and Albinus still on his way. He summoned a council of judges, brought before it the brother of Jesus, the so-called Christ, whose name was James, and some others, on the accusation of breaking the law and delivered them to be stoned. But all who were reputed the most reasonable of the citizens and strict observers of the law were angered at this and sent secretly to the Emperor, begging him to write to Ananus to give up doing such things, for they said that he had not acted rightly from the very beginning. And some of them also went to meet Albinus as he journeyed from Alexandria, and explained that it was illegal for Ananus to assemble the council without his permission. Albinus was influenced by what was said and wrote angrily to Ananus threatening him with penalties, and for this reason King Agrippa deprived him of the High Priesthood when he had held it for three months, and appointed Jesus the son of Dammaeus.' Such is the story of James, whose is said to be the first of the Epistles called Catholic.[101]

One additional question that, to my knowledge, has not been raised in scholarship, is whether Origen influences Eusebius' treatment of John. Eusebius recommends to anyone wishing to understand his own position – anyone with "a genuine love of truth" – to turn to Origen's *Contra Celsum*.[102] Yet for Eusebius, Josephus is a reliable witness, whereas for Origen, Josephus' trustworthiness is in question. Awareness on the part of Eusebius that Origen found Josephus to

---

99 H. J. LAWLOR/J. E. L. OULTON, eds., *Eusebius. Ecclesiastical History and Martyrs of Palestine*, 2 vols.

100 CHADWICK, *Origen: Contra Celsum*, 43 n. 2.

101 Eusebius, *Hist. eccl.* 2.23.21–24; ET: LAKE [LCL]).

102 *Hier.* 1,5. See T. D. BARNES, *Constantine and Eusebius*, 165.

be unreliable may have compelled Eusebius' free rewriting of the source. The fourth-century Christian historian has an open investment in Josephus' historical testimony; the second-century Alexandrian apologist finds history pedantic.

3.4. Summation: Origen and Eusebius as Witnesses to Josephus

Origen is the first to cite Josephus on John the Baptist. His testimony about the passage dated to *ca.* 248 is the first witness to *A.J.* 18 on record unless one regards Luke-Acts as dependent upon *A.J.* That said, this testimony is no more than a hollow reference. The ensuing discussion does not concern John, but James and Jesus. Moreover, Origen does not present Josephus as a credible witness. Eusebius is second to cite Josephus' Baptist passage and is possibly reliant on Origen to do so. However, Eusebius misrepresents or misconstrues *A.J.* 18.109–119, creating from an account about Antipas one about John and claiming that his own new concatenation of sources and ideas corroborates the gospels of Mark and Matthew, even though Josephus does not. Eusebius also mistakes placement of the *Testimonium* in *A.J.* and – although citing the passage about James according to extant versions – includes Origen's otherwise unattested passage about James. At the same time, Eusebius' citation of *Antiquitates* on John the Baptist (*Hist. eccl.* 1.11) matches the three oldest extant manuscript witnesses. A fair assessment of this data is not easily obtained. In short, the three different witness groups to *A.J.* 18.116–119, (1) manuscripts, (2) Origen and (3) Eusebius each *acknowledge*, but *express different versions* of the section under discussion. Scholars' various explanations for the differences have not yet offered a compelling solution to these divergent witnesses and can at times flirt with speculation.

4. Conclusion

Most scholars today endorse the authenticity of Josephus' three paragraphs on John the Baptist on the basis of (1) absence of significant Christian tampering; (2) coherence with the overall *Antiquitates* narrative in which it is embedded; and/or (3) Origen's and/or Eusebius' reference to the passage. In contrast, this essay demonstrates that each of these bases is unsound. Furthermore, there appears at present to be no way beyond the resulting impasse. I have argued that *A.J.*'s multi-author and or multi-source compositional project produced a corpus disposing itself all too well to editorial modification in transmission. Such a variegated base text complicates interminably subsequent analyses of purported redactional strata. This is not to say with strict historicists that no history can be proven such that, for example, we cannot attribute Josephus' works to him. It is only impossible to make a definitive claim about a single brief passage. If translators, co-workers, and sources were exploited which no doubt they were – not to mention possible contributions by interpolators – then the Josephan corpus remains Josephus' collective enterprise from any historical vantage point.

In terms of the historical John the Baptist, the NT gospels offer only vaguely more promise. The canonical gospels possess notable interest in John the Baptist.[103] Luke's account is distinct in part by omission of Markan materials about John. John's account is separated by the addition of new information. In his brief survey of treatments of the historical John, the late John Reumann describes progress on the historical Baptist as "something of a chimera."[104] In the following oft-cited passage Reumann writes:

> All the hazards of the quest for the historical Jesus exist in the search for the history of John, and then some: conflicting sources, canonical and beyond; tendentiousness in sources; the unsettling role of form and redaction criticism; problems of *religionsgeschichtlich* background; the theology of the early Christian church; *plus the fact that*, if we take seriously the possibility of the Baptist provenance for some of the materials (as many scholars named above do), what we have in the New Testament is *separated* from historical actuality *both by Christian usage and by (earlier) Baptist use*. It is as if we were trying to recover the historical Jesus from traditions filtered through a second, later disciple community of another faith, say Islam (save that the separation in time from the event is shorter). If in the Gospels, to use R. H. Lightfoot's oft misunderstood phrase, we hear, in the case of Jesus 'little more than a whisper of his voice,' then in the case of the Baptist we have only an echo (or echoes) of his whisper. In short, there is more diversity in modern studies about the Baptist than assumed, more optimism than warranted about recovering knowledge of him historically, and more reason to suspect we cannot throw real light on him than even in the case of Jesus.[105]

While a number of Reumann's above claims may be disputed, such as whether the Baptist movement and its traditions was necessarily earlier than Jesus' or whether Baptist belief ('faith') was as different from Christian belief as Christian belief is from Islam, *and* while Reumann is thinking only of evidence provided by the NT gospels, his conclusion probably pertains to Josephus' Baptist passage as well: we have only an echo of a whisper.[106]

---

103 See further ROTHSCHILD, Baptist Traditions and Q, 36–46.
104 REUMANN, "The Quest for the Historical Baptist," 181–199, here: 184.
105 REUMANN, "Quest for the Historical Baptist," 187; emphases original.
106 With the phrase "echo of a whisper" Reumann cites R. H. LIGHTFOOT. See explanation to the title of the present essay. Also, a moratorium on authenticity is not equivalent to a moratorium on historicity. Proven composition of *A.J.*'s Baptist passage by Christians, (Eusebius?), Baptists, an intermediate (Thackeray's 'Thucydidean' editor), an ultimate source or Josephus can neither guarantee nor discredit historical reliability of the content. See excellent summaries of status quaestionis by MASON, *Josephus, Judea, and Christian Origins*, 112–113, 134–137. Different from Mason, however, the present essay emphasizes *A.J.*'s textual disparity (whether secretaries or sources) whereas Mason stresses continuity and unity (e.g., p. 121).

As the only corroboration outside of early Christian literature to his life, Josephus' report about the life and work of John the Baptist (*A.J.* 18.116–119) is crucial to any study of John's practice. Thus, the implications of this conclusion for historical reconstructions of John's individual or group baptism for the forgiveness of sin, and/or bodily lustrations are serious. In my view, only the two constructive paths delineated by Steve Mason remain: (1) "hypotheses for heuristic purposes only, abandoning any claim to probability"; and, (2) "shift our sights from the events behind Josephus's accounts to the compositions themselves as historical phenomena, produced in particular circumstances."[107] Investigations of either of these types may help to recover the historical context of individual or group baptism, baptism for the forgiveness of sin and bodily lustration, if not the specific person, John the Baptist. They are, thus, the recommended way forward for projects reconstructing early Christian ablution rites of/or with regard to John's baptism.

Bibliography

BARDY, GUSTAVE, *Eusèbe de Césarée. Histoire Ecclésiastique. Livres I–IV* (SC 31), Paris: Cerf 1952.

BARNES, TIMOTHY D., *Constantine and Eusebius*, Cambridge, Mass./London: Harvard University Press 1981.

BEGG, CHRISTOPHER, *Josephus' Account of the Early Divided Monarchy (AJ 8, 212–420): Rewriting the Bible* (BEThL 108), Leuven: Leuven University Press 1993.

— *Josephus' Story of the Later Monarchy* (BEThL 155), Leuven: Leuven University Press 2000.

BILDE, PER, *Flavius Josephus between Jerusalem and Rome. His Life, His Works, and their Importance* (JSPE.S 2), Sheffield: Journal for the Study of the Old Testament Press 1988.

BAMMEL, E., "The Baptist in Early Christian Tradition," in: *NTS* 18 (1971/72) 95–128.

BECKER, J., *Johannes der Täufer und Jesus von Nazareth*, Neukirchen-Vluyn: Neukirchener Verlag 1972.

BOWEN, C. R., "Prolegomena to a New Study of John the Baptist" and "John the Baptist in the New Testament," in: Robert J. Hutcheon (ed.), *Studies in the New Testament: Collected Papers of Dr. Clayton R. Bowen*, Chicago: University of Chicago Press 1936, 30–76.

---

107 MASON, *Josephus, Judea, and Christian Origins*, 136–137.

BORRET, MARCEL (ed.), *Origène. Contre Celse (Livres I et II)* (SC 132), Paris: Cerf 1967.

CHADWICK, HENRY, *Origen: Contra Celsum*, Cambridge: Cambridge University Press 1953.

COHEN, SHAYE, *Josephus in Galilee and Rome*, Boston/Leiden: Brill 2002.

COLLINS, ADELA YARBRO, "The Origin of Christian Baptism," *StudLit* 19 (1989) 28-46.

CREED, JOHN MARTIN. "The Slavonic Version of Josephus' History of the Jewish War," in: *HThR* 25 (1932) 277-319.

VON DESTINON, J., *Die Quellen des Flavius Josephus in der Jüd. Arch. Buch XII-XVII – Jüd. Krieg. Buch I*, Kiel: Lipsius 1882.

DIBELIUS, MARTIN, *Die urchristliche Überlieferung von Johannes dem Täufer*, Göttingen: Vandenhoeck & Ruprecht 1911.

EISLER, ROBERT, *Iesous Basileus ou Basileusas*, 2 vols. Heidelberg: Carl Winter 1929-1930; in ET: abridged and corrected by Alexander H. Krappe, *The Messiah Jesus and John the Baptist According to Flavius Josephus' Recently Discovered "Capture of Jerusalem" and the Other Jewish and Christian Sources*, London, UK: Methuen 1931.

ERNST, JOSEF, *Johannes der Täufer: Interpretation, Geschichte, Wirkungsgeschichte* (BZNW 53), Berlin: de Gruyter 1989.

Eusebius, Ecclesiastical History Books I-V, Kirsopp Lake (trans.) (LCL), Cambridge, Mass./London, UK: Harvard University Press 1926.

Eusebius. Ecclesiastical History and Martyrs of Palestine, H. J. Lawlor and J. E. L. Oulton, (eds.), 2 vols. London, UK: SPCK 1927-1928 (repr. 1954).

Eusebius Werke, Sechster Band. Die Demonstratio Evangelica, Ivar A. Heikel, (ed.) (GCS 23). Leipzig: Hinrichs 1913.

FELDMAN, LOUIS H., *Josephus, Jewish Antiquities Books XVIII-XIX* (LCL), Cambridge, Mass./London, UK : Harvard University Press 1965.

— "The *Testimonium Flavianum*: The State of the Question," in: R. F. Berkey/S. A. Edwards (eds.), *Christological Perspectives: Essays in Honor of Harvey K. McArthur*, New York: Pilgrim 1982, 179-199.

— *Josephus and Modern Scholarship 1937-1980*, Berlin: de Gruyter 1984.

— *Josephus, Judaism and Christianity*, Detroit, Mich.: Wayne State University 1987.

— "Josephus," in: *ABD* 3:981–998.

— *Josephus' Interpretation of the Bible*, Berkeley: University of California Press 1998.

— *Studies in Josephus' Rewritten Bible*, Leiden: Brill 1998.

FITZMYER, JOSEPH A., *The Gospel According to Luke I–IX* (AB 28), New York: Doubleday 1995.

GEYSER, A. S., "The Youth of John the Baptist: A Deduction from the Break in the Parallel Account of the Lucan Infancy Story," in: *NT* 1 (1956) 70–75.

GOGUEL, M., *Au seuil de l'évangile: Jean-Baptiste*, Paris: Payot 1928.

GOODMAN, MARTIN, *The Ruling Class of Judaea: The Origins of the Jewish Revolt against Rome A.D. 66–70*. Cambridge, UK: Cambridge University Press 1987.

HAGNER, DONALD A., "James," in: *ABD* 3.616–618.

HARWICK, MICHAEL E., *Josephus as a Historical Source in Patristic literature through Eusebius* (BJSt 128), Atlanta: Ga.: Scholars Press 1989.

HEINEMANN, I., "Josephus' Method in the Presentation of Jewish Antiquities," in: *Zion* 5 (1939–1940) 180–203.

HERRMANN, LÉON, *Chrestos. Témoignages paiens et juifs sur le christianisme du premier siècle* (Collection Latomus 109), Brussels: Latomus 1970.

HOLLENBACH, P. W., "Social Aspects of John the Baptist's Preaching Mission in the Contexts of Palestinian Judaism," in: *ANRW* II.19.1, 850–875.

HÖLSCHER, GUSTAV, "Josephus," 1934–2000 in Vol. 18 of *Paulys Realenzyklopädie der Classischen Altertumswissenschaft*, ed. by A. F. Pauly, G. Wissowa et al., Munich: A. Druckenmüller 1916.

FOAKES-JACKSON F. J./LAKE, KIRSOPP, *The Beginnings of Christianity: Part I: The Acts of the Apostles*, 5 vols. Grand Rapids, Mich.: Baker 1979 (orig. 1920–1923).

Josephus, Jewish Antiquities Books I–III, H. St. J. Thackeray (trans.) (LCL), Cambridge, Mass./London, UK, 1930 (repr. [8]1998).

Josephus, Jewish Antiquities, Books IX–XI, Ralph Marcus (trans.) (LCL), Cambridge, Mass.: Harvard University Press/London, UK: Heinemann 1937 (repr. [7]1995).

Josephus, Jewish Antiquities XVIII–XIX, L. H. Feldman (trans.) (LCL), Cambridge, Mass./London, UK: Harvard University Press 1965 (repr. [5]1996).

Josephus, The Jewish War, H. St. J. Thackeray (trans.) (LCL), Cambridge, Mass.: Harvard University Press 1927–1928 (repr. ⁷1997).

Josephus, The Life/Against Apion, H. St. J. Thackeray (trans.) (LCL), Cambridge, Mass.: Harvard University Press 1926 (repr. ⁷1997).

KELHOFFER, JAMES A., *The Diet of John the Baptist* (WUNT 176), Tübingen: Mohr Siebeck 2005.

KENNARD, JR., J. SPENCER, "Gleanings from the Slavonic Josephus Controversy," in: *JQR* 39 (1948–1949) 161–170.

KLOSTERMANN, ERICH (ed.), *Origenes Werke. Zwölfter Band. Origenes Matthäuserklärung. III. Fragmente und Indices, 1. Hälfte* (GCS 41.1), Leipzig: J. C. Hinrichs 1941.

KRAELING, C. H., *John the Baptist*, New York: Scribner 1951.

LICHTENBERGER, H., "Reflections on the History of John the Baptist's Communities," in: *FolOr* 25 (1988) 45–49.

LIGHTFOOT, R. H., *History and Interpretation in the Gospels* (The Bampton Lectures 1934), New York/London, UK: Harper and Brothers 1935.

— "Täufergemeinden und frühchristliche Täuferpolemik im letzten Drittel des 1. Jahrhunderts," in: *ZThK* 84 (1987) 36–57.

LOHMEYER, E., *Das Urchristentum 1: Johannes der Täufer*, Göttingen: Vandenhoeck & Ruprecht 1932.

LUPIERI, E., *Giovanni Battista fra Storia e Leggenda*, Brescia: Paideia 1988.

MASON, STEVE, *Josephus and the New Testament*, Peabody, Mass.: Hendrickson ²2003.

— *Josephus, Judea, and Christian Origins: Methods and Categories*, Peabody, Mass.: Hendrickson 2009.

MCLAREN, JAMES, *Turbulent Times? Josephus and Scholarship on Judaea in the First Century*, Sheffield: Sheffield Academic Press 1998.

MEIER, JOHN P., "John the Baptist in Matthew's Gospel," in: *JBL* 99/3 (1980) 383–405.

— "John the Baptist in Josephus: Philology and Exegesis," in: *JBL* 111 (1992) 225–237.

— *A Marginal Jew: Rethinking the Historical Jesus. Volume Two: Mentor, Message, and Miracles*, New York: Doubleday 1994.

MOEHRING, HORST R., "Novelistic Elements in the Writings of Flavius Josephus," Ph.D. Diss., University of Chicago 1957.

— "Joseph Ben Matthia and Flavius Josephus," in: *ANRW* 2.21.2:864–891, Berlin/New York: de Gruyter 1984.

MURPHY-O'CONNOR, JEROME, "John the Baptist and Jesus: History and Hypothesis," in: *NTS* 36 (1990) 359–374.

NIESE, BENEDICT, *Flavii Josephi Opera*, 7 vols., Berlin: Weidmann ²1955 (¹1885–1895).

NODET, ÉTIENNE, "Jésus et Jean-Baptiste selon Josephe," in: *RB* 92 (1985) 321–348.

— *Flavius Josèphe. Les antiquités juives, Volume I: Livres I à III. A. Introduction et texte*, Paris: Cerf 1990.

— *La Bible de Josèphe*. Paris: Cerf 1996.

OLSEN, KEN, "Eusebius and the *Testimonium Flavianum*," in: *CBQ* 61 (1999) 305–322.

Origen's Commentary on the Gospel of Matthew, A. Roberts/J. Donaldson (eds.), Edinburgh: T&T Clark 1867.

PERVO, RICHARD, I., *Dating Acts: Between the Evangelists and the Apologists*, Santa Rosa, Calif.: Polebridge 2006.

RAJAK, TESSA, *Josephus: The Historian and His Society*, London: Duckworth 1983 (²2002).

REUMANN, JOHN, "The Quest for the Historical Baptist," in: J. Reumann (ed.), *Understanding the Sacred Text: Essays in Honor of Morton S. Enslin on the Hebrew Bible and Christian Beginnings*, Valley Forge, Penn.: Judson 1972, 181–199.

ROTHSCHILD, CLARE K., *Baptist Traditions and Q* (WUNT 190), Tübingen: Mohr Siebeck 2005.

SANDERS, E. P., *Jesus and Judaism*, Philadelphia, Penn.: Fortress 1985.

Schreckenberg, Heinz., *Die Flavius-Josephus-Tradition in Antike und Mittelalter*, Leiden: Brill 1972.

SCHÜTZ, J., *Johannes der Täufer*, Zürich: Zwingli 1967.

SCHWARTZ, DANIEL R., "Josephus and Nicolaus on the Pharisees," in: *JSJ* 14 (1983) 157–171.

— *Agrippa I: The Last King of Judaea* (TSAJ 23), Tübingen: Mohr Siebeck 1990.

SCOBIE, C. H. H., *John the Baptist*, London: SCM 1964.

SHUTT, R. J. H., *Studies in Josephus*, London: SPCK 1961.

STEINMANN, J., *Saint John the Baptist and the Desert Tradition*, New York: Harper 1958.

TATUM, W. B., *John the Baptist and Jesus: A Report of the Jesus Seminar*, Sonoma, Calif., Polebridge 1994.

TAYLOR, JOAN E., *The Immerser: John the Baptist in Second Temple Judaism*, Grand Rapids, Mich.: Eerdmans 1997.

THACKERAY, H. ST. J., *Josephus The Man and The Historian*, New York: Jewish Institute of Religion 1929.

THOMAS, JOSEPH, *Le mouvement baptiste en Palestine et Syrie (150 av. J.C. – 300 ap. J.C.)*, Gembloux: Duculot 1935.

TRILLING, WOLFGANG, "Die Täufertradition bei Matthäus," in: *BZ* (1959) 271–289.

VERMES, GEZA/FERGUS MILLAR (eds.), *The History of the Jewish People in the Age of Jesus Christ*, 4 vols., Edinburgh: T&T Clark 1973–1987.

WEBB, R. L., *John the Baptizer and Prophet: A Socio-Historical Study*, Sheffield: Journal for the Study of the Old Testament Press 1991.

— "John the Baptist and his Relationship to Jesus," in: B. D. Chilton/C. A. Evans (eds.), *Studying the Historical Jesus: Evaluations of the Current State of Current Research*, Leiden: Brill 1994, 214–299.

— "The Activity of John the Baptist's Expected Figure at the Threshing Floor (Matthew 3.12 – Luke 3.17)," in: *JSNT* 43 (1991) 103–111.

WHEALEY, ALICE, *Josephus on Jesus* (Studies in Biblical Literature 36), New York: Lang 2003.

WHISTON, WILLIAM, *The Works of Josephus: Complete and Unabridged*, Peabody, Mass.: Hendrickson 1987.

WINK, W., *John the Baptist in the Gospel Tradition*, Cambridge: Cambridge University Press 1968.

— "Jesus' Reply to John: Matt. 11:2–6/Luke: 7:18–23," in: *Forum* 5 (1989) 121–128.

„Ist er heraufgestiegen, gilt er in jeder Hinsicht als ein Israelit" (bYev 47b)
Das Proselytentauchbad im frühen Judentum

DIETER SÄNGER

1. Hinführung zum Thema

In seinem berühmt-berüchtigten Judenexkurs im 5. Buch der Historien (V 1–13), einem Musterstück antijüdischer Polemik, bemerkt Tacitus, wer zum Kult der Juden übertrete (*transgressi in morem*), gebe den väterlichen Glauben auf und lasse sich beschneiden[1]. Trotz der bissigen Häme, mit der Tacitus den „missachtetsten Teil der Knechtsvölker" (*despectissima pars servientium*, V 8,2) überzieht, wird man dem traditionsbewussten Verteidiger angestammter römischer Werte zumindest an diesem Punkt nicht widersprechen können. Neben dem Christentum kennt die kaiserzeitliche Antike nur noch eine Religion mit Exklusivanspruch: das Judentum. Der Anschluss ist an Bedingungen geknüpft. Zentrale Voraussetzung ist die Akzeptanz eines Wirklichkeitsverständnisses, das zu dem von der Mehrheitsgesellschaft geteilten in Spannung steht. Seine theologischen und anthropologischen Begründungszusammenhänge erscheinen suspekt. Das ihm korrespondierende, als deviant empfundene Ethos schürt Argwohn und mobilisiert Abwehrreaktionen. Wissenssoziologisch haben wir es mit einer gruppenspezifischen „Weltansicht" zu tun, die durch eine „einheitliche Sinnmatrix"[2] gekennzeichnet ist. Ihr Konkurrenzverhältnis zu alternativen Entwürfen etwa aus dem Bereich der klassischen Philosophie, deren metaphysischer und kosmologischer Referenzrahmen vor allem gebildeten Kreisen als Richtschnur für eine religiös fundierte Lebensführung diente, resultiert aus dem exklusiven Anspruch, das menschliche Dasein deuten und ihm Sinn und Orientierung vermitteln zu können. Deshalb verlangt die volle Zugehörigkeit zum Judentum eine umfassende, seine „Weltansicht" zur Anschauung bringende Um- und Neugestaltung des ganzen Lebensvollzugs, d.h. eine Konversion[3]. Sie

---

1   *Hist.* V 5,1f. Vgl. Josephus, *Ant* 11,212; 20,75; *Ap* 2,148.258; Iuv. 14,100–104.
2   TH. LUCKMANN, Die unsichtbare Religion, 93.
3   Vgl. P. L. BERGER/TH. LUCKMANN, Konstruktion, 169: „Die neue Plausibilitätsstruktur muß die Welt des Menschen werden, die alle anderen Welten und besonders die, welche er vor seiner Konversion ‚bewohnte', verdrängt". Von Konversion kann natürlich sinnvoll nur die Rede sein,

stellt gleich in doppelter Hinsicht einen Bruch im biographischen Kontinuum dar. Zum einen impliziert sie die Abkehr von einem religiösen Überzeugungssystem, das seine identitätsstiftende und sozial-integrative Funktion verloren hat; zum anderen markiert sie den Eintritt in eine Gemeinschaft, die sich von der paganen Bevölkerungsmehrheit durch ihre – aus der Fremdperspektive als gesellschaftlicher Störfaktor wahrgenommene, im Binnenraum jedoch kohäsive Kraft entfaltende und stabilisierend wirkende – „observance of the ancestral laws"[4] abgrenzt. Während im Christentum für den rituellen Vollzug des mit der Konversion verbundenen religiösen und sozialen Statuswechsels[5] die Taufe konstitutiv ist[6], und zwar unabhängig vom Geschlecht, ist es im Judentum bei männlichen Konvertiten die Beschneidung[7]. Über eine parallel zur Beschneidung ent-

---

wenn es sich um religionsmündige Konvertiten, d.h. in der Regel um erwachsene Frauen und Männer handelt. Ausschließlich an sie ist im Folgenden gedacht.

4   S. J. D. COHEN, *Beginnings*, 59.

5   Schon aufgrund des differenzierten Beziehungsgefüges von religiös bestimmter Sozialität und sozial legitimierter Religiosität gehören beide Aspekte untrennbar zusammen. Für den jüdischen Bereich vgl. nur Philo, *SpecLeg* 1,52; 4,178; *Virt* 102; bYev 62a; bGit 39a, für den christlichen I Kor 12,13; Gal 3,28; Phlm 10.15f., ferner II Kor 5,17; Gal 6,14f.

6   Wohl von Anfang an. Nirgends wird die Taufe als solche in den neutestamentlichen Schriften problematisiert. Die paulinische Korrespondenz setzt sie als gängige christliche Praxis voraus (Röm 6,3f.; Gal 3,27; I Kor 1,13ff; 6,11; 12,13), und das nicht erst in ihrer Zeit, wie u.a. der Rückgriff auf ältere (antiochenische?) Tauftradition in Gal 3,26–28 erkennen lässt. Sollte Paulus sich in das ἐβαπτίσθημεν von Röm 6,3; I Kor 12,13 einschließen und damit das „Wir" auch im individuell-biographischen Sinn zu verstehen sein, erführen die beiden Notizen in Apg 9,18 und 22,16, deren Historizität umstritten ist, eine zusätzliche Stütze. Der Annahme, die Taufpraxis reiche bis in die Gründungsphase der Christenheit zurück, stehen Apg 18,24–28 und 19,2–7 nicht entgegen. Denn obwohl Lukas weder Apollos noch den Johannesjüngern in Ephesus ihr Christsein abspricht – von Apollos heißt es, er sei ein ἀνὴρ λόγιος, ζέων τῷ πνεύματι und lehre ἀκριβῶς τὰ περὶ τοῦ Ἰησοῦ, die Johannesjünger werden ausdrücklich als μαθηταί und πιστεύσαντες (bei Lukas stets auf Christen bezogen) charakterisiert –, stellen sie für ihn einen Ausnahmefall dar. Gleiches gilt hinsichtlich der Apostel, von denen ebenfalls nicht berichtet wird, sie seien getauft worden, die aber seit Pfingsten den heiligen Geist besitzen (Apg 2,1–4). Vgl. K. ALAND, „Vorgeschichte", 188–194; F. AVEMARIE, *Tauferzählungen*, 68–81. Das Problem der Taufe Unmündiger mag hier auf sich beruhen (vgl. in der vorliegenden Publikation den Beitrag von Hermut Löhr).

7   Vorexilische Belege: Gen 34,13–17.22–24; Ex 4,24–26; Jos 5,2f.8f.; Ri 14,3f.; 15,18; I Sam 14,6; 18,25.27; 31,4; II Sam 1,20; 3,14 u.ö. In exilisch-nachexilischer Zeit wird die Beschneidung zum Bundeszeichen schlechthin, vgl. exemplarisch Gen 17,9–14.23–27; Lev 12,1–3; Dtn 10,12–22; Jes 52,1f.; Ez 44,6–9; Sir 44,19f.; Jdt 14,10; Jub 15,25–29. Dass die Beschneidung vor allem im Bereich der hellenistisch-jüdischen Diaspora an Bedeutung verloren habe, so J. J. COLLINS, „Circumcision and Salvation", 163–186, Übertrittswillige in einzelnen Gemeinden sogar von der Beschneidungsforderung dispensiert worden seien, wie N. J. MCELENEY, „Conversion", 328–333, meint, ist den Quellen nicht zu entnehmen. Trotz seiner Bemerkungen in *SpecLeg* 1,8–11 (vgl. *Quaest in Ex* 2,2) löst auch Philo die Beschneidung nicht symbolisch auf. Gegenüber extremen Allegoristen insistiert er auf ihrem Vollzug (*Migr* 89–94). Grundsätzlich gilt: „This (sc. circumcision) was the only ritual that ... was demanded of all male converts by all non-Christian Jewish communities", COHEN, *Beginnings*, 219. In diesem Sinn u.a. auch J. NOLLAND, „Uncircumcised Proselytes?", 173–194; M. GOODMAN, *Mission and Conversion*, 81; W. KRAUS,

wickelte Ersatzhandlung für Frauen, die sich schon in alttestamentlicher Zeit herausgebildet hat, erfahren wir nichts. Jedenfalls findet sich in den biblischen Texten kein Hinweis darauf[8]. Obwohl Mischehen verpönt waren (Ex 34,14-16) und das Verbot, sich mit anderen Völkern zu verschwägern (Dtn 7,3), besonders Ehen mit deren Frauen sanktioniert (7,4), sind solche Verbindungen keine Seltenheit gewesen. Juda nimmt eine Kanaaniterin zur Frau (Gen 38,2), Joseph eine heidnische Priestertochter (Gen 41,45.50; 46,20), Mose eine Midianiterin (Ex 2,21) und Kuschitin (Num 12,1), David eine Hethiterin (II Sam 11,26f). Von Salomo wird berichtet, er habe eine unbestimmte Zahl von Ausländerinnen geheiratet (I Kön 11,1-3)[9], darunter die Tochter des Pharao (I Kön 3,1; 7,8) und die Ammoniterin Naama (I Kön 14,21). Psalm 45 besingt die Hochzeit eines ungenannten Königs – möglicherweise aus dem Nordreich – mit einer tyrischen Prinzessin (45,12f.). Nirgends hören wir davon, vor ihrer Heirat hätten sich die Frauen dem Volk Israel förmlich angeschlossen und ihre Zugehörigkeit durch einen rituellen Akt besiegelt. Die einfachste Erklärung für diesen Sachverhalt dürfte auch die wahrscheinlichste sein. Heirateten fremdstämmige Frauen einen Israeliten, wurden sie im Normalfall gleichsam automatisch dem Familien- und Sippenverband ihres Mannes eingegliedert und nahmen seine Religion an[10]. Ausnahmen bestätigen die Regel, wie die z.T. scharf kritisierten Folgen (I Kön 9,6-9; 11,4-8.9-11.30-33, vgl. 16,29-33) der von wirtschaftlichen und diplomatischen Überlegungen geleiteten Heirats- und Bündnispolitik Salomos (I Kön 5,15; 9,26-29; 10,11.22) zeigen.

Nach dem Exil veränderten sich die Rahmenbedingungen. Zwar allmählich erst, aber seit dem Übergang von der persischen zur griechischen Vorherrschaft immer deutlicher erkennbar. Nicht zuletzt aufgrund der sich rasch ausbreitenden Diaspora kam es vermehrt zu Übertritten. Mit den zahlreicher werdenden Proselyten gewann auch die Beschneidung als Identitäts- und Differenzmerkmal an Bedeutung. In dieser Phase des sich neu konstituierenden jüdischen Ethnos[11] wird der innere Konnex von Konversion und Beschneidung historisch

---

Volk Gottes, 96-107. Es gibt nur einen Ausnahmetatbestand: akute Gefahr für Leib und Leben (z.B. Hämophilie), bYev 64b; tShab 15,8 [ed. ZUCKERMANDEL 133], vgl. bHul 4b.5a.

8   Erst in talmudischer Zeit wird die Auffassung vertreten, bereits die Stammmütter hätten als Ersatz für die Beschneidung das Tauchbad genommen, bYev 46a.b.

9   Die Vielzahl der Frauen Salomos – nach I Kön 11,3 sollen es insgesamt 1000 gewesen sein, darunter 300 Konkubinen – wird in der rabbinischen Literatur unterschiedlich bewertet. Während etwa R. Jose b. Chalaphta (Tannait um 150 n.Chr.) in bonam partem interpretiert und das ständige Anwachsen des Harems damit erklärt, Salomo habe die ausländischen Frauen unter die Fittiche der Shekhina, d.h. zum Gott Israels bringen wollen, urteilt sein Kontrahent R. Shim'on b. Jochai weit nüchterner: Salomo habe Unzucht getrieben (ySan 2,6 [20c]).

10   Ausführlicher hierzu COHEN, „Conversion to Judaism", 33f.43f.

11   Vgl. Josephus, *Ant* 11,173, und näherhin zum Verhältnis von jüdischem Ethnos und religiös definierter „Jüdischkeit" („Judaeanness") COHEN, *Beginnings*, 109-139.

erstmals fassbar[12]. Deshalb könnte man erwarten, für weibliche Konvertiten habe es analog zur Beschneidung ein Ritual gegeben, das sie von Nichtjüdinnen unterscheidbar machte. Dies umso mehr, als Frauen überproportional vertreten waren und das Gros der Proselyten stellten[13]. Auf dem Hintergrund des unter pharisäischem Einfluss zunehmend ethnisch-religiös geprägten jüdischen Selbstverständnisses erscheint die These zunächst plausibel, etwa seit der Mitte des 1. vorchristlichen Jahrhunderts hätten sich übertrittswillige Frauen einem Tauchbad unterziehen müssen, das ihrer kultischen Reinigung diente und sie als Mitglieder der jüdischen Gemeinschaft auswies[14]. Es wird noch zu prüfen sein, ob die dafür in Anspruch genommenen Belege leisten, was sie leisten sollen, nämlich die Existenz des Proselytentauchbads schon in dieser (vorherodianischen?) Zeit wahrscheinlich zu machen (s.u. unter § 5.)[15].

2. Problemstellung

In der frühchristlichen Taufpraxis spiegelt sich die Missionssituation. Der (erwachsene) Christ wird getauft, nachdem er zum Glauben gekommen ist[16]. Soweit sie sich zum Thema äußert, bildet auch in der Literatur des rabbinischen Judentums das zeitliche Nacheinander von Tauchbad (טבילה) und Opferdarbringung (קרבן [הרצייח]), dem beim Mann die Beschneidung (מילה) voraufgeht, den Abschluss des Konversionsprozesses[17]. Präziser noch, rechtsgültig vollzogen ist der Übertritt auch ohne das (Sühne-)Opfer. Es ist aber erforderlich, um als Pro-

---

12 COHEN, „Conversion to Judaism", 35.

13 Vgl. nur Josephus, Bell 2,560; Ant 18,82, ferner Bell 7,44f.; Ant 14,110.114–118. Hauptsächlich wohl deshalb, weil bei ihnen die Beschneidung entfiel. Auch das (nicht immer strikt befolgte) Verbot der Mischehe wird eine Rolle gespielt haben, vgl. Jub 30,11ff; Philo, SpecLeg 3,29; Josephus, Ant 8,191; 18,340–352; syrBar 42,4; bAZ 36b. Die in den legendarischen Erzählungen Esr 9f. und Neh 9f. und nicht zuletzt im Buch Tobit propagierte Endogamie spiegelt den Versuch frommer Kreise, einem als bedrohlich empfundenen Trend entgegenzuwirken.

14 Vgl. Bill. I, 103.105.112; F. GAVIN, The Jewish Antecedents, 31; J. LEIPOLDT, Die urchristliche Taufe, 2f.; TH. F. TORRANCE, „Proselyte Baptism", 154; D. DAUBE, Rabbinic Judaism, 106f.; J. JEREMIAS, Kindertaufe, 29f.33f. Eine andere Vermutung geht dahin, bis 70 n.Chr. seien Frauen verpflichtet gewesen, im Tempel ein Sühnopfer darzubringen, J. E. TAYLOR, The Immerser, 65.

15 Zweifel sind angebracht. Das gilt z.B. für bKer 9a (vgl. mKer 2,1) ebenso wie für mPes 8,8 (= mEd 5,2); bYev 46a.71a und SifBam 108 zu Num 15,14 [ed. HOROVITZ 112]. Methodisch erscheint es problematisch, unbesehen davon auszugehen, die hier festgelegten (und auf keinen gemeinsamen Nenner zu bringenden) Regularien für das Aufnahmeverfahren seien bereits in der Periode vor 70 n.Chr. praktiziert worden.

16 Apg 2,38.41; 8,12f.36.38; 9,18; 10,47f.; 16,14f.33f.; 18,8; 19,5; 22,16, vgl. Mt 28,19f.; Kol 2,11f.

17 Die Trias מילה, טבילה, קרבן הרצייח begegnet in bKer 9a; bYev 46a; MekhSh zu Ex 12,48 [ed. HOFFMANN 30]; SifBam 108 zu Num 15,14, vgl. MekhSh zu Ex 19,10 [ed. HOFFMANN 97], nicht aber in der Mischna. Das Tauchbad leitet Rabbi aus Ex 24,6.8, das Opfer aus Ex 24,5 ab (bKer 9a). In mPes 8,8 und mEd 5,2 (vgl. Gerim 1.3.5) fehlt das Opfer. Lediglich Beschneidung und Tauchbad werden erwähnt. Noch der aus spät- bzw. nachtalmudischer Zeit stammende Traktat

selyt „Heiliges" (קדשים) essen zu können[18]. Gemeint ist die erstmalige Teilnahme am Opfermahl[19]. Daraus wird ersichtlich, dass die genannten drei Elemente nicht in gleicher Weise als normativ betrachtet wurden. Und selbst wenn dies der Fall wäre, besagt das noch nicht, sie seien bereits zur Zeit des Zweiten Tempels üblich gewesen und hätten einen unverzichtbaren Bestandteil des Aufnahmeverfahrens gebildet.

Inzwischen besteht ein relativ breiter Konsens, dass die christliche Taufe die von Johannes dem Täufer gespendete voraussetzt und sich aus ihr entwickelt hat[20]. Hingegen sind Ursprung, Alter, Eigenart und Bedeutung des Proselytentauchbads nach wie vor umstritten. Besonders hinsichtlich seines Ursprungs und Alters gehen die Meinungen weit auseinander. Sieht man von forschungsgeschichtlich überholten Positionen einmal ab, die das Proselytentauchbad im eigentlichen Sinn, d.h. in seiner disktinkten, von den üblichen rituellen Waschungen zu unterscheidenden Funktion als Aufnahmeritus[21] entweder extrem früh (spätprophetisch) oder extrem spät (Ende des 3. Jahrhunderts n.Chr.) datieren[22], lässt sich die Mehrzahl der übrigen Vorschläge auf die Alternative reduzieren: vortannaitisch oder tannaitisch. Die Erwähnung des Proselytentauchbads in der Mischna und seine wie selbstverständlich vorausgesetzte Existenz in Teilen der übrigen Traditionsliteratur gilt den einen als zureichendes Indiz für eine

---

Gerim 2,5 reflektiert den Dissens in dieser Frage. R. Eliezer b. Jakob hält das Opfer für notwendig, um als Proselyt anerkannt werden zu können, R. Shim'on (b. Jochai) nicht.

[18] mKer 2,1. Vgl. G. F. MOORE, *Judaism I*, 332. Der Widerspruch von B. J. BAMBERGER, *Proselytism*, 45, ist aufgrund seiner alleinigen Orientierung an der in bKer 8a–9b formulierten Gegenposition nur zum Teil berechtigt. Zwar wird dort zunächst gesagt, erst nach Darbringung des Opfers sei der Proselyt geeignet, in die Gemeinde zu kommen. Aber anschließend heißt es von dem ausdrücklich als Proselyt (גר) bezeichneten, d.h. bereits rechtsgültig zum Judentum übergetretenen ehemaligen Nichtjuden, ihm sei solange verwehrt Heiliges zu essen, bis er sein Opfer dargebracht habe (vgl. Lev 12,8; 14,30). Demnach konditionierte das vorgeschriebene Opfer eines Taubenpaares (bKer 8b–9a; tKer 1,11f. [ed. ZUCKERMANDEL 561f]; tSheq 3,21 [ed. ZUCKERMANDEL 179]) bzw. im Notfall nur cincr Taube (mMen 12,5; bKer 8b; tSheq 3,20 [ed. ZUCKERMANDEL 179]) die Mahlteilnahme, nicht jedoch auch die volle Zugehörigkeit zur jüdischen Gemeinde. Vgl. bYev 47b: „Nachdem er untergetaucht und heraufgestiegen ist, gilt er in jeder Hinsicht als Israelit".

[19] Nach der Tempelzerstörung ist diese Forderung natürlich obsolet geworden. Sie wurde auch als anachronistisch begriffen, ySheq 8,4 [51b]. Dass sie dennoch aufrecht erhalten wurde, zeigt die Kontinuität und das Beharrungsvermögen der ursprünglich auf den Tempel bezogenen kultisch-rituellen Vorschriften.

[20] Näheres hierzu im Beitrag von Michael Labahn in der vorliegenden Publikation.

[21] Gelitten hat die Diskussion über weite Strecken hinweg und noch bis in die jüngste Vergangenheit an der mangelnden Trennschärfe zwischen „repeated lustrations for uncleanliness prescribed by the law" und dem „witnessed act of baptism described in the Babylonian Talmud", K. PUSEY/J. HURT, „Proselyte Baptism", 143. Vgl. H. H. ROWLEY, „Jewish Proselyte Baptism", 214; A. YARBRO COLLINS, „Origin", 34.

[22] Die erste Variante vertritt O. BÖCHER, „Wasser und Geist", 62, die zweite M. SCHNECKENBURGER, *Proselytentaufe*, 133–153.185.

bereits vor der Tempelzerstörung in Geltung stehende Praxis[23]. Besonders Vertreter der älteren Forschung tendieren dazu, den Zeitpunkt noch weiter nach hinten zu verschieben. Ihnen zufolge lassen sich die Spuren des Tauchbads bis in die zweite Hälfte des 1. vorchristlichen Jahrhunderts zurückverfolgen. Es sei als notwendig empfunden worden, um die den heidnischen Konvertiten jetzt persönlich zugeschriebene Unreinheit zu beseitigen[24]. Träfe dies zu, könnte das Proselytentauchbad nicht nur auf die Johannestaufe eingewirkt haben, sondern es ließe sich über sie auch eine Verbindung zwischen ihrem jüdischen Vorbild und der christlichen Taufe herstellen[25].

---

23 Exemplarisch E. SCHÜRER, History 3/1, 173: "[E]ven in the absence of definite proof they (sc. Beschneidung, Proselytentauchbad, Opfer) can be considered as prevailing in Second Temple period". Ähnlich argumentieren J. DELORME, „Practice of Baptism", 29f.; G. R. BEASLEY-MURRAY, Taufe, 42–44.53; TAYLOR, The Immerser, 67f., und jetzt wieder T. L. DONALDSON, Judaism and the Gentiles, 490 Anm. 19: „[T]he three requirements are taken sufficiently for granted in the Tannaitic period that it is hard to imagine immersion as a later innovation".

24 Darauf hebt besonders JEREMIAS, Kindertaufe, 30f., ab. Dies habe nicht nur für heidnische Frauen gegolten, denen man die permanente Unreinheit einer Menstruierenden attestiert habe, sondern aufgrund ihres intimen Kontakts auch für deren Männer. Bis heute ist allerdings umstritten, von welcher Zeit an Nichtjuden allgemein als rituell unrein galten. In ihrer ausführlichen Studie zu dieser Frage kommt CH. E. HAYES zu dem Ergebnis, das Konzept der Unreinheit der Heiden sei relativ späten Datums. Es handle sich um eine rabbinische Konstruktion, Gentile Impurities, 107–144.256–268. Jedenfalls reicht es nicht aus, auf Josephus, Bell 2,150; Ant 14,285; 18,93f.; Apg 10,28; Joh 18,28 und mToh 7,6 zu verweisen, um als „a consensus" festzuhalten, „that Gentiles were unclean and needed to be purified at the point of their entrance into Judaism", so TAYLOR, The Immerser, 66. Wäre dies der Fall, bliebe es unverständlich und bedürfte einer Erklärung, warum noch im 3. Jahrhundert (!) von einem Proselyten gesagt wird, dass er „im vorigen Jahr ein Nichtjude und für die Unreinheit nicht empfänglich war, während er jetzt Israelit und für die Unreinheit empfänglich ist" (bPes 92a, vgl. mNeg 7,1). Zwar gilt bereits im Alten Testament das Land der Heiden und alles, was mit fremden Göttern zu tun hat, als unrein (Gen 35,2; Jos 22,19; Am 7,17, vgl. bShab 14a). Darüber hinaus finden sich neben den oben genannten weitere jüdische Texte, die Heiden als solchen Unreinheit attestieren (z.B. Jub 22,16f.; JosAs 7,1, vgl. Dan 1,8; Jdt 12,1f.; I Makk 9,34; II Makk 5,27; Philo, LegGai 212; mKel 1,8 u.ö.). Aber sie dürfen weder pars pro toto genommen und verallgemeinert werden noch geben sie zu erkennen, worin genau diese Unreinheit begründet ist. An levitische Unreinheit kann schwerlich gedacht sein. Heiden sind von den entsprechenden Bestimmungen in Lev 11–15; 19,23–25; Dtn 14,3–21 nicht betroffen, vgl. mNeg 3,1; bNaz 61b und zur Frage E. P. SANDERS, Judaism. Practice and Belief, 72–76.502f. Deshalb ist der Schluss naheliegend: „[I]n principle there was simply no room for purification", DAUBE, Rabbinic Judaism, 107. Vgl. MOORE, Judaism I, 331–335; L. FINKELSTEIN, „Baptism", 208; R. E. WEBB, John the Baptizer, 124–127; V. HAARMANN, JHWH-Verehrer, 30f. (Anm. 58).

25 Für L. H. SCHIFFMAN, „Conversion", 303, ist die christliche Taufe „an imitation of proselyte immersion". Dabei erliegt er der Gefahr, mit einer petitio principii zu operieren, weil er nur unter der Voraussetzung der zeitlichen Priorität des Proselytentauchbads die Taufe des Johannes und die christliche Taufe meint erklären zu können, vgl. IDEM, Who Was a Jew?, 26.29. Zugleich muss er aber zugeben, dass eindeutige Indizien für die Existenz des Proselytentauchbads zur Zeit des Zweiten Tempels fehlen, ibid. 29. Ähnlich wie SCHIFFMAN argumentieren LEIPOLDT, Die urchristliche Taufe, 2 (als Vergleich zur frühchristlichen Taufe komme „vorzugsweise die jüdische Proselytentaufe in Betracht"); O. CULLMANN, Tauflehre, 5.56–58, und TH. F. TORRANCE,

Hingegen beurteilen andere den Aussagewert der rabbinischen Texte wesentlich skeptischer, gerade was den terminus a quo seines usuellen Gebrauchs betrifft. Aus ihrer Sicht sind es vor allem drei Sachverhalte, die in der Summe zu einer erheblich späteren Ansetzung nötigen. Erstens: Die in Frage stehenden Quellen sind für unterschiedliche Interpretationen offen. Allein von ihnen her lässt sich eine Frühdatierung des Proselytentauchbads nicht begründen. Zweitens: Seine geschichtliche Rückführung in die Zeit vor 70 n.Chr. beruht auf dem methodischen Vorentscheid, den Mangel an textbasierter historischer Evidenz mit Hilfe der nicht weiter problematisierten Zusatzannahme „Traditionskontinuum" zu kompensieren. Dadurch geraten alternative Optionen nicht nur aus dem Blick, sondern werden bereits im operativen Vorfeld faktisch suspendiert. Drittens: Erklärt werden muss, warum zeitgenössische jüdische Autoren das Proselytentauchbad ignorieren oder nicht zu kennen scheinen. Ihr Schweigen wäre merkwürdig und bliebe ein Rätsel, sollte es in ihrer Gegenwart bereits gängige Praxis gewesen sein[26]. Folgt man dieser Argumentation, hat das Tauchbad als ein zur Beschneidung hinzutretender ritueller Akt im Konversionsgeschehen erst in der formativen Phase nach 70 n.Chr. die ihm in Mischna und Talmud beigelegte – und durchaus kontrovers diskutierte – Bedeutung erlangt.

Die hier sichtbar werdenden positionellen Differenzen lassen sich auf keinen gemeinsamen Nenner bringen. Sie reflektieren eine gegensätzliche Bewertung des vorhandenen Quellenmaterials und seiner Validität als Ausgangs- und Orientierungspunkt für das rekonstruktive Nachzeichnen historischer Prozesse. Je nach Perspektive und Einschätzung ihrer Interpreten werden sie in einen chronologischen Rahmen eingespannt, dessen Eckdaten zum Teil erheblich voneinander abweichen. Darin erschöpft sich der Dissens aber nicht. Kaum weniger strittig sind die (sozial-)anthropologischen und religiösen Implikationen sowie die normative Geltung des Proselytentauchbads. Zudem wird sein religionsgeschichtliches Profil im Kontext vergleichbarer kultischer Waschungen sehr unterschiedlich bestimmt.

Angesichts der von Kontradiktionen geprägten Debatte, in der die Kritik an vormals konsensfähig erscheinenden Positionen wächst, ohne dass sie schon durchschlagende Wirkung erzielt und zu einer Bereinigung der unübersichtlichen Gesprächslage geführt hätte, ist es weder sinnvoll noch möglich, den diskursiven Prozess auch nur grob nachzuzeichnen und seinen bisherigen Ertrag zu sondieren. Vielmehr sollen im Folgenden die wichtigsten der in Frage kommenden Texte noch einmal vorgestellt und daraufhin geprüft werden, ob und inwieweit sie im Zusammenhang der Diskussion über das Alter und die

---

„Origins", 158–171. Vgl. A. OEPKE, Art. „βάπτω κτλ.", 535; M. BARTH, *Die Taufe – ein Sakrament?*, 14f.

26 Der Einwand, dieses Argument „would be valid only if it could be shown that references to proselyte baptism is absent from passages where it should have appeared, SCHÜRER, *History* 3/1, 174 Anm. 89, ist berechtigt. Nur lässt sich zeigen, dass dies in der Tat der Fall ist.

spezifische Funktion des Proselytentauchbads argumentativ belastbar sind. Diese schon aus Raumgründen erforderliche Konzentration auf das Wesentliche nötigt von vornherein zum Verzicht. Sie bringt es mit sich, dass nicht alle mit dem Thema verbundenen Problemaspekte namhaft gemacht, geschweige denn erörtert werden können.

3. Zur Terminologie

Der im Deutschen geläufige und bis heute verwendete Ausdruck „Proselytentaufe" ist wie sein englisches und französisches Pendant „proselyte baptism / baptême des prosélytes" ungeeignet, den gemeinten Sachverhalt adäquat zur Sprache zu bringen. Wir haben es jeweils mit einem Zuschreibungsbegriff zu tun, der eine bestimmte Perspektive verrät und sich als *interpretatio christiana* zu erkennen gibt. Durch den bewusst oder unbewusst hergestellten Bezug auf die Taufe werden Vorstellungen evoziert, die die nötige Trennschärfe vermissen lassen und sich damit als kontraproduktiv erweisen. Der im rabbinischen Judentum durchweg als טבילה[27] bezeichnete rituelle Akt hat weder sakramentalen Charakter noch ist er in irgend einer Weise soteriologisch konnotiert. Das in der LXX als Wiedergabe der Wurzel טבל gebrauchte Verb βάπτειν[28] – nur in 4Reg 5,14 wird für טבל das durch die Endung -ιζ intensivierte βαπτίζειν eingesetzt[29] – bedeutet wie sein hebräisches Äquivalent „(ein-, unter-)tauchen, baden" (lat. *tingere*), βαπτίζειν kausativ „eintauchen machen" (lat. *mergere*). Um dem Missverständnis vorzubeugen, mit der terminologischen Identifikation von „Proselytentaufe" und „Taufe" sei auch eine inhaltliche Nähe gegeben, empfiehlt es sich, einen neutralen Begriff zu wählen und von „Proselytentauchbad" bzw. „proselyte immersion" zu sprechen.

4. Proselytentauchbad – Johannestaufe – christliche Taufe

In der Diskussion um den Ursprung der christlichen Taufe spielt das Proselytentauchbad insofern eine gewichtige Rolle, als häufig angenommen wird, es habe „wenigstens hinsichtlich der äußeren Form" seines Vollzugs Johannes dem

---

27 Im Alten Testament fehlt dieser Begriff. Zu beachten ist, dass er in Mischna, Talmud und Midrasch jede Art von rituellem Bad bezeichnet und טבל dessen rituellen Vollzug, vgl. mYom 3,2–4.6; bBer 2b; bQid 62b; bSot 12b; bMeg 13a; WaR 1,3 [ed. MIRKIN 12] u.ö.

28 Ex 12,22; Lev 4,6.17; 9,9; 14,6.16.51; Num 19,18; Dtn 33,24; Jos 3,15; Ruth 2,14; I Reg 14,27; IV Reg 8,15; Hi 9,31.

29 Hier begegnet das mediale ἐβαπτίσατο: Naeman „tauchte sich selbst unter". Vgl. ferner Sir 34,25; Jdt 12,7 (jeweils auf das einfache rituelle Reinigungsbad bezogen). In Jes 21,4 steht βαπτίζειν für טבל. Zu den außerbiblischen Belegen und ihrem semantischen Gehalt vgl. S. LÉGASSE, *Naissance du baptême*, 16f., und jetzt ausführlich E. FERGUSON, *Baptism*, 38–59.

Täufer „als Vorbild gedient"[30]. Johannes habe den für heidnische Konvertiten entwickelten Ritus adaptiert und für seine jüdischen Zeitgenossen inhaltlich neu bestimmt, indem er sie mit jenen auf eine Stufe stellte und ihnen so ihr kollektives Versagen als Gottesvolk vor Augen hielt[31]. Zur Begründung werden vier signifikante Merkmale angeführt, die das Proselytentauchbad mit der von Johannes gespendeten Taufe gemeinsam habe: Beide seien einmalig und unwiederholbar. Beide unterschieden sich von sämtlichen anderen jüdischen Tauchbädern dadurch, dass sie a) nicht „für sich allein"[32] und b) durch Untertauchen vollzogen wurden. Ferner sei mit beiden, wiederum in singulärer Weise, der Gedanke der Sündenvergebung verbunden. Doch reichen die wirklichen oder vermeintlichen Konvergenzen als Differenzkriterium nicht aus, um den postulierten Sonderstatus des Proselytentauchbads im Kontext frühjüdischer Ganzkörperwaschungen zu begründen.

In seiner äußeren Form unterschied es sich in nichts von ihnen. Das im Zusammenhang des Übertritts geforderte Untertauchen des ganzen Körpers (bYev 46b; Gerim 1,5, vgl. mMiq 1,7; 2,1) war auch vor dem Betreten des Tempels verbindlich[33]. In gleicher Weise problematisch ist die Behauptung, das Proselytentauchbad habe wesentlich die Funktion gehabt, die zuvor begangenen Sünden des Konvertiten abzuwaschen. Dabei wird zweierlei stillschweigend vorausgesetzt: 1) Das dergestalt symbolisch aufgeladene Tauchbad hat von Beginn an, d.h. nach diesem Verständnis seit dem 1. vorchristlichen Jahrhundert, neben der Beschneidung eine von ihr qualitativ zu unterscheidende eigenständige Bedeutung im Kontext des Aufnahmeritus gehabt[34]. 2) Johannes hat mit seiner

---

30 Bill. I, 112. Ihm folgen LEIPOLDT, *Die urchristliche Taufe*, 26–28; JEREMIAS, „Johannestaufe", 320; IDEM, „Proselytentaufe", 419.421; CULLMANN, *Tauflehre*, 58; BÖCHER, „Wasser und Geist", 63. In die gleiche Richtung tendieren DELORME, „Practice of Baptism", 31, und OEPKE, Art. „βάπτω κτλ.", 533.535. Dagegen hatte bereits SCHNECKENBURGER, eingewandt, dies könne aus zeitlichen Gründen lediglich für die „gewöhnlichen Lustrationen" gelten, *Proselytentaufe*, 185f. In diesem Sinne auch W. MICHAELIS, „Proselytentaufe", 19.

31 Vgl. PUSEY/HURT, „Proselyte Baptism", 143.

32 JEREMIAS, „Proselytentaufe", 427. Das Proselytentauchbad erfordert die Anwesenheit von Zeugen, den „Vätern des Tauchbads" (bYev 47a, vgl. bYev 46b.47b; bQid 62b und Gerim 1,5.8 [auf dem Hintergrund von Dtn 19,15]), die Johannestaufe die aktive Beteiligung des Täufers, Mk 1,5 par. Mt 3,6: ἐβαπτίζοντο ὑπ' αὐτοῦ, vgl. Mt 3,13.

33 Jub 21,16; TestLev 9,11; Philo, *SpecLeg* 1,261.269; 3,89.205; Josephus, *Bell* 4,205; 5,227; *Ant* 8,96; 12,145; *Ap* 2,103f. (vgl. *Ant* 3,318f); mYom 3,3, vgl. mHag 2,5f.; mMid 2,2; tNeg 8,9 [ed. ZUCKERMANDEL 628]. Näheres bei FINKELSTEIN, „Baptism", 203f.; SANDERS, *Judaism. Practice and Belief*, 134f. Der archäologische Befund bestätigt diese Angaben. Bei Ausgrabungen an der Süd- und Westseite des Tempelbergs wurden zahlreiche Tauchbecken (Miqwaot) zutage gefördert, die der kultischen Reinigung dienten. Sie alle datieren in die Zeit vor 70 n.Chr., E. REGEV, „Ritual Baths", 194–204 (vgl. hierzu den Beitrag von SEÁN FREYNE, „Jewish Immersion and Christian Baptism", 221–253 in der vorliegenden Publikation).

34 Vgl. exemplarisch Bill. I, 105: „[D]as Tauchbad als ein selbständiger Akt, als der Hauptakt bei der Konversion ... mußte ... aus seiner bisherigen Verbindung mit der Beschneidung gelöst, d.h. vor allem zeitlich von dieser getrennt werden".

Taufe „von dem jüdischen Doppelakt der Aufnahme der Proselyten nur den einen Teil ... übernommen" und mit ihm den am Tauchbad haftenden Gedanken der Sündenbeseitigung[35]. Die Schwierigkeit ist nur, dass sich in vortannaitischer Zeit kein zweifelsfreier Beleg für das so bestimmte *Proselyten*tauchbad findet. Dessen Sünden tilgende Funktion ergibt sich für Joachim Jeremias aus der Kombination mehrerer Stellen aus Talmud und Midrasch, unter denen er bYev 48a und QohR 1,8 besonders stark gewichtet[36]. Allerdings bezieht sich der in bYev 48a zitierte Ausspruch des R. Jose (um 150 n.Chr.): „Ein Proselyt, der zum Judentum übergetreten ist, gleicht einem (eben) geborenen Kind"[37] gar nicht auf das Proselytentauchbad. Von ihm ist nicht einmal entfernt die Rede. Zudem handelt es sich um einen Rechtssatz. Er besagt: Für Proselyten existiert das vorkonversionelle Leben nicht mehr. Ihre vormaligen Gebotsübertretungen werden ihnen daher nicht angerechnet und bleiben ungestraft. Weder der Wortlaut noch der unmittelbare Kontext legen es nahe, den Vergleich im religiösen Sinne, d.h. im Sinne einer Neuschöpfung zu interpretieren und in einen Zusammenhang mit dem Proselytentauchbad zu bringen[38].

Kritisch ist auch der Verweis auf QohR 1,8 zu beurteilen. Selbst wenn man die Datierungsproblematik einmal ausklammert[39] und mit der Möglichkeit rechnet, dass der Midrasch alte Überlieferung – vielleicht sogar aus tannaitischer Zeit – enthält, lässt sich der fraglichen Stelle nicht entnehmen, bei dem ersten Tauchbad sei ein Sündenbekenntnis gesprochen worden. Denn die R. Jehoschua um Aufnahme bittende Frau wird *vor* dem Übertritt – wiederum ist von einem Tauchbad keine Rede, weder im engeren noch im weiteren Kontext – aufgefordert, ihre Sünden zu bekennen. Überdies wird nicht gesagt, sie seien ihr vergeben worden.

---

35 CULLMANN, *Tauflehre*, 6.57 (Zitat 57).
36 JEREMIAS, *Kindertaufe*, 38f.40 (mit Anm. 7). Vor ihm hatte sich schon DAUBE, *Rabbinic Judaism*, 112f., auf den Midrasch bezogen. Ein weiterer von JEREMIAS genannter Text ist yBik 3,3 [65d]. Abgesehen davon, dass er vereinzelt dasteht und zudem spät datiert, referiert er nicht auf das Tauchbad, sondern hat allgemein die Bekehrung zum Judentum im Blick. Die auch von FERGUSON, *Baptism*, 80, hergestellte Verbindung zwischen „immersion" und „forgiveness of sins" gibt die Stelle gerade nicht her.
37 Vgl. bYev 22a.62a.97b; bBekh 47a.
38 So aber JEREMIAS, „Proselytentaufe", 426; IDEM, *Kindertaufe*, 39. Zur berechtigten Kritik vgl. LEIPOLDT, *Die urchristliche Taufe*, 22f.; MICHAELIS, „Johannestaufe", 112–115; K. G. KUHN/H. STEGEMANN, Art. „Proselyten", 1276; DELORME, „Practice of Baptism", 32; BEASLEY-MURRAY, *Taufe*, 38–40 (Anm. 49); D. SMITH, „Proselyte Baptism", 24f.; PUSEY/HURT, „Proselyte Baptism", 144. Zutreffend formuliert G. G. PORTON, *Stranger*, 166: „[M]isdeeds which the converts performed while they were gentiles do not have any importance after they become members of the Israelite community".
39 Die Endredaktion der Makroform dürfte erst im 8. Jahrhundert erfolgt sein. QohR 5,5 setzt den außerkanonischen Mischnatraktat Avoth voraus, 5,9 die sog. kleinen Traktate Gerim, ʿAbadim, Tzitzit, Tephillin und Mezuza.

Nur Qumran bildet in dieser Hinsicht eine Ausnahme, ohne dass freilich Proselyten in den Blick geraten. Dort wurde den Waschungen, die durch eigenes Untertauchen erfolgten (Josephus, *Bell* 2,129), über ihre Funktion zur Erlangung kultischer Reinheit hinaus auch sühnende Wirkung zugeschrieben, wie 1QS 3,4–12 (vgl. 4QS^a [4Q255] 2,1–4; 4QS^c [4Q257] 1 II 9–13) exemplarisch zu erkennen gibt. Allerdings stellt der Abschnitt klar, dass Sühne und Heiligung nicht von kultischen Reinigungsriten abhängen. Sie sind ausschließlich ein Werk des heiligen Geistes, den Gott der Gemeinde verliehen hat: [Z. 6] „ ... durch den Geist des wahrhaftigen Rates Gottes werden die Wege eines Mannes entsühnt, alle [Z. 7] seine Sünden, ... und durch den heiligen Geist (, der) der Einung in seiner Wahrheit (gegeben ist,) wird er [sc. der Untertauchende] gereinigt von allen [Z. 8] seinen Sünden" (vgl. 1QS 4,21)[40]. Die Reinigung von Sünden bildet demnach die Voraussetzung zur Teilnahme am Tauchbad und ist nicht die effektive Folge seines Vollzugs (1QS 5,13f). „Admission to the regular ablutions ... symbolized the conviction, that those admitted were pure and free of sin and were living in a holy manner and thus widely separated from sinful and impure people"[41].

Der markante Unterschied zwischen Johannestaufe und טבילה – Empfang der Taufe durch Johannes dort, Selbsttauchung hier; innerer Konnex von Taufe und Sündenvergebung bei Johannes, hingegen ist dem Tauchbad die gedankliche Verbindung von kultischer Reinheit und Entsühnung fremd – macht es von vornherein schwierig, beide Handlungen analog zu verstehen oder gar den Täuferritus vom Proselytentauchbad abzuleiten. Abgesehen von dieser häufig marginalisierten Differenz erscheint ihre komplementäre Zuordnung auch insofern problematisch, als sie dem Verdacht unterliegt, in einer das Ergebnis präjudizierenden Vorurteilsstruktur befangen zu sein, die sich letztlich als dysfunktional erweist. Der primär am phänomenologisch Fassbaren orientierte Vergleich impliziert nämlich unter der Hand ein chronologisches Urteil. Er ist erkennbar von dem Interesse geleitet, die Johannestaufe in dem Proselytentauchbad präfiguriert zu sehen, was zugleich heißt, dass sie ihm zeitlich nachgeordnet wird und sein höheres Alter bestätigen soll. Methodisch ist es

---

[40] Vgl. J. GNILKA, „Tauchbäder", 195f.; J. ERNST, *Johannes der Täufer*, 327; AVEMARIE, „Johannestaufe", 401–404; H. LICHTENBERGER/B. JANOWSKI, „Enderwartung und Reinheitsidee", 87–89. Von einem „Messianic baptism through the spirit of holiness", so DELORME, „Practice of Baptism", 45, sollte man aber nicht sprechen.

[41] YARBRO COLLINS, „Origin", 30f. In ihrer Reinigungs- und Sühnefunktion wird sich die beim Eintritt in den Jachad von den Novizen geforderte Waschung (vgl. Josephus, *Bell* 2,138) nicht von den danach regelmäßig wiederholten Waschungen (*Bell* 2,129), die z.T. täglich mehrfach erfolgten, unterschieden haben, auch wenn sie in gewisser Weise einen initiatorischen Akt darstellte und insofern einmalig war, O. BETZ, „Proselytentaufe", 25–28; AVEMARIE, „Johannestaufe", 405. Differenzkriterium ist ihr besonderer Anlass – der vor der ganzen „Einung Gottes" (יחד אל, 1QS 1,12, vgl. 1QM 4,10; 1QSa 1,25) stattfindende Übertritt in die Sphäre der Reinheit und Vollkommenheit, nicht ihre sühnende Kraft für das neue Mitglied.

jedoch unzulässig, von punktuellen Übereinstimmungen auf ein – wenngleich nur indirekt vermitteltes – Interdependenzverhältnis im Sinne der historischen Priorität des Proselytentauchbads zu schließen, zumal ihnen eine Reihe fundamentaler Differenzen entgegenstehen. Zu den gravierendsten gehören: *Erstens*: Das Proselytentauchbad beschränkt sich *per definitionem* auf Heiden. Die von Johannes angebotene Taufe ist vor allem oder gar ausschließlich an Juden adressiert (Q 3,7f.; Mk 1,5; Mt 3,5; Josephus, *Ant* 18,118). *Zweitens*: Der mit der Johannestaufe verbundene eschatologische Aspekt (Q 3,9,17f.; Mk 1,7f., vgl. Apg 13,24) spielt bei dem Proselytentauchbad keine Rolle[42]. *Drittens*: Während die Johannestaufe eine deutliche Distanz zum Tempelkult zeigt[43], ist das Proselytentauchbad eng auf die Darbringung des Opfers bezogen. Jedenfalls in der Theorie[44]. Denn das Opfer soll dargebracht werden, wenn der Tempel wieder aufgebaut sein wird[45]. Zwei weitere Aspekte, die häufig unberücksichtigt bleiben, kommen hinzu. Hinter Johannes steht keine Gemeinde, in die hinein er tauft. Ein initiatorischer Akt, der eine Grenzüberschreitung impliziert, ist die Wassertaufe nicht. Ferner zielt seine Umkehrpredigt nicht auf eine Bekehrung bzw. einen Übertritt. Wer sich zum Zeichen der Umkehr von Johannes taufen lässt, erhält keinen neuen Status – weder im rechtlichen noch im religiösen Sinne –, sondern wird restituiert. Er gewinnt zurück, was er aus Sicht des Täufers verloren hat: Nachkomme Abrahams zu sein, dem die feste Zusage gilt, im eschatologischen Gericht bestehen zu können.

---

42 Er darf nicht aus Sib 4,165 eingetragen werden, gegen OEPKE, Art. „βάπτω κτλ.", 533.535. Denn es dürfte so gut wie ausgeschlossen sein, dass der fragliche Passus 4,162–169 auf das Proselytentauchbad referiert (s.u. § 5.2.). In seiner Notiz über Johannes (*Ant* 18,116–119) spart Josephus das vom Täufer hergestellte Junktim zwischen Taufe und Sündenvergebung und dann konsequenterweise auch dessen eschatologischen Horizont aus. Hinter dieser wohl bewussten Eliminierung des Eschatologischen könnte die Absicht stecken, Johannes von der zelotischen Bewegung und ihren apokalyptisch grundierten theokratischen Vorstellungen zu distanzieren. Auf den Adressatenbezug hebt besonders YARBRO COLLINS, „Origins", 29, ab: Im Blick auf seine aufgeklärte und skeptische heidnische Leserschaft habe Josephus das eschatologische Moment zugunsten eines „rationalizing understanding of John's teaching" unterschlagen.

43 Dafür sprechen das Auftreten des Täufers in der Wüste abseits von Jerusalem und die Taufe im Jordan. Bei G. BARTH, *Taufe*, 26f., bleibt dieser wichtige Aspekt unterbestimmt. Zurückhaltender urteilt AVEMARIE, „Johannestaufe", 407: Man könne allenfalls sagen, dass Johannes „dem Tempelkult … indifferent gegenüberstand". Eine andere Frage ist, ob ein wenn auch indirekter Zusammenhang mit den im Alten Testament vorgeschriebenen priesterlichen Waschungen (Ex 30,17–21; Lev 8; Ps 51,9–13; Ez 36, 25–28 u.ö.) besteht.

44 Vgl. oben die Anm. 17 und 18.

45 Den symbolischen Charakter der Ersatzleistung (ein Viertel Silberdenar) unterstreicht ySheq 8,6 [51b]. Um nicht der Versuchung zu erliegen, die zum Kauf des Opfers vorgesehenen Gelder zwischenzeitlich für profane Zwecke zu verwenden, erklärt R. Shim'on b. Jochai (um 150 n.Chr.) das Opfer für unnötig (bKer 9a; Gerim 2,5, vgl. bRHSh 31b; tSheq 3,22 [ed. ZUCKERMANDEL 179]; SifZ 283 zu Num 15,15). An der zuerst genannten Stelle beruft er sich dabei auf R. Jochanan b. Zakkai (gest. um 80 n.Chr.), der es aus diesem Grund abgeschafft habe. Vielleicht auch deshalb ist R. Aqiba (gest. 135 n.Chr.) der Ansicht, nur die Beschneidung und das Tauchbad seien für einen Proselyten erforderlich, bYev 71a.

Fazit: Die wenigen und zudem recht unspezifischen Berührungspunkte zwischen beiden Riten (Untertauchen im Wasser, Einmaligkeit[46]) reichen nicht aus, um eine über äußerliche Gemeinsamkeiten hinausgehende Verbindung zwischen der Johannestaufe und dem Proselytentauchbad herstellen zu können[47]. „[T]he evidence for its practice before and at the time of John is inconclusive"[48].

5. Die Quellen

Das Quellenmaterial ist überschaubar. Zunächst ist festzustellen: Keine alttestamentliche Schrift bezeugt das Proselytentauchbad[49]. Gleiches gilt für die zwischentestamentliche Literatur (Apokryphen, Pseudepigraphen), Philo und Josephus[50]. Selbst dort, wo Veranlassung bestanden hätte, neben der Beschneidung auf das Tauchbad als weitere *nota Iudaica* einzugehen (vgl. Jdt 14,10 [Achior]; Josephus, *Ant* 13,257f.319; 18,81f.; 20,17–48[51]), bleibt es unerwähnt[52]. Hält man

---

46 In Bezug auf Johannes bestritten von B. CHILTON, „John the Purifier", 260. Doch ist zu beachten, dass nicht nur die neutestamentlichen Texte im Blick auf die Johannestaufe stets den Singular gebrauchen (βάπτισμα), sondern auch Josephus, *Ant* 18,117 (βαπτισμός, βάπτισις). Damit ist freilich nicht behauptet, die von Johannes Getauften hätten sich später keinen rituellen Waschungen mehr unterzogen. Aufgrund seiner intiatorischen und juridischen Funktion ist auch das Proselytentauchbad unwiederholbar.

47 Bezeichnenderweise erwähnt Tertullian in *De bapt.* 10 das Proselytentauchbad nicht, obwohl er dort eigens auf die Johannestaufe und ihren Ursprung zu sprechen kommt.

48 TAYLOR, *The Immerser*, 69.

49 Obwohl Ruth, eine Moabiterin (Ruth 1,4), vom Verfasser des gleichnamigen Buchs zur Urgroßmutter Davids gemacht wird (4,13–20), wird sie allein durch ihre Heirat mit dem Judäer Boas zur rechtmäßigen Ahnfrau.

50 JEREMIAS, „Proselytentaufe", 425 Anm. 30, macht aus der Not eine Tugend, indem er „[d]as Schweigen des Philo und des Josephus … als Zufall" bewertet. Allein der Umfang des Textmaterials lässt daran zweifeln.

51 Die in claudischer Zeit (Tac. *ann.* XII 13,1; 14,1) erfolgte Konversion des Herrscherhauses von Adiabene, der späteren römischen Provinz Assyria, auf das Josephus mit sichtlichem Stolz mehrfach verweist (*Bell* 520; 4,567; 5,55.147; 6,252.355f), war nicht zuletzt politisch motiviert. Das schließt natürlich persönliche Beweggründe nicht aus, vgl. SCHIFFMAN, „Conversion", 293–312; I. BROER, „Konversion", 156–162.

52 Vgl. ferner Josephus, *Bell* 7,45; Iuv. 14,99. Wenigstens anmerkungsweise sei auch an Justin, *Dial. c. Tryphone* 13,1–14,7; 18,2; 19,2 und 29,1 erinnert. Hier wird im Zusammenhang der Taufe kräftig gegen die jüdischen Tauchbäder polemisiert und ihre Nutzlosigkeit betont. Das mit der Taufe strukturell vergleichbare und phänomenologisch ihr entsprechende Proselytentauchbad wird dabei nicht einmal erwähnt (gegen JEREMIAS, „Proselytentaufe", 425 Anm. 30, für den 29,2 darauf anspielt), gerade auch nicht in 19,2. Dort wird allein die Beschneidung mit der „Waschung, die das Leben gibt" (τὸ βάπτισμα τοῦτο τὸ τῆς ζωῆς ἐστι), kontrastiert. Nur durch sie (sc. die Beschneidung) unterscheiden sich die Juden von allen anderen Menschen (16,3). In 23,3f. ist zwar von potentiellen Proselyten und ihrer Beschneidung die Rede (vgl. 24,1; 80,1; 122.1.3–5; 123,1f), darüber hinaus von der Feier des Sabbats, von Festen und vom Opfer. Aber das Tauchbad fehlt in dieser Liste jüdischer Spezifika. Das ist umso bemerkenswerter, als in 122,5 jüdischen Proselyten *christliche* Proselyten („wir Heiden") gegenübergestellt werden, bei

sich an den Grundsatz, als *argumentum e silentio* tauge dieser Negativbefund nur dann, wenn sich zeigen lasse, „that reference to proselyte baptism is absent from passages where it should have appeared"[53], sprechen die Leerstellen, vorsichtig formuliert, eher gegen als für eine Frühdatierung.

Die neutestamentlichen Schriften bieten das gleiche Bild. Obwohl die überwiegende Mehrheit ihrer Verfasser einen jüdischen bzw. judenchristlichen Hintergrund hat, scheinen sie das Proselytentauchbad nicht zu kennen. Im Kolosserbrief wird der christlichen Taufe bezeichnenderweise die „mit Händen vorgenommene Beschneidung" gegenübergestellt (Kol 2,11), nicht jedoch, wie andernfalls zu erwarten wäre, das besser zur Taufe passende Tauchbad. Stets ist es die Beschneidung, die pars pro toto für das ἰουδαΐζειν (Gal 2,14, vgl. 1,14) steht[54].

Hinsichtlich der rabbinischen Literatur hat nach wie vor Gültigkeit, was George F. Moore bereits vor gut achtzig Jahren konstatierte: „The Origin of the requirement of baptism is not known"[55]. Mehr noch: „All the references are disappointing for one trying to prove the antiquity and universality of the proselyte water rite"[56]. Kein einziger Text gibt Auskunft über das Alter, den ursprünglichen Sinn und die älteste Form des Proselytentauchbads. Nirgends findet sich eine Andeutung, die es uns erlaubte, seine Herkunft und Geschichte zu erhellen[57]. Mindestens bis zum Beginn der formativen Periode des Judentums, d.h. seiner zwischen 70 und ca. 100 n.Chr. erfolgten Neukonstitution in Jabne, fehlen überzeugende Indizien, dass Übertrittswillige – sofern männlichen Geschlechts – außer der Beschneidung, die unter Umständen sogar ein Nichtjude

---

denen die Taufe die Zugehörigkeit zur christlichen Gemeinde markiert. Dem entspricht, dass 23,5 die Unmöglichkeit der Beschneidung für Frauen festhält, ohne dass jedoch auch nur angedeutet wird, es habe für sie einen Ersatzritus gegeben. In diesem Zusammenhang lohnt auch ein Seitenblick auf Tertullian. In *De bapt.* 15 ist der gleiche Negativbefund zu verzeichnen. Mit der Taufe in Bezug gesetzt werden einzig die täglichen jüdischen Waschungen: *Semel ergo lavacrum inimus, semel delicta abluuntur, quia ea iterari non oportet. Ceterum Israel [Judaeus] cotidie lavat, quia cotidie inquinatur. Quod ne in nobis quoque factitaretur, propterea de uno lavacro definitum est* [„Nur einmal also steigen wir ins Taufbad, nur einmal werden die Sünden abgewaschen, da man sie nicht wiederum begehen darf. Dagegen vollzieht Israel täglich (rituelle) Waschungen, da es sich täglich verunreinigt. Damit dies nicht auch bei uns dauernd geschehe, darum wurde für das einmalige Taufbad die Bestimmung getroffen"] (15,3).

53 SCHÜRER, *History* 3/1, 174 Anm. 89.
54 Vgl. Gal 2,3.8.12; 5,3.6; 6,12; Phil 3,2f.5; Eph 2,11; Tit 1,10, ferner Apg 10,45; 11,2; 15,1.5; 21,21 u.ö. Bestätigt wird dies durch Josephus, *Bell* 2,454. Dort verspricht der um sein Leben bangende römische Offizier Metilius „Jude zu werden und selbst die Beschneidung auf sich zu nehmen (καὶ μέχρι περιτομῆς ἰουδαΐσειν)". Ein Tauchbad scheint nicht notwendig zu sein.
55 MOORE, *Judaism I*, 332.
56 PUSEY/HURT, „Proselyte Baptism", 142.
57 Zur Recht betont von KUHN/STEGEMANN, Art. „Proselyten", 1274.

vornehmen konnte (bMen 42a; bAZ 27a; Josephus, *Ant* 20,46)[58], weitere rituelle Handlungen zu vollziehen hatten. Kein aus dem Traditionsreservoir der vortannaitischen Zeit schöpfender Text kommt auf die טבילה und das Opfer (הרציית [קרבן]) im Zusammenhang des Konversionsprozesses zu sprechen. Nirgends werden sie verpflichtend gemacht. Wir hören nichts von einer den Übertritt begleitenden oder seine Rechtmäßigkeit beglaubigenden Instanz. Schloss sich eine Frau dem Judentum an, gab es keine förmlich geregelte Prozedur, die sie zu durchlaufen hatte. Daher fiel es schwer, sie von einer Gottesfürchtigen zu unterscheiden[59]. Der vermutlich um die Zeitenwende, vielleicht auch etwas später entstandene jüdisch-hellenistische Roman „Joseph und Aseneth", in dessen Mittelpunkt die Bekehrung der Götzen verehrenden Priestertochter Aseneth zum jüdischen Glauben steht, berichtet nichts von einem Tauchbad seiner Protagonistin. Das Schweigen ist in diesem Fall durchaus beredt.

Auf drei kontrovers diskutierte außerrabbinische Texte gehe ich etwas ausführlicher ein. Ihre Relevanz ergibt sich aus dem hohen Stellenwert, der ihnen zugeschrieben wird. Besonders aus Sicht der älteren Forschung, die bis heute nachwirkt, stützen sie eine frühe Datierung des Proselytentauchbads.

5.1. TestLev 14,6

ἐν πλεονεξίᾳ τὰς ἐντολὰς τοῦ κυρίου διδάξητε, τὰς ὑπάνδρους βεβηλώσητε [καὶ παρθένους Ἰερουσαλὴμ μιανεῖτε], καὶ πόρναις καὶ μοιχαλίσι συναφθήσεσθε, θυγατέρας ἐθνῶν λήψεσθε εἰς γυναῖκας [**καθαρίζοντες αὐτὰς καθαρισμῷ παρανόμῳ**], καὶ γενήσεται ἡ μίξις ὑμῶν Σόδομα καὶ Γόμορρα [ἐν ἀσεβείᾳ] (ed. DE JONGE, PVTG I, 19).

So werdet ihr in Gewinnsucht die Gesetze des Herrn lehren. Verheiratete Töchter werdet ihr schänden [und die Jungfrauen Jerusalems werdet ihr beflecken], mit Huren und Ehebrecherinnen werdet ihr euch verbinden, (ja sogar) Töchter aus den Völkern werdet ihr zu Frauen nehmen [**sie reinigend mit einer ungesetzlichen Reinigung**]. Und (dadurch) wird eure Vermischung wie (in) Sodom und Gomorra sein [in Gottlosigkeit] (Übers. BECKER, JSHRZ III/1, 57).

Für Joachim Jeremias liefert TestLev 14,6 „den bisher vermißten direkten Beleg für die Übung der Proselytentaufe in vorchristlicher Zeit"[60]. Ob es sich tatsäch-

---

58 Die Haltung der Rabbinen in dieser Frage war uneinheitlich, bAZ 26b–27a; yYev 8,1 [9a]; tAZ 3,12f. [ed. ZUCKERMANDEL 464]. Entsprechend strittig wurde diskutiert, ob der Beschneidung *ex opere operato* Effizienz zuzuschreiben sei. Vor das gleiche Problem stellte das Tauchbad, vgl. yQid 3,13 [64d]; bYev 45b einerseits und bYev 47a–b andererseits.

59 Das den Sachverhalt klärende matrilineare Prinzip, wonach das Kind einer jüdischen Mutter, sei sie eine geborene Jüdin oder Proselytin, jüdisch ist (wenngleich bei einer unerlaubten Verbindung ein *mamzer*), begegnet erst in der Mischna, mQid 3,12; mYev 4,13, vgl. bYev 44b–45b.46a; bAZ 59a; yYev 2,6 [4a] (= BerR 7,2 [ed. THEODOR/ALBECK 51f]). Es ist aber schon in Dtn 7,3 grundgelegt.

60 JEREMIAS, *Kindertaufe*, 33.

lich so verhält, hängt von der Beantwortung zweier Fragen ab: Gehört der vor allem interessierende Passus καθαρίζοντες αὐτὰς καθαρισμῷ παρανόμῳ zum ursprünglichen Wortbestand? Referiert er überhaupt auf das Proselytentauchbad? Innerhalb der griechischen Handschriften, die grob gesagt in die beiden Familien α und β zerfallen[61], wird er nur von β geboten. Während Robert H. Charles u.a. ihren textkritischen Wert geringer einschätzten als den von α, kommen neuere Untersuchungen zu einem günstigeren Urteil. Beide Familien sind aufs Ganze gesehen in etwa gleichwertig[62]. Zudem ist der Annahme von Charles, β lasse sich wie α auf eine hebräische Rezension zurückführen, schon früh widersprochen worden. Sie gilt inzwischen als überholt[63]. Da β auch sonst zu Ergänzungen neigt – im engeren Kontext: ἐν ἀσεβείᾳ (V.6fin.) ist mit ziemlicher Sicherheit sekundär; V. 8 nimmt erneut Motive aus V. 5b und V. 7a auf[64] –, unterliegt der Partizipialsatz dem Verdacht, aus zweiter Hand zu stammen. Seine jüdische Herkunft ist zwar kaum zu bestreiten. Doch bleibt unklar, ob er sich auf das Proselytentauchbad bezieht. Joachim Jeremias datiert das nur fragmentarisch erhaltene *aramäische* TestLev ins zweite vorchristliche Jahrhundert („spätestens"[65]), die griechische Version an das Ende des 1. Jahrhunderts v.Chr. Ihr Verfasser bekämpfe mit der von ihm eingefügten Passage καθαρίζοντες αὐτὰς καθαρισμῷ παρανόμῳ das Tauchbad, weil es die Mischehe begünstige und keinen Anhalt an der Schrift habe[66]. Abgesehen davon, dass das Problem der Mischehe kein Novum war, die semantische Valenz des Begriffs καθαρισμός viel zu unbestimmt ist, um einen ausschließlichen Bezug auf das Proselytentauchbad begründen zu können, und auch dessen später erfolgte Herleitung aus der Schrift seitens der

---

61 Ich bleibe der Einfachheit halber bei dieser Einteilung, auch wenn β zunehmend als Familie aufgelöst wird. Mit J. H. ULRICHSEN, *Grundschrift*, 42, rechne ich zu β alle griechischen Hss., die nicht zu α gehören.

62 J. BECKER, *Untersuchungen*, 16–32.

63 Einen guten Überblick über die mit den TestXII verbundenen textgeschichtlichen, quellen- und literarkritischen Probleme bietet R. A. KUGLER, *The Testaments of the Twelve Patriarchs*, 25–38.

64 Vgl. BECKER, *Untersuchungen*, 33f.303f.

65 JEREMIAS, *Kindertaufe*, 33. Je nachdem, auf welcher Materialbasis die aramäische Fassung rekonstruiert wird (zu ihr BECKER, *Untersuchungen*, 69–81; M. DE JONGE, „The Testament of Levi and 'Aramaic Levi'", 180–190; KUGLER, *The Testaments of the Twelve Patriarchs*, 48–50), wird ihr Umfang sehr unterschiedlich bestimmt. Die in Qumran gefundenen Fragmente (1QLevi ar; 4QLevi a–f ar) helfen in der anstehenden Frage m.E. nicht weiter, obwohl einige von ihnen Entsprechungen zum griechischen TestLev aufweisen, vgl. DE JONGE, „Levi in 'Aramaic Levi' and in the Testament of Levi", 71–89.

66 Zustimmend aufgenommen von KRAUS, *Volk Gottes*, 106. Die von JEREMIAS vertretene Datierung ist nicht frei von vorgängigen Setzungen. Eine frühere Entstehungszeit des TestLev scheidet für ihn schon deshalb aus, weil sie mit der von ihm postulierten Funktion des Proselytentauchbads, die den heidnischen Konvertiten persönlich zugeschriebene Unreinheit zu beseitigen, kollidierte (s.o. unter § 2.). Bei einer zeitlich um einiges späteren Ansetzung entfiele TestLev 14,6 als Beleg für die vorchristliche Existenz des Proselytentauchbads.

um eine biblische Fundierung des Ritus bemühten Rabbinen etwas gekünstelt wirkt[67], räumt Jeremias selbst ein, es handle sich lediglich um eine „Vermutung". Freilich gerät sie bei ihm unter der Hand zur Gewissheit mit der Folge, dass TestLev 14,6 nun als *dictum probans* fungiert und argumentativ belastet wird. Sollte die griechische Fassung jedoch um einiges früher entstanden sein – ihre Datierung reicht bis ins erste Drittel des zweiten vorchristlichen Jahrhunderts[68] –, wäre eine Referenz auf das Proselytentauchbad schon aus zeitlichen Gründen nahezu ausgeschlossen. Rechnet man hingegen mit einem Einschub aus späterer Zeit, in der es bereits in Geltung stand, stellt sich die Frage, warum dem metonymisch als „Reinigung" bezeichneten Tauchbad vorgeworfen wird, gesetzeswidrig zu sein[69]. Angesichts der textkritischen, chronologischen und interpretatorischen Probleme, die sich mit TestLev 14,6 verbinden, erscheint es methodisch nicht vertretbar, dem Vers allzu große Beweislast aufzubürden und ihn für das Proselytentauchbad in Anspruch zu nehmen[70].

5.2. Sib 4,162–169[71]

ἆ μέλεοι, μετάθεσθε, βροτοί, τάδε, μηδὲ πρὸς ὀργὴν / παντοίην ἀγάγητε θεὸν μέγαν, ἀλλὰ μεθέντες / φάσγανα καὶ στοναχὰς ἀνδροκτασίας τε καὶ ὕβρεις / ἐν ποταμοῖς λούσασθε ὅλον δέμας ἀενάοισιν, / χεῖράς τ' ἐκτανύσαντες ἐς αἰθέρα τῶν / πάρος ἔργων / συγγνώμην αἰτεῖσθε καὶ εὐλογίαις ἀσέβειαν / πικρὰν ἱλάσκεσθε· θεὸς δώσει μετάνοιαν / οὐδ' ὀλέσει· παύσει δὲ χόλον πάλιν, ἤνπερ ἅπαντες / εὐσεβίην περίτιμον ἐνὶ φρεσὶν ἀσκήσητε (ed. GEFFCKEN, 100f).

---

67 Vgl. oben Anm. 17.

68 Vgl. H. C. KEE, „Testaments of the Twelve Patriarchs", 777f. Auf die Unsicherheit der Datierung der TestXII („virtually impossible to date") und die daraus resultierende Warnung, den Text überzustrapazieren, macht zu Recht YARBRO COLLINS, „Origin", 34, aufmerksam.

69 Diese Frage stellt zu Recht BEASLEY-MURRAY, *Taufe*, 41f. Eine Nähe zur Reinheitshalacha der Qumrangruppe, insbesondere zu 4QMMT B 75–82, sieht HAYES, *Gentile Impurities*, 83 (mit Anm. 67). Hier wie dort gehe es um das Verbot für Priester, fremde Frauen zu heiraten. Der Verfasser von TestLev 14,6 halte eine solche Verbindung für unerlaubt, weil „all Israel is holy seed, which cannot be mixed with the profane seed of Gentiles – *not even converted Gentiles*" (Kursivierung im Orig.). Zum Datierungsproblem äußert sich HAYES allerdings nicht. Wiederum anders akzentuiert A. HULTGÅRD, *L'eschatologie*, 100: „Sous le rite visé en Levi 14:6 se cache selon toute vraisemblance un élément rituel, peut-être d'origine non-juive, introduit par des prêtres hellénisants dans le contexte des mariages mixtes". Ein Bezug auf das Proselytentauchbad liegt auch für Hultgård nicht vor.

70 Ganz ablehnend z.B. W. BRANDT, *Baptismen*, 90; FINKELSTEIN, „Baptism", 203–205; SMITH, „Proselyte Baptism", 19f.; K. RUDOLPH, *Baptismen*, 12; WEBB, *John the Baptizer*, 125 (mit z.T. unterschiedlicher Begründung).

71 Der Neueinsatz beginnt mit Z. 162 und nicht mit Z. 161, wie gewöhnlich zu lesen ist. Vgl. die Ausgabe von J. GEFFCKEN, *Oracula Sibyllina*, 100, und A. KURFESS, *Sibyllinische Weissagungen*, 120.

> Ihr armseligen Menschen, bereut dies; reizt nicht den großen / Gott zu mancherlei Zorn; legt vielmehr ab eure Schwerter / und laßt ab von dem Jammer, vom Männermord und von dem Hochmut! / Reinigt den ganzen Leib in immerfließendem Wasser! / Streckt eure Hände empor zum Himmel und fleht um Verzeihung / für eure Taten und sühnet mit Lobpreis den bittern / Frevelsinn! Dann wird es Gott reuen; er wird euch nicht schlagen. / Nochmal stillt er den Groll, wenn alle ihr übet im Herzen / frommen und gottesfürchtigen Sinn, der bei allen geehrt ist (Übers. KURFESS, Sibyllinische Weissagungen, 121).

Der Abschnitt ist als Bußpredigt zu charakterisieren. Wie die 4. Sibylle insgesamt, deren Kultkritik gegen Idolatrie polemisiert, richtet er sich nicht speziell an Juden. Angesprochen werden alle Menschen, vornehmlich aber Heiden. Auf der makrotextuellen Ebene sind sie die eigentlichen Adressaten (vgl. Z. 4–30). Diese auf den jüdischen Bearbeiter zurückgehende Perspektive hat wohl mit dazu beigetragen, in der Aufforderung ἐν ποταμοῖς λούσασθε ὅλον δέμας ἀεναοισιν (Z. 165) eine Anspielung auf das Proselytentauchbad zu sehen[72]. Doch bereits die motivliche Verknüpfung von Untertauchen – Bitte um Vergebung (συγγνώμην αἰτεῖσθε [Z. 167]) – sühnender Lobpreis (εὐλογίαις ἀσέβειαν πικρὰν ἰάσασθε [Z. 167f]) steht einem Bezug auf die jüdische Reinigungspraxis und speziell auf das Proselytentauchbad entgegen[73]. Nach seiner Einführung markiert es im Verbund mit der Beschneidung den rechtsgültig vollzogenen Übertritt in die neue Gemeinschaft, hat jedoch keine soteriologische Qualität und bewahrt nicht vor dem göttlichen Zorn. Zudem deutet im Text nichts auf eine Konversion zum Judentum hin[74]. Eher wäre eine Affinität zu qumran-essenischen Vorstellungen denkbar. Dafür könnte das strukturelle Ensemble der verwendeten Motivik sprechen[75]. Für die Qumranfrommen hat das Tauchbad sühnende Wirkung. Sie wird durch den heiligen Geist vermittelt und setzt das unbedingte Einhalten der göttlichen Gebote, d.h. eine Umkehr voraus. An die Stelle des an den Tempel gebundenen Opfers tritt der Lobpreis[76]. Aber aus historischen Gründen erscheint diese Möglichkeit äußerst gering. Nach 68 n.Chr. verlieren sich die Spuren der

---

72 LEIPOLDT, *Die urchristliche Taufe*, 18f.; OEPKE, Art. „βάπτω κτλ.", 533; JEREMIAS, *Kindertaufe*, 40f.; SCHÜRER, *History* 3/1, 174 [F. MILLAR] (anders freilich ibid. 642 [GOODMAN]).

73 Der Einwand von JEREMIAS, „Proselytentaufe", 426 Anm. 35, wegen der Aoristform λούσασθε in Z. 165 müsse an ein einmaliges Bad (d.h. für ihn: an das Proselytentauchbad) gedacht sein, sticht nicht. Denn parallel zu diesem Imp. Aorist steht in den Z. 166 und 167 jeweils der Imp. Präsens αἰτεῖσθε bzw. ἱλάσκεσθε. Offensichtlich wird vom Verfasser zwischen den Tempora nicht scharf unterschieden. Im Übrigen trifft es auch nicht zu, dass der Aorist per se etwas Einmaliges ausdrückt. Vielmehr unterstreicht er im Gegensatz zum durativen Präsens das Momentane, ohne dass Wiederholbarkeit ausgeschlossen ist, vgl. BDR §§ 318.335-337.

74 Zu Recht bemerkt J. J. COLLINS, *Between Athens and Jerusalem*, 167: „[T]here is nothing to suggest that anyone is expected to convert to Judaism ... There is no question of circumcision or of any distinctively Jewish observance".

75 Vgl. B. NOACK, „Sibylline Oracles", 94.96-99; V. NIKIPROWETZKY, „Réflections", 37-58.

76 1QS 9,3-6.26; 10,8.14.22; 11,14f.; 11QPsa (11Q05) 18,8-11 u.ö.

im Wesentlichen auf Judäa sich beschränkenden Qumran-Essener[77]. Die jüdische Redaktion der 4. Sibylle[78] setzt die Zerstörung Jerusalems und des Tempels [Z. 115–118.125–127] sowie den Ausbruch des Vesuvs im Jahre 79 n.Chr. voraus [Z. 130–133]. In Z. 138f. spiegelt sich die Erwartung des Nero redivivus. Außerdem ist nicht von regelmäßigen Waschungen, sondern nur von einem einmaligen Bad die Rede, das vor dem Feuergericht rettet [Z. 165]. Als Alternative kommt am ehesten noch ein Zusammenhang mit Vorstellungen in Betracht, die in (jüdischen) Täuferkreisen gepflegt wurden und sich möglicherweise von Johannes dem Täufer herleiten[79]. Seiner Verkündigung korrespondieren das angeprangerte ethische Fehlverhalten, das Glaube und Gerechtigkeit Hohn spricht [Z. 152–156], sowie die eschatologische Perspektive. Christlicher Einfluss ist zwar nicht a limine auszuschließen. Doch fehlt jeder konkrete Anhalt für einen intendierten Bezug auf die Taufe. In diesem Fall wäre eine „Nennung des Getauftwerdens ‚auf den Namen …'" (εἰς τὸ ὄνομα …)"[80] zu erwarten.

Fazit: Der Abschnitt Sib 4,162–169 scheidet als Beleg für das Proselytentauchbad mit an Sicherheit grenzender Wahrscheinlichkeit aus[81].

5.3. Epiktet, Diss II 9,19–21

τί ἐξαπατᾷς τοὺς πολλούς, τί ὑποκρίνῃ ᾽Ιουδαῖον ὢν ῞Ελλην; οὐχ ὁρᾷς, πῶς ἕκαστος λέγεται ᾽Ιουδαῖος, πῶς Σύρος, πῶς Αἰγύπτιος; καὶ ὅταν τινὰ ἐπαμφοτερίζοντα ἴδωμεν, εἰώθαμεν λέγειν „οὐκ ἔστιν ᾽Ιουδαῖος, ἀλλ᾽ ὑποκρίνεται". ὅταν δ᾽ ἀναλάβῃ τὸ πάθος τὸ τοῦ βεβαμμένου καὶ ᾑρημένου, τότε καὶ ἔστι τῷ ὄντι καὶ καλεῖται ᾽Ιουδαῖος (ed. SCHENKL, 144).

---

77 Trotz der neuerlichen Einwände etwa von Y. HIRSCHFELD, Qumran, und J. ZANGENBERG, „Qumran und Archäologie", 262–306, kann das „klassische" Konvergenzmodell, wonach die Textfunde von der Siedlung Chirbet Qumran und ihren Bewohnern nicht zu trennen sind, immer noch große Plausibilität für sich beanspruchen.

78 Sie wird entweder in Kleinasien, Syrien oder dem Jordantal (DELORME, „Practice of Baptism", 33; COLLINS, „Sibylline Oracles", 382), Ägypten (NIKIPROWETZKY, „Réflections", 58; NOACK, „Sybilline Oracles", 97) oder Rom (H. LICHTENBERGER, „Täufergemeinden", 41) lokalisiert.

79 MICHAELIS, „Johannestaufe", 116f.; DELORME, „Practice of Baptism", 43; SMITH, „Proselyte Baptism", 20f.; LICHTENBERGER, „Täufergemeinden", 40f.; YARBRO COLLINS, „Origin", 30; AVEMARIE, „Johannestaufe", 401 (mit Anm. 49). M. HENGEL schreibt das 4. Buch Anhängern einer antirömisch eingestellten jüdischen Täufergruppe zu, „Anonymität, Pseudepigraphie und ‚literarische Fälschung'", 240. Vgl. auch DONALDSON, Judaism and the Gentiles, 169; COHEN, Beginnings, 222 (mit Anm. 56), und GOODMAN, „Jewish Proselytizing", 97: „[T]his … passage may refer not to a baptism for converts but just to a bath for purification". Hingegen schließt LÉGASSE, Naissance du baptême, 54, einen jüdischen Hintergrund aus. Es handle sich um einen „discours aux païens". Als Analogiefall könnte man auf die – von der Johannestaufe beeinflussten? – Tauchbäder des Wüstenasketen Bannus verweisen (Josephus, Vit 11)

80 LICHTENBERGER, „Täufergemeinden", 40.

81 So auch BRANDT, Baptismen, 87–90; ROWLEY, „Jewish Proselyte Baptism", 228f.; RUDOLPH, Baptisten, 12; NIKIPROWETZKY, „Réflexions", 46f.; SCHÜRER, History 3/1, 642 („probably a baptism of repentance like that provided by John the Baptist"); LÉGASSE, Naissance du baptême, 53f.; COHEN, Beginnings, 222; KRAUS, Volk Gottes, 104f.

Warum betrügst du die Menge? Warum gibst du vor, ein Jude zu sein, während du doch ein Grieche bist? Siehst du nicht, in welchem Sinn jemand Jude, Syrer, Ägypter genannt wird? Und wenn wir jemanden sehen, der zwischen (zwei Religionen) hin und her schwankt, dann sagen wir gewöhnlich: ‚Das ist kein Jude, sondern er stellt sich nur so'. Nimmt er aber die Lebensweise (?) dessen auf sich, der getaucht ist und einen Entschluss gefasst hat, dann ist er in Wahrheit ein Jude und heißt auch so.

Der Kontext: In seiner neunten Rede im 2. Buch erklärt Epiktet Aufgabe und Ziel der (stoischen) Philosophie, wobei er anhand mehrerer Beispiele die bereits vorher (I 9) thematisierten praktischen Konsequenzen der Gottesverwandtschaft des Menschen veranschaulicht. Ihm lediglich zu sagen, wer er ist und was ihn von den naturhaft allein sinnlich veranlagten Tieren unterscheidet, genügt nicht. Seiner Bestimmung als Vernunft begabtes Wesen wird der Mensch erst gerecht, wenn er aus der ihm gegebenen Einsicht, am göttlichen Logos teilzuhaben (I 9,5), die richtigen Schlüsse in Bezug auf sein Handeln zieht und beides, Wissen und Tun, in Einklang bringt. Daran zu erinnern ist den Philosophen aufgetragen. Sie „ermahnen uns, dass wir uns nicht mit dem bloßen Lernen zufrieden geben, sondern auch die Praxis hinzunehmen und dann (das Gelernte) anwenden" (II 9,13). Anders formuliert: Es widerspricht dem philosophischen Ethos, wenn das als wahr und richtig Erkannte die ihm gemäßen Konsequenzen vermissen lässt.

Zur Illustration führt Epiktet in unserem Abschnitt einen Stoiker an, der sich wie ein Jude gibt, ohne es jedoch zu sein. Denn Juden zeichnen sich wie Angehörige anderer Ethnien auch – Syrer oder Ägypter[82] – durch distinkte Merkmale aus, die sie als Mitglieder dieser Volksgruppen ausweisen. Epiktets Unterscheidung eines wirklichen von einem scheinbaren Juden, der nicht die beschwerliche Lebensweise (τὸ πάθος)[83] eines Getauchten (βεβαμμένος) auf sich nimmt, lässt vermuten, dass er mit dem Tauchbad – hier im kultischen Sinne als Reinigungsritus verstanden – eines der jüdischen Identitätsmerkmale kennt. Fraglich ist nur, ob dabei an das *Proselyten*taubad gedacht ist. Das Nebeneinander der beiden Perfektpartizipien βεβαμμένου und ᾑρημένου könnte dafür sprechen. Vor allem dann, wenn man das καί nicht kopulativ, sondern explikativ versteht. Unter dieser Voraussetzung lässt sich zwischen dem Untertauchen und dem Entschluss-Fassen ein sachlicher Zusammenhang herstellen. Im Tauchbad realisiert sich der zuvor gefasste Entschluss, zum Judentum

---

[82] In *Diss.* I 11,12 und 22,4 begegnen neben diesen drei Gruppen noch die Römer. Dass Epiktet Juden nicht mit Christen verwechselt, sondern zwischen beiden zu unterscheiden weiß, zeigt IV 7,6: Christen = Galiläer.

[83] Das Verständnis von τὸ πάθος bereitet seit jeher Schwierigkeiten. Entsprechend divergieren die Übersetzungsversuche. OEPKE, Art. „βάπτω κτλ.", 533, schwankt zwischen „unbequeme Lebensweise" und „Verfolgung", RUDOLPH, Baptisten, 13, übersetzt mit „Sinnesart", M. STERN, *Greek and Latin Authors I*, 543, mit „attitude", DONALDSON, *Judaism and the Gentiles*, 390, mit „attitude of mind" bzw. „experienced condition", LÉGASSE, *Naissance du baptême*, 95, mit „épreuve".

überzutreten, und wird von jedermann wahrnehmbar vollzogen. Übersetzt man jedoch τὸ πάθος mit „Missgeschick" und sieht darin eine euphemistische Umschreibung für die Beschneidung[84], ergibt sich eine andere Interpretationsmöglichkeit. Der Betreffende dokumentiert durch das Eintauchen, dass er bereits beschnitten worden ist und sich der jüdischen Gemeinde angeschlossen hat[85]. Selbst wenn man die erste Lesart favorisiert, besagt das lediglich: Mit dem Tauchbad verbindet Epiktet die Zugehörigkeit zum Judentum. Ob er dabei das Proselytentauchbad vor Augen hat, wie häufig vermutet wird[86], oder ob er sich auf die Aktivität jüdischer Täuferkreise bezieht[87], ist nicht mehr auszumachen und muss offen bleiben. Wie immer man auch entscheidet, in keinem Fall lässt sich unter Berufung auf Epiktet (ca. 50–130 n.Chr.) die These erhärten, das Proselytentauchbad habe bereits zur Zeit des Zweiten Tempels ein konstitutives Element im Aufnahmeverfahren gebildet[88].

5.4. Rabbinische Texte

Die frühjüdische Traditionsliteratur habe ich bisher nur am Rande gestreift. Sie erforderte eine eigene Untersuchung. Da in der jüngeren Vergangenheit mehrere thematisch einschlägige Studien erschienen sind, in denen die Konversionspraxis und mit ihr auch das Proselytentauchbad zum Teil ausführlich behandelt werden, kann ich mich auf eine Problemskizze beschränken. Aus Raumgründen finden nur die Texte aus Mischna, Talmud und Tosefta Berücksichtigung, in denen ein Bezug auf das Proselytentauchbad vorliegt oder vorliegen könnte. Zahlreich sind sie nicht.

---

84 G. POLSTER, „Proselyten", 21 (mit Anm. 1); FERGUSON, Baptism, 78 (mit Anm. 99). POLSTER verweist in diesem Zusammenhang auf Ail. var. 5,19. Dort bezieht sich τὸ πάθος auf die Kriegsverstümmelung des Ameinias. Vgl. auch Josephus, Bell 2,454, wo τὸ πάθος im Sinne von „Verlust" gebraucht wird.

85 Vgl. POLSTER, „Proselyten", 21; KRAUS, Volk Gottes, 106.

86 NOLLAND, „Uncircumcised Proselytes?", 178–182; HULTGÅRD, L'eschatologie, 99; L. H. FELDMAN, Jew and Gentile, 33; STERN, Greek and Latin Authors I, 543f.; GOODMAN, Mission and Conversion, 81; COHEN, Beginnings, 60f.222 (aber: „the statement is not without difficulties", ibid. 222); DONALDSON, Judaism and the Gentiles, 391.

87 So RUDOLPH, Baptisten, 13 (vor allem wegen des Ausdrucks παραβαπτισταί, der ihm „als Hinweis auf sektiererische Strömungen" im zeitgenössischen Judentum gilt), und LICHTENBERGER, „Täufergemeinden", 47. Vielleicht ist diese Alternative zu eng gefasst. Es kann auch ganz allgemein an die jüdischen Tauchbäder gedacht sein.

88 Für unser Thema unergiebig sind die Bemerkungen bei Tertullian, De bapt. 5,5, und Justin, Dial. c. Tryphone 122f. (vgl. oben Anm. 52). Anders etwa TORRANCE, „Proselyte Baptism", 154.

5.4.1. mPes 8,8 (= mEd 5,2)[89]

Ein Leidtragender nehme ein Tauchbad (טובל) und esse [dann] sein Pascha am Abend, jedoch nicht von [anderen] heiligen [Opfern]. Wer hört den Tod eines Angehörigen und wer Gebeine [eines Toten] sich sammelt, nehme ein Tauchbad (טובל) und darf von heiligen [Opfern] essen.
Ein Proselyt (גר), der am Vorabend des Paschafestes Proselyt geworden ist, nehme – sagen die Schammaiten – ein Tauchbad (טובל) und esse sein Pascha am Abend. Die Hilleliten aber sagen: ‚Wer sich von der Vorhaut absondert, gilt wie der, der sich vom Grabe absondert' (Übers. G. BEER).

Wir haben es hier mit dem einzigen Beleg in der Mischna zu tun, in dem ein Tauchbad für Proselyten erwähnt wird. Ihre mögliche Teilnahme am Passamahl ist Gegenstand einer Kontroverse zwischen den Schulen Schammais und Hillels. Diskutiert wird der Grenzfall, ob ein am Passa-Rüsttag zum Judentum Konvertierter noch am selben Abend das Passalamm essen darf[90]. Die Schammaiten beantworten die Frage positiv. Es ist erlaubt, wenn er zuvor das Tauchbad genommen hat. Anders die Hilleliten. Ihre Ablehnung begründen sie mit der in Num 19,11f.16 geforderten siebentägigen Karenzzeit, in der sich der Beschnittene zweimal (am 3. und 7. Tag) mit Wasser reinigen muss, um kultfähig zu sein[91]. Wegen der im Text hergestellten Verbindung von Konversion („Absonderung von der Vorhaut") und Tauchbad (טובל) wird die Waschung oft auf das Proselytentauchbad gedeutet[92]. Shaye J. D. Cohen hat jedoch einleuchtend dargelegt, dass mit dem hier zur Debatte stehenden Tauchbad gar nicht das *Proselyten*tauchbad gemeint ist[93]. Vielmehr geht es, wie ein Vergleich mit mHag 3,3 und bPes 59a [Bar.] sowie der Kontext (die Trauernden und mit den Gebeinen eines Toten in Berührung Gekommenen sind *Juden*) deutlich machen, um die Beseitigung eines dem Konvertiten anhaftenden Mangels, der seine Zulassung zum Passamahl verhindert. Das Tauchbad ist notwendig, weil er das vorgeschriebene Opfer (mKer 2,1) noch nicht dargebracht hat und seine vollständige Entsühnung

---

89 Vgl. tPes 7,13 [ed. ZUCKERMANDEL 167]; bPes 92a; yPes 8,8 [36b].

90 Nach Ex 12,48 wurde zum Passamahl nur zugelassen, wer beschnitten war, vgl. Josephus, *Bell* 6,427. Von einem Tauchbad als weitere Voraussetzung ist nicht die Rede.

91 Wer als Proselyt am Passamahl teilnehmen will, muss sich also nach Ansicht der Hilleliten schon in der vorhergehenden Woche beschneiden lassen.

92 Bill. I, 102f.; MOORE, *Judaism I*, 331; TORRANCE, „Proselyte Baptism", 152 (mit Anm. 11); SCHÜRER, *History* 3/1, 173f.; SCHIFFMAN, *Who Was a Jew*, 27–29; FELDMAN, *Jew and Gentile*, 292.

93 COHEN, „Proselyte Baptism", 278–292. So schon TAYLOR, „Beginnings", 195; SMITH, „Proselyte Baptism", 21; WEBB, *John the Baptizer*, 126f., und neuerdings (mit weiteren Argumenten) HAYES, *Gentile Impurities*, 116–122.259–262.

aus diesem Grund noch aussteht[94]. Erst nachdem er sich rituell gereinigt und geopfert hat, ist es ihm gestattet, am Passamahl teilzunehmen.

Hinsichtlich seiner Funktion und Intention entspricht das in mPes 8,8 geforderte Tauchbad des Konvertiten exakt der Waschung, der sich auch die beiden zuvor Erwähnten – der trauernde oder mit Leichenunreinheit behaftete Jude – unterziehen müssen. Daraus ergibt sich, dass „the immersion that precedes the consumption of sacrificial meat is an additional immersion that *follows* the completed purification process". Sie bildet „the transition from a state of being prohibited to a state of being permitted to partake of sacrificial meat"[95]. Gestützt wird dieses Verständnis durch tPes 7,13, einer Ergänzung zu mPes 8,8. Denn hier wird stillschweigend vorausgesetzt, dass die Beschneidung bereits erfolgt ist und der neue Status die – jetzt mit Num 31,19 begründete – Reinigung verlangt (vgl. bPes 92a).

Fazit: Alles spricht dafür, dass es in mPes 8,8 par. mEd 5,2 nicht um „an initiation baptism as a rite for inclusion" geht, sondern um „a simple purification"[96]. Das schließt natürlich nicht aus, dass der Mischnatext zur Vorgeschichte des „eigentlichen" Proselytentauchbads gehört und ein Stadium reflektiert, in dem die Waschung beginnt, sich allmählich zu einem eigenständigen Element im Kontext des Aufnahmeverfahrens zu entwickeln[97].

5.4.2. bYev 46a

R. Eliezer (b. Hyrkanos) sagte: Ein Proselyt (גר), der beschnitten worden und nicht untergetaucht ist, gilt als Proselyt; denn dies finden wir bei unseren Vorfahren, sie waren beschnitten und nicht untergetaucht. R. Jehoschua (b. Chananja) sagte: Ist er untergetaucht, aber nicht beschnitten worden, so gilt er als Proselyt; denn dies finden wir bei unseren Stammüttern, sie waren untergetaucht und nicht beschnitten worden (Übers. GOLDSCHMIDT).

Bis in welche Zeit die von dieser Baraita bezeugten Meinungsunterschiede zwischen R. Eliezer (Schammait, um 90 n.Chr.) und R. Jehoschua (Hillelit) zurückreichen, ist ungewiss. Orientiert man sich an den zitierten Autoritäten (Tannaiten der 2. Generation), spiegeln sie die Auffassungen der beiden führenden Schulen an der Wende vom 1. zum 2. Jahrhundert. Auffällig ist zweierlei. Die Antwort R.

---

94 Hingegen impliziert yPes 8,8 [36b], dass der Betreffende als unrein gilt, weil er in der Zeit vor seinem Übertritt mit Leichen Kontakt gehabt haben konnte.

95 HAYES, *Gentile Impurities*, 260 Anm. 35 (Kursivierung im Orig.). Eine vermittelnde Position nimmt PORTON, *Stranger*, 142, ein: „It appears that the Shammaites believed that immersion was a conversion ritual, so that when the gentiles were immersed they ... were therefore permitted to eat the Passover lamb. The Hillelites, on the other hand, considered the immersion to be part of an extended purification ritual, so that the converts could not eat the lamb because they were not in a state of ritual purity".

96 S. MCKNIGHT, *Jewish Missionary Activity*, 81.

97 So A. BLASCHKE, *Beschneidung*, 252f., im Anschluss an COHEN, „Proselyte Baptism", 278.291.

Jehoschuas unterscheidet sich inhaltlich fundamental von dem, was R. Eliezer behauptet. Jedenfalls dann, wenn man sie beim Wort nimmt und grundsätzlich fasst, also nicht speziell auf Frauen bezieht[98]. Ihre antithetische Gestalt lässt keinen Freiraum für eine Kompromisslösung. Ferner hat der hier formulierte Beschneidungsverzicht hypothetischen Charakter und ist reine Theorie. Während potentielle Konvertiten schon vor dem Übertritt beschnitten sein konnten[99] – in Teilen der jüdischen Tradition gelten prominente biblische Gestalten sogar als beschnitten geboren[100], Engel sind es von Natur aus (Jub 15,27) –, so dass sie sich unter Umständen nur noch dem Tauchbad unterziehen mussten, ist der von R. Jehoschua konstruierte Fall aus halachischer Sicht schlechterdings undenkbar[101]. Aus diesem Grund erscheint die Annahme plausibel, in bYev 46a hätten wir es mit einem Gedankenspiel zu tun[102], das auf eine Aufwertung des Tauchbads, nicht jedoch auf eine Abwertung der Beschneidung zielt. Sie selbst wird nicht einmal probehalber zur Disposition gestellt. Trifft dies zu, unterstreicht der Text, welche Bedeutung dem Proselytentauchbad – präziser: dem ersten Tauchbad eines Proselyten – von Seiten der Hilleliten zu Beginn des 2. Jahrhunderts n.Chr. zugemessen werden konnte. Zugleich gibt er aber auch zu erkennen, wie umstritten dessen Funktion als *nota Iudaica* in dieser Zeit noch war. Sonst hätte es nicht gegen Einwände verteidigt werden müssen. Eine Selbstverständlichkeit ist das Tauchbad demnach nicht gewesen, jedenfalls nicht im Rahmen und als integraler Bestandteil des Aufnahmeprozesses[103]. Wie bei dem zuvor besprochenen Text lässt sich allenfalls sagen, dass sich in der fraglichen Zeit (Ende des 1./

---

98 Dazu neigt FERGUSON, *Baptism*, 80.

99 Beschnittene Araber und Gebirgsbewohner (Gabnuni) werden in bYev 71a und bAZ 27a erwähnt (vielleicht ist aber an der zuletzt genannten Stelle גבעוני [„Gibeonit"] statt גבנוני zu lesen). Aus dem Alten Testament sind weitere Völker bekannt (Jer 9,25; Ez 28,2.10). Auch die Samaritaner (Kutim) waren beschnitten. Zu diesem Personenkreis BLASCHKE, *Beschneidung*, 185–191.

100 Zu ihnen gehören u.a. Adam, Noah, Jakob, Joseph, Moses, Samuel und David, unter den Propheten Jesaja und Jeremia, LAB 9,13.15f.; ARN [A] 2; MTeh 9,7 zu V.6 [ed. BUBER 58]; BerR 84,6 [ed. THEODOR/ALBECK 1006f], vgl. I. KALIMI, „He Was Born Circumcised", 1–12.

101 Vgl. die Korrektur in bYev 47b (mit Verweis auf die den Streit im Sinne R. Eliezers entscheidende Mehrheitsmeinung der Rabbanan). Sie entspricht der gängigen in Mischna, Tosefta und Midrasch vertretenen Auffassung. Neben mPes 8,8 vgl. tShab 15,9 [ed. ZUCKERMANDEL 133]; tPes 7,14 [ed. ZUCKERMANDEL 167]; tAZ 3,12 [ed. ZUCKERMANDEL 464]; SifBam 108 zu Num 15,14 [ed. HOROVITZ 112]. BAMBERGER, *Proselytism*, 47–51, minimiert m.E. das Problem, indem er bYev 46a gegen die Parallelstelle yQid 3,13 [64d] (vgl. 4,7 [66a]) ausspielt und meint, R. Jehoschua vertrete die Ansicht, der Übertritt werde erst nach dem Tauchbad rechtsgültig. So interpretieren auch SCHIFFMAN, *Who Was a Jew?*, 33–36, und BLASCHKE, *Beschneidung*, 249.

102 W. G. BRAUDE, *Jewish Proselyting*, 76 („exegetical game"). MOORE, *Judaism* III, 110 (Nr. 103) spricht von einem „jeux d'esprit", JEREMIAS, „Proselytentaufe", 424, von einem „rein dialektischen Wortgefecht[]", das keinen Rückschluss „auf die tatsächlichen Verhältnisse in Brauch und Lehre" erlaube.

103 Vgl. hierzu die ausführliche Diskussion bei PORTON, *Stranger*, 94–96.290–292.

Anfang des 2. Jahrhunderts n.Chr.) „die Entwicklung zur *allgemeinen* Anerkennung der Proselytentaufe als Aufnahmeritus ... angebahnt"[104] hat.

5.4.3. tPes 7,13 (ed. ZUCKERMANDEL 167)

> In Jerusalem gab es Soldaten und Torwächter, die (während des Tages) ein Tauchbad nahmen und dann am Abend ihr Passa aßen.

Diese Tosefta ist ein Addendum zu mPes 8,8. Der zitierte Text, ein Zusatz zu tPes 7,13, enthält eine historische Reminszenz. Als Quelle wird R. Eliezer b. Jakob (um 150 n.Chr.) genannt[105]. Vorauf geht ein von R. Eleazar b. R. Zadok überlieferter Disput zwischen den Schulen R. Schammais und R. Hillels. Er entzündet sich an der Frage, ob ein am 14. Nisan zum Judentum übergetretener Heide noch am gleichen Abend das Passa essen darf. Für die Schammaiten besteht kein Hindernis, sofern er tagsüber beschnitten wurde und das Tauchbad genommen hat. Hingegen verlangen die Hilleliten analog zu mPes 8,8 eine Wartezeit von sieben Tagen. Die nachgetragene anekdotische Bemerkung lässt sich unterschiedlich deuten. Mit den Soldaten und Torwächtern können Juden oder Nichtjuden gemeint sein. Im ersten Fall läge der gleiche Sachverhalt vor, wie er in den Parallelstellen des Talmud Yerushalmi vorausgesetzt wird. Dort bezieht sich die gleichlautende Notiz zweifellos auf Juden[106]. Im anderen Fall ergäbe sich eine Übereinstimmung mit der schammaitischen Position. Bei den Soldaten handelte es sich um unbeschnittene Heiden. Da der Text zur Auffassung der Schammaiten inhaltlich passt und für „Soldaten" das griechische Lehnwort στρατιῶται (איצטרדיות) gebraucht wird, hat diese Möglichkeit alle Wahrscheinlichkeit für sich. Unterstellt man, dass R. Eliezer b. Jakob, der Tradent des Zusatzes, identisch ist mit dem gleichnamigen Gelehrten, von dem in mKer 2,1 die Rede ist („R. Eliezer b. Jakob sagt: Ein Proselyt erlange Sühne erst, wenn man für ihn das Blut gesprengt hat"), und dieser an seiner Meinung festgehalten hat, hätten die zum Übertritt entschlossenen Soldaten am 14. Nisan in der Tat „a busy day"[107] gehabt. Man muss sich nämlich Folgendes vorstellen: Nach ihrer Beschneidung haben sie ein der Reinigung dienendes Tauchbad genommen, um im Tempel das geforderte Sühnopfer darbringen zu können. Anschließend mussten sie sich er-

---

104 MICHAELIS, „Johannestaufe", 106 (Kursivierung im Orig. gesperrt gedruckt). In Bezug auf die Diskussion zwischen den beiden Rabbinen meint auch TAYLOR, *The Immerser*, 68, sie indiziere die „growing adoption (sc. des Proselytentauchbads) as an integral part of the conversion ritual by the early second century", will aber nicht ausschließen, dass es schon früher praktiziert worden ist, *ibid*. 66.

105 Nach der Erfurter Handschrift ist es sein gleichnamiger Vater (um 90 n.Chr.). Doch yPes 8,8 [36b] stützt die Annahme, dass der Sohn gemeint ist.

106 yPes 8,8 [36d]; yNaz 8,1 [57a].

107 COHEN, „Proselyte Baptism", 291.

neut einem Tauchbad unterziehen[108]. Es fungierte als Zulassungsbedingung zum Passamahl und markierte den Übergang von „verboten" zu „erlaubt". Danach erst durften sie „Heiliges" (קדשים) essen, d.h. an der abendlichen Feier teilnehmen[109]. Wenn die Schammaiten davon ausgehen, ein am 14. Nisan Übergetretener könne noch am gleichen Tag untertauchen und schon am Abend das Passa essen, können sie sich nicht auf das *Proselyten*tauchbad beziehen. Denn das Tauchbad, von dem sie in mPes 8,8 und tPes 7,13 jeweils sprechen, ist ein von der Konversion getrennter und zeitlich auf sie folgender Akt. Insofern ergänzt und bestätigt die Tosefta den aus der Mischna zu erhebenden Befund[110]. Eine ganz andere Frage ist, ob sich aus dem von der Schule R. Schammais geforderten Tauchbad das Proselytentauchbad als nunmehr integraler Bestandteil des Aufnahmeverfahrens entwickelt hat. Diese Möglichkeit ist nicht von der Hand zu weisen. Mit ihr rechnet etwa Shaye J. D. Cohen, räumt aber ein: „*mPesahim* is unaware of this development"[111].

5.4.4. bYev 47a–b; Traktat Gerim

Werfen wir zum Schluss noch einen Blick auf bYev 47a–b und den außerkanonischen Mischnatraktat Gerim. Die in bYev 47a–b überlieferten Bestimmungen für den Übertritt – sie werden durch die Einführungsformel רבנן תנו („unsere Lehrer haben gelehrt") als Baraitot gekennzeichnet – spiegeln die Verhältnisse um die Mitte des 2. Jahrhunderts oder etwas später. Ihre palästinische Herkunft ist sicher. Spätere Ergänzungen und Interpolationen sind nicht ausgeschlossen. Der Traktat Gerim ist wohl irgendwann zwischen dem sechsten und achten Jahrhundert entstanden, enthält aber altes Material. Die beiden ersten Kapitel stellen inhaltlich eine Variante zu bYev 47a–b dar und schreiben den Text fort. Insofern ist der kleine Traktat ein wichtiger Zeuge für die geschichtliche Entwicklung der Konversionspraxis in spättalmudischer bzw. nachtalmudischer Zeit[112].

---

108 Vgl. mHag 3,3: Wer noch nicht entsühnt ist (wörtl.: „Ein der Sühne Ermangelnder") muss, auch wenn er schon das Tauchbad genommen hat, nach Darbringung des Opfers vor dem Verzehr von קדשים untertauchen.

109 Zum Ausschluss von Nichtjuden (ἀλλόφυλοι) und anderen als unrein Geltenden vom Passamahl vgl. Josephus, *Bell* 6,426f.

110 Vgl. oben den Abschnitt § 5.4.1.

111 COHEN, *Beginnings*, 291 (Kursivierung im Orig.). Etwas anders akzentuiert BEASLEY-MURRAY, *Taufe*, 43f., der den Zusatz in tPes 7,13 früh datiert und in ihm eine Erinnerung aus der Zeit des 1. jüdisch-römischen Kriegs aufbewahrt sieht.

112 Vgl. COHEN, *Beginnings*, 211.217. Seine viel zu frühe Datierung des Traktats (4. Jahrhundert) verleitet DELORME, ihn mit den zuvor besprochenen Texten auf eine Stufe zu stellen und sie von ihm her zu interpretieren, „Practice of Baptism", 28–30.

Zunächst zu bYev 47a–b. Das hier geschilderte Procedere ist klar strukturiert[113]. Es besteht aus vier Teilen[114]:

1) Der künftige Proselyt (גר הבא להתגייר) bittet um Aufnahme. Daraufhin wird die Ernsthaftigkeit seiner Absicht geprüft. Gefragt wird nach den Beweggründen („Was veranlasst dich [zu uns] zu kommen, um Proselyt zu werden?") und danach, ob er sich über die Tragweite seines Entschlusses im Klaren ist („Weißt du nicht, dass Israeliten heutzutage gequält, bedrängt, gedemütigt und weggestoßen werden und dass Leiden über sie kommen?").

2) Antwortet er, dies alles zu wissen, steht seiner Aufnahme nichts im Wege. Aus zeitlichen Gründen und um ihn nicht zu überfordern wird er fürs Erste nur mit einer repräsentativen Auswahl von Geboten („einigen der leichteren und einigen der schwereren"[115]) bekannt gemacht sowie auf die Konsequenzen hingewiesen, die ihre Beachtung oder Übertretung nach sich zieht.

3) Stimmt er zu und bleibt bei seiner Entscheidung, wird er gleich beschnitten.

4) Sobald die Wunde abgeheilt ist, steigt er in Gegenwart von drei (bYev 46b; bQid 62b) Zeugen[116] in das Tauchbad. Sie machen nicht das Bad, sondern die Aufnahme ins Judentum rechtsgültig. Dann wird der Proband – er befindet sich immer noch im Wasser – von zwei Schriftkundigen[117] ein weiteres Mal über die Gebote belehrt, aber wiederum in dosierter Form („man rede nicht zuviel auf ihn ein") und auf die für ihn wichtigsten beschränkt. Dahinter steckt die auch sonst belegte Vorstellung, später werde der Konvertit alles weitere lernen (bShab 31a)[118]. Für den Übertritt gilt das Gleiche wie für ein Gerichtsverfahren. Er hat öffentlichen Charakter. Deshalb darf das Tauchbad analog zur

---

113 Ich verzichte auf eine Darbietung des relativ umfangreichen Texts. Eine deutsche Übersetzung findet sich in der Ausgabe von L. GOLDSCHMIDT und bei BILL. I, 110f. Eine englische Fassung bieten MOORE, *Judaism I*, 333f., und BAMBERGER, *Proselytism*, 38f. Für den Traktat Gerim verweise ich auf die kommentierte zweisprachige Ausgabe von POLSTER, „Proselyten". Eine Synopse beider Texte ist abgedruckt bei GAVIN, *The Jewish Antecedents*, 33–35, und COHEN, *Beginnings*, 199–202.

114 Vgl. GAVIN, *The Jewish Antecedents*, 32; COHEN, *Beginnings*, 203–207.

115 Zu dieser Unterscheidung SifBam 115 zu Num 15,41 (ed. HOROVITZ 128).

116 Eine im Namen von R. Jochanan korrigierte Mindermeinung hält zwei für ausreichend (bYev 47b). Nach Gerim 4,3 sind Zeugen verzichtbar, wenn jemand glaubhaft in Israel erklärt, er sei ein Proselyt. Anders wiederum bYev 47a. Vgl. auch yQid 4,7 [66b].

117 In diesem Zusammenhang wird nicht gesagt, ob es sich bei ihnen um zwei der Zeugen oder andere Personen handelt, die eigens mit dieser Aufgabe betraut sind. Gegen die erste Möglichkeit könnte das für Proselytinnen vorgesehene Verfahren sprechen. Dort sind die Rollen verteilt (dazu gleich). Aber diese unterschiedliche Funktionszuweisung dürfte geschlechtsspezifische Gründe haben, so dass im Fall des Übertritts eines Mannes in der Regel mit drei schriftkundigen Zeugen zu rechnen ist.

118 Vgl. PORTON, *Stranger*, 196: „The rabbis ... realized that (the) complete acceptance of the israelite way of life could come only after a period of time". In abgewandelter Form begegnet dieser Gedanke auch im Neuen Testament, vgl. I Kor 3,2; I Petr 2,2; Hebr 5,12f.

Beschneidung (Sifra zu Lev 12,3) auch nur tagsüber stattfinden (bYev 46b.72a–b). Nach dem Heraufsteigen gilt der Proselyt „in jeder Hinsicht als ein Israelit" (הרי הוא כישראל לכל דבריו, bYev 47b).

Ein Anhang regelt das Verfahren für Frauen. Bei ihnen entfällt natürlich die Beschneidung. Das Untertauchen geschieht in Anwesenheit einer nicht näher bezifferten Anzahl von Zeuginnen. Entgegen des ihnen sonst verwehrten Zeugnisrechts[119] sind Frauen hier zugelassen, da es um eine Angelegenheit geht, die speziell sie betrifft (vgl. mKet 7,6; bYev 39b). Während die Konvertitin bis zum Hals im Wasser sitzt, wird sie von zwei männlichen Unterweisern, die sich außerhalb des Badehauses (בית הטבילה[120]) aufhalten, in den Geboten unterrichtet. Dabei dürfte vor allem an solche Mizwot gedacht sein, deren Kenntnis aus halachischer Sicht gerade für Frauen unabdingbar ist, um den Haushalt in Kaschrut und ritueller Reinheit führen zu können[121].

Mit dem Vollzug des Tauchbads, das am Ende des gestuften Aufnahmeverfahrens steht, hat der Proselyt „undergone a change of legal status based on the performance of, and the stated obligation to continue performing, certain legal norms"[122]. Gehörte er von Haus aus zu den Menschen aus der Völkerwelt (גוים), hat diese qua Herkunft sein bisheriges Dasein kennzeichnende biologische Realität jetzt ihre Existenz bestimmende Bedeutung verloren. Der Eintritt in den neuen Sozialverband „Israel" markiert nicht nur den Übergang vom Status ritueller Unreinheit in den der Reinheit, sondern auch einen Identitätswechsel. Durch seine Konversion ist der ehemalige Heide ein Teil des Volkes Israel, ein „gerechter Proselyt" (גר צדק) geworden und besitzt damit eine – nicht allein religiös definierte – neue Identität[123]. Nach rabbinischen Verständnis ist die Integration in das Ethnos der Juden ein zentraler, vielleicht sogar der dominierende Aspekt im Kontext des Übertritts. Seine religiöse Dimension klingt zwar an, erscheint aber nicht sonderlich ausgeprägt. Davon, dass der Proselyt – theologisch gesprochen – eine neue Schöpfung ist, von Schuldenlast befreit ist und ihm seine Sünden vergeben sind, verlautet nichts. Er wird auf kein Bekenntnis

---

119 Dtn 17,6; 19,15; Josephus, *Ant* 4,219; bShevu 30a; SifDev § 190 [ed. FINKELSTEIN 230].

120 Vgl. mMid 1,9; mPar 3,7; mSheq 8,2; mTam 1,1; Gerim 1,3; bYom 11a; bPes 19b.

121 Einen Näherungswert liefert das von jüdischen Mädchen zu lernende Basiswissen, das sie als junge Frauen mit in die Ehe zu bringen hatten: „Was fällt unter ‚Gesetz Mose'? Wenn eine ihm (sc. ihrem Mann) zu essen gibt, was nicht verzehntet ist; oder wenn eine als Menstruierende Beischlaf mit ihm hat; oder wenn sie die Teighebe nicht absondert; oder wenn sie ein Gelübde ablegt und es nicht erfüllt. Was fällt unter ‚jüdische Sitte'? Wenn eine mit unbedecktem Haupt ausgeht; oder wenn eine auf der Straße spinnt; oder wenn eine mit jedermann spricht" (mKet 7,6). Dieses Wissen vermittelte die Mutter (Philo, *Ebr* 54f.; *SpecLeg* 2,125; bKet 63a), für die vertiefte Unterweisung in der jüdischen Tradition war in erster Linie der Vater zuständig (mNed 4,3; mSot 3,4).

122 COHEN, *Beginnings*, 237.

123 Dies betont zu Recht HAARMANN, *JHWH-Verehrer*, 28f. Von „self-transformation" spricht PORTON, *Stranger*, 198.

verpflichtet. Ein ausdrücklicher Bezug auf Gott findet sich ebenfalls nicht, weder in Form einer Doxologie noch zur Begründung der Beschneidung noch im Zusammenhang des Tauchbads. Überhaupt lässt das im Text geschilderte Verfahren jeden Hinweis vermissen, mit dem Übertritt gehe „a change in belief or a change of spirituality"[124] einher.

Zweifellos identifiziert bYev 47a–b das Proselytentauchbad als einen konstitutiven Bestandteil des Aufnahmeritus. Für Männer bildet es den Abschluss des Konversionsprozesses, für Frauen ist es das Kernstück[125]. Die geforderte Präsenz von Zeugen unterstreicht den rechtlichen Aspekt der Handlung. Deshalb erscheint es nur folgerichtig, dass kultische Bezüge wie etwa der Hinweis, nun am Passamahl teilnehmen und „Heiliges" essen zu dürfen, fehlen. Der ansonsten den rituellen Waschungen anhaftende Gedanke der Reinigung wird völlig ausgeblendet[126].

Wie der Traktat Gerim erkennen lässt, hat das Tauchbad später erheblich an Bedeutung gewonnen. Die Ausführlichkeit, mit der selbst Detailfragen behandelt und geregelt werden – und zwar im Blick auf weibliche *und* männliche Konvertiten –, fällt auf. Umso mehr, als von der Beschneidung keine Rede ist. Sie wird ähnlich wie in tPes 7,13 einfach vorausgesetzt (1,3; 2,1f.4)[127]. Möglicherweise steckt die Absicht dahinter, das in bYev 47a–b zu beobachtende Ungleichgewicht von Mann und Frau aufzuheben zugunsten einer mehr kohärenten Form, die auch der Frau gerecht wird. Darüber hinaus wird im Unterschied zur älteren Version Gott gepriesen und der Übergetretene beglückwünscht, dass er nun ein Kind Gottes ist und Gott ihn liebt (1,5).

Die in beiden Textvarianten festgelegten Regularien für den Vollzug des Tauchbads im Zusammenhang des Konversionsprozesses sind ganz auf Er-

---

124 COHEN, *Beginnings*, 238.
125 Die einschlägigen Vorschriften in mMiq 9,1–7; bEr 4b.14b über alles, was zur „Trennung" führt – gemeint ist: das Wasser nicht an den ganzen Körper lässt und damit das Tauchbad ungültig macht – und was nicht, geben zu erkennen: Männer wie Frauen vollziehen das Tauchbad, nachdem sie sich völlig entkleidet haben, aus Gründen der Scham und Schicklichkeit freilich jeweils für sich. Auch Schmuck, sonstige Accessoires und selbst Wundpflaster fallen unter die Rubrik „Trennendes" und müssen entfernt werden (mMiq 9,2; Kizzur Schulchan Aruch 161,1.3f. [ed. GANZFRIED 922f]). Nur die Körperbehaarung ist davon ausgenommen (mMiq 9,3). Vor dem Untertauchen wird in einem gesonderten Raum (בית המרחץ) die Kleidung abgelegt. Anschließend trocknet man sich mit ihr wieder ab. Da aus pharisäischer Sicht die Kleidung von Angehörigen des ʻam ha-aretz als unrein galt (mHag 2,7), hätte sie streng genommen für diesen Zweck keine Verwendung finden dürfen. Die meisten werden sich jedoch über diese Bedenken hinweggesetzt haben. Vgl. SANDERS, *Judaism. Practice and Belief*, 225 (mit Anm. 28 [521]).
126 Vgl. MOORE, *Judaism I*, 334: „In the whole ritual there is no suggestion that baptism was a real or symbolical purification".
127 POLSTER, „Proselyten", 20; COHEN, *Beginnings*, 214f. Daher findet die Gebotsunterweisung im Unterschied zum Paralleltext allein während des Tauchbads statt. Allerdings mit einem die Prozedur erleichternden Zugeständnis an die Konvertiten. Frau und Mann dürfen in dieser Zeit – nur bis zur Scham mit Wasser bedeckt – im Tauchbad stehenbleiben (1,3f.). Erst danach tauchen sie den ganzen Körper unter.

wachsene zugeschnitten. Bis auf eine Ausnahme (Gerim 2,1[128]) werden Kinder nicht erwähnt. Erlaubt dieser Tatbestand den Schluss, für Minderjährige seien die genannten Vorschriften nicht gedacht und auf sie nicht angewandt worden? Angesichts der Quellenlage lässt sich diese Frage weder rundweg bejahen noch verneinen. Sie erfordert eine differenzierte Antwort.

Gerim 2,1 geht davon aus, dass der unmündige Sohn einer Proselytin (גיורת, vgl. mYev 6,5) noch am Tage des Übertritts seiner Mutter beschnitten wird[129]. In Mischna und Talmud findet sich mehrfach die Wendung „Proselytinnen, die (im Alter von) unter drei Jahren und einem Tag bekehrt sind"[130]. Obwohl an keiner dieser Stellen ausdrücklich von einem Tauchbad die Rede ist, durch das die betreffenden Mädchen der jüdischen Gemeinschaft inkorporiert wurden, könnte es als Bedingung vorausgesetzt sein. Gestützt wird diese Annahme durch ein in bYev 78a überliefertes Wort des Raba (= Raba b. Joseph b. Chama, gest. 352 n.Chr.): „Wenn eine schwangere Fremde Proselytin geworden ist, bedarf ihr Kind nicht des Tauchbads". Positiv formuliert: Mit der untergetauchten Mutter ist auch das noch ungeborene Kind als ein Teil von ihr Jude bzw. Jüdin geworden. Daraus lässt sich schließen, dass für den riten Vollzug des Übertritts das Tauchbad auch bei Unmündigen unverzichtbar ist, sofern sie nicht „in Heiligkeit" (mYev 11,2), d.h. nach dem Übertritt der Mutter geboren wurden. Ein weiterer Hinweis findet sich in bKet 11a. Nach dem Tod des Vaters eines offensichtlich sehr jungen und daher noch nicht entscheidungsfähigen Kindes, von dem die Mutter wünschte, es solle Proselyt werden, riet R. Huna (gest. 297 n.Chr.): „Einen minderjährigen Proselyten lasse man auf Veranlassung des Gerichtshofs untertauchen". Dies sei gerechtfertigt, weil es dem Kind zum Vorteil gereiche, und einen Vorteil dürfe man einem Menschen auch in seiner Abwesenheit, d.h. ohne sein Wissen zuwenden. Ein Aufschub oder gar Dispens ist keine ernsthaft erwogene Option. Zugestanden wird lediglich ein wenn auch zeitlich begrenztes Widerrufsrecht. Ist jemand bei seinem Übertritt noch unmündig gewesen, kann er später als Erwachsener die von anderen getroffene Entscheidung rückgängig machen. Wer die eingeräumte Frist – sie endet eine Stunde nach Erreichen der Volljährigkeit – verstreichen lässt, hat den Einspruch verwirkt. Allerdings zeigt bKet 11a auch, dass dieses Zugeständnis auf erhebliche Vorbehalte stieß und Widerspruch provozierte.

---

128 „Ein Proselyt wird am achten Tage beschnitten. Wie ist das möglich? Wenn der Sohn geboren war, bevor seine Mutter getaucht wurde, so wird er am gleichen Tage beschnitten. Wenn er aber nach dem Tauchbad der Mutter geboren wurde, wird er am achten Tage beschnitten". In Gerim 3,8: „Wenn ein Proselyt stirbt und einen Sohn oder eine Tochter hinterlässt, die mit ihm Proselyten geworden sind, ..." bleibt das Alter der genannten Kinder unbestimmt. Sohn (בן) und Tochter (בה) ist man auch als Religionsmündiger.

129 Vgl. mYev 11,2; bShab 135a.b; tYev 12,2 [ed. ZUCKERMANDEL 254].

130 mKet 1,2.4; 3,1; bKet 11a (3x); bYeb 60b; bQid 78a; yQid 4,66a [10]; yYev 8,9b [62f], vgl. mKet 3,2.

Im Ensemble geben die tradierten Äußerungen zu erkennen: Beim Übertritt der Eltern oder – je nach den persönlichen Umständen – lediglich eines Elternteils werden in der Regel auch die noch minderjährigen Kinder ins Judentum aufgenommen. Das Verfahren entspricht dem für Erwachsene üblichen. Söhne werden beschnitten und untergetaucht, Mädchen müssen sich nur dem Tauchbad unterziehen. Freilich ist gleich hinzuzufügen: Keiner der angeführten Belege taugt als Argument für das vermeintlich hohe Alter des Proselytentauchbads[131]. Sie alle sind jüngeren Datums und spiegeln ein fortgeschrittenes Stadium, in dem das Tauchbad allmählich kriteriologische Bedeutung gewann oder bei einzelnen Vertretern der führenden Schulen bereits besaß und neben der Beschneidung die Zugehörigkeit zum Judentum konstituierte. Dies bestätigen nicht zuletzt die Namen der zitierten rabbinischen Gelehrten. Der älteste ist R. Shim'on b. Jochai (um 150 n.Chr.), ein Tannait der dritten Generation[132].

5.5. Ertrag

Ich ziehe ein abschließendes Resümee. Die Annahme, das Proselytentauchbad habe schon in vorrabbinischer Zeit, d.h. lange *vor* dem 2. Jahrhundert n.Chr. existiert und sei neben der Beschneidung das bestimmende Element im Prozess des Übertritts – und deshalb gerade für Frauen unverzichtbar – gewesen, erscheint wenig plausibel. Vielmehr gilt: „There is no explicit reference to proselyte immersion in our period (sc. bis 135 n.Chr.)"[133]. Erst im tannaitischen Midrasch SifBam 108 zu Num 15,14 (Jehuda ha-Nasi) und in bKer 9a wird die grundlegende Funktion von Beschneidung, Tauchbad und Opfer als Zulassungsbedingung für den Eintritt in den „Bund" (bKer 9a) ausdrücklich festgehalten[134]. Dazu passt, dass sich in den Katalogen des Mischnatraktats Miqwaot, in denen die Wassermengen für die rituellen Tauchbäder vorgeschrieben und die Wasserarten je nach ihrer Beschaffenheit und Reinigungskraft qualitativ unterschiedlich eingestuft werden (mMiq 1f)[135], kein Hinweis auf das Proselytentauchbad fin-

---

131 Anders z.B. JEREMIAS, *Kindertaufe*, 44–47, und OEPKE, Art. „παῖς κτλ.", 646f. Weit zurückhaltender als sie urteilt BEASLEY-MURRAY, *Taufe*, 432f., und zwar sowohl im Blick auf die zeitliche Einordnung der entsprechenden rabbinischen Texte als auch hinsichtlich ihrer Verwendbarkeit zugunsten einer frühen Datierung des Proselytentauchbads.

132 Vgl. bQid 78 [Bar.] par. bYev 60b. Mit einer Ausnahme (mHag 1,7) begegnet er in der Mischna sonst immer nur als R. Shim'on.

133 DONALDSON, *Judaism and the Gentiles*, 490 Anm. 19. Vgl. COHEN, „Conversion to Judaisam", 37; COLLINS, *Between Athens and Jerusalem*, 106; HAYES, *Gentile Impurity*, 117: „[S]uch a ritual immersion (sc. of converts) is not specifically stated elsewhere in tannaitic literature", wobei sie das „elsewhere" auf die in dieser Hinsicht von ihr selbst als nicht belastbar eingestufte Stelle mPes 8,8 bezieht.

134 Vgl. Gerim 2,5; MekhSH zu 12,48 [ed. HOFFMANN 30] und zu 19,10 [ed. HOFFMANN 97].

135 Nach mMiq 1,7; 2,1–3; 5,6; bEr 4b.14b sind (mindestens) 40 Se'a (ca. 800 Liter) erforderlich. R. Chanina begründet diese Menge damit, sie verhindere Ehebruch, weil sie nach einem illegiti-

det[136]. Wenngleich der Traktat relativ spät datiert (3. Jahrhundert n.Chr.) und in vielen Fällen mehr die halachischen Vorstellungen der Rabbinen als die real existierenden historischen Verhältnisse widerspiegelt, auf die er referiert, hat diese Negativanzeige als Hilfsargument durchaus Gewicht und fügt sich in das bisherige Ergebnis ein.

6. Das Proselytentauchbad – ein Initiationsritus?

Eine eindeutige Antwort auf die Frage, ob das Proselytentauchbad als ein Initiationsritus zu klassifizieren ist, fällt schwer. Viel hängt davon ab, was man unter „Initiation / Initiationsritus" versteht. Nach der bis heute wirkmächtigen, auf Übergangsriten tribaler Gesellschaften bezogenen ethnologisch-soziologischen Definition Arnold van Genneps haben Initiations- bzw. Transitionsrituale primär die Funktion, die Dynamik individueller Veränderungen (Raum-, Zustands-, Zeitwechsel) innerhalb des weithin als statisch aufgefassten Ordnungsgefüges des sozialen Lebens zu kontrollieren[137]. Der Sozialanthropologe Victor W. Turner knüpft daran an, betont aber stärker den von Konflikten und Antagonismen gekennzeichneten Prozesscharakter sozialer Systeme, deren Widersprüche im rituell dramatisierten Initiationsgeschehen zum Ausdruck gebracht und symbolisch aufgefangen werden[138]. Im Unterschied zu diesen beiden konzeptionell verwandten Modellen begreift Mircea Eliade Initiation als rituell begleiteten individuell-biographischen Übergang von einer Lebensphase in die nächste, verbunden mit einer grundlegenden Umwandlung des Initianden: „[D]ie Initiation (entspricht) einer ontologischen Veränderung der existentiellen Ordnung. Am Ende seiner Prüfung erfreut sich der Neophyt einer ganz anderen Seinsweise als vor der Initiation: er ist ein *anderer* geworden"[139].

Orientiert man sich versuchsweise an dieser – zugegeben recht allgemein gehaltenen – Definition, fehlen dem Proselytentauchbad wesentliche Merkmale eines Initiationsritus. Wir hören nichts davon, dass beim Übertritt der heidnischen Vergangenheit und den bisher verehrten Gottheiten abgeschwo-

---

men – aber auch sonst verunreinigenden – Geschlechtsverkehr nicht immer zur Verfügung stehe (bBer 22a). Im Zweifelsfall gilt der Grundsatz: Die untertauchende Person bzw. die zu reinigende Gerätschaft (z.B. ein Gefäß) oder das Kleidungsstück muss mit Wasser bedeckt sein, vgl. bYev 46a; mMiq 1,7; 5,3; 8,5. Keine Körperstelle darf unberührt bleiben (bEr 4b; Kizzur Schulchan Aruch 161,1 [ed. GANZFRIED 922], an der zuletzt genannten Stelle speziell auf die Frau bezogen).

136 Das gilt auch für tMiq 6,11 [ed. ZUCKERMANDEL 658].
137 A. VAN GENNEP, *Übergangsriten*.
138 Ich verweise nur auf V. W. TURNER, „Betwixt and Between", 93–111. Diese kleine Studie darf für seine weiteren Arbeiten als grundlegend gelten.
139 M. ELIADE, *Mysterium der Wiedergeburt*, 11 (Kursivierung im Orig.). Zum Problemfeld vgl. CH. WETZ, *Eros und Bekehrung*, passim.

ren wird[140]. Nirgends ist von einer Bitte um Vergebung der zuvor begangenen Sünden[141], von Schuldbefreiung, Wiedergeburt oder Erneuerung[142] die Rede. Es wird kein Gebet gesprochen, in dem der Übergetretene sein bisheriges Leben rückschauend betrachtet, für seine Umkehr zum Gott der Juden[143] dankt und den Blick in die Zukunft richtet[144]. Obwohl er in das jüdische Volk aufgenommen wird, fehlt jeder explizite Bezug auf den neuen sozialen Verband. Auch gibt es keine Geschenke, keine Segenswünsche[145], kein gemeinsames Mahl, das die Gemeinde ausrichtet und mit dem sie den Konvertiten in ihrer Mitte begrüßt. Über Formen ritueller Performanz, etwa eine Prozession oder einen Kleiderwechsel, der den Bruch mit dem vorkonversionellen Leben symbolisiert und den religiösen Statuswechsel des Neophyten demonstriert, erfahren wir nichts[146]. Die nach van Genneps Analyse einen Übergangsritus kennzeichnenden drei Phasen – Ablösungsphase (Trennungsriten = rites de séparation), Schwellen- bzw. Umwandlungsphase (Schwellen- bzw. Umwandlungsriten[147] = rites de marge), Integrationsphase (Angliederungsriten = rites d' agrégation)[148] – werden im Zusammenhang des Proselytentauchbads nicht performiert. Mit anderen Worten, es lässt – zumindest in tannaitischer Zeit – alle distinkten Merkmale eines Initiationsritus vermissen. Ob und inwieweit der spät- bzw. nachtalmudische Traktat Gerim erste Ansätze in dieser Richtung erkennen lässt, wie Shaye J. D. Cohen meint[149], sei dahingestellt und mag hier auf sich beruhen.

---

140 Vgl. yYev 8,1 [8d]; bAZ 64b.
141 Vergleichbar dem Gebet Aseneths in JosAs 12,1–13,15 [ed. BURCHARD 154–174].
142 Vgl. JosAs 8,9 [ed. BURCHARD 118–120]. Der wiederholt zitierte Satz, der Proselyt „gleich(e) einem neu geborenen Kind" (bYev 22a.48b.62a.97b; bBekh 47a; mNeg 7,1), ist kein Gegenargument. Er besagt lediglich, dass der Proselyt vor seinem Übertritt keine anrechenbare Sünde begangen hat und deshalb, einem neu geborenen Kind gleich, nicht der Sühne bedarf (vgl. oben das unter 4. Gesagte).
143 Vgl. JosAs 11,10 [ed. BURCHARD 146]; TestJos 12,3; Josephus, Ant 9,20.
144 Solche Gebete gab es. Ein Beispiel dafür ist yBer 4,2 [7d].
145 Bei der Beschneidung eines Kindes respondieren die Anwesenden auf die vom Mohel gesprochene Berakha, bShab 137b [Bar.].138a; bMen 42a, vgl. yBer 9,3 [13a].
146 Erst im Mittelalter wurde der Konvertit aufgefordert, einen jüdischen Namen anzunehmen. Für diesen Brauch gibt es in der rabbinischen Literatur m.W. nur einen Beleg (tGit 6,4 [ed. ZUCKERMANDEL 329], vgl. bEr 62a; bKet 46a; bHul 101b). Jedoch bleibt offen, ob der alte Name durch den neuen konsequent ersetzt oder im Alltag noch verwendet wird. Zu den epigraphischen Belegen vgl. JEREMIAS, Kindertaufe, 39f., und COHEN, Beginnings, 161f.
147 Schwellenriten beziehen sich auf einen Raumwechsel, Umwandlungsriten auf einen Zustandswechsel.
148 VAN GENNEP, Übergangsriten, 21.29 und passim.
149 COHEN, Beginnings, 234–238.

Dennoch erscheint es cum grano salis gerechtfertigt, hinsichtlich des Proselytentauchbads von einem initiatorischen Akt zu sprechen[150]. Und zwar in dem Sinne, dass es – wenn auch erst sukzessive – zu einer habitualisierten Handlung geworden ist, die neben der Beschneidung die Zugehörigkeit zum Judentum sinnenfällig zur Anschauung bringt. Dabei dürfte das ihm innewohnende egalitäre Moment als ein inklusiver, die Geschlechterdifferenz von Mann und Frau transzendierender Ritus eine wesentliche Rolle gespielt haben. Denn für weibliche Konvertiten stellte es die einzige Möglichkeit dar, ihren Übertritt nach außen hin zu dokumentieren, ihn rechtskräftig zu besiegeln und so etwaige Zweifel an ihrer jüdischen Identität zu zerstreuen.

Bündelt man den Ertrag der einzelnen Textuntersuchungen zu einer These, lässt sich abschließend formulieren: Der Stellenwert des ersten Tauchbads für Proselyten, das wie alle, die noch folgten, der rituellen Reinigung diente und sich damit in nichts von ihnen unterschied – weder funktional noch intentional –, hat sich im Laufe der Zeit gewandelt. Aufgrund seiner immer stärker akzentuierten und vermutlich auch aus der Fremdperspektive wahrgenommenen Bedeutung als *nota Iudaica* gewann es im Rahmen des Konversionsprozesses einen eigenen Charakter und verselbstständigte sich[151]. Aus einer zusätzlich zur und neben die Beschneidung tretenden kultisch-religiösen Handlung, die hinsichtlich ihrer Notwendigkeit, Eigenart und Begründungsstruktur lange strittig blieb und zwischen den führenden Schulen zum Teil heftige Diskussionen auslöste, wurde im Zusammenhang des Übertritts ein rituell inszenierter initiatorischer Akt[152].

7. Rückblick und Ausblick

Über Alter, Ursprung und Funktion des Proselytentauchbads sowie über seine geschichtliche Entwicklung bis etwa zur Mitte des 2. Jahrhunderts lassen sich allenfalls begründete Vermutungen anstellen. Dass es zunächst für Frauen eingeführt wurde, um dem – erst in den tannaitischen Quellen propagierten – matrilinearen Prinzip eine Basis zu verschaffen[153], hat einiges für sich. Gut möglich ist auch (das muss keine Alternative sein), dass die Notwendigkeit empfunden

---

150 BAMBERGER, *Proselytism*, 44; PUSEY/HURT, „Proselyte Baptism", 144; FERGUSON, *Baptism*, 79.
151 Zutreffend urteilt m.E. BLASCHKE, *Beschneidung*, 256: „Existierte die zeitliche Absetzung der טבילה von der Beschneidung erst einmal, *mußte* sie als nach der Beschneidung zu vollziehender und den Übertritt erst vollständig machender Konversionsritus zunehmend an Bedeutung gewinnen, während sie früher, gleich nach der Beschneidung vollzogen, als deren bloßes Akzidens erscheinen sein mochte" (Kursivierung im Orig.).
152 Vgl. BRAUDE, *Jewish Proselyting*, 74 Anm. 1: „Originally baptism may have been a purificatory rite; in Talmudic days it had become an initiatory ceremony".
153 Zu diesem Prinzip COHEN, *Beginnings*, 263–307. Die Apokryphen und Pseudepigraphen, Josephus und Philo kennen es nicht, ebenso wenig das Neue Testament und die Qumranschriften.

wurde, eine bis dato „wilde" Praxis[154] zu beenden, sie zu regulieren, zu formalisieren und in geordnete Bahnen zu lenken.

Etwas anderes kommt hinzu. Die Haltung der Rabbinen gegenüber Proselyten ist ambivalent. Zumeist werden sie willkommen geheißen und erfreuen sich besonderer Fürsorge[155]. Vor allem in Gebetstexten wird dies deutlich. So heißt es in der 13. Benediktion des Achtzehngebets: „Über die gerechten Proselyten (גרי הצדק) möge sich dein Erbarmen regen" (pal. Rez.)[156]. Es gibt freilich auch kritische Stimmen. Sie reichen bis zur schroffen Ablehnung. Der vielzitierte, im Talmud gleich mehrfach begegnende Ausspruch R. Helbos: „Proselyten sind für Israel so schlimm wie Aussatz" (bYev 47b.109b; bQid 70b; bNid 13b [Bar.]) stellt zwar einen Extremfall dar. Er fügt sich aber in eine Reihe vergleichbarer Äußerungen ein[157]. Die Reaktionen spiegeln den fragilen sozialen Status der Proselyten innerhalb der jüdischen Gesellschaft, nicht nur im palästinischen Mutterland. Der im Laufe der Zeit zunehmend stärker katechetisch geprägte Rahmen des Proselytentauchbads lässt sich als Versuch verstehen, Vorbehalte zu entkräften und den neuen Status der Konvertiten halachisch zu fundieren. Insofern eignet dem aus der Tora nur mühsam abzuleitenden Tauchbad eine kaum zu überschätzende sozial-integrative und identitätsstiftende Funktion.

Wenn das Proselytentauchbad nicht als Vorbild der Johannestaufe gedient hat, wer oder was dann? Vielleicht ist die Frage aber falsch gestellt. Johannes bewegte sich in einem zeit- und religionsgeschichtlich vertrauten Milieu, so dass jeder Versuch einer genetischen Ableitung seiner Taufe von einem bestimmten Typus jüdischer Waschungen trotz formaler und inhaltlicher Analogien notwendig hypothetisch bleibt. Eher dürfte ihr dezidiert eschatologischer und ethischer Impetus[158] als eine Innovation des Täufers zu begreifen sein. Dafür könnte u.a. der in Joh 3,25 reflektierte Konflikt (Johannestaufe vs. jüdische Reinigungsriten) sprechen. Immerhin ist es eine bedenkenswerte Möglichkeit, dass Johannes sich an diesem Punkt von Qumran beeinflusst zeigt (vgl. nur

---

154 COHEN spricht in diesem Zusammenhang von einem „entirely personal and chaotic process", Beginnings, 236. Vgl. ibid. 218–225 und DONALDSON, Judaism and the Gentiles, 489f.

155 Philo, Virt 20.102–104.179; Josephus, Ap 2,210; mAv 1,12; bShab 145b–146a; Sifra zu Lev 19,34; ShemR 30,12 [ed. MIRKIN 45] u.ö.

156 Vgl. bMeg 17b; yBer 2,4 [5a]; 4,3 [8a]; tBer 3,25 [ed. ZUCKERMANDEL 9].

157 bYev 24b [Bar.]; bBM 59b; bGit 45b; bAZ 3b [Bar.].24a; bMen 44a; ySan 10,2 [29b]; QohR 1,8 u.ö., vgl. Josephus, Ap 2,123. Eine gute Übersicht über das Pro und Contra bieten MOORE, Judaism I, 341–348; BRAUDE, Jewish Proselyting, 26–48.100–107; BAMBERGER, Proselytism, 149–173; HAARMANN, JHWH-Verehrer, 31–36. Ausführlich behandelt das Thema PORTON, Stranger, 16–131.227–323.

158 Die uneschatologische Darstellung bei Josephus, Ant 18,116f., verdankt sich der interpretatio graeca des Täufers und seiner Verkündigung. Johannes erscheint hier als Tugendlehrer. Auch sonst stellt Josephus jüdische Gruppierungen gerne in Analogie zu hellenistischen Philosophenschulen dar, vgl. Bell 2,119–166 (Essener, Pharisäer, Sadduzäer); Ant 15,373–378 (Essener).

1QS 4,18–22)¹⁵⁹, ohne in ihm deswegen einen geistigen Schüler der Qumranfrommen zu sehen. Darüber hinaus ist es eine nach wie vor offene Frage, inwieweit die christliche Taufpraxis auf die Ausgestaltung des Proselytentauchbads eingewirkt und seine Verbreitung und schließliche Akzeptanz gefördert hat¹⁶⁰. Entwicklungsprozesse verlaufen selten linear. Sie verdanken sich nicht nur endogenen, sondern zumeist auch exogenen Faktoren. Leider fehlen eindeutige Indizien, die es uns erlauben, etwaige Wechselwirkungen namhaft zu machen und so über Mutmaßungen hinauszukommen. Doch gibt es zumindest eine wenngleich nur schwache Spur, die in diese Richtung weist.

> Zu den besonders auffallenden Merkmalen der in bYev 47a–b und im Traktat Gerim geschilderten Aufnahmeprozedur gehört die konnektive Struktur von Proselytenkatechese und Tauchbad. Sie begegnet hier zum ersten Mal. In den älteren Traditionsschichten der rabbinischen Literatur ist sie ohne Parallele. An keiner anderen Stelle, an der die טבילה erwähnt und über ihre Bedeutung gestritten wird, erscheint sie mit einer Unterweisung verbunden. Dass die Katechese nunmehr in das Aufnahmeverfahren integriert und mit dem Tauchbad verkoppelt ist – in bYev 47a.b geht sie der Beschneidung schon voraus –, erweckt den Anschein, als handle es sich um ein Novum. Jedenfalls deutet nichts darauf hin, bereits zuvor sei es gängige Praxis gewesen, Übertrittswillige vor dem Tauchbad bzw. der Beschneidung und dann ein zweites Mal während ihres Untertauchens mit den wichtigsten Geboten und Halachot bekannt zu machen, auf die sie sich verpflichteten und an denen sie ihr Leben künftig ausrichten sollten. Ein vergleichbares Verfahren kennt aber das frühe Christentum, und zwar in Gestalt des Taufkatechumenats.

Erste Hinweise finden sich in den neutestamentlichen Schriften. Die von Paulus in I Kor 15,3b–5 zitierte Bekenntnisformel lässt sich als ein katechetisches Summarium verstehen, das den zentralen Inhalt der auf die Taufe vorbereitenden Unterweisung konzentriert zusammenfasst. I Petr 3,18–22 enthält in dichter Form eine Reihe lehrhaft klingender Bekenntnisaussagen, die um das Stichwort „Taufe" (βάπτισμα, V. 21a) gruppiert und darauf bezogen sind. Es spricht m.E. nichts dagegen, sie wie auch „die Bitte an Gott" (oder: „die Verpflichtung gegenüber Gott" [V. 21b]) als Taufhomologie bzw. -versprechen im Kontext des Taufrituals zu interpretieren. Das markanteste Beispiel ist Hebr 6,1f. Zunächst

---

159 Vgl. SMITH, „Proselyte Baptism", 29–32.
160 So u.a. RUDOLPH, *Baptisten*, 13; M. TILLY, Art. „προσήλυτος", 1028. Zu Recht fragen PUSEY/HURT, „Proselyte Baptism", 141f.: „Could it be that missioning Jews copied the Christian initiation act? Its attractiveness as a substitute for circumcision is obvious and while there is little evidence of male converts being allowed to dispense with that requirement, some alternative must have been in use during the time when the circumcision of foreigners was banned". Hier ist vor allem an das von Hadrian (117–138 n.Chr.) erlassene Beschneidungsverbot zu denken (Historia Augusta, *Hadr* 14,2: *moverunt ea tempestate et Judaei bellum, quod vetabantur mutilare genitalia* [„Zu jener Zeit begannen auch die Juden einen Krieg, weil ihnen verboten worden war, ihre Genitalien zu verstümmeln"]). Die Möglichkeit christlicher Beeinflussung hat bereits SCHNECKENBURGER erwogen, *Proselytentaufe*, 166–169.184.

wird in Aufnahme traditioneller Bekehrungsterminologie (vgl. JosAs 11,8; 12,5; Weish 11,23; 12,2; Apg 17,30f.; 20,21 u.ö.) die Konversion als „Umkehr von toten Werken" und Hinwendung zum „Glauben an Gott" beschrieben. Dann folgen Hauptstücke der Lehre (διδαχή), die Bestandteil der präbaptismalen Unterweisung ist: Das Wesen der Taufe, die Bedeutung der Handauflegung (wohl in Verbindung mit der Taufe, vgl. Apg 8,16f.; 19,5f.), die Totenauferstehung, das endzeitliche Gericht. Schließlich bietet die zeitlich nicht viel später anzusetzende Didache in Kap. 1–6 eine primär ethisch ausgerichtete Taufkatechese, um dann unmittelbar zur Taufe überzuleiten (Kap. 7).

Vielfach wird dieser Befund für die Priorität des Proselytentauchbads in Anspruch genommen. Der anfänglich noch nicht geübte Taufunterricht sei erst beim Übergang des Christentums auf außerjüdisches Gebiet notwendig geworden. Dieses praktische Bedürfnis habe dazu geführt, dass „the Jewish scheme (sc. die dem Tauchbad voraufgehende Belehrung) was taken over"[161]. Es könnte aber auch genau umgekehrt sein: Die sich entwickelnde christliche Praxis hat auf die jüdische eingewirkt und zu deren späterer Ausgestaltung beigetragen. Angesichts der Tatsache, dass es keine belastbaren Indizien für eine Frühdatierung des Proselytentauchbads gibt und seine katechetische Rahmung nicht vor Mitte des 2. Jahrhunderts n.Chr. literarisch bezeugt ist, erscheint diese alternative Möglichkeit durchaus plausibel. Sie sollte stärker, als es bisher der Fall ist, bedacht und weiter geprüft werden.

Bibliographie

Quellen

Becker, Jürgen, *Die Testamente der zwölf Patriarchen* (JSHRZ 3/1), Gütersloh: Gütersloher Verlagshaus 1980.

Beer, Georg, *Pesachim (Ostern). Text, Übersetzung und Erklärung. Nebst einem textkritischen Anhang (Die Mischna. Text, Übersetzung und ausführliche Erklärung)*, Gießen: Alfred Töpelmann 1912.

Collins, John J., „Sibylline Oracles", in: J. H. Charlesworth (Hrsg.), *The Old Testament Pseudepigrapha I: Apocalyptic Literature and Testaments*, New York: Doubleday & Company 1983, 317–472.

Der Babylonische Talmud. Nach der ersten zensurfreien Ausgabe unter Berücksichtigung der neueren Ausgaben und handschriftlichen Materials neu übertragen durch Lazarus Goldschmidt, 12 Bde, Frankfurt am Main: Jüdischer Verlag 2007 (= 1930–1936).

---

[161] Daube, *Rabbinic Judaism*, 125. Vgl. Jeremias, *Kindertaufe*, 36; Smith, „Proselyte Baptism", 23f.

GEFFCKEN, JOHANNES, *Die Oracula Sibyllina* (GCS 8), Leipzig: J. C. Hinrichs'sche Buchhandlung 1902.

DE JONGE, MARINUS, *Testamenta XII Patriarcharum* (PVTG 1), Leiden: Brill 1964.

KEE, HOWARD C., „Testaments of the Twelve Patriarchs", in: *The Old Testament Pseudepigrapha I* (s.o.), 775–828.

KURFESS, ALFONS, *Sibyllinische Weissagungen. Urtext und Übersetzungen*, Berlin: Heimeran 1951.

SCHENKL, HEINRICH, *Epicteti Dissertationes. Ab Arriani Digestae* (BSGRT), Stuttgart: Teubner 1965 (= ²1916).

SCHLEYER, DIETRICH, *Tertullian. De Baptismo. De Oratione. Von der Taufe. Vom Gebet* (FC 76), Turnhout: Brepols Publishers 2006.

SEKUNDÄRLITERATUR

ALAND, KURT, „Zur Vorgeschichte der christlichen Taufe", in: idem, *Neutestamentliche Entwürfe* (TB 63), München: Chr. Kaiser Verlag 1979, 183–197.

AVEMARIE, FRIEDRICH, „Ist die Johannestaufe ein Ausdruck von Tempelkritik? Skizze eines methodischen Problems", in: B. Ego u.a. (Hrsg.), *Gemeinde ohne Tempel/Community without Temple. Zur Substituierung und Transformation des Jerusalemer Tempels und seines Kults im Alten Testament, antiken Judentum und frühen Christentum* (WUNT 118), Tübingen: Mohr Siebeck 1999, 395–410.

— *Die Tauferzählungen der Apostelgeschichte. Theologie und Geschichte* (WUNT 139), Tübingen: Mohr Siebeck 2002.

BAMBERGER, BERNARD J., *Proselytism in the Talmudic Period*, New York: KTAV Publishing House ²1968.

BARTH, GERHARD, *Die Taufe in frühchristlicher Zeit*, Neukirchen-Vluyn: Neukirchener Verlag ²2002.

BARTH, MARKUS, *Die Taufe – ein Sakrament? Ein exegetischer Beitrag zum Gespräch über die kirchliche Taufe*, Zollikon-Zürich: Evangelischer Verlag AG 1951.

BEASLEY-MURRAY, GEORGE R., *Die christliche Taufe. Eine Untersuchung über ihr Verständnis in Geschichte und Gegenwart*, Kassel: J. G. Oncken Verlag 1968.

BECKER, JÜRGEN, *Untersuchungen zur Entstehungsgeschichte der Testamente der Zwölf Patriarchen* (AGJU 8), Leiden: Brill 1970.

BERGER, PETER L./LUCKMANN, THOMAS, *Die gesellschaftliche Konstruktion der Wirklichkeit. Eine Theorie der Wissenssoziologie*, Frankfurt am Main: Fischer Verlag ²¹2007.

BETZ, OTTO, „Die Proselytentaufe der Qumrangemeinde und die Taufe im Neuen Testament", in: idem, *Jesus. Der Herr der Kirche. Aufsätze zur biblischen Theologie II* (WUNT 52), Tübingen: Mohr Siebeck 1990, 21–48.

(STRACK, HERMANN L.) – BILLERBECK, PAUL, *Kommentar zum Neuen Testament aus Talmud und Midrasch, I: Das Evangelium nach Matthäus*, München: C. H. Beck'sche Verlagsbuchhandlung ⁵1969 (= 1926).

BLASCHKE, ANDREAS, *Beschneidung. Zeugnisse der Bibel und verwandter Texte* (TANZ 28), Tübingen/Basel: A. Francke Verlag 1998.

BÖCHER, OTTO, „Wasser und Geist", in: idem, *Kirche in Zeit und Endzeit. Aufsätze zur Offenbarung des Johannes*, Neukirchen-Vluyn: Neukirchener Verlag 1983, 58–69.

BRANDT, WILHELM, *Die jüdischen Baptismen oder das religiöse Waschen und Baden im Judentum mit Einschluß des Judenchristentums* (BZNW 18), Gießen: Alfred Töpelmann 1910.

BRAUDE, WILLIAM G., *Jewish Proselyting in the First Five Centuries of the Common Era. The Age of the Tannaim and Amoraim* (Brown University Studies 6), Providence, R.I.: The George Banta Publishing Company 1940.

BROER, INGO, „Die Konversion des Königshauses von Adiabene nach Josephus (Ant XX)", in: C. Meyer u.a. (Hrsg.), *Nach den Anfängen fragen. FS für G. Dautzenberg zum 60. Geb.* (GSTR 8), Gießen: Universitätsverlag 1994, 133–162.

CHILTON, BRUCE, „John the Purifier. His Immersion and His Death", in: *HThR* 57 (2001) 247–267.

COHEN, SHAYE J. D., „Conversion to Judaism in Historical Perspective: From Biblical Israel to Postbiblical Judaism", in: *CJud* 36 (1983) 31–45.

— „Is 'Proselyte Baptism' mentioned in the Misnah? The Interpretation of M. Pesahim 8.8 (= M. Eduyot 5.2)", in: J. C. Reeves/J. Kampen (Hrsg.), *Pursuing the Text. Studies in Honor of Ben Z. Wacholder on the Occasion of his Seventieth Birthday* (JSOT.S 184), Sheffield: Sheffield Academic Press 1994, 278–292.

— *The Beginnings of Jewishness: Boundaries, Varieties, Uncertainties* (Hellenistic Culture and Society 21), Berkeley, Calif. u.a.: University of California Press 1999.

COLLINS, JOHN J., „A Symbol of Otherness. Circumcision and Salvation in the First Century", in: J. Neusner/E. S. Frerichs (Hrsg.), „To See Ourselves as Others See Us". Christians, Jews, „Others" in Late Antiquity, Chico: Scholars Press, Ga. 1985, 163–186.

— Between Athens and Jerusalem. Jewish Identity in the Hellenistic Diaspora, Grand Rapids, Mich.: Eerdmans ²2000.

CULLMANN, OSCAR, Die Tauflehre des Neuen Testaments. Erwachsenen- und Kindertaufe (AThANT 12), Zürich: Zwingli-Verlag 1948.

DAUBE, DAVID, The New Testament and Rabbinic Judaism (JLCR 2), London: The Adlone Press 1956, 106–140.

DELORME, JEAN, „The Practice of Baptism in Judaism at the Beginning of the Christian Era", in: A. George u.a., Baptism in the New Testament. A Symposium, London: Chapman 1964, 25–60.

DONALDSON, TERENCE L., Judaism and the Gentiles. Jewish Patterns of Universalism (to 135 CE), Waco, Tex.: Baylor University Press 2007.

ELIADE, MIRCEA, Das Mysterium der Wiedergeburt. Versuch über einige Initiationstypen, Frankfurt am Main: Insel-Verlag 1988.

ERNST, JOSEF, Johannes der Täufer. Interpretation – Geschichte – Wirkungsgeschichte (BZNW 53), Berlin/New York: Walter de Gruyter 1989.

FELDMAN, LAWRENCE H., Jew and Gentile in the Ancient World. Attitudes and Interactions from Alexander to Justinian, Princeton, N.J.: Princeton University Press 1993.

FERGUSON, EVERETT, Baptism in the Early Church. History, Theology, and Liturgy in the First Five Centuries, Grand Rapids, Mich./Cambridge, U.K.: Eerdmans 2009.

FINKELSTEIN, LOUIS, „The Institution of Baptism for Proselytes", in: JBL 52 (1933) 203–211.

GAVIN, FRANK, The Jewish Antecedents of the Christian Sacraments, New York: KTAV Publishing House 1969 (= London: S.P.C.K 1928).

VAN GENNEP, ARNOLD, Übergangsriten (Les rites de passage), Frankfurt/New York: Campus-Verlag ³2005.

GNILKA, JOACHIM, „Die essenischen Tauchbäder und die Johannestaufe", in: RdQ 3 (1961) 185–207.

GOODMAN, MARTIN, Mission and Conversion. Proselytizing in the Religious History of the Roman Empire, Oxford: Clarendon Press 1994.

— „Jewish Proselytizing in the First Century", in: idem, *Judaism in the Roman World. Collected Essays* (AGJU 66), Leiden u.a.: Brill 2007, 91–116.

Haarmann, Volker, *JHWH-Verehrer der Völker. Die Hinwendung von Nichtisraeliten zum Gott Israels in alttestamentlichen Überlieferungen* (AThANT 91), Zürich: Theologischer Verlag Zürich 2008.

Hayes, Christine E., *Gentile Impurities and Jewish Identities. Intermarriage and Conversion from the Bible to the Talmud*, Oxford: University Press 2002.

Hengel, Martin, „Anonymität, Pseudepigraphie und ‚literarische Fälschung' in der jüdisch-hellenistischen Literatur", in: idem, *Judaica et Hellenistica. Kleine Schriften I* (WUNT 90), Tübingen: Mohr Siebeck 1996, 196–251.

Hirschfeld, Yishar, *Qumran – die ganze Wahrheit. Die Funde der Archäologie – neu bewertet*, Gütersloh: Gütersloher Verlagshaus 2006.

Hultgård, Anders, *L'eschatologie des Testaments des Douze Patriarches I: Interprétation des textes* (AUU.HR 6), Stockholm: Almqvist & Wiksell International 1977.

Jeremias, Joachim, „Der Ursprung der Johannestaufe", in: *ZNW* 28 (1929) 312–320.

— „Proselytentaufe und Neues Testament", in: *ThZ* 5 (1949) 418–428.

— *Die Kindertaufe in den ersten vier Jahrhunderten*, Göttingen: Vandenhoeck & Ruprecht 1958.

de Jonge, Marinus, „The Testament of Levi and 'Aramaic Levi'", in: idem, *Jewish Eschatology, Early Christian Christology, and the Testament of the Twelve Patriarchs. Collected Essays* (SNT 63), Leiden: Brill 1991, 180–190.

— „Levi in 'Aramaic Levi' and in the Testament of Levi", in: E. G. Chazon/M. E. Stone (Hrsg.), *Pseudepigraphic Perspectives. The Apocrypha and Pseudepigrapha in the Light of the Dead Sea Scrolls* (StTDJ 31), Leiden: Brill 1999, 71–89.

Kalimi, Isaac, „'He Was Born Circumcised'. Some Midrashic Sources, Their Concept, Roots and Presumably Historical Context", in: *ZNW* 93 (2002) 1–12.

Kraus, Wolfgang, *Das Volk Gottes. Zur Grundlegung der Ekklesiologie bei Paulus* (WUNT 85), Tübingen: Mohr Siebeck 1996.

Kugler, Robert A., *The Testament of the Twelve Patriarchs* (Guides to Apocrypha and Pseudepigrapha), Sheffield: Sheffield Academic Press 2001.

KUHN, KARL-GEORG/STEGEMANN, HARTMUT, Art. „Proselyten", in: *PRE.S* 9 (1962) 1248–1283.

LÉGASSE, SIMON, *Naissance du baptême* (LeDiv 153), Paris: Les Éditions du Cerf 1993.

LEIPOLDT, JOHANNES, *Die urchristliche Taufe im Lichte der Religionsgeschichte*, Leipzig: Dörffling & Franke 1928.

LICHTENBERGER, HERMANN, „Täufergemeinden und frühchristliche Täuferpolemik im letzten Drittel des 1. Jahrhunderts", in: *ZThK* 84 (1987) 36–57.

LICHTENBERGER, HERMANN/JANOWSKI, BERND, „Enderwartung und Reinheitsidee. Zur eschatologischen Deutung von Reinheit und Sühne in der Qumrangemeinde", in: B. Janowski, *Gottes Gegenwart in Israel. Beiträge zur Theologie des Alten Testaments*, Neukirchen-Vluyn: Neukirchener Verlag ²2004, 70–101.

LUCKMANN, THOMAS, *Die unsichtbare Religion*, Frankfurt am Main: Suhrkamp ⁴2005.

MCELENEY, NEIL J., „Conversion, Circumcision and the Law", in: *NTS* 20 (1974) 319–341.

MCKNIGHT, SCOTT, *A Light Among the Gentiles. Jewish Missionary Activity in the Second Temple Period*, Minneapolis, Minn.: Fortress Press 1991.

MICHAELIS, WILHELM, „Die jüdische Proselytentaufe und die Tauflehre des Neuen Testaments", in: *KBRS* 105 (1949) 17–20.34–38.

— „Zum jüdischen Hintergrund der Johannestaufe", in: *Jud.* 7 (1951) 81–120.

MOORE, GEORGE, F., *Judaism in the first Centuries of the Christian Era. The Age of the Tannaim, Vol. I*, Cambridge (Mass.): Harvard University Press 1966 (= 1927).

— *Judaism in the first Centuries of the Christian Era. The Age of the Tannaim, Vol. III: Notes*, Cambridge, Mass.: Harvard University Press ²1940.

NIKIPROWETZKY, VALENTIN, „Réflexions sur quelques problèmes du quatrième et du cinquième livre des Oracles Sibyllins", in: *HUCA* 43 (1972) 29–76.

NOACK, BENT, „Are the Essenes Referred to in the Sibylline Oracles?", in: *StTh* 17 (1963) 90–102.

NOLLAND, JOHN, „Uncircumcised Proselytes?", in: *JSJ* 12 (1981) 173–194.

OEPKE, ALBRECHT, Art. „βάπτω κτλ.", *ThWNT* 1 (1933) 527–544.

— Art. „παῖς κτλ.", *ThWNT* 5 (1954) 636–653.

— Polster, Gottfried, „Der kleine Talmudtraktat über die Proselyten. Text, Übersetzung, Bemerkungen", in: *Angelos* 2 (1926) 1–38 (zuzügl. zwei Abb., Seiten unpaginiert).

Porton, Gary G., *The Stranger Within Your Gates. Converts and Conversion in Rabbinic Literature* (Chicago Studies in the History of Judaism), Chicago, Ill./London: The University of Chicago Press 1994.

Pusey, Karen/Hurt, John, „Jewish Proselyte Baptism", in: *ET* 95 (1984) 141–145.

Regev, Eyal, „The Ritual Baths near the Temple Mount and Extra-Purification before Entering the Temple Courts", in: *IEJ* 55 (2005) 194–204.

Rowley, Harold H., „Jewish Proselyte Baptism and the Baptism of John", in: idem, *From Moses to Qumran. Studies in the Old Testament*, London: Lutterworth Press ²1964, 211–235.

Rudolph, Kurt, *Antike Baptisten. Zu den Überlieferungen über frühjüdische und -christliche Taufsekten* (SSAW.PH 121/4), Berlin: Akademie Verlag 1981.

Sanders, Ed P., *Judaism. Practice and Belief 63 BCE – 66 CE*, London/Philadelphia, Pa.: SCM Press, Trinity Press International ²1994.

Schiffman, Lawrence, H., *Who Was a Jew? Rabbinic and Halakhic Perspectives on the Jewish-Christian Schism*, Hoboken, N.J.: KTAV Publishing House 1985.

— „The Conversion of the Royal House of Adiabene in Josephus and Rabbinic Sources", in: L. H. Feldman/G. Hata (Hrsg.), *Josephus, Judaism, and Christianity*, Leiden: Brill 1987, 297–312.

Schneckenburger, Matthias, *Über das Alter der jüdischen Proselytentaufe und deren Zusammenhang mit dem johanneischen und christlichen Ritus. Nebst einer Beilage über die Irrlehrer zu Colossä*, Berlin: Ferdinand Dümmler 1828.

Schürer, Emil, *The History of the Jewish People in the Age of Jesus Christ (175 B.C.–A.D. 135). A New English Version revised and edited by G. Vermes u.a.*, Vol 3/1, Edinburgh: T. & T. Clark 1995 (= 1986).

Smith, Derwood, „Jewish Proselyte Baptism and the Baptism of John", in: *RestQ* 25 (1982) 13–32.

Stern, Menahem, *Greek and Latin Authors on Jews and Judaism, Vol. I: From Herodotus to Plutarch*, Jerusalem: The Israel Academy of Sciences and Humanities 1974.

TAYLOR, JOAN E., *The Immerser. John the Baptist within Second Temple Judaism*, Grand Rapids, Mich./Cambridge, U.K.: Eerdmans 1997.

TAYLOR, THEOPHILUS M., „The Beginnings of Jewish Proselyte Baptism", in: *NTS* 2 (1955/56) 193–198.

TILLY, MICHAEL, Art. „προσήλυτος", *TBLNT*² 2 (2000) 1026–1028.

TORRANCE, THOMAS F., „Proselyte Baptism", in: *NTS* 1 (1954) 150–154.

— „The Origins of Baptism", in: *SJTh* 11 (1958) 158–171.

TURNER, VICTOR W., „Betwixt and Between. The Liminal Period in Rites de Passage", in: idem, *The Forest of Symbols. Aspects of Ndembu Rituals*, Ithaca/New York: Cornell University Press 1967, 93–111.

ULRICHSEN, JARL H., *Die Grundschrift der Testamente der Zwölf Patriarchen. Eine Untersuchung zu Umfang, Inhalt und Eigenart der ursprünglichen Schrift* (AUU 10), Uppsala: Almquist & Wiksell International 1991.

WEBB, ROBERT L., *John the Baptizer and Prophet. A Socio-Historical Study* (JSNT.S 62), Sheffield: Sheffield Academic Press 1991.

WETZ, CHRISTIAN, *Eros und Bekehrung. Anthropologische und religionsgeschichtliche Untersuchungen zu „Joseph und Aseneth"* (NTOA/StUNT 87), Göttingen: Vandenhoeck & Ruprecht 2010.

YARBRO COLLINS, ADELA, „The Origin of Christian Baptism", in: *StLi* 19 (1989) 28–46.

ZANGENBERG, JÜRGEN, „Qumran und die Archäologie. Überlegungen zu einer umstrittenen Ortslage", in: S. Alkier/J. Zangenberg (Hrsg.), *Zeichen aus Text und Stein. Studien auf dem Weg zu einer Archäologie des Neuen Testaments* (TANZ 42), Tübingen/Basel: A. Franke Verlag 2003, 262–306.

Part/Teil IV

Earliest Christianity

Urchristentum

Kreative Erinnerung als nachösterliche Nachschöpfung
Der Ursprung der christlichen Taufe

MICHAEL LABAHN

1. Methodische Vorüberlegungen

Die Frage nach dem *Ursprung der christlichen Taufe* bzw. nach einer Kontinuität oder einer Entwicklung, die von der Johannestaufe zur urchristlichen Taufpraxis führt, nötigt zu einer *konstruktiven historischen Methodik*, die die Quellen auf historische Erinnerung befragt und aus den Nachrichten ein plausibles Gesamtbild entwirft. Dabei ist nach einem möglichen „missing link" zwischen diesen beiden, in den frühchristlichen Schriften zumeist unverbunden nebeneinander stehenden Taufpraktiken zu fragen (Abschn. § 3.1.).[1] Eine explizite Verbindung zwischen Johannestaufe und einer im Neuen Testament sonst nicht belegten Taufaktivität Jesu findet sich nur in Joh 3,22; 4,1 (dazu später) – ob diese Nachricht bzw. eine ihr zugrunde liegende historische Erinnerung als Verbindung dienen kann, wird ebenfalls zu klären sein.

Die zeitlich frühsten, der Entstehung der frühchristlichen Taufpraxis am nächsten stehenden Quellen sind primär die neutestamentlichen Schriften. Die frühchristlichen Briefe, insbesondere des Paulus, interpretieren bzw. kontextualisieren im Regelfall den christlichen Taufakt bzw. die durch den Taufakt veränderte Existenz des christlichen Menschen in Bezug auf seine Relation zu Gott, zum Christus und/oder zur Gemeinde. Dabei werden Konsequenzen für das durch die Taufe neu konstituierte Leben gezogen. Erzähltexte berichten hingegen von Taufgeschehen, sei es die Taufe von Jesus oder die Taufe von neubekehrten Christen. Alle diese Texte einschließlich der lukanischen Apostelgeschichte sind nicht an einer Aufklärung darüber interessiert, wie es zur christlichen Taufpraxis gekommen ist. Sie bieten keine kritisch zu würdigende Darstellung der Einsetzung der Taufe, sondern setzen die Taufpraxis weitgehend als Eintrittsakt für die Neophyten in die christliche Gemeinde, sei es als Teil der Argumentation, als Bekenntnis oder als Bericht (vgl. vor allem die Tauferzählungen der

---

1 S.a. G. LOHFINK, „Ursprung", 173: „Bei der Frage nach dem Ursprung der christlichen Taufe steht man sofort vor einem seltsamen, ja rätselhaften Phänomen: Jesus selbst hat nicht getauft – aber schon die Urgemeinde hat die Taufe als kirchliche und theologische Selbstverständlichkeit praktiziert".

Apostelgeschichte),[2] voraus (Abschn. § 3.2.);[3] eine Ausnahme bildet das späte Modell von Mt 28,18–20, eine Episode, die aufgrund ihres besonderen Charakters als „Einsetzungsbericht" der Taufe in unserem Zusammenhang hohe Aufmerksamkeit verdient, auch wenn man ihren matthäischen Kontext bedenken muss, zu dem die rituelle Praxis seiner Gemeinschaft gehört (Abschn. § 4.1.).

Die beschriebene Textbasis ist die Quellenlage, die den Historiker/die Historikerin zu einer konstruierenden bzw. re-konstruierenden Methodik führt, die sich mit der Repräsentanz von Geschehenem in der neugestalteten Erinnerung auseinandersetzt. Die historische Konstruktion[4] bezieht sich auf die dem Historiker/der Historikerin zugänglichen Quellen, auch wenn diese sehr unterschiedlicher inhaltlicher Natur und literarischer Gattung sind, und sucht aus diesen Nachrichten plausible und konsensfähige Zusammenhänge zu bilden, mithin: Geschichte plausibel, methodisch reflektiert und historisch debatierbar zu „erzählen". Die Darstellung des Ursprungs der christlichen Taufe ist „ein hypothetischer, falsifizierbarer Entwurf, der die vorhandenen Quellen als Wirkungen derjenigen Ereignisse, auf die sie sich beziehen, verständlich zu machen versucht".[5] Es stellt sich die Frage, ob sich die Ereignisse und ihre Erinnerungen in neuen Sinnbildungen zu einem möglichen und plausiblen Bild des Ursprungs zurückverfolgen lassen. Die literarischen Eckdaten (Abschn. § 2.1.) haben bislang zu unterschiedlichen Deutungsmodellen (Abschn. § 2.2.) geführt, die auf die Mehrdeutigkeit der Quellen hinweisen.

In dieser Studie wird zu fragen sein, wie die große Verbreitung der christlichen Taufe in unterschiedlichen frühchristlichen Gemeinden zu verstehen ist. Das Modell direkter historischer Abhängigkeit von einem möglichen Urgeschehen (Taufpraxis Jesu oder der Urgemeinde) ist nicht mehr als eine mögliche bzw. wahrscheinliche Option, die aber Auswirkungen auf Zeitpunkt und Ort des Werdens einer frühchristlichen Taufe hat, eben die Verankerung an den Ursprung bzw. die Frühphase der christlichen Bewegung.[6] Hier kommt der Analyse früher Nachrichten Bedeutung für die Frage zu, ob ihr Informationen zum Ursprung der Taufpraxis zu entnehmen sind. Der Schatten der kreativen und ak-

---

2   Vgl. z.B. F. AVEMARIE, *Tauferzählungen*.

3   Vgl. z.B. die Hinweise bei L. HARTMAN, *Namen des Herrn Jesus*, 32.

4   Vgl. zur Terminologie und Methodik z.B. J. SCHRÖTER, „Historizität der Evangelien", 108f. G. HÄFNER, „Konstruktion und Referenz", 93ff., macht in Auseinandersetzung mit narrativen Geschichtstheorien das „Moment der Konstruktion" stark, zielt damit aber anders als Schröter (aaO., 94f.), eigentlich auf Rekonstruktion (Häfner, aaO., schreibt „Re-Konstruktion").

5   Um die Aussagen zur wissenschaftlichen Jesusdarstellung von SCHRÖTER, „Historizität der Evangelien", 190, auf das Problem dieses Beitrages zu übertragen.

6   Vgl. DUNN, *Beginning From Jerusalem*, 186: „… baptism as a feature of the new sect [d.h. die frühchristliche Bewegung; ML.] from the beginning"; s.a. F. HAHN, *Verständnis der Mission*, 41: „Mit der ganzen Urgemeinde hat Petrus von Anfang an die Taufe an allen Glaubenden vollzogen …".

tualisierenden Erinnerung lässt sich zur Annahme einer christlichen Taufpraxis erhellen, die wohl bereits in der frühsten Phase der christlichen Bewegung nach dem Vorbild der Johannestaufe geübt, aber als nachösterlicher Akt des Erhöhten und somit als Neuschöpfung verstanden wurde (Abschn. § 4.2.).

2. Die historische Ausgangslage

2.1. Zwei historische Eckpunkte zum Ursprung der christlichen Taufe in der frühchristlichen Literatur

In den neutestamentlichen Texten sind *zwei Eckpunkte* markiert, die für die Frage nach dem Ursprung der christlichen Taufe von entscheidender Bedeutung sind. Einerseits finden wir Nachricht(en) bzw. Erzählung(en) darüber, *dass Jesus von Johannes (dem Täufer) getauft wurde*: Mk 1,9–11; Mt 3,13–17; Lk 3,21f. (Q 3,[[21f.]]⁷); s.a. Joh 1,29–34.[8] Sie berichten vom Taufen des Johannes, der Taufe Jesu (nicht Joh 1,29–34) und einer Geistverleihung aus dem Himmel wie eine Taube bzw. in Gestalt einer Taube herabkommend. Gemeinsam ist den Belegen der Synoptiker die historisch weitestgehend akzeptierte Information[9], dass ein Taufakt Johannes des Täufer an Jesus am Beginn des öffentlichen Wirkens Jesu

---

7   Zur Frage der literarischen Präsenz einer Tauferzählung in Q vgl. z.B. M. LABAHN, *Der Gekommene als Wiederkommender*, 131–136 (mit Lit.).

8   Die häufig in ihrer (möglichen literarischen oder oralen) Relation zu den synoptischen Tauftexten diskutierte Passage Joh 1,29–34 (vgl. z.B. D.-A. KOCH, „Täufer als Zeuge", 1978ff.; J. ERNST, *Johannes der Täufer*, 198ff.; M. STOWASSER, *Johannes der Täufer*, 109ff.) erzählt gerade nicht die Taufe Jesu; an deren Stelle steht das in Joh 1,7f.15 angekündigte Zeugnis des Täufers über Jesus, das ihn als „Lamm Gottes, das der Welt Sünde trägt", vorstellt. Sprechen Mk 1,6 par Mt 3,5 vom Sündenbekenntnis bei der Johannestaufe, so bewirkt die Taufe nach Lukas die Sündenvergebung (Lk 3,3a; vgl. die Wirkung der christlichen Taufe: Act 2,38); das vierte Evangelium christologisiert das Thema und schreibt das Tragen der Sünde und somit die befreiende Wirkung dem Lamm zu (vgl. mit etwas anderer Argumentation auch C. R. KOESTER, *Symbolism*, 177f.). D.-A. KOCH, „Täufer als Zeuge", 1978 Anm. 48, erwägt sogar eine ‚Richtigstellung' von Mk 1,6.

9   Der entsprechende Konsens lässt sich von z.B. RUDOLF BULTMANN (*Geschichte der synoptischen Tradition*, 263) bis in gegenwärtige Jesusdarstellungen hinein nachzeichnen (vgl. z.B. DUNN, *Jesus Remembered*, 350f.; J. FREY, „Apokalyptik als Herausforderung", 59ff.; J. P. MEIER, *A Marginal Jew 2*, 100–105; s.a. E. FERGUSON, *Baptism*, 99f.). Allerdings gibt es auch vereinzelte Gegenstimmen, von denen aus der jüngeren Forschung beispielhaft auf E. HAENCHEN, *Weg Jesu*, 60–63; B. CHILTON, „John the Baptist", 25–44; L. E. VAAGE, „Bird-Watching", 280–294, zu verweisen ist. Im Rahmen von Ritualtheorien sei nach R. E. DEMARIS, „Taufe Jesu", 43–52, die Geistbesessenheit im Taufbericht das Historische, die Taufe als vom christlichen Ritual beeinflusster Akt das historisch Zweifelhafte. Diese Analyse wirft verschiedenste Fragen auf, insbesondere wenn dann über ein anderes mögliches „Ritual", dem Fasten Jesu mit dem Vorbild von Mk 3,21 als Ersatz (aaO., 49), spekuliert wird.

steht, der Jesus und seine Lehre in einen noch näher zu bestimmenden Zusammenhang mit der Lehre der Täufers[10] stellt.

Der *zweite Eckpunkt* für unser Thema ist die Präsenz eines christlichen Rituals, der Taufe auf den Namen Jesu, in zahlreichen frühchristlichen Schriften, die als ein wirkmächtiger, d.h. als ein im Vollzug des Rituals den Menschen im Selbst-Verständnis wie im Fremdverständnis neu konstruierender Eingang[11] in das christliche Gemeindeleben verstanden wird. Paulus darf hier als frühester literarischer Zeuge genannt werden, der seinerseits auf älteren Tauftraditionen aufruht und auf diese kreativ gestaltend zurückgreift.[12]

Erich Dinkler betont angesichts dieser Überlieferungssituation, dass „die T[aufe; ML.] auf den Namen Christi ... anscheinend von Anbeginn an geübt" wurde.[13] Dieses Modell bildet jedoch keineswegs einen unwidersprochenen Konsens ab. Gerade in der ersten Hälfte des 20. Jh.s wird die Taufe als ein sekundärer Akt der Rückerinnerung gedeutet, der mit dem Einfluss des Hellenismus verbunden wird.[14] Mögliche Einflüsse von religiösen Phänomenen auf die Interpretation und Entwicklung der christlichen Taufpraxis (z.B. die Analogien zu Konzeptionen in hellenistischen Mysterienkulten) sind zweifelsohne zu beobachten, aber in diesem Beitrag nicht zu verfolgen, lediglich die *Frage nach formenden und die Genese der frühchristlichen Taufpraxis erhellenden Phänomenen ist zu beachten*, wobei wir vor allem auf den ersten der benannten Eckpunkte, die Johannestaufe, gewiesen sein dürften (Abschn. § 4.2.).

---

10 Zu den Möglichkeiten und Grenzen, Johannes als „Lehrer" Jesu zu bestimmen bzw. von einer Täuferschule zu sprechen, vgl. z.B. K. BACKHAUS, *„Jüngerkreise" des Täufers Johannes*, 47ff.; ERNST, *Johannes der Täufer*, 349ff.; vermittelnd argumentiert die Zusammenfassung bei U. SCHNELLE, *Theologie des Neuen Testaments*, 64: „Die Überlieferung verweist auf eine geistige Verwurzelung Jesu im Täuferkreis, beide bewegten sich in einem vergleichbaren religiös-sozialen Milieu und Jesus wurde als Parallelgestalt zum Täufer wahrgenommen (vgl. Mk 6,14–16par; 8,28). Zugleich gibt es keine überzeugenden Indizien für eine längere Mitgliedschaft Jesu im Täuferkreis. Man wird Jesus deshalb als einen Täuferschüler für kurze Zeit verstehen müssen".

11 In der Interpretation paulinischer Tauftheologie spricht Schnelle, *Paulus*, 546f., davon, dass die Taufe „heilstatsächlich" ist, und G. THEISSEN, „Taufe", 107ff., arbeitet heraus, dass nach Paulus im Ritual der ‚neue Mensch' in theologischer wie in sozialer Hinsicht konstruiert wird.

12 Vgl. grundlegend SCHNELLE, *Gerechtigkeit und Christusgegenwart*; s.a. z.B. H. D. BETZ, „Transferring a Ritual", 240–271; F. HAHN, „Taufe und Rechtfertigung", 241–270; TH. SÖDING, „Taufe, Geist und neues Leben", 335–345.

13 E. DINKLER, „Art. Taufe", 627; K. ALAND, „Vorgeschichte", 183: „Die christliche Taufe ist so alt wie die christliche Kirche"; G. BARTH, *Taufe in frühchristlicher Zeit*, 11–13. Die Gegenposition markiert die Ausnahme; z.B. E. BARNIKOL, „Fehlen der Taufe", 593–610, oder zuvor das differenzierte Urteil von J. WEISS, *Urchristentum*, 36: aufgrund seiner Analyse der Tauferzählungen der Apostelgeschichte, wonach „nicht überall und daher wohl nicht von Anfang an die Taufe vollzogen wurde" und „die Taufe nicht von je her ein notwendiges Kennzeichen der Jesusanhänger war", sondern „einen Schritt auf dem Wege zu festerer Organisation (war; ML.), und diese wird anfangs gefehlt haben".

14 Nachweise bei DUNN, *Beginning From Jerusalem*, 186 Anm. 62; LOHFINK, „Ursprung", 178f.

2.2. Erklärungsmodelle zum Ursprung der christlichen Taufe in der exegetischen Literatur

Die Forschung stellt unterschiedliche Erklärungsmuster zur Verfügung, wie diese beiden Pole – Jesu Taufe durch Johannes und die frühchristliche Taufe auf den Namen Jesu – in Relation gesetzt werden können.[15] Trotz des mehrheitlichen Schweigens in der frühchristlichen Literatur über eine Taufaktivität Jesu[16] besteht eines der Modelle *in der personalen Kontinuität zu einem Taufen Jesu*. So erwägt Jens Schröter:

> Dass in Jesu Verkündigung die Botschaft von der Gottesherrschaft an die Stelle der Taufe des Johannes tritt, ist zweifellos zutreffend. Dies spricht jedoch nicht dagegen, dass Jesus zunächst ebenfalls getauft und auf diese Weise erste Anhänger gewonnen hat. Das würde … verständlich machen, warum die Taufe sehr bald zu einer zentralen Symbolhandlung der Christen wurde und sogar als Auftrag Jesu selbst ausgegeben werden konnte.[17]

Allerdings wird selbst bei Exegeten, die mit einer (kurzen) Taufpraxis Jesu rechnen, mit dem Argument, dass diese Taufe keine zentrale Rolle in seiner Verkündigung gespielt hat, die Bedeutung jener Praxis zur Erklärung der christlichen Taufe bestritten (pointiert bei Petr Pokorný):

> Es ist wahr, daß Jesus und einige seiner Jünger dem weiteren Kreis der Anhänger Johannes des Täufers angehört haben und daß Jesus noch während seiner selbständigen Tätigkeit zu Leuten aus jenem Kreis Kontakte behielt: Mt 11,2–19 par; Lk 7,29f.; Mk 6,14–29; Joh 3,22f.; 4,1f. Es ist nicht ganz ausgeschlossen, daß er eine kurze Zeit am Anfang seines Wirkens wirklich auch getauft hat. Die Taufe ist für ihn jedoch nicht bezeichnend gewesen, und er hat seine Verkündigung

---

15　Auch die Waschungen in Qumran (hierzu A. LABAHN in der vorliegenden Publikation) oder die jüdische Proselytentaufe (hierzu D. SÄNGER in der vorliegenden Publikation) konnten als genetisch-historische Modelle der christlichen Taufe interpretiert werden: eine Linienführung von der „essenischen Proselytentaufe zur Johannestaufe und damit zur frühchristlichen Taufe zog z.B. O. BETZ, „Die Proselytentaufe der Qumrangemeinde". H. KRAFT, „Anfänge", 410f., verortet den Ursprung der christlichen Taufe im Pfingstgeschehen, nicht in der Johannestaufe, wobei Joel 2,28f. (3,1–5MT) eine entscheidende Rolle spielt.

16　Vgl. z.B. DUNN, *Beginning From Jerusalem*, 185.

17　SCHRÖTER, *Jesus von Nazareth*, 138; s.a. ALAND, „Vorgeschichte", 194f.: „Das Johannesevangelium ist, weil es die Tatsache der Taufe Jesu durch Johannes völlig unterdrückt, freier und kann ganz unbefangen von der Tauftätigkeit Jesu bzw. seiner Begleiter berichten, …"; L. SCHENKE, *Urgemeinde*, 115; TH. M. FINN, *From Death To Rebirth*, 138. 141. Für die Annahme einer (dauerhaften) Tauftätigkeit Jesu plädieren auch: z.B. G. R. BEASLEY-MURRAY, *Baptism*, 68ff.; J. BECKER, *Johannes der Täufer*, 13f.; O. BÖCHER, „Wasser und Geist", A. Y. COLLINS, „Origin of Christian Baptism", 229f.; R. T. FRANCE, „Jesus the Baptist?", 105–107; D. M. SMITH, „Problem of History in John", 317; STOWASSER, *Johannes der Täufer*, 212–214; J. E. TAYLOR, *The Immerser*, 295 Anm. 73: Lit.!

nicht durch die Taufe versiegelt. Die Taufpraxis der ersten Christen kann von der Taufpraxis Jesu nicht abgeleitet werden.[18]

Ein weiteres Modell ist das der *sachlichen Kontinuität, die die frühchristliche Taufpraxis aus der Erinnerung an die eine Taufe Jesu durch Johannes heraus entstanden versteht.* So formuliert Udo Schnelle:

> Grunddatum aller nt.lichen T.aussagen und der mit ihnen verbundenen T.praxis ist das hist. Faktum der T. Jesu durch Johannes den Täufer (vgl. Mk 1,9 par.). ... die T. Jesu am Jordan [dürfte; ML.] erklären, warum von Anfang an in den urchristl. Gemeinden ... die T. als normativer Initiationsritus galt.[19]

Eng verwandt mit der Ableitung aus der Taufe Jesu und bisweilen mit diesem Erklärungsmodell kombiniert ist die Herleitung der frühchristlichen Taufpraxis aus der Johannestaufe, wobei sich genetische und phänomenologische Argumentation verbinden (z.B. Ludger Schenke):

> Die Urgemeinde hat die Taufpraxis von Johannes dem Täufer übernommen. Mit diesem teilte sie auch die Anschauung vom Charakter und von der Wirkung der Taufe. Sie galt als ein eschatologisches ‚Sakrament', durch das dem, der umkehrte und seine Sünden bekannte, die Sünden der Vergangenheit erlassen wurden. So war er vor dem kommenden Gottesgericht sicher. Für die Übernahme der Taufe spielte in der Urgemeinde sicher die Erinnerung daran eine große Rolle, daß Jesus selbst sich von Johannes hatte taufen lassen.[20]

Noch direkter, im Modus der „Fortsetzung" bestimmt Knut Backhaus das Verhältnis zwischen Johannestaufe und frühchristlichem Taufhandeln:

> Daß die Kirche sich als Fortsetzung der palästinischen Täuferbewegung verstand, ist besonders deutlich daraus zu ersehen, daß sie sich von ihren frühesten Anfängen an ohne Verzug und mit barer Selbstverständlichkeit deren zentrale Übung zu eigen machte. Die christliche Taufe war die im Licht des Christus-Ereignisses

---

18 P. POKORNÝ, *Entstehung der Christologie*, 148. Pokorný unterscheidet damit übrigens zwischen einer kurzfristigen, von ihm als völlig akzidentiell betrachteten Tauftätigkeit und einer regulären Taufpraxis – ein differenzierter, aber mir nicht völlig konsequent erscheinender Umgang mit der Quellenlage.

19 SCHNELLE, „Art. Taufe 1", 663; s.a. B. OESTREICH, „Taufe als Symbol", 49ff.; SCHENKE, *Urgemeinde*, 115. Die Rückführung der urchristlichen Taufpraxis ist Aufgabe der Studie „Zur Vorgeschichte der christlichen Taufe" von Kurt Aland. Er listet seine Argumente aaO., 187–196, auf: zeitliche Nähe, Taufe Jesu und einiger seiner Anhänger, die Episode von den Johannesjüngern in Ephesus (Act 19,1ff.) sowie die Nachricht über Priscilla und Aquila in 18,25ff., die johanneische Nachricht von einer Tauftätigkeit Jesu (Joh 3,22; 4,1), einen „Umschmelzungsprozeß" durch Auferstehungserlebnis und Geisterfahrung und Act 2,38 als mögliche „Brücke" zwischen Bußtaufe und christlicher Taufe. Die Argumentation ist eher genetisch, denn phänomenologisch – zu fragen ist jedoch, ob die Johannestaufe als Erklärungsmodell auch gleichzeitig die historische Problematik löst.

20 SCHENKE, *Urgemeinde*, 115; s.a. LOHFINK, „Ursprung", 187ff., für den die „eschatologische Grundsituation" (aaO., 190) der Täufertaufe und frühchristliches Taufverständnis miteinander parallel gehen und so die Rezeption verständlich machen.

reinterpretierte Johannestaufe. Der Täufer war, so gesehen, auch der ‚Anfang' der christlichen Taufpraxis.[21]

Es finden sich jedoch auch deutliche Gegenstimmen, die das Element der Diskontinuität betonen und die Gestaltung der Taufepisode(n) im Dienste der späteren christlichen Taufpraxis verstehen. So sind die Tauferzählungen nach dem Modell von Rudolf Bultmann „Tauflegenden", die die nachösterliche Praxis durch die Verlagerung in die vorösterliche Erzählzeit legitimieren sollen. Die „Legende" nimmt laut Bultmann ihren Ausgangspunkt in der Übertragung der Messiaswürde auf Jesus, die ihren Ausdruck in der Geistverleihung bei der Taufe findet, wie es erst der hellenistischen Tauftheologie entspräche; daher „kann die Tauflegende erst hellenistischen Ursprungs sein".[22] Diese Tauflegende wirkt weiter:

> Wenn so die Tauflegende unter dem Einfluß des christlichen Kults gestaltet wurde, so kann es nicht wundern, daß sie bald unter diesem Einfluß noch weiter ausgestaltet wurde, nämlich in dem Sinne, daß sie nun zur Begründung des christlichen Taufkultes dient und so zur Kultuslegende im eigentlichen Sinne wird.[23]

Im Spiegel der frühchristlichen Literatur finden sich auch andere Modelle für die Herleitung der frühchristlichen Taufpraxis, die ebenfalls ein Element der Diskontinuität und Neugestaltung nahe legen. James Dunn, insbesondere auf Mt. 28,19 bezugnehmend, findet in den frühchristlichen Schriften die Erinnerung wachgehalten, dass

> the first Christian community believed that the risen Christ had so instructed them [die Taufpraxis als frühchristliches Grundmerkmal; ML].[24]

Es wird im Folgenden zu prüfen sein, wie sich die beiden Eckpunkte – Taufe von Jesus und frühchristliche Taufpraxis – im Horizont von Kontinuität und Diskontinuität zueinander verhalten. Lassen die Quellen zudem hinreichend sicher eine Taufpraxis Jesu erkennen, die die spätere christliche Praxis mit der Johannestaufe direkt verbindet? Oder ist das Element der Diskontinuität und der Kreativität wesentlich höher zu veranschlagen, wobei die Erinnerung an die Taufpraxis des Johannes ebenso Einfluss genommen haben kann wie auch die neutestamentliche Erinnerung Spuren der Gestaltung aus der aktuellen Gemeindepraxis tragen kann? Antworten auf diese Fragen kann nur ein erneuter Durchgang durch die

---

21 BACKHAUS, „Jüngerkreise" des Täufers Johannes, 332. Backhaus fragt zugleich nach dem Grund der Wiederaufnahme bzw., in seiner Diktion, „der Unterbrechung in der Zeit der öffentlichen Wirksamkeit Jesu" (aaO., 333).

22 R. BULTMANN, Geschichte der synoptischen Tradition, 263ff.; das Zitat: aaO., 267.

23 BULTMANN, Geschichte der synoptischen Tradition, 269, denkt an die alte Kirche und verweist auf Tertullian; hier gelte: „er [Jesus; ML.] ist der erste, der die Taufe mit Wasser und Geist empfangen und sie damit wirkungskräftig für die Gläubigen inauguriert hat".

24 DUNN, Beginning From Jerusalem, 186.

Quellen bringen, wobei die Elemente der Kontinuität (gestaltende Repräsentanz der Erinnerung im Erinnern) und der Diskontinuität (Gestaltung durch die Sinnbildung, auf die hin das Ereignis erinnert wird) zu beachten sind.

3. Die Suche nach Verbindungslinien und Ausgangspunkten

3.1. Jesus, der Getaufte, aber nicht der Taufende

Wie bereits festgehalten, gehört es zu den sicheren Daten der frühchristlichen Jesuserinnerung, dass Jesus durch Johannes, den Täufer, getauft wurde und dass diese Taufe einen entscheidenden Impuls auf Jesu Wirken als Verkündiger, Bote und Täter der punktuell präsenten Gottesherrschaft ausübt. Die entsprechenden Nachrichten finden sich in *Mk 1,9–11; Mt 3,13–17; Lk 3,21f. (s.a. Q 3,⟦21f.⟧).*[25] Diese synoptischen Texte berichten von der Taufe Jesu durch Johannes, wobei die Johannestaufe als ein Reinigungsgeschehen von Sünden (Lk 3,3, aber s.a. Mk 1,5 par. Mt 3,6) dargestellt wird, das der tätigen[26] Umkehr der Getauften die Vergebung angesichts des Anbruchs des Gottesgerichts zuspricht (vgl. Mk 1,5; Mt 3,6.7–10; Lk 3,3.7–9; s.a. Q 3,7–9[27]).[28]

Fügt sich der Bericht im Markusevangelium als narrative Realisierung von Mk 1,1 in den markinischen Sinnentwurf ein,[29] so spiegelt Matthäus bekanntlich eine christologisch motivierte Diskussion um die Taufepisode, die in der möglichen Problematisierung der Vorrangstellung von Jesus gegenüber dem Täufer durch den Taufakt (Mt 3,14b: ἐγὼ χρείαν ἔχω ὑπὸ σοῦ βαπτισθῆναι [ich bedarf von dir getauft zu werden]) besteht; die matthäische Lösungsstrategie liegt in Jesu vorbildlicher Erfüllung der notwendigen Gerechtigkeit (V.15b: οὕτως γὰρ πρέπον ἐστὶν ἡμῖν πληρῶσαι πᾶσαν δικαιοσύνην [denn nur so ist

---

[25] Außerkanonische frühchristliche Tauferzählungen sammelt und bewertet E. FERGUSON, *Baptism*, 104–112.

[26] Z.B. ERNST, *Johannes der Täufer*, 312.

[27] In Q ist die Taufe als Wassertaufe im Gegensatz zum Kommenden vorgestellt (3,16b), wahrscheinlich auch die Taufe Jesu erwähnt (3,⟦21f.⟧) sowie die Gerichtspredigt überliefert (3,7–9), aber ein Bekennen der Sünden im Taufgeschehen wird nicht berichtet.

[28] S.a. ERNST, *Johannes der Täufer*, 334–336. Nach H. MERKLEIN, „Gericht und Heil", 64, ist die Taufe des Täufers „Vorwegnahme und Vollzug" des Gerichts (s.a. POKORNÝ, *Entstehung der Christologie*, 151); sie „symbolisiert das Todesgericht über den Sünder". In diesem Sinn ist die Taufe „Frucht der Umkehr": IDEM, „Umkehrpredigt", 116f.

Das Josephus-Zeugnis (Ant 18,116–119) betont hingegen die Rolle des Täufers als Tugendlehrer und nimmt so das Handeln der Adressaten als entscheidenden Aspekt in den Blick ausdrücklich zu Ungunsten der Taufe als Akt zur Sündenvergebung; zur Analyse des Josephus-Zeugnisses z.B. BACKHAUS, *„Jüngerkreise" des Täufers Johannes*, 266ff. Die Darstellung des Täufers entspricht dem Anliegen, das Judentum als werteorientierte philosophische Tradition zu beschreiben; vgl. S. MASON, *Flavius Josephus*, 184ff.

[29] S.a. SCHNELLE, „Theologie als kreative Sinnbildung", 129.

es für uns möglich, *die ganze Gerechtigkeit zu erfüllen*]), die die Taufe als im Gotteswillen angelegtes Geschehen bestimmt. Einzig bei Lukas zeichnet sich ein Einfluss der Gemeindepraxis auf die Schilderung der Johannestaufe ab; aus dem Sündenbekenntnis im Taufvollzug (Mk 1,5 par. Mt 3,6) wird die Taufe zur Vergebung der Sünden (Lk 3,3a), was sprachlich seiner Darstellung der christlichen Taufpraxis in der Urgemeinde entspricht (Act 2,38)[30].

Der Bericht von der Taufe Jesu ist also, kurz gesagt, in die jeweilige Sinnbildung der Evangelienerzähler[31] integriert, wobei sich wenigstens im Matthäusevangelium christologische Probleme mit dem Erinnerten zeigen: diese lassen sich wohl am besten mit dem ‚Anstößigkeits-Kriterium'[32] als eine historische Erinnerung verstehen, die nicht allein aus historischen Gründen, sondern aufgrund der gemeindlichen Taufpraxis, die dem erinnerten Geschehen nahe steht, bewahrt und weiter berichtet wird. Lediglich bei Lukas wird eine direkte sprachliche Überformung der Johannestaufe durch die christliche Taufpraxis sichtbar.[33]

Ob auch die jeweils berichtete Geistverleihung an Jesus an die Gabe des Geistes im frühchristlichen Taufverständnis erinnert,[34] kann zumindest erwogen werden, ist aber vielleicht noch immer mit Bultmann bei den synoptischen Traditionen bzw. Erzählungen der Jesustaufe der messianischen Gestaltungstendenz der Erinnerung zuzuschreiben[35] oder eine Erinnerung an ein Geschehen, das zur Eigenart der Gottesreichsverkündigung Jesu führt.[36] Sicherlich sind der Aspekt der Geistbegabung Jesu und die Geistverleihung in der Taufe auch dem Weiterwirken der Erinnerung an die Taufe Jesu und der Ausgestaltung der christlichen Taufe förderlich. Hier ergeben sich wohl Synergieeffekte zwischen Erinnerung und Gestaltung.

Folgt aus dem Bericht von der Taufe Jesu auch eine mögliche Annahme eines eigenen Taufhandelns Jesu? Die später zu behandelnden Notizen Joh 3,22; 4,1 scheinen dies zu belegen, aber gerade die Jesuserzählungen, die Jesu Taufe enthalten, schweigen von seinem Taufen. Es ist also zunächst zu fragen, welche in-

---

30   Vgl. Anm. 47.
31   Zum Stichwort bei Markus vgl. SCHNELLE, „Theologie als kreative Sinnbildung", 128–134.
32   Vgl. z.B. G. THEISSEN/D. WINTER, *Kriterienfrage*, 177–180, 248.
33   Erwogen werden kann auch, dass auch der Taufakt Jesu nach der lukanischen Gemeindepraxis gestaltet wurde; so kann die Akoluthie vom Gebet Jesu hin zum Geistempfang gedeutet werden; so FINN, *From Death To Rebirth*, 144.
34   Andererseits möchte LOHFINK, „Ursprung", 187, hinsichtlich der Entwicklung des frühchristlichen Taufverständnisses die urchristliche Taufpraxis und die Geistverleihung „erst sekundär miteinander verbunden" wissen.
35   S.o. S. 343 mit Anm. 23.
36   Überlegungen zu Visionen im Rahmen der Taufe: z.B. J. MARCUS, „Jesus' Baptismal Vision", 512–521, demzufolge ein prophetischer Ruf, dessen Inhalt in der Vision Lk 10,18 bestehe, gegenüber der Geistverleihung ursprünglicher sei.

haltlichen Berührungspunkte aus der Begegnung und Taufe Jesu bei Johannes für die Verkündigung Jesu zu gewinnen sind und ob diese die Annahme einer, warum auch immer unterdrückten,[37] Tauftätigkeit Jesu stützen.

Zwischen der Gerichtsankündigung Johannes des Täufers (Q 3,7–9.16b–17), die im Vollzug der Bußtaufe mit tätiger Umkehr einen Heilsaspekt beinhaltet,[38] und dem Wirken Jesu besteht eine inhaltliche Differenz, die sachlich dazu führt, dass Jesus eigenständig und parallel zum Täufer lehrte und an Kranken und Besessenen wirkte, nicht aber eine Taufe vollzog. Die Pointe der Verkündigung Jesu liegt im dem sich während des Wirkens Jesu punktuell und wirkmächtig ereignenden Gottesreich (vgl. Q 11,19f.),[39] zu dem Jesus vorbehaltlos und unmittelbar in direkter Anrede einlädt.

Die spannende Frage, warum Jesus trotz seiner Begegnung mit dem Täufer, trotz seiner Taufe und trotz des Aspekts der Umkehr in seiner Verkündigung nicht selbst taufte, muss aus diesem sachlichen Abstand heraus verstanden werden. Die Differenz in der Jesusverkündigung bezeichnet nicht die Alternative zwischen Heilsverkündigung Jesu und der Gerichtsankündigung des Täufers als Schwerpunkt, dem nur durch einen Bußakt (Taufe) mit entsprechendem Wandel zu entgehen ist, sondern das unmittelbare und direkte Kommunikationsgeschehen der Heilsansage und Heilszusage,[40] angesichts deren die theologische und soziale Neukonstruktion der Adressaten direkt und jenseits einer ritualisierten Initiation[41] stattfindet.

---

37 Gerade im Blick auf die historische Plausibilität und die Frage der Erinnerung ist das Erzählen einer christologisch nicht problemlosen Taufe Jesu, aber das Schweigen über eine für die Taufpraxis der christlichen Gemeinde doch grundlegenden Taufe durch Jesus in den synoptischen Jesuviten wiederum beredt; vgl. DUNN, *Jesus Remembered*, 606. Vgl. exemplarisch auch die Erwägungen bei LOHFINK, „Ursprung", 173–175.

38 Vgl. BARTH, „Gesichtspunkte", 141; SCHNELLE, *Theologie des Neuen Testaments*, 65; in Abweichung gegenüber der Deutung von BECKER, *Johannes der Täufer*, 106, der darauf besteht, dass das Gericht „beim Täufer einziges Thema" sei.

39 Vgl. H. WEDER, *Gegenwart und Gottesherrschaft*, 29: „Aus dem Jenseits, wo sie vermutet, geahnt, gefürchtet wird, erstreckt sie sich bis ins Diesseits. Aus der Zukunft, von der sie erhofft und ersehnt wird, dehnt sie sich aus bis ins Jetzt. Durch das exorzistische Wirken gewinnt die Gottesherrschaft eine unvermutete Ausdehnung, sie gewinnt sozusagen Einfluß auf das Jetzt. Dabei geht es nicht primär um die auf der Zeitgeraden gedachte innerzeitliche Beziehung der Gottesherrschaft zur Gegenwart, sondern vielmehr um ihre als Wirksamkeit gedachte Wirklichkeit"; zum Logion Q 11,19f. als Teil der Verkündigung der Gottesreichspredigt Jesu vgl. M. LABAHN, „Jesu Exorzismen", 631f.

40 Vgl. etwa die Seligpreisungen Q 6,20f., wobei die lukanische Form direkter Ansprache dem erkennbaren Charakter der Verkündigung Jesu wie auch der Rekonstruktion für Q (M. LABAHN, *Der Gekommene als Wiederkommender*, 318f. mit Lit.) am ehesten entsprechen dürfte.

41 Nach DUNN, *Jesus Remembered*, 607, wäre die Taufe eine rituelle Barriere für die Umkehrwilligen (ein etwas zu moderner Gedanke, der allerdings die Momente der ungehinderten Unmittelbarkeit zu Recht stark macht). Jesu Umkehrruf begegnet den Adressaten in „acts of loving concern (Mark 10.21 pars.) and restitution for wrong-doing (Luke 19.8)".

Die synoptischen Tauftexte geben den Blick frei auf Jesus als den durch den Täufer Getauften – eine für Erzähler wie Adressaten in unterschiedlichem Maße als anstößig empfundene Episode. Die Berichte werden in die jeweiligen Sinnbildungen integriert, wobei die Taufe Jesu auffällig wenig Einblick auf die spätere christliche Taufpraxis gewährt, sieht man von der Frage nach der Geistverleihung im Rahmen der Tauferzählungen ab. Lediglich das lukanische Doppelwerk zieht eine sprachlich explizite Sinnlinie, die zur frühchristlichen Taufpraxis führt, und mag auch Elemente seiner Taufpraxis in die Jesusszene haben einfließen lassen.[42] Es wäre wohl übertrieben, aus diesen Beobachtungen (1) eine bruchlose Ableitung der frühchristlichen Tauftätigkeit aus der Taufe Jesu durch Johannes zu entwickeln.[43] Die Jesuserinnerung der Synoptiker lässt zudem (2) keinen Raum, diese Taufpraxis aus einem Taufhandeln Jesu abzuleiten. Das Schweigen über solch ein Wirken Jesu wiegt schwer und das schlüssige Porträt der Jesusverkündigung weist solche Differenzen zum Täufer auf, die eine jesuanische Tauftätigkeit unwahrscheinlich machen.

3.2. Die christliche Taufe am Anfang der Urgemeinde

In der Perspektive von Kontinuität und Diskontinuität wird das einmalige Geschehen einer Taufe Jesu durch den Täufer Johannes zum Katalysator für die christliche Taufpraxis und damit in seinen Bestandteilen von Umkehrtaufe und Sündenbekenntnis Modell für einen Eingangsritus in die frühchristliche Gemeinde. Den Umkehrgedanken (vgl. die I Kor 6,11) und die Schuldvergebung spiegeln folgende Tauftraditionen wieder: z.B. I Kor 6,11; Röm 3,25 (s.a. I Kor 1,30c [… ὃς ἐγενήθη σοφία ἡμῖν ἀπὸ θεοῦ, δικαιοσύνη τε καὶ ἁγιασμὸς καὶ ἀπολύτρωσις]), wobei über die genannten Aspekte der Bezug auf Jesus Christus heraustritt: I Kor 1,30a; Gal 3,27. Beide Aspekte verdichten sich in der lukanisch gestalteten Darstellung des Erfolges der Pfingstpredigt des Petrus in *Act 2,38.41*:[44]

> 38 Πέτρος δὲ πρὸς αὐτούς·
> μετανοήσατε, [φησίν,]
> καὶ βαπτισθήτω ἕκαστος ὑμῶν ἐπὶ τῷ ὀνόματι Ἰησοῦ Χριστοῦ
> εἰς ἄφεσιν τῶν ἁμαρτιῶν ὑμῶν

---

42 S.o. S. 345 mit Anm. 33.
43 Pointiert G. KRETSCHMAR, „Geschichte des Taufgottesdienstes", 15: „… die christliche Taufe [kann; ML.] auch historisch nicht einfach als Fortsetzung oder Wiederaufnahme der ursprünglichen Johannestaufe beschrieben werden."
44 Pointiert bucht G. LÜDEMANN, *Das frühe Christentum*, 52. 53, Act 2,38.41 auf das Konto des lukanischen Erzählers, dessen „Sicht" bzw. „Phantasie" greifbar wird. Zur Taufe in der Apostelgeschichte und zu ihren hier verhandelten Taufbelegen s.a. Schröter in der vorliegenden Publikation.

καὶ λήμψεσθε τὴν δωρεὰν τοῦ ἁγίου πνεύματος.
...

⁴¹ Οἱ μὲν οὖν ἀποδεξάμενοι τὸν λόγον αὐτοῦ ἐβαπτίσθησαν·
καὶ προσετέθησαν τῇ ἡμέρᾳ ἐκείνῃ ψυχαὶ ὡσεὶ τρισχίλιαι.

³⁸ Petrus aber sagte zu ihnen:
Kehrt um
Und jeder von euch lasse sich taufen auf den Namen Jesu Christi
zur Vergebung eurer Sünden
und ihr werdet empfangen das Geschenk des heiligen Geistes
...

⁴¹ Die nun, die sein Wort annahmen, ließen sich taufen;
und es wurden an jenem Tage um die dreitausend Menschen hinzugefügt.

Die erste große Rede der Apostelgeschichte schließt mit dem Appell zur Umkehr (μετανοήσατε) und der Aufforderung an jeden einzelnen Zuhörer (ἕκαστος ὑμῶν), als Folge dieser Umkehr sich taufen zu lassen (βαπτισθήτω). Die Taufe erfolgt „auf den Namen Jesu Christi" (ἐπὶ τῷ ὀνόματι Ἰησοῦ Χριστοῦ), was den Akt deutlich von der Johannestaufe unterscheidet. Die Wirkung der Taufe besteht in der Vergebung der Sünden. Mit erneutem καί folgt der Taufaufforderung eine futurische Zusage für den Fall der Taufe. An den Taufakt reiht sich der Empfang der Gabe des heiligen Geistes (λήμψεσθε τὴν δωρεὰν τοῦ ἁγίου πνεύματος; vgl. Act 10,45[45]). V.41 lässt bei denen, die die Petrus-Predigt annehmen, die Taufe folgen. Die Annahme ist als ein Akt der Umkehr zu lesen, dem die Taufe folgt. Abschließend wird ein möglichst großer Erfolg festgestellt.

Ohne Zweifel stellt Lukas in dieser Notiz *sein* Bild der Ausbreitung der Urgemeinde durch die Pfingstpredigt dar, wobei die Möglichkeit besteht, dass seine eigene Gemeindepraxis Einfluss nimmt.[46] Die lukanische Ausformung der Verse[47] schließt jedoch nicht die Verwendung älterer Tradition(en) oder

---

45 Hier ist im lukanischen Bericht die Geistesgabe an die Heiden (10,45) der Taufe (10,47) voraus.

46 Weitreichend J. Zмijewski, *Apostelgeschichte*, 153, der an eine Rückwärtsprojektion der lukanischen Gemeindepraxis in die Darstellung der Urgemeinde denkt.

47 Die lukanische Ausarbeitung ist in der sprachlichen Kohärenz von Lk 3,3; 24,47 und Act 2,38 zu greifen, womit Lukas eine Sinn- und Deutungslinie erzeugt:

Act 2,38 ... **μετανοήσατε**, [φησίν,] καὶ **βαπτισθήτω** ἕκαστος ὑμῶν **ἐπὶ τῷ ὀνόματι Ἰησοῦ Χριστοῦ εἰς ἄφεσιν τῶν ἁμαρτιῶν** ὑμῶν καὶ λήμψεσθε τὴν δωρεὰν τοῦ ἁγίου πνεύματος

Lk 3,3 ... κηρύσσων βάπτισμα *μετανοίας* **εἰς ἄφεσιν ἁμαρτιῶν**

Lk 24,47 καὶ κηρυχθῆναι **ἐπὶ τῷ ὀνόματι** *αὐτοῦ μετάνοιαν* **εἰς ἄφεσιν ἁμαρτιῶν** εἰς πάντα τὰ ἔθνη ...

Erinnerung(en) aus,[48] was sich vor allem auf die erkennbare eingliedrige Taufformel beziehen lässt:[49] die Taufe erfolgt ἐπὶ τῷ ὀνόματι Ἰησοῦ Χριστοῦ. Die Datierung der Taufe in die früheste Gemeinde und ihre Mission sind nicht notwendig ausschließlich lukanische Konstruktion. Lukas hält in seiner Darstellung eine m.E. zutreffende Erinnerung fest[50] und erzählt sie in seiner historischen Sinnbildung neu, dass schon in der ältesten Phase der frühchristlichen Bewegung der Weg in die Gemeinde durch einen Taufakt erfolgt, indem der Täufling durch die Taufe auf (ἐπί[51]) den Namen Jesu durch einen von dem Namensgeber bestimmten Ritus[52] in ein heilbringendes[53] Eigentumsverhältnis[54] zu Jesus Christus übergeht. Funktional wird der Taufakt als Sündenvergebung beschrieben (s.a. die Selbstreflexion des Paulus in Act 22,16) und mit dem Geschehen der Geistverleihung verbunden (in Act s.a. 9,17f.; s.a. 10,47: Präsenz des Geistes als Zeichen, dass die Heiden getauft werden sollen). Act 2,41 lässt erkennen, dass Umkehr als eine aktive Annahme der missionarischen Verkündigung verstanden wird.[55] Die Begleitung der Taufe durch einen Bekenntnisakt[56] lässt „Lukas" auch in Act 22,16b (… ἀναστὰς βάπτισαι καὶ ἀπόλουσαι τὰς ἁμαρτίας σου ἐπικαλεσάμενος τὸ ὄνομα αὐτοῦ [… stehe auf, um dich taufen und von deinen Sünden abwaschen zu lassen, und *rufe seinen Namen an*]) erkennen. Mögliche Taufbekenntnisse oder liturgische Stücke, die in einem Taufgeschehen eingebunden sind und die das Einverständnis des Täuflings dokumentie-

---

Zur Sache vgl. ZMIJEWSKI, *Apostelgeschichte*, 148f.

48 So z.B. ALAND, „Vorgeschichte", 196: „Urgestein".

49 SCHENKE, *Urgemeinde*, 115.

50 Positivistisch, aber im Kern unserer Analyse nahestehend AVEMARIE, *Tauferzählungen*. 213: „Lukas – oder die Tradition, der er die Pfingsterzählung verdankt – dürfte verlässlich gewusst haben, dass die Bekehrungstaufe in den christlichen Gemeinden, einschließlich Jerusalems, von Anfang an geübt wurde".

51 Die Verwendung der Präposition in Act 2,38 kann dem Einfluss des Joel-Zitats (2,32aLXX: καὶ ἔσται πᾶς ὃς ἂν ἐπικαλέσηται τὸ ὄνομα κυρίου σωθήσεται …) in Act 2,21 geschuldet sein; vgl. z.B. HARTMAN, *Namen des Herrn Jesus*, 125 („… die angeführten Zeilen aus Joel werden zu einer Weissagung dessen, was die Menschen dem Text nach tun, wenn sie umkehren und getauft werden: Sie rufen den Herrn an und werden gerettet".); R. PESCH, *Apostelgeschichte 1*, 125.

52 Bes. HARTMAN, „Into the Name of Jesus".

53 In Auseinandersetzung mit anderen Interpretationen ist der Aspekt der Heilsvermittlung durch die Namensformel vor allem von G. DELLING, *Zueignung des Heils*, herausgearbeitet worden.

54 Grundlegend, aber in seinen religionsgeschichtlichen Ableitungen inzwischen ausdifferenziert und erweitert: W. HEITMÜLLER, *„Im Namen Jesu"*. So wurde der Aspekt der Heilsvermittlung durch die Namensformel vor allem von DELLING, *Zueignung des Heils*, herausgearbeitet.

55 S.a. G. SCHNEIDER, *Die Apostelgeschichte I*, 278 Anm. 145; er weist zu Recht darauf hin, dass τὸν λόγον αὐτοῦ „nicht einfach das ‚Wort' oder die ‚Rede' des Petrus, sondern seine Botschaft (mit Forderung), die man akzeptieren oder zurückweisen kann", bedeutet. Nach Schneider, aaO., 277 Anm. 132, ist die Taufe „sichtbare Bekundung der Umkehr".

56 Vgl. z.B. LOHFINK, „Ursprung", 192.

ren, sind in den frühchristlichen Schriften an verschiedenen Stellen indirekt zu erschließen; z.B. Act 8,37D;[57] Röm 10,8–14; Mt 16,16b.17; Mk 16,16.[58]

Die Apostelgeschichte schildert keine Einsetzung der christlichen Taufpraxis. Die Taufe wird von Beginn der Erzählung an *selbstverständlich vollzogen* als ein Akt, *der in einer gewissen sachlichen Kontinuität zur Johannestaufe steht* (Bezeichnung als Taufe, die mit der Umkehr verbunden ist, und in ihrer Funktion εἰς ἄφεσιν τῶν ἁμαρτιῶν); eine klare *Diskontinuität* besteht darin, dass die *Taufe unter der Namensanrufung Jesu Christi* geschieht, die in ein heilsvermittelndes Eigentumsverhältnis führt. Mit der Taufe auf den Namen wird aus Jesus, dem Getauften, die heilsrelevante Bezugsgröße des Taufakts, die für die Neu-Konstruktion des Getauften von entscheidender Bedeutung ist. Aus der Taufe folgt zudem die Gabe des Geistes, deren Darstellung aber deutlich zwischen Jesustaufe und Gemeindetaufe unterschieden ist.[59]

Die Selbstverständlichkeit der Schilderung mag der lukanischen Gemeindepraxis entsprechen, allerdings spricht die Verbindung mit der alten Taufformel dafür, dass diese Gemeindepraxis die Erinnerung an die Praxis in der frühsten Gemeinde wach hielt;[60] für Lukas steht diese Taufe in Kontinuität und Diskontinuität zur Johannestaufe, eine Verhältnisbestimmung, die sachlich zutreffend ist.

3.3. Jesus als Täufer und der Täufer. Johanneische Akzentverschiebungen

Die Erklärungsmodelle, die die Johannestaufe als Vorbild oder die Taufe Jesu als Rückspiegelung christlicher Gemeindepraxis und Wandlung zur Taufätiologie deuten – beide Modelle setzten neben Kontinuität auch eine Distanz zwischen vorösterlichem und nachösterlichem Geschehen voraus. Eine Brücke zwischen beiden Vollzügen könnte eine eigene Taufpraxis Jesu oder seiner Jünger bilden, zumal deutlich ist, dass sich im Kreis der frühen Anhänger Jesu ehemalige Johannesjünger befunden haben dürften (Joh 1,29ff.). Die synoptischen Jesusdarstellungen schweigen jedoch über eine Taufaktivität Jesu, und ihr Bild seiner

---

57 Zu diesem Text: F. W. HORN, „Act 8,37, der Westliche Text und die frühchristliche Tauftheologie".

58 Vgl. H. KLEIN, „Traditionsgeschichte", 129f., der ein dem Taufakt vorausgehendes Taufbekenntnis und die Seligpreisung als Antwort vermutet.

59 Act 2,38   ... καὶ λήμψεσθε τὴν δωρεὰν τοῦ ἁγίου πνεύματος.
   Lk 3,21b–22:   ... καὶ προσευχομένου ἀνεῳχθῆναι τὸν οὐρανὸν καὶ καταβῆναι τὸ πνεῦμα τὸ ἅγιον σωματικῷ εἴδει ὡς περιστερὰν ἐπ' αὐτόν, ...

60 Mit DUNN, *Beginning From Jerusalem*, 186: „Luke is correct in depicting baptism as a feature of the new sect from the beginning".

Verkündigung ist, wie Petr Pokorný zu Recht betont,[61] nicht auf ein derartiges Ritual angelegt. Jesu Verkündigung zielt auf direkte, existenzverändernde Anrede und entsprechendes Handeln.

Dass dennoch das Taufen Jesu als Bindeglied zur frühchristlichen Gemeindepraxis erwogen wird, liegt im Zeugnis des vierten Evangeliums begründet. Erst das Johannesevangelium spricht von einem Tauferfolg Jesu: Joh 3,22; 4,1. Beide Notizen werden vereinzelt als historisch glaubwürdige Angaben beurteilt.[62] Trotz neuerlich positiverer Urteile über die historische Zuverlässigkeit im vierten Evangelium[63] ist auf die sinnbildende und somit auch kreativ gestaltende Kraft des johanneischen Erzählers zu verweisen,[64] der „Erinnerung" an Jesus bewahrt, aber sie zugleich neu gestaltet und aktualisiert.[65] Die Frage spitzt sich also darauf zu, ob die johanneische Sinnbildung Erinnerungsträger eines Taufens Jesu ist oder ob dieses Handeln gänzlich johanneischer Konstruktion zuzurechnen ist.

Dass Letzteres von entscheidender Bedeutung sein wird, kann der Leser/die Leserin bereits daran ablesen, dass die Taufe Jesu nicht berichtet wird, obgleich an die synoptische Taufszene erinnert wird. Der Erzähler signalisiert hiermit eindrücklich, dass die Erinnerung an die Taufe Jesu und damit das in ihr repräsentierte Geschehen seiner theologischen bzw. christologischen Darstellungsintention zu dienen hat.

Joh 1,29–34 berichtet vom Täuferzeugnis, das Jesus als Lamm Gottes bezeichnet. Nach der Erläuterung seiner eigenen Rolle in Bezug auf Jesus mit Hinweis auf sein Taufen (V.31: ἦλθον ἐγὼ ἐν ὕδατι βαπτίζων) spricht der johanneische Täufer davon, dass (1,32):

... τεθέαμαι τὸ πνεῦμα καταβαῖνον ὡς περιστερὰν ἐξ οὐρανοῦ καὶ ἔμεινεν ἐπ᾽ αὐτόν.
... ich sah den Geist aus dem Himmel herabsteigen wie eine Taube und er blieb auf ihm.

Aus den synoptischen Taufberichten ist das Ereignis der Geistverleihung erhalten geblieben, und man kann Spuren der Himmelsöffnung erkennen. Eine Himmelsstimme, die über Jesus und seine Verbindung zu Gott Auskunft gibt, ist nach dem Prolog nicht mehr nötig. Die eigentliche Taufe Jesu ist nur im Reflex auf das Taufhandeln des Täufers zu eruieren, das Offenbarungsfunktion haben soll, wobei das Passiv sogar ein fremdes, ein göttliches Handeln signalisieren kann.[66]

---

61 S.o. S. 341–342.
62 Z.B. SCHRÖTER; s.o. S. 341 mit weiterer Literatur (s. Anm. 17).
63 Vgl. z.B. P. ANDERSON, Fourth Gospel, mit recht weitreichenden literarkritischen Hypothesen; s.a. die Überlegungen von Smith, „Problem of History in John", 315–319.
64 Z.B. SCHNELLE, „Johannesevangelium als neue Sinnbildung", 291–313.
65 Vgl. z.B. die Überlegungen bei M. LABAHN, „John 21", 335–348.
66 So SCHNELLE, Johannes, 61.

Über das Zeugnis des Täufers über Jesus hinaus spielt das Taufgeschehen[67] keine Rolle. Gespielt wird mit Erinnerung, aber *die entstandene Geschichte ist christologisch motivierte Neubildung*. Es wird deutlich, dass das Taufthema im vierten Evangelium ein Raum christologischer Sinn-Konstruktionen wird, das zwar mit einzelnen Traditionen spielt, aber nicht zuverlässig als Quelle zur Rekonstruktion der Taufe von bzw. durch Jesus herangezogen werden kann.

Für das Taufhandeln Jesu ist zunächst die eher lakonisch zu nennende Notiz *Joh 3,22* zu analysieren:

Μετὰ ταῦτα
ἦλθεν ὁ Ἰησοῦς καὶ οἱ μαθηταὶ αὐτοῦ εἰς τὴν Ἰουδαίαν γῆν
καὶ ἐκεῖ διέτριβεν μετ᾽ αὐτῶν
καὶ ἐβάπτιζεν.

Danach
kamen Jesus und seine Jünger in das Land Judäa.
Dort hielt er sich mit ihnen auf
und taufte er.

Mit dem Texttrenner μετὰ ταῦτα eingeleitet berichtet 3,22 einen Ortswechsel Jesu und seiner Jünger nach Judäa, wo er sich mit ihnen eine Zeit lang aufhält (διέτριβεν). Dieser Aufenthalt ist als Zeitraum einer eigenen Tauftätigkeit Jesu beschrieben, wie die Imperfektform ἐβάπτιζεν unterstreicht. Dieser Notiz folgt eine Episode zum Taufen des Täufers, die sein Handeln in Konkurrenz zu dem Jesu stellt (3,23ff.): Jesus hat sehr zum Ärger der Täuferjünger größeren Erfolg, aber der Täufer sieht dies als göttlichen Willen an und unterstreicht seine Unterordnung unter den Christus (V.30): ἐκεῖνον δεῖ αὐξάνειν, ἐμὲ δὲ ἐλαττοῦσθαι (jener muss wachsen, ich jedoch muss abnehmen). Neben der christologischen Relationsbestimmung zwischen dem ‚Christus' (V.28) und seinem Zeugen und der Interpretation Jesu als eschatologischem Bräutigam (V.29) lässt sich 3,22–30 als ein Zeugnis für eine Wertschätzung der Taufe in der johanneischen Gemeinde lesen und damit als ein Hinweis auf eine eigene Taufpraxis. Intendiert ist nicht die historisierende Rückführung der eigenen Taufpraxis auf den irdischen Jesus, sondern ihre Abgrenzung gegenüber der Johannestaufe und die Unterstreichung einer Kontinuität zum Wirken Jesu, das am Kreuz seinen Zielpunkt findet und letztlich dort das johanneische Sakramentsverständnis begründet (vgl. 19,34; dazu Abschn. § 4.1.).[68]

---

67 Informationen über die Johannestaufe sind in 1,19ff. und 3,23ff. verstreut, wobei Taufort, Zustrom der Bevölkerung und der Reinigungsgedanke Erwähnung finden.

68 S.a. SCHNELLE, *Evangelium nach Johannes*, 93: „Der Evangelist setzt die Taufe nicht nur beiläufig voraus, sondern Joh. 3,23.25.30; 4,1 dokumentieren ein eminent theologisches Interesse. Die Taufe ist für Johannes *eine sachgemäße Fortsetzung des Wirkens Jesu* und als konstitutiver Aufnahmeritus in die Gemeinde Conditio sine qua non christlicher Existenz" (Hervorhebung; ML.).

Die größere Wirkung der Taufpraxis Jesu, verglichen mit der des Täufers, unterstreicht in merkwürdig gestelzter Argumentation auch *Joh 4,1*:

Ὡς οὖν ἔγνω ὁ κύριος[69]
    ὅτι ἤκουσαν οἱ Φαρισαῖοι
        ὅτι
            Ἰησοῦς
                πλείονας μαθητὰς ποιεῖ καὶ βαπτίζει ἢ
            Ἰωάννης …

Als nun der Herr erkannte,
    dass die Pharisäer hörten,
        dass
            Jesus
                mehr Jünger macht und tauft **als**
            Johannes …

Die erneute Gegenüberstellung von Täufer und Jesus ist deutlich. Es geht nicht so sehr um eine Erinnerung an Jesu Wirken, sondern um eine Verhältnisbestimmung zwischen Jesus und dem Täufer. Überraschend ist der Appell an die wunderbare Kardiognosie Jesu (ἔγνω ὁ κύριος) und an die die Pharisäer erreichende Fama (ἤκουσαν οἱ Φαρισαῖοι) vom Tauferfolg Jesu. Die Erwähnung der Pharisäer ordnet den Erfolg Jesu gegenüber dem Täufer in das johanneische Konfliktschema ein: die, denen schon das Wirken des Täufers als Boten (1,19ff.) suspekt war (1,24), stellen auch das Wirken des Bezeugten in Frage, um ihn schließlich dem Tode zu überantworten (7,32; 11,47; 18,3 u.ö.). Dies ist als ein Vorausverweis auf den Erzählort, das Kreuz, dem sich johanneisch die Sakramente verdanken, zu lesen.

Joh 4,1 blickt auf später Erzähltes voraus, das sachlich die Voraussetzung des Erzählten, die Taufe in die Gemeinschaft mit Jesus, ist. Der ekklesiologische Aspekt wird deutlich, da das Taufen Jesu (βαπτίζει) als ein „Jünger-Machen" (μαθητὰς ποιεῖ)[70] verstanden wird. Zu Recht sieht Knut Backhaus in dieser Notiz ein weiteres Indiz, dass Joh 4,1 nicht als eine historische Notiz/Erinnerung an das Wirken des historischen Jesus zu lesen ist.[71]

Die Notiz in 4,1 steht damit in einer Linie mit unserer Interpretation von Joh 3,22ff. und ist nicht für eine historische Re-Konstruktion zu verwerten, sondern innerhalb des *plots* des vierten Evangeliums zu verstehen.

---

69 Mit G. Van Belle, „ΚΥΡΙΟΣ or ΙΗΣΟΥΣ", 159–174, den Handschriften P[66.75] A B et al. folgend.

70 Dies steht den Aussagen von Mt 28,19f. (μαθητεύσατε πάντα τὰ ἔθνη, βαπτίζοντες αὐτοὺς εἰς τὸ ὄνομα τοῦ πατρὸς καὶ τοῦ υἱοῦ καὶ τοῦ ἁγίου πνεύματος, διδάσκοντες αὐτοὺς τηρεῖν πάντα ὅσα ἐνετειλάμην ὑμῖν· [hierzu s.u. Abschn. § 4.1.]) nicht fern. Dies ist auch deshalb zu unterstreichen, da eine literarische Abhängigkeit beider Passagen nicht zu vermuten ist. Beide Passagen formulieren ähnliche Erinnerungen aus.

71 Backhaus, *„Jüngerkreise" des Täufers Johannes*, 264.

Wahrscheinlich eine spätere Glosse,[72] wohl im Prozess johanneischer Relecture, stellt in Parenthese – ein beliebtes johanneisches Stilmittel – *Joh 4,2* klar:

- καίτοιγε
Ἰησοῦς αὐτὸς οὐκ ἐβάπτιζεν
ἀλλ᾽
οἱ μαθηταὶ αὐτοῦ. –

– und doch
nicht Jesus selbst taufte,
sondern
seine Jünger. –

Es ist zu wenig, in dieser Notiz nur eine spätere kirchliche oder durch die Lektüre der Synoptiker gesteuerte Korrektur der johanneischen Taufnachricht zu lesen.[73] Werden die Jünger als Ausübende der Taufe vorgestellt, so stellt dies eine singuläre Nachricht innerhalb der Erzählwelt des vierten Evangeliums dar, das eine ähnliche Aktivität der Jesusjünger nicht kennt. Sie verweist mittels der Technik der Horizontverschmelzung[74] eher jenseits der erzählten Zeit auf die nachösterliche johanneische Praxis. Der Erfolg des Taufvollzugs der Jünger illustriert das ‚Mehr' der nachösterlichen Zeit (Joh 1,50: μείζω τούτων ὄψῃ). Die glossierende Relecture von 4,1 durch 4,2 schafft Klärung, indem sie den Blick von der Relationsbestimmung vom Täufer zu Jesus auf die Taufpraxis der Gemeinde verlagert. Sie wird im Horizont der Zusage des Größeren in der nachösterlichen Zeit gelesen, so dass der Erfolg der Taufpraxis der johanneischen Gemeinde die Wirkung des Täufers übersteigt. Auch Joh 4,2 lebt folglich von der Erinnerung, dass die frühchristliche Taufpraxis nicht im Wirken Jesu gründet.

Das vierte Evangelium erzählt ein Taufhandeln Jesu, aber nicht seine Taufe durch Johannes. Dies allein mahnt zur Vorsicht, in den johanneischen Notizen historische Ereignisse re-präsentiert zu finden. Die Nachrichten lassen zudem erkennen, dass *die Taufe in der johanneischen Gemeinde* geübt wurde. Erkennbar ist auch, dass man sich der Nähe der christlichen Taufe zum Taufhandeln des Johannes bewusst war und so Differenzierungen setzen musste. So wird Jesus zum Täufer und die eigene Gemeindepraxis steht in Bezug zum Wirken des Irdischen, das im Kreuz zu ihrem Ziel und der Grundlegung der Taufe kommt. Zugleich aber wird auch hier – wenngleich sekundär präzisierend – deutlich gemacht, dass das eigene Taufhandeln nachösterlich als Werk der Jünger datiert, das auf die Einsetzung der Sakramente im Sterben Jesu bezogen ist (Horizontverschmelzung).

---

72 Zur Sache und zum Verständnis J. ZUMSTEIN, „Prozess der Relecture", 25: Die Glossen „widerspiegeln auf ihre Weise die kontinuierliche Arbeit der joh Schule".

73 Klassisch: BULTMANN, *Johannes*, 128 Anm. 4.

74 Zur ‚johanneischen' Horizontverschmelzung vgl. FREY, *Eschatologie II*, 247ff.

4. Lösungsmodell: Nachösterliche Nachschöpfung als Eingangsritual in die neue Gemeinschaft

4.1. Der nachösterliche Ursprung der christlichen Taufe

(a) Das pointierte Schlusswort des Auferstandenen in *Mt 28,18–20* ist ein beachtenswerter Hinweis, dass noch in der matthäischen Gemeinde eine Erinnerung daran greifbar ist, dass die christliche Taufpraxis in der frühen nachösterlichen Zeit gründet und als ein eigenständiger Akt, eine Art Neuschöpfung (s.u. Abschn. § 4.2.), zu verstehen ist. Die Erinnerung ist in die aktuelle Gemeindepraxis eingefügt[75] und wird zur abschließenden Sinngebung der matthäischen Jesusgeschichte. Die matthäische Gemeinde als Gemeinde der besseren Gerechtigkeit (Mt 5,20) ist eine missionarische Gemeinde in der Gewissheit des Auftrags und Mitseins des Auferstandenen.

Vergegenwärtigen wir uns den abschließenden Auftrag Jesu an seine Jünger:

18		καὶ προσελθὼν ὁ Ἰησοῦς ἐλάλησεν αὐτοῖς λέγων·
	a	**ἐδόθη μοι πᾶσα** ἐξουσία ἐν οὐρανῷ καὶ ἐπὶ [τῆς] γῆς.
19	b	πορευθέντες οὖν μαθητεύσατε πάντα τὰ ἔθνη,
	c	βαπτίζοντες αὐτοὺς
		εἰς τὸ ὄνομα τοῦ πατρὸς καὶ τοῦ υἱοῦ καὶ τοῦ ἁγίου πνεύματος,
20	b'	διδάσκοντες αὐτοὺς τηρεῖν πάντα ὅσα ἐνετειλάμην ὑμῖν·
	a'	ἰδοὺ **ἐγὼ μεθ' ὑμῶν εἰμι πάσας** τὰς ἡμέρας ἕως τῆς συντελείας τοῦ αἰῶνος.
18		Da kam Jesus herbei und sprach zu ihnen:
	a	**Mir wurde alle Macht** im Himmel und auf der Erde **gegeben**.
19	b	Geht nun hin und macht zu Jüngern alle Völker,
	c	*tauft sie* auf den Namen des Vaters und des Sohnes und des Heiligen Geistes,
20	b'	und lehrt sie zu bewahren alles, was ich euch geboten habe;
	a'	und siehe, **ich bin bei euch alle** Tage bis an das Ende der Ewigkeit.

---

75 So betont durch Barth, *Taufe in frühchristlicher Zeit*, 13ff., für den damit aber auch die Möglichkeit, dass hinter der Konstruktion und Aktualisierung Erinnerung steht, ausgeschlossen ist.

Am Ende des Evangeliums begegnet Jesus seinen verbliebenen elf Jüngern, die nicht ohne Zweifel waren ([28,17] – ein Blick auf die matthäische Gemeinde?). Jesus tritt in V.18 auf sie zu (προσελθών), um ihnen einen abschließenden Auftrag zu geben (feierliches [s.a. die Einleitung zur Gleichnisrede, 13,3, und die feierliche Selbstvorstellung des Seewandelnden, 14,27]: ἐλάλησεν αὐτοῖς λέγων). Aufbau und Struktur der matthäisch-redaktionellen Szene[76] sind verständnisleitend. Der Auftrag an die Jünger ist in Jesus fundiert und von ihm her ermöglicht: so stellt sich der Auftraggeber als Inhaber quantitativ und räumlich universell beschriebener Macht (πᾶσα ἐξουσία ἐν οὐρανῷ καὶ ἐπὶ [τῆς] γῆς) vor (a). Diese Selbstvorstellung zielt nicht auf christologische Erkenntnis, sondern auf ekklesiologische Zuversicht (a'): betont kommt sie im ἐγὼ μεθ᾽ὑμῶν εἰμι zum Ziel. Der Mächtige ist als Mächtiger der Mitseiende und zwar beständig (τὰς ἡμέρας ἕως τῆς συντελείας τοῦ αἰῶνος), wodurch der räumlichen eine chronologisch universelle Komponente an die Seite gestellt wird.

Drei Partizipien (πορευθέντες, βαπτίζοντες und διδάσκοντες) und ein Aorist Imperativ charakterisieren den Auftrag, der sich aus der Mächtigkeit des Sprechers und Auftraggebers ergibt. Lässt sich der Rahmen gut vom Auftrag abheben und chiastisch verstehen, so ist die Struktur des Auftrags komplexer. Die finite Verbform des Imperativs μαθητεύσατε ist der Leitbegriff,[77] dem das Partizip Aorist πορευθέντες näher steht als die Partizipien in Präsens: βαπτίζοντες und διδάσκοντες. Die Leitvorstellung ist die des Hingehens und Zu-Jüngern-Machens – ein missionarischer Auftrag, der sich in Taufe und Unterweisung konkretisiert. Das Adjektiv πάντα verbindet nun aber b und b', Lehre und Unterweisung, so dass die Taufe mit triadischer Formel in die Zentralposition rückt (c). Die „Mission" zielt auf alle Völker und hat die Unterweisung der Bewahrung aller Gebote Jesu zum Inhalt. Das Adjektiv πᾶς und die christologische Zuspitzung (ὅσα ἐνετειλάμην ὑμῖν) verbinden den Auftrag mit seinem Rahmen. Hier scheint das zu Begründende zu liegen, das mit der Autorität der universellen Macht und des zeitlosen Mitseins ausgestattet ist. Die Taufe in Zentralstellung (c) ist hingegen das Unstrittige, die Erinnerung an eine Praxis, die bereits der Gemeinde voraus ist.

Auffällig ist lediglich die triadische Formel εἰς τὸ ὄνομα τοῦ πατρὸς καὶ τοῦ υἱοῦ καὶ τοῦ ἁγίου πνεύματος (s.a. Did 7,1),[78] die die im Neuen Testament

---

76 Eine ausführliche Analyse muss im Rahmen der Fragestellung dieses Beitrages unterbleiben. Einen Überblick über die zahlreiche Literatur zu Mt 28,18ff. gibt U. Luz, *Matthäus (Mt 26–28)*, 427f., der auch die Merkmale matthäischer Redaktion überzeugend herausarbeitet: aaO., 430–432. Luz macht darauf aufmerksam, dass V.18b und die triadische Formel V.19b sich aus der matthäischen Sprachwelt abheben, was aber über den weitgehend als traditionell angesehenen Charakter der Taufformel nicht hinausführt.

77 S.a. J. Gnilka, *Matthäusevangelium II*, 508; Luz, *Matthäus (Mt 26–28)*, 443.

78 Die aus der teilweise verkürzenden Aufnahme von Mt 28,19f. bei Euseb resultierende These der sekundären Einfügung des Taufauftrags samt trinitarischer Formel ist angesichts der matthäischen Textüberlieferung, der Uneinheitlichkeit und Eigenart der Rezeption bei Euseb wie

häufigere und wohl zugleich ältere[79] Formel „auf (mit den Präpositionen ἐπί, εἰς und ἐν) den Namen Jesu" (Act 2,38; 8,16; 10,48; 19,5; I Kor 1,13 [auch im Hintergrund von V.15: ἵνα μή τις εἴπῃ ὅτι εἰς τὸ ἐμὸν ὄνομα ἐβαπτίσθητε]; verkürzt zu εἰς Χριστὸν [Ἰησοῦν]: Gal 3,27; Röm 6,3) erweitert. Sie setzt gegenüber der eingliedrigen Formel ein reflektierteres Stadium von Taufliturgie voraus,[80] bestätigt zugleich als Differenz zur Johannestaufe den konstitutiven Jesusbezug, mit dem die Zuordnung des Täuflings in eine neue konstitutive und heilsbegründete Relation durch den Taufvollzug beschrieben wird.

Dass in Mt 28,19f. die matthäische Gemeindepraxis und ihre Sinngebung am Ende des 1.Jh. n.Chr. entfaltet werden,[81] bedarf also keiner weitergehenden Erläuterung. Auch wenn die Taufe im Zentrum von Mt 28,19f. (c) steht und durch eine wohl bereits auf die matthäische Gemeindepraxis verweisende ‚trinitarische' Taufformel bezogen wird, so steht der Missionsauftrag (vgl. b und b') als in Vollmacht und Mit-Sein be- und gegründete Aktivität der Gemeinde (a und a') im Zentrum der matthäisch-redaktionellen Pragmatik und nicht die Taufe. Wie Kurt Aland zu Recht bemerkt: „Die Taufe ist auch hier eine vorgegebene, feststehende Tatsache".[82]

Sieht man von der Taufformel ab, so gelingt es kaum in diesem wohlgestalteten Schlussabschnitt, literarkritisch oder traditionsgeschichtlich separierbare Traditionsstücke zu isolieren. Dennoch ist zwischen matthäischer Redaktion und der Repräsentanz historischer Erinnerung zu unterscheiden, auch wenn Letztere nicht anders als im Vollzug der Sinngebung greifbar ist.[83]

Die matthäische Taufpraxis versteht sich im Wort des Auferstandenen begründet, was aus Erinnerung lebt. Sie weiß um den nachösterlichen Ursprung der christlichen Taufpraxis, die in Mt 28,19 auf einen Stiftungsakt des auferstandenen Christus zurückgeführt wird – ist der nachösterliche Ursprung des christlichen Taufakts authentische Erinnerung, so stellt sich wenigstens die Frage, ob die „Einsetzung" nicht schon früh in der Autorität des Erhöhten verankert wurde.[84]

---

auch dem Zeugnis der Didache (hierzu A. LINDEMANN in der vorliegenden Publikation) für die triadische Formel nicht zu halten; vgl. z.B. GNILKA, *Matthäusevangelium II*, 504f.; BARTH, *Taufe in frühchristlicher Zeit*, 13ff. FERGUSON, *Baptism*, 134f.

79 Z.B. HARTMAN, „Early Baptism", 192ff.; KRETSCHMAR, „Geschichte des Taufgottesdienstes", 32.
80 Mit Hinweis Did 7; IgnMagn 13,2; OdSal 23,33 verweist LUZ, *Matthäus (Mt 26–28)*, 431, nach Syrien, wo sie um 100 n. Chr. verbreitet war. Gegen eine chronologische Differenzierung zwischen der eingliedrigen und der dreigliedrigen Formel H. VON CAMPENHAUSEN, „Taufen", 1–16.
81 Z.B. betont durch Dinkler, „Art. Taufe", 629.
82 ALAND, „Vorgeschichte", 185.
83 Anders W. REINBOLD, *Propaganda und Mission*, 278.
84 So DUNN, *Beginning From Jerusalem*, 186.

(b) Von *Mk 16,15f.* sind keine ergänzenden Informationen zu erwarten, da der lange Markusschluss, Mk 16,9–20, als textgeschichtlich sekundärer aus den Evangelien kompilierter Text gilt, mit dem das offene Ende des Markusevangeliums an die kanonischen Jesusviten inhaltlich herangeführt werden sollte.[85] Mk 16,15f. entspricht Mt 28,19f.:

Mt 28,19f.	Mk 16,15f.
πορευθέντες οὖν μαθητεύσατε πάντα τὰ ἔθνη,	πορευθέντες εἰς τὸν κόσμον ἅπαντα κηρύξατε τὸ εὐαγγέλιον πάσῃ τῇ κτίσει.
	ὁ πιστεύσας
βαπτίζοντες αὐτοὺς εἰς τὸ ὄνομα τοῦ πατρὸς καὶ τοῦ υἱοῦ καὶ τοῦ ἁγίου πνεύματος,	καὶ βαπτισθεὶς
	σωθήσεται,
	ὁ δὲ ἀπιστήσας κατακριθήσεται.
διδάσκοντες αὐτοὺς τηρεῖν πάντα ὅσα ἐνετειλάμην ὑμῖν·	
Geht nun hin und macht zu Jüngern alle Völker,	Geht hin in die ganze Welt, verkündigt das Evangelium der gesamten Schöpfung.
	Wer glaubt
tauft sie auf den Namen des Vaters und des Sohnes und des Heiligen Geistes,	und getauft wurde,
	soll gerettet werden.
	Wer aber nicht glaubt, soll verurteilt werden.
und lehrt sie zu befolgen alles, was ich euch geboten habe;	

Der Vergleich lässt erkennen, dass Mk 16,15f. keine Kopie, sondern zumindest gestaltete Reproduktion von Mt 28,19f. ist.[86] In dieser Gestaltung wird nicht die Aufforderung zum Taufen, sondern die Aufgabe bzw. die Heilskondition der Taufe bedacht, der Glaube; dies entspricht dem Kontext des sekundären Schlus-

---

85 Wichtigste Textzeugen: A, C, D. Vgl. zum textgeschichtlichen Problem grundlegend Aland, „Schluß des Markusevangeliums", 246–283. Eine neuere Interpretation mit Forschungsgeschichte: J. A. Kelhoffer, *Miracle and Mission*.

86 Ferguson, *Baptism*, 133, erwägt „early independent tradition" oder zumindest eine frühe Unterstützung der matthäischen Behauptung der Einsetzung der Taufpraxis durch den Auferstandenen.

ses, der zunächst den Unglauben der Jünger nach der Auferstehung kritisiert. Mk 16,15f. ist ein interessanter Text für das Taufverständnis seiner Erzähler, aber nicht für die Entstehung der christlichen Taufe.

(c) Informationen, dass *die Taufe Teil der missionarischen Anstrengung der christlichen Gemeinde(n) seit ihren Anfängen* war, lassen sich der Apostelgeschichte entnehmen. Act 2,38.41 (s.o.) zeigt, dass der lukanische Erzähler die Taufpraxis in der Urgemeinde verankert findet.[87] Dass hier eine idealisierende Sichtweise vorliegt, die Aspekte der eigenen Gemeindepraxis spiegelt, muss nicht bestritten werden. Dennoch wird hinter dem lukanischen Gestaltungswillen historische Erinnerung greifbar. Wenn die paulinischen Taufaussagen von I Kor 12,13 (… ἡμεῖς πάντες εἰς ἓν σῶμα ἐβαπτίσθημεν …), Gal 3,27 (ὅσοι γὰρ εἰς Χριστὸν ἐβαπτίσθητε, …) und Röm 6,3 (ἢ ἀγνοεῖτε ὅτι, ὅσοι ἐβαπτίσθημεν εἰς Χριστὸν Ἰησοῦν …) die Gesamtheit der Getauften betonen (s.a. Eph 4,5), so lassen diese Aussagen nicht erkennen, dass Raum für die Erinnerung an eine Periode ohne Taufe als Eingangsakt in die christliche Gemeinde besteht; eine Praxis, die auch die autobiographische Erfahrung des Paulus einschließt.[88] Auch die lukanische Szene lässt keinen Zweifel daran, dass der Autor die Taufe mit dem Anfang der urchristlichen Missionspredigt verbunden sieht. Der Verfasser des lukanischen Doppelwerks zeigt, dass die Taufe an den Anfang der christlichen Bewegung und ihrer missionarischen Jesusverkündigung gehört und hier als einmaliger Akt des Eintritts in die frühchristliche Gemeinde praktiziert wurde.

Diese Texte lassen keinen mikroskopischen Blick auf die Frühgeschichte der Taufe oder ein Ursprungsdatum zu; sie sind Sinnbildungen, die vergangene Ereignisse für eine neue Zeit verdichten und gestalten. Sie repräsentieren eine kreative Erinnerung daran, dass die Taufe zur christlichen Bewegung so grundsätzlich hinzu gehört, dass man *chronologisch für ihren Ursprung auf die Anfangsphase dieser Bewegung zurückverwiesen* ist. Wenn die Verfasser des Matthäusevangeliums und des lukanischen Doppelwerkes keine Taufpraxis Jesu oder seiner Jünger berichten, so bedeutet dies, dass die christliche Taufpraxis in die Urgemeinde datiert und nicht davor. Dies bestreitet auch nicht die Sinnlinie, die der Verfasser des lukanischen Doppelwerkes zwischen Johannestaufe und frühchristlicher Taufe zieht, vielmehr gibt sie zu erkennen, dass und

---

[87] Act 1,5 berichtet in Gegenüberstellung zur Johannestaufe von der Geisttaufe der Apostel: ὑμεῖς δὲ ἐν πνεύματι βαπτισθήσεσθε ἁγίῳ. Sie ist keine Wassertaufe, sondern ein spezieller Akt für das Zeugnis der Apostel; vgl. SCHRÖTER in der vorliegenden Publikation; nach Schröter zeichnet diese Notiz dennoch das lukanische Taufverständnis aus: „Lukas kennzeichnet auf diese Weise die an den Auferstandenen und Erhöhten gebundene Taufe als ein Geschehen, das mit der Geistmitteilung verbunden ist und deshalb die neue Qualität der Kirche in nachösterlicher Zeit bestimmt". Erinnert auch diese Sinnbildung daran, dass die christliche Taufe einen nachösterlichen Ursprung hat?

[88] Vgl. DUNN, *Beginning From Jerusalem*, 186; s.a. HARTMAN, *Namen des Herrn Jesus*, 32, mit Bezug auf I Kor 12,13.

wie die frühchristliche Taufe in Kontinuität und Diskontinuität zur Johannestaufe steht.

(d) Die *johanneische Sakramentspraxis*[89] verlegt die Stiftung der Sakramente in die Zeit des Sterbens Jesu, präziser *nach dem Sterben Jesu* (19,34) und ermöglicht damit eine erst nachösterliche Taufpraxis der Gemeinde (s.a. Joh 4,2[90]):

ἀλλ' εἷς τῶν στρατιωτῶν λόγχῃ αὐτοῦ τὴν πλευρὰν ἔνυξεν,
καὶ ἐξῆλθεν εὐθὺς αἷμα καὶ ὕδωρ.

sondern einer der Soldaten stieß mit einer Lanze in seine Seite,
und sogleich ergossen sich Blut und Wasser.

Es ist der am Kreuz Gestorbene, nachdem er am Kreuz sein Werk zum Ziel gebracht hat (19,28–30),[91] der nach johanneischem Verständnis als Ursprung von Herrenmahl und Taufe zu gelten hat. Der narrative Rahmen berichtet, dass die verunreinigenden Leichname der Gekreuzigten zum Passafest entfernt werden sollen. Zur Beschleunigung des Prozesses des Sterbens werden den Mitgekreuzigten die Knochen gebrochen, was schriftgemäß dem bereits gestorbenen johanneischen Jesus nicht widerfährt. Einer der Soldaten sticht zum Beweis des Todes Jesu die Lanze in die Seite Jesu καὶ ἐξῆλθεν εὐθὺς αἷμα καὶ ὕδωρ. Nach Jean Zumstein begegnet das johanneische Motiv des ‚produktiven Verlustes', das die Frage beantwortet: „Wie vermag Christi Tod eine neue Gemeinschaft zu schaffen?"[92] Der exegetische Streit, ob die Tatsächlichkeit des Todes des Menschen Jesus im Herausfließen des sogenannten Blutwassers belegt werden soll oder doch Blut als Hinweis auf das Herrenmahl und Wasser als Hinweis auf die Taufe[93] als Begründung der johanneischen Sakramentspraxis im Sterben Jesu

---

89   Die Rolle und Funktion der Taufe und des Herrenmahls im Text des vierten Evangeliums bzw. in der johanneischen Literaturgeschichte sind ebenso strittig wie die Frage nach möglichen Referenzen: vgl. einführend: F. J. MOLONEY, „When is John Talking about Sacraments?", 10ff.; SCHNELLE, *Antidoketische Christologie*, 195f.; speziell zur Taufe: aaO., 196ff.

90   S.o. S. 355.

91   Vgl. M. LABAHN, „‚Verlassen' oder ‚Vollendet'", 136–150.

92   ZUMSTEIN, „Johannes 19,25–27", 265f.

93   Z.B. MOLONEY, *John*, 505f. („The author presupposes the readers' knowledge and experience of the 'water' of Baptism (cf. 3:5) and the 'blood' of Eucharist (cf. 6:53, 54, 55–56), and links them with the cross."); erst im Lektürevollzug der bei C. R. KOESTER, *Symbolism*, 202, recht weitreichend bestimmten Taufbezüge (neben 1,19–34; 3,5 auch 2,1ff. und 13,1ff.) kann der Taufbezug des Wassers in 19,34 verstanden werden: „The water from Jesus' side is not primarily a baptismal symbol, but when related to the comments about baptism earlier in the Gospel, it shows that baptism becomes significant through association with the Spirit that engenders faith in Jesus, who was 'lifted up' in death (3:5, 14–15, 22–30)". Alternativinterpretationen von αἷμα καὶ ὕδωρ schließen die Deutung auf die Heilsbedeutung des Todes Jesu (z.B. H. THYEN, *Johannesevangelium*, 751f.) bis zur Gabe des Geistes (C. S. KEENER, *John*, 1153, der sich auf die „anomaly of water" konzentriert) ein.

dienen, ist wohl damit nicht im Sinne einer ausschließlichen Alternative zu klären.[94]

Der sakramentale Bezug der knappen Wendung ἐξῆλθεν εὐθὺς αἷμα καὶ ὕδωρ ist durch die johanneische Sprachwelt (s.a. I Joh 5,6–8) angeleitet,[95] die αἷμα außer in 1,13 jeweils in Referenz auf das Herrenmahl verwendet (so in der sakramentalen *relecture* in 6,53.54.55.56[96]). Weniger eindeutig ist der Sachverhalt für ὕδωρ, das nicht allein für die Johannestaufe (1,26.31.33; 3,23) und die christliche Taufe (3,5), sondern beispielsweise auch zur metaphorischen Umschreibung des von Jesus ausgehenden Lebens verwendet wird (4,10ff.; 7,38), wodurch zwei wichtige Bezüge zum Taufwasser ergänzt werden: der der Geistgabe (3,5: ... ἐὰν μή τις γεννηθῇ ἐξ ὕδατος καὶ πνεύματος ...[97]) und der der Lebensvermittlung.

Der als Mensch wirklich gestorbene Gottessohn, der in seinem Tod sein Leben nach dem göttlichen Willen für die Seinen hingibt und es – so steht der Tod auch im Licht von Ostern – sich wieder nimmt,[98] konstituiert nach johanneischem Verständnis die christliche Taufe. Es ist ein Moment, der auf Ostern zuschreitet, dem sich johanneisch die Taufe verdankt. Anders als in Mt 28,18–20 ist es damit nicht der Auferstandene, der die Taufpraxis initiiert, aber die an Jesus gebundene Stiftung des Taufrituals verweist auf eine Praxis der nachösterlichen Gemeinde und der Stiftungsakt drängt auf das Ostergeschehen hin.

Vor diesem Hintergrund lässt sich die bisherige Erklärungslinie dahingehend ausziehen, dass das Kreuz in seiner Perspektive auf Ostern hin nach johanneischem Verständnis Ort der Einsetzung der Taufe ist, die Geistes- und Lebensgabe beinhaltet. An die Wassertaufe des Johannes ist so erinnert, dass eine Kontinuität in der Konkurrenz des Taufens des Johannes und Jesu transparent wird. Entscheidend ist jedoch das theologische Konzept der Diskontinuität, das in der Sündenbefreiung durch Jesus (1,29), der Überbietung durch eine – innerjohanneisch nicht unumstrittene (4,2) – Darstellung einer Taufpraxis Jesu (3,22; 4,1), der Verbindung mit Geist- (3,5) und Lebensgabe (4,11ff.; 7,38) und letztlich der ‚Einsetzung' durch den am Kreuz hängenden Jesus selbst besteht.

---

94 S.a. SCHNELLE, *Johannes*, 317f; IDEM, *Antidoketische Christologie*, 229f.; SMITH, *John*, 363. Z.B. auch E. LOHSE, „Wort und Sakrament", 198, der auf dem literarkritisch sekundären Charakter von 19,34b–35 besteht.

95 Vgl. z.B. M. LANG, *Johannes und die Synoptiker*, 244.

96 Zur Begründung einer sakramentalen Interpretation von Joh 6,51c–58 und ihres literarischen Charakters als relecture vgl. z.B. M. LABAHN, *Offenbarung*, 68–78.

97 Vgl. hierzu TH. POPP, *Grammatik des Geistes*, 122–127: „In Beziehung zum Ganzen des JohEv gesetzt zeigt 3,5 somit eindrücklich, wie sich in pneumatologischer Perspektive die Christologie mit der Soteriologie und Ekklesiologie verbindet" (aaO., 127).

98 M. LABAHN, „‚Verlassen' oder ‚Vollendet'", 150, in Aufnahme von Joh 10,17.

Das johanneische Taufkonzept, das hier im Blick auf die Erinnerungsleistung hinsichtlich des Ursprungs der christlichen Taufe befragt wurde, lässt eine Transparenz zur Johannestaufe als Vorbild der christlichen Taufe erkennen. Zugleich wird ein Konzept der Abgrenzung und Überbietung entwickelt, in das sich auch das Taufen Jesu einreiht; es ist konzeptionell gebunden und keine Re-präsentanz historischen Handelns (s.o. Abschn. § 3.3.). Zudem ist auffällig, dass trotz der Notiz über das Taufen Jesu die christliche Taufe als Handeln der Jünger (4,2) und im Kreuz fundiert wird. Ist Letzteres ebenfalls im theologischen Konzept begründet, so ist in Summe auch hier eine Erinnerung daran fixiert, dass die Einsetzung der frühchristlichen Taufe nach Tod und Auferstehung Jesu datiert.

(e) Als eine Negativprobe, wie tragbar das Bild einer starken Erinnerung an den *nachösterlichen Ursprung* der christlichen Taufe ist, könnten die verschiedenen Versionen der *Aussendungsrede* gelten (Q 10,2–16; Mk [3,14f.;] 6,7–13; Mt 9,37f.; 10,5–16; Lk 9,1–6; 10,1–12). Alle Varianten erzählen die Aussendung der Jünger durch Jesus zur Zeit seines irdischen Wirkens. Ihr Handeln besteht nach der Version in Q 10,5ff. in der Darbietung des Friedens, der Heilung der Kranken unter Verkündigung der Nähe des Gottesreiches ohne Hinweis auf ein Taufhandeln.[99] Gerade wenn wir „das Schema [der Aussendungsreden; ML.] der Urgemeinde zuschreiben müssen",[100] so unterstreicht dies die Erinnerung daran, dass während des irdischen Wirkens Jesu keine Taufpraxis geübt wurde.

4.2. Überlegungen zu Kontinuität und Diskontinuität von der Johannestaufe zur christlichen Taufe: Die Johannestaufe als Modell in gewandelter Zeit

Folgende der Johannestaufe und der frühchristlichen Taufe gemeinsamen Merkmale lassen sich den verschiedenen Traditionen und Texten über die frühchristliche Taufpraxis entnehmen, ohne hierdurch die Vielfalt frühchristlicher Taufinterpretationen in Abrede zu stellen: die Johannestaufe wie die christliche Taufe wurden im Unterschied zu Waschungen der Umwelt als *einmaliger Vorgang* wahrscheinlich zunächst *in fließendem Wasser* (vgl. Act 8,38; Did 7,1ff.)[101] und durch Untertauchen,[102] nicht durch eigene Aktivität, sondern *passiv durch eine weitere Person* vollzogen (vgl. I Kor 1,14.16; Act 8,38; 10,48). Der Akt zielt auf

---

99 S.a. KRETSCHMAR, „Geschichte des Taufgottesdienstes", 15; LOHFINK, „Ursprung", 175.
100 HAHN, Verständnis der Mission, 36.
101 Did 7,1b–3 diskutiert in absteigender Linie auch andere Wasserarten, die zur Taufe geeignet sind (vgl. die Erörterung bei K. NIEDERWIMMER, Didache, 163), so dass Did 7 nicht eine Entwicklung abbildet oder gar das dreimalige Wassergießen auf den Kopf als gebräuchlichste Praxis zu erkennen gibt (zu TAYLOR, The Immerser, 52f.).
102 Vgl. die Argumentation bei BARTH, Taufe in frühchristlicher Zeit, 38f.

die *Befreiung von Sünden* (so Mk 1,4 bzw. I Kor 6,11; Röm 3,25; Eph 5,26; Hebr 10,22; II Petr 1,9; Act 2,38), wobei die Getauften zu *Umkehr* und *entsprechendem Handeln* bzw. *Wandel* (vgl. Mt 3,7-10 par. Lk 3,7-9 [Q] bzw. Act 2,38.41) gerufen werden.[103]

Die wesentliche *Differenz des urchristlichen Taufkonzepts* liegt in der christologischen Zuspitzung; wie gesehen, erfolgt die Taufe auf den Namen Jesu Christi, so dass die Christen durch Christus in ein heilsrelevantes, durch den Namensgeber bestimmtes Eigentumsverhältnis[104] zu Jesus Christus übergehen bzw. paulinisch formuliert „in Christus" sind (mit der Tauftradition I Kor 1,30[105]). Mit der Taufe verbunden ist ein Akt der Geistverleihung (vgl. I Kor 12,13; s.a. I Kor 6,11b; II Kor 1,22; Eph 1,13; Hebr 6,4;[106] Tit 3,5; Mk 1,8 parr. lässt der Taufe Jesu die Herabkunft des Geistes folgen[107]). Stimmen beide Taufkonzepte darin überein, dass sie eschatologische und soteriologische Bedeutung haben (s.a. I Petr 1,3.23), so ist für die christliche Taufe auch ein ekklesiologischer, gemeindeintegrierender Zug zu vermerken.[108] Die Taufe wird zum generellen Eingliederungsritual, das aus einem anderen Leben (vgl. I Kor 6,9-11 [zum Lasterkatalog stellt Paulus fest: καὶ ταῦτά τινες ἦτε; V.11a]; I Petr 3,21; II Petr 1,9, s.a. I Thess 1,9, wenn es sich um ein Tauffragment handelt) in ein neues Leben,[109] in die neue, christliche Gemeinde hineinführt (I Kor 12,13 [καὶ γὰρ ἐν ἑνὶ πνεύματι ἡμεῖς πάντες εἰς ἓν σῶμα ἐβαπτίσθημεν[110]]; vgl. Act 2,41).

Es kann folglich festgehalten werden, dass der Vergleich der christlichen Taufpraxis und ihres frühchristlichen Verständnisses mit Elementen und Strukturen der Johannestaufe die Einsicht untermauert, dass die Johannestaufe für das frühchristliche Taufritual Pate gestanden hat (am deutlichsten in der lukanischen Sinnlinie von Lk 3,3a zu Act 2,38 auch den frühchristlichen Adressaten angezeigt), die ihrerseits nach ihren Vorbildern zu befragen ist. Allerdings ist aufgrund der zentralen Differenzen, die sich allerdings primär auf ihre Begründung und ihre Ausdeutung beziehen, die Relation nicht im Sinne einer chronologisch-genetischen Ableitung zu sehen, sondern als Akt einer

---

103 Gefolgt wird weitgehend der Aufstellung bei SCHNELLE, „Art. Taufe 1", 663; s.a. BARTH, „Gesichtspunkte", 140-142. 148f.; IDEM, *Taufe in frühchristlicher Zeit*, 38-41.

104 Hierzu s.o. S. 349.

105 Zur Interpretation vgl. SCHNELLE, *Gerechtigkeit und Christusgegenwart*, 44-46.

106 Zum Taufbezug von Hebr 6,4 z.B. H.-F. WEISS, *Hebräer*, 342 u.ö.

107 In Act 10,48 folgt die Taufe auf die Geistverleihung, aber diese Reihenfolge von der Gabe des Geistes zur Taufe belegt Gottes Annahme des Cornelius, „now the church of Jews and circumcised must ratify their acceptance of these Gentiles by baptism" (DUNN, *Beginning From Jerusalem*, 400).

108 LOHFINK, „Ursprung", 195.

109 THEISSEN, *Erleben und Verhalten*, 359f.

110 Zur ekklesiologischen Dimension der Tauftradition vgl. z.B. SCHNELLE, *Gerechtigkeit und Christusgegenwart*, 140f.

nachösterlichen Nachschöpfung.[111] Diese Nachschöpfung wird dort, wo eine Reflexion oder eine Begründung der als allgemein erkannten Taufpraxis erfolgt, auf den Auferstandenen (Mt 28,19) oder den bereits Verstorbenen, der sich das Leben zurücknehmen wird (Joh 19,34), zurückgeführt.

Man wird diesen Akt im frühen Wirken der Urgemeinde verankern müssen, wo eine Praxis entstanden ist, die offensichtlich weitgehende Akzeptanz erfahren hat. Die Überlegungen, dass die Erinnerung an Jesu eigene Taufe dieser Akzeptanz förderlich war, sind angemessen. Eine bruchlose Kontinuität zwischen den Taufhandlungen des Johannes und der frühchristlichen Praxis vermittelt durch eine Taufaktivität Jesu selbst ist jedoch nicht zu begründen.

4.3. Die frühchristliche Taufe als Eingang in die neue Gemeinschaft

Dort, wo in den Quellen Auskunft über die Entstehung der Taufe gegeben wird, und dies geschieht nur an wenigen Stellen in den frühchristlichen Schriften, scheint die Erinnerung durch, dass es sich um ein sehr früh entstandenes nachösterliches Phänomen handelt, das aufgrund der Struktur des Taufgeschehens der Johannestaufe nachgebildet ist. Für eine befriedigende Erklärung des Ursprungs der frühen christlichen Taufpraxis sind diese Quellen nach den Bedürfnissen zu befragen, die zu dieser Nachschöpfung geführt haben. Gerade wenn es keine bruchlose Kontinuität von der Johannestaufe zur christlichen Taufe gegeben hat, muss sich das Erklärungsmodell der nachösterlichen Entstehung an der Beantwortung der Frage nach Anlass und Bedürfnissen der frühen Gemeinde bewähren.

Ein Erklärungsmuster, das in Kombination mit den vorgenannten Überlegungen soziologisch bzw. theologiegeschichtlich nach den Bedürfnissen fragt, die zur Entstehung der frühchristlichen Taufe geführt haben, bietet Gerhard Lohfink. Er sucht den Ursprung der christlichen Taufe in phänomenologischen Kohärenzen in Milieu und Funktion der Taufe bei Johannes dem Täufer und in den frühchristlichen Gemeinden; seine Antwort ist „die Parallelität der eschatologischen Grundsituation":[112]

> Die Urgemeinde greift auf das eschatologische Versieglungsgeschehen des Johannes zurück, weil in diesem Zeichen gerade das sinnenfällig wird, worum es ihr

---

111 S.a. BARTH, „Gesichtspunkte", 159, der allerdings die Kontinuität innerhalb der Neuschöpfung m.E. zu stark akzentuiert: „Die Urgemeinde übernahm also den ganzen Ritus der Johannestaufe, verstand aber deren Gabe der Sündenvergebung als allein durch das Heilsgeschehen in Jesu Tod und Auferstehung begründet"; POKORNÝ, *Entstehung der Christologie*, 150: „Die christliche Taufe ist mit der Taufe des Johannes durch ihre rituelle Gestalt und durch ihren eschatologischen Hintergrund verbunden. Die Begründung ist jedoch neu. Sie ist mit der Person und der Geschichte Jesu verbunden".

112 LOHFINK, „Ursprung", 190.

geht und was ihr Auftrag ist: die Sammlung und Zurüstung Israels angesichts des nahen Endes.[113]

Lohfink legt damit den Finger auf die wichtige Aufgabe, den möglichen Katalysator für die Nachschöpfung der Taufe in den christlichen Gemeinden zu bestimmen.[114] Seine Antwort, die in der Begründung einer eschatologischen Gemeinschaft liegt, ist sachlich überzeugend. Allerdings sind die Parallelen zur Johannestaufe nicht überzustrapazieren.[115]

Ist die theoretische Reflexion über den Sinn der christlichen Taufe und ihrer Theologie der religiösen Praxis des Urchristentums chronologisch nachgeordnet, so zeigen die späteren Erinnerungen an die frühchristliche Taufpraxis sowie die Modelle von der Einsetzung der Taufe nach Jesu Tod oder Auferstehung, dass die frühchristliche Taufe den Eintritt in die neue, christologisch bestimmte (Taufe auf den Namen Jesu) Gemeinschaft der frühsten Gemeinde markiert (vgl. bes. Act 2; s.a. Mt 28,18ff.). Historische Re-konstruktion kann diesen aktualisierenden Erinnerungen plausible Hinweise auf Ursprungssituationen der urchristlichen Taufpraxis entnehmen.

Sobald die urchristliche Verkündigung zu einer religiös wie soziologisch unterscheidbaren Bewegung innerhalb des zeitgenössischen Judentums wurde, was aufgrund der einzigartigen Verkündigung vom eschatologischen Gotteshandeln in der Auferweckung Jesu, des gekreuzigten Messias, sehr früh geschah, mussten sich identitätsstiftende Merkmale herausbilden. Mithilfe solcher Gruppenmarker werden die Umkehrenden als Glieder der Bewegung nach innen wie nach außen bestimmt. Die Umkehrtaufe des Johannes, der sich Jesus selbst unterzogen hat, wie sie das kollektive Gedächtnis der Bewegung bezeugte, bot sich als sinn-volles Modell an. Wie die Johannestaufe kennzeichnet die christliche Taufe eine Gemeinschaft im Angesicht des erwarteten Gotteshandelns, das auf die Vollendung des mit dem Auferstehungskerygma verbundenen Gotteshandelns hin wartet, der Parusie des Auferweckten.

---

113 LOHFINK, „Ursprung", 190.

114 Einen ähnlichen Weg beschreibt BARTH, Taufe in frühchristlicher Zeit, 43. Er bestimmt als Katalysator für die Aufnahme des Taufhandelns „die Erfahrung der heilschaffenden Nähe und der Gnade Gottes in der Begegnung mit Jesus, durch die Ereignisse von Karfreitag und Ostern erst in ihrer letzten, äonenwendenden Relevanz offenbart". Es ist also wie bei Lohfink die eschatologische Situation, die zur Aufnahme der Taufpraxis führt, allerdings um die Zuspitzung auf das Heilsgeschehen erweitert; s.a. BACKHAUS, „Jüngerkreise" des Täufers Johannes, 333f. Doch muss die Argumentation eher bei der Funktion der Taufe in dieser eschatologischen (Grund-)Situation ansetzen, auch wenn diese nur in Form späterer Reflexion und Interpretation zugänglich ist.

115 LOHFINK, „Ursprung", 195, bestimmt die historische Kontinuität zwischen Täufergruppe und Urchristentum sehr eng; die „Macht und das Nachwirken der Täuferbewegung, die mit der Urgemeinde noch stark verknüpft war", wird zu einem wichtigen Interpretament der frühchristlichen Taufe und ihrer Funktion.

Die frühchristliche Verkündigung über Jesus zielt auf die Umkehr des Einzelnen als Antwort auf die Mission/Verkündigung über Jesus. Die Taufe ist ein sinnfälliges Ritual, das die Umkehr durch die Waschung anschaubar macht und die Aufnahme in die neue Gemeinschaft (Sündenvergebung und Geistgabe) markiert. Sie ist wie die Johannestaufe ein einmaliges Geschehen. Will der Täufer keine neue Gemeinschaft begründen, sondern die ursprüngliche Gemeinschaft mit Gott für einen Rest in Israel durch einen Reinigungs- und Gerichtsakt wieder herstellen, so verbindet das frühchristliche Taufverständnis den Akt von Umkehr und Eingliederung in die Gemeinschaft durch die sie begleitende Sündenvergebung und Geistverleihung und somit mit wichtigen weiteren Identitätskennzeichen. Spätere Interpretationen reflektieren in neuen religiösen Kontexten das Woher als Abkehr von Götzen und das Wohin des Täuflings. Weiteres theologisches, christologisches und anthropologisches Bedenken kann Sündenvergebung und Geistgabe konsequent und folgerichtig, wie Gerd Theißen treffend zeigte,[116] als Neu-Konstruktion des Getauften verstehen. Die Einbindung des Umkehrenden durch eine einmalige Untertauchtaufe, die in eine neue eschatologische Gemeinschaft führt, bereitet diese Sinnbildung vor. Auch hier entwickeln aktualisierte Erinnerungen das Gedächtnis an die Ursprünge fort.

Die Frage nach den zur christlichen Taufpraxis führenden Faktoren bestätigt, dass die Praxis keine bruchlose Fortsetzung der Johannestaufe ist, sondern kann die Übernahme als in den Quellen im Medium der Erinnerung erkennbare Nach-Schöpfung lesen, die an der Funktion ihres Vorbilds der Taufe zur Umkehr anknüpft.

5. Zusammenfassung: Nachösterliche Nachschöpfung in Kontinuität zur Johannestaufe

Die Quellenlage hinsichtlich der Frage nach dem Ursprung der frühchristlichen Taufe bleibt diffizil und verlangt eine hohe Sensibilität der Konstruktionsbemühungen des Exegeten/der Exegetin. Die Suche nach dem Ursprung der christlichen Taufe findet keine direkte Antwort. Die historische Konstruktion wird nicht monokausal argumentieren können, da die Kombination unterschiedlicher Linien und Gründe die frühchristliche Taufpraxis initiiert haben wird. Auch lässt sich der Ursprung nicht durch das Auffinden alter Einzeltraditionen erklären. Erklärungshinweise lassen sich vielmehr interpretierten und aktualisierten Erinnerungsfragmenten entnehmen.

Die Texte setzen allesamt eine frühzeitig verbreitete und weiträumig akzeptierte frühchristliche Taufpraxis voraus. Die in den späteren Texten erkennbare Sinnbildung muss die Taufpraxis nicht neu begründen, sondern will

---

116 S.o. Anm. 11.

im jeweiligen narrativen und/oder rhetorischen Kontext aus der Taufpraxis Sinn, d.h. Verstehens- und Handlungsspielräume für die Adressaten in ihrer jeweiligen Gegenwart generieren. Dies widerspricht nicht der Vermutung, dass Sinnbildung durch historische Erinnerung erfolgt und Impulse für historische Konstruktionen vernehmbar sind. Allerdings lassen sich nur Eckpunkte und Grundannahmen für die Re-Konstruktion eines Anfangs der frühchristlichen Taufpraxis erstellen. Dazu gehören:

a. die historisch akzeptable Nachricht von der Taufe Jesu durch den Täufer, die der Neuaufnahme des Taufaktes als normativem Eingangsritus in die christliche Gemeinde förderlich war,

b. die Johannestaufe als Modell für den neuen, frühchristlichen Taufritus, wie eine Reihe sachlicher und struktureller Parallelen belegen,

c. die Beobachtung sachlicher und inhaltlicher Differenzen zwischen Johannestaufe und frühchristlicher Taufe, insbesondere die konstitutive Bezugnahme auf Jesus, die einen phänomenologischen, aber keinen direkten genetischen Zusammenhang begründet,

d. eine weder durch die Verkündigung und ihr Porträt bei den Synoptikern noch durch Joh 3,22; 4,1 historisch zu begründende Taufpraxis Jesu, die somit nicht als kontinuitätsstiftendes Moment zwischen beiden Taufhandlungen betrachtet werden kann,

e. die fehlende Erinnerung frühchristlicher Tauftexte an eine Einsetzung der Taufe durch den irdischen Jesus und

f. das Konzept der Einsetzung der Taufe nach dem Sterben Jesu oder als Akt des Auferstandenen, die ein deutliches Signal der Erinnerung an die Taufpraxis als nachösterliche Bildung beinhaltet, die sich möglicherweise frühzeitig auf die Autorität des Erhöhten gründete.

Nimmt man diese Eckpunkte zusammen, so ergibt sich folgendes Bild: in den frühchristlichen Gemeinden hat sich zu einem keineswegs fixierbaren, aber wahrscheinlich sehr frühen Zeitpunkt das Bedürfnis herausgebildet, den Eintritt in die frühchristliche Gemeinde durch einen rituellen Akt zu vollziehen. Dieser Akt fixiert den Wechsel in die neue Gemeinschaft, der sich Stiftung und Wirken des Christus ebenso verdankt, wie diese neue Existenz als Existenz im heilsbringenden Eigentumsbereich des Christus durch Aussprechen seines Namens im Taufakt vollzogen wird. Die Bußtaufe des Täufers, dessen Erinnerung als Entschuldigungsakt im Verständnis der Taufe des Gottessohnes Jesus problematisch war, ist als ritueller Vollzug der Abkehr von dem vorherigen Leben (vgl. für den Täufer Mt 3,7–10 par. Lk 3,7–9 [Q]; für die christliche Taufe: I Kor 6,9–11; Act

2,38.41) hin zu Gott ein inspirierendes Modell, das nunmehr im Kontext der frühchristlichen Sinnbildung verankert wird.

Bibliographie

ALAND, KURT, *Neutestamentliche Entwürfe* (TB 63), München: Chr. Kaiser 1979. Daraus:

— „Zur Vorgeschichte der christlichen Taufe", 183–197.

— „Der Schluß des Markusevangeliums", 246–283.

— ANDERSON, PAUL, *The Fourth Gospel and the Quest for Jesus. Modern Foundations Reconsidered* (LHJS = LNTS 321), London/New York, N.Y.: T&T Clark 2007.

AVEMARIE, FRIEDRICH, *Die Tauferzählungen der Apostelgeschichte. Theologie und Geschichte* (WUNT 139), Tübingen: Mohr Siebeck 2002.

BACKHAUS, KNUT, *Die „Jüngerkreise" des Täufers Johannes. Eine Studie zu den religionsgeschichtlichen Ursprüngen des Christentums* (Paderborner theologische Studien 19), Paderborn et al.: Schöningh 1991.

BARNIKOL, ERNST, „Das Fehlen der Taufe in den Quellenschriften der Apostelgeschichte und in den Urgemeinden der Hebräer und Hellenisten", in: *WZ(H)* 6 (1956/57) 593–610.

BARTH, GERHARD, „Zwei vernachlässigte Gesichtspunkte zum Verständnis der Taufe im Neuen Testament", in: *ZThK* 70 (1973) 137–161.

— *Die Taufe in frühchristlicher Zeit* (BThSt 4); Neukirchen-Vluyn: Neukirchener Verlag 1981.

BEASLEY-MURRAY, GEORGE R., *Baptism in the New Testament*, London: Macmillan 1962.

BECKER, JÜRGEN, *Johannes der Täufer und Jesus von Nazareth* (BSt 63), Neukirchen-Vluyn: Neukirchener Verlag 1972.

BETZ, HANS DIETER, „Transferring a Ritual: Paul's Interpretation of Baptism in Romans 6", in: idem, *Paulinische Studien. Gesammelte Aufsätze III*, Tübingen: Mohr Siebeck 1994, 240–271.

BETZ, OTTO, „Die Proselytentaufe der Qumrangemeinde und die Taufe im Neuen Testament", in: idem, *Jesus. Der Herr der Kirche. Aufsätze zur biblischen Theologie II* (WUNT 52), Tübingen: Mohr Siebeck 1990, 21–48.

BÖCHER, OTTO, „Wasser und Geist", in: idem, *Kirche in Zeit und Endzeit. Aufsätze zur Offenbarung des Johannes*, Neukirchen-Vluyn: Neukirchener Verlag 1983, 58–69.

BULTMANN, RUDOLF, *Die Geschichte der synoptischen Tradition* (FRLANT 29), Göttingen: Vandenhoeck & Ruprecht [9]1979.

— *Das Evangelium des Johannes* (KEK 2), Göttingen: Vandenhoeck & Ruprecht [20]1985.

VON CAMPENHAUSEN, HANS, „Taufen auf den Namen Jesu?", in: *VigChr* 25 (1971) 1–16.

CHILTON, BRUCE, „John the Baptist. His Immersion and His Death", in: Stanley E. Porter/A. R. Cross (Hgg.), *Dimensions of Baptisms. Biblical and Theological Studies* (JSNTS 234), London – New York, NY: Sheffield Academic Press 2002, 25–44.

COLLINS, ADELA YARBRO, „The Origin of Christian Baptism", in: eadem, *Cosmology and Eschatology in Jewish and Christian Apocalypticism* (JSJS 50); Leiden et al.: Brill 1996, 218–238.

DELLING, GERHARD, *Die Zueignung des Heils in der Taufe. Eine Untersuchung zum neutestamentlichen „Taufen auf den Namen"*, Berlin: Evangelische Verlagsanstalt 1961.

— *Die Taufe im Neuen Testament*, Berlin: Evangelische Verlagsanstalt 1963.

DEMARIS, RICHARD E., „Die Taufe Jesu im Kontext der Ritualtheorie", in: Wolfgang Stegemann/Bruce J. Malina/Gerd Theißen (Hgg.), *Jesus in neuen Kontexten*, Stuttgart et al.: Kohlhammer 2002, 43–52.

DINKLER, ERICH, „Art. Taufe II. Im Urchristentum", in: RGG^3 6 (1962. ND 1986) 627–637.

DUNN, JAMES D. G., *Jesus Remembered* (Christianity in the Making 1), Grand Rapids, Mich./ Cambridge: W. B. Eerdmans 2003.

— *Beginning From Jerusalem* (Christianity in the Making 2), Grand Rapids, Mich./Cambridge: W. B. Eerdmans 2009.

ERNST, JOSEF, *Johannes der Täufer: Interpretation – Geschichte – Wirkungsgeschichte* (BZNW 53), Berlin – New York: de Gruyter 1989.

FERGUSON, EVERETT, *Baptism in the Early Church. History, Theology, and Liturgy in the First Five Centuries*, Grand Rapids, Mich./Cambridge, UK: W. B. Eerdmans 2009.

FINN, THOMAS M., *From Death To Rebirth. Ritual and Conversion in Antiquity*, Mahwah, N.J.: Paulist Press 1997.

FRANCE, R. T., „Jesus the Baptist?", in: Joel B. Green/Max Turner (Hgg.), *Jesus of Nazareth: Lord and Christ. Essays on the Historical Jesus and New Testament Christology*, Grand Rapids, Mich.: Eerdmans 1994, 94–111.

FREY, JÖRG, *Die johanneische Eschatologie II. Das johanneische Zeitverständnis* (WUNT 110), Tübingen: Mohr Siebeck 1998.

— „Die Apokalyptik als Herausforderung der neutestamentlichen Wissenschaft. Zum Problem: Jesus und die Apokalyptik", in: Michael Becker/Marcus Öhler (Hgg.), *Apokalyptik als Herausforderung neutestamentlicher Theologie* (WUNT 2/214), Tübingen: Mohr Siebeck 2006, 23–94.

GIESEN, HEINZ, „Die Johannestaufe. Religions- bzw. traditionsgeschichtliche Einordnung und Bedeutung für die christliche Taufe", in: idem, *Jesu Heilsbotschaft und die Kirche. Studien zur Eschatologie und Ekklesiologie bei den Synoptikern und im ersten Petrusbrief* (BEThL 179), Leuven: Peeters 2004, 279–293.

GNILKA, JOACHIM, *Das Matthäusevangelium II. Kommentar zu Kap. 14,1–28,20 und Einleitungsfragen* (HThK I/2), Freiburg et al.: Herder 1988.

— *Die frühen Christen. Ursprünge und Anfang der Kirche* (HThK.S 7), Freiburg i.B.: Herder 1999.

HÄFNER, GERD, „Konstruktion und Referenz. Impulse aus der neueren geschichtstheoretischen Reflexion", in: Knut Backhaus/Gerd Häfner, *Historiographie und fiktionales Erzählen. Zur Konstruktivität in Geschichtstheorie und Exegese* (BThSt 86); Neukirchen-Vluyn: Neukirchener-Verlag 2007, 67–96.

HÄKKINEN, SAKARI, „The Baptism of Jesus", in: Antti Mustakallio/Heikki Leppä (Hgg.), *Lux Humana, Lux Aeterna. Essays on Biblical and Related Themes in Honour of Lars Aejmelaeus* (SFEG 89), Göttingen: Vandenhoeck & Ruprecht 2005, 73–91.

HAENCHEN, ERNST, *Der Weg Jesu. Eine Erklärung des Markus-Evangeliums und der kanonischen Parallelen* (GLB), Berlin: de Gruyter ²1968.

HAHN, FERDINAND, *Das Verständnis der Mission im Neuen Testament* (WMANT 13), Neukirchen-Vluyn: Neukirchener Verlag 1963.

HARTMAN, LARS, „'Into the Name of Jesus'. A Suggestion concerning the Earliest Meaning of the Phrase", in: *NTS* 20 (1973/74) 432–440.

— *Auf den Namen des Herrn Jesus. Die Taufe in den frühchristlichen Schriften* (SBS 148), Stuttgart: Katholisches Bibelwerk 1992.

— „Art. Baptism", in: *ABD 1* (1992) 583-594.

— „Early Baptism – Early Christology", in: A. J. MALHERBE/W. A. MEEKS (Hgg.), *The Future of Christology. Essays in Honor of L. E. Keck*, Minneapolis, Minn.: Fortress Press 1993, 191-201.

HELLHOLM, DAVID, „The Impact of the Situational Contexts for Paul's Use of Baptismal Traditions in his Letters", in: David E. Aune/Torrey Seland (Hgg.), *Neotestamentica et Philonica. Studies in Honor of Peder Borgen* (NT.Sup 106), Leiden et al.: Brill 2003, 147-175.

HEITMÜLLER, WILHELM, *„Im Namen Jesu". Eine sprach- u. religionsgeschichtliche Untersuchung zum Neuen Testament, speziell zur altchristlichen Taufe* (FRLANT 2), Göttingen: Vandenhoeck & Ruprecht 1903.

HORN, FRIEDRICH WILHELM, „Apg 8,37, der Westliche Text und die frühchristliche Tauftheologie", in: Tobias Nicklas/Michael Tilly (Hgg.), *The Book of Acts as Church History. Apostelgeschichte als Kirchengeschichte. Text, Textual Traditions and Ancient Interpretations. Text, Texttraditionen und antike Auslegung* (BZNW 120), Berlin et al.: de Gruyter 2003, 225-239.

KEENER, CRAIG S., *The Gospel of John. A Commentary*, Peabody, Mass.: Hendrickson 2003.

KLEIN, HANS, „Zur Traditionsgeschichte von Mt 16,16b.17. Zugleich ein Beitrag zur Frühgeschichte der christlichen Taufe", in: Karl Kertelge/Traugott Holtz (Hgg.), *Christus bezeugen. FS Wolfgang Trilling* (Erfurter theologische Studien 59), Freiburg et al.: Herder 1990, 124-135.

KOCH, DIETRICH-ALEX, „Der Täufer als Zeuge des Offenbarers. Das Täuferbild von Joh 1,19-34 auf dem Hintergrund von Mk 1,2-11", in: Frans Van Segbroeck/Christopher M. Tuckett/Gilbert Van Belle/Josef Verheyden (Hgg.), *The Four Gospels 1992. FS Frans Neirynck* (BEThL 100), Leuven: Peeters 1992, 1963-1984.

KOESTER, CRAIG R., *Symbolism in the Fourth Gospel. Meaning, Mystery, Community*, Minneapolis, Minn.: Fortress Press 2003.

KRAFT, HEINRICH, „Die Anfänge der christlichen Taufe", in: *ThZ* 17 (1961) 399-412.

KRETSCHMAR, GEORG, „Die Geschichte des Taufgottesdienstes in der alten Kirche", in: Karl Friedrich Müller/Walter Blankenburg (Hgg.), *Der Taufgottesdienst* (Leiturgia 5), Kassel: Johannes-Stauda-Verlag 1970, 1-348.

LABAHN, MICHAEL, *Offenbarung in Zeichen und Wort. Untersuchungen zur Vorgeschichte von Joh 6,1-25a und seiner Rezeption in der Brotrede* (WUNT 2/117), Tübingen: Mohr Siebeck 2000.

- „Jesu Exorzismen (Q 11,19–20) und die Erkenntnis der ägyptischen Magier (Ex 8,15): Q 11,20 als bewahrtes Beispiel für Schrift-Rezeption Jesu nach der Logienquelle", in: Andreas Lindemann (Hg.), *The Sayings Source Q and the Historical Jesus* (BEThL 153), Leuven: Peeters 2001, 617–633.

- „‚Verlassen' oder ‚Vollendet'. Ps 22 in der ‚Johannespassion' zwischen Intratextualität und Intertextualität", in: Dieter Sänger (Hg.), *Ps 22 und die Passionsgeschichten der Evangelien* (BThSt 88), Neukirchen-Vluyn: Neukirchener Verlag 2007, 111–153.

- *Der Gekommene als Wiederkommender. Die Logienquelle als erzählte Geschichte*, (Halle/Wittenberg: masch. Habilitationsschrift 2008) [in Vorbereitung für den Druck: AGB 32; Berlin: Evangelische Verlagsanstalt 2010].

- „John 21 and the Adoption of Sinners", in: PAUL N. ANDERSON/FELIX JUST/ TOM THATCHER (Hgg.), *John, Jesus, and History, Vol. 2: Aspects of Historicity in John* (SBL. Early Christianity and Its Literature 2), Atlanta, Ga.: Society of Biblical Literature 2009, 335–348.

LANG, MANFRED, *Johannes und die Synoptiker. Eine redaktionsgeschichtliche Analyse von Joh 18–20 vor dem markinischen und lukanischen Hintergrund* (FRLANT 182), Göttingen: Vandehoeck & Ruprecht 1999.

LOHFINK, GERHARD, „Der Ursprung der christlichen Taufe", in: idem, *Studien zum Neuen Testament* (SBAB 5), Stuttgart: Katholisches Bibelwerk 1989, 173–198.

LOHSE, EDUARD, „Wort und Sakrament im Johannesevangelium", in: idem, *Die Einheit des Neuen Testaments. Exegetische Studien zur Theologie des Neuen Testaments*, Göttingen: Vandenhoeck & Ruprecht ²1973, 193–208.

LÜDEMANN, GERD, *Das frühe Christentum. Nach den Traditionen der Apostelgeschichte. Ein Kommentar*, Göttingen: Vandenhoeck & Ruprecht 1987.

LUZ, ULRICH, *Das Evangelium nach Matthäus (Mt 26–28)* (EKK I/4), Düsseldorf und Zürich: Benzinger/Neukirchen-Vluyn: Neukirchener Verlag 2002.

MARCUS, JOEL, „Jesus' Baptismal Vision", in: *NTS* 41 (1995) 512–521.

MASON, STEVE, *Flavius Josephus on the Pharisees. A Composition-Critical Study* (Studia Post-Biblica 39), Leiden et al.: Brill 1991.

MEIER, JOHN P., *A Marginal Jew. Rethinking the Historical Jesus 2: Mentor, Message, and Miracles* (ABRL), New York, N.Y., et al.: Doubleday 1994.

MERKLEIN, HELMUT, „Die Umkehrpredigt bei Johannes dem Täufer und Jesus von Nazaret", in: idem, *Studien zu Jesus und Paulus* (WUNT 43), Tübingen: Mohr Siebeck 1987, 109–126.

— „Gericht und Heil. Zur heilsamen Funktion des Gerichts bei Johannes dem Täufer, Jesus und Paulus", in: idem, *Studien zu Jesus und Paulus II* (WUNT 105), Tübingen: Mohr Siebeck 1998, 60–81.

MOLONEY, FRANCIS J., „When is John Talking about Sacraments?", in: *ABR* 30 (1982) 10–33.

— *John* (SP 4), Collegeville, Minn.: Liturgical Press 1998.

NIEDERWIMMER, KURT, *Die Didache* (KAV 1), Göttingen: Vandenhoeck & Ruprecht 1989.

OESTREICH, BERNHARD, „Die Taufe als Symbol für das eschatologische Gericht", in: Roberto Badenas (Hg.), *Die Taufe: Theologie und Praxis* (Studien zur adventistischen Ekklesiologie 3), Hamburg: Advent-Verlag 2002, 31–55.

PESCH, RUDOLF, *Die Apostelgeschichte 1. Teilband: Apg 1–12* (EKK V/1), Zürich et al.: Benzinger/Neukirchen-Vluyn: Neukirchener Verlag 1986.

POKORNÝ, PETR, *Die Entstehung der Christologie. Voraussetzungen einer Theologie des Neuen Testaments*, Stuttgart: Calwer Verlag 1985.

POPP, THOMAS, *Grammatik des Geistes. Literarische Kunst und theologische Konzeption in Johannes 3 und 6* (ABG 3), Leipzig: Evangelische Verlagsanstalt 2001.

REINBOLD, WOLFGANG, *Propaganda und Mission im ältesten Christentum. Eine Untersuchung zu den Modalitäten der Ausbreitung der frühen Kirche* (StUNT 188), Göttingen: Vandenhoeck & Ruprecht 2000.

RIESNER, RAINER, „Taufkatechese und Jesus-Überlieferung (2Tim 2,11–13; Röm 6,3–11; Jak 1,2–27; 1Petr 1–4; 1Joh 2,7–29; 2Kor 1,15–22)", in: Volker A. Lehnert/Ulrich Rüsen-Weinhold (Hgg.), *Logos – Logik – Lyrik. Engagierte exegetische Studien zum biblischen Reden Gottes. FS Klaus Haacker* (ABG 27), Leipzig: Evangelische Verlagsanstalt 2007, 305–339.

ROTHSCHILD, CLARE K., *Baptist Traditions and Q* (WUNT 190), Tübingen: Mohr Siebeck 2005.

SCHENKE, LUDGER, *Die Urgemeinde. Geschichte und theologische Entwicklung*, Stuttgart et al.: Kohlhammer 1990.

SCHNEIDER, GERHARD, *Die Apostelgeschichte I. Teil: Einleitung, Kommentar zu Kap. 1,1–8,40* (HThK V/1); Freiburg et al.: Herder 1980.

SCHNELLE, UDO, *Gerechtigkeit und Christusgegenwart. Vorpaulinische u. paulinische Tauftheologie* (Göttinger theologische Arbeiten 24) Göttingen: Vandenhoeck & Ruprecht ²1986.

— *Antidoketische Christologie im Johannesevangelium. Eine Untersuchung zur Stellung des vierten Evangeliums in der johanneischen Schule* (FRLANT 144), Göttingen: Vandenhoeck & Ruprecht 1987.

— „Art. Taufe 1. Biblisch", in: *EKL*³ 4 (1996) 663–665.

— „Art. Taufe II. Neues Testament", in: *TRE* 32 (2001) 663–674.

— *Paulus. Leben und Denken* (GLB), Berlin et al.: de Gruyter 2003.

— „Theologie als kreative Sinnbildung: Johannes als Weiterbildung von Paulus und Markus", in: Thomas Söding (Hg.), *Das Johannesevangelium – Mitte oder Rand des Kanons? Neue Standortbestimmungen* (QD 203), Freiburg i. Br. et al.: Herder 2003, 119–145.

— *Das Evangelium nach Johannes* (ThHK 4), Leipzig: Evangelische Verlagsanstalt ³2004.

— „Das Johannesevangelium als neue Sinnbildung", in: Gilbert Van Belle/Jan G. Van der Watt/Petrus Maritz (Hgg.), *Theology and Christology in the Fourth Gospel. Essays by the Members of the SNTS Johannine Writings Seminar* (BEThL 184), Leuven: Peeters 2005, 291–313.

— *Theologie des Neuen Testaments* (UTB 2917), Göttingen: Vandenhoeck & Ruprecht 2007.

SCHRÖTER, JENS, *Jesus von Nazareth. Jude aus Galiläa – Retter der Welt* (Biblische Gestalten 15), Leipzig: Evangelische Verlagsanstalt 2006.

— *Von Jesus zum Neuen Testament. Studien zur urchristlichen Theologiegeschichte und zur Entstehung des neutestamentlichen Kanons* (WUNT 204), Tübingen: Mohr Siebeck 2007). Daraus:

— „Konstruktion von Geschichte und die Anfänge des Christentums. Reflexionen zur christlichen Geschichtsdeutung aus neutestamentlicher Perspektive", 37–54.

— „Von der Historizität der Evangelien. Ein Beitrag zur gegenwärtigen Diskussion um den historischen Jesus", 105–146.

SMITH, DWIGHT MOODY, *John* (ANTC), Nashville, Tenn.: Abingdon Press 1999.

— „The Problem of History in John", in: Tom Thatcher (Hg.), *What We Have Heard from the Beginning. The Past, Present, and Future of Johannine Studies*, Waco, Tex.: Baylor University Press 2007, 311–320.

SÖDING, THOMAS, „Taufe, Geist und neues Leben. Eine Orientierung an Paulus", in: idem, *Das Wort vom Kreuz. Studien zur paulinischen Theologie* (WUNT 93), Tübingen: Mohr Siebeck 1997, 335–345.

STOWASSER, MARTIN, *Johannes der Täufer im Vierten Evangelium. Eine Untersuchung zu seiner Bedeutung für die johanneische Gemeinde* (ÖBS 12), Klosterneuburg: Katholisches Österreichisches Bibelwerk 1992.

STRECKER, CHRISTIAN, „Macht – Tod – Leben – Körper. Koordinaten einer Verortung der frühchristlichen Rituale Taufe und Abendmahl", in: Gerd Theißen/Petra von Gemünden (Hgg.), *Erkennen und Erleben. Beiträge zur psychologischen Erforschung des frühen Christentums*, Gütersloh: Gütersloher Verlagshaus 2007, 133–153.

TAYLOR, JOAN E., *The Immerser. John the Baptist within Second Temple Judaism* (Studying the Historical Jesus), Grand Rapids, Mich.: Eerdmans 1997.

THEISSEN, GERD, „Die urchristliche Taufe und die soziale Konstruktion des neuen Menschen", in: Jan Assmann/Guy G. Stroumsa (Hgg.), *Transformations of the Inner Self in Ancient Religions* (SHR 83), Leiden et al.: Brill 1999, 87–114.

— *Erleben und Verhalten der ersten Christen. Eine Psychologie des Urchristentums*, Gütersloh: Gütersloher Verlagshaus 2007.

THEISSEN, GERD/WINTER, DAGMAR, *Die Kriterienfrage in der Jesusforschung. Vom Differenzkriterium zum Plausibilitätskriterium* (NTOA 34), Freiburg, CH: Universitäts-Verlag/Göttingen: Vandenhoeck und Ruprecht 1997.

THYEN, HARTWIG, *Das Johannesevangelium* (HNT 6), Tübingen: Mohr Siebeck 2005.

VAAGE, LEIF E., „Bird-Watching at the Baptism of Jesus. Early Christian Mythmaking in Mark 1:9–11", in: Elizabeth A. Castelli/Hal Taussig (Hgg.), *Reimaging Christian Origins. A Colloquium Honoring Burton L. Mack*, Valley Forge, Penn.: Trinity Press 1996, 280–294.

VAN BELLE, GILBERT, „ΚΥΡΙΟΣ or ΊΗΣΟΥΣ in John 4,1?", in: Adelbert Denaux (Hg.), *New Testament Textual Criticism and Exegesis. Festschrift J. Delobel* (BEThL 161), Leuven: Peeters 2002, 159–174.

WEBB, ROBERT L., „Jesus' Baptism: Its Historicity and Implications", in: *BBR* 10 (2000) 261–309.

WEDER, HANS, *Gegenwart und Gottesherrschaft. Überlegungen zum Zeitverständnis bei Jesus und im frühen Christentum* (BThSt 20), Neukirchen-Vluyn: Neukirchener Verlag 1993.

WEISS, HANS-FRIEDRICH, *Der Brief an die Hebräer* (KEK 13), Göttingen: Vandenhoeck & Ruprecht 1991.

WEISS, JOHANNES, *Das Urchristentum*. Hg. v. Rudolf Knopf, Göttingen: Vandenhoeck & Ruprecht 1917.

ZMIJEWSKI, JOSEF, *Die Apostelgeschichte* (RNT), Regensburg: Pustet 1994.

ZUMSTEIN, JEAN, „Der Prozess der Relecture in der johanneischen Literatur", in: idem, *Kreative Erinnerung. Relecture und Auslegung im Johannesevangelium* (AThANT 84), Zürich: Theologischer Verlag ²2004, 15–30.

— „Johannes 19,25–27", in: *aaO.*, 253–275.

Jesus' Baptism and the Origins of the Christian Ritual

Hans Dieter Betz

The early history of Christian baptism in the New Testament follows two tracks of tradition that appear to have little or no contact.[1] First, there is the epistolary tradition in the letters of Paul and the deutero-Pauline epistles. I have pursued this tradition in an earlier essay which does not need to be restated at this point.[2] Second, there is the narrative tradition in the Gospels, beginning with Mark and continuing with Mark's interpreters in Matthew, Luke/Acts, and John. It is this narrative tradition that will be investigated in the following paper.[3]

The origin of Christian baptism is anchored in Jesus' baptism by John the Baptist in a coarse statement in Mark 1:9: "And it happened in those days that Jesus came from Nazareth of Galilee and was baptized in the Jordan by John [the Baptist]."[4]

The sentence looks like it has been taken from a longer historical narrative, but which narrative could it have been? It could only have been narrative material connected with John the Baptist, from which Mark also derived 1:4–8. If this was a pre-Markan source, Mark breaks it off after 1:9, so that we do not learn what this earlier source had to say about the consequences of Jesus' baptism. The coarse sentence of 1:9, however, is left standing with all its ambiguities. This seems to express Mark's intention rather than incompetence or superficiality, and for his later interpreters it had the force of a bombshell. To make this effect plausible, sufficient reasoning had to be provided, and to this we will turn next.

---

1 The following paper is intended to serve the purposes of the symposium to which it was submitted. Surveying adequately the vast body of literature on early Christian baptism has to be left to others. See G. Alles, F. Avemarie, et al., "Taufe," 50–92; "Baptism," 572–598; E. Ferguson, *Baptism*.

2 See H. D. Betz, "Transferring a Ritual, 240–271; also D. Hellholm's essay (in this publication).

3 For extra-canonical amplifications see W. Bauer, *Das Leben Jesu*, 110–141; H.-J. Klauck, *Apokryphe Evangelien*, 51–52, 59–60, 66, 74, 173–174, 242.

4 καὶ ἐγένετο ἐν ἐκείναις ταῖς ἡμέραις ἦλθεν Ἰησοῦς ἀπὸ Ναζαρὲτ τῆς Γαλιλαίας καὶ ἐβαπτίσθη εἰς τὸν Ἰορδάνην ἀπὸ Ἰωάννου.

1. Preliminary Historical Questions

1.1. Issues of Historiography

Undeniably, Mark knew of the enormous consequences Jesus' baptism by John the Baptist had for the complicated history of Christian baptism. As it stands, the statement in 1:9 was implausible and embarrassing, given the Christian context of Mark. Rather than omitting it from his Christian story, however, Mark leaves it in and lets it play its role as a powerful provocation. The fact that Mark as well as the other gospel writers offer completely different interpretations means that they all felt the sting, but also, curiously, allow it to stand. Thus, the first question is, How can this phenomenon be explained?

It may be helpful to take seriously a remark of Tacitus, the Roman historian, who discusses the problem of how the historian should deal with events of profound importance which have resulted in farreaching changes. Tacitus calls them "grand events" (*magna*). Such events are *eo ipso* "ambiguous" and cause compositional problems for the historian. Accordingly, on the one hand historians need to emphasize the magnitude of subject matter to justify their work in principle, while on the other hand the conspicuousness of such events is easily compromised by excessive rhetorical flourish. This dilemma is captured by Tacitus in a brief statement of principle: "The point is that the great events are ambiguous, because there are those who listen to all hearsay, whatever its kind, and admit it as ascertained facts, and there are others who turn what is truth into the opposite; in each case, by posterity they increase and magnify."[5] The historian, therefore, is advised to leave the "grand events" in their ambiguities, whereby the varieties of interpretations are allowed to flourish. This is necessary because, even if he were personally an eye-witness, the historical author has no direct access to the events themselves, but only to secondary documents or oral reports, all of them interpretations. Leaving the ambiguities as they are stimulates sources to report divergent stories, among which the critical historian can choose what may be the most probable.

Since, as we suggested, Mark follows the recommendation of the historians, he intended to write as a historian, and his Gospel of Mark is, in this respect, a piece of historiography.[6] He left the ambiguous sentence of 1:9 in its place, precisely to provoke alternative interpretations, such as those represented by the other gospel writers.

---

5 Tac. Ann. 3.19: *Adeo maxima quaeque ambigua sunt, dum alii quoque modo audita pro compertis habent, alii vera in contrarium vertunt; et gliscit utrumque posteritate.* (The translation is mine.) For commentary see A. J. WOODMAN, *Annals of Tacitus*, vol. 3, 196–198, who also points to the close parallel in Dio Cass. *Roman History*, 53.19.1–6.

6 This is not, of course, to suggest that Mark read Tacitus, but that the latter formulates a general principle.

As a concrete example of such ambiguity Jesus' last cry on the cross might be mentioned. Mark (15:37) leaves the cry without articulation: "Then Jesus gave a very loud cry and breathed his last."[7] The other gospel writers did not leave it at that. Matthew (27:50) makes Jesus' last cry the second following a first articulated one (v. 46): "Then Jesus again cried with a loud voice and gave off his spirit."[8] Again different, Luke (23:46) articulates the cry by having Jesus quote a verse from Ps 31:6: "Then Jesus, crying with a loud voice, said: 'Father, into your hands I commend my spirit'."[9] Finally, John's Gospel (19:30) gives the voice a characteristically Johannine meaning. "When Jesus had received the wine, he said, 'It is finished [or: fulfilled]'. Then he bowed his head and gave up his spirit."[10] This version has greatly expanded the possibilities for further interpretation ranging from victory cry to abysmal dejection.[11]

Turning to baptism, all four gospel authors agree that the Christian ritual of baptism was introduced by John the Baptist's baptism of Jesus. Taken by itself, in Mark's coarse sentence of 1:9 John the Baptist stands in the center, not Jesus. The focus is changed from John to Jesus first by Mark in 1:10–11, and then by all subsequent gospels. Rather than removing the complications, Mark has in fact evoked the variety of versions in the other gospels. These other versions differ on the very substance, the event itself and what occurred in it. Paradoxically, for the modern historian this variety constitutes the historicity of the event.

The question, therefore, is, Why do the gospel writers, Mark included, retain the embarrassment, instead of removing it? The answer is that apparently they all regard it as an indispensable factor in claiming historical veracity. This also raises the question of the literary genre of Mark as a work of historiography. If Mark indicates the genre by the title in 1:1 as "origin of the gospel of Jesus Christ [son of God]" (ἀρχὴ τοῦ εὐαγγελίου Ἰησοῦ Χριστοῦ [υἱοῦ θεοῦ]), the other gospel writers substitute other titles, but they do not deny the fact as such.[12] Mark was the first who seems to have recognized the need for a biography of Jesus, and he met that need by his gospel. How did he get this idea? The issue as such, however, was not new. Paul included biographical data concerning Jesus

---

7   Mark 15:37: ὁ δὲ Ἰησοῦς ἀφεὶς φωνὴν μεγάλην ἐξέπνευσεν.

8   Matt 27:50: ὁ δὲ Ἰησοῦς πάλιν κράξας φωνῇ μεγάλῃ ἀφῆκεν τὸ πνεῦμα.

9   Luke 23:46: καὶ φωνήσας φωνῇ μεγάλῃ ὁ Ἰησοῦς εἶπεν· πάτερ, εἰς χεῖράς σου παρατίθεμαι τὸ πνεῦμά μου.

10 John 19:30: [ὁ] Ἰησοῦς εἶπεν· τετέλεσται, καὶ κλίνας τὴν κεφαλὴν παρέδωκεν τὸ πνεῦμα.

11 See R. Bultmann, *Das Evangelium des Johannes*, 523; ET: *The Gospel of John*, 674–675; R. E. Brown, *The Gospel according to John*, vol. 2, 930–931. For an impressive literary example, using John 19:30, see Mephistopheles' nihilistic comments on Faust's death, according to Goethe, *Faust II*, part 5, lines 11587–11603, in: A. Schöne (ed.), vol. 1, 446–447; with the commentary vol. 2, 761–763.

12 Matt 1:1,18 speaks of (ἡ) γένεσις Ἰησοῦ Χριστοῦ υἱοῦ Δαυὶδ υἱοῦ Ἀβραάμ; Luke 1:1: διήγησις περὶ τῶν πεπληροφορημένων ἐν ἡμῖν πραγμάτων; John 1:1: ὁ λόγος, but they retain the notion of origin (see ἀρχή Luke 1:2; John 1:1).

in his statements of self-definition as apostle in 1 Cor 15:3–11 and Rom 1:1–7, and foremost in his hymn to Christ in Phil 2:6–11.[13] Whether Mark knew of Paul's letters is uncertain, to be sure, but he understood the challenge implicit in Paul's concept of the gospel (εὐαγγέλιον). Both Mark and Paul speak of "the gospel of Jesus Christ" (τὸ εὐαγγέλιον Ἰησοῦ Χριστοῦ), and both address the biographical as well as the historical implications: Where did the gospel come from, how did Jesus get connected with it, and what was the historical impact?[14] If Christ was a historical figure of divine significance, a biography of his life as a human being was needed. However, since Paul states that the gospel was "proclaimed before by the prophets in holy scriptures",[15] this would not include John the Baptist whom Paul never mentions in his letters. Instead Paul lets the gospel begin with Abraham.[16] Mark, on the other side, while never mentioning Abraham attributes a high status to John and has him introduce his message (Mark 1:7–8), by a citation (1:2–3) of the prophet Isaiah (40:3 LXX), thus making him a mediator figure between Isaiah and Jesus.

This conclusion, therefore, points to the question of the literary genre of Mark. This question has been hotly debated by New Testament scholars especially in the 20th c. However, as various surveys of the debates show, the many attempts at genre definition have thus far remained inconclusive. Recent proposals have come from Hubert Cancik, a classicist specializing in Roman historiography,[17] and the New Testament scholars Eve-Marie Becker[18] and Adela Yarbro Collins.[19] There seems to be broad agreement about Mark being a

---

13 See Phil 2:7–8: ἐν ὁμοιώματι ἀνθρώπων γενόμενος· καὶ σχήματι εὑρεθεὶς ὡς ἄνθρωπος ἐταπείνωσεν ἑαυτὸν γενόμενος ὑπήκοος μέχρι θανάτου, θανάτου δὲ σταυροῦ.

14 The concept of gospel (εὐαγγέλιον) is extraordinarily complicated, as the gospel authors and Paul demonstrate by their explanations. See the overview, with further literature, by H. Koester, "Evangelium I.II," 1735–1741; ET, 528–532.

15 Rom 1:2: ὃ προεπηγγείλατο διὰ τῶν προφητῶν αὐτοῦ ἐν γραφαῖς ἁγίαις.

16 Gal 3:6–29; 4:21–31; Rom 4:1–17; 9:7; 11:1; 2 Cor 11:22.

17 Cancik's article first appeared in 1984 and was republished in 2008: "Die Gattung Evangelium", 100–130. He offers a wealth of pertinent observations and points in a certain direction: "Die auf das Publikum bezogene Gattungsbestimmung führt einerseits auf das Prophetenbuch, andererseits of den βίος eines θεῖος ἀνήρ." (126).

18 E.-M. Becker, Das Markus-Evangelium. This wide-ranging survey of 20th century research features Mark 1:1 as the beginning (ἀρχή) of Christian historiography: "*Das Markus-Evangelium markiert den historischen und literaturgeschichtlichen Beginn christlicher Geschichtsschreibung*" (400; italics). Biographical elements are subordinated to historiography, and Paul is mentioned merely in passing.

19 A. Y. Collins new Hermeneia Commentary on Mark: *A Commentary*, includes a detailed survey on the genre discussions (15–43), in which she combines reports on a variety of perspectives without reaching a clear result about genre: "I will discuss the genre of Mark from several points of view: Mark as a 'gospel', that is a new and unique genre; Mark as a 'biography', and Mark as 'history'. Finally, I will argue that Mark is best understood as an eschatological historical monograph." (18).

work of historiography as well as biography, but there is no explanation of the relationship between these two categories as regards Mark' gospel. Whatever its genre may be, it is called new and unique, and somehow it is claimed to belong to the Graeco-Roman historiographical literature[20]. However, this result is not more than a summary of the complexities.

Regarding the literary genre, in the Graeco-Roman era a rigid separation of biography and historiography is not supported by the sources. Instead, both are nearly always connected in some ways, differing from author to author or even among the works of the same author. There is also a trend in imperial historiography towards becoming more and more biographical. Authors like Sallustius, Tacitus, Suetonius, Plutarch, and Dio Cassius, write history as sequences of biographies, whereby each of these authors follows various concepts of what history and biography is supposed to be.[21]

A similar diversity can be observed among the four gospels of the New Testament. If Mark's Gospel is primarily biographical, its title of ἀρχὴ τοῦ εὐαγγελίου Ἰησοῦ Χριστοῦ expresses a historical interest. Matthew's Gospel, while enforcing the biographical focus, also contains a historical perspective with the history of the early church in mind.[22] Luke's Gospel goes even further by turning the biography of Jesus in the Gospel into the first part of a history of the early church by adding the Book of Acts (Luke 1:1–4; 3:1–2; Acts 1:1–8).[23] In quite the opposite way, the Gospel of John sharply centers on the biography of the divine redeemer Jesus, for which the foundation is the myth of the Logos prefaced as a hymnic prologue (John 1:1–18).

1.2. Issues of Comparative Religion

One of the implications of Mark 1:9 is that Jesus' baptism by immersion in the river Jordan occurs in the religious context of Judaism. This reminds Mark's readers that Christianity originated within Judaism. If it was John the Baptist who provided the impetus toward Christianity, the question arises whether John or Jesus was the "founder" of Christianity.[24] The New Testament texts show that

---

20　It is agreed that this includes the Hellenistic-Jewish literature as well.

21　Not without interest for New Testament scholarship, E. LÖFSTEDT, "On the Style of Tacitus," has observed that Tacitus' *Annales* consist of a series of biographies, each ending with a catastrophic event and together pointing to the great tragedy of Rome.

22　See BETZ, "The Sermon on the Mount in Matthew's Interpretation," 258–275; repr. in: my *Synoptische Studien*, 270–289.

23　It is worth mentioning that Luke's sequence of biography and history has a parallel in Tacitus: He wrote first the "Agricola", a biography of his father-in-law, and then his "Histories" and "Annals".

24　For an earlier discussion of the background in the history of scholarship see BETZ on "Wellhausen's Dictum 'Jesus was not a Christian, but a Jew' in Light of Present Scholarship," 83–110, reprinted in my *Antike und Christentum*, 1–31.

each of the gospel writers answered the question by locating the two figures of John and Jesus in their place, attributing to them ranks and functions. Accordingly, John is shown not to be the founder of a new religion but the prophetic announcer of Jesus as the messiah and founder. Together, John and Jesus provide the irrevocable link between Judaism and Christianity, John being the herald and mentor of "the coming one" (ὁ ἐρχόμενος),[25] the messiah Jesus of Nazareth. Thus, Jesus began his own career and mission as a disciple of John within Judaism. After John's assassination, however, this disciple came into his own as a Jewish teacher whose teachings both agreed with and differed from those of his mentor.[26] In fact, Jesus taught his own disciples new teachings, not only those of John. Within the plurality of Jewish movements at the time, Jesus offered a new variety of teaching and lifestyle.

This situation gives rise to the next question: How could Jesus figure as the founder of Christianity, if what he founded was just another "school" within Judaism? Whatever the answer, the embarrassment was increased by a Christianity not able to claim that it appeared as a new religion. Indeed, there was no spectacular break between the old and the new. Whatever differences may have existed between Jesus and John, they amounted to no more than varieties within the same movement. Jesus is not reported to have abandoned what he learned from John, nor to have simply continued it. None of the gospel writers seems capable of precisely distinguishing between the teachings of the two masters, and they left their readers with plenty of ambiguities. It belonged to later interpreters who worked out the differences and magnified them. In the New Testament accounts, the ranks of John and Jesus became clearly differentiated in that John assumed second place as prophetic herald and precursor, while Jesus was ranked as the Christian messianic redeemer. Beyond this, there seems to have existed considerable confusion and overlap of the traditions even in the Synoptic traditions themselves.[27]

How then did Jesus' teaching and lifestyle express his rank and purpose as messianic redeemer? This question is not easy to answer. Sharing a similar fate of catastrophic end, both the historical John and Jesus failed to reach whatever their goals may have been. Both were murdered by the ruling authorities without due process because they were denounced as political and religious subversives. Neither John nor Jesus, however, conspired to form a military insurgency, but in the eyes of the authorities it sufficed that they were verbal opponents to the Jewish and Roman overlords. Consequently, John and Jesus shared the destiny of prophets and righteous men of old, but at this point the similarities between them ended. Jesus was crucified not as a prophet but as the messianic

---

25 See Mark 1:7; Matt 3:11; Luke 3:16; John 1:15,27,30.

26 See, esp., Mark 6:14–29 and parr., and the commentary by Yarbro Collins, *Mark*, 303–314.

27 See the recent investigations by J. A. Kelhoffer, *The Diet of John the Baptist*, and C. K. Rothschild, *Baptist Traditions and Q*.

King of the Jews.[28] This fact, startling again, was first stated by an outsider, that is no less a person than the Roman governor Pilate who had the charge fixed to the cross: "The King of the Jews" (ὁ βασιλεὺς τῶν Ἰουδαίων, Mark 15:26, and parr.). In comparison, neither Jesus' disciples nor his adversaries had drawn this conclusion. To the Jews, even including his disciples, friends and relatives, Jesus' crucifixion was a humiliating blow, to the Christian readers of Mark the salvation event.[29]

The further question the author of Mark's Gospel had to answer was, What messianic qualifications were revealed by Jesus' preaching, teaching, and conduct? The gospels agree that to outsiders and insiders alike Jesus appeared as a mysterious figure. The people admired him as a miracle-worker, and his followers as a wise teacher and leader, but they all failed to see in him the expected messiah of Israel. The general failure of his contemporaries to comprehend his true nature was caused by the fact that Jesus did not conform to the traditional criteria of a messiah. This lack of understanding even on the part of his disciples is described by the gospels in painful detail. Written from the perspective of post-Easter Christian faith, however, the gospel writers left no doubt that Jesus was the messiah, but at the same time they made it clear to their readers that, paradoxically, a degree of incomprehension remains a constant element of the Christian faith itself. While the gospel writers redefined the fundamental criteria of messiahship, they presented Jesus' ambiguous appearance as a disguise which kept the truth about his messianic nature hidden from his disciples, not to mention all others, until it was revealed to them by his post-resurrection epiphanies.[30] Thus the Christian readers of the gospels were enabled to deal creatively with Jesus' messiahship. On the one hand the believers were to expect Jesus' return at the eschatological *parousia* as the victorious redeemer, while on the other hand by retaining the ambiguity of Jesus' appearance in the texts the non-believing readers were kept guessing.

Modern scholarship, moreover, has addressed the history-of-religions questions raised by Jesus' early response to the appeal of John the Baptist. According to Mark, the prophet challenged the Jewish people to repent and obtain God's forgiveness of their sins in view of the impending end of the world and the Last Judgment (Mark 14:61–62). It so happened that John baptized in the desert,

---

28 According to 1 Thess 2:14–16, however, Jesus is seen in line with the prophets of old, but would Paul include here also John the Baptist? There is no indication of this in Paul; even in passages mentioning Apollos who was connected with the movement of John the Baptist (1 Cor 1:12; 3:4–9, 22; 4:6; 16:12; but cf. Acts 18:24–25; 19:1–7).

29 This is highlighted by Jesus' predictions of his passion and resurrection (Mark 8:31–33; 9:30–32; 10:32–34; 16:6).

30 On the "messianic secrecy" of Jesus see G. THEISSEN, "Die pragmatische Bedeutung der Geheimnismotive im Markusevangelium", 225–245.

"proclaiming a baptism of repentance for the forgiveness of sins."[31] If so, the young man Jesus had responded favorably to John's call, but Mark does not give a reason why Jesus reacted in this way. The fact is that information about Jesus' growing up into the life of an adult is extremely sparse. It is, however, reasonable to infer that like many other young people he was looking for better education than was available in the village of Nazareth. Electing the famous John the Baptist as teacher speaks for Jesus' high expectations and goals. Jesus was certainly not the only young man who left home and walked down to the Jordan valley, got baptized and joined the group of like-minded disciples of John the Baptist. Concerning John's learning and teaching little information is available. Josephus describes him in Hellenistic terms and sees in him a Stoic philosopher.[32] The example of Qumran shows that even out in the desert scholarship and teaching could be substantial. Apart from a desire to advance in education no other reasons are suggested in the sources. Speculations, therefore, are unwarranted, if they suggest that Jesus suffered from pathological remorse about his sinfulness, or that he may have become disgusted by the simple life in the home village, or that he separated from his parents because of disagreements. Rather, a good example is that of young Josephus who left home and studied in the Judean desert with a respected sage by the name of Bannus; after three years he left Bannus and studied the doctrines of the three major Jewish schools, in order then to join the Pharisees whom he associated with the Stoics.[33]

From a Jewish perspective there is nothing inordinate in Jesus' acceptance of John's call. Repentance and prayers for forgiveness of sins belong to the daily life of every faithful Jew. God's demand of righteousness is met by asking for his mercy. Since Jesus fully participated in the Jewish religion, he shared in its daily way of life.

There are, however, indications that Jesus differed in some respects from John's priorities of religious convictions. Notably, Jesus did not become another ascetic prophet living in the desert. Instead, he returned to the towns and villages, where he shared the life of ordinary people. Together with his disciples he took up a life of an itinerant teacher, wandering through the country preaching and teaching the gospel.[34] Educating his disciples became Jesus' proverbial mark of distinction. Different from John the Baptist and his baptism, Jesus' signature was his oral teaching through parables, examples, and sayings composi-

---

31 Mark 1:4: ἐγένετο Ἰωάννης [ὁ] βαπτίζων ἐν τῇ ἐρήμῳ καὶ κηρύσσων βάπτισμα μετανοίας εἰς ἄφεσιν ἁμαρτιῶν.

32 Josephus, *AJ* 18.116–19.

33 See Josephus, *Vit.* 11.

34 The label "Wandercharismatiker", now a popular cliché, should be used with caution because it conveys notions of instability, restlessness, and anti-intellectualism, all too appealing to certain modern trends. See M. N. EBERTZ, "Charisma, II.,"113–115; ET, 493–495.

tion. The prayer called "The Lord's Prayer" and the teachings of "The Sermon on the Mount" even became "world literature."[35]

Finally, the question can be raised whether these accomplishments of Jesus were in effect taught him by John the Baptist, his teacher and mentor. Interestingly, there is no evidence in the sources that this was the case. Instead the sources convey the message that Jesus' teaching was his own, or better to say, he was divinely inspired (θεοδίδακτος). If John's teaching had any effect, it enabled Jesus to develop his own distinctive style of life and work. The traditional claim that John was the first to detect Jesus' messianic potential may not be without its historical foundation. That such a situation is the ordinary to expect in antiquity is shown by important analogies, most notably the students of Socrates, all of whom became quite different from their master, and from each other as well.

2. The Earliest Account (Mark 1:9–11)

Textually, the oldest account of Jesus' baptism is found in Mark 1:9–11. Apart from its older historical information (v. 9), the passage is the result of Mark's secondary expansion and Christian interpretation.[36]

(9) And in those days, Jesus came from Nazareth in Galilee and was baptized in the Jordan by John.

(10) And immediately, while he was coming out of the water, he saw the heavens split and the Spirit coming down in(to) him like a dove.

(11) And a voice came from the heavens, "You are my beloved son, I take delight in you."

(9) Καὶ ἐγένετο ἐν ἐκείναις ταῖς ἡμέραις ἦλθεν Ἰησοῦς ἀπὸ Ναζαρὲτ τῆς Γαλιλαίας καὶ ἐβαπτίσθη εἰς τὸν Ἰορδάνην ὑπὸ Ἰωάννου.

(10) καὶ εὐθὺς ἀναβαίνων ἐκ τοῦ ὕδατος εἶδεν σχιζομένους τοὺς οὐρανοὺς καὶ τὸ πνεῦμα ὡς περιστερὰν καταβαῖνον εἰς αὐτόν·

(11) καὶ φωνὴ ἐγένετο ἐκ τῶν οὐρανῶν, Σὺ εἶ ὁ υἱός μου ὁ ἀγαπητός, ἐν σοὶ εὐδόκησα.

Two scenes and their interpretation are clearly discernable. As mentioned already, the first scene contains general historical information (v.9). The second scene represents an expansion (v.10–11), by which the original event of an historical narrative is turned into a biographical legend concerning Jesus' inaugura-

---

35 See Betz, *The Sermon on the Mount*, 2–3.

36 For a detailed comparison of the different versions of the story, see H. Braun, "Entscheidende Motive," 39–53, reprinted in his *Gesammelte Studien*, 168–172.

tion as the messiah.[37] While the first scene of v. 9 by itself presupposes a Jewish situation, the second scene of v. 10–11 requires a Christian context of Mark's christology. This combination unites John the Baptist's earlier messianology (1:2–8) with Mark's later christology of Jesus as messiah.[38]

When v. 10 picks up the narrative of v. 9, the adverb εὐθύς adds to the story a miraculous twist. The new turn is that Jesus at the moment of his emerging from the water experiences a sudden vision of the heavens split open, out of which revelations come forth. Jesus being the subject of εἶδεν means that only Jesus has this experience. The revelations in effect change the event of the first scene into a quite different second one, of which only Jesus is aware. According to the new scene Jesus is being inaugurated as the messiah. Two divinatory events make up this *inauguration*. In the first event in v. 10 the spirit descends in the form of a dove, and designates Jesus, whereby εἰς αὐτόν can mean different things: "toward him," "pointing to him," "settling down on him," or "entering into him." At any rate, the event associates designation and inspiration, two traditional elements of inauguration.[39]

The second element follows in v. 11. A voice, identified as God's voice, sounds out of the heavens and proclaims Jesus' adoption as his beloved son. The traditional adoption formula is cited from Scripture (Ps 2:7 LXX).[40] Wide-ranging parallels from the ancient world (Near East, Old Testament, and Graeco-Roman sources) point to the fact that important elements of royal inauguration occur in Mark's story.[41] The Baptist's prediction of Jesus' messiahship, the prophetic oracles from Scripture, the cosmic sign of the open heavens, the desig-

---

37   Cf. BULTMANN, *Geschichte*, 263–270, 264: "Die Legende erzählt Jesu Weihe zum Messias, ist also im Grunde nicht eine biographische, sondern eine Glaubenslegende." Bultmann's comment, however, should not be taken as contrasting the two notions, but as both belonging together.

38   See YARBRO COLLINS, *Mark*, 146–151.

39   For an interesting example see Cicero's dream according to Plutarch's *Life of Cicero* 44.2–5. During the time when Pompey and Iulius Caesar were still alive, people were wondering who the next ruler would be. Thus, someone invited the promising sons of senators to come to the Capitol, where Iupiter would designate the future ruler. Eagerly, the young men ran up, and stationed themselves in their purple-bordered robes at the Temple, when the door suddenly opened and the youths came inside in front of the god. They walked around the statue and the god inspected them, but sent them away in sorrow. Yet, when the young Octavianus advanced, the god stretched out his hand and said, "O Romans, ye shall have an end of civil wars when this youth has become your ruler." The next day, when Cicero who had not met Octavianus before came into the Campus Martius, he suddenly recognized the youth of the dream to be Octavianus, and finding out who he was he talked to him. And this explains why there was later that cordial relationship between Augustus and Cicero. Cited according to the LCL edition and translation by B. PERRIN, *Plutarch's Lives*, vol. 7, 1919, 195–197.

40   See on this point BULTMANN, *Geschichte*, 264, n. 1; YARBRO COLLINS, *Mark*, 150–151.

41   This interpretation as inauguration was first proposed in BETZ, "Plutarch's Life of Numa", 44–61; reprinted in my, *Paulinische Theologie*, 166–190.

nation by the divine spirit in form of a bird (*auspicium*), and God's own voice pronouncing the adoption of the messiah as son of God are those elements.[42] As mentioned in my article, strange is the omission of the anointing and the enthronement.[43] Wellhausen's suggestion that the baptism took the place of the anointment may explain the oddity.[44] Adding two further rituals, anointment and enthronement, would be in conflict with Jesus' personal vision of the whole event.[45] Apart from the inauguration, ritual baptism plays no role in Mark's Gospel. In other words, for Mark baptism is not the entrance ritual for the Christian church.[46]

3. The Interpretation in Other Gospels

3.1. Matthew 3:13–17

The Gospel of Matthew represents a thorough revision of Mark, its major source. While the author did not remove the historical fact that Jesus was baptized by John the Baptist, he changed what that fact was all about. Actually, Mark's ambiguities caused Matthew to first change the entire context for the event. Before turning to Mark's text, Matthew supplies more information about John the Baptist and his message (Matt 3:1–12), after which the narrative continues:

(13) Then Jesus comes from Galilee to the Jordan to John to be baptized by him.

(14) But John tried to prevent him and said: "I need to be baptized by you, and you come to me?"

(15) But Jesus answered and said to him: "Let it be so now, for it is thus appropriate for us to fulfill all righteousness." Then he permitted him.

---

42 For literature and passages see J. LINDERSKI, "The Augural Law," 2146–2312, especially 2215–2296.

43 See BRAUN, "Entscheidende Motive," 54–55; for later additions of anointment, see KLAUCK, *Apokryphe Evangelien*, 173–174, 185–186.

44 J. WELLHAUSEN, *Das Evangelium Marci*, 5: "An Stelle der Salbung, die zum Begriff des Messias gehört, tritt bei Jesus die Taufe. Mit ihr beginnt seine Messianität."

45 In his critique of Bultmann, PH. VIELHAUER in an important article ("Erwägungen zur Christologie des Markusevangeliums," 199–214) proposes a background in an "enthronement ritual" in three stages, as shown by E. NORDEN, *Die Geburt des Kindes*, 116–134. However, it seems to be Mark's intention precisely to avoid the language of royal enthronement in application to Jesus; indeed it would be incompatible with the "messianic secret."

46 Correctly observed by M. WERNER, *Der Einfluss paulinischer Theologie im Markusevangelium*, 138: "… dass Markus in seiner Schrift keine einzige Aussage über die christliche Taufe bietet." However, the real problem begins here; cf. also Mark 10:38–39; [16:16: not the original Mark]. See J. A. KELHOFFER, *Miracle and Mission*, 101–102; YARBRO COLLINS, *Mark*, 497, 810–811.

(16) And after he was baptized Jesus immediately went up from the water; and behold, the heavens were opened to him, and he saw the Spirit of God descending as a dove and coming on him.

(17) And behold, a voice spoke from the heavens: "This one is my beloved son, in whom I have taken delight."

(13) Τότε παραγίνεται ὁ Ἰησοῦς ἀπὸ τῆς Γαλιλαίας ἐπὶ τὸν Ἰορδάνην πρὸς τὸν Ἰωάννην τοῦ βαπτισθῆναι ὑπ' αὐτοῦ.

(14) ὁ δὲ Ἰωάννης διεκώλυεν αὐτὸν λέγων, Ἐγὼ χρείαν ἔχω ὑπὸ σοῦ βαπτισθῆναι, καὶ σὺ ἔρχῃ πρός με;

(15) ἀποκριθεὶς δὲ ὁ Ἰησοῦς εἶπεν πρὸς αὐτόν, Ἄφες ἄρτι, οὕτως γὰρ πρέπον ἐστὶν ἡμῖν πληρῶσαι πᾶσαν δικαιοσύνην. τότε ἀφίησιν αὐτόν.

(16) βαπτισθεὶς δὲ ὁ Ἰησοῦς εὐθὺς ἀνέβη ἀπὸ τοῦ ὕδατος· καὶ ἰδοὺ ἠνεῴχθησαν [αὐτῷ] οἱ οὐρανοί, καὶ εἶδεν [τὸ] πνεῦμα [τοῦ] θεοῦ καταβαῖνον ὡσεὶ περιστερὰν [καὶ] ἐρχόμενον ἐπ' αὐτόν·

(17) καὶ ἰδοὺ φωνὴ ἐκ τῶν οὐρανῶν λέγουσα, Οὗτός ἐστιν ὁ υἱός μου ὁ ἀγαπητός, ἐν ᾧ εὐδόκησα.

While in Mark John is not aware about who the one is who is coming to get baptized, in Matthew he is informed. From Matt 1:1 onwards Jesus' identity is made clear through portents and prophetic revelations, the genealogy (1:1–17), and the stories about his birth (1:18–2:23). The story about John the Baptist (3:1–12) serves to announce "the stronger who is coming after me" (3:11). Given this new context, Jesus' baptism is not as in Mark a secret known only to Jesus, but it becomes the occasion of the public proclamation of Jesus as the messianic Son of God (3:17). Apart from this christological significance, Matthew also sees Jesus' baptism as the institution of baptism as the entrance ritual into the Christian church.

If Matthew maintains this interpretation, he must explain why Jesus needs to be baptized at all. Indeed, given Matthew's Christian perspective the act of baptism seems to be redundant, and to avoid that conclusion he provides the following explanations:

3.1.1. Jesus himself gives the answer (3:15): "Let it be so now, for it is proper for us in this way to fulfill all righteousness." Thus, Matthew underscores that Jesus' baptism was at his own initiative.

3.1.2. There are a ritual and a theological reason. Writing as a Christian, Matthew acknowledges that both Jesus and John were Jews under the obligation of fulfilling Jewish law. Under those terms, accepting John's baptism was ritually appropriate (πρέπον), that is, it complied with the criterion of θεοπρέπεια, which is part of Jewish δικαιοσύνη. Thus, on this issue Matthew explains Mark by a comparative-religion argument.

3.1.3. As a Christian writer Matthew knows baptism as the entrance ritual into the church. Thus, the mission program revealed by Christ in his post-Easter appearance (Matt 28:16–20) stipulates: "Go out and make disciples among all the nations, baptizing them in the name of the Father and the Son and the Holy Spirit."[47] Therefore, the new reason for Jesus' baptism is that he thereby institutes the entrance ritual for the Christian church. Since Christian baptism includes the gift of the holy spirit, the appearance of the spirit of God receives added emphasis (3:16; cf. 3:11).

3.2. Luke 3:21–22

Although Luke's Gospel is the longest, his section on Jesus' baptism is the briefest. He does not rely on sources other than Mark. Not knowing Matthew's explanations, Luke avoids the problems rather than explaining them.[48] Also in his scheme of things, Jesus' baptism is redundant, so that he simply cuts Mark short at this point.

(21) Now it happened that, when all the people were baptized, and when Jesus also had been baptized and was praying, the heavens opened,

(22) and the holy spirit descended on him in bodily form like a dove, and a voice came from heaven, "You are my beloved Son, with you I am well pleased."

(21) Ἐγένετο δὲ ἐν τῷ βαπτισθῆναι ἅπαντα τὸν λαὸν καὶ Ἰησοῦ βαπτισθέντος καὶ προσευχομένου ἀνεῳχθῆναι τὸν οὐρανὸν

(22) καὶ καταβῆναι τὸ πνεῦμα τὸ ἅγιον σωματικῷ εἴδει ὡς περιστερὰν ἐπ᾽ αὐτόν, καὶ φωνὴν ἐξ οὐρανοῦ γενέσθαι, Σὺ εἶ ὁ υἱός μου ὁ ἀγαπητός, ἐν σοὶ εὐδόκησα.

Luke does not expressly say that John baptized Jesus, but that he lets him join the crowds and get baptized along with them. He also clarifies that Jesus sees the open heaven while he is praying afterwards and not during the baptism. Moreover, it is in line with Luke's theology that it is the "holy spirit" (τὸ πνεῦμα τὸ ἅγιον) that is descending on him. Mark's somewhat vague expression ὡς περιστεράν becomes a physical object that settles on him. The heavenly voice is identical with that of Mark. The episode says nothing new because readers know that Jesus has the holy spirit since his origin (Luke 1:35) and that he is the Son of God since 1:32 and 2:49. Thus, Luke's interest is focused on the gift of the spirit, which is then tested in the story of the temptation (4:1, 18). The main reason why Luke keeps Jesus' baptism is that it becomes the Christian ritual with its core being the dispensation of the spirit to all Christian believers.[49] How precisely John the Baptist's baptism becomes the Christian ritual Luke explains by the separate event of the outpouring of the holy Spirit at Pentecost (Acts 2:1–13; cf. 19:1–7).

---

47 28:19: πορευθέντες οὖν μαθητεύσατε πάντα τὰ ἔθνη, βαπτίζοντες αὐτοὺς εἰς τὸ ὄνομα τοῦ πατρὸς καὶ τοῦ υἱοῦ καὶ τοῦ ἁγίου πνεύματος.
48 See H. Klein, *Das Lukasevangelium*, 169–171.
49 See Acts 1:5; 2:38–41; 8:12–16, 36–38; 9:18; 10:47–48; 16:15, 33; 18:8; 19:3–7; 22:16.

3.3. John 1:19–34

The relationship of the Gospel of John to the synoptic tradition poses one of the most difficult problems of New Testament scholarship. These problems are particularly acute with regard to the traditions concerning John the Baptist.[50] On the whole, the situation of the Gospel of John is different from the Gospels of Matthew and Luke in the following respects:

3.3.1. The Gospel of John suppresses Jesus' baptism by John the Baptist altogether. When Jesus comes to John (John 1:29), it is not to get baptized (cf. also the dialogue in Matt 3:14–16). Why Jesus comes to John remains ambiguous. The name ὁ βαπτιστής is never mentioned, although his activity (βαπτίζειν) is attested (1:25, 30; 3:22, 23, 26; 4:1–2). The author of this gospel seems to be familiar with the synoptic tradition in some form, perhaps even with the Markan version. However, instead of holding on to this tradition he transforms it radically in light of his new interpretation.

3.3.2. The principles of the new interpretation are introduced in the Prologue, which identifies John as the one who brings the μαρτυρία (1:6–9). His witness is that of the forerunner (1:15), and he is not himself the χριστός (1:19–28). He announces and identifies Jesus as the messianic "lamb of God that takes away the sin of the world" (1:29–31). Since John merely testifies, the tradition is reworked accordingly (1:32–34).

(32) And John testified saying, "I saw the Spirit descending like a dove from heaven, and it remained on him.

(33) I myself did not know him, but the one who sent me to baptize with water said to me: 'He on whom you see the Spirit descend and remain is the one who baptizes with the Holy Spirit'.

(34) And I myself have seen and have testified that this is the Son of God.

(32) Καὶ ἐμαρτύρησεν Ἰωάννης λέγων ὅτι Τεθέαμαι τὸ πνεῦμα καταβαῖνον ὡς περιστερὰν ἐξ οὐρανοῦ καὶ ἔμεινεν ἐπ' αὐτόν.

(33) κἀγὼ οὐκ ᾔδειν αὐτόν, ἀλλ' ὁ πέμψας με βαπτίζειν ἐν ὕδατι ἐκεῖνός μοι εἶπεν, Ἐφ' ὃν ἂν ἴδῃς τὸ πνεῦμα καταβαῖνον καὶ μένον ἐπ' αὐτόν, οὗτός ἐστιν ὁ βαπτίζων ἐν πνεύματι ἁγίῳ.

(34) κἀγὼ ἑώρακα καὶ μεμαρτύρηκα ὅτι οὗτός ἐστιν ὁ υἱὸς τοῦ θεοῦ.

Since the author of the Fourth Gospel was probably familiar with the Markan tradition in some form, he omits altogether the first scene, when John the Baptist baptizes Jesus (Mark 1:9). He then transforms the second scene (1:10–11) into the Baptist's "witness" (μαρτυρία). Because, according to Mark, Jesus was

---

50 For a survey of the present state of research, see J. FREY, "Das Vierte Evangelium auf dem Hintergrund der älteren Evangelientradition," 60–118, especially 93–100; ROTHSCHILD, *Baptist Traditions and Q*, 46–52.

personally unknown to John (John 1:31, 33), the Fourth Gospel has the Logos reveal in advance who Jesus was (1:6–18). In this way the synoptic source is being reduced to the Baptist's "witness". Also the Fourth Gospel distinguishes between John's and Jesus' baptism, so that Jesus baptizes with the Spirit, not with water as John does. In this way, a later usage of the water ritual by Jesus is ruled as inconsistent (4:1–2; 1:26, 31, 33). While the author of the Fourth Gospel seeks to eliminate discrepancies in the sources, he shows awareness of a competing tradition promoted by disciples of John apparently arguing in favor of Jesus as continuing the water baptism of John the Baptist. Although the Fourth Gospel is not interested in historiographical details, precisely some of such details show up in what is probably source material adapted from John the Baptist's movement.[51] This material claims that before John the Baptist's death (cf. 3:24), both John and Jesus baptized (3:22–23). In 3:25–4:3 it is assumed that there was competition between the two movements and that Jesus made more converts and baptized them (4:1). Some manuscripts at 4:1–2 try to correct this view by arguing that it was not Jesus but his disciples who baptized with water. Seemingly to avoid a conflict was to make Jesus leave Judea for Galilee (4:3), thus dividing the field: Judea goes to the movement of John the Baptist, Galilee to the Jesus movement (cf. 3:22). Apparently, this conflict continues in the Jewish-Christian gospels of the second century. That the Jewish-Christian movements bequeathed water baptism to the church is also reflected in Paul's letters, when he hesitates to baptize Gentiles (1 Cor 1:13–17) and makes the ritual fully conform to his theology only in Gal 3:26–28 and Rom 6–8. Also Acts reports that in Paul's (and Luke's) view John the Baptist's baptism, practiced by the Alexandrian Apollos, was not fully "Christian" (Acts 18:24–28; 19:2–7).

4. Conclusion

How then is the tradition concerning Jesus' baptism by John the Baptist to be assessed? The earliest information presented in Mark 1:9–11 is indeed startling. Joachim Jeremias was certainly right when he concluded: "So ärgerniserregende Nachrichten hat man nicht erfunden."[52] Indeed, since all of the later revisions in one way or another attempt to explain it away, this information must be historically authentic. However, this conclusion does not fully answer the question. Why did Mark choose precisely the brief sentence in 1:9 as signifying "the beginning of the gospel of Jesus Christ [Son of God]"? Bultmann's intuition seems to point in the right direction: "Es bleibt für das Verständnis der Legende ein Rest, nämlich die Frage, wie die Überlieferung dazu kam, Jesu Taufe als die Stunde

---

51   See ROTHSCHILD, *Baptist Traditions and Q*, 46–63.

52   J. JEREMIAS, *Neutestamentliche Theologie*, 52. ET: *New Testament Theology*, 1971, 45: "Such a scandalizing piece of information cannot have been invented."

der Messiasweihe zu wählen?"[53] He also identified the expression of τὸ πνεῦμα as pointing to the Hellenistic church as the origin, rather than Palestinian Jewish Christianity.[54] This is affirmed by the fact that Matthew and Luke modified the term to [τὸ] πνεῦμα [τοῦ] θεοῦ (Matt 3:16), or τὸ πνεῦμα τὸ ἅγιον (Luke 3:22), while the Fourth Gospel kept τὸ πνεῦμα, without attribute, for the Spirit descending on Jesus, and ἐν πνεύματι ἁγίῳ for Jesus' own baptism (John 1:32–33).

Assuming that the other Gospels did their best in their struggle to come to terms with Mark, they used no other sources from which to retrieve additional information. Rather, we see them "correcting" Mark, that is, bringing Mark's Gospel in line with their own different perspectives. Therefore, the crucial question remains: For what reason did Mark decide to let John the Baptist's baptism of Jesus be the key note at "the beginning of the gospel of Jesus Christ"? Scholars have long ago proposed that the reason must be Mark's christology. In other words, Bultmann was right suggesting that Mark was a Hellenistic Christian belonging to the Pauline sphere.[55] Recently, the old hypothesis of Mark the Paulinist[56] was persuasively argued by Margaret Mitchell.[57]

In the hymn in Phil 2:6–11 the divine Christ is incarnated in Jesus: ἐν ὁμοιώματι ἀνθρώπων γενόμενος· καὶ σχήματι εὑρεθεὶς ὡς ἄνθρωπος ἐταπείνωσεν ἑαυτὸν γενόμενος ὑπήκοος μέχρι θανάτου, θανάτου δὲ σταυροῦ. (v.7–8). If Jesus' messianic inauguration by the Spirit is not mentioned either in the Philippian hymn, or in the pre-Pauline christological formulae in Rom 1:3–4, Mark's account brought it into conformity with Paul's christology of the "Christ according to the flesh",[58] as well as the "Son of God according to the Spirit".[59] According to Mark[60] awareness of his messianic status is reserved for

---

53 Bultmann, *Geschichte*, 267; ET: *History*, 250: "But there still remains something for the understanding of the legend, viz. the question how the tradition came to light on the baptism as the time for the consecration of the Messiah."

54 Bultmann, *Geschichte*, 268: "Ein entscheidendes Indizium dafür, dass Mk 1,9–11 nicht aus der palästinensischen Gemeinde stammen kann, ist der absolute Gebrauch von τὸ πνεῦμα." ET: *History*, 251: "The use of τὸ πνεῦμα absolutely is a decisive pointer to the conclusion that Mk. 1:9–11 could not have come from the Palestinian Church."

55 Bultmann, *Geschichte*, 270; idem, *Theologie*, 28–29, 477–478, 494–95.

56 For the older literature see G. Volkmar, *Evangelien*; repudiated by Werner, *Einfluss*; A. Lindemann, *Paulus im ältesten Christentum*, 151–154.

57 M. M. Mitchell, "Epiphanic Evolutions in Earliest Christianity," *ICS* 29 (2004) 183–201; Eadem, "The emergence of the written record," 177–194, especially 185–190.

58 Paul speaks of the Χριστὸς κατὰ σάρκα in Gal 4:4–5; 1 Cor 15:3–4; 2 Cor 5:16; Rom 1:3–4; 8:3–4; 9:4–5; Phil 2:7–8; cf. also 1 Tim 3:16; cf. Ἰησοῦς 1 Thess 1:10; 4:14; Gal 6:17; 1 Cor 12:3; 2 Cor 4:3, 10–11, 14; 11:4; Rom 8:11.

59 In Pauline christology, the risen Christ is identical with the divine Spirit (2 Cor 3:17). See for other main passages Gal 4:6; 1 Cor 15:45; Rom 8:3–17; cf. Phil 2:7–11; Rom 1:3–4.

60 The terms of ἐν ὁμοιώματι ἀνθρώπων and ὡς ἄνθρωπος in Phil 2:7 provide the opening for the "messianic secret" (see above, n. 30).

Jesus, while it is withheld from the Jewish people, including his family and disciples.

As mentioned already, Mark's provocative sentences are not limited to 1:9. They are found also at the end of his Gospel, when it ends with the acclamation of the first person to recognize the divinity of Jesus. He is a Roman centurion and certainly meant to be a pagan, but enigmatic when he says "Truly, this man was a son of God."[61] The concluding statement about the women is just as enigmatic. When in the grip of tremor and bewilderment, they fled and said nothing to anyone: "For they were afraid." (ἐφοβοῦντο γάρ).[62] This conclusion is to be seen in juxtaposition with the sentence in 1:9.

In conclusion, when the author of Mark undertook the audacious task of writing the first biography of Jesus of Nazareth, he appears to have designed it on the basis of what Paul calls the λόγος τοῦ σταυροῦ (1 Cor 1:18). Hard to comprehend for the early church, Jesus "secret messiahship" had to include his entire life as a Jew. Indeed, Mark concludes, the "scandal of the cross" (σκάνδαλον τοῦ σταυροῦ, Gal 5:11; 1 Cor 1:23)[63] unfolded in Jesus' life on earth, beginning with his baptism by John the Baptist.[64]

Bibliography

ALLES, GREGORY; FRIEDERICH AVEMARIE, ET AL., "Taufe," *RGG*[4], vol. 8 (2005) 50–92; ET: "Baptism," *RPP* vol. 1 (2007) 572–598.

BAUER, WALTER, *Das Leben Jesu im Zeitalter der neutestamentlichen Apokryphen*, Tübingen: Mohr Siebeck 1909; reprinted Darmstadt: Wissenschaftliche Buchgesellschaft 1967.

BECKER, EVE-MARIE, *Das Markusevangelium im Rahmen antiker Historiographie* (WUNT 194), Tübingen: Mohr Siebeck 2006.

BETZ, HANS DIETER, "Transferring a Ritual: Paul's Interpretation of Baptism in Romans 6," in: TROELS ENGBERG-PEDERSEN (ed.), *Paul in His Hellenistic Context*, Minneapolis: Fortress Press 1995, 84–118; reprinted in BETZ, *Paulinische Studien*, 240–271.

---

61 Mark 15:39: Ἀληθῶς οὗτος ὁ ἄνθρωπος υἱὸς θεοῦ ἦν. The statement can be translated in several ways. The pagan centurion correctly emphasizes the tragic end of an heroic human being, a worthy son of deity. Believers, however, can easily read it as a Christian confession, made unawares. See on these issues YARBRO COLLINS, *Mark*, 764–771.

62 For intentionally strange endings of literary works see F. KERMODE, *The Genesis of Secrecy*, 66–73.

63 See also Gal 3:1; 5:24; 6:14; 1 Cor 1:13, 23; 2:2, 8; 2 Cor 13:4.

64 Cf. also Mark 4:17; 6:3.

— "The Sermon on the Mount in Matthew's Interpretation," in: BIRGER A. PEARSON ET AL. (eds.), *The Future of Early Christianity. Essays in Honor of Helmut Koester*, Minneapolis: Fortress Press 1991, 258–275; reprinted in BETZ, *Synoptische Studien*, 270–289.

— *The Sermon on the Mount. A Commentary on the Sermon on the Mount, Including the Sermon on the Plain (Matthew 5:3–7:27; Luke 6: 20–49)* (Hermeneia), Minneapolis: Fortress Press 1995.

— "Wellhausen's Dictum 'Jesus was not a Christian, but a Jew' in Light of Present Scholarship," in: StTh 45 (1991) 83–110; reprinted in BETZ, *Antike und Christentum*, 1–31.

— "Plutarch's Life of Numa: Some Observations on Graeco-Roman 'Messianism,'" in: MARKUS BOCKMUEHL and JAMES CARLTON PAGET (eds.), *Redemption and Resistance: The Messianic Hopes of Jews and Christians in Antiquity*, London & New York: Clark 2007, 44–61; reprinted in BETZ, *Paulinische Theologie*, 166–190.

— *Synoptische Studien. Gesammelte Aufsätze II*, Tübingen: Mohr Siebeck 1992.

— *Paulinische Studien. Gesammelte Aufsätze III*, Tübingen: Mohr Siebeck 1994.

— *Antike und Christentum. Gesammelte Aufsätze IV*, Tübingen: Mohr Siebeck 1998.

— *Paulinische Theologie und Religionsgeschichte. Gesammelte Aufsätze V*, Tübingen: Mohr Siebeck 2009.

BRAUN, HERBERT, "Entscheidende Motive in den Berichten über die Taufe Jesu von Markus bis Justin," in: ZThK 50 (1953) 39–53; reprinted in IDEM, *Gesammelte Studien zum Neuen Testament und seiner Umwelt*, Tübingen: Mohr Siebeck ²1967, 168–172.

BROWN, RAYMOND E., *The Gospel acording to John*, 2 vols. (AB 29), Garden City, NY: Doubleday 1970.

BULTMANN, RUDOLF, *Das Evangelium des Johannes* (KEK 2), Göttingen: Vandenhoeck & Ruprecht ¹³1953; ET: *The Gospel of John: A Commentary*, trans. G. R. Beasley-Murray, Oxford: Blackwell 1971.

— *Die Geschichte der synoptischen Tradition* (FRLANT 12), Göttingen: Vandenhoeck & Ruprecht ³1957; ET: *The History of the Synoptic Tradition*, trans. by John Marsh, Oxford: Blackwell ²1968.

— *Theologie des Neuen Testaments*, Tübingen: Mohr Siebeck ⁹1984.

CANCIK, HUBERT, "Die Gattung Evangelium. Das Evangelium des Markus im Rahmen antiker Historiographie," in: IDEM, *Religionsgeschichten*, 100–130.

— *Religionsgeschichten: Römer, Juden und Christen im römischen Reich. Gesammelte Aufsätze II*, Tübingen: Mohr Siebeck 2008.

EBERTZ, MICHAEL N., "Charisma, II: Neues Testament und älteres Christentum," in: *RGG*[4] 2 (1999) 113–115; *RPP* 2 (2007) 493–495.

FERGUSON, EVERETT, *Baptism in the Early Church: History, Theology, and Liturgy in the First Five Centuries*, Grand Rapids, MI: Eerdmans 2009.

FREY, JÖRG, "Das Vierte Evangelium auf dem Hintergrund der älteren Evangelientradition," in: THOMAS SÖDING (ed.), *Johannesevangelium – Mitte oder Rand des Kanons? Neue Standortbestimmungen* (QD 203), Freiburg: Herder 2003.

JEREMIAS, JOACHIM, *Neutestamentliche Theologie, I: Die Verkündigung Jesu*, Gütersloh: Mohn, 1971; ET: *New Testament Theology*, vol. 1: *The Proclamation of Jesus*, London: SCM Press 1971.

KELHOFFER, JAMES A., *Miracle and Mission: The Authentication of Missionaries and Their Message in the Longer Ending of Mark* (WUNT 2.112), Tübingen: Mohr Siebeck 2000.

— *The Diet of John the Baptist: 'Locusts and Wild Honey' in Synoptic and Patristic Tradition* (WUNT 176), Tübingen: Mohr Siebeck 2005.

KERMODE, FRANK, *The Genesis of Secrecy. On the Interpretation of Narrative*, Cambridge MA: Harvard University Press 1979.

KLAUCK, HANS-JOSEF, *Apokryphe Evangelien. Eine Einführung*, Stuttgart: Katholisches Bibelwerk [3]2008.

KLEIN, HANS, *Das Lukasevangelium* (KEK I/3), Göttingen: Vandenhoeck & Ruprecht 2006.

KOESTER, HELMUT, "Evangelium I.II.," in: *RGG*[4] 2 (1999) 1735–1741; ET: *RPP* V (2009) 528–532

LINDEMANN, ANDREAS, *Paulus im ältesten Christentum. Das Bild des Apostels und die Rezeption der paulinischen Theologie in der frühchristlichen Literatur bis Marcion* (BHTh 58), Tübingen: Mohr Siebeck 1979.

LINDERSKI, JERZY, "The Augural Law," in: *ANRW* II, 16, 3 (1986) 2146–2312.

LÖFSTEDT, EINAR, "On the Style of Tacitus," in: *JRS* 38 (1948) 1–8.

MITCHELL, MARGARET M., "Epiphanic Evolutions in Earliest Christianity," in: *ICS* 29 (2004) 183–201.

— "The Emergence of the Written Word," in: MARGARET M. MITCHELL and FRANCES M. YOUNG (eds.), *The Cambridge History of Christianity*, vol. 1: *Origins to Constantine*, Cambridge: Cambridge University Press 2006, 177–194.

NORDEN, EDUARD, *Die Geburt des Kindes. Geschichte einer religiösen Idee*, Stuttgart: Teubner 1924.

PERRIN, BERNADOTTE, *Plutarch's Lives*, LCL, London: Heinemann; Cambridge MA: Harvard University Press, 1914ff.

ROTHSCHILD, CLARE K., *Baptist Traditions and Q* (WUNT 194), Tübingen: Mohr Siebeck 2005.

SCHÖNE, ALBRECHT, *Goethe, Faust II*, 2 vols., Frankfurt a. M.: Deutscher Klassiker Verlag 1994.

THEISSEN, GERD, "Die pragmatische Bedeutung der Geheimnismotive im Markusevangelium. Ein wissenssoziologischer Versuch," in: HANS KIPPENBERG & GUY G. STROUMSA (eds.), *Secrecy and Concealment. Studies in the History of Mediterranean and Near Eastern Religions* (SHR 65), Leiden: Brill 1995, 225–245.

VIELHAUER, PHILIPP, "Erwägungen zur Christologie des Markusevangeliums," in: IDEM, *Aufsätze zum Neuen Testament*, Munich: Kaiser Verlag 1965, 199–214.

VOLKMAR, GUSTAV, *Die Evangelien oder Marcus und die Synopsis der kanonischen und ausserkanonischen Evangelien nach dem ältesten Text mit exegetischhistorischem Commentar*, Leipzig: Fues, Reisland 1870.

WELLHAUSEN, JULIUS, *Das Evangelium Marci*, Berlin: Reimer ²1909.

WERNER, MARTIN, *Der Einfluss paulinischer Theologie im Markusevangelium. Eine Studie zur neutestamentlichen Theologie* (BZNW 1), Giessen: Töpelmann 1923.

WOODMAN, A. J., *The Annals of Tacitus*, vol. 3, Cambridge: Cambridge University Press 1972.

YARBRO COLLINS, ADELA, *Mark: A Commentary* (Hermeneia), Minneapolis, MN: Fortress Press 2007.

Usages — Some Notes on the Baptismal Name-Formulae[1]

Lars Hartman

In 1903 Wilhelm Heitmüller published an impressive study of 347 pages, "*Im Namen Jesu*".[2] The amount of pages of that volume is an indication that a discussion of the topic mentioned in the above headline can cover wide fields. The following considerations have, however, a limited scope and are precisely "notes." They will mainly focus on the linguistic surface of the texts referred to, and will accordingly deal less with the contents and the exegesis of the passages in question.

1. The Formulae

In the New Testament the baptismal name-formula appears in the following forms:

- "into the name of the Lord Jesus" (εἰς τὸ ὄνομα τοῦ κυρίου Ἰησοῦ): Acts 8:16; 19:5
- "in the name of Jesus Christ" (ἐν τῷ ὀνόματι Ἰησοῦ Χριστοῦ): Acts 10:48
- "because of the name of Jesus Christ" (ἐπὶ τῷ ὀνόματι Ἰησοῦ Χριστοῦ): Acts 2:38[3]
- "into the name of the Father and the Son and the Holy Spirit" (εἰς τὸ ὄνομα τοῦ πατρὸς καὶ τοῦ υἱοῦ καὶ τοῦ ἁγίου πνεύματος): Matt 28:19

The first formula is echoed in 1 Cor 1:13, "into the name of Paul" (εἰς τὸ ὄνομα Παύλου) and in 1 Cor 1:15, "into my name" (εἰς τὸ ἐμὸν ὄνομα). The sentence in 1 Cor 6:11 reminds of the second formula: "(you were washed …, you were justified) in the name of Jesus Christ the Lord" (ἐν τῷ ὀνόματι τοῦ κυρίου Ἰησοῦ Χριστοῦ). Also Rom 6:3 should be taken into account, ("we were baptized into

---

1 To a large extent the deliberations of 2.1. below make use of material and discussions advanced in a few earlier works of mine, especially L. Hartman, "'Into the Name of Jesus.' A Suggestion concerning the Earliest Meaning of the Phrase" and *'Into the Name of the Lord Jesus. Baptism in the Early Church*, especially 37–50.

2 W. Heitmüller, "*Im Namen Jesu*." *Eine religionsgeschichtliche Untersuchung zum Neuen Testament*.

3 The codices Vaticanus and Bezae and some minuscules read ἐν, a reading often encountered in the patristic texts.

Christ Jesus" [εἰς Χριστὸν Ἰησοῦν]), as well as Gal 3:27, ("you were baptized) into Christ [εἰς Χριστόν]"), and 1 Cor 10:2, ("baptized into Moses").

In *Didache* 9:5 baptism takes place "into the name of the Lord" (εἰς τὸ ὄνομα τοῦ κυρίου), and so also in Hermas, *Vis.* 3.7.3. In *Did.* 7:1 the same formula is used as in Matt 28:19.

The "into the name" construction in Matt 18:20 is similar to the one in the baptismal contexts in that the sentence concerns worship: two or three persons gather "into the name" of Jesus. The phrase also occurs in Matt 10:41–42, where, however, the usage is different: it is about being received "into the name" of a prophet and "into the name" of a righteous person, respectively, that is, "as being" or "because he/she is" a prophet etc. Otherwise the phrase does not appear in the New Testament in this more or less prepositional usage. Unlike the other two "name"-phrases the one with "into" neither appears in the Greek OT, nor in other Greek Jewish texts. (There are some constructions in which the verb + "into the name" etc. functions in another way and which therefore need not be taken into account here; see for example "utter blasphemies against — 'into' — his name," 2 Macc 8:4, and "believe into the name of ...," e.g., John 1:12.)

In contrast, the phrase "in the name of ..." is common in the New Testament and is used with verbs of different meanings, e.g., Matt 23:39 (come in the name of the Lord; quoting Ps 118:26); Mark 9:38 (receive a child in my name); John 10:25 (works done in the name of my Father); 1 Cor 5:4 (judge in the name of Jesus the Lord); Phil 2:10 (kneeling in the name of Jesus).

Also the phrase "because of the name of ..." is rather common in the New Testament, although not so frequent as the "in"-construction: for example, Matt 18:5 (receive a child because of my name); Matt 24:5 (many appear because of my name); Mark 9:39 (perform a mighty deed because of my name); Mark 13:6 (many come because of my name, saying ...); Acts 4:17 (speak because of this name).

The constructions "in the name of ... " and "because of the name of ..." represent a relatively established early Christian usage, and no doubt they have been taken over, directly or indirectly, from the Greek Old Testament. There are a few examples of them in Jewish pseudepigrapha, but in comparison with the Greek texts we still have at our disposal from Early Judaism these two formulae are much more common in the New Testament.[4]

On the other hand, as already mentioned, the "into the name" construction does not appear in the Greek Old Testament, and is a bit peculiar also as regarded within a wider framework of Greek literature — it mainly appears in documents using banking terminology and there refers to the "name" of the person who disposes an account in a bank.[5] We will return to this problem below.

---

[4] "In the name": *Joseph and. Aseneth* 9:1; 15:7; *Testament of Solomon* 67 and 115; *Prayer of Joseph.* fragm. 190. "Because of the name": *1 Enoch* 10:2; *Testament of Asher* 2:4.

[5] The classic study is HEITMÜLLER, *"Im Namen Jesu"*.

2. Different Communication Situations

2.1. The Enigmatic Beginning

Very early in the history of the church the Christians have apparently practiced a rite of initiation that meant that neophytes entered the church via accepting ("believing") the message about Christ and undergoing a rite of immersion.[6] The similarities between the baptism of John and this Christian baptism suggest that the first Christians have taken over John's baptism and, so to speak, have christianized it; this ought to have taken place during a short, formative period under the influence of experiences and convictions that are reflected in the resurrection traditions. When Paul was baptized some five years after the end of Jesus' earthly career,[7] this was a sign that at least by then baptism was an established Christian rite of initiation.

What has happened in this early phase of the history of the Christian church is hidden behind the oldest traditions. However, to these traditions belong the name-formulae connected to baptism, and it is a common scholarly opinion that at least the "into the name of ..." phrase is very old.[8] The "in the name of ..." construction appears in 1 Cor 6:11, where the whole sentence can represent tradition taken over by Paul.[9]

There are various scholarly suggestions as to the linguistic and cultural background of the formula/the formulae, and they have led to different assumptions concerning which were the meaning and the interpretation of baptism and of the person of Jesus in this hidden phase of early Christianity.[10] Thus Wilhelm Heitmüller built his argument on what baptism meant on the fact, already mentioned, that the "into the name" phrase was common in banking documents; there it was used referring to the procedure that a sum of money was transferred to somebody whose "name" was the name over a bank account.[11]

---

6   See HARTMAN, *Into the Name of the Lord Jesus*, 29–35; G. BARTH, *Die Taufe in frühchristlicher Zeit*, 9–39. Further references can be found in both of these books. In my book just mentioned I had the opportunity to refer very often to the first edition of Barth's study, and to do so in agreeing with him.

7   For a Pauline chronology see H. KOESTER, *Introduction to the New Testament II*, 99–106.

8   See already HEITMÜLLER, "*Im Namen Jesu*", 120, etc.

9   E.g., F. HAHN, "Taufe und Rechtfertigung. Ein Beitrag zur paulinischen Theologie in ihrer Vor- und Nachgeschichte", 105f.; U. SCHNELLE, *Gerechtigkeit und Christusgegenwart. Vorpaulinishe und paulinische Tauftheologie*, 39–42.

10 JENS SCHRÖTER's contribution to this volume, "Die Taufe in der Apostelgeschichte", has an excursus, "Zur Bedeutung der präpositionalen Taufformulierungen", which contains a sober discussion of the debate. Schröter discusses more in detail the history of religions aspects of Heitmüller's ideas than I do on these pages.

11 Passages of such contents are also adduced to explain 1 Cor 1:13 in P. ARZT-GRABNER ET. AL., *Papyrologische Kommentare zum Neuen Testament: 1. Korinther*, 70–72.

He concluded that to Greek speaking Christians baptism meant that the person baptized became the property of the Lord Jesus like a sum of money paid to a person's bank account. In addition Heitmüller assumed that this manner of speaking about baptism was embedded in a belief in the magical power of names, not least those of divine figures.

Heitmüller's understanding has been widely accepted,[12] but it has also been criticized, not least on linguistic grounds. Thus it has been doubted how far it is justified to insulate the adverbial expression "into the name" from verbs denoting payments, debts, etc. and then combine it with a verb belonging to a totally different semantic field but still let the prepositional phrase retain the associations with banking practice.[13] In addition, one has noted, in order to function as imagery the usage should presuppose that in the linguistic milieu — the communication situation — there existed a convention according to which a deity was compared to a rich person who was the owner of his/her adherents like money on his/her banking account. Certainly one could claim that Israel was God's "heritage," his flock, etc., but the step is long from that imagery to that of the banking-language.[14]

So another suggestion has been launched as to how to explain the "into the name" phrase as used concerning baptism. The scholars in question assume that the phrase is a literal translation of a Hebrew expression *l^{e}shem* (or its Aramaic equivalent *l^{e}shum*). Thus the communication situation is supposed to be an early Hebrew/Aramaic speaking community, whose terminology has been literally translated into Greek. Normally the expression means "with regard to ...," "having in mind ..." and the like.

The following Mishnah passage has played an important role for the scholars who have defended this interpretation:[15]

> An offering must be slaughtered into the name of (with regard to) six things: into the name of the offering (which offering category?), into the name of the offerer (who presents the offering?), into the name of the Name (the offering is to Almighty God, nobody else), into the name of the altar-fire (be conscious of its being a burnt offering), into the name of the fragrance, into the name of the pleasure (both: bear in mind that the offering shall please God) (*m. Zebahim* 4:6).

---

12   E.g. R. BULTMANN, *Theologie des Neuen Testaments*, 42; J. A. FITZMYER, *Romans*, 430.

13   The criticism is well developed in the new edition of Barth's study, referred to above.

14   HEITMÜLLER refers to the seal-image to support his interpretation (*"Im Namen"*, 150f., 171, 175, etc.), but it seems to the present writer that the connections between sealing and transferring to a bank account are not obvious enough. Cf. the article "Seal and Baptism" by KARL OLAV SANDNES in this publication.

15   H. L. STRACK/P. BILLERBECK, *Kommentar zum Neuen Testament aus Talmud und Midrasch I*, 591, 1005; H. BIETENHARD, "ὄνομα", 275. The idea had earlier been launched by A. J. H. W. BRANDT, "Onoma en de Doopsformule in het Nieuwe Testament," and G. DALMAN, *Die Worte Jesu I*.

In the interpretation of the scholars who take this passage as a point of departure for their understanding of baptism in the early church, the "into the name" formula meant that the sacrifice in question was presented to God. They then assumed that the formula indicated something similar when used about baptism: the person baptized was given to Jesus and became his property. Consequently, the result is very much the same as Heitmüller's.

There seems, however, to have existed a usage of the "into the name" phrase about ritual matters that suggests that God, "into" whose "name" the rite was performed, plays another role than to receive something — or somebody — to be his property. It may be instructive briefly to consider the saying of R. Jose (around 150 C.E.) that follows immediately after the lines quoted above: "Even if somebody in his heart were not mindful of one 'name' of all these, the offering is valid." This demonstrates that the "name" nuance of the noun "name" is very weak and that the *l*ᵉ*shem* also here has a vaguer meaning of "with respect to," "having in mind," etc.[16] Thus to be mindful of God (in *Zebahim* 4 "the Name") when performing the rite, did not so much focus on God as being the receiver of the sacrifice as rather the fundamental referent of the rite, the one who stands for a meaningful presupposition of the cultic act.

This is further illustrated by the following examples of the phrase as used about rituals. *M. Niddah* 5:6 deals with the validity of religious vows: young people may be too rash in giving vows, although they say, "We know into whose name (*lᵉshem mi*) we have vowed."

In the Tosephta tractate on idolatry it is stated apropos of circumcision as practiced by the Samaritans that it is performed "into the name of Mount Gerizim" (*t. Abodah Zarah* 3:13). Here the Gerizim stands for the religious system that forms the basic ideological frame of the rite. Furthermore, when *m. Hullin* 2:8 discusses how to apply the biblical rules for slaughter (for food), the possible case is introduced that if somebody slaughters "into the name of mountains or into the name of hills or into the name of seas or into the name of wildernesses, his slaughter is invalid," i.e., the slaughter is assumed to take place under the presupposition of idolatry (cf. Deut 12:2).

Such a key to a rite is radically different from what is ruled, for example, in *m. Aboth* 4:11: "R. Johanan the Sandal Maker (around 140 C.E.) said: 'Every assembly that is into the name of heaven (i.e., God) will be established in the end, the one that is not into the name of heaven will not be established in the end'." A statement in S. Num § 13.6 makes a similar distinction: "There are two ways

---

16 I would suggest that this is also what the phrase means in the first line of the following magic amulet from late antiquity and said to have been found south of Bethlehem: "With regard to (to the name of, *lᵉshem*) Marten daughter of Qoriel. [Period added by L.H.] I adjure against Marten daughter of Qoriel. In the name of *(bᵉshem)* Agirat, my lady, ... I destroy ..." (J. NAVEH/SH. SHAKED, *Amulets and Magic Bowls*, 78f.).

of drawing near (that is, to one's god in worship), one into the name of heaven, one not into the name of heaven."

In order to strengthen the relevance of this rabbinic material for an assessment of the original meaning of the "into the name" phrase as a characterization of early Christian baptism one may have wanted to find it represented in other early Jewish texts, indeed earlier than the passages so far cited. Particularly it would have been an advantage if the Qumran material could provide us with something similar. This is, however, not so,[17] and the only relatively certain example locating the usage in the first century C.E. is Matt 18:20 (gathering into Jesus' name); however, it is a Jewish-Christian one and thus of some importance.

A couple of further details should be mentioned in this context: It is often maintained that the three prepositional expressions as such mean the same thing;[18] if there are any differences in their respective contents, these should be sought in the genitives added to the "name" and in the nuances effected by the context. So, as so often is the case with established phrases in ritual contexts, the phrase should be capable of several applications.[19] Another aspect of this flexibility is that the expression can be varied: this was so in the rabbinic material too: people may, e.g., vow "into the name of" God (see above), but it can also be stated that an idolator vows "*in* the name of" his god (*m. Sanhedrin* 7:6).[20] Such variations may be analogous to the variety of prepositions in our formulae as well as with the cases where Paul seems to replace an "into the name" with a mere "into" (Rom 6:3; Gal 3:27).

We now turn to the formula "in the name of Jesus (etc.)" as used in connection with baptism. As intimated above this use may be traditional and as such belong to the same early period as the "into the name" formula. If this is so, it means using a phrase with biblical roots. In the Old Testament it is used with several meanings. Thus one may, for example, walk in the name of the Lord (Micah 4:5), but in our context it is of interest to note that the formula is also used as characterizing ritual actions.[21] Thus one may praise God rejoicing in his name (Ps 89:13, 17), one prays in God's name and invokes (in) it (1 Kgs 18:24) as well as Baal's prophets do "in the name of" their god (1 Kgs 18:24).

---

17 I would not be prepared to regard 1Q20 XXI.2 as an example: "praise (the verb is *halal* piel) (into) God's name."

18 E.g. C. F. D. MOULE, *An Idiom Book of New Testament Greek*, 50.

19 Rightly emphasized by BARTH, *Die Taufe in frühchristlicher Zeit*, 52f. See also HARTMAN, "'Into the Name of Jesus'", 436f.

20 Similarly the *l^eshem* of *m. Abodah Zarah* 3:6 is taken up in the Gemara as a simple *l^e* (*b. Abodah Zarah* 48a). In this context it may also be worthwhile to note that the translators of the Peshitta do not bother to try to imitate the into" (*eis*) in e.g. Matt 28:19 and 1 Cor 1:13 but have "in (*b^e*) the name" instead. Similarly the Vulgate says *in nomine*.

21 BIETENHARD, "ὄνομα", 259f.,

Furthermore, one may swear by ("in") God's name (Deut 6:13), bless and curse in it (Deut 10:8, 2 Kgs 2:24, respectively). Likewise Elijah builds an altar in the name of the Lord (1 Kgs 18:3). We also come across the formula in the deuterocanonical writings: see Sir 47:18; 50:20.

Thus the "in the name"-formula is part of a religious language also in early Judaism, and so appears also in the Qumran texts: "All" boast in God's name (4Q 292, fragm. 3), the priests bless in God's name (11Q14, 1.1 and 3) as do also the angels (*Songs of the Sabbath Sacrifice*, 4Q403, 1.9 and 12). Another, also biblical usage is represented by *Temple Scroll* 61.3: the prophets spoke in God's name (cf., e.g., Deut 18:20; Jer 11:21; 14:14; 23:25).

Above we have encountered other instances of the formula in the rabbinic material, where it could be used more or less as a synonym of "into the name," as well as a couple of passages from the pseudepigrapha (*Joseph and Aseneth, Testament of Solomon,* and *Prayer of Joseph*).[22]

The meaning of the phrase is also in this case rather vague, but when used in the characterization of a rite the one behind the "name" is of basic importance for the rite and its meaning.

2.2. Outside the New Testament

The purpose of the following few paragraphs is to give the present-day exegete an idea of what the linguistic soil was like in which our formulae appeared. In other words, we will look for possible different communication presuppositions in terms of linguistic usage after the enigmatic beginning.

When Heitmüller elaborated the linguistic basis for his contention, he claimed that such a transferred usage was "hellenistische Umgangssprache."[23] Very briefly I now present some examples that show different possibilities of using the three prepositional phrases. Unlike the aim of Heitmüller but also going farther than I have done in earlier studies of the topic,[24] this means taking into regard that the formulae can get different nuances of meaning not only because of their vagueness but also because of differences between reading contexts: it is, for example, not self-evident that the original meaning discussed above, Paul's individual understanding, and, e.g., the reading of some Gentile-Christian Corinthians were identical. An essential part of the presuppositions of such differences should be the various linguistic associations of those who used the formulae or encountered them in a communication.

---

22 Cf. also *1 Enoch* 50.2: the righteous ones will be victorious in God's name.
23 Heitmüller, *"Im Namen Jesu"*, 102.
24 Particularly in the works mentioned in footnote 1.

2.2.1. "Into the Name …"

It was mentioned above that this construction is not found in the Septuagint. So we now ask for a possible communication situation in which the question may arise how to understand the "into the name" formula in relation to existing Greek usage. A search in the collections of papyri and ostraca[25] reveals that there is a great number of examples in those texts of the banking usage mentioned above. This usage includes instances where the phrase does not refer to a concrete banking account or an official register of real estate, but also passages where the phrase has a more general meaning of "to be the property of …" or the like. In general, however, also in these cases the contents concern economical matters.

A few examples may be enough. A typical topic is dealt with in P.Meyer 8.13 (151 C.E.): a man orders that "it all" be registered "into the name" of his wife. BGU 15.2495 (3rd cent. C.E.) is a testament in favor of ("into the name") of two persons. P.Mert. I 8,8–9 (3–4 C.E.) is also typical: the named person is officially registered as the one who shall cultivate a piece of public land. A similar topic is dealt with in P.Lond. 3.908 (139 C.E.) about a fortune transferred to be the property of the person mentioned.[26]

BGU 15.2495 (3rd cent. C.E.) concerns a contract made "into the name" of somebody and P.Lond. 2.180 (228 C.E.) refers to a certain amount of wheat that has been measured out "into the name" of a priest. We come across a slightly different usage in P.Mert. 1.23 (2nd cent. C.E.), where it is prescribed that a person shall deliver "this letter," and if he wants to do certain negotiations "into the name" of the sender, he may do so, although, if he would prefer so, he may as well do it "into your (own) name." The meaning of the phrase seems to come close to "on my (your) behalf," "being commissioned by me."

It should, however, be noted that the phrase "into the name" is not exclusively bound to economical language.[27] Some texts represent a not uncommon terminology when they tell that people name children, places, etc. "into the name" of a person. Thus according to Pausanias somebody gave a city its name "into the name" of his daughter (*Fragment* 407, line 107), and Diodorus Siculus mentions that somebody was called Hermes "into the name" of the planet (*Bibliotheca historica* 6.5.2). So also the founders of Thebae are said to have

---

25 I have used the CD *Greek Documentary Texts*, compiled by The Packard Humanities Institute. For other Greek literature I have used the CD *Thesaurus Linguae Graecae*, ed. University of California at Irvine.

26 These two texts are also quoted in ARZT-GRABNER ET. AL., *Papyrologische Kommnentare*, 71. A rich material is found in the ὄνομα-article in F. PREISIGKE, *Wörterbuch der griechischen Papyrusurkunden*.

27 The following Plutarch passage is a weak witness to the non-monopoly of the economical associations: Damon seemed to "slink away into the name of music" to conceal his power as a sophist (*Pericles* 4). It should rather be classed in the same category as the above-mentioned John 1:18 ("believe into the name …") etc.

named the city "into the name of their father" (Cephalion, *Fragment* 6). In examples like these the meaning of the expression might contain a nuance of "with respect to" or even "to the honor of."

Already Heitmüller mentioned an exception to the circumstance that the "into the name" phrase was not represented in the Greek literary language of New Testament times, namely Herodianus, *History* 2.2.10 and 2.13.2, where the phrase is used in connection with the verb "to swear."[28] There are a few more examples that suggest that to a Greek ear of the times the "into the name" phrase was not automatically associated with transferring goods of economical value. Thus according to Aelianus a person writes to another that either he is serious (σπουδάζεις) "about (into) my name" or he is making sport (*Epistulae* 8.1), and an inscription from the Aegean Islands (IG 12.7, 409) deals with persons who have "served" their native city in many offices personally (on their own costs) and "into the name of" their children. The meaning of the passage may not be too lucid — they may have rendered the service "on the children's behalf" — but anyway the inscription can serve as another sign that the adverbial phrase "into the name" was not necessarily bound to economical language or to imagery inspired by such terminology.

One further detail should not be forgotten, namely that at this stage of the development of the Greek language the usage of the preposition εἰς as referring to direction was weakened and could come close to ἐν.[29] This circumstance may be related to the fact that in the Peshitta translation of the formula the preposition used is b^e-, and similarly Jerome uses *in*+ablative in the Vulgate.

Thus, if we assume a communication situation in which people are not acquainted with a Christian usage colored by the Hebrew-Aramaic idiom as also represented by Matt 18:20, the persons in question might feel a bit bewildered. They might vaguely come to think of banking terminology, but other associations could be possible. They might even suspect that in this context the use of the Greek "into the name" phrase represented "a particular Christian usage."[30] Insofar as the communication situation also contained a use of a baptismal "in the name …" formula it may have colored the understanding of the "into the name" phrase (cf. 1 Cor 1:13–15 and 6:11).

2.2.2. "In the Name …" and "Because of the Name …"

As already mentioned, the phrase "in the name …" is common in the Septuagint, both with and without the definite article. Thus the examples from the Old Testament mentioned above under 2.2.1. are topical also when we focus on Greek

---

[28] HEITMÜLLER, *"Im Namen Jesu"*, 101. Heitmüller notes that others have referred to Herodianus before him.
[29] See F. BLASS/A. DEBRUNNER/F. REHKOPF, *Grammatik des neutestamentlichen Griechisch*, § 206.
[30] U. SCHNELLE, "Taufe", 665.

texts, although the Septuagint uses both ἐν and ἐπί + dative to translate *bᵉshem*. This means that to Greek speaking Christians there existed a collection of texts that formed a sounding-board under the communication when they used and/ or encountered turns of phrase concerning baptism as being a rite performed "in the name of" Jesus Christ (etc.).

One may ask whether this sounding-board has been the only one, and, as a matter of fact, it seems that there are no good analogies in the profane literature to this religious/ritual usage.[31] There are, however, some papyri that represent the same category as the texts we encountered above which dealt with economical matters like registration of property, delivery of crops, etc. Thus one example is P.Col. 8.209 (3rd cent. C.E.) according to which some fields are cultivated by a man "in his name," and another is P.Oslo 107 (2nd cent. C.E.), which states that a certain cottage that is registered as a woman's heritage must not be (unlawfully) disposed "in her name." Similarly P.Oxy. 45.3242 (185–187 C.E.) concerns some fields that have been registered "in the name of my forefathers."

Thus, if in this case somebody's ear was not used to catch the biblically inspired idiom but stayed with "profane" associations, he/she might have found the usage a bit peculiar.[32]

Lastly, as to the third phrase, ἐπὶ τῷ ὀνόματι, we noted above that it only appears in Acts 2:38, and that there are no echoes of it in traditional material. Rather it may be assessed as representing Luke's tendency to take to biblical turns of phrase, that is, to give his Greek a flavor of the Greek style of the LXX.[33] Here also Luke's choice of preposition may have been influenced by the ἐπί component of the verb in the Joel quotation in v. 21.[34]

The deliberations so far concerning different possible "sounding-boards" under the production and reception of the baptismal name-phrases may bring to mind some suggestions concerning the linguistic usage of Greek speaking Jews in antiquity, namely that it represents a so-called diglossia, that is, persons using a certain language are able to use different linguistic codes or registers

---

31 J. H. MOULTON/G. MILLIGAN, *The Vocabulary of the Greek Testament Illustrated from the Papyri and Other Non-Literary Sources*, 451; W. BAUER, *Griechisch-deutsches Wörterbuch zu den Schriften des Neuen Testaments und der frühchristlichen Literatur*, 1160. —The wording of a magical papyrus may be inspired by Jewish usage: "Come, O Lord ..., save me and this boy unharmed, in the name (ἐν ὀνόματι) of the most high god, samas phreth" *Papyri graecae magicae I*, ed. K. PREISENDANZ, 5.45. See also the exorcism "in the name of" a certain spirit, quoted in footnote 16 above.

32 A "normal" Christian usage appears in a great number of somewhat later papyri: contracts and similar documents begin by "in the name of God ..." and similar phrases. The custom is continued in documents written by Muslims.

33 HARTMAN, *Into the Name of the Lord Jesus*, 38.

34 H. CONZELMANN, *Die Apostelgeschichte*, 36; J. A. FITZMYER, *The Acts of the Apostles*, 264: a "Lucan composition."

that exist beside each other. The term was introduced by C. A. Ferguson,[35] and J. M. Watt has analyzed the phenomenon in Luke and Acts, thereby noting how Luke switches between two registers of *koine*, one semitizing and one more standard Greek.[36] G. Walser has applied these insights in a broader study of the Greek of the ancient synagogue[37] and concludes that "the speech community of the ancient synagogue was polyglossic, i.e., there existed several varieties of Greek side by side" (note his broadening of the diglossia concept!).[38] It seems to the present writer that the usage of the baptismal name-formulae can be taken as an example of such polyglossia among the early Christians — they used formulae and phrases about baptism that were different from the phraseology of everyday language. One may compare this usage with their way of taking over the biblical concept of "flesh": in normal Greek it meant meat etc., and a Greek-speaking person who converted to Judaism or Christianity had to learn that in the context of their new religion the word sometimes had a quite different meaning.

2.3. Some Christian Greek Texts after the New Testament

We now turn to a type of communication situation in which Christian writers in the patristic era represent what becomes an established usage in terms of the baptismal formulae.

2.3.1. "Into the Name …"

The textual material for a discussion of the usage of the baptismal formulae after the New Testament is rich *and* poor. It is rich in so far as there are many passages that quote or allude to a baptismal formula, but it is poor in other respects. On the one hand practically only one formula appears, namely the one characterizing baptism as one "into the name of" the Trinity, on the other, the formula is taken for granted to such an extent that the writers do not seem to think that they need to explain what it means.

As to the predominance of the "into the name of" the Trinity, in the *Didache* it still appears together with a shorter formula. The longer formula appears in 7:1 and 7:3, that is, in the instruction concerning how baptism shall be performed. On the other hand, in 9:5 we hear the echo of a shorter formula when it is stated who are allowed to share the Eucharist, namely those who are "baptized into the name of the Lord." We may assume that the longer formula is

---

35 C. A. FERGUSON, "Diglossia".
36 J. M. WATT, *Code-Switching in Luke and Acts*.
37 G. WALSER, *The Greek of the Ancient Synagogue. An Investigation on the Greek of the Septuagint, Pseudepigrapha and the New Testament*.
38 WALSER, *The Greek of the Ancient Synagogue*, 183.

used at the baptismal rite, whereas the other can function as a short characterization of Christian baptism.

One might regard Hermas *Vis.* 3.7.3 in a similar manner: the interpreter of the vision characterizes a certain group of possible converts: they have heard the word and "want to be baptized into the name of the Lord."

The longer form is used at the rite of baptism according to the First Apology of Justin Martyr. He reports that those who are "born anew" "receive the washing with water in the name (ἐπ' ὀνόματος) of God the Father and the Lord of the All and of our Savior Jesus Christ and of the Holy Spirit" (*Apology* I. 61.3). We may note that Justin, turning to outsiders, uses a less awkward preposition than "into."

This tendency in terms of the use of our prepositional phrases becomes the norm in the texts of the ecclesiastical writers of the following centuries. The fact that according to Matt 28:19 the risen Jesus has ordered that baptism should be performed "into the name of" the Three Persons has apparently had the effect that this is how one expresses oneself. As mentioned above, the formula seems to be so established that the fathers normally do not care to explain what they think it means. One exception is when John Chrysostom more or less in passing says that in principle it is not the baptizer who baptizes but the Father, the Son and the Holy Spirit "whose name is called upon by the one who is baptized when he/she answers "I believe" (*Catechesis ultima* 170). Quite often, however, the formula is used as an argument in defending or exposing the Trinitarian dogmas (e.g., Epiphanius, *Ancoratus* 7.1; 81.2: Eusebius, *Contra Marcellum* 1.1.9).

With regard to the deliberations above on the meaning of the "into the name" formula in the earliest church we may state that at least a relatively quick reading of the passages where it appears in the patristic texts there seems to be no clear examples of an understanding of the formula that implies an imagery that compares the one baptized with a sum of money or with a piece of land that is transferred to a new owner.

So this baptismal formula is also the most common context in which the "into the name" construction appears. Some figures can illustrate the distribution: the ecclesiastical writers included in the CD-Rom Thesaurus Linguae Graecae quote or refer to the baptismal formula of Matt 28 about 140 times, to the name-phrases of Matt 10 ("into the name of a prophet") and Matt 18 ("gather into my name") some 20 times, and a little more seldom to "into the name" phrases in connection with baptism in First Corinthians and Acts.[39] Remains a small number of passages, say around a dozen, in which "into the name of ..." occurs; it is there combined with verbs like "swear," "talk nonsense," "prophecy," "seal" (thus Epiphanius, *Panarion* 1.192), "exorcise" (thus

---

39 The around 40 passages containing the phrase "believe into the name ..." of course represent another category of adverbial phrases.

Fragmentum alchemicum 299.3r). Ignatius of Antioch praises the churches that have received him "into the name of Jesus Christ," not as a mere passer – by (*Rom.* 9:3; cf. Matt 18:5, receive a child "in — ἐπί — my name"). There are also some cases where an author uses "into the name" when telling that one names a house or a temple after a person — cf. the "profane" examples of, e.g., Pausanias, quoted above.[40] There are also some examples in which a writer repeats "into the name" using instead a simple "into" (e.g., John the Damascene, *Expositio fidei* 82; Basilius, *Prologus* 8, 31.688).

The dominating use of the "into the name" phrase in the trinitarian baptismal formula does not render much support to an assumption that the fathers understood the formula in the light of the banking terminology, of which we saw a few examples under 2.2.1. above.[41] The relatively few instances of a use with other verbs do it even less.[42]

2.3.2. "In the Name …" and "Because of the Name …"

As to these two formulae we can be brief. The fact that they are well established phrases in the Septuagint and often appear in New Testament texts determines their usage in the texts of the fathers. The two phrases seem to be more or less synonymous and a further reason to deal with them together is the text-critical situation in Acts 2:38: beside the best reading with ἐπί there is namely a variant

---

40 The texts of Epiphanius may represent a particular case. HEITMÜLLER (*"Im Namen Jesu"*, 108f.) intimates that when quoting Epiphanius he does so taking him as a representative of the patristic literature — which then is said to support his particular views on the "into the name" phrase and its background. Searchings on the *Thesaurus Linguae Graecae* CD show that this is hardly a fair assessment of Epiphanius' style, which actually is a bit peculiar (see J. QUASTEN, *Patrology III*, 385f.). His style includes a richer use of "into the name" phrases than with other writers. These phrases seem, however, rather inspired by a kind of biblical style than by banking language. Thus, e.g., when Epiphanius writes that a temple was built "into" God's name (*Panarion* 1.373), the expression is found in 2 Sam 7:13, where the Hebrew text says "to my name" (*lishmi*), whereas the LXX uses plain dative; similarly when he reports that certain saints, particularly the Virgin Mary, were revered and that offerings were brought "into" their "name," the style reminds of, e.g., Mal 1:11 (*Ancoratus* 13.8; *Panarion* 1.159 etc,). Epiphanius also uses "into the name" when reporting on books as being ascribed to or written by certain persons; thus John's gospel is "into the name of John" (*Panarion* 2.275) and similar turns of phrase are used about books ascribed to Moses (*Panarion* 1.209), Eve (*Panarion* 1.278), Seth (*Panarion* 1.284), or Philip (*Panarion* 1.292).

41 See the beginning of the preceding footnote.

42 This should also hold true of a few passages that mention a $ "into the name" of the Divinity: Epiphanius, *Ancoratus* 8.8; *Panarion* 1.231 (but according to *Ancoratus* 22.6 "we receive the seal" "*in* the name" of the three Persons); John Chrysostom, *Catechesis ad illuminandos* 2.22: one receives the seal whereby the minister says "So and so is anointed into the name of the Father, the Son and the Holy Spirit." Cf. HEITMÜLLER, who claims that the sealing rite supports his idea that the into the name phrase is rooted in banking language (*"Im Namen Jesu"*, 150f., 171, 175, etc.).

reading with ἐν, and it has a relatively good manuscript support.[43] Both readings are represented in the writings of the fathers.

The two phrases are very common in the patristic material, although it is particularly true in the case of "in the name." There is no need to go into detail, but "in the name" of somebody one speaks or prophecies, performs miracles, comes, or blesses; two more examples chosen at random from a vast material: in Jesus' name one drinks poison without being harmed (Papias, fragment 11.2) and is delivered from this evil age (Epiphanius, *Panarion* 2.36). On the other hand it was noted above that the two phrases appear rather seldom in "profane" texts.

Concerning the three prepositional expressions it was pointed out under 2.3.1. that in the texts of the fathers a dominating position was held by "into the name," more precisely in the form encountered in Matt 28:19. Consequently, in spite of the frequent use of the two phrases with ἐν and ἐπί, especially the former, there are few passages in which baptism is characterized by one of these two expressions. In most of the cases it seems that the phrase appears in the text because the writer refers to or comments on a New Testament passage which makes use of the ἐν or ἐπί phrase.[44] In some of these cases the author raises the question whether the shorter formula means anything else than the "normal" one, viz., the Matt 28 form. Thus, e.g., Basilius claims that the reference to the Lord in the shorter form is no problem, "for at the rebirth the Son does the same work as the Father and the Spirit" (*Adv. Eunomium* 29.720).

There are, however, some instances where an author refers to baptism as performed "in the name" without any connection to a specific New Testament passage. Thus Epiphanius mentions baptism "in" the name of the Trinity (*Panarion*, 3.299) and Cyrillus can write about baptism in general as one "in" Christ's name (*Catechesis* 17.21). Furthermore, Didymus Caecus, *De trinitate* 39.733 (probably spurious) deals with some non-orthodox Christians who baptize "in" the name of the three Persons; the text reminds of Matt 28:19 (which, as we remember uses "into"), and this is a sign that the three prepositional expressions were regarded as more or less synonymous.[45]

---

[43] The variant reading is supported by Codices Vaticanus and Bezae and by a few minuscules.

[44] Thus with "in the name": Epiphanius, *Panarion* 1.202; John Chrysostom, *Hom. in Acta* 60.63; *Hom. in 2 Cor* 61.458; 61.608; Cyrillus, *Catechesis* 3.4; 17.30; Theodoretus, *Explanatio in Canticum Canticorum* 81.204. "Because of the name": John Chrysostom, *Hom. in Acta* 60.65; Procopius, *Comm. in Is* 2244.

[45] There are other indications to this effect: thus Basilius quotes Matt 28:19 and then repeats its contents in writing "in the name of the Trinity" (*Adv. Eunomium* 29.720).

3. Conclusion

In the introduction to these "notes" it was stressed that they were precisely "notes" and that they would not deal much with the contents of the passages where the formulae appeared. The reader can by now state that this has been true, both as to the biblical texts and those from post-New Testament Christian authors. If, on the other hand, the above deliberations could to some extent be termed lexicographical, they still are "notes" and leave lots of material and aspects without consideration.

A couple of terms have, however, played a certain role in the above discussion, namely (linguistic) usage and communication situation. These concepts cover linguistic aspects that are interrelated in a way that can be a challenge to the student of the texts concerned. Thus we have been able to note how the different name-formulae appear in several usages, partly very different from each other. We have also noted how our phrases are used in different communication situations; this is true for the Christian texts, but also for the comparative material. So the interpreter of a given text has to come to grips with the interrelationship of usage and communication situation. In other words, the context of a given document calls for attention, both the literal context (the co-text) and the social one. To get an idea of the more precise meaning of a given passage, in our case one containing a baptismal name-formula, we have to analyze carefully the literal unit with its linguistic, rhetorical etc. properties, but also, and not least, try to get an idea of cultural, theological, ecclesiastical and pastoral preconditions of the text. So it may be appropriate at the end of a discussion like this one to remind us of the need to combine investigation of vocabulary and grammar with the texts themselves with their manifold aspects as textual communication.

Bibliography

Texts

Greek texts are quoted according to the CD *Thesaurus Linguae Graecae*, compiled 1999, ed. University of California, Irvine, and *Greek Documentary Texts*, compiled 1991–1996 by The Packard Humanities Institute.

Literature

Arzt-Grabner, Peter/Kritzer, Ruth Elisabeth/Papathomas, Amphilochios/Winter, Franz (eds.), *1. Korinther* (Papyrologische Kommentare zum Neuen Testament 2), Göttingen: Vandenhoeck & Ruprecht 2006.

Barth, Gerhard, *Die Taufe in frühchristlicher Zeit*, Revised ed., Neukirchen-Vluyn: Neukirchener ²2002.

BAUER, WALTER, *Griechisch-deutsches Wörterbuch zu den Schriften des Neuen Testaments und der frühchristlichen Literatur*, ed. by K. Aland, Berlin – New York: de Gruyter ⁶1988.

BIETENHARD, HANS, "ὄνομα", in: *ThWNT* 5 (1954) 242–283.

BLASS, FRIEDRICH/DEBRUNNER, ALBERT/REHKOPF, FRIEDRICH, *Grammatik des neutestamentlichen Griechisch* (revised by F. Rehkopf), Göttingen: Vandenhoeck & Ruprecht ¹⁴1975.

BRANDT, A. J. H. W., "Onoma en de Doopsformule in het Nieuwe Testament," in: *ThT* 25 (1891) 565–610.

BULTMANN, RUDOLF, *Theologie des Neuen Testaments*, Tübingen: Mohr Siebeck ⁴1968.

CONZELMANN, HANS, *Die Apostelgeschichte* (HNT 7), Göttingen: Mohr Siebeck ²1972.

DALMAN, GUSTAF, *Die Worte Jesu I. Einleitung und wichtige Begriffe*, Leipzig: Hinrichs 1898.

FERGUSON, CHARLES A., "Diglossia", in: *Word* 16 (1959) 325–340.

FITZMYER, JOSEPH A., *Romans* (AncB 33), New York etc.: Doubleday 1993.

— *The Acts of the Apostles* (AncB 41), New York etc: Doubleday 1998.

HAHN, FERDINAND, "Taufe und Rechtfertigung. Ein Beitrag zur paulinischen Theologie in ihrer Vor- und Nachgeschichte", in: J. Friedrich/W. Pöhlmann/P. Stuhlmacher (eds.), *Rechtfertigung* (FS E. Käsemann), Tübingen: Mohr Siebeck and Göttingen: Vandenhoeck & Ruprecht 1976, 95–124.

HARTMAN, LARS, "'Into the Name of Jesus.' A Suggestion concerning the Earliest Meaning of the Phrase", in: *NTS* 20 (1973/74) 432–444.

— *Into the Name of the Lord Jesus. Baptism in the Early Church*, Edinburgh: T&T Clark 1997.

HEITMÜLLER, WILHELM, *"Im Namen Jesu." Eine religionsgeschichtliche Untersuchung zum Neuen Testament* (FRLANT 1.2), Göttingen: Vandenhoeck & Ruprecht 1903.

KOESTER, HELMUT, *Introduction to the New Testament II*, Philadelphia, Pa. – Berlin – New York: Fortress 1982.

MOULE, CHARLES F. D., *An Idiom Book of New Testament Greek*, Cambridge: Cambridge University Press ²1959.

MOULTON, JAMES HOPE/MILLIGAN, GEORGE, *The Vocabulary of the Greek Testament Illustrated from the Papyri and Other Non-Literary Sources*, Grand Rapids, Mich.: Eerdmans 1985 (first edition 1930).

NAVEH, JOSEPH/SHAKED, SHAUL, *Amulets and Magic Bowls. Aramaic Incantations of Late Antiquity*, Leiden: Magnes Press, Hebrew University 1985.

PREISENDANZ, KARL (ed.), *Papyri Graecae Magicae. Die Griechischen Zauberpapyri I*, Stuttgart: Teubner ²1973.

PREISIGKE, FRIEDRICH, *Wörterbuch der griechischen Papyrusurkunden mit Einschluss der griechischen Inschiften, Aufschriften, Ostraka, Mumienschilder u.s.w. aus Ägypten*, ed. W. Kiessling, vol. 1–4 and suppl., Berlin – Marburg: Selbstverlag 1925–1971.

QUASTEN, JOHANNES, *Patrology III: The Golden Age of Greek Patristic Literature*, Utrecht: Spectrum/Westminster Md.: Newman 1960.

SCHNELLE, UDO, *Gerechtigkeit und Christusgegenwart. Vorpaulinishe und paulinische Tauftheologie* (GTA 24), Göttingen: Vandenhoeck & Ruprecht 1983.

— "Taufe II. Neues Testament", in: *TRE* 32 (2001) 663–674.

STRACK, HERMANN L./BILLERBECK PAUL, *Kommentar zum Neuen Testament aus Talmud und Midrasch I: Das Evangelium nach Matthäus*, Munich: Becksche 1922.

WALSER, GEORG, *The Greek of the Ancient Synagogue. An Investigation on the Greek of the Septuagint, Pseudepigrapha and the New Testament* (Studia Graeca et Latina Lundensia 8), Stockholm: Almqvist & Wiksell 2001.

WATT, JONATHAN M., *Code-Switching in Luke and Acts* (Berkeley Insights in Linguistics and Semiotics 31), New York etc.: Lang 1997.

Vorgeformte Tauftraditionen und deren Benutzung in den Paulusbriefen[1]

David Hellholm

Drei Aspekte müssen berücksichtigt werden, wenn wir ernsthaft versuchen wollen, eine Antwort auf die Frage nach vorgeformten Tauftraditionen in den Paulusbriefen zu finden[2].

(1) Die Einschätzung der Bedeutung der *inter-textuellen* Ko-Texte, besonders in den paulinischen Homologoumena, aber auch in einigen der Antilegomena[3];

(2) Die Bewertung des jeweilgen *Situationskontextes* als Teil der dahinterliegenden Argumentation in den Briefen[4];

---

1   Stark erweiterte und überarbeitete deutsche Fassung eines Vortrags gehalten an den Evangelisch-Theologischen Fakultäten in Sibiu-Hermannstadt am 18. Mai 2001, in Kiel am 28. Juni 2002 und in Münster am 17. Juni 2003. Erstfassung in englischer Sprache unter dem Titel „The Impact of the Situational Contexts for Paul's Use of Baptismal Traditions in His Letters" erschienen in: *Neotestamentica et Philonica. Studies in Honor of Peder Borgen*, 147–175. Ergänzt durch eine erweiterte Fassung meiner Abschiedsvorlesung an der Theologischen Fakultät der Universität Oslo am 19. November 2008 und publiziert unter dem Titel „Paulus och den urkristna doptraditionen" in: *NTT*, 132–151.

2   Mit dem neutralen Begriff „vorgeformt" ersetze ich im Anschluss an J. Weiss, *Urchristentum*, 310, die gewohnten Begriffe „vorliterarisch" oder „vorpaulinisch", um erstens anzugeben, dass es sich nicht ausschließlich um literarische und zweitens nicht lediglich um „vorpaulinische" Traditionen handelt. Hierzu auch A. Lindemann, *Paulus*, 116: „vorformuliert"; W. Schenk, *Philipperbriefe*, 336: „vorgeprägte".

3   Zur Intertextualität siehe z.B. U. Broich/M. Pfister (Hg.), *Intertextualität*; H. F. Plett (Hg.), *Intertextuality*; S. Holthuis, *Intertextualität*; S. Alkier, „Intertextualität", 1–26. Siehe auch die theoretische Darstellung bei A. Merz, *Selbstauslegung*, 1–71; ferner M. M. Mitchell, „Corinthian Correspondence", 17–53.

4   Vgl. *mutatis mutandis* einerseits F. von Kutschera, *Erkenntnistheorie*, 144 Anm. 78: „Wie wir eine Sache erleben, hängt auch davon ab, welche Informationen wir über sie schon haben. Die Aspekte, unter denen man das Bild von Goya [sc. Die Erschießung des 3. Mai] betrachtet, und das, was man dabei erfaßt, ergeben sich auch aus dem, was man über dieses Bild weiß (z.B. über seine Entstehungszeit, Komposition und kunstgeschichtliche Bedeutung), über Goya und sein Werk, über die Erhebung der Spanier gegen die Franzosen und die grausame Unterdrückung des Aufstands in Madrid durch Murat, die zu den Erschießungen am 2. und 3. Mai 1808 führte"; andererseits W. Raible, „Textwissenschaft", 102: „Sprachsysteme müssen dominant auf die Interessen der Hörer ausgerichtet sein. … Insofern ist es von vornherein äußerst erfolgversprechend, bei der Analyse von sprachlichen Äußerungen und Sprachsystemen die Perspektive des Hörers zu wählen". Hierzu jetzt auch K. M. Hartvigsen, *„Prepare the Way"*, bes. 6–113. Siehe ferner unten § 2.

(3) Die Beurteilung des Gewichts der Bedeutung des *intra-textuellen* Ko-textes bei der jeweiligen Analyse des paulinischen Argumentationsganges[5].

Zuerst möchte ich mich in einer diachronen Analyse den inter-textuellen Ko-texten widmen; danach werde ich als Teil eines pragmatischen Vorgehens dem Situationskontext nachgehen; schließlich soll, unter Berücksichtigung der intra-textuellen Ko-texte, eine synchrone Analyse durchgeführt werden.

1. Vorgeformte Tauftraditionen bei Paulus – Die inter-textuellen Ko-texte

Es ist sicherlich korrekt, wenn Hans Dieter Betz meint, dass „Paulus Lehre von der Taufe in Römer 6 charakteristisch anders ist als in anderen seiner Briefe"[6]. Er bezieht sich hierbei besonders auf I Kor 1,13–17 und Gal 3,26–28 sowie auf die Feststellung, dass die Taufe im 1. Thessalonicherbrief nicht erwähnt wird – jedenfalls nicht direkt in diesem ältesten der Paulusbriefe[7]. Nun wird die Taufe aber auch im Philipperbrief nicht erwähnt, was besonders auffallend ist, wenn das Schreiben in Rom als letzter Brief des Paulus (nach dem Römerbrief) abgefasst worden wäre[8].

---

5   Vgl. hierzu die ähnlichen Annäherungen bezüglich des Jakobusbriefes bei W. POPKES, *Jakobus*, 6: „Anzusetzen ist vielmehr bei internen Gesichtspunkten der Kommunikation zwischen Jak und seinen Adressaten"; IDEM, „Christologie", 64–83. Siehe ferner Anm. 156.

6   H. D. BETZ, „Ritual", 85 [241].

7   Siehe bereits BETZ, *Galatians*, 186f., 189; IDEM, *Galaterbrief*, 320–327. Wenn die Aussage „wie Christus – so die Seinen", sich zuerst im I Thess 4,14ff. findet (siehe U. SCHNELLE, *Gerechtigkeit*, 79), so ist hier direkt von der Taufe nicht die Rede; allerhöchstens lediglich indirekt. Die Denkstruktur ist allerdings schon vorhanden und geht womöglich auf vorgeformte Tradition zurück.

8   So der *Markionitische Prolog*: „*Philippenses sunt Machedones. ... hos apostolus conlaudat scribens eis a Roma de carcere per Epaphroditum*" („Die Philipper sind Makedonier. ... Der Apostel lobt sie durch Epaphroditus, wenn er aus dem Gefängnis in Rom schreibt") als auch Euthalius, *Argumenta*: Ταύτην ἐπιστέλλει ἀπὸ ῾Ρώμης („Er sendet diesen [sc. Brief] aus Rom"; PG 85: 764) und Theodoret (PG 82: 560A) sowie Theophylakt (PG 124: 1140A). Für Rom als Abfassungsort und -zeit plädieren: J. B. LIGHTFOOT, *Philippians*, 1–46: 58; WEISS, *Urchristentum*, 294–298; IDEM, *History* I, 385–389: Ende der Gefangenschaft; A. JÜLICHER/E. FASCHER, *Einleitung*, 120–122: 62–63; G. LÜDEMANN, *Heidenapostel*, 142f. mit Anm. 80: ca. 59–64; W. A. MEEKS, *Urban Christians*, 63: ca. 59–64; J. T. FITZGERALD, „Philippians", 322–323: 58–62; SCHNELLE, *Einleitung*, 153–156: ca. 60; IDEM, *Paulus*, 408–411: ca. 60; G. D. FEE, *Philippians*, 34–37: 60–62; G. W. PETERMAN, *Philippi*, 19–20: 60–62. Für Ephesus treten ein: H. KOESTER, *Introduction II*, 135–138: 54–55; SCHENK, *Philipperbriefe*, 338: 53–54; U. B. MÜLLER, *Philipperbrief*, 16–23: 55; R. MARTIN/G. F. HAWTHORNE, *Philippians*, xxxix–l: 52–54; H.-M. SCHENKE/K. M. FISCHER, *Einleitung I*, 127–129: 54–55; W. G. KÜMMEL, *Einleitung*, 284–291: 53–55; PH. VIELHAUER, *Geschichte*, 166–170: 54–55?; C. R. HOLLADAY, *Introduction: Expanded CD Version*, 523: ca. 55; R. E. BROWN, *Introduction*, 493–496: 54–56; H. OMERZU, *Prozess*, 324–331: „Frühdatierung"; J. REUMANN, *Philippians*, 13–18: 53–55; P. POKORNÝ/U. HECKEL, *Einleitung*, 287f.: ca. 55.

Betz ist der Meinung, dass wir eine Entwicklung der Tauflehre bei Paulus feststellen können[9]. Er bezieht sich dabei besonders auf die Äußerung in I Kor 1,13ff., wo Paulus schreibt:

> (13) Ist Christus zerteilt? Ist etwa Paulus für euch gekreuzigt worden? Oder seid ihr auf den Namen des Paulus getauft worden? (14) Ich danke Gott, dass ich keinen von euch getauft habe, ausgenommen Krispos und Gaios, (15) damit ja nicht jemand sage, dass ihr auf meinen Namen getauft worden wäret. (16) Ich habe allerdings auch das Haus des Stephanas getauft; im übrigen weiß ich nicht, ob ich irgendeinen anderen getauft habe. (17) Christus hat mich nämlich nicht gesandt zu taufen, sondern (das Evangelium) zu verkündigen ... .

Es scheint tatsächlich ein langer Weg von dieser scheinbar negativen Äußerung im 1. Korintherbrief zu der positiven, ja fast mysterienhaften Darstellung in Römer 6 zu sein.

Die *inter-textuelle* Analyse braucht – wie allzu oft angenommen wird – nicht nur Ähnlichkeiten festzustellen, sondern kann indessen auch Differenzen herausstellen. Die Validität dieser Art von Analyse bleibt in beiden Fällen jedoch dieselbe!

Eine Reihe verschiedener Taufformeln im Neuen Testament hat Lars Hartman besprochen[10]. Einige davon spielen für meine Zwecke in diesem Zusammenhang eine bedeutende Rolle; alle fünf Taufformeln aus dem 1. Korintherbrief, dem Galaterbrief sowie dem Römerbrief werde ich in meiner *intertextuellen* Ko-textanalyse behandeln[11].

1.1. Der Taufspruch bei der Taufe – Die „Namensformel"

Die Formel „Auf den Namen des Herrn Jesus" oder ähnliche Taufformeln finden sich öfters in Act (8,16; 19,5: εἰς τὸ ὄνομα τοῦ κυρίου Ἰησοῦ; 10,48: ἐν τῷ ὀνόματι Ἰησοῦ Χριστοῦ; 2,38: ἐπὶ τῷ ὀνόματι Ἰησοῦ Χριστοῦ)[12].

---

9 Dagegen vgl. *mutatis mutandis* E. LOHSE, „Christus, des Gesetzes Ende?", 25f.: „Für die rechte Einordnung der verschiedenen Ausführungen in den Ablauf des apostolischen Wirkens ist es wichtig, sich über die geschichtliche Abfolge klar zu werden. [...] Sieht der Apostel die für sein Leben und Wirken schlechthin entscheidende Wende in seiner Bekehrung und Berufung begründet, dann gehen Überlegungen fehl, die meinen, Paulus habe seine Theologie der Rechtfertigung erst allmählich entwickelt". Siehe ferner unten Anm. 166.

10 L. HARTMAN, „*Auf den Namen*"; IDEM, '*Into the Name*'. Siehe auch G. STRECKER, *Theologie*, 171–176.

11 Auf II Kor 1,21f. gehe ich nicht ein, sondern verweise auf die Beiträge von U. SCHNELLE, „Salbung, Geist und Taufe im 1. Johannesbrief" (§ 3.) und K. O. SANDNES, „Seal and Baptism in Early Christianity" (§ 3.1.) in vorliegender Publikation, 629–654 bzw. 1439–1479.

12 Hierzu in dieser Publikation die Beiträge von HARTMAN, „Usages – Some Notes on the Baptismal Formulae", 397–413 und J. SCHRÖTER, „Taufe in der Apostelgeschichte", 557–586. Vgl. ferner HARTMAN, „*Auf den Namen*", 39–46; IDEM, '*Into the Name*', 37–44 und 127–145. Weiter, siehe die Kommentare *ad loc.*, sowie besonders F. AVEMARIE, *Tauferzählungen*, bes. 26–43.

Laut Hartman hat diese Formel zwei Zwecke oder Funktionen: Erstens wird dadurch die christliche Taufe von der johanneischen unterschieden[13]; zweitens stellt die Taufe hier den Täufling in den Dienst des Herrn[14].

Gleich ob die Formula auf die hellenistische Bankterminologie („auf ein Konto setzen") wie Wilhelm Heitmüller meinte[15], oder auf das hebräische/aramäische *l*ᵉ*shem/l*ᵉ*shum* („mit Rücksicht auf" oder „im Hinblick auf") zurückzuführen ist, bleibt als Tatsache jedoch, dass wir es hier mit der vermutlich ältesten Tauformel des Urchristentums zu tun haben[16]. Hartman, der sich entschieden für den semitischen Ursprung der Namensformel einsetzt, versteht sie jedoch nicht als Bezeichnung für die getauften Christen als Eigentum des Herrn Jesus[17], d.h. in ähnlicher Weise wie Heitmüllers Interpretation[18], sondern als Verweis auf „eine größere Autorität [...], die ihr Sinn und Bedeutung verlieh"[19]. Die beiden Deutungen stellen m.E. aber keine wirklichen Alternativen dar. Im Hinblick auf die unterschiedliche *Kommunikationssituation* sind sie wohl eher komplementär: Selbst wenn die Formula εἰς τὸ ὄνομα (τοῦ κυρίου Ἰησοῦ) ursprünglich semitischer Herkunft sein sollte, die sich wahrscheinlich mit der christlichen Taufe der ältesten jüdisch-christlichen Phase in Verbindung bringen ließe[20], ist sie in hellenistisch-christlichen Gemeinden – etwa in Korinth als Finanz- und Bankzentrum – verwendet und dort höchstwahrscheinlich in Analogie zu der Bank-Terminologie εἰς τὸ ὄνομά τινος der hellenistischen Wirtschaftssprache verstanden worden[21] (vgl. II Kor 10,7).

Hartman selber gibt zu, dass „die Phrase ‚auf den Namen' ... unbiblisch (ist) in dem Sinne, daß sie in der Septuaginta nicht vorkommt. Außerdem ist es eigenartiges Griechisch, indem der Ausdruck im damaligen Griechisch eigent-

---

13 So auch H. Thyen, *Sündenvergebung*, 145–152.

14 Hartman, „*Auf den Namen*", 43f., 46–52; idem, '*Into the Name*', 41, 44–50.

15 W. Heitmüller, '*Im Namen Jesu*', bes. 95–126; siehe jetzt auch das Material bei P. Arzt-Grabner/R. E. Kritzer/A. Papathomas/F. Winter, *1. Korinther*, 70–71.

16 Siehe z.B. G. Barth, *Taufe*, 40f.; Hartman, „*Auf den Namen*", 45; idem, '*Into the Name*', 43. Gegen H. von Campenhausen (siehe Anm. 37 und Anm. 70).

17 So H. Bietenhard, „ὄνομα", 275.

18 So z.B. F. J. Leenhard, *Le baptême chrétien*, 36; G. R. Beasley-Murray, *Baptism*, 90–92, 100.

19 Hartman, „*Auf den Namen*", 46; idem, '*Into the Name*', 45. Vgl. auch die Diskussion in W. Schrage, *1. Korinther (VII/1)*, 154f.

20 So Hartman, „*La formule*", bes. 733f.; idem, „*Auf den Namen*", 44f., 49; idem, '*Into the Name*', 42f., 47. Siehe aber die Warnung von J. A. Fitzmyer, *Acts*, 266: „[...] but beware of the late date of the rabbinic evidence adduced [...]"; idem, *First Corinthians*, 146.

21 Heitmüller, '*Im Namen Jesu*', 104f.; D. Hellholm, „Impact", 149f.; Jetzt auch Arzt-Grabner et alii, *1. Korinther*, 71: „Selbst wenn der Vorstellungshintergrund des Paulus ein anderer wäre (z.B. das AT), was nicht ausgemacht ist, so ist doch davon auszugehen, dass die Briefempfänger den Ausdruck in diesem ... banktechnischen Sinn verstanden und ihn dann erst als Metapher begriffen: Taufen ‚auf den Namen Jesu' bedeutet also eine kultische Übereignung an ihn in einem Akt des Sich-Bekennens zu ihm". Vgl. ferner unten ad und in Anm. 26.

lich als Fachausdruck im Bankverkehr vorkommt, wo der ‚Name' den Inhaber eines Kontos bezeichnet"[22].

Die Polysemie eines Syntagmas wie εἰς τὸ ὄνομα kann und ist wahrscheinlich in unterschiedlichen pragmatischen Situationen, in denen es verwendet wurde, verschiedenartig monosemiert[23].

Interessanterweise taucht nun diese Taufformel bei Paulus ausschließlich im 1. Korintherbrief auf, v.a. ganz am Anfang in 1,13-17. Hier handelt es sich, laut Margaret Mitchell, um ein Textsegment, „das eine kurze Narration bringt, die dazu dient, Paulus' eigene rhetorische Frage zu widerlegen, eine Frage, dessen Ziel es ist, die Zersplitterung der Gemeinde direkt zu bekämpfen ..."[24].

I Kor 1,13c   εἰς τὸ ὄνομα Παύλου ἐβαπτίσθητε;
I Kor 1,15   (ἵνα μή τις εἴπῃ ὅτι) εἰς τὸ ἐμὸν ὄνομα ἐβαπτίσθητε.
[I Kor 1,13b μὴ Παῦλος ἐσταυρώθη ὑπὲρ ὑμῶν;]
I Kor 6,11   ἐδικαιώθητε ἐν τῷ ὀνόματι τοῦ κυρίου Ἰησοῦ Χριστοῦ.

I Kor 1,13c   Wurdet ihr auf den Namen des Paulus getauft?
I Kor 1,15   (Damit niemand sagen kann,) ihr wäret auf meinen Namen getauft.
[I Kor 1,13b Wurde etwa Paulus für euch gekreuzigt?]
I Kor 6,11   Ihr seid gerechtfertigt worden im Namen des Herrn Jesus Christus.

Wie Gerhard Barth richtig feststellt, „ist freilich eine Taufformel ‚auf den Namen Christi' [es müsste eigentlich heißen ‚des Herrn Jesus (Christus)'] nicht direkt genannt" in I Kor 1,13-15, „aber sie ist doch deutlich vorausgesetzt. Wie die rhetorische Frage ‚Ist etwa Paulus für euch gekreuzigt worden?' (μὴ Παῦλος ἐσταυρώθη ὑπὲρ ὑμῶν;) nur deshalb sinnvoll ist und nur deshalb ihr argumentatives Ziel erreichen kann, weil in der Tat nicht Paulus, sondern Christus für uns gekreuzigt wurde, so gilt gleichfalls von der zweiten Frage, daß sie nur deshalb ihr Ziel erreichen kann, weil es unbestritten ist, daß die Taufe eben ‚auf den Namen Christi [des Herrn Jesus (Christus)]' vollzogen wird". Barth stellt außerdem fest, dass „das Argument ... noch um so überzeugender (ist), je stärker Paulus sich an einen feststehenden liturgischen Brauch anlehnt, den jeder kennt und den niemand bestreitet"[25]. „Mit dem Genitiv der Zugehörigkeit ordnen sich die einzelnen exklusiv einer Autorität zu", wie Dieter Zeller mit Recht hervorhebt[26]. Deswegen tadelt Paulus nicht lediglich die „Bindung des jeweils einzelnen an

---

22 HARTMAN, ‚Auf den Namen', 40; IDEM, 'Into the Name', 38.
23 So auch SCHRAGE, 1. Korinther (VII/1), 155; vgl. HARTMAN, „Baptism", 586. Siehe nunmehr bes. HARTMANS Beitrag, „Usages – Some Notes on the Baptismal Formulae" in vorliegender Publikation, 397-413.
24 MITCHELL, Reconciliation, 201 (meine Übers.). Vgl. HARTMAN, „Auf den Namen", 60-64; IDEM, 'Into the Name', 59-63; LINDEMANN, 1. Korinther, 41, 140f.
25 Siehe hierzu bes. BARTH, Taufe, 41f. Vgl. außerdem J. SPRUTE, Enthymemtheorie, 57: ἔνδοξα; MITCHELL, Reconciliation, 87; F. HAHN, Theologie I, 281; HELLHOLM, „Argumentation", bes. 128f.: ἔνδοξα.
26 D. ZELLER, 1. Korinther, 91; FITZMYER, First Corinthians, 142; BDR, 132 [§ 162,7].

eine Leitfigur"[27], sondern außerdem „die dadurch hervorgerufene Fraktionierung der Gemeinde, wie aus der Fortsetzung V. 13a hervorgeht"[28].

Auch in I Kor 6,11 findet sich innerhalb einer vorgeformten Taufformel die „Namensformel", was auf die enge Beziehung zwischen den beiden Formeln hindeutet: ἐν τῷ ὀνόματι τοῦ κυρίου Ἰησοῦ Χριστοῦ[29]. Betz bemerkt, dass diese „Namensformel" nur hier bei Paulus Verwendung findet, ist aber der Meinung, dass Paulus diese Formel nur widerstrebend akzeptiert, u.a. deswegen weil sie von Anfang an mit Petrus in Verbindung gebracht war (vgl. z.B. Act 2,38; 8,16; 10,48) und weiterhin weil die Streitigkeiten in Korinth dadurch verursacht waren, dass Anhänger von Petrus und Apollos offenbar die Bedeutung der Täufer hervorgehoben hatten[30]. Im übrigen habe Paulus zur Zeit der Abfassung des 1. Korintherbriefes im Frühjahr 53–55 n.Chr. wenig Interesse an der Taufe gehabt[31]. Zu der „merkwürdigen" Aussage von Paulus, dass er Gott dafür dankt, „dass er in Korinth nur wenige Personen eigenhändig getauft hat!", bemerkt aber Adolf von Harnack[32]:

> Als eine Nichtachtung der Taufe ist das natürlich nicht zu verstehen …, sondern er erinnert sich, und zwar in diesem Falle mit Freude, an die Schranke des Apo-

---

27 LINDEMANN, *1. Korinther*, 38.

28 ZELLER, *ibid.*; BETZ unten ad Anm. 30; MITCHELL, Zitat ad Anm. 24; Tertullian, Zitat unten ad Anm. 34. Anders LINDEMANN, *1 Korinther*, 41: „… auch scheinen die ἔριδες nichts mit der Taufe zu tun zu haben", und Vos, „Argumentation", 32.

29 Diese Taufformel wird unten näher analysiert. Vgl. die in das „Christuslied" (Phil 2,6–11) eingefügte Akklamation (ἵνα ἐν τῷ ὀνόματι Ἰησοῦ … πᾶσα γλῶσσα ἐξομολογήσεται ὅτι κύριος Ἰησοῦς Χριστός [V. 11]); siehe unten § 1.3.mit Anm. 106.

30 BETZ, „Ritual", 86–100, 103–105 [242–254, 257–259]; IDEM, „Magic and Mystery", bes. 220ff. mit Bezug auf *PGM* IV. 172, 2254 und Philo, *Virt.* 185; *Vita Mos.* 1.71; *Cherub.* 49; *Spec. leg.* 1.319; ähnlich H. CONZELMANN, *1. Korinther*, 51–54; M. WOLTER, „Apollos", 66 [anders 419]; FEE, *First Corinthians*, 61; CHR. WOLFF, *1. Korinther*, 30f.; S. VOLLENWEIDER, *Freiheit*, 328; SCHNELLE, *Einleitung*, 86; siehe CHR. RIEDWEG, *Mysterienterminologie*, 26, 59f., 126f., bes. 59: „Interessanterweise spielen dabei (sc. in den eleusinischen Mysterien) gemäß dieser athenischen Inschrift (sc. SIG 885) die Mystagogen eine wichtige Rolle: Sie sind für ihre Mysten verantwortlich, ὅπως ἐν τάξει καὶ κοσμίως [πορείαν ποιῶσι] wie sinnvoll ergänzt wird (LSS 15,27f.)"; F. GRAF, „Mystagogos", 611. H.-J. KLAUCK, „Mysterienkulte", bes. 184f. So schon W. BOUSSET, „1. Korinther", 77. Kritisch dagegen vor allem G. WAGNER, *Das religionsgeschichtliche Problem*; J. M. WEDDERBURN, *Baptism and Resurrection*; ZELLER, *1. Korinther*, 94. Siehe Anm. 221 unten.

31 BETZ, „Ritual", 104 [258]. Für das Datum des 1. Korintherbriefes, siehe KOESTER, *Introduction*, 126: 53–54; KÜMMEL, *Einleitung*, 242: 54/55; VIELHAUER, *Geschichte*, 141: 54–56; CONZELMANN, *1. Korinther*, 18: 55; FEE, *First Corinthians*, 4f.: 54–55; BETZ/MITCHELL, „Corinthians, First Epistle to the", 1140: 53–55; SCHRAGE, *1. Korinther (VII/1)*, 36: 51–54/52–55; SCHNELLE, *Einleitung*, 75: 55; WOLFF, *1. Korinther*, 12f.: ca. 54; LINDEMANN, *1. Korinther*, 17: 54–56; FITZMYER, *First Corinthians*, 43: „early in the year 57 (but the end of 56 is also possible)"; ZELLER, *1. Korinther*, 47: 53–54.

32 A. VON HARNACK, *Mission*, 399. Ferner E. FERGUSON, *Baptism*, 149: „A depreciation of baptism … is not to be concluded from this passage, only a depreciation of the administrator of the baptism".

stelberufs. Dieser Beruf legt ihm nur das Predigen des Wortes Gottes auf; das Taufen gehört strenggenommen nicht zu seiner Kompetenz; er kann es ausüben, aber in der Regel ist es Sache anderer; denn es setzt bei den meisten eine längere Unterweisung und Prüfzeit voraus.

So schon in der alten Kirche Tertullian[33]:

> Aber auch auf den Apostel selbst kommen sie immer wieder zurück, weil er gesagt hat: ‚Denn nicht, um zu taufen hat mich Christus gesandt'. Als ob durch dieses Argument der Taufe der Boden entzogen würde! (*Quasi hoc argumento baptismum adimatur!*) Warum taufte er also Gaius und Krispus und zugleich die Familie des Stephanas? Und doch hatte Christus, obwohl er ihn nicht dazu gesandt hatte, gleichwohl anderen Aposteln geboten zu taufen (*attemen aliis apostolis praeceperat tinguere*).

Dass die Verwendung dieser Formel in I Kor 1,13/15 *situationsbedingt* ist, hat wiederum Tertullian hervorgehoben[34]:

> Allerdings wurde dies im Hinblick auf die damaligen Zeitumstände (*pro condicione tunc temporis*) an die Korinther geschrieben, weil ja Spaltungen und Parteiungen unter ihnen entstanden, als der eine sich den Anhängern des Paulus, der andere denen des Apollos zurechnete. Deswegen sagt der Apostel als Friedensstifter (*pacificus apostolus*), um sich nicht den Anschein zu geben, alles für sich zu beanspruchen, er sei nicht gesandt um zu taufen, sondern um zu verkünden. Denn die Verkündigung ist das Frühere (*prius est praedicare*), die Taufe das Spätere (*posterius tinguere*), wenn zuvor verkündigt wurde. Ich glaube aber, daß dem, der verkündigen durfte, auch gestattet war zu taufen[35].

Formgeschichtlich kann diese Tauformel „Namensformel" genannt werden. Sie wurde aller Wahrscheinlichkeit nach in der Liturgie im Zusammenhang mit dem Taufakt verwendet (vgl. hierzu Jak 2,7: οὐκ αὐτοὶ βλασφημοῦσιν τὸ καλὸν ὄνομα τὸ ἐπικληθὲν ἐφ᾽ ὑμᾶς;[36] [„Lästern nicht sie den guten Namen, der über

---

33 Tertullian, *De bapt.* 14,1. Lat. Text und deut. Übers. D. Schleyer, *Tertullian, De baptismo, De oratione*, 198f. Neben Tertullian Johannes Chrysostomos, *Hom. in I Cor* (PG 61. III,17–18): „Denn er (Paulus) hat viele getauft; aber dies war nicht die Frage, von wem sie getauft, sondern auf wessen Namen sie getauft wurden" (ἐβάπτισε γὰρ πολλούς· ἀλλ᾽ οὐ τὸ ζητούμενον τοῦτο ἦν, ὑπὸ τίνος ἐβαπτίσθησαν, ἀλλὰ τὸ εἰς τίνος ὄνομα ἐβαπτίσθησαν). In der Moderne, neben von Harnack, Weiss, *1. Korinther*, 21: „Der Grund dafür, daß P[aulus] wenige Mitglieder der Gemeinde getauft hat, ist natürlich nicht in einer Geringschätzung der rituellen Handlung zu suchen [...]"; F. W. Horn, *Angeld*, 142f.; Wolff, *1. Korinther*, 32.

34 Tertullian, *De bapt.* 14,2; Schleyer, *ibid.*

35 Vgl. Weiss, *1. Korinther*, 22: Charakteristik des Paulus: „Ein Erweckungsprediger von Gottes Gnaden, aber kein Liturg"; ähnlich jetzt auch Fitzmyer, *First Corinthians*, 147.

36 Siehe Weiss, *1. Korinther*, 19; M. Dibelius/H. Greeven, *Jakobus*, 175f., sowie G. Strecker, *Theologie*, 700; W. Popkes, *Jakobus*, 169–171; Mitchell, „The Letter of James", 86; J. Schröter, „Taufe in der Apostelgeschichte" in dieser Publikation, 557–586, § 4. Anm. 91. Anders z.B. Hartman, „*Auf den Namen*", 51 Anm. 48; idem, '*Into the Name*', 49 Anm. 52; H. Frankemölle, *Jakobus*, 395–399; Chr. Burchard, *Jakobusbrief*, 102, die den „Namen" auf Gott beziehen.

euch angerufen wurde?"]). Sie lautete wohl entweder βαπτίζω σε εἰς τὸ ὄνομα τοῦ κυρίου Ἰησοῦ oder eher noch βαπτίζεται ὁ δεῖνα εἰς τὸ ὄνομα τοῦ κυρίου Ἰησοῦ[37]. Dieser mutmaßliche „Sitz im Leben" bestätigt sich nun durch die später entwickelte triadische ὄνομα-Formel, die hier anderswo behandelt wird[38].

1.2. Die Taufaffirmation der Neugetauften – Die „Eingliederungsformel"

Außer der oben angeführten „Namensformel" gibt es im I Kor. noch eine Textsequenz, die wahrscheinlich ebenfalls auf eine vorgeformte Tradition zurückgeht, nämlich I Kor 12,13. „This verse is one of the fundamental Pauline texts that teach the incorporation of baptized believers into Christ"[39]. Dieser Text erinnert an die noch zu behandelnde „Bekleidungsformel" von Gal 3,26–28 und lautet[40]:

1. Καὶ γὰρ[41] [ἐν[42] ἑνὶ πνεύματι] ἡμεῖς πάντες εἰς ἓν σῶμα ἐβαπτίσθημεν,
2.   εἴτε Ἰουδαῖοι εἴτε Ἕλληνες,
3.   εἴτε δοῦλοι εἴτε ἐλεύθεροι
[[3a?]]   [[εἴτε ἄρσεν εἴτε θῆλυ·]]
4. καὶ   πάντες (εἰς[43]) ἓν πνεῦμα ἐποτίσθημεν.

---

37   Johannes Chrysostomos, *Cat. bapt.*, 2/3,3 (R. Kaczynski, *Johannes Chrysostomos, Catecheses baptismales II*, 86, 236); so auch Theodor von Mopsuestia, *hom. cat.*, 14,15 (P. Bruns, *Theodor von Mopsuestia, Katechetische Homilien II*, 373). Siehe in dieser Publikation J. Day, „Catechetical Lectures", 1179–1204, § 4.5. Vgl. Barth, *Taufe*, 42f.; G. J. Steyn, „Reflections", 484. Vgl. ferner Anm. 70. Für die Bedeutung der Anrufung des Namens bei der Debatte um die Wiedertaufe in der Alten Kirche, siehe das Material bei Ferguson, *Baptism*, 380–399. Gegen von Campenhausen, „Taufe", 197–216, der verneint, dass die Neophyten ursprünglich „auf den Namen des Herrn Jesus" getauft wurden; kritisch dazu Barth, *Taufe*, 42–45; Hartman, „Baptism", 586f. und Conzelmann, *1. Korinther*, 54 Anm. 37; so schon Bousset, „1. Korinther", 77: „… daß die christliche Taufe zu des Paulus Zeit eine Taufe auf den Namen Christi war, …".

38   S. K. M. Hartvigsen, „Matt 28:9-20 and Mark 16:9-20" in dieser Publikation, 655–716, § 2.1.

39   Fitzmyer, *First Corinthians*, 478. M. V. Lee, *Paul, the Stoics and the Body of Christ*, 129–138.

40   Zur Struktur dieser Formel siehe vor allem Betz, *Galatians*, 182; idem, *Galaterbrief*, 321f.; ferner Meeks, „Androgyne", hier 180; M. Bouttier, „Complexio Oppositorum", 1; A. Eriksson, *Tradition*, 127–134, bes. 128.

41   Siehe BDR, 382 [§ 452,3.4]: „καὶ γάρ 'denn' (*etenim*) …". Falls καὶ γάρ = *etenim*, dann ist die Vermutung einer Hinzufügung, um eine Verbindung mit dem Kontext herzustellen (so Betz, *Galatians*, 182; idem, *Galaterbrief*, 322) nicht zwingend und καὶ γάρ kann somit der Formel zugerechnet werden.

42   Vgl. Weiss, *1. Korinther*, 303: „Es fragt sich, ob wir ἐν streng von ἐβαπτίσθημεν abhängig machen sollen: ‚wir sind in einen Geist hineingetaucht'. Hierfür würde die Parallele ἓν πνεῦμα ἐποτίσθημεν sprechen, wo ja der Geist ausdrücklich als eine Art Fluidum erscheint. Jedenfalls ist dies besser als die instrumentale Deutung ‚vermittelst'". Die lokale Deutung vertritt auch Fee, *First Corinthians*, 605. Die instrumentale vertritt u.a. R. Schnackenburg, *Heilsgeschehen*, 23–25, 77–86; Schrage, *1. Korinther (VII/3)*, 216; Wolff, *1. Korinther*, 298; A. C. Thiselton, *First Corinthians*, 997. Fitzmyer, *First Corinthians*, 477: „… the prep. *en* is not clear …". Diese Alternative ist „müßig" (H. Merklein/M. Gielen, *1. Korinther III*, 139).

43   Einige wenige Handschriften lesen εἰς ἓν πνεῦμα ἐποτίσθημεν. Siehe dazu Weiss, *1. Korinther*, 304 Anm. 1: „εἰς ἓν πνεῦμα ἐποτίσθημεν, wo ποτίζω = βαπτίζω gebraucht zu sein scheint …".

1. Denn [durch/in einen/m Geist] sind wir alle in einen Leib getauft worden,
2. ob Juden oder Griechen,
3. ob Sklaven oder Freie,
⟦3a?⟧ ⟦ob männlich oder weiblich,⟧
4. und alle sind wir (in einen) mit einem Geist getränkt worden/wir bekamen alle den einen Geist über uns gegossen.

Diese Formel ist unterschiedlich behandelt worden auch bezüglich der *Gliederungsstruktur*. Da bislang m.W. keine rhetorisch-stilistische Analyse vorliegt, soll eine solche vorangestellt werden:
Eine Reihe „Wiederholungsformen" (*repetitio*) unterschiedlicher Art finden sich in dieser Formel[44]:

(1) Inclusio   Z. 1 – 4   (καί ... καί; πάντες ... πάντες; ἕν ... ἕν; ἐβαπ. ... ἐποτ.)
(2) Anaphora   Z. 1 – 4   (καί ... καί; πάντες ... πάντες; ἕν ... ἕν; ἐβαπ. ... ἐποτ.)
                   Z. 2 – 3   (εἴτε ... εἴτε *bis*)
(3) Epiphora   Z. 2 – 3   (εἴτε ... εἴτε *bis*; Ἰουδαῖοι ... δοῦλοι)
                   Z. 3 *bis* (δοῦλοι ... ἐλεύθεροι)
                   Z. 1 – 4   (σῶμα ... πνεῦμα; ἐβαπτίσθημεν ... ἐποτίσθημεν)
(4) Monostichon   Z. 2 – 3   (εἴτε ... εἴτε *bis*)
    auf Distanz
(5) Distichon   Z. 1 – 4   (καί ... καί; εἴτε ... εἴτε *bis*; πάντες ... πάντες; ἕν ... ἕν; σῶμα ... πνεῦμα; ἐβαπτίσθημεν ... ἐποτίσθημεν)
(6) Assonanz   Z. 1 – 4   (ἐβαπτίσθημεν ... ἐποτίσθημεν)
(7) Homoiotel.   Z. 1 – 4   (ἐβαπτίσθημεν ... ἐποτίσθημεν)

Die meisten Kommentatoren unterlassen die Fragestellung, ob hier vorgeformte Tradition vorliegt oder nicht[45], oder bezweifeln die Existenz eines Traditionsstückes[46]. Andere, wie Wayne A. Meeks und ihm folgend Anders Eriksson bezeichnen die vorgeformte Tradition als „Reunification Formula", wobei das Gewicht auf die Zeilen 2 und 3 gelegt wird[47].
(1.) Mit dem Wechsel von der 3. Pers. Sing. (τὸ σῶμα/ὁ Χριστός) zur 1. Pers. Pl. (ἡμεῖς πάντες) ist indessen ein erstes Indiz für die Einarbeitung eines vorgeformten Traditionsstücks gegeben[48].

---

44 Zu den morphologischen Figuren siehe PLETT, *Einführung*, 41–53; IDEM, *Systematische Rhetorik*, 87, 120–124; H. LAUSBERG, *Handbuch*, 311–321 [§§ 612–634]; J. MARTIN, *Rhetorik*, 297–315. Dieselbe Wiederholung kann, wie in der Analyse durchgeführt wird, natürlich verschiedenen Figuren zugerechnet werden. Siehe ferner HELLHOLM, „Funktion", 389 mit Anm. 22 (Lit.); IDEM, „Universalität", 259–264.

45 Z.B. HORN, *Angeld*, 172; CHR. STRECKER, *Die liminale Theologie*, 320 mit Anm. 93; M. KONRADT, *Gericht*, 434; FITZMYER, *First Corinthians*, 477f.

46 So z.B. WOLFF, *1. Korinther*, 299; KONRADT, *Gericht*, 428 Anm. 1221.

47 MEEKS, „Androgyne", 180–183; IDEM, *Urban Christians*, 88; ERIKSSON, *Traditions*, 127–134; MERKLEIN/GIELEN, *1. Korinther III*, 138.

48 Vgl. ERIKSSON, *Traditions*, 127 Anm. 261; LINDEMANN, *1. Korinther*, 270.

(2.) Vorhandensein einer Reihe morphologischer Figuren ein anderes.
(3.) Die *inklusive* Parallelität zwischen den Gliedern 1 und 4, mit dem καί explicativum im 4. Glied, ist ein weiteres Indiz dafür. Ob ἐν ἑνὶ πνεύματι ein paulinischer Zusatz, wie etwa διὰ τῆς πίστεως in Gal 3,26 und Röm 3,25, wahrscheinlich ist[49], kann diskutiert werden, ist aber keineswegs zwingend. Dann wäre die Parallelität zwischen den Zeilen allerdings lediglich von πάντες εἰς in Zeile 1 und πάντες (εἰς) in Zeile 4 sowie womöglich auch von ἐβαπτίσθημεν und ἐποτίσθημεν abhängig[50]. Die Parallelität zwischen ἐν ἑνὶ πνεύματι und ἓν πνεῦμα fiele dann in der Formel weg, aber gewiss nicht im paulinischen Text[51].
(4.) Die Parallelität im „sozialen Urbekenntnis"[52] bzw. in der „unification formula" (εἴτε ... εἴτε) ist ein viertes Indiz für ein vorgeformtes Traditionsstück[53]. Ob „angesichts der Glosse in 14,33b–35" das dritte Begriffspaar in Zeile [[3a εἴτε ἄρσεν εἴτε θῆλυ]] o.ä. „sekundär getilgt worden sein könnte", lässt sich ebenfalls vermuten[54], schwerlich aber schlüssig nachweisen. Eine andere, aber ebenso hypothetische Erklärung für das Fehlen des dritten Glieds hat mit der korinthischen Situation zu tun, weswegen Paulus „den Enthusiasmus korinthischer Frauen (vgl. 11,2ff.) nicht begünstigen" möchte[55], als er diese Formel in den Brief einfügte. Also: im ersten Falle obliegt die angenommene Tilgung einem Redaktor, im zweiten Falle Paulus selber[56]. Wie man erstens den intra-textuellen Ko-text im I Kor, zweitens den Situationskontext innerhalb der korinthischen Gemeinde, drittens aber auch die Entstehungsgeschichte des überlieferten Textes versteht, führt zu zwei unterschiedlichen Erklärungen der einen oder der anderen Tilgungshypothese. Als Exegeten sind wir immer genötigt, uns auf Wahrscheinlichkeitsdeutungen zu verlassen, und zwar mit

---

49 So als Möglichkeit Betz, *Galatians*, 182; idem, *Galaterbrief*, 322; R. Bultmann, *Theologie*, 49; E. Käsemann, „Zum Verständnis von Röm 3,24–26", 96–100; Kl. Wengst, *Formeln*, 88; Vielhauer, *Geschichte*, 22; D.-A. Koch, „Crossing the border", 213 und 221; Hahn, „Taufe und Rechtfertigung", 259; Lohse, *Römer*, 133; R. Jewett, *Romans*, 269–271.

50 So offenbar Weiss, *1. Korinther*, 303, der in V. 13 mit einem „Vierzeiler (abba, reimartiger Anklang in a a, Anaphora in b b)" rechnet; aufgenommen von Eriksson, *Traditions*, 128. Es handelt sich in den Zeilen 1 und 4 um Epiphora, die die Inclusio (Klauck, *Herrenmahl*, 335) der beiden Zeilen noch stärker hervorhebt.

51 Hierzu bes. I. Hermann, *Kyrios und Pneuma*, 76–85.

52 G. Sellin, „Die Armen und die Reichen", 40.

53 Vgl. jedoch Weiss, „Beiträge zur paulinischen Rhetorik", 179: „Recht beliebt ist die Teilung mit εἴτε – εἴτε, wodurch er (sc. Paulus) schöne Wirkungen erzielt". Unter seinen vielen Beispielen verzeichnet Weiß, wenn ich recht sehe, allerdings I Kor 12:13 nicht!

54 So die zögernde Vermutung von Lindemann, *1. Korinther*, 272.

55 Vgl. Wolff, *1. Korinther*, 299, dem Konradt, *Gericht*, 429 Anm. 1224 folgt; so auch J. A. Harrill, „Paul and Slavery", 598.

56 Vgl. Zeller, *1. Korinther*, 398: Unter Verweis auf die Variabilität der Tradition (Gal 3,28; I Kor 12,13 und Kol 3,11) „... wird man nicht sicher behaupten können, dass Paulus in I Kor 12,13 die Vergleichgültigung der Geschlechter bewusst unterschlägt ...".

Hilfe von Rekonstruktionen, die auf text-externen Präsuppositionen und textinternen Implikturen basieren[57].

(5.) Ein abschließendes Indiz dafür, dass ein vorgeformtes Traditionsstück vorliegt, ist die Beobachtung, dass in der Formel alles Gewicht auf der Einheit liegt (πάντες zweimal und ἕν dreimal), während im umgebenden Ko-Text der Nachdruck auf den μέλη πολλά im Verhältnis zu dem ἓν σῶμα liegt[58].

Ein weiteres Problem stellt die Bedeutung von ποτίζειν im Aktivum wie im Passivum dar. Bezieht sich das ἐποτίσθημεν im Glied 4 auf die Taufe und steht somit parallel zu ἐβαπτίσθημεν im Glied 1[59], oder bezieht sich das Verb auf das Abendmahl?[60] (Vgl. 10,4: καὶ πάντες τὸ αὐτὸ πνευματικὸν ἔπιον πόμα [„und alle denselben geistlichen Trank tranken"]) Joh. Weiß vertritt die Meinung, dass „[d]as Wort ἐποτίσθημεν … mehr aus rednerischen Gründen im Gegensatz zu ἐβαπτίσθημεν gewählt (ist)" (vgl. die Stilanalyse o. S. 423) und folglich auf die Taufe zu beziehen ist[61], und Dieter Zeller verweist außerdem auf den „Aorist wie bei ἐβαπτίσθημεν", was auf ein „einmaliges Geschehen" hinweist[62].

---

57 Vgl. KL. W. HEMPFER, „Präsuppositionen", 317. G. STRECKER/T. NOLTING, „Der vorchristliche Paulus", 718: „Historisch-kritisches Arbeiten heißt immer auch Hypothesen unterschiedlicher Wahrscheinlichkeit gegeneinander abwägen zu müssen".

58 Vgl. LINDEMANN, 1. Korinther, 270; ferner M. KONRADT, Gericht, 434; FITZMYER, First Corinthians, 479.

59 So schon in der alten Kirche: Johannes Chrysostomos, Hom. in Ep. 1 ad Cor 30.2 (PG 61. XLIV: 251). Neuzeitlich u.a.: WEISS, 1. Korinther, 303f.; SCHRAGE, 1. Korinther (VII/3), 217f.; LINDEMANN, 1. Korinther, 272; MITCHELL, Reconciliation, 141 Anm. 456; 254 Anm. 379; H. UMBACH, In Christus getauft, 262; SCHNELLE, Paulus, 234 mit Anm. 106; MERKLEIN/GIELEN, 1. Korinther III, 139; FERGUSON, Baptism, 153; ZELLER, 1. Korinther, 398; FITZMYER, First Corinthians, 478: „… nowhere in the NT or early patristic writers is the Spirit ever said to be bestowed through the Eucharist". Unentschieden: CONZELMANN, 1. Korinther, 258 mit Anm. 17. Auf die Taufe deutet G. WIDENGREN OdSal 6 (Religionsphänomenologie, 224): „Wie real die lebensspendende Kraft der Taufe gedacht wurde, geht aus den Oden Salomos hervor …"; OdSal 6:12–16, 18: „Denn vom Höchsten wurde der Trank gegeben. Heil darum den Dienern jenes Trankes, ihnen, denen sein Wasser anvertraut ist. … Denn jedermann hat sie erkannt im Herzen [Herrn!], und sie leben durch das Wasser ein Leben bis in die Ewigkeit". Keine Beziehung zur Taufe: M. LATTKE, Oden Salomos, 86–93: Rückübersetzung von V. 18 ins Griechische: παντῶν δὲ γνόντων αὐτοὺς ἐν κυρίῳ, σεσῳσμένοι καὶ ὕδατι ζωῆς αἰωνίου („Denn sie alle haben sie/sich erkannt im Herrn, und sie sind erlöst durch Wasser des Lebens in Ewigkeit" (92–93); IDEM, Odes of Solomon, 82–87.

60 So schon in der alten Kirche z.B. Theophylakt, PG 124. 561–794: 716; Johannes Damascenus, PG 95. 570–706: 669. Neuzeitlich u.a.: G. HEINRICI, 1. Korinther, 385; E. PETERSON, 1. Korinther, 293; KÄSEMANN, „Anliegen", 16–17; KLAUCK, Herrenmahl, 334f.; HORN, Angeld, 172–175; CHR. STRECKER, Die liminale Theologie, 320 mit Anm. 93; KONRADT, Gericht, 433f. Vgl. auch das Fragezeichen bei CONZELMANN, 1. Korinther, 258 Anm. 17; und das Zitat aus FITZMYER, First Corinthians, oben in Anm. 59. – W. BAUER/K. ALAND/B. ALAND, Wörterbuch, 1394, s.v. ποτίζω übersetzen mit „wir haben alle einunddenselben Geist zu trinken bekommen".

61 WEISS, 1. Korinther, 304; so auch ERIKSSON, Traditions, 130. Siehe oben im Text (3.1.): καὶ explicativum (so mündlich auch D. Sänger).

62 ZELLER, 1. Korinther, 398 mit Anm. 109.

Inhaltlich stellt sich die Frage, wie βαπτισθῆναι zu verstehen ist: konkret als die Wassertaufe oder metaphorisch als eine zusätzliche Geisttaufe[63] oder aber als eine Geisttaufe bei der Bekehrung[64]. Für den Bezug auf die Taufe spricht (1.) „der die Einmaligkeit des Geschehens bezeichnende Aor[ist]", was nicht der Fall ist bezüglich des Abendmahls[65]; (2.) „die formale Verschränkung beider Versteile"; (3.) „die inhaltliche Parallelität"[66]. Den Lexem-Wechsel erklärt Christian Wolff folgendermaßen: „Der Ausdrucksweise ,tränken' (vgl. 3,2.6) liegt dann die Vorstellung zugrunde, daß der Glaubende bei der Taufe Gottes Geist in sich aufnahm, von ihm durchdrungen wurde ..." und betont somit „das Wirksamwerden des Geistes bei der Taufe"[67]. Ähnlich auch Hartman: „Der letzte Satz, ,alle wurden wir mit dem einen Geist getränkt' könnte ebensowohl mit ,wir bekamen alle den einen Geist über uns gegossen' wiedergegeben werden"[68]. Unter Hinweis auf den Sprachgebrauch in zahlreichen Papyrustexten unterstreicht auch Peter Arzt-Grabner, dass ποτίζειν durchgehend die Bedeutung „bewässern" hat[69]. Diese Verwendung des Lexems kann möglicherweise den Umstand, dass die Taufe nicht nur durch Untertauchen[70], sondern zuweilen durch Übergießen

---

63 So z.B. E. Best, *Body*, 73; H. Hunter, *Spirit-Baptism*, 39–42.

64 So Fee, *First Corinthians*, 603–605; J. D. G. Dunn, *Baptism*, 127–131; idem, *Theology of Paul*, 450–452.

65 Hervorgehoben von C. K. Barrett, *First Corinthians*, 289 und Zeller (siehe Anm. 62). Anders H.-J. Klauck, *Herrenmahl*. Siehe jetzt G. Theissen, *Religion*, 174: „Die urchristliche Taufe ist ... ein Initiationsritus. ... Das urchristliche Abendmahl ist ... ein (immer wiederholter) Integrationsritus, der den Zusammenhalt der Gemeinschaft erneuert".

66 So Schrage, *1. Korinther (VII/3)*, 217.

67 Wolff, *1. Korinther*, 299; so schon H. Lietzmann, *An die Korinther I/II*, 63; jetzt auch Fitzmyer, *First Corinthians*, 479; Zeller, *1. Korinther*, 398.

68 Hartman, *„Auf den Namen"*, 68; ähnlich Ferguson, *Baptism*, 153–154.

69 Arzt-Grabner et alii, *1. Korinther*, 138: „In seiner geläufigen Bedeutung ... ,bewässern' begegnet ποτίζω anschließend in I Kor 3,6–8. Diese Bedeutung trägt das Verb auch durchgehend in den zahlreichen Papyrusbelegen".

70 Bousset, *„1. Korinther"*, 134: „Die Taufe ist ein Untertauchen in das Wasser nach dem äußeren Geschehen; nach dem inneren ein Hineingetauchtwerden in Christus ... daher auch ein Eingegliedertwerden in seinen Leib, die Gemeinde". Siehe *Did. apost.* III 12,2–3: „... *cum mulieres in aquam descendunt*" („... wenn die Frauen in das Wasser hinabsteigen) [2] „*Et cum ascendit ex aqua, quae baptizatur*" („.... Und wenn die Frau, die getauft wird, aus dem Wasser heraussteigt ...) [3]"; Zu *Did. apost.* siehe Lindemann, „Zur frühchristlichen Taufpraxis", in dieser Publikation, 767–816. Vgl. Pap. Bodmer XLI (koptisches Fragment der Paulusakten), siehe R. Kasser/P. Luisier, „Le Papyrus Bodmer XLI", 319–323: Auf dem Weg nach Jericho begegnet Paulus einem schrecklichen Löwen, der auf Paulus' Frage, was er will, antwortet, dass er getauft werden möchte. Paulus steigt mit dem Löwen in einen nahegelegenen Fluss herab; er berichtet: „Ich nahm den Löwen bei seiner Mähne und *im Namen Jesu Christi tauchte ich ihn dreimal unter*. Als er dem Wasser wieder entstieg, schüttelte er seine Mähne zurecht und sagte zu mir: ,Gnade sei mit dir!' und ich sagte ihm: ,Desgleichen mit dir!'" (meine Hervorhebung). Der Löwe ist natürlich Symbol für die „Triebkraft schlechthin". Zitiert nach H.-J. Klauck, *Apokryphe Bibel*, 111–115.

bzw. Überschütten[71] durchgeführt wurde, widerspiegeln (Did 7,3: ... ἔκχεον εἰς τὴν κεφαλὴν τρὶς ὕδωρ εἰς ὄνομα πατρὸς καὶ υἱοῦ καὶ ἁγίου πνεύματος [„... gieße über den Kopf dreimal Wasser aus auf den Namen des Vaters, des Sohnes und des Heiligen Geistes"]; zum Taufwasser siehe andererseits Tertullian, *De bapt.*, 4,3: „... Es gibt keinen Unterschied, ob jemand im Meer (*mare*) oder in einem Teich (*stagnum*), in einem Fluß (*flumen*) oder in einer Quelle (*fons*), in einer Zisterne (*lacus*) oder in einem Becken (*alveus*) getauft wird"[72]. TA 21,1: *Sit aqua fluens in fonte (*κολυμβήθρα*) vel fluens de alto*[73] [„Es soll Wasser sein, das aus einer Quelle fließt oder von oben herabfließt".]). Diese Art des Taufens wird später in der altkirchlichen Kunst wiedergegeben[74]. Das Übergießen als Taufform könnte auch indirekt durch die Ausformung der Taufbecken in späterer Zeit bestätigt werden, da diese oft zu klein waren, um Untertauchen zuzulassen[75]. Allerdings konnte das Untertauchen durch „Hinunterbeugung des Kopfes" (ἀπὸ τῆς κεφαλῆς κατεῖχεν) zuwege gebracht werden, wozu keine großen Taufbecken benötigt wurden[76] (Siehe Fig. 25 und Fig. 26).

---

71   So G. J. CUMING, „ΕΠΟΤΙΣΘΗΜΕΝ (I Corinthians 12.13)", 285: „We all had the one holy Spirit poured over us". Bezweifelt von WOLFF, *1. Korinther*, 299; E. R. ROGERS, „ΕΠΟΤΙΣΘΗΜΕΝ Again", 139–142: „cause to drink"; FITZMYER, *First Corinthians*, 479.

72   D. SCHLEYER, *De baptismo*, 169. Siehe NORDERVAL, „Simplicity and Power. Tertullian's *De Baptismo*" in vorliegender Publikation, 947–972, § 4. mit Anm. 71.

73   Texte: G. SCHÖLLGEN/W. GERLINGS, *Didache/Traditio Apostolica*, 118 bzw. 256. Siehe K. NIEDERWIMMER, *Didache*, 163; A. EKENBERG, *Hippolytos*, 53; IDEM, „Initiation in the *Apostolic Tradition*" in dieser Publikation, 1011–1050; vgl. B. KLEINHEYER, *Sakramentliche Feiern 1*, 58–63; H. EMMINGHAUS, „Der gottesdienstliche Raum", 400–403.

74   Siehe die Darstellungen auf dem Sarkophag in Sancta Maria Antiqua in Rom (vor 313 n.Chr.) sowie auf dem Sarkophag im Benedictus Museum (*Moseo Pio Christiano*) in Rom (300–330 n.Chr.), oder die Wandmalereien in den Sankt Peter und Marcellinus Katakomben (etwa Ende des 4. Jhs n.Chr.), oder auf einem Grabstein eines Kindes (aus dem 5. Jh. n.Chr.): hierzu F. VAN DER MEER & C. MOHRMANN, *Bildatlas*, 41 Abbildung 45; 126 Abbildungen 396 und 397.

75   Siehe den Ausgrabungsbericht von A. H. S. MEGAW, *Kourion*, 71, 75, 98 (Pl. 1.22c), 107–118. Zum Taufritual: Untertauchen oder Übergießen, siehe auch J. NEIJENHUIS, „Taufbecken", 49.

76   Johannes Chrysostomos, *Cat. bapt.* 2/3,3; IDEM, *De S. Babyla* II,25. Ebenso Ps-Athanasius, *virg.* 11 (καταδῦσαι/ἀναδῦσαι); Theodor von Mopsuestia, Dritte Homilie über die Taufe (= *Hom. cat.* 14): „Rituale" sowie 14,18–19 (Übers. BRUNS, *Theodor von Mopsuestia, Katechetische Homilien II*, 359, 376–378). Vgl. Cyrill von Jerusalem, *Cat. ill.*, 3,4; 3,17; 17,14 (PG 33); sowie *Myst. cat.*, 2,4: καταδύω. Text und Übers. G. RÖWEKAMP, *Cyrill von Jerusalem, Mystagogicae Catecheses*, 114–115; siehe in dieser Publikation die Beiträge von J. DAY, „The Catechetical Lectures of Cyril of Jerusalem", 1179–1204, § 4.5., CHR. STRECKER, „Tauftrituale im frühen Christentum und in der Alten Kirche", 1381–1438, § 2.1. und H. Schneider, „Die Entwicklung der Taufbecken in der Spätantike", 1695–1718, § 3.1.; vgl auch oben Anm. 70. Ferner FERGUSON, *Baptism*, 438: „The text (*Didascalia Apostolorum*) is not explicit about the dipping, but presumably the male administrator who anointed the head also dipped it under the water". Zu undifferenziert THEISSEN, „Urchristliche Taufe", 105 mit Anm. 26; IDEM, *Religion*, 185 mit Anm. 14. Die Behauptung RÖWEKAMPS, *Myst. Cat.*, 33: „Erst im 4. und 5. Jahrhundert finden sich literarische Zeugnisse für ein ganzes Untertauchen des Täuflings ...", ist nachweislich falsch, siehe Tertullian, *De bapt.*, 7,2: „... *quod in aqua mergimur* ..." („.... weil man uns im Wasser untertaucht");

Die Bedeutung der Präpositionen ἐν im mitunter vermuteten „paulinischen Zusatz" ἐν ἑνὶ πνεύματι und εἰς im präformulierten Traditionsstück εἰς ἓν σῶμα ἐβαπτίσθημεν ist lebhaft diskutiert worden. Was den eventuellen „paulinischen Zusatz" betrifft, stellt sich die Alternative wie folgt: Wird der Glaubende „in einen Geist", d.h. modal als Gabe[77] oder „durch einen Geist", d.h. instrumental mit dem Geist als Mittel[78] getauft. Die instrumentale Deutung ist unter den Kommentatoren die vorherrschende, welche auch dann ein nahes Verhältnis zwischen Taufe und Geist bedeutet, aber dann nicht als Gabe bei der Taufe, sondern als Instrument, das bei der Eingliederung in den Leib Christi, also in die Gemeinde wirksam ist. Wolfgang Schrage sieht hier kein „entweder ... oder", sondern betont wohl zurecht, dass bei der Taufe der Geist gleichzeitig vermittelt wird und wirksam ist[79].

Bezüglich des präformulierten Traditionsstücks sehen die Alternativen wie folgt aus: (a) Wird der Gläubige lokal in einen schon existierenden präexistenten Leib getauft[80], oder (b) um in finaler oder konsekutiver Hinsicht diesen Leib zu bilden[81] oder (c) lediglich als „Herstellung einer Beziehung" in Analogie zur „ὄνομα-Formel" (I Kor 1,13c)?[82]. Die Parallele mit ἐνδύσασθαι in Gal 3,27 spricht m.E. am ehesten für die lokale Bedeutung. Was das „soziale Urbekenntnis" angeht, so gilt, dass dieses hier, wie in Gal 3,28, das ethnisch-religiöse sowie das sozial-kulturelle Umfeld umfasst[83]. Ursprünglich war wohl, wie oben erwogen, auch in I Kor 12,13 das genus-relatierte Feld repräsentiert. Die Taufe, die die Einverleibung in den Leib Christi bewirkte, führte, gemäß dieser Formel, zwar nicht zur Gleichartigkeit, wohl aber zur Gleichwertigkeit

---

ferner IDEM, *Adv. Prax.*, 26,9: „*Nam nec semel sed ter ad singula nomina in personas singulas tinguimur.*" („Denn nicht nur einmal, sondern dreimal werden wir eingetaucht zu jedem der drei Namen und auf jede der drei Personen"). Text und Übers. in H. J. SIEBEN, Tertullian, *Adversus Praxean*, 232–233.

77 So PETERSON, *1. Korinther*, 293; FEE, *First Corinthians*, 603; E. DINKLER, „Taufaussagen", 88f.

78 So schon BOUSSET, „1. Korinther", 134: „Das Wunder aber wird gewirkt durch den Geist, der bei der Taufe wirksam gegenwärtig ist und das Wasser mit seinen Kräften füllt"; ferner BEASLEY-MURRAY, *Baptism*, 167; HARTMAN, ‚*Auf den Namen'*, 67f.; IDEM, *'Into the Name'*, 66–68; WOLFF, *1. Korinther*, 298; LINDEMANN, *1. Korinther*, 272.

79 SCHRAGE, *1. Korinther (VII/3)*, 216; ähnlich HORN, *Angeld*, 173.

80 So z.B. HERMANN, *Kyrios*, 79–81; H. HALTER, *Taufe*, 590 Anm. 9; CONZELMANN, *1. Korinther*, 258: „Der Christusleib ist in Beziehung auf die ‚Glieder' präexistent"; SCHRAGE, *1. Korinther (VII/3)*, 216; vgl. SCHNELLE, *Gerechtigkeit*, 121, 141; HORN, *Angeld*, 173.

81 So z.B. SCHNACKENBURG, *Heilsgeschehen*, 23–25; WOLFF, *1. Korinther*, 298; O. HOFIUS, „Gemeinschaft", 211 Anm. 39; LINDEMANN, *1. Korinther*, 271, zitiert unten in Anm. 85.

82 So ZELLER, *1. Korinther*, 397.

83 Vgl. KOCH, „Christen als neue Randgruppen", 361: „Wenn für diese neue religiöse Bewegung der Grundsatz galt: Hier ist weder Jude noch Grieche (Gal 3,28, vgl. 1Kor 12,13), dann bedeutet das den programmatischen Verzicht auf den Zusammenhang von ethnischer und religiöser Identität, der für jüdische Synagogengemeinden, jedenfalls in ihrer bisherigen Gestalt, schlechterdings unverzichtbar war". Vgl. ferner H. MOXNES, „From Theology to Identity", 271–273.

zwischen den verschiedenen, bisweilen oppositionellen Gruppen innerhalb der Gemeinde[84].

Formgeschichtlich kann diese Taufformel „Wiedervereinigungsformel" („Reunification Formula") genannt werden, wenn man den Nachdruck auf die Glieder 2–3/[3a] legt. Legt man aber das Gewicht auf die einschließenden Zeilen 1 und 4, dürfte die Bezeichnung „Eingliederungsformel" der übergreifenden Funktion besser entsprechen, weil hier von der Eingliederung (aller Glieder) εἰς ἓν σῶμα durch die Taufe die Rede ist[85]. Inhaltlich und strukturell steht sie der „Bekleidungsformel" (Gal 3,26–28) nahe. Bezüglich des „Sitzes im Leben" der vorgeformten Tauformeln, ist es methodisch notwendig mit Udo Schnelle festzustellen, dass der primäre „Sitz im Leben" in der Liturgie nicht identisch sein muss mit dem „Sitz in der Literatur"[86], d.h. in diesem Falle mit dem Argumentationsgang im 1. Korintherbrief. Der konkrete text-externe „Sitz im Leben" dürfte genau wie der der „Bekleidungsformel" (Gal 3,26–28) in der vorgeprägten Taufliturgie beheimatet sein[87]. Die Funktion der Formel war allerdings anders als in der „Bekleidungsformel": Sie war nicht an die Neugetauften gerichtet, sondern wie die „Identifikationsformel" deren *eigene* Taufaffirmation. Sie ist somit als ihr „soziales Urbekenntnis" auszusprechen, und zwar in diesem Fall als Bestätigung des Empfangs der Gabe bzw. der Mitwirkung des Geistes bei der Taufe, und bringt so die Eingliederung der Neugetauften in den Leib Christi (εἰς ἓν σῶμα), d.h. in die Kirche[88], bzw. ihren eschatologischen Status vor Gott zum Ausdruck[89].

Wir haben also folgende *Differenzen* gegenüber der „Namensformel" festzustellen: (1.) eine ganz andere Struktur, (2.) eine andere Terminologie, (3.) eine andere Konzeption von der Taufe und ihrem Zweck, und (4.) einen anderen spezifischen „Sitz im Leben", nämlich als Affirmation der Neophyten nach dem Taufakt.

---

84 Vgl. SCHNELLE, *Gerechtigkeit*, 140f.; SELLIN, „Die Armen und die Reichen", 41.

85 Siehe BULTMANN, *Theologie*, 312: „Das ἐν Χριστῷ ... ist primär eine ekklesiologische Formel und bezeichnet das Eingefügtsein in das σῶμα Χριστοῦ durch die Taufe ..."; vgl. auch LINDEMANN, *1. Korinther*, 271: „εἰς bezeichnet jetzt das Ziel und möglicherweise zugleich die Folge: Taufe bedeutet Eingliederung in das σῶμα, zugleich aber auch das Entstehen jenes dann im folgenden beschriebenen Leibes"; dass diese Formel an die Taufformel βαπτίζειν εἰς τὸ ὄνομα anklingt, wie LINDEMANN, *ibid.* meint, scheint mir wenig wahrscheinlich zu sein, denn hier handelt es sich um eine „Eingliederungsformel" und nicht um eine „Namensformel". Eher steht wohl εἰς τὸ σῶμα parallel zu εἰς Χριστόν (Gal 3,27) bzw. εἰς Χριστὸν Ἰησοῦν (Röm 6,3).

86 SCHNELLE, *Gerechtigkeit*, 33.

87 Vgl. BETZ, *Galatians*, 184; IDEM, *Galaterbrief*, 325; ERIKSSON, *Traditions*, 129.

88 Vgl. SCHRAGE, *1. Korinther*, 216: „Daß ὁ Χριστός tatsächlich den Christusleib bezeichnet und dieser eine Einheit bildet, wird begründet (γάρ) mit der durch den *einen* Geist erfolgten Eingliederung in den *einen* Leib. Der Christusleib ist damit als solcher vorgegeben und nicht erst das Resultat menschlichen Sozialisations- und Einheitsstrebens der einzelnen Glieder".

89 Siehe HARTMAN, *„Auf den Namen"*, 68.

1.3. Die Bestätigung an die Neugetauften – Die „Rechtfertigungsformel"

Auch in I Kor 6,11 findet sich eine vorgeprägte Taufformel, die hinsichtlich ihrer Form dem „soteriologischen Kontrast-Schema" zugerechnet werden kann und die nach einer leichten Rekonstruktion aufgrund des Ko-Textes etwa wie folgt aussieht[90]:

1. [*ἄδικοι ἦτε,*[91]]
2. ἀλλὰ ἀπελούσασθε[92],
3. ἀλλὰ ἡγιάσθητε,
4. ἀλλὰ ἐδικαιώθητε
5. ἐν τῷ ὀνόματι τοῦ κυρίου Ἰησοῦ Χριστοῦ[93]
6. καὶ ἐν τῷ πνεύματι τοῦ θεοῦ ἡμῶν.

1. [*Ihr wart Ungerechte*]
2. aber ihr habt euch abwaschen lassen,
3. ja, ihr seid geheiligt worden,
4. ja, ihr seid gerechtgesprochen worden
5. im Namen des Herrn Jesus Christus
6. und im Geist unseres Gottes.

Auch diese Formel zeigt, zusätzlich zum „Kontrastschema", einige „Wiederholungsformen" (*repetitio*) auf, wenn auch nicht so variierend wie in 12,13:

---

90 Dieser Taufformel liegt das „soteriologische Kontrast-Schema zugrunde: ... ‚Ihr wart einst – jetzt aber seid ihr/... hat Gott (Christus) euch'", vgl. dazu N. A. DAHL, „Formgeschichtliche Beobachtungen", 5f.; vgl. schon BULTMANN, *Theologie*, 107; ferner P. TACHAU, ‚*Einst' und ‚Jetzt'*, 83f., 86, 120f.; Tachau zeigt, dass dieses Schema auch ein „stilistisches Mittel in der klassischen Antike und im Hellenismus" war (*ibid.*, 71–78). Ferner HELLHOLM, „„Revelation – Schema'", 233–248; vgl. auch H.-U. WEIDEMANN, „Titus, der getaufte Heide", 43.

91 Die vorgeschlagene mögliche Ergänzung [*...*] entstammt den VV. 9a + 11a. Bezüglich der vorgeprägten Taufformel gilt, dass es sich bei dem Imperfekt ἦτε (vgl. Röm 6,17) nur um die „vorchristliche Existenz" (ZELLER, *1. Korinther*, 218, der allerdings „keine überlieferte Formel" annimmt) handelt. Im Kontext ändert dies sich allerdings, siehe unten ad und in Anm. 310. Vgl. SCHNELLE, *Gerechtigkeit*, 38; SCHRAGE, *1. Korinther (VII/1)*, 433: „Alles liegt am Kontrast zwischen dem *Imperfekt* ἦτε und den dreifachen ἀλλά-Sätzen [„mit den drei *Aoristformen*"], die diese Zäsur begründen" (meine Hervorhebung); ferner WEIDEMANN, „Titus, der getaufte Heide", 43.

92 Ἀπελούσασθε ist Medium in der Bedeutung „abwaschen lassen" und deutet „den freiwilligen Entschluss des Täuflings, ins Wasser zu steigen" an; so SCHRAGE, *1. Korinther (VII/1)*, 427; BDR, 262f. [§ 317]; BAUER/ALAND/ALAND, *Wörterbuch*, 192; WEISS, *1. Korinther*, 155; BOUSSET, „*1. Korinther*", 95; WOLFF, *1. Korinther*, 121; LINDEMANN, *1. Korinther*, 134; anders LIETZMANN, *1. Korinther*, 26; CONZELMANN, *1. Korinther*, 136. Die Passivform von ἀπολούω ist selten und kommt im NT nicht vor; siehe A. OEPKE, „λούω, ἀπολούω κτλ.", 306; J. YSEBAERT, *Terminology*, 63, der auch feststellt, dass hier bereits technische Taufsprache vorliegt.

93 W. KRAMER, *Christos*, 217–219: Diese „Onoma-Wendung" gehört „zum Sprachmaterial der vorpaulinischen Gemeinde". Vgl. HARTMAN „Usages – Some Notes on the Baptismal Formulae" in vorliegender Publikation, 397–413, § 2.

(1) Amplificatio   Z. 1 – 2   (*ἄδικοι ἦτε* ... ἀλλά κτλ.)
                   Z. 2 – 4   (ἀλλὰ ἀπελούσασθε, ἀλλὰ ἡγιάσθητε,
                              ἀλλὰ ἐδικαιώθητε)
(2) Anaphora   Z. 2 – 4   (ἄδικοι ... ἀλλά ... ἀλλά ... ἀλλά)
(3) Epiphora   Z. 2 – 3   (ἀλλά ... ἀλλά ... ἀλλά)
                   Z. 1 – 4   (*ἦτε* ... ἡγιάσθητε ... ἐδικαιώθητε)[94]
                   Z. 5   (τοῦ κυρίου Ἰησοῦ Χριστοῦ)
(4) Tristichon   Z. 2 – 4   (ἀλλά ... ἀλλά ... ἀλλά)
(5) Assonanz[95]   Z. 5 – 6   (ἐν τῷ ὀνόματι ... ἐν τῷ πνεύματι)

Strukturell sprechen folgende Beobachtungen für eine präformulierte Tradition:
(1.) Die dreifache ἀλλά-Konstruktion mit ihrer anaphorischen Struktur und synthetischem Parallelismus hebt sich vom Kontext ab[96]. (2.) Der lexikalische Befund mit dem bei Paulus einmaligen Verbum (ἀπολούεσθαι)[97], mit dem in der kultisch-liturgischen Tradition beheimateten Begriff ἁγιάζειν[98] und vor allem mit der eingeschobenen „Namensformel" ἐν τῷ ὀνόματι τοῦ κυρίου Ἰησοῦ Χριστοῦ weist in dieselbe Richtung. Diese Merkmale zeigen an, erstens, dass wir es aller Wahrscheinlichkeit nach mit einer vorgeformten Tradition zu tun haben, und zweitens, dass diese Formel mit der Taufe zusammengehört, obwohl hier nicht direkt von der Taufe die Rede ist[99]. Joseph Ysebaert vermutet, dass mit ἀπολούεσθαι bereits technische Taufsprache vorliegt[100]. Dies dürfte, in Ergänzung zur Seltenheit des Passivums, erklären, warum die Passivform ἀπελούθητε, die zu Epiphora bzw. Tristichon/Distichon mit *ἦτε* ... ἡγιάσθητε ... ἐδικαιώθητε vorzüglich gepasst hätte, nicht zur Verwendung kommen konnte. (3.) Das Aorist-Tempus des Verbs zeigt auf einen abgeschlossenen Akt in der

---

94   Unterbrochen von ἀπελούσασθε in Z. 2; siehe die Erklärung dafür unten.
95   Zur Assonanz siehe HELLHOLM, „Funktion", 389 Anm. 22 mit Lit.
96   Vgl. HORN, *Angeld*, 143; ZELLER, *1. Korinther*, 218 lässt unglücklicherweise die Abweichung vom Kontext unberücksichtigt.
97   Zur verbalen Taufterminologie (ἀπολούεσθαι) siehe Act 22,16; Eph 5,26; Tit 3,5; Apk 1,5; ferner zum entsprechenden substantivischen Gebrauch (ἀπολύτρωσις) siehe Röm 3,24; Kol 1,14; Eph 1,7; Hebr 9,15.
98   Vgl. H. BALZ, „ἅγιος κτλ.", 38–48. Ferner Eph 5,26a, s. E. BEST, *Ephesians*, 542; bzw. I Petr 1,2, siehe L. GOPPELT, *1. Petrusbrief*, 86.
99   Auf die Taufe deutet schon Joh. Chrys., Cat. bapt., 2/1,11 (R. KACZYNSKI, *Johannes Chrysostomos, Cat. bapt.,* 166–169). Siehe auch SCHNACKENBURG, *Heilsgeschehen*, 1–3; BULTMANN, *Theologie*, 138f.; BEASLEY-MURRAY, *Baptism*, 163; CONZELMANN, *1. Korinther*, 137; SCHNELLE, *Gerechtigkeit*, 39; HORN, *Angeld*, 143–147. Vgl. LINDEMANN, *1. Korinther*, 140, der auf OrSib VIII 315f. verweist: ἀθανάτου πηγῆς ἀπολουσάμενος ὕδατεσσιν τὰς πρότερον κακίας ἵνα γεννηθέντες ἄνωθεν („tilgend im Wasser unsterblichen Quells ihrer früheren Bosheit, all der Vergangenheit Schmutz, auf dass sie, aufs neue geboren"; Text: A. KURFESS/ÜBERS.: J.-D. GAUGER, in: IIDEM, *Sibyllinische Weissagungen*, 190–191).
100 Siehe Anm. 92.

Vergangenheit, was die Taufe ja war, hin[101]. (4.) Aus formaler Hinsicht bilden die drei Verben eine Einheit und beschreiben das Taufgeschehen in seiner Totalität[102]. Dabei ist das erste ἀλλά-Glied antithetisch im Verhältnis zur negativen Vergangenheit, während die beiden folgenden ἀλλά-Glieder amplifikatorisch sind, d.h. sie bilden eine Steigerung mit ἐδικαιώθητε als Klimax[103]; deswegen auch die Übersetzung mit „aber ... ja ... ja"[104]. (5.) Die beiden abschließenden Adverbialsätze gehören je auf ihre Weise zur Traditionsschicht[105]: (a) teils durch die „Namensformel" (ἐν τῷ ὀνόματι τοῦ κυρίου Ἰησοῦ Χριστοῦ), die hier in die „Rechtfertigungsformel" integriert ist[106]; (b) teils aber auch durch die ungewöhnliche Formulierung ἐν τῷ πνεύματι τοῦ θεοῦ ἡμῶν, die sonst bei Paulus nur in I Thess 2,2 vorkommt[107]. Die Präposition ἐν hat entweder in beiden Fällen dieselbe Bedeutung, d.h. die instrumentale „durch", „vermittelst" bzw. ist als „Angabe eines Begleitumstandes" zu verstehen[108], oder sie hat verschiedene Bedeutungen, d.h. „unter Nennung des Namens"[109] in der eingefügten „Namensformel" und „in" (lokal) bzw. „durch" (instrumental) in der „Rechtfertigungsformel".

Inhaltlich baut das Traditionsstück deutlich auf dem „soteriologischen Kontrastschema von ‚Einst – Jetzt'" auf[110]. Als Kontrastbegriff zur vorchristlichen Statusangabe ἄδικοι[111] kann δικαιωθῆναι auch ethische Bedeutung haben und infolge einer Reihe von Exegeten „in *keinem* Zusammenhang mit der

---

101 Vgl. schon HEITMÜLLER, ‚*Im Namen Jesu*‘, 74; BEASLEY-MURRAY, *Baptism*, 163; SCHRAGE, *1. Korinther (VII/1)*, 433.

102 Vgl. WEISS, *1. Korinther*, 155; SCHNELLE, *Gerechtigkeit*, 39.

103 Siehe WEISS, *1. Korinther*, 156; SCHNELLE, *Gerechtigkeit*, 40; WOLFF, *1. Korinther*, 121.

104 So auch WEISS, *1. Korinther*, 156; WOLFF, *1. Korinther*, 112; LINDEMANN, *1. Korinther*, 134.

105 Vgl. SCHRAGE, *1. Korinther (VII/1)*, 428.

106 Vgl. ferner den sog. Hymnus Phil 2,11, wo die „Namensformel" (ἐν τῷ ὀνόματι Ἰησοῦ) in der Akklamation: ἵνα ... πᾶσα γλῶσσα ἐξομολογήσηται ὅτι κύριος Ἰησοῦς Χριστός aufgenommen und in diesen Hymnus integriert ist. Siehe KRAMER, *Christos*, 61–67; WENGST, *Formeln*, 132–133; VIELHAUER, *Geschichte*, 3–24. Zuletzt VOLLENWEIDER, „Hymnus", 224–225: „hymnisches Christuslob".

107 Siehe LINDEMANN, *1. Korinther*, 141; ferner HORN, *Angeld*, 144–147; vgl. BOUSSET, „1. Korinther", 95: „Daß der ‚Geist Gottes' bei der Taufe wirksam ist, war allgemein christliche Überzeugung. Die christliche Taufe ist keine einfache Wasser-Taufe, sondern eben Geistes-Taufe".

108 Instrumental: z.B. BEASLEY-MURRAY, *Baptism*, 166; SCHRAGE, *1. Korinther (VII/1)*, 434; WOLFF, *1. Korinther*, 122; THISELTON, *First Corinthians*, 455; begleitumständlich: WEISS, *1. Korinther*, 156.

109 BAUER/ALAND/ALAND, *Wörterbuch*, 1161.

110 Siehe Anm. 90.

111 Vgl. HEITMÜLLER, *Taufe*, 12: „[A]us Ungerechten wurden die korinthischen Christen Gerechte ..."; BULTMANN, *Theologie*, 138f.: Charakterisierung der sündvollen heidnischen Vergangenheit der Adressaten.

paulinischen Rechtfertigungslehre des Gal und Röm steh[en]"[112], sondern „in dem gemeinchristlichen Sinne der Sündentilgung"[113]. Die nächste Parallele zu ἀπολούεσθαι findet sich in Act 22,16: „Steh auf! Lass dich taufen (βάπτισαι) und dir deine Sünden abwaschen (ἀπόλουσαι τὰς ἁμαρτίας σου) …". Die beiden medialen Imperative haben hier kausative Bedeutung und die Reinwaschung betrifft die Sünden[114]. Eine naheliegende Parallele ist die in Eph 5,26a-b: „… um sie (d.h. die Kirche) zu heiligen (ἵνα αὐτὴν ἁγιάσῃ) durch ein Reinigungsbad im Wasser (καθαρίσας τῷ λουτρῷ τοῦ ὕδατος) und durch das Wort (ἐν ῥήματι)". Ob damit das „Taufwort"[115] oder das „Verkündigungswort"[116] gemeint ist, ist umstritten. In jedem Fall gilt die Formulierung von Nils Alstrup Dahl: „It is clear that baptism was accompanied by words (it was not a silent ritual)"[117].

Dass sich, im Kontext des 1. Korintherbriefs, das volle paulinische Rechtfertigungsverständnis einstellt, ist selbstverständlich[118]. Schon in der Formel beschreibt allerdings auch δικαιωθῆναι einen „Gnadenakt Gottes" mit der Bedeutung „ihr seid durch die in der Taufe vollzogene Reinigung wirklich ‚Gerechte' geworden, … es ist jetzt möglich, ein neues Leben in der δικαιοσύνη zu beginnen"[119]. Hier zeigt sich deutlich das Verhältnis zwischen ko-textloser und ko-textbedingter Interpretation und damit zwischen diachroner und synchroner Annäherung zu einem Text[120].

Umstritten ist die Deutung der medialen Form ἀπελούσασθε, die kausativ aufgefasst werden kann: „ihr habt euch rein waschen lassen"[121]; hierdurch wird die eigene Entscheidung ins Wasser zu steigen, um gereinigt zu werden, her-

---

112 So z.B. SCHNELLE, *Gerechtigkeit*, 40; HEITMÜLLER, *Taufe*, 12.
113 Z.B. BULTMANN, *Theologie*, 139; THYEN, *Sündenvergebung*, 147 mit Anm. 2. Anders aber offenbar BULTMANN, „ΔΙΚΑΙΟΣΥΝΗ ΘΕΟΥ", 472 bzw. „Apokalyptik", 479 (siehe Zitat unten Anm. 132);
114 Siehe CONZELMANN, *Apostelgeschichte*, 134; C. K. BARRETT, *Acts*, Vol. II, 1042f.; AVEMARIE, *Tauferzählungen*, 127f.
115 So H. HÜBNER, *An Philemon etc.*, 247; E. BEST, *Ephesians*, 543f.
116 So SELLIN, *Epheser*, 448f.
117 Siehe DAHL, „Baptism in Ephesians", bes. 420-424; BOUSSET, *Kyrios Christos*, 227: „Der Name Jesu ist geradezu das bei der Taufe (neben dem Wasser) wirksame Gnadenmittel"; G. STRECKER, *Theologie*, 96: „Es ist nicht allein das Wasser, dass in der Verbindung mit dem Geist eine eschatologische Qualität besitzt, sondern das Anrufen des Namens Jesu setzt einen neuen Tatbestand". So auch Tertullian, *De bapt.*, 2,1: „*inter pauca verba*". Vgl. FERGUSON, *Baptism*, 380-399.
118 Siehe SCHRAGE, *1. Korinther (VII/1)*, 433.
119 WEISS, *1. Korinther*, 155; ferner *ibid*.: „So enthält auch hier das rein passivische ἡγιάσθητε eine unausgesprochene Mahnung, die Heiligkeit nun auch zu verwirklichen". Vgl. SCHRAGE, *1. Korinther (VII/1)*, 433: „Dabei sind gerade hier die ‚ethischen Nebentöne und Implikationen' (BARRETT, *First Corinthians*, 142) nicht zu übersehen"; so auch ZELLER, *1. Korinther*, 219.
120 Dazu HELLHOLM, „Beatitudes", bes. 286-290, 343f.; K. BALDINGER, *Theorie*, 15-16; U. ECO, *Lector*, 17-21, 83-106 *et passim*.
121 So jetzt auch ZELLER, *1. Korinther*, 218.

vorgehoben[122]. In Übereinstimmung mit den beiden Passivformen, ziehen eine Reihe von Exegeten es jedoch vor, die Medium-Form als Passivum (genauer als *passivum divinum*) zu verstehen, was zu der Übersetzung führt: „ihr seid [von Gott] rein gewaschen worden"[123]; damit fällt der Hinweis auf die eigene Entscheidung weg und Gott wird der allein Handelnde.

Bei der medialen Deutung führt dies zur *Steigerung*: vom menschlichen Beschluss, sich taufen zu lassen, zur göttlichen Heiligung mit deren ethischen Implikationen und Konsequenzen und zur Rechtfertigung als Klimax[124].

Dies folgt aus der strukturellen Reihenfolge der Verben ἀπολούεσθαι, ἁγιασθῆναι, δικαιωθῆναι[125]. Mit Johannes Weiß kann festgestellt werden: „Das Medium (mit der Bedeutung sich abwaschen lassen) ist hier ausgezeichnet am Platze, da es sich um die Taufe handelt, bei der man sich untertaucht. ... Ebenso notwendig ist das Passivum bei ἡγιάσθητε und ἐδικαιώθητε, da es sich hier um wunderbare Wirkungen Gottes handelt"[126]. Wenn eine Steigerung vorliegt, dann gilt folgendes: Abgesehen vom medialen oder vom passivischem Verständnis von ἀπελούσασθε enthält dieser Terminus die Bedeutung „Reinigung von den Sünden des Vergangenen", also von den „*Sündenschulden*"[127]; ἡγιάσθητε (*passivum divinum*) dagegen schließt in sich eine Einverleibung in die Heiligkeitssphäre, d.h. in „die Gemeinde der Heiligen" und folglich eine Befreiung von der „*Sündenmacht*", also von der Macht, die zur weiteren Sklaverei unter der Macht der Sünde führt[128]; diese Befreiung bringt aber zugleich eine Verpflichtung zur Heiligung mit sich (vgl. Röm 6,19.22; 15,16)[129]; ἐδικαιώθητε ist wie schon oben dargelegt am schwierigsten zu deuten: Eine Reihe von Exegeten ist der Meinung, dass das Verb hier nicht die gewöhnliche forensische Bedeutung – „als gerecht hinstellen" – hat wie im Galater- und im Römerbrief[130].

---

122 So interpretieren auch WEISS, *1. Korinther*, 155; A. ROBERSTON/A. PLUMMER, *First Corinthians*, 119; SCHNACKENBURG, *Heilsgeschehen*, 2; BEASLEY-MURRAY, *Baptism*, 163; BARRETT, *First Corinthians*, 141; SCHNELLE, *Gerechtigkeit*, 39; SCHRAGE, *1. Korinther (VII/1)*, 427; WOLFF, *1. Korinther*, 121; LINDEMANN, *1. Korinther*, 134. Heruntergespielt von ZELLER, *1. Korinther*, 218, der die amplifikatorische Struktur übersieht.
123 H. LIETZMANN, *An die Korinther I/II*, 26; CONZELMANN, *1. Korinther*, 136; HARTMAN, ‚*Auf den Namen*‘, 64; IDEM, ‚*Into the Name*‘, 63; HORN, *Angeld*, 143.
124 Siehe SCHRAGE, *1. Korinther (VII/1)*, 427; ferner auch THEISSEN, „Urchristliche Taufe", 110 (zitiert unten ad Anm. 134).
125 Siehe hierzu und zum Folgenden, SCHRAGE, *1. Korinther (VII/1)*, ibid.
126 WEISS, *1. Korinther*, 155; richtiger wäre: „... bei der man sich untertauchen lässt".
127 Siehe HARTMAN, ‚*Auf den Namen*‘, 64; IDEM, ‚*Into the Name*‘, 64.
128 SCHRAGE, *1. Korinther (VII/1)*, 427–428; WOLFF, *1. Korinther*, 121; vgl. P. VON GEMÜNDEN, „Urchristliche Taufe", 130 unter Verweis auf die ‚Taufparänese ([Röm] 6,12)'.
129 Vgl. HELLHOLM, „Argumentation", 175.
130 BULTMANN, *Theologie*, 271–275; SCHNELLE, *Gerechtigkeit*, 40; HEITMÜLLER, *Taufe*, 12.

Vielmehr sei hier der „gemeinchristliche Sinn der Sündentilgung" gemeint[131]. Dadurch, dass im letzten Glied des synthetischen Parallelismus innerhalb der „Rechtfertigungsformel" das mediale ἀπελούσασθε mit dem passivischen ἐδικαιώθητε als *passivum divinum*-Formulierung ersetzt ist, wird klargestellt, dass hier nicht mehr lediglich der Beschluss des Gläubigen, sich von den Sünden reinigen zu lassen, sondern vielmehr der Beschluss Gottes, die Sündenmacht zu brechen und den Ungerechten (ἄδικος) gerecht (δίκαιος) zu machen, ins Zentrum gerückt wird[132]. Hierdurch wird offenbar, dass wir es mit einer *Steigerung* innerhalb der dreistelligen Anapher dieser präformulierten „Rechtfertigungsformel" zu tun haben: von der Tilgung früherer Sünden zur Befreiung von der Sünde als Machtfaktor bis hin zur Gerechtsprechung Gottes[133]. Auf diese Weise kommt nun auch lexikalisch das „soteriologische Kontrastschema" (μὲν ποτέ … νυνὶ δέ), also: „vorher wart ihr Ungerechte … jetzt aber seid ihr Gerechtgemachte" klar zum Ausdruck. In dieser Formel bestätigt sich somit die Formulierung Gerd Theissens: „Obwohl allen bewusst ist, dass sie [sc. die Taufe] auf einem Willensakt des Menschen basiert, wird sie zugleich als ‚Erwählung', ‚Berufung', kurz als ein unverfügbares Handeln Gottes gedeutet"[134].

Formgeschichtlich handelt es sich um eine hellenistisch-judenchristliche „Rechtfertigungsformel"[135], die bestätigend über die gerade getauften Neophyten ausgesprochen wurde. Hierdurch wird ihre neugewonnene Situation *coram Deo* deutlich gemacht, d.h. Reinigung der Sündenschuld, Befreiung von der Sündenmacht, Einverleibung in die Gemeinschaft der Heiligen (οἱ ἅγιοι) sowie die endgültige Bekräftigung ihrer von Gott erteilten Rechtfertigung.

Wir haben folgende *Differenzen* gegenüber der „Namensformel" bzw. der „Eingliederungsformel" festzustellen: (1.) eine ganz andere Struktur mit Steigerung und eingebauter „Namensformel", (2.) eine andere ungewöhnliche Terminologie, (3.) eine andere Konzeption von der Taufe und ihrem Zweck und (4.) einen anderen spezifischen „Sitz im Leben", nämlich eine Anrede nach dem Taufakt mit Adresse an die Neugetauften seitens des Täufers oder eines Helfers.

---

131 BULTMANN, *Theologie*, 139; LOHSE, „Taufe und Rechtfertigung" 323; IDEM, *Römer*, 80; THYEN, *Sündenvergebung*, 147 mit Anm. 2. So anscheinend auch WEIDEMANN, „Titus, der getaufte Heide", 43, wenn er im Kommentar zur Synopse von 1 Kor 6,11 und Tit 3,3 schreibt: „Auffällig ist, dass in Tit 3 – anders als in 1 Kor 6,11 – Taufe, Geistgabe, Rechtfertigung und Erbschaft mit einer Variante des (vor-)paulinischen ‚Basissatzes' [‚Gerechtfertigt ohne Werke' (42) –DH] kombiniert sind (meine Hervorhebung).

132 Siehe auch BULTMANN, „ΔΙΚΑΙΟΣΥΝΗ ΘΕΟΥ", 472: „Entsprechend bedeutet δικαιωθῆναι von Gott gerechtgesprochen bzw. gerecht gemacht worden sein …"; IDEM, „Apokalyptik" 479: „Das δικαιωθῆναι der Glaubenden ist nach Röm 5,1; 8,30; 1Kor 6,11 doch schon erfolgt".

133 Siehe LOHSE, „Taufe", 323; ferner oben zu Anm. 132. Gegen FITZMYER, *First Corinthans*, 258, der die Ansicht vertritt, dass „[t]he three effects are simply mentioned with no chronological or logical order among them".

134 THEISSEN, „Urchristliche Taufe", 110.

135 Siehe HORN, *Angeld*, 144, 257; SCHNELLE, *Gerechtigkeit*, 42.

1.4. Der Heilszuspruch an die Neugetauften – Die „Bekleidungsformel"

Im Galaterbrief, dessen Datierung von etwa 50/51 bis 55/56 n.Chr. schwankt[136], finden wir noch eine andere Taufformel vor, nämlich 3,26–28, die Paulus offenbar zitiert[137]. Die Struktur dieser Formula hat Hans Dieter Betz sehr schön herausgearbeitet[138]:

1. πάντες γὰρ υἱοὶ θεοῦ ἐστε [διὰ πίστεως] ἐν Χριστῷ Ἰησοῦ·
2. ὅσοι γὰρ εἰς Χριστὸν ἐβαπτίσθητε, Χριστὸν ἐνεδύσασθε.
3. οὐκ ἔνι Ἰουδαῖος οὐδὲ Ἕλλην,
4. οὐκ ἔνι δοῦλος οὐδὲ ἐλεύθερος,
5. οὐκ ἔνι ἄρσεν καὶ θῆλυ·
6. πάντες γὰρ ὑμεῖς εἷς ἐστε   ἐν Χριστῷ Ἰησοῦ.

1. Denn ihr alle seid Söhne/Kinder Gottes [durch den Glauben] in Christus Jesus.
2. Denn ihr alle, die ihr auf Christus getauft seid, habt Christus angezogen.
3. Da ist nicht Jude noch Grieche,
4. Da ist nicht Sklave noch Freier,
5. Da ist nicht männlich und weiblich;
6. Denn ihr alle seid einer   in Christus Jesus.

Auch diese Formel zeigt mehrere „Wiederholungsformen" (*repetitio*) auf, wenn auch etwas anders angeordnet als diejenigen in I Kor 6,11 und 12,13.

(1) Inclusio   Z. 1 – 6 (πάντες γάρ … ἐν Χριστῷ Ἰησοῦ)
(2) Anaphora   Z. 3 – 4 (οὐκ ἔνι … οὐδέ *bis*)

---

136 Siehe Betz, *Galatians*, 12 und 103; idem, *Galaterbrief*, 51 und 196f.: Also vor oder etwa gleichzeitig mit dem 1. Korintherbrief; ähnlich D. Lührmann, „Galaterbrief", 451; Koester, *Introduction*, 122: Am Anfang des Aufenthalts in Ephesus etwa 52–53, vor dem 1. Korintherbrief; Kümmel, *Einleitung*, 266: 54–55; Vielhauer, *Geschichte*, 110: 54–56; J. L. Martyn, *Galatians*, 19f.: Vor dem 1. Korintherbrief; Vouga, *Galater*, 11: 49–52 oder 52–54. Für ein späteres Datum nach dem 1. und 2. Korintherbrief und kurz vor dem Römerbrief, siehe z.B. G. Luedemann, *Paul Apostle*, 85, 90–92, 99, 263: 50/53 aber nach dem I Kor und gleichzeitig mit dem II Kor; H. W. Boers, „Context for Interpreting Paul", 434f.: Nach dem 1. und 2. Korintherbrief und kurz vor dem Römerbrief; D. Sänger, „Adresse", 39: „… später als die korinthische Korrespondenz"; Schnelle, *Einleitung*, 114: „unmittelbar vor dem Röm im Spätherbst 55"; J. Becker, *Galater*, 16: 55–56; Koch, „Barnabas", 316f.: Nach dem 1. Korintherbrief; Wolff, *1. Korinther*, 429: I Kor 16,1f. ist eine frühere Instruktion als der Brief an die Galater.

137 Siehe Betz, „The Literary Composition", 371 [87]; idem, „Ritual", 107 [261]; idem, *Galatians*, 181–185; idem, *Galaterbrief*, 320–327. Hartman, „*Auf den Namen*", 8–10; idem, '*Into the Name*', 1–3. Vgl. auch Bouttier, „Complexio Oppositorum", 1–19; Schnelle, *Gerechtigkeit*, 57–62, 191–195; Martyn, *Galatians*, 378–380. Zu den divergierenden Deutungen in der alten Kirche siehe M. Meiser, *Galater*, 165–175.

138 Betz, „Spirit, Freedom, and Law", bes. 147f.; deutsche Fassung als „Geist, Freiheit und Gesetz", 80–81 [48–50]; idem, *Galatians*, 181f.; idem, *Galaterbrief*, 320f.; Schnelle, *Gerechtigkeit*, 58f.; Hartman, „*Auf den Namen*", 8–10; idem, '*Into the Name*', 1–3; Martyn, *Galatians*, 378–380; Hellholm, „Impact", 152; Becker, *Galater*, 59f.; Koch, „Crossing the border", 213. Anders, aber nicht überzeugend, H. Paulsen, „Einheit und Freiheit", bes. 77 [24]; kritisch dazu Schnelle, *Gerechtigkeit*, 192 Anm. 227.

		Z. 1 – 6	(πάντες γάρ ... πάντες γάρ)
(3)	Epiphora	Z. 1 – 6	(Ἰησοῦ ... Ἰησοῦ)
(4)	Monostichon	Z. 2 – 2	(Χριστόν ... Χριστόν)
	auf Distanz	Z. 3 – 4	(οὐκ ἔνι ... οὐδέ *bis*)
(5)	Distichon	Z. 3 – 4	(οὐκ ἔνι ... οὐδέ)
(6)	Tristichon	Z. 3 – 5	(οὐκ ἔνι ... οὐκ ἔνι ... οὐκ ἔνι)
(7)	Assonanz	Z. 1 – 6	(ἐν Χριστῷ Ἰησοῦ ... ἐν Χριστῷ Ἰησοῦ)
(8)	Homoiotel.	Z. 1 – 6	(ἐν Χριστῷ Ἰησοῦ ... ἐν Χριστῷ Ἰησοῦ)

Diese Formel ist sicherlich älter als der Galaterbrief selbst, was (1.) durch den unmotivierten Wechsel von der 1. Pers. Pl. in V. 25 zur 2. Pers. Pl. in V. 26, (2.) durch die *Inclusio* zwischen den Zeilen 1 und 6, (3.) durch die spezifische Terminologie (ἐνδύεσθαι) sowie (4.) durch die beiden aus argumentativer Sicht überflüssigen Zeilen 4 und 5 bestätigt wird[139]. (5.) Jürgen Becker hat außerdem auf ähnliche Formulierungen in I Kor 7,18–22; 12,13; Kol 3,11 und Joh 17,21 hingewiesen[140]. Im Gegensatz zu Lars Hartman[141] muss festgestellt werden, dass wir es hier nicht mit der Formula „im oder auf den Namen des Herrn Jesus" zu tun haben[142]; ferner können wir auch beobachten, dass hier kein Hinweis auf einen Täufer, weder auf Paulus noch auf irgendjemanden sonst, vorliegt. Die Kurzformel εἰς Χριστὸν ἐβαπτίσθημεν könnte möglicherweise als Kurzform der Formulierung ἐν τῷ σώματι Χριστοῦ ἐβαπτίσθημεν, der wir in I Kor 12,13 begegnen, interpretiert werden[143], sollte jedoch wohl eher als traditionelle Formulierung mit polysemischer Bedeutung angesehen werden[144]. In diesem Heilszuspruch wird von Christus „anziehen" im Zusammenhang mit der Taufe gesprochen[145]. Alle diejenigen, die auf Christus getauft sind, haben Christus angezogen. Hier wird Christus als der kosmische Mantel, oder der kosmische Mensch verstanden[146]. Dieser kosmische Mensch ist gewissermaßen auch als die Kirche (vgl. allerdings hierzu den oben erwähnten Begriff σῶμα) interpretiert. Also gilt: alle diejenigen, die auf Christus getauft sind, haben eine göttliche Transformation

---

139 MARTYN, *Galatians*, 376.

140 BECKER, *Galater*, 60.

141 HARTMAN, „*Auf den Namen*", 57; IDEM, '*Into the Name*', 56.

142 Siehe BULTMANN, *Theologie*, 311f.; BETZ, *Galatians*, 186; IDEM, *Galaterbrief*, 328; MARTYN, *Galatians*, 375f.; VOUGA, *Galater*, 90f.; HELLHOLM, „Argumentation", 151–153.

143 SCHRAGE, *1. Korinther (VII/3)*, 216. Anders LINDEMANN, *1. Korinther*, 271: „In der Formulierung klingt die Tauformel βαπτίζειν εἰς τὸ ὄνομα an [...]."

144 Siehe Anm. 229.

145 Vgl. BETZ, *Galatians*, 188; IDEM, *Galaterbrief*, 332: „Die übertragene Sprache des Bekleidens findet sich schon im Alten Testament, aber Parallelen für das ‚Anziehen' eines Erlösers gibt es nur in den Mysterienreligionen und im Gnostizismus".

146 S. mit reichem religionsgeschichtlichen Parallelmaterial bes. DAHL, „Kleidungsmetaphern", 389–411. Englische Übers. als N. A. DAHL/D. HELLHOLM, „Garment-Metaphors", 139–158.

und Inkorporation in Christus[147], d.h. in die Kirche erlebt; deshalb gilt: „Alle seid ihr *einer* in Christus Jesus" (πάντες γὰρ ὑμεῖς εἷς ἐστε ἐν Χριστῷ Ἰησοῦ)[148]. Dieser „Bekleidungsformel" zufolge hat also die Taufe eine „einheitsstiftende Funktion" ἐν Χριστῷ Ἰησοῦ; als Kinder Gottes haben sie „einen Status, der unabhängig von ihrem Status in der Gesellschaft ist"[149].

Formgeschichtlich ist diese vorgeformte Komposition von Betz[150] als „Makarismus" bezeichnet worden. Aber im Hinblick darauf, dass ausgerechnet das Word μακάριος/οι oder ihre Äquivalente (z.b. ὄλβιος/οι) fehlen, möchte ich die Formel lieber als „Taufruf"[151] oder baptismalen „Heilszuspruch"[152] oder möglicherweise als „Taufmakarismus" bezeichnen. Dieser „Taufruf" oder „Heilszuspruch" wurde, wie die Vergangenheitstempora zeigen, erst nach dem Taufakt gesprochen und zwar vom *Täufer* oder von assistierenden *Diakonen/Diakoninnen* bzw. *Presbytern* (vgl. I Kor 1,14–16[153]; *Didasc. Apost.*, III 12[154]; *TA* 21.16–17; Epiphanius, *Panarion*, III 79.3,6 = PG 42:744D), wie die 2. Pers. Pl. (ὑμεῖς) anzeigt[155]. Was über dem Täufling ausgesprochen wurde, ist mit Gerhard Sellin

---

147 Bezüglich der Transformation als Teil eines Christwerdens, siehe HELLHOLM, „Funktion", 395f., 407, 411, MOXNES, „From Theology to Identity", 271–273 und CHR. STRECKERS Beitrag in dieser Publikation, „Taufrituale im frühen Christentum und in der Alten Kirche", 1381–1438, § 3.1.

148 Das maskuline Pronomen εἷς mag auf Christus, auf den lebendigen Menschen Bezug nehmen, siehe BETZ, *Galatians*, 200f.; IDEM, *Galaterbrief*, 352; MARTYN, *Galatians*, 377; VOUGA, *Galater*, 92; DAHL/HELLHOLM, „Kleidungsmetaphern", 392f.; IIDEM, „Garment-Metaphors", 144f. Siehe ferner Eph 4,22.24; Kol 3,9f.; NHC II.3: *EvPhil* 75,21–24: „Das lebendige Wasser ist ein Leib. Es ist nötig, daß wir den lebendigen Menschen anziehen. *Zu dem Zweck* entkleidet sich, wer zum Wasser herabsteigt, daß er jenen anziehe" (Übers. H.-M. SCHENKE in: *Nag Hammadi Deutsch*. 1. Band, 207); *ActThom* 48: καὶ ἀποδύσωνται τὸν παλαιὸν ἄνθρωπον σὺν ταῖς πράξεσιν αὐτοῦ, καὶ ἐνδύσωνται τὸν νέον κτλ. („und sie mögen den alten Menschen mit seinen Taten aus- und den neuen Menschen anziehen etc.").

149 THEISSEN, „Urchristliche Taufe", 104.

150 BETZ, *Galatians*, 183; IDEM, *Galaterbrief*, 323f.

151 SCHNELLE, *Gerechtigkeit*, 58f.: „Es handelt sich [...] auch bei Gal 3,26–28 um einen Taufruf, der die neue Situation des Getauften vor Gott definiert".

152 BECKER, *Galaterbrief*, 60.

153 Vgl. die Vermutung von WEISS, *1. Korinther*, 21: „Im allgemeinen scheint also P[aulus] den Vollzug der Taufe seinen Genossen (Silvanus und Timotheus) überlassen zu haben".

154 Text: F. X. FUNK (Hg.), *Didascalia et constitutiones apostolorum*, Vol. I, 208ff. Lat. Text und deut. Übers. in: P. GUYOT/R. KLEIN, *Das frühe Christentum*, Band II, 10–11, 241; FERGUSON, *Baptism*, 436–440. Siehe den Beitrag von A. LINDEMANN, „Zur frühchristlichen Taufpraxis" in dieser Publikation, 767–816, § 3.2.

155 Siehe BETZ, *Galatians*, 181f., 184; IDEM, *Galaterbrief*, 320f., 325f.: „In der Liturgie mag der Spruch dazu gedient haben, die neu Initiierten zu belehren, ihnen von ihrem eschatologischen Status vor Gott im Vorgriff auf das Jüngste Gericht zu erzählen und ihnen mitzuteilen, welchen Einfluß dieser Status auf ihr soziales, kulturelles und religiöses Selbstverständnis und ihre Verantwortung im Hier und Jetzt hat bzw. welche Veränderungen er herbeiführt"; BECKER, *Galater*, 59: „[...] Der Apostel (bedient sich) eines festgeprägten gottesdienstlichen Zuspruchs, wie er wohl nach Bekenntnis (etwa 1. Kor 8,6) und Taufe den soeben Getauften zugesprochen wurde"; so auch MARTYN, *Galatians*, 379.

aller Wahrscheinlichkeit nach „eine ekklesiologische Maxime der antiochenischen Urgemeinde"[156], was in der Tat auch ein „soziales Urbekenntnis" als Teil der Inkorporation der Neophyten in die Kirche darstellt[157].

Wir haben also folgende *Differenzen* gegenüber der „Namensformel" bzw. der „Eingliederungsformel" und der „Rechtfertigungsformel" festzustellen: (1.) eine ganz andere Struktur, z.T. abgesehen von der „Eingliederungsformel", (2.) eine andere Terminologie, z.T. abgesehen von der „Eingliederungsformel", (3.) eine andere Konzeption von der Taufe und ihrem Zweck und (4.) einen anderen spezifischen „Sitz im Leben", nämlich nach dem Taufakt mit Adresse an die Neugetauften seitens des Täufers oder eines Helfers.

Von einer Entwicklung des Taufverständnisses bei Paulus[158] kann allein aus chronologischen Gründen kaum die Rede sein, da beide Briefe etwa gleichzeitig geschrieben worden sind und die chronologische Reihenfolge sich nicht eindeutig feststellen lässt[159].

1.5. Die Taufaffirmation der Neugetauften – Die „Identifikationsformel"

In seinem Beitrag zum Sammelband *Paul in His Hellenistic Context* hebt Betz hervor, dass die exegetische Diskussion der letzten Jahre gezeigt hat, dass die Interpretation der Taufe in Römer 6 immer noch große Probleme von außerordentlicher Komplexität mit sich bringt[160]. Seine These ist es, dass Paulus erst hier sein volles Verständnis der christlichen Taufe entwickelt hat: „My thesis is that he did not fully develop it before Romans"[161]. Dies setzt zweierlei voraus: (1.) dass der Römerbrief viel später als I Kor und Gal anzusetzen ist[162] und (2.) dass man wohl mit keinen vorgeformten Tauftraditionen im Römerbrief rechnen kann[163],

---

156 Diese ‚ekklesiologische Maxime' passt gut zu den Verhältnissen in der Gemeinde in Antiochien, ehe die von Jakobus Gesandten dort eintrafen und Petrus und Barnabas sich von Paulus abgrenzten. Siehe BECKER, *Paulus*, 110–119, 283; N. WALTER, „Vorstellungen", 173–195; KOCH, „Crossing the border", 213–231.

157 SELLIN, „Armen", 29–44, 40; bezüglich des antioch. Ursprungs, siehe bes. BECKER, *Galater*, 60.

158 So BETZ, „Ritual", 106 [260].

159 Vgl. CONZELMANN, *1. Korinther*, 18 Anm. 31: „Das zeitliche Verhältnis von 1Kor und Gal ist nicht sicher festzustellen". Siehe ferner oben Anm. 136.

160 BETZ, *ibid.*, 84 [240].

161 BETZ, *ibid.*, 107 [261]. Vgl. schon SCHNACKENBURG, „Todes- und Lebensgemeinschaft", 42.

162 Zur Datierung des Römerbriefs, siehe z.B. KÜMMEL, *Einleitung*, 272: Frühjahr 55–56; KOESTER, *Introduction*, 111, 142: Winter 55–56; VIELHAUER, *Geschichte*, 175: Frühestens 56, spätestens 59; SCHNELLE, *Einleitung*, 130: Frühjahr 56; DUNN, *Romans 1–8*, xliii: „late 55/early 56 or late 56/early 57"; FITZMYER, *Romans*, 87: „the mid or the late fifties"; LOHSE, *Römer*, 42: Im Jahr 56; JEWETT, *Romans*, 21: 56–57; POKORNÝ/HECKEL, *Einleitung*, 303: 56.

163 BETZ, „Ritual", 107 [261]: „In fact, what Paul presents in Romans 6 is a complete reinterpretation of the older formula of Gal 3.26–28".

was mir allerdings wenig wahrscheinlich scheint[164]. Klar ist auf alle Fälle, dass in Römer 6 die Taufe als eine „Schicksalsgemeinschaft mit Christus" dargestellt wird[165]. Dies ist im Zusammenhang mit der Taufe in der Tat neu! Insofern ist Betz's Beurteilung korrekt. Bedeutet dies aber, dass wir hier mit einer Entwicklung bei Paulus rechnen müssen? Auch in diesem Falle denke ich wohl kaum[166], selbst dann – bzw. gerade dann –, wenn Paulus, wie ich für wahrscheinlich halte, an der Entstehung der zu rekonstruierenden Taufformel selber beteiligt war[167].

Die „Schicksalsgemeinschaft" hat ihren Grund in der doppelten christologischen *Pistis*-Formel, die Paulus in I Kor 15,3–5 zitiert[168]:

(1) ὅτι Χριστὸς ἀπέθανεν ὑπὲρ τῶν ἁμαρτιῶν ἡμῶν κατὰ τὰς γραφὰς
(1a) καὶ ὅτι ἐτάφη καὶ
(2) ὅτι ἐγήγερται τῇ ἡμέρᾳ τῇ τρίτῃ κατὰ τὰς γραφὰς
(2a) καὶ ὅτι ὤφθη Κηφᾷ (εἶτα τοῖς δώδεκα)·

(1) Dass Christus gestorben ist für unsere Sünden gemäß den Schriften
(1a) und dass er begraben worden ist, und
(2) dass er auferweckt wurde am dritten Tage gemäß den Schriften
(2a) und dass er erschienen ist dem Kephas (danach den Zwölf).

Diese Formel ist ein Zweizeiler (1+2) und gibt den Tod und die Auferstehung Christi als den wesentlichen Inhalt des christlichen Glaubens an. Hinzugefügt sind zwei komplementäre Zeilen (1a+2a), die interkaliert sind. Diese komple-

---

164 So bereits HEITMÜLLER, „Paulus", 335 [141]; BULTMANN, *Theologie*, 142–146; so auch N. GÄUMANN, *Taufe*, 47ff., 73ff.; SCHNELLE, *Gerechtigkeit*, 80f., und G. STRECKER, *Theologie*, 174.

165 Zur ausführlichen Analyse von Röm 6, siehe meine Studie HELLHOLM, „Argumentation". Siehe nunmehr auch THEISSEN, „Kreuz als Sühne", 451–453: „Conformitas der Christen mit Chrisus"; A. DETTWILER, „Enthousiasme", 279–296, bes. 281–289. Zur Auslegung von Römer 6 im Frühchristentum, siehe R. SCHLARB, *Wir sind mit Christus begraben*.

166 Vgl. in Bezug auf die Rechtfertigung das Zitat aus Lohse oben in Anm. 9 und in Bezug auf das Gesetzesverständnis BECKER, *Paulus*, 419: „Weil Paulus sich sogleich bei seiner Berufung vor einen Grundsatzentscheid in der Gesetzesfrage gestellt sah, wird man also beim Gesetzesverständnis dem Apostel keine Entwicklung unterstellen können. Seine Position ist im wesentlichen anfangs seiner antiochenischen Jahre ausgebildet. Man kann hinzufügen: Es hat auch wenig Sinn, zwischen Gal und Röm noch Spuren einer Entwicklung angezeigt zu sehen. Die Unterschiede bestehen wohl nur aus polemischen Akzenten, wie sie den Gal prägen, und Vertiefungen, wie sie der Röm enthält". Ebenso SÄNGER, „Adressaten", 272: „Der in Gal 2,16 zum Ausdruck gebrachte Kerngedanke der Rechtfertigungslehre … hatte sich Paulus schon lange vor der Zeit seiner literarischen Wirksamkeit erschlossen …"; *ibid.*, 273: die „rechtfertigungstheologisch grundierte Erstverkündigung in den galatischen Gemeinden … ha[t] für den Apostel konstitutive Bedeutung und gehör[t] zur Tiefenstruktur des paulinischen Denkens"; ferner HAHN, *Theologie I*, 245f.

167 Zur Ausbildung und Bildung des Paulus, siehe T. VEGGE, *Paulus und das antike Schulwesen*.

168 Siehe z.B. KRAMER, *Christos*, 15–40; WENGST, *Formeln*, 92–104; CONZELMANN, „Zur Analyse", 131–141; IDEM, *1. Korinther*, 305–309; IDEM, *Grundriß*, 50f.; THYEN, *Sündenvergebung*, 152–154; G. STRECKER, *Theologie*, 80–82; WOLFF, *1. Korinther*, 355–370; LINDEMANN, *1. Korinther*, 328–333; SCHRAGE, *1. Korinther (VII/4)*, 18ff.; E. BRADSHAW AITKEN, *Jesus' Death*, 28–33; FITZMYER, *First Corinthians*, 541–549; ZELLER, *1. Korinther*, 461–469.

mentären Zeilen von Christi Begräbnis und Erscheinung sind da, um seinen Tod und seine Auferweckung zu bekräftigen. Auf diese Weise entsteht ein augenscheinlicher Vierzeiler[169].

Diese *Pistis*-Formel wurde aller Wahrscheinlichkeit nach im *Taufunterricht* verwendet[170] und ist demzufolge natürlich älter als der 1. Korintherbrief. Im 1. Korinther dient diese essentielle (ἐν πρώτοις) Tradition (ὁ καὶ παρέλαβον)[171] als Erinnerungsangabe (γνωρίζω) von dem, was Paulus den Korinthern bei der Gründung der Gemeinde mitgeteilt hatte (παρέδωκα ὑμῖν ἐν πρώτοις)[172]. Im Ko-text des Briefes wird sie als gemeinchristliche Basis der paulinischen Argumentation für den Glauben an die Auferstehung von den Toten gebraucht[173].

Wenn wir nun diese *Pistis*-Formel dem Text von Römer 6,3–4 gegenüberstellen, wird die Parallelität beider Texte ersichtlich[174]. Mit Werner Kramer stellen wir demzufolge fest, dass „[d]ie Erörterung der Bedeutung der Taufe in R[öm] 6,2–9 [...] ja nichts anderes als die Aufarbeitung der Pistisformel (ist)"[175].

---

169 Vgl. einerseits LINDEMANN, *1. Korinther*, 329, der aus formalen Gründen die Formel mit ὤφθη Κηφᾷ enden lässt; so auch H. CONZELMANN/A. LINDEMANN, *Grundriß*, 50; G. STRECKER, *Theologie*, 80; FITZMYER, *First Corinthians*, 541, 549f.; andererseits SCHRAGE, *1. Korinther (VII/4)*, 20, der εἶτα τοῖς δώδεκα als Teil der ursprünglichen Formel rechnet; so auch CONZELMANN, *1. Korinther*, 301; WOLFF, *1. Korinther*, 358; VIELHAUER, *Geschichte*, 18; W. PRATSCHER, *Herrenbruder Jakobus*, 31; ZELLER, *1. Korinther*, 468. Unentschieden FEE, *First Corinthians*, 723: Paulus habe vielleicht ein ursprüngliches καί in εἶτα geändert.

170 So KRAMER, *Christos*, 59f.; VIELHAUER, *Geschichte*, 21f.; WOLFF, *1. Korinther*, 360f.; KOCH, „Zwölferkreis", 112: „katechetische Fundamentalaussage"; SÄNGER, „Ewiges Leben", 49; ZELLER, *1. Korinther*, 461f.: In der judenchristlich-hellenistischen Gemeinde formuliert (462) und Paulus im Taufunterricht in Damaskus überliefert (461). So schon HEITMÜLLER, „Paulus", 331f. [136–137]; ferner B. HEININGER, „Von der Jugendweihe zur Taufe", 252: Did 7,1–4; Justin, 1. Apol. 61,2; Hebr 6,1–2. Für Damaskus plädiert auch STRECKER/NOLTING, „Der vorchristliche Paulus", *passim*. Anders LINDEMANN, *1. Korinther*, 330; unentschieden SCHRAGE, *1. Korinther (VII/4)*, 18.

171 So bes. SCHRAGE, *ibid.*, 31f.

172 So auch LINDEMANN, *ibid.*, 329–330.

173 Vgl. SCHRAGE, *ibid.*, 27, 72; SÄNGER, „Ewiges Leben", 50 mit Anm. 6.

174 So bereits A. SEEBERG, *Katechismus*, 52ff., 176; ferner E. LARSSON, *Christus als Vorbild*, 56, und G. WAGNER, *Das religionsgeschichtliche Problem*, 302; ferner GÄUMANN, *Taufe*, 61–65; LOHSE, „Wort und Sakrament", 50; IDEM, *Römer*, 187; THYEN, *Sündenvergebung*, 202f.; HELLHOLM, „Argumentation", 157, 161; H. KLEIN, „Gegenwart des neuen Lebens", 64. Anders KÄSEMANN, *Römer*, 156: „Wunschdenken".

175 KRAMER, *Christos*, 60, ferner *ibid.*, 24: „Im Hintergrund von R[öm] 6,3–9 steht eine analoge Formel (sc. 1K[or] 15,3–5), allerdings *aufgesplittert und elementweise in den Verlauf der Argumentation eingestreut*" (meine Hervorhebung).

1 Kor 15,3–5	Römer 6,3–4/[8]
(1) ὅτι Χριστὸς ἀπέθανεν ...	εἰς τὸν θάνατον αὐτοῦ ἐβαπτίσθημεν
(1a) καὶ ὅτι ἐτάφη καὶ	συνετάφημεν αὐτῷ διὰ τοῦ βαπτίσματος
	εἰς τὸν θάνατον,
(2) ὅτι ἐγήγερται ...	ἵνα ὥσπερ ἐγέρθη Χριστὸς ἐκ νεκρῶν
(2a) καὶ ὅτι ὤφθη Κηφᾷ	οὕτως καὶ [*συζῶμεν αὐτῷ*][176]
(εἶτα τοῖς δώδεκα)	{ἡμεῖς ἐν καινότητι ζωῆς
	περιπατήσωμεν}[177].

Aufgrund dieser Synopse sind wir in der Lage, die Parallelität der Aussagen in beiden Texten zu erkennen. Diese Parallelität findet sich aber ausschließlich in den Passagen im Römer 6, wo Paulus *explizit* von der Taufe spricht, d.h. in den Versen 3–4 sowie in den Versen 5 und 8. Besonders hervorzuheben ist hier die spezielle Formulierung der Zeile 2a. Die Bekräftigungszeilen (1a) und (2a) der *Pistis*-Formel finden sich auch in Römer 6, aber hier weicht die zweite Bekräftigungszeile vom Credo-Text ab, insofern als sich die Bestätigung nicht im ontologischen, sondern im ethischen Bereich ereignet. Der Beweis dafür, dass der Christ an der Auferstehung Christi teil hat, ist in der Tat sein neues Leben hier und jetzt[178]. Die rekonstruierte ontologische Formulierung *συζῶμεν αὐτῷ*, hier ergänzend eingetragen, ist dem vorgeformten V. 8b entnommen.

Wenn Paulus argumentiert, ob im 1. Korinther- oder im Galaterbrief, legt er – wie wir schon gesehen haben – seiner Argumentation Traditionsformeln zugrunde. Nun entsteht deshalb die Frage, ob das auch für seine Argumentation in Römer 6 gilt[179]. Diese Frage ist nicht so einfach zu beantworten, denn anscheinend hat Paulus hier eine eventuelle Taufaffirmation aus argumentativen Gründen zerlegt, sodass diese Traditionsformel rekonstruiert werden muss[180].

Im Folgenden soll versucht werden, eine solche Rekonstruktion zu unternehmen. Ein erster allumfassender Versuch wurde von Walter Schmithals in seinem Römerbriefkommentar vorgelegt[181]:

---

176 Eine alternative Ergänzung findet sich bei SCHNELLE, *Gerechtigkeit*, 77: οὕτως καὶ ἡμεῖς ἐκ νεκρῶν ἐγερθῶμεν, in Anlehnung an BULTMANN, *Theologie*, 143.

177 { ... } gibt paulinisches Interpretament *ad hoc* an.

178 Vgl. SELLIN, „Auferstehung", 228–230 [44–45].

179 Vgl. LINDEMANN, *Paulus*, 116: „... Röm 6,1–11 macht – wie andere Abschnitte des Röm auch – den Eindruck eines nicht ad hoc geschriebenen, sondern bereits vorformulierten Textes".

180 So auch S. VOLLENWEIDER, *Freiheit*, 328, der freilich bezweifelt, dass Paulus hier eine einheitliche Formel zitiert. Vgl. die ähnlich komplizierte Verfahrensweise des Paulus beim Zitieren der Formel in Röm 3,2(4)5–26a; siehe hierzu z.B. BULTMANN, *Theologie*, 49; VIELHAUER, *Geschichte*, 22; WENGST, *Formeln*, 87–91; DUNN, *Romans 1–8*, 163f.; W. KRAUS, *Heiligtumsweihe*, 20, 92; LOHSE, *Römer*, 133; JEWETT, *Romans*, 270f.; KOCH, „Crossing the border", 221f.; ferner in Bezug auf die Zersplitterung der Pistisformel siehe KRAMER, *Christos*, 24 (Zitat in Anm. 175).

181 W. SCHMITHALS, *Römerbrief*, 191: „Jede der vier Zeilen dieses Textes besteht aus 5 griechischen Wörtern, wie sonst ein Hinweis auf ein festes Traditionsstück. ... Unter dieser Voraussetzung aber bekommen V.3 + V.(5)8 den Charakter eines Zitats, und wir begegnen damit einem → 1,2f.;

(1) Wie viele wir getauft sind in Christus Jesus, in seinen Tod sind wir getauft. (V. 3)
(2) Wenn wir aber gestorben sind mit Christus, so glauben wir, dass wir auch leben werden mit ihm. (V. 8)

Mein Versuch ist einerseits komplizierter, demzufolge natürlich auch hypothetischer[182], andererseits einfacher, weil ohne Zählung von Wörtern, und besteht aus den unten angegebenen Strophen, wobei ich zur Annahme geneigt bin, dass πιστεύομεν ὅτι im Argumentationsverlauf des Paulustextes getilgt worden ist[183]. Dann käme in der ursprünglichen „Identifikationsformel" πιστεύομεν ὅτι in beiden Strophen in Form einer durch Inklusion entstandenen *amplificatio* vor (πιστεύομεν ὅτι ... bzw. πιστεύομεν ὅτι καὶ ...).

Nach diesem im Argumentationsverlauf getilgten meta-kommunikativen Satz[184] fährt die Formel mit dem korrelativen Pronom. ὅσος fort und lautet[185]:

(Ia) 1. 〚*πιστεύομεν ὅτι*〛 ὅσοι
2. ἐβαπτίσθημεν
3. εἰς Χριστὸν Ἰησοῦν,
4. εἰς τὸν θάνατον αὐτοῦ
5. ἐβαπτίσθημεν· (V. 3)[186]

→ 3,25; → 4,24b.25; → 5,21 vergleichbaren Phänomenen: Paulus greift Lehrgut auf, das seinen Adressaten in Rom aus ihren östlichen Heimatgemeinden vertraust ist, und er legt es seiner eigenen Ausführung als verbindlich zugrunde ...".

182 Vgl. HELLHOLM, „Argumentation", 161. Für 6,3a und/oder 6,3b als Teil einer vorgeformten Tradition, siehe, u.a., BULTMANN, *Theologie*, 143f.; THYEN, *Sündenvergebung*, 202; KÄSEMANN, *Römer*, 157; P. SIBER, *Mit Christus leben*, 191ff., 217f.; SCHNELLE, *Gerechtigkeit*, 76. Für 6,8 als eine vorgeprägte Tradition, siehe HAHN, „Taufe und Rechtfertigung", 109 [255]; IDEM, *Theologie I*, 281f.; so auch DUNN, *Romans 1–8*, 322. – Siehe ferner oben Anm. 176.

183 Siehe z.B. Röm 10,9 in der Rekonstruktion der Pistisformel von VIELHAUER, *Geschichte*, 15: πιστεύομεν ὅτι ὁ θεὸς ἤγειρεν Ἰησοῦν ἐκ νεκρῶν. Vgl. CONZELMANN, „Christenheit", 107–119; ferner WENGST, *Lieder*, 45f.; KRAMER, *Christos*, 25, der auf I Thess 4,14 aufmerksam macht: „εἰ γὰρ πιστεύομεν ὅτι Ἰησοῦς ἀπέθανεν καὶ ἀνέστη, ... Dass wir auch diese sachlich analoge Formel Pistisformel nennen dürfen, wird bewiesen durch das 1Th[ess] 4,14 gegebene Stichwort πιστεύομεν ὅτι: Sterben und Auferstehen (bzw. Auferwecktwerden) stellen den Inhalt des Glaubens dar"; ferner T. HOLTZ, *1. Thessalonicher*, 190.

184 Dass Paulus bei der Einfügung vorgeformter Traditionen kurze Aussagen, u.a. von meta-kommunikativem Charakter, die vorangestellt waren, tilgen musste, ist nicht nur wahrscheinlich, sondern öfters geradezu erforderlich; vgl. zu Röm 3,25 etwa LOHSE, *Römer*, 133: „Ursprünglich muß eine kurze Aussage vorangegangen sein, an die der Relativsatz dann angehängt werden konnte, etwa: Gelobt sei Jesus Christus o. ä." Siehe ferner oben Anm. 180 und Anm. 183.

185 Vgl. die ähnliche Formulierung in der „Bekleidungsformel" Gal 3,27: ὅσοι γὰρ εἰς Χριστὸν ἐβαπτίσθητε. Siehe BDR, 252 [§ 304,1]: ὅσοι = πάντες οἵ. VIELHAUER, *Geschichte*, 12. Ein weiterer Versuch, eine vorgeformte Tradition in Röm 6 zu rekonstruieren, stammt von H. KLEIN, der allerdings auf die präsentischen Aussagen in Kol 2,12 und 3,1 rekurriert (IDEM, „Gegenwart", 78 Anm. 8).

186 In V. 3 ist eine chiastische Struktur erkennbar, wie JEWETT, *Romans*, 392 im Anschluss an J. D. HARVEY, *Listening*, 128 und P. A. HOLLOWAY, „Paul's Pointed Prose", 51 bemerkt.

(Ib) 6. συνετάφημεν οὖν αὐτῷ
      7. διὰ τοῦ βαπτίσματος
      8. εἰς τὸν θάνατον·[187] (V. 4a)

(IIa) 9. εἰ γὰρ σύμφυτοι γεγόναμεν
      10. τῷ ὁμοιώματι τοῦ θανάτου αὐτοῦ,
      11. ἀλλὰ[188] καὶ [τῷ ὁμοιώματι][189]
      12. τῆς ἀναστάσεως ἐσόμεθα. (V. 5)

(IIb) 13. εἰ δὲ ἀπεθάνομεν σὺν Χριστῷ,
      14. πιστεύομεν ὅτι καὶ συζήσομεν αὐτῷ· (V. 8)

(I)   ⟦*Wir glauben, dass*⟧
      wir alle, die wir in Christus Jesus getauft worden sind,
      in seinen Tod getauft worden sind. (V. 3)
      Wir sind also mit ihm durch die Taufe
      in Bezug auf den Tod begraben. (V. 4a)

(II) Wenn wir nämlich verbunden sind mit der Gleichgestalt seines Todes,
      werden wir es gewiss auch mit [der] seiner Auferstehung sein. (V. 5)
      Wenn wir aber mit Christus gestorben sind,
      dann glauben wir auch, dass wir mit ihm leben werden. (V. 8)

Auch in dieser Formel finden sich einige rhetorische Stilmittel wie *Inclusio*, Steigerung (*amplificatio*), Chiasmus und „Wiederholungsformen" (*repetitio*), wenn auch z.T. anderer Art und in anderem Ausmaß als in den vorher behandelten.

(1) Amplificatio Z. I – II   (Tod ... Auferstehung)
                  Z. IIa – IIb ([τῷ ὁμοιώματι] τῆς ἀναστάσεως ἐσόμεθα ...
                                συζήσομεν αὐτῷ)
                  Z. 4 – 6   (Tod ... Begräbnis)
                  Z. 9 – 12   (Tod ... Auferstehung: ἀλλὰ καί)

---

187 Die Präposition εἰς versteht CHR. STRECKER, *Liminale Theologie*, 185 im *finalen* Sinne „zum Tod", wobei „die Aussage συνετάφημεν ... εἰς τὸν θάνατον [...] auf den Tod als Zielpunkt des Begrabenwerdens an[spielt]". Vom Kontext her liegt m.E. allerdings eine *relationale* Bedeutung näher: „mit Rücksicht auf", „in Bezug auf", „hinsichtlich", „wegen" (vgl. BAUER/ALAND/ALAND, *Wörterbuch*, 463 s.v. 5; *LSJ*, 491 s.v. VI; MENGE/GÜTHLING, *Wörterbuch*, 210, s.v. 3 c). In diesem Falle führt nicht das Begräbnis zum Tod, sondern der Tod zum Begräbnis; vgl. SCHNELLE, *Gerechtigkeit*, 82; B. FRID, „Römer 6", 197; THEISSEN, *Religion*, 189 Anm. 17. Die Liminalität wird teils durch den metaphorischen Gebrauch von θάνατος, teils durch die Futurformen ἐσόμεθα und συζήσομεν trotzdem zum Ausdruck gebracht! Siehe unten ad Anm. 211.

188 Zu ἀλλὰ in der Bedeutung „ja sogar", „erst recht", siehe BDR, 378 [§ 448,6]; BAUER/ALAND/ALAND, *Griechisch-deutsches Wörterbuch*, 75, s.v. ἀλλά 4; hier mit „gewiss" wiedergegeben. Ferner J. D. G. DUNN, *Romans 1–8*, 318; R. JEWETT, *Romans*, 401; SELLIN, „Auferstehung", 44 Anm. 17: „ ... ,wenn nämlich ... dann aber *auch*' ...".

189 Die meisten Kommentatoren verstehen V. 5b als eliptisch und setzen τῷ ὁμοιώματι ergänzend voraus, siehe z.B. GÄUMANN, *Taufe*, 79; DUNN, *Romans 1–8*, 318; HAHN, *Theologie II*, 514; LOHSE, *Römer*, 190; R. JEWETT, *Romans*, 401.

		Z. 1 - 14	(Tod ... Auferstehung: πιστεύομεν ὅτι ...πιστεύομεν ὅτι καί)
		Z. 13 -14	(ἀπεθάνομεν σὺν Χριστῷ ... καὶ συζήσομεν αὐτῷ)
(2)	Inclusio	Z. 1 - 14	(*πιστεύομεν ὅτι* ... πιστεύομεν ὅτι καί)
(3)	Chiasmus	Z. 2 - 5	(ἐβαπτίσθημεν ... εἰς ... εἰς ... ἐβαπτίσθημεν)
(4)	Anaphora	Z. 2 - 5	(ἐβαπτίσθημεν ... ἐβαπτίσθημεν)
		Z. 3 - 4	(εἰς ... εἰς)
(5)	Epiphora	Z. 2 - 5	(ἐβαπτίσθημεν ... ἐβαπτίσθημεν)
		Z. 13 - 14	(σὺν Χριστῷ ... συζήσομεν αὐτῷ)
(6)	Distichon	Z. 4 - 8	(εἰς τὸν θάνατον ... εἰς τὸν θάνατον)
		Z. 9 - 13	(εἰ γάρ ... εἰ δέ)
(7)	Tristichon	Z. 2 - 7	(ἐβαπτίσθημεν ... ἐβαπτίσθημεν ... βαπτίσματος)

Im Unterschied zu Schmithals habe ich zuerst in Ergänzung zu V. 3 auch V. 4a in die vorgeformte Tradition aufgenommen, weil hier die Rede vom Begräbnis vorkommt (συνετάφημεν)[190]. Außerdem habe ich in Bezug auf das Auferstehungsmotiv nicht nur V. 8 berücksichtigt, sondern auch V. 5 aufgenommen[191] aufgrund der auffälligen Futurformen in beiden Versen: ἐσόμεθα (V. 5) und συζήσομεν (V. 8)[192]. Diese beiden Verbformen haben immer wieder Probleme bei der Exegese bereitet, bes. im Hinblick auf die paulinische Argumentation im Römerbrief. Außerdem finden sich zwei auffällige Lexeme in V. 5: σύμφυτοι ist im NT singulär und ὁμοίωμα kommt ausgerechnet in dem vorgeformten Hymnus Phil 2,6–11, V. 7[193] sowie in der „urchristliche(n) Bekenntnisaussage", der

---

[190] Für V. 4a als traditionelles Gut, siehe auch SCHNELLE, *Gerechtigkeit*, 76; H. UMBACH, *In Christus getauft*, 242, 247.

[191] V. 5a ist auch Teil von H. Kleins Rekonstruktion, siehe oben Anm. 185.

[192] Siehe U. WILCKENS, *Römer (VI/2)*, 15; SELLIN, „Auferstehung", 44. Vgl. auch die liturgische Formel II Tim 2,11(-13): εἰ γὰρ συναπεθάνομεν, καὶ συζήσομεν mit dem futuralen Tempus συζήσομεν; hierzu siehe z.B. L. R. DONELSON, *Pseudepigraphy*, 150. G. LOHFINK, „Vermittlung", 177–180 und I. H. MARSHALL, *Pastoral Epistles*, 732f., der der Meinung sind, dass das Traditionsstück unabhängig von Röm 6,8 ist. L. OBERLINNER, *Pastoralbriefe (I/2)*, 82–85, der allerdings auf die Futurform nicht eingeht, sowie A. WEISER, *2. Timotheus*, 153–154, 172–173 denken beide an eine Verschmelzung von unterschiedlichen Traditionen, die z.T. durch Röm 6,8 beeinflußt sind; vgl. schon LINDEMANN, *Paulus*, 139: „Das einleitende πιστὸς ὁ λόγος läßt den nachfolgenden Text als autoritatives Traditionsgut erscheinen; diese Tradition aber ist eine Mischung vor allem aus Röm 6,3f.8 und Röm 3,3". Siehe auch I Thess 4,17 und 5,10 mit den Bemerkungen von HAHN, „Taufe und Rechtfertigung", 110 mit Anm. 58 [256 Anm. 58]; IDEM, *Theologie I*, 282: „Der eschatologische Horizont von Röm 6,5.8 ist auch kennzeichnend für den sonstigen Gebrauch der Wendung ‚mit Christus' (σὺν Χριστῷ) die aus dem Zusammenhang der Aussagen über die Heilsvollendung stammt (vgl. dazu 1 Thess 4,14fin. 17b; 5,10b; 2 Kor 4,14; 13,4; Phil 1,23; 3,21), und dann auf die Taufe und das Leiden mit Christus bezogen wurde (vgl. Röm 8,17; 2 Kor 7,3; Gal 2,19)". Vgl. den Beitrag von TOR VEGGE, „Baptismal Phrases in the Deuteropauline Epistles" in vorliegender Publikation, 497–?, § 4.2.

[193] Siehe R. C. TANNEHILL, *Dying and Rising*, 35–39; LOHSE, *Römer*, 231.

sog. „Sendungsformel", in Röm 8,3 vor[194]. Entgegen meinem früheren Versuch[195] habe ich hier die Reihenfolge der Verse 5 und 8 beibehalten: (1.) weil die zukünftige Verbindung mit Christi Auferstehungsgestalt dem Leben mit ihm logisch vorangeht (*amplificatio* in Form einer *Epiphrase*[196]), (2.) weil die σύν-Aussagen eine abschließende Steigerung bedeuten und (3.) weil der meta-kommunikative Satz πιστεύομεν ὅτι eine *Inclusio* mit dem entsprechenden aber im Kontext getilgten meta-kommunikativen Satz am Anfang der Formel bildet. Durch diese *Inclusio* wird auch lexikalisch an die *Pistis*-Formel angeknüpft[197]. Durch die Beibehaltung der Reihenfolge wird außerdem die hypothetische Rekonstruktion um einen Schritt reduziert.

Im Übrigen sollte nicht übersehen werden, dass der Begriff „Sünde" (ἁμαρτία) in der rekonstruierten Formel *nicht* begegnet[198]. In Paulus' eigener Argumentation spielt ἁμαρτία gewiss eine äußerst bedeutungsvolle, ja sogar auslösende Rolle (vgl. 6,1), in der „Identifikationsformel" dagegen überhaupt nicht[199]. Das Thema der Formel ist – wie die σύν-Aussagen nicht nur in den VV. 5a und 8b, sondern auch in V. 4a bzw. V. 3 (ἐβαπτίσθημεν εἰς τὸν θάνατον αὐτοῦ) anzeigen – die „Schicksalsgemeinschaft zwischen Christus und den Getauften", nicht aber die „Vergebung der Sünden", eine Aussage, die in der „Identifikationsformel" den Parallelismus zwischen Christus und den Christen (Phil 2,8; Röm 5,19[200]; II Kor 5,2[201]) kompliziert, wenn nicht sogar unmöglich gemacht hätte. Die aoristischen bzw. perfektischen (Tod) wie eschatologischen (Auferstehung) σύν-Aussagen sowohl im *negativen* ersten Teil (1) als auch im *positiven* zweiten Teil (2) sind ein zusätzlicher Grund für die oben gegebene Rekonstruktion[202]. Das Verhältnis zwischen V. 3 und V. 4a ist amplifikatorisch,

---

194 Siehe TANNEHILL, *ibid.*; LOHSE, *ibid.*; zur vorgeformten „Sendungsformel", siehe KRAMER, *Christos*, 108–112; E. SCHWEIZER, „Zum religionsgeschichtlichen Hintergrund", 83–95; IDEM, „Was meinen wir eigentlich", 204–224; VOLLENWEIDER, *Freiheit*, 302f., 359f.

195 HELLHOLM, „Impact", 157f.

196 Vgl. PLETT, *Einführung*, 37.

197 KRAMER, *Christos*, 15–40.

198 Vgl. TH. ZAHN, *Römer*, 297: Er bemerkt zutreffend, was ausschließlich auf die „Identifikationsformel", nicht aber auf die Paulusargumentation zutrifft, nämlich „daß der Tod Jesu hier nicht unter dem Gesichtspunkt seiner Bedeutung als Sühnemittel und Bedingung des Schulderlasses betrachtet wird, sondern unter dem Gesichtspunkt des Gedankens, daß er sowohl für Jesus selbst als rücksichtlich seiner Wirkung auf die Christen das Ende eines bisherigen und den Übergang zu einem neuen Leben bedeutet".

199 Hier zeigt sich nochmals deutlich das Verhältnis zwischen ko-textloser und ko-textbedingter Interpretation und damit zwischen diachroner und synchroner Annäherung an einen Text; siehe ferner oben ad Anm. 120 und unten ad Anm. 312.

200 HELLHOLM, „Universalität", 246–252.

201 BULTMANN, *2. Korinther*, 166–167.

202 Bezüglich der σύν-Aussagen und ihrer traditionshistorischen Differenzierung in eschatologische, sakramentale, und Leidenskonzepte, siehe die Feststellung in SCHNELLE, *Gerechtigkeit*,

insofern als die σύν-Aussage in V. 4a (συνετάφημεν) die Todes-Aussage (εἰς τὸν θάνατον αὐτοῦ) in V. 3b verstärkt, ganz in Analogie zu I Kor 15,4[203].

Wenn Schmithals' oder meine Rekonstruktion einigermaßen zutreffen, dann würden wir ein zusätzliches Zeugnis für die Verwendung von Traditionsmaterial bei Paulus an Stellen besitzen, wo er es für nötig hält, sich auf ein Einverständnis mit seinen Adressaten zu berufen, wie in Gal 3 und in I Kor Kapp. 1, 6, 11, 12 und 15[204].

Bemerkenswert in Römer 6 ist die Sprache von der Schicksalsgemeinschaft zwischen Christus und den getauften Christen. In dem direkt vorangehenden Ko-text hat Paulus schon herausgestellt, dass alle die, die der Sünde gestorben sind, nicht mehr (ἔτι) in der Sünde leben (V. 2). Wenn Paulus in den VV. 3ff. die Tauftradition aufbringt, dann wechselt er von der 2. Pers. Pl. (ἢ ἀγνοεῖτε) zurück zur 1. Pers. Pl. (ὅσοι ἐβαπτίσθημεν) und erwähnt außerdem – wie schon bemerkt – die Sünde nicht, bis er in V. 6 auf sie wieder zu sprechen kommt.

Laut des *ersten Teils* der Tauffaffirmation funktioniert offenbar die Taufe zu allererst als Bestätigung für den Tod der Christen, genauso wie Christi Begräbnis als ein *signum necessarium* für seinen Tod dient (VV. 3–4a). Dieses *signum* kann allerdings kaum als αἴτιον bzw. *causa* aufgefaßt werden[205]. Vielmehr ist die Taufe ein Zeichen dafür, dass der alte Mensch, was sein *vorheriges Leben* ohne Schicksalsgemeinschaft mit Christus betrifft, tot ist, genauso wie Christi Begräbnis ein Zeichen seines Todes ist, nicht aber die Ursache dafür: jedesmal wenn jemand getauft worden ist, kann man also schließen, dass diese Person tot ist von ihrem früheren Leben, da ihr Tod durch die Taufe bekräftigt worden ist[206]. Es kommt also implizit zu einem doppelten Todesverständnis: Tod der Christen bezüglich des Lebens ohne Christus, ohne Gabe des Geistes – leiblicher Tod am Ende des Lebens[207]. In V. 4a folgt die Implikation, dass

---

206 Anm. 397: „Die Überführung und damit Ausweitung der Vorstellung als Bezeichnung der bereits gegenwärtigen Teilhabe an der Auferstehung ist nicht einfach organisch aus der apokalyptischen Vorstellung abzuleiten …, sondern muß als eigenständige theologische Leistung des vor- bzw. nebenpaulinischen Christentums angesehen werden, was insbesondere die Exegese von Röm 6 zeigt".

203 Siehe H. Umbach, *In Christus getauft*, 243; gegen Gäumann, *Taufe*, 74f.

204 Siehe Kl. Wegenast, *Verhältnis*, bes. 51–92 und Conzelmann, „Paulus und die Weisheit", bes. 178; Conzelmann/Lindemann, *Grundriß*, 46–57, 178–181; U. Luz, „Aufbau", 172f.

205 Gegen Schnelle, *Gerechtigkeit*, 206 Anm. 396; begrenzt Chr. Strecker, *Liminale Theologie*, 185. Siehe Hellholm, „Argumentation", 156.

206 Vgl. K. Niederwimmer, „*Pax Dei*", 296: Die Christen sind zum „inneren Frieden" gelangt „durch den Gehorsamsakt des Glaubens und ratifiziert durch das Sakrament der Taufe"; Theissen, „Kreuz als Sühne und Ärgernis", 453: „Der Tod wird … durch das Begräbnis definitiv"; idem, „Urchristliche Taufe", 105: „Das Begräbnis aber ist nicht der Tod selbst, sondern bestätigt ihn. Der Tod ist schon vorausgesetzt".

207 Vgl. Johannes Chrysostomos, *Cat. bapt.*, 2/2, 5. Bezüglich Röm 6,5 erklärt Johannes: „Er (sc. Paulus) sagt nicht ‚in seinem Tod', sondern ‚in der Ähnlichkeit (ὁμοίωμα) mit seinem Tod'. Denn beides ist Tod, aber nicht Tod derselben Sache: Das eine nämlich ist Tod des Leibes, das

der Tod und das Begräbnis der Christen nicht möglich wären, wenn Christus nicht gestorben und begraben worden wäre. Dies ist der *negative* Aspekt der Affirmation!

Erst im *zweiten Teil* der Affirmationsformel begegnen wir dem *positiven* Aspekt, dem Leben der Christen mit Christus[208]. Wiederum können wir feststellen, dass die Schicksalsgemeinschaft zwischen Christus und den Getauften durch die σύν-Aussagen hervorgehoben wird. An dieser Stelle aber bricht die Parallelität zwischen Christus und den Christen auseinander, insofern als Christus von den Toten erweckt worden ist, während die Christen noch in der Hoffnung harren, dass sie einst mit ihm in seiner Auferstehung vereint werden (V. 5) bzw. mit ihm leben werden (V. 8)[209]. Auch hier liegt indirekt ein doppeltes Verständnis vor: „Gegenwärtig ist das neue Leben seit der Taufe. Zukunft hingegen bleibt die ἀνάστασις der Christen. ‚Auferstehung der Leiber' wird nun zu einem zweiten Akt nach der Verleihung von Leben, nach der Gabe des Geistes"[210]. Oder, wie Petra von Gemünden es zum Ausdruck bringt, der Christ befindet sich „im Zustand der Liminalität – er ist nach Rom 6:3–5 zwar in der Taufe mit Christus begraben, jedoch steht für ihn – anders als für Christus – die Auferstehung von den Toten noch aus"[211].

Dieser Bruch im Parallelismus ist verschiedenartig erklärt worden: (1) Die Futurformen seien als logische zu beurteilen[212]; dann aber liegt kein Bruch vor. (2) Die Futurformen seien im Hinblick auf die pneumatisch-enthusiastischen

---

andere Tod der Sünde; deswegen spricht er von der Ähnlichkeit mit seinem Tod" (Text und Übers. KACZYNSKI, *Johannes Chrysostomus, Cat. bapt.*, 206f.). Ähnlich Cyrill von Jerusalem, *Myst. Cat.*, II,5: „Wir starben nicht wirklich, wir wurden nicht wirklich begraben, wir sind auch nicht wirklich als Gekreuzigte auferstanden, sondern die Nachahmung geschah im Bild, das Heil aber in Wirklichkeit" – οὐκ ἀληθῶς ἀπεθάνομεν, οὐδ' ἀληθῶς ἐτάφημεν, οὐδ' ἀληθῶς σταυρωθέντες ἀνέστημεν, ἀλλ' ἐν εἰκόνι ἡ μίμησις, ἐν ἀληθείᾳ, δὲ ἡ σωτηρία. (Text und Übers. RÖWEKAMP, *Cyrill von Jerusalem, Mystagogicae Catecheses*, 116–117). Siehe das analoge Verhältnis in der positiven Bewertung in und ad Anm. 209–211.

208 Siehe unten ad Anm. 324.
209 Vgl. CHR. STRECKER, *Liminale Theologie*, 187: „Diese liminale Bewährungssituation, in der das Alte vergangen ist und das Neue lediglich proleptisch in der Erneuerung der Lebensführung greifbar wird, endet erst mit der vollen Teilhabe an Christi Auferstehung bei der Parousie, ..."; ferner N. R. PETERSEN, „Baptism", 226.
210 SELLIN, „Auferstehung", 229–230 [45].
211 VON GEMÜNDEN, „Urchristliche Taufe", 135.
212 So z.B. SCHNACKENBURG, *Heilsgeschehen*, 33; J. SCHNEIDER, *Taufe*, 47; LARSSON, *Christus als Vorbild*, 70f.; BEASLEY-MURRAY, *Baptism*, 139; THYEN, *Sündenvergebung*, 206ff.; H. SCHLIER, *Römer*, 196; FITZMYER, *Romans*, 435. JEWETT, *Romans*, 406 versteht die Futurform συζήσομεν in V. 8 als eine logische, die Futurform ἐσόμεθα in V. 5 aber als eine eschatologische (*ibid.*, 402).

Phänomene, die Paulus in Korinth, wovon er den Brief schreibt, erfahren hat, in erster Linie als „eschatologische Vorbehalte" zu verstehen[213].

Keine dieser Erklärungen ist zufriedenstellend[214]. Die Begründung dafür werde ich bei der Erörterung der paulinischen Argumentationsstrategie in Römer 6 vorlegen. Falls Schmithals' oder eher noch meine Rekonstruktion einer vorgeformten Tauftradition in diesem Kapitel zutrifft, dann waren die Futurtempora Teil einer schon existierenden Tauftradition, einer Tradition, die von eschatologischen Vorstellungen beeinflusst war und welche eine Differenz zwischen Christi Auferstehung und der der Christen zu gewahren wusste[215]. Dies ist nun in der Tat ein schwieriges Problem für Paulus bei seiner Argumentation im Römerbrief.

Auch in diesem Falle halte ich den antiochenischen Ursprung der Formel für wahrscheinlich, denn dort ist Paulus, wie Eduard Lohse zutreffend bemerkt, „mit dem hellenistischen Christentum des syrischen Raumes in Berührung gekommen (Gal 1,17). Dort wurde die Taufe zwar gleichfalls (sc. wie in der palästinensischen Urgemeinde) geübt, aber in der Bedeutung verstanden, daß der Täufling mit dem Geschick des Todes und der Auferstehung Christi verbunden werde. Mit diesem Verständnis suchten die frühchristlichen Gemeinden den Sinn der Taufe so zu beschreiben, daß sie in der synkretistischen Welt verständlich gemacht werden konnte"[216]. Das würde wohl bedeuten, dass Paulus mit solchen theologischen Überlegungen schon zu Beginn seiner Tätigkeit in Berührung gekommen war bzw. sich selber daran beteiligt hatte[217].

Wenn die Taufe, d.h. der *Ritus*, ein Teil des Christwerdens war, dann kann kein Zweifel daran bestehen, dass die jeweiligen Tauformeln als *Mythus* das Gegenstück dazu ausmachten[218]. Das nahe Verhältnis zwischen den beiden Teilen des Kultes ist nach meiner Darstellung oben hoffentlich deutlich gewor-

---

213 So schon PETERSON, *Römer*, 189; bes. aber CONZELMANN, „Die Schule des Paulus", 91. A. STANDHARTINGER, *Studien*, 139f. rechnet zwar mit „vorliegende[r] Tradition", meint aber *ibid.* sowie 145, dass Paulus die traditionsgeschichtlich ursprünglichere Form mit der „Tradition der vollständigen Analogie" ... „(ὥσπερ οὕτως καὶ ἡμεῖς ἐκ νεκρῶν ἐγερθῶμεν)", wie sie in Kol 2,11f. zu finden ist, ins Futurische verändert hat. Dies ist m.E. wenig wahrscheinlich, siehe unten Anm. 330. Eine eher korrekte Beurteilung findet sich in den Ausführungen von HAHN, „Taufe und Rechtfertigung", auf die oben in Anm. 192 hingewiesen wurde.
214 Siehe auch SELLIN, „Auferstehung", 229 [45].
215 So z.B. N. GÄUMANN, *Taufe*, 79; SCHNELLE, *Gerechtigkeit*, 83; WILCKENS, *Römer (VI/2)*, 15, 18; KÄSEMANN, *Römer*, 161; DUNN, *Romans 1–8*, 318; LOHSE, *Römer*, 192; JEWETT, *Romans*, 402.
216 LOHSE, *Römer*, 188; vgl. ferner unten Anm. 220–221.
217 Anders BETZ, „Ritual", bes. 86–100 [242–254].
218 Vgl. hierzu nur HARTMAN, „Auf den Namen", 10–13; IDEM, „Into the Name", 3–8. Zur Definition siehe WIDENGREN, *Religionsphänomenologie*, 150: „Der Mythus ist das natürliche Kompliment des Ritus. Während der Ritus die heilige Handlung ist, ist der Mythus das heilige Wort, das der Handlung folgt und diese erklärt".

den[219]. Wie Betz richtig festgestellt hat, besteht in dieser Hinsicht eine große Ähnlichkeit mit den Mysterienkulten[220]. Wenn Schnelle, nach Verweis auf zwei Goldblättchen aus dem 4. Jh. v.Chr. sowie auf Apuleius, *Metamorphosen* XI 23,8 und Firmicus Maternus, *De Errore Profanarum Religionum* 22,1, feststellt, dass „eine Verbindung zwischen diesen Texten und Röm 6,3f. ... in der Vorstellung einer Identifikation des Mysten mit dem Schicksal der Gottheit (besteht)", so zeigt dies, dass die in Röm 6 verarbeitete „Identifikationsformel" zwar keine genealogische, wohl aber zumindest eine teilweise (weil ohne *Tauf*rituale!) analoge Vorstellung in den „Mysterienkulte(n) als kulturgeschichtliches Umfeld" hat[221].

Viel diskutiert ist die Bedeutung des Lexems ὁμοίωμα. Am wahrscheinlichsten ist die Deutung James D. G. Dunns, die das Faktum wahrnimmt, dass „[ὁμοίωμα] is regularly used to denote the form of transcendent reality perceptible to man"[222], was heißt, dass der Ausdruck εἰ γὰρ σύμφυτοι γεγόναμεν τῷ ὁμοιώματι τοῦ θανάτου αὐτοῦ impliziert, dass das Verbundensein (σύμφυτοι) „is with the likeness of Christ's death (which is equivalent to fusion with Christ in his death ..., but not to fusion with Christ by means of the likeness of his death)"[223]. Noch stringenter Gerd Theißen, der feststellt, dass Paulus mit der „‚Gleichgestalt' nicht etwa die Taufe als Abbild des Todes Jesu (meint). Vielmehr denkt er an eine *conformitas* zwischen einem inneren Geschehen in den Christen und dem Sterben und Auferstehen des Christus"[224]. Diese Interpretation bedeutet auch, dass ein *direkter* Bezug zum rituellen Taufvorgang im negativen wie im positiven Auferstehungsteil der „Identifikationsformel" fehlt; ein *indirekter* ist des Mythus wegen jedoch unbestreitbar. In der späteren kreuzförmigen Gestaltung der Taufbecken wird auch im Ritus dieser Bezug dargestellt (siehe Fig. 25 und Fig. 26).

---

219 Vgl. hierzu das Zitat aus Dahl, „Baptism in Ephesians", 420 oben ad Anm. 117, wo auch andere Autoren inklusive Tertullian erwähnt sind.

220 Betz, „Ritual", 86–100, bes. 97f. [242–254, bes. 251–253].

221 Schnelle, *Paulus*, 364f.; siehe ferner G. Strecker et alii, *Neuer Wettstein, Teilband 1*, 122f., 125f.; Lohse, *Römer*, 188f. Siehe besonders den Beitrag von F. Graf, „Baptism in the Graeco-Roman Mystery Cults" in vorliegender Publikation, 101–118.

222 Dunn, *Romans 1–8*, 316f. mit Hinweis u.a. auf Plato, *Parm.* 1321 und *Phaed.* 250B, auf LXX Exod 20,4; Deut 4,12; Ezek 1,4–5 usw., sowie auf Philo, *Migr.* 48–49.

223 Dunn, *Romans 1–8*, 318; ähnlich Schmithals, *Römerbrief*, 192 und Lohse, *Römer*, 191: „So weist auch an unserer Stelle die Begriffsverbindung ὁμοίωμα τοῦ θανάτου αὐτοῦ auf den Gekreuzigten hin, mit dem die Seinen fest verbunden sind – und nicht auf die Taufe"; so auch Hahn, *Theologie I*, 282; siehe schon G. Bornkamm, „Taufe und neues Leben bei Paulus", 34–50; Schnackenburg, „Todes- und Lebensgemeinschaft", 33–37. Anders Betz, „Ritual", 115f.: „This ritual is a ὁμοίωμα" (115); so schon V. Warnach, „Taufe und Christusgeschehen", 42f. und ferner Schnelle, *Gerechtigkeit*, 82f.; Fitzmyer, *Romans*, 435.

224 Theissen, „Urchristliche Taufe", 106. Weiss, *Urchristentum*, 500: „Nachbildung".

Die Aussage des Taufspruchs hat ein doppeltes Ziel: *a simile* und *a modo*[225]. Als Aussage der *Similarität* signifiziert sie den Parallelismus: Christus ist gestorben – wir sind gestorben; Christus ist auferweckt – wir werden auferweckt werden. Als Aussage der *Relation* signifiziert sie, in welcher Weise Christi und unser Schicksal in Beziehung stehen: Christus ist gestorben – und wir *mit ihm* (σὺν αὐτῷ); Christus ist auferweckt – und wir werden *mit ihm* (σὺν αὐτῷ) auferweckt werden. Zur Identitätsrelation kommt noch die Differenz hinzu, die ausdrücklich durch das Lexem ὁμοίωμα zur Sprache gebracht wird: „So zeigt auch hier das Wort Identität und Distanz an"[226]. Dieses Identität–Distanz–Verhältnis betrifft zweierlei: (1.) die Gleichgestalt mit dem Gekreuzigten und Auferstandenen sowie (2.) „... den in Verkündigung und Bekenntnis begegnenden Tod Jesu selbst, wie die parallele Erwähnung der Auferstehung in V. 5b zeigt"[227].

In diesem Text findet sich kein Hinweis auf die „Namensformel" (vgl. I Kor 1,13.15), auch gibt es keine direkte Beziehung zur „Bekleidungsformel" (Gal 3,27)[228]. Das was Galater und Römer vereinigt, ist lediglich die Formulierung βαπτισθῆναι εἰς Χριστόν[229]. Zwar sind die Formeln sehr unterschiedlich, aber sie stehen nicht in Kontradiktion zu einander, weder inhaltlich noch funktional[230], sondern sind eher komplementär!

Formgeschichtlich ist die „Identifikationsformel" in Römer 6 als „Taufaffirmation" zu charakterisieren[231]. In Bezug auf den spezifischen Sitz im Leben können wir feststellen: Wenn die *Pistis*-Formel wie in I Kor 15,3–5 Teil des

---

225 Siehe HELLHOLM, „Argumentation", 161f. Vgl. auch MEEKS, *Urban Christians*, 154: „... The image of dying and rising with Christ. This is expressed not only in the language of analogy ... but also in the language of participation ...".

226 T. HOLTZ, „ὁμοίωμα", 1254; ähnlich auch WILCKENS, *Römer (VI/2)*, 13f.; SCHNELLE, *Gerechtigkeit*, 82; G. STRECKER, *Theologie*, 174; LOHSE, *Römer*, 190f. Dies gilt m.E. auch für das „conformitas"-Verständnis, wie es von THEISSEN, *ibid.*, gebraucht wird. Siehe das Zitat aus Johannes Chrysostomos, *Cat. bapt.* oben in Anm. 207: Differenz zwischen „innerem" und „äußerem" Tod; ferner Cyrill von Jerusalem, *Myst. Cat.* II,7: „Denn wirklich war bei Christus der wirkliche Tod ... . Für uns aber gibt es ein Gleichbild des Todes und der Leiden – vom Heil jedoch kein Gleichbild, sondern die Wirklichkeit" (Ἀληθῶς γὰρ ἐπὶ Χριστοῦ θάνατος ἀληθής ... . Ἐπὶ δὲ ἡμῶν θανάτου μὲν καὶ παθημάτων ὁμοίωμα· σωτηρίας δὲ οὐχ ὁμοίωμα, ἀλλὰ ἀλήθεια). Text und Übers., RÖWEKAMP, *Cyrill von Jerusalem, Mystagogicae Catecheses*, 120–121.

227 SCHMITHALS, *Römerbrief*, 192 mit Hinweis auf J. KÜRZINGER, „Zur Taufaussage von Röm 6", 95. So auch HOLTZ, *ibid*.

228 Anders BETZ, *Galatians*, 187; IDEM, *Galaterbrief*, 329–333.

229 Eine m.E. richtige Interpretation wird von I. DE LA POTTERIE, „Discussion", 106 vertreten: „Pour bien comprendre la formule βαπτίζειν εἰς Χριστὸν Ἰησοῦν ..., il est nécessaire de s'interroger sur sa provenance. Elle serait la transposition d'une ancienne formule de foi: πιστεύειν εἰς Χριστόν. ... La foi nous unit au Christ; le sens de εἰς n'est donc pas local mais personnel. Il en va de même pour la formule baptismale. ... L'expression a donc tout ensemble un sens dynamique et personnel: tout comme la foi, le baptême unit au Christ".

230 Siehe hierzu DE LA POTTERIE, *ibid.*, 113.

231 Siehe unten Anm. 233.

katechetischen Unterrichts war, die „Namensformel" beim Taufakt verwendet wurde und die „Bekleidungsformel" nach der Taufe an die Neugetauften gesprochen wurde, dann ist anzunehmen, dass die „Taufaffirmation" von Römer 6,3–4a und 5/8 vermutlich vor der versammelten Gemeinde direkt nach der Taufe von den Neugetauften aufgesagt wurde: „Wir alle, die wir auf Christus getauft worden sind usw." (vgl. *TA* 21,33). Signifikant ist der Unterschied zum „Taufspruch"/„Taufmakarismus" in Galater 3,26–28, der ja in zweiter Person formuliert ist. War der „Taufspruch" von Galater 3 vom Täufer oder einem Begleiter nach der Taufe an die Neugetauften adressiert[232], so ist die "Taufaffirmation" von Römer 6 wohl von den Neugetauften selber gesprochen[233]. Wenn meine Analyse stimmen würde, dann bekämen wir zusätzlich einen näheren Einblick in die Taufliturgie der allerältesten christlichen Gemeinden.

Das aber heißt, dass wir in dieser Formel folgende *Differenzen* gegenüber den anderen Formeln beobachten können: (1.) eine ganz andere Struktur, (2.) eine ganz andere Terminologie, (3.) ganz andere theologische Inhalte und Zwecke und (4.) einen anderen spezifischen *Sitz im Leben*, möglicherweise abgesehen von dem der „Eingliederungsformel", nämlich eine *affirmatio* seitens der Neugetauften nach dem Taufakt.

1.6. Vorläufige Reflexion hinsichtlich der Textanalyse

Eine Frage, die zum Schluss der oben durchgeführten Textanalysen gestellt werden muss, ist, warum diese vorformulierten Traditionsstücke so schwer interpretierbar sind, m.a.W. semantisch so polysemisch, obwohl sie text-syntaktisch sehr wohlstrukturiert sind? Die Antwort darauf kann zumindest vorläufig nur lauten, dass die Ursache davon herrührt, dass ihre ursprünglich konkreten „Sitze im Leben" für uns nahezu unzugänglich sind. Wir besitzen lediglich die vorgeformten Formeln in ihren jeweiligen „Briefkontexten", also ihre „Sitze in der Literatur", aber meistens sind die Riten uns nicht mehr zugänglich. Diejenigen Texte und Abbildungen, welche die Riten beschreiben, sind alle leider jüngeren Datums.

In einer Anzahl von Teiltexten in den paulinischen Briefen finden sich öfters rhetorisch-stilistische Passagen[234]. In den oben analysierten Traditionsstücken zeigt sich indessen eine Ballung von ungewöhnlichem Ausmaß. Diese Verdichtung spricht entschieden dafür, dass hier vorgeformte Traditionen vorliegen. Aufgrund der durchgehenden Verwendung von rhetorischen Stilmitteln

---

232 Siehe oben Anm. 153 und 155.

233 Vgl. die tentative Vermutung von SCHMITHALS, *Römerbrief*, 191: „Anscheinend haben wir es mit einem ‚Taufspruch' zu tun, vielleicht mit einem liturgischen Stück aus dem Taufgottesdienst, das etwa nach vollzogener Taufe von den Täuflingen gesprochen worden sein könnte".

234 Siehe WEISS, „Beiträge zur Paulinischen Rhetorik"; HELLHOLM, „Universalität und Partikularität", bes. 259–264 (mit Lit.); SELLIN, „Ästhetische Aspekte der Sprache in den Briefen des Paulus", 411–426 [148–163]; FITZMYER, *First Corinthians*, 66–67.

in seinen Briefen kann nicht ausgeschlossen werden, dass Paulus – zusammen mit seinen Mitarbeitern – an der Formulierung zumindest einiger dieser Traditionsstücke selber beteiligt war.

2. Die Situationskontexte der drei Paulusbriefe – Die pragmatischen Präsuppositionen

In diesem Teil werde ich mich kurz den pragmatischen Situationen der jeweiligen Gemeinden zuwenden, die zur Abfassung der drei erwähnten Briefe führten. Wie ich anderswo nachdrücklich betont habe, gilt in Bezug auf antike Literatur, dass in den meisten Fällen die *situativen Kontexte* durch Interpretation von Texten aus zweierlei Sicht etabliert werden müssen, nämlich in Bezug auf *inter-* sowie auf *intra-*textuelle Ko-texte[235].

Wir müssen uns folglich mit dem Problem der *Rekonstruktion* pragmatischer Briefpräsuppositionen befassen[236]. In der ursprünglichen Kommunikationssituation war dies weniger ein Problem, da Sender, Adressat und Gegner in den meisten Fällen die gegenseitigen Positionen kannten oder zumindest meinten, sie zu kennen. Bei der Etablierung von Präsuppositionen muss der/die moderne Interpret/in methodologisch sowohl *text-interne* Indikationen als auch *text-externe* Informationen berücksichtigen[237]. Folglich werde ich bei der Rekonstruktion der situativen Kontexte text-interne wie text-externe Angaben berücksichtigen[238].

---

[235] Vgl. HELLHOLM, „Beatitudes", 286.

[236] Vgl. HEMPFER, „Präsuppositionen", bes. 317; ECO, *Lector*, 28–30 *et passim*. Ferner KOESTER, *Introduction*, 123; siehe auch C. J. CLASSEN, „Paulus und die antike Rhetorik", 7f. Dies muss zur behutsamen Verteidigung von dem, was zuweilen „mirror reading" genannt wird, hervorgehoben werden; vgl. hierzu nunmehr auch W. POPKES, *Jakobus*, 17. Gegen z.B. MITCHELL, *Reconciliation*, 54f., besonders aber gegen G. LYONS, *Autobiography*, 96–105.

[237] Für diese Unterscheidung, siehe HELLHOLM, *Visionenbuch*, 43, 80ff.; ferner RAIBLE, „Gattungen", 335: „Die Situation und der Zweck, der vom Sprecher durch ein komplexes sprachliches Zeichen verfolgt wird, also die textexternen Merkmale, können nun auch die Gestalt des Textes entscheidend determinieren"; K. BRINKER, „Textfunktionen", 135f.: „Texte sind immer eingebettet in eine Kommunikationssituation; sie stehen immer in einem konkreten Kommunikationsprozeß, in dem Emittent und Rezipient mit ihren sozialen und situativen Voraussetzungen und Beziehungen die wichtigsten Faktoren darstellen". Siehe ferner die Zitate von F. von Kutschera und W. Raible oben in Anm. 4.

[238] Vgl. in Bezug auf die text-*interne* Annäherung, MITCHELL, *Reconciliation*, 72; in Bezug auf die text-*interne* und *-externe* Annäherung, J. S. VOS, „Argumentation", 87 [29]: „Wenn man die rhetorische Situation bestimmen will, kommt man deshalb kaum umhin, dies aufgrund von Rückschlüssen aus der Argumentation des Apostels und zur Not auch mit Hilfe anderer Texte zu tun".

2.1. Die Situation in der korinthischen Gemeinde

Um die pragmatische Situation in der korinthischen Gemeinde zu rekonstruieren, ist es – unter Voraussetzung der Einheitlichkeit des Ersten Korintherbriefes[239] – erforderlich, zuerst die Frage nach der Briefgattung zu stellen, um dann der Frage nach Form und Funktion der ersten vier Kapitel sowie der Gesamtproblematik dieses Briefes nachzugehen.

Was die Gattungsfrage betrifft, scheint sich ein Konsensus zu etablieren, dass es sich generisch-rhetorisch entweder um eine deliberative[240] oder eine gemischte[241] Gattung handelt. In beiden Fällen ist in diesem Brief der deliberative Aspekt dominierend, und demzufolge weist der funktionale Zweck auf eine *Veränderung der Situation* in der korinthischen Gemeinde hin, die mittels hortativer und ermahnender Textteile[242] herbeigeführt werden soll. Wie Margaret Mitchell hervorgehoben hat, ist es äußerst bedeutsam, die Gattung eines Textes als Ganzes festzustellen[243]. Dies heißt aber nicht, dass die Möglichkeit anderer generischer Textteile auszuschließen ist. Die rhetorischen Gattungen treten nämlich selten in reiner Form, sondern überwiegend gemischt auf[244].

In einer komplexen Kommunikationssituation wird der Verfasser es für nötig halten, unterschiedliche Gattungen zu gebrauchen, um sein Ziel zu erreichen; je befähigter ein Autor ist, um so wahrscheinlicher ist es, dass er so viele rhetorische Mittel verwendet, wie er für erforderlich hält und die ihm hierzu zur Verfügung stehen[245]. Die rhetorischen Gattungen waren in der an-

---

239 Im Hinblick auf die unterschiedlichen Teilungshypothesen, siehe CONZELMANN, *1. Korinther*, 15–17; BETZ/MITCHELL, „Corinthians, First Epistle to", 1142f.; MITCHELL, „Korintherbriefe", 1688–1694; EADEM, „Corinthian Correspondence", 17–53; vgl. D. TROBISCH, *Entstehung*, 119–128; IDEM, *Paulusbriefe*, 83–136; LINDEMANN, *1. Korinther*, 3–6; FITZMYER, *First Corinthians*, 48–53; ZELLER, *1. Korinther*, 52–58.

240 So MITCHELL, *Reconciliation*, bes. 20–64 (= Kap. II) *et passim*; G. A. KENNEDY, *Interpretation*, 87.

241 SCHRAGE, *1. Korinther (VII/1)*, 86–90. Siehe Ps.-Libanios, „Epistolary Styles", in: A. J. MALHERBE, *Epistolary Theorists*, 72f.,6 [45]: Μικτὴ δὲ ἦν ἐκ διαφόρων χαρακτήρων συνιστῶμεν („The mixed type is that which we compose from many characteristics/styles"); siehe außerdem die dargebrachten Spezifizierungen in *ibid.*, 80f., 37–41 [92]. Vgl. insbesondere R. BRUCKER, ,Christushymnen', 174–210; weiterhin auch Betz's Charakterisierung von II Kor 8, wobei die VV. 1–15 „beratende", während hingegen die VV. 16–22 „administrative" genannt werden (BETZ, *2 Corinthians 8 and 9*, 139).

242 So auch SCHRAGE, *ibid.*, 88ff.

243 So MITCHELL, *Reconciliation*, 16; vgl. RAIBLE, „Gattungen", 335, zitiert oben in Anm. 237.

244 Quintilian, *Inst.*, III. 8, 55: *Solent in scholis fingi materiae ad deliberandum similiores controversiis et ex utroque genere commixtae* ... („In den Schulen ist es üblich, Stoffe für die Beratungsrede zu erfinden, die eher Kontroversien und aus beiden Gattungen gemischt sind"). Siehe ferner [Cicero], *Rhet. Her.*, III. 4,7. Vgl. S. K. STOWERS, *Letter Writing*, 51f.; HELLHOLM, „Argumentation", 129f.; LAUSBERG, *Handbuch*, 132 [§ 243]; D. E. AUNE, „Review", 325; BETZ, *Galaterbrief*, 2; BRUCKER, ,Christushymnen', 300 *et passim*.

245 Vgl. auch BETZ, *2 Corinthians 8 and 9*, 130f.

tiken Praxis weniger strickt von einander getrennt als in der Theorie[246]. Ein bedeutungsvoller Aspekt in der deliberativen Rhetorik war die Qualifikation des Orators[247], was unter bestimmten Verhältnissen zur Selbstverteidigung und Apologie führen konnte.

Der nächste Ko-Text der vorgeformten „Namensformel" in I Kor 1,14–17 ist die Textsequenz 1,10–4,21 mit ihren anfänglichen und abschließenden παρακαλῶ-Sätzen in 1,10 und 4,16[248]. Die Integrität des 1. Korintherbriefs vorausgesetzt, muss jetzt versucht werden, die Funktion dieser Text-Sequenz innerhalb dieses Briefes zu etablieren. Mit Nils Dahl verstehe ich diese Sequenz als „eine Introduktion", in der Paulus „zu allererst klarstellen musste, dass er nicht als Vertreter einer Gruppe, sondern als Apostel Jesu Christi, als Gründer und geistlicher Vater der ganzen Gemeinde auftritt. Der erste Teil, Kapitel 1–4, ist deshalb ein notwendiger Teil der Totalstruktur des Briefes und hat eine vorbereitende Funktion … Paulus musste zuerst die Korinther dazu nötigen, sich zu vertragen und eines Sinnes zu sein"[249]. Eine Reihe von Forschern, vor und nach Dahl, haben diese Textsequenz als apologetisch charakterisiert. Diese Charakterisierung erfolgt zu Recht und zwar in Bezug auf die ἔριδες und σχίσματα (vgl. 1,10f.; 4,1–6.18)[250], weil die σχίσματα nicht nur das Resultat der ἔριδες zwischen verschiedenen Gruppen innerhalb der korinthischen Gemeinde, sondern auch

---

246 Siehe z.B. Quintilian, *Inst.*, III. 4,15–16. Vgl. J. ENGELS, „Genera causarum", 702; BRUCKER, ‚Christushymnen', 174–252.

247 Quintilian, *Inst.*, III. 8, 12, 13, 48; Aristoteles, *Rhet.*, I. 2, 3–4; Cicero, *De orat.* 2. 333. Siehe auch HELLHOLM, „Argumentation", 127, 129; MITCHELL, *Reconciliation*, 45f.; H.-J. SCHILD, „Beratungsrede", bes. 1443f.

248 Die Abgrenzung dieses Abschnitts ist allgemein anerkannt, siehe z.B. DAHL, „Paul and the Church at Corinth", 313–335; CONZELMANN, *1. Korinther*, 48ff.; SCHRAGE, *1. Korinther (VII/1)*, 90, 127ff., 133; WOLFF, *1. Korinther*, 24ff.; LINDEMANN, *1. Korinther*, VIIf., 7f., 33ff. Eine etwas abweichende Textabgrenzung aus rhetorischer Sicht wird von MITCHELL, *Reconciliation*, 198–202, 207–225 vertreten; ebenso von BETZ/MITCHELL, „Corinthians, First Epistle to", 1143. ZELLER, *1. Korinther*, 85–86. Anders FITZMYER, *First Corinthians*, 54–58. SELLIN, „Geheimnis"', 72f. [12–13]: Kap. 1–4 stellen einen separaten Brief dar.

249 DAHL, „Paul and the Church at Corinth", 317, 326 (meine Übers.). Siehe auch L. L. WELBORN, „Discord in Corinth", 6; MITCHELL, *ibid.*, 66f.

250 So z.B. DAHL, „Paul and the Church at Corinth", passim, bes. 317, 320; VIELHAUER, „Paulus und die Kephaspartei", 171; SELLIN, „Geheimnis"', 74–79 [13–19]; SCHRAGE, „Das apostolische Amt", 103; IDEM, *1. Korinther (VII/1)*, 93, 128–133; Vos, „Argumentation", 88ff. [30–33], 119 [62–64]; etwas zurückhaltend LINDEMANN, *1. Korinther*, 33; als deliberativ eingeschätzt von WELBORN, „Discord in Corinth", 7 und MITCHELL, *Reconciliation*, 16 Anm. 54. Die Zurückweisung von Dahls Interpretation von I Kor 4,1–5 als apologetisch (Dahl, *ibid.*, 321) seitens MITCHELL, *ibid.*, 55 ist unberechtigt; siehe die begründete Kritik an Mitchell von Vos, „Argumentation", 89 mit Anm. 4 [31 Anm. 4]; apologetisch auch SELLIN, „Geheimnis"', 75 [15]; ähnlich LINDEMANN, *ibid.*, 95. Keine Apologie: FITZMYER, *First Corinthians*, 211: 4,1–5 sollte vom nachfolgenden Abschnitt VV. 6–16/21 nicht isoliert werden: "For in vv. 1–16 Paul sees no need to defend himself or to refute any opposite claims".

zwischen diesen Gruppen und Paulus darstellen[251]. Das Problem hat zum Teil mit der mangelnden Authorität des Apostels zu tun[252]. Aus 4,18 ist zu erkennen, dass Paulus, obwohl er die ganze Gemeinde anredet, offenbar einige Mitglieder (τίνες) als besonders „arrogant" (ἐφυσιώθησαν) ansieht[253]. In diesem Zusammenhang ist nach Dahl auch das Schlagwort von 1,12 zu verstehen, wenn er schreibt: „Da der ganze Teiltext eine Apologie für Paulus enthält und der Streit in Korinth mit der Opposition gegen ihn zusammenhängt, ist es ziemlich einfach, das in 1,12 erwähnte Schlagwort zu interpretieren"[254]. Dahls Interpretation des Schlagwortes ist m.E. immer noch der überzeugendste Versuch, diese Wendungen zu explizieren[255]: „Diejenigen, die sagten, ‚ich gehöre zu Paulus' waren stolz auf ihn und meinten, seine hervorragende Qualität übertraf diejenige von Apollos oder Kephas. Die anderen Slogans sind alle als Unabhängigkeitserklärungen von Paulus zu verstehen. Apollos ist erwähnt als der hervorragendste christliche Lehrer, der Korinth nach Paulus besucht hat. Kephas ist die berühmte Säule, der erste Zeuge der Auferstehung Jesu und Apostel vor Paulus. Das Schlagwort ‚Ich gehöre zu Christus' ist nicht ein Motto einer spezifischen ‚Christus-Partei', sondern heißt einfach ‚Ich selbst gehöre zu Christus – und bin von Paulus unabhängig'"[256]. Eindrucksvoll bei Dahls Interpretation ist die Tatsache, dass dadurch „alle Schlagworte [inklusive des Christus-Slogan –DH] eine klare Bedeutung sowohl im literarischen Ko-text als auch im situativen Kontext bekommen"[257].

Die offizielle Haltung der Gemeinde ist durch einen Brief charakterisiert, in dem einerseits die Loyalität dem Apostel gegenüber (11,2), andererseits aber auch die Bitte um Stellungnahme zu verschiedenen Angelegenheiten zum Ausdruck gebracht wird. Der Brief ist wahrscheinlich durch Stephanas, Fortunatus und Achaicus als offizielle Delegaten der korinthischen Gemeinde überreicht worden[258]. Inoffiziell aber konnten die Leute der Chloe von Streitigkeiten in Korinth sowie von einer gewissen Opposition gegen Paulus berichten[259]. Die

---

251 Vgl. Vos, *ibid.*, 88 [30f.]: „Bei den Streitigkeiten in der Gemeinde geht es nicht so sehr um Spaltungen zwischen den Mitgliedern der Gemeinde unter sich als vielmehr um Spaltungen zwischen den Gemeindemitgliedern und ihrem Verhältnis zu den Aposteln".
252 Siehe z.B. Vos, *ibid.*, 89 [32].
253 Vgl. Dahl, „Paul and the Church at Corinth", 318.
254 Dahl, *ibid.*, 322 (meine Übers.).
255 Vgl. Fitzmyer, *First Corinthians*, 137ff.: „I am following basically the analysis of Dahl" (137).
256 Dahl, *ibid.* (meine Übers.).
257 Dahl, *ibid.*, (meine Übers.); vgl. II Kor 10,7: „Wenn jemand überzeugt ist, Christus zu gehören, dann soll er doch auch bedenken, dass nicht nur er, sondern auch wir Christus gehören" (Χριστοῦ [εἶναι]: Genitiv der Zugehörigkeit; vgl. BDR, 132–134 [§ 162] bzw. 106 [§ 1282]).
258 So auch Conzelmann, *1. Korinther*, 369; Wolff, *1. Korinther*, 436; Zeller, *1. Korinther*, 543. Anders allerdings Horn, „Stephanas und sein Haus", 96.
259 Vgl. Dahl, *ibid.*, 323.

Art und Weise, wie Stephanas erwähnt wird, zuerst am Anfang in Kap. 1, wo Paulus sich selbst durch Hinzufügung, dass er auch den Haushalt des Stephanas getauft hat, korrigiert, und dann auch die Aufforderung, die im letzten Kap. gebracht wird, sind von Bedeutung. Paulus nötigt ja in 16,15–18 die Korinther, „sich solchen Menschen unterzuordnen" wie Stephanas, Fortunatus und Achaicus und ihnen ihre „Anerkennung zu gewähren". Dahl folgert mit Recht, dass diese „doppelte Emphase zur Annahme berechtigt, dass nicht jeder in Korinth bereit war, gebührend Anerkennung an Stephanas, seinen Haushalt und seine Gefolgschaft, [die ‚die Erstlingsfrucht von Achaja ist'] zu billigen". Er erwägt sogar die Hypothese, dass „die streitenden Korinther ebensosehr gegen Stephanas opponiert haben wie gegen Paulus selber"[260].

Ein anderer strittiger Punkt in der korinthischen Gemeinde betrifft das Verhältnis zwischen Gemeindemitgliedern, die vor weltlichen Gerichten gegeneinander Prozesse führen (6,7–11). Bei diesen Streitigkeiten, geht es offenbar um finanzielle bzw. materielle Angelegenheiten[261]. Die begüterten Gemeindeglieder führen Prozesse gegen die ärmeren Mitchristen im Bewusstsein dessen, dass in der römischen Rechtspraxis „für die Parteilichkeit zugunsten der Bessersituierten eher charakteristisch als die Ausnahme war"[262]. Wegen der Unangemessenheit solcher Aktionen führt Paulus einen Lasterkatalog an. „Die katalogische Aufzählung von Lastern hat dabei die Funktion, prägnant Verhaltensweisen zu markieren, die für ‚heidnisches' Leben kennzeichnend sein mögen, mit christlicher Existenz aber unvereinbar sind ..."[263].

Das Verhältnis von Einheit und Vielfalt liegt hinter den Problemen in Kap. 12. Dies kommt in der Darstellung der Gemeinde durch Paulus als einem einzigen Leib (ἓν σῶμα) aber mit vielen Gliedern (μέλη πολλά) zum Ausdruck. Wie am Anfang des Briefes steht in diesem Abschnitt die Einheit der Gemeinde auf dem Spiel, was durch den Ko-text deutlich hervorgeht, wo die Zersplitterung innerhalb der korintischen Gemeinde in Bezug auf die Geistesgaben thematisiert wird und Paulus hervorheben muss, dass „es verschiedene Gnadengaben gibt, aber nur den einen Geist" (Διαιρέσεις δὲ χαρισμάτων εἰσίν, τὸ δὲ αὐτὸ πνεῦμα [v. 4]). Er erlaubt es den Korinthern nicht, die verschiedenen Gaben gegeneinander auszuspielen. Paulus argumentiert zuerst mit dem Bild vom Leib und seinen Gliedern, wenn er schreibt: „Denn wenn der Leib einer ist und doch viele Glieder hat, alle Glieder des Leibes aber, obwohl sie viele sind, doch ein

---

260 DAHL, ibid., 324 (meine Übers.). Ähnlich LINDEMANN, *1. Korinther*, 385; ferner HORN, „Stephanas und sein Haus", 90 *et passim*.

261 KONRADT, *Gericht*, 336; vgl. WOLFF, *1. Korinther*, 113; LINDEMANN, *1. Korinther*, 136; THEISSEN, „Soziale Schichtung", 258.

262 KONRADT, *Gericht*, 337.

263 KONRADT, *Gericht*, 339. Vgl. auch das Verhältnis zwischen Taufe und Lasterkatalogen in den Deuteropaulinen; siehe hierzu den Beitrag von TOR VEGGE, „Baptismal Phrases in the Deuteropauline Epistles", *passim* in vorliegender Publikation, 497–?.

Leib sind: so ist es auch mit Christus" (καθάπερ γὰρ τὸ σῶμα ἕν ἐστιν καὶ μέλη πολλὰ ἔχει, πάντα δὲ τὰ μέλη τοῦ σώματος πολλὰ ὄντα ἕν ἐστιν σῶμα, οὕτως καὶ ὁ Χριστός); wir erblicken also, wie Paulus hier vom Bild des Leibes zur Sache selbst, d.h. zum σῶμα Χριστοῦ hinüberwechselt. Das Gewicht liegt hier auf dem *positiven Aspekt der Vielfalt* im Rahmen der Ganzheit, wie aus dem Bild vom Leib in V. 14 deutlich hervorgeht: „Auch der Leib besteht nicht nur aus einem Glied, sondern aus vielen Gliedern" (Καὶ γὰρ τὸ σῶμα οὐκ ἔστιν ἓν μέλος ἀλλὰ πολλά). Dies wird in dem nachfolgenden Ko-text weiter ausgeführt, um in V. 27 wieder „zum eigentlichen Sinn (‚Christusleib', → V. 13)" zurückzukommen[264]: Ὑμεῖς δέ ἐστε σῶμα Χριστοῦ καὶ μέλη ἐκ μέρους („Ihr aber seid [der] Leib Christi und als einzelne Glieder").

2.2. Die Situation in den galatischen Gemeinden

Der Brief an die Galater ist m.E. mit Recht als hauptsächlich apologetisch bezeichnet worden[265]. Das ist der Fall schon bei Johannes Chrysostomos, wie Margaret Mitchell gezeigt hat[266]. Dies ist sicherlich eine korrekte Beurteilung, was die übergreifende Struktur des Galaterbriefes betrifft, schließt aber keinesfalls die Existenz deliberativer Textteile aus, wie Betz schon längst hervorgehoben und später noch bestätigt hat[267]. Im Gegensatz zum 1. Korintherbrief, der einen deliberativen Brief mit apologetischen Elementen darstellt, ist der Galaterbrief ein apologetischer Brief mit deliberativen Elementen[268].

---

264 CONZELMANN, *1. Korinther*, 261; ähnlich WEISS, *1. Korinther*, 307; SCHRAGE, *1. Korinther (VII/3)*, 216, 230; MERKLEIN/GIELEN, *1. Korinther III*, 141; LEE, *Paul, the Stoics, and the Body of Christ*, 125–129, 138. Anders WOLFF, *1. Korinther*, 301–305, LINDEMANN, *1. Korinther*, 275–277 und ZELLER, *1. Korinther*, 397.

265 So bes. BETZ, „Literary Composition", 353–379; IDEM, *Galatians*, 24–25 et passim; IDEM, *Galaterbrief*, 68–72 et passim; ähnlich BECKER, *Galater*, 11f. Zu den Einwänden dagegen und der Behauptung, dass es sich um eine deliberative Gattung handelt, siehe, u.a., D. E. AUNE, „Review", 323–328; G. HALLBÄCK, „Jerusalem og Antiokia i Gal. 2", *passim*. Vgl. auch MARTYN, *Galatians*, 21; SCHNELLE, *Einleitung*, 118–220. Ferner HÜBNER, *Theologie*, 57f.

266 MITCHELL, „Reading Rhetoric", bes. 349f. In seinem Kommentar zum Galaterbrief verwendet Johannes Chrysostomos regelmäßig die Lexeme ἀπολογεῖσθαι und ἀπολογία, siehe MITCHELL, ibid., 350–353. Vgl. S. A. COOPER, „*Narratio* and *Exhortatio*", 107–135, der zwar beobachtet wie „Victorinus' exegesis could seem to support a reading of Galatians as deliberative rhetoric" (ibid., 112), jedoch „the unwillingness" des Victorinus „to identify Galatians with a specific rhetorical genre" zugibt (ibid., 133). Vorsichtig äußert sich, trotz seiner Kritik an Betz, G. LYONS, *Autobiography*, 112–121.

267 BETZ, „Galatians, Epistle to the", 873: „The rhetoric of the letter is, on the whole, of the judicial type (*genus iudiciale*), but the element of dissuasion is also present (*genus deliberativum*). The two genres correlate here as they do in other texts"; IDEM, *Galaterbrief*, 2: „Im Blick auf den Galaterbrief sei wenigstens soviel gesagt, daß das Genre des apologetischen Briefes Elemente beratender Funktion keineswegs ausschließt". Vgl. bereits IDEM, *Galatians*, 213: Paulus' „goal is, of course, to change the Galatians's mind and to reverse their present plans".

268 Siehe oben Anm. 241–247.

Anscheinend durch Zufall, d.h. durch seine Erkrankung (Gal 4,13), ist Paulus nach Galatien gekommen und hat dort das Evangelium verkündigt und Gemeinden gegründet[269]. Nachdem Paulus Galatien verlassen hatte, änderte sich die Situation sehr rasch durch das Eindringen von Judaisten, die verlangten, dass die galatischen Christen das Gesetz halten und sich beschneiden lassen sollten. Folglich drohte das Eindringen dieser Judaisten, die Gemeinde von ihrem Gründer, Paulus, wegzureissen[270].

In Anbetracht ihres Abwendens von ihm und seinem Evangelium, belegt Paulus sie sogar mit einem Fluch in 1,9: „Wenn euch jemand ein Evangelium bringt entgegen dem, was ihr empfangen habt, der sei verflucht"[271]. Offenbar waren die Galater auf dem Wege, sich von Paulus und seinem gesetzesfreien Evangelium abzuwenden und der paulinischen Opposition zu folgen. Deshalb kann Paulus, wie er sonst in allen Briefen zu pflegen tut, keine Danksagung für die Galatergemeinden geben, sondern bricht in Verwunderung darüber aus, dass sie „so schnell von dem abfallen, der sie durch die Gnade Christi berufen hat" (1,6) und bezeichnet die Galater als „Unverständige" und „Verzauberte" (3,1)[272]. Der Brief als ganzer ist eine Apologie des Paulus, nicht als Individuum, sondern als Apostel Christi mitsamt seinem Kerygma. Das Evangelium ist nicht nur für Juden, sondern auch für Griechen, d.h. ein Nicht-Jude braucht nicht erst Jude zu werden, um Christ zu werden[273]. Die judaistische Propaganda wird von Paulus auf das Schärfste zurückgewiesen. Dabei nötigt er die Galater bei dem Kerygma, das sie gehört und akzeptiert haben und durch welches sie den Heiligen Geist empfangen haben, zu bleiben[274]. Dies ist der knappe Hintergrund für den Gebrauch des „baptismalen Heilszuspruchs" in Galater 3,26–28.

2.3. Die Situation in den Romgemeinden

Der Brief an die Römer ist an eine Gemeinde bzw. an mehrere Hausgemeinden geschrieben worden, die Paulus nur bedingt kennt und in denen er selbst für die Mehrheit unbekannt ist. Wenn Kapitel 16 einen originalen Teil des Briefes

---

269   Vgl. VIELHAUER, *Geschichte*, 109; SCHLIER, *Galater*, 210; BETZ, *Galatians*, 224; IDEM, *Galaterbrief*, 388. Unentschieden BECKER, *Galater*, 68. Anders VOUGA, *Galater*, 108.

270   Vgl. VIELHAUER, *Geschichte*, 113–124; SCHENKE/FISCHER, *Einleitung*, 81–84; BETZ, *Galatians*, 5–9; IDEM, *Galaterbrief*, 40–47; SCHNELLE, *Einleitung*, 121–23; KOESTER, *Introduction*, 123–126; MARTYN, *Galatians*, 18f., 117–126, 302–306; BECKER, *Galater*, 12f.; SÄNGER, „Strategien", 155–181; ferner VOUGA, *Galater*, 159–162.

271   Siehe bes. BETZ, *Galatians*, 50–52; IDEM, *Galaterbrief*, 108–111.

272   Vgl. z.B. BETZ, *Galatians*, 128–132; IDEM, *Galaterbrief*, 236–242; VOUGA, *Galater*, 65–69; MARTYN, *Galatians*, 282–286. LOHSE, „Christus, des Gesetzes Ende?", 27f.

273   Vgl. I Kor 7,17–20 und hierzu bes. CONZELMANN, *1. Korinther*, 157–160; LINDEMANN, *1. Korinther*, 168–171.

274   Siehe BETZ, „Spirit", 145–160; IDEM, „Geist", 46–62; IDEM, „In Defense of the Spirit", 99–114 [98–109].

darstellt[275], dann werden gewisse Informationen über die Verhältnisse in der Romgemeinde (oder wohl richtiger: in den römischen Hausgemeinden) für ihn zugänglich gewesen sein[276]. Auch in diesem Brief liegen Spuren antipaulinischer Propaganda seitens seiner judaistischen Opponenten vor. Also hat Paulus es nötig gehabt, sich selbst in diesem Brief zu verteidigen. Der Römerbrief gehört offensichtlich der gemischten rhetorisch-literarischen Gattung an. Zumindest in den Kapiteln drei und sechs liegen apologetische Teiltexte vor[277].

Das Hauptproblem bei der Sicherstellung der Position, die hinter den Gegenargumenten in Kap. 6 liegt, wird dadurch kompliziert, dass der moderne Interpret die Contra-Argumente sowie die paulinischen Pro-Argumente vom selben semantischen Standpunkt her evaluieren muss, nämlich dem Libertinismus. Dieser kann, pragmatisch gesehen, entweder der paulinischen Opposition oder ihrer Auffassung von Paulus zugeschrieben werden[278]:

(1) Die Gegner vertreten einen libertinistischen Standpunkt[279] – eine Position, die Paulus bekämpft.
(2) Die Gegner klagen Paulus wegen Libertinismus an[280] – eine Anklage, die Paulus zurückweist.

Aus text-internen Gründen ist es offenkundig, dass die zweite Option die einzig mögliche ist; dies ist klar, wenn Paulus in 3,8 ein Zitat aus der Anklage der Gegner bringt, wo ihm eine vorgebliche blasphemisch-libertinistische (καθὼς βλασφημούμεθα) Aufforderung: „Lasst uns das Böse tun, damit das Gute komme" (ποιήσωμεν τὰ κακά, ἵνα ἔλθῃ τὰ ἀγαθά) unterschoben wird[281]. Diese Anklage wird – wie im Galaterbrief – von Paulus zurückgewiesen mit einem Eid: „Deren Verdammnis ist gerecht" (3,8b: ὧν τὸ κρίμα ἔνδικόν ἐστιν). Die gleiche

---

275 So z.B. H. Y. GAMBLE, *History*, 1977; W.-H. OLLROG, „Abfassungsverhältnisse", 221–244; P. LAMPE, „Roman Christians of Romans 16", 216–230; A. REICHERT, *Römerbrief*, 335–342; LOHSE, *Römer*, 50–53; JEWETT, *Romans*, 8–9. Anders, z.B. PETERSEN, „Ending(s)", 337–347; SCHMITHALS, *Römerbrief*, 543–562; TROBISCH, *Paulusbriefsammlung*, 118.
276 Siehe LAMPE, *Stadtrömische Christen*, 58, 129, 160–162.
277 Siehe unten Anm. 286.
278 Das Folgende stützt sich auf HELLHOLM, „Argumentation", 142–146. Siehe ferner DETTWILER, „Enthousiasme", 283.
279 So W. LÜTGERT, *Römerbrief*, 72ff., 111; C. E. B. CRANFIELD, *Romans, Vol. I*, 297 Anm. 1; ähnlich GÄUMANN, *Taufe*, 69 Anm. 7; TACHAU, ‚*Einst' und ‚Jetzt'*, 122. So wieder ohne jedwede Begründung VON GEMÜNDEN, „Urchristliche Taufe", 132.
280 So KÄSEMANN, *Römer*, 157: „Doch ist Pls nach 3,5ff. tatsächlich der Verführung zum Libertinismus beschuldigt worden, so daß man eher mit Verteidigung gegenüber einer Missdeutung der Rechtfertigungslehre zu rechnen hat"; SCHLIER, *Römerbrief*, 190; WILCKENS, *Römer (VI/2)*, 8f.; CONZELMANN, „χάρις κτλ.", 386; CONZELMANN/LINDEMANN, *Grundriß*, 326; SCHMITHALS, *Römerbrief*, 110; LAMPE, *Stadtrömische Christen*, 55; VOLLENWEIDER, *Freiheit*, 328; JEWETT, *Romans*, 250f., 391, 394–396. Sehr zurückhaltend LOHSE, *Römer*, 186.
281 Vgl. U. LUZ, „Aufbau", 169, 175; ferner SCHNELLE, *Gerechtigkeit*, 74; THEISSEN, *Psychologische Aspekte*, 183; FRID, „Römer 6,4–5", 188; SCHMITHALS, *Römerbrief*, 110.

Anklage wird gerade in 6,1 wiederholt, wo er schreibt: ἐπιμένωμεν τῇ ἁμαρτίᾳ, ἵνα ἡ χάρις πλεονάσῃ; („Sollen wir bei der Sünde bleiben, damit sich die Gnade mehre?" – als deliberativer Konjunktiv, oder „Laßt uns bei der Sünde bleiben, damit sich die Gnade mehre!" – als hortativer Konjunktiv). Dies ist die Art der Opposition, die Paulus von den judaistischen Gegnern erwartet, welche – wie Philipp Vielhauer vorgeschlagen hat – entweder die Gemeinden in Rom schon infiltriert haben oder von denen Paulus erwartet, dass sie demnächst die Gemeinde infiltrieren werden[282]. Dies ist auch der Grund, warum Paulus sich selbst und sein Evangelium im Proömium dieses Briefes so akribisch präsentiert[283].

Die text-*externen* Überlegungen weisen in die gleiche Richtung, nämlich von judaisierender und/oder jüdisch-synagogaler Propaganda gegen Paulus und seine gesetzesfreie Verkündigung, die angeblich zu einer laxen Lebensführung anleiten werde. Die Gründe für die Annahme einer judaisierenden bzw. synagogalen Propaganda als Hintergrund der Argumentation des Paulus sind kurz gefasst folgende: (a) während seines Aufenthaltes in Ephesus hat Paulus erfahren, wie seine Gemeinden in Galatien und Korinth von judaistischen Gegnern bedroht worden waren[284]; (b) als er den Römerbrief in Korinth schrieb, war er gerade auf dem Wege nach Jerusalem, um dort die Kollekte zu übergeben. Wie ernst seine Lage in der Tat war, können wir aus Röm 15,30–32 ersehen: er befürchtet erstens seine Liquidierung durch die „Ungehorsamen in Judaea" und zweitens die Verweigerung der Annahme der Kollekte seitens der Jüdisch-Christlichen Gemeinschaft in Jerusalem. Dieser Aspekt ist zu Recht – wenn auch etwas einseitig – von Jacob Jervell vertreten worden[285]; (c) offenbar befürchtet Paulus z.Z. der Abfassung des Römerbriefes, dass die judaistischen Gegner, die ihm im Osten schon Schwierigkeiten bereitet hatten, nun auch in Rom gegen ihn auftreten würden[286]; (d) die Absicht des Paulus mit dem Römerbrief war vermutlich u.a., die römischen Hausgemeinden für sich zu gewinnen, so dass er von ihnen Unterstützung für seine geplante Mission in Spanien erhalten könne (15,28)[287].

---

282 VIELHAUER, *Geschichte*, 183: „Paulus mußte damit rechnen, daß die Feindschaft seiner Gegner, die ih[m] mit ihrer Agitation auf seinen Missionsfeldern und in Jerusalem das Leben schwer gemacht hatte, auch in Rom Einfluß gewonnen hatte; und er mußte diesem Einfluß, falls schon vorhanden, entgegenwirken oder, falls noch nicht vorhanden, vorbeugen, wenn sein Spanien-Plan gelingen sollte".

283 Zusätzlich zu den Kommentaren, siehe REICHERT, *Römerbrief*, 108–118.

284 Vgl. z.B. BETZ, *Galatians*, passim; IDEM, *Galaterbrief*, passim; VIELHAUER, *Geschichte*, 113–124.

285 See J. JERVELL, „The Letter to Jerusalem", 53–64.

286 Siehe das Zitat aus VIELHAUER, *Geschichte*, 183 oben in Anm. 282; ferner vgl. auch WILCKENS, *Römer (VI/1)*, 33–48: „Aus der Polemik des Galaterbriefs ist im Römerbrief eine umfassende Apologie geworden ..." (48); IDEM, *Römer (VI/2)*, 10; ferner BORNKAMM, „Römerbrief als Testament", 138; BECKER, *Paulus*, 367; LAMPE, „Roman Christians", 221.

287 Vgl. E. BRANDENBURGER, „Paulinische Schriftauslegung", 8; siehe ferner VIELHAUER, *Geschichte*, 183; JEWETT, *Romans*, 80–91.

Von diesen Voraussetzungen, die auf text-internen sowie auf text-externen Beobachtungen ruhen, muss man einerseits versuchen, die These des Römerbriefes im allgemeinen und die Argumentationsweise in Kapitel 6 im besonderen zu verstehen[288]. Andererseits wird die Argumentationsweise in diesem Kapitel die Annahme judaistischer (oder sogar jüdischer) Gesprächspartner in diesem Brief bekräftigen.

3. Der Gebrauch von Tauftraditionen in der Argumentation – Die intra-textuellen Ko-Texte

Haben wir bis jetzt zunächst die Tauftraditionen in den drei Paulusbriefen (I Kor, Gal, Röm) herausgearbeitet und danach knapp die verschiedenen Situationskontexte hinter den drei Briefen skizziert, so wollen wir nun nach der paulinischen Verwendung dieser unterschiedlichen Tauftraditionen im Rahmen der jeweiligen Argumentationsstrategie angesichts der verschiedenartigen Gemeindesituationen fragen[289]. Dies kann indessen aus Raumgründen nur in begrenztem Umfang geschehen[290].

3.1. Die Argumentation des Paulus im 1. Korintherbrief

3.1.1. Die „Namensformel" als Argument (I Kor 1,13.15)

Angesichts der Zersplitterung in der korinthischen Gemeinde geht Paulus auf die Probleme direkt am Anfang, d.h. in den ersten vier Kapiteln seines Briefes, ein. Im Zusammenhang mit den ἔριδες und σχίσματα in Korinth[291] spielte offensichtlich die Taufe eine bedeutende Rolle[292]. Dies ist neuerdings verneint u.a. von

---

288 Vgl. CONZELMANN, „χάρις κτλ.", 386, der allerdings meint: „Paulus weist ihn (sc. den Libertinismus) nur formal-pauschal, nicht argumentierend zurück". Siehe dagegen HELLHOLM, „Argumentation", *passim*.

289 Vgl. hierzu auch C. J. BJERKELUND, „„Nach menschlicher Weise rede ich"", bes. 307: „So viel steht auf jeden Fall fest, der Apostel nimmt in seinen Briefen Rücksicht auf die Situation und entscheidet von daher, auf welche Weise er argumentieren wird"; IDEM, „The Concept of 'Sin' in the New Testament", in: *ibid.*, 439: „The contents of the letters are determined to a large degree by the situations in which they are written; words and expressions are chosen in view of the specific intention of the letters".

290 In Bezug auf Römer 6 ist dies ausführlich behandelt in HELLHOLM, „Argumentation".

291 Siehe MITCHELL, *Reconciliation*, 87: „Thus μερίζειν in 1 Cor 1:13 is perfectly synonymous with σχίσματα in 1:10 and ἔριδες in 1:11", und das Zitat oben ad Anm. 24 und unten Anm. 299.

292 Siehe das Zitat aus Tertullian, *De bapt.* 14 oben ad Anm. 34. Vgl. FITZMYER, *First Corinthians*, 147: „Paul thus insists that no matter what relationship the Paul-group of Corinth might be claiming to him, it does not stem from him as their baptizer. Some interpreters have argued that this was the nature of the rival groups, that Corinthians who had been baptized by a certain preacher developed a bond of allegiance to him. Now Paul would be countering that claim".

Wolfgang Schrage, Andreas Lindemann und Dieter Zeller[293], aber kaum überzeugend im Hinblick auf ihre Erwähnung direkt im Anschluß an die „Namens-Frage" am Anfang des Briefes und weiterhin im Hinblick auf die Interpretation des Abendmahls in Kapitel 11 und die Einschätzung der Vikariatstaufe in Kapitel 15. In den Mysterienkulten spielte der Mystagoge – der allerdings kein Täufer war! – eine entscheidende Rolle bei der Einweihung der Mysten, weil er während der Zeremonie Verantwortung für die Initianden trug[294]. In der christlichen Gemeinde in Korinth (nicht weit von Eleusis [Demeter-Kult] und Kenchreai [Isis-Kult] entfernt!) hielten sich offenbar die getauften Neophyten besonders an ihre „Mystagogen", d.h. ihre Täufer. Einige hielten sich an Paulus, andere an Petrus (vgl. auch 9,5[295]), und wieder andere an Apollos[296]. Diese drei oder vielleicht deren Repräsentanten[297] waren offenbar die hervorragendsten Vollbringer der Taufe in Korinth. – Christus war natürlich kein Täufer! Wie früher bemerkt, hat Dahl bei seiner Interpretation des Schlagwortes „Ich gehöre zu Christus" m.E. recht, dass damit gemeint ist: „Ich bin unabhängig von Paulus"[298]. Wir können somit negativ schlussfolgern, dass einige Gemeindeglieder die originale Taufformel missverstanden bzw. missbraucht haben. Also war diese „Namensformel" in Korinth im Gebrauch! Wohl nicht gegen diese Formel als solche opponiert Paulus, sondern gegen ihren Missbrauch, weshalb er froh ist, nicht allzuviele getauft zu haben. Gert J. Steyn hat dieses Verhältnis geradezu positiv formuliert, wenn er schreibt: „Paul's appeal for unity is based on the implicit baptismal formula which binds all of them together, i.e., that they were baptised 'in the name of the Lord, Jesus Christ'. ... This binds them closely together, so that when looking back on their divisions based on other 'names', that way of reasoning looks incorrect"[299]. Diese Interpretation wird durch die Erklärung von Gerhard Barth verstärkt, wenn es bei ihm, wie schon oben zitiert, heißt: „Das Argument ist dazu noch um so überzeugender, je stärker Paulus sich an einen feststehenden liturgischen Brauch anlehnt, den jeder kennt und den niemand bestreitet"[300].

---

293 SCHRAGE, *1. Korinther (VII/1)*, 149, 155; LINDEMANN, *1. Korinther*, 41; ZELLER, *1. Korinther*, 94.

294 Siehe oben Anm. 30; ferner SELLIN, „‚Geheimnis' der Weisheit", 74 [14].

295 Vgl. hierzu LINDEMANN, *1. Korinther*, 202f.

296 Für Petrus, siehe F. C. BAUR, „Christuspartei", 61–206; VIELHAUER, „Kephaspartei", 169–182; für Apollos: SELLIN, „‚Geheimnis' der Weisheit", *passim*; WOLTER, „Apollos", *passim*; KONRADT, „Weisheit", 192–194.

297 DAHL, „Paul and the Church at Corinth", 323. Vgl. N. WALTER, „Nikolaos", 207; siehe auch das Zitat aus Tertullian, *De bapt.* 14,1 oben ad Anm. 34.

298 DAHL, „Paul and the Church at Corinth", 322.

299 STEYN, „Reflections", 484. HARTMAN, „Commentary", 391: „These queries [1,13] reflect aspects of Paul's views on Christ, …, and on baptism, but they primarily function as elements of his argument for a message with a precise purpose in a very precise situation".

300 BARTH, *Taufe*, 46; ferner HELLHOLM, „Argumentation", 128f., 141; SPRUTE, *Enthymemtheorie*, 57: „Ganz wesentlich ist daher für den Rhetoriker das Auffinden der zu dem jeweiligen Fall passenden ἔνδοξα".

3.1.2. Die „Eingliederungsformel" als Argument (I Kor 12:13)

Bei der Behandlung der Vielfalt der Geistesgaben in Kap. 12 argumentiert Paulus zuerst mit dem Bild vom Leib und seinen Gliedern, wenn er schreibt: „Denn wenn der Leib einer ist und doch viele Glieder hat, alle Glieder des Leibes aber, obwohl sie viele sind, doch ein Leib sind: so ist es auch mit Christus".

Nun begnügt sich aber Paulus in seiner Argumentation nicht mit dem Bild von einem Leib mit vielen Gliedern, sondern begründet die Bedeutung und Notwendigkeit der Einheit mit Hilfe der Tauftradition, in diesem Falle mit der „*Eingliederungsformel*"[301]. Mit der Verwendung dieser Formel erinnert[302] er die Korinther daran, wie sie den Geist (ἐν ἑνὶ πνεύματι ... ἓν πνεῦμα) im Zusammenhang mit der Taufe empfingen und wie sie dadurch in einen Leib, d.h. in die Gemeinde Christi einverleibt wurden. Mit Hilfe dieser Taufformel, abgefasst in 1. Pers. Pl., bezieht er die Korinther in seine Argumentation ein. Die Taufe ist also für Paulus die objektive Wirklichkeit, angesichts derer die Korinther zu verstehen haben, was Einheit in Christus und was Zersplitterung bedeutet. Sie sind alle, abgesehen von weltlichem Status (εἴτε Ἰουδαῖοι εἴτε Ἕλληνες, εἴτε δοῦλοι εἴτε ἐλεύθεροι, [[εἴτε ἄρσεν εἴτε θῆλυ·]][303]), durch die Taufe in den Leib Christi eingegliedert und haben alle den selben Geist (τὸ αὐτὸ πνεῦμα [v. 4]) der Heiligkeit empfangen. Alle haben sie, jede(r) auf ihre/seine Weise, eine Aufgabe in der Gemeinde Christi. In der vorliegenden Diskussion mit der Korinthergemeinde war die Benutzung der „Eingliederungsformel" anstatt der „Bekleidungsformel" dadurch bedingt, dass die Konstruktion „εἴτε ... εἴτε" die positive *Bedeutung der Verschiedenheit* im Rahmen der Einheit betont, während die „Bekleidungsformel" das Gewicht auf die Gleichheit mit der *Aufhebung* der Unterschiede „οὐκ ἔνι ... οὐδὲ/καὶ" legt[304].

3.1.3. Die „Rechtfertigungsformel" als Argument (I Kor 6,11)

Diese Formel befindet sich in einem Textabschnitt, in dem das Verhältnis zwischen Christen und dieser Welt behandelt wird. Zuerst fragt Paulus die Korinther: „Wie kann jemand von euch wagen, wenn er einen Streit mit einem anderen hat, sein Recht vor den Ungerechten (ἄδικοι) und nicht vor den Heiligen (ἅγιοι) zu suchen?" (6,1). Gibt es niemanden in der Gemeinde, der zwischen Bruder und Bruder schlichten könnte, so dass der Prozess nicht vor den Ungläubigen (ἄπιστοι) geführt werden muss? Schon die Tatsache, dass ihr mit einander Pro-

---

301 So auch HORN, *Angeld*, 172: „In der jetzt vorliegenden Form dient V. 13 als ein Argument, den vorausgehenden V. 12 zu begründen"; ferner ERIKSSON, *Traditions*, 130; SCHRAGE, *1. Korinther (VII/3)*, 216; WOLFF, *1. Korinther*, 298; FITZMYER, *First Corinthians*, 477f.: „He (sc. Paulus) is making use of such traditional teaching to advance his argument ...".

302 Vgl. BARTH, *Taufe*, 110.

303 Siehe oben § 1.2.

304 Siehe LINDEMANN, *1. Korinther*, 272.

zesse führt, ist ein Versagen (V. 6), betont der Apostel. Als Argument für seine Stellungnahme gibt er zuerst ein *eschatologisches* an: „Wisst ihr nicht (οὐκ οἴδατε …), dass die Heiligen (οἱ ἅγιοι) die Welt richten werden?" … „Wisst ihr nicht (οὐκ οἴδατε …), dass wir über Engel richten werden? Erst recht über alltägliche Dinge?" (VV. 3–4). Die Argumentation wird hier aus einem *a maiore ad minus-Prinzip* her geführt! Diese Art des Argumentierens geschieht aufgrund eines *jüdischen* Rechtssystems[305]. Ein noch rigoroserer Weg bietet sich an durch das *griechische* und *christliche* Prinzip[306], das in den VV. 7–8 zum Ausdruck kommt: „Nun ist es überhaupt ein Versagen für euch, dass ihr Prozesse gegeneinander führt. Weshalb leidet ihr nicht lieber Unrecht? Weshalb lasst ihr euch nicht lieber berauben? Stattdessen begeht ihr Unrecht, und ihr begeht Raub – und das an Brüdern!"[307]. Hier liegt, wie so oft bei Paulus, eine amplifikatorische Struktur der Argumentation zugrunde[308]. Nach einer erneuten rhetorischen Frage in V. 9a: „Oder wisst ihr nicht (ἢ οὐκ οἴδατε …), dass Ungerechte (ἄδικοι) Gottes Herrschaft nicht erben werden?", folgt in den VV. 9b–10 ein Lasterkatalog[309]. Wenn Paulus anschließend betont: „Und solche sind einige von euch gewesen" (καὶ ταῦτά τινες ἦτε), dann stellt er wenigstens einige Mitglieder der korinthischen Gemeinde als Ungerechte (ἄδικοι) dar, d.h. sie sind zurückgefallen in ihren vorchristlichen Status als ἄδικοι, oder wie Johannes Weiß es treffend formuliert: „Und nun kamen all die alten Sünden wieder"[310]. In direktem Anschluss daran verwendet Paulus als endgültiges Argument die sakramentale „Rechtfertigungsformel" mit ihrem „soteriologischen Kontrastschema"[311]. Wiederum zeigt sich die divergierende Bedeutung bei ko-textloser („Sitz im Leben") bzw. ko-textbedingter („Sitz in der Literatur") Interpretation: ἄδικοι als vorchristlicher Status und ἄδικοι als Rückfall in diesen vorchristlichen Status[312].

Die im vorgeprägten Traditionsstück verwendeten Verben ἡγιάσθητε und ἐδικαιώθητε knüpfen an die Begriffe ἅγιοι und ἄδικοι im vorhergehenden Kotext, bes. an V. 1 an[313], was die Funktion der Formel als äußerste *Begründung*

---

305 Vgl. LINDEMANN, *1. Korinther*, 141f.
306 Vgl. CONZELMANN *1. Korinther*, 135 mit Anm. 28.
307 Vgl. LINDEMANN, *1. Korinther*, 141f.
308 Siehe z.B. HELLHOLM, „Universalität und Partikularität".
309 Siehe oben ad und in Anm. 263.
310 WEISS, *1. Korinther*, 154. Vgl. DINKLER, „Problem der Ethik", 204–240: 210: „1. Die ἄδικοι als ἄπιστοι und 2. die durch ἀδικεῖν verschiedener Äußerungsformen ihr Christsein infragestellenden korinthischen Gemeindeglieder, welche somit trotz Getauftseins zu ἄδικοι und ἄπιστοι werden"; *ibid.*, 227: „… Warnung vor den ἄδικοι draußen und vor der ἀδικία in den eigenen Reihen …".
311 SCHNELLE, *Gerechtigkeit*, 38f., 43; CONZELMANN, *1. Korinther*, 137.
312 Gegen ZELLER, *1. Korinther*, 218.
313 Vgl. WEISS, *1. Korinther*, 155: „So enthält auch hier das rein passivische ἡγιάσθητε eine unausgesprochene Mahnung, die Heiligkeit nun auch zu verwirklichen"; LINDEMANN, *1. Korinther*,

des Argumentationsganges in diesem Kapitel des 1. Korintherbriefes gewährleistet[314].

Hier liegt also auch ein ethisch-paränetisches Moment vor[315]: lebt nun gemäß euerem Status als neue Geschöpfe (II Kor 5,17), also als solche, die ihr durch die Taufe euch habt reinigen lassen, von Gott geheiligt und von ihm gerecht gemacht seid!

3.1.4. Bilanz

Das bedeutet nun, dass die Verwendung der verschiedenen Taufformeln mit ihren unterschiedlichen Akzentsetzungen, denen wir im 1. Korintherbrief begegnen, jeweils *situationsbedingt* ist und demzufolge kein Anzeichen für eine Entwicklung bezüglich der Tauftheologie des Paulus darstellen muss. Es kann aber auch kein Hinweis auf ein Desinteresse des Paulus an der Taufe sein, was durch Act 18,8 noch bestätigt wird[316]. Vielmehr wurde, wie wir gesehen haben, die „Namensformel" vom Vollzieher der Taufe in der Liturgie im Zusammenhang mit dem Taufakt verwendet, und gerade diese Formel war diejenige, die am ehesten von den Zersplittergruppen missverstanden bzw. missbraucht werden konnte.

Im ersten und im letzten Teil des 1. Korintherbriefes war besonders deutlich zu erkennen, wie Streit und Zersplitterung in der Gemeinde entstanden sind und zur Bedrohung ihrer Existenz geführt haben. Die Fraktionsbildung ist verheerend und Paulus muß sich im ganzen Brief mit korinthischen Separatisten auseinandersetzen, gleich ob es um Götzenopferfleisch, Abendmahlsfeier, Gemeindeordnung oder Auferstehungsglaube geht. Dies ist der Zusammenhang, in dem wir die Verwendung der „Namensformel", der „Eingliederungsformel" sowie der „Rechtfertigungsformel" zu verstehen haben.

134.

314 Vgl. SCHRAGE, *1. Korinther (VII/1)*, 433: „Gerade weil Paulus die Taufe nicht nur kognitiv, sondern effektiv-kausativ versteht, kann sie ihm zur Begründung der durchgreifenden Erneuerung und Verpflichtung dienen".

315 Vgl. vor allem WOLFF, *1. Korinther*, 121: „Durch die Taufe sind die Christen von Gott (passivum divinum) geheiligt, d.h. von Gott und für Gott aus dem Machtbereich der gottfernen Welt ausgesondert (vgl. 3,17). Darum können sie dann auch nicht mehr so leben wie früher (V.9f.) ...."; BEASLEY-MURRAY, *Baptism*, 166.

316 Siehe VON HARNACK, *Mission*, 399; zitiert oben ad Anm. 32. Vgl. auch AVEMARIE, *Tauferzählungen*, 441: „Von daher ist anzunehmen, dass auch bei den vorangehenden Gemeindegründungen in Makedonien die Bekehrungstaufe reguläre paulinische Praxis war".

3.2. Die Argumentation des Paulus im Galaterbrief

3.2.1. Die „Bekleidungsformel" als Argument (3,26–28)

Wenn Paulus die judaistischen Christen wegen ihrer Forderung, dass die Galater sich nicht damit begnügen sollten, den Geist empfangen zu haben, sondern dazu noch das Gesetz halten und sich beschneiden lassen sollten, rügt, dann hat die Zeile 3 der „Bekleidungsformel" (οὐκ ἔνι Ἰουδαῖος οὐδὲ Ἕλλην) Sinn, während die Zeilen 4 (οὐκ ἔνι δοῦλος οὐδὲ ἐλεύθερος) und 5 (οὐκ ἔνι ἄρσεν καὶ θῆλυ) nicht viel zum aktuellen Streitthema beitragen. Dadurch bestätigt sich unsere traditionsgeschichtliche Analyse oben. Außerdem sind die parallelen Zeilen 1 (πάντες γὰρ υἱοὶ θεοῦ ἐστε [διὰ τῆς πίστεως] ἐν Χριστῷ Ἰησοῦ) und 6 (πάντες γὰρ ὑμεῖς εἷς ἐστε ἐν Χριστῷ Ἰησοῦ), die eine *Inclusio* darstellen, für die Wirkung der Argumentation des Paulus bedeutungsvoll, denn hier wird *positiv* auf die Gemeinschaft *aller* Christen volles Gewicht gelegt. Im Hinblick auf die judaistische Propaganda in den galatischen Gemeinden, die Paulus mit aller Härte bekämpft, ist es nicht verwunderlich, dass er auch mit der Taufe argumentiert. Besonders wichtig dabei ist, dass er sich auf eine alte, in Galatien und in mehreren Gemeinden anerkannte und gebrauchte Tauformel, die gewissermaßen als „Erinnerungshilfe" dient[317], beziehen kann. Dass die Formel, die wir in Gal 3,26–28 vorfinden, für seine Entgegnung den Propagandisten gegenüber außerordentlich gut passt, kommt ja – wie soeben dargelegt – explizit durch die Zeile 3 zum Ausdruck!

Wiederum zeigt sich, dass der Gebrauch der jeweiligen Tauftradition, die Paulus für seine argumentativen Zwecke verwendet, *situationsbedingt* ist. Deshalb kann auch hier diese Formel nicht für eine Entwicklung des paulinischen Taufverständnisses in Anspruch genommen werden. Als vorgeformte Tradition kann sie außerdem nicht ohne weiteres als Grundlage eines *exklusiv* paulinischen Taufverständnisses gelten.

3.2.2. Ermahnung als Argumentationsmittel

Schon im Galaterbrief – wie später auch im Römerbrief – verwendet Paulus zusätzlich zur „Bekleidungsformel" Ermahnungen als Argumentationsmittel. Dies ist die nächstliegende Interpretation des paränetischen Teils im Galaterbrief, eines Teils, dem ein apologetischer Teiltext 1,6–2,21 bzw. 4,31 vorausgegangen ist, und dem eine polemische Konklusion in 6,11–17 folgt[318]. Der argumentative Beweis des sogenannten paränetischen Textteils (5,13–6,10) unterstreicht den moralischen Charakter des Verfassers und seine Rechtfertigungsbotschaft mit

---

317 Betz, „Literary Composition", 371 [87]; idem, „Ritual", 107 [261]; idem, *Galatians*, 184f.; idem, *Galaterbrief*, 325–27; ähnlich Martyn, *Galatians*, 374f.

318 Siehe Becker, *Galater*, 11 und *ad loc.*

Hilfe von Ermahnungen, die im Text selber gegeben sind. Dadurch verfehlt die Propaganda der Gegner ihr Ziel; dies ist m.E. der wirkliche und strategische Grund für den paränetischen Teil in Gal 5–6.[319]

3.3. Die Argumentation des Paulus im Römerbrief

3.3.1. Die „Identifikationsformel" als Argument (Röm 6,3–4a, 5/8)

Im Blick auf die schon eingetretene oder unmittelbar bevorstehende Bedrohung der paulinischen Rechtfertigungsbotschaft durch Vertreter der Synagoge oder durch judaistische Propagandisten argumentiert Paulus in Kap. 6 besonders ausführlich, und angesichts der absurden Anklage des Libertinismus tut er es – wie wir schon gesehen haben – gewiss schon in 3,8, aber jetzt in Kap. 6 in voller Intensität.

Grund für die Anklage des Libertinismus ist die These des Paulus, die er am Ende von Kap. 5 darlegt[320]. Diese These konstituiert die unmittelbare thematische Voraussetzung für seine Argumentation in Kap. 6[321], und zwar in doppelter Weise: (1.) In *negativer* Hinsicht heißt es: „Das Gesetz hat sich dazwischengedrängt, damit die Übertretung zunimmt". (2.) In *positiver* Hinsicht heißt es aber: „Da wo (οὗ δὲ κτλ.; nicht ὅτι δὲ κτλ.[322]) die Sünde sich mehrte, da strömte die Gnade über und über". Daraufhin stellt Paulus in 6,1 eine Frage (*genus deliberativum*) oder zitiert eine Aufforderung (*genus hortativum*), die ihm seine Gegner unterschieben: „Sollen wir bei der Sünde bleiben, damit sich die Gnade mehre?" oder „Laßt uns bei der Sünde bleiben, damit sich die Gnade mehre!" Paulus weist diese Interpretation seiner Position scharf zurück durch ein μὴ γένοιτο (Auf keinen Fall!). Dies wäre der reine Anachronismus! (V. 2).

Damit ist eigentlich genug gesagt! Aber Paulus begnügt sich nicht damit, sondern fährt mit seiner Entgegnung fort, jetzt eben gerade mit Hilfe der Tauftradition. Dabei knüpft er an eine von allen akzeptierte Tradition an: ἢ ἀγνοεῖτε; („oder wisst ihr nicht?")[323].

Im Anschluß an die vorgeprägte Tauftradition zieht Paulus, teils in negativer, teils in positiver Weise, seine Argumentation durch[324]:

(1.) Der *negative* Aspekt ist klarer und einfacher zu erfassen. Der Christ ist mit Christus (jetzt aufgrund der Auseinandersetzung in *paulinischer* Sicht

---

319 Hellholm, „Argumentation", 176; bezüglich Römer 6,15–23, siehe, *ibid.*, 170–179.
320 Siehe Hellholm, „Universalität", 217–269.
321 So jetzt auch Ph. F. Esler, *Conflict*, 202f.
322 Siehe Schlier, *Römerbrief*, 191.
323 Siehe Hellholm, „Argumentation", 124f., 128f.; idem, „Römer 7.1–6", 387f. So auch Standhartinger, *Studien*, 139 und Hahn, *Theologie I*, 281.
324 Bezüglich des Verhältnisses zwischen den beiden Strophenteilen (1) und (2) der rekonstruierten vorgeformten Tauftradition, siehe Hellholm, „Argumentation", 158f.

von den *Sünden!*) gestorben und begraben worden. Dieses Argument dient der Zurückweisung der gegnerischen Vorwürfe einer libertinistischen Lebensführung (6,1). Dabei ist ‚Tod' hier natürlich metaphorisch gemeint, deswegen aber nicht weniger real[325]!

(2.) Der *positive* Aspekt bereitet Paulus indessen von der Taufformel her Schwierigkeiten. Denn die futurischen Verbformen (συζήσομεν/ἐσόμεθα in VV. 5 und 8) sagen nur etwas über die künftige Auferstehung und das daraus resultierende Leben mit Christus aus, nicht jedoch etwas über die Relevanz für die Gegenwart. Aus diesem Grunde modifiziert Paulus die Tradition οὕτως καὶ *συζῶμεν αὐτῷ* und formuliert anstelle in V. 4c: ἵνα ὥσπερ ἠγέρθη Χριστός … οὕτως καὶ ἡμεῖς ἐν καινότητι ζωῆς περιπατήσωμεν („damit, wie Christus auferweckt wurde … so auch wir in [der] neuen Lebenswirklichkeit wandeln"). Hier, in V. 4c, verändert Paulus die futurischen Formulierungen in präsentisch-ethische[326]. Somit kann er sich auch die positive Seite der Taufe für seine argumentativen Zwecke zu Nutze machen, denn hiermit geht es nun um ein neues Leben, d.h. einen neuen Lebenswandel aller Getauften[327], und nicht erst um ein neues Leben mit Christus im Eschaton. Von Libertinismus bei Paulus kann deswegen keine Rede sein!

Diese ethischen Implikationen der Taufe sind übrigens in Übereinstimmung mit den ethischen Forderungen in den Mysterien, besonders im Isis-Kult, wie Herbert Braun schön herausgestellt hat, wenn er bemerkt: „die Weihe nimmt den Mysten in eine ausgesprochene Verpflichtung hinein" und mit der Beobachtung fortfährt, „[a]uch die Verpflichtung, also das Verständnis solch einer engen Verbindung mit der Gottheit als Dienst, hat bis in die militanten Ausdrücke hinein bei Paulus (besonders Röm 6,12–23; auch schon 6,4c) ihre Analogien …"[328].

3.3.2. Die ethischen Implikationen

Nochmals zeigt sich, dass Paulus eine wohlbekannte Tauftradition benutzt, um eine Anklage zurückzuweisen. Diese Tradition ist – wie oben herausgestellt – älter als der Römerbrief. Paulus nimmt sie indessen auf, um sie als Grundlage für seine Entgegnung zu gebrauchen. Dieses Taufverständnis ist also nicht neu und geht wahrscheinlich nicht allein auf Paulus selbst zurück, sondern ist wohl ein Produkt einer Gemeinde/Schule in Antiochien und wird von ihm bei dieser

---

325 Siehe oben in und ad Anm. 207.
326 Vgl. wenn auch etwas einseitig H. BRAUN, „Das ‚Stirb und Werde'", 154: „Das ‚Stirb und Werde' der Taufe interessiert im NT ausschließlich unter dem Gesichtspunkt der Konsequenzen, welche für die Getauften aus der Taufe folgen: sie sollen sich der Sünde gegenüber für tot erachten und in Neuheit des Lebens wandeln (Röm 6,4–11)".
327 Siehe HELLHOLM, „Argumentation", 157–159; auch oben ad Anm. 176–177.
328 BRAUN, „Das ‚Stirb und Werde'", 148 bzw. 153. Ferner HELLHOLM, „Argumentation", 159, 170–179.

Gelegenheit aufgenommen[329]. Auch in diesem Falle ist die Verwendung der benutzten Tauftradition *situationsbedingt*, weil gerade diese mysterienhafte/sakramentale Tauftradition sich für die Zurückweisung der judaistischen bzw. synagogalen Propaganda gegen Paulus sehr wohl eignete: wir sind tot von den *Sünden*, wie Paulus hier ergänzend darlegt, und, wieder ergänzend bzw. modifizierend, zum *neuen Lebenswandel* hier und jetzt befreit! In die Formel selbst wollte Paulus anscheinend nicht eingreifen, sondern ließ die Futurformen (συζήσομεν bzw. ἐσόμεθα) stehen[330].

Auch abgesehen von seiner Argumentationsstrategie kann man mit großer Wahrscheinlichkeit vermuten, dass Paulus das Taufverständnis der Formel grundsätzlich bejahen konnte, sonst „hätte er sie ja seinem Brieftext nicht einverleiben müssen"[331]. Mit Eduard Lohse kann festgestellt werden: „Der Apostel Paulus hat nicht eine systematische Entfaltung der Tauftheologie vorgenommen, sondern jeweils in der Begegnung mit konkreten Fragen und in Auseinandersetzung mit den in den Gemeinden vorhandenen Anschauungen dargelegt, was die christliche Taufe bedeutet"[332].

3.4. Die Argumentationsstrategie des Paulus

Charakteristisch für seine Argumentationsweise ist, wie Ernst von Dobschütz schon längst festgestellt hat, dass „Paulus ..., wie er das immer gerne tut, aus dem Zentrum des christlichen Glaubens heraus (argumentiert)"[333]. Dies gilt z.B. einmal für die christologisch-soteriologischen πίστις-*Formeln* wie Röm 4,24; 4,25; 5,8; 10,9b; I Kor 15,3–5; I Thess 4,14; für die *Homologien* wie *Kyrios-Akklamationen* Röm 10,9a; Phil 2,11; I Kor 12,3; für die *liturgischen Texte* wie die *Εἷς-Akklamationen* I Kor 8,6 bzw. für die *Kultformeln* des Herrenmahls I Kor 11,23–26; sowie für die *Lieder* Phil 2,6–11[334].

Dies gilt aber in gleicher Weise auch für die unterschiedlichen *Taufformeln*, die oben zum einen separat, zum anderen aber auch in ihren jeweiligen Zusammenhängen im brieflichen Argumentationsverlauf analysiert wurden. Of-

---

329 Siehe das Zitat von Lohse oben ad Anm. 216.

330 Dies tut Paulus, weil für ihn „die Auferstehung der Christen ganz apokalyptisch ein zukünftiges und postmortales Geschehen [bleibt]"; SELLIN, *Der Brief and die Epheser*, 162. Dies könnte auch dafür sprechen, dass – wie oben erwogen – Paulus bei der Ausarbeitung dieser „Identifikationsformel" selber beteiligt war.

331 WALTER, „Alttestamentliche Bezüge" 249; siehe auch BETZ, „Ritual", 107 [261]: „If he [sc. Paul] had not fully approved of it, he would not have given baptism the high status in the argument which it has in the letter".

332 LOHSE, „Taufe und Rechtfertigung", 315. Vgl. ferner HARTMAN, „*Auf den Namen*", 53; IDEM, '*Into the Name*'. 52.

333 E. VON DOBSCHÜTZ, 1. *Thessalonicher*, 189.

334 Vgl. zusammenfassend VIELHAUER, *Geschichte*, 9–49, wo aber die „vorgeformten" Taufformeln in den paulinischen Homologoumena unberücksichtigt geblieben sind.

fensichtlich argumentiert Paulus in seinen Briefen ganz bewusst vom Zentrum des christlichen Glaubens, also von der christologisch-soteriologischen sowie der kultischen Tradition her[335], und zwar immer dann, wenn er diese „vorgeprägten" Formeln als abschließende Begründungen seiner Argumentation benötigt.

Diese vorgeformten Traditionsstücke zeigen zum einen, wie in der Urkirche ein großer Variationsreichtum an vorgeprägten Formeln existierte und diese in wechselnden liturgischen Zusammenhängen zur Verwendung gekommen sein mögen, zum anderen aber auch, dass Paulus diese vielleicht unter seiner Mitwirkung in unterschiedlichen Zusammenhängen entwickelten Formeln bei seiner jeweiligen Argumentationslage verwenden konnte.

4. Abschluss – Ertrag

Als Abschluss können folgende Ergebnisse der diachronen, pragmatischen und synchronen Untersuchung kurz zusammengefasst werden: (1.) In den drei behandelten Paulusbriefen ist Traditionsmaterial aus der ältesten Zeit des Christentums erhalten. (2.) Dies gilt sowohl für christologisch-soteriologische Formeln als auch für Taufformeln. (3.) Paulus verwendet diese Traditionsformeln nicht nur als Basis für seine Argumentation, sondern auch als abschließende Begründungen, besonders dann, wenn er in seiner Argumentationsstrategie die „Erinnerungstechnik" benutzt. (4.) Die behandelten Taufformeln sind unterschiedlich in Bezug auf Struktur, Terminologie und spezifischen Sitz im Leben. (5.) Alle analysierten Formeln sind von Paulus im Zusammenhang mit je unterschiedlichen Konflikten gebraucht worden; jedesmal wählt er die dafür geeignete Formel aus. (6.) Es ist deshalb signifikant, zu beobachten, dass in jedem Einzelfall, in dem eine Taufformel von Paulus verwendet und adaptiert wurde, diese in einem apologetischen oder deliberativen Teiltext auftaucht. (7.) Die Formeln, wie sie in den vorliegenden Briefen von Paulus verwendet werden, tragen dazu bei, ein besseres Verständnis der Probleme in den adressierten Gemeinden zu gewinnen. (8.) Die Argumentationsstrategie des Paulus kommt meistens gerade in den Fällen zu ihrer Klimax, in denen er auf vorformuliertes Material zurückgreift. (9.) Gerade diese traditionellen Texte lassen nur bedingt eine Rekonstruktion einer Entwicklung der paulinischen Tauftheologie zu. (10.) Ebensowenig läßt die paulinische Verwendung des Traditionsmaterials Schlüsse auf eine mögliche Entwicklung der paulinischen Theologie zu, da die jeweilige Verwendung in den Texten von den situativen Zusammenhängen bedingt ist. (11.) Die hier durchgeführte Analyse kann bei einer vorsichtigen Rekonstruktion einer baptismalen Liturgie in den ältesten Schichten der Alten Kirche behilflich sein: (a)

---

335 Siehe hierzu O. LINTON, „Paulus och juridiken", 173–192, bes. 187; vgl. ferner HELLHOLM, „Funktion", 404.

beim Taufakt selbst wurde wohl die eingliedrige (später wohl eher – aber nicht ausschließlich – die dreigliedrige) „Namensformel" vom Täufer bei der Taufe verwendet; (b) nach vollzogener Taufe wurde der „baptismale Heilszuspruch" über die neugetauften Neophyten vom Täufer selbst oder von einem Assistenten ausgesprochen; (c) in ähnlicher Weise schließlich sprachen gegebenenfalls die Neugetauften nach dem Taufakt vor der anwesenden Gemeinde ihre alternativen „Taufaffirmationen" aus.

Bibliographie

Textausgaben – Lexica – Grammatiken – Archäologie

Novum Testamentum Graece, eds. E. NESTLE/B. ALAND/K. ALAND, Stuttgart: Deutsche Bibelgesellschaft [27]1996.

Aristotle, The "Art" of Rhetoric. With an English Translation by JOHN HENRY FREESE (LCL XXII), Cambridge, Mass.: Harvard University Press/London: Heinemann 1975.

Aristoteles, Rhetorik. Übersetzt und erläutert von CHRISTOF RAPP (Aristoteles Werke in deutscher Übersetzung 4: Erster und Zweiter Teilband), Darmstadt: Wissenschaftliche Buchgesellschaft 2002.

Cicero, De oratore. Über den Redner. Lateinisch/Deutsch. Übersetzt und herausgegeben von HARALD MERKLIN (Reklam), Stuttgart: Reklam [2]1976.

[Cicero], Rhetorica ad Herennium. Lateinisch-Deutsch. Herausgegeben und übersetzt von THEODOR NÜSSLEIN (Tusculum), Düsseldorf/Zürich: Artemis & Winkler 1998.

Cyrill von Jerusalem, Mystagogicae Catecheses/Mystagogische Katechesen. Übersetzt und eingeleitet von GEORG RÖWEKAMP (FC 7), Freiburg i. Br. etc.: Herder 1992.

Didache/Zwölf-Apostel-Lehre – Traditio Apostolica/Apostolische Überlieferung. Übersetzt und eingeleitet von GEORG SCHÖLLGEN/WILHELM GEERLINGS (FC 1), Freiburg i. Br. etc: Herder 1991.

Didascalia et constitutiones apostolorum, Vol. I, hg. von F. X. FUNK, Paderborn: Schöningh 1905.

Johannes Chrysostomus, Catecheses Baptismales/Taufkatechesen, Erster Teilband. Übersetzt und eingeleitet von REINER KACZYNSKI (FC 6/1), Freiburg i. Br. etc.: Herder 1992.

Johannes Chrysostomus, Catecheses Baptismales/Taufkatechesen, Zweiter Teilband. Übersetzt und eingeleitet von REINER KACZYNSKI (FC 6/2), Freiburg i. Br. etc.: Herder 1992.

Quintilianus, Institutionis oratoriae Libri XII. Ausbildung des Redners, Zwölf Bücher. Herausgegeben und übersetzt von HELMUT RAHN. Erster und zweiter Teil (TzF 2/3), Darmstadt: Wissenschaftliche Buchgesellschaft 1972/1975.

Sibyllinische Weissagungen. Griechisch-deutsch. Herausgegeben und übersetzt von A. KURFESS/J.-D. GAUGER (Tusculum), Darmstadt: Wissenschaftliche Buchgesellschaft 1998.

Tertullian, Adversus Praxean/Gegen Praxeas. Übersetzt und eingeleitet von HERMAN-JOSEPH SIEBEN (FC 34), Freiburg i.Br. 2001.

Tertullian, De Baptismo – De Oratione/Von der Taufe – Vom Gebet. Übersetzt und eingeleitet von DIETRICH SCHLEYER (FC 76), Turnhout: Brepols 2006.

Theodor von Mopsuestia, Katechetische Homilien. Erster Teilband. Übersetzt und eingeleitet von PETER BRUNS (FC 17/1), Freiburg i. Br. etc.: Herder 1994.

Theodor von Mopsuestia, Katechetische Homilien. Zweiter Teilband. Übersetzt und eingeleitet von PETER BRUNS (FC 17/2), Freiburg i. Br. etc.: Herder 1995.

ARZT-GRABNER, P./KRITZER, R. E./PAPATHOMAS, A./WINTER, F., *1. Korinther* (PKNT 2), Göttingen: Vandenhoeck & Ruprecht 2006.

BAUER, W., *Griechisch-deutsches Wörterbuch*, K. & B. Aland (Hg.), Berlin – New York: de Gruyter [6]1988.

BLASS, F./DEBRUNNER, A./REHKOPF, F., *Grammatik des neutestamentlichen Griechisch*, Göttingen: Vandenhoeck & Ruprecht [14]1976 [= BDR].

GUYOT, P./KLEIN, R., *Das frühe Christentum bis zum Ende der Verfolgungen. Band II: Die Christen in der heidnischen Gesellschaft* (TzF 62), Darmstadt: Wissenschaftliche Buchgesellschaft 1994.

KASSER, R./LUISIER, PH., „Le Papyrus Bodmer XLI en édition princeps. L'épisode d'Éphèse des *Acta Pauli* en copte et traduction", in: *Muséon* 117 (2004) 281–384.

LATTKE, M., *Oden Salomos. Text, Übersetzung, Kommentar. Teil 1: Oden 1 und 3–14* (NTOA 41/1), Göttingen: Vandenhoeck & Ruprecht/Freiburg, CH: Universitätsverlag 1999.

— *Odes of Solomon* (Hermeneia), Minneapolis, Minn.: Fortress 2009.

LIDDELL, H. G,/SCOTT, R./JONES, H. S., *A Greek–English Lexicon,* Oxford: Clarendon Press [9]1940 [= Reprint 1966; LSJ].

MALHERBE, A. J., *Ancient Epistolary Theorists* (SBLSBS 19), Atlanta, Ga.: Scholars Press 1988.

VAN DER MEER, F./MOHRMANN, C., *Bildatlas der frühchristlichen Welt*. Deutsche Ausgabe von H. Kraft, Gütersloh: Gerd Mohn 1959.

MEGAW, A. H. S., *Kourion. Excavations in the Episcopal Precinct*, Washington, DC: Dumbarton Oaks/Harvard University Press 2007.

MENGE, H./GÜTHLING, O., *Enzyklopädisches Wörterbuch der griechischen und deutschen Sprache*, Erster Teil: Griechisch–Deutsch, Berlin/München/Zürich: Langenscheidt [19]1965.

SCHENKE, H.-M./BETHGE, H.-G./KAISER, U. U. (Hg.), *Nag Hammadi Deutsch*. Band I: NHC I,1-V,1 (Koptisch-Gnostische Schriften II; GCS 8), Berlin – New York: de Gruyter 2001.

PHILOSOPHISCHE UND SPRACHWISSENSCHAFTLICHE ARBEITEN

ALKIER, S., „Intertextualität – Annäherungen an ein texttheoretisches Paradigma", in: D. Sänger (Hg.), *Heiligkeit und Herrschaft. Intertextuelle Studien zu Heiligkeitsvorstellungen und zu Psalm 110* (BThSt 55), Neukirchen–Vluyn: Neukirchener Verlag 2003, 1–26.

BALDINGER, K., *Semantic Theory. Towards a Modern Semantics*, London: Blackwell/New York: St. Martin's Press 1980.

BRINKER, K., „Textfunktionen. Ansätze zu ihrer Beschreibung", in: *Zeitschrift für Germanistische Linguistik* 11 (1983) 127–148.

BROICH, U./PFISTER, M. (Hg.), *Intertextualität. Formen, Funktionen, anglistische Fallstudie* (Konzepte der Sprach- und Literaturwissenschaft 35), Tübingen: Niemeyer 1985.

ECO, U., *Lector in fabula. Die Mitarbeit der Interpretation in erzählenden Texten* (dtv 30141), München: Deutscher Taschenbuch Verlag [3]1998.

ENGELS, J., „Genera causarum", in: *HWR*, Band 3; Darmstadt: Wissenschaftliche Buchgesellschaft 1996, 701–721.

HEMPFER, KL. W., „Präsuppositionen, Implikaturen und die Struktur wissenschaftlicher Argumentation", in: Th. Bungarten (Hg.), *Wissenschaftssprache. Beiträge zur Methodologie, theoretischen Fundierung und Deskription*, München: Fink 1991, 309–342.

HOLTHUIS, S., *Intertextualität. Aspekte einer rezeptionsorientierten Konzeption* (Stauffenburg Colloquium 28), Tübingen: Stauffenburg Verlag 1993.

von Kutschera, F., *Grundfragen der Erkenntnistheorie* (DGS), Berlin: de Gruyter 1982.

Lausberg, H., *Handbuch der literarischen Rhetorik*, München: Hueber ²1973.

Martin, J., *Antike Rhetorik* (HAW II.3), München: Beck 1974.

Plett, H. F., *Einführung in die rhetorische Textanalyse*, Hamburg: Buske ⁹2001.

— *Systematische Rhetorik. Konzepte und Analysen* (UTB 2127), München: Fink 2000.

— (Hg.), *Intertextuality* (RTT 15), Berlin – New York: de Gruyter 1991.

Raible, W., „Was sind Gattungen? Eine Antwort aus semiotischer und textlinguistischer Sicht", in: *Poetica* 12 (1980) 320–349.

— „Phänomenologische Textwissenschaft", in: M.-E. Conte (Hg.), *Kontinuität und Diskontinuität in Texten und Sachverhalts-Konfigurationen* (Papiere zur Textlinguistik 50), Hamburg: Buske Verlag 1989, 101–110.

Schild, H.-J., „Beratungsrede", in: *HWR*, Band 1, Darmstadt: Wissenschaftliche Buchgesellschaft 1992, 1441–1454.

Sprute, J., *Die Enthymemtheorie der aristotelischen Rhetorik* (AAWG.PH 124), Göttingen: Vandenhoeck & Ruprecht 1982.

Exegetisch-Theologische Arbeiten

Aitken, E. Bradshaw, *Jesus' Death in Early Christian Memory. The Poetics of the Passion* (NTOA 53), Göttingen: Vandenhoeck & Ruprecht/Fribourg: Academic Press 2004.

Aune, D. E., „Review H. D. Betz, Galatians …", in: *RSR* 7 (1981) 323–328.

Avemarie, F., *Die Tauferzählungen der Apostelgeschichte. Theologie und Geschichte* (WUNT 139), Tübingen: Mohr Siebeck 2002.

Balz, H., „ἅγιος κτλ.", in: *EWNT*, Band I, H. Balz/G. Schneider (Hg.), Stuttgart: Kohlhammer 1980, 38–48.

Barrett, C. K., *The First Epistle to the Corinthians* (BNC), London: Black ²1971.

— *The Acts of the Apostles*, Vol. II (ICC), Edinburgh: T & T Clark 1998.

Barth, G., *Die Taufe in frühchristlicher Zeit*, Neukirchen-Vluyn: Neukirchener Verlag ²2002.

BAUR, F. C., „Die Christuspartei in der korinthischen Gemeinde, der Gegensatz des paulinischen und petrinischen Christentums in der ältesten Kirche, der Apostel Petrus in Rom", in: *TZTh* 4 (1831) 61–206.

BEASLEY-MURRAY, G. R., *Baptism in the New Testament*, London: Macmillan 1962.

BECKER, J., *Paulus. Der Apostel der Völker*, Tübingen: Mohr Siebeck 1989.

— *Der Brief an die Galater* (NTD 8/1), Göttingen: Vandenhoeck & Ruprecht 1998.

BEST, E., *One Body in Christ: A Study in Relationship of the Church of Christ in the Epistles of the Apostel Paul*, London: SPCK 1955.

— *Ephesians* (ICC), Edinburgh: T & T Clark 1998.

BETZ, H. D., „Spirit, Freedom, and Law. Paul's Message to the Galatian Churches", in: *SEÅ* 39 (1974) 145–160. (Deutsche Fassung: „Geist, Freiheit und Gesetz", in: *ZThK* 71 (1974) 78–93 [= in: IDEM, *Paulinische Studien. Gesammelte Aufsätze III*, Tübingen: Mohr Siebeck 1994, 46–62]).

— „The Literary Composition and Function of Paul's Letter to the Galatians", in: *NTS* 21 (1975) 353–379 (= in: IDEM, *Paulinische Studien. Gesammelte Aufsätze III*, 63–97).

— „In Defense of the Spirit: Paul's Letter to the Galatians as a Document of Early Christian Apologetics", in: E. Schüssler-Fiorenza (Hg.), *Aspects of Religious Propaganda in Judaism and Early Christianity*, Notre Dame, Ind.: University of Notre Dame Press 1976, 99–114 (= in: IDEM, *Paulinische Studien. Gesammelte Aufsätze III*, 98–109).

— *Galatians* (Hermeneia), Philadelphia, Pa.: Fortress 1979.

— *2 Corinthians 8 and 9* (Hermeneia), Philadelphia, Pa.: Fortress 1985.

— *Der Galaterbrief. Ein Kommentar zum Brief des Apostels Paulus an die Gemeinden in Galatien* (Ein Hermeneia-Kommentar), München: Kaiser 1988.

— „Magic and Mystery in the Greek Magical Papyri", in: IDEM, *Hellenismus und Urchristentum. Gesammelte Aufsätze I*, Tübingen: Mohr Siebeck 1990, 209–229.

— „Geist, Freiheit und Gesetz", in: IDEM, *Paulinische Studien. Gesammelte Aufsätze III*, 46–62.

— „Galatians, Epistle to the", in: *ABD*, Vol. II, New York: Doubleday 1992, 872–875.

— „Transferring a Ritual: Paul's Interpretation of Baptism in Romans 6", in: T. Engberg-Pedersen, (Hg.), *Paul in His Hellenistic Context*, Edinburgh: T & T Clark/Minneapolis, Minn.: Fortress 1994/95, 84–118 (= in: IDEM, *Paulinische Studien. Gesammelte Aufsätze III*, 240–271).

BETZ, H. D./MITCHELL, M. M., „Corinthians, First Epistle to the", in: *ABD*, Vol. I, New York: Doubleday 1992, 1139–1148.

BIETENHARD, H., „ὄνομα κτλ.", in: *ThWNT*, Band 5, Stuttgart: Kohlhammer 1954, 242–283.

BJERKELUND, C. J., „'Nach menschlicher Weise rede ich'. Funktion und Sinn des paulinischen Ausdrucks", in: IDEM, *Form und Funktion paulinischer Argumentation. Parakalô und sieben kleinere Paulusstudien* (WUNT), hg. von D. Hellholm/R. Aasgaard/V. Blomkvist, Tübingen: Mohr Siebeck in Vorbereitung, 257–307.

— „The Concept of 'Sin' in the New Testament", in: IDEM, *Form und Funktion*, 425–446.

BOERS, H. W., „A Context for Interpreting Paul", in: T. Fornberg/D. Hellholm (Hg.), *Texts and Contexts. Biblical Texts in Their Textual and Situational Contexts*. FS Lars Hartman, Oslo: Scandinavian University Press 1995, 429–463.

BORNKAMM, G., „Taufe und neues Leben bei Paulus", in: IDEM, *Das Ende des Gesetzes. Paulusstudien. Gesammelte Aufsätze Band I* (BEvTh 16), München: Kaiser ³1961, 34–50.

— „Der Römerbrief als Testament des Paulus", in: IDEM, *Geschichte und Glaube. Zweiter Teil. Gesammelte Aufsätze Band IV* (BEvTh 53), München: Kaiser 1971, 120–139.

BOUSSET, W., „Der erste Brief an die Korinther", in: J. Weiß (Hg.), *Die Schriften des Neuen Testaments*, Zweiter Band, Göttingen: Vandenhoeck & Ruprecht ²1908, 72–161.

— *Kyrios Christos. Geschichte des Christusglaubens von den Anfängen des Christentums bis Irenaeus*, Göttingen: Vandenhoeck & Ruprecht ⁵1965 (= ²1921).

BOUTTIER, M., „*Complexio Oppositorum*. Sur les formules de I Cor. XII.13; Gal. III.26–8; Col. III. 10,11", in: *NTS* 23 (1977) 1–19.

BRANDENBURGER, E., „Paulinische Schriftauslegung in der Kontroverse um das Verheißungswort Gottes", in: *ZThK* 82 (1985) 1–47.

BRAUN, H., „Das ‚Stirb und Werde' in der Antike und im Neuen Testament", in: IDEM, *Gesammelte Studien zum Neuen Testament und seiner Umwelt*, Tübingen: Mohr Siebeck ²1967, 136–158.

BROWN, R. E., *An Introduction to the New Testament* (ABRL), New York etc.: Doubleday 1997.

BRUCKER, R., *‚Christushymnen' oder ‚epideiktische Passagen'?* (FRLANT 176), Göttingen: Vandenhoeck & Ruprecht 1997.

BULTMANN, R., „ΔΙΚΑΙΟΣΥΝΗ ΘΕΟΥ", in: IDEM, *Exegetica. Aufsätze zur Erforschung des Neuen Testaments*, hg. von E. Dinkler, Tübingen: Mohr Siebeck 1967, 470–475.

— „Ist die Apokalyptik die Mutter der christlichen Theologie", in: IDEM, *Exegetica*, 476–482.

— *Zweiter Korintherbrief* (KEK Sonderband), hg. von E. Dinkler, Göttingen: Vandenhoeck & Ruprecht 1976.

— *Theologie des Neuen Testaments*, Tübingen: Mohr Siebeck ⁹1984.

BURCHARD, CHR., *Der Jakobusbrief* (HNT 15/I), Tübingen: Mohr Siebeck 2000.

VON CAMPENHAUSEN, H., „Taufe auf den Namen Jesu?", in: IDEM, *Urchristliches und Altkirchliches. Vorträge und Aufsätze*, Tübingen: Mohr Siebeck 1979, 197–216.

CLASSEN, C. J., „Paulus und die antike Rhetorik", in: *ZNW* 82 (1991) 1–33.

CONZELMANN, H., *Die Apostelgeschichte* (HNT 7), Tübingen: Mohr Siebeck ²1972.

— „χάρις κτλ.", in: *ThWNT*, Band 9, Stuttgart: Kohlhammer 1973, 363–366, 377–393.

— „Was glaubte die frühe Christenheit?", in: IDEM, *Theologie als Schriftauslegung. Aufsätze zum Neuen Testament* (BEvTh 65), München: Kaiser 1974, 107–119.

— „Zur Analyse der Bekenntnisformel 1. Kor. 15,3–5", in: IDEM, *Theologie als Schriftauslegung*, 131–141.

— „Paulus und die Weisheit", in: IDEM, *Theologie als Schriftauslegung*, 177–190.

— „Die Schule des Paulus", in: C. Andresen/G. Klein (Hg.), *Theologia Crucis – Signum Crucis*. FS E. Dinkler, Tübingen: Mohr Siebeck 1979, 85–96.

— *Der erste Brief an die Korinther* (KEK 5), Göttingen: Vandenhoeck & Ruprecht ²1981.

CONZELMANN, H./LINDEMANN, A., *Grundriß der Theologie des Neuen Testaments* (UTB 1446), Tübingen: Mohr Siebeck ⁵1992.

COOPER, S. A., „*Narratio* and *Exhortatio* in Galatians According to Marius Victorinus Rhetor", in: *ZNW* 91 (2000) 107–135.

CRANFIELD, C. E. B., *The Epistle to the Romans*, Vol. I (ICC), Edinburgh: T & T Clark 1977.

CUMING, G. J., „ΕΠΟΤΙΣΘΗΜΕΝ (I Corinthians 12.13)", in: *NTS* 27 (1981) 283–285.

DAHL, N. A., „Formgeschichtliche Beobachtungen zur Christusverkündigung in der Gemeindepredigt", in: W. Eltester (Hg.), *Neutestamentliche Studien für Rudolf Bultmann* (BZNW 21), Berlin: Töpelmann ²1957, 3–9.

— „Paul and the Church at Corinth according to 1 Corinthians 1:10–4:21", in: W. R. Farmer/C. F. D. Moule/R. R. Niebuhr (Hg.), *Christian History and Interpretation: Studies Presented to John Knox*, Cambridge, UK: Cambridge University Press 1967, 313–335.

— „Kleidungsmetaphern: der alte und der neue Mensch", in: IDEM, *Studies in Ephesians. Introductory Questions, Text- & Edition-Critical Issues, Interpretation of Texts and Themes*, hg. von D. Hellholm/V. Blomkvist/T. Fornberg (WUNT 131), Tübingen: Mohr Siebeck 2000, 389–411.

— „The Concept of Baptism in Ephesians", in: IDEM, *Studies in Ephesians* 2000, 413–439.

DAHL, N. A. & HELLHOLM, D., „Garment-Metaphors: The Old and New Human Being", in: A. Y. Collins & M. M. Mitchell (Hg.), *Antiquity and Humanity. Essays on Ancient Religion and Philosophy Presented to Hans Dieter Betz on His 70th Birthday*, Tübingen: Mohr Siebeck 2001, 139–158.

DAY, J., „The Catechetical Lectures of Cyril of Jerusalem", in vorliegender Publikation, 1179–1204.

DETTWILER, A., „Enthousiasme religieux dans Rm 6?", in: U. Schnelle (Hg.), *The Letter to the Romans* (BEThL 226), Leuven: Peeters 2009, 279–296.

DIBELIUS, M./GREEVEN, H., *Der Brief des Jakobus* (KEK 15), Göttingen: Vandenhoeck & Ruprecht ¹¹1964.

DINKLER, E., „Zum Problem der Ethik bei Paulus. Rechtsnahme und Rechtsverzicht (1Kor 6,1–11)", in: IDEM, *Signum Crucis. Aufsätze zum Neuen Testament und zur Christlichen Archäologie*, Tübingen: Mohr Siebeck 1967, 204–240.

— „Die Taufaussagen des Neuen Testaments", in: F. Viering (Hg.), *Zu Karl Barths Lehre von der Taufe*, Gütersloh: Mohn 1971, 60–153.

VON DOBSCHÜTZ, E., *Die Thessalonicher-Briefe* (KEK 10), Göttingen: Vandenhoeck & Ruprecht 1974 (= 1909).

DONELSON, L. R., *Pseudepigraphy and Ethical Argument in the Pastoral Epistles* (HUTh 22), Tübingen: Mohr Siebeck 1986.

DUNN, J. D. G., *Baptism in the Holy Spirit* (SPT 2:15), London: SCM 1970.

— *Romans 1–8* (WBC 38A), Dallas, Tex.: Word Books 1988.

— *The Theology of Paul the Apostle*, Grand Rapids, Mich.: Eerdmans 1998.

EKENBERG, A., *Hippolytos. Den Apostoliska Traditionen*, Uppsala: Katolska Bokförlaget 1994.

— „Initiation in the *Apostolic Tradition*", in vorliegender Publikation, 1011–1050.

EMMINGHAUS, J. H., „Der gottesdienstliche Raum und seine Ausstattung ... ‚Der Taufort'", in: R. Berger et alii, *Gestalt des Gottesdienstes. Sprachliche und nichtsprachliche Ausdrucksformen* (GdK 3), Regensburg: Pustet ²1990, 353–425.

ERIKSSON, A., *Traditions and Rhetorical Proof. Pauline Argumentation in 1 Corinthians* (CB.NT 29), Stockholm: Almqvist & Wiksell 1998.

ESLER, PH. F., *Conflict and Identity in Romans. The Social Setting of Paul's Letter*, Minneapolis, Minn.: Fortress 2003.

FEE, G. D., *The First Epistle to the Corinthians* (NICNT), Grand Rapids, Mich.: Eerdmans 1987.

— *Paul's Letter to the Philippians* (NICNT), Grand Rapids, Mich.: Eerdmans 1995.

FERGUSON, E., *Baptism in the Early Church. History, Theology, and Liturgy in the First Five Centuries*, Grand Rapids, Mich.: Eerdmans 2009.

FITZGERALD, J. T., „Philippians, Epistle to the", in: *ABD*, Vol. V, New York etc.: Doubleday 1992, 318–326.

FITZMYER, J. A., *Romans. A New Translation with Introduction and Commentary* (AncB 33), New York: Doubleday 1993.

— *The Acts of the Apostles. A New Translation with Introduction and Commentary* (AncB 31), New York: Doubleday 1998.

— *First Corinthians. A New Translation with Introduction and Commentary* (Anchor Yale Bible 32), New Haven, Conn./London: Yale University Press 2008.

FRANKEMÖLLE, H., *Der Brief des Jakobus. Kapitel 2–5* (ÖTK 17/2), Gütersloh: Mohn/Würzburg: Echter 1994.

FRID, B., „Römer 6,4–5", in: *BZ* 30 (1986) 188–203.

GÄUMANN, N., *Taufe und Ethik. Studien zu Römer 6* (BEvTh 47), München: Kaiser 1967.

GAMBLE, H. Y., *The Textual History of the Letter to the Romans* (SD 42), Grand Rapids, Mich.: Eerdmans 1977.

VON GEMÜNDEN, P., „Die urchristliche Taufe und der Umgang mit den Affekten", in: J. Assmann/G. Stroumsa (Hg.), *Transformations of the Inner Self in Ancient Religions* (Numen.BS), Leiden: Brill 1999, 115–136.

GOPPELT, L., *Der Erste Petrusbrief* (KEK 12/1), Göttingen: Vandenhoeck & Ruprecht 1978.

GRAF, F., „Mystagogos", in: *DNP*, Band 8, Stuttgart – Weimar: Metzler/Darmstadt: Wissenschaftliche Buchgesellschaft 2000, 611.

— „Baptism and Graeco-Roman Mystery Cults", in vorliegender Publikation, 101–118.

HAHN, F., „Taufe und Rechtfertigung. Ein Beitrag zur paulinischen Theologie in ihrer Vor- und Nachgeschichte", in: J. Friedrich/W. Pöhlmann/P. Stuhlmacher (Hg.), *Rechtfertigung*. FS E. Käsemann, Tübingen: Mohr Siebeck 1976, 95–124 (= in: IDEM, *Studien zum Neuen Testament*, Band II [WUNT 192], Tübingen: Mohr Siebeck 2006, 241–270).

— *Theologie des Neuen Testaments*, Band I, Tübingen: Mohr Siebeck 2002.

— *Theologie des Neuen Testaments*, Band II, Tübingen: Mohr Siebeck 2002.

HALLBÄCK, G., „Jerusalem og Antiokia i Gal. 2. En historisk hypotese", in: *DTT* 53 (1990) 300–316.

HALTER, H., *Taufe und Ethos. Paulinische Kriterien für das Proprium christlicher Moral* (FThSt 106), Freiburg i. Br.: Herder 1977.

VON HARNACK, A., *Mission und Ausbreitung des Christentums in den ersten drei Jahrhunderten*, Leipzig: Hinrichs'sche ⁴1924/Wiesbaden: VMA Verlag o.J.

HARRILL, J. A., „Paul and Slavery", in: J. P Sampley (Hg.), *Paul in the Greco-Roman World. A Handbook*, Harrisburg, Pa.: Trinity Press 2003, 575–607.

HARTMAN, L., „La formule baptismale dans les Actes des Apôtres: Quelques observations relatives au style de Luc", in: *À cause de L'Évangile. Mélanges offerts à Dom Jacques Dupont* (LeDiv 123), Paris: Cerf 1985, 727–738.

— „Baptism", in: *ABD*, Vol. 1, New York: Doubleday 1992, 583–594.

— ,Auf den Namen des Herrn Jesus'. *Die Taufe in den neutestamentlichen Schriften* (SBS 148), Stuttgart: Katholisches Bibelwerk 1992.

— *'Into the Name of the Lord Jesus'. Baptism in the Early Church* (SNTW), Edinburgh: T & T Clark 1997.

— „A Commentary: A Communication about a Communication", in: *NT* 51 (2009), 389–400.

— „Usages — Some Notes on the Baptismal Name-Formulae", in vorliegender Publikation, 397–413.

HARTVIGSEN, K. M., *'Prepare the Way of the Lord'. Towards a Cognitive Poetic Analysis of Audience Involvement with Characters and Events in the Markan World*, PhD Diss. Oslo Universität 2009 (Erscheint in BZNW 2011).

— „Matthew 28:9–20 and Mark 16:9–20. Different Ways of Relating Baptism to the Joint Mission of God, John the Baptist, Jesus, and their Adherents", in vorliegender Publikation, 655–716.

HARVEY, J. D., *Listenting to the Text: Oral Patterning in Paul's Letters* (ETSSt), Grand Rapids, Mich.: Baker 1998.

HEININGER, B., „Von der Jugendweihe zur Taufe. Initiationsriten in der Antike und im frühen Christentum", in: IDEM, *Die Inkulturation des Christentums. Aufsätze und Studien zum Neuen Testament und seiner Umwelt* (WUNT 255), Tübingen: Mohr Siebeck 2010, 231–255.

HEINRICI, G., *Der erste Brief an die Korinther* (KEK 5), Göttingen: Vandenhoeck & Ruprecht 1896.

HEITMÜLLER, W., *,Im Namen Jesu'. Eine sprach- u. religionsgeschichtliche Untersuchung zum Neuen Testament, speziell zur altchristlichen Taufe* (FRLANT 1), Göttingen: Vandenhoeck & Ruprecht 1903.

— *Taufe und Abendmahl bei Paulus. Darstellung und religionsgeschichtliche Beleuchtung*, Göttingen: Vandenhoeck & Ruprecht 1903.

— „Zum Problem Paulus und Jesus", in: *ZNW* 13 (1912) 320–337 (= in: K. H. Rengstorf (Hg.), *Das Paulusbild in der neueren deutschen Forschung* [WdF 24], Darmstadt: Wissenschaftliche Buchgesellschaft 1964, 134–143).

HELLHOLM, D., *Das Visionenbuch des Hermas als Apokalypse. Formgeschichtliche und texttheoretische Studien zu einer literarischen Gattung* (CB.NT 13), Lund: Gleerup 1980.

— „Enthymemic Argumentation in Paul: The Case of Romans 6", in: T. Engberg-Pedersen (Hg.), *Paul in His Hellenistic Context*, Edinburgh: T & T Clark/ Minneapolis, Minn.: Fortress 1994/95, 119–179.

— „Die argumentative Funktion von Römer 7.1–6", in: *NTS* 43 (1997) 385–411.

— „The 'Revelation – Schema' and Its Adaptation in the Coptic Gnostic Apocalypse of Peter", in: *SEÅ* 63 (1998) 233–248.

— „Beatitudes and Their Illocutionary Functions", in: A. Y. Collins (Hg.), *Ancient and Modern Perspectives on the Bible and Culture*. FS H. D. Betz (Scholars Press Homage Series 22), Atlanta, Ga.: Scholars Press 1998, 286–344.

— „The Impact of the Situational Contexts for Paul's Use of Baptismal Traditions in His Letters", in: D. E Aune/T. Seland/J. H. Ulrichsen (Hg.), *Neotestamentica et Philonica. Studies in Honor of Peder Borgen* (NT.S 106), Leiden: Brill 2003, 147–175.

— „Universalität und Partikularität. Die amplifikatorische Struktur von Römer 5,12–21", in: D. Sänger/U. Mell (Hg.), *Paulus und Johannes. Exegetische Studien zur paulinischen und johanneischen Theologie und Literatur* (WUNT 198), Tübingen: Mohr Siebeck 2006, 217–269.

— „Paulus och den urkristna doptraditionen", in: *NTT* 110/3 (2009) 132–151.

HERMANN, I., *Kyrios und Pneuma. Studien zur Christologie der paulinischen Hauptbriefe* (StANT 2), München: Kösel 1961.

HOFIUS, O., „Gemeinschaft am Tisch des Herrn", in: IDEM, *Exegetische Studien* (WUNT 223), Tübingen: Mohr Siebeck 2008, 203–217.

HOLLADAY, C. R., *A Critical Introduction to the New Testament. Interpreting the Message and Meaning of Jesus Christ*, Nashville, Tenn.: Abingdon Press 2005.

HOLLOWAY, P. A., „Paul's Pointed Prose: The *Sententia* in Roman Rhetoric and Paul", in: *NT* 40 (1998) 32–54.

HOLTZ, T., „ὁμοίωμα/ὁμοίωσις", in: *EWNT*, Band II, Stuttgart: Kohlhammer 1981, 1254–1255.

HORN, F. W., *Das Angeld des Geistes. Studien zur paulinischen Pneumatologie* (FRLANT 154), Göttingen: Vandenhoeck & Ruprecht 1992.

— „Stephanas und sein Haus – die erste christliche Hausgemeinde in der Achaia. Ihre Stellung in der Kommunikation zwischen Paulus und der korinthischen Gemeinde", in: D. Bienert/J. Jeska/Th. Witulski (Hg.), *Paulus und die antike Welt. Beiträge zur zeit- und religionsgeschichtlichen Erforschung des paulinischen Christentums*. FS D.-A. Koch (FRLANT 222), Göttingen: Vandenhoeck & Ruprecht 2008, 83–98.

HÜBNER, H., *Biblische Theologie des Neuen Testaments*, Band 2, Göttingen: Vandenhoeck & Ruprecht 1993.

— *An Philemon, An die Kolosser, An die Epheser* (HNT 12), Tübingen: Mohr Siebeck 1997.

HUNTER, H., *Spirit-Baptism, A Pentecostal Alternative*, Lanham, Md.: University Press of America 1983.

JERVELL, J., „The Letter to Jerusalem", in: K. P. Donfried (Hg.), *The Romans Debate*. Revised and Expanded Edition, Peabody, Mass.: Hendrickson 1991, 53–64.

JEWETT, R., *Romans* (Hermeneia), Minneapolis, Minn.: Fortress 2007.

JÜLICHER, A./FASCHER, E., *Einleitung in das Neue Testament*, Tübingen: J. C. B. Mohr (Paul Siebeck) [7]1931.

KÄSEMANN, E., „Anliegen und Eigenart der paulinischen Abendmahlslehre", in: IDEM, *Exegetische Versuche und Besinnungen*, Band I-II: Erster Band, Göttingen: Vandenhoeck & Ruprecht 1964, 11–34.

— „Zum Verständnis von Röm 3,24–26", in: IDEM, *Exegetische Versuche und Besinnungen*, Erster Band, 96–100.

— *An die Römer* (HNT 8a), Tübingen: Mohr Siebeck [3]1974.

KENNEDY, G. A., *New Testament Interpretation Through Rhetorical Criticism*, Chapel Hill, N.C.: University of North Carolina Press 1984.

KLAUCK, H.-J., *Herrenmahl und hellenistischer Kult. Eine religionsgeschichtliche Untersuchung zum ersten Korintherbrief* (NA 15), Münster: Aschendorff 1982.

— „Die antiken Mysterienkulte und das Urchristentum. Anknüpfung und Widerspruch", in: IDEM, *Religion und Gesellschaft im frühen Christentum. Neutestamentliche Studien* (WUNT 152), Tübingen: Mohr Siebeck 2003, 171–193.

— *Die Apokryphe Bibel. Ein anderer Zugang zum Frühen Christentum* (Tria Corda 4), Tübingen: Mohr Siebeck 2008.

KLEIN, H., „Die Gegenwart des neuen Lebens in der Sicht des Apostels Paulus", in: H. Klein/H. Pitters (Hg.), *Im Kraftfeld des Evangeliums*. FS H. Binder, (Beihefte der „Kirchlichen Blätter" 3), Sibiu-Hermannstadt: Landeskonsistorium der Evangelischen Kirche in Rumänien 1981, 61–80.

KLEINHEYER, B., *Sakramentliche Feiern 1. Die Feiern der Eingliederung in die Kirche* (GdK 7/1), Regensburg: Pustet 1989.

KOCH, D.-A., „Zwölferkreis und Gottesvolk. Überlegungen zur Frühgeschichte neutestamentlicher Ekklesiologie", in: IDEM, *Hellenistisches Christentum. Schriftverständnis – Ekklesiologie – Geschichte* (NTOA 65), Göttingen: Vandenhoeck & Ruprecht 2008, 111–125.

— „Crossing the border: The 'Hellenists' and their way to the Gentiles", in: IDEM, *Hellenistisches Christentum*, 213–231.

— „Barnabas, Paulus und die Adressaten des Galaterbriefs", in: IDEM, *Hellenistisches Christentum*, 299–317.

— „Die Christen als neue Randgruppen in Makedonien und Achaia im 1. Jahrhundert n.Chr.", in: IDEM, *Hellenisisches Christentum*, 340–368.

KOESTER, H., *Introduction to the New Testament, Vol. 2: History and Literature of Early Christianity*, Berlin – New York: de Gruyter [2]2000.

KONRADT, M., *Gericht und Gemeinde. Eine Studie zur Bedeutung und Funktion von Gerichtsaussagen im Rahmen der paulinischen Ekklesiologie und Ethik im 1 Thess und 1 Kor* (BZNW 117), Berlin – New York: de Gruyter 2003.

— „Die korinthische Weisheit und das Wort vom Kreuz. Erwägungen zur korinthischen Problemkonstellation und paulinischen Intention in 1 Kor 1–4", in: *ZNW* 94 (2003) 181–214.

KRAMER, W., *Christos – Kyrios – Gottessohn. Untersuchungen zu Gebrauch und Bedeutung der christologischen Bezeichnungen bei Paulus und den vorpaulinischen Gemeinden* (AThANT 44), Zürich: Zwingli 1963.

KRAUS, W., *Der Tod Jesu als Heiligtumsweihe. Eine Untersuchung zum Umfeld der Sühnevorstellung in Römer 3,25–26a* (WMANT 66), Neukirchen-Vluyn: Neukirchener Verlag 1991.

KÜMMEL, W. G., *Einleitung in das Neue Testament*, Heidelberg: Quelle & Meyer [17]1973.

KÜRZINGER, J., „Zur Taufaussage von Röm 6", in: L. Lenhart (Hg.), *Universitas. Dienst an Wahrheit und Leben. FS A. Stohr*, Mainz: Grünewald 1960, 93–98.

LAMPE, P., *Die stadtrömischen Christen in den ersten beiden Jahrhunderten. Untersuchungen zur Sozialgeschichte* (WUNT 2/18), Tübingen: Mohr Siebeck [2]1989.

— „The Roman Christians of Romans 16", in: K. P. Donfried (Hg.), *The Romans Debate*. Revidierte und erweiterte Aufl., Peabody, Mass.: Hendrickson 1991, 216–230.

— *From Paul to Valentinus. Christians at Rome in the First Two Centuries*, Minneapolis, Minn.: Fortress 2003.

LARSSON, E., *Christus als Vorbild. Eine Untersuchung zu den paulinischen Tauf- und Eikontexten* (ASNU 23), Lund: Gleerup 1962.

LEE, M. V., *Paul, the Stoics, and the Body of Christ* (MSSNTS 137), Cambridge, UK: Cambridge University Press 2006.

LEENHARDT, F. J., *Le baptême chrétien* (CThAP 4); Neuchâtel: Delachaux & Niestlé 1944.

LIETZMANN, H./KÜMMEL, W. G., *An die Korinther I/II* (HNT 9), Tübingen: Mohr Siebeck ⁵1969.

LIGHTFOOT, J. B., *St. Paul's Epistle to the Philippians*, London: Macmillan 1913 (Reprint Grand Rapids, Mich.: Zondervan 1953/1978).

LINDEMANN, A., *Paulus im ältesten Christentum. Das Bild des Apostels und die Rezeption der paulinischen Theologie in der frühchristlichen Literatur bis Marcion* (BHTh 58), Tübingen: Mohr Siebeck 1979.

— *Der Erste Korintherbrief* (HNT 9/I), Tübingen: Mohr Siebeck 2000.

LINTON, O., „Paulus och Juridiken", in: *SvTK* 21 (1945) 173–192.

LOHFINK, G., „Die Vermittlung des Paulinismus zu den Pastoralbriefen", in: *BZ* 32 (1988) 169–188.

LOHSE, E., „Taufe und Rechtfertigung bei Paulus", in: *KuD* 11 (1965) 308–324 (= in: IDEM, *Die Einheit des Neuen Testaments. Exegetische Studien zur Theologie des Neuen Testaments*, Band I, Göttingen: Vandenhoeck & Ruprecht 1973, 228–244).

— „Wort und Sakrament in der paulinischen Theologie", in: F. Viering, (Hg.), *Zu Karl Barths Lehre von der Taufe*, Gütersloh: Mohn 1971, 44–59.

— *Der Brief an die Römer* (KEK 4), Göttingen: Vandenhoeck & Ruprecht 2003.

— „Christus, des Gesetzes Ende? Die Theologie des Apostels Paulus in kritischer Perspektive", in: *ZNW* 99 (2008) 18–32.

LÜDEMANN, G., *Paulus der Heidenapostel. Band I: Studien zur Chronologie* (FRLANT 123), Göttingen: Vandenhoeck & Ruprecht 1980.

LUEDEMANN, G., *Paul Apostle to the Gentiles. Studies in Chronology*, Philadelphia, Pa.: Fortress 1984.

LÜHRMANN, D., „Galaterbrief", in: *RGG*⁴, Band III, Tübingen: Mohr Siebeck 2000, 451–453.

LÜTGERT, W., *Der Römerbrief als historisches Problem*, Gütersloh: Bertelsmann 1913.

LUZ, U., „Zum Aufbau von Röm. 1–8", in: *ThZ* 25 (1969) 161–181.

LYONS, G., *Pauline Autobiography. Toward a New Understanding* (SBL.DS 73), Atlanta, Ga.: Scholars Press 1985.

MARSHALL, I. H., *The Pastoral Epistles* (ICC), Edinburgh: T & T Clark 1999.

MARTIN, R./HAWTHORNE, G. F., *Philippians* (WBC 43), Nashville, Tenn.: Thomas Nelson 2004.

MARTYN, J. L., *Galatians. A New Translation with Introduction and Commentary* (AncB 33A), New York: Doubleday 1997.

MEEKS, W. A., „The Image of the Androgyne: Some Uses of a Symbol in Earliest Christianity", in: *HR* 13 (1974) 165–208.

— *The First Urban Christians. The Social World of the Apostle Paul*, New Haven, Conn.: Yale University Press 1983.

MEISER, M., *Galater* (Novum Testamentum Patristicum 9), Göttingen: Vandenhoeck & Ruprecht 2007.

MERKLEIN, H./GIELEN, M., *Der erste Brief an die Korinther. Kapitel 11,2–16,24* (ÖTK 7/3), Gütersloh: Gütersloher Verlag 2005.

MERZ, A., *Die fiktive Selbstauslegung des Paulus. Intertextuelle Studien zur Intention und Rezeption der Paulusbriefe* (NTOA/StUNT 52), Göttingen: Vandenhoeck & Ruprecht/Fribourg, CH: Academic Press 2004.

MITCHELL, M. M., *Paul and the Rhetoric of Reconciliation. An Exegetical Investigation of the Language and Composition of 1 Corinthians* (HUTh 28), Tübingen: Mohr Siebeck 1991.

— „Korintherbriefe", in: *RGG*[4], Band 4, Tübingen: Mohr Siebeck 2001, 1688–1694.

— „Reading Rhetoric with Patristic Exegetes. John Chrysostom on Galatians", in: A. Y. Collins/M. M. Mitchell (Hg.), *Antiquity and Humanity. Essays on Ancient Religion and Philosophy*. FS H. D. Betz, Tübingen: Mohr Siebeck 2001, 333–355.

— „The Corinthian Correspondence and the Birth of Pauline Hermeneutics", in: T. J. Burke/J. K. Elliott (Hg.), *Paul and the Corinthians. Studies on a Community in Conflict. Essays in Honour of Margaret Thrall* (NT.S 109), Leiden: Brill 2003, 17–53.

— „The Letter of James as a Document of Paulinism?", in: R. L. Webb/J. S. Kloppenborg (Hg.), *Reading James with New Eyes. Methodological Reassessments of the Letter of James*, London: T & T Clark 2007, 75–98.

MOXNES, H., „From Theology to Identity: The Problem of Constructing Early Christianity", in: T. Penner/C. Vander Stichele (Hg.), *Moving Beyond New Testament Theology? Essays in Conversation with Heikki Räisänen* (Publication of the Finnish Exegetical Society 88), Helsinki: Finnish Exegetical Society/Göttingen: Vandenhoeck & Ruprecht 2005, 264–281.

MÜLLER, U. B., *Der Brief des Paulus an die Philipper* (ThHK 11/I), Leipzig: Evangelische Verlagsanstalt ²2002.

NEIJENHUIS, J., „Taufbecken", in: *RGG*⁴, Band 8, Tübingen: Mohr Siebeck 2005, 49.

NIEDERWIMMER, K., *Die Didache* (KAV 1), Göttingen: Vandenhoeck & Ruprecht 1989.

— „Pax Dei custodia cordis (Phil 4,7)", in: *WZTh* 7 (2008) 293–311.

OBERLINNER, L., *Die Pastoralbriefe. Zweite Folge: Kommentar zum Zweiten Timotheusbrief* (HThK X I/2), Freiburg i. Br.: Herder 1995.

OEPKE, A., „λούω, ἀπολούω κτλ.", in: *ThWNT*, Band 4, Stuttgart: Kohlhammer 1942, 297–309.

OLLROG, W.-H., „Die Abfassungsverhältnisse von Röm 16", in: D. Lührmann/ G. Strecker (Hg.), *Kirche*. FS G. Bornkamm, Tübingen: Mohr Siebeck 1980, 221–244.

OMERZU, H., *Der Prozeß des Paulus. Eine exegetische und rechtshistorische Untersuchung der Apostelgeschichte* (BZNW 115), Berlin – New York: de Gruyter 2002.

PAULSEN, H., „Einheit und Freiheit der Söhne Gottes – Gal 3,26–29", in: *ZNW* 71 (1980) 74–95 (= in: IDEM, *Zur Literatur und Geschichte des frühen Christentums. Gesammelte Aufsätze*, hg. von U. E. Eisen [WUNT 99], Tübingen: Mohr Siebeck 1997, 21–43).

PETERMAN, G. W., *Paul's Gift from Philippi. Conventions of Gift Exchange and Christian Giving* (MSSNTS 92), Cambridge, UK: Cambridge University Press 1997.

PETERSEN, N. R., „Pauline Baptism and 'Secundary Burial'", in: G. W. E. Nickelsburg/G. W. MacRae (Hg.), *Christians among Jews and Gentiles*. FS K. Stendahl, Philadelphia, Pa.: Fortress 1986, 217–226.

— „On the Ending(s) of Paul's Letter to Rome", in: B. A. Pearson (Hg.), *The Future of Early Christianity*. FS H. Koester, Minneapolis, Minn.: Fortress 1991, 337–347.

PETERSON, E., *Der erste Brief an die Korinther und Paulus Studien* [E. Peterson, Ausgewählte Schriften 7], Aus dem Nachlass hg. von H.-U. Weidemann, Würzburg: Echter 2006.

POKORNÝ, P./HECKEL, U., *Einleitung in das Neue Testament. Seine Literatur und Theologie im Überblick* (UTB 2798), Tübingen: Mohr Siebeck 2007.

POPKES, W., *Der Brief des Jakobus* (ThHK 14), Leipzig: Evangelische Verlagsanstalt 2001.

— „1Kor 2,2 und die Anfänge der Christologie", in: *ZNW* 95 (2004) 64–83.

DE LA POTTERIE, I., „Discussion", in: L. de Lorenzi (Hg.), *Battesimo e giustizia in Rom 6 e 8* (Serie Monografica di 'Benedictina'. Serie biblico-ecumenica 2), Roma: Abbazia 1974, 103–126.

PRATSCHER, W., *Der Herrenbruder Jakobus und die Jakobustradition* (FRLANT 139), Göttingen: Vandenhoeck & Ruprecht 1987.

REICHERT, A., *Der Römerbrief als Gradwanderung. Eine Untersuchung zur Abfassungsproblematik* (FRLANT 194), Göttingen: Vandenhoeck & Ruprecht 2001.

REUMANN, J., *Philippians. A New Translation with Introduction and Commentary* (Anchor Yale Bible 33B), New Haven, Conn. – London: Yale University Press 2008.

RIEDWEG, CHR., *Mysterienterminologie bei Platon, Philon und Klemens von Alexandrien* (UaLG 26), Berlin – New York: de Gruyter 1987 (Englische Ausgabe in Vorbereitung).

ROBERTSON, A./PLUMMER, A., *First Epistle of St Paul to the Corinthians* (ICC), Edinburgh: T & T Clark ²1914.

SÄNGER, D., „Ewiges Leben mit und ohne Auferstehung – Transmortale Vorstellungen im frühen Judentum", in: Ph. David/H. Rosenau (Hg.), *Auferstehung. Ringvorlesung der Theologischen Fakultät Kiel* (Kieler Theologische Reihe 10), Berlin – Münster: Lit 2009, 49–80.

— „Die Adressaten des Galaterbriefs und das Problem einer Entwicklung in Paulus' theologischem Denken", in: W. KRAUS (Hg.), *Beiträge zur urchristlichen Theologiegeschichte* (BZNW 163), Berlin – New York: de Gruyter 2009, 247–275.

— „Die Adresse des Galaterbriefs. Neue (?) Überlegungen zu einem alten Problem", in: M. Bachmann/B. Kollmann (Hg.), *Umstrittener Galaterbrief. Studien zur Situierung und Theologie des Paulus-Schreibens* (BThSt 106), Neukirchen-Vluyn: Neukirchener Verlag 2010, 1–53.

— „Literarische Strategien der Polemik im Galaterbrief", in: O. Wischmeyer/L. Scornaienchi (Hg.), *Polemik in der frühchristlichen Literatur* (BZNW 170), Berlin – New York: de Gruyter 2011, 155–181.

SCHENK, W., *Die Philipperbriefe des Paulus. Kommentar*, Stuttgart etc.: Kohlhammer 1984.

SCHENKE, H.-M./FISCHER, K. M., *Einleitung in die Schriften des Neuen Testaments. I: Die Briefe des Paulus und Schriften des Paulinismus*, Berlin: Evangelische Verlagsanstalt 1978.

SCHLARB, R., *Wir sind mit Christus begraben. Die Auslegung von Römer 6,1–11 im Frühchristentum bis Origenes* (BGBE 31), Tübingen: Mohr Siebeck 1990.

SCHLIER, H., *Der Brief an die Galater* (KEK 7), Göttingen: Vandenhoeck & Ruprecht ^{12}1962.

— *Der Römerbrief* (HThK 6), Freiburg i. Br.: Herder 1977.

SCHMITHALS, W., *Der Römerbrief. Ein Kommentar*, Gütersloh: Mohn 1988.

SCHNACKENBURG, R., *Das Heilsgeschehen bei der Taufe nach dem Apostel Paulus. Eine Studie zur paulinischen Theologie* (MThS 1), München: Zink 1950.

— „Todes- und Lebensgemeinschaft mit Christus. Neue Studien zu Röm 6,1–11", in: *MThZ* 6 (1955) 32–53.

SCHNEIDER, H., „Die Entwicklung der Taufbecken in der Spätantike", in vorliegender Publikation, 1695–1718.

SCHNEIDER, J., *Die Taufe im Neuen Testament*, Stuttgart: Kohlhammer 1952.

SCHNELLE, U., *Gerechtigkeit und Christusgegenwart. Vorpaulinische und paulinische Tauftheologie* (GThA 24), Göttingen: Vandenhoeck & Ruprecht 1983.

— *Einleitung in das Neue Testament* (UTB 1830), Göttingen: Vandenhoeck & Ruprecht ^{4}2002.

— *Paulus. Leben und Denken* (GLB), Berlin – New York: de Gruyter 2003.

SCHRAGE, W., „Das apostolische Amt des Paulus nach 1Kor 4,14–17", in: A. Vanhoye (Hg.), *L'Apôtre Paul. Personnalité, style et conception du ministère*, (BEThL 78), Leuven: University Press/Peeters 1986, 103–119.

— *Der Erste Brief an die Korinther (1Kor 1,1–6,11)* (EKK VII/1), Zürich: Benziger/Neukirchen-Vluyn: Neukirchener Verlag 1991.

— *Der Erste Brief an die Korinther (1Kor 11,17–14,40)* (EKK VII/3), Zürich: Benziger/Neukirchen-Vluyn: Neukirchener Verlag 1999.

— *Der Erste Brief an die Korinther (1Kor 15,1–16,24)* (EKK VII/4), Zürich: Benziger/Neukirchen-Vluyn: Neukirchener Verlag 2001.

SCHWEIZER, E., „Zum religionsgeschichtlichen Hintergrund der ‚Sendungsformel' Gal 4,4f; Röm 8,3f; Joh 3,16f; 1 Joh 4,9", in: IDEM, *Beiträge zur Theologie des Neuen Testaments*, Zürich: Zwingli 1970, 83–95.

— „Was meinen wir eigentlich, wenn wir sagen ‚Gott sandte seinen Sohn'?", in: *NTS* 37 (1991) 204–224.

SEEBERG, A., *Der Katechismus der Urchristenheit*, Leipzig: Deichert 1903 (Neudruck: München: Kaiser 1966).

SELLIN, G., „Das ‚Geheimnis' der Weisheit und das Rätsel der ‚Christuspartei' (zu 1 Kor 1–4)", in: *ZNW* 73 (1982) 69–96 (= in: IDEM, *Studien zu Paulus und zum Epheserbrief* [FRANT 229], hg. von D. Sänger, Göttingen: Vandenhoeck & Ruprecht 2009, 9–36).

— „‚Die Auferstehung ist schon geschehen'. Zur Spiritualisierung apokalyptischer Terminologie", in: *NT* 25 (1982) 220–237 (= in: IDEM, *Studien zu Paulus und zum Epheserbrief*, 37–52).

— „Die Armen und die Reichen in Korinth. Vom Umgang einer urchristlichen Großstadtgemeinde mit den sozialen Problemen", in: *Die Armen und die Reichen. Soziale Gerechtigkeit in der Stadt?* (Kirche in der Stadt 3), Hamburg: E.B.-Verlag Rissen 1993, 29–44.

— „Ästhetische Aspekte der Sprache in den Briefen des Paulus", in: D. Sänger/U. Mell (Hg.), *Paulus und Johannes. Exegetische Studien zur paulinischen und johanneischen Theologie und Literatur* (WUNT 198), Tübingen: Mohr Siebeck 2006, 411–426 (= in: IDEM, *Studien zu Paulus und zum Epheserbrief*, 148–163).

— *Der Brief an die Epheser* (KEK 8), Göttingen: Vandenhoeck & Ruprecht 2008.

SIBER, P., *Mit Christus leben. Eine Studie zur paulinischen Auferstehungshoffnung* (AThANT 61), Zürich: Theologischer Verlag 1971.

STANDHARTINGER, A., *Studien zur Entstehungsgeschichte & Intention des Kolosserbriefs* (NT.S 94), Leiden: Brill 1999.

STEYN, G. J., „Reflections on TO ONOMA TOY KYPIOY in 1 Corinthians", in: R. Bieringer (Hg.), *The Corinthian Correspondence* (BEThL 125), Leuven: University Press/Peeters 1996, 479–490.

STOWERS, S. K., *Letter Writing in Greco-Roman Antiquity* (LEC), Philadelphia, Pa.: Westminster 1986.

STRECKER, CHR., *Die liminale Theologie des Paulus. Zugänge zur paulinischen Theologie aus kulturanthropologischer Perspektive* (FRLANT 185), Göttingen: Vandenhoeck & Ruprecht 1999.

STRECKER, G., *Theologie des Neuen Testaments* (GLB), Berlin – New York: de Gruyter 1996.

STRECKER, G./NOLTING, T., "Der vorchristliche Paulus. Überlegungen zum biographischen Kontext biblischer Überlegungen", in: T. Fornberg/D. Hellholm/ Chr. Hellholm (Hg.), *Texts and Contexts. Biblical Texts in their Textual and Situational Contexts*. FS Lars Hartman, Oslo etc.: Scandinavian University Press 1995, 713–741.

STRECKER, G./SCHNELLE, U./SEELIG, G. (Hg.), *Neuer Wettstein. Texte zum Neuen Testament aus Griechentum und Hellenismus. Band II: Texte zur Briefliteratur und zur Johannesapokalypse. Teilband 1*, Berlin – New York: de Gruyter 1996.

TACHAU, P., *‚Einst' und ‚Jetzt' im Neuen Testament* (FRLANT 105), Göttingen: Vandenhoeck & Ruprecht 1972.

TANNEHILL, R. C., *Dying and Rising with Christ* (BZNW 32), Berlin: Töpelmann 1966.

THEISSEN, G., "Soziale Schichtung in der korinthischen Gemeinde. Ein Beitrag zur Soziologie des Hellenistischen Urchristentums", in: *ZNW* 65 (1974) 232–272 (= in: IDEM, *Studien zur Soziologie des Urchristentum* [WUNT 19], Tübingen: Mohr Siebeck 1979, 231–271).

— *Psychologische Aspekte paulinischer Theologie* (FRLANT 131), Göttingen: Vandenhoeck & Ruprecht 1983.

— "Die urchristliche Taufe und die soziale Konstruktion des neuen Menschen", in: J. Assmann/G. Stroumsa (Hg.), *Transformations of the Inner Self in Ancient Religions* (Numen.BS), Leiden: Brill 1999, 87–114.

— *Die Religionen der ersten Christen. Eine Theorie des Urchristentums*, Gütersloh: Chr. Kaiser & Gütersloher Verlag/Darmstadt: Wissenschaftliche Buchgesellschaft ³2003.

— "Das Kreuz als Sühne und Ärgernis. Zwei Deutungen des Todes Jesu bei Paulus", in: D. Sänger/U. Mell (Hg.), *Paulus und Johannes. Exegetische Studien zur paulinischen und johanneischen Theologie und Literatur* (WUNT 198), Tübingen: Mohr Siebeck 2006, 427–455.

THISELTON, A. C., *The First Epistle to the Corinthians* (NIGTC), Grand Rapids, Mich.: Eerdmans/Carlisle, UK: Paternoster 2000.

THYEN, H., *Studien zur Sündenvergebung im Neuen Testament und seinen alttestamentlichen und jüdischen Voraussetzungen* (FRLANT 96), Göttingen: Vandenhoeck & Ruprecht 1970.

TROBISCH, D., *Die Entstehung der Paulusbriefsammlung* (NTOA 10), Freiburg, CH: Universitätsverlag/Göttingen: Vandenhoeck & Ruprecht 1989.

— *Die Paulusbriefe und die Anfänge der christlichen Publizistik* (KT 135), Gütersloh: Kaiser 1994.

UMBACH, H., *In Christus getauft – von der Sünde befreit. Die Gemeinde als sündenfreier Raum bei Paulus* (FRLANT 181), Göttingen: Vandenhoeck & Ruprecht 1992.

VEGGE, T., *Paulus und das antike Schulwesen. Schule und Bildung des Paulus* (BZNW 134), Berlin/New York: de Gruyter 2006.

VEGGE, T., „Baptismal Phrases in the Deuteropauline Epistles" in vorliegender Publikation, 497–?.

VIELHAUER, PH., *Geschichte der urchristlichen Literatur. Einleitung in das Neue Testament, die Apokryphen und die Apostolischen Väter* (GLB), Berlin – New York: de Gruyter 1975.

— „Paulus und die Kephaspartei in Korinth", in: IDEM, *Oikodome. Aufsätze zum Neuen Testament* (ThB 65), München: Kaiser 1979, 169–182.

VOLLENWEIDER, S., *Freiheit als neue Schöpfung. Eine Untersuchung zur Eleutheria bei Paulus und in seiner Umwelt* (FRLANT 147), Göttingen: Vandenhoeck & Ruprecht 1989.

— „Hymnus, Enkomion oder Psalm. Schattengefechte in der neutestamentlichen Wissenschaft", in: *NTS* 56 (2010) 208–231.

VOS, J. S., „Die Argumentation des Paulus in 1 Kor 1,10–3,4", in: R. Bieringer (Hg.), *The Corinthian Correspondence* (BEThL 125), Leuven: University Press/Peeters 1996, 87–119 (= in: IDEM, *Die Kunst der Argumentation bei Paulus. Studien zur antiken Rhetorik* [WUNT 149], Tübingen: Mohr Siebeck 2002, 29–64).

VOUGA, F., *An die Galater* (HNT 10), Tübingen: Mohr Siebeck 1998.

WAGNER, G., *Das religionsgeschichtliche Problem von Römer 6,1–11* (AThANT 39), Zürich: Zwingli 1962.

WALTER, N., „Ekklesiologische Vorstellungen bei Paulus. Mitbringsel aus Antiochien?", in: U. Mell/U. B. Müller (Hg.), *Das Urchristentum in seiner literarischen Geschichte*. FS J. Becker (BZNW 100), Berlin – New York: de Gruyter 1999, 173–195.

— „Alttestamentliche Bezüge in christologischen Ausführungen des Paulus", in: U. Schnelle/Th. Söding (Hg.), *Paulinische Christologie. Exegetische Beiträge*. FS Hans Hübner, Göttingen: Vandenhoeck & Ruprecht 2000, 246–271.

— „Nikolaos, Proselyt aus Antiochien, und die Nikolaiten in Ephesus und Pergamon. Ein Beitrag auch zum Thema: Paulus und Ephesus", in: *ZNW* 93 (2002) 200–226.

WARNACH, V., „Taufe und Christusgeschehen nach Römer 6", in: *ALW* 3 (1954) 34–50.

WEDDERBURN, J. M., *Baptism and Resurrection. Studies in Pauline Theology against Its Graeco-Roman Background* (WUNT 44), Tübingen: Mohr Siebeck 1987.

WEGENAST, K., *Das Verhältnis der Tradition bei Paulus und in den Deuteropaulinen* (WMANT 8), Neukirchen-Vluyn: Neukirchener Verlag 1962.

WEIDEMANN, H.-U., „Titus, der getaufte Heide – Überlegungen zu Tit 3,1–8", in: H.-U. Weidemann/W. Eisele (Hg.), *Ein Meisterschüler. Titus und sein Brief* (SBS 214), Stuttgart: Katholisches Bibelwerk 2008, 31–54.

WEISER, A., *Der Zweite Brief an Timotheus* (EKK XVI//1), Zürich: Benziger/ Neukirchen-Vluyn: Neukirchener Verlag 2003.

WEISS, J., „Beiträge zur Paulinischen Rhetorik", in: C. R. Gregory et alii (Hg.), *Theologische Studien*, FS für B. J. Weiß, Göttingen: Vandenhoeck & Ruprecht 1897, 165–247.

— *Der erste Korintherbrief* (KEK 5), Göttingen: Vandenhoeck & Ruprecht 1970 [= 1910].

— *Das Urchristentum*, Göttingen: Vandenhoeck & Ruprecht 1917.

— *The History of Primitive Christianity*, Vol. I, New York: Wilson-Erickson 1937.

WELBORN, L. L., „Discord in Corinth: First Corinthians 1–4 and Ancient Politics", in: IDEM, *Politics and Rhetoric in the Corinthian Epistles*, Macon, Ga.: Mercer 1997, 1–42.

WENGST, KL., *Christologische Formeln und Lieder des Urchristentums* (StNT 7), Gütersloh: Mohn 1972.

WIDENGREN, G., *Religionsphänomenologie* (GLB), Berlin: de Gruyter 1969.

WILCKENS, U., *Der Brief an die Römer (Röm 1–5)* (EKK VI/1), Zürich: Benziger/ Neukirchen-Vluyn: Neukirchener Verlag 1978.

— *Der Brief an die Römer (Röm 6–11)* (EKK VI/2), Zürich: Benziger/Neukirchen-Vluyn: Neukirchener Verlag 1980.

WOLFF, CH., *Der erste Brief des Paulus an die Korinther* (ThHNT 7), Leipzig: Evangelische Verlagsanstalt 1996.

WOLTER, M., „Apollos und die ephesinischen Johannesjünger", in: *ZNW* 78 (1987) 49–73 (Unter dem Titel „Apollos und die Johannesjünger von Ephesus (Apg 18,24 – 19,7)", in: IDEM, *Theologie und Ethos im frühen Christentum* [WUNT 236], Tübingen: Mohr Siebeck 2009, 402–426).

YSEBAERT, J., *Greek Baptismal Terminology. Its Origin and Early Development* (GCP 1), Nijmegen: Dekker & van de Vegt 1962.

ZAHN, TH., *Der Brief des Paulus an die Römer* (KNT 6), Leipzig/Erlangen: Deichert ³1925.

ZELLER, D., *Der erste Brief an die Korinther* (KEK 5), Göttingen: Vandenhoeck & Ruprecht 2009.

Baptismal Phrases in the Deuteropauline Epistles

Tor Vegge

In the letter to Titus, we read that all believers were once foolish and slaves to various passions and pleasures. But when the goodness and philanthropy of God appeared, he saved them through the bath of rebirth and renewal by the Holy Spirit. In Ephesians the readers are encouraged to maintain the unity of the Spirit, knowing that there is one Lord, one faith and one baptism, while in Colossians the reader learns that he/she was buried with Christ in baptism and raised with him through faith. While baptism may be reflected in all the letters considered to be Deuteropauline, in certain passages references to baptism seem more articulated. In this essay, I intend to make several remarks on the function of these references in selected passages of Colossians, Ephesians, 2 Timothy and Titus.

1. Introduction

1.1. Theory – Baptism and the Texts Referring to Baptism

Baptism may be referred to in the texts that are to be commented upon here; however, baptism itself is not treated as a separate topic. It is possible to relate several conceptions, motifs and texts found in early Christian literature to baptism, and this may be appropriate if our intuitive impression is sustainable, this being that many factors in early Christianity were related to baptism. I hold this to be true, at any rate from a theoretical point of view. As sympathetic observers, we assume that the believers presupposed coherence in their religious beliefs and practices. Beliefs concerning baptism were associated with those concerning Christ and salvation. This is not to say that this coherence was identical for all believers, or that all texts represent an identical coherence – the problems concerning the presentation of a Biblical or New Testament theology attest to this fact; however, it seems reasonable to presuppose a general conviction that all this in principal should be coherent: for example, baptism in its capacity of initiation rite was harmonically related to the identity and self-conception of the believers, and that this self-conception was grounded in a social reality with this same group (the church) as meeting place and social point of orientation. Briefly, it means that coherence between beliefs, rites, social context and behaviour in principle existed.

Such presuppositions seem to imply that everything is related to everything, e.g. baptism is related to everything else in the Christian religion. In as much as this seems reasonable from one point of view, we need some theoretical guidelines to help us discuss how the references to baptism in the texts function more specifically. With respect to this essay's particular point of discussion, I seek support in a fairly broad semiotic approach that regards different religious dimensions in interrelation with one another. For instance, G. A. Lindbeck's approach states that "religions are seen as comprehensive interpretive schemes, usually embodied in myths or narratives and heavily ritualized, which structure human experience and understanding of self and world".[1] The schemes consist of both cognitive and behavioural dimensions: doctrines, cosmic stories or myths, ethical directives, rituals practised, sentiments evoked, actions recommended, and institutional forms developed.[2] Assuming a broad religious studies perspective, one can take interest in the coherence between all doctrinal, mythical, social, experiential and behavioural dimensions. These dimensions are interacting, explaining and justifying, interpreting and motivating one another reciprocally, together constituting a universe.[3] Nonetheless, this does not mean that each individual believer is capable of giving a linguistic account for a supposed coherence, but she or he reasons that coherence is existent, and that someone else (one of the experts among the fellow believers) is able to give such an account.[4]

---

[1] G. A. Lindbeck, *The Nature of Doctrine*, 32. Lindbeck's approach seems, at least in some ways, to correspond to C. Geertz' semiotic approach to culture (Geertz, *The Interpretation of Cultures*, 24–30). See also W. A. Meeks, *The Moral World of the First Christians*, 11–17; G. Theissen, *The Religion of the Earliest Churches*.

[2] Lindbeck, *The Nature of Doctrine*, 33. See also N. Smart, *The World's Religions*, 10–21.

[3] "As a language (or 'language game' to use Wittgenstein's phrase) is correlated with a form of life, and just as culture has both cognitive and behavioral dimensions, so it is also in the case of a religious tradition. Its doctrines, cosmic stories or myths, and ethical directives are integrally related to the rituals it practices, the sentiments or experiences it evokes, the actions it recommends, and the institutional forms it develops. All this is involved in comparing a religion to a cultural-linguistic system" (Lindbeck, *The Nature of Doctrine*, 33). See also Geertz, *The Interpretation of Cultures*, 126–130. Geertz, however, discussing analysis of culture warns against assuming complete coherence: "coherence cannot be the major test of validity for cultural description. Cultural systems must have a minimal degree of coherence, else we would not call them systems; and, by observation they normally have a great deal more" (Geertz, *The Interpretation of Cultures*, 17f.).

[4] See Geertz, *The Interpretation of Cultures*, 126–130. It should, however, be considered that individuals in the course of their lives tend to live with some inconsistencies in beliefs or between world view and ethos. See also H. Moxnes, "From Theology to Identity" where the emphasis is more on boundary demarcation than on the comprehensiveness of beliefs. By Moxnes the focus is on "the pragmatic function of boundaries within Paul's argumentation, not on their general function as parts of a construction of a worldview or a belief 'system'" (279). Moxnes' "interpretation represents an attempt to read the thought world of early Christians, but with a view also to how this thought world *functioned*" (280). Further Theissen, *The Religion of the Earliest Churches*, 5.

The discussion below will not only briefly elaborate upon several perspectives concerning the interpretation of early Christian letters, but will also try to see the references to baptism in relation to such comprehensive interpretive schemes, by so doing attempting to utilise the perspective in illuminating the function of such references within the overall rhetorical structure of a written work. Early Christian literature may be seen as concerned with doctrines, stories and moral instruction. Texts are, however, also the prominent medium for interpreting the different dimensions of human life and experience, so that in a sense the different dimensions of religious beliefs and experiences can be represented in the semantic dimension of the language. Moreover, close examination of the texts will make us able to study the comprehensive interpretive schemes of the users of these very texts.

1.2. The Deuteropauline Letters within the History of Early Christian Literature

Even if the question of the authorship of these writings is still under discussion, and even though this discussion is not without relevance for the issues treated in this article, the fairly established view that Colossians, Ephesians, 2 Thessalonians, 1 Timothy, 2 Timothy and Titus were not written by Paul, but rather by persons who viewed themselves as disciples/successors of Paul, is presupposed.

The close resemblances between Colossians and Ephesians can be explained by either regarding the two writings as belonging to the same milieu using common traditions[5] or seeing one as being dependent on the other in a literary sense. Furthermore, if this is the case, it seems reasonable to assume that the author of Ephesians used a copy of the letter to the Colossians.[6] The suppositions of the present author tends to view the two writings as belonging to the same milieu, this being a Pauline school,[7] where one worked with teaching and literary texts, among them the teachings and written works of Paul. L. Hartman assumes that the Pauline school kept copies of Paul's letters and did so in accordance with Paul's own intentions.[8] While the question of authorship and literary dependence will not be discussed further here, it seems reasonable to assume literary interdependence in this type of school setting, and the present author favours the view that Colossians is the older of the two. The Let-

---

[5] E. BEST, *Ephesians*, 20ff. and 613f.

[6] F. MUSSNER, "Epheserbrief", 743; R. SCHNACKENBURG, *Der Brief an die Epheser*, 26–30; A. LINDEMANN, *Der Epheserbrief*, 11f.; H. HÜBNER, *An Philemon. An die Kolosser. An die Epheser*, 10f.; U. SCHNELLE, *Einleitung in das Neue Testament*, 350. 355f.

[7] For a discussion of the character of a Pauline school see P. MÜLLER, "Zum Problem der Paulusschule". See also HÜBNER, *An Philemon. An die Kolosser. An die Epheser*, 16f.

[8] HARTMAN, *Kolosserbrevet*, 200f. Further HARTMAN, *Into the Name of the Lord Jesus*, 95.

ter to Titus can thus be viewed as belonging to another branch of the Pauline school along with the two other so-called Pastoral Epistles.

If the writings discussed here are truly Deuteropauline (meaning written in the school of Paul), one would suppose that the authentic letters (protopauline letters) were known and used by the authors. We cannot, however, be sure which letters were known and in which literary form they existed. The authors may have known other letters of Paul, and they may have used teachings of Paul not present in the letters known to us. The authors are supposed to consider themselves as being pupils of Paul, and the figure/persona of Paul dominates the implied authors. Among the actual audience some may have had only superficial knowledge of Pauline writings or Pauline teaching, while other more competent readers may have studied Pauline teaching more thoroughly.

Additionally, the question of literary relationship/dependence is quite naturally of interest regarding the paragraphs related to baptism and the development of baptismal practice and theology. We can assume that the deuteropauline letters were written during the same period as other early Christian writings came into being. Even if none of the Gospels were known to the authors, we take for granted that the synoptic tradition was known and used in several communities. These specific questions will not be discussed further here. Interestingly enough, however, the synoptic stories of John the Baptist and of Jesus' baptism as well as Johannine teaching on new birth and living water,[9] and the baptismal language found in Acts regarding being baptised so that sins may be forgiven (Acts 2:38), or of being baptised into the name of the Lord Jesus (Acts 8:16), do not seem to be at all reflected in the Deuteropauline epistles.

1.3. Which Texts Contain References to Baptism?

As outlined in the introduction, the question of which texts are relevant depends on one's chosen perspective. It is no easy task to determine the importance of baptism as it relates to the believers' identity or for early Christian teaching. Moreover, factors not explicated on the textual surface are not easily recognised by modern readers. For instance, regarding the letter to the Ephesians (which may contain only one clear reference to baptism), N. A. Dahl states that "in a sense all the conceptions used about the transition from the sphere of sin and death to a new life in Christ can be regarded as baptismal motifs".[10]

Next, while the letters commented upon here place themselves in a Pauline tradition, it should be noted that in his writings Paul never speaks of his own

---

9   The conception of "cleansing water" is used in Eph 5:26 and may denote "baptism", and the language of bath and rebirth is found in Titus 3:5.

10 Dahl, "The Concept of Baptism in Ephesians", 413. See also the texts chosen and shortly commented in E. Ferguson, *Baptism in the Early Church*, 158–164; Schnelle, "Taufe", 670; F. Avemarie, "Taufe", 56f.

baptism, not even in the passages where he presents himself and the transition from his former life to his present one as a believer in Christ (Phil 3:1–11; Gal 1:11ff.). The author of Acts reports that Paul was baptised (9:18), and lets Paul narrate his encounter with Ananias in Damascus, who invites him to be baptised (22:16). However, it does not present Paul as a baptiser, even if he did lay his hands on the disciples who had first been baptised using John's baptismal ceremony and then were baptised "in the name of the Lord Jesus" (Acts 19:1–7).[11]

Simply stated, Paul was no baptiser and, when faced with the disagreements at Corinth, Paul is grateful for not having baptised anyone except Crispus and Gaius (1 Cor 1:14). The readers would not perceive Paul to be a baptiser, but rather a teacher. The fictional setting for Pauline literary communication would thus hardly be some sort of baptismal liturgy, baptismal service or even baptismal catechesis.

2. Baptismal Language in Colossians

In one section of the writing in which readers are encouraged to lead their lives "in Christ" as they have received Christ, they are both warned against deceiving philosophy and reminded of what they have in Christ, with whom they are symbolically buried in baptism and also raised with through faith (2:6–12). The writing imparts teaching including both world view and ethos, and the reference to baptism functions within this comprehensive teaching.

2.1. Structure and Genre

The function of each utterance needs to be seen within the dominant line of argument of the writing in its entirety. It is somehow conventional to see the letter to the Colossians – like a typical Pauline letter – divided into a teaching (descriptive) section and a paraenetic (prescriptive) section.[12] There is, however, a discussion of where one should see the beginning of the paraenetic section, either in 2:6, 2:20, 3:1 or 3:5.[13] In an outline like the one suggested by E. Schweizer, the reference to baptism falls into the descriptive section.[14] Instead of pursu-

---

11   See H. D. BETZ, "Transferring a Ritual", 103ff.
12   See e.g. E. LOHSE, Kolosser und Philemon, 29f.
13   See D. HELLHOLM, "Die Gattung Haustafel im Kolosser- und Epheserbrief", 104f.
14   Schweizer sees the structure as follows: I Briefeingang (1:1–8), II Die Grundlegung (1:9–2:23), III Leben aus Glauben (3:1–4:6), IV Briefschluß (4,7–18) (SCHWEIZER, *Der Brief an die Kolosser*). Similarly LINDEMANN, *Der Kolosserbrief* and J. ERNST, "Kolosserbrief". Somewhat different J. D. G. DUNN, *The Epistles to the Colossians and to Philemon*, 41f. M. Wolter identifies 2:6–4:6 as the "Briefcorpus", that has two main parts: *argumentatio* (2:9–23) and *exhortatio* (3:5–4:6) (WOLTER, *Der Brief an die Kolosser. Der Brief an Philemon*, 114ff.) Similarly MÜLLER, "Gegner

ing a discussion of such divisions, it would perhaps be more beneficial to first regard the letter as deliberative, subsequently considering its overall intended function as being a guiding one, which, in this context – as far as physics is the framework of ethics –, includes seeing oneself in relation to a world view. In an early Christian context this would imply framing one's self-understanding in a Christian theological world view. Teaching in a descriptive form can be taken as an invitation to position oneself in this particular world view, which then results in a certain way of leading your life. Deliberative rhetoric does not work without a foundation in view of the communicative context; that is, in some recognised truth claims[15] (even world view), and in a shared view of the purpose of being occupied with the subject matter at hand established between speaker and recipient.

Accordingly, it seems appropriate to recognise paraenesis[16] all the way through the letter, as done by Hartman. After the address (1:1–2) follows the main section (1:3–4:6), the sermon containing "softer exhortation with Christological basis" (1:3–23), a "direct exhortation with Christological basis" (1:24–2:23), and then "ethical prescriptions" based on the previous section (3:1–4:6).[17] Dunn states that the letter body (2:6–4:6) "cannot be simply analyzed into doc-

---

im Kolosserbrief", 368. B. Witherington III proposes a rhetorical analysis and divides it as follows: Epistolary Prescript (1:1–2), Exordium/Thanksgiving Prayer (1:3–14), Narratio – The Pattern of Christ (1:15–20), Propositio/Partitio (1:21–23), Probatio – Argument One (1:24–2:5), Probatio – Argument Two (2:6–3:4), Probatio – Argument Three (3:5–4:1), Peroratio (4:2–6), Epistolary Closing (4:7–18) (WITHERINGTON, *The Letters to Philemon, the Colossians and the Ephesians*, 115ff.).

15 Such celebration of what is already true or existing can be perceived as epideictic rhetoric (WITHERINGTON, *The Letters to Philemon, the Colossians and the Ephesians*, 7). G. A. Kennedy emphasises the often deliberative function of epideictic rhetoric (KENNEDY, *New Testament Interpretation Through Rhetorical Criticism*, 73ff.). See also Betz: "Paraensis, therefore, consists of more than free-standing moral commandments or recommendations. It implies an appeal to reason, claiming that the exhortation, whatever it may be, stands upon a rational framework as well as practical experience" (BETZ, "Paraenesis and the Concept of God", 227). My reasoning in this paragraph should not be taken as intending to diminish the syntactic and pragmatic differences between descriptive and prescriptive language, but rather to meet another presupposition that I find reasonable, namely that an author/speaker has but one main purpose or one main function in mind when assuming the labour of composing a written work or speech, which in its turn should lead us to consider only one genre for one written work/speech. This does not mean that an author always succeeds in making such a purpose visible or that he/she succeeds in writing the perfect text according to such ideals, even if his/her text was included among the sacred texts of the Christian church. For a brief discussion of rhetorical genres in literary texts, see T. VEGGE, *Paulus und das antike Schulwesen*, 349–352.

16 In the use of "paraenesis" I favour a functional understanding of the concept. See W. POPKES, "Paraenesis in the New Testament", 17; 34; 42. The point here is not a clear-cut definition of paraenesis in relation to e.g. exhortation (παράκλησις), but the relations between doctrines and ethics. See T. ENGBERG-PEDERSEN, "The Concept of Paraenesis", 54ff.; J. M. STARR, "Was Paraenesis for Beginners?", 79–81.

17 HARTMAN, *Kolosserbrevet*, 195f.

trinal and practical parts."[18] Hartman holds the letter with regard to genre to be a *letter* and a *sermon*.[19] It seems reasonable to regard the letter as having an overall guiding function, i.e. as belonging to the deliberative genre.[20] The suggestion may be forwarded that the letter was not supposed to be read as an actual sermon when the whole congregation was gathered, but rather was meant for a smaller circle including persons who could use the text for their own learning as well as further their own teaching and guidance of other believers.[21] If, however, the address "in Colossae" is fictitious, one could suppose the intended function of the letter to be of a more general kind.[22]

2.2. The Function of the Writing

In view of genre and the letter's function, a search for a *propositio* or *partitio/divisio* (in which the speech's content is briefly described) may be undertaken.[23] I will point to a couple of passages that could also be seen as specifying the intention of the letter. This is 1:9f., which follows the thanksgiving section, expressing the wish that readers "may be filled with the knowledge of God's will in all spiritual wisdom and understanding, so that you may lead lives worthy of the Lord...." The direct reference here is, however, the constant prayers the implied authors make for the implied readers. Further, in 2:1–2 we meet a clear metacommunicative utterance that could be seen as revealing the intention of the entire letter:

> For I want you to know how much I am struggling for you and for those in Laodicea […]. I want their hearts to be encouraged and united in love, so that they may have all the riches of assured understanding and have the knowledge of God's mystery, that is, Christ himself.

---

18 Dunn, *The Epistles to the Colossians and to Philemon*, 136. See also Popkes, "Paraenesis in the New Testament", 16; Hellholm, "Die Gattung Haustafel im Kolosser- und Epheserbrief", 104f.

19 Hartman, *Kolosserbrevet*, 195.

20 Hübner is reluctant to assign the letter to a certain rhetorical genre, also to evaluate it as deliberative because there is no direct appeal to a "deliberative act" in the letter (Hübner, *An Philemon. An die Kolosser. An die Epheser*, 22f.). My own evaluation rests probably on a somewhat different view of the functions of the deliberative genre.

21 4:16 seems however to indicate that the letter was intended to be read when the congregation was gathered, and maybe even in the worship service, see Hartman, *Kolosserbrevet*, 193; Betz, "Paul's 'Second Presence'", 515.

22 Lindemann supposes the address to be fictitious, but that the letter nevertheless was addressed to a certain congregation, the congregation in Laodicea (Lindemann, *Der Kolosserbrief*, 12f. The extensive reasoning may be found in Lindemann, "Die Gemeinde von ‚Kolossä'").

23 Witherington finds the *propositio/partitii* in 1:21–23. As the thesis that is going to be argued is complex, "the propositio is divided in several parts" mentioning the parts that will be treated in the discourse (Witherington, *The Letters to Philemon, the Colossians and the Ephesians*, 137).

This is not very different from 1:9f. in which encouragement and knowledge are signified. "The knowledge of God's mystery, that is, Christ himself" is sketched in the passage 1:15–20, praising Christ with statements of his cosmic power and status. This type of knowledge is the framework of moral guidance. The same passage (2:4) also comments on the communicative function: "I am saying this so that no one may deceive you with plausible arguments". These statements, communicating the intention of imparting knowledge/understanding merged with moral exhortation,[24] appear (regardless of how they are classified in view of the *dispositio*) to be important in the evaluation of the function of the letter and, further, in the assessment of the function of the reference to baptism in the reasoning. According to Hartman, the main purpose of the letter is "to warn the addressees of a certain 'philosophy'".[25] Wolter identifies 2:6–8 as the *partitio* of the letter. 2:6 ("As you therefore has received Christ Jesus the Lord") may allude to the Christ confession in the service of the first believers. The author puts this confession up against the philosophy, and the confession is supposed to find an expression in a corresponding conduct of life.[26]

In light of the metacommunicative statements referred to above, I am inclined to formulate the main purpose in the following manner: The author intends to impart knowledge of the cosmic power and status of Christ as a framework for the exhortations. Such teaching could be perceived as intended to consolidate the identity of the believers.

2.3. Line of Reasoning in Colossians 2

Hartman points to the fact that while Col 2:11 and its context do not present a theology of baptism, the author does write about baptism as a component of reasoning standing in opposition to this philosophy.[27] This relates to the function of the reference to baptism, and the comprehension of such function is related to a view regarding the structure of the text passages. Moreover, there seems

---

24 Such connection of knowledge and moral guidance corresponds to the concept of paraenesis discussed in Engberg-Pedersen/Starr, *Early Christian Paraenesis in Context*. In a suggested definition "Paraenesis is [1] clear, concrete, benevolent guidance that [...], [3] expresses a shared, articulated world view " (Popkes, "Paraenesis in the New Testament", 42f.) Further Starr, "Was Paraenesis for Beginners?", 111. I perceive the discussion of the concept "paraenesis" in these contributions to be held in a hermeneutical context that is comparable to the theoretical framework outlined in the introduction to this essay.

25 Hartman, *Into the Name of the Lord Jesus*, 95. See also Lohse, *Kolosser und Philemon*, 28.

26 Wolter, *Der Brief an die Kolosser. Der Brief an Philemon*, 117f. If the expression refers to the Christ confession, the baptismal event may also be alluded to (Wolter, *Der Brief an die Kolosser. Der Brief an Philemon*, 117). Dunn identifies the main thrust of the letter thematically stated in 2:6–7 as being "a passage which indicates clearly the integration of faith and praxis." (Dunn, *The Epistles to the Colossians and to Philemon*, 136).

27 Hartman, *Kolosserbrevet*, 99.

to be a transition in the text in 2:6. After a section in which the implicit author presents himself follows a passage containing a direct address to the audience (in 2:6) with the exhortation to "walk in Christ Jesus the Lord". The extent to which the following passages are prescriptive language will not be discussed in depth here.[28] Certainly, the guidance in 2:6ff. is of a somewhat different nature than the exhortations in 3:5ff.; however, the form and function of both may be seen as falling within the category of deliberative rhetoric.

While scholars have supposed a confessional tradition or a hymn to be behind 2:9–15, it seems difficult to recognise a clear structure (rhythm and lines) in the supposed hymn.[29] It seems more beneficial to regard the elements of rhythmic repetition as being a rhetorical application of style. Such style elements can be seen in the formulation ἐν αὐτῷ repeated twice and then twice again in its relative counterpart ἐν ᾧ introducing the sentences that include the phrase on baptism. These four expressions appearing first in four elements of reasoning are subordinated the κατὰ Χριστόν (2:8):

(8) ... κατὰ Χριστόν
(9) ὅτι **ἐν αὐτῷ** κατοικεῖ πᾶν τὸ πλήρωμα τῆς θεότητος σωματικῶς,
(10) καὶ ἐστὲ **ἐν αὐτῷ** πεπληρωμένοι, ὅς ἐστιν ἡ κεφαλὴ πάσης ἀρχῆς καὶ ἐξουσίας,
(11) **ἐν ᾧ** καὶ περιετμήθητε περιτομῇ ἀχειροποιήτῳ ἐν τῇ ἀπεκδύσει τοῦ σώματος τῆς σαρκός, ἐν τῇ περιτομῇ τοῦ Χριστοῦ,
(12) συνταφέντες αὐτῷ ἐν τῷ βαπτισμῷ,
ἐν ᾧ καὶ συνηγέρθητε διὰ τῆς πίστεως τῆς ἐνεργείας τοῦ θεοῦ τοῦ ἐγείραντος αὐτὸν ἐκ νεκρῶν (Col 2:9–12)[30]

(8) ... according to Christ
(9) For in him the whole fullness of deity dwells bodily,
(10) and you have come to fullness in him, who is the head of every ruler and authority.
(11) In him also you were circumcised with a spiritual circumcision, by putting off the body of the flesh in the circumcision of Christ;
(12) when you were buried with him in baptism,
you were also raised with him through faith in the power of God, who raised him from the dead.

---

28 As mentioned above, certain scholars believe the paraenetic (prescriptive) section of the letter to begin either with 2:6, 2:20, 3:1 or 3:5. See HELLHOLM, "Die Gattung Haustafel im Kolosser- und Epheserbrief", 104f. Related to this discussion is the abovementioned question of the nature of exhortation/paraenesis. See ENGBERG-PEDERSEN/STARR, *Early Christian Paraenesis in Context*.

29 See ERNST, "Kolosserbrief", 371; DUNN, *The Epistles to the Colossians and to Philemon*, 146.

30 Similarly structured by DUNN, *The Epistles to the Colossians and to Philemon*, 146. See also LINDEMANN, *Der Kolosserbrief*, 38.

In each instance the formulation means "in Christ"[31] and is always followed by a finite verb, the first of which has "the whole fullness of deity" (πᾶν τὸ πλήρωμα τῆς θεότητος) as the subject, the following three the implied readers (2.p.pl.). This suggests a structure in 2:9–12 with a fundamental worldview statement (theological/Christological) (2:9) followed by an application on the implied readers in three sequences.

This application of the "fullness of deity" on the implied reader (2:9–12, which could be extended to verse 15) is preceded by the exhortation to "walk in him [Christ] …" (2:6–8). In this passage ἐν αὐτῷ occurs twice. The implied readers have received Christ Jesus the Lord and are exhorted to "walk in him" (ἐν αὐτῷ περιπατεῖτε) (2:6), and they are also "rooted and built up in him" (ἐν αὐτῷ) (2:7). Furthermore, they are "established when it comes to the faith". This established faith is founded in teaching (καθὼς ἐδιδάχθητε) (2:7). This encouragement is followed by a warning, and the phrasing relates to teaching and learning. It is a warning against another teaching labelled "philosophy", a philosophy that the implied author claims to be in accordance with human tradition and the elements of the world and not in line with Christ (κατὰ Χριστόν) (2:8).[32] This exact κατὰ Χριστόν is then elaborated upon in the following sentences (2,9ff.). The transmission is brought about through the relative sentence ὅτι ἐν αὐτῷ κατοικεῖ …. The contents of the philosophy that are in accordance with human tradition and the elements of the world mentioned in 2:8a are also indicated in 2:16–23, after the teaching according to Christ. Thus a chiastic structure can be seen in 2:8–23.[33]

The addressees hear this encouragement to walk in Christ Jesus the Lord (2:6) just after hearing the implied author communicate clearly metacommunicative utterances: "For I want you to know how much I am struggling for you […] and for all who have not seen me face to face" (2:2). The implied author is a construction of the person of Paul, and the readers have of course not met him. A few lines later it is stressed that "Paul", although "absent in body", is with them in spirit. Moreover, "Paul" rejoices over their morals and firmness of faith in Christ. Having created this intimate and personally demanding atmosphere, the speaker communicates the exhortation to walk in Christ Jesus the Lord.

---

31 In 2:12 the relative pronoun could relate to baptism (so SCHWEIZER, *The Letter to the Colossians*, 145f., differently: HÜBNER, *An Philemon. An die Kolosser. An die Epheser*, 83), but if this were the case, the later formulation of the same sentence (τοῦ θεοῦ τοῦ ἐγείραντος αὐτὸν ἐκ νεκρῶν) would have the proper name of Christ and not the pronoun.

32 Lohse points to baptism referred to in the subsequent sentences as foundation for the reader's affiliation with Christ (LOHSE, *Kolosser und Philemon*, 141).

33 Dunn outlines this chiastic structure: 8a and 16–23 containing polemical denunciation, 8b and 9–15 the teaching in accordance with Christ, with 2:8 functioning "as a heading and initial statement of the section's theme" (DUNN, *The Epistles to the Colossians and to Philemon*, 144).

2.4. The Attitude of the Implied Author

Through the utterances in 2:1–4, ones having strong metacommunicative signals, the implied author signifies the role he intends to establish in the imagined communicative situation created through the letter's text. The situation is fictive; "he" is absent in body but present in spirit (2:5). He presents himself as an orator working with arguments, ones concerning understanding and possessing knowledge of God's mystery (2:2–3 and 1:26–28). He also teaches about the fullness of deity that dwells bodily in Christ (2:9). These are the themes more reminiscent of a philosopher than an orator, and he also consequently contrasts himself to others teaching other forms of philosophy. In 1:28 he also says that he "teaches everyone in all wisdom". The implied author therefore presents himself as being a moral teacher and philosopher who wants to impart encouragement and unity (2:2), and the knowledge of God's hidden mystery to the implied readers. An established picture of Paul is the model for this person, and in this role the implied author then comes to speak of baptism, drawing on traditions authorised by Paul (Rom 6) and developing Paul's teaching, but also as Paul himself applying the remembrance of baptism on moral exhortation (2:16ff.).

2.5. Baptismal References in Colossians 2

Baptism figures in the third of the κατὰ Χριστόν subordinated elements, as indicated in the structure outlined above. The sentences in this third element can be read as seeing baptism (τῷ βαπτισμῷ) as the only expression to be taken in a literal sense, while the others are to be taken in a metaphorical sense, transferring meaning to the concept of baptism:

ἐν ᾧ καὶ περιετμήθητε περιτομῇ ἀχειροποιήτῳ
ἐν τῇ ἀπεκδύσει τοῦ σώματος τῆς σαρκός,
ἐν τῇ περιτομῇ τοῦ Χριστοῦ,
συνταφέντες αὐτῷ ἐν τῷ βαπτισμῷ (2:11–12a)

In him also you were circumcised with a spiritual circumcision,
by putting off the body of the flesh
in the circumcision of Christ;
when you were buried with him in baptism.

The closest qualification of the word baptism is συνταφέντες αὐτῷ ("when you were buried with him"). "Baptism" understood literally and referring to the baptismal rite that the readers have experienced is thus interpreted symbolically as signifying a burial with Christ, an interpretation that implies an application of his significant death. "Being buried with him in baptism" appears once again to be an interpretation/explication of the foregoing formulation ἐν τῇ περιτομῇ τοῦ Χριστοῦ ("in the circumcision of Christ"), the prominent meaning of which in this context is thereby not the death of Christ, but rather the "circumcision" bestowed on the believer in baptism.[34] "The circumcision of Christ" is again a definition/qualification of a statement concerning the readers, which constitutes the first part of this third element ("in whom you were also circumcised with a circumcision not made with hands in the undressing of the body of the flesh" [my translation]). The reader learns in the subsequent textual flow that this metaphorical speech of their having been circumcised may be qualified in a related metaphor, "the circumcision of Christ", which again is a metaphorical way of speaking of baptism.[35]

Such articulate use of circumcision imagery suggests that circumcision was a topic with which the audience was familiar. Col 1:21.27 and 3:5–7 seem to envisage the audience as believers having a Gentile background, even if a mention of the Gentiles as found in 1:27 and the vice list in 3:5 identifying one or more of the vices as being idolatry could also function with readers having a Jewish background. The readers seem in any case imagined as being familiar with circumcision as a Jewish mark of identity.[36] One possibility is to assume that the "philosophy" warned against (2:8) emphasised circumcision, another that circumcision was a topic of discussion in the contact with Jewish groups, including proselytes and God-fearers.[37] This problem will not be further dis-

---

34 So LINDEMANN, *Der Kolosserbrief*, 41.; HÜBNER, *An Philemon. An die Kolosser. An die Epheser*, 81f.; 83. Differently: DUNN, *The Epistles to the Colossians and to Philemon* 157f. See the next footnote.

35 The references of the sentences could be interpreted in a somewhat different way, seeing the first and the last part of the element as referring to the experiences of the reader, and the middle section – ἐν τῇ ἀπεκδύσει τοῦ σώματος τῆς σαρκός, ἐν τῇ περιτομῇ τοῦ Χριστοῦ –referring to the cross and death of Christ, which is explicitly mentioned in the following sentences (2:14f.), where also the word ἀπέκδυσις is taken up again (so DUNN, *The Epistles to the Colossians and to Philemon*, 157f.). Studied in this manner, the "circumcision of Christ" is not one given by Christ e.g. in baptism, but the "circumcision" given to Christ, in a literal sense the execution on the cross. This reading emphasises that it is the death of Christ that has brought about the "circumcision not made by hands" for the believers, and that baptism is the unifying with the death of Christ. This aspect is, however, not absent in the first rendered reading as far as baptism is qualified as a burial with Christ.

36 Dunn supposes "a church made up initially of Jews and God-fearing Gentiles or proselytes (mostly the latter if 1:12, 27 and 2:13 are any guide)" (*ibid.*, 29). For the question of circumcision as a Jewish mark of identity, see *ibid.*, 154.

37 Lohse supposes circumcision to have been a theme in the philosophy, denoting a sacramental act of consecration in a group resembling mystery cults. If περιτομή only designated the sacramental act or if circumcision was actually performed cannot be accounted for (LOHSE, *Kolosser und Philemon*, 153f.). Hartman doubts that we are dealing with a philosophy practicing circumcision, but rather that the representatives of this philosophy may have been God-fearing Gentiles associated with the synagogue without having become proselytes, but sharing Jewish monotheism and observing Jewish purity rules, without, however, having been circumcised (HARTMAN, *Kolosserbrevet*, 119 and 121). Dunn supposes that "circumcision was indeed a factor in the threatening situation in Colossae. Moreover, the evidence clearly indicates that this factor included Jews as such, with their distinctive attitude to Gentiles as 'the uncircumcision'

cussed here.[38] The implied reader is familiar with circumcision and its religious and identity-marking significance. The question of circumcision seems at any rate not to be as urgent a question as it was when e.g. the letter to the Galatians was written (Gal 5:2–12).[39] The topic of circumcision occurs less frequently in the deuteropauline writings, which suggests that the question had to a certain extent been clarified.

2.5.1. "Circumcision not Made with Hands" and Virtue

The figure of speech "circumcision not made with hands" should most likely be taken as denoting ethical quality,[40] where the "not made with hands" connotes divine agency.[41] Denoting ethical quality is the traditional manner of applying this figure of speech. The figurative speech of the "circumcision not made with hands" is no Christian invention inspired by the practice of baptism. On the contrary, when Paul writes about circumcision in a figurative way as a "circumcision of heart" (Rom 2:29), this refers to Deut 30:6; Jer 4:4; 9:25f., and further texts could be included.[42] "In NT days the figurative and spiritualised view of circumcision was by no means unknown in Palestinian Judaism."[43] From Qumran we learn that the circumcision of the foreskin of the "lower nature" promotes virtuous conduct:

> They are to practice truth together with humility, (4) charity, justice, loving-kindness, and modesty in all their ways. Accordingly, none will continue in a willfull heart and thus be seduced, not by his heart, (5) neither by his eyes, nor yet by his lower nature. Together they shall circumcise the foreskin of this nature, this stiff

---

(2:13; 3:11)" (DUNN, *The Epistles to the Colossians and to Philemon*, 155). Lindemann also assumes the philosophy to have demanded circumcision, however that we have to do with a Gnostic conviction that "die körperliche Beschneidung als einen sinnfälligen Akt der Beseitigung irdischer Weltbindungen gedeutet haben" (LINDEMANN, *Der Kolosserbrief*, 42).

38 The problem is discussed at length in the commentaries, see LOHSE, *Kolosser und Philemon*, 153f.; SCHWEIZER, *The Letter to the Colossians*, 125–134; HARTMAN, *Kolosserbrevet*, 117–125; DUNN, *The Epistles to the Colossians and to Philemon*, 23–35.

39 DUNN, *The Epistles to the Colossians and to Philemon*, 156.

40 HARTMAN, *Into the Name of the Lord Jesus*, 96; LINDEMANN, *Der Kolosserbrief*, 41f. Wolter interprets the expression in a somewhat broader sense: "Weil sie [die Taufbeschneidung] von Gott vorgenommen ist, wird der einzelne in seiner gesamten Existenz umgestaltet" (WOLTER, *Der Brief an die Kolosser. Der Brief an Philemon*, 130).

41 LOHSE, *Kolosser und Philemon*, 154; WOLTER, *Der Brief an die Kolosser. Der Brief an Philemon*, 129f.; DUNN, *The Epistles to the Colossians and to Philemon*, 156; HÜBNER, *An Philemon. An die Kolosser. An die Epheser*, 81f.

42 See R. JEWETT, *Romans*, 236.

43 R. MEYER, "Peritemno", 79.

neck, and so establish a foundation of truth for Israel – that is to say, for the *Yahad* of the Eternal (6) Covenant.⁴⁴ (1QS 5:3–6) (See also 1QS 5:24–26)

Philo equals "being uncircumcised in heart" with not having undertaken the labours of virtue and being ignorant of the taste of moral excellence.⁴⁵ The figurative speech of circumcision in these passages focuses on morality and virtues.

This type of ethical reading of the expression "being circumcised with a circumcision not made with hands in the undressing of the body of the flesh" corresponds to the prescriptive sections of the writing as well as to other texts in which baptism as initiation marks the transition to a new way of leading one's life (Rom 6).⁴⁶

2.5.2. Truth Claims of Christ and the Status of the Believers

This third element mentioning baptism is preceded by two others having the same relation to the superordinate κατὰ Χριστόν (2:9–10). The first makes a statement referring to Christ, and the second states the application to the readers of the content of the first. The expressions are not metaphorical in the same sense as the following are, but rather are religious truth claims about Christ and the status of the believers. These two elements make several references to 1:15–20, a passage in refined prose style (a prose hymn) expressing the deeds, qualities and roles of Christ in God's history with the existent reality and his power in all the domains of this reality. A sentence from the final passage of 1:15–20 is nearly literally cited in the first part of the section containing the baptismal language:

ὅτι ἐν αὐτῷ εὐδόκησεν πᾶν τὸ πλήρωμα κατοικῆσαι (1:19)
ὅτι ἐν αὐτῷ κατοικεῖ πᾶν τὸ πλήρωμα τῆς θεότητος σωματικῶς (2:9)

For in him all the fullness of God was pleased to dwell (1:19)
For in him the whole fullness of deity dwells bodily (2:9)

With regard to our discussion of baptism, the addition in 2:9 – σωματικῶς – seems significant, but should be taken in a fairly straightforward manner as denoting bodily presence or "the accessibility (come-at-ableness) of the divine epiphany",⁴⁷ or the reality ("Wirklichkeit") of God's presence in Christ.⁴⁸ In rela-

---

44 Translation according to *The Dead Sea Scrolls. Translated and with a Commentary by Michael Wise, Martin Abegg Jr., and Edward Cook*, 122.
45 Philo, *Spec. Leg.* I.304f.
46 For the argumentative structure of Rom 6, see HELLHOLM, "Enthymemic Argumentation in Paul".
47 DUNN, *The Epistles to the Colossians and to Philemon*, 152.
48 LINDEMANN, *Der Kolosserbrief*, 41; LOHSE, *Kolosser und Philemon*, 151f.; WOLTER, *Der Brief an die Kolosser. Der Brief an Philemon*, 126. See also the discussion in HÜBNER, *An Philemon. An die Kolosser. An die Epheser*. Hübner prefers the meaning "incarnate" ("leibhaft") (79f.).

tion to baptism, it could refer to the concrete "bodily" performance of the rite itself.

Further, the word πλήρωμα is significant in this context. In 1:15–20 the "fullness" seems to incorporate what is said in the foregoing statements about how everything is created in him, how he existed before everything and how everything is held together in him (τὰ πάντα ἐν αὐτῷ συνέστηκεν).[49] The concentration of these motifs is carried over in the passage (2:8–15) through the adapted citation, and is even explicated in 2:10 (ὅς ἐστιν ἡ κεφαλὴ πάσης ἀρχῆς καὶ ἐξουσίας) (also 2:15). In the second of the four elements (2:10), this concentration of truth claims about the reality in its totality is applied on the readers/believers in a striking formulation καὶ ἐστὲ ἐν αὐτῷ πεπληρωμένοι, ὅς ἐστιν ἡ κεφαλὴ πάσης ἀρχῆς καὶ ἐξουσίας ("and you have come to fullness in him, who is the head of every ruler and authority"), which simply means "that in Christ they have been granted a completeness and fulfillment which they could not find or achieve anywhere else."[50]

The text also presents a significant conjunction of the cosmos and all the powers and authorities with the church. Christ is the head of both entities. The readers/believers know that they belong to a church, and they have learned (or been reminded of the fact) in 1:18 and 1:24 that the church is the body of Christ. Now the believers are filled with him also being the head of all powers and authorities (καὶ ἐστὲ ἐν αὐτῷ πεπληρωμένοι, ὅς ἐστιν ἡ κεφαλὴ πάσης ἀρχῆς καὶ ἐξουσίας). Thus they belong to a body whose head is also the head of all powers and authorities in the cosmos. So these are the cosmological truth claims identifying the church being the social place where the believers meet. The believer has entered the church through baptismal initiation into a social space having such an all-embracing framework. Seen from the perspective of baptism, this ritual has granted recipients entrance into a room, a context carrying the potential of the qualities that have belonged to Christ since before time began, and that are at his disposal in all spheres of reality.

The fourth of the κατὰ Χριστόν subordinated elements – ἐν ᾧ καὶ συνηγέρθητε διὰ τῆς πίστεως τῆς ἐνεργείας τοῦ θεοῦ τοῦ ἐγείραντος αὐτὸν ἐκ νεκρῶν ("you were also raised with him through faith in the power of God, who raised him from the dead") – completes this sequence of elements explicating the expression κατὰ Χριστόν that in light of the antithesis in 2:8 should be understood as teaching κατὰ Χριστόν (see 2:7), as opposed to the disadvantageous philosophy. In the following sentences the expression ἐν ᾧ καὶ συνηγέρθητε is continued in a parallel expression: συνεζωοποίησεν ("made alive together with"),[51] which is contrasted with a symbolic description of the former existence of the readers

---

49 See Hartman, *Kolosserbrevet*, 47.

50 Dunn, *The Epistles to the Colossians and to Philemon*, 152. See also Müller, "Gegner im Kolosserbrief", 368.

51 For the concept σὺν Χριστῷ see Lohse, *Kolosser und Philemon*, 157f.

being "dead in trespasses and the uncircumcision of your flesh" (2:13). In light of the above interpretation of 2:11–12, this symbolic description denotes life before baptism. Two semantic schemes are in turn applied to the baptismal motifs here: the "dead – alive" and the "once – now" scheme, schemes that reappear in Col 3:7f. These schemes are also used in other exhortative passages.[52]

2.5.3. Baptismal Motifs Continued

The formulation ἀπεθάνετε σὺν Χριστῷ (2:20) picks up the motif of having "been buried with him" (συνταφέντες αὐτῷ) (2:12) and "being dead" (ὑμᾶς νεκροὺς ὄντας) (2:13). According to the structure outlined by Dunn,[53] 2:20 with ἀπεθάνετε σὺν Χριστῷ occurs in the last section of the chiastic structure in 2:8–23, this last section corresponding to 2:8a: βλέπετε μή τις ὑμᾶς ἔσται ὁ συλαγωγῶν διὰ τῆς φιλοσοφίας καὶ κενῆς ἀπάτης κατὰ τὴν παράδοσιν τῶν ἀνθρώπων, κατὰ τὰ στοιχεῖα τοῦ κόσμου ("See to it that no one takes you captive through philosophy and empty deceit, according to human tradition, according to the elemental spirits of the universe, and not according to Christ"). Accordingly, the motif of "having died with Christ" marks the more concrete development of the warning against the philosophy "according to human traditions and the elements of the world", while the συνηγέρθητε τῷ Χριστῷ (3:1) introduces a short passage containing strongly positive encouragements to the believer to "*seek* the things that are above" and to "*set your minds* on things that are above", that is "where Christ is seated at the right hand of God". Moreover, the passage contains the assurance that the believer will be revealed in glory with Christ. This short passage states both the orientation of beliefs and that of ethos.

This passage introduced by "having been raised with Christ" (3:1) also motivates the more concrete exhortations that are abundant in the remainder of the writing. This section contains lists of vices and virtues. Furthermore we encounter the scheme "once – now" again (3:7–8) now in an exhortative passage, and as already indicated, the motifs of death and life that interpret baptism in descriptive language in the above text are applied in the following prescriptive passages.[54] The word νεκρώσατε (3:5) introduces a vice catalogue and continues the baptismal images from 2:11ff.

In 3:9 the motif of "stripping off garment" and "clothing" (ἀπεκδυσάμενοι τὸν παλαιὸν ἄνθρωπον σὺν ταῖς πράξεσιν αὐτοῦ καὶ ἐνδυσάμενοι τὸν νέον) is used in a prescriptive context. The image of stripping off has already been used as it relates to baptism in 2:11 (ἐν τῇ ἀπεκδύσει τοῦ σώματος τῆς σαρκός). In Paul, the motif of clothing is used in the baptismal text Gal 3:27f. (ὅσοι γὰρ εἰς

---

52 For a further discussion of those schemes, see below to Eph 2:1–10.
53 Dunn, *The Epistles to the Colossians and to Philemon*, 144.
54 See Lohse, *Kolosser und Philemon*, 192.

Χριστὸν ἐβαπτίσθητε, Χριστὸν ἐνεδύσασθε).[55] It is significant that the continuation in Col 3:11 – ὅπου οὐκ ἔνι Ἕλλην καὶ Ἰουδαῖος ("there is no longer Greek and Jew …") – has its closest parallel in the same text in Gal 3:28 – οὐκ ἔνι Ἰουδαῖος οὐδὲ Ἕλλην ("there is no longer Jew or Greek") –, which in Galatians states the spiritual and intended social status of those persons initiated through baptism.[56] The formula is also present in 1 Cor 12:13 as a baptismal formula.[57] Hence it is reasonable to see these images in Colossians also related to baptism. Stated briefly, the subsequent passages in Col 2:16ff. impart exhortation based on baptismal motifs.

2.5.4. Colossians 2 and Romans 6

Formulations, motifs and patterns of argumentation in Col 2 and 3 have close resemblances to Romans 6. The passages are different, yet have characteristic similarities.[58]

Baptism is a central textual topic, and is used in the overall argumentative strategy. For instance, the formulation ἀποθνῄσκειν σὺν Χριστῷ is found in both texts, and the striking figurative use of συνθάπτειν (aor. pass. συνετάφην) is found only in these two texts in the NT (Rom 6:4; Col 2:12). The word that continues the argumentative line in Col 2:12, the aorist passive συνηγέρθητε, is not found in Romans; instead, it is stated that as Christ was raised from the dead (ὥσπερ ἠγέρθη Χριστὸς ἐκ νεκρῶν – 6,4b) so shall we walk in the newness of life (οὕτως καὶ ἡμεῖς ἐν καινότητι ζωῆς περιπατήσωμεν) (future tense; 6:4c). Further, Romans contains εἰ δὲ ἀπεθάνομεν σὺν Χριστῷ, πιστεύομεν ὅτι καὶ συζήσομεν αὐτῷ (6:8), and the parallel continuation in Colossians shows the same difference in verbal tense: ὑμᾶς νεκροὺς ὄντας [ἐν] τοῖς παραπτώμασιν καὶ τῇ ἀκροβυστίᾳ τῆς σαρκὸς ὑμῶν, συνεζωοποίησεν ὑμᾶς σὺν αὐτῷ (2:13). How these differences are to be explained and the significance they have for the relations between Romans and Colossians (and further Ephesians 2) is a topic of debate. One can suppose literary dependence or the use of common traditions.[59]

---

55 Regarding the image see HARTMAN, *Into the Name of the Lord Jesus*, 56; BETZ, *Galatians*, 188f.; DAHL, "Kleidungsmetaphern".

56 To the formula See BETZ, *Galatians*, 189–201; in the present publication: HELLHOLM, "Vorgeformte Tauftraditionen", § 1.4.

57 Refer to the present publication: HELLHOLM, "Vorgeformte Tauftraditionen", § 1.2.

58 The relations between the texts are also briefly discussed in the ensuing discussion of Eph 2:1–10.

59 A. Standhartinger (STANDHARTINGER, *Studien zur Entstehungsgeschichte*) supposes that both Paul and the author of Colossians use a tradition already common in the Hellenistic communities (139). Paul is responsible for the future perspective of the identification with the resurrection in Romans 6 (139f.), while Colossians cites the tradition in its more original form (145f.). Similarly SCHWEIZER, *The Letter to the Colossians*, 143ff. Such considerations lead

What is important to the present discussion is that baptismal motifs present in Colossians 2:12–13 in a line of reasoning *combining the Christ myth with the baptismal ritual* is known to us as being distinctively Pauline,[60] and the combination, or at least the literate interpretation of this combination in a descriptive language, could be assumed to be Paul's own invention. It can, however, be argued (as Hellholm does) that the text in Romans 6 incorporates preformed baptismal traditions where this combination of myth and ritual is already present.[61]

I would nonetheless assume that the author of Colossians considers this tradition to be a Pauline one, and that he applies it in the writing intending the ideal reader to recognise the teaching as being Pauline in nature. "Paul" is the figure of the implied author, and the text shows familiarity with the teaching of Paul known to us in his letters, both through characteristic formulations and coherence in the doctrines. I assume the author is familiar with Romans, but even in the case of literary dependence, the author might deal with the particular literary text in a fairly autonomous manner in order to serve his rhetorical intentions.

Assuming that the author knew and used the Pauline teaching as we know it in Romans 6, why does the clear modification in verbal tense in the formulations expressing the unification with Christ appear? One intention could be to construct a more continuous line of reasoning. The future verbal forms in the identification of the baptised with the resurrection of Christ in Romans

---

Standhartinger to doubt a literary dependence between Colossians and the letters written by Paul. On the contrary, she considers oral sermons and discussions in the group around Paul as explanations for the similarities between the writings (134). Hübner, however assuming literary dependence on Romans 6, considers the possibility that the author of Colossians "in der Tat die paulinische Aussageintention in die vorpaulinische ‚re-modifiziert' [hat]" (HÜBNER, *An Philemon. An die Kolosser. An die Epheser*, 83f.). In his reconstruction of preformed material in Romans 6, Hellholm is inclined to see the future tense as already extant in the preformed tradition (in the present publication: HELLHOLM, "Vorgeformte Tauftraditionen", § 1.5.). Similarly G. SELLIN, *Der Brief an die Epheser*, 162. This view makes the aorist formulation in Colossians stand out as a specific characteristic in comparison with Paul. For a discussion of intertextuality related to the Pauline writings and the question of a Pauline school see MÜLLER, "Zum Problem der Paulusschule", 190ff.

60 Jewett comments on the word συνταφέντες in Col 2:12 and points to the fact that "Rom 6:4 is the first instance of religious use of this term in Greco-Roman or Jewish culture" (JEWETT, *Romans*, 398).

61 HELLHOLM, "The Impact of the Situational Contexts", 157; 174, and in the present publication: HELLHOLM, "Vorgeformte Tauftraditionen", § 1.5. See also JEWETT, *Romans*, 396ff. who tends to see these motifs as an invention of Paul worked out for the letter to the Romans. Betz proposes that this is a Pauline development and, further, that the focus in the passage of Romans 6 is on the new identity motivating a new way of leading one's life, and the same focus may be found in Colossians (BETZ, "Transferring a Ritual").

seem to imply a break in the reasoning's logic with regard to parallelism.[62] I am, however, inclined to see – not the logical parallelism but rather – the modification in relation to the main purpose of Colossians being one of arguing that the cosmic power and status of Christ is in fact available to the believer,[63] and is fundamental for his/her identity as believers. It also concerns the manner in which the believer is to lead his/her life (see above). Stating that "the believer is raised with Christ" corresponds with both the world view and the perceived status of the believer within the reality that the implied author imparts to his ideal reader.

Would the readers notice these significant modifications? Competent readers would do so, readers engaged in studying and elaborating on the teachings of Paul. Others with merely a superficial knowledge of Paul would recognise the motifs as being characteristically Pauline, but would perhaps not notice the modifications. Another question is how different readers would perceive and interpret the modifications. The assumption that literary interdependence included interpretation, innovation and transformation might have been at hand.[64]

Leaving the question of modifications aside, one could further assume that recognised and characteristic Pauline motifs displaying Pauline authority play a role in the warning against the "philosophy". Hartman writes the following on this subject:

> This text contains several echoes from Paul, and if we consider the recipient's side of the communication, it is a fair assumption that they recognised the echoes; if this is correct, it reinforced the polemics against the 'philosophy'.[65]

Finally, there is the point important within the scope of this essay, this being the structure combining descriptive and prescriptive language. There is descriptive language in both Romans 6 and Colossians 2 combining the Christ myth with the baptismal ritual of initiation. The identification of myth and ritual is existent in the significant death and resurrection of Christ being resembled in the baptismal rite, although in a manner in which the performative details and the concrete symbolism of the rite are unknown to us. Furthermore, the "dead – alive" scheme, carrying the sounding board of the experienced ritual, is carried

---

62 See Hellholm's discussion in the present publication: HELLHOLM, "Vorgeformte Tauftraditionen", § 1.5.

63 See WOLTER, *Der Brief an die Kolosser. Der Brief an Philemon*, 131ff.; DUNN, *The Epistles to the Colossians and to Philemon*, 161. H. Merklein assumes that the author integrates the Pauline baptismal concept into a traditional conversion scheme and so makes an innovative change to the Pauline statement. The Pauline death – resurrection concept is integrated in a thought pattern where the contrast below – above gets more attention than the present – future contrast (MERKLEIN, "Paulinische Theologie in der Rezeption des Kolosser- und Epheserbriefes", 44f.).

64 MERKLEIN, "Eph 4,1 – 5,20 als Rezeption von Kol 3,1–17", 196.

65 HARTMAN, *Into the Name of the Lord Jesus*, 99.

over in consecutive prescriptive passages and not merely the dead – alive scheme in itself, but also the very identification of the believer with the mythical fate of Christ. This particular combination of descriptive and prescriptive language is found both in Romans and in Colossians. The exhortations in Col 3:1ff. continue to demonstrate the baptismal language of the former passages in a similar way as the exhortations in Rom 6:12ff. Thus, in both Romans and in Colossians, the language of baptism as being incorporated into Christ's death and resurrection is the foundation for moral progress. These similarities suggest comparable interrelations between the dimensions of comprehensive interpretive schemes, and the structure itself is significant for the Pauline version of a Christian comprehensive interpretive scheme.

2.6. Concluding Remarks

Col 2:9ff. can be read as an elaboration on the learning /teaching according to Christ (κατὰ Χριστόν [2:8]). This teaching consists of both cognitive and behavioural dimensions. Colossians contains deliberative rhetoric aimed at what will be beneficial for the audience, and "Paul" figures as its implicit author, giving authority to the reasoning therein.

In Colossians we meet a brave integration of moral advice with a grand description of reality. Colossians 2 assimilates the concepts of the Christ eulogy in Chapter 1 and the exhortations given in other parts of the writing. The myth of Christ (as outlined in 1:15–20) is the conceptual essence of both worldview and ethos, and baptism represents the "door", or transition into a space where these things make sense in the broader context. Baptismal motifs are related to the Christ myth and are applied in the exhortations. Such integration has a model in Paul. Assuming that Romans 6 expresses the more original version of these motifs, Colossians could be said to represent a brave new interpretation, stating as it does the presence of the powers of the exalted Christ in the space where the believers live their lives.

The texts we are dealing with are linguistic expressions of conceptual relations, representing comprehensive interpretive schemes as indicated in the introduction of this essay. At the same time, when regarded from a rhetorical and pragmatical perspective, texts apply these schemes – and when it comes to deliberative texts, such as Colossians – apply this type of scheme containing identity-building intentions and functions. The texts express how different dimensions are represented in a scheme of interpretation. Moreover, the argumentation functions well if the audience finds the scheme informative, as in creating meaning and motivation. Such analysis of course expands on the presupposition that people are inclined to apply such schemes without having first been trained to do so.

This literate application of comprehensive interpretive schemes may function in formation understood as "Bildung" or, using a somewhat different terminology, as identity formation. One feature of such formation is remembrance.[66] Exhortation applies remembrance, referring to both doctrines already known and moral values already shared, in Colossians: 1:5; 1:23; 2:7. This function of remembrance intends to create a perception of broader coherences. The reasoning therefore mentions, reminds, and creates a linguistic presence of different elements and religious dimensions, integrating them to a comprehensive interpretive scheme. The anamnesis of experiences related to ritually marking the transition from old to new activate sentiments that other dimensions of the comprehensive scheme are not able to accomplish.

On another note, Colossians as a deliberative text functions as religious or philosophical guidance. The implicit author presents himself as a teacher. Other philosophies are identified as contrasts, alternatives to the teaching presented by himself. His teaching integrates doctrines and moral advice as well as remembrance of the initiation rite. The comprehensive interpretive scheme in its totality serves as motivation for leading a new way of life and as a context for assuming a Christian identity.

3. Baptismal Language in Ephesians

Several motifs and passages in Ephesians may contain references to baptism,[67] e.g. in Eph 1:13 where the motif of the seal is applied, stating "when you […] had believed in him, were marked with the seal of the promised Holy Spirit" (1:13).[68] Eph. 2:1–10 bears resemblance to Rom 6 and Col 2 where baptism is explicitly mentioned. Baptism is mentioned in a list articulating Christian core concepts in Eph 4:5, and in Eph 5:26 we hear that Christ made the church holy "by cleansing her with the washing of water by the word." This might be a reference to baptism,[69] and it occurs in a Haustafel where the imagined relationship between Christ and the church is applied as an analogy that is thought to have a function

---

66 See A. J. Malherbe, "Paraenesis in the Epistle to Titus", 309–311.

67 See Dahl, "The Concept of Baptism in Ephesians".

68 The reference to baptism should not be taken as obvious, even if it is possible that the author and certain readers could have related the expression to baptism. See the discussion in Schnackenburg, *Der Brief an die Epheser*, 64f.; Lindemann, *Der Epheserbrief*, 25f.; Best, *Ephesians*, 150; Sellin, *Der Brief an die Epheser*, 115–117. See also in the present publication: K. O. Sandnes, "Seal and Baptism", § 3.

69 Schnackenburg supposes that the expression is meant to refer to baptism (Schnackenburg, *Der Brief an die Epheser*, 255) as does Lindemann (Lindemann, *Der Epheserbrief*, 103f.) and Hübner, *An Philemon. An die Kolosser. An die Epheser*, 246f. Sellin assumes the wedding images to be more prominent, but does not exclude the idea that the image field of baptism is activated (Sellin, *Der Brief an die Epheser*, 448f.). Hartman remarks that the author probably refers to baptism in 5:26 (Hartman, *Into the Name of the Lord Jesus*, 102).

in motivating the exhortation to the husband to maintain a correct attitude towards his wife. In the present essay I intend to discuss the (possible) baptismal references in Eph 2 and Eph 4.

3.1. Structure and Genre

As stated above, the following discussion presupposes that Ephesians is both a Deuteropauline letter and is literary dependent of Colossians. According to Dahl, Sellin and others, Ephesians, like most of the Pauline letters, is divided into two main sections, one descriptive, or in rhetorical terms *epideictical* (1:3–3:21), and one prescriptive, or *symbouleutical* (4:1–6:9). Regarding function, the first epideictical section can be defined more specifically as eulogistic, and the second symbouleutical section can be specified as *exhortatio* or *paraenesis*.[70] According to H.-J. Klauck, "the first main part in 2:1–3:21 expands themes from the thanksgiving (1:15–23), partly in the language of prayer".[71] This outline places the first passage to be commented on in the descriptive section, and the second in the prescriptive one. In accordance with the discussion above of the structure and genre of Colossians, the descriptive and prescriptive passages should be seen as being interdependent of one another also in Ephesians.

In terms of genre, the writing seems difficult to classify.[72] Common to more of the suggested designations – theological teaching, wisdom discourse, medi-

---

70 SELLIN, *Der Brief an die Epheser*, 52. Similarly SCHNELLE, *Einleitung in das Neue Testament*, 354 and LINDEMANN, *Der Epheserbrief*, 15. For a thorough discussion of the composition, see DAHL, "Einleitungsfragen zum Epheserbrief", 3–12 and 16f. According to Dahl, Ephesians has few, if any, features of symbouleutic rhetoric (DAHL, "Einleitungsfragen zum Epheserbrief", 16). One could agree if symbouleutic rhetoric is defined in a more restricted sense as having the political sphere as its subject. However, arguments advocating the unity of the believers could be defined as political argumentation, see M. M. MITCHELL, *Paul and the Rhetoric of Reconciliation*, 68ff.; 76ff.; O. M. BAKKE, *Concord and peace*. What is more, if the prescriptive sections are seen as important regarding form and function of the writing, and further, if the prescriptive part along with the descriptive part as a whole could be evaluated as some sort of (moral-) philosophical letter, symbouleutic rhetoric seems to be the obvious category. See MALHERBE, "Paraenesis in the Epistle to Titus", 297f.; B. FIORE, *The Pastoral Epistles*, 12; VEGGE, *Paulus und das antike Schulwesen*, 225–229 with references to further literature. For the discussion of the concept *paraenesis*, which is of interest for the discussion in this essay, see the volume ENGBERG-PEDERSEN/STARR, *Early Christian Paraenesis in Context*.

71 KLAUCK, *Ancient Letters and the New Testament*, 316. Similarly SELLIN, *Der Brief an die Epheser*, 98.

72 See the discussion in BEST, *Ephesians*, 59–63; DAHL, "Einleitungsfragen zum Epheserbrief", 3f. Furthermore, according to Mußner, Ephesians is no letter "sondern eine ‚Epistle', genauer: ein theologisches ‚Lehrschreiben'" (MUSSNER, "Epheserbrief", 743). Schnelle emphasises that the letter should not be considered as situational, but rather as a circular letter to the Pauline congregations in Asia Minor (SCHNELLE, *Einleitung in das Neue Testament*, 354). Sellin points to its homiletic function and mentions that it has been classified as a sermon (SELLIN, *Der Brief an die Epheser*, 53).

tation, liturgical homily, theological treatise, letter of prayer[73] – is the cognitive and instructional function of the letter. The writing is recognised as some sort of teaching or sermon given an epistolary frame. It has even been suggested that the writing is either a baptismal liturgy or sermon first given at the baptism of new converts and then slightly altered in order to function as the corpus of a circular letter.[74] Personally speaking, I am reluctant to see baptism as the main topic of the writing. C. Caragounis remarks that there is only "a single bald mention of that term [baptism]".[75] Moreover, according to Best, the references to baptism are too few to point to such a classification, and further: "since baptism would have been seen as a significant event in their lives by Christians who had been converted from paganism, it would not be surprising to find some references to it in any Christian writing".[76] Sellin supposes the text to have been difficult to understand for newly converted Gentiles.[77] Regarding genre, I would suggest the broad category of "philosophical letter", which in terms of the traditional rhetorical genera can be evaluated as being symbouleutical,[78] and in terms of character concerned with moral guidance.

3.2. The Function of the Writing

The letter has a universal character in terms of reasoning, and the implied author is general in addressing the audience.[79] Similar to the proto-Pauline letters, Ephesians imparts religious-philosophic teaching and, more specifically, both the *epideictical* worldview aspect and the *symbouleutical* ethos aspect of such education. In Ephesians it is communicated by a student of Paul's who wishes

---

73 See BEST, *Ephesians*, 61; SCHNELLE, *Einleitung in das Neue Testament*, 354f.; DAHL, "The Letter to the Ephesians: Its Fictional and Real Setting", 451.

74 For an introduction to the discussion and a critical assessment of the importance of baptism in the letter see CARAGOUNIS, *The Ephesian Mysterion*, 46, footnote 83. Shortly also in BEST, *Ephesians*, 61. See further the discussion in DAHL, "The Concept of Baptism in Ephesians", 414–416. Dahl is inclined to attach greater importance to baptism in the letter, and states, "one can characterize the contents with the catchwords 'baptismal anamnesis' and 'baptismal paraenesis'" (416).

75 CARAGOUNIS, *The Ephesian Mysterion*, 46, footnote 83.

76 BEST, *Ephesians*, 61.

77 SELLIN, *Der Brief an die Epheser*, 62.

78 See MALHERBE, *Moral Exhortation*, 79–85; VEGGE, *Paulus und das antike Schulwesen*, 225–229 with reference to additional literature. For a short description of philosophical letters relevant to the topics discussed in the present essay, see also FIORE, *The Pastoral Epistles*, 12–14. See also the paragraphs on the Pastoral Epistles below.

79 J. BECKER/U. LUZ, *Die Briefe an die Galater, Epheser und Kolosser*, 108; SCHNELLE, *Einleitung in das Neue Testament*, 350; SELLIN, *Der Brief an die Epheser*, 57f. The general character of the writing is commented upon in detail by Dahl: DAHL, "Einleitungsfragen zum Epheserbrief", 12–14. See also 80.

to consolidate the latter's teaching. "Paul" figures as the fictional author[80] and, furthermore, the writing reveals a thorough familiarity with what – through existing proto-Pauline letters – is known to us as the teachings of "Paul",[81] and demonstrates a particular interdependence with Colossians.[82] In addition the author reveals an extensive acquaintance with Jewish Hellenistic theology and antique philosophy.[83]

A clear-cut statement of the writing's intention (a *propositio* or *partitio/divisio*) is absent in the introductory passages. There are, however, passages and utterances with a metacommunicative function scattered throughout the writing. For instance, in the passage from 1:15, the implicit author presents himself and his intentions for the implicit audience. He reports on his prayers asking God to give them a spirit of wisdom and revelation (1:17). In 3:1 he once again tells them about both his prayers and the mystery revealed to him. He has written about the mystery above (1:9), and when the audience hears this passage read, they will perceive his insight into the mystery. In 4:1 he says that he exhorts them (παρακαλῶ οὖν ὑμᾶς), and in 4:17 "This I then say and confess in the Lord ..." (τοῦτο οὖν λέγω καὶ μαρτύρομαι ἐν κυρίῳ). According to these passages, the implicit author is concerned with the teaching of the revealed mystery which, when performed, will impart readers with wisdom and insight.

Dahl suggests that the composition character and writing content can be summarised "unter den Stichwörtern Taufanamnese und Taufparänese".[84] Based on this summary, he suggests that the letter was addressed to newly established churches. However, the supposition of a later date and the summary warning against heresies in 4:14 points toward another explanation.[85] Similarly Mußner considers the models for the paraenetic teaching in the letter to originate in the oral missionary sermon and "Taufunterweisung".[86] He finds the cen-

---

80 Regarding the fictional setting, see DAHL, "The Letter to the Ephesians: Its Fictional and Real Setting", 452f.

81 BECKER/LUZ, *Die Briefe an die Galater, Epheser und Kolosser*, 111–113; MUSSNER, "Epheserbrief", 743f.; SCHNELLE, *Einleitung in das Neue Testament*, 361f.; SELLIN, *Der Brief an die Epheser*, 58; DAHL, "Einleitungsfragen zum Epheserbrief", 39. Dahl also writes: "Man muß annehmen, daß der Verfasser nicht nur mit dem literarischen Nachlaß des Apostels, sondern auch mit der mündlichen Form seiner Sprache vertraut war" (*ibid.*, 52).

82 Luz supposes that the author wanted to stay as close as possible to the words of his teacher and probably assumed Colossians to be written by Paul himself (BECKER/LUZ, *Die Briefe an die Galater, Epheser und Kolosser*, 111). See the detailed comparison of the two writings in DAHL, "Einleitungsfragen zum Epheserbrief", 39–48.

83 "Sein Verfasser hat umfassende Kenntnisse der paulinischen Briefe und ihrer Theologie, der jüdisch-hellenistischen Theologie und der antiken Philosophie" (SELLIN, *Der Brief an die Epheser*, 57).

84 DAHL, "Einleitungsfragen zum Epheserbrief", 64.

85 *Ibid.*, 64.

86 MUSSNER, "Epheserbrief", 748.

tral sentence of the letter in 2:18, stating that both Gentiles and Jews have access in one Spirit to the Father.[87] Agreeing with this statement, Sellin emphasises that the main topic is "das Motiv der 'Ein(s)heit', das auch terminologisch vor allem die Abschnitte 2,14–18; 4,1–6.13–16 beherrscht."[88] Furthermore, Sellin points to 2:11–22 as the centre of the writing's epideictic main section,[89] and the striking elaborateness of the paraenetic section 4:1–6:9.[90]

Assessments like "missionary sermon" and "Taufunterweisung" suggest that the implied readers are newly converted Gentiles. Sellin remarks that the text presupposes Christian families, and assumes the terminology and the line of thought to be difficult to understand for newly converted Gentiles:

> Besonders im epideiktischen Hauptteil Kap. 1–3 wird eine Theologie vorausgesetzt, die mit ihren hellenistisch-jüdischen religiösen und philosophischen Grundlagen und Anspielungen die Verstehensmöglichkeiten frisch bekehrter Heiden bei weitem übersteigen würde.[91]

My own evaluation follows this direction of seeing the text as envisaging readers more competent than the average newly converted believer. Caragounis offers some – in my opinion – spot on comments when he refers to Paul's remarks in 1 Corinthians "that they neither were nor are at present sufficiently mature to receive proper food (βρῶμα). Instead, they had to be given milk …. Could it be rightly claimed that Eph is but spiritual milk? Is it not rather στερεά τροφή of the highest kind?"[92] Starr argues that paraenesis as understood in e.g. Plutarch "is written for mature readers who were already well established in their philosophical and theological convictions."[93] I suppose that a similar evaluation is adequate for Ephesians in its entirety.

Such considerations on function and certain remarks made above concerning genre may suggest that the letter could be seen in a school setting where the conceptual world of the believers is considered and developed in a literate form. The implicit author has the characteristics of a teacher, and the implied readers are advanced in Christian formation and identifying themselves with the school of Paul. This constructed fictive setting does not exclude the possi-

---

87 *Ibid.*, 743.
88 SELLIN, *Der Brief an die Epheser*, 61.
89 "Das Zentrum des epideiktischen Hauptteils bildet […] der Abschnitt 2,11–22: der Entwurf einer neuen Menschheit, in der Frieden, Versöhnung (mit Gott und dadurch mit allen Menschen) und metaphysische 'Ein(s)heit' verwirklicht sein werden. Demonstriert wird das an der Vereinigung von Juden und Heiden, die den 'Bau' der Kirche bilden (2,19–22)" (*ibid.*, 62).
90 *Ibid.*, 62.
91 *Ibid.*, 303. See also 62.
92 CARAGOUNIS, *The Ephesian Mysterion*, 46, note 83.
93 STARR, "Was Paraenesis for Beginners?", 88, and the conclusions, page 111.

bility that the writing was read in other settings with larger groups of believers present.

3.3. Ephesians 2:1–10

This passage is commented upon here because it bears strong resemblance to other texts in which baptism is explicitly mentioned, and because it can be seen as being dependent in a literary sense on the particular texts in Rom 6 and Col 2.[94] I intend to discuss to which degree the passage can be considered to contain baptismal phrases.

3.3.1. Line of Reasoning

The passage, being part of the first (epideictic section, 1:3–3:21) of two main sections in the letter's main body, follows upon the thanksgiving passage ending in the form of a Christ doxology, 1:15–23. The passage 2:1–10 is singled out as being a separate unit by showing a transition from this doxology (1:20–23) into addressing the audience/readers directly in 2:1 (καὶ ὑμᾶς …), and by means of an *inclusio*:[95]

ταῖς ἁμαρτίαις ὑμῶν, ἐν αἷς ποτε περιεπατήσατε (2:1f.)
ἔργοις ἀγαθοῖς … ἐν αὐτοῖς περιπατήσωμεν (2:10)

sins in which you once lived (2:1f.)
good works … to be our way of life (2:10)

The passage has a clear antithetical structure,[96] contrasting the former life of "being dead in the trespasses and sins" and "walking according to the realm of this world" (2:1–2) with the new existence of walking in good deeds, an existence made possible by being made alive in Christ. The formulation introducing the first section – ὄντας νεκροὺς τοῖς παραπτώμασιν – is repeated at the beginning of the second (2:5). Based on this formulation, the two sections are figured to be approximately equal in length (82 and 83 words).

This passage appears once again to establish a foundation for the subsequent passage (2:11–22) where an argument is made for the unity and equality of those once called "foreskin" and those called "circumcised", a passage that can be seen as clearly expressing the writing's key issue.[97] The ideal reader in these

---

94　See SELLIN, *Der Brief an die Epheser*, 162f.
95　Similarly HÜBNER, *An Philemon. An die Kolosser. An die Epheser*, 155, who, however, sees a paraenetic arrangement of the section emphasised through the *inclusio*.
96　So *ibid.*, 155f.
97　See DAHL, "Einleitungsfragen zum Epheserbrief", 71; SELLIN, *Der Brief an die Epheser*, 61f.; SELLIN, "Die Paränese des Epheserbriefes", 180.

passages seems to be a Gentile believer[98] who is encouraged to see himself/herself being par with Jews in his/her relationship with God.[99]

The antithetical structure of the passage concurs with two semantic schemes, the scheme "once – now" and the scheme of "dead – alive", which are put into a reasoning strategy advocating unity. Both schemes seem appropriate for interpreting an initiation rite. They are used not only in relation to baptism in our sources, but also in paragraphs where baptism is not mentioned.

3.3.2. The Schemes "Once – Now" and "Dead – Alive"

The scheme "once – now"[100] occurs in Rom 3:21 and 25–26; 5:6–11; 7:4–6 the focus at times falling more on the salvation revealed by God at a chosen time in history, and at other times on the believers' life histories. In Eph 5:8 this occurs in a paraenetic context and combined with the contrasting notion of "darkness – light".

The "dead – alive" scheme is the prominent scheme of early Christian doctrines concerning Jesus Christ (1 Cor 15:3–5). It is obvious that it is not always directly related to baptism (Rom 8:10.13; 11:15). An interesting note to our discussion is that the scheme in several Pauline texts is combined with the "once – now" scheme (Rom 5:6–11; 7:4–6; 1 Cor 15:20–22; 2 Cor 5:14–17, and perhaps Gal 2:19–21 as well). Phil 3 highlights the contrast between Paul's present and former life. The reasoning is antithetical and is based on a "once – now" contrast. Righteousness through having faith in Christ is mentioned as a positive aspect of being in the present, as are the power of his resurrection and of becoming like Christ in his death and, further, the hope of attaining resurrection from the dead (Phil 3:4–11). The "dead – alive" scheme is thus connected to his reasoning contrasting his present and former life. In the Deuteropauline Col 1:21–22 the former life (ποτε ὄντας) is contrasted with being holy and blameless, and the change is brought about by the death of Christ. The schemes are combined in these instances; however, there is no obvious reference to baptism, also not in Phil 3, even if circumcision is regarded as being one of the advantages of Paul's former life.

Finally, we arrive at texts where the schemes are connected with baptism. In 1 Cor 6:11 the scheme "once – now" seems to be combined with baptism

---

98   See Luz in BECKER/LUZ, *Die Briefe an die Galater, Epheser und Kolosser*, 108.
99   This does not exclude the fact that actual Jewish readers could find positive meaning in the passage.
100 See DAHL, "Formgeschichtliche Beobachtungen" and HELLHOLM, "The 'Revelation-Schema'". For a discussion of the tradition and application of the scheme, see P. TACHAU, ‚Einst' und ‚Jetzt' im neuen Testament. Tachau discusses Sitz im Leben with regard to the scheme, and shows the close relations to baptism. However, he also refers to the many passages where the scheme does not seem connected to baptism (130f.) and concludes that the "sermon" (Predigt) can be assumed as Sitz im Leben without offering any closer definition of sermon (133).

(καὶ ταῦτά τινες ἦτε· ἀλλὰ ἀπελούσασθε …)[101] as it is in Tit 3:3–7. The tradition in 1 Cor 15:3–4 contains the "dead – alive" scheme. While baptism is not directly mentioned, there are reasons to believe that the traditions imparted here belonged to settings related to baptism.[102] The "once – now" scheme is not extant. The prominent passage concerning the combination of both schemes with baptism is found in Rom 6, where "dead – alive" (the death and resurrection of Christ applied on the existence of the believers) is the prominent motif, both related to the baptismal rite and combined with the "once – now" scheme through the verbal forms in aorist and future tense, and through adverbials such as μηκέτι (6:6) and οὐκέτι (6:9). In the paraenetic application of the baptism sentences, the "once – now" is further pronounced (6:19–22). Furthermore, both schemes are combined in Col 2:13 (ὑμᾶς νεκροὺς ὄντας … συνεζωοποίησεν ὑμᾶς), in a baptismal context. The two schemes are interwoven in the elaborate paraenetic passage Col 3:1–17, expanding on the descriptive baptismal sentences in Col 2, the passage itself applying motifs that in other Pauline texts are related to baptism.[103]

We are dealing with schemes that can either be used separately or combined, as they are here in Ephesians. They can also be used in a variety of contexts, such as baptismal contexts. The "once - now" scheme is prominent in Ephesians. It supports the structure in 2:11–22 where the key issue in the writing appears to be clearly stated (ποτὲ ὑμεῖς [2:11] … ἦτε τῷ καιρῷ ἐκείνῳ [2:12] … νυνὶ δὲ ἐν Χριστῷ Ἰησοῦ ὑμεῖς οἵ ποτε ὄντες …[2:13]). The "dead – alive" scheme is applied (2:13.16) here as well. In addition it seems to be present in the paraenesis section of the writing[104] and is outspoken in 5:8 (ἦτε γάρ ποτε σκότος, νῦν δὲ φῶς ἐν κυρίῳ), combined with the contrast "darkness – light". In 5:14 the contrast "darkness – light" is combined with the "dead – alive" scheme in a citation of unknown origin:[105] πᾶν γὰρ τὸ φανερούμενον φῶς ἐστιν. διὸ λέγει, Ἔγειρε, ὁ καθεύδων, καὶ ἀνάστα ἐκ τῶν νεκρῶν, καὶ ἐπιφαύσει σοι ὁ Χριστός (for everything that becomes visible is light. Therefore it says, "Sleeper, awake! Rise from the dead, and Christ will shine on you").[106]

---

101 See in the present publication: Hellholm, "Vorgeformte Tauftraditionen", § 1.3.

102 A reconstructed pistis-formula behind 1 Cor 15:3–5 may have been used in the baptism catechesis, and may be closely related both linguistically (conceptually) and in terms of setting to formulas belonging to the baptismal rite, which again may be reconstructed from Rom 6 (*Ibid.*, 1.5).

103 See above to Colossians 2.

104 See Sellin, *Der Brief an die Epheser*, 302; Tachau, *"Einst" und "Jetzt" im neuen Testament*, 125f.

105 Sellin, *Der Brief an die Epheser*, 411f.

106 G. Barth assumes the three line citation has the baptismal service as its Sitz im Leben (Barth, *Die Taufe in frühchristlicher Zeit*, 121), and according to Best "Eph 5.14 is probably a passage from a baptismal hymn" (Best, *Ephesians*, 80, further 497ff.).

The "once – now" scheme shapes the antithetical structure in the passage commented upon here, and where it is also combined with the "dead – alive" scheme. The brief discussion above indicates the motifs' flexibility. It also indicates that the motifs themselves (and even the combination of the two schemes) are not exclusively connected to baptism. 1 Cor 15:22 (ὥσπερ γὰρ ἐν τῷ Ἀδὰμ πάντες ἀποθνῄσκουσιν, οὕτως καὶ ἐν τῷ Χριστῷ πάντες ζῳοποιηθήσονται) appears to come close to Eph 2:5 (καὶ ὄντας ἡμᾶς νεκροὺς τοῖς παραπτώμασιν συνεζωοποίησεν τῷ Χριστῷ) in wording and structure; however, it does so with no reference to baptism. The connection exists most likely in that Eph 2 cites Col 2:13, which in turn may be inspired by 1 Cor 15:22.[107] In Colossians baptism is found in the close context. The word ζῳοποιέω occurs with the "dead - alive" scheme in Rom 8:10, with neither the "once – now" scheme nor any reference to baptism (see also Rom 4:17).

This discussion suggests that references to baptism are not obvious in Eph 2:1–10. A definite application to baptism would for most readers need a clear instruction on the textual surface. The close resemblances with Rom 6 and Col 2, however, need further comment.

3.3.3. On the Relation to Romans 6 and Colossians 2

Even if baptism is not mentioned explicitly in this passage (Eph 2:1–10), its structure and motifs have parallels in Col 2:6–13 and in Rom 6, texts with distinct references to baptism. The similarities suggest that a competent reader would link the texts together. The phrases "being made alive with Christ" even if "we were dead" and, further, that God has "raised us from death with him" are quite similar to the sentences in Romans 6 and Col 2. The words "you being dead because of the transgressions" (ὑμᾶς ὄντας νεκροὺς τοῖς παραπτώμασιν) (Eph 2:1) could be read as a citation from Colossians (ὑμᾶς νεκροὺς ὄντας [ἐν] τοῖς παραπτώμασιν) (Col 2:13). This wording returns in Eph 2:5, altering only the person and order of the first two words (ὄντας ἡμᾶς νεκροὺς τοῖς παραπτώμασιν). In Colossians (but not in Ephesians) the τοῖς παραπτώμασιν is combined with the "uncircumcision of your flesh" (τοῖς παραπτώμασιν καὶ τῇ ἀκροβυστίᾳ τῆς σαρκὸς ὑμῶν). In Ephesians although the speech about ἀκροβυστία and περιτομή follows in the next paragraph, the firm sense of "Gentile" and "Jew" seems more prominent there.

Additionally, the continuation is almost identical:

συνεζωοποίησεν ὑμᾶς σὺν αὐτῷ, χαρισάμενος ἡμῖν πάντα τὰ παραπτώματα (Col 2:13)
συνεζωοποίησεν τῷ Χριστῷ, - χάριτί ἐστε σεσῳσμένοι (Eph 2:5)

made you alive together with him, when he forgave us all our trespasses (Col 2:13)

---

107 SELLIN, *Der Brief an die Epheser*, 176.

made us alive together with Christ – by grace you have been saved (Eph 2:5)

The word συζωοποιέω occurs only in these two instances in the NT, and is not found elsewhere in Greek, non-Christian literature. The close similarities in sequence and concepts, although showing differences, could be explained as Ephesians reworking Colossians, or that both authors were familiar with the structure of Pauline teaching of the believer being dead and made alive together with Christ, known to us most prominently in Rom 6, and formulated the argumentation independent of one another.

Several features of Ephesians suggest that the author used Colossians, and that he was presumably familiar with both Pauline teaching and other Pauline writings. I have already briefly discussed issues, which are relevant for the identity of the intended reader. We could suggest that the reader is assumed to be a competent reader familiar with Pauline writings. If the address is more general, the author may have supposed a superficial knowledge of Pauline teaching. The competent readers acquainted with Rom 6 and/or Col 2 could make a reference to baptism when listening to this text. On the other hand, the competent reader might also notice the modifications in relation to Romans and Colossians. I will therefore briefly mention three such modifications that might be of significance:

(1) The sentences expressing being raised with Christ (Eph 2:5f.) may be seen as a development of Col 2:12, which in turn represents a development of Romans 6:4f.[108] Paul writes in Romans that we are buried with him by baptism, and having grown together [with him] in the likeness/analogy of his death, we shall also do so in the resurrection. According to Colossians, we are buried with him in baptism and have already been raised with him, and eventually, according to Ephesians, we are made alive with Christ, raised with him and even placed with him in heaven.[109] This further development in Ephesians (καὶ συνήγειρεν καὶ συνεκάθισεν ἐν τοῖς ἐπουρανίοις ἐν Χριστῷ Ἰησοῦ, 2:6) is terminologically and conceptually prepared in 1:20 (ἣν ἐνήργησεν ἐν τῷ Χριστῷ ἐγείρας αὐτὸν ἐκ νεκρῶν καὶ καθίσας ἐν δεξιᾷ αὐτοῦ ἐν τοῖς ἐπουρανίοις).[110] In comparison with those other texts the absence of any direct reference to baptism and the συνεκάθισεν would stand out as distinctive features in Ephesians.

(2) Sellin emphasises the fact that the conception of "having been buried with him" in Col 2:12 (and originating in Rom 6:4)[111] is missing in Ephesians. These formulations express the idea that baptism signifies a symbolic unifica-

---

108 So Hübner, *An Philemon. An die Kolosser. An die Epheser*, 161.

109 See Merklein, "Paulinische Theologie in der Rezeption des Kolosser- und Epheserbriefes", 42f.; Hübner, *An Philemon. An die Kolosser. An die Epheser*, 161f.

110 Sellin, *Der Brief an die Epheser*, 176.

111 συνετάφημεν οὖν αὐτῷ διὰ τοῦ βαπτίσματος (Rom 6:4); συνταφέντες αὐτῷ ἐν τῷ βαπτισμῷ (Col 2:12).

tion with the death and burial of Christ. Death and burial symbolism is, according to Sellin, an essential motif in baptismal symbolism, and it is noticeable that they are obliterated in Ephesians,[112] which might suggest that a reference to baptism is not intended here. The competent reader would notice a diminution of baptismal motifs.

(3) A further characteristic of the intertextual relationship appears to be a process of condensation. The lengthy passage in Rom 6 elaborating on the "dead – alive" scheme and baptism seems condensed in Colossians, but then expanded in certain characteristic ways. If these texts inspired Eph 2, they are further condensed in Ephesians, as expressed in 2:5–6 (and obliterating certain motifs as well). However, the scope of this particular essay does not allow for commenting upon this condensation.

Summing up: The reasoning in Eph 2:1–10 appears to be linked to a cluster of motifs found in the Pauline writings that were also presumably central in Pauline teaching and belonging to the core of the Pauline gospel and, as such, could be applied in different contexts. Likewise, the schemes "dead – alive" and "once – now" are not alien to other early Christian writings, and the metaphorical "dead – alive" as a description of religious-philosophic status is found in Hellenistic Judaism (Philo), originating in the Stoa.[113] The metaphor was and is assumed to be quite adaptive. The reasoning applying the two contrastive schemes and demonstrating the new status of the believers supports the following passage in 2:11ff., one describing a Jewish perceived difference in religious status between Jews and Gentiles once extant; however the two have now been united. This passage takes up the motif of circumcision that is connected to baptism in Colossians 2, while in Eph 2:11 the more concrete sense of "Gentile" and "Jew" seems dominant in the formulations "those once called foreskin" and "those called circumcised". In 2:14ff. (ὁ ποιήσας τὰ ἀμφότερα ἓν …) the motif of oneness/unity appears, a motif that is also present in the baptismal sentences in Galatians 3 and 1 Cor 12 (which is also the predominant motif in Eph 4, where baptism is mentioned explicitly).

3.3.4. Concluding Remarks

The passage is structured by two schemes that are central in the baptismal texts of Rom 6 and Col 2. There are prominent elements in the passage that in other texts are linked directly to baptism, both the rite and its interpretation, and the rite as initiation, a transition from an old to a new context. The contrastive schemes and the passage's antithetical structure correspond to the conception of such a transition having taken place previously in the lives of believers in Christ. However, to general believers attending churches in Asia Minor and hearing

---

112 SELLIN, *Der Brief an die Epheser*, 176f.
113 *Ibid.*, 165.

this text, a reference to baptism would in my opinion be rather accidental and dependent on the individual reader. Some of these readers might have been familiar with Rom 6 and/or Col 2, or with the line and form of the argumentation, as far as these topoi (lines of reasoning) were in use in oral teaching and preaching inspired by Paul.[114] Such readers would recognise the expressions as being Pauline, and remember that in comparable passages, baptism is drawn upon. If the intended reader were more competent and supposed to have engaged himself/herself more thoroughly with Pauline writings and teaching, he/she would notice that the explicit reference to baptism is downplayed or even absent in the text. The motif of unity is expressed clearly in the context of this passage, and is accentuated in the subsequent passage to be commented on where baptism is mentioned explicitly.

3.4. Ephesians 4:5

The expression referring to baptism occurs in the following context:

(3) ... σπουδάζοντες τηρεῖν τὴν ἑνότητα τοῦ πνεύματος ἐν τῷ συνδέσμῳ τῆς εἰρήνης·
(4) ἓν σῶμα καὶ ἓν πνεῦμα, καθὼς καὶ ἐκλήθητε ἐν μιᾷ ἐλπίδι τῆς κλήσεως ὑμῶν·
(5) εἷς κύριος, μία πίστις, ἓν βάπτισμα,
(6) εἷς θεὸς καὶ πατὴρ πάντων, ὁ ἐπὶ πάντων καὶ διὰ πάντων καὶ ἐν πᾶσιν (Eph 4:3–6)

(3) ... making every effort to maintain the unity of the Spirit in the bond of peace.
(4) There is one body and one Spirit, just as you were called to the one hope of your calling,
(5) one Lord, one faith, one baptism,
(6) one God and Father of all, who is above all and through all and in all.

The text is styled as an argumentative accumulation of expressions that can be comprehended as an amplification of the phrase τὴν ἑνότητα τοῦ πνεύματος τῆς εἰρήνης (4:3). Baptism is not the main topic of the passage starting with 4:1. While from certain perspectives the other contextual concepts could be said to relate to baptism, in my judgement it would be misleading to say that baptism is the core concept of the passage. Rather, the concept of baptism is brought into a line of reasoning in a row with other loaded Christian concepts. The text presents no elaboration on baptism, and if we (or someone at that time) would explore the potential semantic references of the concept, this would soon include

---

114 At least I would assume that Paul used the topoi found in his letters in other communication situations, and to the degree that they found resonance and were taught by associates of Paul, they were used and spread in the churches.

far more notions than can be mobilised in the reader/listener during the actual oral communication of the text.

3.4.1. Line of Reasoning

3:14–21 gives an account of the implied author's prayer. The passage functions as an ethos argument showing the author's commitment to his audience. The content, or what he wants to pray for, is assimilated into the other topics found in the writing. 4:1 introduces a textual component which, according to general opinion, is the second main section (out of two) in the writing. This prescriptive, exhortative section is, in comparison to other Pauline writings, extensive.[115] The reference to baptism is found in the paragraphs 4:1–16, initiating this prescriptive main section, where motifs from the first descriptive section of the writing recur as well: the motif of unity, the power and authority of Christ, the spatial dimensions of his authority and the motif of Christ as the head of his body, which, according to 1:22, is the ἐκκλησία. The compilation of these motifs seems intended to assure the believers that they belong to a unity that has cosmic dimensions.

4:1 sets the paraenetic/appellative[116] tone for the following passages. The expression παρακαλῶ οὖν ὑμᾶς / "I therefore beg you" should be heard as a metacommunicative utterance; the author states what kind of function he intends in relation to the readers of the ensuing sentences. A metacommunicative utterance appears again in 4:17 (τοῦτο οὖν λέγω καὶ μαρτύρομαι / "now this I affirm and insist on") that in effect seems to recapitulate the utterance in 4:1. The passages in between are in fact mainly instructive (epideictical) except for the exhorting sentences in 4:2–3 (and the exhortative tone in 4:14f.), so a renewal of the metacommunicative utterance is needed after 4:4–17 as far as the speaker considers the main function of the remaining passages to be prescriptive (symbouleutical). The baptismal phrase (ἓν βάπτισμα, 4,5) is found within a text passage that remains mainly descriptive, yet within a greater part of the writing that is mainly prescriptive. The metacommunicative utterances in 4:1 and 4:17 suggest that 4:1–16 should be taken as a delimited text component. Features of form and content make it natural to see three sections within the component: 4:1–6, 4:7–10 and 4:11–16.[117]

---

115 "Auffällig ist die Ausführlichkeit des paränetischen Teils 4,1–6,9 (fast die Hälfte des ganzen Schreibens)" (SELLIN, *Der Brief an die Epheser*, 62).

116 Sellin remarks that the paraenetic sections in the Pauline letters are appellative texts intended for those already baptised. They are not protreptic or catechetical teaching (SELLIN, "Die Paränese des Epheserbriefes", 184).

117 SELLIN, *Der Brief an die Epheser*, 306f.

3.4.2. Form

4:1–3 marks the transition to the prescriptive section of the writing, containing sentences in an appellative form; however, as previously stated, 4:4–16 is mainly descriptive before the main line becomes once again prescriptive. The form of the sentences in 4:4–6 is outstanding in a prose text. Some scholars explain the rhythmic repetitive form by the existence of a supposed textual prehistory, in a catechetical and baptismal context,[118] or as a tradition originating in the Pauline school.[119] According to Sellin, the passage has most likely been formulated by the author freely choosing elements and combining them.[120] Sellin points to the formative function of a row of triads in the passage 4:1–6.[121] Regarding 4:4–6, he comments:

> V.4 enthält die Trias ἓν σῶμα ('ein Leib') – ἓν πνεῦμα ('ein Geist') – μία ἐλπίς ('eine Hoffnung'). [...] V.5 enthält die Trias εἷς κύριος ('ein Herr') – μία πίστις ('ein Glaube') – ἓν βάπτισμα ('eine Taufe') – wobei die drei unterschiedlichen Genera εἷς – μία – ἕν ein weiteres triadisches Element darstellen. [...] Zu εἷς θεός ('ein Gott'), der den beiden letztgenannten Triaden als siebente Einheit übergeordnet ist, werden die drei präpositionalen Attribute mit ἐπι, διά und ἐν gesetzt.[122]

As stated previously, the focus of this article is to discuss the function and meaning of the phrases as they occur in the letter to the Ephesians. If in fact a formula existed, which was recognised by the audience and related to baptism (rite or interpretation) as the writing was being read, this would make baptism a main topic of the passage. I am inclined to see the passage as formulated and rhetorically styled by the author, with baptism not being the main topic of the passage, but rather an element in a line of reasoning emphasising the believers' unity. The entire piece of writing refers to "Paul" through his role as the fictive author. Regarded in this context, the idea should be considered that Paul most likely did not have any reputation as a baptiser (1 Cor 1:14).[123] The fictional setting for

---

118 SCHNACKENBURG, *Der Brief an die Epheser*, 162; 168. Schnackenburg emphasises however, the uncertainty in the assumption that the euphonic triad was already a constituent of the celebration of baptism. Lindemann supposes that the author is in fact citing a formula, one known to his readers. The origin of the formula is, however, unknown to us (LINDEMANN, *Der Epheserbrief*, 70–73).

119 BEST, *Ephesians*, 358f.

120 See the discussion in SELLIN, *Der Brief an die Epheser*, 308–313. Hartman is doubtful to the suggestion that "fragments of baptismal instruction and/or baptismal confessions" are represented in the passage and holds that "it is wholly possible that the heptad simply has its origin in a wish to begin a new section with rhetorical elegance" (HARTMAN, *Into the Name of the Lord Jesus*, 104 and 104, footnote 24).

121 Sellin refers to HÜBNER, *An Philemon. An die Kolosser. An die Epheser*, 203 for this observation.

122 SELLIN, *Der Brief an die Epheser*, 313.

123 See BETZ, "Transferring a Ritual", 104.

Pauline literary communication would for this reason hardly be a service related to baptism. On the contrary, the readers of Ephesians would be more inclined to perceive Paul as a teacher, and the competent readers would be familiar with Pauline teachings related to baptism.

3.4.3. Baptism in Ephesians 4:4–6

The key issue of Ephesians – unity – is prominent in the passage Eph 4:4–6.[124] As already stated, the metacommunicative utterance in 4:1 marks the transition to the prescriptive second main part of the writing. The passage 4:4–16 retains, however, a mostly descriptive mode of speaking. Lindemann refers aptly to the function of this section within the larger prescriptive part when writing that the author first mentions "'Rahmenbedingungen' für das Verhalten der Christen."[125] Lindemann maintains further that the keyword "unity" initiates several formulaic expressions in 4:4–6 that in rhetorically styled form emphasise the concept of unity.[126]

This rhetoric stylisation is effectively demonstrated by Sellin in his rendering of the several triads that structure the section (see above).[127] In this argumentative sequence several Christian core concepts are intertwined in a very compact and compelling form. It is a rhetorically well-formed *amplificatio* that by its mere form expresses a harmonic totality. After mentioning basic core virtues, such as ταπεινοφροσύνη (humility), πραΰτης (gentleness), μακροθυμία (patience), ἀγάπη (love) (4:2), then combining the key issue ἑνότης (unity) with the quality of εἰρήνη (peace) (4:3), follows the amplificatory sequence of core concepts: σῶμα (meaning the body of Christ), πνεῦμα (spirit), ἐλπίς (hope), κλῆσις (call), κύριος (Lord), πίστις (belief), βάπτισμα (baptism), θεὸς καὶ πατήρ (God and father) each of them determined by the emphatic numeral "one" that ultimately – via the syntagm εἷς θεὸς καὶ πατὴρ πάντων (one God and Father of all) – is associated with the concept of "all", meaning complete reality.

The question is now how the reference to baptism functions in this sequence. I will try to indicate how the concept of baptism functions in an *amplificatio* argument outlining the comprehensiveness of the believers' identity. We have already touched upon the question of setting for this text's use and communication. As indicated above, I favour the notion that the implied readers are competent readers advanced in Christian formation as taught within the school of

---

124 See Hübner, *An Philemon. An die Kolosser. An die Epheser*, 202 ("Einheit der Kirche") and Sellin: "Das Hauptthema des Eph ist das Motiv der ‚Ein(s)heit', das auch terminologisch vor allem die Abschnitte 2,14–18; 4,1–6.13–16 beherrscht." (Sellin, *Der Brief an die Epheser*, 61. See also 62). Further Hartman, *Into the Name of the Lord Jesus*, 104.

125 Lindemann, *Der Epheserbrief*, 70.

126 Ibid., 70.

127 Sellin, *Der Brief an die Epheser*, 313.

Paul. This type of fictional setting does, however, not exclude the fact that the writing was read in other settings with larger groups of believers present.

The term βάπτισμα, which is the most common word for baptism in The New Testament,[128] refers to both the baptismal rite and its interpretation. Such reference to baptism in a text has the potential of recreating the image of the rite's performance and of reactivating experiences from one's own baptism, or from being present as others were baptised. Such sentiments might be extended and differentiated in a linguistic account of the rite, but cannot exist in the same form independent of it. The interpretation of the rite is a unit of teaching that integrates baptism in a comprehensive system of beliefs, proposing in turn a rationale as to how the baptismal rite functions within such a comprehensive scheme. Different dimensions of this scheme could be seen as being represented in the text, and we can suppose that these expressions refer to a corresponding, comprehensive scheme within which author and reader interpret and live their lives.[129] The scheme consists of both cognitive and behavioural dimensions: doctrines, cosmic stories or myths, ethical directives, rituals practised, sentiments evoked, actions recommended, and institutional forms developed.[130] The words in the condensed linguistic form of 4:4–6 refer to different dimensions of such a scheme, the contents of which can only be briefly mentioned here.

Σῶμα (body) refers to the body, which can be the body of Christ or the body of which Christ is the head (4:16). This body at the same time designates the church (1:22–23)[131] where Jews and Gentiles are one body (2:16). So σῶμα, a central term with complex connotations, also denotes the social context, the institution of the church; furthermore, since it is the body of Christ, it refers to the central myths and the central mythological figure in Christian belief. As found in other NT writings, πνεῦμα (spirit) appears not only frequently in Ephesians (and may have different connotations), but it also denotes experiences and sentiments evoked (as e.g. in Gal 3:5). In Eph 3:16 the author says that he prays for the readers that "you may be strengthened in your inner being with power through his Spirit".

Ἐλπίς (hope) refers to eschatological expectations[132] and as such, to cosmic stories or myths expressing a world view, explicated further in other parts of the writing (1:3–23). Nonetheless, it is also related to faith, expressing as it does the attitude of the church members. Κλῆσις (call) refers to God's engagement vis-à-vis the believer, his initiative (1:18, here combined with hope as well), and

---

128 βαπτισμός occuring once in Mark, once in Colossians and twice in Hebrews.

129 See LINDBECK, *The Nature of Doctrine*, 32; 35.

130 GEERTZ, *The Interpretation of Cultures*, 126–129; LINDBECK, *The Nature of Doctrine*, 33. See also SMART, *The World's Religions*, 10–21.

131 HÜBNER, *An Philemon. An die Kolosser. An die Epheser*, 202.

132 SELLIN, *Der Brief an die Epheser*, 323; HÜBNER, *An Philemon. An die Kolosser. An die Epheser*, 202.

the adequate reaction from the believer; there are recommended actions, as stated in the immediate context (4:1). It has already been emphasised that the literary context of this conceptual amplification is one of exhortation, expressing ethical directives and recommended actions. The word/concept is Pauline and denotes thus the identity of the religious traditions.[133]

Κύριος (Lord) refers to the central mythological figure and the stories of his earthly life integrated in mythological stories of his presence in the different spheres of reality referred to in other parts of the writing (1:3–23; 4:8–10). Πίστις (belief) refers directly to the beliefs, doctrines and narratives (the doctrinal and philosophical dimension), of which the final elements for the amplification express a synthesis of the world view in the statements of the εἶς θεὸς καὶ πατὴρ πάντων (one God and Father of all). God embraces everything and secures the unity in the cosmos and, furthermore, the coherence in the comprehensive interpretive scheme, which the implied author knows the audience shares with him in principle. However, through his writing he now wishes to strengthen and activate the scheme, using it as the argumentative framework for the exhortation to unity.

How does the reference to baptism function in this sequence which, according to the above reasoning, represents a comprehensive interpretive scheme used by members of the groups of "Christ-believers"? This scheme could be observed from the perspective of baptism, and the elements make sense in relation to baptism as indicated in the scientific writings whose authors regard baptism as a central topic. The particular perspective of this article is to see baptism as comprising only one part of an *amplificatio* argument. As indicated above, the reasoning seems – in its condensed form – to sketch something near a comprehensive, interpretative scheme applied by the believers for the interpretation of their own identity, here supporting the exhortative argumentation, with unity being its central motif ("the unity of the Spirit in the bond of peace," 4:3). Baptism, then, contributes to the scheme's comprehensiveness, by presenting a dimension of a nature slightly different from the cognitive presuppositions (doctrines) bringing in the dimension of rite and experience. The reference to the rite, functioning as a reminder, is – as no other word – capable of activating experience and sentiments that are important in rhetorical reasoning.[134]

---

133 See K. L. Schmidt, "Καλέω", 492–494.

134 It is presupposed that such sentiments are distinguishable from the kind of emotions that are seen as destructive in several educational traditions in antiquity, also by Paul and his pupils (Rom 7:8; 1 Cor 7:9; Col 3:8; Eph 2:3). See P. v. Gemünden, "Die urchristliche Taufe"; D. B. Martin, "Paul Without Passion". For the function of remembering the rite see Dahl, "Einleitungsfragen zum Epheserbrief", 81: "Der Brief ruft Christen auf, zu gedenken was ihnen in Christus geschenkt worden ist. Ein gedenkendes Erinnern setzt aber vorhergehende Erfahrung voraus, die zwar geklärt und vertieft, aber nicht durch das zum Gedenken rufende Wort allein gestaltet werden kann."

Furthermore, baptism refers to the rite of initiation and has as such a distinctive function in the comprehensive scheme in as much as it marks the entrance into the social domain characterised and identified by the scheme. Continuing the line of the present reasoning, one important aspect would be that Jews and Gentiles have a different past, one which includes different conditions for their relation to God, although they have now experienced the same initiation rite. They have passed the same "door" and belong to same "room" "with free access to the Father".[135] According to Dahl, such a "door" may be important for symbolising the transition from outside to inside, even if the "door" itself is not mentioned or elaborated on.[136] Theissen writes about baptism as the initiation rite into the new social context with its particular "symbolische Welt". Theissen emphasises that – even if the content of the rite itself and the social and religious conditions in the new context were the same – the contrast between old and new were different for Jews and Gentiles. Regarding Jews, one could speak of

> einen systemimmanenten Wechsel und einen Übergang innerhalb derselben symbolischen Welt [...]. Die grundlegenden Normen und Werte bleiben dieselben [...]. Anders ist das bei Heidenchristen: Sie müssen sich von ihren bisherigen Normen und Werten trennen, ja, müssen sie als Götzendienst verurteilen.[137]

Regarding Gentile Christians, baptism signifies a transition "von einer symbolischen Welt in eine ganz andere."[138] To put it slightly differently: According to Jews, the initiation into the Christian context implies a reorganisation of a familiar scheme, while to Gentiles it implies the adoption of a new scheme. According to Gentiles, several elements in the scheme are substituted with new: the doctrines of God, conceptions of his relation to the world, of the salvation figure, and of the exclusiveness in the relation to God. The ethical and experiential dimensions, however, had to be altered to a lesser degree. In the conceptual framework of Ephesians, the unity of Gentiles and Jews is integrated in a world view where Christ guarantees unity through the authority and power given to him by God.

We have in the foregoing discussion used a theory that views different religious dimensions in a comprehensive entirety. A written work like Ephesians is communicated in a setting fit for cognitive communication of different textual types, and yet, the situation is definitely a setting where it is a literary text that is communicated, and not the performance of a rite. Moreover, even if the reasoning

---

135 DAHL, "The Concept of Baptism in Ephesians", 416.
136 *Ibid.*, 416.
137 THEISSEN, "Die urchristliche Taufe", 100. See also the discussion of identity and boundaries related to baptism in MOXNES, "From Theology to Identity", 271–273.
138 THEISSEN, "Die urchristliche Taufe", 100.

is prescriptive in intention, it is not an ethical situation depicting conflict. Communicative potentials of the text are to be found in the ability of the audience to envisage other settings to which the utterances may be referring. While these are the general conditions of text communication, it seemed convenient in this context to indicate that different religious aspects may interact in a semantic dimension as a text is being communicated.

It should further be noted that the audience members listening to the text have no possibility to dwell on the possible meanings of each single word. For example, in Eph 4:4–6 the word "one" completely dominates the textual appearance. In the oral communication, the other words cannot accomplish more than to sketch a picture where the audience can perceive the greater comprehensive scheme – as indicated above –, and may perceive the multiplicity in the dimensions, although the reasoning through its very aesthetic composition imparts harmony, interaction and unity.[139]

Summing up: The reference to baptism in this passage is supposed to function interactively with the other concepts in sketching the comprehensive, interpretive scheme. It does so from a rhetorical perspective that is to contribute to the argumentative amplification, which in turn shapes an aesthetic and conceptual frame for the exhortation in the second main section of the writing. Baptism is an element in a rhetorical *amplificatio* that draws a grand conceived world view as a framework for the ethos and identity of the believers.

3.4.4. Concluding Remarks

The anamnesis of the baptismal rite could be seen as convenient in moral exhortation in its ability to activate sentiments created by the experience of the rite and, further, as a symbol for the transition into a new social and conceptual context.[140] Baptism seems, however, not to be explicated to such a degree that it is obvious it functions directly in the writing's exhortation. The contrast "once – now", "old – new", is prominent both in the descriptive and the prescriptive part of the writing. Baptism is the initiation ritual marking the transition from once to now. My impression is that while the contrast itself is central to the reasoning,

---

139 No other word – notwithstanding its conceptual importance or weight – seem to stand out as the central theme of the passage, including the first word in the row ("body") as suggested by Best. Best emphasises that the formula "has 'body' as its initial element, and this suits [the author's] context, for in vv. 7–16 he proceeds to expound "body". Moreover, Best continues to stress that "body" is "indeed the only word in the whole formula which is important at this point in his argument. Vv. 5, 6 are not strictly relevant to what he is about to say, and it is difficult to see why they should have been introduced unless they already formed part of a statement known to his readers and therefore could not easily have been omitted." (BEST, *Ephesians*, 359).

140 On exhortation motivated with the rite of initiation see SELLIN, "Die Paränese des Epheserbriefes", 185f. See also DAHL, "Einleitungsfragen zum Epheserbrief", 81.

the baptismal rite is not applied explicitly in this function. It seems doubtful that the audience would think of the baptismal rite other than in short glimpses during the mentioning of the word.

The character of the implied readers is still an open question. It seems to me that they are expected to be able to "digest solid food", and in this case, we can envisage a minor group seeing themselves as disciples of Paul, competent readers that are able to develop in a literate form the different dimensions of Christian identity, and are capable of teaching in the churches. Such readers would be familiar with Pauline teaching related to baptism, and would in another setting be able to elaborate on the meaning of the expression "one baptism".

4. Baptismal Language in the Pastoral Epistles

In a passage in Second Timothy where "Timothy" is encouraged to remember "Jesus Christ, raised from the dead", he is reminded of a reliable doctrine: "If we have died with, we will also live with". In a passage where "Titus" is told to remind the believers of the virtues of a good life, as contrasted to the vices of a former life, the audience is also encouraged to remember the philanthropy of God, who saved through the bath of rebirth. The last utterance seems to contain a clear reference to baptism, while the one in 2 Timothy is not so clear. 1 Timothy does not appear to contain any direct references to baptism.

4.1. Setting, Genre and Key Issue

The Pastoral letters are in this essay seen as being Deuteropauline. They may be perceived as a small collection within what later became the larger collection of Pauline letters. Additionally, the authors of the Pastoral Epistles place themselves in a Pauline school tradition,[141] a tradition, however, that was not uniform in itself. Colossians and Ephesians seem to represent one direction and the Pastoral Epistles another.[142] According to J. Roloff, a conservative wing in the school of Paul is making its statements through the Pastoral Epistles that might even be considered as an intentional reaction against a theological development articulated in Colossians and Ephesians.[143] The author(s) might have been (a) Gentile Christian(s) of the second[144] or third generation[145] and, according to Schnelle, the author of the Pastoral Epistles was an unknown member of the Pauline

---

141 ROLOFF, "Pastoralbriefe", 55.

142 H.-U. WEIDEMANN, "Titus, der getaufte Heide", 44f.

143 ROLOFF, "Pastoralbriefe", 56. See also SELLIN, "Vom Kolosser- zum Epheserbrief", 151.

144 FIORE, The Pastoral Epistles, 19.

145 ROLOFF, "Pastoralbriefe", 56. L. T. Johnson argues for a Pauline authorship (JOHNSON, The First and Second Letters to Timothy, 55–99), as do G. W. KNIGHT, The Pastoral Epistles, 4–52.

school, and the epistles were probably written about 100 AD in Ephesus, which was "Sitz der Paulusschule".[146] It should be noted that 1 Timothy and Titus are quite similar to one another, while 2 Timothy differs from the two both formally and as regards content.[147]

The Pastoral letters are exhortatory in outline and strategy. Belonging to the second or third generation, they may be closely associated with the administration of communities that had been under Pauline influence. Regarding genre, 1 Timothy and Titus may be classified as "church orders" and 2 Timothy as Paul's "last will and testament".[148] With respect to my own point of view, I would rather emphasise the paraenetic dimensions of the writings that can be viewed in a school setting[149] with parallels in philosophical schools, a setting more inde-

---

146 SCHNELLE, *Einleitung in das Neue Testament*, 379f. Roloff assumes that the author was situated in Ephesus as well (ROLOFF, "Pastoralbriefe", 56), and Lindemann also suggests a date about 100 AD (LINDEMANN, *Paulus im ältesten Christentum*, 45).

147 WOLTER, *Die Pastoralbriefe als Paulustradition*, 155; ROLOFF, "Pastoralbriefe", 58; SCHNELLE, *Einleitung in das Neue Testament*, 383; FIORE, *The Pastoral Epistles*, 8.

148 For the question of function and genre see the discussion in e.g. M. DIBELIUS/H. CONZELMANN, *The Pastoral Epistles*, 5–8; WOLTER, *Die Pastoralbriefe als Paulustradition*; JOHNSON, *The First and Second Letters to Timothy*, 96f.; SCHNELLE, *Einleitung in das Neue Testament*, 383; FIORE, *The Pastoral Epistles*, 5–14. Regarding 1 Timothy and Titus Dibelius/Conzelmann writes of an "amalgamation of church order and rules for the household" while "in 2 Tim the personal elements become prominent to a remarkable extent". The content and "manner of exhortation […] indicate that this piece of writing belongs to the genre of paraensis" (DIBELIUS/CONZELMANN, *The Pastoral Epistles*, 6f.). I read L. Oberlinner as placing the writings within a discussion of administration of the communities in a situation with controversies over the preaching of the gospel. Oberlinner characterises the Pastorals as "kirchenamtliche Lehr- und Mahnschreiben" (OBERLINNER, *Kommentar zum ersten Timotheusbrief*, XXVI). Having presented several literary parallels Wolter concludes: "1 Tim und Tit lassen sich geschlossen verstehen als briefliche Instruktionen an weisungsbefugte Amts- und Mandatsträger durch ihren Mandaten" (WOLTER, *Die Pastoralbriefe als Paulustradition*, 196). 2 Timothy differs from the two others in the collection and stands out with its strong emphasis on the unity between author and reader that has parallels in letters of friendship (213). Wolter characterises 2 Timothy as "testamentarische Mahnrede" (236). Similarly OBERLINNER, *Kommentar zum zweiten Timotheusbrief*, 1f. For 2 Timothy A. Weiser discusses letters of friendship and testament literature. He concludes "dass 2Tim ein *testamentarisches Mahnschreiben in Form eines Freundschaftsbriefes* ist" (WEISER, *Der zweite Brief an Timotheus*, 40). L. T. Johnson assuming the letters to be written by Paul, judges 2 Timothy to be "our most perfect example from antiquity of the *personal paraenetic* letter". 1 Timothy and Titus, in turn, fit the form of royal correspondence called the *mandata principis* (literally, "commandment of a ruler") letter" (JOHNSON, *The First and Second Letters to Timothy*, 97). I. H. Marshall similarly evaluates 2 Tim as a "personal paraenetic letter" and "both Tit and 1 Tim […] fits into the genre of mandates" (MARSHALL/TOWNER, *The Pastoral Epistles*, 12). Marshall remarks on the recipients that "the letters are intended for church leaders as the primary audience, although they are to hear them, as it were, in the presences of the congregation who are intended to apply some of what is said to themselves" (76).

149 Also Fiore (FIORE, *The Pastoral Epistles*) holds "the nature and aim of the Pastoral Epistles" to be "somewhat clarified by reference to testamentary letters and also to official memoranda or 'appointment charters'" (12) but supposes "literary, exhortatory epistles in classical antiquity" to "provide more comprehensive parallels to the Pastoral Epistles" (12). They are related to

pendent and with looser ties to the communities. The author and addressees have seen themselves belonging to a Pauline school, which, for the purpose of the writings, is more important than the positions of author and addressees in the communities. However, this does not rule out the possibility that the letters were read in other contexts. The letters appear in a collection[150] as do the Cynic Epistles.[151]

4.2. Baptismal Language in Second Timothy

2 Timothy 2:11 could be assumed to refer to baptism:

⁽¹¹⁾ πιστὸς ὁ λόγος·
εἰ γὰρ συναπεθάνομεν, καὶ συζήσομεν
⁽¹²⁾ εἰ ὑπομένομεν, καὶ συμβασιλεύσομεν·
εἰ ἀρνησόμεθα, κἀκεῖνος ἀρνήσεται ἡμᾶς·
⁽¹³⁾ εἰ ἀπιστοῦμεν, ἐκεῖνος πιστὸς μένει,
ἀρνήσασθαι γὰρ ἑαυτὸν οὐ δύναται. (2 Tim 2:11–13)

⁽¹¹⁾ The saying is sure:
If we have died with (him), we will also live with (him);[152]
⁽¹²⁾ if we endure, we will also reign with him;
if we deny (him), he will also deny us;
⁽¹³⁾ if we are faithless, he remains faithful –
for he cannot deny himself

4.2.1. Line of Reasoning

The writing contains no clear statement of the key issue or intention of the writing (*propositio*). But the letter is exhortatory,[153] and there are statements commenting on the function of the writing scattered throughout the letter, more of

---

philosophical schools and the teaching letter "became a surrogate for the dialogue between the heads of the schools and their far-flung pupils" (12). The Cynic Epistles of Socrates and the Socratics are such letters (12). Malherbe finds friendship language also in Titus and sees Titus as a paraenetic letter rather than a church order (MALHERBE, "Paraenesis in the Epistle to Titus", 298f.; 317). See also M. L. J. STIREWALT, *Studies in Ancient Greek Epistolography*.

150 LINDEMANN, *Paulus im ältesten Christentum*, 44; WOLTER, *Die Pastoralbriefe als Paulustradition*, 131. The letters also appear together in the manuscripts. See WOLTER, *Die Pastoralbriefe als Paulustradition*, 20ff.; ROLOFF, *Der erste Brief an Timotheus*, 46ff.

151 For similar letter collections in philosophical contexts, see S. K. STOWERS, *Letter Writing*, 40; K. BERGER, *Formgeschichte*, 366f.

152 As argued in the following I would have preferred the omition of "him": "If we have died with, we will also live with". See the translation in the Lutherbibel (revidierte Fassung von 1984): "Sterben wir mit, so werden wir mit leben".

153 See above § 4.1.

them communicated more indirectly through the exhortative sayings (1:6; 1:13; 2:7–8; 3:1). 2:7 advices the reader to "think over" in order to gain understanding.

The letter opens in close resemblance with 1 Timothy and Titus, addressing Timothy as the "beloved child" (1:2), and continues reminding of the close relationship between author and addressee,[154] containing as its does a reminder about God's gift given by the laying on of hands by "Paul" (1:6). Then the author narrates his suffering for the gospel (1:8), which leads to a condensed account of the Pauline gospel, applying Pauline clauses expressing concepts known to us through the authentic Pauline letters (1:9–10), the reason for which "Paul" suffers (1:12). This gospel is then referred to as "sound teaching" (1:13) and a "good treasure entrusted to you" (1:14). The scheme "once – now"[155] occurs in this gospel account. These first passages also contain the motif of "Paul" the teacher (1:13) and the motif of tensions; former associates have turned away (1:15), which indicates that the responsibility now rests on "Timothy", that is, on those who read the letter and perhaps see themselves as Paul's pupils. The following passages have references to tradition (2:2) and to reflection that imparts knowledge (νόει ὃ λέγω· δώσει γάρ σοι ὁ κύριος σύνεσιν ἐν πᾶσιν, 2:7). 2:8 reminds again of the Pauline gospel introducing the passage with the clause in 2:11 that is the focus of the discussion here. The passages following in 2:14ff. are predominantly prescriptive, encouraging the addressee to remind his fellow believers of the gospel and to warn against "wrangling over words" (2:14) and the aberration from the truth, for example the opinions of Hymenaeus and Philetus, who claim "that the resurrection has already taken place" (2:18). Further passages contain lists of vices and virtues as well as a mirror of virtues for the teacher (2:24–25). The encouragements are motivated in claims regarding the reliability of the sound teaching (3:10–17). At the end "Paul" talks of his own imminent death (4:6–8) and urges the addressee to come to him as fast as possible, giving some concrete instructions concerning his journey. The passage 2:8–13 can be seen as a unit framed by the encouragement to the addressee in 2:8 to "remember" (μνημόνευε), and the exhortation in 2:13 to remind others of what is just mentioned (ταῦτα ὑπομίμνῃσκε).[156]

4.2.2. On the Function and Meaning of 2 Timothy 2:11

The passage 2:8–13 starts with an exhortation to remember Jesus Christ (2:8). What is to be remembered is the Christian myth of Christ and its relevance for

---

154 WOLTER, *Die Pastoralbriefe als Paulustradition*, 213.

155 See above § 3.3.2.

156 Also Oberlinner takes 8–13 as a unit referring, however, to content and also to form as far as 1–7 is paraenetic and 8–13 is based in the confession (v 8) and is Christologically coined (OBERLINNER, *Kommentar zum zweiten Timotheusbrief*, 75). Marshall is less inclined to divide formally between the two sections (MARSHALL/TOWNER, *The Pastoral Epistles*, 36 and 732).

the believers that has already been stated in the gospel account in 1:9–10. These reminders of the gospel refer to core concepts that are developed in other settings and contexts. This is a recurring feature in philosophical letters.[157] The pupils of Paul (implied readers) are supposed to be familiar with the Pauline gospel in its extended form, and do not need the elaboration of the teaching in a letter, as they need only the reminders through characteristic phrases. 2:8 displays reminiscences of Romans, where Paul already in the extended greeting (1:1–7) presents a condensation of his gospel.[158] The expressions εὐαγγέλιον and ἐκ σπέρματος Δαυὶδ and the reference to the resurrection of Christ also occur there. The encouragement to remember Christ in 2 Tim 2:8 seems to contain a strong encouragement to bring the teaching ("gospel") of Paul to mind. If the readers knew Romans, a reference to the opening of Romans could include a reference to the teaching as it is elaborated in Romans.[159]

2:9–10 once again relates the gospel to "Paul's" suffering (as in 1:9–12). While the function is partly to impart the ethos of the speaker and his intentions, the motif of suffering is recurring in the writing and seems more like a central theme. Here the expression "chained like a criminal" might refer to the sufferings of Jesus before his death[160] and further to Paul's self-presentation (as in 2 Cor 11:23).[161] The intention and motivation is the salvation in Christ. Accounts of the sufferings of the apostle are a known feature in Paul's letters (2 Cor 4:7–18; 6:3–10; 11:16–12:10).

This attitude is then based in some fundamental claims (2:11–13), introduced through a metacommunicative utterance as reliable teaching (πιστὸς

---

157 See BERGER, "Hellenistische Gattungen", 1134; STIREWALT, "The Form and Function of the Greek Letter-Essay", 148; FIORE, The Pastoral Epistles, 13.

158 Dibelius/Conzelmann evaluate 2:8 as "a kerygmatic formulation. The source is probably a two-part formula of the same type as Rom 1:3f." (DIBELIUS/CONZELMANN, The Pastoral Epistles, 108). Others emphasise the direct literary dependence on Paul. See JOHNSON, The First and Second Letters to Timothy, 374 (who assumes 2 Timothy to be written by Paul), and further Oberlinner who remarks: "literarische Abhängigkeit von Röm 1,3f [ist] als höchst wahrscheinlich anzunehmen" (OBERLINNER, Kommentar zum zweiten Timotheusbrief, 76), and especially Weiser who lists the direct literary references in 2 Timothy to other Pauline letters. References to Romans dominate the list by far (WEISER, Der zweite Brief an Timotheus, 66).

159 For remarks on the teaching of Paul in Romans with reference to his students, see STOWERS, The Diatribe, e.g. 183–184.

160 JOHNSON, The First and Second Letters to Timothy, 374; FIORE, The Pastoral Epistles, 149.

161 For a discussion of the interpretation of Paul's sufferings in 2 Timothy see OBERLINNER, Kommentar zum zweiten Timotheusbrief, 79–82.

ὁ λόγος),[162] and formulated here in a clear, rhythmic form,[163] one that makes them stand out in the flow of speech, completing the argument with the help of an *amplificatio*, and functioning as a pointed reminder of Paul's teaching. The first phrase is distinctively recognisable as denoting Pauline concepts, those following (2:12–13) are not as clear and might have been formulated in analogy with the first.[164] 2:11 is reminiscent of Romans 6:3ff. in particular 6:8 (εἰ δὲ ἀπεθάνομεν σὺν Χριστῷ, πιστεύομεν ὅτι καὶ συζήσομεν αὐτῷ) that have the same form: conditional clause and verbs in the indicative form. Regarding the discussion mentioned above concerning the elaboration of Romans 6 in Colossians 2 and Ephesians 2, it is notable that the concept "live with" here as in Rom 6 is formulated in the future tense. The future tense is logical here as far as the context contains warnings against aberrations from the truth: the opinions of Hymenaeus and Philetus, who claim, "that the resurrection has already taken place" (2:18).[165]

In view of Romans 6, which might represent the prominent elaboration of the teaching that is referred to here, the "συν-" in the short expression συναπεθάνομεν, καὶ συζήσομεν would denote "together with Christ", a unifica-

---

[162] For the formula πιστὸς ὁ λόγος see DIBELIUS/CONZELMANN, *The Pastoral Epistles*, 28f. Dibelius/Conzelmann considers the formula to be a quotation formula and a formula of affirmation. "As a rule, this formula is either preceeded or followed by a clause whose content goes beyond the particular context" (28); similarly U. WAGENER, *Die Ordnung des ‚Hauses Gottes'*, 70f. Wagener remarks that the formula is specific for the Pastorals (70). Further WEISER, *Der zweite Brief an Timotheus*, 170f.; MARSHALL/TOWNER, *The Pastoral Epistles*, 326–330.

[163] Dibelius/Conzelmann, regarding πιστὸς ὁ λόγος as a quotation formula, evaluate 11–13 as being a "quotation of unknown origin, in the style of a hymn" (DIBELIUS/CONZELMANN, *The Pastoral Epistles*, 28 and 109). Oberlinner supposes "in diesen Versen wird wieder ein in sich geschlossenes Traditionsstück zitiert" and he evaluates the section as "hymnusartig" and the short sentences as "bekenntnishaft" (OBERLINNER, *Kommentar zum zweiten Timotheusbrief*, 82). Also Weiser assumes a section "dessen größter Teil sowohl inhaltlich als auch in seiner sprachlichen Formung aus *Traditionsgut* stammt" evaluates, however, its character as being "lehrhaft" and the section as "ein katechetisches Traditionsstück paränetischen Inhalts" (WEISER, *Der zweite Brief an Timotheus*, 153f.). Marshall assumes the influence of traditional language, including Pauline language, "but the material is adapted to the needs of the author" (MARSHALL/TOWNER, *The Pastoral Epistles*, 732f.). As indicated in the reasoning above I am inclined to see the form as dependent of the author's work with rhetorical style.

[164] According to Johnson, "we find a series of statements that resemble a number of balanced or antithetical statements found elsewhere in Paul" (JOHNSON, *The First and Second Letters to Timothy*, 378), but see the discussion by Oberlinner, where the parallelism with Rom 6:8 is emphasised regarding the first phrase (OBERLINNER, *Kommentar zum zweiten Timotheusbrief*, 83–88).

[165] Oberlinner sees the future tense as consequent in light of v 10 where it says that the elect may "obtain the salvation that is in Christ Jesus, with eternal glory" (OBERLINNER, *Kommentar zum zweiten Timotheusbrief*, 85). According to Sellin the author argues against a spiritualising of the Pauline concept (ὡσεὶ ἐκ νεκρῶν ζῶντας/"brought from death to life", Rom 6:13) deflating it of its apocalyptic content in a time when the apocalyptic dimension of comfort expecting reward for present suffering gained importance (SELLIN, "‚Die Auferstehung ist schon geschehen'", 49).

tion initiated in the rite of baptism. The very short expression could be due to the function as rhythmic, pointed reminders of core concepts. One could, however, consider a possible presence of the – to the letter important – friendship topic expressing the community of author and addressee in the sufferings.[166] This is immediately expressed before these sentences: "You then, my child ... share in the suffering (συγκακοπάθησον)" (2:1 and 3) (see also συγκακοπάθησον τῷ εὐαγγελίῳ in 1:8). The short formulations, leaving out the dative form (Χριστῷ / αὐτῷ), could indicate a double meaning, including and emphasising the common and shared sufferings of implied author and readers.[167] Also the next three phrases in 2:11-13 are, in my view, intended as reminders of teaching. References to Pauline teaching seem not so clear as in the first phrase[168] but the wording in 2:12 may recall phrases in Romans 8:17 that also have the same conditional form, and 2:13 may recall formulations as the ones in Romans 3:3f.[169] and 1 Cor 10:13.

The intention of these remarks is to suggest an interpretation of the phrases focussing on the function of reminding pupils in a short and condensed form of teaching known in a more elaborate form in other texts or from other contexts,[170]

---

166 WOLTER, *Die Pastoralbriefe als Paulustradition*, 213.

167 The scholarly discussion has, as indicated above, focussed on the presence of preformed tradition(s), the character of the supposed tradition(s), the relation of the expression (2:11b) to Romans 6, and if the meaning of "to die with" in the course of tradition has shifted from baptism to denoting martyrdom. Hartman states that "nothing in the text indicates that this refers to a baptismal death with Christ [...]. What in Romans 6 was the existential realisation or re-enactment in baptism of Christ's suffering has become a community of fate between martyrs" (HARTMAN, *Into the Name of the Lord Jesus*, 112f.). Johnson suggests a reference to the "deep pattern of Christian existence, imprinted on believers through their initiation into Christ in baptism" (JOHNSON, *The First and Second Letters to Timothy*, 376), and according to Fiore, "the context indicates here and in Romans that the exhortation is not to martyrdom, but to death to sin by all Christians in their being crucified with Christ in the baptismal ritual (FIORE, *The Pastoral Epistles*, 150). Oberlinner discusses the possible references to the martyrdom of Paul but maintains that the reference is to baptism here as in Rom 6 (OBERLINNER, *Kommentar zum zweiten Timotheusbrief*, 83–85). Weiser writes of a relocation of meaning from baptism in Rom 6 to martyrdom in the tradition and eventually in 2 Timothy to, by referring to Paul, denoting the "Ausübung des Lehr- und Leistungsdienstes der *Gemeindevorsteher*" that is associated with struggle and suffering and that even might require death. „Dabei ist der Gedanke an die Taufe und an das Martyrium auch im jetzigen Textzusammenhang mitgemeint" (WEISER, *Der zweite Brief an Timotheus*, 172), and Marshall reasons that "the reference could be to spiritual identification with Christ in baptism and the Christian life, i.e. to dying to sin or to self and safety", and further that it is likely, "that the reference is to a past death to self which may involve readiness even for martyrdom." (MARSHALL/TOWNER, *The Pastoral Epistles*, 739).

168 For the references in the phrases see OBERLINNER, *Kommentar zum zweiten Timotheusbrief*, 86–88.

169 See *Ibid.*, 87.

170 A reasoning as the one undertaken by Oberlinner, where the section is evaluated as hymnic and the sentences as confessions, places the section more in a context of worship. Oberlinner further assumes the section to be a "Traditionsstück" that might be an interpretation and a

contexts that presumably would include oral teaching.[171] The question in the scope of this essay is if the expression εἰ γὰρ συναπεθάνομεν, καὶ συζήσομεν is intended to remind of baptism, and if so, the cognitive interpretation of baptism. The direct dependence on Romans 6:8 and the reference to baptism are by no means obvious according to scholarly interpretations.[172] Before making some concluding remarks on this question, I will refer to another text elaborating on the same motifs as 2 Timothy.

In 2 Corinthians 4 Paul talks about the gospel, a knowledge of the glory of God (4:6) that is a treasure. Because of the gospel the apostle and his associates are suffering, and this suffering is interpreted as "carrying in the body the death of Jesus, so that the life of Jesus may also be made visible in our bodies" (πάντοτε τὴν νέκρωσιν τοῦ Ἰησοῦ ἐν τῷ σώματι περιφέροντες, ἵνα καὶ ἡ ζωὴ τοῦ Ἰησοῦ ἐν τῷ σώματι ἡμῶν φανερωθῇ, 4:10). These images are further developed and continued in an elaboration of the hope for the future God will provide: "this slight momentary affliction is preparing us for an eternal weight of glory beyond all measure" (τὸ γὰρ παραυτίκα ἐλαφρὸν τῆς θλίψεως ἡμῶν καθ' ὑπερβολὴν εἰς ὑπερβολὴν αἰώνιον βάρος δόξης κατεργάζεται ἡμῖν, 4:17). Here the sufferings are interpreted as unification with the death of Christ, which also implies a life that is, in fact, the life of Jesus. The short claim in 2 Tim 2:11 might thus be read as a reminder of an elaborate sequence of teaching known to us through 2 Corinthians. 2 Corinthians may be a collection of more letters, but in the form known to us, Timothy is mentioned as sender together with Paul (1:1), and the passage referred to above is styled in 1. p. Plur.[173] 2 Timothy could be read as Paul and Timothy – the fictitious author and addressee of 2 Timothy – suffering together because of the gospel.

Among texts of Paul known to us, there are therefore at least two passages that could function as the elaborate teaching to which 2 Tim 2:11 refers. If we were to decide among the two, our text shares with 2 Corinthians the prominent motif of suffering interpreted as unification with the significant death of Christ. Regarding Romans: The motif of having "been buried with" which, according to Sellin is the essential motif in this baptism symbolism,[174] is absent in 2 Timothy. On the other hand, our text does not only share the phraseology

---

transformation of Rom 6:8 (*ibid.*, 82–85). Also Weiser sees the section as traditional but evaluates its character as "lehrhaft" and paraenetical (WEISER, *Der zweite Brief an Timotheus*, 153f.)

171 For the question of literary dependance on other Pauline letters and on Pauline traditions not present in the letters see WEISER, *Der zweite Brief an Timotheus*, 64–66.

172 See above footnote 167. E.g. by Dibelius/Conzelmann baptism is not mentioned in the comments on the phrase (DIBELIUS/CONZELMANN, *The Pastoral Epistles*, 109).

173 In another extended account of the sufferings of Paul, 2 Cor 11:16–12:10, the sufferings are said to be for the sake of Christ (12:10).

174 SELLIN, *Der Brief an die Epheser*, 176f. Sellin however maintains that 2 Tim 2:11 is an echo of Rom 6:8 (SELLIN, ",Die Auferstehung ist schon geschehen", 49)

with Romans 6, but also the form of the expression: conditional clauses expressing objective circumstances through verbal forms in the indicative:

εἰ δὲ ἀπεθάνομεν σὺν Χριστῷ, πιστεύομεν ὅτι καὶ συζήσομεν αὐτῷ (Rom 6:8)
εἰ γὰρ συναπεθάνομεν, καὶ συζήσομεν (2 Tim 2:11)

4.2.3. Concluding Remarks

The motif of the death and resurrection of Christ made relevant for the believer is, of course, central in the gospel of Paul and not always combined with baptism. The presupposition that the letter contains brief references to teaching does not imply that this teaching is known to us. Its prominent medium may have been oral teaching. Nonetheless, it includes the assumption that the elaborate teaching is also reflected in other writings so that we may get an idea of its form and contents. It seems probable that competent readers, including those regarding themselves as pupils of Paul, would recognise the phrase γὰρ συναπεθάνομεν, καὶ συζήσομεν as a phrase used by Paul in his interpretation of baptism.

In the context of 2 Timothy, however, baptism (both the rite and its interpretation) does not seem to be important. The laying on of hands (1:6) is probably not related to baptism.[175] The "once – now" scheme in 1:9–10 is applied to God's history with mankind and not to the lives of the individual believers where baptism signified the transition from "once" to "now". With respect to comprehensive, interpretive schemes drawn upon above, the perspectives in 2 Timothy seem limited, the focus being on attitudes and behavioural dimensions. A cognitive dimension is presupposed as already formulated and settled; the doctrines and teaching – the gospel – are referred to as known. Although certain readers of 2 Tim 2:11 may be reminded that Paul talked similarly about baptism, neither the sentiments evoked by the rite of baptism, nor the doctrines interpreting baptism, or baptism as initiation motivating a life of morally high standards are employed by the author regarding the formation of the identity and character of the second letter to Timothy's intended reader.

4.3. Baptismal Language in the Epistle to Titus

In the imaginary setting of the Epistle to Titus, "Paul" first presents himself as author, "an apostle of Jesus Christ, for the sake of the faith of God's elect and the knowledge of the truth that is in accordance with godliness", and then he both greets Titus and gives him his instructions (1:1–4). This fictive setting gives the audience insight into a fictitious internal communication between "Paul" and one of his close standing disciples one concerning themselves and regarding how

---

[175] See 1 Tim 4:14 and the comments in Fiore, *The Pastoral Epistles*, 136f.; Johnson, *The First and Second Letters to Timothy*, 353f.

they are to be organised (Chap 1) and what teaching they are to live by (Chap 2–3). This teaching ("the truth that gives faith …, 1:1–2) predominantly contains exhortations, although including a couple of shorter, descriptive passages (1:2–3; 2:11–14; 3:3–8a). In one of these passages, the reference to the "bath of rebirth and the renewal" appears, which we interpret as denoting baptism. The fact that the "bath" (λουτρόν) here denotes baptism is indicated by the close combination with the Spirit.[176] Further, in Acts 22:16 the effect of baptism is the washing away of sins (ἀπόλουσαι τὰς ἁμαρτίας), and in Eph 5:26 "the washing of water by the word" (λουτρόν τοῦ ὕδατος ἐν ῥήματι) may refer to baptism.[177] The reference to baptism occurs in a context of exhortation, a sort of double or indirect moral guidance. The communication is from the (implied) author calling on the (implied) reader to exhort other members of the community.

In the outline of the entire written work, the passage 3:3–8[178] appears towards the conclusion, and is preceded by exhortative passages warning against different unwanted attitudes and encouraging readers to live by the sound teaching (2:1), demonstrate self-control (2:6) and so forth. In a short descriptive passage about the grace and salvation of God (2:11–14), it says that the grace revealed to salvation for all people "educates us to renounce impiety and worldly passions and […] to live lives that are self-controlled, upright and godly" (2:11–12). Furthermore, in a statement reiterating common Christian beliefs of Christ ("who gave himself for us"), we learn that the purpose of all this was that we should be his own people eagerly doing good deeds (2:14). A short metacommunicative phrase (πιστὸς ὁ λόγος, 3:8a)[179] stating that the imparted truth claims are reliable teaching, marks the transition from the descriptive language of 3:4–7 to a subsequently brief passage expressing that the point of learning this is that those who believe in God shall concentrate on showing good deeds (3:8). This emphasis on the educative function of God's grace is indeed characteristic for the epistle to Titus.[180] Thereafter follows another sequence of warnings against stupid controversies and against heretics (3:8–10). The descriptive statements regarding Christ and God and containing the reference to baptism seem embedded in the writing's overall exhortative intention.

---

176 BARTH, *Die Taufe in frühchristlicher Zeit*, 70.

177 DIBELIUS/CONZELMANN, *The Pastoral Epistles*, 148; FIORE, *The Pastoral Epistles*, 219. Regarding Ephesians, DAHL, "The Concept of Baptism in Ephesians", 420–424.

178 The metacommunicative phrase πιστὸς ὁ λόγος (3:8a) functions as a transition from the descriptive language of 3:3ff to the exhortations in 3:8ff.

179 For the formula πιστὸς ὁ λόγος see DIBELIUS/CONZELMANN, *The Pastoral Epistles*, 28f. Dibelius/Conzelmann considers the formula to be a quotation formula and a formula of affirmation. Further WAGENER, *Die Ordnung des "Hauses Gottes"*, 70f.; WEISER, *Der zweite Brief an Timotheus*, 170f.; MARSHALL/TOWNER, *The Pastoral Epistles*, 326–330. Here the function as formula of affirmation should be preferred (DIBELIUS/CONZELMANN, *The Pastoral Epistles*, 150).

180 See MALHERBE, "Paraenesis in the Epistle to Titus", 314.

4.3.1. On the Function and Meaning of Titus 3:5

The utterance in 3:1 – ὑπομίμνῃσκε αὐτούς – serving as a "double" metacommunicative utterance (one directed at both Titus as the reader in the fictive setting and the intended readers) defines the function of 3:1ff. as being one of reminding.[181] Likewise, the descriptive language imparting the truth claims about God reminds readers of truths with which they are supposed to be familiar.[182] At first in Chap 3, they are reminded of general positive attitudes: to obey the authorities, be ready for every good work etc. They are then reminded of their past (or rather by the contrast between the past and their present status), the contrast being strengthened through the amplificatory and hyperbolic listing of vices (foolishness, disobedience, slavery to various passions and pleasures, the passing of days in malice and envy, despise, the hating of one another) that can hardly be read as an accurate description of the ethos and values of the believers' former lives. This somber background prepares the way for reminding the believers of the conditions surrounding their new status that has been established by God. The author uses a scheme that we have encountered in other contexts, including baptismal contexts (see above), the scheme "once – now" (ἦμεν γάρ ποτε … ὅτε δέ) (3:3f.). Here the past is articulated in a vice list, and in the writing as a whole, the present is characterised by the sound attitude and good deeds of the believers. However, it is in Chapter 3 that the reminder of the past (through presenting the list of vices) leads to a development of a cognitive (doctrinal) frame of reference – how good and philanthropic God our Saviour is (3:4) –,[183] which is interwoven with an exemplary testimony of the saved human being (3:5), testifying that the salvation occurred "through the regenerative bath and renewal by the Holy Spirit". This text sequence then marks the transition from the former status by stating the doctrinal framework of such a transition,[184] and by referring

---

181 For the function of remembrance in paraensis, and in Titus see *Ibid.*, 309ff. Further STARR, "Was Paraenesis for Beginners?", 79.

182 See above to 2 Timothy.

183 See the discussion of "The Soteriological Terminology of Titus 2:11–14 and 3:4–7" in DIBELIUS/CONZELMANN, *The Pastoral Epistles*, 143–146. According to Dibelius/Conzelmann the terms "prove to be […] technical terms from Hellenistic cults, especially from the cult of the ruler" (144). The terms seem to be introduced by the author as if he "is passing on what he has received" (145) and the expressions may "derive from the usage of the Judaism of the Diaspora" (145). If the author himself has developed this cognitive frame of reference, that does of course not rule out the usage of traditional material.

184 See WOLTER, *Die Pastoralbriefe als Paulustradition*, 66f., who classifies the passage 3:3–7 as "soteriologische Aussagen" coloured by the "once – now" scheme. "Sie machen diese Weisungen zu postconversionalen Mahnreden, die die Intention haben, das geforderte Verhalten als zwangsläufige Konsequenz des durch das Heilsgeschehen bewirkten Umbruchs darzustellen." Dibelius/Conzelmann observe, when compared to Rom 6:17f.; 1 Cor 6:9–11; Col 3:7, 8; Eph 2:2ff., 2*Clem.* 1.6–8, a significant train of thought in the passage: "Such a presentation of a person's past before becoming a Christian, followed by a description of his condition as a Christian, was one of

to baptism as the rite of transition (initiation);[185] or, stated somewhat differently: the text sequence expresses the adoption of a new identity with reference to rite (the experience of the ritual) and to the existential and cognitive meaning of the ritual. This new status and identity form the basis for the abundant number of exhortations found in the writing.

In the passages in Colossians and Ephesians discussed above, the motifs related to baptism are distinctively Pauline, while motifs used in other early Christian writings (e.g. the baptismal language in Acts) of being baptised so that sins are forgiven (Acts 2:38), or of being baptised into the name of the Lord Jesus (Acts 8:16), do not seem reflected. The epistle to Titus places itself in a Pauline tradition, and yet the imagery used of baptism is not the distinctive Pauline images of being buried with Christ,[186] and the exhortations are not explicitly based on an identification with the burial and resurrection of Christ (as is the case in Romans 6 and Colossians 2).[187]

---

the most common topics of early Christian preaching" (DIBELIUS/CONZELMANN, *The Pastoral Epistles*, 147). See also MARSHALL/TOWNER, *The Pastoral Epistles*, 306. Oberlinner comments: "vielmehr wird davon gesprochen, wie bzw. warum [Gott] gehandelt hat. Gottes ‚Güte' und seine ‚Menschenfreundlichkeit' sind der Grund dafür, daß sich die Bedingungen ‚für uns' entscheidend geändert haben" (OBERLINNER, *Kommentar zum Titusbrief*, 168). The question of "traditional material" in the passage will not be discussed here. See DIBELIUS/CONZELMANN, *The Pastoral Epistles*, 147f.; MARSHALL/TOWNER, *The Pastoral Epistles*, 306. See further the outline suggested by Marshall maintaining, "the statement is entirely concerned with soteriology". God's mercy (τὸ αὐτοῦ ἔλεος) constitutes the "basis" for the "Main action", the salvation (ἔσωσεν ἡμᾶς), that is effected through "Means" (διὰ λουτροῦ παλιγγενεσίας ...) (MARSHALL/TOWNER, *The Pastoral Epistles*, 307).

185 Dibelius/Conzelmann comment, "again the salvation is made a present reality, in this case by the reference to the sacrament" (DIBELIUS/CONZELMANN, *The Pastoral Epistles*, 148). Similarly OBERLINNER, *Kommentar zum Titusbrief*, 172f. Hartman writes, "thus baptism became a station on the boarder between the old and the new" (HARTMAN, *Into the Name of the Lord Jesus*, 109).

186 See HARTMAN, *Into the Name of the Lord Jesus*, 111. Oberlinner assumes "die Past und ihre Gemeinden stehen in einem traditionellen Verständnis der christlichen Taufe" (OBERLINNER, *Kommentar zum Titusbrief*, 174). Dibelius/Conzelmann maintain, however, "the understanding of baptism as rebirth expressed in Tit 3:5ff is similar to that of Rom 6:4". The link between them is found in an understanding of rebirth "analogous to certain concepts of the mysteries. It is an understanding related to the image of baptism as death or burial" (DIBELIUS/CONZELMANN, *The Pastoral Epistles*, 148). F. Büchsel argues, though, that a derivation from the mysteries would presuppose "daß παλιγγενεσία in den Mysterien früher nachweisbar wäre, als es ist" (BÜCHSEL, "Γίνομαι etc.", 688). Büchsel assumes rather that παλιγγενεσία in Tit 3:5 can be explained as "christliche Weiterbildung der jüdischen Ausgestaltung des stoischen Begriffs [der stoischen (kosmischen) Wiedergeburtsvorstellung]" (688). See also the discussion in MARSHALL/TOWNER, *The Pastoral Epistles*, 319f., and in FIORE, *The Pastoral Epistles*, 220.

187 Weidemann, however, notes the association of justification and baptism in Tit 3 and finds the same association in 1 Cor 6:11. Weidemann argues that the author of Titus uses an old baptismal tradition or that he applies 1 Cor 6:9–11 directly. Significant is the connection of the "once/ now" scheme with a vice catalogue, baptism understood as washing, the gift of the Holy Spirit, and the entrance in the heirship (WEIDEMANN, "Titus, der getaufte Heide", 43). Regarding 1 Cor

The language of rebirth is not found in Paul but resembles that of John 3:3–8 (γεννηθῆναι ἄνωθεν ... ἐξ ὕδατος καὶ πνεύματος) and 1 Pet 1:3.23 (ἀναγεννάω). In 1 Peter rebirth is not directly related to baptism[188] whereas it seems to be in the version we know of the Gospel of John. It is merely speculative to assume literate relations between the Gospel of John and the letter to Titus, while 1 Peter might be associated with the school of Paul.[189] In the time of early Christianity, the language of rebirth was widespread religious language,[190] and the author of Titus could have invented the language of baptism as regeneration without a direct model in either Paul or other Christian writings known to him. If the metaphor is not Pauline, there are motifs in Paul that could support the application of the metaphor in the present context in Titus. In 2 Cor 5:17 Paul writes, "if anyone is in Christ, there is a *new creation*". In Rom 12:2 the readers are encouraged to "be transformed by the *renewing* of your minds" (ἀνακαίνωσις τοῦ νοός) and in the deuteropauline Col 3:10 the readers are reminded that they have "clothed themselves with the *new, which is being renewed*" (ἐνδυσάμενοι τὸν νέον τὸν ἀνακαινούμενον).[191] The word ἀνακαίνωσις is equated with παλιγγενεσία in Titus 3:5. The context for the renewal is one of exhortation in Romans and Colossians as in Titus.

In addition, the Holy Spirit is closely related to baptism in early Christian texts.[192] In Paul the Spirit is not explicitly related to baptism in Gal 3:26–28 and Romans 6, as it is in 1 Cor 12:13. While the Spirit is not mentioned in Colossians 2:6ff., it is present in Ephesians 4. Titus 3:5 could be said to render common early Christian concepts of the close relationship between Spirit and baptism. The renewal of the Holy Spirit that is poured out on believers can be read as a reference to the prophecy in Joel 2:28 (3:1), the prophetic promise now

---

6:11 as a baptismal text see Hellholm, "Vorgeformte Tauftraditionen", § 1.1. and § 1.3. According to Weidemann the author avoids the reference to Romans 6 because he wants to counteract interpretations of Romans 6 like the ones in Col 2:12; 3:1; Eph 2:6 where the resurrection with Christ is stated to be a present reality (See 2 Tim 2:18) (Weidemann, "Titus, der getaufte Heide", 44f.).

188   See in the present publication: Moxnes, "Because of the 'Name of Christ'". Moxnes indicates that the metaphor may here be associated with baptism. R. Feldmeier supposes that a reference to baptism is not intended. "Rebirth" emphasises "die Wirksamkeit des göttlichen Wortes" (Feldmeier, *Der erste Brief des Petrus*, 85).

189   Feldmeier, *Der erste Brief des Petrus*, 19, footnote 95.

190   See *Ibid.*, 16; 84–86; further Büchsel, "Γίνομαι etc.", 685ff.; Dibelius/Conzelmann, *The Pastoral Epistles*, 148–150; Hartman, *Into the Name of the Lord Jesus*, 109f.; Fiore, *The Pastoral Epistles*, 220.

191   See Fiore, *The Pastoral Epistles*, 220.

192   See *Ibid.*, 219; Barth, *Die Taufe in frühchristlicher Zeit*, 60–72; Hartman, *Into the Name of the Lord Jesus*, 66–68, 81.

having been fulfilled in the lives of believers as an occasion connected to the saving act of God and closely related to the "bath of rebirth".[193]

4.3.2. Baptism and Its Contexts in Titus

The reference to baptism occurs in one of the short descriptive passages in Titus. These passages are embedded in the main line of reasoning in the letter: the order of the churches, and the good and beneficial conduct of the believers. This reasoning can be seen in relation to presupposed comprehensive interpretive schemes of author and audience and it combines cognitive and behavioural dimensions. The truth claims about God – God being the saviour and showing his goodness and philanthropy – are related to the life experience of the believer: the bath of rebirth and renewal by the Holy Spirit. This descriptive language states the beliefs that are the framework motivating moral advice.[194] The social dimension is in view inasmuch as the writing is concerned with internal relations in the groups. The eucharist is not mentioned, and the rite of baptism itself and its experiential dimensions appear not to be emphasised, but rather the cognitive interpretation of it.

As far as an interpretive scheme can be labelled as being Christian in nature, it can be related to identity. At first sight (exhortation being so dominant in the writing) one could be lead to believe that it is the concrete virtues that are intended to signify Christian identity. But a closer look reveals the virtues to be generally accepted ones as they were taught and imparted in philosophical and rhetorical schools.[195] Hence the conduct of life in itself is not suitable for showing the believers' characteristic Christian identity – the conduct is to be approved by the outsiders (2,5; 2:8; 3:2; 3:8) –, but rather the totality in religious dimensions corresponding to a comprehensive interpretive scheme.[196] The list of vices in 3:3 is not a realistic description of the believers' lives before the baptismal initiation, nor a realistic rendering of the normative morals of those existing outside the community of believers, but rather serving as a contrast to

---

[193] See FIORE, *The Pastoral Epistles*, 221; HARTMAN, *Into the Name of the Lord Jesus*, 110.

[194] For the integration of beliefs and moral advice see Malherbe's discussion of conceptual world and paraenesis in philosophical schools and in Titus (MALHERBE, "Paraenesis in the Epistle to Titus", 311–317).

[195] See *Ibid.*, 298ff., 317.

[196] Malherbe remarks that "while some of the language, paraenetic devices, and the way the argument holds together in Titus are similar to the moral philosophical traditions we have observed, there are considerable differences between the two. The cognitive element in Titus is not human reason reaching for the truth, but is knowledge derived from apostolic tradition and Scripture" (*Ibid.*, 316). See also how Malherbe outlines the interrelation between the "theological warrant" in 2:11–14 and baptism through which "God saved in a single, past event", and the precepts. God saved through baptism, and "God's saving grace continues to train us", the grace has an "educative function" (314). See also FIORE, *The Pastoral Epistles*, 13f.

show the significant impact of the belief in Christ, the renewal of the Spirit and the initiation of baptism interpreted as rebirth.

Finally, in the comprehensive scheme baptism has its function. If the virtues referred to represent those commonly accepted among educators, the rite and its interpretation displayed Christian characteristics, and even more so the dogmatic and mythical dimensions being thought of as exclusive (none other than the one God should be worshipped) and supreme. Baptism was the rite marking the transition, and fulfilled a function in the comprehensive interpretive scheme, including when this scheme was applied in a written work like the Epistle to Titus, which was intended to promote the identity formation of believers.

Bibliography

Texts

Bible texts are cited according to *The Harper Collins Study Bible* (NRSV), New York: Harper Collins 2006.

Greek (and German) Bible texts are cited according to Nestle-Aland, *Das neue Testament. Griechisch und Deutsch*, Stuttgart: Deutsche Bibelgesellschaft/Katholische Bibelanstalt 2003.

The Dead Sea Scrolls. Translated and with a Commentary by Michael Wise, Martin Abegg Jr., and Edward Cook, San Francisco, Calif.: Harper Collins 2005.

Literature

Avemarie, F., "Taufe II. Neues Testament", in: *RGG*[4] 8 (2005) 52–59.

Bakke, O. M., *"Concord and peace". A Rhetorical Analysis of the First Letter of Clement with an Emphasis on the Language of Unity and Sedition* (WUNT 141), Tübingen: Mohr Siebeck 2001.

Barth, G., *Die Taufe in frühchristlicher Zeit* (BthSt 4), Neukirchen-Vluyn: Neukirchener Verlag 1981.

Becker, J./Luz, U., *Die Briefe an die Galater, Epheser und Kolosser* (NTD 8/1), Göttingen: Vandenhoeck & Ruprecht 1998.

Berger, K., *Formgeschichte des Neuen Testaments*, Heidelberg: Quelle & Meyer 1984.

— "Hellenistische Gattungen im Neuen Testament", in: *ANRW*, 2.25/2 (1984) 1031–1432 and 1831–1885.

BEST, E., *A Critical and Exegetical Commentary on Ephesians* (ICC), London/New York: T & T Clark 1998.

BETZ, H. D., *Galatians. A Commentary on Paul's Letter to the Churches in Galatia* (Hermeneia), Philadelphia: Fortress Press 1979.

— "Paraenesis and the Concept of God", in: J. M. Starr/T. Engberg-Pedersen (eds.), *Early Christian Paraenesis in Context* (BZNW 125), Berlin/New York: Walter de Gruyter 2004, 217–234.

— "Paul's 'Second Presence' in Colossians", in: D. Hellholm/T. Fornberg (eds.), *Texts and Contexts. Biblical Texts in Their Textual and Situational Contexts. Essays in Honor of Lars Hartman*, Oslo: Scandinavian University Press 1995, 507–518.

— "Transferring a Ritual: Paul's Interpretation of Baptism in Romans 6", in: T. Engberg-Pedersen (ed.), *Paul in His Hellenistic Context*, Minneapolis: Fortress Press 1995, 84–118.

BÜCHSEL, F., "Γίνομαι etc.", in: *ThWNT* 1 (1933), 680–688.

CARAGOUNIS, C. C., *The Ephesian Mysterion. Meaning and Content* (CB.NT 8), Lund: Gleerup 1977.

DAHL, N. A., "Formgeschichtliche Beobachtungen zur Christusverkündigung in der Gemeindepredigt", in: W. Eltester (ed.), *Neutestamentliche Studien für Rudolf Bultmann*, Berlin: Töpelmann [1]1954; [2]1957, 3–9.

— "The Concept of Baptism in Ephesians", in: N. A. Dahl, *Studies in Ephesians. Introductory Questions, Text- & Edition-Critical Issues, Interpretation of Texts and Themes*, ed. by D. Hellholm/V. Blomkvist/T. Fornberg (WUNT 131), Tübingen: Mohr Siebeck 2000, 413–439.

— "Einleitungsfragen zum Epheserbrief", in: N. A. Dahl, *Studies in Ephesians*, 3–105.

— "Kleidungsmetaphern: der alte und der neue Mensch", in: N. A. Dahl, *Studies in Ephesians*, 389–411.

— "The Letter to the Ephesians: Its Fictional and Real Setting", in: N. A. Dahl, *Studies in Ephesians*, 441–459.

DIBELIUS, M./CONZELMANN, H., *The Pastoral Epistles. A Commentary on the Pastoral Epistles* (Hermeneia), Philadelphia: Fortress 1972.

DUNN, J. D. G., *The Epistles to the Colossians and to Philemon. A Commentary on the Greek Text* (NIGTC), Grand Rapids/Carlisle: Eerdmans 1996.

ENGBERG-PEDERSEN, T., "The Concept of Paraenesis", in: J. M. Starr/T. Engberg-Pedersen (eds.), *Early Christian Paraenesis in Context* (BZNW 125), Berlin/New York: Walter de Gruyter 2004, 47–72.

ENGBERG-PEDERSEN, T./STARR, J. M., *Early Christian Paraenesis in Context* (BZNW 125), Berlin: Walter de Gruyter 2004.

ERNST, J., "Kolosserbrief", in: *TRE* 19 (1990) 370–376.

FELDMEIER, R., *Der erste Brief des Petrus* (ThHK 15/I), Leipzig: Evangelische Verlagsanstalt 2005.

FERGUSON, E., *Baptism in the Early Church. History, Theology, and Liturgy in the First Five Centuries*, Grand Rapids, Mich.: Eerdmans 2009.

FIORE, B., *The Pastoral Epistles: First Timothy, Second Timothy, Titus* (Sacra Pagina Series 12), Collegeville, Minn.: The Liturgical Press 2007.

GEERTZ, C., *The Interpretation of Cultures. Selected Essays*, New York: Basic Books 2000.

VON GEMÜNDEN, P., "Die urchristliche Taufe und der Umgang mit den Effekten", in: J. Assmann/G. G. Stroumsa (eds.), *Transformations of the Inner Self in Ancient Religions* (SHR 83), Leiden/Boston/Köln: Brill 1999, 115–136.

HARTMAN, L., *"Into the Name of the Lord Jesus": Baptism in the New Testament* (SNTW), Edinburgh: T&T Clark 1997.

— *Kolosserbrevet* (KNT[U] 12), Uppsala: EFS-förlaget 1985.

HELLHOLM, D., "Enthymemic Argumentation in Paul: The Case of Romans 6", in: T. Engberg-Pedersen (ed.), *Paul in His Hellenistic Context*, Minneapolis, Minn.: Fortress Press 1995, 119–179.

— "The 'Revelation-Schema' and Its Adaptation in the Coptic Gnostic Apocalypse of Peter", in: *SEÅ* 63 (1998) 233–248.

— "The Impact of the Situational Contexts for Paul's Use of Baptismal Traditions in his Letters", in: D. E. Aune, et al. (eds.), *Neotestamentica et Philonica. Studies in Honor of Peder Borgen*, Leiden: Brill 2003, 147–175.

— "Die Gattung Haustafel im Kolosser- und Epheserbrief. Ihre Position innerhalb der Paränese-Abschnitte und ihr Hintergrund in der spätantiken Gesellschaft", in: P. Müller (ed.), *Kolosser-Studien* (Biblisch-theologische Studien 103), Neukirchen-Vluyn: Neukirchener 2009, 103–128.

— "Vorgeformte Tauftraditionen und deren Benutzung in den Paulusbriefen", in *the present publication,* 415–423.

HÜBNER, H., *An Philemon. An die Kolosser. An die Epheser* (HNT 12), Tübingen: Mohr Siebeck 1997.

JEWETT, R., *Romans. A Commentary* (Hermeneia), Minneapolis, Minn.: Fortress Press 2007.

JOHNSON, L. T., *The First and Second Letters to Timothy. A New Translation with Introduction and Commentary* (AncB 35A), New York: Doubleday 2001.

KENNEDY, G. A., *New Testament Interpretation Through Rhetorical Criticism*, Chapel Hill, N.C.: The University of North Carolina Press 1984.

KLAUCK, H.-J., *Ancient Letters and the New Testament. A Guide to Context and Exegesis*, Waco, Tex.: Baylor University Press 2006.

KNIGHT, G. W., *The Pastoral Epistles. A Commentary on the Greek Text* (NIGTC), Grand Rapids, Mich./Carlisle: Eerdmans/The Paternoster Press 1992.

LINDBECK, G. A., *The Nature of Doctrine. Religion and Theology in a Postliberal Age*, Philadelphia, Pa.: Westminster Press 1984.

LINDEMANN, A., *Der Epheserbrief* (ZBK.NT 8), Zürich: Theologischer Verlag 1985.

— *Der Kolosserbrief* (ZBK.NT 10), Zürich: Theologischer Verlag 1983.

— "Die Gemeinde von ‚Kolossä'. Erwägungen zum ‚Sitz im Leben' eines pseudopaulinischen Briefes", in: *WuD* 16 (1981) 111–134.

— *Paulus im ältesten Christentum. Das Bild des Apostels und die Rezeption der paulinischen Theologie in der frühchristlichen Literatur bis Marcion* (BHTh 58), Tübingen: Mohr Siebeck 1979.

LOHSE, E., *Die Briefe an die Kolosser und an Philemon* (KEK IX/2), Göttingen: Vandenhoeck & Ruprecht 1977.

MALHERBE, A. J., *Moral Exhortation, A Greco-Roman Sourcebook* (LEC 4), Philadelphia, Pa.: The Westminster Press 1986.

— "Paraenesis in the Epistle to Titus", in: J. M. Starr/T. Engberg-Pedersen (eds.), *Early Christian Paraenesis in Context* (BZNW 125), Berlin/New York: Walter de Gruyter 2004, 297–317.

MARSHALL, I. H./TOWNER, P. H., *A critical and exegetical commentary on the Pastoral Epistles* (ICC), London: T&T Clark International 2004.

MARTIN, D. B., "Paul Without Passion. On Paul's rejection of desire in sex and marriage", in: H. Moxnes (ed.), *Constructing Early Christian families. Family as social reality and metaphor*, London: Routledge 1997, 201–215.

MEEKS, W. A., *The Moral World of the First Christians* (LEC 6), Philadelphia, Pa.: The Westminster Press 1986.

MERKLEIN, H., "Eph 4,1–5,20 als Rezeption von Kol 3,1–17", in: P.-G. Müller/W. Stenger (eds.), *Kontinuität und Einheit. Für Franz Mußner*, Freiburg i. Br.: Herder 1981, 194–210.

— "Paulinische Theologie in der Rezeption des Kolosser- und Epheserbriefes", in: K. Kertelge (ed.), *Paulus in den neutestamentlichen Spätschriften*, Basel: Herder 1981, 25–69.

MEYER, R., "Peritemno, peritomê, aperitmêtos", in: *TDNT* 6 (1968) 72–84.

MITCHELL, M. M., *Paul and the Rhetoric of Reconciliation. An Exegetical Investigation of the Language and Composition of 1 Corinthians*, Tübingen/Louisville Ky.: Mohr Siebeck/Westminister John Knox Press 1992.

MOXNES, H., "Because of the 'Name of Christ'. Baptism and the Location of Identity in 1 Peter", in *the present publication.*, 605–628.

— "From Theology to Identity: The Problem of Constructing Early Christianity", in: T. Penner/C. V. Stichele (eds.), *Moving Beyond New Testament Theology* (SESJ 88), Göttingen: Vandenhoeck & Ruprecht 2005, 264–281.

MUSSNER, F., "Epheserbrief", in: *TRE* 9 (1982) 743–753.

MÜLLER, P., "Gegner im Kolosserbrief. Methodische Überlegungen zu einem schwierigen Kapitel", in: W. Kraus/U. B. Müller (eds.), *Beiträge zur urchristlichen Theologiegeschichte* (BZNW 163), Berlin/New York: Walter de Gruyter 2009, 365–394.

— "Zum Problem der Paulusschule. Methodische und sachliche Überlegungen", in: P. Müller (ed.), *Kolosser-Studien* (BThSt 103), Neukirchen-Vluyn: Neukirchener 2009, 171–197.

OBERLINNER, L., *Die Pastoralbriefe. Erste Folge: Kommentar zum ersten Timotheusbrief* (HThK XI/2), Freiburg/Basel/Wien: Herder 1994.

— *Die Pastoralbriefe. Zweite Folge: Kommentar zum zweiten Timotheusbrief* (HThK XI/2), Freiburg/Basel/Wien: Herder 1995.

— *Die Pastoralbriefe. Dritte Folge: Kommentar zum Titusbrief* (HThK XI/3), Freiburg/Basel/Wien: Herder 1996.

POPKES, W., "Paraenesis in the New Testament", in: J. M. Starr/T. Engberg-Pedersen (eds.), *Early Christian Paraenesis in Context* (BZNW 125), Berlin/New York: Walter de Gruyter 2004, 1–46.

Roloff, J., *Der erste Brief an Timotheus* (EKK 15), Neukirchen-Vluyn: Neukirchener/Zürich: Benziger 1988.

— "Pastoralbriefe", in: *TRE* 26 (1996) 50–68.

Sandnes, K. O., "Seal and Baptism in Early Christianity", in: *the present publication*, 1439–1479.

Schmidt, K. L., "Καλέω", in: *ThWNT* 3 (1938) 428–439.

Schnackenburg, R., *Der Brief an die Epheser* (EKK 10), Neukirchen-Vluyn: Neukirchener/Zürich: Benziger 1982.

Schnelle, U., *Einleitung in das Neue Testament* (UTB 1830), Göttingen: Vandenhoeck & Ruprecht 2002.

— "Taufe II. Neues Testament", in: *TRE* 32 (2001) 663–674.

Schweizer, E., *Der Brief an die Kolosser* (EKK 12), Zürich: Benziger/Neukirchen-Vluyn: /Neukirchener Verlag 1976/1989(3).

— *The Letter to the Colossians. A Commentary*, Minneapolis, Minn./London: Augsburg Pub. House/SPCK 1982.

Sellin, G., *Der Brief an die Epheser* (KEK 8), Göttingen: Vandenhoeck & Ruprecht 2008.

— "‚Die Auferstehung ist schon geschehen'. Zur Spiritualisierung apokalyptischer Terminologie", in: D. Sänger (ed.), *Studien zu Paulus und zum Epheserbrief* (FRLANT 229), Göttingen: Vandenhoeck & Ruprecht 2009, 37–52.

— "Die Paränese des Epheserbriefes", in: D. Sänger (ed.), *Studien zu Paulus und zum Epheserbrief* (FRLANT 229), Göttingen: Vandenhoeck & Ruprecht 2009, 180–198.

— "Vom Kolosser- zum Epheserbrief. Eine Entwicklung im Deuteropaulinismus", in: P. Müller (ed.), *Kolosser-Studien* (BThSt 103), Neukirchen-Vluyn: Neukirchener 2009, 151–170.

Smart, N., *The World's Religions. Old Traditions and Modern Transformations*, Cambridge: Cambridge University Press 1989.

Standhartinger, A., *Studien zur Entstehungsgeschichte und Intention des Kolosserbriefs* (NT.S 94), Leiden: Brill 1999.

Starr, J. M., "Was Paraenesis for Beginners?", in: J. M. Starr/T. Engberg-Pedersen (eds.), *Early Christian Paraenesis in Context* (BZNW 125), Berlin/New York: Walter de Gruyter 2004, 73–111.

STIREWALT, M. L. J., "The Form and Function of the Greek Letter-Essay", in: K. P. Donfried (ed.), *The Romans Debate*, Peabody, Mass.: Hendricson 1991, 147–171.

— *Studies in Ancient Greek Epistolography* (SBL Resources for Biblical Study 27), Atlanta, Ga.: Scholars Press 1993.

STOWERS, S. K., *The Diatribe and Paul's Letter to the Romans* (SBL.DS 57), Chico Calif.: Scholars Press 1981.

— *Letter Writing in Greco-Roman Antiquity* (LEC 5), Philadelphia, Pa: Westminster Press 1986.

TACHAU, P., *‚Einst' und ‚Jetzt' im neuen Testament. Beobachtungen zu einem urchristlichen Predigtschema in der neutestamentlichen Briefliteratur und zu seiner Vorgeschichte* (FRLANT 105), Göttingen: Vandenhoeck & Ruprecht 1972.

THEISSEN, G., "Die urchristliche Taufe und die soziale Konstruktion des neuen Menschen", in: J. Assmann/G. G. Stroumsa (eds.), *Transformations of the Inner Self in Ancient Religions* (SHR 83), Leiden/Boston/Köln: Brill 1999, 87–114.

— *The Religion of the Earliest Churches. Creating a Symbolic World*, Minneapolis, Minn.: Fortress Press 1999.

VEGGE, T., *Paulus und das antike Schulwesen. Schule und Bildung des Paulus* (BZNW 134), Berlin/New York: Walter de Gruyter 2006.

WAGENER, U., *Die Ordnung des ‚Hauses Gottes'. Der Ort von Frauen in der Ekklesiologie und Ethik der Pastoralbriefe* (WUNT 65), Tübingen: Mohr Siebeck 1994.

WEIDEMANN, H.-U., "Titus, der getaufte Heide – Überlegungen zu Tit 3,1–8", in: H.-U. Weidemann/W. Eisele (eds.), *Ein Meisterschüler. Titus und sein Brief* (SBS 214), Stuttgart: Katholisches Bibelwerk 2008, 31–54.

WEISER, A., *Der zweite Brief an Timotheus* (EKK 16/1), Düsseldorf und Zürich: Benziger/Neukirchen-Vluyn: Neukirchener 2003.

WITHERINGTON, B., *The Letters to Philemon, the Colossians and the Ephesians. A Socio-rhetorical Commentary on the Captivity Epistles*, Grand Raphids, Mich.: Eerdmans 2007.

WOLTER, M., *Die Pastoralbriefe als Paulustradition* (FRLANT 146), Göttingen: Vandenhoeck & Ruprecht 1988.

— *Der Brief an die Kolosser. Der Brief an Philemon* (ÖTBK 12), Gütersloh: Gütersloher Verlagshaus Gerd Mohn/Würzburg: Echter Verlag 1993.

Die Taufe in der Apostelgeschichte[1]

Jens Schröter

1. Die Taufe im Rahmen der lukanischen Geschichtstheologie

Das lukanische Doppelwerk schildert die Entstehung einer neuen Gemeinschaft durch das Wirken Jesu, ihr Anwachsen und ihre geographische Ausbreitung bis nach Rom.[2] Zu den wichtigsten Ereignissen dieser Geschichte gehört die Trennung vom Judentum, die sich von Beginn an abzeichnet und durch das letzte Wort des Paulus über die künftige Hinwendung des Heils zu den Heiden besiegelt wird.[3] Diese Trennung bedeutet zugleich, dass sich die Geschichte Israels künftig auf zwei Wegen fortsetzen wird, nämlich im Judentum und in der Kirche.[4] Dass darüber hinaus das „Ende der Erde" (Act 1,8) in den Blick genommen wird, zeigt an, dass Lukas nur den Beginn dieser Ausbreitung erzählt, deren Fortsetzung er für die Zukunft erwartet und die bis zur Wiederkunft des Menschensohnes Jesus am Ende der Zeit andauern wird.[5]

Die Tauferzählungen der Act erhalten ihre spezifische Funktion innerhalb dieses Geschichtskonzeptes.[6] Ihre Bedeutung wird bereits daran erkennbar, dass die Wortgruppe βαπτίζειν/βάπτισμα innerhalb des Neuen Testaments in

---

1 Für Hilfe bei den Korrekturen und der Formatierung danke ich meiner studentischen Mitarbeiterin Juni Hoppe sehr herzlich.

2 Die Diskussion über die lukanische Geschichtstheologie und das darin entwickelte Verhältnis von Israel und Kirche hat in der neueren Actaforschung große Aufmerksamkeit erfahren. Vgl. dazu J. Schröter, *Actaforschung seit 1982. III: Die Apostelgeschichte als Geschichtswerk; IV: Israel, die Juden und das Alte Testament*. Besonders hervorzuheben sind: R. I. Denova, *The Things Accomplished Among Us. Prophetic Tradition in the Structural Pattern of Luke-Acts*; G. Wasserberg, *Aus Israels Mitte – Heil für die Welt. Eine narrativ-exegetische Studie zur Theologie des Lukas*; D. P. Moessner (Hg.), *Jesus and the Heritage of Israel. Luke's Narrative Claim upon Israel's Legacy (Luke the Interpreter of Israel 1)*.

3 Vgl. E. Plümacher, *Rom in der Apostelgeschichte*.

4 Vgl. M. Wolter, *Das lukanische Doppelwerk als Epochengeschichte*, bes. 284–287; W. S. Kurz, *Reading Luke-Acts. Dynamics of Biblical Narrative*.

5 Auf den geographischen Horizont verweist Act 1,8, auf den zeitlichen 1,11. Dass dabei mit dem in 1,8 erwähnten „Ende der Erde" nicht etwa Rom gemeint ist, hat W. C. van Unnik bereits vor längerer Zeit gezeigt. Vgl. idem, „Der Ausdruck ἙΩΣ ἘΣΧΑΤΟΥ ΤΗΣ ΓΗΣ (Apostelgeschichte I 8) und sein alttestamentlicher Hintergrund".

6 Die grundlegende Monographie zum Thema ist die Arbeit von F. Avemarie, *Die Tauferzählungen der Apostelgeschichte. Theologie und Geschichte*. Vgl. weiter M. Quesnel, *Baptisés dans l'Esprit. Baptême et Esprit Saint dans les Actes des Apôtres*; H.-S. Kim, *Die Geisttaufe des Messias*

der Act am häufigsten begegnet und die beiden für die Entstehung der Kirche grundlegenden Ereignisse – das Pfingstgeschehen in Jerusalem (Act 2) und die Geistausgießung auf die Heiden im Haus des Kornelius (Act 10–11) – Tauferzählungen sind: Die Ausgießung des Geistes auf die Apostel zu Jerusalem ist Act 1,5 zufolge ein Taufgeschehen, dessen Deutung durch die Rede des Petrus zur Taufe von weiteren etwa 3000 Menschen führt (2,41); auf die im Haus des Kornelius Versammelten fällt während der Rede des Petrus der Geist, woraufhin sie ebenfalls getauft werden (10,44.47f.; 11,15–17).

Der in diesen Texten begegnende Zusammenhang von Geistausgießung und Taufe zeigt bereits, dass die Ausbreitung der Christusbotschaft für Lukas eng mit der Gabe des Geistes verbunden ist. Der Zusammenhang von Geistvermittlung und Taufe wird dabei durch zwei weitere Texte unterstrichen: Da die Taufe von Samaritanern durch Philippus – obwohl sie eine Taufe εἰς τὸ ὄνομα τοῦ κυρίου Ἰησοῦ ist – Lukas zufolge nicht den Geist vermittelt, wird dieser durch Handauflegung von Petrus und Johannes nachträglich verliehen.[7] Die etwa zwölf Jünger, die Paulus in Ephesus antrifft, kennen nur die Taufe des Johannes und werden deshalb von Paulus auf den Namen des Herrn Jesus getauft, wobei sie ebenfalls durch Handauflegung den Geist erhalten.[8] Das Verhältnis von Taufe und Geistempfang ist demnach ein für die lukanischen Tauferzählungen zentrales Thema, wenngleich genauer zu fragen sein wird, wie dieser Zusammenhang zu verstehen ist.[9] Deutlich ist jedenfalls, dass der Geistbesitz für Lukas konstitutiv mit der Entstehung christlicher Gemeinschaft verbunden ist und mit der Taufe in einen engen Zusammenhang gerückt wird.

Neben den genannten sind zwei weitere Tauferzählungen der Act zu nennen, die an der Taufe von Einzelpersonen orientiert sind: Die Taufe des Äthiopiers in Act 8,26–40 stellt eine bemerkenswerte Einzelepisode dar, deren Bedeutung für den lukanischen Erzählzusammenhang gesondert zu betrachten ist. Auch

---

sowie jetzt E. FERGUSON, *Baptism in the Early Church. History, Theology, and Liturgy in the First Five Centuries*, 166–185.

7   Act 8,14–17.

8   Act 19,1–7.

9   Dieses Thema berührt die Diskussion über die lukanische Pneumatologie, was hier nur angedeutet werden kann. Strittig ist dabei bekanntlich, ob Lukas das πνεῦμα als Begabung zu prophetischer Rede und außergewöhnlichen Machttaten versteht, ihm jedoch keine soteriologischen Funktionen beimisst – so pointiert E. SCHWEIZER, πνεῦμα κτλ., 401–413, bes. 409f., dann auch R. P. MENZIES, *The Development of Early Christian Pneumatology* – oder ob ihm bei Lukas eine grundlegende Bedeutung für die Schaffung des Gottesvolkes aus Juden und Heiden und also durchaus eine soteriologische Bedeutung zukommt – so in neuerer Zeit vor allem M. TURNER, *Power from on High. The Spirit in Israel's Restoration and Witness in Luke-Acts*. Für die hier verfolgte Fragestellung ist das lk Geistverständnis insofern von Bedeutung, als es die Frage nach dem durch die Taufe begründeten neuen Status der Christen betrifft.

die Taufe des Saulus ist Bestandteil einer individuell ausgerichteten Erzählung.[10] Anders als bei derjenigen des Äthiopiers geht hier allerdings eine Erscheinung des erhöhten Jesus voraus, die eine Bekehrung des Verfolgers der „Jünger des Herrn" (9,1) bewirkt. Zudem handelt es sich hier um eine Episode, die für den Fortgang der in der Act berichteten Ereignisse grundlegende Bedeutung besitzt, wogegen der Äthiopier nach seiner Taufe aus der Erzählwelt der Act abtritt.

Dieser erste Überblick zeigt bereits, dass sich in der Act ein facettenreiches Spektrum von Tauferzählungen findet. Darauf weisen die variable Zuordnung von Geistempfang, Handauflegung und Taufe, der mehrfach herausgestellte Unterschied von Wasser- und Geisttaufe sowie die in verschiedene Erzählzusammenhänge eingebundenen Taufvorgänge hin. Diese zeigen, dass Lukas in den Tauferzählungen Überlieferungen aufgenommen hat, die an unterschiedlichen Orten und Personen hafteten. Um das in der Act entwickelte Taufverständnis zu erheben, ist deshalb nicht zuletzt auf das Verhältnis von Lukas bereits vorliegenden Überlieferungen und deren Einarbeitung in die lukanische Geschichtsdarstellung zu achten. Dabei ist auch danach zu fragen, wie sich die sprachlich variierenden Formeln εἰς τὸ ὄνομα, ἐν τῷ ὀνόματι und ἐπὶ τῷ ὀνόματι (κυρίου) Ἰησοῦ Χριστοῦ erklären.

2. Aspekte der Tauferzählungen in der Apostelgeschichte

2.1. Taufe als Befähigung zur Zeugenschaft: Die Ankündigung der Geistausgießung in Act 1,4–8 als Taufgeschehen

Die Texte, in denen die Taufe für die von der Act erzählte Geschichte des frühen Christentums besondere Bedeutung erlangt, sind die Pfingsterzählung, die Taufe der Samaritaner und des Simon Magus sowie des Äthiopiers durch Philippus, diejenige des Saulus sowie schließlich die Taufe der im Haus des Kornelius Versammelten. Die ausführlichen Tauferzählungen konzentrieren sich demnach im ersten Teil der Act, der die Ausbreitung des Christuszeugnisses bis nach Antiochia zum Inhalt hat. Danach gibt es nur noch knappe und summarische Notizen darüber, dass sich Lydia aus Philippi mit ihrem Haus taufen ließ (16,15), ebenso wie später der dortige Gefängnisaufseher (16,33), sowie dass viele der Korinther zum Glauben kamen und sich taufen ließen (18,8). Eine gewisse Sonderstellung nimmt die Taufe der Johannesjünger in Ephesus ein, die – sieht man von dem Rückblick des Paulus auf seine Taufe in 22,16 ab – zugleich die letzte Erwähnung einer Taufe in der Act darstellt.[11] Daraus lässt sich entnehmen, dass die Taufer-

---

10 Die Taufe wird in 9,18; 22,16 erwähnt. In dem dritten Bekehrungsbericht in Kap. 26 wird die Taufe nicht erwähnt.

11 In 22,16 berichtet Paulus im Rückblick von der Aufforderung des Hananias an ihn, sich taufen zu lassen. Es handelt sich dabei um einen Rückgriff auf bereits früher Erzähltes, weshalb diese

zählungen der Act in den Kontext der numerischen und geographischen Ausbreitung der Kirche gehören. Die verschiedenen Aspekte, die Lukas dabei mit den Tauferzählungen verbindet, sind im Folgenden näher zu betrachten.

Das erste Vorkommen des Verbums βαπτίζειν begegnet unmittelbar am Beginn der Act in 1,4–8 innerhalb des Dialogs des Auferstandenen mit seinen Jüngern.[12] In Aufnahme von Lk 24,49 werden die Jünger angewiesen, in Jerusalem zu bleiben und auf die Verheißung des Vaters zu warten. Die Formulierung ἐπαγγελία τοῦ πατρός in 1,4 wird dabei durch ἣν ἠκούσατέ μου mit den letzten Anweisungen des Auferstandenen in Lk 24 verbunden. In beiden Texten wird mit dieser Wendung metonymisch auf den heiligen Geist verwiesen, den der Vater senden wird und der in Lk 24,49 und Act 1,8 auch als δύναμις bezeichnet werden kann.

Der explizite Bezug zur Taufe wird sodann in V.5 hergestellt: Der Empfang der ἐπαγγελία τοῦ πατρός wird nunmehr als βαπτίζεσθαι ἐν πνεύματι ἁγίῳ bezeichnet, das der Wassertaufe des Johannes gegenübersteht. Lukas nimmt dazu Bezug auf das Wort des Johannes, mit dem dieser seine eigene Taufe von derjenigen des nach ihm kommenden Stärkeren unterschieden hatte. Dieses Wort aus Lk 3,16 begegnet hier allerdings als Wort des Auferstandenen, als welches es in Act 11,16 von Petrus auch ausdrücklich zitiert wird. Zudem ist es gegenüber dem Johanneswort aus Lk 3,16 in mehrfacher Hinsicht modifiziert.[13] Die für die neue Verwendung markanteste Veränderung ist, dass es sich nunmehr um ein Wort *Jesu* an seine Jünger handelt, die damit zugleich als Adressaten der Geisttaufe in Erscheinung treten.

Die Unterscheidung von Wassertaufe des Johannes und Geisttaufe durch den erhöhten Jesus erhält dadurch für das Taufverständnis der Act grundlegende Bedeutung. Sie wird durch ein Jesuswort begründet, das auf das Pfingstgeschehen vorausverweist. Dort wird diese Ankündigung dergestalt aufgenommen, dass in 2,4 vom Erfülltwerden mit dem heiligen Geist gesprochen wird und in 2,33 in der Petrusrede der Ausdruck ἐπαγγελία τοῦ πνεύματος τοῦ ἁγίου παρὰ τοῦ πατρός begegnet. Auf Johannes selbst wird dagegen in Act 13,25 innerhalb einer Paulusrede nur der Satz über seine Unwürdigkeit, die Schuhriemen des nach ihm Kommenden zu lösen, zurückgeführt. Damit ist die Geistausgießung zu Pfingsten als Taufgeschehen gedeutet, das die Wassertaufe des Johannes qualitativ überbietet. Der Empfang des Geistes ist dabei zugleich die Befähi-

---

    Stelle hier außer Betracht bleiben kann.

12 Wie das (wohl am besten als „zusammen essen" aufzufassende) συναλιζόμενος anzeigt, handelt es sich um eine Mahlszene in Anknüpfung an die Mähler des Auferstandenen in Lk 24,30f.41–43. Zur Diskussion vgl. F. J. FOAKES-JACKSON/K. LAKE, *The Beginnings of Christianity, Volume IV: English Translation and Commentary*, 4–6; C. K. BARRETT, *A Critical and Exegetical Commentary on the Acts of the Apostles*, 71f.

13 Das ἰσχυρότερος aus Lk 3,16 fehlt in Act 1,5 und 11,16; statt des dortigen ἱκανός heißt es hier ἄξιος; die Taufe der Apostel erfolgt nur ἐν πνεύματι ἁγίῳ, das καὶ πυρί aus Lk 3,16 fehlt.

gung zur Zeugenschaft. Darum wird er in 1,8 als δύναμις bezeichnet, was auf die Kraft zum Wunderwirken hindeutet[14], die im weiteren Verlauf von den Aposteln, aber auch von Stephanus, Philippus und Paulus, berichtet wird.[15]

Im Blick auf die Bedeutung der Taufe in der Act lassen sich daraus folgende Merkmale ableiten. Zunächst wird unmittelbar am Beginn der Act die in Lk 24,29 angedeutete narrative Fortsetzung der Jesusgeschichte[16] aufgenommen und dahingehend konkretisiert, dass die bereits in Lk 24,48 genannte Zeugenschaft der Jünger eine solche bis ans Ende der Erde sein wird. Des Weiteren wird deutlich, dass die an Jesus gebundene Geisttaufe an die Stelle der Wassertaufe des Johannes tritt, die damit als für die Ausbreitung der Christusbotschaft unzureichend charakterisiert wird. Dies geschieht ungeachtet der Tatsache, dass Lukas den Vollzug der christlichen Taufe als Wassertaufe voraussetzt, was bei der Taufe des Äthiopiers in 8,36 sowie derjenigen der im Haus des Kornelius versammelten Heiden in 10,47f. deutlich wird, aber auch für die anderen Stellen vorauszusetzen ist, an denen Menschen durch die Taufe in die christliche Gemeinschaft aufgenommen werden.[17] Demgegenüber wird die Taufe der Apostel ausschließlich als Geisttaufe ohne Wasser beschrieben. Es handelt sich bei der Ausgießung des Geistes zu Pfingsten demnach um eine spezifische, auf die Apostel beschränkte[18] Form der Taufe durch den erhöhten Jesus.[19]

Dass Lukas dieses Geschehen mit dem Verbum βαπτίζεσθαι charakterisiert, könnte seinen Grund in der Gegenüberstellung von Wasser- und Geisttaufe in der in Act 1,5 aufgenommenen Überlieferung haben. Für das Taufverständnis der Act liegt darin jedoch eine darüber hinausgehende Bedeutung. Das zeigt sich bereits an dem schon genannten Rekurs auf dieses Wort des Auferstandenen in Act 11,16 sowie an der ausdrücklichen Gegenüberstellung von Johannestaufe und Taufe auf den Namen des Herrn Jesus in 19,1–7. Lukas kennzeichnet auf diese Weise die an den Auferstandenen und Erhöhten gebundene Taufe als

---

14 Vgl. E. HAENCHEN, *Die Apostelgeschichte*, 150, Anm. 4; C. K. BARRETT, *A Critical and Exegetical Commentary on the Acts of the Apostles*, 79.

15 Vgl. Act 3,12; 4;7.33; 6,8; 8,13; 19,11. Die δυνάμεις der Zeugen sind dabei Ausweis des Wirkens Gottes, der durch sie ebenso wirkt, wie er dies zuvor in der Geschichte Israels (7,36) und durch Jesus (2,22) getan hat.

16 Vgl. M. WOLTER, *Das Lukasevangelium*, 794.

17 Auffällig ist dies insbesondere bei den im Haus des Kornelius Getauften. In 10,47 erwähnt Petrus ausdrücklich das Wasser, mit dem die mit dem Geist begabten Heiden getauft werden sollen, in 11,16 stellt er dagegen zur Interpretation dieses Geschehens Wasser- und Geisttaufe ausdrücklich einander gegenüber. Die Wassertaufe als christlicher Ritus stellt hier demnach die logische Konsequenz des vorausgegangenen Geistempfangs dar.

18 Die Hellenisten werden in Act 6,6 durch Handauflegung eingesetzt, ohne dass eine Taufe oder Geistvermittlung genannt würde.

19 Vgl. 2,33: Der zur Rechten Gottes Erhöhte hat die ἐπαγγελία τοῦ πνεύματος τοῦ ἁγίου empfangen, um sie auf die Apostel auszugießen.

ein Geschehen, das mit der Geistmitteilung verbunden ist und deshalb die neue Qualität der Kirche in nachösterlicher Zeit bestimmt.

2.2. Taufe als Eintritt in die Gemeinschaft der Glaubenden: Die Grundlegung des Taufverständnisses in Act 2,37–41

Von der Geistausgießung auf die Apostel charakteristisch unterschieden ist die Darstellung derjenigen Taufen, die auf das Pfingstgeschehen und die anschließende Rede des Petrus folgen. Für den narrativen Kontext ist zunächst wichtig, dass sich diese Rede ausschließlich an jüdische Hörer aus jedem ἔθνος richtet.[20]

Die Rede des Petrus führt zur Frage der Zuhörer τί ποιήσωμεν, die eine Betroffenheit der Hörer durch die Petrusrede anzeigt (2,37). In der Antwort auf diese Frage wird ein von der Geistverleihung in 1,4–8 deutlich verschiedenes Taufverständnis entwickelt. Die Taufe wird nunmehr als regelrechter „Initiationsritus" dargestellt: Sie hat das μετανοεῖν zur Voraussetzung, die Sündenvergebung zum Inhalt und den Empfang des Heiligen Geistes zur Folge.[21] Dabei ist die individuell ausgerichtete Aufforderung zur Taufe (βαπτισθήτω ἕκαστος ὑμῶν) von dem allgemeinen, im Plural formulierten μετανοήσατε abgesetzt. Auf diese Weise wird die Aneignung der Botschaft des Petrus von der Auferweckung und Erhöhung Jesu als subjektiver Akt dargestellt, der durch die Taufe besiegelt wird.[22] Anders als bei der Ausgießung des Geistes auf die Apostel ist die Taufe hier demnach Bestandteil eines Bekehrungsvorgangs, der zur Aufnahme in die christliche Gemeinschaft führt. Dementsprechend wird dann auch die Aufnahme von etwa 3000 Menschen als Ergebnis dieses Geschehens geschildert (2,41).

---

20 Die Formulierungen, mit denen Lukas in 2,5.14 die beim Pfingstereignis Anwesenden beschreibt, sind nicht ganz eindeutig. Nach 2,5 scheint es sich um in Jerusalem ansässige Juden ἀπὸ παντὸς ἔθνους τῶν ὑπὸ τὸν οὐρανόν zu handeln, in der Völkerliste 2,9–11 ist dagegen von Juden und Proselyten und sogar Kretern und Arabern die Rede (2,11), die man sich kaum als in Jerusalem wohnende Juden vorstellen wird. Vielmehr scheint die Völkerliste darauf zu zielen, einen möglichst weiten Kreis von Gebieten und Völkerschaften aufzuzählen, aus denen Juden kommen, die zu Zeugen des Pfingstgeschehens werden. In 2,14 werden schließlich Juden und alle Einwohner Jerusalems nebeneinander aufgezählt, wobei nicht ganz deutlich ist, worin sich diese Gruppen unterscheiden, da ja nach 2,5 auch die Juden aus den anderen Völkern nunmehr Einwohner Jerusalems zu sein scheinen. Vgl. dazu D.-A. Koch, „Proselyten und Gottesfürchtige", 251–258. Die Intention des Lukas dürfte darin bestehen, das weltweite Judentum als Zeugen des Pfingstgeschehens darzustellen. Das wird nicht zuletzt durch die Wendung πᾶσιν τοῖς εἰς μακράν in 2,39 nahegelegt, die den Adressatenkreis über die Anwesenden hinaus räumlich und zeitlich ausdehnt.

21 Der Satz dürfte so aufzufassen sein, dass μετανοήσατε καὶ βαπτισθήτω ἕκαστος ὑμῶν als aufeinander folgende, unmittelbar zusammenhängende Vorgänge vorgestellt sind. Die εἰς-Formulierung beschreibt die unmittelbare Wirkung der Taufe, wogegen das zweite καί konsekutiv aufzufassen ist und den Geistempfang als Folge der Taufe beschreibt. Vgl. BDR § 442,2 zum καί consecutivum.

22 Dem entspricht dann auch 2,41: οἱ μὲν οὖν ἀποδεξάμενοι τὸν λόγον αὐτοῦ ἐβαπτίσθησαν.

Die Gabe des heiligen Geistes als Folge der Taufe ist von deren unmittelbarer Wirkung, nämlich der Sündenvergebung, unterschieden. Das wird damit begründet, dass die ἐπαγγελία den hier Versammelten, ihren Kindern und allen εἰς μακράν gelte (2,39). Die ἐπαγγελία ist demnach nicht auf die Gabe des Geistes beschränkt.[23] Vielmehr wird mit der Formulierung ὅσους ἂν προσκαλέσηται κύριος ὁ θεὸς ἡμῶν auf die Formulierung οὓς κύριος προσκέκληται in Joel 3,5b angespielt, die Fortsetzung des von Petrus in 2,17–21 angeführten Zitates.

Mit der Wendung ἐπὶ τῷ ὀνόματι Ἰησοῦ Χριστοῦ εἰς ἄφεσιν τῶν ἁμαρτιῶν ὑμῶν wird die Taufe inhaltlich charakterisiert. Mit der finalen εἰς-Wendung wird das Ziel der Taufe angegeben: Sie befreit von Sünden und begründet damit ein neues Gottesverhältnis. Die präpositionale Wendung ἐπὶ τῷ ὀνόματι ist dagegen eine derjenigen Formulierungen, mit denen Lukas die Taufe zu Jesus Christus in Beziehung setzt. Innerhalb der Act steht sie in Korrespondenz zu ἐν τῷ ὀνόματι (10,48) sowie zu εἰς τὸ ὄνομα in 8,16 und 19,5. Wie der semantische Gehalt dieser Wendungen und ihr Verhältnis zueinander zu bestimmen ist, wird seit langem diskutiert.

Exkurs: Zur Bedeutung der präpositionalen Taufformulierungen

Für die inhaltliche Bestimmung der christlichen Taufe spielen die präpositionalen Wendungen, mit denen sie zu Jesus Christus bzw. zu seinem Namen in Beziehung gesetzt wird, eine wichtige Rolle. Wilhelm Heitmüller hatte die Diskussion über diese Wendungen und die darin möglicherweise zum Ausdruck kommenden Taufverständnisse seinerzeit durch eine von der Perspektive der Religionsgeschichtlichen Schule auf das Urchristentum inspirierte Untersuchung angestoßen.[24] Er führte die Wendungen auf unterschiedliche religionsgeschichtliche Ursprünge zurück und sah darin das Gegenüber eines semitisch-jüdisch geprägten und eines pagan-hellenistisch beeinflussten Bereichs der urchristlichen Theologiegeschichte. Die ἐπί- bzw. ἐν-Wendungen hätten demnach ihren Hintergrund in semitisch geprägten griechischen Formulierungen und seien auf entsprechende hebräische Formulierungen (לשם bzw. בשם) zurückzuführen. Sie würden den Vorgang der Taufe beschreiben, die unter Nennung des Namens Jesu vollzogen worden sei. Inhaltlich käme darin der Glaube an die numinose Kraft göttlicher Namen zum Ausdruck, durch deren Anrufung man Dämonen vertreibt und Geister bezwingt. In dieser Weise sei auch die jüdische Auffassung über den Namen Gottes aufzufassen, dessen Aussprechen oder Schreiben besondere Kräfte verleihe.[25] Die εἰς τὸ ὄνομα-Wendungen, die in der LXX und auch in der literarischen Profangräzität (fast) völlig fehlen,[26] entstammten dagegen

---

23 Vgl. C. K. Barrett, *Acts*, 155; J. Roloff, *Die Apostelgeschichte*, 63.
24 Vgl. W. Heitmüller, *„Im Namen Jesu"*.
25 So Heitmüllers religionsgeschichtliche Herleitung, a.a.O., 128–222.
26 Ausnahmen sind die nicht zur Übersetzungsliteratur gehörigen Stellen 2 Makk 8,4; 3 Makk 2,9, sowie im paganen Bereich Herodian, II 2,10; 13,2. Vgl. Heitmüller, *„Im Namen Jesu"*, 111 bzw. 101.

der hellenistischen Umgangssprache und bezeichneten die Übereignung von Geld oder Besitz.[27] In den Taufwendungen würden sie entsprechend nicht den Vorgang beschreiben, sondern dessen Zweck bzw. Erfolg angeben, nämlich dass der Täufling „in das Verhältnis der Zugehörigkeit, des Eigentums zu Jesus tritt".[28] Diese Bedeutung von εἰς τὸ ὄνομα in der Profangräzität hatte zuvor bereits Adolf Deißmann in zwei kurzen Abschnitten herausgestellt, auf die Heitmüller ausdrücklich hinweist.[29]

Ob diese strikte Differenzierung religionsgeschichtlicher Kontexte im Blick auf die präpositionalen Taufwendungen tragfähig ist, wurde allerdings schon bald zweifelhaft. Problematisch ist bereits, dass Heitmüller seine These über die jüdische Auffassung von der numinosen, exorzistischen Wirkung des Gottesnamens im Wesentlichen aus späteren, rabbinischen Texten gewinnt und mit Hilfe babylonischer, persischer und mandäischer Analogien einem synkretistischen Milieu zuordnet, das auch für die entsprechenden Taufformeln vorauszusetzen und entsprechend von den εἰς τὸ ὄνομα-Formulierungen abzugrenzen sei.[30] Diese These lässt sich jedoch angesichts der neutestamentlichen Texte schwer durchhalten. So hatte bereits Heitmüller selbst die Wendung εἰς τὸ ἐμὸν ὄνομα in Mt 18,20 sowie die Entsprechungen in 10,41f.[31] auf hebräisches לשם zurückgeführt und darin eine semitische Entsprechung zu den εἰς τὸ ὄνομα-Formulierungen gesehen.[32] Diese Wendung begegnet innerhalb des MtEv jedoch neben der auf die Taufe bezogenen εἰς τὸ ὄνομα-Formulierung in 28,19,[33] was einen strikten Bedeutungsunterschied, der auf unterschiedliche sprachliche und kulturelle Milieus zurückzuführen sei, unwahrscheinlich macht. Des Weiteren begegnen in I Kor 1,13.15 εἰς τὸ ὄνομα und εἰς τὸ ἐμὸν ὄνομα unmittelbar hintereinander, wobei die zweite Formulierung eine Variation der ersten darstellt. Damit ist fraglich, ob sich mit den genannten Wendungen tatsächlich verschiedene Taufverständnisse (Anrufung des Namens in exorzistischer Absicht bzw. Übereignung des Täuflings an Jesus) verbinden, die sich einem semitischen bzw. einem hellenistischen Milieu zuweisen ließen. Schwierigkeiten bereitet schließlich auch die These, die Verwendung von εἰς τὸ ὄνομα in der Geschäftssprache sei zugleich der für die entsprechende Taufformel maßgebliche Vorstellungshorizont.[34]

---

27 Das Material ist zusammengestellt bei HEITMÜLLER, „Im Namen Jesu", 102–109.

28 HEITMÜLLER, „Im Namen Jesu", 127.

29 A. DEISSMANN, Bibelstudien, 143–145; IDEM, Neue Bibelstudien, 25f. Vgl. auch IDEM, Licht vom Osten, 97f. Deißmann zufolge handelt es sich um eine „in der hellenistischen Welt ganz geläufige Rechtsformel". Vgl. den Hinweis auf Deißmann bei HEITMÜLLER, „Im Namen Jesu", 101, Anm. 4.

30 Heitmüller sieht dies sehr wohl, hält dem aber entgegen, es handle sich um eine „zu allen Zeiten" und „bei allen Völkern" verbreitete Vorstellung, die er dem Bereich „des Aberglaubens und der Zauberei" zuweist. Vgl. a.a.O., 147.

31 εἰς ὄνομα προφήτου bzw. εἰς ὄνομα μαθητοῦ.

32 HEITMÜLLER, „Im Namen Jesu", 112f.

33 Vgl. Did 7,1.3, wo εἰς τὸ ὄνομα und εἰς ὄνομα als synonyme Formulierungen unmittelbar hintereinander in einem Taufkontext begegnen.

34 Vgl. G. DELLING, Die Zueignung des Heils in der Taufe, 31–34; L. HARTMAN, „Into the Name of Jesus", 433.

Eine Alternative zu dieser Unterscheidung religionsgeschichtlicher Bereiche war die Herleitung der εἰς τὸ ὄνομα-Wendung aus dem semitisch geprägten Griechisch. So vermerkt Paul Billerbeck im ersten Band seines großen Kommentars zu Mt 10,41 und 28,19, die Wendungen εἰς ὄνομα προφήτου sowie εἰς τὸ ὄνομα seien gleichermaßen als Entsprechungen zu לשׁם aufzufassen.[35] Diese Interpretation wurde dann auch von Hans Bietenhard in seinem ὄνομα-Artikel für das Theologische Wörterbuch vertreten.[36] Die Taufformel sei demnach als Übersetzungsgriechisch aufzufassen, die ein finales Moment zur Geltung bringe und darin von der ebenfalls semitisch gefärbten, jedoch kausal zu deutenden Formulierung in Mt 18,20 (10,41f.) unterschieden sei. Mit der Herkunft aus dem Giroverkehr lasse sie sich dagegen nur schwer vereinbaren, da es in der Taufe um die Zueignung gehe, jedoch nicht um die Vorstellung einer Einschreibung.

In einer eingehenden Untersuchung der Wendung „taufen auf den Namen" erklärte Gerhard Delling sodann die neutestamentlichen Kontexte selbst zum maßgeblichen Kriterium der inhaltlichen Bestimmung der Formel.[37] Delling analysiert zunächst den Hintergrund der Wendung „auf den (im) Namen" in der LXX und in außerbiblischen jüdischen Schriften, ihren sachlichen Hintergrund im Neuen Testament und angrenzenden Schriften sowie schließlich „Form und Inhalt der neutestamentlichen Wendung ‚taufen auf den (im) Namen'". Sein Fazit lautet: Indem die Taufe im Urchristentum auf den bzw. im Namen Jesu Christi erfolgt, fügt sie den Getauften in das an diesen Namen gebundene Heilsgeschehen ein. Ableitungen aus der LXX sowie aus dem pagan-hellenistischen Bereich seien deshalb unzureichend, um das Spezifikum des christlichen Taufvorgangs zu erfassen. Dieses ergebe sich vielmehr erst aus dem jeweiligen Kontext der neutestamentlichen Wendung selbst.[38]

Im Blick auf die Act stellt Delling die Verbindung zu anderen Aussagen über den Namen Jesu und Handlungen, die in diesem Namen geschehen, heraus.[39] Der Name Jesu bzw. des Herrn wird auch im Zusammenhang des Redens, also der Verkündigung (4,18; 5,40; 9,27f.), des machtvollen Wirkens von Zeichen und Wundern (4,30) sowie von Heilungen und Exorzismen (3,6; 4,10; 16,18) verwendet. Die mit verschiedenen Präpositionen verbundenen Taufaussagen erklärten sich vor diesem Hintergrund. Mit ihnen würde „die Heilswirklichkeit, die sich mit diesem Namen verbindet, in einer Sigle zusammengefaßt".[40]

Lars Hartman legte in seiner Untersuchung sodann die Bedeutungsbreite der Formulierung im Hebräischen dar, als deren gemeinsamen Nenner er „die Kategorie, die Absicht, ja die grundlegende Beziehung eines Ritus" bestimmt.[41] Auch wenn der in der pagan-hellenistischen Verwendung enthaltene Gedanke der

---

35   H. L. STRACK/P. BILLERBECK, *Das Evangelium nach Matthäus*, 590f. 1054f.
36   H. BIETENHARD, „ὄνομα κτλ.", hier 274f.
37   G. DELLING, *Die Zueignung des Heils in der Taufe*.
38   A.a.O., 97.
39   A.a.O., 83–94. Vgl. auch IDEM, *Die Taufe im Neuen Testament*, 58–74.
40   A.a.O., 89.
41   HARTMAN, "Into the Name of Jesus"; IDEM, *"Into the Name of the Lord Jesus"*, 37–50; IDEM, „ὄνομα", hier 1276.

Übereignung nicht ausgeschlossen zu werden brauche[42], gehe die Verwendung in der Taufformel kaum darin auf. Die Nennung des Jesusnamens könne zu einem wesentlichen Teil darauf zurückzuführen sein, dass die christliche Taufe auf diese Weise von der Johannestaufe unterschieden werden sollte.

Das legt auch die Verwendung an den neutestamentlichen Stellen nahe. Die triadische εἰς τὸ ὄνομα-Wendung in Mt 28,19 beschreibt nicht nur die neue Zugehörigkeit, sondern – wie die umliegenden Verbalausdrücke μαθητεύσατε und διδάσκοντες zeigen – auch den Taufvorgang selbst, der demnach die Ausrufung des dreifachen Namens über dem Täufling beinhaltete.[43] In I Kor 1,13 begegnet die εἰς τὸ ὄνομα -Wendung ebenfalls im Zusammenhang der Taufe, obwohl Paulus nur negativ sagt, die Korinther seien nicht εἰς τὸ ὄνομα Παύλου getauft. Auch hier macht der Kontext deutlich, dass die Formulierung nicht auf den Übereignungsaspekt einzugrenzen ist, sondern den inhaltlichen Bezug des Taufgeschehens insgesamt beschreibt. Sowohl der vorausgehende Hinweis, Paulus sei nicht für die Korinther gekreuzigt worden, als auch die von Paulus herausgestellte Unmöglichkeit der Taufe auf den Namen eines Menschen zeigen, dass die Taufe eine umfassende Einbeziehung in das durch Christus bewirkte Heil darstellt.[44]

Die Verwendung bei Lukas bestätigt diesen Befund. Mit den ἐπί- bzw. ἐν-Wendungen in 2,38 und 10,48 greift er auf den Sprachgebrauch der LXX zurück, die εἰς τὸ ὄνομα τοῦ κυρίου Ἰησοῦ-Wendungen in 8,16 und 19,5 nehmen dagegen eine geprägte Formel des Urchristentums auf. Wesentliche inhaltliche Unterschiede sind damit kaum verbunden.[45] Lukas kommt es vor allem darauf an, die Taufe durch den Namen Jesu Christi zu qualifizieren, zwischen den Präpositionen bestehen dabei allenfalls Bedeutungsnuancen.[46] Für die jeweilige Verwendung könnte das sprachliche Kolorit ausschlaggebend sein: Die mit Petrus verbundenen Taufen in Jerusalem und Cäsarea sind an LXX-Wendungen orientiert, die das hebräische לשׁם bzw. בשׁם wiedergeben, die Taufen durch Philippus in Samaria und Paulus in Ephesus werden dagegen mit der εἰς τὸ ὄνομα-Wendung ausgedrückt, die den urchristlichen Taufritus beschreibt.[47]

Von dem Sonderfall des Pfingstgeschehens abgesehen, kann für die Schilderung der ersten Taufen in der Act demnach festgehalten werden: Lukas bindet die Taufe in ein umfassenderes Geschehen ein, das die Bekehrung aufgrund der

---

42 Vgl. G. BARTH, Die Taufe in frühchristlicher Zeit, 75–78.
43 Vgl. auch Did 7,13; Herm vis III 7,3; Jak 2,7: τὸ καλὸν ὄνομα τὸ ἐπικληθὲν ἐφ᾽ ὑμᾶς, sowie die Beschreibung des Taufritus in TA 21.
44 Vgl. CHR. WOLFF, Der erste Brief des Paulus an die Korinther, 30; H. MERKLEIN, Der erste Brief an die Korinther, 163.
45 Das zeigen auch diejenigen Wendungen, in denen andere Präpositionen wie ὑπέρ (9,16; 15,26; 21,13) und διά (4,30; 10,43) mit einer ὄνομα -Formulierung verbunden sind. Die Namensformeln sind zudem nicht auf die Taufe beschränkt, sondern können sich auch auf Reden, Lehren, Heilen oder Leiden beziehen. Dies deutet darauf hin, dass mit dem ὄνομα κυρίου Ἰησοῦ Χριστοῦ ein durch Jesus Christus qualifizierter Bereich gekennzeichnet ist.
46 So auch BARRETT, Acts, 154.
47 Zu einem ähnlichen Ergebnis kommt AVEMARIE, Tauferzählungen, 26–43.

Christusverkündigung zur Voraussetzung und die Sündenvergebung zum Ziel hat und Anteil an der Verheißung Gottes gibt, wie sie sich in den prophetischen Schriften Israels findet. Wie sich die Taufe konkret vollzieht, wird dabei nicht geschildert. Darüber geben jedoch andere Stellen näheren Aufschluss.

2.3. Taufe auf den Namen Jesu, Johannestaufe und Geistverleihung: Act 8,4–25 und 19,1–7

Weitere Charakteristika des lk Taufverständnisses lassen sich der Erzählung über die Ausbreitung der Christusbotschaft nach Samarien entnehmen. Lukas hat hier offenbar Überlieferungen über die Samarienmission des Urchristentums, bei der Philippus eine herausragende Rolle spielte, eine an dem Magier Simon Magus haftende Personaltradition, möglicherweise auch eine Überlieferung vom Auftreten des Petrus (und Johannes) in Samarien verarbeitet.[48] Deutlich ist dabei, dass er dem jetzt vorliegenden Gesamtzusammenhang sein eigenes sprachliches und inhaltliches Gepräge verliehen hat. Im Blick auf die Taufthematik treten dabei folgende Aspekte in den Blick.

Wie bereits in 2,37–41 wird die Taufe auch hier als Folge der Annahme der Christusverkündigung – in diesem Fall des Philippus – dargestellt. Deren Inhalt wird nicht eigens geschildert – Philippus gehört also nicht zu den „Rednern" in der Act – sondern mit der Formulierung κηρύσσειν τὸν Χριστόν (8,5) bzw. εὐαγγελίζεσθαι περὶ τῆς βασιλείας τοῦ θεοῦ καὶ τοῦ ὀνόματος Ἰησοῦ Χριστοῦ (8,12) summarisch bezeichnet.[49] Daneben wird Philippus ausdrücklich als Vollbringer staunenswerter σημεῖα καὶ δυνάμεις dargestellt (8,6.13).

Auffälligstes Merkmal der Erzählung ist zweifellos, dass die Taufe des Philippus nachträglich durch die Geistvermittlung ergänzt werden muss, die die Jerusalemer Apostel durch Gebet und Handauflegung vollziehen. Das ist um so bemerkenswerter, als 8,16 zufolge die Taufe des Philippus ausdrücklich als eine solche εἰς τὸ ὄνομα τοῦ κυρίου Ἰησοῦ bezeichnet wird. Geradezu im Gegensatz zu 19,5f., wo die Charakterisierung der Taufe mit der gleichen Wendung dazu dient, das „Defizit" der Johannestaufe zu beheben, da mit der Taufe auf den Namen Jesu Handauflegung und Geistverleihung unmittelbar verbunden sind, treten in 8,15–17 Taufe auf den Namen des Herrn Jesus und Geistempfang durch Handauflegung personal und zeitlich auseinander.

---

[48] Die genaue Gestalt dieser vorlk Überlieferungen ist freilich umstritten. Denkbar ist zudem auch, dass Lukas die Episode vom Kommen des Petrus und Johannes nach Samarien selbst ergänzt hat, um dadurch die Philippusmission seinem Konzept von der Ausbreitung der Christusbotschaft einzufügen. Vgl. zur Diskussion der verschiedenen Vorschläge AVEMARIE, *Tauferzählungen*, 233–243.

[49] Vgl. auch 8,35; 5,42; 11,20; 17,18. Lukas kann mit diesen Formulierungen die Christusverkündigung der Zeugen insgesamt bezeichnen. Χριστός (Ἰησοῦς) steht dabei als direktes Objekt zu den Verben des Verkündigens und fasst deren Inhalt zusammen.

Daraus lässt sich entnehmen, dass für Lukas Taufe und Geistempfang zwei Ereignisse darstellen, die zwar zusammenfallen können, dabei aber gleichwohl ihre Eigenständigkeit behalten. Sieht man von dem Sonderfall in 1,4–8 ab, stellte auch bereits in 2,38 der Geistempfang einen selbständigen Akt dar, der auf die mit der Sündenvergebung verbundene Taufe folgt. In 8,15–17 und 19,5f. wird die Geistverleihung mit der Handauflegung verbunden und dadurch ebenfalls vom Akt der Taufe selbst unterschieden. Lukas kennt demnach den urchristlichen Ritus der Handauflegung, den er mit dem Geistempfang verbinden kann, der daran allerdings nicht notwendig gebunden ist.[50] Die Taufe ist dagegen derjenige Ritus, der mit Umkehr, Annahme der Christusbotschaft und Sündenvergebung verbunden ist und in die Christusgemeinschaft aufnimmt, der zudem mit der Geistverleihung in einem engen Zusammenhang steht, die von der Taufe jedoch als eigenständiger Akt unterschieden bleibt.

Dieser Befund wird durch die Episode über die Taufe der Johannesjünger (19,1–7) bestätigt. Der Grund für die ausdrückliche Bindung des Geistes an die Handauflegung des Paulus ist dabei unschwer zu erkennen. Wie bereits in 1,5 und 11,16 deutlich wurde, ist die Johannestaufe darin defizitär, dass sie als Wassertaufe ohne Geist auf die vorösterliche Zeit beschränkt war, wogegen die Aufnahme in die christliche Gemeinschaft an die Taufe auf den Namen Jesu und den durch den Erhöhten ausgegossenen Geist gebunden ist. Die Johannestaufe, die Lukas als vorösterliche Umkehrtaufe zur Vergebung der Sünden durchaus anerkennt[51], ist für die erst nachösterlich mögliche Aufnahme in die Gemeinschaft der Glaubenden unzureichend und muss darum durch die an den Namen Jesu gebundene Taufe ersetzt bzw. ergänzt werden. Wie 2,38 zeigt, geht dabei auch die Funktion der Sündenvergebung an die Taufe auf den Namen Jesu über. Bei den Johannesjüngern, die diese bereits bei ihrer ersten Taufe erhalten haben, kann die Wirkung dagegen auf den Geistempfang beschränkt werden. Was immer historisch hinter der Episode über die ephesinischen Johannesjünger stehen mag[52], deutlich ist, dass Lukas hier den Zusammenhang

---

50 In Act 6,6 wird der Kreis der Sieben durch Handauflegung eingesetzt, in 28,8 heilt Paulus durch Handauflegung einen Kranken.

51 Vgl. Lk 3,3.

52 Nach E. KÄSEMANN verbergen sich dahinter Johannesjünger, die Lukas zu „Christen im embryonalen Zustand" erhoben habe. Vgl. IDEM, „Die Johannesjünger zu Ephesus", 167. H. v. CAMPENHAUSEN sah dagegen in Apollos und den ephesinischen Christen „Zeugen einer ersten Ausbreitungswelle des Christentums, in der die Christentaufe und die Johannestaufe noch als identisch galten". Vgl. IDEM, „Taufen auf den Namen Jesu?", 206. Ein weiterer Vorschlag lautet, Lukas habe in Apollos wie den Johannesjüngern eine „Vorstufe der christlichen Gemeinde" gesehen, was aber historisch unzutreffend sei, weil es sich tatsächlich um einen jüdischen Schriftgelehrten und eine Gruppe von Johannesjüngern gehandelt habe, die von Lukas im Sinne der heilsgeschichtlichen Kontinuität in einem „Übergangsstadium zwischen Judentum und Christentum" angesiedelt worden seien. Vgl. SCHWEIZER, „Die Bekehrung des Apollos", 79. M. WOLTER sieht die Intention des lk Berichtes von Act 18,24–19,7 dagegen in der Klärung des Verhältnisses von Paulus und Apollos. Im Blick auf die Johannesjünger ergibt sich für ihn

von Handauflegung, Geistmitteilung und Taufe thematisiert und damit den Unterschied der Taufe auf den Namen Jesu zur Johannestaufe narrativ ausgestaltet. Dies wird durch das Johanneswort über den nach ihm Kommenden, mit dem er die Bedeutung seiner Umkehrtaufe selbst begrenzt und auf das in 19,4 angespielt wird, deutlich.[53]

Dass der Philippustaufe die Geistvermittlung mangelt, ist dagegen schwieriger zu erklären. Die von Philippus gespendete Taufe erfolgt auf den Namen des Herrn Jesus und ist als solche zweifellos eine „legitime" christliche Taufe. Dass sie nicht den Geist vermittelt, hängt offenbar damit zusammen, dass Lukas von den Hellenisten ein eigenes Profil zeichnet, das sich sowohl von demjenigen der Apostel als auch von Paulus unterscheidet.[54] Die Hellenisten werden einerseits als Männer πλήρεις πνεύματος καὶ σοφίας (Act 6,3) dargestellt, was anhand der geisterfüllten Rede des Stephanus konkretisiert wird.[55] Sie sind jedoch nicht in das an die Apostel gebundene Geschehen der Weitergabe des Geistes eingebunden. Dass sich darin die Kenntnis einer Taufpraxis ohne Geistvermittlung spiegelt[56], wird vor allem anhand der noch zu besprechenden Episode der Taufe des Äthiopiers wahrscheinlich. Für die vorliegende Erzählung ist indes entscheidend, dass christliche Taufe und Geistempfang zusammengehören, auch wenn sie zeitlich auseinander treten können.

Das komplexe Verhältnis von Taufe und Geistempfang lässt sich demnach folgendermaßen zusammenfassen. Lukas liegt zum einen daran, die Wassertaufe des Johannes und die Taufe ἐν πνεύματι ἁγίῳ einander gegenüberzustellen. Das zeigt sich bereits daran, dass er die in 1,5 erwähnte Begrenztheit der Johannestaufe an zwei entscheidenden Stellen – nämlich zur Interpretation des Pfingstereignisses sowie bezüglich der Öffnung des Gottesvolkes für die Heiden – wieder aufnimmt. Auch die explizite Begrenzung seiner Taufe durch Johannes selbst in 19,4 gehört in diesen Kontext. Zum anderen wird der Inhalt der Taufe vom Pfingstereignis her entwickelt und bestimmt auch diejenige Taufe, die selbst den Geist noch nicht vermittelt.

Dieser Befund lässt sich am besten so erklären, dass Lukas die ihm bekannte Taufpraxis des Urchristentums mit Hilfe seiner Konzeption vom Wirken

---

daraus, dass „die Erzählung von der Belehrung und Taufe der Johannesjünger durch Paulus insgesamt eine lukanische Konstruktion ist", mit der Lukas die Dominanz von Paulus über Apollos zum Ausdruck bringe. Vgl. IDEM, „Apollos und die Johannesjünger von Ephesus (Apg 18,24–19,7)", 421.

53   In Lk 3,16 verweist Johannes auf die Taufe mit Geist und Feuer durch den kommenden Stärkeren, was in 19,4 auf Jesus bezogen wird, an den man glauben soll.

54   Zu den sogenannten „Hellenisten" vgl. jetzt die Monographie von M. ZUGMANN, „Hellenisten" in der Apostelgeschichte. Grundlegend auch M. HENGEL, „Zwischen Jesus und Paulus".

55   Vgl. 6,5.10; 7,55.

56   So etwa ROLOFF, Apostelgeschichte, 142.

des Geistes Gottes interpretierte. Für letztere ist kennzeichnend, dass der Geist diejenige Größe ist, durch die Gott die Geschichte lenkt, Menschen zum Zeugnis befähigt und durch die Christusverkündigung die Gestalt des Gottesvolkes aus Juden und Heiden schafft. Die lukanische Sicht auf das Wirken des Geistes Gottes ist demnach umfassender als diejenige auf die Taufe, was auch die unterschiedlichen Zuordnungen von Taufe und Geistempfang erklärt. Tragend dabei ist die Vorstellung, dass Menschen durch Taufe und Geistempfang in das Gottesvolk aufgenommen werden. Dies ist an das Wirken des erhöhten Herrn, die Apostel bzw. Paulus gebunden. Wird der Geist dagegen nachträglich verliehen, wie in Samarien und bei den Johannesjüngern, so erklärt sich dies daraus, dass hier offenbar eigene urchristliche Tauftraditionen vorliegen, die nunmehr in die an der Taufe auf den Namen Jesu orientierte Geisttaufe integriert werden.

2.4. Taufe als Öffnung des Gottesvolkes für die Heiden: Act 10,1–11,18

Die Erzählung über die Taufe der im Haus des Kornelius Versammelten erweist sich schon durch ihre ausführliche Gestaltung sowie durch die Wiederholung im unmittelbar anschließenden Bericht des Petrus als für den Erzählverlauf der Act überaus bedeutsames Geschehen.[57] In ihrem Zentrum steht die Öffnung des Gottesvolkes für die Heiden, die durch Gott selbst ins Werk gesetzt wird, der dazu den Widerstand des toratreuen Petrus überwindet und ihm mit Hilfe einer Vision die Aufhebung der Trennung reiner und unreiner Speisen kundtut.

Kennzeichnend für die lukanische Geschichtstheologie ist dabei, dass – sehen wir von dem Sonderfall des äthiopischen Beamten vorläufig ab – die erste Bekehrung eines Nichtjuden diejenige eines Römers ist, der als εὐσεβὴς καὶ φοβούμενος τὸν θεόν σὺν παντὶ τῷ οἴκῳ αὐτοῦ (10,2) charakterisiert wird. Er gehört demnach zu denjenigen Heiden, die dem Judentum zugeneigt sind und den Gott Israels anerkennen. Dieses Phänomen lässt sich, wie in zahlreichen Untersuchungen herausgestellt wurde, auch historisch konkretisieren.[58] Für

---

57 Zur Analyse des Textes aus narratologischer Perspektive vgl. W. S. Kurz, „Effects of Variant Narrators in Acts 10–11".

58 Die Diskussion über heidnische Sympathisanten mit dem Judentum und die sogenannten „Gottesfürchtigen" kann sich vornehmlich auf Notizen bei paganen griechischen und römischen Autoren (Epiktet, Seneca, Horaz, Juvenal, Petronius), einige Bemerkungen bei Josephus über Heiden, die er als σεβόμενοι τὸν θεόν bzw. als θεοσεβής (so die Charakterisierung der Gattin Neros Poppaea Sabina in Ant. 20,195) beschreibt, die bekannte, in ihrer Bedeutung jedoch nicht ganz eindeutige Theaterinschrift von Milet, die ΤΟΠΟΣ ΕΙΟΥΔΕΩΝ ΤΩΝ ΚΑΙ ΘΕΟΣΕΒΙΟΝ lautet (vgl. Deissmann, Licht, 391f.) sowie die (in der Datierung umstrittenen) Inschriften von Aphrodisias stützen. Zu letzteren vgl. die Analyse von Koch, „The God-fearers between facts and fiction". Zum Phänomen insgesamt vgl. I. Levinskaya, The Book of Acts in Its Diaspora Setting; B. Wander, Gottesfürchtige und Sympathisanten sowie die bereits ältere, jedoch überaus instruktive Studie von F. Siegert, „Gottesfürchtige und Sympathisanten". Insgesamt ergibt sich daraus das Bild einer Attraktivität des Diasporajudentums für das nicht-jüdische Umfeld, die zu verschiedenen Formen der Annäherung (Affinität zum monotheistischen Glau-

die lk Geschichtsdarstellung gewinnen diese Heiden besondere Bedeutung.[59] Sie werden von Lukas in der Weise beschrieben, dass ihre Gottesfurcht und Frömmigkeit die Voraussetzung für die Annahme der christlichen Verkündigung darstellen. Damit stehen sie in gewisser Weise am Übergang zur heidenchristlichen Kirche: Sie glauben an den Gott Israels und öffnen sich zugleich der Einsicht, dass dieser durch das Wirken, Auferweckung und Erhöhung Jesu Christi in neuer Weise gehandelt hat. Darin unterscheiden sie sich von denjenigen Juden, die letzteres gerade zurückweisen und sich dadurch als von Gott verstockt erweisen.[60]

Innerhalb der Kornelius-Episode wirkt sich dies so aus, dass Petrus anhand seiner Vision erkennt, dass Gott fürchten und Tun der Gerechtigkeit jeden Menschen, unabhängig davon, aus welchem ἔθνος er stammt, vor Gott angenehm macht (10,35). Das φοβεῖσθαι τὸν θεόν wird damit, gemeinsam mit dem Tun der Gerechtigkeit, zum allgemeinen Kriterium für die Zugehörigkeit zu Gott.

Damit ist zugleich die Voraussetzung für die Aufnahme der gottesfürchtigen Heiden im Haus des Kornelius ins Gottesvolk gegeben. Diese vollzieht sich so, dass der Geist während der Rede des Petrus auf diese herabfällt[61], wodurch die Verkündigung der Christusbotschaft und die Aufnahme ins Gottesvolk unmittelbar zusammenfallen.

Das eigentliche Taufgeschehen[62] ergänzt gegenüber demjenigen im Zusammenhang des Pfingstereignisses vor allem zwei Aspekte: Zum einen wird

---

ben, Teilnahme am Synagogengottesdienst, Sabbatbeachtung, Einhaltung von Speisevorschriften) führen konnte, ohne dass damit ein Übertritt zum Judentum verbunden war. Vgl. dazu S. COHEN, „Crossing the Boundary and Becoming a Jew". Die – aus jüdischer Sicht heidnischen – Sympathisanten oder Gottesfürchtigen stellen jedoch keinesfalls eine fest umrissene Gruppe dar, die zwischen Judentum und heidnischer Religiosität stehen würde. In eine solche Position werden sie allenfalls durch polemische Äußerungen paganer Autoren gerückt, die in deren Verhalten eine Gefahr für die Aufrechterhaltung des mos maiorum sehen. Vgl. dazu D. SÄNGER, „Heiden – Juden – Christen. Erwägungen zu einem Aspekt frühchristlicher Missionsgeschichte", 185–212.

59 Vgl. J. G. GAGER, „Jews, Gentiles, and Synagogues in the Book of Acts"; M. C. DE BOER, „God-Fearers in Luke-Acts".

60 Auch für Lukas sind diese φοβούμενοι bzw. σεβόμενοι τὸν θεόν also Heiden, die dem Glauben an den Gott Israels bereits zugeneigt sind. Auf keinen Fall handelt es sich für ihn dagegen um „semi-Jews", die von „full Gentiles" zu unterscheiden wären (so jedoch J. JERVELL, „The Church of Jews and Godfearers", 11–20.138–140). Sie repräsentieren für Lukas vielmehr einen Typ von Heiden, der die entscheidende Voraussetzung für die Annahme der Christusbotschaft – den Glauben an den Gott Israels – bereits mitbringt.

61 Nach 10,44 ereignet sich die Geistausgießung ἔτι λαλοῦντος τοῦ Πέτρου. In 11,15 heißt es etwas abweichend ἐν δὲ τῷ ἄρξασθαί με λαλεῖν κτλ. Deutlich ist in beiden Fällen, dass die Rede des Petrus und die Geistausgießung unmittelbar zusammenfallen.

62 Die Taufe geschieht 10,48 zufolge ἐν τῷ ὀνόματι Ἰησοῦ Χριστοῦ. Zur Bedeutung der präpositionalen Wendungen vgl. den Exkurs oben unter § 2.2.

die Taufe mit Wasser ausdrücklich erwähnt[63], zum anderen wird das Reden in Zungen (nicht: in Fremdsprachen, wie in 2,4) als Wirkung des Taufgeistes herausgestellt.[64] Die Zuordnung von Geistempfang und Taufe gestaltet sich zudem etwas anders als in 2,38: Wird dort der Empfang des Geistes als Folge der Taufe dargestellt, so erfolgt er hier bereits während der Petrusrede und wird im Anschluss durch die Taufe besiegelt.

Die Bedeutung des Ereignisses wird durch die (rhetorische) Frage des Petrus, ob irgendjemand oder er selbst es hindern könne, dass die mit dem Geist beschenkten Heiden getauft werden, hervorgehoben.[65] Des Weiteren wird sie durch zwei Bemerkungen herausgestellt, in denen Lukas an späterer Stelle darauf rekurriert: In 11,16f. wird das Geschehen ausdrücklich auf dieselbe Stufe wie das Pfingstgeschehen gestellt[66], auf dem Apostelkonzil stellt es die Begründung dafür dar, dass den Heiden keine Forderungen außer den vier von Jakobus genannten Bedingungen auferlegt werden (15,7–11.14). Damit ist deutlich, dass es sich innerhalb der lk Geschichtsdarstellung um eine für die Konstitution des Gottesvolkes grundlegende Begebenheit handelt, die das Pfingstgeschehen in eine neue Dimension stellt: Die dort innerhalb des Judentums verbleibende Geistausgießung wird nunmehr dahingehend erweitert, dass sie Menschen aus jedem ἔθνος zugedacht ist, die die in 10,35 formulierten Voraussetzungen erfüllen.

3. Die Taufe des Äthiopiers und des Saulus als individuelle „Sonderfälle"

3.1. Taufe ohne Geist: Der äthiopische Eunuch

Die Taufe des äthiopischen Eunuchen erweist sich im Rahmen der lk Geschichtstheologie als die am schwierigsten einzuordnende Tauferzählung.[67] Sie schließt in 8,26–40 als zweite Episode über das Wirken des Philippus unmittelbar an die oben besprochene Samarienepisode an. Sowohl dieser gegenüber als auch im

---

63   Bei der Taufe des Äthiopiers findet sich hierzu insofern eine Analogie, als hier Täufer und Täufling gemeinsam in ein am Weg liegendes Wasser steigen (8,36).

64   Vgl. 2,4: Die Apostel reden nach dem Herabkommen des Geistes ἑτέραις γλώσσαις, sowie 19,6: Zungenreden und Prophezeien sind Befähigungen, die den Johannesjüngern durch die Geistverleihung vermittelt werden.

65   Vgl. 10,47; 11,17. Das in beiden Versen verwendete Verbum κωλύειν begegnet auch in 8,36 im Zusammenhang der Taufe des Äthiopiers. Zur Diskussion seiner Bedeutung in den Tauferzählungen vgl. den nächsten Abschnitt.

66   Petrus bezeichnet die Geistausgießung ausdrücklich als ἡ ἴση δωρεά wie diejenige beim Pfingstereignis.

67   Vgl. zu dieser Episode A. LINDEMANN, „Der ‚äthiopische Eunuch' und die Anfänge der Mission unter den Völkern nach Apg 8–11".

Vergleich zu den anderen bislang betrachteten Tauferzählungen weist sie Besonderheiten auf, die nach ihrer Funktion im Rahmen der Act fragen lassen.

Markant ist zunächst, dass es sich um die Taufe einer Einzelperson handelt, die keine Auswirkungen auf den Fortgang der von Lukas berichteten Ereignisse besitzt. Die Frage nach dem Status des Äthiopiers ist dabei in der Forschung umstritten.[68] Lukas gibt die Informationen, es handle sich um einen ἀνὴρ Αἰθίοψ, der als εὐνοῦχος eine Stellung als „Hofbeamter" (δυνάστης) am Hof der Kandake, der Königin der Äthiopier, innehatte.[69] Das lässt auf einen Heiden schließen, dessen Affinität zum jüdischen Gottesglauben sich darin zeigt, dass er nach Jerusalem gereist war, um dort anzubeten. Dafür spricht weiter, dass Philippus ihn im Buch des Propheten Jesaja lesend antrifft. Die Kennzeichnung als εὐνοῦχος ist schließlich nicht so aufzufassen, als wolle Lukas damit die Unmöglichkeit, der Äthiopier könne zum jüdischen Volk gehören, zum Ausdruck bringen.[70] Gleichwohl beschreibt ihn Lukas nicht als zum jüdischen Volk gehörig und kennzeichnet ihn auch nicht als „Gottesfürchtigen". Es handelt sich in seiner Perspektive vielmehr um einen Heiden, der sich dem Glauben an den Gott Israels und den Schriften gegenüber aufgeschlossen zeigt und damit auch die Voraussetzungen für die Annahme der Christusverkündigung des Philippus und damit auch für die Taufe mitbringt. Zugleich unterscheidet ihn Lukas von denjenigen Heiden im Haus des Kornelius, die mit dem Geist begabt werden und mit denen deshalb die Öffnung des Gottesvolkes für die Heiden beginnt. Die Taufe des Äthiopiers bleibt dagegen eine Einzelepisode, die im weiteren von Lukas erzählten Geschichtsverlauf nicht wieder aufgenommen wird.

Die Sonderstellung der Erzählung zeigt sich nicht zuletzt daran, dass von einer Ergänzung der Taufe des Philippus durch eine nachträgliche Geistverleihung wie in 8,14–17 nichts verlautet, obwohl die Taufe auch hier nicht mit einer Geistmitteilung verbunden ist. Dagegen wird an dieser Stelle zum ersten Mal der *Vorgang* der Taufe geschildert: Auslöser für das Taufbegehren ist, dass Philippus und der Eunuch ἐπί τι ὕδωρ gelangen (8,36); beide steigen sodann zur Taufe in das Wasser. Wie die Taufe selbst konkret vollzogen wird, sagt Lukas nicht, auch wird nicht deutlich, um welche Art von „Wasser" es sich handelt,

---

68 Vgl. dazu die Analyse bei AVEMARIE, *Tauferzählungen*, 54–67.

69 Κανδάκη war der Titel der äthiopischen Königin. Er wurde aber von antiken Autoren, so offenbar auch von Lukas, häufig als Eigenname aufgefasst.

70 Die entsprechende Bestimmung aus Dtn 23,2, keiner, dem die Hoden zerquetscht wurden oder das Glied abgetrennt wurde, dürfe in die Gemeinde des Herrn hineinkommen, wurde offensichtlich in dem für Lukas maßgeblichen Zeitraum jüdischerseits keineswegs als Hinderungsgrund für die Aufnahme von Zeugungsunfähigen betrachtet. Dies hat AVEMARIE, *Tauferzählungen*, 57–61, anhand rabbinischer Belege sowie entsprechender Stellen aus den Qumranschriften und bei Philo, die auf Dtn 23,2 rekurrieren, gezeigt.

in dem die Taufe stattfindet.[71] Auszugehen ist vermutlich von einem Untertauchen des Täuflings durch den Täufer.

Die Eigentümlichkeit der Episode ist schon früh bemerkt worden und hat sich auch in der Textüberlieferung niedergeschlagen. So wird in einem Teil der Manuskripte der fehlende Geistempfang nachgetragen.[72] Ein weiterer markanter Zug der Textüberlieferung ist der in einem Teil der Textüberlieferung[73] in 8,37 eingefügte Dialog zwischen Philippus und dem Äthiopier.[74] Dieser wird durch den Hinweis des Philippus eingeleitet, das πιστεύειν des Täuflings sei die Voraussetzung für seine Rettung, dem das Bekenntnis des Äthiopiers zu Jesus Christus als dem Sohn Gottes folgt.[75] Damit ist das eigentliche Defizit der Erzählung, nämlich die fehlende Notiz über eine inhaltliche Bestimmung der Taufe durch Nennung des Namens Jesu Christi sowie Glauben und Geistempfang des Täuflings, behoben.[76]

Die Ergänzung der Taufe erfolgt allerdings nicht unter dem Einfluss der frühchristlichen Taufpraxis und -liturgie. Das wird schon daran deutlich, dass weder eine triadische Taufformel vorliegt, wie sie in anderen Schriften des späten 1. sowie des 2. Jahrhunderts bezeugt ist[77], noch eine Geistverleihung erwähnt wird. Auch finden sich keine Hinweise auf eine präbaptismale Unterweisung, *renuntio* oder Tauffragen, die vom Täufer an den Täufling gerich-

---

71 Anders als in Did 7,1f., wo ausdrücklich die Taufe mit fließendem Wasser (ὕδωρ ζῶν) angeordnet wird und nur falls dieses nicht vorhanden ist in absteigender Reihenfolge kaltes und warmes Wasser (ψυχρόν, θερμόν) als Ersatz genannt werden, erfolgt hier keine nähere Beschreibung des Wassers.

72 In der längeren Lesart von V.39, die sich als Ergänzung im Codex Alexandrinus, einigen Minuskeln sowie lateinischen, syrischen und armenischen Übersetzungen findet, fällt das πνεῦμα ἅγιον auf den Eunuchen, als er mit Philippus aus dem Wasser steigt. Dieser wird anschließend von einem ἄγγελος κυρίου, nicht vom πνεῦμα, entrückt. Auf diese Weise wird das Defizit der fehlenden Geistverleihung behoben.

73 Der Vers findet sich zuerst im griechisch-lateinischen Codex Laudianus (E, Bibliotheca Bodleiana, Oxford) aus dem 6. Jahrhundert, der nur die Act enthält. Außerdem überliefern ihn eine Reihe von Minuskeln sowie ein Teil der altlateinischen und syrischen Überlieferung. Bei Irenäus, *Haer.* III 12,8, wird nur das Bekenntnis des Äthiopiers zitiert. Dieses war also gegen Ende des 2. Jahrhunderts als Teil des Act-Textes bekannt, auch wenn Irenäus deshalb nicht automatisch als Zeuge des Textes aus dem Laudianus und anderer Manuskripte gelten kann. Im Codex Bezae fehlt der Text von Act 8,29–10,14 nahezu vollständig.

74 Vgl. F. W. HORN, „Apg 8,37, der Westliche Text und die frühchristliche Tauftheologie".

75 Eine Abbildung der entsprechenden Stelle im Codex Laudianus findet sich bei B. M. METZGER, *Der Text des Neuen Testaments*, Tafel 6a.

76 Daraus zu schließen, dass die christliche Taufe ursprünglich überhaupt ohne Nennung des Namens Jesu Christi erfolgte und von der Johannestaufe nicht unterschieden wurde, wie dies VON CAMPENHAUSEN, „Taufen", tut, ist kaum überzeugend. Der nachtägliche Einschub zeigt vielmehr, dass der Bezug zu Jesus Christus durch die Glaubensformel nachgetragen wurde, die sachlich der Namensformel korrespondiert.

77 Mt 28,19; Did 7,1; Justin, 1 *Apol.* 61.

tet und von diesem mit dem dreigliedrigen Bekenntnis beantwortet werden.[78] Stattdessen wird ein Bekenntnis eingefügt, das den Glauben an Jesus Christus als den Sohn Gottes zum Ausdruck bringt. Dies zeigt, dass es der Ergänzung der Episode von der Taufe des äthiopischen Eunuchen darauf ankommt, den in der Erzählung fehlenden Bezug der Taufe zum Glauben an Jesus Christus herauszustellen und sie dadurch inhaltlich zu charakterisieren.[79] Der Akzent liegt also auf dem πιστεύειν, jedoch nicht auf einer bestimmten Taufpraxis oder einem Taufbekenntnis.[80]

Ein weiterer markanter Zug der Erzählung ist schließlich die Frage des Eunuchen angesichts des plötzlich auftauchenden Wassers:[81] τί κωλύει με βαπτισθῆναι; Aus dem hier sowie in 10,47 und 11,17[82] im Zusammenhang der Taufe begegnenden κωλύειν ist mitunter auf ein im Kontext der frühen Taufliturgie begegnendes Problem möglicher Taufhindernisse geschlossen worden.[83] Das ist jedoch kaum wahrscheinlich. Die umgangssprachliche Wendung bedeutet kaum mehr als „Warum sollte ich nicht getauft werden?"[84], zumal der Kontext der neutestamentlichen Stellen in keiner Weise die Praxis eines Ausschlusses von Taufhindernissen nahe legt.[85] Eher wird dadurch – gerade im Gegenteil – betont, dass es *keinen* Hinderungsgrund für die Taufe gibt. Damit wird die Gleichwertigkeit der Taufe des Äthiopiers und der im Haus des Kornelius versammelten Heiden gegenüber den Taufen der Juden zu Pfingsten herausgestellt: Wie diesen durch die Taufe das durch Jesus Christus vermittelte Heil zuteil wurde, so ist dies nunmehr auch bei Heiden der Fall.

Die Taufe des Äthiopiers gehört zu den Überlieferungen über das Wirken des Philippus. Im Geschichtsentwurf des Lukas ist daraus die Erzählung über einen dem Glauben an den Gott Israels zugeneigten Heiden geworden, der von den später in den Blick tretenden Gottesfürchtigen unterschieden bleibt. Es handelt sich um eine Taufe ohne Geistvermittlung, die darum auch nicht die

---

78 In dieser Weise wird die Taufhandlung in TA 21 beschrieben.
79 Vgl. auch von Campenhausen, „Taufen", 202f.
80 Vergleichbar ist der sekundäre Mk-Schluss. Auch hier wird das πιστεύειν in den Vordergrund gerückt und in Mk 16,16 auf mit Act 8,37 vergleichbare Weise mit Taufe und Gerettetwerden verbunden: ὁ πιστεύσας καὶ βαπτισθεὶς σωθήσεται, ὁ δὲ ἀπιστήσας κατακριθήσεται.
81 Nach Plümacher hat „die providentia specialissima" für das zur Taufe notwendige Wasser gesorgt. Vgl. idem, *Lukas als hellenistischer Schriftsteller*, 91. Damit ist zutreffend erfasst, dass es Lukas nicht um Informationen über geographische Umstände geht (wiewohl man deshalb nicht auszuschließen braucht, dass Lukas um Wasser in der Gegend wusste), sondern darum, die für die Erzählung notwendigen Begleitumstände herauszustellen.
82 Vgl. auch das διακωλύειν in Mt 3,14.
83 So vor allem O. Cullmann, *Die Tauflehre des Neuen Testaments*, 65–73. Vgl. auch J. Jeremias, *Die Kindertaufe in den ersten vier Jahrhunderten*, 65–67. Vorsichtige Zustimmung äußert u.a. Haenchen, *Apostelgeschichte*, 302.
84 Vgl. Barrett, *Acts*, 432; Avemarie, *Tauferzählungen*, 90–92.
85 So zu Recht Horn, „Apg 8,37", 232–235.

Öffnung des Gottesvolkes für die Heiden markiert. Sie zeigt, wie die Christusbotschaft über die von Lukas beschriebene Hauptrichtung ihrer Ausbreitung hinaus auch zu solchen Menschen und in deren Heimatländer gelangt, die sich dem Glauben an den Gott Israels verbunden wissen. Es handelt sich demnach um eine Missionsgeschichte mit eigenem Profil.

3.2. Die Taufe des Saulus

Eine weitere an einer Einzelperson orientierte Taufe ist diejenige des Saulus. Sie wird als Bestandteil seiner Bekehrung erwähnt und dann noch einmal in seinem ersten Selbstbericht über dieses Ereignis genannt.[86] In der zweiten Rede in Kap. 26, die sich vor allem auf den künftigen Auftrag des Paulus konzentriert, die Umstände seiner Bekehrung dagegen nur am Rande erwähnt, wird sie dagegen nicht mehr genannt.[87]

In Kap. 9 und 22 steht die Taufe des Saulus im Kontext derjenigen Ereignisse, durch die er in die christliche Gemeinschaft aufgenommen wird: In Kap. 9 gehen die Handauflegung durch Hananias und die damit verbundene Geisterfüllung voraus; die Blindheit, mit der Paulus geschlagen war, wird beendet. Die Taufe durch Hananias markiert die hierauf folgende Aufnahme in die Christusgemeinschaft. In der knappen Aufforderung in 22,16 ἀναστὰς βάπτισαι καὶ ἀπόλουσαι τὰς ἁμαρτίας σου ἐπικαλεσάμενος τὸ ὄνομα αὐτοῦ wird die Taufe dagegen mit dem Abwaschen der Sünden und dem Anrufen des Namens des Gerechten verbunden.

Die Taufe des Saulus hat damit diejenigen Züge, die bereits in 2,38 zur Sprache gekommen waren. Dort war von Bekehrung, Sündenvergebung und Geistverleihung die Rede. Alle diese Aspekte begegnen auch bei der Taufe des Saulus, die damit eine für das lukanische Verständnis charakteristische Darstellung einer Einzeltaufe ist. Innerhalb der Act gewinnt sie darüber hinaus dadurch besondere Bedeutung, dass die Bekehrung diejenige eines „Drohung und Mord schnaubenden" Verfolgers zu einem Jünger des Herrn ist[88], der im weiteren Verlauf zur zentralen Gestalt der Ereignisse avanciert. Paulus wird dabei zu demjenigen, mit dem sich die Ausbreitung der Christusbotschaft zu den Heiden verbindet, der aber, angefangen von seiner Taufe, zugleich eine paradigmatische Funktion des zu Christus bekehrten und für seinen Namen leidenden Zeugen besitzt.[89] Darin unterscheidet sich dieser Bericht, obwohl es sich ebenfalls um

---

86 Act 9,18; 22,16.
87 Zu den drei Berichten vgl. D. MARGUERAT, „La conversion de Saul", sowie J. KREMER, „Die dreifache Wiedergabe des Damaskuserlebnisses Pauli in der Apostelgeschichte".
88 Vgl. Act 9,1 und zur Analyse der Wendung P. W. VAN DER HORST, „Drohung und Mord schnaubend".
89 Vgl. J. SCHRÖTER, „Kirche im Anschluss an Paulus".

eine Erzählung über eine individuelle Taufe handelt, grundsätzlich von demjenigen über die Taufe des Äthiopiers durch Philippus.

Die Bedeutung der Taufe des Saulus wird nicht zuletzt daran deutlich, dass er seinerseits Menschen dazu bringen wird, sich taufen zu lassen und dadurch des an Christus gebundenen Heils teilhaftig zu werden. Das geschieht zuerst bei Lydia und ihrem Haus in Philippi (16,15), sodann, ebenfalls in Philippi, bei dem Kerkermeister und allen, die zu ihm gehören (16,33), schließlich bei dem Synagogenvorsteher Krispus und seinem Haus sowie vielen weiteren in Korinth (18,8). In den entsprechenden Bemerkungen wird der Taufvorgang selbst nicht geschildert, vielmehr ist stets vorausgesetzt, dass die Annahme der Christusbotschaft die Voraussetzung für die Taufe bildet, durch die Taufe selbst dagegen die Aufnahme in die Gemeinschaft der Glaubenden vollzogen wird.

Der dargestellte Befund zeigt, dass die Tauferzählungen der Act durch das in 1,8 formulierte Programm der Ausbreitung des Christuszeugnisses zusammengehalten werden. Die in 1,5 formulierte Unterscheidung von Wasser- und Geisttaufe ist dabei insofern von besonderer Bedeutung, als die Geistverleihung zu einem für die Ausbreitung des Christuszeugnisses und die Entstehung der neuen, auf der Annahme dieses Zeugnisses gründenden Gemeinschaft konstitutiven Merkmal wird. Darum wird die Geistausgießung zu Pfingsten in besonderer Weise herausgestellt und diejenige im Haus des Kornelius in Analogie hierzu gesetzt und auf diese Weise zu einem grundlegenden Geschehen für die Gestalt der Kirche erklärt: Entscheidendes Kriterium für die Zugehörigkeit zum an Christus gebundenen Heil ist der Glaube, der sich in Umkehr und Annahme der Christusbotschaft manifestiert. Taufe und Geistvermittlung, die in einem engen, wenngleich variablen Zusammenhang miteinander stehen, sind dem korrespondierende Vorgänge der Zueignung dieses Heils. Sprachlich kommt das dadurch zum Ausdruck, dass die mit wechselnden Präpositionen begegnenden Wendungen stets die Bindung der Taufe an den Namen Jesu Christi zum Ausdruck bringen.

Jenseits dieses übergreifenden narrativen Konzeptes ist innerhalb der Tauferzählungen eine Disparatheit zu konstatieren. Diese zeigt sich zum einen an den mit den Taufen verbundenen Bestandteilen des Christwerdens. Nur im Zusammenhang der Bekehrung der in Jerusalem versammelten Juden wird das μετανοεῖν erwähnt, die Sündenvergebung wird in 2,38 und 22,16 genannt, zusätzlich zur Anerkenntnis Jesu Christi als κύριος bzw. zur Anrufung seines Namens. Bei den Taufen des Philippus wird dagegen nur das Zum-Glauben-Kommen als Reaktion auf sein εὐαγγελίζειν genannt. Eine Bindung der Taufe an bestimmte Personen ist nicht zu erkennen. Taufen können die Apostel, Philippus, Hananias sowie Paulus. Des Öfteren wird passivisch formuliert, dass Menschen getauft wurden oder sich taufen ließen, oder es wird der Auftrag erteilt, Menschen zu taufen.

Komplex ist der Befund bezüglich Taufe, Handauflegung und Geistverleihung. In 2,38 gibt es einen unmittelbaren Zusammenhang von Taufe und Sündenvergebung bzw. Geistempfang, in 8,16f. wird der Geist nachträglich durch die Handauflegung verliehen, in 9,17f. folgt die Taufe auf die zuvor durch Handauflegung bewirkte Geistverleihung, in 10,44–48 fällt der Geist auf die Hörer der Petrusrede, die daraufhin getauft werden, und in 19,5f. wird der Geist durch Handauflegung nach der Taufe verliehen. Darin zeigt sich, dass es sich für Lukas um selbständige Akte handelt, die in enger Beziehung stehen, ohne jedoch miteinander identifiziert zu werden.

Schließlich zeigt Lukas wenig Interesse, den Vorgang der Taufe selbst zu schildern. In bestimmten Fällen kann sie sich mit der Handauflegung verbinden, die gleichwohl als selbständige Handlung vorgestellt ist. Aus der Erwähnung des Ins-Wasser-Steigens von Täufer und Täufling bei der Taufe des äthiopischen Eunuchen sowie aus der Nennung des Wassers in 10,47 lässt sich entnehmen, dass die christliche Taufe ungeachtet der Entgegensetzung von Wassertaufe des Johannes und christlicher Geisttaufe im konkreten Vollzug ebenfalls eine Wassertaufe war. Es werden jedoch nirgendwo konkrete Regelungen genannt, wie das Taufritual zu vollziehen ist. So begegnet weder eine triadische Taufformulierung noch ein Hinweis darauf, mit welcher Art von Wasser getauft werden soll oder wer zur Taufe berechtigt ist. Das Interesse des Lukas an der Taufe konzentriert sich demnach auf deren Bedeutung im Zusammenhang der Entstehung der Kirche aus Juden und Heiden. An der Regelung des liturgischen Vollzugs der Taufe zeigt er dagegen kein Interesse, ebensowenig wie der Vorgang des Hinabsteigens ins Wasser und Heraufsteigen aus diesem symbolisch ausgedeutet wird.[90]

4. Die Traditionsgrundlage der Tauferzählungen

Der dargestellte Befund zeigt, dass Lukas in den Tauferzählungen in verschiedener Weise auf urchristliche Überlieferungen zurückgegriffen hat. Dazu gehört zunächst die Taufe „auf den Namen", die auch in I Kor 1,13.15; Mt 28,19 sowie Did 7,1.3 belegt ist. Sachlich verwandt sind das Getauftsein εἰς Χριστὸν Ἰησοῦν (Röm 6,3) bzw. εἰς Χριστόν (Gal 3,27) sowie die Formulierung εἰς τὸν Μωϋσῆν ἐβαπτίσθησαν in I Kor 10,2. Die deutlichste Nähe besteht demnach zu Paulus, wogegen Mt und Did eine triadische Formel verwenden. Zu vergleichen ist auch

---

90 Vgl. zum Hinabsteigen ins Wasser und Heraufsteigen daraus Barn 11,11; Herm mand IV 3,1; sim IX 16,4; EvPhil 59; 101; 109a. Der Vorgang wird symbolisch als Abwaschen der Sünden (Barn; Herm mand) bzw. als Tot- und wieder Lebendigwerden (Herm sim) gedeutet. In EvPhil wird mit der Taufe der Empfang des Geistes bzw. das Anziehen des lebendigen Menschen verbunden (59; 101), die Deutung als Hinabsteigen in den Tod dagegen ausdrücklich abgelehnt (109a).

die Wendung τὸ καλὸν ὄνομα τὸ ἐπικληθὲν ἐφ' ὑμᾶς in Jak 2,7, die vermutlich ebenfalls auf die Taufe anspielt.[91]

Bei der Darstellung der Paulusbekehrung sind markante terminologische Berührungen mit den Paulusbriefen – wie etwa σκεῦος ἐκλογῆς, πορθεῖν oder ἐπικαλεῖν τὸ ὄνομα τοῦ κυρίου – festzustellen. Diese deuten darauf hin, dass Lukas hier Traditionen von der Bekehrung und Berufung des Paulus verarbeitet hat. Zugleich sind diese Erzählungen von einem spezifisch lukanischen Erzählinteresse geprägt. Sie machen deutlich, wie Paulus von dem erhöhten Herrn als auserwähltes Werkzeug in den Dienst genommen und zum Zeugen vor Juden und Heiden wird. Dieses in 9,15f. angekündigte Programm wird dann u.a. in den Selbstberichten des Paulus in Kap. 22 und 26 eingelöst. Die Taufe des Paulus wird dabei in 9,18 und 22,16 eher en passant erwähnt, ist aber insofern von Bedeutung, als sie Paulus zum vollwertigen Christuszeugen macht und damit die Voraussetzung für sein künftiges Wirken bildet.

Sodann hatte Lukas offenbar Zugang zu Philippustraditionen. Ohne dass die Traditionsgrundlage der mit seinem Wirken verbundenen Episoden hier genauer untersucht werden kann, ist deutlich, dass Philippus durch die Tätigkeit des Verkündigens (κηρύσσειν, εὐαγγελίζεσθαι) charakterisiert und in 21,8 mit der seltenen Bezeichnung ὁ εὐαγγελιστής benannt wird. Anzunehmen ist des Weiteren, dass Lukas Personal- und Lokalüberlieferungen über die Samarienmission, die Person des Simon Magus sowie die Bekehrung eines höherstehenden Nicht-Israeliten durch Philippus vorlagen, die von Lukas bearbeitet und in das erzählerische Konzept der Act eingepasst wurden.

Im Blick auf die Tauftätigkeit des Philippus ist dabei bemerkenswert, dass sie nicht explizit mit der Geistverleihung verbunden, sondern seiner Verkündigungstätigkeit untergeordnet ist. Liest man, wie oben dargestellt, in 8,39 mit der Mehrzahl der Handschriften den kürzeren Text πνεῦμα κυρίου ἥρπασεν τὸν Φίλιππον und nicht mit dem Codex Alexandrinus sowie verschiedenen Minuskeln πνεῦμα ἅγιον ἐπέπεσεν ἐπὶ τὸν εὐνοῦχον, ἄγγελος δὲ κυρίου ἥρπασεν τὸν Φίλιππον, fehlt der Philippustaufe in beiden Erzählungen das Element der Geistverleihung. Das könnte auf eine eigene Taufpraxis des Philippus zurückzuführen sein. Bemerkenswert dabei ist, dass es Lukas nur im Fall der Samarienmission für notwendig hält, die durch Petrus und Johannes bewirkte Geistmitteilung ausdrücklich zu berichten, wogegen in der Erzählung von dem Äthiopier von der Behebung eines „pneumatischen Defizits" nichts verlautet. Der Grund dafür dürfte darin zu suchen sein, dass Samarien auf diese Weise in den Bereich der von der urchristlichen Mission erreichten Gebiete eingegliedert wird. Die Entsendung von Petrus und Johannes wird entsprechend damit

---

91 Der „gute Name" dürfte sich auf den Namen Jesu Christi, nicht Gottes, beziehen. Die Stelle wäre dann ein Beleg dafür, dass dieser Name beim Taufakt tatsächlich genannt wurde. Das ließe sich dann entsprechend auch auf die εἰς τὸ ὄνομα- bzw. die ἐπὶ τῷ ὀνόματι-Formeln übertragen.

begründet, ὅτι δέδεκται ἡ Σαμάρεια τὸν λόγον τοῦ θεοῦ (8,14). Die lukanische Intention bei der Darstellung der Philippustaufen lässt sich demnach so beschreiben, dass damit zum einen die in 1,8 antizipierte Ausbreitung des Zeugnisses nach Samaria eingelöst, zum anderen die grundsätzliche Möglichkeit der Taufe von Heiden dargestellt wird, wobei der äthiopische Eunuch allerdings nicht dem Bereich entstammt, der von der Ausbreitung der Kirche erfasst wird und folglich nach seiner Taufe auch wieder aus dem Blickfeld verschwindet.

Die Traditionsgrundlage der Episode über Apollos und die Johannesjünger in Ephesus ist schwer zu erheben. Ob es in Ephesus tatsächlich eine Gruppe von Johannesanhängern gegeben hat, ob zwischen diesen und der von Apollos praktizierten Taufe eine Beziehung bestand und wie das Verhältnis einer solchen Gruppe zu den christlichen Gemeinden zu beschreiben wäre, lässt sich kaum aufhellen. Innerhalb der lukanischen Konzeption nimmt diese Gruppe jedenfalls den Platz zwar getaufter, aber nicht zur christlichen Kirche gehöriger Jünger ein. Damit besteht eine gewisse Analogie zu den von Philippus getauften Samaritanern. Diese Analogie wird freilich erst durch die lukanische Darstellung hergestellt. In historischer Hinsicht lässt sich dagegen vermuten, dass es sich um urchristliche Gruppen mit unterschiedlichem Tauf- und Geistverständnis handelt, die in der lukanischen Erzählung in ein bestimmtes geschichtstheologisches Konzept integriert werden.

Bei der Pfingsterzählung sowie derjenigen von der Taufe in Cäsarea ist die lukanische Gestaltung am deutlichsten zu erkennen. Die Taufe in Kap. 2 ist die Reaktion auf die große Rede des Petrus, in der er, ausgehend von dem Joel-Zitat, das Ereignis der Geistausgießung erläutert. In Kap. 10 werden in einer kunstvollen Komposition Petrus und Kornelius mittels zweier Visionen zusammengeführt, damit Petrus im Haus des Kornelius die Rede über die Zuwendung Gottes zu allen Menschen halten kann. Dementsprechend gibt auch die Darstellung der Taufen in 2,38 und 10,44–48 am deutlichsten zu erkennen, was Lukas für den „Normalfall" der christlichen Taufe hält: Sie ist die Konsequenz der Bekehrung, die durch die Ausrichtung des Christuszeugnisses bewirkt wurde. Sie bewirkt Sündenvergebung und hat die Geistverleihung zur Folge. Sie kann im Prinzip an jedem Menschen vollzogen werden, der den Gott Israels fürchtet und zum Glauben an Jesus Christus kommt. Dieses Verständnis ist auch für die Notizen über die Taufe der Lydia und des Krispus in 16,15 und 18,8 vorauszusetzen. Lukas kann sich hier auf die knappen Erwähnungen der Taufen beschränken, weil er bereits dargelegt hat, was sich damit inhaltlich verbindet.

5. Fazit: Die Tauferzählungen als Bestandteil der Geschichtstheologie der Act

Der Beitrag der Act zum Thema „Taufe im frühen Christentum" lässt sich folgendermaßen zusammenfassen:

Die Geschichtstheologie der Act zielt auf die Entstehung des Gottesvolkes aus allen Menschen, die die Christusverkündigung annehmen und zum Glauben kommen. Die Tauferzählungen sind diesem Konzept eingeordnet. Die Hauptlinie der lukanischen Darstellung ist deshalb in der durch die explizite Korrespondenz von Pfingst- und Korneliuserzählung herausgestellten Öffnung des Gottesvolkes für die Heiden zu erkennen, die dann durch die knappen Notizen über die Taufen der Lydia und des Krispus fortgesetzt wird. Dabei setzt Lukas voraus, dass die christliche Taufe eine Wassertaufe ist, mit der sich Umkehr, Sündenvergebung und Geistempfang verbinden.

An der Darstellung des Ritus ist Lukas – wie die meisten anderen urchristlichen Autoren auch – nicht interessiert. Benötigt wird, wie die Taufe des Eunuchen und diejenige der im Haus des Kornelius Versammelten zeigen, lediglich Wasser, ohne dass Lukas – anders als die Didache – eigens ausführen würde, um welche Art von Wasser es sich dabei handelt. Erforderlich ist weiter, dass ein bereits zur christlichen Gemeinschaft Gehöriger die Taufe vollzieht. Dabei muss es sich nicht um Personen mit besonderer Autorität oder in leitender Stellung handeln, vielmehr kann im Prinzip jeder Gläubige zum Täufer werden.

Ein weiteres Merkmal der Act besteht darin, dass sich die Tauferzählungen häufiger auf „Sonderfälle" beziehen: die nicht mit Geistmitteilung verbundene Taufe der Samaritaner; die Taufe eines Äthiopiers mit einer Affinität zum Gott Israels, der aus einer Region stammt, die ansonsten nicht im Blickfeld der Act liegt und in der in 1,8 skizzierten geographischen Ausbreitung des Christuszeugnisses auch nicht genannt wird; die Taufe des Christenverfolgers Saulus, der zum maßgeblichen Zeugen für die Ausbreitung der Christusbotschaft zu den Heiden wird; schließlich die Taufe einer Gruppe von Jüngern, die bislang nur die Taufe des Johannes kannten.

Diese „Sonderfälle" haben ihre Grundlage in Überlieferungen aus der Frühzeit des Christentums, die Lukas aufgenommen und seinem Gesamtkonzept integriert hat. Dabei verfolgt er zum einen das Interesse, eine sich kontinuierlich vom Pfingstereignis her entwickelnde Gestalt der Kirche zu zeichnen, in die auch Gruppen mit eigenem Taufverständnis aufgenommen werden. Zum anderen macht er auf diese Weise deutlich, dass die Offenheit für den Glauben an den Gott Israels und die christliche Verkündigung eine notwendige und zugleich hinreichende Voraussetzung für die Taufe darstellt.

Dieser Befund differenziert sich dadurch aus, dass einerseits die im Haus des Kornelius Versammelten, obwohl der Geist auf sie in gleicher Weise ausgegossen wurde wie auf die Apostel, zusätzlich getauft werden müssen, andererseits im Fall des Philippus auch eine Taufe auf den Namen Jesu ohne Geistverleihung existiert. Zudem geht aus der Taufe des Eunuchen explizit hervor, was auch für die anderen Tauferzählungen – mit Ausnahme des Pfingstgeschehens – vorauszusetzen ist, dass nämlich auch die christliche Taufe eine Wassertaufe ist.

Vor diesem Hintergrund erklärt sich auch die mehrfache Gegenüberstellung von Wassertaufe und Geisttaufe. Ist diese zunächst darin auffällig, dass auch die Taufe auf den Namen Jesu eine Wassertaufe ist, so erklärt sie sich daher, dass Lukas von der durch den Auferstandenen selbst angekündigten Geistausgießung nicht erfasste Taufpraktiken als unzureichend aufweisen will. Das gilt sowohl für die Johannestaufe als auch für diejenige des Philippus.

Die Taufe ist demnach für Lukas derjenige Ritus, der die Zugehörigkeit zur christlichen Kirche begründet. Sie basiert auf Bekehrung und Annahme der Christusbotschaft, dient der Sündenvergebung und ist verbunden mit der Vermittlung des zu Pfingsten ausgegossenen Geistes. Auf diese Weise gliedert sie ein in die vom Geist Gottes bestimmte Gemeinschaft der an Christus Glaubenden. Zwar ist – wie der Fall des äthiopischen Eunuchen zeigt – eine Taufe, die ohne Geistmitteilung bleibt, prinzipiell möglich. Eine solche Taufe bindet jedoch nicht in die Kirche ein. Gerade daran zeigt sich, dass Taufe und Geistmitteilung erst gemeinsam zur Aufnahme in die christliche Gemeinschaft führen.

Bibliographie

AVEMARIE, F., *Die Tauferzählungen der Apostelgeschichte. Theologie und Geschichte* (WUNT 139), Tübingen: Mohr Siebeck 2002.

BARRETT, C. K., *A Critical and Exegetical Commentary on the Acts of the Apostles* (ICC). Volume I: Preliminary Introduction and Commentary on Acts I-XIV, Edinburgh: T & T Clark 1994.

BARTH, G., *Die Taufe in frühchristlicher Zeit* (BThS 4), Neukirchen-Vluyn: Neukirchener Verlag 1981.

BIETENHARD, H., „ὄνομα κτλ.", in: *ThWNT* V (1954) 242–283.

BLASS, F./DEBRUNNER, A./REHKOPF, F., *Grammatik des neutestamentlichen Griechisch*, Göttingen: Vandenhoeck & Rupecht [17]1990 (BDR).

DE BOER, M. C., „God-Fearers in Luke-Acts", in: C. Tuckett (Hg.), *Luke's Literary Achievement. Collected Essays* (JSNT.SS 116), Sheffield: Sheffield Academic Press 1995, 50–71.

VON CAMPENHAUSEN, H., „Taufen auf den Namen Jesu?", in: DERS., *Urchristliches und Altkirchliches. Vorträge und Aufsätze*, Tübingen: Mohr Siebeck 1979, 197–216.

COHEN, S., „Crossing the Boundary and Becoming a Jew", in: *HThR 82* (1989) 13–33.

CULLMANN, O., *Die Tauflehre des Neuen Testaments. Erwachsenen- und Kindertaufe*, Zürich: Zwingli ²1958.

DEISSMANN, A., *Neue Bibelstudien. Sprachgeschichtliche Beiträge, zumeist aus den Papyri und Inschriften, zur Erklärung des Neuen Testaments*, Marburg: Elwert 1897.

— *Bibelstudien. Beiträge, zumeist aus den Papyri und Inschriften, zur Geschichte der Sprache, des Schrifttums und der Religion des hellenistischen Judentums und des Urchristentums*, Marburg: Elwert 1895.

— *Licht vom Osten. Das Neue Testament und die neuentdeckten Texte der hellenistisch-römischen Welt*, Tübingen: Mohr Siebeck ⁴1923.

DELLING, G., *Die Taufe im Neuen Testament*, Berlin: Evangelische Verlagsanstalt 1963.

— *Die Zueignung des Heils in der Taufe. Eine Untersuchung zum neutestamentlichen „taufen auf den Namen"*, Berlin: Evangelische Verlagsanstalt 1961.

DENOVA, R. I., *The Things Accomplished Among Us. Prophetic Tradition in the Structural Pattern of Luke-Acts* (JSNT.S 141), Sheffield: Sheffield Academic Press 1997.

FOAKES-JACKSON, F. J. /LAKE, K., *The Beginnings of Christianity. Part I: The Acts of the Apostles, Volume IV: English Translation and Commentary* (by K. Lake and H. J. Cadbury), Grand Rapids, Mich. Baker, repr. 1979.

GAGER, J. G., „Jews, Gentiles, and Synagogues in the Book of Acts", in: *HThR 79* (1986) 91–99.

HAENCHEN, E., *Die Apostelgeschichte* (KEK III), Göttingen: Vandenhoeck & Ruprecht ⁷1977.

HARTMAN, L., „'Into the Name of Jesus'. A Suggestion concerning the Earliest Meaning of the Phrase", in: *NTS 20* (1973/74) 432–440.

— *'Into the Name of the Lord Jesus'. Baptism in the Early Church*. Edinburgh: T & T Clark 1997.

— „ὄνομα", in: *EWNT* II (²1992) 1268–1277.

HEITMÜLLER, W., *„Im Namen Jesu". Eine sprach- u. religionsgeschichtliche Untersuchung zum Neuen Testament, speziell zur altchristlichen Taufe* (FRLANT 1), Göttingen: Mohr Siebeck 1903.

HENGEL, M., „Zwischen Jesus und Paulus: Die ‚Hellenisten', die ‚Sieben' und Stephanus", in: ders., Paulus und Jakobus (Kleine Schriften III; WUNT 141), Tübingen: Mohr Siebeck 2002, 1–67.

HORN, F. W., „Apg 8,37, der Westliche Text und die frühchristliche Tauftheologie", in: T. Nicklas/M. Tilly (Hgg.), *The Book of Acts as Church History/Apostelgeschichte als Kirchengeschichte* (BZNW 120), Berlin/New York: de Gruyter 2003, 225–239.

VAN DER HORST, P. W., „Drohung und Mord schnaubend (Acta IX 1)", in: *NT* 12 (1970) 257–269.

JEREMIAS, J., *Die Kindertaufe in den ersten vier Jahrhunderten*, Göttingen: Vandenhoeck & Ruprecht 1958.

JERVELL, J., „The Church of Jews and Godfearers", in: J. B. Tyson (Hg.), *Luke-Acts and the Jewish People. Eight Critical Perspectives*, Minneapolis, Minn.: Augsburg 1988, 11–20.138–140.

KÄSEMANN, E., „Die Johannesjünger zu Ephesus", in: DERS., *Evangelische Versuche und Besinnungen I*, Göttingen: Vandenhoeck & Ruprecht 1964, 158–168.

KIM, H.-S., *Die Geisttaufe des Messias. Eine kompositionsgeschichtliche Untersuchung zu einem Leitmotiv des lukanischen Doppelwerks. Ein Beitrag zur Theologie und Intention des Lukas* (Studien zur klassischen Philologie 81), Frankfurt/M. u.a.: Peter Lang 1993.

KOCH, D.-A., „Proselyten und Gottesfürchtige als Hörer der Reden von Apostelgeschichte 2,14–39 und 13,16–41", in: DERS., *Hellenistisches Christentum. Schriftverständnis – Ekklesiologie – Geschichte* (NTOA 65), Göttingen: Vandenhoeck & Ruprecht 2008, 250–271.

— „The God-fearers between facts and fiction. Two theosebeis-inscriptions from Aphrodisias and their bearing for the New Testament", in: DERS., *Hellenistisches Christentum*, 272–298.

KREMER, J., „Die dreifache Wiedergabe des Damaskuserlebnisses Pauli in der Apostelgeschichte. Eine Hilfe für das rechte Verstehen der lukanischen Osterevangelien", in: J. Verheyden (Hg.), *The Unity of Luke-Acts* (BEThL 142), Leuven: Peeters 1999, 329–355.

KURZ, W. S., *Reading Luke-Acts. Dynamics of Biblical Narrative*, Louisville, Ky.: Westminster/John Knox 1993.

— „Effects of Variant Narrators in Acts 10–11", in: *NTS* 43 (1997) 570–586.

LEVINSKAYA, I., *The Book of Acts in Its Diaspora Setting* (The Book of Acts in its First Century Setting, Volume 5), Grand Rapids, Mich.: Eerdmans/Carlisle: Pater Noster 1996.

LINDEMANN, A., „Der ‚äthiopische Eunuch' und die Anfänge der Mission unter den Völkern nach Apg 8–11", in: DERS., *Die Evangelien und die Apostelgeschichte. Studien zu ihrer Theologie und zu ihrer Geschichte* (WUNT 241), Tübingen: Mohr Siebeck 2009, 231–251.

MARGUERAT, D., „La conversion de Saul (Ac 9; 22; 26)", in: DERS., *La première histoire du christianisme. Les Actes des Apôtres* (LeDiv 180), Paris: Editions du Cerf/Geneva: Labor et Fides ²2003, 275–306.

MENZIES, R. P., *The Development of Early Christian Pneumatology with Special Reference to Luke-Acts* (JSNT.S 54), Sheffield: JSOT Press 1991.

MERKLEIN, H., *Der erste Brief an die Korinther*, Kapitel 1–4 (ÖTK 7/1), Gütersloh: Gütersloher Verlag 1992.

METZGER, B. M., *Der Text des Neuen Testaments. Einführung in die neutestamentliche Textkritik*, Stuttgart u.a.: Kohlhammer 1966.

MOESSNER, D. P. (Hg.), *Jesus and the Heritage of Israel. Luke's Narrative Claim upon Israel's Legacy* (Luke the Interpreter of Israel 1), Harrisburg, Penn.: Trinity Press International 1999.

PLÜMACHER, E., *Lukas als hellenistischer Schriftsteller. Studien zur Apostelgeschichte* (StUNT 9), Göttingen: Vandenhoeck & Ruprecht 1972.

— „Rom in der Apostelgeschichte", in: DERS., *Geschichte und Geschichten. Aufsätze zur Apostelgeschichte und zu den Johannesakten* (WUNT 170), Tübingen: Mohr Siebeck 2004, 135–169.

QUESNEL, M., *Baptisés dans l'Esprit. Baptême et Esprit Saint dans les Actes des Apôtres* (LeDiv 120), Paris: Edition du Cerf 1985.

ROLOFF, J., *Die Apostelgeschichte* (NTD 5), Göttingen: Vandenhoeck & Ruprecht 1981.

SÄNGER, D., „Heiden – Juden – Christen. Erwägungen zu einem Aspekt frühchristlicher Missionsgeschichte", in: DERS., *Von der Bestimmtheit des Anfangs. Studien zu Jesus, Paulus und zum frühchristlichen Schriftverständnis*, Neukirchen-Vluyn: Neukirchener Verlag 2007, 185–212.

SCHRÖTER, J., „Actaforschung seit 1982. III: Die Apostelgeschichte als Geschichtswerk", in: *ThR* 72 (2007) 383–419. IV: „Israel, die Juden und das Alte Testament", in: *ThR* 73 (2008) 1–59.

— „Kirche im Anschluss an Paulus. Aspekte der Paulusrezeption in der Apostelgeschichte und in den Pastoralbriefen", in: *ZNW* 98 (2007) 77–104.

SCHWEIZER, E., „Die Bekehrung des Apollos", in: DERS., *Beiträge zur Theologie des Neuen Testaments*, Zürich: Zwingli 1970, 71–79.

— „πνεῦμα κτλ.", in: *ThWNT* VI (1959) 330–453.

SIEGERT, F., „Gottesfürchtige und Sympathisanten", in: *JSJ* 4 (1973) 109–164.

STRACK, H. L./BILLERBECK, P., *Kommentar zum Neuen Testament aus Talmud und Midrasch. Erster (Doppel-) Band: Das Evangelium nach Matthäus*, München: C. H. Beck [10]1994.

TURNER, M., *Power from on High. The Spirit in Israel's Restoration and Witness in Luke-Acts* (JPT.SS 9), Sheffield: Sheffield Academic Press 1996.

VAN UNNIK, W. C., „Der Ausdruck ἙΩΣ ἘΣΧΑΤΟΥ ΤΗΣ ΓΗΣ (Apostelgeschichte I 8) und sein alttestamentlicher Hintergrund", in: DERS., *Sparsa Collecta I* (NT.S 29), Leiden: Brill 1973, 386–401.

WANDER, B., *Gottesfürchtige und Sympathisanten. Studien zum heidnischen Umfeld von Diasporasynagogen* (WUNT 104), Tübingen: Mohr Siebeck 1998.

WASSERBERG, G., *Aus Israels Mitte – Heil für die Welt. Eine narrativ-exegetische Studie zur Theologie des Lukas* (BZNW 92), Berlin/New York: de Gruyter 1998.

WOLFF, C., *Der erste Brief des Paulus an die Korinther* (ThKNT 7), Leipzig: Evangelische Verlagsanstalt 1996.

WOLTER, M., „Apollos und die Johannesjünger von Ephesus (Apg 18,24–19,7)", in: DERS., *Theologie und Ethos im frühen Christentum. Studien zu Jesus, Paulus und Lukas* (WUNT 236), Tübingen: Mohr Siebeck 2009, 402–426.

— „Das lukanische Doppelwerk als Epochengeschichte", in: DERS., *Theologie und Ethos im frühen Christentum* (WUNT 236), Tübingen: Mohr Siebeck 2009, 261–289.

— *Das Lukasevangelium* (HNT 3), Tübingen: Mohr Siebeck 2008.

ZUGMANN, M., *„Hellenisten" in der Apostelgeschichte* (WUNT II/264), Tübingen: Mohr Siebeck 2009.

Baptism in the Letter to the Hebrews

Samuel Byrskog

1. Introduction

Most scholars have considered baptism to be a rather peripheral theme in the letter to the Hebrews.[1] The discussion on this subject during last century was indeed meagre. In the English speaking world, W. F. Flemington, to take an early example, treated it briefly on two pages in his book *The New Testament Doctrine of Baptism* from 1948, though noticing that it is of both eschatological and Christological importance in the letter.[2] The German contributions were equally slim. In his well-known book *Die Taufe – Ein Sakrament? Ein exegetischer Beitrag zum Gespräch über die christliche Taufe* from 1951,[3] Markus Barth argued that the Christian baptism was of no significance in Hebrews. Similarly, to take another example, Gerhard Delling, in his booklet *Die Taufe im Neuen Testament* from 1963, gave only sporadic references to it and failed to relate it to the general thrust of the letter.

The most extensive discussion was provided by the Baptist New Testament scholar George Beasley-Murray in his book *Baptism in the New Testament* from 1962. The discussion is however limited to a few pages in a chapter discussing baptism in both Hebrews and 1 Peter. Beasley-Murray focuses on Heb 6:1–6 and 10:22–23 and maintains, to be sure, that the importance of the Christian baptism is not to be left in doubt. It reinforces, according to Beasley-Murray, the crucial link to the Kingdom in face of apostasy in the last times (6:1–6) and constitutes the sacramental meeting place of the sanctifying power of Christ's

---

1   I will use the conventional designation "the letter to the Hebrews" or simply "Hebrews" without any implication as to the precise genre of the composition. To the author it was a "word of consolation/exhortation" (13:22), which indicates that it was a form of oral speech. For the present purposes, I may also leave open questions of authorship and date. On the basis of the masculine singular self-reference in 11:32, I only assume male authorship. As for the recipients and first hearers/readers of the letter, the discussion that follows implies that they were Christ-believers thoroughly acquainted with the Old Testament. For further discussion of the historical setting of Hebrews, see, besides the commentaries, B. Lindars, *The Theology of the Letter to the Hebrews*, 1–25.

2   W. F. Flemington, *The New Testament Doctrine of Baptism*, 97–98.

3   Cf. similarly J. Schneider, *Die Taufe im Neuen Testament*.

death and the individual, pointing the hearers/readers to the hope which they confessed at their baptism (10:22-23).[4]

The situation is still much the same. Everett Ferguson, in his large volume *Baptism in the Early Church: History, Theology, and Liturgy in the First Five Centuries* from 2009, gives only scant attention to what the author of Hebrews has to say about baptism.[5] The sole exception in recent times to this random treatment of the Christian baptism in Hebrews is Peter J. Leithart's article on Heb 10:19–22.[6] Leithart holds the opinion that baptism, according to Hebrews, fulfils and replaces the Old Testament ordination of priests. It confers to the believer several tasks and privileges in a way that is similar to what the priestly ordination did in the Old Testament. The expression "our bodies washed with pure water" in Heb 10:22 implies in context, according to Leithard, that it initiates into the Christian priesthood.

The lack of a more wide-ranging discussion of baptism in Hebrews has to do with the sparse references to it in the letter. There are only three passages mentioning some kind of immersion in water. They either use the term βαπτισμός in plural (6:2; 9:10) or point to the washing with pure water (10:22). To this should be added a reference to enlightenment (6:4). Not all of them, as we will see, refer to the Christian baptism.

In what follows each of the texts will be examined separately. Rather than trying to delineate a specific theology of baptism in Hebrews or to reconstruct the practice of baptism in the communities that were familiar to the author and the hearers/readers, I will focus on how the references to immersion in water function in the author's argument as it was performed for the first time to the intended audience. This approach is informed by several recent studies which have shown that Hebrews is a thoroughly rhetorical composition.[7] Rhetoric, in turn, is an out-growth of a culture dominated by various forms of orality. Together with several stylistic features of the text,[8] the rhetorical character of the

---

4 G. R. BEASLEY-MURRAY, *Baptism in the New Testament*, 242–250.

5 E. FERGUSON, *Baptism in the Early Church*, 186–188.

6 P. J. LEITHART, "Womb of the World: Baptism and the Priesthood of the New Covenant in Hebrews 10.19–22," 49–65.

7 For an early pioneering study of the rhetorical strategies in Hebrews, see W. ÜBELACKER, *Der Hebräerbrief als Appell: I. Untersuchungen zu* exordium, narratio *und* postscriptum *(Hebr 1–2 und 13, 22–25)*; B. LINDARS published in the same year his article "The Rhetorical Structure of Hebrews," 382–406. These studies have been followed by many others in the same vein. For a commentary using the approach of classical rhetoric, cf. C. R. KOESTER, *Hebrews: A New Translation with Introduction and Commentary*.

8 L. T. JOHNSON (*Hebrews: A Commentary*, 10) mentions four stylistic features that indicate the oral character of Hebrews: the use of the first person plural, the references to speaking and hearing, the alternation of exposition and exhortation, and the manner in which the author puts forth themes that are only later developed more fully. To be sure, some of these features may also occur in texts which were not aimed for oral performance.

letter implies that it was aimed for persuasive oral reading and aural reception. While not entering into a technical analysis of different rhetorical strategies in the letter, I will point graphically to the immediate argumentative context of each text-unit mentioning some kind of immersion in water and indicate how its hierarchical structure affected the recipients' experience of the text when they heard it being performed for the first time. When this has been done, we will be in a better position to discern what notions about baptism and what baptismal practices that the author took for granted, where he put his emphases, and how he wished the intended hearers/readers to experience the performance of the pericopees of interest here.

2. The Texts

2.1. Hebrews 6:1–6

The first occurrence of baptismal references is found in 6:1–6. The crucial expressions are βαπτισμῶν διδαχῆς in verse 2 and ἅπαξ φωτισθέντας in verse 4. They appear within a larger hierarchy of arguments that can be illustrated as follows:

1 Διὸ
    ἀφέντες τὸν τῆς ἀρχῆς τοῦ Χριστοῦ λόγον
    ἐπὶ τὴν τελειότητα φερώμεθα,
    μὴ πάλιν θεμέλιον καταβαλλόμενοι
        μετανοίας ἀπὸ νεκρῶν ἔργων,
        καὶ πίστεως ἐπὶ θεόν,
2   **βαπτισμῶν διδαχῆς**,[9]
        ἐπιθέσεώς τε χειρῶν,
        ἀναστάσεώς τε νεκρῶν,
        καὶ κρίματος αἰωνίου.
3 καὶ τοῦτο ποιήσομεν
    ἐάνπερ ἐπιτρέπῃ ὁ θεός.
4 Ἀδύνατον γὰρ τοὺς   **ἅπαξ φωτισθέντας**,
        γευσαμένους τε τῆς δωρεᾶς τῆς ἐπουρανίου
        καὶ μετόχους γενηθέντας πνεύματος ἁγίου
5   καὶ καλὸν γευσαμένους θεοῦ ῥῆμα δυνάμεις τε
        μέλλοντος αἰῶνος,
6   καὶ παραπεσόντας,

---

9 Some early mss (P46, B, d) read διδαχήν instead of διδαχῆς. But διδαχῆς has a wider external support and should be preferred. Differently H. W. ATTRIDGE, *The Epistle to the Hebrews*, 155.

πάλιν ἀνακαινίζειν εἰς μετάνοιαν,
ἀνασταυροῦντας ἑαυτοῖς τὸν υἱὸν τοῦ θεοῦ
καὶ παραδειγματίζοντας.

1 Therefore,
   leaving the word of the beginning of Christ,
   let us carry on to perfection,
      not laying again a foundation
         of repentance from dead works
         and faith in God
2   instruction about "baptisms,"
         laying on of hands,
         resurrection of (the) dead ones,
         and judgement of the age.
3 And we will do this,
   if God permits.
4 For it is impossible to restore again to repentance [from v. 6] those
   who have once been enlightened,
   tasted the heavenly gift
   and become sharers in the Holy Spirit,
5 and tasted the good word of God and the powers
   of the age to come,
6 and then have fallen away,
   on their own crucifying (again) the Son of God
   and making an example.

As is evident from the argumentative structure of the text, the expression βαπτισμῶν διδαχῆς is part of the author's exhortation that the hearers/readers should carry on to perfection.[10] The exhortation is introduced with διό. Together with the fact that the text shifts from the accusatory second person plural of 5:11–12 to the hortatory first person plural, the particle indicates that the author now wishes to address the situation of the audience more directly.[11] He thus develops and applies the previous argument that the immature can only mature when they are fed and learn to assimilate solid food.

---

10 For a discussion of the theme of perfection in Hebrews, see D. Peterson, *Hebrews and Perfection: An Examination of the Concept of Perfection in the 'Epistle to the Hebrews'*, here especially pp. 183–186.

11 Cf. H.-F. Weiss, *Der Brief and die Hebräer*, 335; Johnson, *Hebrews*, 157.

They should, consequently, leave "the word of the beginning of Christ." While the expression τῆς ἀρχῆς τοῦ Χριστοῦ can be understood as an objective or a subjective genitive, the context leads the hearers/readers to think of the elementary word about Christ.[12] That word could have been brought to them either as mission preaching – when they first heard about Christ – or as specific teaching to them when they were new converts. Possibly they retrospectively thought of the mission preaching and the catechetical teaching as one comprehensive event related to the beginning of the Christian life.[13] In any case, we have to do with basic teaching about Christ. As the author had previously pointed out, they ought now themselves to be teachers rather than people who need someone to teach them again the basic elements of the word of God (5:12).

As part of the elementary word about Christ, there was instruction about "baptisms." The reference to "baptisms" is closely related to other doctrines mentioned in 6:1b–2. These doctrines can be divided into three pairs: (1) repentance from dead works and faith in God, (2) "baptisms" and laying on of hands, and (3) resurrection of the dead and eternal judgement. The last two pairs are separated from the first one by the introductory "instruction about" (διδαχῆς), with "baptisms" emphatically put first, and thus belong closely together as crucial items of the teaching familiar to the author and his audience. The fact that they are mentioned immediately after the first pair indicates however also that the hearers/readers might understand the appeal for repentance and faith to be integral to the Christian initiation.

What does "baptisms" refer to? The author uses βαπτισμός instead of the usual βάπτισμα and puts it in the plural.[14] The question at stake is if the term points to Christian baptism or, in accordance with its occurrence elsewhere (Mark 7:4; Heb 9:10), to repeated levitical ablutions practised by the Jews.[15] George Buchanan reminds us that such ablutions probably continued among some groups of Christians, while others objected to them. Justin attacks these practices in 1 *Apol.* 62. Although there was only one Christian baptism for ad-

---

12 Differently ATTRIDGE, *The Epistle to the Hebrews*, 162. Attridge's argument is that there is no explicit Christological element in the following summary. This is true only if we regard the summary as a full account of the teaching and empty it of its implicit Christology, as Attridge is inclined to do (cf. *ibid.*, 163–164). The alternative idea, that Christ himself preached about baptisms and other doctrines mentioned in the summary, cannot be supported from any other texts in the New Testament. KOESTER (*Hebrews*, 303–305) strangely takes the subjective genitive for granted and refers to a number of texts concerning the teaching of Jesus' followers.

13 E. Gräßer calls it "Missionskatechese." See GRÄSSER, *An die Hebräer*, 1:335.

14 For βαπτισμός, cf. also Col 2:12. Several mss to Col 2:12 give the more familiar word βάπτισμα. FERGUSON (*Baptism*, 160) thinks that Paul might have borrowed the term from the language of the opponents, who were treating baptism as they did other ritual ordinances. Josephus, *Ant.* 18.117, uses βαπτισμός for the baptism administered by John.

15 For an account of different interpretations of the term from patristic times to the present, see A. R. CROSS, "The Meaning of 'Baptisms' in Hebrews 6.2," 163–186 (163–166).

mission into the Christian community, continued observance of levitical laws was basic to the Christians ethical code of behaviour in the temple, Buchanan argues. The author of Hebrews and his addressees belonged, according to this view, to some such group and understood the term accordingly.[16]

The main problem with this interpretation is that while it makes sense of the plural it neglects the argumentative flow of the text. The author discusses the beginning of the Christian life and the instruction that was given to the addressees at the time of their conversion. It is likely that he intends to remind them of the teaching concerning baptisms that was given to them as they heard the basic message about Christ and were to be admitted into the community. Moreover, repentance and laying on of hands were not normally associated with levitical ablutions, while we may assume that they were related to the Christian baptism.[17] The author regards the ablutions as inferior regulations of the flesh (9:10).[18] Yet the fact that he uses βαπτισμός rather than βάπτισμα, and puts it in plural, suggests that he recalled and wished to communicate the baptismal instruction as containing an element where the Christian baptism was seen in connection to other religious washings with which he and the hearers/readers were familiar.[19] These washings could be of different kinds and need not only have included Jewish practices.[20] The Christian baptism, the initiates were presumably taught, was similar and yet distinctively and decisively dissimilar from other well-known ancient washings and baptisms. In view of the deeply rooted practice of such ablutions among the Jews, it comes as no surprise that the recipients of the letter – themselves called "Hebrews" – needed such teaching already from the beginning. The specifically Christian use of water had to be grasped by the new adherents. The exhortation in 6:1–2 might indicate that they had not entirely understood it, or that they were turning back to old practices. The hearers/readers should realize that this instruction about baptisms was given to them already at their conversion. Now they are to move on to perfection.

The expression ἅπαξ φωτισθέντας in verse 4 is also of interest. In Hebrews the term "once" (ἐφάπαξ or ἅπαξ) indicates a temporal perspective of once-for-all and the unique quality of what is described. The verb "illuminate" (φωτίζειν)

---

16   G. BUCHANAN, *To the Hebrews: Translation, Comment and Conclusions*, 104.
17   So FERGUSON, *Baptism*, 187.
18   So GRÄSSER, *An die Hebräer*, 1:342. Gräßer however goes too far in rejecting any indication of levitical ablutions and maintains that the plural refers to an unknown Christian initiation practice including several repeated baptisms.
19   Similarly WEISS, *Der Brief and die Hebräer*, 339.
20   JOHNSON (*Hebrews*, 159) mentions that an individual might have undergone a proselyte baptism, circumcision, John's baptism, and baptism into the Jesus movement. CROSS ("The Meaning of 'Baptisms'") suggests that baptism in blood, that is, martyrdom, be included in the "baptisms" and traces this understanding back to Tertullian.

carries connotations that relate to instruction and salvific revelation. In view of other New Testament passages using the metaphor of enlightenment to describe an important occurrence in the life of the believer,[21] it probably here refers to the experience of baptism.[22] It is of interest that Justin writes of the Christian baptism in similar terms in 1 *Apol.* 61.12: "And this washing (τοῦτο τὸ λουτρόν) is called illumination (φωτισμός), as they who learn these things are illuminated (φωτιζομένων) in their understandings."[23] He identifies both baptism as well as teaching about baptism as illumination. The Syriac versions paraphrase the verb in Heb 6:4 in order to make this meaning explicit. The Peshitta has "who have once descended to baptism"; the Haraclean Syriac renders it "who have once been baptized."[24]

While the author has previously in the letter reminded the hearers/readers of the instruction about baptisms that was given to them at their conversion and urged them to move on to perfection, he now has the specifically Christian baptism in mind. In verse 4 he explains or develops (γάρ) the preceding two verses and, as the overview of the argumentative structure shows, puts the expression ἅπαξ φωτισθέντας at top of several parallel occurrences of aorist verbs (φωτισθέντας, γευσαμένους, γενηθέντας, γευσαμένους). Together they describe the most important aspects of the beginning of the Christian life, wherein people tasted the heavenly gift, became sharers in the Holy Spirit, and tasted the good word of God and the powers of the age to come. Since these parallel expressions describe a crucial experience at a decisive moment in the past, we may assume that the hearers/readers understood also ἅπαξ φωτισθέντας as a reference to the once-for-all experience of being baptized, not only to the instruction mentioned in verse 1. The four lines in verses 4–5 might in fact describe the singular grand event of becoming a Christian. Baptism as a once-for-all experience is closely linked to other central aspects of the beginning of the Christian life and seen as an event where the persons being baptized gained insight into the spiritual realities which they at that moment tasted and received, and now tend to abandon.

---

21 E.g. Rom 13:12; 2 Cor 4:6; Eph 5:14 (perhaps a fragment of a baptismal hymn); Heb 10:32; 1 Pet 2:9.

22 This is not to say that it was a technical term for baptism.

23 Cf. also 1 *Apol.* 65.1 ("... in order that we may offer prayers in common for ourselves and for the illuminated [τοῦ φωτισθέντος] person"); *Dial.* 122.5 ("... us who have been illumined [πεφωτισμένους] by Jesus"). Cf. also Clement of Alexandria, *Paed.* 1.6.26.

24 So according to Beasley-Murray, *Baptism*, 244–245.

2.2. Hebrews 9:9–10

The second occurrence of baptismal references is in 9:9–10. The crucial expression is διάφοροι βαπτισμοί in verse 10. Again, it appears within a larger hierarchy of arguments that came to the fore at the oral performance:

> ⁹ ἥτις παραβολὴ εἰς τὸν καιρὸν τὸν ἐνεστηκότα,
> καθ' ἣν δῶρά τε καὶ θυσίαι προσφέρονται
> μὴ δυνάμεναι κατὰ συνείδησιν τελειῶσαι τὸν λατρεύοντα,
> ¹⁰ μόνον ἐπὶ βρώμασιν καὶ πόμασιν καὶ **διαφόροις βαπτισμοῖς**,
> δικαιώματα σαρκὸς
> μέχρι καιροῦ διορθώσεως ἐπικείμενα.

> ⁹ This (lit. which) is a parable for the present time,
> according to which both gifts and sacrifices are offered
> that cannot perfect the worshipper according to conscience,
> ¹⁰ only on the level of food and drink and various "baptisms,"
> regulations of the flesh
> imposed until the time of setting straight.

The author mentions διάφοροι βαπτισμοί without reference to the Christian baptism. The hearers/readers are here probably led to experience an echo of the ablutions in the tent of meeting mentioned in Lev 16:23–28 in connection with references to the regulations for offerings on the Day of Atonement. The whole section of 9:1–10 is framed by an inclusion marked by the word "regulations" (δικαιώματα) in verses 1 and 10, presenting a description of the parts of the tent where the priests alone were admitted and the ways in which these parts were used and by whom.

This description or tent is said to be a "parable" – probably in the sense of being an illustration (cf. 11:19) – for the present time.[25] The term ἥτις, literally "which," refers either to "the first tent" (τῆς πρώτης σκηνῆς) in verse 8 or to the whole preceding section.[26] It indicates that the various levitical "baptisms" were heard/read as regulations of the flesh that were inefficient, to be sure, but that also functioned as illustrations for the present situation of the author and his audience. They were temporarily imposed until the decisive καιρός and inferior to the time when Christ came as a high priest (9:11).

---

25 For discussion of the extent and meaning of the "parable," cf. S. STANLEY, "Hebrews 9:6–10: The 'Parable' of the Tabernacle," 385–399. Stanley prefers the meaning "illustration."

26 Grammatically it could refer also to "the way of [viz. into] the sanctuary" (τὴν τῶν ἁγίων ὁδόν) in verse 8 or to "standing" (στάσιν) in verse 8.

2.3. Hebrews 10:21–23

The third instance of baptismal references is the expression τὸ σῶμα ὕδατι καθαρῷ in 10:22. The hierarchy of the argumentation that was expressed at the performance may be illustrated as follows:

21   … καὶ ἱερέα μέγαν ἐπὶ τὸν οἶκον τοῦ θεοῦ,
22   προσερχώμεθα
     μετὰ ἀληθινῆς καρδίας
     ἐν πληροφορίᾳ πίστεως
     ῥεραντισμένοι τὰς καρδίας ἀπὸ συνειδήσεως πονηρᾶς
     καὶ λελουσμένοι **τὸ σῶμα ὕδατι καθαρῷ**·
23   κατέχωμεν τὴν ὁμολογίαν τῆς ἐλπίδος ἀκλινῆ,
     πιστὸς γὰρ ὁ ἐπαγγειλάμενος·

21   … and (since we have) a great priest over the house of God,
22   let us approach
     with a true heart
     in fullness of faith
     (our) hearts sprinkled (clean) from evil conscience
     and (our) body washed with pure water.
23   Let us hold fast to the confession of hope without wavering,
     for he who has promised is faithful.

This passage contains strong cultic imagery. Chapter 10 portrays the old and inefficient sacrifices prescribed in the law and contrasts them with Christ's sacrifice once and for all. The exhortation to "approach" maintains the cultic connotations, viz. to approach the altar or the house of God (cf. 10:21),[27] and describes the circumstances of the approach with two parallel participles (ῥεραντισμένοι, λελουσμένοι) stating that the Christians must have the hearts sprinkled (clean) from evil conscience and their body washed with pure water.

The language in verse 22 creates an echo of the regulations for the Day of Atonement in Lev 16:3–19. In that text Aaron is exhorted to bathe his body in water (LXX Lev 16:4: λούσεται ὕδατι πᾶν τὸ σῶμα αὐτοῦ) and sprinkle (LXX Lev 16:14: ῥανεῖ … ῥανεῖ) the blood of the bull on the front of the mercy seat as an offering for himself. In Lev 8, where Aaron and his sons are washed with water as part of their ordination (8:6), Moses takes some of the blood of the

---

27   Cf. W. Thüsing, "'Lasst uns hinzutreten' (Hebr 10,22). Zur Frage nach dem Sinn der Kulttheologie im Hebräerbrief," 1–17. Thüsing minimizes however the more metaphorical sense of the cultic images used in Hebrews.

second ram and puts it on Aaron and his sons (8:23-24; cf. 8:30), thus following the regulations of Exod 29:4, 20-21. The description in Heb 10:1-17 and the term προσερχώμεθα in 10:22 created among the hearers/readers who knew the Greek Bible a primary echo of the Day of Atonement,[28] but that echo was probably blended with allusions to the consecration for priestly ministry.[29] Just as the hearers/readers in the previous verses were reminded of the confidence they have to enter (παρρησίαν εἰς τὴν εἴσοδον) into the sanctuary by the blood of Jesus and the way he opened for them through the curtain (10:19-20), the believers, it is now suggested, are as consecrated priests to enter into the presence of God.

The sprinkling of the hearts and the washing of the body are presented in two parallel phrases. The parallel might express a contrast or it might point to one and the same reality. The former alternative suggests that the heart is contrasted with the body and indicates a reference first to the internal cleansing through the sacrifice of Christ and then to the external cleansing through baptism.

This view is problematic, because in a cultic setting distinctions between inner and outer cleansings are irrelevant. What seems to be an outwardly practice carries in a cultic setting an effectively consecrating function. The fact that the author describes the water as "pure" indicates instead that there is more at stake than the mere washing of the body and produces an echo of Ezek 36:25.[30] After describing how the Lord God promises to "sprinkle clean water upon you," thus cleaning the house of Israel from all uncleannesses and idols, the prophet declares God's promise of a new heart and a new spirit to be put within them. Here the sprinkling of clean water and the rendering of a new heart express parallel divine actions.[31]

The author of Hebrews will not have meant to communicate less to the audience and used the term "hearts" because of its previous occurrence in the singular in the same verse.[32] The two parallel clauses therefore express one and the same reality.[33] As we saw, the hearers/readers were led to understand baptism

---

28 W. Lane suggests that the echo is to the blood and water of the Sinai covenant, but these allusions are far more remote. Cf. W. LANE, *Hebrews*, 2:287.

29 For an emphasis on the imagery of ordination, cf. LEITHART, "Womb of the World," 53-55.

30 Cf. also *T. Levi* 8:4-5.

31 JOHNSON (*Hebrews*, 258) maintains that the washing of the body with pure water extends the image of purification to the body as the outward symbol and instrument of faithful obedience. Johnson downplays however the parallel character of the two participial clauses and neglects the allusion to Ezek 36:25.

32 Cf. FERGUSON, *Baptism*, 188: "That the sprinkling here does not refer to baptism is indicated by the fact that it is applied to the hearts." Ferguson fails to see the rhetorical finesse of the author's reference to the hearts.

33 N. A. DAHL suggested that the sprinkling of the hearts identifies the inner significance of the reality that baptism ritually signifies. See his article "A New and Living Way: The Approach to

as a decisive experience closely linked to other central aspects of the beginning of the Christian life and as a moment when the persons being baptized gained decisive insight into the spiritual realities (6:1–6). It was much more than an external cleansing of the body. They are by means of cultic images exhorted to draw near to God, just like the High Priest of ancient times did, but now on the basis of a superior cleansing afforded by the sacrifice of Christ. The cleansing with water effectively purifies them through the power of Christ's death and gives them confidence to enter into the presence of God.

3. Thematic Implications

It is easy to read too much into a strongly rhetorical text. Yet baptism emerges indeed as a concept that is of more significance to the author of Hebrews and his hearers/readers than might have been expected from a first glance at the letter. From the hierarchical structure of the oral performance of the text, certain thematic and fundamental convictions emerge. The references to the Christian baptism in 6:1–6 and 10:22–23, in particular, are set within a larger framework and imply in spite of their strongly rhetorical character certain fundamental views of baptism and its practice.

3.1. Baptism as Initiation

The first and most evident observation is that the author regarded and portrayed baptism as a vital experience of initiation belonging to the beginning of the addressees' life as Christians. It is unclear precisely when he believed they were baptised, at their conversion or soon after it, but 6:1–2 suggests that they received instruction about baptisms after their repentance and faith in God. That instruction was part of the foundation of the Christian life. The fact that the author reminded them of several other fundamental Christian doctrines about which they had been instructed and that the instruction about the Christian baptism probably included a clarification of its distinctive feature in comparison with other religious washings, might indicate that they now – at the time of hearing/reading the letter for the first time – looked back upon their baptism as a rite which was part of that repentance from dead works about which they had needed proper instruction before it was carried out.

This does not mean that baptism was secondary to conversion. The hearers/readers were reminded of baptism as a decisive initiatory event which in effect made them sharers in the heavenly realities. Whenever it took place, it was more than a symbolic act of obedience. The parallel occurrences of four aorist participles (φωτισθέντας, γευσαμένους, γενηθέντας, γευσαμένους) in

---

God According to Hebrews 10:19–25," 401–412.

6:4–5 shows that the enlightenment of baptism was seen as a comprehensive experience at a specific moment of time. The repeated aorists point to one and the same event in the past, an event that had different dimensions. The author makes no indication that he wished the hearers/readers to think of a number of successive events, as he could have done by inserting temporal markers in the text. Although he shows little explicit interest in the idea known from Paul that baptism means incorporation into a community of believers,[34] he formulates with rhetorical skill the notion that the experience of baptism effectively and once and for all mediates a new life and brings the baptized person into the realm of the Holy Spirit. In 10:22 he communicates the same understanding of baptism. Employing Old Testament cultic language extensively, he adds a dimension of the initiatory rite which symbolically points to the ordination for a new Christian priesthood and explicates the truly purifying cleansing with water as a means to enter like priests into the presence of God.[35] To be baptized is to move into a new relationship with God and the whole transcendent reality.

3.2. Baptism as a Christological Event

This effective function of baptism or cleansing with water has further important corollaries. Baptism is also a profoundly Christological event in Hebrews. Perhaps it was precisely this Christological aspect that needed to be pointed out to the newly converted as they were taught about various baptisms (6:1). But not only is instruction about baptisms part of the elementary teaching about Christ. The Christological aspect is even more fundamental to what baptism is.

In particular, Jesus' death is central. Those who reject the heavenly realities that baptism mediated in effect crucify (again) the Son of God on their own (6:6).[36] The expression ἀνασταυροῦντας ἑαυτοῖς, here translated as "on their own crucifying (again)," has been understood variously, such as indicating, for instance, that they crucify to their own loss or that they crucify in order to end the relationship with Christ. In any event, it indicates that while not in a position to literally crucify Jesus, they do something that has Christological implications and themselves symbolically participate in Christ's execution. What is at stake here is not so much his death as such as the notion that they make a spectacle of him (παραδειγματίζοντας) and put him to shame (cf. 12:2). To be

---

34 For an attempt to read Hebrews as a pseudepigraphon imitating Paul, cf. C. K. ROTHSCHILD, *Hebrews as Pseudepigraphon: The History and Significance of the Pauline Attribution of Hebrews*. It is however difficult to maintain that the first hearers/readers experienced the allusions to the Pauline letters throughout the oral performance, especially as the imitative indication of Pauline authorship is only vaguely communicated at the very end of Hebrews.

35 Cf. LEITHART, "Womb of the World," 49–65.

36 The prefix ἀνα in ἀνασταυροῦντας may mean "again" or refer to "the lifting" up in crucifixion. Since the discussion concerns believers who have accepted the once-for-all character of Jesus' death, the meaning "again" might be implied here.

baptized is so intimately linked with Christ that its rejection is equivalent with the most disgraceful act done towards him.[37]

There is a further, even more fundamental Christological dimension to baptism in the letter. The death of Christ is not only used as a point of reference for the shameful act which those who reject baptism make themselves guilty of, but it is also the essential power of baptism. The link between baptism and the death of Jesus is drawn almost to the extreme in the strongly cultic language of the letter. This emphasis has its own distinctive character in the New Testament. Whereas Paul stresses the importance of Jesus' death using the imagery of immersion and identification (Rom 6:4–5), the author of Hebrews finds his analogy in the ceremonial of the sanctuary.[38] The immediate basis for the exhortation that the hearers/readers shall approach the house of God with sprinkled hearts and washed body is that the blood of Jesus gives them confidence to enter into the sanctuary (10:19). The exhortation in fact builds on the entire argument so far developed in chapter 10 and draws the conclusion from the emphasis on Christ's sacrifice once and for all. The implication for baptism is that it is effective only through Jesus' obedient offering of himself in death. It is the blood of his sacrificial death that gives power to baptism and makes it into a truly purifying experience.

3.3. Baptism as an Eschatological Event

Baptism is also an eschatological event in Hebrews.[39] Intersected with references to baptism are notions that made the hearers/readers think of it as something that brings them into contact with what they have since long waited for and now finally become part of. The typological pattern of relating to cultic realities depicted in the Old Testament as well as the element of spatial thinking of what is above and what is below are in Hebrews supplemented with references to a two-age eschatology that is expressly future-oriented.[40]

---

37 L. SABOURIN takes εἰς μετάνοιαν and ἀνασταυροῦντας together and argues that ἀδύνατον goes with ἀνασταυροῦντας: "it is impossible to crucify afresh the Son of God for the sake of one's repentance." See his article "Crucifying Afresh for One's Repentance (Heb 6:4-6)," 264–271. Sabourin's suggestion, while increasing the importance of Christ's death, does not do justice to the syntactical balance of the sentence. For critique of Sabourin, see A. H. SNYMAN, "Hebrews 6.4–6: From a Semiotic Discourse Perspective," 354–368 (363–364).

38 Cf. similarly FLEMINGTON, *The New Testament Doctrine of Baptism*, 98.

39 In his treatment of baptism in Hebrews, Lars Hartman points precisely to its Christological and eschatological dimensions. See HARTMAN, *'Into the Name of the Lord Jesus': Baptism in the Early Church*, 123–126.

40 The classic study pointing to the role of Jewish eschatology and not only Platonic cosmology in Hebrews is C. K. BARRETT, "The Eschatology in the Epistle to the Hebrews," 363–393. For a more recent statement following Barrett, see S. D. MACKIE, *Eschatology and Exhortation in the Epistle to the Hebrews*, 54–58, 124–135.

The instruction about baptisms is thus presented in a way that relates to teaching about events of the end-time, such as resurrection of the dead and judgement (6:2). Moreover, the enlightenment of baptism is closely connected to the tasting of the heavenly gift, of becoming sharers in the Holy Spirit, and it is parallel to the tasting of the powers of the age to come (6:4). As the author somewhat later in the same passage expresses his confidence that the hearers/readers will not fall away but eventually reach their salvation and inherit the promises, he points them earnestly to the zeal for the fullness of hope (πληροφορίαν τῆς ἐλπίδος) until the end (6:11). This accords with the fact that the hearers/readers are in chapter 10 reminded of the fullness of faith (πληροφορία πίστεως) and the confession of hope.[41] Thus they might in view of the reference to baptismal sprinkling and washing have interpreted the cultic imagery in terms of what they fully believed and confessed about their eschatological hope at baptism and now should hold fast to on the basis of Christ's faithfulness (10:22–23) and in view of the Day that is approaching (10:25). What they had experienced, and what was described by means of typological comparison with cultic practices, was in essence a decisive eschatological event.

3.4. Baptism as a Non-Repeatable Event

Linked especially to the Christological and eschatological character of baptism is the author's well-known insistence on the impossibility of repentance for apostates and, by implication, that baptism is a unique, non-repeatable event.[42] On both occasions where baptism is mentioned, the author directs the attention of the hearers/readers to the inevitable condemnation and judgement of those who have sinned and fallen away from their new Christ-centered faith (6:4–9; 10:26–31).[43] There is no indication that the apostates have any hope of redemption or that they could repeat or again claim the reality of baptism that they once truly experienced. To be sure, there is no formulation of a carefully considered doctrine on the impossibility of post-baptismal repentance and the author certainly wished to emphasize to his hearers/readers the more hopeful parts of his exhortations. But while later Christian authors maintained different views on

---

41 As is well-known, the connection between faith and hope in Hebrews is quite intimate. Cf. 11:1, 13–16. See ATTRIDGE, *The Letter to the Hebrews*, 288.

42 For English-speaking literature on this much discussed subject, see D. MATHEWSON, "Reading Heb 6:4–6 in Light of the Old Testament," 209–225 (209 n. 1). To his list could be added R. B. COMPTON, "Persevering and Falling Away: A Reexamination of Hebrews 6:4–6," 135–167. For a survey of research including also German (and other) literature, see I. GOLDHAHN-MÜLLER, *Die Grenze der Gemeinde. Studien zum Problem der Zweiten Buse im Neuen Testament unter Berücksichtigung der Entwicklung im 2. Jh. bis Tertullian*, 3–23. To her discussion could be added H. LÖHR, *Umkehr und Sünde im Hebräerbrief.*

43 So-called warning passages appear also elsewhere in Hebrews. Cf. 2:1–4; 3:7–4:13; 12:14–29.

the possibility of a second repentance,[44] the author's stance in Hebrews is a rigorous and non-negotiable one.[45]

The Christological aspect of baptism implies that baptism is non-repeatable by linking apostasy to the act of crucifying and dishonouring the Son of God a second time (6:6). The author lets his hearers/readers assume that the apostates had like all other converts at their baptism accepted the once-for-all character of Christ's sacrificial death but now, by falling away from all that which they had experienced in connection with baptism, make his crucifixion null and void and put him to shame. In Hebrews there is a strong sense of sin as refusal of both the gift and the giver and a corresponding sense both of the need for conversion and of the impossibility of converting when the Christological ground of conversion has itself been rejected.[46] The underlying conviction is that since Christ's death which gives baptism its salvific force cannot be repeated, the baptism which mediated salvation on the basis of that death is also non-repeatable. When the converts become apostates, they in effect make his death into mockery and nullify any possibility of experiencing the real power of baptism again.

The eschatological character of baptism points to its urgency and significance at the end-time and also suggests that it cannot be repeated. While the author occasionally seems to think that there is no time to repent (10:25; 12:17), he does not use the argument of the immanence of the end in any extensive way to preclude a time for second repentance.[47] In the passages of exhortation following closely upon the references to baptism, it is rather the fact that baptism belongs to and mediates those gifts which God has bestowed on the believers that is of significance. Baptism is eschatological in view of its greatness. When the author warns the hearers/readers against wilfully persisting in sin after having received the knowledge of truth (10:26), he therefore directs their attention to the previous references to baptism and depicts the fearful prospect of the apostate in eschatological terms of eternal destruction (10:27–31), before reminding them of those earlier days when they had been enlightened (10:32). Thus, to suppose that they could take or leave what was mediated in baptism or that they could repeat or reclaim such a grand gift at any time after having rejected it would be to minimize its significance. The baptism of the believers

---

44 See e.g. GOLDHAHN-MÜLLER, *Die Grenze der Gemeinde*.

45 COMPTON ("Persevering and Falling Away," 136–145) provides a survey of the major views concerning the spiritual status of those addressed in 6:4–6 (and elsewhere in the letter) and the nature of the warning. I follow those scholars who interpret them to be true believers – not least in view of the author's view of baptism – and the apostasy to mean loss of salvation. See e.g. S. MCKNIGHT, "The Warning Passages of Hebrews: A Formal Analysis and Theological Conclusions," 21–59 (24–25, 43–48).

46 So JOHNSON, *Hebrews*, 163.

47 This is pointed out by ATTRIDGE, *The Epistle to the Hebrews*, 169.

was in distinction to other baptisms of such great importance for the new life of the believer that its rejection would mean nothing else but final destruction.

Bibliography

ATTRIDGE, HAROLD W., *The Epistle to the Hebrews* (Hermeneia), Philadelphia, Pa.: Fortress 1989.

BARRETT, C. K., "The Eschatology in the Epistle to the Hebrews," in: *The Background of the New Testament and Its Eschatology: Essays in Honour of C. H. Dodd*, ed. W. D. Davies and David Daube, Cambridge: Cambridge University Press 1956, 363–393.

BARTH, MARKUS, *Die Taufe – Ein Sakrament? Ein exegetischer Beitrag zum Gespräch über die christliche Taufe*, Zürich: Zollikon 1951.

BEASLEY-MURRAY, GEORGE R., *Baptism in the New Testament*, Exeter: Paternoster Press 1962.

BUCHANAN, GEORGE, *To the Hebrews: Translation, Comment and Conclusions* (AB 36), Garden City, NY: Doubleday & Company ²1976.

COMPTON, R. BRUCE, "Persevering and Falling Away: A Reexamination of Hebrews 6:4–6," in: *Detroit Baptism Seminary Journal* 1 (1996) 135–167.

CROSS, ANTHONY R., "The Meaning of 'Baptisms' in Hebrews 6.2," in: *Dimensions of Baptism: Biblical and Theological Studies* (JSNTSup 234), ed. Stanley E. Porter and Anthony R. Cross, Sheffield: Sheffield Academic Press 2002, 163–186.

DAHL, NILS ALSTRUP, "A New and Living Way: The Approach to God According to Hebrews 10:19–25," in: *Int* 5 (1951) 401–412.

DELLING, GERHARD, *Die Taufe im Neuen Testament*, Berlin: Evangelische Verlagsanstalt 1963.

FERGUSON, EVERETT, *Baptism in the Early Church: History, Theology, and Liturgy in the First Five Centuries*, Grand Rapids, Mich.: Eerdmans 2009.

FLEMINGTON, W. F., *The New Testament Doctrine of Baptism*, London: SPCK 1948.

GOLDHAHN-MÜLLER, INGRID, *Die Grenze der Gemeinde. Studien zum Problem der Zweiten Buse im Neuen Testament unter Berücksichtigung der Entwicklung im 2. Jh. bis Tertullian* (GTA 39), Göttingen: Vandenhoeck & Ruprecht 1989.

GRÄSSER, ERICH, *An die Hebräer* (3 vols.; EKK 17:1–3), Zürich: Benziger Verlag and Neukirchen-Vluyn: Neukirchener Verlag 1990–1997.

HARTMAN, LARS, 'Into the Name of the Lord Jesus': Baptism in the Early Church (Studies of the New Testament and Its World), Edinburgh: Clark 1997.

JOHNSON, LUKE TIMOTHY, Hebrews: A Commentary (The New Testament Library), Louisville, Ky.: Westminister John Knox Press 2006.

KOESTER, CRAIG R., Hebrews: A New Translation with Introduction and Commentary (AB 36), New York: Doubleday 2001.

LANE, WILLIAM, Hebrews (2 vols.; WBC 47A-B), Dallas, Tex.: Word 1991.

LEITHART, PETER J., "Womb of the World: Baptism and the Priesthood of the New Covenant in Hebrews 10.19-22," in: *JSNT* 78 (2000) 49-65.

LINDARS, BARNABAS, *The Theology of the Letter to the Hebrews* (New Testament Theology), Cambridge: Cambridge University Press 1991.

— "The Rhetorical Structure of Hebrews," in: *NTS* 35 (1989) 382-406.

LÖHR, HERMUT, *Umkehr und Sünde im Hebräerbrief* (BZNW 73), Berlin: de Gruyter 1994.

MACKIE, SCOTT D., *Eschatology and Exhortation in the Epistle to the Hebrews* (WUNT 2/223), Tübingen: Mohr Siebeck 2007.

MATHEWSON, DAVE, "Reading Heb 6:4-6 in Light of the Old Testament," in: *WTJ* 61 (1999) 209-225.

McKNIGHT, SCOT, "The Warning Passages of Hebrews: A Formal Analysis and Theological Conclusions," in: *TJ* 13 (1992) 21-59.

PETERSON, DAVID, *Hebrews and Perfection: An Examination of the Concept of Perfection in the 'Epistle to the Hebrews'* (SNTSMS 47), Cambridge: Cambridge University Press 1982.

ROTHSCHIELD, CLAIRE K., *Hebrews as Pseudepigraphon: The History and Significance of the Pauline Attribution of Hebrews* (WUNT 235), Tübingen: Mohr Siebeck 2009.

SABOURIN, LEOPOLD, "Crucifying Afresh for One's Repentance (Heb 6:4-6)," in: *BTB* 6 (1976) 264-271.

SCHNEIDER, JOHANNES, *Die Taufe im Neuen Testament*, Stuttgart: Kohlhammer 1952.

SNYMAN, ANDRIES H., "Hebrews 6.4-6: From a Semiotic Discourse Perspective," in: *Discourse Analysis and the New Testament: Approaches and Results*, ed. Stanley E. Porter and Jeffrey T. Reed (JSNTSup 170), Sheffield: Sheffield Academic Press 1999, 354-368.

STANLEY, STEVE, "Hebrews 9:6–10: The 'Parable' of the Tabernacle," in: *NovT* 37 (1995) 385–399.

THÜSING, WILHELM, ",Lasst uns hinzutreten' (Hebr 10,22). Zur Frage nach dem Sinn der Kulttheologie im Hebräerbrief," in: *BZ* 9 (1965) 1–17.

ÜBELACKER, WALTER, *Der Hebräerbrief als Appell: I. Untersuchungen zu* exordium, narratio *und* postscriptum *(Hebr 1–2 und 13, 22–25)* (ConBNT 21), Stockholm: Almqvist & Wiksell International 1989.

WEISS, HANS-FRIEDRICH, *Der Brief and die Hebräer* (KEK 13), Göttingen: Vandenhoeck & Ruprecht 1991.

Because of "The Name of Christ"
Baptism and the Location of Identity in 1 Peter

Halvor Moxnes

Baptism is a central theme underlying much of the exhortations in 1. Peter, it is understood as the basis for the life and identity for the addressees, but it is only one passage where it is explicitly mentioned, viz. 3:18–22. This is therefore the best place to start to gain an insight in the way 1 Peter understands baptism. This text uses and integrates traditions and material from Jewish and other early Christian literature; this raises the question if the letter has its own specific understanding of baptism.

The central role of baptism, illustrated by 3:18–22, has been a main cause for many suggestions that 1 Peter as a whole should be understood as related to baptism in some way or other, either as a baptismal homily or catechesis, or as composed of material from liturgical or creedal traditions used in exhortations and paraenesis. Several of these homiletic or paraenetical forms build on a model oriented in time, for instance, "return to baptism", or the transition form "before" to "now." On the basis of a discussion of some of these proposals, I will suggest a reading of 1 Peter where the baptismal identity of the audience is addressed in spatial categories.

1. Baptism in 1 Peter: The Central Text 3:18–22

The main baptismal passage in 1 Peter, 3:18–22, is part of a larger section, 3:13–4:6 that speaks of the suffering of the Christians. The close context is 1 Peter 3:13–17 that discusses the sufferings of the readers, in the form of abusive speech and shaming from those who "revile your good behaviour in Christ" (3:16). The section ends with the comfort that "it is better to suffer for doing right, if such should be the will of God, than for doing wrong." In the introduction to 3:18, Christ's suffering is invoked but in contrast to other exhortations to endure suffering, e.g. 2:21, *not* as an example. Instead it is Christ's suffering for sins and the redemptive effects of that suffering in the lives of the addressees that is emphasized. The purpose of Christ's death was that "he might bring you to God," and that was a result of Christ being put to death "in the flesh" but made alive "in the spirit." (3:18). "Spirit" may serve as a catchword and introduction to the following section, "In the spirit also he went and made his proclamation to the imprisoned spirits" (3:19) that marks the rather abrupt transition to a section that may seem as a separate tradition, with its combination of Christ's proclamation to the spirits, the story of Noah who was saved through water, as an antitype to baptism that now saves (3:19–21). Finally, at the end of v. 21–22, the text returns to the resurrection of Jesus Christ as that which brings salvation. Therefore it has been suggested that the text in 3:18–22 has been put together from different sources, and that 3:18 and 22 serve as a frame for traditional material in 3:19–21.[1]

Here I will draw attention to the central elements in these traditions and their use in 1 Peter. The "imprisoned spirits, those who had refused to obey in the past," refer to the Enoch tradition of the fallen angels, also called spirits in I Enoch 6–16.[2] This is a central aspect of the reworking of the Genesis tradition in 6:1–4. I Enoch transforms the idea of the sons of God having intercourse with the daughters of the people, and makes it into a theology of fallen angels, who produced giants who corrupted people and led them into sin. God determined to send a flood to punish the giants, while the angels were to be held in bondage until the final judgment. Enoch was sent by the angels to plead their case before God, but their plea was rejected. This tradition of the angels, the flood and judgment is found in many versions in Jewish and early Christian texts, of special interest for 1 Peter, in the related traditions of 2 Peter 2:4–5 and Jude 6.[3]

Christ's proclamation upon his ascension of judgement for the angels introduces the theme of the deluge, with destruction of the unrighteous,[4] in contrast to the salvation of the righteous Noah. Noah was found as a model of the exemplary and righteous man in Jewish literature,[5] and in early Christianity also in 2 Peter 2:5 and Hebrew 11:7, as an example of faith and righteousness. The explicit mention of "a few, eight" emphasizes the small number who were saved διά water. This preposition should be understood not in an instrumental

---

1   See the review of previous research in J. H. ELLIOTT, *1 Peter*, 647–68, 693–710. R. BULTMANN, "Bekenntnis- und Liedfragmente im ersten Petrusbrief," is a classic study of 3:18–22; the most comprehensive is W. J. DALTON, *Christ's Proclamation to the Spirits*; still valuable is BO REICKE, *The Disobedient Spirits and Christian Baptism*.

2   A. ISAAC, "I Enoch. Introduction," 9.

3   J. C. VANDERKAM, "1 Enoch, Enochic Motifs, and Enoch in Early Christian Literature."

4   The notion that Jesus went and proclaimed for the imprisoned spirits (3:19), has sometimes been interpreted in light of a much later tradition of Jesus' descent to the underworld, Hades, in the period between his death and resurrection (see the late apocryphal *Gospels of Bartholomew* and *Nicodemus*), later understood as Jesus preaching salvation to the righteous of the old covenant. However, this tradition should not be read back into 1 Peter, which speaks of Jesus going "in the spirit," i.e. after his resurrection, so that it refers to his ascension, and the proclamation is judgment upon the evil angels; see DALTON, *Christ's Proclamation to the Spirits*, 177–84; ELLIOTT, *1 Peter*, 706–709.

5   A few examples from writers close in time to 1 Peter: Philo, *Abr.* 27–46; *Migr.* 125; Josephus, *Ant.* 1.75–79; further references, see ELLIOTT, *1 Peter*, 663.

sense, it was not the water that saved, but Noah and his family were saved *from* the deluge, or while "passing through" water, as in Wis 14:5.[6] It is this saving act that now is the *antitypos* for baptism, that now saves "you." This is the central phrase that establishes the place and an identity for the readers of 1 Peter. *Antitypon* establishes a correspondence between the salvation of Noah and his family at the beginning of time and the eschatological salvation of the believers through baptism and the resurrection of Christ.[7] 1 Peter here presents the first example of an association between Noah, the Flood and baptism, a theme that should become popular in Early Christian literature.[8]

Whereas the references to the imprisoned spirits, the deluge and Noah showed how 1 Peter stood in a cultural context with contemporary Jewish and Early Christian adaptations of ancient Israelite traditions,[9] the rest of v. 21 shows 1 Peter as an original and independent interpreter of baptism. The expression "baptism saves you" is unique in the New Testament,[10] and is qualified with the phrase "through the resurrection of Jesus Christ." This is similar to the way Paul speaks of baptism, linking it to the resurrection of Christ, although he does not explicitly say that baptism saves. 1 Peter introduces also another qualification that defines baptism: it is "not (as) a removal of filth from the body but (as) a pledge to God of a sound mindfulness of God's will."[11] This is a contrast between an external activity and an internal commitment, similar to Jesus' exhortations in the Sermon on the Mount, Matt 6:1–18, and Paul on circumcision, Rom 2:28–29. The negative reference may be to ritual cleansings as practised by Jews.[12] In contrast baptism is a moral action, a pledge of commitment to follow God's will. This understanding of baptism is followed up in the paraenesis throughout the letter, that can be characterised as *reditus ad baptismum*.[13]

But it is "through the resurrection of Jesus Christ" that baptism saves; the contrast between external cleansing and internal commitment serves as a par-

---

6   Elliott, *1 Peter*, 667.

7   The grammatical construction as well as text-critical problems cause difficulties for the interpretation here. It seems most coherent with the understanding that it is not the water, but the whole act that saves, that the reference for *antitypon* is the preceding saving event; G. R. Beasley-Murray, *Baptism in the New Testament*, 259–260; Elliott, *1 Peter*, 670–672. For an argument that the correspondence is between water and baptism, see J. D. G. Dunn, *Baptism in the Holy Spirit*, 216.

8   J. Daniélou, "Déluge, Baptême, Jugement;" J. Daniélou, *The Bible and the Liturgy*, 70–85.

9   J. Achtemeier (*1 Peter*, 70–73) emphasizes the importance of "the language of Israel" as the "controlling metaphor" in the theology of 1 Peter.

10 Elliott, *1 Peter*, 674.

11 Translation from Elliott, *1 Peter*, 637.

12 Beasley-Murray, *Baptism*, 260–261.

13 K. Berger, *Formgeschichte des Neuen Testaments*, 130.

enthetical explanation of the moral significance of baptism.[14] It is the explicit combination of the eschatological event, through the resurrection of Christ, and the total moral commitment to this event that makes 1 Peter's explanation of baptism in 3:21 so central to many of the arguments in the letter.[15]

2. Baptism and the Structure and Composition of 1 Peter

On the basis of the central role of baptism and new birth in the letter there have been many attempts to see the form and function of the letter directly related to baptism.[16] This has been part of form critical studies of the letter that have emphasized the compositional character of the letter. Many of these suggestions were made in an initial form at the beginning of the 20th century and then taken up and developed in mid-century. The suggestion that main parts of the letter formed a baptismal homily was made by Perdelwitz in 1911,[17] and followed up by Bornemann in 1920.[18] Various theories of the possibility of constructing a baptismal liturgy on the basis of 1 Peter were launched by Preisker[19] and Cross.[20] Starting with suggestions by Seeberg from 1903,[21] Selwyn has undertaken a very detailed investigation suggesting that 1 Peter was a baptismal catechism.[22] More recent studies have, however, questioned both the compositional character of the letter and the focus on baptism as a determining factor. There is therefore now a questioning of the suggestions that the letter was based on larger units, e.g. of catechetical character, and more emphasis on the letter as composed by a single author using smaller units of traditional elements.[23]

Klaus Berger has made a suggestion for how smaller elements make up larger paraenetical units in the letter where the addressees are admonished to hold onto the change that has occurred in their lives.[24] He uses the term "post

---

14 BEASLEY-MURRAY, *Baptism*, 260–61; ELLIOTT, *1 Peter*, 677; contra DUNN (*Baptism*, 219) who holds that the position of 1 Peter is that "baptism is the means by which men come to God rather than by which God comes to men."

15 O. S. Brooks has even tried to argue, not quite convincingly, that 3:21 represents a key to the structure of 1 Peter as a whole, "1 Peter 3:21 – literary structure."

16 For presentations and critical evaluations of these theories, see ACHTEMEIER, *1 Peter*, 58–62; ELLIOTT, *1 Peter*, 7–12.

17 E. R. PERDELWITZ, *Die Mysterienreligionen und das Problem des 1. Petrusbriefes*.

18 W. BORNEMANN, "Der erste Petrusbrief – eine Taufrede des Silvanus?"

19 H. PREISKER, see H. WINDISCH, *Die katholischen Briefe*.

20 J. L. CROSS, *1 Peter. A Paschal Liturgy?*

21 A. SEEBERG, *Der Katachismus der Ur-Christenheit*.

22 E. G. SELWYN, *The First Epistle of St. Peter*.

23 For a criticism and ultimate rejection of the hypothesis of the composite nature of 1 Peter, see ACHTEMEIER, *1 Peter*, 60–62; ELLIOTT, *1 Peter*, 10–12, and HORRELL, *1 Peter*. 7–8.

24 BERGER, *Formgeschichte des Neuen Testaments*, 130–135.

conversional admonition" for this form because it is oriented towards the moment ("Zeitpunkt") of this change, when it happened, and he therefore speaks of a *reditus ad baptismum*. This is based on the understanding that conversion and baptism represented a drastic change in the lives of the addressees and established their new status and identity. The challenge which the paraenesis addresses is to fulfil in their daily lives as Christ believers what happened in this moment of change. Berger finds that this form of paraenesis has its roots in Hellenistic Judaism and that it was associated with conversion.[25] There are many common elements in this form for paraenesis, for instance catalogues of vices and virtues, patterns of contrast between "once" and "now", "darkness" and "light", "old" and "new"; distancing from "outsiders" and close, family like relations to "insiders". But there are also elements that are not based on the contrast model, but on positive descriptions of their new status, e.g. call to holiness, to follow the will of God, to reject power, love of the "brothers." Berger finds that this pattern can be found in large parts of 1 Peter and mentions especially 1:3–3:12; 4:7–11; 5:6–9.

Berger does not mention 1 Peter 3:18–22 in this context, probably since it is not a paraenetical text, but that text exactly represents this moment of change that the post-conversional paraenesis refers to. The statement that baptism saves through the resurrection of Jesus Christ in 3:21 holds together many expressions about transitions from life to death, from the old to the new reflected in other parts of the letter. In 1:3–10 salvation is something which the believers wait for, together with the revelation of Christ in his glory (1:7). The new birth to a living hope is based on the resurrection of Jesus Christ (1:3). Even if these expressions are not explicitly identified with baptism, they are associated with baptism as the main act in this process. Baptism is so to speak the crystallizing point for all the other ways to speak of this transition.[26] It can have this function because it unites the baptised with the resurrected Christ and brings them into contact with God and the saving power of God manifested in the resurrection of Jesus Christ (1:3; 3:21). This association between baptism and resurrection is similar to that in Paul and the Pauline tradition, where baptism meant to be included "in Christ," that is in the crucified and resurrected Christ (Rom 6:4–5, 8–11; 1 Cor 15:20–28, 29–34; Col 2:12).

3. Placed "in Christ" as a Spatial Metaphor in 1 Peter

When Berger points to a reference point for the post-conversional paraenesis, he speaks of it as the "moment" of change, that is, in temporal categories. Cullmann, however, in his *Baptism in the New Testament,* has a very perceptive way of see-

---

25 BERGER, *Formgeschichte des Neuen Testaments*, 135.
26 HARTMAN, *Into the Name of the Lord Jesus*, 120.

ing this change or transition not just in temporal but also in spatial categories. He speaks of baptism as "This *once-for-all character of being set at this specific place*, i.e. within the Church of Christ."[27] In the following he focuses on how Paul uses spatial terms to describe what happens in baptism: "the person baptised is 'planted' with the dead and risen Christ,"[28] and "what happens in the act of Baptism is clearly defined in the decisive Pauline texts I Cor. 12.13 and Gal. 3.27–28 as a setting within the body of Christ." Moreover, Cullmann emphasizes that this is not a mere idea, but a real act: "God sets a man within, not merely informs him that he sets him within, the Body of Christ."

It is this spatial perspective on the new status of the baptised as being set "in Christ" that I will apply to 1 Peter. This perspective is developed by Bonnie Howe in *Because you Bear This Name,* where she studies the relations between conceptual metaphors and the moral meaning of 1 Peter.[29] I will take the spatial perspective in a different direction, and look at how 1 Peter uses it to establish identity. I suggest that 1 Peter uses "in Christ" with its associations to baptism as a spatial metaphor that provides a response to the experience of Christians who were displaced as "strangers" and "aliens" within the local communities of Asia Minor.

I will start with how 1 Peter speaks of being "in Christ," and how his use of this terminology can be related to questions of the social location of the presumed addressees of the letter, and then develop the role of this new place "in Christ" as a central metaphor in the letter. Two uses of this expression, 1 Peter 4:14 followed up by 4:16, serve to introduce this issue of challenged identities:

> If you are reproached for the name of Christ (ἐν ὀνόματι Χριστοῦ),
> You are blessed, Because the spirit of glory and of God rests upon you.
>
> If one suffers as a Christian (ὡς Χριστιανός),
> Let him not be ashamed, But under that name let him glorify God.

The passage in 1 Peter 4:12–19 is unique in that it combines these two types of designations for the addressees of the letter. It first applies a term that speaks from an "inside" perspective to "you" who are reproached "for the name of Christ (ἐν ὀνόματι Χριστοῦ)," and secondly it adopts a term reflecting an outsider's perspective, speaking of one who suffers as a Christian (ὡς Χριστιανός).[30] This combination of speaking as an insider and at the same time accepting and using an outsider terminology on the identity of the group is characteristic of 1 Peter. The tension and partly ambiguity that this double usage creates is reflected

---

27 O. Cullmann, *Baptism*, 30.
28 Cullmann, *Baptism*, 30; the following quotations from p. 31.
29 Bonnie Howe, *Because you Bear This Name*.
30 See the use of the terminology "insider" and "outsider" in D. G. Horrell, "The Label *Christianos*: 1 Peter 4:16 and the Formation of Christian Identity," 362–363, 367–370.

in the letter at large, and has caused some of the conflicts about how to place the letter. Does 1 Peter represent an accommodation to the surrounding dominating society, or does it take a strong stand for a distinct identity and separation from the larger society?[31]

First let us take a look at the terms themselves and their usage. The term "Christian" (Χριστιανός) is very rare in the New Testament. Except for the occurrence in 1 Peter 4:16 it is only used twice in Acts. The first instance is in Luke's comment that it was in Antioch that the believers were first called Christians (11:26), and then in Agrippa's ironical comment that Paul will make him a Christian (26:28). There is general agreement that this is a term that has been created by non-Christians, the Latinized form suggests a Latin background, and it is likely that it has been forged by pagan outsiders, maybe even including Roman authorities, as a derogatory name.[32] David Horrell has taken up the investigation of the possible context for this usage, with special focus on 1 Peter and Pliny's letter to Trajan.[33] Pliny reports that Christians are brought to trial (by other people) for their faith, and that the focus of his investigation is their allegiance to Christ. Thus, the test case is whether they are willing to renounce and to revile Christ. And Pliny asks Trajan if Christians shall be judged even if they have not committed any other crimes, so that their only crime is the allegiance to Christ, that is, the mere carrying of the name "Christian."[34]

David Horrell suggests that there are significant similarities between the situation described in Pliny's letter and 1 Peter. Both are dealing with the situation for Christians in the same general region, Pliny from Bithynia, 1 Peter with all the provinces in Asia Minor.[35] Other scholars have made similar suggestions, but have been criticized by John H. Elliott on the grounds that there is in 1 Peter no indication of official persecution or punishment of Christians.[36]

---

31 The central debate on this issue was between David L. Balch and John H. Elliott, starting in 1986 with D. L. BALCH, "Hellenization/Acculturation in 1 Peter;" and J. H. ELLIOTT, "1 Peter, Its Situation and Strategy." Cf. also the summary of the debate in HORRELL, *1 Peter*, 78–81, and his attempt to go beyond that debate by arguing that 1 Peter is both conforming to and resisting its surrounding society, *1 Peter*, 92–95.

32 ELLIOTT (*1 Peter*, 789–91) suggests translations as "partisans of Christ", and in the case of the derogatory comment by Agrippa in Acts 26:28 even "Christ-lackeys, shameful sycophants of Christ."

33 HORRELL, "The Label *Christianos*." 370–376; Pliny, *Ep.* 10. 96.

34 Pliny, *Ep.*10.96: "Whether any difference is to be made on account of age, or no distinction allowed between the youngest and the adult; whether repentance admits to a pardon, or if a man has been once a Christian it avails him nothing to recant; whether the mere profession of Christianity, albeit without crimes, or only the crimes associated therewith are punishable? In all these points I am greatly doubtful (*an ei, qui omnino Christianus fuit, desisse non prosit, nomen ipsum, etiamsi flagitiis careat, an flagitia cohaerentia nomini puniantur*)."

35 Cf. the address in 1:1: "the chosen, strangers in the world of the Diaspora in Pontus, Galatia, Cappadocia, Asia and Bithynia,"

36 *1 Peter*, 792–794.

And Horrell has difficulties in finding proofs of such links,[37] mention of sufferings may of course refer also to public acts, not just to slander or ostracism for neighbours, but it remains arguments from silence. What does seem plausible, however, is that also in 1 Peter Χριστιανός refers to a term used by outsiders, so that it presents an outside criticism, and is comparable to accusations for serious crimes, of being a murderer or a thief. Thus 1 Peter reveals a situation where the Christ believers live in a hostile environment, where they have been given a name that makes its possible for outsiders to identify them, and where they experience sufferings because of that name.

4. Conflict with the World as Dislocation of Identity

The main question that is raised by 1 Peter's use of these two designations of Christian identity, one external, inimical, and one internal, positive, is therefore in what critical situation they are used. Recent studies of 1 Peter have discussed what place the addressees of 1 Peter had within these provinces of the Roman Empire in Asia Minor; what their situation was in relation to society and political authorities, and finally – what type of a response the reference to baptism might represent in this situation.

The present discussions on the social and political context for 1 Peter are to a large extent influenced by the studies by David L. Balch and John H. Elliott in the last part of the 20th century. In a dissertation from 1974 Balch studied the household codes in 1 Peter in a comparison with similar codes in classical antiquity.[38] The similarities with the classical codes led Balch to an investigation of the possible social function of these codes when they were used by early Christians living in a pagan environment. Balch' hypothesis was that the household codes served the purpose of association and integration into society, and he argued that this hypothesis was relevant for the general situation of the letter as well.

Elliott presented a strong challenge to this proposal with his *Home for the Homeless* from 1981.[39] At the time his study represented a new approach not only to the study of 1 Peter, but to New Testament writings in general. Elliott employed sociological models in his interpretation (later termed social-scientific[40]) to investigate the life-situation behind literary texts. Based on the typology of sect to identify the situation and strategies of the letter he argued that

---

37 "The Label *Christianos*," 373.

38 D. L. BALCH, *Let Wives be Submissive. The Domestic Code in 1 Peter.*

39 J. H. ELLIOTT, *A Home for the Homeless. A Sociological Exegesis of 1 Peter, Its situation and Strategy.*

40 The subtitle of the 2.ed. of the book from 1990 was *A Social-Scientific Criticism of 1 Peter, Its situation and Strategy.*

the purpose of the letter was not assimilation, but to strengthen the self-identity of the group and to distinguish it from the outside. An important part of his interpretation was that Elliott did not follow the common view that the terms πάροικοι and παρεπίδημοι (1:1; 2:11) used of the addressees referred to their being aliens in this world, in contrast to heaven. Instead Elliott suggested that the terms had kept their socio-political meaning and referred to the social situation of Christians as in fact being among the resident aliens in Asia Minor.[41] Since they experienced homeless-ness in the society within which they lived, 1 Peter presented their life as Christians in terms of a *home*, as belonging to the household of God.

This approach initiated by Elliott has proved very influential, even if many of the individual points in Elliott's presentation have met with criticism, especially the hypothesis that the addressees of 1 Peter were "resident aliens" in a socio-political sense.[42] 25 years after the Balch – Elliott debate the question of the social context of 1 Peter has been taken up anew, in studies that also have been concerned with new theoretical and methodological approaches in biblical studies.[43] Especially fruitful are the attempts to use post-colonial theories.[44] Post-colonial perspectives have recently been used in many biblical studies.[45] Theories developed in modern societies with colonial or imperial histories do not represent a blueprint for studies of texts from the Roman Empire, but they may provide perspectives and suggest lines of approach. Using post-colonial theory takes into account the context of the Roman Empire in the provinces of Asia Minor, its power structures, and also the emperor worship which was an important factor of life.[46] Horrell suggests that "the most relevant social-scientific resources for appreciating the community-world relationship in 1 Peter are likely to be those which concern themselves specifically with contexts of imperial/colonial domination and with the ways in which subaltern groups produce and sustain their identity in such context."[47] Thus, from another perspective this approach confirms that the "community-world" relationship must be seen within a structure of marginality and domination. Achtemeier suggests

---

41 ELLIOTT, *A Home for the Homeless* (1990), 21–58.

42 See the review of the discussion in HORRELL, *1 Peter*, 48–52, 59, and further T. W. MARTIN, *Metaphor and Composition in 1 Peter*; S. R. BECHTLER, *Following in His Steps*, 64–83; T. SELAND, *Strangers in the Light*, 39–78.

43 See especially R. L. WEBB and B. BAUMAN-MARTIN (eds.), *Reading First Peter with New Eyes*.

44 In the volume mentioned above, see B. BAUMAN-MARTIN, "Speaking Jewish: Postcolonial Aliens and Strangers in First Peter," and D. HORRELL, "Between Conformity and Resistance."

45 In addition to studies of individual texts, see especially R. S. Sugirtharajah (ed.), *The Postcolonial Biblical Reader*, and S. D. MOORE and F. F. SEGOVIA (eds.), *Postcolonial Biblical Criticism*.

46 See S. R. F. PRICE, *Rituals and Power. The Roman Imperial Cult in Asia Minor*; S. J. FRIESEN, *Imperial Cults and the Apocalypse of John*.

47 HORRELL, "Between Conformity and Resistance," 117.

that 1 Peter's use of the terminology of alienation should be seen in light of Jewish metaphors of a Diaspora situation,[48] rejecting Elliott's proposal to see it as a Greco-Roman political terminology; but even so the terminology suggests a marginal social location, if not necessarily economically deprived.

I will suggest some perspectives from post-colonial studies that can be adapted to the study of 1 Peter and its use of baptism metaphors to establish an identity for its addressees.

The discussion of whether 1 Peter encourages accommodation or resistance vis-à-vis society at large raises the question of how they experienced their place within that society. The importance of place for human identities in its spatial, mental and ideological perspectives has recently gained recognition in studies in humanities and social sciences.[49] Place and displacement are prominent features in post-colonial literature.[50] This concern reflects the post-colonial crisis of identity: how to develop or recover a relationship between self and place. If we take as a starting point that all identities are placed, many people living in colonized or oppressive situations have suffered loss of identity through *dislocation*. Such dislocations may have happened in different ways, by migration, enslavement or forced removal from the land of inhabitancy. It may also happen by cultural denigration, for instance by oppression of local cultures by a supposedly superior racial or cultural model. Thus post-colonial societies are often characterised by a dialectic of belonging to a place and the experience of displacement. This dialectic is found in the introduction of 1 Peter where he addresses the recipients as "the chosen, strangers in the world of the Diaspora in Pontus, Galatia, Cappadocia, Asia and Bithynia" (1:1).

Addressing his readers in this way 1 Peter creates an image of a displaced community. The terms "strangers (παρεπίδημοι)" and Diaspora point to displacement, and even the list of provinces may in itself indicate a transition from geographical space to imaginary space. At the time of 1 Peter the Roman provinces Pontus and Bithynia had long been united, so the mention of both of them may point to the fictitious character of the rhetoric of place in 1 Peter.[51] This place description was central for Elliott's suggestion that the addressees of 1 Peter really were πάροικοι, that is "resident aliens" in Asia Minor, without a secure place in the land. Even if his suggestion that the Christians were recruited from resident aliens in a political sense have received mixed reviews, the importance of his observation lies in its focus on the situation of displacement in the letter and the experience of Christians of being in a Diaspora, as aliens. This is a displacement not (or not only) in the sense of being aliens in a metaphorical sense

---

48 Achtemeier, 1 Peter, 55–58.
49 H. Moxnes, "Landscape and Spatiality. Placing Jesus."
50 B. Ashcroft, G. Griffiths and H. Tiffin, *The Empire Writes Back*, 8–11.
51 Howe, *Because you Bear This Name*, 265–66.

of being "in the world" in contrast to "in heaven," but in relation to society.[52] "Place" is not only a geographical locality, it can also be a discursive practice that constructs places. Therefore we shall see what alternative places 1 Peter creates.

Elliott focused on the "homelessness" of the resident aliens, and saw 1 Peter's use of οἶκος (home/household) as a central metaphor for the Christian community, understanding itself as the household of God.[53] In light of the above discussion of place and identity I will suggest that 1 Peter also uses "in Christ" with its associations to baptism as a spatial metaphor that provides a response to the experience of displacement in the letter. It is this perspective Howe develops in *Because you Bear This Name*. She argues that the cluster of conceptual metaphors "in Christ" constitutes "a certain kind of 'living space' wherein moral (or immoral) behaviour is displayed and constrained."[54] Howe starts with the description of the addressees in the letter opening as Diaspora sojourners and exiles in Asia Minor, and raises the question: "where *do* they belong?"[55] She finds the response given by 1 Peter to be the term "in Christ." As a distinct identification it does not appear until 3:16, but it has been prepared through many instances of the use of a spatial ἐν (1:2, 6, 15b; 3:2; 4:19). On that basis Howe argues that "in Christ" has a spatial meaning in the exhortation in 3:16: "keep your conscience clear, so that, when you are abused, those who revile your good behaviour in Christ may be put to shame." The physical experience of being spatially located helps to conceptualize how one can think of one's relation to another. Howe suggests that the metaphor ἐν Χριστῷ evokes the image of a bounded region in space, with a boundary, an inside and an outside. It is a conceptual schema that evokes the experience of containment as protection from outside forces. And into this conceptual container is put everything the reader associates with Christ: "stories of his life, his sayings, his character, even his manner of death."[56] The "good behaviour in Christ" therefore refers to how they live within the spatial boundary of Christ and the associations of his character.[57] Howe suggests that 1 Peter evokes four additional overlapping conceptual spaces that represent "living spaces" for his readers: 1) time and events, 2) a nation or people group, 3) households, and 4) human body. With this mapping of living spaces 1 Peter "has outlined how he thinks

---

52 Howe, *Because you Bear This Name*, 265–78, esp. 271–72; against T. W. Martin, *Metaphor and Composition in 1 Peter*.

53 Cf. the use of *oik-* terminology in 1 Peter: 2:5, 18; 3:7; 4:10, 17; and see also terminology reflecting family relations: 1:22–23; 2:17; 3:8; 5:9, 12; Elliott, *Home for the Homeless*, 200–37.

54 Howe, *Because you Bear This Name*, 233.

55 Howe, *Because you Bear This Name*, 241.

56 Howe, *Because you Bear This Name*, 239.

57 Howe, *Because you Bear This Name*, 249–308.

readers could live "in Christ" as ordinary citizens (and non-citizens) vis-à-vis non-Christian society."[58]

5. Displacement as Stigmatization and Shame

A reading of 1 Peter along these lines suggests that the situation of the addressees vis-à-vis the larger society was filled with conflicts, where the small groups of Christ believers were in a weak position. The very existence of the label Χριστιανός as an outsider's term in 1 Peter indicates a negative evaluation of its addressees from the larger society, something that discredits its bearers. Within a context of very unequal power relations we might analyse such a situation in terms of the social categories stigma and stigmatization.[59] There is a large theoretical discussion of stigmatization, especially within social psychology, and it has also been applied within biblical studies.[60] Research on stigmatization has both dealt with the groups that stigmatize, their reasons and attitudes and various forms of stigmatization, and with the response from the groups or individuals that suffer stigmatization. Stigmatization has largely been studied in terms of social processes and structures, but it also has a spatial aspect, and can be studied as an interaction in space. Libelling and stigmatizing is a way of making boundaries around a person, of ejecting somebody from her/his place in society, i.e. displacing or dislocating.

Stigmatization can be the result of activities and attitudes from dominant groups, as well as by official policy of that society. A stigma is a characterization that marks a person as "deviant, flawed, limited, spoiled, or generally undesirable."[61] Studies of social psychology have pointed to the unequal power relations that lie behind stigmatization:

> Whenever an individual, a class or a nation wishes to maintain a hierarchical relationship, or to maintain aloofness it will have resort to contempt of the other. Contempt is the mark of the oppressor. The hierarchical relationship is maintained either when the oppressed assumes the attitude of contempt for himself or hangs his head in shame.[62]

This quotation also links the contempt inherent in stigmatization with shame. To shame implies the power to take away respect and recognition from somebody.

---

58   Howe, *Because you Bear This Name*, 248.
59   Horrell, "The Label *Christianos*," 376–80. The classical study of stigmatization is E. Goffman, *Stigma: Notes on the Management of Spoiled Identity*.
60   E. S. Mligo, *Jesus and the Stigmatized*.
61   E. E. Jones et al. *Social Stigma: The Sociology of Marked Relationships*, 6.
62   E. K. Sedgwick and A. Frank, *Shame and its Sisters: A Silvan Tomkin Reader*, 139.

As a result, those who are exposed in this way experience being shamed, of losing both the respect of others and self- respect.

The perspective of stigmatization is particularly useful to study power structures and hierarchical relations within Roman societies as honour-shame cultures.[63] The dominant masculine values were associated with honour, the value of a person in the eyes of the society, especially powerful persons, and the corresponding self-evaluation. Lack of honour or loss of honour resulted in shame, a situation in which a man was not able to defend his position or to stand up for himself. The competition for honour and to fend off attempts by opponents to inflict shame was central in an agonistic society. The honour-shame competition is linked to the perspective we started with, of place and displacement. To have honour meant to be in one's proper place, to lose honour meant to be displaced.

In 1 Peter the relations between Christians and the outsiders are described in honour-shame categories.[64] This competition to gain honour and to avoid shame is reflected in 4:16, "yet if one suffers in the name of Christ, let him not be ashamed (*me aischynesto*), but under that name let him glorify (δοξαζέτω) God." In this statement it is those who made the Christians suffer who are the implied shaming agents.[65] When the Christians were exposed to suffering they experienced shame in the eyes of the observers. But 1 Peter encourages his addressees not to accept outsiders as judges or evaluators of honour and shame. Instead God is the judge, indicated by the exhortation to "glorify God" and thereby to transform the values, turning shame into honour. This transvaluation takes place also in statements about the future hope, where the opponents of the Christians no longer can act as shaming agents, but themselves will be exposed to shame by God (2:6; 3:16).

The term Χριστιανός was used by the dominant society as a characterization that designed the bearers as deviant or undesirable. However, we do not have direct access to the attitudes and actions of the Roman administrators or the local population who used this expression. In 1 Peter we get the perspective from a group that suffers stigmatization, and the letter can be analysed as a strategy of how to cope with it. A theoretical approach for such an analysis is provided by studies of socially based coping with stigmatizing situations.[66] One way is to try harder to be accepted within the dominant group, another is to seek alternative relationships and to establish a stronger group affection within a new group. These social strategies are combined with conceptual strategies that affect the stigmatizing categorisation as such. It can take the form of a re-

---

63 H. Moxnes, "Honor and Shame."
64 B. L. Campbell, *Honor, Shame and the Rhetoric of 1 Peter;* J. H. Elliott, *Conflict, Community and Honor.*
65 Elliott, *1 Peter*, 794–95.
66 Mligo, *Jesus and the Stigmatized*, 57–62.

socialization where language is used to identify themselves in a way different from the larger society. This resocialization into a new group can also take the form of redefining the values that society has used to exclude and stigmatize them.

1 Peter provides examples of all of these strategies. The author encourages his readers to behave in such a way that the opponents/the outsiders will recognize that the believers are righteous (2:11–12). Here there is an attempt to find a common ground with the outsiders who put blame on them and reproach them for being wrongdoers.[67] 1 Peter pretends that there is a shared agreement between the society at large and the insider group about what is morally right and wrong. Therefore the author emphasizes that he does not speak of or condone suffering for crimes like murder, theft, or other types of wrongdoing, 4:15. In 2:14–15 he exhorts his addressees to subject themselves under human authorities, especially the governors who were sent by the emperor to punish wrongdoers and to praise "the one who does right" (ἀγαθοποιῶν). The audience of 1 Peter ought to belong to this group, the letter emphasizes that it is the will of God that they shall "do right." Thus, it appears that 1 Peter tones down conflicts with the authorities, and instead puts the blame on opponents among their neighbours who wrongly accuse them of wrong doings. But the goal to be accepted by the outsiders for their good behaviour represents a hope that most likely only will be fulfilled in the distant future (1:3–9; 4:1–6; 5:6–11). The main strategy of the letter is to strengthen the group cohesion through a re-socialization, to provide a new, secure place for people who have been socially and conceptually displaced, and to redefine the central values of honour and shame held by of the dominant society.[68]

6. From Displacement to Place "in Christ"

The central metaphor for this re-socialization is ἐν Χριστῷ, either with explicit use of the term or employing the conceptual schema of being in Christ, as being within a bounded space and sharing the fate of Christ.[69] The author describes the experience of stigmatization with different words, one of the central terms used are "suffer" or "suffering" (πάσχω/πάθημα).[70] In the letter these terms are used both of the addressees and of Christ, and when used of the addressees they

---

67 Cf. Horrell's suggestion (*1 Peter*, 92–95) that 1 Peter combines a strategy of conformity and resistance.
68 BECHTLER, *Following in His Steps*, 202–04.
69 HOWE, *Because you Bear This Name*, 240–46.
70 πάσχω, 2:19, 20, 21, 23; 3:14, 17, 18; 4:1, 15, 19; 5:10; πάθημα, 1:11; 4:13; 5:1, 9. With 19 occurrences of these terms, 1 Peter has by far the largest number among New Testament writings; no other has more than 6.

are always placed in a context of the sufferings of Christ. There are three central passages of sufferings "in Christ;" the first concerning slaves, 2:19–21; then the passage introducing the baptism narrative, 3:13–18; and finally the most explicit discussion of suffering in 4:12–19. All passages are introduced with phrases of re-socialization, which will reinterpret the experience of suffering and make it meaningful within a new conceptual universe (2:20; 3:13; 4:12). The author also emphasizes the conditions under which this cognitive re-socialization can take place: it does not apply to those who have done wrong, who are "wrongdoers" (2:20; 3:17; 4:15), but only to those who have been doing good, who are "good-doers" (2:20; 3:17; 4:19). "To do good" is essential for those who "bear the name of Christ", this is so to speak the expected result of being included "in Christ."[71] Here we see an example of a "post conversional admonition" that brings the addressees back to the moment when they became included in Christ and made the commitment to follow the will of God. It is their position "in Christ" that makes a re-evaluation of their sufferings possible.

That is, sufferings that cause displacement from their position of recognition and honour are given a new place and re-placed "in Christ." The slaves in 2:18–20 do not have any honour in the eyes of society; suffering in a physical form is part of their daily experience.[72] But what is unique is that they are addressed as subjects,[73] called to suffer patiently and to see Christ's suffering as a model for them. Their own suffering is put in a new light when it is said that "Christ suffered for you". Christ is portrayed in a similar way as the slaves when they were beaten, he was also exposed to power in a hierarchical system of domination: he was insulted and he suffered (2:20, 23), although in the same way as the slaves, he had not done anything wrong (2:20, 22). The description of Christ's suffering combines elements from the passion narrative in the gospels with the portrait of the "suffering servant" in second Isaiah chapter 53. Christ's behaviour in face of cruel suffering is given a new meaning with the phrase that "he trusted him (i.e. God) who judges justly" (2:23). This provides a security that suffering will not be the final result for those who suffer and trust in God.

1 Peter 3:13–17 again discusses the sufferings of the readers, this time not the physical abuse that the house slaves experienced, but abusive speech and shaming from those who "revile your good behaviour in Christ" (3:16).[74] This expression does not refer to slander of "good behaviour" in a general sense, but specifically their "good in-Christ behaviour."[75] They may have been accused by

---

71 Howe, *Because you Bear This Name*, 234–235.

72 J. A. Glancey, *Slavery in Early Christianity*, 16–24, 55–60.

73 In this way slaves might become symbols of the new identity in Christ; cf. J. Vogt, *Ancient Slavery and the Ideal of Man*, 142–145.

74 Elliott, *I Peter*, 631.

75 Bechtler, *Following in His Steps*, 195.

opponents in the community for being "Christians" and for behaviour associated with that (cf. 4:16), but the author of 1 Peter turns that accusation around to a positive identification with their being "in Christ." Likewise, the abuse and shaming from their opponents are turned against them, the author expresses the conviction that they will be put to shame (3:16d). As in 2:21 Christ's suffering is invoked as the warrant for the exhortation to suffer when "doing good," but this time not as an example. Instead it is Christ's suffering for sins and the redemptive effects of that suffering in the lives of the addressees that is emphasized.

It is significant that Christ's suffering is this time not invoked as an ideal to be followed.[76] Instead the focus is on Christ's suffering "for them," that "he might bring you to God." Thus, there is a transition from the moral implications of being included "in Christ" to a reminder of the meaning of the act when this inclusion took place, and how that created their new identity in the resurrected Christ. The frame of the baptismal passage in 3:19–21 in 3:18 and 22 portrays Christ as going from death to life in the spirit, entering the location at the right hand of God. It was into this Christ they were placed at their baptism, who himself went from the shame of suffering and death to a life in the spirit and the seat of honour at the right hand God. Therefore this passage serves to bring the recipients of the letter back to baptism, this "moment of change," but now not primarily with the purpose of paraenesis, but as a basis for confidence. In a temporal perspective, baptism provided a certainty that they would go from suffering and shame to sharing a place of honour with Christ (3:22).[77] In terms of identity expressed as a spatial location, they were reminded that baptism included them "in Christ."

We can now return to the designations of the addresses as being reproached for "the name of Christ" and suffering as "Christian" in 4:14 and 16. The passage 4:12–19 is the most explicit attempt by the author of 1 Peter to build an alternative symbolic universe around the sufferings of his readers.[78] He starts by presenting an alternative understanding of the very fact that they are exposed to suffering: it is not something unexpected, to be surprised at (4:12). This approach confronts the normal reaction to unjust suffering, that it is illogical and that it should be avoided. In this confrontation 1 Peter goes further than in his previous explanations that they are called to suffer and that Christ provides an example to follow. Here he says that they actually share in (κοινωνέω) the sufferings of Christ.[79] This goes beyond a comparison, κοινωνέω implies a sharing,

---

76 ACHTEMEIER, *1 Peter*, 245.

77 ACHTEMEIER (*1 Peter*, 274) sees 3:22 as providing assurance to the readers of Christ's victory over evil forces and his protection of the community.

78 BECHTLER, *Following in His Steps*, 199–200.

79 BECHTLER, *Following in His Steps*, 199).

a participation that reminds of the phrase, being "in Christ."[80] Here the author enters into a conflict with the societal context and presents a total reversal of the values of that society when he addresses his audience with their internal designation: "if you are reproached for the name of Christ, you are blessed," 4:14. This exhortation is addressed to the readers as members of the new family of God who bear the name of Christ: "This *name* is the pivot point, the crux, of the whole matter – it expresses the central Christian moral motivation and identity."[81] It is followed up with an encouragement to the one who suffers as Christian not to be ashamed, but to glorify God, 4:16.

The exhortation "let him not be ashamed," is more than en encouragement to an individual feeling, it represents a protest, not to be subdued, not to accept the power of the powerful. Here the values of society are reversed, suffering is a cause of rejoicing, and the shame of public punishment is negated. This is a way of creating a separate symbolic world where everything is viewed from the perspective of Christ and his sufferings, and where none of the values of the larger society are accepted. The honour/shame system of Roman society is turned upside down. The ordeals from outside, the shaming and slandering do not have power over them. Therefore in their sufferings they can be confident that "the divine Spirit of Glory" rests upon them (4:14). There is an emphasis on glory (δόξα) in this section (4:13, 14, 16) which points to the glory, i.e. honour of God as the ground for the honour of the believers.[82] Their honour does not come from the powers of the society where they live, but from God. And being "in Christ" and sharing in the sufferings of Christ they can trust that they will participate when his glory is revealed (4:13).

7. Conclusion

7.1. "In Christ" as a New Place

1 Peter addresses its readers as exiles and strangers, within the Roman regions of Asia Minor. Some may have been technically resident aliens, but more importantly, they all appear to have had an experience of being outsiders in society. Their situation appears to be precarious, it is frequently described with words for reviling, slandering, that is with a terminology for stigmatization, exclusion and displacement, and summed up as suffering. The challenge for 1 Peter and his addressees was to find a new location for identity, to establish a secure basis.

---

80   Elliott, *1 Peter*, 774–776. Paul does not have the same terminology, but the idea of sharing the sufferings of Christ, see 2 Cor 1:5; Phil 3:10; see also Col 1:24.

81   Howe, *Because you Bear This Name*, 291. But see Elliott (*1 Peter*, 779) who argues that "in the name of Christ" here functions as an idiom and translates it "because of Christ."

82   Elliott, *1 Peter*, 796.

In the three main passages where 1 Peter discusses the challenges its readers face from the sufferings they experience, Christ is presented as the new location of identity. Christ is presented in a way that makes sense in light of the precarious situation the readers encounter. 1 Peter 2:18–25 deals with the suffering of slaves, and here Jesus is presented as suffering in a similar type of situation, exposed to slander. The slaves are exhorted to follow his example, in peaceful and quiet obedience that might become a model for other Christians as well.

The next passage, 3:13–22, explains how the life of Christ could become a model for the Christians. This is explained through the purpose or effect of his death: to bring the Christians to God, i.e. Christ's death made possible a placement of them that was much more privileged than the position of the majority. It is in this context that narratives about the judgment of fallen angels and the salvation of Noah are brought in to serve as images of what baptism has provided. The addressees are under obligation to live the life into which they have been placed. But facing the suffering of marginalisation and displacement of identity, they need to be brought back to what God has done in baptism, through the resurrection of Jesus Christ. In this context Christ is not a moral example, but the one who facilitates the new place, with God and eventually in the heavens with him (3:18, 22).

These spatial categories merge with identity categories in 4:12–19. The close relationship to Christ is expressed by stating that the readers do more than imitate Christ, they actually share in the sufferings of Christ. They are reproached and suffer "in the name of Christ" and as a "Christian."

In the concluding verse of the letter, 5:13, "all of you that are in Christ" is an inclusive term; it includes everybody who shares "the name of Christ," and is a "Christian." In the introduction to the letter the addressees were named as "strangers of the Diaspora", that is, as displaced persons. The letter ends with a declaration of their new place,[83] "in Christ" as a spatial category that includes all who are included in Christ through baptism.

1 Peter is one of the earliest examples of use of the term Χριστιανός as a category of identity, and it receives a specific meaning from its immediate context. It is used of those who "share Christ's sufferings" and who are "reproached for the name of Christ." The basis for this identity was their inclusion "in Christ," which happened in baptism. In 1 Peter it is a terminology used of persons living in a situation of suffering, under pressure and as a minority. It is used to give a positive identification for their situation as exiles, strangers and foreigners, and a justification for their situation of suffering: this was a Christ-like suffering, and as such not a surprise or mistake, but something that was the will of God. With this interpretation 1 Peter rejected the frame of interpretation given by the stigmatizers and provided a new interpretation of identity and locality as

---

83 Howe, *Because you Bear This Name*, 239–240.

well: they were not a displaced minority among an oppressive majority, instead, they were embodied "in Christ" and in a new locality with God.

7.2. "In Christ" – An Ethnic Identity?

The metaphor "in Christ" is associated with other metaphors that respond more explicitly to the social and political context of the addressees of 1 Peter. Howe suggests that there are four additional conceptual spaces that are associated with the space "in Christ."[84] The four spaces are 1) time and events, 2) a nation or people group, 3) household, and 4) the human body. These conceptual spaces serve to explicate the meaning of the central conceptual space "in Christ": "Each domain becomes, in effect, a *living space* – an arena in which one lives "in Christ." Especially the first part of 1 Peter 1:3–2:10 have many motives that are recognized as associated with baptism e.g. rebirth (1:3, 23; 2:2), conversion and transformation (2:9), hope (1:3, 21), inheritance (1:4), etc. These allusions to baptism emphasize the new dignity of the baptized and the contrast between their former situation, allegiances, and modes of behaviour, and their present status.[85] Among these descriptions of their new situation, in contrast to their previous situation as "strangers" and "no people" (1:1; 2:10), is the broad description in ethno-racial categories in 2:9: "But you are a chosen race, a royal priesthood, a holy nation, God's own people."[86]

The importance of this category, nation or people, is that it responds directly to the question posed by the salutation, who are "the strangers of the Diaspora"? As mentioned above there has been a long discussion whether there is a socio-political or metaphorical meaning to this terminology. Howe argues that terms can be both metaphorical and contain a socio-political meaning,[87] and holds up "the primary social understandings that arise from people's experience of peoplehood itself – of belonging to a nation or ethnic group. The way such experiences constrain identity and behaviour is a central component of Peter's message."[88] Howe therefore concludes that what remains, regardless that various words for "people" are used (γένος, ἔθνος, λαός), "is the notion that the Christians' new set of relationship with one another and with God – their group identity – is like that of a distinctive people group, ... they are encour-

---

84 Howe, *Because You Bear This Name*, 248.
85 Elliott, *1 Peter*, 351.
86 Cf. the translation by Elliott, *1 Peter*, 406: "But you are an "elect stock," a "royal residence," a "priestly community," a "holy people," a "people for (God's) possession."
87 Howe, *Because You Bear This Name*, 271–273, nn. 10, 11.
88 Howe, *Because You Bear This Name*, 265.

aged to think of themselves *as* a distinctive People, a legitimate Nation, even a nation located in an imaginary geo-political region."[89]

The conceptual space of people, nation and race seem to be associated with the spatial metaphor "in Christ,"[90] and 1 Peter developed that space in its relation to the exile and Diaspora situation of its readers. In her investigation of ethnic reasoning in early Christianity Denise K. Buell finds that 1 Peter represents a very early expression of Christian identity in ethno-racial categories.[91] This shows the strength of the baptismal metaphor of being "in Christ" in the argument of 1 Peter. It builds on the presupposition that ethnic identity is fluid and can be changed, at the same time it presupposes that through baptism one is placed in an identity that is stable and stronger than previous ethnic identities.

A post-colonial perspective on 1 Peter identified the experience of dislocation and displacement in the address to readers as "exiles" and "aliens" in the Diaspora. This reflected the experiences of the Christ believers who suffered verbal attacks, stigmatization, maybe even accusations before the authorities because they were Χριστιανοί, a negative term used by outsiders. 1 Peter presented a response with a spatial interpretation of the baptismal experience as establishing their identity "in Christ." We have tried to follow the way 1 Peter expressed this baptismal identity of his addressees through the spatial metaphor "in Christ." It was the image of the suffering and resurrected Christ that made it possible to turn around the negative experiences of displacement as "Christians" and "strangers and aliens" and turn it into a location of hope.

Bibliography

ACHTEMEIER, P. J., *1 Peter* (Hermeneia), Minneapolis, Minn.: Fortress 1996.

ASHCROFT, B., GRIFFITHS, G., AND TIFFIN, H., *The Empire Writes Back. Theory and Practice in Post-Colonial Literatures*, London: Routledge ²2002.

BALCH, D. L., *Let Wives be Submissive. The Domestic Code in 1 Peter* (SBLMS 26), Chico, Calif.: Scholars Press 1981.

— "Hellenization/Acculturation in 1 Peter," in: Charles H. Talbert (ed.), *Perspectives on First Peter*, Macon, Ga.: Mercer University Press 1986, 79–101.

---

[89] HOWE, *Because You Bear This Name*, 267.

[90] The transition into this space was described in terms used of conversion and transformation, SELAND, *Strangers in the Light*, 64–67.

[91] DENISE K. BUELL, *Why This New Race?* 45–46. Studies of ethnicity represent a recent approach in New Testament studies, see MARK G. BRETT (ed.), *Ethnicity and the Bible*.

BAUMAN-MARTIN, B., "Speaking Jewish: Postcolonial Aliens and Strangers in First Peter," in: Webb, R. L. and Bauman-Martin, B. (eds.), *Reading First Peter with New Eyes*, London: T & T Clark 2007, 144–177.

BEASLEY-MURRAY, G. R., *Baptism in the New Testament*, Exeter: Paternoster 1976.

BECHTLER, S. R., *Following in His Steps. Suffering, Community, and Christology in 1 Peter* (SBLDS 162), Atlanta: Scholars Press 1998.

BERGER, K., *Formgeschichte des Neuen Testaments*, Heidelberg: Quelle & Meyer 1984.

BORNEMANN, W., "Der erste Petrusbrief – eine Taufrede des Silvanus?" in: *ZNW* 19 (1919–20) 143–165.

BRETT, M. G. (ed.), *Ethnicity and the Bible* (Biblical Interpretation Series 19), Leiden: Brill 1996.

BROOKS, O. S., "1 Peter 3:21 – the clue to the literary structure of the Epistle," in: *NovT* 16 (1974) 290–305.

BUELL, D. K., *Why This New Race? Ethnic Reasoning in Early Christianity*, New York: Columbia University Press 2005.

BULTMANN, R., "Bekenntnis- und Liedfragmente im ersten Petrusbrief," in: *Coniectanea Neotestamentica XI in honorem Antonii Fridrichsen sexagenarii* (ConBNT 11), Lund: Gleerup 1947, 1–14 [= idem, *Exegetica. Aufsätze zur Erforschung des Neuen Testaments*, ed. by E. Dinkler, Tübingen: Mohr Siebeck 1967, 285–297].

CAMPBELL, B. L., *Honor, Shame and the Rhetoric of 1 Peter* (SBLDS 160), Atlanta, Ga.: Scholars Press 1998.

CROSS, J. L., *1 Peter. A Paschal Liturgy?*, London: Mowbray 1954.

CULLMANN, O., *Baptism in the New Testament*, London: SCM 1950.

DALTON, W. J., *Christ's Proclamation to the Spirits: A Study of 1 Peter 3.18–4:6* (AnBib 23), Rome: Pontifical Biblical Institute 1965.

DANIÉLOU, J., "Déluge, Baptême, Jugement chez les Pères de l'Église," in: idem, *Sacramentum Futuri*, Paris: Beauchesne 1950, 69–94.

— *The Bible and the Liturgy*, Notre Dame: Notre Dame University Press 1956.

DUNN, J.D.G., *Baptism in the Holy Spirit*, London: SCM 1970.

ELLIOTT, J. H., "1 Peter, Its Situation and Strategy: A Discussion with David Balch," in: Talbert, Ch. H., (ed.), *Perspectives on First Peter*, Macon, Ga.: Mercer University Press 1986, 61–78.

— *A Home for the Homeless. A Social-Scientific Criticism of 1 Peter, Its situation and Strategy*, With a new Introduction, Minneapolis, Minn.: Fortress 1990. (1st ed. 1981 as *A Home for the Homeless. A Sociological Exegesis of 1 Peter, Its situation and Strategy*).

— *1 Peter* (AB 37 B), New York: Doubleday 2000.

— *Conflict, Community and Honor: 1 Peter in Social-Scientific Perspective*, Eugene, Or.: Cascade 2007.

FELDMEIER, REINHARD, *Der Erste Brief des Petrus* (THKNT 15/1), Leipzig: Evangelische Verlagsanstalt 2005.

FRIESEN, S. J., *Imperial Cults and the Apocalypse of John*, Oxford: Oxford University Press 2001.

GLANCEY, J. A., *Slavery in Early Christianity*, Oxford: Oxford University Press 2002.

GOFFMAN, E., *Stigma: Notes on the Management of Spoiled Identity*, Hammondsworth: Penguin 1963.

GREEN, J. B., *1 Peter*, Grand Rapids, Mich.: Eerdmans 2007.

HARTMAN, L., *'Into the Name of the Lord Jesus': Baptism in the Early Church*, Edinburgh: T & T Clark 1997.

HORRELL, D. G., "The Label *Christianos:* 1 Peter 4:16 and the Formation of Christian Identity," in: *JBL* 126 (2007) 361–381.

— "Between Conformity and Resistance: Beyond the Balch – Elliott Debate Towards a Post-Colonial Reading of First Peter," in: Webb, R. L. and Bauman-Martin, B. (eds.), *Reading First Peter with New Eyes*, London: T & T Clark 2007, 111–143.

— *First Peter* (New Testament Guides), London: T & T Clark 2008.

HOWE, B., *Because you Bear This Name. Conceptual Metaphor and the Moral Meaning of 1 Peter* (Biblical Interpretation Series 81), Leiden: Brill 2006.

ISAAC, A., "Introduction, 1 Enoch," in: Charlesworth, J. H. (ed.), *The Old Testament Pseudepigrapha* vol.1, London: Darton, Longman and Todd 1983, 5–12.

JONES, E. E. ET AL., *Social Stigma: The Sociology of Marked Relationships*, New York: Freeman 1984.

Martin, T. W., *Metaphor and Composition in 1 Peter* (SBLDS 131), Atlanta: Scholars Press 1992.

Mligo, E. S., *Jesus and the Stigmatized. Reading the Gospel of John in a Context of HIV/AIDS-Related Stigmatization in Tanzania* (Acta Theologica 30), Diss. Submitted to the faculty of Theology, University of Oslo 2009.

Moore, S. D. and Segovia, F. F. (eds.), *Postcolonial Biblical Criticism: Interdisciplinary Intersections*, London: T & T Clark 2005.

Moxnes, H., "Honor and Shame," in: *BTB* 23 (1993) 167–176.

— "Landscape and Spatiality. Placing Jesus," in: Neufeld, D. and Rohrbaugh, R. (eds.) *Social World of the New Testament*, New York: Routledge 2010, 93–109.

Perdelwitz, E. R., *Die Mysterienreligionen und das Problem des 1. Petrusbriefes* (RVV 11/3), Giesen: Töpelmann 1911.

Price, S. R. F., *Rituals and Power. The Roman Imperial Cult in Asia Minor*, Cambridge: Cambridge University Press 1984.

Reicke, B., *The Disobedient Spirits and Christian Baptism: A study of 1 Peter III.19 and its Context* (ASNU 13), Copenhagen: Munksgaard 1946.

Sanders, E. P., *Paul and Palestinian Judaism. A Comparison of Patterns of Religion*, London: SCM 1977.

Sedgwick, E. K. and Frank, A., *Shame and its Sisters: A Silvan Tomkin Reader*, Durham, N.C.: Duke University Press 1995.

Seeberg, A., *Der Katechismus der Ur-Christenheit*, Leipzig: Deichert 1903.

Seland, T., *Strangers in the Light. Philonic Perspectives on Christian Identity in 1 Peter* (Biblical Interpretation Series 76), Leiden: Brill 2005.

Selwyn, E. G., *The First Epistle of St. Peter*, London: MacMillan ²1955.

Sugirtharajah, R. S. (ed.), *The Postcolonial Biblical Reader*, Malden, Mass.: Blackwell 2006.

VanderKam, J. C., "1 Enoch, Enochic Motifs, and Enoch in Early Christian Literature," in: VanderKam, J. C. and Adler, W. (eds.), *The Jewish Apocalyptic Heritage in Early Christianity*, Assen: Van Gorcum 1996, 60–88.

Vogt, J., *Ancient Slavery and the Ideal of Man*, Oxford: Blackwell 1974.

Webb, R. L. and Bauman-Martin, B. (eds.), *Reading First Peter with New Eyes* (Library of New Testament Studies 364), London: T & T Clark 2007.

WINDISCH, H., *Die katholischen Briefe*, rev. and ed. by Preisker, H. (HNT 15), Tübingen: Mohr Siebeck ³1951.

Salbung, Geist und Taufe im 1. Johannesbrief

Udo Schnelle

1. Die historische Situation des 1. Johannesbriefes

Richtet sich der II Joh an eine Einzelgemeinde und der III Joh an eine Einzelperson, so fehlen im I Joh die wesentlichen äußeren Kennzeichen eines wirklichen Briefes (Briefpräskript und Schlussgrüße)[1]. Andererseits lassen sich briefliche Merkmale nachweisen, so das Auseinandertreten von Schreiber und Adressaten sowie die Anrede der Leser/Hörer mit τεκνία („Kinder"; vgl. I Joh 2,1.12.28; 3,7.18; 4,4; 5,21) oder ἀγαπητοί („Geliebte"; vgl. I Joh 2,7; 3,2.21; 4,1.7.11). Auch das häufige γράφειν („schreiben") scheint auf eine Briefsituation hinzuweisen (vgl. I Joh 1,4; 2,1.7f.12–14.21.26; 5,13), wobei der Verweis auf die Freude in I Joh 1,4 den üblichen Segenswunsch abgelöst haben könnte. Für den brieflichen Charakter des Schreibens spricht auch, dass der Verfasser auf die konkreten Probleme der Hörer und Leser eingeht: 1) Die Frage nach der Sündlosigkeit des Christen stellte offenkundig ein akutes dogmatisches und ethisches Problem dar (vgl. I Joh 1,8ff.; 3,4ff.; 5,16ff.). 2) Wie im II/III Joh ist auch im I Joh die Auseinandersetzung mit den aus der Gemeinde hervorgegangenen Falschlehrern ein zentrales Thema (vgl. I Joh 2,22f.; 4,2ff; 5,6ff.). Der Umfang der Falschlehrerpolemik zeigt, dass der Einfluss der Gegner innerhalb der johanneischen Schule keineswegs zurückgegangen war (vgl. zuvor II Joh 7), sondern nach wie vor eine ernste Gefahr darstellte. 3) Die durchgängige Ermahnung zur Bruderliebe/Geschwisterliebe in Verbindung mit der Aufforderung zu konkreter sozialer Hilfe für den notleidenden Bruder in I Joh 3,17f. lässt vermuten, dass es innerhalb der johanneischen Schule relevante soziale Unterschiede gab. Der Verfasser des I Joh versucht diese Problematik durch die fortwährende Ermahnung zu tatkräftiger Bruderliebe bis hin zu sozialer Unterstützung zu lösen bzw. zu entschärfen.

Nach I Joh 5,13 sind diejenigen Leser des Schreibens, die ‚an den Namen des Sohnes Gottes glauben'. Somit richtet sich der I Joh nicht an eine bestimmte Ortsgemeinde der johanneischen Schule, sondern spricht die Gesamtgemeinde an[2]. Der I Joh darf weder als Gelegenheitsbrief noch als theologisch abstraktes Traktat oder situationsgelöste Meditation verstanden werden, vielmehr als eine Schrift, die lehrhafte, paränetische und polemische Abschnitte enthält, um die

---

1 Zu den Einleitungsfragen vgl. U. Schnelle, *Einleitung*, 471–503.
2 Zur vorausgesetzten Gemeindestruktur vgl. D. Rusam, *Gemeinschaft der Kinder Gottes*, 210ff.

Gemeinde in einer konkreten historischen Bedrohungssituation in grundlegenden Fragen zu unterweisen, zu beraten, ihr abzuraten, sie zu warnen und zu stärken. Die schlüssige Zuordnung des I Joh zu einer Gattung will nicht gelingen, denn das Fehlen wichtiger brieflicher Merkmale, die Erörterung grundlegender Glaubensfragen (z. B. die Sündenthematik), die durchgängige ethische Prägung und die Falschlehrerpolemik lassen sich nicht widerspruchsfrei harmonisieren. Deshalb sollte der I Joh *als theologischer Diskurs* (in einem Schreiben mit brieflichen Elementen) bezeichnet werden. Ein Diskurs ist eine durch Argumentation gekennzeichnete Kommunikationsform, die mit Rechtfertigungs- und Geltungsansprüchen verbunden ist und auf Zustimmung aus ist[3].

2. Die Auseinandersetzung mit der Falschlehre

Die Verwendung und das Verständnis von χρῖσμα in I Joh 2,20.27 lassen sich nur sachgemäß erfassen, wenn die Einbettung dieses Begriffes in die Auseinandersetzung mit der Falschlehre gesehen wird. Nicht zufällig erfolgt die erste Erwähnung von χρῖσμα in I Joh 2,20 unmittelbar nach der Erwähnung des Schismas in I Joh 2,19 und seine maßgebliche Entfaltung in I Joh 2,27 genau vor dem endzeitlichen Szenario in I Joh 2,28ff., wo es um nicht weniger geht als um Lüge und Wahrheit, Heil und Unheil. Der Verwirrung und Verführung der Antichristen wird das wahre Wissen der gesalbten Gemeinde entgegengestellt. Deshalb gilt es zunächst die Auseinandersetzung mit der Falschlehre in ihren Grundzügen darzustellen, die bereits mit dem Prolog I Joh 1,1–4 einsetzt, in 2,22 und 4,1–3 fortgesetzt wird und in deren innere Logik auch die Erwähnungen des Chrisma in I Joh 2,20.27 gehören.

Der *Prolog 1,1–4* ist ein kraftvoller Anfang, der keiner textexternen Verstehenshilfen bedarf[4]. Er präsentiert nicht nur das theologische Programm des Schreibens, sondern verbindet damit unüberhörbar und unübersehbar einen massiven Anspruch: Die theologische Augenzeugenschaft der johanneischen Schule. Sie schließt vom Selbstanspruch her eine historische Augenzeugenschaft und die soziale Kontinuität innerhalb der johanneischen Schule mit ein, hört aber unmittelbarer und blickt tiefer, indem sie die wahre Bedeutung der Offenbarung des Logos Jesus Christus erfasst. Die Dominanz der johanneischen Epiphanie- und Offenbarungssprache (2mal ἀκούω; 3mal ὁράω, θεάομαι, φανερόω, μαρτυρέω) und das Umgreifen/Begreifen des Logos in V. 1 lassen

---

[3] Zum Diskursbegriff vgl. die Forschungsüberblicke und Darstellungen bei R. Keller, *Diskursforschung*, 13–60; A. Landwehr, *Historische Diskursanalyse*, 60–90.

[4] Gegen Th. K. Heckel, „*Historisierung*", 436, der behauptet: „Die Adressaten des Briefes sollen an den Prolog des Evangeliums denken und erst unter dieser Voraussetzung werden sie an das besondere Thema des 1Joh herangeführt."

deutlich erkennen, dass es dem I Joh um die Realität des Heilsgeschehens geht, d.h. der Briefprolog eröffnet bereits die Auseinandersetzung mit der Falschlehre[5]. Dabei zeigt die Voranstellung des Hörens in V. 1 in Verbindung mit dem zweifachen ἀπαγγέλλω in V. 2f., dass diese Auseinandersetzung vor allem auf der Ebene der Verkündigung in den johanneischen Gemeinden geführt wird. Das johanneische Hören und Sehen ist ein Erkennen, das zum Glauben an den wirklich ins Fleisch gekommenen Gottessohn Jesus Christus führt; es erreicht sein Ziel, wenn es in der Gestalt des Irdischen zugleich den Sohn Gottes erkennt und umgekehrt (vgl. I Joh 2,22; 4,1–3). Damit leistet I Joh 1,1–4 genau das, worauf es bei einem Diskurs ankommt: Es wird eine Wirklichkeit hergestellt, mit der die Argumentation bestimmt und die eigenen Ansprüche legitimiert werden[6].

In *I Joh 2,22* und *4,1–3* wird die Kontroverse mit der Falschlehre explizit weitergeführt. Mit I Joh 2,18ff. verändert sich der Ton des Schreibens, die Bildsprache wird drastischer und die Worte mit warnendem Signalcharakter nehmen zu. Der Autor appelliert an die Emotionen seiner Hörer/Leser: Die Endzeit hat begonnen, eschatologische Gegenspieler treten auf und es geht um nicht weniger als um Lüge und Wahrheit, Heil und Unheil. Die Gemeinde wird nicht mehr wie in I Joh 1,6ff. vom Autor in einen breit gefächerten Argumentationsgang mit hineingenommen, sondern er greift ehemalige Gemeindeglieder (V. 19) und ihre falsche Lehre direkt an (V. 22f.). Nicht Argumentation und Motivation, sondern Abgrenzung, Konfrontation und massive Warnung herrschen vor.

Diese Verschiebungen lassen zwei mögliche Erklärungen zu: a) Der Autor wendet sich gegen reale Gegner, die aus seiner Gemeinde hervorgingen und eine christologische Falschlehre vertreten. b) Der Autor konstruiert einen Gegnerkonflikt[7], um so in der Gemeinde eine Reflexion über die christologischen und vor allem ethischen Dimensionen des Christusgeschehens auszulösen[8]. Inner-

---

[5] Ein Bezug auf die gegnerische Lehre in I Joh 1,1–4 wird von den meisten Exegeten gesehen, vgl. die Darstellung bei W. UEBELE, *„Viele Verführer sind in die Welt ausgegangen"*, 125–128; anders z.B. D. NEUFELD, *Reconceiving Texts as Speech Acts*, 71, der eine selbstreferentielle Funktion annimmt: „Therefore what we had heard, seen and touched is not directed against Gnostics who denied the reality of Christ, but the attempt of an author to establish the credibility of his message before an audience unknown to him."

[6] Vgl. LANDWEHR, *Historische Diskursanalyse*, 117.

[7] Vgl. H. SCHMID, *Gegner im 1. Johannesbrief?*, 137: „Erinnerung und Vergangenheitsbezug des Gegnermotivs haben infolgedessen eine handlungspragmatische Dimension. Das Konstrukt des Gegnerkonfliktes erzeugt eine Entscheidungsnotwendigkeit und eine Handlungskompetenz für Gegenwart und Zukunft. Die Narrativität des Gegnermotivs kann somit als ein Element des Gegnertopos verstanden werden und ist kein Beleg für die reale Existenz der Gegner." Ohne Gegnerbezug versteht den Abschnitt auch NEUFELD, *Reconceiving Texts as Speech Acts*, 96–112.

[8] Vgl. SCHMID, *Gegner im 1. Johannesbrief?*, 140f.: „Die Gegner dienen als Exemplum der Negativität, das der Autor dem Leser vorhalten kann … Das sinnlose, bedrohliche antithetische

halb dieser beiden Thesen sind vielfältige Akzentuierungen möglich, zu klären ist aber zunächst die Frage, ob ein realer oder ein konstruierter Gegnerkonflikt vorliegt. Gegen die Annahme eines inszenierten Konfliktes sprechen m. E. folgende Argumente: 1) Der Autor nimmt in I Joh 2,19 Gemeindewissen auf und setzt es argumentativ ein („Von uns sind sie ausgegangen, aber sie waren nicht von uns"). Läge ein rein fiktiver Konflikt vor, dann wüsste die Gemeinde, dass diese sie unmittelbar berührende Information nicht stimmt und dem Autor des I Joh wäre die Überzeugungskraft entzogen. Können reale Adressaten beeinflusst, zu zentralen Erkenntnissen geführt und die Gruppengrenzen gefestigt werden, wenn sie wissen, dass gerade die sie betreffenden Behauptungen eines Autors nicht zutreffen? 2) Die gesamte endzeitliche Inszenierung in V. 18 würde deshalb bei der Annahme eines fiktiven Konfliktes ebenso an Überzeugungskraft verlieren wie die christologische Argumentation in V. 22f. und ihre Variationen in I Joh 4,1–3; 5,6–8. 3) Ist es möglich, den christologischen Konflikt für konstruiert, den ethischen aber für real zu erklären? Für eine solche Differenzierung gibt es keinerlei Anzeichen im Text. 4) Die These einer aus textpragmatischer Intention konstruierten Gegnerfront[9] und eines rein selbstreferentiellen Argumentationssystems ist selbst ein neuzeitliches Konstrukt, das (umstrittene) neuzeitliche Theorien[10] zum Interpretationsmaßstab antiker Texte macht. Theoretisch kann nicht ausgeschlossen werden, dass auch antike Texte polemische Konstruktionen vornehmen. Dann müssen sich dafür aber im Text selbst (und nicht erst durch das Interpretationsmodell *konstruiert*!) eindeutige Hinweise finden. Nur wenn der Text des I Joh zu erkennen gibt, dass er konstruierte Aussagen enthält und die Adressatengemeinde diese auch verstehen und akzeptieren würde, wäre die Hypothese einer konstruierten Gegnerfront plausibel. Dies ist aber nicht der Fall! 5) Der II/III Joh zeigen vielmehr, dass es reale theologische und persönliche Konflikte in der johanneischen Schule gab, so dass dies auch für den I Joh angenommen werden kann.

Fazit: Das textpragmatische Ziel einer Gemeindefestigung in zentralen Fragen des Denkens (Christologie) und Handelns (Ethik) kann nur erreicht werden, wenn es sich bei dem in die Argumentation einfließenden Gemeindewissen um reales Wissen handelt, das vom Autor modelliert in die aktuelle Situation wieder eingespeist wird. Dem Autor und den Adressaten ist bewusst, dass es ethische Probleme in der Gemeinde gibt, und sie wissen, dass aus ihrer Mitte eine starke Gruppe hervorgegangen ist, die eine alternative Christologie entwickelte und so eine Spaltung in der johanneischen Schule hervorrief. Damit wird die Gegner-

---

Szenario stiftet und erhält damit selbst Sinn, indem es zum einen in den Rahmen der übergreifenden Konzeption göttlicher Geschichte eingeordnet, zum anderen für die Paränese funktionalisiert wird."

9 Vgl. SCHMID, *Gegner im 1. Johannesbrief?*, 282: „Die Gegner spielen folglich keine eigenständige Rolle, sondern sind eine mehrfach auf das Grundanliegen von I Joh hin funktionalisierte Größe."

10 Als Metatheorien für Wirklichkeitserklärung fungieren vor allem die Sprechakt Theorie (D. Neufeld, H. Schmid) und die Systemtheorie N. Luhmanns (H. Schmid).

frage/Falschlehre nicht zum Interpretationsschlüssel des gesamten I Joh, sie ist aber dort zu berücksichtigen, wo der Textbefund es erfordert.

In *I Joh 2,22* lässt die Wendung ‚Jesus ist nicht der Christus' (Ἰησοῦς οὐκ ἔστιν ὁ Χριστός) vier ernsthafte Interpretationsmöglichkeiten zu[11]: 1) Es könnte sich um eine jüdische Leugnung der Messianität Jesu handeln[12]. Dagegen sprechen aber vor allem zwei Gründe: a) Die Parallelität von Χριστός („Gesalbter/ Christus") und υἱός („Sohn") am Ende von V. 22a und 22b macht eine einseitige Konzentration auf die Messiasproblematik unwahrscheinlich. b) Nach I Joh 2,19 gehörten die Falschlehrer zur johanneischen Gemeinde, kamen also nicht von außen. 2) Dieses Problem wäre hinfällig, wenn es sich um Judenchristen handelte, die Jesu Messianität infrage stellten. Sollten sie die johanneische Christologie als Verletzung des jüdischen Monotheismus abgelehnt haben?[13] Warum aber sollten sie dies getan haben? Sie schlossen sich der johanneischen Gemeinde doch sehr wahrscheinlich an, weil sie in Jesus von Nazareth die jüdischen Messiashoffnungen erfüllt sahen, in ihm den Messias und Gottessohn erblickten (vgl. Ps 2,7; 110)[14]. Zudem dürfte es in der johanneischen Schule nie eine andere als die uns in den Briefen und dem Evangelium vorliegende ‚hohe' Christologie (mit der Einheit von Vater und Sohn) gegeben haben, worauf nicht zuletzt V. 22d.23 hinweisen! Wer sich als geborener Jude einer johanneischen Gemeinde anschloss, muss von Anfang an mit solchen Vorstellungen konfrontiert worden sein und sie auch akzeptiert haben. Die Vermutung, diese judenchristliche Gruppe sei zur Synagoge zurückgekehrt und habe von dort aus agitiert[15], überzeugt ebenfalls nicht, denn offenkundig handelt es sich um einen anhaltenden Konflikt *innerhalb* der johanneischen Schule. Nur diese Annahme erklärt die Vehemenz der Argumentation, denn nach der Rückkehr zur Synagoge wäre diese Gruppe nur da, wo sie vor ihrem Anschluss an eine johanneische Gemeinde auch schon war, was den I Joh kaum zu einer

---

11   Eine Forschungsübersicht bietet H.-J. KLAUCK, *Die Johannesbriefe*, 127–151.
12   So A. WURM, *Irrlehrer*, 24f. u.ö.; H. THYEN, *Art. „Johannesbriefe"*, 194, bezeichnet (im Anschluss an Wurm) die Gegner als ‚orthodoxe Juden', die die Notwendigkeit eines himmlischen Offenbarers zur Gotteserkenntnis bestreiten. Von einem ‚innerjüdischen Konflikt' sprechen auch E. STEGEMANN, *„Kindlein, hütet euch vor den Götterbildern!"*, 294; K. ERLEMANN, *„1Joh und der jüdisch-christliche Trennungsprozess"*, 291 („zwischen Juden und Judenchristen ist vor der Abfassung des Briefes noch nicht klar zu unterscheiden, die Grenze ist fließend").
13   So vor allem U. WILCKENS, *„Gegner"*, 90: „Diese Gegner sind Christen der johanneischen Gemeinde (2,19), die deren emphatisches Bekenntnis zu Jesus als Gottes Sohn, wie es im Johannesevangelium ausgearbeitet ist (vgl. 10,30!), als Verletzung des jüdischen Grundmonotheismus im Sinne von Dtn 6,4 und Ex 20,2ff. abgelehnt haben und demgemäß beanspruchten, als Christen ‚orthodoxe Juden' zu sein."
14   Zu den jüdischen ‚Sohn-Gottes'-Konzeptionen vgl. M. HENGEL, *Der Sohn Gottes*, 35–89.
15   So RUSAM, *Gemeinschaft der Kinder Gottes*, 192f.; vgl. auch T. GRIFFITH, *Keep Yourselves from Idols*, 175: „I wish to argue that 2.19 describes a situation where ethnic Jews who had become Christians were returning to the synagogue and thereby denying their formerly held belief that the Messiah was Jesus."

solchen Polemik bewegt hätte. 3) Es könnte sich bei den Falschlehrern (wie in Korinth) um Pneuma-Enthusiasten handeln, die ein Vollendungsbewusstsein hatten und für die Zukunft „keinen ‚Gesalbten' im herausragenden und heilsvermittelnden Sinne, also keinen ‚Christus' mehr brauchen."[16] Bei diesem primär anthropologischen Ansatz wird zumeist auch der Konflikt um die Sünde/ Sündlosigkeit miteinbezogen[17]. Dagegen spricht allerdings die 1. Pers. Pl. in I Joh 1,6–2,2; sie zeigt, dass diese Auseinandersetzung zuallererst den Autor und die aktuelle Gemeinde des I Joh betrifft und mit den Falschlehrern nur indirekt etwas zu tun hat. Zudem lässt sich ein (anthropologischer und ethischer) Heilsenthusiasmus für die Falschlehrer kaum nachweisen, zumal der Streit um die ‚Fleischwerdung' des Jesus Christus (vgl. I Joh 4,2) damit überhaupt nicht erklärt werden kann. 4) Die Falschlehrer vertraten eine doketische Christologie[18], d.h. sie leugneten aus der Sicht des Briefschreibers die soteriologische Identität zwischen dem irdischen Jesus und dem himmlischen Christus (Ἰησοῦς οὐκ ἔστιν ὁ Χριστός; vgl. ferner die Identitätsaussagen in I Joh 4,15; 5,1.5). Offenbar waren für die Gegner nur der Vater und der himmlische Christus heilsrelevant, nicht jedoch das Leben und Sterben des geschichtlichen Jesus von Nazareth, das sie nur als ein unwesentliches Scheingeschehen einstuften. Diese Interpretation ergibt sich (neben dem Zusammenspiel mit II Joh 7; I Joh 4,2f.; 5,6) in V. 22 aus der Unterscheidung von Ἰησοῦς und Χριστός, vor allem aber aus der Synonymität von Christus und Gottessohn. Sie zeigt wie V. 23, dass nicht – isoliert – die Messianität Jesu zur Debatte steht, sondern das Verständnis des Sohnes in seinem Verhältnis zum Vater, so dass der Χριστός-Titel inhaltlich dem υἱός-Titel zuzuordnen ist[19]. Die Falschlehrer beanspruchten Gott ebenso für sich wie der I Joh, für den allerdings der den Vater nicht hat, der das Wirken des Sohnes falsch lehrt. Vater und Sohn, Sohn und Vater gehören für den I Joh untrennbar zusammen; er sieht die irdische und himmlische Existenz des Sohnes als Einheit und versteht den Vater vom Sohn her.

In *I Joh 4,1–3* wird die Endzeitperspektive aus I Joh 2,18 wieder aufgenommen und zugleich verschärft. Angesichts des Auftretens des Antichristen und des Wirkens seiner Pseudopropheten ist die Prüfung der Geister angesagt. Es geht um nicht weniger als um das rechte Verständnis der Person und des Werkes Jesu Christi. Damit stehen zugleich das Verhältnis zu Gott und die eigene

---

16 J. BEUTLER, *Die Johannesbriefe*, 23; ähnlich bereits K. WEISS, *„Die ‚Gnosis' im Hintergrund und im Spiegel der Johannesbriefe"*, 356.

17 Vgl. BEUTLER, *Die Johannesbriefe*, 74.

18 Für eine dezidiert doketische Interpretation von I Joh 2,22 votieren U. SCHNELLE, *Antidoketische Christologie*, 74f.; G. STRECKER, *Die Johannesbriefe*, 137f.; M. HENGEL, *Die johanneische Frage*, 170–185; J. FREY, *Die johanneische Eschatologie III*, 72; W. VOGLER, *Die Briefe des Johannes*, 17f.; UEBELE, *„Viele Verführer sind in die Welt ausgegangen"*, 133–136. Bewusst unpräzis ist KLAUCK, *Der erste Johannesbrief*, 162; eine wirkliche Festlegung vermeidet auch J. M. LIEU, *I, II, & III John*, 105–108.

19 Vgl. R. SCHNACKENBURG, *Die Johannesbriefe*, 157.

Existenz auf dem Spiel. Wie in 2,18–27 findet sich auch hier die für jeden erfolgreichen Diskurs notwendige Verbindung zwischen Gefühlsstimulation (2,18f.; 4,1) und Sachlogik (2,22.23; 4,2.3); im Kontext des Endzeitszenariums vermittelt der I Joh fundamentale theologische Einsichten.

Die Gemeinde wird aufgefordert zu prüfen, ob die auftretenden Geister eine Individuation Gottes oder seines Widersachers, des Teufel sind (I Joh 4,1). Diese Prüfung ist nach 4,2 ein erkennbarer Vorgang[20]; möglicherweise als öffentlicher Akt im Gottesdienst, denn es geht nicht um ein inwendiges Bejahen, sondern um ein erkennbares, d.h. hörbares Bekenntnis. Neben das sichtbare Verhalten tritt das hörbare Bekenntnis als Ausdruck der Gottesgemeinschaft. Das Bekenntnis zeigt, ob jemand den Geist Gottes hat oder nicht. Auf den theologischen folgt mit der Wendung πᾶν πνεῦμα („jeder Geist" = jeder) ein anthropologischer Geistbegriff. Das Verb ὁμολογεῖν („bekennen") bezieht sich in I Joh 1,9 auf das Sündenbekenntnis und in II Joh 7; I Joh 2,23; 4,2.15 auf das christologische Bekenntnis. Im hörbaren Bekenntnis gewinnt der Glaube seine Gestalt, was bereits Paulus in Röm 10,9f. programmatisch formuliert[21]: „Denn wenn du mit deinem Mund bekennst, dass Jesus der Herr ist, und in deinem Herzen glaubst, dass Gott ihn von den Toten auferweckt hat, wirst du gerettet. Mit dem Herzen nämlich glaubt man zur Gerechtigkeit, mit dem Munde aber bekennt man zur Rettung!" Für Paulus gilt wie für die johanneische Literatur: Der Mensch kann sich gegenüber dem Glaubensinhalt nicht neutral verhalten, sondern ihn nur bekennen oder ablehnen. Das Bekenntnis wird in einem antithetischen Parallelismus in V. 2b–3a formuliert, auf eine positive folgt eine negative Aussage. Der positive Inhalt des Bekenntnisses lautet: Ἰησοῦν ἐν σαρκὶ ἐληλυθότα („Jesus Christus als im Fleisch gekommen" = Jesus Christus ist im Fleisch gekommen). Es handelt sich dabei um einen doppelten Akkusativ[22], wobei das Perfekt „einen Zustand als Resultat einer vergangenen Handlung"[23] bezeichnet und das inhaltliche Schwergewicht deutlich auf ἐν σαρκί liegt. Es geht hier nicht wie in I Joh 2,22 um das Verhältnis des Ἰησοῦς zum Χριστός, denn I Joh 3,23 gebraucht Ἰησοῦς Χριστός als formelhaften Doppelnamen, der hier wieder aufgenommen wird. Zudem wäre wie in I Joh 2,22; 5,1.5 ein Artikel vor Χριστός zu erwarten. Es geht in I Joh 4,2 allein um die Fleischwerdung und d.h. das wirkliche und wahre Menschsein Jesu Christi, des Gottessohnes (vgl. I Joh 3,23; 4,9)[24]. Die starke Betonung der Inkarnation (vgl. I Joh 1,1f.; 5,6)

---

20 Die Form γινώσκετε kann auch als Imperativ interpretiert werden, was allerdings wegen I Joh 3,24 (und 3,16.20) unwahrscheinlich ist; vgl. STRECKER, *Die Johannesbriefe*, 210 Anm. 15.

21 Vgl. dazu H. CONZELMANN, *„Was glaubte die frühe Christenheit?"*, 106–119.

22 Vgl. SCHNACKENBURG, *Die Johannesbriefe*, 220f; KLAUCK, *Die Johannesbriefe*, 228.

23 BLASS/DEBRUNNER/REHKOPF, *Grammatik,* § 319.4.

24 GRIFFITH, *Keep Yourselves from Idols*, 184, wird dem sprachlichen Befund des I Joh nicht gerecht, wenn er mit Hinweis auf Barn 5,6–7.10–11 behauptet: „The phrase 'came into the flesh' describes the fact of Jesus' presence in the *sphere* in which humanity lives."

lässt auf die Bestreitung der heilsrelevanten Fleischwerdung des präexistenten Christus durch die Falschlehrer schließen. Wiederum wird deutlich, dass der Sühnetod des geschichtlichen Jesus von Nazareth (vgl. I Joh 1,9; 2,2; 4,10) für sie keine Heilsbedeutung hatte. Sie unterschieden strikt zwischen dem allein heilsrelevanten himmlischen Christus und dem irdischen Jesus, während dem I Joh alles an deren Identität liegt. Wie aber stellten sich die Falschlehrer das Verhältnis zwischen dem irdischen Jesus, dessen pure Existenz sie als Christen nicht verneinen konnten, und dem himmlischen Christus vor? Hier schweigt der I Joh, aber es spricht nichts gegen die Vermutung, dass die Gegner Jesus Christus wesenhaft ausschließlich als Gott ansahen, der seiner irdischen Erscheinung nach nur einen nicht heilsrelevanten Scheinleib haben konnte. Sie hätten dann eine doketische Christologie vertreten.

Für diese Interpretation spricht der negative Teil des Bekenntnisses in V. 3: „und jeder Geist, der Jesus zunichte macht, ist nicht aus Gott" (καὶ πᾶν πνεῦμα, ὃ λύει τὸν Ἰησοῦν ἐκ τοῦ θεοῦ οὐκ ἔστιν)) Die Gegner „eliminierten Jesus aus ihrer Lehre, leugneten die menschliche Seite des Erlösers"[25]. Diese Verkürzung des gesamten Heilswerkes Jesu Christi und die damit verbundene Aufhebung des einzigartigen Verhältnisses von Vater und Sohn kennzeichnet den Antichrist. Die Gemeinde hatte von seinem Auftreten gehört, nun erkennt sie ihn in der Falschlehre seiner Pseudopropheten, die ehemals zur Gemeinde gehörten (vgl. I Joh 2,19).

Schon die Identitätsaussage in I Joh 2,22 (vgl. I Joh 5,1.5) ließ sich nicht überzeugend auf eine jüdische oder judenchristliche Position der Falschlehrer beziehen. In I Joh 4,1–3 geht es nicht um eine (wie auch immer zu bestimmende) Identität zwischen Ἰησοῦς und Χριστός, sondern um die wirkliche Fleischwerdung Jesu Christi, wobei auf dem ἐν σαρκί der Ton liegt[26]. Gottes Heil erschien in der Gestalt des Menschen Jesus von Nazareth, der zugleich Gottessohn und Messias ist. Was sollten Juden oder (ehemalige) Judenchristen an der Fleischwerdung Jesu Christi auszusetzen gehabt haben? Warum insistiert der I Joh so vehement auf die Begriffe Fleisch, Wasser und Blut (vgl. I Joh 5,6)? Sieht man in den Falschlehrern die Vertreter einer intellektuell anspruchsvollen und

---

25 P. WEIGANDT, Doketismus, 105. Für die LA λύει plädieren u. a. SCHNACKENBURG, Die Johannesbriefe, 222; R. BULTMANN, Die Johannesbriefe, 67; R. E. BROWN, The Epistles of John, 494–496; WEIGANDT, Doketismus, 104; KL. WENGST, Der erste, zweite und dritte Brief des Johannes, 171; U. B. MÜLLER, Die Geschichte der Christologie in der johanneischen Gemeinde, 60. Für die LA μὴ ὁμολογεῖ sprechen sich z. B. aus: STRECKER, Die Johannesbriefe, 213; F. VOUGA, Die Johannesbriefe, 63; KLAUCK, Der erste Johannesbrief, 237; BEUTLER, Die Johannesbriefe, 103.

26 Vgl. KLAUCK, Der erste Johannesbrief, 233; UEBELE, „Viele Verführer sind in die Welt ausgegangen", 120; die Bedeutung von ἐν σαρκί, minimieren alle Ausleger, die auch hier allein einen jüdischen Hintergrund haben wollen (so WURM, Irrlehrer, 57; THYEN, Art. „Johannesbriefe", 193; WILCKENS, „Gegner", 106, „wonach die Gegner die Gottessohnschaft Jesu im Sinne der Einheit Jesu mit Gott bestreiten, nicht aber die Inkarnation des Himmelswesens Christus in dem Menschen Jesus").

offenbar in der Gemeinde erfolgreichen doketischen Christologie[27], ergibt die Polemik des I Joh einen religionsgeschichtlich und theologisch fassbaren Sinn.

Der kulturgeschichtliche Ausgangspunkt und Hintergrund des Doketismus sind Grundannahmen des platonischen Denkens[28], die mit dem Mittelplatonismus des 1./2. Jh. n. Chr. von großem Einfluss waren (Philo von Alexandrien, Plutarch, Apuleius, Maximus von Tyros)[29]. Weil das Gewordene aus dem Ungewordenen erklärt werden muss, ist die platonische Wirklichkeitsauffassung von dem Gegensatz εἶναι–δοκεῖν (vgl. Politeia II 361b.362a u.ö.) geprägt. Das eigentliche Sein ist das geistig-ideelle Sein (οὐσία, ὄντως ὄν, ὃ ἔστιν ὄν), die Welt der Ideen. Sie liegen als eigentliche Wirklichkeit allen sinnlichen Wahrnehmungen zugrunde, während die Welt der Wahrnehmungen (aus der Sicht der Doketen das leibliche Sein Jesu) dem Wandel, der Täuschung, dem Vergehen, dem Schein (δοκεῖν/ δόκησις) unterworfen ist.

Der Doketismus ist eine eigenständige Christologieform[30], die sich religionsphilosophisch an der platonischen Grundeinsicht orientiert, dass der (vergängliche) Leib nicht heilsrelevant, sondern nur heilshinderlich sein kann; für die die soteriologisch relevante Menschwerdung einer Gottheit ebenso unvorstellbar war wie das Leiden Gottes ‚für andere'. Besonders griechisch gebildete Gemeindeglieder dürften sich für diese (im damaligen Weltbild) rationale Argumentation geöffnet haben, wobei vor allem die Polemik des I Joh zeigt, wie erfolgreich der Doketismus in den johanneischen Gemeinden war. Weil der Doketismus und spätere gnostische Systeme ihre weltanschaulichen Grundlagen/ihr Wirklichkeitsverständnis gleichermaßen dem Platonismus entnehmen, ist es nur folgerichtig, wenn doketische Anschauungen vielfach bei Gnostikern erscheinen.

---

27 Für eine doketische Interpretation der Falschlehre votieren u. a.: SCHNELLE, *Antidoketische Christologie*, 75; HENGEL, *Die johanneische Frage*, 184f; STRECKER, *Die Johannesbriefe*, 212f.; C. COLPE, Art. „Gnosis II", 611; G. SCHUNACK, *Die Johannesbriefe*, 75 (Vorstufe ausgeprägter doketischer Vorstellungen); FREY, *Eschatologie III*, 72; UEBELE, *„Viele Verführer sind in die Welt ausgegangen"*, 120f.; P. POKORNÝ/U. HECKEL, *Einleitung*, 581. SCHNACKENBURG, *Die Johannesbriefe*, 221, sieht in I Joh 4,2 keine antidoketische Tendenz und fragt, ob überhaupt eine Inkarnationsformel vorliegt; eine antidoketische bzw. antignostische Stoßrichtung lehnt auch VOUGA, *Die Johannesbriefe*, 63, ausdrücklich ab.

28 Zur platonischen Theologie und ihrer überragenden Wirkungsgeschichte in der Antike vgl.: H. DÖRRIE/M. BALTES/CHR. PIETSCH (Hg.), *Die philosophische Lehre des Platonismus. Theologia Platonica*, passim.

29 Vgl. dazu vor allem W. MAAS, *Die Unveränderlichkeit Gottes*, 34–118 (Die Unveränderlichkeit Gottes in der griechischen Philosophie).

30 Umfassende Begründung und Literatur bei: U. SCHNELLE, *Die Johannesbriefe*, 138–146.

3. Das Chrisma im kulturgeschichtlichen Vor- und Umfeld des 1. Johannesbriefes

Bevor das Verständnis und die Funktion von Chrisma in I Joh 2,20.27 näher in den Blick genommen werden kann, müssen die kulturellen Verstehensvoraussetzungen betrachtet werden. Was ist mit χρῖσμα gemeint? Zunächst bedeutet τὸ χρῖσμα *das Aufgestrichene, das mit der Hand Aufgetragene*[31] (abgeleitet von χρίειν = bestreichen; vgl. auch τὸ χρῖσμα = Salbe zum Einreiben).

In der *LXX* findet sich χρῖσμα 9mal (Ex 29,7; 30,25 [2x]; 35,[14].19; 38,25; 40,9.15; Sir 38,30; Dan 9,26), zumeist für hebr. מִשְׁחָה (außer Sir und Dan). In Verbindung mit ἔλαιον bezeichnet es das Salböl: Ex 30,25; vgl. ἔλαιον τοῦ χρίσματος (Ex 29,7; 35,14.19 u.ö.). Gesalbt werden die Priester (Ex 29,7; 30,25), der König (I Sam 16,13) oder der Prophet (Jes 61,1), wobei mit der Salbung in der Regel auch die Geistverleihung verbunden ist[32]. *Josephus* verwendet χρῖσμα im Zusammenhang der Einsetzung des aaronitischen Priestertums; die Hütte und die Priester werden mit einer wohlriechenden Salbe gereinigt, die aus Myrrhe, Iris, verschiedenen Gewürzen sowie Olivenöl besteht (Ant 3,197). *Philo* erwähnt χρῖσμα als wohlriechendes Salböl im Zusammenhang der Einsetzung der Priester am Sinai (Vit Mos II 146.152). Besonders aufschlussreich ist der Gebrauch von χρῖσμα in *Joseph und Aseneth*, wo es deutlich eine metaphorische Bedeutung im Sinne einer göttlichen Gabe/Ausstattung bekommt:

> Nicht ist es geziemend einem gottverehrenden Manne, der segnet (mit) seinem Munde Gott den lebenden und ißt gesegnetes Brot (des) Lebens und trinkt gesegneten Kelch (der) Unsterblichkeit und salbt sich (mit) gesegneter Salbe (der) Unverweslichkeit (καὶ χρίεται χρίσματι εὐλογημένῳ ἀφθαρσίας), (zu) küssen eine fremde Frau, welche segnet (mit) ihrem Munde (Götzen)bilder tot und stumm und ißt von ihrem Tisch Brot (der) Erwürgung und trinkt aus ihrem Trankopfer Kelch (des) Hinterhalts und salbt sich (mit) Salbe (des) Verderbens (Jos As 8,5)[33].

> Siehe doch, von dem (Tage) heute (an) wirst du wieder erneuert und wieder geformt und wieder lebendig gemacht werden und wirst essen gesegnetes Brot (des) Lebens und trinken gesegneten Kelch (der) Unsterblichkeit und dich salben (mit) gesegneter Salbe (der) Unverweslichkeit (καὶ χρισθήσῃ χρίσματι εὐλογημένῳ ἀφθαρσίας) (Jos As 15,5)[34].

---

31 Vgl. F. Passow, *Handwörterbuch der griechischen Sprache II/2*, 2514; χρῖσμα gehört zu den griechischen Substantiven auf -μα, „welche meistens das Ergebnis der Handlung bedeuten" (R. Kühner/B. Gerth, *Grammatik I/2*, 272).

32 Vgl. hier umfassend E.-J. Waschke, *Der Gesalbte*, 3–155; für die Entwicklung in jüdisch-hellenistischer Zeit vgl. M. Karrer, *Der Gesalbte*, 95–267.

33 Übers.: Chr. Burchard, *Joseph und Aseneth*, 649f.

34 A.a.O., 675.

Im *griechisch-römischen Bereich* wird χρῖσμα für alles Aufgetragene bzw. Aufgestrichene gebraucht, vor allem für *kosmetische und medizinische Salben* (vgl. Hippocrates, De medico 1,1; De diaeto II 30; III 9.14; De alimento 16; De humoribus 5; vgl. ferner Rufus med., De renumet vesicae morbis 11,12; 15,5; De satyriasmo 23,3.32f; 47,3; Quaest. medic. 52,2)[35]. Vor einem Gastmahl pflegt man sich zu reinigen und zu salben; vgl. Xenophon, Symposion I 7, wo von einer Einladung des Kallias an Sokrates und seine Freunde berichtet wird:

> Bald darauf fanden sich die Gäste bei ihm ein, nachdem sie zuvor noch ein wenig Sport getrieben und sich gesalbt (καὶ χρισάμενοι) oder auch ein Bad genommen hatten.

Aber auch andere Akzente sind möglich; so berichtet Philostrat von dem Brauch der Inder, das Brautpaar mit einer Hochzeitssalbe zu besprengen, damit es den Segen der Aphrodite erhält (Vita Apollonii III 1). Lukian, Anarchasis 1,18, spottet gegenüber einem Skyten über die Griechen:

> Wenn du dich, wie ich hoffe, länger unter den Griechen aufhalten solltest, so gedenke ich es noch bald genug zu erleben, dass du selbst einer von diesen Besalbten und Eingepuderten sein wirst, so angenehm und nützlich wirst du die Sache finden.

Ähnlich ironisch Theophrast, Charak 5,6, über den, der immer gut aussehen und allen gefallen will:

> Überaus häufig geht er zum Friseur, hält seine Zähne weiß, wechselt seinen Mantel, so dass er immer sauber aussieht, und schmiert sich mit Salben ein.

Für die Mysterienreligionen bezeugt lediglich Firmicus Maternus, Err 22,1, eine Salbung im Rahmen einer Mysterienhandlung[36]:

> Darauf wird der Hals derer, die weinten, vom Priester gesalbt (tunc a sacerdote omnium qui flebant fauces unguentur), und nachdem sie gesalbt wurden (quibus perunctis), flüstert der Priester in langsamem Gemurmel: Seid guten Mutes, ihr Mysten; da der Gott gerettet ist, wird auch euch Rettung von den Mühen zuteil werden (θαρρεῖτε μύσται τοῦ θεοῦ σεσωσμένου· ἔσται γὰρ ὑμῖν ἐκ πόνων σωτηρία).

Die Salbung erfolgt hier im Rahmen der Vorbereitung auf die Teilhabe am Schicksal der Gottheit, so dass ihr durchaus eine besondere Funktion und Bedeutung beizumessen ist. Allerdings sind wir über die Einzelheiten dieser Zere-

---

35 Vgl. auch die Texte in: NEUER WETTSTEIN I.1.1, 663–672.
36 Vgl. W. BURKERT, *Antike Mysterien*, 86: „Im übrigen ist ein weiterer Ritus der Ehrung, Heilung, Integration, der im Judentum eine große Rolle spielt, in den griechischen Mysterien praktisch unbekannt: die Salbung."

monie nicht wirklich unterrichtet und die Überlieferungsbasis ist zu schmal, um daraus allgemeine Folgerungen für die Mysterienreligionen zu ziehen[37].

Der religionsgeschichtliche Befund für χρῖσμα ist relativ eindeutig: 1) Es benennt Salben und Salbungen in der antiken Medizin[38]; es bekommt 2) als Vorbereitungsritus (im Kontext eines Symposions) eine begrenzte Erkenntnisfunktion und erhält 3) vor allem bei Joseph und Aseneth eine religiös–philosophische Dimension, indem es die Erkenntnis und die Gabe des wahren, ewigen Lebens benennt.

Im *Neuen Testament* erscheint χρῖσμα nur I Joh 2,20.27; eine Sachparallele mit dem Verb χρίειν findet sich in *II Kor 1,21f*: „Der uns aber mit euch auf Christus fest gegründet hat und uns gesalbt hat, der uns versiegelt und das Angeld des Geistes in unsere Herzen gegeben hat."[39] Paulus betont hier gegenüber den Korinthern, dass es Gott selbst ist, der in der Taufe die Gemeinde und den Apostel mit Christus verband und so das Fundament schuf, auf dem beide stehen. Den in der Taufe sich vollziehenden rechtlichen Akt der Übereignung bringt Paulus besonders mit σφραγίζειν zum Ausdruck[40]. Σφραγίζειν bezeichnet das Versiegeln mit dem Siegel des Eigentümers[41]. Innerhalb des Taufgeschehens werden damit die Versiegelung des Täuflings und die Obergabe an den neuen Herrn Jesus Christus beschrieben. Unübersehbar sind dabei die Momente der Unantastbarkeit und des Schutzes für den Täufling durch dieses Geschehen. Für Paulus ist zwar σφραγίζειν noch nicht Synonym für die Taufe, aber er bereitet diese Entwicklung vor[42]. Wiederum auf einen Terminus des griechischen Handelsrechtes greift der Apostel mit der Wendung δοὺς τὸν ἀρραβῶνα τοῦ πνεύματος zurück[43]. Mit ἀρραβών wird eine Werthinterlegung bezeichnet, bei

---

37 In Apuleius, Met XI 23,1–9, ist lediglich von besonderen Waschungen die Rede, ebenso bei Justin Apologie I, 62. Zu Besprengungen in Mysterienreligionen vgl. W. D. BERNER, *Initiationsriten*, 15.95–98; BERNER, a.a.O., 224f. listet insgesamt als mögliche Initiationsriten in Mysterienreligionen acht Handlungen auf: „1) Rituelle Handlungen, in deren Verlauf Kultsymbole mit kathartischer Bedeutung verwendet werden. 2) Auf einen bestimmten Zeitraum beschränkte Askese, insbesondere Fasten. 3) Rituelle Besprengungshandlung. 4) Tauchbad. 5) Siegelung an der Stirn. 6) Übergießen mit Honig. 7) Rituell vollzogene Belehrung. 8) Die ‚zentrale kultische Handlung', die bereits den Charakter des Hauptsakramentes trägt, sowie die ‚Begrüßung des Mysten als Gott'."

38 Zu Ölen vgl. B. KRANEMANN, Art. „ Krankenöl", 915–965.

39 Zur umfassenden Analyse von II Kor 1,21f. vgl. U. SCHNELLE, *Gerechtigkeit und Christusgegenwart*, 124–126.

40 Zu σφραγίζειν vgl. W. HEITMÜLLER, ΣΦΡΑΓΙΣ, in: A. DEISSMANN/H. WINDISCH (Hg.), Neutestamentliche Studien, 40–59; G. KRETSCHMAR, *Die Geschichte des Taufgottesdienstes in der Alten Kirche*, 36ff.

41 So auch Röm 15,28.

42 Vgl. Eph 1,13f.; 4,30; II Klem 7,6; 8,6; Herm sim VIII 6,3; IX 16,2ff.; 17,4.

43 Vgl. E. DINKLER, „Taufterminologie in 2Kor 1,21f", 113ff.

deren Vollzug ein Abschluss perfekt ist[44]. Paulus will hiermit die Gewissheit des Taufgeschehens und der damit verbundenen Geistverleihung betonen, so wie er in II Kor 5,5 mit der gleichen Wendung die Gewissheit der Totenauferstehung unterstreicht. Die feste Verbindung zwischen Taufe und Geistverleihung bezeugen auch I Kor 6,11; 10,1ff.; 12,13; Gal 5,24.25; Röm 5,5, wobei insbesondere I Kor 6,11; 12,13 und II Kor 1,21f. darauf hinweisen, dass schon auf vorpaulinischer Ebene Taufe und Geist fest miteinander verknüpft waren. Besonders eindrücklich wird die gegenseitige Bezogenheit von Taufgeschehen und Geistverleihung durch die bewusste Zuordnung von Gal 2,19.20 zu Gal 3,2–5; Gal 3,26–28 zu Gal 4,6.7 und Röm 6 zu Röm 8 belegt: Die pneumatische Existenz ist Folge und Wirkung des Taufgeschehens, das wiederum als Heilsgeschehen ein Geschehen in der Kraft des Geistes ist. Alle Texte machen deutlich, dass diese Geistverleihung bei der Taufe nicht als individuelle Übereignung zu verstehen ist, sondern Paulus immer die Gemeinde auf ihr Getauftsein anspricht.

Bei den Zitaten oder Zitatanspielungen (Lk 4,18; Act 4,27; 10,38; Hebr 1,9) ist χρίειν vor allem im Kontext von Taufe und Geistbegabung Jesu von Bedeutung (vgl. Lk 4,18; Act 10,38), denn von hieraus war die Bezeichnung des Jesus von Nazareth als Χριστός („Gesalbter/Messias") im Kontext antiker Salbungsriten rezipierbar. Die im gesamten Mittelmeerraum verbreiteten Salbungsriten zeugen von einem gemeinantiken Sprachgebrauch, wonach gilt: „wer/was gesalbt ist, ist heilig, Gott nah, Gott übergeben"[45]. Sowohl Judenchristen als auch Christen aus griechisch-römischer Tradition konnten Χριστός als Prädikat für die einzigartige Gottnähe und Heiligkeit Jesu verstehen, so dass Χριστός (bzw. Ἰησοῦς Χριστός) gerade als Titelname zum idealen Missionsbegriff wurde. Ebenso konnte der neue Status der getauften Christen mit χρῖσμα und χρίειν zum Ausdruck gebracht werden, denn auch sie waren von Gott auserwählt und mit der Gabe des Geistes ausgezeichnet worden und unterschieden sich so grundlegend von ihrer Umwelt. Dabei wurde kaum noch exakt zwischen ‚Salböl' und ‚Salbung' unterschieden, sondern Handlung und Sache gehören zusammen, so dass χρῖσμα die Salbung mit Salböl im Kontext von Taufe und Geistempfang meint.

4. Das Chrisma im 1. Johannesbrief

Die Platzierung des Chrisma in I Joh 2,20.27 im Kontext der Falschlehrerkontroverse ist kein Zufall, sondern theologisches Programm. In *I Joh 2,20* („Und ihr habt das Salböl/die Salbung vom Heiligen und seid alle Wissende") führt der Autor ein grundlegendes Unterscheidungsmerkmal zwischen den Schisma-

---

[44] Zu den Belegen aus der Profangräzität vgl. A. DEISSMANN, *Bibelstudien*, 100ff.; ἀρραβών ist ein Lehnwort aus dem Semitischen, vgl. Gen 38,17–20.
[45] KARRER, *Der Gesalbte*, 211.

tikern (I Joh 2,19) und der angesprochenen Gemeinde ein: Nur sie hat ‚vom Heiligen' (= Christus) das Chrisma/das Salböl/die Salbung empfangen und deshalb sind alle Gemeindeglieder ‚Wissende'. Der I Joh steht damit in Kontinuität zu frühchristlichen Vorstellungen, indem er den Taufakt samt Geistverleihung mit einer rituellen Salbung verbindet[46]. Für eine solche Interpretation spricht vor allem die Vorstellung, dass mit dem χρῖσμα ein umfassender Abwaschungs- und Erneuerungsvorgang verbunden ist, der im frühen Christentum in der Taufe seinen Ort hat. Hinzu kommen die Nähe zu II Kor 1,21f. und die sachlichen Übereinstimmungen mit den Paraklet- und damit Geistaussagen im Johannesevangelium (vgl. V. 27). Darin geht die Chrisma-Vorstellung aber nicht auf! Es dürfte kein Zufall sein, dass die Aussagen über das χρῖσμα genau dort erscheinen, wo es um Wahrheit und Lüge (V. 21.22.26.27) und um falsche Lehre geht (V. 22). Das Chrisma lehrt, Wahres und Falsches zu unterscheiden (V. 27), so dass ihm eine noetische Funktion zukommt. Hierin zeigt sich das exklusive Selbstverständnis des I Joh und seiner Gemeinde; sie sind rituell gereinigt/gesalbt und wissen sich so in besonderer Weise von Gott gelehrt, denn sie sind ‚alle Wissende'. Während die Falschlehrer – wie alle Christen – den Geist empfangen haben, lebt und urteilt die Gemeinde des I Joh im Besitz des Chrisma[47]. Die Funktionen des Chrisma zeigen deutlich (vgl. vor allem V. 27!), dass nicht die Salbung als solche, sondern die mit der Taufe verbundene Geistverleihung die eigentliche Basis des gesamten Vorstellungskomplexes ist, so dass durchaus von einem ‚Geist-Chrisma' gesprochen werden kann. Zugleich beansprucht aber der I Joh (wie das Johannesevangelium mit dem Parakleten) ein superadditum, das bewusst mit einem Ritus verbunden wird. Rituale (wie Taufe und Salbung) als Verdichtungen von Wirklichkeit können kollektive Identitäten herstellen, stabilisieren und erhalten. Rituale sind wie Symbole eine zentrale Kategorie religiöser Sinnvermittlung und Lebensdeutung[48] und die johanneische Schule bedient sich ihrer in vielfacher Form (vgl. I Joh 5,6–8; Joh 3,5; 13,1–20)[49]. Taufe, Geist

---

[46] Anders KLAUCK, *Der erste Johannesbrief*, 157, der im χρῖσμα „eine figurative Verschlüsselung" dessen sieht, „was sich in der Sehweise des Glaubens bei der Taufe mit Wasser ereignet."

[47] Gegen KLAUCK, *Der erste Johannesbrief*, 159, der behauptet: „Vom ‚Chrisma' ist nur positiv die Rede; es erscheint als etwas, das allen Gläubigen unbestritten eignet, damit allerdings auch denen, die inzwischen ihren eigenen Weg gesucht haben." Dagegen sprechen neben dem Gesamtkontext vor allem das direkte ὑμεῖς χρῖσμα ἔχετε („ihr habt das Chrisma bekommen") und das betonte ‚ihr seid alle Wissende', womit jeweils ein Gegensatz behauptet wird. WENGST, *Häresie und Orthodoxie*, 48, vermutet, dass die Gegner das Chrisma exklusiv für sich beanspruchten.

[48] Vgl. C. GEERTZ, *Dichte Beschreibung*, 90: „Jemand, der beim Ritual in das von religiösen Vorstellungen bestimmte Bedeutungssystem ‚gesprungen' ist, ... und nach Beendigung desselben wieder in die Welt des Common sense zurückkehrt, ist – mit Ausnahme der wenigen Fälle, wo die Erfahrung folgenlos bleibt – verändert. Und so wie der Betreffende verändert ist, ist auch die Welt des Common sense verändert, denn sie wird jetzt nur noch als Teil einer umfassenderen Wirklichkeit gesehen, die sie zurechtrückt und ergänzt."

[49] Vgl. dazu die Auslegung von I Joh 5,6–8.

und Chrisma müssen nach dem I Joh unterschieden, können aber auch nicht getrennt werden; sie bilden eine wirkmächtige Einheit, ohne identisch zu sein[50].

Mit dem Schreib-Motiv in I Joh 2,26 wird das Ende des Abschnitts eingeleitet; die Gemeinde soll die falsche Lehre der Verführer/Verwirrer[51] erkennen, beurteilen und sich von ihr distanzieren können. Nach *I Joh 2,27* ist sie dazu durch die Gabe des Chrisma/der Salbung in besonderer Weise in der Lage:

> Und für euch gilt: Die Salbung/das Salböl, das ihr von ihm empfangen habt, bleibt in euch und ihr habt es nicht nötig, dass euch jemand belehrt, sondern sein Salböl lehrt euch über alles; und so ist es wahr und keine Lüge ist und so, wie es euch belehrt hat, bleibt in ihm.[52]

Das von Jesus gewährte und mit der Taufe/Geistverleihung verbundene Chrisma ‚bleibt' in den Glaubenden, so dass sie an der Ursprungslehre festhalten und keinerlei Belehrung (durch die Falschlehrer) nötig haben. Die Bezüge in V. 27fin sind unübersichtlich; indem das Chrisma die Gemeinde lehrt, befähigt es sie, in Christus zu bleiben, d.h. μένετε ἐν αὐτῷ bezieht sich wie ἀπ' αὐτοῦ in V. 27a auf Christus[53]. Auffallend sind die Parallelen zum Parakleten im Johannesevangelium, denn auch er ist bei den Glaubenden „in Ewigkeit" (Joh 14,16) und von ihm gilt: „denn er bleibt bei euch und wird in euch sein" (Joh 14,17). Die nachösterliche Lehre ist ebenfalls eine Grundfunktion des Parakleten:

> Der Paraklet, der Heilige Geist, den der Vater in meinem Namen senden wird, jener wird euch alles lehren und euch an alles erinnern, was ich euch gesagt habe (Joh 14,26).

Schließlich belehrt der Paraklet als „Geist der Wahrheit" (Joh 14,17) wie das Chrisma über ‚die Wahrheit' bzw. ‚was wahr ist'. Die Funktionen, die im I Joh das Chrisma wahrnimmt, kommen im Johannesevangelium dem Parakleten zu. Offenbar haben Brief und das Evangelium eine unterschiedliche Parakletkonzeption; während der Paraklet in I Joh 2,1 mit Jesus gleichgesetzt wird und ihm nur eine begrenzte Funktion zukommt, liegen im Evangelium breit gefächerte Parakletaussagen vor.

Der endzeitlichen Gefährdung aus der Mitte der eigenen Gemeinde setzt der I Joh die mit dem Chrisma von Gott/Christus gewährte Erkenntnis des

---

50 Anders LIEU, *I, II & III John*, 103, die Chrisma und Pneuma nicht nur unterscheiden, sondern trennen will.

51 Das Wortfeld πλανάω/πλάνη (=„verführen/täuschen/Betrug") gehört traditionell in den Kontext der Polemik gegen Falschpropheten (Dtn 13,6), falsche Messiasanwärter (Mk 13,5f.22) oder das Wirken des Satans (Apk 12,9).

52 Während bei χρῖσμα in V. 20 und V. 27a zwischen der Handlung, dem Mittel der Handlung und dem Effekt der Handlung nicht wirklich unterschieden werden kann (deshalb die Übersetzung: *Salbung/Salböl*), entfernt sich in V. 27b der Akzent deutlich von der Handlung (deshalb nur: *Salböl*).

53 Vgl. KLAUCK, *Der erste Johannesbrief*, 167.

Wahren und Falschen entgegen[54]. Er führt so eine neue Form des Wissens in den Diskurs ein und verbindet damit einen unmittelbaren Erkenntnisanspruch. Das Chrisma geht nicht in den geläufigen Vorstellungen von Taufe und Geistempfang auf, denn es gewährt wahre Erkenntnis/wahres Wissen und ist somit ein superadditum, das im Ritus der mit der Taufe verbundenen Salbung übermittelt wird. Das Chrisma gewährt eine besondere Erkenntnisfähigkeit, es ist so etwas wie ein ‚innerer' Lehrer. Durch das Chrisma hat die an der wahren Tradition festhaltende Gemeinde eine eigene Unmittelbarkeit der Gottesbeziehung und damit auch der Erkenntnis des Sohnes und des Vaters. Hier könnte die johanneische Vorstellung der unmittelbaren Gottgelehrtheit ihren Ursprung haben (vgl. Joh 6,45: διδακτοὶ θεοῦ). Das Bleiben in der Tradition, im Wort und somit im Vater und im Sohn ist unmittelbar mit dem Chrisma verbunden, dem somit eine Schlüsselrolle für das Anliegen des I Joh zukommt, gleichermaßen durch Argumentation und scharfe Grenzziehungen Identität zu stiften und zu sichern.

5. Chrisma und Geist im 1. Johannesbrief

Im I Joh erscheint πνεῦμα („Geist") 12mal, wobei fünf Belege in I Joh 4,1.2.3.6 im Sinn von ‚jede Person, die' auf Repräsentanten der Falschlehre bezogen ist. Demgegenüber steht der ‚Geist Gottes' (I Joh 4,2) bzw. der ‚Geist der Wahrheit' (I Joh 4,6), die zur sachgemäßen Erkenntnis Jesu Christi anleiten. Nach I Joh 3,24; 4,13 vollendet sich Gottes Liebe in der Gemeinde, weil sein Geist als Kraft der Liebe in den Glaubenden bleibt (vgl. 3,24). Der Geist ist als Medium der reziproken Immanenz zwischen den Glaubenden und Gott zugleich der Erkenntnisgrund und der sichtbare Ausdruck der Gottesgemeinschaft. Bereits Paulus kann davon sprechen, dass Gott seine Liebe ausgegossen hat „in unsere Herzen durch den Heiligen Geist, den er uns gab" (Röm 5,5). Bemerkenswert ist in I Joh 3,24; 4,13 die Formulierung ἐκ τοῦ πνεύματος („aus dem Geist/vom Geist"), die erkennen lässt, dass der Geist Gottes nicht in diesem gemeindebezogenen Geschehen aufgeht, sondern weitaus größer ist[55].

Mit *I Joh 5,6-8* wird eine neue Dimension massiv in den Diskurs eingeführt[56]: Die Sakramente. Damit stellt der Autor einen unmittelbarer Bezug zur

---

54 Weshalb I Joh 2,18–27 „mit einem christologischen Schwerpunkt innerhalb seines Umfelds erst einmal thematisch fremd erscheint" (so SCHMID, *Gegner im 1. Johannesbrief?*, 95), erschließt sich mir nicht.

55 Vgl. STRECKER, *Die Johannesbriefe*, 241.

56 Zur Auslegung von I Joh 5,6–8 vgl. neben den Kommentaren: J. BEUTLER, *Martyria*, 276–281; M. C. DE BOER, „*Jesus the Baptizer*", 87–106; W. NAUCK, *Die Tradition und der Charakter des ersten Johannesbriefes*, 147–182; G. RICHTER, „*Blut und Wasser aus der durchbohrten Seite Jesu (Joh 19,34b)*", in: DERS., *Studien*, 120–142; H.-J. VENETZ, „*»Durch Wasser und Blut gekommen«*", 345–361.

Gemeinderealität her. Er appelliert an die Gefühle, Erfahrungen und Erinnerungen seiner Hörer/Leser und erhöht so durch die Verbindung von Emotionalität und Sachlogik die Wirkmächtigkeit seiner Argumentation. Schon aus rituaItheoretischer Sicht ist es unhaltbar, der johanneischen Theologie jegliches Interesse an den Sakramenten abzusprechen[57]. Rituale wie die Taufe, Geist-/Chrismagabe und die Eucharistie als Verdichtungen von Wirklichkeit können kollektive Identitäten stabilisieren und erhalten. Ihre lebensweltliche Funktion besteht darin, eine Brücke „von einem Wirklichkeitsbereich zum anderen"[58] zu schlagen. Rituale und Symbole verfügen über die Kraft, religiöse Sinnvermittlung zu bewirken, was von der johanneischen Theologie genutzt wird (vgl. I Joh 2,27; 5,6–8; Joh. 3,3–5; 6,30–58; 13,1–20; 19,34–35), um den zentralen Gedanken ihrer Sinnbildung ein unverkennbares Profil zu geben: Der inkarnierte, gekreuzigte und auferstandene, in der Taufe und der Eucharistie gegenwärtige Jesus Christus ist der wahre Lebensspender.

Nach I Joh 5,6 ist Jesus Christus durch Wasser und Blut gekommen, womit auf Jesu Taufe und die im blutigen Kreuzestod gründende Eucharistie angespielt wird. Innerhalb der johanneischen Theologie waren durch die rituell-liturgische Praxis ὕδωρ („Wasser") und αἷμα („Blut") schon gefüllte Begriffe, bevor der I Joh und das Johannesevangelium geschrieben wurden, und in beiden Schriften verbinden sie sich mit einem christologischen Konzept.

Die Darstellung der Taufe Jesu in Joh 1,32–34 weist drei Besonderheiten auf: 1) Allein Gott vermag Jesus mit dem Geist zu ‚taufen'; Johannes d. T. hingegen bezeugt nur, dass Jesus der Geistempfänger, der Geistträger und der Geistübermittler ist. 2) Weil der Geist bleibend auf Jesus ruht, zu einem Attribut seiner Person wird, kann das gesamte Auftreten Jesu, seine Taten und Reden, als ein Geschehen in der Kraft des Geistes verstanden werden. 3) In Joh 1,34 und damit unmittelbar mit der Taufe Jesu verbunden, erscheint zum ersten Mal der zentrale christologische Titel des 4. Evangeliums im vollen offenbarungstheologischen Sinn: ὁ υἱὸς τοῦ θεοῦ („Sohn Gottes"). Dem entspricht die Bedeutung der Taufe der johanneischen Gemeinde; in ihr vollzieht sich der Übergang von der Sphäre der Sarx in den Lebensbereich Gottes durch die Pneumagabe (Joh 3,3.5), die ihrerseits aus der Inkarnation, dem Tod und der Verherrlichung Jesu Christi hervorgeht. Mit ihrer Taufpraxis erweist sich die johanneische Schule in zweifacher Hinsicht als legitime Fortsetzerin des Wirkens Jesu: a) Sie führt mit der Taufe das Werk

---

57 So aber die einflussreiche Position von R. Bultmann, der alle sakramentalen Texte seiner ‚kirchlichen Redaktion' zuschreibt und in Bezug auf das Johannesevangelium konstatiert, „daß auch die Sakramente keine Rolle spielen" (R. Bultmann, Theologie, 411; vgl. ferner: ders., Theologie, 443: „Es fehlt auch jedes spezifisch ekklesiologische Interesse, jedes Interesse an Kultus und Organisation").

58 A. Schütz/Th. Luckmann, Strukturen der Lebenswelt II, 95.

des geschichtlichen Jesus weiter (Joh 3,22.26; 4,1). b) Zugleich gewährt sie in der Taufe Anteil am Heilswirken des erhöhten Jesus Christus[59].

Zugespitzt artikuliert sich der inkarnatorische Grundzug der johanneischen Theologie im eucharistischen Abschnitt Joh 6,51c–58. Er wurde vom Evangelisten verfasst und an die traditionelle Lebensbrotrede Joh 6,30–35.41–51b angefügt[60], um eine zentrale christologische Aussage zu formulieren: In der Eucharistie erkennt die joh. Schule die Identität des erhöhten Menschensohnes mit dem Inkarnierten und Gekreuzigten. Der Präexistente und Erhöhte ist kein anderer als der wahrhaft Mensch gewordene und am Kreuz gestorbene Jesus von Nazareth. Gerade bei der Eucharistie verdichten sich christologische, soteriologische und ekklesiologische Momente, denn als Ort der heilvollen Gegenwart des Inkarnierten, Gekreuzigten und Verherrlichten lässt das Herrenmahl dem Glaubenden die Gabe des ewigen Lebens zuteil werden. Die vom Evangelisten Johannes eingeführte Erwähnung von αἷμα καὶ ὕδωρ ("Blut und Wasser") in Joh 19,34b und das Zeugnis des Lieblingsjüngers in 19,35 unterstreichen diese Zusammenhänge[61]. Jesu wahrer Tod hat seine wahre Menschwerdung zur Voraussetzung, beides wiederum ist die Ermöglichung der Heilsbedeutung des Todes und der Auferstehung Jesu Christi, die sich in Taufe und Eucharistie realisiert[62].

Die Bedeutung von Taufe und Eucharistie für das johanneische Denken ergibt sich sachgemäß aus dem Grundbekenntnis des johanneischen Glaubens: In Jesus Christus wurde Gott Mensch und ist Gott gegenwärtig. Taufe und Eucharistie verleihen diesem Gedanken unmittelbaren Ausdruck, denn sie sind im Leben und Sterben des geschichtlichen Jesus von Nazareth begründet und gewähren durch den Auferstandenen zugleich im Raum der Gemeinde die Gaben der Neuschöpfung (I Joh 2,27; 3,9f.; Joh 3,5) und des ewigen Lebens (I Joh 5,11f.; Joh 6,51c–58). Zugleich war dieses Konzept in der johanneischen Schule offenbar umstritten, denn aus V. 6b ist eine Ablehnung der Heilsbedeutung der Passion Jesu und der damit verbundenen Eucharistie durch die Falschlehrer zu erkennen. Wenn hier betont wird, Jesus Christus sei ‚nicht nur im Wasser allein (μόνον), sondern im Wasser und im Blut' gekommen, darf daraus gefolgert werden, dass die Falschlehrer wohl der Taufe Jesu einen soteriologischen Sinn abgewinnen konnten, nicht aber seinem wirklichen Kreuzestod[63]. Offensichtlich kam der Taufe als Ort der Geistverleihung an Jesus (Joh 1,32–34) und an die Glaubenden (I Joh 2,27; 3,24; 4,1–3.13; Joh 3,5) innerhalb der johanneischen Schule eine

---

59 Vgl. zum johanneischen Taufverständnis SCHNELLE, *Antidoketische Christologie*, 196–213; TH. POPP, *Grammatik des Geistes*, 233–255.

60 Vgl. zur ausführlichen Begründung und Auseinandersetzung mit der Literatur SCHNELLE, *Antidoketische Christologie*, 214–228; ferner POPP, *Grammatik des Geistes*, 360–386.

61 Vgl. zur Einzelbegründung U. SCHNELLE, *Das Evangelium nach Johannes*, 317–319.

62 Vgl. W. BAUER, *Das Johannes-Evangelium*, 226, der zu Recht bemerkt, dass der Bezug auf die Sakramente „auch durch die Voranstellung des Blutes" nicht hinfällig wird.

63 Vgl. SCHNACKENBURG, *Die Johannesbriefe*, 258.

große Bedeutung zu. Von dort begründeten die Falschlehrer ihr Pneumatikertum, während sie das Kreuz und wahrscheinlich auch die Eucharistie verwarfen. Dazu passen die Überlieferungen, dass die Doketen der Eucharistie fernblieben (IgnSm 7,1) oder nur mit Wasser feierten (Johannesakten 46.84–86.109f.; Epiphanius, Pan XLII 3,3). Der Sohn Gottes konnte aus der Logik der doketischen Falschlehrer wohl geistbegabt sein, nicht aber wirklich sterben und eine auf das Blut Christi begründete Eucharistiepraxis rechtfertigen. Demgegenüber betont der I Joh die Heilsbedeutung von Taufe *und* Abendmahl. Zwar ist in I Joh 5,6 von den Sakramenten noch nicht explizit die Rede, aber die Argumentation läuft auf V.7f. zu, wobei aus johanneischer Sicht das Heilsereignis und seine Vergegenwärtigung nicht getrennt werden können, weil Wasser und Blut die Elemente der Sakramente sind[64]. Zudem sind Begriffe wie ὕδωρ („Wasser") und αἷμα („Blut") immer mehrschichtig, für verschiedene, einander nicht ausschließende Bedeutungsebenen offen. Es ist geradezu ein Kennzeichen der gesamten johanneischen Theologie, durch literarische Kunstmittel wie Repetition, Variation, Zahlensymbolik (vgl. V. 7!), mehrschichtige Ausdrucksweise und Leitworte den Lesern/ Hörern neue Einsichten zu eröffnen oder bereits Erkanntes zu stabilisieren[65].

Eine neue Argumentationsebene wird mit V. 6c erreicht; der Geist tritt nicht nur zu Wasser und Blut hinzu, sondern er bezeugt die Wahrheit des Gesamtgeschehens, d.h. Taufe und Abendmahl sind nur in ihrer Verbindung mit dem Geist wahres Zeugnis. Während der Geist von den Falschlehrern wahrscheinlich nur mit der Taufe verbunden wurde, bezieht der I Joh die Eucharistie mit ein und bindet die gesamte Glaubwürdigkeit an das Zeugnis des Geistes. Damit werden dem Pneuma Funktionen zuerkannt, die weit über die Taufe (Jesu und der Glaubenden) hinausgehen. Vom Chrisma wird in I Joh 2,27b gesagt, es belehre die Glaubenden über alles „und so ist es wahr und keine Lüge ist und so, wie es euch belehrt hat, bleibt in ihm"; der Parakleten heißt auch ‚Geist der Wahrheit' (Joh 14,17; 15,26) und wird die Glaubenden ‚in alle Wahrheit führen' (Joh 16,13). Schließlich wird über den Lieblingsjünger unter dem Kreuz (vgl. Joh 19,25–27) gesagt: „Und der es gesehen hat, hat es bezeugt, und sein Zeugnis ist wahr, und jener weiß, dass er die Wahrheit sagt, damit auch ihr glaubt" (Joh 19,35). Das Chrisma kann von Christus (I Joh 2,27) und der Geist kann von Gott (I Joh 3,24) gesandt sein, d.h. aus ihrer Fülle senden der Vater und/oder der Sohn den Geist (vgl. Joh 14,16.26.15,2616,7), der in seinem Ursprung ganz

---

64 Gegen SCHNACKENBURG, *Die Johannesbriefe*, 257f.; BULTMANN, *Die Johannesbriefe*, 82f.; NAUCK, *Die Tradition und der Charakter*, 147; WENGST, *Der erste, zweite und dritte Johannesbrief*, 207; SCHUNACK, *Die Johannesbriefe*, 94; KLAUCK, *Der erste Johannesbrief*, 297f., die ὕδωρ und αἷμα (nur) auf die geschichtlichen Daten der Taufe und des Kreuzestodes Jesu beziehen. Einen Bezug auf die Sakramente sehen bereits in V. 6: SCHNELLE, *Antidoketische Christologie*, 81f.; BROWN, *The Johannine Epistles*, 577f.; VENETZ, *„»Durch Wasser und Blut gekommen«"*, 354; STRECKER, *Die Johannesbriefe*, 273.

65 Vgl. dazu POPP, *Grammatik des Geistes*, 457–491.

auf den Vater und den Sohn bezogen ist, indem er das Offenbarungsgeschehen immer neu vergegenwärtigt und bezeugt, weil in ihm der Sohn und der ihn sendende und beglaubigende Vater immer gegenwärtig sind.

Während zuvor nur der Geist bezeugt, erscheinen nun in I Joh 5,7.8 alle drei Größen als Zeugen, wobei die Voranstellung des Geistes seine besondere Stellung unterstreicht. Im Hintergrund steht die u. a. in Dtn 19,15 („Nur auf die Aussage von zwei oder drei Zeugen hin soll eine Sache gültig sein") bezeugte jüdische Tradition, wonach allein das übereinstimmende Zeugnis zweier oder dreier Menschen wahr ist (vgl. ferner Num 35,30; Dtn 17,6). Diese Tradition findet sich auch in Joh 8,17f.: „Auch steht in eurem Gesetz geschrieben, dass das Zeugnis zweier Menschen wahr ist. Ich bin es, der von mir selbst Zeugnis gibt, und es zeugt für mich der Vater, der mich gesandt hat."[66] Aus johanneischer Sicht kann sich gerade Jesus auf diesen Grundsatz berufen, denn das Verhältnis von Vater und Sohn zeichnet sich nicht durch eine äußerliche, sondern eine innere, vollständige Übereinstimmung aus. Als Gesandter Gottes repräsentiert Jesus den Vater in der Welt, seine Präsenz in der Welt macht zugleich den Vater als Sendenden offenbar.

Was bezeugen Geist, Wasser und Blut und sind darin ‚auf das eine hin ausgerichtet'? Wasser und Blut sind nun selbst Zeugen, d.h. zumindest jetzt hat gegenüber V. 6 ein Bedeutungswandel stattgefunden[67]. Geist, Wasser und Blut stimmen nicht nur in ihrem Zeugnis überein, sondern als theologisch und rituell geprägte Begriffe stehen sie für etwas, nämlich für die Sakramente. In den Sakramenten von Taufe und Abendmahl wird das eine Heilsereignis durch den Geist vergegenwärtigt und damit bezeugen alle drei die Wahrheit des Einen (vgl. Joh 10,30: „Ich und der Vater sind eins"). Die Voranstellung des Geistes in der Bezeugung des Heilshandelns des Vaters im Sohn zeigt zudem, dass die Anfänge eines bewussten trinitarischen Denkens innerhalb des frühen Christentums in der johanneischen Schule liegen; es deutet sich im I Joh an und ist im Johannesevangelium schon deutlich entfaltet[68].

In der Auseinandersetzung mit den Falschlehrern geht der I Joh über christologische Verhältnisbestimmungen hinaus und führt die rituelle Wirklichkeit der Gemeinde ins Feld. Taufe, Geistverleihung/Salbung und Eucharistie sind nicht nur Verdichtungen grundlegender theologischer Zusammenhänge, sondern auch soziale und emotionale Orte von bleibender Prägung. Weil der inkarnierte, gekreuzigte und auferstandene Jesus Christus in Taufe und Eucharistie gegenwärtig ist, schmälern die Falschlehrer mit ihrer einseitigen Ausrichtung auf die Göttlichkeit des Sohnes die Heilswirklichkeit und verfehlen sie zugleich. Sowohl in der Taufe als auch in der Eucharistie erschließt sich der

---

66 Vgl. im NT ferner: Mt 18,16; II Kor 13,1; Hebr 10,28.

67 Gegen WENGST, *Der erste, zweite und dritte Johannesbrief*, 210, der einen Bedeutungswandel leugnet; vgl. hingegen SCHNACKENBURG, *Die Johannesbriefe*, 261f.

68 Vgl. dazu U. SCHNELLE, *„Trinitarisches Denken im Johannesevangelium"*, 367–386.

Gekreuzigte und Auferstandene als Inbegriff des Lebens den Glaubenden und gewährt ihnen Anteil an seiner eigenen Lebensfülle.

6. Fazit

Das Chrisma ist mehr als ein Synonym für Taufe oder Geist, denn mit diesem schillernden Begriff verbindet der I Joh ein erkennbares theologisches Programm und textpragmatisches Ziel: Er führt in seiner Kontroverse mit den Schismatikern die Vorstellung einer rituellen Geistsalbung ein, um so der Gemeinde ihren besonderen Status und ihre exklusive Erkenntnisfähigkeit zu verdeutlichen. Damit stellt der Autor einen unmittelbaren Bezug zur Gemeinderealität her; er appelliert an die Gefühle, Erfahrungen und Erinnerungen seiner Hörer/Leser und erhöht so durch die Verbindung von Emotionalität und Sachlogik die Wirkmächtigkeit seiner Argumentation. Das Chrisma lehrt die Glaubenden alles Wissen und schenkt den göttlichen Blick, der im Gegensatz zum Antichristen in Jesus Christus den fleischgewordenen Sohn des Vaters erkennt (vgl. I Joh 2,22–24; 4,1–3). Weil die johanneischen Christen vom erhöhten Christus und damit auch von Gott gelehrt sind (vgl. I Joh 2,20), ihnen das Chrisma Gleichzeitigkeit vermittelt, haben sie gegenüber den ‚historischen' Augenzeugen keinen Nachteil, sie erkennen sogar aus nachösterlicher Perspektive tiefer und wahrer die vielfältigen Dimensionen des Christusgeschehens. Es geht dabei um ein Erkennen, das eine intellektuelle Dimension miteinschließt, denn das Bekenntnis der Gemeinde unterscheidet sich in einem entscheidenden Punkt von der (erfolgreichen) Verkündigung der Falschlehrer. Während in der Gemeinde der Geist Gottes wirkt, der mit dem Chrisma als superadditum alles lehrt (vgl. I Joh 2,20.27), täuschen und verwirren die Falschlehrer, so dass sich der Geist der Wahrheit und der Geist des Irrtums/der Lüge gegenüberstehen.

Während der Geist von den Falschlehrern wahrscheinlich nur mit der Taufe verbunden wurde, bezieht der I Joh die Eucharistie mit ein und bindet so die Gegenwart und auch die Glaubwürdigkeit des Heilsgeschehens an das Zeugnis des Geistes. Damit werden dem Pneuma Funktionen zuerkannt, die weit über die Taufe (Jesu und der Glaubenden) hinausgehen. Aus der Verbindung von Geist und Zeugnis ergibt sich ein theologisches Gesamtmotiv: Der Geist, der in seinem Ursprung ganz auf den Vater und den Sohn bezogen ist, vergegenwärtigt und bezeugt immer neu das Offenbarungsgeschehen, weil in ihm der Sohn und der ihn sendende und beglaubigende Vater stets gegenwärtig sind.

Das Chrisma geht über die mit der Taufe und dem Geistempfang verknüpften geläufigen Vorstellungen hinaus, weil es wahre Erkenntnis und wahres Wissen ermöglicht, die im Ritus der mit der Taufe verbundenen Salbung übermittelt werden. Das Chrisma fungiert als ein ‚innerer' Lehrer, der das Bleiben in der Tradition, im Wort, in der Liebe und somit im Vater und im Sohn gewährt und dem so eine Schlüsselrolle für das Grundanliegen des I Joh zukommt, Identitätsstiftung und Identitätssicherung durch Zuspruch, Aufklärung und Abgrenzung vorzunehmen.

Bibliographie

BAUER, WALTER, *Das Johannes-Evangelium* (HNT 6), Tübingen: Mohr Siebeck ³1933.

BERNER, WOLF DIETRICH, *Initiationsriten in Mysterienreligionen, im Gnostizismus und im antiken Judentum*, Diss. theol., Göttingen 1972.

BEUTLER, JOHNANNES, *Martyria* (FTS 10), Frankfurt: Verlag Josef Knecht 1972.

— *Die Johannesbriefe* (RNT), Regensburg: Pustet 2000.

BLASS, FRIEDRICH/DEBRUNNER, ALBERT/REHKOPF, FRIEDRICH, *Grammatik des neutestamentlichen Griechisch*, Göttingen: Vandenhoeck & Ruprecht ¹⁶1984.

BROWN, RAYMOND E., *The Johannine Epistles* (AncB 39), London: Geoffrey Chapman 1982.

BULTMANN, RUDOLF, *Theologie des Neuen Testaments*, Tübingen: Mohr Siebeck ⁷1977.

— *Die Johannesbriefe* (KEK 14), Göttingen: Vandenhoeck & Ruprecht 1967.

BURCHARD, CHRISTOPH, *Joseph und Aseneth* (JSHRZ II/4), Gütersloh: Gütersloher Verlagshaus 1983.

BURKERT, WALTER, *Antike Mysterien*, München: Beck ²1991.

COLPE, CARSTEN, Art. „Gnosis II", in: *RAC* 11, Stuttgart: Anton Hiersemann 1981, 537–659.

CONZELMANN, HANS, „Was glaubte die frühe Christenheit?", in: ders., *Theologie als Schriftauslegung* (BEvTh 65), München: Kaiser 1974, 106–119.

DE BOER, MARTIN C., „Jesus the Baptizer: 1 John 5:5–8 and the Gospel of John", in: *JBL* 107 (1988) 87–106.

DEISSMANN, ADOLF, *Bibelstudien*, Marburg: N. G. Elwert'sche Verlagsbuchhandlung 1895.

DEISSMANN, ADOLF/WINDISCH, HANS (Hg.), *Neutestamentliche Studien* (FS G. Heinrici), Leipzig: J. G. Hinrich'sche Buchhandlung 1914.

DINKLER, ERICH, „Taufterminologie in 2Kor 1,21f", in: DERS., *Signum Crucis. Aufsätze zum Neuen Testament und zur christlichen Archäologie*, Tübingen: Mohr Siebeck 1967, 99–117.

DÖRRIE, HEINRICH/BALTES, MATTHIAS/PIETSCH, CHRISTIAN (Hg.), *Die philosophische Lehre des Platonismus* (Theologia Platonica, Der Platonismus der Antike 7.1), Stuttgart: Frommann-Holzboog 2008.

ERLEMANN, KURT, „1Joh und der jüdisch-christliche Trennungsprozess", in: *ThZ* 55 (1999) 285–302.

FREY, JÖRG, *Die johanneische Eschatologie III* (WUNT 117), Tübingen: Mohr Siebeck 2000.

GEERTZ, CLIFFORD, *Dichte Beschreibung*, Frankfurt: Suhrkamp 1987.

GRIFFITH, TERRY, *Keep Yourselves from Idols* (JSNT.SS 233), London/New York: T&T Clark 2002.

HECKEL, THEO K., „Die Historisierung der johanneischen Theologie im Ersten Johannesbrief", in: *NTS* 50 (2004) 425–443.

HENGEL, MARTIN, *Der Sohn Gottes*, Tübingen: Mohr Siebeck ²1977.

— *Die johanneische Frage* (WUNT 67), Tübingen: Mohr Siebeck 1993.

KELLER, REINER, *Diskursforschung*, Wiesbaden: Verlag für Sozialwissenschaften ²2004.

KARRER, MARTIN, *Der Gesalbte. Die Grundlagen des Christustitels* (FRLANT 151), Göttingen: Vandenhoeck & Ruprecht 1991.

KLAUCK, HANS-JOSEF, *Die Johannesbriefe* (EdF 276), Darmstadt: Wissenschaftliche Buchgesellschaft 1991.

— *Der erste Johannesbrief* (EKK XXIII/1), Neukirchen: Neukirchener Verlag 1991.

KLEIN, WASSILOS, Art. „Salbung I", in: *TRE* 29, G. Müller (Hg.), Berlin: de Gruyter 1998, 707–709.

KRANEMANN, BENEDIKT, Art. „Krankenöl", in: *RAC* 21, Stuttgart: Anton Hiersemann, 2006, 915–965.

KRETSCHMAR, GEORG, *Die Geschichte des Taufgottesdienstes in der Alten Kirche* (Leiturgia V), Kassel: Johannes Stauda Verlag 1970.

KÜHNER, RAPHAEL/GERTH, BERNHARD, *Ausführliche Grammatik der griechischen Sprache I/2*, Hannover: Hahnsche Buchhandlung ⁴1955.

LANDWEHR, ACHIM, *Historische Diskursanalyse*, Frankfurt: Campus Verlag 2008.

LIEU, JUDITH M., *I, II, & III John. A Commentary* (NTL), Louisville, Ky./London: Westminster/John Knox 2008.

MAAS, WILHELM, *Die Unveränderlichkeit Gottes*, Paderborn: Schöningh 1974.

MÜLLER, ULRICH B., *Die Geschichte der Christologie in der johanneischen Gemeinde* (SBS 77), Stuttgart: Katholisches Bibelwerk 1975.

NAUCK, WOLFGANG, *Die Tradition und der Charakter des ersten Johannesbriefes* (WUNT 3), Tübingen: Mohr Siebeck 1957.

NEUFELD, DIETMAR, *Reconceiving Texts as Speech Acts* (BIS 7), Leiden: Brill 1994.

PASSOW, FRANZ, *Handwörterbuch der griechischen Sprache II/2*, Leipzig: Fr. Chr. Wilh. Vogel ^{5}1857.

POKORNÝ, PETR/HECKEL, ULRICH, *Einleitung in das Neue Testament*, Tübingen: Mohr Siebeck 2007.

POPP, THOMAS, *Grammatik des Geistes* (ABG 3), Leipzig: Evang.Verlagsanstalt 2001.

RICHTER, GEORG, *Studien zum Johannesevangelium* (BU 13), Regensburg: Pustet 1977.

RUSAM, DIETRICH, *Gemeinschaft der Kinder Gottes* (BWANT 133), Stuttgart: Kohlhammer 1993.

SCHMID, HANSJÖRG, *Gegner im 1Johannesbrief?* (BWANT 159), Stuttgart: Kohlhammer 2002.

SCHNACKENBURG, RUDOLF, *Die Johannesbriefe* (HThK XIII/3), Freiburg: Herder ^{6}1979.

SCHNELLE, UDO, *Gerechtigkeit und Christusgegenwart* (GTA 24), Göttingen: Vandenhoeck & Ruprecht ^{2}1986.

— *Antidoketische Christologie im Johannesevangelium* (FRLANT 137), Göttingen: Vandenhoeck & Ruprecht 1987.

— „Trinitarisches Denken im Johannesevangelium", in: *Israel und seine Heilstraditionen im Johannesevangelium* (FS J. Beutler), hg. v. M. Labahn/K. Scholtissek/A. Strothmann, Paderborn: Schöningh 2004, 367–386.

— *Einleitung in das Neue Testament* (UTB 1830), Göttingen: Vandenhoeck & Ruprecht ^{6}2007.

— *Das Evangelium nach Johannes* (ThHK 4), Leipzig: Evang. Verlaganstalt ^{4}2009.

— (Hg.), *Neuer Wettstein I.1.1: Texte zum Markusevangelium*, in Zusammenarb. m. M. Labahn u. M. Lang, Berlin: de Gruyter 2008.

— *Die Johannesbriefe* (ThHK 17), Leipzig: Evang. Verlagsanstalt 2010.

SCHÜTZ, ALFRED/LUCKMANN, THOMAS, *Strukturen der Lebenswelt II*, Frankfurt: Suhrkamp ³1994.

SCHUNACK, GERD, *Die Johannesbriefe* (ZBK), Zürich: TVZ 1982.

STEGEMANN, EKKEHARD W., „Kindlein, hütet euch vor den Götterbildern!". Erwägungen zum Schluss des 1. Johannesbriefes, in: *ThZ* 41 (1985) 284–294.

STRECKER, GEORG, *Die Johannesbriefe* (KEK XIV), Göttingen: Vandenhoeck & Ruprecht 1989.

THYEN, HARTWIG, Art. „Johannesbriefe", in: *TRE* 17, G. Müller (Hg.), Berlin: de Gruyter 1988, 186–200.

UEBELE, WOLFRAM, *„Viele Verführer sind in die Welt ausgegangen"* (BWANT 151), Stuttgart: Kohlhammer 2001.

VENETZ, HERMANN-JOSEF, „»Durch Wasser und Blut gekommen«. Exegetische Überlegungen zu 1 Joh 5,6", in: *Die Mitte des Neuen Testaments* (FS E. Schweizer), hg. v. U. Luz/H. Weder, Göttingen: Vandenhoeck & Ruprecht 1981, 345–361.

VOGLER, WERNER, *Die Briefe des Johannes* (ThHK 17), Leipzig: Evang. Verlaganstalt 1993.

VOUGA, FRANCIS, *Die Johannesbriefe* (HNT 15/3), Tübingen: Mohr Siebeck 1990.

WASCHKE, ERNST-JOACHIM, *Der Gesalbte* (BZAW 306), Berlin: de Gruyter 2001.

WEIGANDT, PETER, *Der Doketismus im Urchristentum und in der theologischen Entwicklung des zweiten Jahrhunderts*, Diss. theol. Heidelberg 1961.

WEISS, KONRAD, „Die ‚Gnosis' im Hintergrund und im Spiegel der Johannesbriefe", in: *Gnosis und Neues Testament*, hg. v. K.-W. Tröger, Berlin: Evang. Verlagsanstalt 1973, 341–356.

WENGST, KLAUS, *Häresie und Orthodoxie im Spiegel des ersten Johannesbriefes*, Gütersloh: Gütersloher Verlagshaus 1976.

— *Der erste, zweite und dritte Brief des Johannes* (ÖTK 16), Gütersloh: Gütersloher Verlagshaus 1978.

WILCKENS, ULRICH, „Die Gegner im 1. und 2. Johannesbrief, ‚die Juden' im Johannesevangelium und die Gegner in den Ignatiusbriefen und den Sendschreiben der Apokalypse", in: DERS., *Der Sohn Gottes und seine Gemeinde. Studien zur Theologie der johanneischen Schriften* (FRLANT 200), Göttingen: Vandenhoeck & Ruprecht 2003, 89–125.

WURM, ALOIS, *Die Irrlehrer im ersten Johannesbrief*, Freiburg: Herdersche Verlagshandlung 1903.

ZAGER, WERNER, Art. „Salbung III", in: *TRE* 29, G. Müller (Hg.), Berlin: de Gruyter 1998, 711–714.

Matthew 28:9–20 and Mark 16:9–20
Different Ways of Relating Baptism to the Joint Mission[1] of God, John the Baptist, Jesus, and their Adherents

Kirsten Marie Hartvigsen

1. Introduction

In Matthew 28:16–20 and Mark 16:14–20, the risen Lord encounters the eleven and charges them to continue his mission. Their assignment is presented in different manners in these two endings. In Matthew 28:18–20, Jesus defines their task in terms of the following activities: formation of disciples, baptism, and teaching. Besides this, he promises his addressees that he will be with them "to the end of the age" (Matthew 28:20). In Mark 16:15–18, Jesus highlights proclamation, two responses to this proclamation – belief and baptism versus unbelief – and the signs that will accompany those who believe (Mark 16:17). As these brief summaries suggest, both endings associate the command to baptize with Jesus' final resurrection appearance and his last assignment to his adherents, but the immediate contexts of these commissions are slightly different in the two Gospels. Furthermore, Jesus focuses on dissimilar aspects of the primary task of the eleven in these narratives.

Both the Gospel of Mark and Matthew present Jesus' mission as a prolongation of the activities of the prophets of old and John the Baptist, and in these Gospels the assignments of these characters are all anchored in the initiative and the authority of God.[2] Even at the beginning of Mark and Matthew, Jesus'

---

1 See note 2.
2 In the latter part of this article, I will also employ the terms goal, sub-goal, plan, sub-plan, project, and joint project to refer to different aspects of the mission of these characters. This terminology is drawn from the realm of cognitive science. I will merely sketch some important aspects of this approach here. For a more thorough presentation, see K. M. Hartvigsen, 'Prepare the Way of the Lord:' Towards a Cognitive Poetic Analysis of Audience Involvement with Characters and Events in the Markan World. On the basis of goals and beliefs, sub-goals, plans, and projects are designed to help us reach our own goals, or goals that we share with other people. These plans or goals may be conscious or unconscious. K. Oatley, *Best Laid Schemes: The Psychology of Emotions*, 24–25. If plans made with other people are based on the division of labor, they are called joint plans, whereas the mutual incorporation of goals is labeled shared or joint projects. See P. C. Hogan, *Cognitive Science, Literature, and the Arts: A Guide for Humanists*, 147–148. After plans, projects, and goals have been established, events and circumstances are systematically evaluated by cognitive systems. Vicissitudes are appraised in order to per-

disciples are delegated the responsibility to participate in his mission (Mark 3:13ff.; 6:7ff.; 6:30; Matthew 10:1ff.) and as the Gospels are coming to an end, Jesus' adherents are given the primary responsibility for carrying on this task with the support of the risen Lord (Mark 16:14–20; Matthew 28:16–20).

From a hermeneutical point of view the conclusions of these two Gospels are of vital importance, because they may inspire readers and audience members to reflect on their own commitment to the Christian movement, to its founder, and to previous and subsequent members of this community of believers. In that connection, baptism plays an important, but not the most vital role. In the Gospel of Matthew, the primary emphasis is on the formation of disciples through baptism *and* teaching, whereas the Longer Ending of Mark (Mark 16:9–20) focuses on proclamation and its divergent results, one of which encompasses baptism. In both endings, the expansion of the community is thus the main objective; however, these endings stress different aspects of this aim.

In this article, I will primarily focus on how audience members may interpret the role of baptism during an oral performance of these respective endings and the manner in which they may relate the significance of baptism to their own lives, but first I will touch upon some issues which have played an important role in previous discussions of Jesus' commissions, in particular with regard to the directive to baptize.

2. The Authenticity and Genre of Matthew 28:16–20

A vast amount of scholarly books and articles present dissimilar arguments concerning the authenticity of Matthew 28:16–20.[3] In the following paragraphs, I will treat two aspects of the genuineness of this pericope. (1) Was the command to baptize originally a part of the Gospel of Matthew? (2) Was this directive point uttered by Jesus himself, or were these words put in his mouth by the author of Matthew?

---

ceive how likely they are to contribute to the realization of goals of current plans and projects. If success seems imminent, positive emotions will be elicited, whereas indications of failure will bring about negative emotions. See OATLEY, *Best Laid Schemes*, 47–50. HOGAN, *Cognitive Science, Literature and the Arts*, 146–148.

3   In his book *Baptism in the New Testament*, G. R. Beasley-Murray presents the following four traditional arguments against the authenticity of Matthew 28:18–20 and answers these objections. (1) This tradition is found only in the Gospel of Matthew. (2) Baptism was probably not mentioned in the original text. (3) The Trinitarian formula was adopted late. (4) The manner in which the church coped with the Gentile mission cannot be reconciled with the commission to make disciples of all nations. G. R. BEASLEY-MURRAY, *Baptism in the New Testament*, 78. On the difficulty of accepting Matthew 28:19–20 as an authentic saying, see also P. F. BRADSHAW, *Early Christian Worship*, 2.

2.1. Did the Reference to Baptism and the Triadic Phrase Belong to the Original Version of Matthew 28:16–20?

Some scholars suggest that the commission to baptize and the triadic phrase in Matthew 28:19b (βαπτίζοντες αὐτοὺς εἰς τὸ ὄνομα τοῦ πατρὸς καὶ τοῦ υἱοῦ καὶ τοῦ ἁγίου πνεύματος/"baptizing them into the name of the Father and of the Son and of the Holy Spirit") did not belong to the earliest version of Matthew 28:16–20.[4] Their argument is based on the fact that Eusebius cites the commission in different ways, often without mentioning baptism or the triadic phrase.[5] Nevertheless, the shortened form, "[g]o, make disciples of all the nations in my name," is attested in contexts where the reference to baptism would be superfluous to the argument of Eusebius.[6] Moreover, all textual witnesses to the Gospel of Matthew present the full text "[g]o therefore, make disciples of all nations, baptizing them into the name of the Father and of the Son and of the Holy Spirit" (Matthew 28:19). This version is consequently regarded as original by most textual critics and by this author.[7]

Scholars also consider the triadic phrase to be inauthentic because Matthew 28:19 is the only example in the New Testament which indicates that baptism is related to the Father, the Son, and the Holy Spirit.[8] Other New Testament sources rather associate baptism with the following phrases: "in [ἐπί] the name of Jesus Christ" (Acts 2:38), "into [εἰς] the name of the Lord Jesus" (Acts 8:16; 19:5), "in [ἐν] the name of Jesus Christ" (Acts 10:48), "into [εἰς] Christ Jesus" (Rom 6:3), and "into [εἰς] Christ" (Gal 3:27).[9] Because of these variations, William

---

4   See for instance, F. C. CONYBEARE, "The Eusebian Form of the Text Matth. 28,19." For an overview of different scholars who assert that the commission did not contain the reference to baptism nor the triadic phrase, see BEASLEY-MURRAY, *Baptism*, 81. U. LUZ, *Das Evangelium nach Matthäus (Mt 26–28)*, 431, note 15.

5   E. FERGUSON, *Baptism in the Early Church*, 134. For an overview of the different arguments, see Ferguson note 6 and 8; BEASLEY-MURRAY, *Baptism*, 81–82; LUZ, *Matthäus IV*, 431, note 15; G. BARTH, *Die Taufe in frühchristlicher Zeit*, 11–12. For different citations of Matthew 28:19, see CONYBEARE, "The Eusebian."

6   FERGUSON, *Baptism in the Early Church*, 134. On related views, see BEASLEY-MURRAY, *Baptism*, 82.

7   FERGUSON, *Baptism in the Early Church*, 134–135. On the authenticity of this phrase, see also LUZ, *Matthäus IV*, 431, BARTH, *Die Taufe*, 11–12; L. HARTMAN, *'Into the Name of the Lord Jesus': Baptism in the Early Church*, 147–148; R. T. FRANCE, *The Gospel According to Matthew: An Introduction and Commentary*, 415; J. NOLLAND, "'In Such a Manner It Is Fitting for Us to Fulfil all Righteousness:' Reflections on the Place of Baptism in the Gospel of Matthew," 77. Cf. H. B. GREEN, *The Gospel According to Matthew in the Revised Standard Version*, 230–231.

8   BEASLEY-MURRAY, *Baptism*, 82–84.

9   See the overview provided by W. D. DAVIES/D. C. ALLISON, *The Gospel According to Saint Matthew*, 685.

David Davies and Dale C. Allison are reluctant to speak of baptismal formulas,[10] but Ulrich Luz argues that the triadic phrase may stem from the liturgy of the Matthean church.[11]

Early parallels to the triadic phrase in Matthew 28:19b are Didache 7.1 and 7.3.[12] Luz asserts that the Didache and other texts of Syrian origin may indicate that the triadic baptismal formula was widespread in Syria before 100 CE,[13] and Everett Ferguson suggests that the triadic phrase in the Didache was a formula which was employed, probably by the administrator, when baptism was administered.[14] The presence of the triadic phrase in the Didache may imply dependence on Matthew 28:19b, but it may also be regarded as an independent textual witness to the possible liturgical practice referred to in Matthew 28:19b.[15]

The triadic phrase is later employed in texts that originated in different milieus, such as Justin Martyr's *1 Apology* 61,[16] Tertullian's, *De baptismo*, 6:1–2; 13:3,[17] the Pseudo-Clementine *Homilies* 11:26–27,[18] the *Tripartite Tractate* NHC

---

10   DAVIES/ALLISON, *Matthew*, 685. According to Maxwell E. Johnson, such formulas are a later development. M. E. JOHNSON, *The Rites of Christian Initiation: Their Evolution and Interpretation*, 27–28. He suggests that this phrase could be an interpretation of the meaning of baptism.

11   LUZ, *Matthäus IV*, 431. See also H. FRANKEMÖLLE, *Matthäus Kommentar*, 548. On the fact that the commission may reflect the Syrian/Matthean church, see BARTH, *Die Taufe*, 14. HARTMAN, 'Into the Name of the Lord Jesus', 30–31, 147. On this formula as a reflection of a liturgical tradition, see also K. MCDONNEL/G. T. MONTAGUE, *Christian Initiation and Baptism in the Holy Spirit: Evidence from the First Eight Centuries*, 19. Some scholars have argued that the triadic phrase is developed on the basis of Daniel 7. See for instance, J. SCHABERG, *The Father, the Son and the Holy Spirit: The Triadic Phrase in Matthew 28:19b*. On allusion to Daniel 7:13–14, see DAVIES/ALLISON, *Matthew*, 682–683. Cf. LUZ, *Matthäus IV*, 453.

12   "Didache: The Teaching of the Twelve Apostles," 428–429.

13   LUZ, *Matthäus IV*, 431. On related views, see BARTH, *Die Taufe*, 14.

14   FERGUSON, *Baptism in the Early Church*, 203. On related insights, see LUZ, *Matthäus IV*, 453, including note 138. Cf. JOHNSON, *The Rites of Christian Initiation*, 37. On the triadic formula in the Didache and its relationship with Matthew 28:19, see A. LINDEMANN, "Zur frühchristlichen Taufpraxis" in the present publication, 767–816.

15   See also FERGUSON, *Baptism in the Early Church*, 135.

16   *Justin Martyr*, "Apologia I," 162–169. Ferguson suggests that these words may be uttered by the candidate as an elementary baptismal confession. Alternatively, these words may constitute a formula, or a prayer voiced by the administrator of the baptism over the candidate. FERGUSON, *Baptism in the Early Church*, 238–239. On the triadic phrase in Justin, see also LINDEMANN, in this publication. Lindemann states that the triadic phrase could be cited during baptism, but it is not explicitly mentioned in the text.

17   Tertullian, *De baptismo, De oratione*, trans. and introduced by D. SCHLEYER, 176–179, 196f. See also Ø. NORDERVAL, "Simplicity and Power", in this publication, 947–972.

18   FERGUSON, *Baptism in the Early Church*, 255–256. J. WEHNERT, "Taufvorstellungen in den Pseudoklementinen" in this publication, 1071–1114.

I, 5, 127:25,[19] the *Gospel of Philip* NHC II,3 67:19–22,[20] Irenaeus' *Demonstration* 3 and 7,[21] Shenoute's *There is Another Foolishness* XE 82,[22] John Chrysostom's *Baptismal Catecheses* I 2/3,3,[23] and Theodore of Mopsuestia's, *Catechetical Homilies*, hom. 12–14 *passim*.[24] These examples indicate that the triadic phrase played an important role in different communities of believers in the first centuries AD.[25] One may interpret the widespread use of this phrase in different ways. It may reflect the fact that these congregations or the authors of these texts regarded the Gospel of Matthew as an authoritative text, it may reflect liturgical practises or oral traditions, or it may reflect a combination of these alternatives.

2.2. The Historicity of the Commission to Baptize

On the basis of the vocabulary and style of Matthew 28:16–20, some scholars suggest that these verses were a Matthean creation, whereas others argue that the author drew on previous traditions when he wrote this part of the Gospel.[26] The first alternative implies that Matthew 28:16–20 is editorial[27] and primarily

---

19   In this text, baptism is related to a confession of faith in God the Father, the Son, and the Holy Spirit. "The Tripartite Tractate," 97.

20   H. LUNDHAUG, *Images of Rebirth: Cognitive Poetics and Transformational Soteriology in the Gospel of Philip and the Exegesis on the Soul*, 500–501. The Gospel of Philip refers to the pronouncing of the name of the Father, the Son, and the Holy Spirit.

21   FERGUSON, *Baptism in the Early Church*, 304.

22   LUNDHAUG, "Baptism in the Monasteries of Upper Egypt" in this publication, 1345–1378.

23   Διὰ τοῦτο καὶ ὁ ἱερεὺς βαπτίζων οὐ λέγει »βαπτίζω τὸν δεῖνα«, ἀλλὰ »βαπτίζεται ὁ δεῖνα εἰς τὸ ὄνομα τοῦ Πατρὸς καὶ τοῦ Υἱοῦ καὶ τοῦ ἁγίου Πνεύματος«, δεικνὺς ὅτι οὐκ αὐτός ἐστιν ὁ βαπτίζων, ἀλλ' ὁ Πατὴρ καὶ Υἱὸς καὶ τὸ Πνεῦμα τὸ ἅγιον, ὧν καὶ τὸ ὄνομα ἐπικέκληται. "Deshalb sagt auch der Priester bei der Taufe nicht: ‚Ich taufe den und den', sondern: ‚Der und der wird getauft im Namen des Vaters und des Sohnes und des Heiligen Geistes'. Dadurch macht er deutlich, daß nicht er selbst es ist, der tauft, sondern der Vater und der Sohn und der Heilige Geist, deren Namen auch angerufen werden." Text and trans. R. KACZYNSKI, *Johannes Chrysostomus: Catecheses Baptismales: Taufkatechesen*, Vol. I, 236–237.

24   See Theodor von Mopsuestia, *Katechetische Homilien*, Vol. II, trans. and introduced by P. BRUNS, e.g., 319f., 339, 344f., 353f., 359, 372–378, 381, 384, 386.

25   On the trinitarian formula in connection with baptism, see also JULIETTE DAY, "The Catechetical Lectures of Cyril of Jerusalem" in this publication, 1179–1204.

26   J. P. MEIER, "Two Disputed Questions in Matt 28:16–20," 411. Meier claims that Matthew 28:16–17 is mostly redactional, but previous tradition may be glimpsed in v. 16 and in the theme of seeing Jesus. With regard to Matthew 28:18–20, 18a, 19a, and 20a are redactional, whereas 18b, 19b and perhaps 20b constitute pre-Matthean tradition. For an overview of scholars who try to reconstruct previous traditions, who think that the author draws on the liturgical tradition or singular logia, see LUZ, *Matthäus IV*, 431, note 12–14. DAVIES/ALLISON, *Matthew*, 677–678.

27   J. D. KINGSBURY, "The Composition and Christology of Matt 28:16–20," 574–579. D. J. HARRINGTON, *The Gospel of Matthew*, 415. For an overview of other scholars holding this position, see LUZ, *Matthäus IV*, 431, note 11. DAVIES/ALLISON, *Matthew*, 677.

reflects the theology of second-generation Christianity. The second alternative means that Matthew 28:16–20 is constituted by traditions which echo directives given by Jesus after his resurrection.[28] Below I will present both alternatives, but I will first and foremost focus on the authenticity of those parts of Matthew 28:16–20 that are closely related to baptism per se.

The historicity of Matthew 28:18–20 is widely dismissed by scholars. In this context, the term historicity refers to the question of whether the earthly Jesus or the risen Lord, respectively, commanded the eleven to baptize. In opposition to the frequent rejection of the attribution of this utterance to Jesus, Ferguson claims that the universal practice of baptism in the early church is best explained if this custom was authorized by Jesus himself. He suggests that a post-resurrection setting was the probable occasion for such an instruction.[29]

According to Gerhard Barth, one cannot assume that the commission to baptize in Matthew 28:19 originated just after Easter. He claims that a synoptic comparison indicates that it is impossible to trace the commission to baptize behind the Gospel of Matthew.[30] Barth recognizes that there are structural similarities between Matthew 28:16–20, Luke 24:36–49, and John 20:19–23, which have also influenced Mark 16:14–18, but he proposes that these parallels refer to the appearance of the risen Lord to the disciples, the mission command, and the promise of Jesus' continued presence.[31] These similarities point to an older tradition[32] on which the author of Matthew, Luke, and John drew, but Barth advocates that this tradition did not entail a command to baptize. Rather, Barth deduces that baptism was introduced by the author of the Gospel of Matthew, based on the baptismal practice in his church.[33]

If Jesus actually commissioned the disciples to baptize after his resurrection, the seeming absence of this theme in the original endings of most Gospels must be explained. Both George R. Beasley-Murray and Ferguson attempt to elucidate why the commission to baptize is missing from the other New Testament Gospels. Beasley-Murray claims that the reason why the Gospel of Mark and Q did not contain a baptismal commission was that the former omitted the resurrection narratives, whereas the latter neither narrated the passion nor the resurrection of Jesus. In the case of the Gospel of Luke, he suggests that the author of the Gospel chose to present the missionary commission "as a ful-

---

28 According to Harrington, the triadic phrase indicates that Jesus' language has been influenced by "the experience of the early Church, in this case by a baptismal formula (see *Didache* 7:1–3)." HARRINGTON, *Matthew*, 415. On related views, see BARTH, *Die Taufe*, 14.

29 FERGUSON, *Baptism in the Early Church*, 133. For related views, see also BEASLEY-MURRAY, *Baptism*, 77–92. Cf. BARTH, *Die Taufe*, 11–14.

30 BARTH, *Die Taufe*, 12–14. Cf. G. BORNKAMM, "Der Auferstandene und der Irdische," 175.

31 BARTH, *Die Taufe*, 13.

32 See also BORNKAMM, "Der Auferstandene und der Irdische," 171.

33 BARTH, *Die Taufe*, 14.

filment of Old Testament prophecy."[34] In that particular context it would be inappropriate to mention Christian baptism, but the focus on repentance and forgiveness of sins in Luke 24:46–47 resembles Luke 3:3b (κηρύσσων βάπτισμα μετανοίας εἰς ἄφεσιν ἁμαρτιῶν/"proclaiming a baptism of repentance for the forgiveness of sins"), where the work of John the Baptist was summarized. If one examines Luke 24:47 against the backdrop of Luke 3:3b, proclamation and baptism seem to be indirectly related through the language employed.[35] ("Thus it is written, that the Messiah is to suffer and to rise from the dead on the third day, and that repentance and forgiveness of sins are to be proclaimed in his name to all nations, beginning from Jerusalem," Luke 24:46b–47.)[36] Ferguson points out that the link between baptism and the forgiveness of sins "suggests that there is a parallel between the connection made in Matthew and the long ending of Mark of the commission with baptism and the parallel connection in Luke and John of the commission with the forgiveness of sins."[37] In this manner, the endings of Luke and John may imply an interest in baptism even though it is not explicitly mentioned.

On the basis of the arguments sketched above, it is plausible that the commission to baptize reflects oral traditions that influenced all the canonical Gospels in different manners. It is of course impossible to determine whether Jesus actually uttered this commission and if so which elements it contained.

2.3. The Genre of Matthew 28:16–20

Scholars do not agree on the form-critical category to which Matthew 28:16–20 belongs; furthermore, most scholars focus on Matthew 28:18–20, not the entire pericope. John P. Meier provides the following overview of the different proposals concerning Matthew 28:18–20:[38] The text in question follows the schema of (1) a missionary command with mythic character, (2) a ritual of royal enthronement, (3) the Schema, (4) the OT pattern of divine speech, (5) the royal decree of Cyrus (2 Chr 36:23), or (6) the covenant formula.

---

34 BEASLEY-MURRAY, *Baptism*, 79.

35 IDEM, *Baptism*, 79–80. See also Acts 2:38 and John 20:21ff. Ferguson has suggested that Luke 24:47 and John 20:21–23 may allude to baptism in their accounts of the commissions. FERGUSON, *Baptism in the Early Church*, 133. Davies and Allison also recognize baptismal language in Luke 24:47. DAVIES/ALLISON, *Matthew*, 684.

36 Οὕτως γέγραπται παθεῖν τὸν Χριστὸν καὶ ἀναστῆναι ἐκ νεκρῶν τῇ τρίτῃ ἡμέρᾳ, καὶ κηρυχθῆναι ἐπὶ τῷ ὀνόματι αὐτοῦ μετάνοιαν εἰς ἄφεσιν ἁμαρτιῶν εἰς πάντα τὰ ἔθνη, ἀρξάμενοι ἀπὸ Ἰερουσαλήμ.

37 FERGUSON, *Baptism in the Early Church*, 133.

38 MEIER, "Two Disputed Questions," 417–420. See also the paragraph on structure in DAVIES/ALLISON, *Matthew*, 676–677.

With reference to Matthew 28:16–20, the following form-critical categories are proposed:[39] (1) Jewish-Christian community rule, (2) Easter story/cult legend, missionary commission, resurrection proof, ich-Wort (Bultmann), (3) Christological revelation, (4) resurrection narrative, and (5) commissioning of patriarchs and prophets/apostolic commissioning.

As the two lists indicate, it is extremely difficult to propose a genre for Matthew 28:18–20, or for Matthew 28:16–20 in its entirety. On the one hand, scholars do not agree on the form-critical category of traditional motives because they are so thoroughly incorporated into the Matthean narrative. On the other hand, the integration of these motives has made it difficult to discern the genre of Matthew 28:16–20 as a whole, because the existence of all these elements makes the Matthean ending so complex. As a result, it is hard to determine the purpose of these pericopes prior to their current function in the Gospel. Since the previous proposals tend to focus on some features of the Matthean ending at the expense of others, I will refrain from suggesting a specific form-critical category for this passage.[40] Instead, I will focus on the hermeneutical function of Matthew 28:16–20 in its current context.

2.4. Implications – Baptism in Relation to Christology, Ecclesiology, and Eschatology

In this section, I will draw attention to three themes that are mentioned by Meier in his analysis of the genre proposals, namely the interrelationship between Christological, ecclesiological, and eschatological motives in this ending.[41] It is my suggestion that the underlying oral traditions of a post-resurrectional commission uttered by Jesus to the disciples, as reflected in the canonical Gospels,[42] are modified due to the Christological, ecclesiological, and eschatological ideas characterizing each Gospel.[43] Because it is virtually impossible to reconstruct a plausible genre and thus the *Sitz im Leben* of Matthew 28:16–20 or of the traditions that constitute this ending, I will approach this text from a different angle, i.e. as the culmination of an oral performance of the Gospel. Accordingly, Matthew 28:16–20 and Mark 16:14–20 are examined in this article in order to dis-

---

39 MEIER, "Two Disputed Questions," 420–422.

40 See also D. A. HAGNER, *Matthew 14–28*, 883 and LUZ, *Matthäus IV*, 433. MEIER, "Two Disputed Questions," 424.

41 MEIER, "Two Disputed Questions," 418, 424. For related insights, see BORNKAMM, "Der Auferstandene und der Irdische," 175–178.

42 According to Davies and Allison, the parallels of form and content between 28:16–20 and the endings of the other canonical Gospels indicate that traditions are being passed on. See DAVIES/ALLISON, *Matthew*, 678. See also their overview on p. 677.

43 On the fact that the divergent versions of the commission in the different Gospels reflect the theology of each author, see also BARTH, *Die Taufe*, 13.

cern how a performance of these endings may influence audience members, in particular through the manner in which baptism is related to different aspects of the Christology, the ecclesiology, and the eschatology of each Gospel.

3. The Authenticity of Mark 16:9–20

In this section, the term authenticity refers to two areas of research. (1) Did this ending belong to the original version of the Gospel of Mark? (2) Did this ending draw on independent, oral sources, or did it primarily utilize material from the canonical Gospels and Acts?[44]

Even though the Longer Ending is present in a vast number of manuscripts, it is generally regarded as secondary because it is not attested in the two oldest Greek manuscripts (א and B), in Codex Bobiensis, in the Sinaitic Syriac manuscript, in one hundred Armenian manuscripts, or in the two oldest Georgian manuscripts. Moreover, several manuscripts contain scribal notes or other signs indicating that these verses were added to the document. Eusebius and Jerome also attested to the fact that almost all Greek copies of the Gospel of Mark known to them lacked this pericope. Last, but not least, these verses are not mentioned by Clement of Alexandria and Origen.[45] On this basis, many scholars refrain from commenting on this part of the Gospel of Mark, but the Longer Ending has been investigated by several scholars, among them James A. Kelhoffer.[46]

In the second and the third chapter of *Miracle and Mission: The Authentication of Missionaries and Their Message in the Longer Ending of Mark*, Kelhoffer claims that the author of the Longer Ending intentionally imitated traditional material found in the synoptic Gospels, John, and Acts.[47] Kelhoffer states that even though

> [i]n principle, the author of the LE could have consulted independent oral traditions, written traditions other than copies of the Gospels, oral traditions stemming from the reading of the Gospels in the Christian communities, MSS of the

---

44   Cf. K. M. Hartvigsen, "Canon, Fanon and The Markan Endings as Rewritten Scripture".

45   B. M. Metzger, *A Textual Commentary on the Greek New Testament*, 102–106. See also K. Aland, "Der Schluß des Markusevangeliums." A. Y. Collins, *Mark: A Commentary*, 806–807. J. Marcus, *Mark 8–16: A New Translation with Introduction and Commentary*, 1088–1090. On the interpretation of different versions of the Markan endings, see B. G. Upton, *Hearing Mark's Endings: Listening to Ancient Popular Texts through Speech Act Theory*, 125–200. D. C. Parker, *The Living Text of the Gospels*, 124–147.

46   For an overview of these scholars, see J. A. Kelhoffer, *Miracle and Mission: The Authentication of Missionaries and Their Message in the Longer Ending of Mark*, 5–46.

47   Kelhoffer, *Miracle and Mission*, 48–156. See the lists of parallel passages on p. 121–122 and 138–139. Collins supports this argument, Collins, *Mark*, 807. For related views, see Marcus, *Mark 8–16*, 1090.

Gospels themselves, or all of these. It turns out that literary dependence upon actual copies of the four NT Gospels and probably of Acts best explains the numerous similarities between the LE and various parts of the NT.[48]

According to Kelhoffer, the Longer Ending was composed after the New Testament Gospels were collected in order to establish harmony between the ending of the Gospel of Mark and the endings of Matthew, Luke, and John. He argues that the Gospel of Matthew offers the closest literary parallel to the Longer Ending, with regard to the length and the missionary focus of these texts.[49] Kelhoffer points out that even though the structure of the Longer Ending resembles Matthew 28:8–20, the author of the Longer Ending incorporated motifs from for instance Luke and John as well. Drawing on Luke 24 he included the motif of disbelief and Jesus' appearance to two disciples, whereas dependence on John 20 led him to incorporate Jesus' appearance to Mary Magdalene and the focus on belief.[50] Into these motifs, other motifs from Mark, Luke, John, and Acts were integrated.[51]

On the basis of the available evidence, Beasley-Murray and Fergusson draw conclusions which diverge from the one proposed by Kelhoffer. Beasley-Murray points out the parallel between Matthew 28:16–20 and the Longer Ending of the Gospel of Mark. He claims, however, that the tradition of baptism preserved in the Longer Ending probably was independent of the Gospel of Matthew,[52] because in his opinion the author primarily drew on the Gospel of Luke and Acts.[53] This means that the author of the Longer Ending could have incorporated oral tradition at this point.[54] Ferguson suggests that the author of the Longer Ending could have brought into play early, independent traditions.[55]

---

48 KELHOFFER, *Miracle and Mission*, 123.

49 IDEM, *Miracle and Mission*, 243.

50 IDEM, *Miracle and Mission*, 243. In his commentary on the Gospel of Matthew, Luz suggests that Jesus' appearance before Mary Magdalene (Matt 28:9f.) could have been created by the author of the Gospel of Matthew. Alternatively, this information could reflect oral traditions. Luz refers to John 20:14–18, where Jesus appears to Mary Magdalene at exactly this point in the narrative as an indication that this part of the Gospel could draw on oral traditions. Luz admits that the narratives are different, but both Gospels mention a task, a speech act, which Mary should perform. LUZ, *Matthäus IV*, 417.

51 See tables in KELHOFFER, *Miracle and Mission*, 121–122, 138–139.

52 BEASLEY-MURRAY, *Baptism*, 80. Cf. KELHOFFER, *Miracle and Mission*, 140–141, 243. Kelhoffer suggests that Matthew 28 has influenced word choices and the structure of the Longer Ending.

53 BEASLEY-MURRAY, *Baptism*, 80. See also HARTMAN, *Markusevangeliet 8:27–16:20*, 590–591. He provides an overview of the texts on which he thinks the author of the Longer Ending primarily drew, i.e. the Gospel of Luke, Acts, and the Gospel of John.

54 BEASLEY-MURRAY, *Baptism*, 80.

55 FERGUSON, *Baptism in the Early Church*, 133. According to Aage Pilgaard, the Longer Ending drew on the same or similar traditions that were employed in the other Gospels. AA. PILGAARD, *Kommentar til Markusevangeliet*, 388.

He claims that if the author of the Longer Ending drew on Matthew 28:16–20, this author could be regarded as an early witness to the authenticity of this account.[56] Both these arguments thus underscore the authenticity of the tradition which related the command to baptize to a resurrection appearance.

Whether the author of Mark 16:9–20 drew on written manuscripts of the New Testament Gospels or on oral traditions, is difficult to determine. The similarities observed between the Longer Ending and the ending of the Gospel of Matthew are less profound than the resemblances that are perceived when one carries out a comparison with other parts of the synoptic Gospels. This phenomenon could be explained, though, by the compositional techniques employed by the different authors. With regard to the structural dependence of the Longer Ending on Matthew 28:8–20, Kelhoffer makes the following point:

> All parallels to this Gospel are to material occurring *after* Mark 16:8, that is to Matt 28:8–20. The only part of Matt 28:8–20 not incorporated in some way into the LE is the plot to foil reports about the resurrection (Matt 28:11–15). This leaves Matt 28:8–10 and 16–20, which concern the obedience of the three women to relate the message of the resurrection, the appearance to the eleven and the great commission. No major part of these eight verses has been left out of the LE. Therefore, knowledge of a text of Matthew 28 influenced both numerous word choices and the general structure of Mark 16:9–20. Although an oversimplification, a large part of the use of other Gospel texts by the LE's author consists of (re-)inserting the element of disbelief into the LE's Matthean framework.[57]

Whether the author of the Longer Ending employed the structure of Matthew 28:8–20 as a point of departure is difficult to decide on the basis of the available evidence. The results of a comparison between these texts will be determined by the abstraction level on which the comparison is performed. Furthermore, structural similarities may reflect direct dependence on similar oral traditions, or indirect influence from such sources through other written traditions, that is, the Gospel of Luke or John. Due to the theme of this article, I will focus on a comparison between Mark 16:8–20 and Matthew 28:8–20, not the other Gospels. Verse 8 is included in the comparison because it constitutes the point of departure for the two subsequent endings. First I will treat the main features of Matthew 28:8–15 and Mark 16:8–13, then I will provide a synopsis of Matthew 28:16–20 and Mark 16:14–20.

---

56 Ferguson, *Baptism in the Early Church*, 133.
57 Kelhoffer, *Miracle and Mission*, 141.

4. Comparison of Matthew 28:8–20 and Mark 16:8–20

4.1. Comparison of Matthew 28:8–15 and Mark 16:8–13

In Mark 16:8, the women leave the tomb frightened, and they say nothing to anyone. In Matthew 28:8 this fear is balanced with joy, and they run to tell the disciples. These divergent responses to the empty tomb have led to two different endings. In both the Gospel of Matthew and Mark's Longer Ending, Jesus subsequently appears to women. In Matthew 28:9, he shows himself to "Mary Magdalene and the other Mary" (cf. Matt 28:1) and in Mark 16:9, he appears to "Mary Magdalene, from whom he had cast out seven demons."[58] However, the subsequent structure of the narrative is developed in divergent manners because the Gospels deal with narratological and theological problems in slightly different ways. The differing attempts to cope with these problems reflect divergent emphasis on theological subjects, such as Christology, ecclesiology, and eschatology.

In Matthew 28:9–10 the women worship Jesus, and he gives them a task reminiscent of the one given earlier by the angel (Matthew 28:7).[59] The extradiegetic narrator[60] subsequently relates that the women are on their way (Matthew 28:11a), presumably to the disciples, but he never explicitly mentions the encounter between the women and the disciples. Audience members may infer that this meeting took place on the basis of Matthew 28:16, where they learn that the disciples went to Galilee, but between these two scenes, the extradiegetic narrator of the Gospel of Matthew focuses on how an alternative interpretation of the empty tomb originated (Matthew 28:11b–15).[61]

The extradiegetic narrator of the Longer Ending does not focus on a specific task given to Mary Magdalene. Instead, he stresses the fact that she informs the disciples, but they refuse to believe her (Mark 16:10–11). In Mark 16:12–13 a similar scene is related.[62] This time the witnesses to Jesus' appearance are two of those characters who refused to believe Mary in the previous scene. When they report to the others, they too are met with unbelief.

---

58 Μαριὰμ ἡ Μαγδαληνὴ καὶ ἡ ἄλλη Μαρία (Matthew 28:1) Μαρίᾳ τῇ Μαγδαληνῇ, παρ' ἧς ἐκβεβλήκει ἑπτὰ δαιμόνια (Mark 16:9).

59 According to Davies/Allison, "[t]his short Christophany sets forth the proper response to the risen Lord – worship – and, because Jesus' words about Galilee repeat those of the angel, throws additional emphasis upon the climax to come." DAVIES/ALLISON, *Matthew*, 668.

60 The extradiegetic narrator is external to the story, like for instance third-person omniscient narrators. M. BORTOLUSSI/P. DIXON, *Psychonarratology: Foundations for the Empirical Study of Literary Response*, 63.

61 On related views, see DAVIES/ALLISON, *Matthew*, 670.

62 See also UPTON, *Hearing Mark's Endings*, 161.

On one level, one might say that both versions consist of two scenes of approximately the same length, but the characters and the problems with which these scenes are dealing are different. This results in two distinct structures. In Mark 16:9–13, two parallel scenes coping with the unbelief of Jesus' adherents are preparing for the final scene (Mark 16:14–20),[63] at which point Jesus addresses the problem of lack of faith before he commissions the eleven.[64] In Matthew 28:9–15, the problem of unbelief is related to other characters, i.e. outsiders, which results in another narratological structure. Matthew 28:11–15 shifts the focus from the scene depicting the obedient women on their way to the disciples to the scene dealing with the guards, chief priests, and elders. The latter scene suggests why the Jews will believe the explanation of the empty tomb that was created by their leaders and presumably not the version presented in the Gospel of Matthew. Because this scene does not relate the unbelief to Jesus' closest adherents, it becomes a digression which separates the assignment given to the women from the completion of their task.

In consequence, the structural link between the first two scenes and the commission is much looser in Matthew 28:9–20 than in Mark 16:9–20. The structure of the Longer Ending may reflect the redaction of the author, but in that case he did not simply introduce new themes into the Matthean outline. If the author drew on the structure of Matthew 28 and incorporated elements from the Gospels and Acts into this framework,[65] these components have actually resulted in a novel structure of three parallel scenes, i.e. appearances of the risen Jesus.[66] In the third and final scene previous problems are addressed before the commission is uttered by Jesus. Because the present version of the Longer Ending can be interpreted in different manners, it does not provide us with sufficient evidence to argue concerning the intentions of the author nor does it disclose his sources.

---

63 On related views, see also COLLINS, *Mark*, 807.

64 According to Upton, this scene resolves the problem of disbelief. UPTON, *Hearing Mark's Endings*, 163.

65 See KELHOFFER, *Miracle and Mission*, 243.

66 Collins has divided the Longer Ending into three scenes (16:9–11; 16:12–13; 16:14–18) apart from the conclusion in 16:19–20. COLLINS, *Mark*, 807.

4.2. Synopsis of Matthew 28:16–20 and Mark 16:14–20

Matthew 28:16–20	Mark 16:14–20
(16) Οἱ δὲ **ἕνδεκα** μαθηταὶ ἐπορεύθησαν εἰς τὴν Γαλιλαίαν εἰς τὸ ὄρος οὗ ἐτάξατο αὐτοῖς ὁ Ἰησοῦς, (17) καὶ ἰδόντες **αὐτὸν** προσεκύνησαν, οἱ δὲ ἐδίστασαν. (18) καὶ προσελθὼν ὁ Ἰησοῦς ἐλάλησεν **αὐτοῖς** λέγων· ἐδόθη μοι πᾶσα ἐξουσία ἐν οὐρανῷ καὶ ἐπὶ [τῆς] γῆς. (19) **πορευθέντες** οὖν μαθητεύσατε πάντα τὰ ἔθνη, βαπτίζοντες αὐτοὺς εἰς τὸ ὄνομα τοῦ πατρὸς καὶ τοῦ υἱοῦ καὶ τοῦ ἁγίου πνεύματος, (20) διδάσκοντες αὐτοὺς τηρεῖν πάντα ὅσα ἐνετειλάμην ὑμῖν. καὶ ἰδοὺ ἐγὼ μεθ' ὑμῶν εἰμι πάσας τὰς ἡμέρας ἕως τῆς συντελείας τοῦ αἰῶνος.	(14) Ὕστερον [δὲ] ἀνακειμένοις αὐτοῖς τοῖς **ἕνδεκα** ἐφανερώθη καὶ ὠνείδισεν τὴν ἀπιστίαν αὐτῶν καὶ σκληροκαρδίαν ὅτι τοῖς θεασαμένοις **αὐτὸν** ἐγηγερμένον οὐκ ἐπίστευσαν. (15) καὶ εἶπεν **αὐτοῖς**· **Πορευθέντες** εἰς τὸν κόσμον ἅπαντα κηρύξατε τὸ εὐαγγέλιον πάσῃ τῇ κτίσει. (16) ὁ πιστεύσας καὶ βαπτισθεὶς σωθήσεται, ὁ δὲ ἀπιστήσας κατακριθήσεται. (17) σημεῖα δὲ τοῖς πιστεύσασιν ταῦτα παρακολουθήσει· ἐν τῷ ὀνόματί μου δαιμόνια ἐκβαλοῦσιν, γλώσσαις λαλήσουσιν καιναῖς, (18) [καὶ ἐν ταῖς χερσὶν] ὄφεις ἀροῦσιν κἂν θανάσιμόν τι πίωσιν οὐ μὴ αὐτοὺς βλάψῃ, ἐπὶ ἀρρώστους χεῖρας ἐπιθήσουσιν καὶ καλῶς ἕξουσιν. (19) Ὁ μὲν οὖν κύριος Ἰησοῦς μετὰ τὸ λαλῆσαι αὐτοῖς ἀνελήμφθη εἰς τὸν οὐρανὸν καὶ ἐκάθισεν ἐκ δεξιῶν τοῦ θεοῦ. (20) ἐκεῖνοι δὲ ἐξελθόντες ἐκήρυξαν πανταχοῦ, τοῦ κυρίου συνεργοῦντος καὶ τὸν λόγον βεβαιοῦντος διὰ τῶν ἐπακολουθούντων σημείων.

Matthew 28:16–20	Mark 16:14-20
(16) Now the **eleven** disciples went to Galilee, to the mountain to which Jesus had directed them. (17) And when they saw **him**, they worshiped him; but some doubted.	(14) Later he appeared to the **eleven** themselves as they were reclining at the table; and reproached their unbelief and hardness of heart, because they had not believed those who saw **him** after he had risen.
(18) And Jesus came and said to **them**, "All authority in heaven and on earth has been given to me.	(15) And he said to **them**,
(19) **Go** therefore, make disciples of all nations,	"**Go** into all the world and proclaim the good news to the whole creation.
baptizing them	(16) The one who believes and is baptized will be saved; but the one who does not believe will be condemned.
into the name of the Father and of the Son and of the Holy Spirit, (20) teaching them to observe everything that I have commanded you.	(17) And these signs will accompany those who believe: in my name they will cast out demons; they will speak in new tongues; (18) they will pick up snakes [in their hands], and if they drink something deadly, it will not at all hurt them; they will lay their hands on the sick, and they will recover."
	(19) So then the Lord Jesus, after he had spoken to them, was taken up into heaven and sat down at the right hand of God.
And see, I am with you all days, to the end of the age."	(20) And they went out and proclaimed everywhere, while the Lord worked with them and confirmed the word by the accompanying signs.

Matthew 28:16–20 and Mark 16:14–20 contain many parallel themes, but the synopsis shows that in the strictest sense these two texts do not have many words in common. Besides this, the settings that are mentioned by the extradiegetic narrators diverge. Matthew 28:16 locates the eleven disciples in Galilee, on a mountain, whereas Mark 16:14 positions them at the table at an undisclosed location.

By situating the disciples in Galilee, Matthew 28:16 indirectly stresses the obedience of the women and the eleven. The presence of the eleven in Galilee suggests that they have met the women and chosen to follow Jesus' directions. When Jesus appears, these characters worship him (Matthew 28:17); however, the element of reverence is balanced with doubt.[67] In contrast, Mark 16:14b connects the final scene in the Longer Ending to the previous two by explicitly focusing on the lack of belief and hardness of heart which characterized the eleven in the preceding scenes, and letting Jesus address it explicitly.

As a result, the situations in which Jesus utters the final commissions in the two endings are quite different. In the Gospel of Matthew, the favourable circumstances allow Jesus to introduce the subsequent commission by means of an assertion about the nature of his power, which seems to be enough to overcome the doubts of the eleven.[68] In the Longer Ending of Mark, though, Jesus proceeds directly from severe scolding to the commission. In this ending, Jesus' reprimand presupposes that he has sufficient authority to voice this speech act, but Jesus' power and authority are not mentioned at this point. They are accentuated later by the extradiegetic narrator in a quite visual manner (Mark 16:19–20). The narratological frameworks in which the commissions are uttered thus generate Christology in different ways. In Matthew 28:16–20, Jesus' authority and power seem to be a fact that the extradiegetic narrator does not have to elucidate (Matthew 28:18). In Mark 16:14–20, the extradiegetic narrator draws attention to the source of Jesus' authority and power by connecting it to Jesus' position in the heavenly realm as the risen Lord (Mark 16:19). Such an explanation could be motivated by the earlier negative characterization of the eleven. Because audience members will process this information as if it is directed to them, they may regard this utterance as an attempt to convince them about the power and authority of Jesus, which transcends the narrative world (Mark 16:20).

---

67 On related insights, see Luz, *Das Evangelium nach Matthäus (Mt 1-7)*, 438–440. According to Harrington, the grammar indicates that some of the eleven worshipped Jesus, whereas others doubted. HARRINGTON, *Matthew*, 414. See also DAVIES/ALLISON, *Matthew*, 681–682. Bornkamm relates this theme to the early church. BORNKAMM, "Der Auferstandene und der Irdische," 172.

68 Bornkamm suggests that the doubts of the eleven are overcome by the word of Jesus. BORNKAMM, "Der Auferstandene und der Irdische," 172.

The verb μαθητεύω is employed with reference to the task given to Jesus' adherents in the Gospel of Matthew, whereas the Markan focus on proclamation is reflected in the Longer Ending. In Matthew 28:19–20a, the imperative μαθητεύσατε constitutes the main phrase, which is interpreted by means of the subsequent commands to baptize εἰς τὸ ὄνομα τοῦ πατρὸς καὶ τοῦ υἱοῦ καὶ τοῦ ἁγίου πνεύματος/"into the name of the Father and of the Son and of the Holy Spirit" and to teach αὐτοὺς τηρεῖν πάντα ὅσα ἐνετειλάμην ὑμῖν/"them to observe everything that I have commanded you."[69] In this way, baptism and teaching form the two main elements involved in expanding the group of followers. The first of these constituents stresses the importance of the baptismal ritual as an initiation rite, the authority behind the rite (the triadic phrase), and it mentions explicitly those with regard to whom the rite is performed (the triadic phrase).[70] The subsequent focus on Jesus' teaching indicates that Jesus is the founder of the community into which new people are baptized. The sequence of baptism and teaching may furthermore suggest that teaching refers to the continued teaching of the church after baptism has taken place. Jesus' utterance on baptism is hence directly linked with ecclesiology, that is, with the incorporation of new members into the community of believers and their subsequent, persistent education.

In the Longer Ending, baptism is connected with proclamation, an act which in the Gospel of Mark aims at expanding the community. Accordingly, baptism is associated with a missionary context and thus one aspect of ecclesiology, namely incorporation into the community of believers. At this point, the emphasis is first and foremost on two distinct responses to the proclamation and their respective outcomes: (1) Belief, baptism, and salvation. (2) Unbelief and condemnation. In Mark 16:16a, the sequence of the words employed may point out that baptism succeeds belief, presumably in the proclamation. Moreover, belief and baptism are both regarded as conditions for salvation.[71] Baptism therefore constitutes one of several steps that lead from proclamation to salvation. In this particular case, salvation probably refers to eternal salvation, which relates baptism directly to eschatology.[72] This inference is supported by the subsequent reference to condemnation. Consequently, the Gospel of Matthew focuses on the expansion and maintenance of the worldly community of

---

69 See also Luz, *Matthäus IV*, 429 (esp. note 6) 443, 452, 454.

70 On the meaning of the phrase εἰς τὸ ὄνομα τοῦ πατρὸς καὶ τοῦ υἱοῦ καὶ τοῦ ἁγίου πνεύματος and related phrases, see Hartman, *'Into the Name of the Lord Jesus'*, 37–50. L. Hartman, "Usages — Some Notes on the Baptismal Name-Formulae" in this publication, 397–413.

71 On baptism as a requirement for salvation, see also Kelhoffer, *Miracle and Mission*, 151. On the fact that this interpretation of salvation diverges from the approach to baptism in the rest of the Gospel of Mark, see idem, *Miracle and Mission*, 101.

72 According to Collins, it seems likely "that the future tenses also allude to the future, definitive judgement of all." Collins, *Mark*, 810.

believers, whereas the Longer Ending of the Gospel of Mark stresses the expansion of the community of believers and connects this directly with the life to come.

The main difference pertaining to baptism in these two endings is constituted by the fact that the Longer Ending of the Gospel of Mark does not mention the triadic phrase or a name formula.[73] If the author of the Longer Ending drew on Matthew 28:8–20, it seems strange that the triadic phrase is not mentioned in connection with baptism in Mark 16:16. This phenomenon may indicate that the author came from a community where the triadic phrase was not employed with reference to baptism, it may suggest that he was not interested in mentioning those with regard to whom the rite was performed, or it may imply that the author did not utilize Matthew 28:8–20 when he composed the Longer Ending. In the last case, it is likely that the author employed independent, oral traditions. Dependence on such traditions could explain both similarities and differences in relation to material drawn from the Gospels and Acts.[74]

After the commission proper, the Longer Ending deviates from the Gospel of Matthew in several regards. First of all, Jesus mentions the characteristics of those who believe (Mark 16:17–18).[75] Then audience members learn that Jesus is taken up into heaven and is seated at the right hand of God (Mark 16:19). If Jesus' speech acts in Mark 12:36 and 14:62 are activated by this event,[76] audience members may interpret this situation as the fulfillment of scripture. Through

---

73   See § 4.1. Comparison of Matthew 28:8–15 and Mark 16:8–13.
74   See § 2.2. The Historicity of the Commission to Baptize.
75   On the lack of this information in Matthew, see also BORNKAMM, "Der Auferstandene und der Irdische," 181–182.
76   On priming or activation, see HARTVIGSEN, *"Prepare the Way of the Lord"*, 51–52. Personal associations and reactions are elicited by narratives because experiences, literary or in real life, contain elements which tie them to traces of experiences stored in long-term memory. These traces are usually latent, but they may also be fully activated or semi-activated. If these traces are fully activated, one might say that memories are recalled and emotions reexperienced. HOGAN, *Cognitive Science, Literature and the Arts*, 156–158. HOGAN, *The Mind and Its Stories: Narrative Universals and Human Emotion*, 52–53. Semi-activation, labeled "priming" in cognitive science, is "[a] process whereby the recall of a particular memory causes the low-level activation of other associated memories (a context), without this process necessarily becoming conscious." B. SNYDER, *Music and Memory: An Introduction*, 262. See also LUNDHAUG, *Images of Rebirth*, 39. The process of activation and priming may be summarized in the following manner with regard to all elements of the memory system: Activation and, thus, recall of one element may prime others. Because primed items of long-term memory are in a state of low-level activation, they are more easily activated than latent items. SNYDER, *Music and Memory*, 48. When literature is performed or read, elements from memory are activated and primed: "the activated memory fragments are brought into the task at hand, the ongoing synthesis of the literary work. These memory fragments, then, become part of that literary synthesis, contributing to our understanding of characters, our concretization of scenes, our inference to the unstated causes of events." HOGAN, *Cognitive Science, Literature and the Arts*, 162. On related views, see K. OATLEY, "Emotions and the Story Worlds of Fiction," 52.

Mark 16:19 Jesus is established as a true prophet, and the source of his authority is likewise confirmed.

In the Gospel of Matthew, the women and the disciples are first and foremost characterized as obedient, believing characters. In the Gospel of Mark and the Longer Ending, the disciples are more reluctant to obey and they do not believe. As a result, Jesus can state his authority before he utters the commission in the Gospel of Matthew.[77] In the Longer Ending, however, Jesus proceeds from scolding to the commission. Only after the commission is the source of Jesus' authority explicitly established. Jesus' authority is thus presented in a manner which primarily reflects forwards in connection with the commission in the Gospel of Matthew and backwards with reference to the commission in the Longer Ending.

In Matthew 28:20b, Jesus merely proclaims that he will be with them "all days, to the end of the age." Through the description in Mark 16:20, the extradiegetic narrator allows audience members to "witness" the success of Jesus' earlier command ("they went out and proclaimed everywhere"), and the previously mentioned signs characterizing those who believe (Mark 16:17–18) are now reinterpreted as manifestations that confirm the message of these characters as well as the continued presence of the Lord. In both Gospels, Jesus' continued presence may indicate the efficacy of baptism as one of many activities performed by Jesus' adherents.

All in all, the divergent ways in which the women and the disciples deal with the empty tomb result in different presentations of the authority of the risen Lord. The Christology is thus established in dissimilar manners in the two endings. Moreover, the way in which baptism is presented in the commissions reflects different ecclesiological focal points, i.e. missionary activity (Mark) or missionary activity in combination with maintenance of the community (Matthew). Last but not least, eschatology is implied by the manner in which the author of the Longer Ending relates baptism to eternal salvation, a point which is not mentioned in the Gospel of Matthew. I will return to these aspects below and in the conclusion.

4.3. Hermeneutical Implications

The approach chosen by Kelhoffer focuses on the decisions which the author reached when he composed the Longer Ending. The choices made by the author in turn determined the texts that are considered by Kelhoffer in his analysis.[78]

---

77 According to Bornkamm, "[d]ie Erhöhung des Auferstandenen zum Herrn ist selbst nicht direkt ausgesagt, so deutlich der Text sie auch voraussetzt. Sie ist in Jesu Selbstaussage eingegangen und wird als seine Vollmacht über Himmel und Erde verkündet." BORNKAMM, "Der Auferstandene und der Irdische," 174.

78 KELHOFFER, *Miracle and Mission*, 50.

In this article I have chosen a different approach, which is not completely incompatible with many of the results presented by Kelhoffer. Below, I highlight similarities which audience members (and readers) may recognize between the Longer Ending and traditional material found in the Gospels and Acts. Accordingly, it is not the choices of the author, but the perceptions of audience members which are in focus. As contemporary scholars, neither Kelhoffer nor I have access to oral traditions etc. that could have influenced the author when he wrote the Longer Ending, nor do we have access to the author's consciousness. Our respective analyses of the Longer Ending are determined by the manner in which these verses remind us of, that is, activate New Testament traditions which we have read or in some cases heard. In my analysis, I have chosen not to employ this knowledge to reconstruct the possible intentions of the author. Instead, I will focus on the manner in which the endings of these Gospels during an oral performance of the Gospels of Matthew and of Mark may communicate with audience members who have been baptized, or are candidates for baptism.

Because the analysis below takes an oral performance situation as its point of departure, the authenticity/historicity of these pericopes will not be of particular importance. Whether the traditions told reflect the theology of the early Church or Jesus' own commands will not influence audience members, because in the *narrative world* these speech acts are uttered by the character Jesus, who established the community. By experiencing the performance of these endings, audience members may be transported to the Matthean and the Markan world, respectively. In these worlds, they play the part of invisible witnesses to the events taking place. In this manner, they become connected with Jesus, the founder of the group, and the formative events of the community. By observing events taking place in these narrative worlds, audience members are offered scripts which will enable them to perceive the continuity between the history of the group and their current experiences, but also their future ones.[79] They furthermore learn how they can secure the continued existence of the community. Consequently, baptism becomes integrated into the formative narrative of the group which transmits knowledge and defines the identity of the community of believers. This is in fact the hermeneutical process implied in my cognitive poetic approach to Gospel analyses.

5. Oral Performance of Gospels

Most manuscripts conclude the Gospel of Matthew and the Longer Ending by means of the word ἀμήν. According to Bruce M. Metzger, this ending reflects "the liturgical usage of the text." Even though this word was not present originally,[80] it

---

[79] HARTVIGSEN, *"Prepare the Way of the Lord"*, 602.
[80] METZGER, *A Textual Commentary*, 61, 107. Citation from p. 61.

may be regarded as an indication of the subsequent practice in the Christian communities.[81] Several scholars have recently focused on how the Gospels were communicated, i.e. by means of oral performance.[82] Some of these researchers have suggested different settings in which the Gospels could have been performed, such as worship, liturgy, and missionary activity.[83] David Rhoads lists a number of different settings such as the synagogue, the village market place, an ancient theater, a house, or an open space between villages.[84] Joanna Dewey makes a similar suggestion by claiming that Christian storytellers probably belonged to all of the four classes of storytellers she considered to be common in antiquity: (1) street performers, (2) those who told religious and secular stories either outside temples or inside and outside synagogues, (3) storytellers who had a local reputation but did not earn their living as storytellers, and (4) women, mothers and nursemaids. In view of that, "[s]tories such as Mark's would have been told both during and outside of Christian worship settings."[85] Whitney Shiner claims that "[t]he most likely situation for the performance of the Gospel is a gathering in a house church."[86] He states that a performance which took place in a house church might be "connected with other church ritual, such as

---

81 With regard to manuscripts of the Gospel of Luke and John, see METZGER, *A Textual Commentary*, 164, 221. Early sources which indicate Christian access to literacy and public reading are scarce, but some texts confirm that written sources were read aloud (Matthew 24:15; Mark 13:14; Acts 15:22–31; Colossians 4:16; 1 Thessalonians 5:27; 1 Timothy 4:13–16; Revelation 1:3; Shepherd of Hermas, *Vis.* II.4.3). See also H. Y. GAMBLE, *Books and Readers in the Early Church: A History of Early Christian Texts*, 203–231. W. SHINER, *Proclaiming the Gospel: First-Century Performance of Mark*, 44–45. D. HELLHOLM, "Universalität und Partikularität: Die amplifikatorische Struktur von Römer 5,12–21," 257–258. For the fact that these texts were made for oral delivery, see W. BUJARD, *Stilanalytische Untersuchungen zum Kolosserbrief*, 166.

82 Among these are J. DEWEY, "The Gospel of Mark as an Oral-Aural Event: Implications for Interpretation." R. A. HORSLEY, *Hearing the Whole Story: The Politics of Plot in Mark's Gospel*. SHINER, *Proclaiming the Gospel*. W. D. SHIELL, *Reading Acts: The Lector and the Early Christian Audience*. D. RHOADS, "Performance Criticism: An Emerging Methodology in Second Testament Studies – Part I." IDEM, "Performance Criticism: An Emerging Methodology in Second Testament Studies – Part II." R. A. HORSLEY, J. A. DRAPER, and J. M. FOLEY (eds.), *Performing the Gospel: Orality, Memory, and Mark*. UPTON, *Hearing Mark's Endings*. HARTVIGSEN, *"Prepare the Way of the Lord"*.

83 On oral performance, see HARTVIGSEN, *"Prepare the Way of the Lord"*, 10–22. On these settings, see L. HARTMAN, "Das Markusevangelium ‚für die lectio sollemnis im Gottesdienst abgefaßt'?" C. A. BOBERTZ, "Prolegomena to a Ritual/Liturgical Reading of the Gospel of Mark." Kümmel proposes that the Gospels were read in worship and that they are missionary writings. See W. G. KÜMMEL, *Introduction to the New Testament*, 37. On different settings, see M. A. BEAVIS, *Mark's Audience: The Literary and Social Setting of Mark 4:11–12*, 45–67. Beavis argues "against those who set Mark in the context of early Christian worship and liturgy that the Gospel was written by an early Christian missionary/teacher for the instruction of his audience, which was made up of other missionaries or even non-Christians." BEAVIS, *Mark's Audience*, 66.

84 See RHOADS, "Performance Criticism: Part I", 130.

85 J. DEWEY, "The Survival of Mark's Gospel: A Good Story?," 497–498. Citation from 498.

86 SHINER, *Proclaiming the Gospel*, 27. See also 51.

the Lord's Supper, prayer, or the singing of hymns."[87] Alternatively, Shiner suggests that the Gospel of Mark could have been performed in an outdoor setting, before baptisms.[88] The setting in which one presumes that the Gospels were performed will obviously influence the interpretation of the texts on baptism, but scholars have not agreed upon a specific performance situation for the Gospels. In this article, I will therefore presume that these Gospels were performed during Christian worship in a house church.

6. Baptism in the Gospel of Matthew and Mark

Because this article examines the culmination of an oral performance of the Gospel of Mark, including the Longer Ending, and the Gospel of Matthew, I have chosen to present my analysis of baptism in Matthew before my examination of Mark. Even though Mark 1:1–16:8 was written prior to the Gospel of Matthew, the version of the Gospel of Mark which comprises Mark 16:9–20 probably originated between 120 and 150 CE.[89] On the basis of that information, one may conclude that this variant was first performed at a later stage than the Gospel of Matthew.

6.1. Baptism in the Gospel of Matthew Prior to 28:16–20

During a performance of the Gospel of Matthew, audience members come across numerous references to baptism before they hear Jesus' commission to the eleven. When audience members hear Matthew 28:19, the verb βαπτίζω may prime or activate these pericopes. Matthew 28:19 may first of all prime or activate events that are presented in Matthew chapter 3.[90] In Matthew 3:5–6, John

---

87 IDEM, *Proclaiming the Gospel*, 51. Shiell has similar reflections: "In private settings, the majority of recitations took place in *symposia*. If, as Jerome Neyrey has surmised, the Christian meals functioned similarly to these *symposia*, then the function of texts at meals in Acts took on even greater significance. The issues of Acts 10 and Acts 15 should be read in light of the information about performances in Greco-Roman *symposia*. The recitations of letters (Acts 15) or prophetic texts would be key events in the church. Most believers gathered in *koinonia* meals held in domestic settings and participated either in the remembrance of the Lord's Supper or a gathering for worship or both. These recitations, whether it took place following the eucharist or not, were held privately and would have largely imitated other similar meals in the society." SHIELL, *Reading Acts*, 127.

88 See SHINER, *Proclaiming the Gospel*, 51.

89 KELHOFFER, *Miracle and Mission*, 169–177, 474–475. COLLINS, *Mark*, 807.

90 Because lexical entries are content addressable, this verb may also prime or activate references to John the Baptist (Ἰωάννης ὁ βαπτιστής) in general (Matthew 3:1; 11:11–12; 14:2.8; 16:14 and 17:13). On these references, see also NOLLAND, "In Such a Manner," 64. The fact that lexical entries are also content addressable makes verbatim correspondence unnecessary. This phenomenon implies that a word can be accessed "from a meaning, a meaning from a referent, the

baptizes people from Jerusalem, Judea, and the region around the Jordan, who confess their sins, in the river Jordan. Through Matthew 3:11, John the Baptist contrasts his baptism with water for repentance with the baptismal practice of a subsequent character, who is going to baptize with the Holy Spirit and fire. In Matthew 3:13–17, Jesus is baptized by John. Because lexical entries are content addressable,[91] the verb βαπτίζω may also prime or activate events where the noun τὸ βάπτισμα is employed, such as Matthew 3:7, at which point many Pharisees and Sadducees come for baptism, and Matthew 21:25, where the origin of John's baptism is discussed. If these pericopes on baptism are activated by Matthew 28:19, they may affect the manner in which audience members understand Jesus' speech acts in Matthew 28:19. In order to establish how this previous information may influence interpretation of Jesus' commission, I must provide a brief analysis of these preceding events. Whether these pericopes on baptism will be activated by Matthew 28:19 or not, will depend on the specific situations in which the Gospel is performed and the particular interests of audience members. If this performance takes place in connection with preparations for baptism, or audience members are interested in this theme, preceding events dealing with baptism will be more easily remembered and they may to a greater extent influence the way in which audience members interpret Matthew 28:19.

When audience members hear Matthew 3:5–6, they learn that John the Baptist attracts a crowd of people from Jerusalem, Judea, and the Jordan region who want to be baptized by him. In the Matthean world, these characters seemingly respond to John's previous proclamation "[r]epent, for the kingdom of heaven has come near" (Matthew 3:2). If the actions of these characters (Matthew 3:5–6) are interpreted as the perlocutionary effect of John's former directive point (Matthew 3:2), audience members may regard their baptism as an act of repentance. In that case, they will consider John's speech acts and mission to be successful. That John's baptism is related to repentance is indicated by John's own speech acts in Matthew 3:7–8 and 3:11 as well.[92]

In Matthew 3:6, the extradiegetic narrator provides a summary of the baptismal act per se, which points out that those who are baptized in the Jordan confess their sins. Even though this is not directly stated by the extradiegetic narrator or John the Baptist, audience members may therefore deduce that John's baptism purifies from sin.[93] Through the passive voice, Matthew 3:6 sug-

---

rest of a meaning from part of a meaning and so on." HOGAN, *Cognitive Science, Literature and the Arts*, 43.

91 See previous note.

92 On baptism and repentance, see also H. STEGEMANN, *Die Essener, Qumran, Johannes der Täufer und Jesus*, 307.

93 According to Harrington, "[t]he confession of sins accompanying the baptism relates to the repentance demanded by John and to God's willingness to forgive sins." HARRINGTON, *Matthew*, 52. Luz discusses whether the author of Matthew wanted to distinguish between John's

gests that John's baptism is an administered rite, and according to Hartmut Stegemann, John actually represents God during baptism.[94] Audience members may recognize that this procedure distinguishes this baptism from purification rites and proselyte baptism, both of which are carried out by means of self-immersion.[95]

Audience members may interpret Matthew 3:6 on the basis of the preceding information. In Matthew 3:1–4, John the Baptist and his proclamation are explicitly presented as the fulfillment of a prophecy uttered by Isaiah:

> This is the one of whom the prophet Isaiah spoke when he said, "The voice of one crying out in the wilderness: 'Prepare the way of the Lord, make his paths straight'" (Matthew 3:3).

John thus embodies the voice who is crying out in the wilderness, but his actions also suggest that he prepares the way of the Lord, that is God.[96] By staging John as a prophet (Matthew 3:4),[97] the extradiegetic narrator links him to the line of God's messengers to his people. In this way, John the Baptist plays the part of one of God's slaves (Matthew 21:33ff.),[98] who participates in God's saving project, in this case by proclaiming and baptizing.[99]

Both the proclamation of John the Baptist and the voice in the wilderness contain directive points, i.e. imperatives in the second person plural. During the performance, audience members may process these speech acts as if they

---

baptism as a sign of repentance and Christian baptism which was related to forgiveness of sin. He concludes that such a distinction is unwarranted. Luz, *Matthäus I*, 146–147. According to Nolland, "[i]t is probably too much to say that Matthew in 3.1 withholds from John's baptism the forgiveness of sins with which it is associated in Mk 1.4 and Lk 3.3, but Matthew does want to focus the eschatological forgiveness of the new covenant on the role of Jesus and not on that of John (9.2, 5, 6; 26.28; cf 1.21)." Nolland, "In Such a Manner," 69. According to Hartman, Matthew "indirectly denies that John's baptism was for the forgiveness of sins; instead, it is presented only as a baptism 'in water for repentance' (3.11)." Hartman, *'Into the Name of the Lord Jesus'*, 17. On related views, see H. Thyen, "ΒΑΠΤΙΣΜΑ ΜΕΤΑΝΟΙΑΣ ΕΙΣ ΑΦΕΣΙΝ ΑΜΑΡΤΙΩΝ," 101–103. On baptism and the forgiveness of sins, see Stegemann, *Die Essener*, 302–303, 307.

94   Stegemann, *Die Essener*, 304.
95   On this distinction, see Ferguson, *Baptism in the Early Church*, 86, 88. Nolland, "In Such a Manner," 68–69. D. Sänger, "‚Ist er heraufgestiegen, gilt er in jeder Hinsicht als ein Israelit' (bYev 47b)" in this publication, 291–334. Stegemann, *Die Essener*, 302. According to Stegemann, baptisms in the early church were probably influenced by John the Baptist's procedure.
96   Harrington proposes that the Lord denotes Jesus. Harrington, *Matthew*, 51. Stegemann suggests that with regard to John the Baptist, the Lord referred to God. Stegemann, *Die Essener*, 299.
97   See also Stegemann, *Die Essener*, 298.
98   The focus on bearing fruit is an important aspect of John's utterance in Matthew 3:8. In this way, he may exemplify one of God's slaves who is sent to collect the produce (Matthew 21:33ff.).
99   On the term project, see note 2.

were addressed to them as well, because they are able to carry out the actions requested by John and the voice in the wilderness. Both speech acts refer to actions that should be performed because of the imminent presence of the Lord. If audience members are familiar with Isaiah 40:3 (Matthew 3:3), they may interpret John's proclamation (Matthew 3:2) as a prediction which indicates that God is about to save his people by means of a new Exodus. Matthew 3:2–3 furthermore suggests that the Lord will come. As a result, audience members may interpret baptism in the river Jordan as the proper response to John's proclamation of repentance due to the imminent inauguration of the kingdom of heaven.[100] Such an interpretation may be reinforced by John's speech acts in Matthew 3:7.

In Matthew 3:7, baptism is associated with "the wrath to come." John's question suggests that baptism is a way to avoid this wrath.[101] Through the subsequent directive point "[b]ear fruit worthy of repentance" (Matthew 3:8), John the Baptist employs a metaphor which may encourage his addressees to produce actions that reflect genuine repentance. At this point, it seems that the appropriate acts go beyond baptism: to be exact, they may refer to good deeds which reflect the will of God.[102] Because those who are baptized by John confess their sins, audience members may also infer that John indirectly encourages his addressees to refrain from sinning. Failure to produce the appropriate actions is illuminated by John's speech acts in Matthew 3:10. "Even now the ax is lying at the root of the trees; every tree therefore that does not bear good fruit is cut down and thrown into the fire." Accordingly, John's utterances relate baptism to the final judgment and thus to eschatology.

Through John's speech acts in Matthew 3:11, audience members learn of a new type of baptism, which is contrasted with the baptism that was performed

---

100 On related views, see HARRINGTON, *Matthew*, 51. The location of these baptisms may relate John the Baptist and these characters to the way in which Joshua led Israel into the Holy Land. They are located in the wilderness, the entry into the Promised Land, (or in this case, the kingdom of heaven). STEGEMANN, *Die Essener*, 296–297. According to Stegemann, salvation was at the other side of the river Jordan, which symbolized the final judgment. Against this backdrop, baptism symbolized the anticipation of the final judgment, an event which was bypassed by those who underwent baptism. In this manner, the baptizer guaranteed the symbolic crossing of Jordan and thus salvation. Accordingly, the focus is both on the final judgment and on salvation. STEGEMANN, *Die Essener*, 304–305.

101 See also HARRINGTON, *Matthew*, 55; NOLLAND, "In Such a Manner," 66; STEGEMANN, Die Essener, 304. According to Day, Cyril regards John's words to the people in Matthew 3:7 as warnings to the catechumens. He interprets John's question as an indication of "salvation from the eternal fire for those who believe and are baptized with John's baptism." DAY, "The Catechetical Lectures of Cyril of Jerusalem" in this publication, 1179–1204.

102 See also LUZ, *Matthäus I*, 147. He points out that the criterion in judgment is human deeds. On good deeds that reflect genuine repentance, see HARRINGTON, *Matthew*, 55–56. According to Stegemann, repentance involves acting in accordance with the will of God. STEGEMANN, *Die Essener*, 297.

earlier by John.¹⁰³ John's baptism was carried out by means of water for repentance, but through a prediction, John introduces a mightier character, who will baptize by means of the Holy Spirit and fire.¹⁰⁴ In the Matthean world, this character may refer to God or Jesus.¹⁰⁵ The same character is seemingly associated with "the wrath to come" (Matthew 3:7), because John the Baptist employs metaphors comparable to the ones he used in Matthew 3:10 in order to interpret the role of this coming character. "His winnowing fork is in his hand, and he will clear his threshing floor and will gather his wheat into the granary; but the chaff he will burn with unquenchable fire" (Matthew 3:12). Because the actions of this mightier character are described along these lines, audience members may perceive that the baptism which will be performed by this character is related to eschatology as well. Daniel J. Harrington clearly infers that the character mentioned in Matthew 3:11 is Jesus. He suggests that, "[t]he context of repentance is preparation for the eschaton; the baptism in the Holy Spirit and fire signals the presence of the eschaton, thus underscoring the superiority of Jesus' baptism."¹⁰⁶ Alternatively, if audience members deduce that the character mentioned in Matthew 3:11 denotes God, this event may suggest to them that God is the future judge, but also the true agent of Christian baptism.

If audience members are familiar with Christian baptismal liturgy, as indicated for instance by the Didache, they may link baptism with the Holy Spirit with Christian baptism. During an oral performance of Matthew 3:11b, this inclination may be enhanced by the pronoun ὑμᾶς, because the oral medium may collapse the membrane separating the text-internal and the text-external communication situations.¹⁰⁷ In that case, they may think that John's prediction that "[h]e will baptize you with the Holy Spirit and fire" (Matthew 3:11b)¹⁰⁸ may refer to their own baptism,¹⁰⁹ which may be upcoming or already performed.

Audience members may, however, interpret baptism with fire in different manners, two of which are mentioned here. (1) If audience members are familiar with Acts 1:2–9; 2:1–38 or related oral traditions, they may think that fire refers to the Holy Spirit too. (2) The context suggests that fire may denote the

---

103 On the manner in which one can interpret the preposition ἐν, see FERGUSON, *Baptism in the Early Church*, 90–91.

104 According to Nolland and Ferguson, Holy Spirit and fire may refer to two different baptisms. NOLLAND, "In Such a Manner," 71. FERGUSON, *Baptism in the Early Church*, 91.

105 On the fact that this character may refer to God, see STEGEMANN, *Die Essener*, 299, 305. On the idea that it may represent Jesus, see DAY, "The Catechetical Lectures of Cyril of Jerusalem" in this publication, 1179–1204. See also HARRINGTON, *Matthew*, 59.

106 HARRINGTON, *Matthew*, 59.

107 See my comments on Mark 1:8.

108 αὐτὸς ὑμᾶς βαπτίσει ἐν πνεύματι ἁγίῳ καὶ πυρί.

109 On related views, see HARTMAN, *'Into the Name of the Lord Jesus'*, 18.

annihilating judgment,[110] especially because the metaphors in Matthew 3:12 suggest that God or Jesus may function as the coming judge.[111] In both cases, audience members may relate baptism to eschatology, but in the first case, they may regard the outpouring of the Holy Spirit in the last days (Acts 2:17–21) as an empowerment so that they may prophesy, see visions, and have dreams (Acts 2:17–18). They also know that the Holy Spirit is conveyed through baptism (Acts 2:38). The second alternative indicates that fire is the destructive response to the failure to produce the expected fruit (Matthew 3:10.12), that is, repentance, baptism, and actions that reflect the will of God. In Matthew 3:11, the fact that both the Holy Spirit and the fire are mentioned may suggest to audience members, who appreciate the context of this utterance and know the traditions in Acts, that both aspects of God's/Jesus' activities during the last days may be referred to by John the Baptist (empowerment and judgment).[112] If audience members are not familiar with Acts 1:2–9; 2:1–38 or related traditions, the reference to the Holy Spirit may rather prime or activate notions of purification or ethical holiness in this context,[113] whereas the fire may refer to the final judgment.

Through the assertive point constituting Matthew 3:13, audience members learn that Jesus goes to the Jordan in order to be baptized by John the Baptist,[114] but the subsequent introduction of a speech act uttered by John informs audience members of the following problem: John wants to prevent Jesus from being baptized by him (Matthew 3:14). John's speech act may prime or activate John's prediction in Matthew 3:11. If audience members assume that the character who was mentioned in Matthew 3:11 was Jesus, they may suppose that John attempts to stop Jesus because he regards him as the one who is more powerful than he.[115] The more powerful should not be baptized by an inferior.

On the basis of how the baptismal act was presented in Matthew 3:6, Matthew 3:13–14 may also suggest another problem to audience members. Earlier, in Matthew 1:18–21, they heard that Jesus was conceived by the Holy Spirit and that he would save his people from their sins. Because John's baptisms seem-

---

110 See also Matthew 7:19; 13:40.42.50; 18:9. On related views, see Luz, *Matthäus I*, 148–149. Hartman, *'Into the Name of the Lord Jesus'*, 17–18. On alternatives with regard to the reference to Holy Spirit and fire, see Nolland, "In Such a Manner," 70–71.

111 On the Son of Man as this judge, see Luz, *Matthäus I*, 149. M. Davies, *Matthew*, 42. On God as the coming judge, see Stegemann, *Die Essener*, 299.

112 According to Stegemann, the reference to God as the one who baptizes with the Holy Spirit and fire indicates that salvation and the final judgment are both in focus. Stegemann, *Die Essener*, 305.

113 On these connotations, see McDonnel/Montague, *Christian Initiation and Baptism*, 15. With regard to purification, see also Nolland, "In Such a Manner," 71.

114 On different ways of understanding why Jesus came to John for baptism, see Nolland, "In Such a Manner," 73.

115 On related insights, see Luz, *Matthäus I*, 151.

ingly presupposed that those who were baptized were sinners in need of repentance (Matthew 3:6; 3:11), audience members may recognize that conflicting themes are suggested by Matthew 3:13–14. The Gospel of Matthew does not explicitly claim that Jesus is without sin,[116] but the above-mentioned elements of the narrative may imply this to audience members. If Jesus is sinless, it should not be necessary for him to undergo baptism, but Jesus responds to John's utterance in Matthew 3:14 by means of a speech act which indicates that his baptism is the will of God (Matthew 3:15).[117] Consequently, Jesus' choice to be baptized by John and John's baptism of Jesus "are identified as having their part to play in the unfolding of God's purpose."[118] Because John consents to Jesus' petition, the problem is solved in the Matthean world, but this event has continued to pose problems for interpreters of the Gospel of Matthew.[119]

Audience members are not informed about the details of the baptism of Jesus. For instance, they do not hear whether Jesus confesses his sins, a fact that may contribute to the idea of Jesus' sinlessness. Yet the way in which Jesus exits the water (ἀνέβη ἀπὸ τοῦ ὕδατος) suggests that his baptism is carried out by means of submersion or immersion (Matthew 3:16a).[120]

The interrelationship between Jesus' baptism and the succeeding event (Matthew 3:16–17) is intricate and it determines how audience members may interpret these actions. During the relation of Matthew 3:16b–17, the extradiegetic narrator attributes perceptual access to Jesus to audience members so that they may perceive that the Spirit of God descends on Jesus through his eyes.[121] Besides this, Jesus is presented to witnesses in the narrative world as

---

116 According to Luz, the author of Matthew does not mention the idea of Jesus' sinlessness. LUZ, *Matthäus I*, 153.

117 See also IDEM, *Matthäus I*, 154–155. HARTMAN, *'Into the Name of the Lord Jesus'*, 24. Harrington suggests that the words "to fulfill all righteousness" may refer to "the way of life appropriate to one baptized by John ('producing good fruit')." HARRINGTON, *Matthew*, 62.

118 NOLLAND, "In Such a Manner," 74.

119 According to Barth, Matthew 3:14–15 indicates that the author of the Gospel regarded Jesus' baptism by John as an inappropriate action. Barth suggests that the author would not interpret Jesus' baptism in this manner, if he regarded it as the basis of Christian baptism. He claims that "[e]rst vom zweiten Jahrhundert an begegnet der Gedanke, daß die Taufe Jesu durch Johannes im Jordan selbst schon die Begründung und Einsetzung der christlichen Taufe gewesen sei." BARTH, *Die Taufe*, 16–20. Citation from p. 19. According to Harrington, "John's baptism served as the prototype for Christian baptism. The chief difference is that Christian baptism is 'in the name of Jesus' and takes its direction and meaning especially from Jesus' death and resurrection." HARRINGTON, *Matthew*, 60.

120 On different manners in which baptisms were administered, see JOHNSON, *The Rites of Christian Initiation*, 26–27.

121 Cf. HARRINGTON, *Matthew*, 62. Harrington does not regard this as a private vision, but rather as a public event.

the Son of God.[122] Through the performance situation, Jesus is, however, also introduced as such to audience members.[123] They may interpret these events as part of Jesus' baptism, or they may think that the baptism prepares Jesus for this occasion.

If audience members choose the first alternative, those who are acquainted with the practice reflected in Acts 2:38 or in the Didache may regard the endowment with the Spirit as a model for their own, Christian baptism.[124] Audience members who are familiar with the idea that Christians may be regarded as sons of God (Matthew 5:45) may moreover understand Jesus' baptism as an indication that this status is conferred on them through baptism.[125] If audience members choose to interpret the endowment with the Spirit and the declaration of sonship as a separate occasion, they may think this incident is a Christological event, which focuses on the particular role of Jesus.[126]

In Matthew 4:17, Jesus' proclamation is presented in exactly the same manner as the message of John the Baptist (Matthew 3:2). Accordingly, the projects of Jesus and John are interrelated in several ways at the beginning of this Gospel.[127] (1) Jesus is baptized by John, which means that Jesus sympathizes with John's mission and presumably wants to join him in his efforts.[128] (2) They proclaim the same message, i.e. repentance.[129] On the basis of Jesus' baptism,

---

122 See also GREEN, *Matthew*, 64–65. Cf. FRANCE, *Matthew*, 95. According to France, "[t]he third-person form of the proclamation in v. 17 suggests a public revelation, but this is hard to reconcile with the fact that Jesus' Messianic status was not publicly stated throughout his ministry, and was only grasped by his closest disciples much later (16:13–20); Matthew therefore, while assimilating the words to those at the transfiguration (17:5), probably intends them to be understood as addressed to Jesus only. The whole focus of the account is on Jesus' 'commissioning', not on a public revelation of his mission."

123 On related insights, see HARTMAN, *'Into the Name of the Lord Jesus'*, 24.

124 According to Johnson, it is the presence and gift of the "Holy Spirit that distinguishes Jesus' own and subsequent Christian baptism from that of John." JOHNSON, *The Rites of Christian Initiation*, 15. On Jesus' baptism in the Jordan as a paradigm for understanding baptism in Syria, see IDEM, *The Rites of Christian Initiation*, 47–49. On related views, see P. F. BRADSHAW, *The Search for the Origins of Christian Worship*, 149–150. On the interrelationship between Jesus' baptism and Christian baptism, see MCDONNEL/MONTAGUE, *Christian Initiation and Baptism*, 19–22.

125 On Jesus' baptism and baptismal candidates, see DAY, "The Catechetical Lectures of Cyril of Jerusalem" in this publication, 1179–1204. "[T]he Holy Spirit comes down upon you, and a fatherly voice comes over you: not, 'This is my Son', but, 'This has now become my son'. For upon that one 'is', ... since he is always 'Son of God'; but upon you 'has now become', since you do not have it by nature, but receive sonship by adoption. (PG 33:445)"

126 On related views, see NOLLAND, "In Such a Manner," 76.

127 On related insights, see FRANKEMÖLLE, *Matthäus Kommentar*, 549–550.

128 On related views, see NOLLAND, "In Such a Manner," 74. TH. M. FINN, *From Death to Rebirth: Ritual and Conversion in Antiquity*, 137. Stegemann suggests that Jesus never distanced himself from John the Baptist, see STEGEMANN, *Die Essener*, 316–317.

129 See also NOLLAND, "In Such a Manner," 65–66. FRANCE, *Matthew*, 90. GREEN, *Matthew*, 62. HARRINGTON, *Matthew*, 51–52. According to Stegemann, the fact that they proclaim the same

through which he was empowered by the Spirit of God, audience members may think that Jesus was the character referred to in Matthew 3:11. In that case, the main difference between John and Jesus is that Jesus' power is sanctioned by and derives from the Holy Spirit (Matthew 3:11). Because Jesus received this Spirit in connection with his baptism, John's baptism prepared Jesus for the endowment with the Spirit of God and for the affirmation of his identity.[130] Audience members may therefore recognize the value of John's baptism with regard to Jesus.[131]

After Jesus is empowered by the Spirit, he is able to perform mighty deeds, such as exorcisms, healings etc. (Matthew 12:22–32).[132] In Matthew 9:2–8, Jesus' healings are related to the forgiveness of sins,[133] which is one of Jesus' primary tasks (Matthew 1:21). On the basis of this information, audience members may associate John's speech acts on the Holy Spirit (Matthew 3:11) with these activities.[134] In that case, they may realize that John's prediction pertaining to the Holy Spirit and fire refers to Jesus' cleansing activities and to his function as a coming judge.[135] If audience members relate the Holy Spirit to the outpouring of this Spirit in the last days and thus to empowerment, their focus may be on Jesus' ability to establish the kingdom of heaven. This aspect is probably enhanced by Matthew 11:2–6.[136]

In Matthew 21:23–27, Jesus' authority and its basis are contested by the chief priests and the elders. Jesus replies by asking them about the origin of John's baptism. Through the performance of the Gospel of Matthew, audience members have probably deduced that John the Baptist proclaims and baptizes in order to prepare the way of the Lord. Hence, they know that his baptism is connected with heaven and that John succeeds the prophets of old. John's baptism of Jesus develops this inference further by indicating that Jesus accepts John's mission. Furthermore, Jesus' authority as the Son of God and bearer of the Holy Spirit is declared in relation to that event. In this manner, audience members will probably recognize that both Jesus' authority and John's baptism

---

    message reflects a later stage. STEGEMANN, *Die Essener*, 317.

130 NOLLAND, "In Such a Manner," 75.

131 On the interrelationship between John's baptism and Christian baptism, see NOLLAND, "In Such a Manner," 70. See also DAY, "The Catechetical Lectures of Cyril of Jerusalem" in this publication, 1179–1204.

132 On related insights, see NOLLAND, "In Such a Manner," 64–65.

133 On the relationship between sins and healing, see STEGEMANN, *Die Essener*, 334–335. Along these lines, forgiveness of sins was not associated only with John's baptisms.

134 See also Matthew 11:2–6. MCDONNEL/MONTAGUE, *Christian Initiation and Baptism*, 16.

135 On related insights, see NOLLAND, "In Such a Manner," 70–75, esp. 75.

136 According to Stegemann, Jesus differentiated between the inauguration of the kingdom of God and its future consummation. However, the kingdom of God was also associated with the final judgment. STEGEMANN, *Die Essener*, 332.

are sanctioned by God and that these characters are participating in the same mission.[137]

6.2. Baptism in the Context of Matthew 28:16–20

During the performance of the Gospel of Matthew, Jesus' speech act on baptism (Matthew 28:19) is uttered as soon as the risen Lord is reunited with his disciples.[138] At that juncture, he commissions them to carry on his project (Matthew 28:16–20). Through his other speech acts, Jesus relates baptism to his authority "in heaven and on earth" (Matthew 28:18b), to the formation of disciples, to teaching, and to his presence "to the end of the age" (Matthew 28:20b). Below, Jesus' commission to baptize will be analyzed against this broad backdrop. In Matthew 28:16–20, Jesus' directive point on baptism constitutes the centre of his direct discourse,[139] through which the performance of the Gospel culminates. Although baptism is located in this position, it does not constitute the central theme of this pericope, because the participles βαπτίζοντες and διδάσκοντες are both subservient to the imperative μαθητεύσατε,[140] which forms the main subject matter of this scene.

Before Jesus expresses his directive points to the eleven (Matthew 28:19–20a), he utters an assertive point through which he claims that "[a]ll authority in heaven and on earth has been given to me" (Matthew 28:18).[141] This statement indicates Jesus' opinion about the extent of his authority and the divine passive points out its origin.[142] The intended perlocutionary effect of this speech act is probably that Jesus' addressees form or hold a similar belief. This speech act may function in an analogous manner in connection with the text-internal and text-external communication situation. Those who believe in Jesus' identity as the Son of God, who died and was raised by God, may consider this

---

137 On the authority of John's baptism, see also FERGUSON, *Baptism in the Early Church*, 90.

138 Matthew 28:16–20 constitutes the fulfilment of many prophecies that were previously uttered in the Matthean world (Matthew 16:21; 17:22–23; 20:18–19; 26:31–32; 28:7; 28:10). When Jesus appears to the eleven in Galilee, he is established as a true prophet through an event which both implies that Jesus was raised by God and that he is committed to carrying on his relationship with his disciples. On related views, see HARRINGTON, *Matthew*, 414. DAVIES/ALLISON, *Matthew*, 680, 687.

139 See M. LABAHN, "Kreative Erinnerung als nachösterliche Nachschöpfung" in this publication, 337–376.

140 See LUZ, *Matthäus IV*, 429, esp. note 6. FRANKEMÖLLE, *Matthäus Kommentar*, 545.

141 According to Barth, focus on Jesus' authority is an important aspect of Matthean theology. BARTH, *Die Taufe*, 13. See also BORNKAMM, "Der Auferstandene und der Irdische."

142 See also HARTMAN, *'Into the Name of the Lord Jesus'*, 148. Luz claims that the disciples are the instrument of Jesus' power. LUZ, *Matthäus IV*, 442.

speech act on Jesus' authority as a confirmation of their belief.[143] Those who doubt that Jesus is the Son of God, whose authority was extended as a consequence of his risen state, may regard this assertive point as an attempt to change their opinion.

Jesus' powerful claim forms the point of departure of his subsequent directive points.[144] All of Jesus' addressees in the Matthean world, even those disciples who originally doubted, are commanded to go and "make disciples [μαθητεύσατε] of all nations" (Matthew 28:19a). The verb μαθητεύειν is an imperative inflected in the second person plural. During the performance event, this fact may collapse the membrane separating the Matthean and the real world. Because audience members are able to carry out the requested deed in the real world, that is, to make disciples, they may process this speech act as if it is uttered to them as well as to the eleven.[145] For that reason, the chief command voiced by Jesus connects upcoming activities in the Matthean world with actions which audience members may perform in the real world.

Because Matthew 28:19a serves as Jesus' key utterance,[146] it will determine the manner in which audience members interpret the secondary directive points, i.e. the commands to baptize (Matthew 28:19b) and to teach (Matthew 28:20a). On the basis of the previous statement about Jesus' authority "in heaven and on earth" (Matthew 28:18), audience members may deduce that Jesus has sufficient power to utter these speech acts. The aim of these commands is to expand and sustain the community of Jesus' adherents, who participate in bringing about the goal of the joint projects of God, John the Baptist, and Jesus, i.e. the establishment of the kingdom of heaven.

During the performance, the command "[g]o therefore, make disciples of all nations" (Matthew 28:19a) may prime or activate Matthew 10:5-6. If these speech acts are activated, audience members may recognize that Jesus' previous directive points, which aimed at restricting the activities of the twelve to the house of Israel (Matthew 10:5-6), are set aside by Matthew 28:19a. Hence, the eleven, and indirectly audience members, are now commanded to make disciples of all nations, not primarily Israel. Israel is, however, also included

---

143 According to Hartman, "[t]he evangelist does not, however, connect the death and resurrection of Jesus with baptism; instead, they become stages on his way to the dominion into which people are to be incorporated through becoming disciples, a process which, *inter alia*, includes being baptized." HARTMAN, *'Into the Name of the Lord Jesus'*, 152.

144 On similar insights, see LUZ, *Matthäus IV*, 442.

145 See also LUZ, *Matthäus IV*, 443-444. The commissioning is, according to Luz, "für die Gegenwart transparent: Er richtet sich nicht nur an die elf Apostel am Anfang der Kirchengeschichte; vielmehr sind die Apostel Identifikationsgestalten für alle Jünger/innen Jesu zu allen Zeiten, denen der Auftrag des Auferstandenen ebenso gilt."

146 According to Barth, focus on discipleship is an important aspect of Matthean theology. BARTH, *Die Taufe*, 13. See also BORNKAMM, "Der Auferstandene und der Irdische," 182.

in their mission.¹⁴⁷ Because this speech act is uttered as a directive point, Jesus' addressees may recognize that Jesus believes they are capable of carrying out this task.

Since the speech acts voiced by Jesus in Matthew 28:19–20a are directive points, i.e. commands, emphasis is put on the activities which Jesus demands from his addressees. They are requested to make disciples through baptism and teaching. As I pointed out above, Jesus' addressees are the eleven, but audience members may also process Jesus' speech acts as if they were addressed to them, thanks to the imperative μαθητεύσατε. If they do, audience members may recognize that Jesus' commands relate their behavior to the activities of the eleven who have advanced the joint project of God, John the Baptist, Jesus, and their adherents by making disciples through baptism and teaching. Because the perlocutionary effect of these speech acts concerns the behavior of Jesus' addressees, this utterance does not draw attention to the activities of those individuals who are baptized and taught by the eleven or audience members. This means that emphasis is put on instructions pertaining to how those who already belong to the community of believers can expand this group. The opposite process, that is, instructions on how to join the community, is not the primary focus of Jesus. Audience members may, however, deduce criteria for joining the group on the basis of Jesus' commands.

Because Jesus concentrates on the act of baptizing in Matthew 28:19b, the baptismal activities of John and Jesus in Matthew 3:6; 3:11 and 3:13–17 may be primed or activated at this point. As the commands in Matthew 28:19–20a stress the actions through which disciples are made, audience members may regard John the Baptist and possibly Jesus as figures whom they should imitate. The emulation of John's actions may function particularly well with regard to audience members who have already responded to Jesus' command by baptizing others. These members of the audience may realize that their actions are in accordance with John's project as well as with Jesus' commission. Audience members who have been baptized themselves, but who have not baptized others, may first and foremost realize that their own baptism was performed in line with Jesus' command.¹⁴⁸ They may in addition recognize the interrelationship between their baptism and Jesus' own baptism.¹⁴⁹ If they do, their personal experiences take precedence over the nature of Jesus' speech acts as commands.

---

147   See DAVIES/ALLISON, *Matthew*, 684; HAGNER, *Matthew14–28*, 887; FRANKEMÖLLE, *Matthäus Kommentar*, 546–547. On different ways in which one can interpret "πάντα τὰ ἔθνη," see LUZ, *Matthäus*, 447–452. According to Harrington, this phrase refers to Gentiles only. HARRINGTON, *Matthew*, 414–417.

148   See also HARTMAN, *'Into the Name of the Lord Jesus'*, 147.

149   On the relationship between Christian baptism and Jesus' baptism, see § 6.1. Baptism in the Gospel of Matthew Prior to 28:16–20.

During the performance of the Gospel of Matthew, some members of the audience may decide to join the project constituted by God's saving purposes. These audience members may first and foremost regard baptism as an act through which they gain entrance into the community of believers.[150]

Jesus' subsequent speech acts specify that expanding the group of his adherents involves "baptizing them into the name of the Father and of the Son and of the Holy Spirit" (Matthew 28:19b). From a literary perspective, audience members may interpret Jesus' speech acts in a more profound way than the eleven, because they were present as "invisible witnesses" when John baptized ordinary people and Jesus (Matthew 3), a baptism which in the Gospel of Matthew took place before Jesus called his disciples. From a historical perspective, however, some of the eleven probably started out as disciples of John. They were thus most likely present when Jesus was baptized by John, but we do not know what they actually heard and saw and what theological implications they may have drawn on the basis of this event. From a literary perspective, though, the way in which the extradiegetic narrator relates the event points out at least some important theological aspects of Jesus' baptism to audience members.

When Jesus was baptized by John, the extradiegetic narrator drew attention to the presence of the Spirit of God and he quoted the voice from heaven to audience members (Matthew 3:16–17).[151] If this previous event is activated by Jesus' speech act on baptism,[152] audience members may interpret Jesus' command to baptize against the backdrop of Jesus' own baptism, where the Spirit of God and God the Father were present. In that case, they may realize that subsequent disciples will imitate the baptism of the founder of the community.[153] Because baptism is associated with the Father, the Son, and the Holy Spirit in Matthew 28:19b, audience members may recognize that those who are baptized enter into a new relationship with God.[154] If audience members regard Jesus' baptism as a model for Christian baptism,[155] they may interpret this new affiliation in terms of sonship and empowerment. After they have been baptized, audience members will take part in the joint project of God, John the Baptist, Jesus, and their adherents, and through their baptism these audience members will be empow-

---

150 On baptism as "the door into a new human community," see HARTMAN, 'Into the Name of the Lord Jesus', 46–47. Citation from p. 47.
151 See also § 6.1. Baptism in the Gospel of Matthew Prior to 28:16–20.
152 On related views, see DAVIES/ALLISON, Matthew, 687–688.
153 On similar insights, see LUZ, Matthäus IV, 452. See also DAVIES/ALLISON, Matthew, 685. MCDONNEL/MONTAGUE, Christian Initiation and Baptism, 19–22. On Jesus' baptism as an example for readers, see HARTMAN, 'Into the Name of the Lord Jesus', 147. On the Syrian church, see the article by S. SEPPÄLÄ, "Baptismal Mystery in St. Ephrem the Syrian and Hymnen de Epiphania" in this publication, 1139–1177.
154 On related views, see JOHNSON, The Rites of Christian Initiation, 28.
155 See § 6.1. Baptism in the Gospel of Matthew Prior to 28:16–20.

ered by the Holy Spirit in order to continue their mission (Matthew 3:11; 3:16; 10:20).[156] Audience members may therefore consider baptism "into the name of the Father and of the Son and of the Holy Spirit" as a confirmation of their commitment to the main figures of the community of believers.

If Matthew 28:19b activates baptisms that were carried out by John the Baptist and their meaning, i.e. repentance and possibly the forgiveness of sins, audience members may deduce that baptism signifies repentance and causes the forgiveness of sins in this context as well.[157] They may thus view baptism as a way to escape the final judgment. Activation of these previous baptisms and their meaning is more likely to occur if audience members are preoccupied with baptism from the outset of the performance. If audience members are not particularly interested in baptism, they may not reflect on the interrelationship between baptism, repentance, forgiveness of sins, and escape from the final judgment when they hear Matthew 28:19b.

All in all, Jesus' utterances on baptism may function in different manners with reference to audience members who baptize, audience members who have been baptized, candidates for baptism, and non-believers. Those who perform baptisms will probably imitate the example of John the Baptist, whereas those who have been baptized or are candidates for baptism "into the name of the Father and of the Son and of the Holy Spirit" (Matthew 28:19b) will most likely emulate the example of Jesus. Through their baptism in the name of the Father, the Son and the Holy Spirit, these audience members have become or will become intimately related to the main characters who aim at realizing God's mission. Non-believers may be convinced by the performance and seek to join the community of believers by being baptized into it, or they may continue their life as outsiders.

Through Jesus' speech act in Matthew 28:20a, the verb μαθητεύω is also related to teaching. The focus of Jesus' speech act is on the perlocutionary effect of the teaching which Jesus commands the eleven disciples to conduct, i.e. the addressees of the disciples should obey everything that Jesus had commanded the eleven. This command corresponds to the emphasis put on Jesus' teaching

---

156   See also § 6.1. Baptism in the Gospel of Matthew Prior to 28:16–20.

157   According to Hartman, "there are no distinct signs that in Matthean thinking forgiveness was given in baptism. Nevertheless it is reasonable to assume that it was the case. For when people were received into the new covenant (26.28) or into the dominion which had been established through the divine salvation, it would be natural to believe that they were purified from the sins of the past." HARTMAN, *'Into the Name of the Lord Jesus'*, 152. Stegemann suggests that "während die christliche Taufe im sakramentalen Akt selbst die Tilgung aller zuvor begangenen Sünden bewirkt, geschah die Taufe des Johannes nur *zur* Vergebung der Sünden. Sie war die – ebenfalls sakramentale – Gewährleistung dafür, daß *Gott selbst* den Getauften im *künftigen* Endgericht die bis zur Taufe begangenen Sünden nicht anrechnen werde." STEGEMANN, *Die Essener*, 303.

in the Gospel of Matthew in general,[158] but because this event takes place on a mountain, Jesus' Sermon on the Mount may be activated.[159] In that case, audience members may assume that teaching primarily denotes ethical teaching in this context, but in the Gospel of Matthew Jesus' proclamation is introduced in the following manner: "Repent, for the kingdom of heaven has come near" (Matthew 4:17). For that reason, the kingdom of heaven constitutes an important aspect of Jesus' teaching too.[160] In the Sermon on the Mount Jesus links his ethical teaching to the kingdom on many occasions (Matthew 5:3; 5:10; 5:19–20; 6:33; 7:21).[161] Viewed against this backdrop, Jesus' ethical instructions and his teaching on the kingdom of heaven are interrelated.

According to Matthew 28:20a, Jesus insists that his adherents impart the content of his teaching to their addressees.[162] In that they teach others, the disciples are now given a task which was earlier reserved to Jesus (Matthew 23:8–10).[163] Because Jesus, the founder of the community, focuses on the transmission of his teaching,[164] the communication of the goal and project of the group, as reflected in the values constituting Jesus' teaching, may aim at creating a homogenous community of adherents who focus on implementing the same project and goal. Because Jesus' teaching and deeds are interrelated in the Gospel, teaching may refer to both aspects of Jesus' activities.[165] If the previous imperative, μαθητεύσατε, collapsed the membrane separating the text-internal and the text-external communication situations, Jesus' instructions to teach "them to observe everything that I have commanded [ἐνετειλάμην] you" (Mat-

---

158 On the fact that the Gospel of Matthew contains Jesus' teaching, which makes this book indispensable, see Luz, *Matthäus IV*, 455. S. Byrskog, *Jesus the Only Teacher*, passim.

159 See also Byrskog, *Jesus the Only Teacher*, 209. Davies and Allison suggest that this location indicates parallels to the life of Moses. Davies/Allison, *Matthew*, 679–680. See also France, *Matthew*, 412.

160 On related views, see Luz, *Matthäus IV*, 454. According to Luz, Jesus' five discourses "enthalten Jesu für die Gegenwart gültiges εὐαγγέλιον τῆς βασιλείας." *Ibid.*, 455.

161 See H. D. Betz, *The Sermon on the Mount*.

162 See also Luz, *Matthäus IV*, 454. According to Harrington, "[t]he disciples are commanded to carry on what was a major task of the earthly Jesus in the Gospel. The content of their teaching ('all that I have commanded you') and what is expected of them ('to observe') treats the teaching of Jesus as authoritative." Harrington, *Matthew*, 415.

163 Davies/Allison, *Matthew*, 688.

164 According to Bornkamm, Jesus' teaching continues to be binding. Bornkamm, "Der Auferstandene und der Irdische," 183.

165 See Davies/Allison, *Matthew*, 686. "The resurrection – the full meaning of which only becomes apparent in 28:16–20 – makes Jesus himself an illustration of his own teaching. He is, like the prophets before him, wrongly persecuted because of his loyalty to God, and he gains great reward in heaven. He finds his life after losing it. He is the servant who becomes great, the last who becomes first." Iidem, *Matthew*, 673. See also Frankemölle, *Matthäus Kommentar*, 550.

thew 28:20) become binding for the eleven, but also for the church to the end of the world.[166]

Provided that Jesus' speech acts on baptism and teaching (Matthew 28:19b–20a) have activated previous baptisms carried out by John the Baptist (with their connotations of repentance, forgiveness of sins, and escape from the final judgment) and the Sermon on the Mount (with its focus on ethical teaching and the kingdom of heaven), audience members may remember Matthew 16:27 and interpret Matthew 28:20a against this backdrop. "For the Son of Man is to come with his angels in the glory of his Father, and then he will repay everyone for what has been done" (Matthew 16:27). In that case, audience members may realize that their actions will play an important role with regard to the final judgment. Moreover, Matthew 12:46–50 points out the importance of correct conduct in order to become and remain a member of Jesus' fictive family, which in a text-external communication situation may refer to the community of believers.[167] If audience members interpret Jesus' speech act on this basis, they may conclude that baptism constitutes the entrance to the community of believers, but continued teaching and conduct which reflects Jesus' instructions are also necessary in order to maintain one's membership in this community, to avoid being condemned during the final judgment and to enter into the kingdom of heaven (Matthew 3:7–10.12; 25:31–46).

In Matthew 28:19–20, baptism thus constitutes one of two conditions that are involved in turning people into disciples.[168] Because baptism is mentioned first, audience members may deduce that baptism precedes teaching.[169] In this way, baptism may function as an initiation rite that occurs soon after people become convinced by the initial proclamation of repentance and the kingdom. The teaching mentioned in Matthew 28:20a, would then refer to the continued teaching of the church.[170] If emphasis is put on teaching, this sequence may sug-

---

166 On related views, see BORNKAMM, "Der Auferstandene und der Irdische," 187.
167 On related views, see FRANKEMÖLLE, Matthäus Kommentar, 550–551.
168 On the fact that these speech act are subordinate to the previous imperative μαθητεύσατε, see also LUZ, Matthäus IV, 429, esp. note 6. FRANCE, Matthew, 414. Cf. DAVIES/ALLISON, Matthew, 677. Their view is later nuanced, IIDEM, Matthew, 686.
169 Bornkamm points out that this order does not correspond to the sequence in Didache 7.1, where teaching precedes baptism. BORNKAMM, "Der Auferstandene und der Irdische," 185.
170 See also LUZ, Matthäus IV, 454–455. Davies and Allison discuss the order of the verbs in Matthew 28:19–20. "[P]erhaps one first hears the call to discipleship (μαθητεύσατε) then enters the community through baptism (βαπτίζοντες) and finally learns instruction (διδάσκοντες) with a view towards obedience (τηρεῖν). In this case μαθητεύσατε could refer to pre-baptismal instruction. But it is better to regard μαθητεύσατε not as the first in a series but as a general imperative which is filled out (although not exhausted) by what follows: baptism and instruction in obedience belong to discipleship." DAVIES/ALLISON, Matthew, 686. On other aspects of the order of these verbs, see FRANKEMÖLLE, Matthäus Kommentar, 545. "Setzt man im jüdischen und frühchristlichen Kontext die Erwachsenentaufe als übliche Praxis voraus [...], dann haben vermutlich die ersten Leser die Abfolge von Taufe (19b) und Belehrung (20a) als auffällig beur-

gest that Matthew 28:18ff. primarily focuses on the continued life of the church, not on its mission.[171] However, by stressing baptism as well as teaching, two elements of ecclesiology are in focus, i.e. the expansion of the community of believers and the maintenance of this community. The education of new members by transmitting Jesus' teaching to them also constitutes an important aspect because it passes on the main values of the leader of the group to subsequent members of the community of believers, which in turn will encourage them to proclaim in order to recruit, baptize, and teach new disciples.

Jesus' direct speech is concluded by means of the following directive and commissive points: "And see, I am with you all days, to the end of the age" (Matthew 28:20b).[172] Through the first speech act, Jesus encourages his addressees to keep in mind his following promise. In his second speech act, he commits himself to being with his addressees. Because the end of the age is still to come, this speech act may enhance the inclination of audience members to process Jesus' previous utterances as if they were addressed to them as well.[173] The intended perlocutionary effect of Jesus' speech act is probably to convince his addressees that he will be able to keep his promise. Whether the actual perlocutionary effect will correspond to the intended one or not, depends on the extent to which Jesus' addressees in the Matthean world and audience members believe that Jesus has been given all authority "in heaven and on earth" (Matthew 28:18). This aspect will become increasingly important with regard to audience members who attend a performance situation which aims at connecting them with the distant past of the community and thus with its formative figures.

If audience members believe that Jesus is able to keep his promise, they may think that he will be with them as well as the eleven when they carry on his mission through making new disciples by baptizing and teaching them.[174] Nonbelievers, who are not convinced by Jesus' speech acts, will probably not be persuaded to continue Jesus' mission by performing these actions. As a result,

---

teilt, da jeglicher Hinweis auf einen Unterricht vor der Taufe fehlt. Liest man auch diese Verse im Kontext und läßt man sich dabei vom Auftrag ‚Macht zu Jüngern!' leiten, dann läßt sich eine grundlegende Parallele zwischen den Jünger–Berufungs–Geschichten (s. zu 4,18–22; 9,9; 10,1–4) und der erst darauf folgenden Belehrung feststellen."

171 See BORNKAMM, "Der Auferstandene und der Irdische," 185. See also Luz, who claims: "Das Ziel der Missionsverkündigung der Jünger ist also nicht die Bekehrung, sondern die Praxis der für Jesus neu gewonnenen Jünger/innen." LUZ, *Matthäus IV*, 455.

172 On the fact that this speech act may prime or activate Matthew 1:23, see DAVIES/ALLISON, *Matthew*, 688. LUZ, *Matthäus IV*, 456. GREEN, *Matthew*, 232.

173 According to Luz, the church may recognize that the experiences of the disciples with the earthly Jesus may parallel the experiences of the church with the risen Lord. LUZ, *Matthäus IV*, 456.

174 On the presence of the risen Lord in the church, see BARTH, *Die Taufe*, 14. Davies and Allison point out that the focus may be more on divine assistance than on divine presence. DAVIES/ALLISON, *Matthew*, 687.

the continuation of Jesus' project will be determined by the perlocutionary effects of his final speech.

6.3. Baptism in the Gospel of Mark Prior to the Longer Ending

During an oral performance of the Gospel of Mark, audience members hear numerous references to baptism before Jesus utters the commission to the eleven. The verb βαπτίζω (Mark 16:16) may first and foremost prime or activate events that are presented in Mark chapter 1. Through Mark 1:4–8a, audience members hear of John's baptisms, whereas Mark 1:8b–11 presents the future baptismal activities carried out by God or Jesus and John's baptism of Jesus.[175] In the Gospel of Mark the verb βαπτίζω is also employed in other contexts, i.e. to characterize John (Mark 6:14; 6:24), with reference to ritual washings of persons or things after one has come from the market (Mark 7:4),[176] and as a metaphor for Jesus' suffering and death (Mark 10:38–39). Baptism is accordingly connected with ritual purity, and the way in which baptisms are performed may symbolize the overwhelming character of Jesus' suffering and death. He is "drenched" in suffering.[177] Below, I will focus on the events related in Mark 1.

In Mark 1:4, John the Baptist is introduced to audience members as a character who proclaims "a baptism of repentance for the forgiveness of sins".[178] On the basis of this knowledge, audience members may deduce that John's proclamation and actions are interrelated, i.e. the aim of his proclamation is that people decide to be baptized. Audience members may interpret the phrase βάπτισμα μετανοίας in different manners.[179] (1) The goal of this baptism is to persuade God to change his decision to punish his people. (2) The baptism proclaimed by John refers to an act through which human beings ask for forgiveness of their sins. (3) This action is regarded as "a positive response to the initiative of God taken through the agency of John." In order to evaluate these alternatives, it is vital to emphasize the linear aspect of oral performances.[180] This means that audience members will relate John's proclamation of "a baptism of repentance for the forgiveness of sins" (Mark 1:4) to the preceding information in Mark 1:1–3.

Through Mark 1:1–3, a mission, which throughout the relation of the Markan narrative involves different characters, such as God, the initiator, and his

---

175 On the possibility that these activities are carried out by God, see STEGEMANN, *Die Essener*, 299.
176 The object of the verb is not mentioned.
177 See also J. R. DONAHUE/D. J. HARRINGTON, *The Gospel of Mark*, 62.
178 βάπτισμα μετανοίας εἰς ἄφεσιν ἁμαρτιῶν.
179 On the different interpretations of this phrase, see COLLINS, *Mark*, 140–142. Citation from p. 142.
180 On the linear aspect of oral performances and an analysis of Mark 1:1–3 based on this principle, see HARTVIGSEN, "Prepare the Way of the Lord", 42, 126–135.

associates (prophets of old, John the Baptist, Jesus, and their adherents), is presented to audience members. By means of the prologue to the Gospel of Mark, audience members are encouraged to join and thus promote this project by performing actions which aim at establishing the kingdom of God. I will now present the most important implications of this approach.

Audience members are introduced to the main character, Jesus, in Mark 1:1. When they hear this verse, the noun εὐαγγέλιον may prime or activate Isaiah 40:9; 52:7 and 61:1–2 (LXX). If these traditions are activated, audience members may associate the good news announced with "God's presence, the day of salvation, healing, liberty etc."[181] These themes are probably accentuated by the subsequent settings, i.e. the wilderness and the river Jordan. After the Exodus, the river Jordan constituted the entry to the Promised Land, and this means that these settings symbolize God's saving purposes and new beginnings.[182]

In Mark 1:2–3 several speech acts are uttered, but audience members are not aware of any listeners in the Markan world. Accordingly, they may view themselves as the addressees of these speech acts. This approach is facilitated by the pronouns and imperatives employed in Mark 1:2–3, which may collapse the membrane separating the Markan world and the real world of audience members.

Even though Mark 1:2–3 is introduced as a quotation from a written manuscript of the prophet Isaiah, the content of this quotation may prime or activate Exodus 23:20; Malachi 3:1, and Isaiah 40:3 (LXX). If Exodus 23:20 and its context are activated,[183] audience members may interpret Mark 1:2 in the following manner: "God promises to send his messenger, ahead of his people," i.e. us.[184] Provided that Isaiah 40:9; 52:7 and 61:1–2 were activated by Mark 1:1, audience members may regard Jesus as the messenger in Mark 1:2.[185]

---

181 EADEM, *"Prepare the Way of the Lord"*, 126.

182 EADEM, *"Prepare the Way of the Lord"*, 128. On the role of the wilderness, see E. C. STEWART, *Gathered around Jesus: An Alternative Spatial Practice in the Gospel of Mark*, 203–210. PILGAARD, *Markusevangeliet*, 58. On the river Jordan, see STEGEMANN, *Die Essener*, 296–297. B. M. F. VAN IERSEL, *Mark: A Reader-Response Commentary*, 63. PILGAARD, *Markusevangeliet*, 60. On the fact that "God's revelation of his saving purpose begins in the wilderness," see J. MARCUS, *The Way of the Lord: Christological Exegesis of the Old Testament in the Gospel of Mark*, 23–26. Citation from p. 23.

183 Καὶ ἰδοὺ ἐγὼ ἀποστέλλω τὸν ἄγγελόν μου πρὸ προσώπου σου, ἵνα φυλάξῃ σε ἐν τῇ ὁδῷ, ὅπως εἰσαγάγῃ σε εἰς τὴν γῆν, ἣν ἡτοίμασά σοι (Exodus 23:20).

184 HARTVIGSEN, *"Prepare the Way of the Lord"*, 131. If Exodus 23:20 is activated, the pronoun σου (Mark 1:2), refers to God's people as a corporate personality. If this verse is not activated, audience members may assume that they are addressed as individuals. See also M. A. TOLBERT, *Sowing the Gospel: Mark's World in Literary-Historical Perspective*, 242. SHINER, *Proclaiming the Gospel*, 184. Cf. VAN IERSEL, *Mark*, 94. PILGAARD, *Markusevangeliet*, 56.

185 Later, Mark 12:1–11 indicates that Jesus prepares the way of the Lord by demanding the fruits of the inhabitants of Israel (see also the parable of the sower). When Jesus is killed, like the

Because Malachi 3:1 employs the phrase πρὸ προσώπου μου instead of πρὸ προσώπου σου (Mark 1:2), this verse is probably not fully activated by Mark 1:2, but it may be primed or activated to a low degree.[186] In that case, it may prepare audience members for the speech acts which are uttered in Mark 1:3. In Malachi 3:1, the messenger prepares the way of the Lord who comes suddenly to his temple. Given that the context of Malachi 3:1 is primed or activated to a low degree at this point, audience members may relate the arrival of the Lord, which is suggested by Mark 1:3, to judgment.[187] However, the subject of final judgment is not explicitly developed in the Gospel of Mark.

The interrelationship between Mark 1:2 and Mark 1:3 indicates that the voice in the wilderness corresponds to the messenger in the previous verse. This character utters two directive points, commanding his addressees to "[p]repare the way of the Lord, make his paths straight" (Mark 1:3). Through these speech acts, a goal is presented (the arrival of the Lord) as well as two plans to achieve this goal (the actions requested in Mark 1:3). Against this framework, the Lord for whom the way is prepared is God, Jesus is the messenger, and audience members are requested to prepare for the arrival of the Lord. These verses thus seem "to encourage audience members to take part in God's plan to initiate a new Exodus and possibly a new covenant that prepares for and probably coincides with the arrival of God."[188] Along these lines, Mark 1:2–3 engages audience members in two manners. (1) They are involved in God's saving purposes as the ones who are guarded and cared for on their way to the Promised Land. (2) They are encouraged to join God's project by preparing his way so that he may come. When audience members hear the Longer Ending of the Gospel of Mark, they may interpret Jesus' commission against this backdrop. In that case, proclamation, which may lead to belief and baptism, constitutes one manner in which God's project is implemented.[189]

When audience members hear Mark 1:4, they may realize that John the Baptist embodies the messenger and the voice in the wilderness too,[190] but through his proclamation and baptisms John also performs actions that prepare the way of the Lord. In this manner, John fuses the roles of sender and receiver in Mark 1:3.[191] Audience members may realize that John's proclamation consti-

---

prophets and John the Baptist, the Lord arrives to destroy those who killed his son. See also TOLBERT, *Sowing the Gospel*, 236, 240. HARTVIGSEN, *"Prepare the Way of the Lord"*, 456.

186 On further details, see my analysis of Mark 1:2–3 in HARTVIGSEN, *"Prepare the Way of the Lord"*, 128–135.
187 On related views, see COLLINS, *Mark*, 136.
188 HARTVIGSEN, *"Prepare the Way of the Lord"*, 134.
189 See below.
190 See also DONAHUE/HARRINGTON, *Mark*, 61. COLLINS, *Mark*, 136–137.
191 On this approach to the role of John the Baptist, see HARTVIGSEN, *"Prepare the Way of the Lord"*, 135–139.

tutes a sub-plan related to God's main project.[192] John's sub-plan enables him to reach his sub-goals, i.e. repentance and baptism, which in turn entail forgiveness of sins. These sub-goals all contribute to realization of the ultimate goal, i.e. the arrival of God.[193] As a result, audience members may interpret βάπτισμα μετανοίας εἰς ἄφεσιν ἁμαρτιῶν (Mark 1:4) as a response to God's initiative through John the Baptist (interpretation 3 of the phrase βάπτισμα μετανοίας, which was presented previously). When audience members hear that people confess their sins in Mark 1:5, they may realize, however, that those who are baptized ask for forgiveness of their sins as well. Interpretations 2 and 3 of the phrase βάπτισμα μετανοίας, which were presented previously, are therefore probably combined. This interpretation is supported by the prepositional phrase εἰς ἄφεσιν ἁμαρτιῶν, which indicates the purpose of the baptism.[194]

Through Mark 1:5, audience members are informed about the success of John's sub-plan and the immediate realization of his sub-goals.[195] "And people from the whole Judean countryside and all the people of Jerusalem were going out to him, and were baptized by him in the river Jordan, confessing their sins."[196] On the basis of Mark 1:4–5, audience members learn that John's baptisms require that those who are baptized confess their sins and repent so that their sins will be forgiven.[197] What is more, the passive ἐβαπτίζοντο ὑπ' αὐτοῦ points out that this rite is administered by John the Baptist.[198] If Malachi 3:1

---

192 The subsequent description of John the Baptist (Mark 1:6) may underscore that John continues the work of God's previous slaves, the prophets. (See Mark 9:11–13; 12:1–11). See also TOLBERT, *Sowing the Gospel*, 244. On John the Baptist as a prophet and eschatological agent, see COLLINS, *Mark*, 142.

193 On the fact that John the Baptist prepared the way of God, see STEGEMANN, *Die Essener*, 299. Audience members may later realize that they are also urged to prepare the way for Jesus when he returns (Mark 8:38; Mark 13). See HARTVIGSEN, *"Prepare the Way of the Lord"*, 133, note 594.

194 See DONAHUE/HARRINGTON, *Mark*, 62. COLLINS, *Mark*, 139.

195 On the popularity of John the Baptist, see DONAHUE/HARRINGTON, *Mark*, 62.

196 καὶ ἐξεπορεύετο πρὸς αὐτὸν πᾶσα ἡ Ἰουδαία χώρα καὶ οἱ Ἱεροσολυμῖται πάντες, καὶ ἐβαπτίζοντο ὑπ' αὐτοῦ ἐν τῷ Ἰορδάνῃ ποταμῷ ἐξομολογούμενοι τὰς ἁμαρτίας αὐτῶν.

197 Collins points out different manners in which one can interpret the phrase ἐξομολογούμενοι τὰς ἁμαρτίας αὐτῶν (Mark 1:5). "It could refer to a communal or an individual confession; the confession may be public, in the hearing of all present, or private, in the hearing of John alone. It could be a confession of general sinfulness, of specific sins for which the people as a whole considered themselves accountable, of specific but unnamed sins, or of specific sins described in more or less detail." COLLINS, *Mark*, 142. See also p. 143–145. On the private and public confession of sin, see also DONAHUE/HARRINGTON, *Mark*, 63. According to Donahue and Harrington, this confession precedes baptism. IIDEM, *Mark*, 62. However, this chronology is not explicitly stated in Mark 1:5.

198 See also COLLINS, *Mark*, 142. According to Collins, "[t]he ritual administered by John, immersion in the Jordan River, has its model, as a ritual action, in the commandments in the book of Leviticus that those to be cleansed of various kinds of ritual impurity are to bathe their bodies in water." EADEM, *Mark*, 138. Cf. DONAHUE/HARRINGTON, *Mark*, 62. According to Donahue

and subsequent verses were activated by Mark 1:2, audience members may regard this baptism as a way to join the project of God and thus escape God's judgment and subsequent punishment,[199] but the final judgment is not explicitly mentioned by John.

In Mark 1:7–8, John the Baptist introduces a more powerful character who is coming after him. Through this speech act, audience members may realize that this character may also embody the role of the Lord who is coming to his temple. John contrasts his own baptisms with water in the Jordan River with the upcoming baptisms that will take place by means of the Holy Spirit. John's utterance may evoke Ezekiel 36:25–27.[200]

> I will sprinkle clean water upon you, and you shall be clean from all your uncleannesses, and from all your idols I will cleanse you. A new heart I will give you, and a new spirit I will put within you; and I will remove from your body the heart of stone and give you a heart of flesh. I will put my spirit within you, and make you follow my statutes and be careful to observe my ordinances.

If these verses are activated, audience members may realize that God is about to restore his people through a new act of salvation. At this point, the kingdom of God has not yet been introduced to audience members. When they subsequently hear Jesus' proclamation in Mark 1:15, they may realize that John's speech acts have eschatological implications, because in Mark 1:15 repentance is related to the establishment of the kingdom of God.[201] Yet in the Gospel of Mark, John does not mention eschatological judgment.[202]

If audience members later realize the link between the projects of God, John the Baptist, and Jesus, and their aim, i.e. the arrival of the Lord, John's speech act in Mark 1:8 may refer to two phases in the eschatological mission initiated by God. The first stage is connected with John the Baptist; the second is related to the stronger character, which may refer to God or Jesus.[203] The first phase is characterized by baptism with water and confession of sins, the second is dis-

---

and Harrington, it is problematic to regard water rituals of purification or proselyte baptism as the backdrop of John's baptism. "Ritual washings are self-administered and repeated frequently, while John is the agent of a baptism that is not repeated, prepares for the eschaton, and implies moral conversion."

199 On confession of sins as a plea for being spared from/in the eschatological judgment, see COLLINS, *Mark*, 144–145.

200 On this pericope, see DONAHUE/HARRINGTON, *Mark*, 64. COLLINS, *Mark*, 139. PILGAARD, *Markusevangeliet*, 61.

201 On the eschatological implications of Ezekiel 36, see COLLINS, *Mark*, 139. According to Pilgaard, the command to repent is a central feature of the proclamation of John the Baptist, Jesus, and his disciples (Mark 1:4; 1:15; 6:12). On the basis of the last two verses, he concludes that the request to repent is an encouragement to turn back to God. PILGAARD, *Markusevangeliet*, 59.

202 DONAHUE/HARRINGTON, *Mark*, 63.

203 See IIDEM, *Mark*, 63. They evaluate both alternatives.

tinguished by baptism with the Holy Spirit. In this case, the first stage prepares for the second.[204]

Audience members who are familiar with Christian baptismal liturgy, Acts 1:2–9; 2:1–38, or related oral traditions may associate baptism with the Holy Spirit (Mark 1:8b) with Christian baptism.[205] During an oral performance of Mark 1:8b, this inclination may be encouraged by the pronoun ὑμᾶς,[206] because this pronoun may collapse the membrane separating the text-internal and the text-external communication situations during an oral performance of the Gospel. The future tense of the verb (βαπτίσει) may furthermore facilitate this tendency. It follows that audience members may think that they are addressed by John's prediction and that it may refer to their own upcoming or previously performed baptism.[207]

Through Mark 1:9 audience members learn that Jesus is baptized by John.[208] On the basis of Mark 1:4, audience members may infer that Jesus' baptism is an act of repentance, but audience members do not hear Jesus confess his sins. They may therefore tend to view this action as an indication that Jesus acknowledges John's sub-plan and sub-goals.[209] Against this backdrop, Jesus' baptism can be considered as a sign that Jesus makes a joint project with John the Baptist in order to prepare the way of the Lord (Mark 1:2–3). Indirectly, Jesus' baptism implies that he commits himself to the mission initiated by God. Jesus' commitment to God's undertaking is probably confirmed by the following events.

---

204 On the two stages, see COLLINS, *Mark*, 146. PILGAARD, *Markusevangeliet*, 61. Both Collins and Pilgaard think the stronger character refers to Jesus. STEGEMANN, *Die Essener*, 299: "Der überaus Starke [...] war für den *historischen* Täufer allerdings weder Jesus noch irgendeine messianische Gestalt, sondern kein anderer als Gott selbst, als dessen Vorboten und Wegbereiter Johannes sich betrachtete" (italics mine).

205 See also § 6.1. Baptism in the Gospel of Matthew Prior to 28:16–20.

206 See also SHINER, *Proclaiming the Gospel*, 185–186. Citation from p. 185. "The first half of John's proclamation is addressed to those listening to John in the narrative world. It is unlikely any of us in the audience were baptized by John. The second half erupts from the story world into the present. Nobody in John's audience was baptized with the Holy Spirit. Within the Gospel, Jesus does not baptize anyone with the Holy Spirit. It is only in the post-story-world reality of the Christian audience that Jesus baptizes with Holy Spirit."

207 According to Collins, "[t]he reference to baptism in the Holy Spirit in v. 8 would have called to mind the ritual of initiation into the community of the followers of Jesus (1 Cor 6:11; Acts 2:38)." COLLINS, *Mark*, 147. On related views, see also D. LÜHRMANN, *Das Markusevangelium*, 36. Cf. VAN IERSEL, *Mark*, 98. According to van Iersel, this utterance does not refer to Christian baptism, nor to the outpouring of the Holy Spirit at Pentecost. Furthermore, the pronoun does not denote Jesus' followers, but people from Judea or Jerusalem who were baptized by John.

208 Regarding Jesus' baptism, see H. D. BETZ, "Jesus' Baptism and the Origins of the Christian Ritual" in this publication, 377–396.

209 According to Donahue and Harrington, this portrait of Jesus indicates that he has a feeling of solidarity with the sinful human condition. DONAHUE/HARRINGTON, *Mark*, 65. See also PILGAARD, *Markusevangeliet*, 63.

In Mark 1:10, the extradiegetic narrator focuses on actions that take place when Jesus comes up out of the water.[210] Audience members observe this event through Jesus' eyes, i.e. they experience that the Holy Spirit descends upon him (Mark 1:10). In Mark 1:11, the same perspective is kept when the voice from heaven announces the identity of Jesus. For that reason, audience members seemingly hear what Jesus hears. As I mentioned with regard to the Gospel of Matthew, audience members may interpret this event as a model for their own baptism, where they were endowed with the Holy Spirit. Moreover, if audience members are familiar with the idea that Christians may be considered sons of God, the pronouns σὺ εἶ ὁ υἱός μου ὁ ἀγαπητός, ἐν **σοὶ** εὐδόκησα/"**You** [sg.] are my Son, the Beloved; with **you** [sg.] I am well pleased'" (Mark 1:11, my emphasis) may substantiate the idea that this status is conferred on them through baptism.[211]

If audience members regard Jesus' baptism and the subsequent vision as two separate incidents, they will probably interpret the latter episode primarily as a Christological event, focusing on Jesus' appointment as the Messiah (Psalm 2:7).[212] However, Jesus' baptism and the surrounding occurrences are interrelated. By being baptized by John, Jesus acknowledges John's and God's joint project. God's speech act may thus confirm that God is pleased with Jesus' commitment to implement his goal, and the endowment with the Holy Spirit can be viewed as a way of equipping Jesus so that he is able to promote their common goal, i.e. the arrival of the Lord.[213] Similarly, audience members may realize that they, through their baptism, show their obligation to God, and that they are endowed with the Holy Spirit so that they may promote God's mission (Mark 13:11).

The projects of Jesus and John the Baptist are interrelated in the Markan world, i.e. they have both committed themselves to God, but their proclamation is not identical.[214] John proclaims "a baptism of repentance for the forgiveness of sins" (Mark 1:4), whereas Jesus' proclamation is cited in the following manner: "The time is fulfilled, and the kingdom of God has come near; repent, and

---

210 Similar to Matthew 3:16, the phrase ἀναβαίνων ἐκ τοῦ ὕδατος may indicate that Jesus was baptized by means of submersion or immersion. On the fact that the focus "is on Jesus' vision and the voice from heaven," see also DONAHUE/HARRINGTON, *Mark*, 64. On related views, see LÜHRMANN, *Das Markusevangelium*, 36.

211 Cf. Matthew 3:17 οὗτός ἐστιν ὁ υἱός μου ὁ ἀγαπητός, ἐν ᾧ εὐδόκησα/"This is my Son, the Beloved, with whom I am well pleased." On the idea that this status was associated with baptism, see COLLINS, *Mark*, 147.

212 See also EADEM, *Mark*, 150.

213 If Mark 1:10 activates Mark 1:8, audience members may realize that Jesus is baptized with the Holy Spirit, not the one who baptizes with the Holy Spirit. See TOLBERT, *Sowing the Gospel*, 110. On related views, VAN IERSEL, *Mark*, 99.

214 Mark 1:4; 1:15. See also STEGEMANN, *Die Essener*, 317. Cf. Matthew 3:2; 4:17. In Matthew the proclamation is identical.

believe in the good news" (Mark 1:15). Accordingly, John the Baptist focuses on repentance as it is manifested in confession of sins and baptism. In the Gospel of Mark Jesus does not baptize. He presents repentance and belief as the proper response to the impending kingdom of God.[215] When audience members hear the Longer Ending, they may realize that these elements are interrelated, because baptism and belief are both presented as necessary conditions for salvation (Mark 16:16).

In the Markan world, the consequences of the endowment with the Holy Spirit are elaborated in different ways. The Holy Spirit guides Jesus' actions (Mark 1:12–13) and Jesus presents himself as a person who is "possessed" by the Holy Spirit (3:20–30). If Isaiah 61:1–2 (LXX) was primed or activated by Mark 1:1, audience members may interpret Jesus' baptism and subsequent actions against the following backdrop:

> The Spirit of the Lord is upon me, because he has anointed me; He has sent me to proclaim good news to the poor, To heal those whose hearts are broken, To proclaim release to the captives, The recovery of sight to the blind, To announce the year of the Lord's favor, And the day of recompense of our God, To comfort all who mourn … (Isaiah 61:1–2).[216]

Activation of these verses may also occur because the quotation attributed to the prophet Isaiah in Mark 1:2–3 drew attention to the prophecies in this book. In this way, audience members may associate the activities of Jesus (and John) with prophecies found in Isaiah.[217] Along these lines, the Spirit is put upon Jesus during his baptism so that he may proclaim the good news of the kingdom of God (Mark 1:14–15) and do mighty deeds, such as healings and exorcisms, which illustrate the imminent kingdom of God.[218] It appears that the endowment with the Holy Spirit during his baptism makes Jesus superior to John the Baptist.[219]

6.4. Baptism in the Context of Mark 16:14–20

When audience members hear Jesus' speech act on baptism in Mark 16:16, "[t]he one who believes and is baptized will be saved,"[220] they may recall previous statements on baptism in the Gospel of Mark, above all if they have been preoccu-

---

215 Collins states that Isaiah 40:3 and Jesus' pronouncement in Mark 1:15 both imply a final visitation. "According to Mark, the expected response is twofold: the acceptance of the baptism of repentance proclaimed by John and the repentance and trust in the good news called for by Jesus." COLLINS, *Mark*, 138.
216 Translation by EADEM, *Mark*, 149.
217 On related views, see EADEM, *Mark*, 149.
218 On related views, see STEGEMANN, *Die Essener*, 323–330.
219 See also VAN IERSEL, *Mark*, 100.
220 ὁ πιστεύσας καὶ βαπτισθεὶς σωθήσεται.

pied with baptism from the outset of the performance. Furthermore, audience members will most likely relate this utterance to the immediate context of Mark 16:16.

In Mark 16:14, Jesus is reunited with the eleven and he reproaches them for their unbelief. In the Gospel of Mark, belief, or lack of such, constitutes an important theme. Faith forms the central ingredient of Jesus' proclamation of the good news of God, but it also comprises the intended perlocutionary effect of this proclamation (Mark 1:14–15). In addition, belief is related to mighty deeds (Mark 5:36; 9:23–24, both including contexts, and 11:23–24).[221] In the Gospel of Mark, it seems to be an underlying idea that people may respond to Jesus' mighty deeds, which illustrate the kingdom of God, in two manners, i.e. with belief or unbelief. Despite their close association with Jesus, the disciples may thus nevertheless display lack of faith when they experience one of his mighty deeds (Mark 4:40). In the Longer Ending, the belief/unbelief of Jesus' adherents once more constitutes a major theme,[222] but as indicated by Mark 16:14b this aspect now refers to the manner in which the eleven respond to information about the ultimate mighty deed, namely the resurrection.[223]

After Jesus reproaches the disciples for their lack of belief (Mark 16:14), he immediately commissions them (Mark 16:15–18).[224] Audience members may infer that Jesus' appearance to the disciples convinces them that he was actually raised from the dead. Jesus' emergence in the narrative world may on another level also prove the reality of his resurrection to audience members who function as invisible witnesses in the Markan world.[225] The summary of Jesus' directive points assumes that he has authority to utter this reprimand. It follows that Jesus re-establishes his presence and authority in the Markan world through

---

221 The verb πιστεύω was also employed in Mark 9:42; 11:31; 13:21 and 15:32.

222 On belief/unbelief as a major theme, see UPTON, *Hearing Mark's Endings*, 157. KELHOFFER, *Miracle and Mission*, 79. According to Collins, "[t]he censuring of the disciples' unbelief and hardness of heart is harsh but does not go far beyond the characterization of the disciples in Mark." COLLINS, *Mark*, 808–809.

223 See also PILGAARD, *Markusevangeliet*, 390. Parker disagrees on this point. "This persistent unbelief and hardness of heart may seem to be in accord with the disciples' lack of belief (4.40) and particularly with the women's response to the announcement of the resurrection at 16.8. But this is not so. In the first place, as has just been said, it is an important theme of Mark that everything will make sense for the disciples only after the resurrection. In the second, the Markan disciples' problem is not that [...] they are unbelieving, but that they do not understand what it is they are to believe." PARKER, *The Living Text*, 140.

224 In Codex W, the disciples reply to Jesus' scolding and he answers them. See also UPTON, *Hearing Mark's Endings*, 164. Thus, the transition between Mark 16:14 and 16:15 is less abrupt.

225 According to Upton, "[t]he audience, cast into doubt by the lack of faith of the disciples in the earlier sections, can now experience some relief as they finally accept from the authoritative Jesus the reality of the resurrection. For the implied audience of the Markan community such information would be both vital and well known, the very basis of their faith." UPTON, *Hearing Mark's Endings*, 163.

Mark 16:14,[226] and these two elements serve as the foundation for the subsequent commission of the eleven. In other words, Jesus has sufficient authority to utter these commands.[227]

The noun εὐαγγέλιον in Mark 16:15 may prime or activate Mark 1:1; 1:14–15; 8:35; 10:29; 13:10; 14:9 and their contexts. The verb κηρύσσω may furthermore prime or activate Mark 1:4; 1:7; 1:14; 1:38–39; 1:45; 3:14; 5:20; 6:12; 7:36; 13:10; 14:9 and their surrounding verses. If these verses are activated, they evoke the idea of different characters who contribute to the establishment of the kingdom of God in diverse manners. It is against this backdrop audience members hear Jesus commission his adherents for the last time (cf. Mark 3:14ff., 6:7–12).

The verb κηρύσσω is inflected in the second person plural, which may collapse the membrane separating the text-internal and the text-external communication situation. Audience members may hence process this speech act as if it is directed to them as well as to the eleven.[228] This effect is probably enhanced by the fact that audience members are able to perform the requested action in the real world ("Go into all the world and proclaim the good news to the whole creation," Mark 16:15b).[229] In this fashion, audience members may consider themselves to be commissioned by Jesus to continue his undertaking by proclaiming the good news (of God) (Mark 1:14–15) to the whole creation (Mark 16:15). If audience members take on this task and hear the Gospel of Mark several times, they may focus on Jesus and try to emulate him and his actions.

Through Mark 16:16, Jesus utters two speech acts, one promise and one warning or threat,[230] which at the same time predict the following two perlocutionary effects of the proclamation of his adherents:[231] (1) Belief and baptism will lead to salvation. (2) Lack of belief will lead to condemnation.[232] In this context, audience members may think that salvation refers to eternal salva-

---

226 See also EADEM, *Hearing Mark's Endings*, 164.

227 See also EADEM, *Hearing Mark's Endings*, 165.

228 On the fact that these speech acts can be interpreted on two levels, see EADEM, *Hearing Mark's Endings*, 165.

229 On this approach, see HARTVIGSEN, *"Prepare the Way of the Lord"*, 75.

230 COLLINS, *Mark*, 810.

231 According to Collins, Jesus utters a prophetic saying with regard to the responses the disciples will encounter. She claims that "the saying functions to reassure the disciples that their proclamation will be effective, bringing salvation to those who respond favourably and judgment to those who reject their message." Upton suggests that "[t]he perlocutionary effect on the audience could be intended to reinforce the rebuke of the earlier verses, by laying down rather stringent ground rules for inclusion in the Markan community. Such a response would be supported by the view of Mary Ann Beavis that 'since the Gospel is patently the production of an early Christian missionary/teacher, it might originally [have] been used ("performed") in missionary preaching' (189:175)." UPTON, *Hearing Mark's Endings*, 166.

232 According to Pilgaard, the reference to baptism may indicate that the context of this utterance is missionary activity. PILGAARD, *Markusevangeliet*, 390.

tion, an assumption which is probably sustained by the subsequent focus on condemnation. In the Gospel of Mark, the final judgment is not mentioned alongside baptism; but it was indicated by Mark 9:43–50. In these verses, fire was mentioned, and going to hell was presented as the contrast to entering the kingdom of God. On the basis of the wording of Mark 16:16, audience members will probably infer that the final judgment constitutes the circumstance to which Jesus' utterance refers. Eschatology thus appears to be an important backdrop of baptism in the Longer Ending.[233] Audience members who perceive this connection may regard belief and baptism as the key to entering into the kingdom of God and possibly the community of believers, but eschatology is the primary focus of Mark 16:16.

If audience members remember the prologue and the rest of the Gospel of Mark, they may realize that Jesus' adherents are encouraged to perform actions which combine the efforts of Jesus and John the Baptist in order to save people from condemnation. They will proclaim like Jesus and John, and baptize like John. In the Gospel of Mark, belief is viewed as one of the proper responses to the good news of God (Mark 1:14–15). This news pertains to the imminent kingdom of God, which manifests itself through Jesus' mighty deeds in the Holy Spirit (Mark 3:20–30). Repentance, another aspect of Jesus' proclamation, is also an integral part of John's proclamation (Mark 1:4–5). If these facets are activated by Mark 16:15, audience members may interpret Jesus' utterance on baptism in Mark 16:16a in the following manner: Baptism entails repentance, it requires confession of sins, and it transmits forgiveness of sins (Mark 1:4–5). Repentance and belief constitute the proper response to the news about the impending kingdom of God (Mark 1:15). If Jesus' baptism (Mark 1:9–11) is activated by Mark 16:16a, audience members may associate baptism with the endowment of the Holy Spirit and sonship too.

Baptism is not regarded as a prerequisite for salvation in the Gospel of Mark,[234] but in the Longer Ending this ritual is highlighted because it is presented as one of two conditions for salvation.[235] As the contrasting responses to the proclamation indicate (Mark 16:16), belief and baptism will provide rescue from condemnation. Audience members may therefore infer that baptism will save them from the wrath of God at the final judgment. Against this backdrop, Jesus' promise may function differently with regard to individual audience

---

233 On related views, see IDEM, *Markusevangeliet*, 390.

234 On the salvific implications of baptism, see KELHOFFER, *Miracle and Mission*, 101. See also UPTON, *Hearing Mark's Endings*, 166.

235 Drawing on KELHOFFER, *Miracle and Mission*, 101–102, Collins claims that "[t]he linking of believing and being baptized reflects widespread practice in the communities of those who accepted Jesus as the messiah or as Lord. According to Luke-Acts, baptism is the means by which acceptance of the proclamation and repentance are expressed, sins are forgiven, and the gift of the Holy Spirit is granted (Acts 2:37–38)." COLLINS, *Mark*, 810. On baptism as a condition for salvation, see UPTON, *Hearing Mark's Endings*, 166.

members. If audience members have responded by belief and baptism to previous proclamation, they may think that Jesus' promise guarantees their eternal salvation. If audience members believe, but have not yet been baptized, Jesus' commissive point may encourage them to carry out this act of commitment. If audience members do not believe, they may change their minds, become believers and be baptized. If audience members resist believing, they will neither be persuaded to get baptized nor acknowledge the threat of condemnation.

In the Longer Ending, the proclamation of Jesus' adherents and the divergent responses to their message are in focus. On the basis of their experiences of baptism in the real world, audience members may, however, infer that belief and baptism will incorporate new members into the community of Jesus' adherents, especially if they regard Jesus' baptism (Mark 1:9–11) as an act of commitment to God's and John's joint project. In that case, those who emulate Jesus' baptism will confirm their commitment to the mission of Jesus, John the Baptist, and their previous adherents, a joint project that was initiated by God and carried out by earlier prophets. Accordingly, Jesus' utterance on baptism is associated with ecclesiology, and specifically with the manner in which the community is expanded. However, this aspect is not the main focus of this speech act.

If audience members are familiar with Acts 1:2–9; 2:1–38 or related oral traditions, the theme of eschatology may influence their interpretation of Jesus' promises in Mark 16:17–18 as well. In that case, these signs will be regarded as evidence of the outpouring of the Holy Spirit in the last days (Acts 2:17–21), which empowers Jesus' adherents to speak in different languages etc. On the basis of Mark 1:8–11 and Acts 2:38, audience members may believe that these characters were empowered by the Holy Spirit during their baptism so that they will be capable of performing these deeds. Many of these mighty deeds may prime or activate actions that were performed earlier by Jesus, such as exorcisms (Mark 1:23–27; 1:32–34; 1:39; 5:1–20; 7:24–30; 9:14–27; 16:9) and healings (Mark 1:29–34; 1:40–45; 2:1–12; 3:1–6; 3:10; 5:21–43; 6:5; 6:53–56; 7:31–37; 8:22–26; 10:46–52). Because these actions were carried out earlier by Jesus in the Holy Spirit, audience members may consider these signs as evidence that these characters continue Jesus' mission.[236] This aspect is also supported by the phrase ἐν τῷ ὀνόματί μου (Mark 16:17), which indicates that these characters represent Jesus and may perhaps utter his name when they perform these actions.[237]

On the basis of the future tense of the verbs in Mark 16:16–18, audience members may assume that the mission of these characters will take place in the future. This tense may moreover lead audience members who believe and are

---

[236] Kelhoffer and Collins assert that in Acts the ability to speak in various languages is associated with the Holy Spirit, but in the Longer Ending, Jesus empowers his adherents in this fashion. KELHOFFER, *Miracle and Mission*, 267–268. COLLINS, *Mark*, 814.

[237] On the latter aspect, see PILGAARD, *Markusevangeliet*, 390.

baptized to think about themselves and members of their community as the addressees of Jesus' speech acts. If they do, Jesus' predictions in Mark 16:16 may function in the following ways: (1) As a prediction of the twofold response to their missionary activity. (2) As an assurance of eternal salvation for those who believe and are baptized.[238] In the same manner as Jesus promoted the kingdom of God through mighty deeds, Jesus' adherents, who are baptized with the Holy Spirit, are empowered to promote the kingdom of God by speaking "in new tongues" and by mighty deeds (Mark 16:17–18).

In Mark 16:19, the extradiegetic narrator relates an event which underscores the authority of Jesus and its origin. Christology is therefore in focus. This happening reflects back on Jesus' previous speech acts. The phrase ἐκάθισεν ἐκ δεξιῶν τοῦ θεοῦ may prime or activate Jesus' teaching in Mark 12:35–37. At that point, audience members noticed that Jesus claimed the position at God's right hand.[239] Through Mark 16:19, the extradiegetic narrator indicates that Jesus' former teaching was accurate. Audience members may furthermore view this event as a partial fulfillment of Jesus' prediction in Mark 14:62.[240] If audience members are familiar with traditions related in for instance Psalm (LXX) 17:36; 19:7; 43:4; 47:11, they may interpret Jesus' location as a position which allows him access to the power of God. Through this verse, Jesus' relation to God and hence the origin of his authority are emphasized.[241]

Through Mark 16:20, the extradiegetic narrator relates the actual perlocutionary effect of Jesus' command in Mark 16:15. Audience members will probably conclude that Jesus' previous directive point was successful because "they went out and proclaimed everywhere" (Mark 16:20a). In this manner, the eleven show commitment and enthusiasm concerning the assignment given by Jesus. At the beginning of the Longer Ending, this outcome was not easy to predict. The disciples did not believe those who had seen Jesus, and audience members could for that reason regard them as being at risk of condemnation (Mark 16:16b). Yet audience members may infer that the encounter with the risen Lord turned their unbelief into belief,[242] which together with baptism will secure their salvation.

Through an assertive point, audience members are informed that "the Lord worked with them and confirmed the word by the accompanying signs" (Mark 16:20b). In this way, the missionary activities of the eleven are affirmed by the Lord, whose power and authority were illustrated through the previous descrip-

---

238 According to Upton, "the implied author is attempting to carry out a dual function – of encouraging and teaching the faithful within the community, and welcoming those outside who are showing interest in learning 'the way' of Jesus." UPTON, *Hearing Mark's Endings*, 167.
239 HARTVIGSEN, *"Prepare the Way of the Lord"*, 476.
240 See COLLINS, *Mark*, 816–817.
241 For related views, see UPTON, *Hearing Mark's Endings*, 168.
242 See also COLLINS, *Mark*, 817.

tion of the enthronement in heaven. Jesus' continued power on earth is in turn verified through the signs accompanying the missionary activity of his adherents. The perlocutionary effect of the proclamation, i.e. belief and baptism, is not mentioned at this point. However, by connecting the missionary activities of these characters to Jesus' ability to support his adherents, ecclesiology and Christology are interrelated.

7. When the End is Not the End

7.1. Baptism as a Link between the Gospel Worlds and the Real World of Audience Members

Through Matthew 28:16–20 and Mark 16:14–20, oral performances of the Gospel of Matthew and Mark come to an end. At these moments, the extradiegetic narrator reunites Jesus and the disciples, but the performances of these endings also constitute two crucial points where the membrane separating the Gospel worlds from the real world of audience members collapses. On the basis of this experience, audience members may perceive their own lives in the real world as the logical continuation of the way of life demonstrated by Jesus and his adherents in the Gospel worlds. If they recognize this link, audience members may endeavour to carry out actions which are in keeping with the joint project, plan, goal, and values of these formative figures.[243]

As I pointed out in the previous analysis, Jesus' commissions encourage the eleven disciples situated in the Gospel worlds, and indirectly audience members, to join or to continue his mission. I have earlier suggested that these commissions may communicate in different ways with audience members, depending on their status as non-believers, catechumens, baptized, or office holders. Interpretations of the function of baptism in these commissions may moreover rely on the recollection of previous references to baptism in the Gospels or in oral traditions, but these interpretations may also reflect the personal experiences of audience members with baptisms in the real world. Consequently, the concept of baptism integrates what audience members learn about baptism through the oral performances of the Gospels with their individual experiences of baptisms

---

[243] "The resurrection marks the end of Jesus' earthly time and inaugurates the time of the post-Easter church. In accord with this our pericope (i) looks back to summarize Jesus' ministry as a whole ('all I have commanded you') and (ii) looks forward to the time of the church to outline a programme. So 28:16–20 relates two periods which, although different, have the same Lord and so the same mission." DAVIES/ALLISON, *Matthew*, 678. See also p. 688–689. According to Bornkamm, "[d]ie Szene bleibt vielmehr völlig offen auf die Gegenwart hin, die bis zur Vollendung der Welt währen wird, und auch Jesu Worte Mt 28:18–20 haben nicht den Character einer Abschiedsrede." BORNKAMM, "Der Auferstandene und der Irdische," 172. On related insights, see also FRANKEMÖLLE, *Matthäus Kommentar*, 537–538.

in the real world. Last but not least, baptism functions in divergent ways when the two commissions are performed, on the basis of the type of speech acts which contain the phrase, the contexts in which it is uttered, and how it is related to theological topics such as Christology, ecclesiology, and eschatology.

In the two Gospels, baptism is connected to the joint mission of God, John the Baptist, Jesus, and their adherents in divergent ways. In the comparison below, I will first point out an important similarity concerning how baptism is integrated into this mission, and then I will indicate the main differences.

7.2. Comparison of Baptism in Matthew 28:16–20 and Mark 16:14–20

According to Thomas M. Finn, "[t]he Christians to whom Mark, Matthew, and John addressed themselves tended to emphasize the baptism of Jesus in the Jordan as the way in which Christians entered the kingdom."[244] Although this statement is not directly verified by the manner in which baptism is presented in the endings of the Gospel of Matthew and Mark, my analysis from the perspective of audience members has indicated that it is plausible to view baptism as a way of entering into the community of believers and the kingdom of God. In the following paragraph, I will elaborate on this point.

Because mighty deeds performed by Jesus (and his adherents) in the Gospel worlds illustrate the imminent kingdom of God/heaven, audience members will probably conclude that this kingdom is manifested wherever Jesus and his followers gather.[245] This kingdom is also associated with the impending arrival of the Lord, at which time the kingdom will be fully materialized. The kingdom of God/heaven thus constitutes fluid, sacred space which is present wherever Jesus and his adherents are,[246] but it is conceived as a place which one can enter in the future as well. The community of believers and the kingdom of God/heaven are therefore interrelated.

In the Gospels of Mark and Matthew, baptism relates characters and audience members to both aspects of the kingdom, but the Gospels focus on different features. Matthew 28:19–20 emphasizes the worldly characteristics of the kingdom by relating baptism to the creation of disciples and their education. In this way, the expansion and sustenance of the community of believers are in focus. Mark 16:16 primarily links baptism with eternal salvation and hence the future entry into the kingdom. Furthermore, the phrase ὁ πιστεύσας καὶ βαπτισθεὶς σωθήσεται (Mark 16:16a) indicates that emphasis is put on individual salvation, not primarily on incorporation into the community of believers. Interpretations which indicate that baptism may function as an initiation rite

---

244 FINN, *From Death to Rebirth*, 146.
245 See HARTVIGSEN, *"Prepare the Way of the Lord"*, 600–601; STEWART, *Gathered around Jesus*, 210–219.
246 See HARTVIGSEN, *"Prepare the Way of the Lord"*, ibid.

may still suggest themselves on the basis of the focus on proclamation in Mark 16:15[247] and individual experiences audience members have had of the function of baptisms in the real world.

As I have indicated, the main differences between baptisms in Matthew 28:16–20 and Mark 16:14–20 reflect the manner in which these Gospels associate baptism with ecclesiology, eschatology, and Christology. In what follows, I will first deal with ecclesiology.

In Matthew 28, baptism is related to two aspects of ecclesiology, that is, the incorporation of new members into the community of believers and the sustenance of this community. (1) New disciples are created through baptism. (2) These disciples must learn to abide by the teaching of Jesus, the founder of the community. Because the membrane separating the real world of audience members from the Matthean world collapses during performances of this ending, Jesus' speech act on baptism indicates how audience members may continue the joint project of God, Jesus, John the Baptist, and their adherents in the real world by baptizing new members into the community of believers and by educating them.

In contrast, Mark's Longer Ending merely focuses on one aspect which connects baptism with ecclesiology, i.e. proclamation of the good news (Mark 16:15). On the basis of this Gospel, audience members may thus carry on the joint project of God, Jesus, John the Baptist, and their adherents in the real world through proclamation and baptism. In the Gospel of Mark, proclamation aims at expanding the community, and this means that baptism is connected with missionary activity. Baptism and belief constitute one of two possible responses to this proclamation (Mark 16:16a). In this context, ecclesiology will primarily be inferred by audience members on the basis of the common function of proclamation in the Gospel, but Jesus does not refer to discipleship or the like. Nor is the transmission of teaching that secures the continued existence of the community of believers in focus. It is rather the individual fate of the addressees which forms the main topic of this speech act. This leads to my subsequent reflections on the interrelationship between baptism and eschatology.

When audience members hear the Longer Ending of Mark, they may primarily regard the speech act on baptism as a confirmation of the importance of baptism in order to experience eternal salvation. Because of the imperative κηρύξατε in the second person plural and the future tense of the verb σῴζω, audience members may deduce that Jesus' promise encompasses their addressees as well as the addressees of the eleven. If they consider the propositional content of Jesus' promise as a universal fact, they may also include themselves in the promise of eternal salvation. The eschatology characterizing the Longer Ending of Mark indicates that this way of continuing the joint project of God,

---

247 See the paragraph on ecclesiology below.

Jesus, John the Baptist, and their adherents in the real world does not primarily aim at creating and sustaining a community of believers in the real world. Rather, it emphasizes the criteria of eternal salvation, that is, belief and baptism. In the Gospel of Mark, eternal salvation seems to be related to entry into the kingdom of God (Mark 9:40–50).

In the Longer Ending of Mark, baptism is primarily associated with eschatology because the apparent focus on eternal salvation or condemnation indicates that the final judgment constitutes the backdrop of Jesus' speech act on baptism, which promises salvation to those who believe and are baptized. In contrast, Jesus does not explicitly mention eschatology in Matthew 28:19. In the Gospel of Matthew, eschatology was primarily connected with the baptisms that were performed by John the Baptist and the powerful character in chapter 3. Against this backdrop, audience members may indirectly relate baptism to eschatology in Matthew 28:19, but Jesus seems to focus on the current and future life of the church.

The authority of Jesus' utterances on baptism intersects with the manner in which the Christology of these endings is presented in these Gospels. In Matthew 28:16–20, Jesus takes his authority for granted, a fact which may communicate convincingly with characters in the Matthean world and audience members who already believe that Jesus was raised by God. In the Longer Ending of the Gospel of Mark, Jesus seemingly takes for granted that he may proceed directly from a reprimand to a commission. However, the efforts of the extradiegetic narrator in Mark 16:19–20, which aim at establishing or re-establishing Jesus' authority, indicate that this narrator thinks it is necessary to convince his addressees, that is, audience members, about the nature of the authority of Jesus, the founder of the community. Jesus' utterance on baptism in the Longer Ending of Mark is voiced in a context which may reflect the previous lack of belief exhibited by Jesus' adherents in the Markan world. Against this backdrop, the description of the event taking place in heaven may confirm or re-establish the authority of the founder of the community of believers into which audience members are baptized or possibly will be baptized in the future.

In sum, the manner in which Jesus' adherents responded to the news of the empty tomb situated Jesus' utterances on baptisms in different contexts. These contexts generated divergent ways to construe the function of baptism, Jesus' continued role in the church, and the primary task of his adherents.

Bibliography

Aland, Kurt, "Der Schluß des Markusevangeliums," in: M. Sabbe (ed.), *L'Évangile selon Marc: Tradition et rédaction*, Leuven: Leuven University Press 1974, 435–470.

BARTH, GERHARD, *Die Taufe in frühchristlicher Zeit*, 2. verbesserte Auflage, Neukirchen-Vluyn: Neukirchener Verlag 2002.

BEASLEY-MURRAY, GEORGE R., *Baptism in the New Testament*, London: Macmillian 1963.

BEAVIS, MARY ANN, *Mark's Audience: The Literary and Social Setting of Mark 4:11–12* (JSNT.S 33), Sheffield: JSOT Press 1989.

BETZ, HANS DIETER, *The Sermon on the Mount: A Commentary on the Sermon on the Mount, Including the Sermon on the Plain (Matthew 5:3–7:27 and Luke 6:20–49)*, (Hermeneia), Minneapolis, Minn.: Fortress 1995.

BOBERTZ, CHARLES A., "Prolegomena to a Ritual/Liturgical Reading of the Gospel of Mark," in: Charles A. Bobertz/David Brakke (eds.), *Reading in Christian Communities: Essays on Interpretation in the Early Church*, Notre Dame: University of Notre Dame Press 2002, 174–187.

BORNKAMM, GÜNTHER, "Der Auferstandene und der Irdische Mt 28:16–20," in: Erich Dinkler (ed.), *Zeit und Geschichte: Dankesgabe an Rudolf Bultmann zum 80. Geburtstag*, Tübingen: J. C. B. Mohr 1964, 171–191.

BORTOLUSSI, MARISA and DIXON, PETER, *Psychonarratology: Foundations for the Empirical Study of Literary Response*, Cambridge: Cambridge University Press 2003.

BRADSHAW, PAUL, *Early Christian Worship: A Basic Introduction to Ideas and Practice*, Collegeville, Minn.: The Liturgical Press 1996.

BRADSHAW, PAUL F., *The Search for the Origins of Christian Worship: Sources and Methods for the Study of Early Liturgy*, revised and enlarged ed., London: SPCK 2002.

BRUNS, PETER, *Theodor von Mopsuestia. Katechetische Homilien*, Zweiter Teilband (FC 17/2), Freiburg i.B.: Herder 1995,

BUJARD, WALTER, *Stilanalytische Untersuchungen zum Kolosserbrief als Beitrag zur Methodik von Sprachvergleichen* (StUNT 11), Göttingen: Vandenhoeck & Ruprecht 1973.

BYRSKOG, SAMUEL, *Jesus the Only Teacher: Didactic Authority and Transmission in Ancient Israel, Ancient Judaism and the Matthean Community* (CB.NT 24), Stockholm: Almqvist & Wiksell International 1994.

COLLINS, ADELA YARBRO, *Mark: A Commentary* (Hermeneia), Minneapolis, Minn.: Fortress 2007.

CONYBEARE, FRED. C., "The Eusebian Form of the Text Matth. 28,19," in: *ZNW* 2 (1901) 275–288.

DAVIES, MARGARET, *Matthew* (Readings: A New Biblical Commentary), Sheffield: JSOT Press 1993.

DAVIES, WILLIAM DAVID and ALLISON, DALE C., *The Gospel According to Saint Matthew*, vol. III (ICC), Edinburgh: T & T Clark 1997.

DEWEY, JOANNA, "The Gospel of Mark as an Oral-Aural Event: Implications for Interpretation," in: Elizabeth Struthers Malbon/Edgar V. McKnight (eds.), *The New Literary Criticism and the New Testament* (JSNT.S 109), Sheffield: Sheffield Academic Press 1994, 145–163.

— "The Survival of Mark's Gospel: A Good Story?", in: *JBL* 123, no. 3 (2004) 495–507.

"Didache: The Teaching of the Twelve Apostles," in: Bart D. Ehrman (ed.), *The Apostolic Fathers: I Clement, II Clement, Ignatius, Ploycarp, Didache* (LCL 24), London: Harvard University Press 2003, 403–443.

DONAHUE, JOHN R. and HARRINGTON, DANIEL J., *The Gospel of Mark* (SP 2), Collegeville, Minn.: The Liturgical Press 2002.

FERGUSON, EVERETT, *Baptism in the Early Church: History, Theology, and Liturgy in the First Five Centuries*, Grand Rapids, Mich.: Eerdmans 2009.

FINN, THOMAS M., *From Death to Rebirth: Ritual and Conversion in Antiquity*, New York: Paulist Press 1997.

FRANCE, RICHARD THOMAS, *The Gospel According to Matthew: An Introduction and Commentary* (TNTC), Leicester: Inter-Varsity Press 1985.

FRANKEMÖLLE, HUBERT, *Matthäus Kommentar*, vol. 2, Düsseldorf: Patmos Verlag 1997.

GAMBLE, HARRY Y., *Books and Readers in the Early Church: A History of Early Christian Texts*, New Haven, Conn.: Yale University Press 1995.

GREEN, H. BENEDICT, *The Gospel According to Matthew in the Revised Standard Version* (NCB [NT]), London: Oxford University Press 1975.

HAGNER, DONALD A., *Matthew 14–28* (WBC 33B), Dallas, Tex.: Word Books 1995.

HARRINGTON, DANIEL J., *The Gospel of Matthew* (SP 1), Collegeville, Minn.: The Liturgical Press 1991.

HARTMAN, LARS, "Das Markusevangelium ‚für die lectio sollemnis im Gottesdienst abgefaßt'?" in: D. Hellholm (ed.), *Text-Centered New Testament Studies: Text-Theoretical Essays on Early Jewish and Early Christian Literature* (WUNT 102), Tübingen: Mohr Siebeck 1997, 25–51.

— *'Into the Name of the Lord Jesus:' Baptism in the Early Church* (SNTW), Edinburgh: T & T Clark 1997.

— *Markusevangeliet 8:27–16:20*, vol. 2b (KNT[U]), Stockholm: EFS-förlaget 2005 (Eng. ed. *Mark for the Nations. A Text- and Reader-Oriented Commentary*, Eugene, Ore.: Pickwick Publications [Wipf and Stock Publishers] 2010).

HARTVIGSEN, KIRSTEN MARIE, "'Prepare the Way of the Lord:' Towards a Cognitive Poetic Analysis of Audience Involvement with Characters and Events in the Markan World," PhD diss., University of Oslo 2009 (To be published by Walter de Gruyter (Berlin) in BZNW 2011).

— "Canon, Fanon, and the Markan Endings as Rewritten Scripture. Simulations of the Diverse Denouements of the Markan Plots on the Basis of the Manuscript Tradition", forthcoming.

HELLHOLM, DAVID, "Universalität und Partikularität: Die amplifikatorische Struktur von Römer 5,12–21," in: D. Sänger/U. Mell (eds.), *Paulus und Johannes: Exegetische Studien zur paulinischen und johanneischen Theologie und Literatur* (WUNT 198), Tübingen: Mohr Siebeck 2006, 217–269.

HOGAN, PATRICK COLM, *Cognitive Science, Literature, and the Arts: A Guide for Humanists*, New York: Routledge 2003.

— *The Mind and Its Stories: Narrative Universals and Human Emotion* (Studies in Emotion and Social Interaction), Cambridge: Cambridge University Press 2003.

HORSLEY, RICHARD A., *Hearing the Whole Story: The Politics of Plot in Mark's Gospel*, Louisville, Ky.: Westminster John Knox Press 2001.

HORSLEY, RICHARD A., DRAPER, JONATHAN A. and FOLEY, JOHN MILES (eds.), *Performing the Gospel: Orality, Memory, and Mark*, Minneapolis, Minn.: Fortress 2006.

VAN IERSEL, BAS M. F., *Mark: A Reader-Response Commentary*, London: T & T Clark 2004.

JOHNSON, MAXWELL E., *The Rites of Christian Initiation: Their Evolution and Interpretation*, Collegeville, Minn.: The Liturgical Press 1999.

KACZYNSKI, REINER, *Johannes Chrysostomus: Catecheses Baptismales: Taufkatechesen* (FC 6:1), Freiburg i.Br.: Herder 1992.

KELHOFFER, JAMES A., *Miracle and Mission: The Authentication of Missionaries and Their Message in the Longer Ending of Mark* (WUNT 2/112), Tübingen: Mohr Siebeck 2000.

Kingsbury, Jack Dean, "The Composition and Christology of Matt 28:16-20," in: *JBL* 93, no. 4 (1974) 573-584.

Kümmel, Werner Georg, *Introduction to the New Testament*, revised ed. (NTL), London: SCM Press 1975.

Lundhaug, Hugo, *Images of Rebirth: Cognitive Poetics and Transformational Soteriology in the Gospel of Philip and the Exegesis on the Soul* (NHMS 73), Leiden: Brill 2010.

Luz, Ulrich, *Das Evangelium nach Matthäus (Mt 1-7)*, (EKK I/1). Zurich: Benziger Verlag/Neukirchen-Vluyn: Neukirchener Verlag 1985.

— *Das Evangelium nach Matthäus (Mt 26-28)*, (EKK I/4), Düsseldorf/Zurich: Benziger Verlag/Neukirchen-Vluyn: Neukirchener Verlag 2002.

Lührmann, Dieter, *Das Markusevangelium* (HNT 3), Tübingen: J. C. B. Mohr (Paul Siebeck) 1987.

Marcus, Joel, *Mark 8-16: A New Translation with Introduction and Commentary* (Anchor Yale Bible 27A), New Haven, Conn.: Yale University Press 2009.

— *The Way of the Lord: Christological Exegesis of the Old Testament in the Gospel of Mark*, London: T & T Clark 2004.

Martyr, Justin, "Apologia I," in: Johann Carl Theodor Eqves de Otto (ed.), *Corpus Apologetarum Christianorum Saeculi Secundi*, Wiesbaden: Dr. Martin Sändig 1969, 1-193.

McDonnel, Kilian and Montague, George T., *Christian Initiation and Baptism in the Holy Spirit: Evidence from the First Eight Centuries*, 2nd revised editon, Collegeville, Minn.: The Liturgical Press 1994.

Meier, John P., "Two Disputed Questions in Matt 28:16-20," in: *JBL* 96, no. 3 (1977) 407-424.

Metzger, Bruce M., *A Textual Commentary on the Greek New Testament*, Stuttgart: Deutsche Bibelgesellschaft ²1994.

Nolland, John, "'In Such a Manner It Is Fitting for Us to Fulfil all Righteousness:' Reflections on the Place of Baptism in the Gospel of Matthew," in: Stanley E. Porter/Anthony R. Cross (eds.), *Baptism, the New Testament and the Church: Historical and Contemporary Studies in Honour of R. E. O. White* (JSNT.S 171), Sheffield: Sheffield Academic Press 1999, 63-80.

Oatley, Keith, *Best Laid Schemes: The Psychology of Emotions* (Studies in Emotion and Social Interaction), Cambridge: Cambridge University Press 1992.

— "Emotions and the Story Worlds of Fiction," in: Melanie C. Green, Jeffrey J. Strange and Timothy C. Brock (eds.), *Narrative Impact: Social and Cognitive Foundations*, Mahwah, N.J.: Lawrence Erlbaum Associates 2002, 39–69.

PARKER, DAVID C., *The Living Text of the Gospels*, Cambridge: Cambridge University Press 1997.

PILGAARD, AAGE, *Kommentar til Markusevangeliet* (Dansk kommentar til Det nye Testamente [DKNT 5]), Aarhus: Aarhus Universitetsforlag 2008.

RHOADS, DAVID, "Performance Criticism: An Emerging Methodology in Second Testament Studies – Part I," in: *BTB* 36, no. 3 (2006) 118–133.

— "Performance Criticism: An Emerging Methodology in Second Testament Studies – Part II," in: *BTB* 36, no. 4 (2006) 164–184.

SCHABERG, JANE, *The Father, the Son and the Holy Spirit: The Triadic Phrase in Matthew 28:19b* (SBL Dissertation Series), Chico: Scholars Press 1982.

SCHLEYER, DIETRICH, Tertullian, *De baptismo – De oratione* (FC 76), Turnhout: Brepols 2006.

The Shepherd of Hermas, in: BART D. EHRMAN (ed.), *The Apostolic Fathers: Epistle of Barnabas, Papias and Quadratus, Epistle to Diognetus, The Shepherd of Hermas* (LCL 25), Cambridge: Harvard University Press 2003.

SHIELL, WILLIAM DAVID, *Reading Acts: The Lector and the Early Christian Audience*, (Biblical Interpretation Series), Leiden – Boston: Brill 2004.

SHINER, WHITNEY, *Proclaiming the Gospel: First-Century Performance of Mark*, Harrisburg, Pa.: Trinity Press International 2003.

SNYDER, BOB, *Music and Memory: An Introduction*, Cambridge, Mass.: The MIT Press 2000.

STEGEMANN, HARTMUT, *Die Essener, Qumran, Johannes der Täufer und Jesus: Ein Sachbuch*, Herder/Spektrum, Freiburg: Herder 1993 (Eng. trans. as *The Library of Qumran. On the Essenes, Qumran, John the Baptist, and Jesus*, Grand Rapids, Mich./Cambridge, UK – Leiden/New York/Köln: Brill: 1998).

STEWART, ERIC C., *Gathered around Jesus: An Alternative Spatial Practice in the Gospel of Mark (Matrix)*, Eugen, Oreg.: Cascade Books 2009.

THYEN, HARTWIG, "ΒΑΠΤΙΣΜΑ ΜΕΤΑΝΟΙΑΣ ΕΙΣ ΑΦΕΣΙΝ ΑΜΑΡΤΙΩΝ," in: Erich Dinkler (ed.), *Zeit und Geschichte: Dankesgabe an Rudolf Bultmann zum 80. Geburtstag*, Tübingen: J. C. B Mohr (Paul Siebeck) 1964, 97–125.

TOLBERT, MARY ANN, *Sowing the Gospel: Mark's World in Literary-Historical Perspective*, Minneapolis, Minn.: Fortress 1996.

The Tripartite Tractate (Transl. Einar Thomassen), in: Marvin Meyer (ed.), *The Nag Hammadi Scriptures: The International Edition*, New York: HarperOne 2007, 57–101.

UPTON, BRIDGET GILFILLAN, *Hearing Mark's Endings: Listening to Ancient Popular Texts through Speech Act Theory* (Biblical Interpretation Series), Leiden: Brill 2006.

Baptismal Reflections in the Fourth Gospel

Turid Karlsen Seim

1. Introductory Remarks on Methodology

In the Fourth Gospel water symbolism is abundant and highly significant. However, it plays on a wide register of symbolic meaning. By tracing the expanding meaning of water through the Gospel narrative, Craig Koester shows how each successive appearance of water interprets others until blood and water flow from the body of Jesus on the cross.[1] Alan Culpepper rather underscores the diversity of applied meaning so that as the narrative progresses, water represents Jesus, revelation, new life, and the Spirit, which is the means of access to them all.[2] However, it remains a matter of dispute whether the Johannine preoccupation with water symbolism should be taken to indicate that baptism was an important water rite in the gospel's immediate context.

There is a vast literature debating sacraments or sacramentalism in the Fourth Gospel.[3] The various positions often reflect a particular ecclesiastical frame of reference whereby a sacrament is defined and ecclesiologically located. As Robert Kysar notes: "In the history of scholarship, one can easily recognize that interpreters writing out of a sacramental orientation ... tend to identify both the Eucharist and Baptism in Johannine passages, while those who are affiliated with non-sacramental traditions are inclined to deny and minimize such identifications".[4] True as this might be in many cases, there is a greater theological complexity at work. Rudolf Bultmann notably claimed that in an earlier phase of the development of the present text, the Fourth Gospel did not hold any mention of baptism. Possible references to baptism such as "water" in John 3:5 and "blood and water" in 19:34, were in his view due to the editorial work of an ecclesiastical hand who conformed the original discourse of union

---

[1] C. Koester, *Symbolism in the Fourth Gospel*, 155–183. He finds, not surprisingly, that the water motif is mostly connected to washing and drinking but nevertheless it is less consistent than the motif of light and darkness. See also L. P. Jones, *The Symbol of Water*, 20–33.

[2] A. Culpepper, *Anatomy of the Fourth Gospel*, 192–195.

[3] See G. M. Burge, *The Anointed Community*, 150–156 for an overview.

[4] R. Kysar, "The Sacraments and Johannine Ambiguity", 247–250. The article was first presented as a response to Raymond E. Brown's view on the sacraments in the Introduction to his commentary on the Gospel of John, at the presentation of Francis Moloney's updated version of Brown's commentary in 2003.

with Christ to a sacramental one.[5] Oscar Cullmann, another Lutheran, notably held the position that if a Johannine passage could be understood sacramentally, it most likely should. With good reason, he regarded himself as representing the vast majority of interpreters and argued that Rudolf Bultmann "allzu ausschliesslich nur das eine Motiv der Offenbarung durch das Wort im Johannevangelium durchgeführt sieht".[6] In fact, they are both equally captured by their diverse theological presuppositions although within the same ecclesiastical tradition. Nevertheless and almost ironically, Oscar Cullmann's claim that his own position is in line with that of most exegetes including the ancient fathers, might in fact be said to close the hermeneutical circle beginning with Rudolf Bultmann's ecclesiastical editor. There is hardly any reason to believe that patristic exegesis, however interesting it may be in its own right, necessarily had privileged access to the true or originally intended meaning of the Johannine text. Once the sacraments were institutionalized, one should not be surprised that interpreters found these rites evidenced by all of Scripture. A sacramental interpretation by later readers of any generation only tells that someone interpreted the Fourth Gospel as sacramental but it does not provide evidence that this also was the original intention whether this is to be found in the authorial intention behind the text or somehow in the text itself.

It is, however, interesting that in most recent literature on the gospel, the question of possible sacramental reflections is less prominent, often even marginal. As Robert Kysar perhaps too categorically but again pertinently comments: "The aged distinction between sacramental and non-sacramental interpretations, along with speculations about the evangelist and some redactor, are now tiresome, exhausted, and largely irrelevant". The methods that informed and guided this approach have, Robert Kysar claims, been replaced by a literary criticism/reader's criticism with all of its interest in metaphor, polyvalence, and ambiguity, leaving the question of the author's original intention inaccessible. It does not make sense to work through assumed false meanings in order to arrive at the true meaning.[7] Rather, it is intrinsic to symbolism that it harbors a potential of polyvalence which cannot be limited by insisting on an original intention and/or a univocal meaning. The polyvalence is, however, not without textual limits, and the reader's programmatic involvement in the meaning-making does not necessarily lead to different or contrary results in relation to previous interpretations engaged with authorial intention or historical, original meaning. Rather, it makes it possible to be less absolute and more inclusive of various possibilities such as when Craig Koester concludes that most readers familiar with lustrations could find baptismal imagery in the Fourth Gospel

---

5   See R. BULTMANN's commentary, *Das Evangelium des Johannes*, ad loc.
6   O. CULLMANN, *Urchristentum und Gottesdienst*, 59.
7   KYSAR, "Sacraments and Johannine Ambiguity", 248.

whereas others might not.[8] Thus any interpretation will have to remain in the tension of possible and diverse meanings, while being cautiously aware of any personal presuppositions – be they ecclesiastical or not.

2. The Baptismal Practices of John and Jesus

In the Fourth Gospel, neither the noun βάπτισμα nor the epithet βαπτιστής are used, whereas the verb βαπτίζειν are found thirteen times, a greater number of occurrences than in any other gospel. However, ten of them cluster in the passages 1:22–33 and 3:22–26. The focus is thus on baptismal activity, and in these two passages the baptismal practice of the person John provides a frame of reference. In the Synoptic Gospels he is called ὁ βαπτιστής, but this epithet is not used of him in the Fourth Gospel[9] – even if he also here is portrayed as practicing water baptism. However, the verb βαπτίζειν has never any direct object, and the purpose or meaning of John's baptism remains unclear as there in the Fourth Gospel is no mention of what a person achieves by undergoing this baptism. Since it is a water rite, purification and repentance or forgiveness of sins might seem likely and the brief mention in 3:25 of a discussion between John's disciples and a Jew περὶ καθαρισμοῦ might be taken to support this.[10] However, Craig Koester may well be right when he claims that John's introductory declaration in 1:29: about Jesus as the Lamb of God who takes away the sin of the world, seems to exclude the idea that sin could be removed in other ways including the baptism of John.[11]

John himself is, somewhat awkwardly,[12] introduced already in the Prologue but without any reference to his baptismal activity; he is sent from God as a witness and a forerunner for one who is greater than him. This portrayal is affirmed by 1:19–42, where the witness John renounces any claim to the three messianic titles he is invited to assume; he is neither the Messiah, nor Elijah redivivus, nor the Prophet. His role and mission, apparently including also his baptismal practice, is rather to be a forerunner and a witness to the people so

---

8   KOESTER, *Symbolism*, 164–165. 257–262. However, he also thinks that "the Gospel intimates that the water used by Jesus and his followers should be connected with the baptismal practices of the early church" (p.165) and that baptism is integral to the Gospel's imagery whereas the Lord's Supper/Eucharist is not (p.258).

9   This is why I do not call him John the Baptist in this essay. In order to avoid a possible confusion with the evangelist, I use the designations Fourth Gospel and Fourth Evangelist and not, as I normally would prefer, The Gospel of John.

10 See the multitude of possibilities mentioned in L. P. JONES, *Symbol of Water*, 49.

11 KOESTER, *Symbolism*, 157. Also the Gospel of Matthew keeps the forgiveness of sins as the prerogative of Jesus.

12 The present text of the Fourth Gospel is a result of a complex editorial history, that some supply with an alleged ecclesial hand at a late stage. At certain points in this essay I refer to positions which claim an earlier version or redactional moves in support of their interpretation, but on the whole I assume the present text as the one to be interpreted.

that Jesus, whom neither he nor they did know, might be revealed.[13] The sign by which John is able to recognize the one unknown is the descent of the spirit as a dove that remains over him.[14] This, he had been told, was the sign whereby a person would be designated as Son of God – or perhaps rather as "the Chosen One" (1:34).[15] In the Fourth Gospel, the descent of the spirit is not accompanied by a heavenly voice or any other form of declaration. It is not even made clear whether this happens as Jesus is being baptized in water by John – or not. In fact, there is in the Fourth Gospel no narrative account of a baptism of Jesus by John, and Jesus is never subject to John's agency. In stead there is an indirect report by John about what he saw happening when the Spirit descended on Jesus without any explicit mention of a baptismal setting.

It is likely that the Fourth Evangelist was aware of traditions about Jesus' baptism by John, but whatever these may have been, they were probably radically and emphatically changed.[16] In the Synoptic Gospels, the fact that Jesus was baptized in water by John causes difficulties since it might easily be taken to challenge the assumed hierarchical order between the two – casting Jesus as the dependent figure. The Synoptic Gospels counterbalance the problem by introducing apologetic explanations and by having John on the occasion of Jesus' baptism testify to his own subordinate role and the absolute superiority of Jesus. Some of these humble sayings by John are included also in the Fourth Gospel. (John 1:15–17) but otherwise, this gospel "avoids the difficulty by backgrounding baptism and foregrounding John's role a witness to Jesus".[17]

The fact that the narrative about Jesus' baptism is missing in the Fourth Gospel even if it – or rather particularly because it – may have been known to the evangelist, has significance beyond easing the embarrassment of an invert event where the greater may seem to be inferior. The missing story means John's subservient statements no longer serve the same apologetic purpose but rather

---

13　For further discussion about the provenance of Messiah and an "unknown" Messiah, see J. ASHTON *Understanding the Fourth Gospel*, 304–312.

14　According to KOESTER, *Symbolism*, 157–161, the descent of the Spirit marks Jesus as God's anointed in a manner similar to prophets and kings in the Hebrew Bible. Like these earlier figures, Jesus bore the Spirit of God; but unlike them, he bore it permanently.

15　HARTMAN, '*In the Name of the Lord Jesus*', 27, argues in favor of the reading "the Chosen One", supported by some manuscripts. See also JOHN ASHTON's reconstructed text of the passage, *Understanding the Fourth Gospel*, 252, 257–258. This title, ὁ ἐκλεκτός, is elsewhere in the New Testament only used in Luke 23:35.

16　See, M. DAVIES, *Rhetoric and Reference*, 317–318. L. HARTMAN, '*In the Name of the Lord Jesus*', 20, observes that "the evangelist attaches still less significance to the Baptist and his baptism than the Synoptics do". He explains this as due to the ecclesiastical environment, and follows Raymond Brown in assuming that it may have included people who regarded themselves as the disciples of the Baptist. The passage in 1:29–34 serves "to tell them that their master requested that they turn from him to Jesus".

17　DAVIES, *Rhetoric and Reference*, 316.

is part of his role as a witness sent by God to testify to him who is the Son of God. The more radical consequence is the fact that Jesus in the Fourth Gospel actually does not undergo water baptism. The only feature which is maintained of a possible baptismal narrative is the descent of the Spirit upon him – the sign by which the unknown is to be recognized.[18] The descent of the Spirit further signifies that Jesus himself will baptize with the Holy Spirit.

The relationship between John and Jesus or rather the hierarchical order between the two is also spelled out in terms of baptismal practice: "I did not know him but he who sent me to baptize with water said to me, "He on whom you see the Spirit descend and remain this is he who baptizes with the Holy Spirit" (1:33). John may baptize in water, but only he on or in whom the Spirit abides, can bestow the spirit. The distinction between water and spirit may constitute a contrast or it may imply a ranking of elements where the spirit exceeds or changes the water but not necessarily replaces it. These alternatives represent an interpretative dilemma that repeats itself again and again in the Fourth Gospel.

A potential rivalry between the activity of John and that of Jesus is further addressed in John 3:22–36 and 4:1–2. The most striking feature in the first of these passages is the unique information in 3:22 that Jesus baptized as he spent time with his disciples on Judean territory. The imperfect ἐβάπτιζεν is iterative; this is what Jesus used to do or did over a period of time. At the same time, John who had not yet been imprisoned, also baptized but in a different place. The implication is that the two were regarded as competing practitioners of the same ritual. However, John's choice of location is explicitly determined by an abundance of water.[19] This emphasis on John's need of water for his baptism invites the surmise that water in Jesus' case was not required in the same way or to the same degree – he being the one who baptizes with the Holy Spirit.[20] Thus the contrast in this narrative section between the activity of John and that of Jesus depends on and further displays the distinction made by John in 1:33.[21] John's baptism is with water, whereas Jesus is the one from above and sent by God, and he gives the Spirit without measure (3:34).

---

18 It is nevertheless common to allege that, even if it is not explicitly told, one cannot possibly imagine that Jesus in the Fourth Gospel not "as usual" was baptized in water by John. A very clear example is GEORG STRECKER, *Johannesbriefe*, 272.

19 The precise location is uncertain but the name Aenon is from the Aramaic plural of the word for "spring" (R. E. BROWN, *John*, 151.)

20 JONES, *Symbol of Water*, 84–85, makes much of this piece of information and states that "Jesus replaces any purification John may have offered with his "much water" with what he offers in and of himself". He takes it, however, too far when he bluntly spells it out as a shortcoming on John's part: John has nothing to offer but water. This is not necessarily wrong but it is interesting that the text itself is far more subtle and leaves it to John himself to identify his role.

21 See C. H. DODD, *Interpretation*, 310–311.

In the odd transitional passage 4:1–2, the information already divulged in 3:22–26 about Jesus being successful in baptizing and recruiting disciples is repeated but now only as hearsay: Jesus learns that this is what the Pharisees have heard. The content matter is thus simultaneously reiterated and refuted as a rumor, and immediately further modified by a narrator's commentary claiming that "it was not Jesus himself but his disciples who baptized". In the larger context this may serve as a modification of 3:22 as well.[22] Furthermore, the incident induces Jesus to leave Judean territory – perhaps also because John now has been arrested, and there is a need of creating a distance. It may even be subtly indicated that since Jesus' departure from the area was caused by threatening rumors about an alleged successful baptismal activity, his baptismal practice, to the degree it ever happened, now ceased.

3. Generation from Above (3:1–21)

Jesus' nocturnal conversation with Nicodemus, John 3:1–21, which now precedes the account of Jesus' baptismal activity in 3:22–30, is often made to serve as a major baptismal text and a main source for the understanding of baptism as (re)birth.[23] It has been suggested that in some form the passage 3:22–30 was transposed from the beginning of the Gospel and adapted to its present site in order to bring out the baptismal potential in Jesus' conversation with Nicodemus in 3:1–21.[24] Thus, even if baptism is not mentioned in John 3:1–21 and may not have been the original frame of reference, it nevertheless lends itself to baptismal interpretation or represents a mine from which baptismal reflections might be extracted – as an editor at one stage assumed and a host of later interpreters affirm. However, on quite another key Klyne Snodgrass doubts "that there is even a secondary reference to baptism" in John 3:1–21 and adds that "in the end, many who see a reference to baptism still do not know what to do with the water".[25]

The baptismal potential in John 3:1–21 is primarily due to the juxtaposition ὕδωρ καὶ πνεῦμα in 3:5: ἐὰν μή τις γεννηθῇ ἐξ ὕδατος καὶ πνεύματος οὐ δύναται εἰσελθεῖν εἰς τὴν βασιλείαν τοῦ θεοῦ. The simple use of the preposition ἐκ means that it governs both water and spirit; the two belong together and form a hendiadys.[26] Nevertheless, in the remainder of the dialogue πνεῦμα

---

22 BROWN, *John*, 165–66, aptly comments that the modifying remark in 4:2 serves as almost indisputable evidence of the presence of several hands in the composition of the Gospel of John. He also points to the unusual wording.

23 Thus HARTMAN focuses almost exclusively on this passage in his chapter on the Gospel of John in *'Into the Name of the Lord Jesus'*, 155–159.

24 BROWN, *John*, 155. See also DODD, *Historical Tradition*, 286.

25 K. SNODGRASS "Rebirth and Spirit", 189–192.

26 See L. E. KECK, "Derivation as Destiny", 276.

remains a key term whereas ὕδωρ is never again mentioned and may therefore seem to be dispensable beyond the context of v.5. For this and other reasons, the authenticity of ὕδατος καί has been challenged.[27] The textual evidence that might be taken to support a deletion is, however, marginal and the proposal remains a convenient conjecture.[28] The question should rather be: To what does the whole phrase γεννηθῇ ἐξ ὕδατος καὶ πνεύματος refer? It may serve as a cross-reference to 1:26 and 33, but since there in 3:5 is no indication of a contrast or ranking between water and spirit, one might take that to imply that whereas John's baptism was in water only, Jesus baptized in water and spirit.[29] However, since baptism in 3:1–21 is at best presumed, it is necessary to explore further the various fields of reference which the many sayings of Jesus in 3:1–21 compound.

The passage exemplifies a much-used literary strategy in the Fourth Gospel where ambiguity, misunderstanding, and irony are key devices. A character is cast in the role of misunderstanding the meaning of Jesus' word or act, leading Jesus to communicate fuller and deeper truths while still remaining enigmatic. Like several of the dialogues in this gospel, the conversation flows almost seamlessly into a revelatory monologue during which the conversation partner is being disengaged or almost evaporates from the scene. Jesus no longer speaks to Nicodemus but to a general audience or even more specifically to the readers/listeners of the gospel narrative who may possess the hermeneutical key which the dialogue partners in the gospel text do not know and cannot know. In this passage this is reflected in a fluctuation between second and third person singular in v. 3–7b and the unexpected second person plural in v. 7b when Nicodemus is fading into the shadows. It may therefore well be that a strategy is at work whereby the gospel audience would hear/read this passage as referring to baptism, whereas Nicodemus is left in confusion.[30]

---

27 Notoriously by Bultmann, see above note 5. For a survey of positions see, BURGE, *Anointed Community*, 157–160.

28 The words are missing only in one Vulgate codex and in a vague reference by Justin (Apol 1:61) which, however, primarily is interesting because it seems to allude to a textual version which reads ἀναγεννάω in place of γεννηθῇ ἄνωθεν.

29 As does E. FERGUSON, *Baptism*,144. Thus, according to Ferguson "The water is the means or the occasion whereas the Spirit is the Mediator".

30 R. SCHNACKENBURG, *Johannesevangelium* I, 304, has an intriguing solution when he claims: "Der Evangelist setzt aber sicherlich das christliche Verständnis voraus, dass Jesus die ‚Zeugung aus wasser und Geist' (3,5) d.h. das Taufsakrament bringt", while adding (383) "dass nicht die Wassertaufe (als äusserer Ritus und äußerliches Erfordernis) der eigentliche Blickpunkt ist, sondern die ‚Zeugung aus dem Geiste (Gottes)', also jener grundlegende Heilsvorgang der für die Urkirche (nach Anordnung ihres Herrn) nur eben an das Taufsakrament gebunden war. Deswegen zieht die Belehrung Jesu gegenüber Nikodemus nicht unmittelbar auf die Taufe, sondern auf die Neuschaffung durch den Geist Gottes". This entails that "das Judentum. ... eine genügende Grundlage für Jesu Ausführungen gegenüber Nikodemus bietet". He refers also to "andere parallele Ideen in hellenistische oder hermetische Gnosis." (384).

The saying by Jesus in 3:5, where he speaks of γεννηθῇ ἐξ ὕδατος καὶ πνεύματος οὐ δύναται, is an amplification of his first retort to Nicodemus in 3:3: ἐὰν μή τις γεννηθῇ ἄνωθεν οὐ δύναται ἰδεῖν τὴν βασιλείαν τοῦ θεοῦ. Against this statement Nicodemus reasonably objects that a grown man cannot possibly return to his mother's womb in order to be born again. Nicodemus has heard Jesus speak of rebirth, taking ἄνωθεν to mean 'again' and γεννηθῇ to refer to physical birth from the mother's κοιλία. Indeed the impossibility of the proposition is already clear from the fact that the Greek presupposes a negative answer. In responding, Jesus advances his argumentation by a longer, explanatory statement, vv. 5–8, whereby the ambiguous term ἄνωθεν is clarified by the juxtaposition ἐξ ὕδατος καὶ πνεύματος. This is followed in v. 6 by a binary opposition between σάρξ and πνεῦμα in an epigrammatic formulation of the principle that like produces like.[31] Thereby γεννηθῇ ἄνωθεν is further explained as γεννηθῇ ἐκ πνεύματος leading to the concluding statement in v. 8: "So is everyone γεγεννημένος ἐκ τοῦ πνεύματος" – without any mention of water.

In relation to the wording of Jesus' response in 3:5 γεννηθῇ is the only term that later is not replaced or explained by another term but simply reiterated, as a key term in the discourse. In common Greek usage γεννάω concerns the origin of life and refers mostly to the procreative, engendering function of the father rather than the mother's birthing process.[32] However, it may be used of both parents and also of the mother alone, meaning birthing rather than begetting. Whenever it is used without the agent being mentioned, a decision as to its meaning will therefore have to be made, if possible, from the context. In the Fourth Gospel the passive form is common and the implied subject is often difficult to determine. If it is God, the figurative use of language adds to the difficulty in that God Father still might be seen to assume a maternal capacity thus moving beyond the assignment of gender. An attractive alternative may even be to leave the question of its precise referential meaning open and allow the ambiguity to resonate in the interpretation. However, not only is this difficult to maintain when the Greek is translated, it also does not provide an excuse for not examining each individual case carefully.

---

31 According to Snodgrass, "Rebirth and Spirit", 194, predicative nouns without article prior to the verb are qualitative, that is, they point to the character or nature of the subject – as in John 1:1. See also Keck, 'Derivation as Destiny', 276. He sees in this passage a Johannine equivalent to 1 Cor 15:50. Keck also convincingly contends Trumbower's advocacy for patterns of predestination in the Fourth Gospel: "The function of the stark contrast between flesh and spirit in verse 6 is not to explain why Nicodemus is in a hopeless situation but rather to underscore the necessity of being begotten ἄνωθεν" (p. 277).

32 Keck, 'Derivation as Destiny' 275–276. Also Raymond Brown claims that γεννάω here as also elsewhere has the male connotation of begetting rather than the female of giving birth (John, 29); and Ferguson, Baptism, 142–143.

In the context of the Fourth Gospel procreative language is introduced already in 1:12–13, where term γεννάω occurs for the first time. Also this verse is a possible baptismal reference since it refers to the generation of the children of God: He (the Logos or the True Light) gave those who believe in him the right γενέσθαι τέκνα θεοῦ – οἳ οὐκ ἐξ αἱμάτων οὐδὲ ἐκ θελήματος σαρκὸς οὐδὲ ἐκ θελήματος ἀνδρὸς ἐγεννήθησαν. The constellation of terms is unusual; the precise meaning of each is not easy to determine, and it is not evident how they relate to one another.[33] However, they are all being negated as not being required in the divine process of generation, and a contradiction is implicitly established between divine and human procreation and divine and human life.

Also the juxtaposition ἐξ ὕδατος καὶ πνεύματος in 3:5 may have generational connotations. Interpreters have drawn attention to occurrences where water is used of fluids involved in procreation and birth such as amniotic fluid and sperm.[34] This observation has been further pursued in two different but not necessarily contrary directions. One set of proposals develop 'water' as related to human parturition and birth. Whereas spirit might refer to spiritual or divine birth, water represents the first birth out of the mother's κοιλία, which might be further characterized as a birth κατὰ σάρκα. Thus a double yet parallel contrast is made in Jesus' response to Nicodemus in that the juxtaposition ὕδωρ καὶ πνεῦμα is taken to correlate to σάρξ versus πνεῦμα. Jesus thus explains that it is not enough for human beings to be born in an ordinary human way, of water and of flesh. A second birth is necessary, from above or from spirit. This might seem to agree with 1:12–13, and to support that Jesus differently from John baptizes with the spirit.

However, in 3:5–8 the grammatical difference between the hendiadys ἐξ ὕδατος καὶ πνεύματος and the binary opposition of σάρξ versus πνεῦμα, makes it less likely that σάρξ equals or replaces ὕδωρ. Thus Dorothy Lee regards natural birth as a source domain for interpreting or charging spiritual birth/baptism symbolically.[35] A similar position is held by Judith Lieu. She claims that Johannine irony should not be seen as a form of dualism. Earthly experience is rather a sign that points to and enfleshes divine truth without encompassing it. In this case that means that birth again/from above is not "alien to and contrasted to the mundane birth from a mother. On the contrary, the latter enfleshes and is a sign and carrier of the former".[36] Like Nicodemus in the story, both Lee and Lieu assume that γεννηθῇ refers to a mother's birth-giving, and

---

33 See S. VAN TILBORG, *Imaginative Love*, 41–47. D. LEE, *Flesh and Glory*, 143, sees this "somewhat ponderous phraseology" to be overlapping,

34 LEE, *Flesh and Glory*, 70, summarizes various proposals. See also, B. WITHERINGTON, "Waters of Birth" and M. STOL, *Zwangerschap en Geboorte*, 59–61.

35 LEE, *Flesh and Glory*, 68–71.

36 J. LIEU, "Mother of the Son", 76.

join those who read John 3:3–7 as advancing an understanding of baptism as a form of (re)birth.[37]

Already in 1929 Hugo Odeberg drew attention to some Jewish texts where the Hebrew term הפיט, which he took to mean 'water', was used about sperm (Niddah 16b; Abot 3.1). He therefore proposed that in John 3:5 ὕδωρ might refer to male semen, as a metonymy for σάρξ in 3:6 and in opposition to πνεῦμα both in 3:5 and 3:6.[38] Scrutinizing the evidence further Sjef van Tilborg found that הפיט refers to a drop of whatever fluid and also that the rabbis were well aware that semen was not water. He claimed that "the combination 'water and spirit' appears in this (classical) physiology precisely as indicating the male sperm".[39] Tilborg concludes that despite differences the common element is that πνεῦμα is seen as the most important principle in male sperm.[40]

More recently, Adele Reinhartz has shown how the 'father-son' language in the Fourth Gospel is impregnated with the Aristotelian theory of *epigenesis*.[41] According to this theory, both animals and human beings grow organically from the sperm of the male as set within the medium of growth provided by the female. Integral to the form as supplied by the male seed, is the sentient soul, which resides in the πνεῦμα, and the sperm is viewed as the vehicle for both the λόγος and the πνεῦμα of the father, who alone provides the form and the essence of the offspring. Applied to John 3:5 this would imply that water in conjunction with spirit signifies the father's seed.

---

37 This is also how Justin understands the passage in his First Apology 61,3–5: "Then they (the baptizands) are brought by us where there is water and they are regenerated in the same manner (τρόπον ἀναγεννήσεως) in which we were ourselves generated." He supports this by quoting what Christ said: "ἂν μὴ ἀναγεννηθῆτε, you will not enter into the kingdom of heaven". That this particularly refers to John 3:5 is clear from the fact that he immediately continues by referring to Nicodemus' bewilderment: "Now that it is impossible for those who have once been born to enter into their mothers' wombs, is obvious to all".

38 H. ODEBERG, *The Fourth Gospel Interpreted*, 48–69. According to VAN TILBORG, *Imaginative Love*, 49, Odeberg was followed by Barrett in his commentary edition of 1967, but in his *Essays on John* of 1982 Barrett had changed his mind. Interestingly, SCHNACKENBURG *Johannesevangelium* I, 77, mentions Odeberg's proposal but rejects it as "nicht sehr naheliegend" apparently because he took Odeberg to defend the "Gnostic" idea of *sperma pneumatikon*, which, of course, is a possible reading.

39 VAN TILBORG, *Imaginative Love*, 49–52. A major source is Aristotle (*De Gen. Anim.* II 735a-b) who explicitly states that "semen is a compound of spirit and water". Further evidence covers the period form 4th century BC to 2nd century AD, including Philo of Alexandria (*De Opif. Mundi* 67) and Clement of Alexandria (*Paed.* I.6.49.1)

40 VAN TILBORG, *Imaginative Love*, 41–47. The role and understanding of πνεῦμα may, however, vary: Aristotle sees it as the principle of movement; for the Stoics it participates in the heavenly fire; Philo sees it as a participation in the divine breath; and the pneumatic medical school considers it the active principle which transforms and gives form.

41 A. REINHARTZ, "Divine Epigenesis", 83–103. Cf. also the indication by M. THEOBALD, *Fleischwerdung des Logos*, 243.

Water alone may cleanse and purify, but it has in itself no procreational potential. Laced with spirit, however, water may work as sperm. Without the spirit generation cannot take place, and the emphasis is therefore on spirit rather than on water. Also other passages in the Fourth Gospel affirm that whereas the transmission of spirit is indispensable, the presence of water may be negotiable.

4. Life-Giving Spirit

In John 7:37–39 water and spirit are yet again combined when Jesus refers to a nebulous scriptural reference saying that "out of his κοιλία rivers of living water shall flow forth". The term κοιλία is strange and suggestive and commentators followed by translators tend to upgrade this to "heart" or "inner parts". However, none of the biblical passages which might resonate in this saying in John 7:36–39, seems to include a Hebrew term that indisputably might translate as κοιλία.[42] The term κοιλία therefore represents an intriguing element in the passage as does the peculiar association of κοιλία and the living water/spirit that will flow from it. Although κοιλία is not a common word for womb in classical Greek, it is used in this sense in the LXX (Gen 25:24; Deut 28:4 and 11:1: Ruth 1:11) and elsewhere in the New Testament (Matt 19:12; Luke 11:27; Gal 1:15) – most often determined as κοιλία τῆς μητρός. So also in John 3:4 with which the choice of words in 7:37–39 seems to resonate.

Depending on the punctuation, the one who in John 7:37–39 is the source from whose κοιλία rivers of living water will flow, can be Jesus himself or the

---

[42] It has proven difficult to identify its source with any certainty. Ex 17:5–6; Num 20:7–16; Ps 46:5–8; 105 (104):41; Joel 4:18 (= 3:18[LXX]); Isa 12:3; Ezek 47:1–2 and Zech 14:8, which may be seen to bring some of the others together, have all been mentioned – as has a Targum reading of Ps 78:16. For a survey until 1991, see W. H. BROWNLEE, "Whence the Gospel According to John", 186. M. COLOE, *God Dwells*, 130–131, has helpfully but too categorically distributed the possible scriptural references according to the two textual variants. She herself favors the position that the quotation is from the Targums since ἐκ τῆς κοιλίας should be explained as an Aramaic idiom.

However, none of the suggestions has gained general support and neither has the position that the reference should represent some kind of blended florilegium. M. J. J. MENKEN's proposal (*Old Testament Quotations*, 201–202) that the most probable source is Ps 77:16, 20 LXX, is the one that to my mind comes closest to carry conviction. But also Menken struggles to explain κοιλία and recurs to claiming that it is a substitute of πέτρα in 77:16 LXX and obtained by way of Ps 114:8.

J. MARCUS, "Rivers of Living Water from Jesus' Belly (John 7:38)", 328–330 has tried to make a possible case of Isa 12:3 ("with joy you will draw water from the wells of salvation"), which in several Talmudic passages (b.Sukk 48b; 50b; y.Sukk 5.1) is associated with Tabernacles. He finds that the word for "well" in this passage is very close consonantally to *meim*, that the LXX translates more than twenty times with κοιλία. But again it depends on a possible misspelling, for which there is no evidence, and neither is there in this passage as Marcus himself admits, any mention of rivers of living waters.

believer. Both versions are grammatically possible and are also supported by the textual tradition,[43] and it may well be that in the original text with no punctuation, the saying was equally open to both readings. This ambiguity is in accordance with similar sayings about living water in Jesus' conversation with the Samaritan woman in John 4.[44] Here Jesus is said to be the source or provider of living water and he also promises that in those to whom he gives it, it will become a spring of water gushing up to eternal life (4:10–14). In neither passage, however, is the believer regarded as an independent source of water; he/she depends on the water they have received from Jesus as its original source.

Whereas the term κοιλία in 3:4 is indicative of Nicodemus' misunderstanding, there is no negative association attached in 7:38. It rather serves as a prolepsis to the events in chapter 19-20 when water and blood will flow from the pierced side of Jesus and the spirit, which in 7:38–39 has not yet been given, will be communicated to those who may now call Jesus' Father their Father and his God their God.

In an editorial comment in 7:39, the living water which shall flow from the κοιλία of Jesus is explicitly said to be the Spirit. Thus speaking of water, Jesus actually speaks of the spirit. Furthermore, in the same comment, it is oddly emphasized that because Jesus not yet is glorified, the spirit is not yet there to be received by the believers. Thereby a chronological or narrative, sequential dimension is introduced indicating that the availability of the water/spirit is kept pending until Jesus' glorification has taken place. The passage in 7:37–39 thus functions as a prediction of later incidents in connection with the glorification of Jesus through crucifixion and resurrection.[45] Thus from Jesus' dead

---

43 Most of the early Latin translations and Vulgata support the second non-Christological reading, together with a majority of the Greek Fathers probably depending originally on Origen. SCHNACKENBURG, *Johannesevangelium* II, 212, provides a list of the fathers. J. HEER, *Der Durchgebohrte*, 58–60, refers to Lagrange, who assumed that the preference for the non-Christological version might depend on the Trinitarian position that the Spirit processed from the Father alone. Heer himself is strongly in favor of the Christological reading.

44 KOESTER, *Symbolism*, 13–15, 173–180, therefore sees this ambiguity as apparent or intentional and yet another instance of a two-level image with a primary level referring to Jesus and a secondary level referring to the disciples.

45 This is also one of the reasons why I am not persuaded that the account of the footwashing in John 13 is an allusion to baptism. See also KOESTER, *Symbolism*, 118, for a critical assessment. A cautious support of a baptismal resonance is found in M. E. JOHNSON, *Rites of Christian Initiation*, 20–23, who also refers to MARTIN F. CONNELL's suggestion that rather than baptism, footwashing, especially as this is captured in 13:6–10, may have been the initiatory rite in some Johannine communities, "Nisi Pedes", 20–30. It might also support that baptism could not be repeated. When ultimately at least part of the Johannine community came into communion with "the more dominant Synopticised or Petrine-led churches", its own unique theological traditions and structures ... "became either excised and made subservient to those other communities as the Fourth Gospel itself is further redacted along these interpretative lines. Footwashing does not go away but, at most, remains either as a mere supplement to baptism or as an occasional dramatic rite demonstrating Christian service and humility" (p. 22).

body exalted on the cross, blood and water flow as his πλευρά is pierced (19:34). The lack of verbal correlation between 7:38 (κοιλία) and 19:34 (πλευρά) is a difficulty but may depend on a different set of scriptural associations. Fathers like Origen (Homilies on Exodus 11:2) associate the two loci by saying that as the rock was struck for it to yield life-giving water, so Christ, when he was struck, caused streams to flow. Even if it is not immediately transferable to an interpretation of John 19:34, it is also worth noting that Paul in 1 Cor 10:13 speaks typologically of baptism as drinking the same spiritual drink from the spiritual rock which was Christ.

The question is therefore perhaps not as much to what the passages refer as of whom they speak. It has already been mentioned how Nicodemus almost silently fades away from the narrative in John 3. Even in the first phase of the dialogue, the language stays generic or neutral; third person singular τις is used until it is being applied in v. 7c, and then not to Nicodemus but to a second person plural. In fact, Jesus never speaks to Nicodemus directly in the second person and Nicodemus does not specifically apply Jesus' words to himself.[46] The statements are general and hence endlessly applicable until Jesus from v. 12 enters into a monologue speaking of himself. Thus Jesus' initial statements could equally well refer to himself as the one who has been ἄνωθεν γεννηθῇ. Indeed, the only one of whom we at this stage in the gospel narrative know that he ἄνωθεν γεννηθῇ, is Jesus himself.[47] At the same time Jesus is the agent by whom others may become children of God. In his conversation with the Samaritan woman in John 4, the woman is directed away from (the water in) the well and towards Jesus who is the source of living water. Water is therefore not an external vehicle; it is an intrinsic quality of Jesus in whom the Spirit abides. Thus in his uniqueness Jesus imparts the living water/spirit they would not be able to find elsewhere or draw from a well.

Whether the flow of blood and water in 19:34 is meant as proof against docetic views or whether it rather is ecclesiological and either refers more generally to the generation of the church or more particularly alludes to baptism and eucharist or only to one or the other, is a matter of much dispute in the history of interpretation.[48] Without exploring the further implications of the

---

46 I find that this makes Schnackenburg's suggestion (see above n. 30) about a limited non-sacramental Jewish discourse targeted particularly at Nicodemus even less likely.

47 The ambivalence concerning Jesus' heavenly origin and his life in the flesh as son of Joseph of Nazareth is discussed in SEIM, "Descent and Divine Paternity".

48 SCHNACKENBURG suggests (*Johannesevangelium* III, 345): "ein einziger Lebensstrom". A connection to 1 John 5:6–8 might, however, be taken to emphasise the blood, and thereby possibly an anti-docetic position, cf. *ibid.*, *Johannesevangelium* III, 341: "Hier – auf redaktioneller Ebene – ist ein Zusammenhang mit 1 John 5, 6 zu erwägen .... Es scheint dass der Verf[asser] von 1 John hier zu einer symbolischen Deutung (auf die Sakramente), wenigstens zu einer weiterreichenden Bedeutung der Ereignisse im Raum der Kirche übergeht". As always Schnackenburg has the ability to adopt a critical assessment while in the end leaving the case open.

various possibilities, it is intriguing that blood and water represent fluids of generation so that a generational perspective again is indicated. Jesus exalted on the cross is instrumental in generating from above. As he gives up the spirit, and exhausts his earthly life in water and blood, new children of God are generated. Thus in the resurrection narratives when the risen Lord has made himself known to Mary Magdalene at their encounter in the garden, he tells her to go πρὸς τοὺς ἀδελφούς μου[49] – using for the first time kinship language as a shared frame of reference both for himself and the disciples. He also speaks in an unprecedented manner of "my father and your father" and "my God and your God", marking a distinction but more remarkably also a commonality. The friends whom Jesus loves, have become his 'brothers and sisters', also they are now children of God – οἳ οὐκ ἐξ αἱμάτων οὐδὲ ἐκ θελήματος σαρκὸς οὐδὲ ἐκ θελήματος ἀνδρὸς ἐγεννήθησαν. In the immediately following encounter they are sent by Jesus as he himself was sent by the Father. This commission is accompanied by the rendering of the spirit which Jesus breaths into/on them like God made the earth creature come to life in the Garden of Eden by breathing it into life (20:22). In the Fourth Gospel πνεῦμα is a divine principle or quality also referred to as τὸ ζῳοποιοῦν (5:21; 6:63). Thus, sharing in the Father's life-giving capacity the Son sent by the Father, fulfils his mission by generating and empowering further children of God through the spirit-sperm which shapes and forms them in an act where creation and procreation converge.

5. Concluding Intimations

Beyond the baptismal activity of John, forerunner and witness, and his message that also Jesus will baptize but with the Holy Spirit, the Fourth Gospel is alone in relating that also Jesus somehow baptized until John was arrested. However, whereas availability of water was important for John, this is at best tacitly understood in the case of Jesus who seemingly did not himself undergo water baptism. Moreover, the episode where Jesus is said to baptize, is in its present position framed by a primarily procreational discourse whereby the role of water in relation to spirit is renegotiated.[50] More generally in the gospel, the natural element of water seems not so much to be adopted symbolically as to be counterbalanced by the living water that Jesus has in himself and which is released when he is glorified. Narratively, this happens after he on the cross both has given up the

---

49 Μου is missing in a couple of major manuscripts, but the text with μου represents a *lectio difficilior*.

50 JOHNSON, *Rites of Christian Initiation*, 20, claims that the Fourth Evangelist's "understanding of baptism as a divine and pneumatic 'birth from above', combined with similar implications for baptism from the similar accounts of Jesus' own baptism, will become a central focus and paradigm for the practice and paradigm of Christian baptism especially within the Syrian, and some other, early Christian liturgical traditions".

spirit and his dead and still exalted body is pierced so that blood and water flow forth. When the resurrected but yet not ascended Jesus transmits the spirit to the disciples, water is not involved – he breathes the new life into them as God at creation did to the earthcreature Adam. They are empowered to γενέσθαι τέκνα θεοῦ – οἳ οὐκ ἐξ αἱμάτων οὐδὲ ἐκ θελήματος σαρκὸς οὐδὲ ἐκ θελήματος ἀνδρὸς ἐγεννήθησαν and are made to become his brothers and sisters calling his Father also their Father.

Which kind of baptismal practices does the Fourth Gospel reflect, support or encourage? When it speaks of such practices, other than by John, the emphasis is on spirit rather than on water. At the same time as water symbolism is predominant in the gospel, it is profoundly charged with Christological meaning and carries associations to procreative and life sustaining processes rather than purification. From sources within himself, Jesus provides living water, and this living water is the spirit. Do we in the Fourth Gospel see allusions to a baptismal theology for a dry land or desert communities where water was scarce? Do we see the contour of a Christian group to whom some kind of anointing whereby the Spirit was given, was a primary or preceding rite to water baptism?[51] Or did the water, perhaps a small amount of it, simply signify the Spirit? Crucial was at all events the understanding that the believers thereby was (pro)created to become God's children.

When speaking of baptism in the Fourth Gospel it is therefore important not to be confined by the ritualization of water baptism as it established itself in a more or less unified practice from the Third and Fourth Century onward. Before this time, especially in the East, there seems to have been no established understanding or archetypical pattern or sequence of ritual elements. Rather, there is a growing awareness among liturgy historians that in the earliest centuries there was variety and diversity not only in the theological interpretations of Christian initiation but in the performance of the rites, some of them no longer clearly known to us. All the more intriguing are the questions and insights that the Fourth Gospel poses to the understanding of Christian baptism both historically and theologically, and it is not difficult to understand that the Gospel of John, when integrated in the ecclesiastical mainstream, lent itself to interpret and symbolically charge an established rite of baptism.

Bibliography

Ashton, John, *Understanding the Fourth Gospel*, Oxford: Clarendon Press 1991.

---

51 It is well established that anointing features occur predominently in 1 John. For prebaptismal anointing as an independent and central element in the ritualization of baptism in the East, see Gabriele Winkler, "The Original Meaning of the Prebaptismal Anointing and Its Implications", 58–81.

BARRETT, C. K., *The Gospel According to St John. An Introduction with Commentary and Notes on the Greek Text*, London: SPCK 1967.

— *Essays on John*, London: SPCK/Philadelphia, Pa.: Westminster 1982.

BROWN, RAYMOND, *The Gospel According to John* (AncB 29), Garden City, NY: Doubleday 1966.

BROWNLEE, WILLIAM H., "Whence the Gospel According to John", in: J. H. Charlesworth (ed.), *John and the Dead Sea Scrolls*, New York: Crossroad 1991, 166–194.

BULTMANN, RUDOLF, *Das Evangelium des Johannes* (KEK 2), Göttingen: Vandenhoeck & Ruprecht 1941.

BURGE, GARY M., *The Anointed Community. The Holy Spirit in the Johannine Tradition*, Grand Rapids, Mich.: Eerdmans 1987.

COLOE, MARY, *God Dwells with Us. Temple Symbolism in the Fourth Gospel*, Collegeville, Minn.: The Liturgical Press 2001.

CONNELL, MARTIN F., "Nisi Pedes, Except for the Feet: Footwashing in the Community of John's Gospel", in: *Worship* 70 (1996) 20–30.

CULLMANN, OSCAR, *Urchristentum und Gottesdienst* (AThANT 3), Zürich: Zwingli-Verlag 1950.

CULPEPPER, R. ALAN, *Anatomy of the Fourth Gospel. A Study in Literary Design*, Philadelphia, Pa.: Fortress Press 1983.

DAVIES, MARGARET, *Rhetoric and Reference in the Fourth Gospel*, Sheffield: JSOT Press 1992.

DODD, CHARLES H., *Historical Tradition in the Fourth Gospel*, Cambridge: The University Press 1963.

— *The Interpretation of the Fourth Gospel*, Cambridge: The University Press 1968.

FERGUSON, EVERETT, *Baptism in the Early Church. History, Theology, and Liturgy in the First Five Centuries*, Grand Rapids, Mich.: Eerdmans 2009.

HARTMAN, LARS, *'Into the Name of the Lord Jesus.' Baptism in the Early Church*, Edinburgh: T&T Clark 1997.

HEER, J., *Der Durchgebohrte. Johanneische Begründung der Herz-Jesu-Verehrung*, Roma: Casa Editrice Herder 1966.

JOHNSON, MAXWELL E., *The Rites of Christian Initiation. Their Evolution and Interpretation*. Collegeville, Minn.: The Liturgical Press 2007.

— *Living Water, Sealing Spirit. Readings on Christian Initiation*, Collegeville, Minn.: The Liturgical Press 1995, 58–81.

JONES, LARRY PAUL, *The Symbol of Water in the Gospel of John* (JSNTS.S 145), Sheffield: Sheffield Academic Press 1997.

KECK, LEANDER E., "Derivation as Destiny; 'Off-ness' in Johannine Christology, Anthropology, and Soteriology", in: R. A.Culpepper/C. C. Black (eds.), *Exploring the Gospel of John. In Honor of D. Moody Smith*, Louisville, Ky.: Westminster John Knox Press 1996, 274–288.

KOESTER, CRAIG R., *Symbolism in the Fourth Gospel. Meaning, Mystery, Community*, Minneapolis, Minn.: Fortress Press 1995.

KYSAR, ROBERT, "The Sacraments and Johannine Ambiguity", in: *Voyages with John. Charting the Fourth Gospel*, Waco, Tex.: Baylor University Press 2005.

LEE, DOROTHY, *Flesh and Glory. Symbolism, Gender and Theology in the Gospel of John*, New York: A Herder and Herder Book/The Crossroad Publishing Company 2002.

LIEU, JUDITH, "Mother of the Son in the Fourth Gospel," in: *JBL* 117 (1998) 61–77.

MARCUS, JOEL, "Rivers of Living Water from Jesus' Belly (John 7:38)," in: *JBL* 117/2 (1998) 328–330.

MENKEN, MAARTEN J. J., *Old Testament Quotations in the Fourth Gospel. Studies in Textual Form*, Kampen: KOK Pharos Publishing House 1996.

ODEBERG, HUGO, *The Fourth Gospel Interpreted in Its Relation to Contemporaneous Religious Currents in Palestine and the Hellenistic-Oriental World*, Uppsala: Almqvist & Wiksell 1929.

REINHARTZ, ADELE, "And the Word Was Begotten: Divine Epigenesis in the Gospel of John," in: *Semeia* 85 (1999) 83–103.

SCHNACKENBURG, RUDOLF, *Das Johannesevangelium I-11* (HThK IV/1), Freiburg i.Br.: Herder 1971.

SEIM, TURID KARLSEN, "Descent and Divine Paternity in the Gospel of John: Does the Mother Matter?", in: *NTS* 51 (2005) 361–375.

SNODGRASS, KLYNE R., "That which is born from ΠΝΕΥΜΑ is ΠΝΕΥΜΑ: Rebirth and Spirit in John 3:5–6", in: R. Sloan/M. C. Parsons (eds.), *Perspectives on John: Method and Interpretation in the Fourth Gospel*, Leviston/Lampeter: Edwin Mellen Press 1993, 181–205.

STOL, M., *Zwangerschap en Beoorte Bij de Babiloniers en in de Bijbel* (Ex Oriente Lux XXIII), Leiden: Brill 1983.

STRECKER, GEORG, *Die Johannesbriefe* (KEK 14), Göttingen: Vandenhoeck & Ruprecht 1989.

THEOBALD, MIKAEL, *Fleischwerdung des Logos. Studien zum Corpus des Evangeliums und zu 1 Joh.* (NTA NF 30), Münster: Aschendorff 1988.

VAN TILBORG, SJEF, *Imaginative Love in John*, Leiden: Brill 1993.

WINKLER, GABRIELE, "The Original Meaning of the Prebaptismal Anointing and Its Implications", in: M. E. Johnsen, *Living Water, Sealing Spirit. Readings on Christian Initiation*, Collegeville, Minn.: The Liturgical Press 1995, 58–81.

WITHERINGTON, BEN III, "The Waters of Birth: John 3.5 and I John 5.6–8," in: *NTS* 35 (1989), 155–160.

Hermeneutische Aspekte der Taufe im Neuen Testament

ODA WISCHMEYER

1. Methodische Vorüberlegungen

Die Taufe, βάπτισμα[1], wird in den einzelnen frühchristlichen Schriften, die später zum Neuen Testament zusammengestellt wurden, von Anfang an mit großer Selbstverständlichkeit und in einer gewissen Breite der Bezeugung[2] erwähnt. Über die Taufe wird von ihrem Vollzug, dem βαπτίζειν, her, narrativ oder argumentativ gehandelt. Ihre Kenntnis wird überall vorausgesetzt. Dabei finden wir nirgends eine eigentliche Tauf*lehre*, die die Taufe erklärte und über die Bedeutung der Tauf*handlung* Auskunft gäbe. Wohl aber stoßen wir auf verschiedene *Deutungen*, Deutungszusammenhänge und Deutung spendende Sachbereiche und Metaphern. Denn die Taufe, sei sie religionswissenschaftlich als Lustrationsritual[3], als Initiationsritual oder als *rite de passage*[4], kultursemiotisch als Symbolhandlung[5], kulturwissenschaftlich als *identity marker*[6] oder theologisch als Sakrament[7] beschrieben, kann, sofern sie eine rituelle[8] Handlung ist, nicht ohne

---

1 Vgl. dazu Art. „βάπτω κτλ.", in: *ThWNT* 1, 527–544. βάπτω begegnet im NT wie in LXX nur als „eintauchen" in Lk 16,24; Joh 13,26; Apk 19,13, βάπτισμα und βαπτίζειν (in LXX ebenfalls als „eintauchen") dagegen fast ausschließlich in der Spezialbedeutung von „Taufe, taufen" (βαπτίζειν in Bezug auf Waschungen Mk 7,4 und Lk 11,38). βαπτισμός begegnet nur in Mk 7,4 (dort u. ö. auch das Verb in der allgemeinen Bedeutung) und Hebr 6,2 und 9,10 im Sinne von Reinheitswaschungen. Hebr 6,2 bezieht sich wohl auf den Taufritus, der allerdings im Plural angesprochen wird. Hebr 6,2 zeigt eine gewisse Distanz des Autors zur Taufe an. Deutungspotentiale finden sich hier höchstens indirekt aus der Zusammenstellung mit den aus Act und dem sekundären Markusschluss bekannten Vorstellungen von Umkehr, Glauben und Händeauflegen.

2 Paulus: Galaterbrief, 1. Korintherbrief, Römerbrief. Spätere Briefe: Kolosserbrief, Epheserbrief, Hebräerbrief, (Titusbrief); 1. Petrusbrief. Synoptische Evangelien. Johannesevangelium. Apostelgeschichte. Vgl. auch die Schriften der Apostolischen Väter: Didache, Barnabasbrief, 2. Klemensbrief, Ignatiusbriefe, Hirt des Hermas. Einführend: Art. „Taufe", in: *RGG*[4] 8, 50–96; Art. „Taufe", in: *TRE* 32, 659–741.

3 Vgl. einführend den Art. „Taufe I. Religionsgeschichtlich", in: *RGG*[4] 8, 50–52.

4 Art. Rites de passage, in: *RGG*[4] 7, 534f.

5 Prominent G. THEISSEN, *Die Religion der ersten Christen*.

6 Vgl. Art. „Identität", in: *Lexikon der Bibelhermeneutik*, 275f.

7 Art. „Sakramente", in: *RGG*[4] 7, 752–770.

8 Der religionswissenschaftliche Begriff des „Ritus" wird hier formal im Sinn von „‚kleinster Baustein' eines Rituals" verstanden, inhaltlich als gottesdienstliche Teilhandlung: M. STAUSBERG,

Deutungen stattfinden, die ihr eine *Bedeutung* zuschreiben, die über die bloße Wasserübergießung oder -untertauchung und deren primäre Effekte von Säuberung und Erfrischung hinausgeht[9].

Hans Dieter Betz unterschied dementsprechend in seinem großen Beitrag zu Röm 6 in Bezug auf die Taufe zwischen *performance* und *meaning*: „The entire emphasis is on the meaning of baptism, and indeed this meaning changed considerably, given the respective theological and social contexts in which it was interpreted. Therefore, while the performance was apparently transferred without much change, the interpretation had to be recontextualized"[10]. Entsprechend greift Adela Yarbro Collins jüngst in einem Beitrag zur Taufe bei Paulus den Gedanken von John Scheid auf, „that, among the Romans, it was only *ritual praxis* that was obligatory and normative. Many *interpretations* could be and often were in circulation, but none of theses were authoritative". Sie bezieht diesen Sachverhalt auf Paulus: „This approach illuminates Paul's letters. The *ritual* is well known and normative. *Interpretations* may be invented, each for a particular rhetorical occasion and purpose"[11]. In der Differenz von *performance* oder *ritual* einerseits und *meaning* oder *interpretation* auf der anderen Seite finden wir den Ausgangspunkt, der nicht nur für Paulus, sondern für alle frühchristlichen Schriften eine hermeneutische Untersuchungsbasis darstellt.

Die Begriffe *meaning* oder *interpretation* sind allerdings nicht identisch oder auswechselbar. Sie müssen vielmehr ihrerseits in ihrer hermeneutischen Leistung definiert und differenziert werden. *Meaning* oder Bedeutung[12] bezeichnet unabhängig von der semantischen Differenz zu *sense* oder Sinn[13] die Relation zwischen einem Bezeichneten und einem Zeichen: Zeichen – in unserem Zusammenhang sowohl rituelle Handlungen als auch Wörter und Texte – beziehen sich auf eine wie immer philosophisch konstruierte Wirklichkeit und kommunizieren diese in Textform. *Interpretation* ist demgegenüber die selbständige Verstehens- und Erklärungsleistung eines Interpreten und führt zu einem eigenen neuen Text[14]. Eine zweite Differenzierung ist notwendig: beson-

---

Art. „Ritus/Ritual I. Religionswissenschaftlich", in: *RGG*[4] 7, 547–549; vgl. auch Art. „Ritus/Ritual II. Religionsgeschichtlich. 4. Christentum a) Neues Testament", in: *RGG*[4] 7, 552f.

9   Zu der Materie bzw. dem Medium Wasser im Frühjudentum vgl. K.-H. Ostmeyer, *Taufe und Typos. Elemente der Tauftypologien in 1. Korinther 10 und 1. Petrus 3*, 53–106.

10 H. D. Betz, „Transferring a Ritual: Paul's interpretation of Baptism in Romans 6", 271.

11 A. Yarbro Collins, „Baptism as Transformation", 6.

12 Vgl. Art. „Bedeutung", in: *Lexikon der Bibelhermeneutik*, 67–73.

13 Vgl. Art. „Sinn", in: *Lexikon der Bibelhermeneutik*, 548–555.

14 Vgl. Art. „Interpretation/Interpretieren/Interpret", in: *Lexikon der Bibelhermeneutik*, 289–296. Dort besonders Art. „Interpretation usw. II. Neutestamentlich", 292: Die Interpretation ist „auf den Text bezogen. Sie benutzt ihn nicht. Sie stellt selbst eine Gesamtleistung dar, die sich in einem eigenen kohärenten Text, der ‚I', vergegenständlicht. Die eigene Leistung einer I. ntl. Texte, die über die exegetische Erklärung hinausgeht, liegt in der Möglichkeit, unter Offenlegung des eigenen historischen und biographischen Ausgangspunktes einen neuen eigenen Posttext zu

ders bei traditionalen, geschichteten Texten[15] sowie bei überwiegend argumentativen Texten[16] muss zwischen *textinterner* und *textexterner Interpretation*[17] unterschieden werden. Schon die neutestamentlichen Autoren arbeiten mit den Bedeutungen (*meanings*) der Taufe, wie sie in ihren Traditionen oder Gemeinden vorliegen, und weiten diese unter Umständen zu eigenen Interpretationen aus. Diese Interpretationen fungieren im Rahmen der neutestamentlichen Texte dann als *textinterne Interpretationen*. Die Exegese fügt ihnen weitere – nun *textexterne* – Interpretationen hinzu. Die exegetischen Interpretationen sind ihrerseits in den gegenwärtigen wissenschaftlichen Disziplinen, Methoden, Theorien und Konzepten kontextualisiert. *Mein Konzept ist die historische Hermeneutik, die der Beschreibung der primären textinternen Deutungen gilt, ohne religions- oder kulturwissenschaftliche Theorien anzuwenden*[18]. Meine Fragestellung konzentriert sich auf die Beschreibung des eigenen, textinternen Deutungspotentials der neutestamentlichen Schriften, das sich als Zusammenhang von (1) ritueller Handlung, (2) Semantik der Terminologie, mit der die Handlung belegt wird, und (3) sachlichen und metaphorischen Deutungsmöglichkeiten darstellen lässt. Darüber hinaus werde ich auch (4) die literarischen Zusammenhänge, in denen die Taufe Erwähnung findet, auf ihre hermeneutischen Implikationen befragen. Damit ergibt sich der strukturelle Aufbau der einzelnen thematischen Abschnitte des Beitrags, der die relevanten Schriftengruppen und Einzeltexte in der Folge ihrer Entstehungszeit untersucht[19].

---

einem Prätext zu verfassen, der den Prätext nicht nur erklärt oder als Basis einer Theoriebildung benutzt, sondern in seiner spezifischen formalen und sachlichen Eigenart würdigt und das jeweilige zeitgenössische Gespräch mit ihm ermöglicht und eröffnet".

15 J. A. LOADER, „Intertextualität in geschichteten Texten des Alten Testaments", 99–119.

16 Ähnliches gilt aber auch für die narrative Strategie der Evangelien.

17 Vgl. dazu theoretisch E.-M. BECKER, „Text und Hermeneutik am Beispiel textinterner Hermeneutik", 193–215.

18 Ich werde daher anders als Hans Dieter Betz weder die Begriffe der *Immersion* oder *Initiation* oder als Adela Yarbro Collins den Begriff der *Identität* verwenden, weil sie Teil der Theoriebildung und des methodischen Vokabulars der Religions- und Sozialwissenschaft sind. Ihre Verwendung in einer historisch-hermeneutischen Darstellung würde eine vertiefe Theoriediskussion erfordern, die hier nicht geführt werden kann.

19 Welche Erkenntnisperspektive eine neutestamentliche Studie zur Taufe im Neuen Testament einnehmen will, hängt von der jeweiligen Fragestellung bzw. dem jeweiligen Erkenntnisinteresse der textexternen Interpretation ab. Eine kultursemiotische Analyse antwortet auf andere Fragen als eine vergleichende religionsgeschichtliche Perspektive. Sehr zu begrüßen ist die deutliche Unterscheidung zwischen historischer und theologischer (d.h. systematischer) Perspektive bei F. HAHN, *Theologie des Neuen Testaments*, Bd. 1: passim; Bd. 2: 507–532. Schwierig sind Importe einzelner Theorieelemente – z.B. des Identitätstheorems – in eine primär historische Fragestellung. Hier entsteht leicht der Eindruck, erst durch eine theoriegestützte Fragestellung wie eben die Identitätsproblematik sei eine sinnvolle Erklärung der Taufe möglich. Dann muss aber geklärt werden, weshalb gerade die Taufe diese identitätsstiftende Funktion erfüllt. Dasselbe gilt für die einseitige Prämierung anderer Erklärungszusammenhänge. Ist erst die religions- bzw. kulturwissenschaftliche theoriegeleitete Erklärung im Zusammenhang „liminaler

2. Taufe bei Paulus

2.1. Rituelle Handlung

Die rituelle Handlung der Taufe findet zwischen dem Taufenden und dem Getauften statt. Täufer, Täufling und Taufhandlung bilden ein primäres Dreieck. Die Taufhandlung stellt sich ihrerseits wieder als Dreieck von Medium des Wassers, Vorgang des Untertauchens, Eintauchens oder Übergießens und schließlich der Taufformel dar. In diesen beiden Dreiecken kann jede der jeweils drei Größen problematisch werden. Bei Paulus tritt die rituelle Seite der Taufe nur im 1. Korintherbrief in Erscheinung, und hier erweist sich die Person des Taufenden, also der *Täufer*, in 1,13–17 als mögliches Problem, während weder die Taufhandlung noch die Täuflinge in den Paulusbriefen als problematische Größen erscheinen[20]. Paulus kommt gleich zu Beginn des Briefes auf einen wichtigen Aspekt der Taufpraxis in Korinth zu sprechen: auf den Umstand, dass die Taufe der Gemeindeglieder von leitenden Personen vollzogen wird, denen sich – wie offensichtlich in Korinth – die von ihnen getauften Gemeindeglieder besonders verbunden fühlen[21]. Die Namen der genannten Personen: Paulus, Apollos, Kephas, könnten darauf hinweisen, dass „Apostel" in den Missionsgemeinden taufen und damit – gewollt oder nicht gewollt – die Täuflinge als „Partei" an sich binden. Die verschiedenen historischen Implikationen dieser Frage können uns hier nicht beschäftigen[22]. Zwei Gesichtspunkte sind dagegen in hermeneutischer Hinsicht wichtig. *Erstens* stellt die Formel εἰς τὸ ὄνομα, die Paulus hier in V. 13 und 15 polemisch oder ironisch mit seiner eigenen Person in Verbindung bringt, auf jeden Fall im Verständnis der korinthischen Gemeinde ein persönliches Gefolgschafts- oder Beziehungsverhältnis[23] zwischen Täufer und Getauftem her. Das gilt paradoxerweise auch für den Namen Christi. Möglicherweise gibt es eine „Partei" in Korinth, die Christus analog zu den taufenden Aposteln versteht. Wie auch immer die Situation in Korinth im Einzelnen gewesen sein mag, so muss die Person des *Taufenden* – wie ja auch bei Johannes dem Täufer – für die Getauften in Korinth eine eigene Bedeutung gehabt haben. Paulus selbst be-

---

Theologie" hinreichend (vgl. CHR. STRECKER, *Die liminale Theologie des Paulus*). Und was ist mit dem Sakramentsbegriff? Kann dieser Begriff überhaupt noch eine erschließende Funktion haben?

20 Allerdings stellt sich bereits für Paulus die Frage nach der ethischen Nachhaltigkeit der Taufe für die Lebensführung der Getauften: s.u. Paulus kann sich offensichtlich auch eine Taufe schon verstorbener Personen vorstellen: I Kor 15, vgl. dazu A. LINDEMANN, *Der Erste Korintherbrief*, 350f.

21 Zum Problem vgl. LINDEMANN, *Der Erste Korintherbrief*, 34–43.

22 Vgl. dazu die Überlegungen bei Art. „Ritual", in: *RGG*[4] 7, 259f. Dasselbe gilt für die komplexen Probleme einer möglichen „Christuspartei" und ihres vielleicht durch die Taufformel entstandenen Selbstverständnisses.

23 Vgl. dazu Anm. 30.

kämpft diese Deutung und spielt in diesem Zusammenhang seine eigene Person als eines Taufenden herunter. Diese Haltung dürfte allerdings eher theologisch als realistisch sein! Denn er erinnert sich sehr genau an die Personen, die er getauft hat, – ein Vorgang, der im Rahmen der Gründung neuer Gemeinden verständlich ist und zugleich darauf hinweist, dass doch wohl eine Beziehung zwischen Gemeindegründer[24] und Getauften bestanden hat[25]. *Zweitens* könnte sich dem Text auch eine grundsätzliche Distanz des Paulus zum Taufvorgang und seiner Bedeutung entnehmen lassen, jedenfalls stellt er in diesem Text die Wortverkündigung sachlich deutlich über die Taufe (1,17). Ob diese Distanz zur Bedeutung der Taufe eher seiner Argumentation im 1. Korintherbrief zuzuschreiben ist oder auf ein frühes Stadium seines Taufverständnisses hindeutet[26], kann hier offen bleiben[27].

2.2. Semantik

Paulus benutzt die bereits bestehende Wortbedeutung von Verb und Substantiv aus den griechischsprachigen christusgläubigen Gemeinden: βαπτίζω bzw. βάπτισμα als term. techn.[28] für eine rituelle Handlung in den Gemeinden, die mit der Materie des Wassers arbeitet. Die Bedeutung von „untertauchen", „versenken" (Aktiv) bzw. „versinken", „ertrinken" (Passiv oder Medium) bezieht sich auf das Medium „Wasser" und wird als *primärer* Bedeutungsspender gedient haben. Die *übertragene* Bedeutung von „untergehen", „zugrunde gehen" entfernt sich von dem Medium des Wassers, wird für die Taufsemantik bei Paulus aber sehr wichtig.

2.3. Deutungsmöglichkeiten

Ausgangspunkt für Überlegungen zu den Deutungsmöglichkeiten bei Paulus müssen die folgenden Wendungen sein: (1) βαπτίζειν εἰς τὸ ὄνομα Παύλου, (2) βαπτίζειν εἰς τὸ ὄνομα τοῦ Χριστοῦ, (3) βαπτίζειν εἰς Χριστὸν Ἰησοῦν, (4) εἰς τὸν Μωυσῆν βαπτισθῆναι, (5) εἰς τὸν θάνατον (Ἰησοῦ) βαπτισθῆναι, (6) εἰς ἓν σῶμα

---

24 Vgl. dazu die grundlegenden Ausführungen bei BETZ, Art. „Ritual", in: *RGG*[4] 7, 259f.
25 Das mag besonders für Crispus gegolten haben. Zum Titel „Archisynagogos" vgl. T. RAJAK/D. NOY, „ARCHISYNAGOGOI: Office, Title and Social Status in the Graeco-Jewish Synagogue".
26 Zu der Entwicklung der paulinischen Taufdeutung vgl. Art. „Ritual", in: *RGG*[4], 7, 261–270.
27 I Kor 10,1–5 spricht allerdings dafür, dass Paulus bereits vielfältige Deutungsmöglichkeiten zu Gebote standen.
28 So A. OEPKE im Art. „βάπτω κτλ.", in: *ThWNT* 1, 527–544, 528. Vgl. dort auch die Überlegungen zu hebr. *tabal/tᵉbila*. Weiteres bei OSTMEYER, *Taufe und Typos*, 71–75, zum Wasser des Schilfmeeres.

βαπτισθῆναι, (7) ὑπὲρ τῶν νεκρῶν βαπτισθῆναι[29], (8) Χριστὸν ἐνδύσασθαι und (9) ἐν ἑνὶ πνεύματι βαπτισθῆναι.

Die vier ersten der mit εἰς eingeleiteten Wendungen beziehen sich direkt auf Personen und drücken, wie für I Kor 1,13 schon erwähnt, eine Beziehung[30], ein Autoritäts- oder Zugehörigkeitsverhältnis bzw. ein Partizipationsverhältnis aus. Der letztgenannte Aspekt dürfte die Wendung am ehesten treffen. Eine Person wird durch die Taufe mit der Person und der Autorität einer anderen Person verbunden. Dies wird an den sachlich uneigentlichen Wendungen: „Seid ihr auf den Namen des Paulus getauft?" (I Kor 1,13) und: „Unsere Väter sind in Mose getauft worden" (I Kor 10,2) deutlich[31]. Hans Dieter Betz unterscheidet weiter zwischen der Namensformel und der „Taufe in Christus". Er ordnet die Wendung εἰς τὸ ὄνομα τοῦ Χριστοῦ der Taufe, wie Petrus sie vollzog, zu und versteht diese Wendung als insuffizient, weil sie lediglich magisch agiere: „Kephas' concept created a link between the baptized and their Lord Jesus Christ only through the ὄνομα, that is, by 'magical' application of the name of Christ. Such a link merely *more magico* failed to spell out the ethical and communal obligations entered into by the baptized"[32]. Der magischen Interpretation möchte ich mich nicht anschließen, weil sie weder für die Paulus- noch für die Mosewendung passt[33]. Aber die Probleme in Korinth zeigen in der Tat,

---

29 Auf die Frage der Taufe für Verstorbene kann ich hier nicht eingehen (s.o. Anm. 21). Die Formulierung macht aber deutlich, dass auch hier personale Beziehungen eine Rolle spielen, diesmal bei den Täuflingen. Offensichtlich kann eine Person für die andere eintreten.

30 OEPKE, Art. „βάπτω κτλ.", in: *ThWNT* 1, 537, erklärt die Formel εἰς τὸ ὄνομα im Anschluss an W. Heitmüller aus dem Zusammenhang des hellenistischen Geldverkehrs: W. HEITMÜLLER, *Im Namen Jesu*. Dagegen G. DELLING, *Die Zueignung des Heils in der Taufe*, der bei seiner Deutung auf die Heilszuweisung abhebt. L. HARTMAN, „*Into the Name of the Lord Jesus*", 37–55, übersetzt die εἰς τὸ ὄνομα-Formel in Herleitung aus dem Hebräisch-Aramäischen bᵉ*shem* einfacher mit „with regard to" (40). Hartmans Deutung der Formel ist plausibel: „As a technical, ritual formula, the baptismal formula presupposed more: its ‚name' referred to an authority behind the rite, who conferred significance on the rite and made the formula meaningful" (45). Vgl. die Darstellung der Diskussion bei F. AVEMARIE, *Die Tauferzählungen der Apostelgeschichte*, 26–43. Avemarie schließt sich Hartman an: „Mit L. Hartmans Bestimmung der ὄνομα-Formel als sinngebender Referenz lässt sich dieser Fall am treffendsten erfassen: Durch den Bezug auf einen übergreifenden symbolischen Zusammenhang wird der Ritus identifizierbar, die christologische Signatur macht die Taufe zu einer *christlichen* Taufe" (30). Siehe ferner HARTMANS Beitrag in der vorliegenden Publikation.

31 Vgl. dazu LINDEMANN, *Der Erste Korintherbrief*, 218: „Der Sinn scheint zu sein, eine betont enge Bindung der ‚Väter' an Mose auszusprechen". BETZ, „Transferring a Ritual", 263ff. stellt die Partizipation der Getauften am Schicksal Christi im Einzelnen dar.

32 Art. „Ritual", in: *RGG*⁴ 7, 260. Die historische Rekonstruktion der korinthischen Situation in Bezug auf die taufenden Apostel kann hier nicht diskutiert werden.

33 Außerdem hat sich die Namensformel in trinitarischer Ausformung am Ende des Matthäusevangeliums und in der Didache sowie im sekundären Markusschluss durchgesetzt. Wenn hier auch von Magie gesprochen werden soll, müsste man den Ausdruck „magisch" religionsgeschichtlich genauer zuordnen.

dass die Taufe auf die Namensformel, von Betz wieder mit einem religionsgeschichtlichen Begriff als bloßes *„conversion ritual"* interpretiert[34], den christologischen hermeneutischen Anforderungen nicht entsprach, die Paulus an die Taufe richtete bzw. mit ihr verbinden wollte. Nach Betz ging es Paulus um „interpretation of baptism as initiation"[35], und diese Bedeutung der Taufe als Inkorporation in Christus brachte die einfache Wendung βαπτίζειν εἰς Χριστὸν Ἰησοῦν besser zum Ausdruck. Auch hier übernehme ich nicht die religionsgeschichtliche Terminologie, stimme aber Betz im Ergebnis zu: nach Paulus verbindet die Taufe die Getauften direkt mit der Person und dem Schicksal Jesu. Die beiden weiteren εἰς-Wendungen: „in den Tod taufen", „in einen Leib taufen" haben metaphorische Qualität, ebenso das Bild „Jesus anziehen".

Diese drei metaphorischen Wendungen, die Leibmetapher (I Kor 12,13), die Todesmetapher (Röm 6,3–5), die sich, wie schon gesagt, von der Semantik her nahe legt[36], und die Kleidmetapher (Gal 3,27) eröffnen einen gemeinsamen Deutungsraum. Das Medium des Wassers dient hier nicht als primärer Deutungsgeber, obgleich Paulus in I Kor 6,11 das Verb ἀπελούσασθε setzt und in 10,1.2 das Rote Meer mit der Taufe assoziiert[37]. Zusammengehalten werden diese Metaphern aber nicht durch ihre Beziehung zum Medium Wasser, sondern durch ihre Beziehung auf die Person und das Schicksal Christi einerseits und die Teilhabe der Getauften an diesem Schicksal andererseits. Die Taufe „in" den Tod Jesu und „in" seinen Leib sowie die Taufe als das Anziehen Christi als eines Gewandes[38] sind *partizipatorisch* und *christuszentriert*. Hier finden wir eine eigene Deutung des bereits erwähnten Dreiecks von *Täufer*-Taufvorgang-Täufling. Paulus konstruiert das Dreieck von *Christus*-Taufvorgang-Täufling, ohne allerdings Christus als den Täufer zu verstehen. Der Täufer verliert vielmehr bei Paulus seine konstitutive Rolle in dem Dreieck.

Anhand der Taufmetaphern ergibt sich eine kohärente *Deutung* der Taufe bei Paulus. Die Taufe als eigene Größe verbindet zwei Größen unauflöslich: Christus und die getaufte Person. Die Täuflinge haben Christus wie ein Gewand angezogen, ja sie bilden das σῶμα Christi[39]. Das bedeutet: sie leben in einer neuen somatischen und relationalen Qualität – in einer neuen personalen und sozialen Wirklichkeit, die besonders deutlich in Gal 3,26ff. und in I Kor

---

34 Art. „Ritual", in: *RGG*[4] 7, 262.

35 Art. „Ritual", in: *RGG*[4] 7, 261.

36 Für Kleid und Leib gilt das nicht. Zum Kleid vgl. die Überlegungen bei YARBRO COLLINS, „Baptism as Transformation", 7.

37 Vgl. dazu die Studie von OSTMEYER, *Taufe und Typos*. Ostmeyer weist S. 140 auf das Fehlen der Vokabel ὕδωρ bei Paulus hin und führt fort: „Dort, wo in der paulinischen Korrespondenz Wasser ungenannt im Hintergrund steht, handelt es sich niemals um die Materie als solche … Wasser ist für Paulus immer wirkendes Wasser".

38 Steht hier das „Taufkleid" im Hintergrund?

39 Dazu jetzt L. SCORNAIENCHI, *„Sarx und Soma bei Paulus"*, 167–230.

12,13 ausgedrückt wird. Logisch gesehen schließen sich die Bilder vom Gewand und vom Leib gegenseitig aus, aus der Perspektive der personalen Teilhabe bilden sie eine Klimax der Nähe bis zur Identifizierung. Die Leibmetapher betont das *kommunitäre* Element der Taufe. Die *personale* Sichtweise auf die Taufe findet ihren Ausdruck in der schon genannten Vorstellung, die Israeliten seien „in Mose", ihren Führer und Retter, getauft worden, und in der Abwehr der möglicherweise in Korinth vertretenen Ansicht, man werde „auf den jeweiligen taufenden Apostel" getauft.

Hans Dieter Betz hat besonders auf die sinnstiftenden Begriffe σύμφυτος (verbunden, zusammengewachsen) und ὁμοίωμα (Gleichheit, Gleichgestalt) im Zusammenhang mit Jesu Tod in Röm 6 hingewiesen[40], die beide das historische Ereignis des Todes Jesu mit der Gegenwart der Täuflinge verbinden. Hinzu kommen die Verben συνετάφημεν und συσταυρώθη. Diesen Aspekt möchte ich vertiefen. Es ist nicht selbstverständlich, dass sich diese Begriffe nicht auf Jesus Christus als den himmlischen κύριος, sondern auf Jesu *Todesschicksal* beziehen, mit dem die Täuflinge in der Taufe verbunden (σύν und ὅμοιος) werden. Das „Mitbegrabenwerden" (Röm 6,4), das „Mitsterben" (Röm 6,5) sowie das „Mitgekreuzigtwerden" (Röm 6,6) der Täuflinge orientiert sich sprachlich an der Gemeindetradition von I Kor 15,3f. Sachlich wird hier die oben genannte übertragene Bedeutung von „untergehen", „zugrunde gehen" von βαπτίζειν aufgerufen[41]. Dies geschieht aber nicht im Sinne der bloßen Zerstörung (des alten Lebens) und eines Neuanfangs, d.h. in Diskontinuität[42], sondern in Verbindung mit dem Tod Jesu. Genau hier liegt die eigene interpretatorische Leistung des Paulus, der den Ritus des Eintritts in die christusgläubige Gemeinde[43] in somatischer (personenbezogen) und eschatologischer (epochenbezogen) Perspektive mit dem historischen Todesschicksal Jesu verbindet[44]. Die theologische Fachterminologie spricht hier von Soteriologie. Paulus selbst verwendet verbale Metaphern, die den Taufvorgang mit den einzelnen Aspekten des Todes Jesu zusammenschließen[45]. Er löst die Frage nach dem *Wie* nicht auf. Das *Wie* dieser Teilhabe bleibt unausgesprochen, es ist im Ritus verborgen, genauer

---

40   Art. „Ritual", in: *RGG*[4] 7, 267–269.

41   Vgl. auch das Rote Meer: Wasser in seiner tödlichen Qualität. Es handelt sich allerdings in I Kor 10 um eine gelehrte Allegorie, die an die Vokabel θάλασσα anknüpft. In der Exoduserzählung kommen die Israeliten ja gerade nicht mit dem Meer in Berührung! Vgl. OSTMEYER, *Taufe und Typos*, 71, zur Exoduserzählung: „Das Wasser des Schilfmeers ist nicht Medium, mittels dessen Gott rettet, sondern Medium des Gerichts, aus dem Gott rettet".

42   Dieser Aspekt spielt bei Paulus ebenfalls eine wichtige Rolle: vgl. II Kor 5,17.

43   Ich möchte weder von Konversions- noch von Initiationsritus sprechen. Diese Begriffe sind Teil religionswissenschaftlicher und sozialwissenschaftlicher Theoriebildung, die meinem Beitrag nicht zugrunde liegt.

44   Zu den zeitlichen Aspekten vgl. Art. „Ritual", in: *RGG*[4] 7, 169.

45   Daraus ergibt sich die sperrige Metapher, die Taufe sei ein Mitgekreuzigtwerden mit Jesus.

gesagt: im Handeln Gottes im Ritus, und in der christozentrischen verbalen Metaphorik kodiert.

I Kor 10,1–13 macht die Deutung der Taufe auf das „Sterben mit Christus" besonders plausibel. K.-H. Ostmeyer interpretiert die typologische Beziehung zwischen der „Taufe in Mose" und der „Taufe in Christus" folgendermaßen: „Die alte Existenz beider Gruppen (sc. der Israeliten und der Christen) ist vernichtet durch die tötenden Wasser. Rettung wurde beiden durch göttliche Gegenwart und göttliches Wirken zuteil ... Israeliten und Korinther ... wurden durch ihre Taufe einer neuen prägenden Herrschaft unterstellt"[46].

In diesem Zusammenhang erhält nun ein weiteres Motiv aus I Kor 12,13 seine Bedeutung: ἐν ἑνὶ πνεύματι ἐβαπτίσθημεν. Weder die Materie, das Wasser, noch der Täufer, welcher Apostel oder Gemeindeleiter auch immer, ist entscheidend, sondern das Handeln Gottes, der hier als Geist angesprochen wird. Diese Verbindung von Taufe und Geist, die in den Paulusbriefen nur hier explizit begegnet[47], wird in anderen frühchristlichen Texten sehr wichtig werden.

Zugleich macht den Täufling seine Bindung an das Todesschicksal Jesu aber auch frei zu einem neuen Leben „für Gott in Jesus Christus" (Röm 6,11), und damit treffen wir auf eine weitere hermeneutische Figur der Taufinterpretation bei Paulus, die sich nicht aus den bisher behandelten εἰς-Wendungen und aus dem Rückbezug auf Jesu Todesschicksal ergibt, sondern aus der somatisch verstandenen Teilhabe an Christi himmlischer Existenz in eschatologischer Brechung. Im Römerbrief ist das Sinnpotential der Taufe nämlich nicht abgeschlossen, sondern nach vorn *offen*, ausgedrückt durch das futurische συζήσομεν (Röm 6,8). Die *epochale* Sinnkomponente bezieht sich nicht nur auf die Vergangenheit, d.h. das Mitgestorbensein mit Jesus, sondern auch auf die Zukunft des Mit-Christus-Lebens. Spätestens hier wird deutlich, dass Begriffe wie Identitätsfindung, Konversion, Initiation oder auch die von H. D. Betz bevorzugte Inkorporation (Gal 3) die Deutung der Taufe bei Paulus verkürzen, sofern sie die Taufe als abgeschlossenen Akt verstehen, dessen Bedeutung mit dem Vollzug bereits ausgeschöpft ist. In Röm 6 interpretiert Paulus die Taufe aber als Eröffnung einer neuen Lebensform und damit als Initial von christusförmigem[48] Ethos. Diese hermeneutische Öffnung der Taufe vom Ritual zur Ermöglichung einer Lebensform verbindet die Taufthematik mit der Ethik – eine Verbindung, die die christliche Theologie später unter den Begriffen von Sakrament und Ethik verhandeln wird.

Ich halte fest, dass Paulus seine eigene Deutung der Taufe nicht primär der Materie des Wassers entnimmt, dass er jede besondere Bedeutung der Person des Taufenden verneint und dass er stattdessen die Taufe und den Täufling an

---

46 OSTMEYER, *Taufe und Typos*, 144.
47 Vgl. aber Texte wie I Kor 6,11; II Kor 1,21f.
48 Vgl. Phil 2.

das Todesschicksal Jesu bindet. Daneben haben sich drei weitere bedeutunggebende Bereiche für das Taufverständnis des Paulus ergeben: die Geistbegabung, die kommunitäre Qualität der Teilhabe am σῶμα Χριστοῦ und die Eröffnung einer neuen Lebensform. I Kor 10,1–4 bindet demgegenüber die Taufe an das vorgängige Handeln des Geistes an Israel zurück. In 10,4 und 9 macht Paulus deutlich, dass Christus in diesem Handeln des Geistes bereits anwesend und wirksam war. Er bezieht die Taufe also nicht auf Johannes den Täufer zurück, sondern verbindet sie typologisch mit Mose.

2.4. Literarische Zusammenhänge

Adela Yarbro Collins hat erneut nachdrücklich auf die Bedeutung der jeweiligen rhetorischen Situation und des jeweiligen argumentativen Zwecks hingewiesen, die die einzelnen Aussagen des Paulus zur Bedeutung der Taufe bestimmen[49]. Darüber hinaus muss auch die Gattungsfrage berücksichtigt werden. Allgemein gilt, dass sich die Taufaussagen des Paulus in drei seiner Gemeindebriefe finden. Sie beziehen sich also ausschließlich auf das, was wir beschreibend „Gemeindetheologie" und Paränese nennen können. Die Taufe tritt – unabhängig von den Deutungspotentialen, die Paulus ihr gibt – faktisch als rituelle Eintrittshandlung in die christusgläubigen Gemeinden in den Blick. Das heißt auch, dass die Deutungskoordinaten innerhalb der kommunitären Strukturen der ἐκκλησίαι τοῦ θεοῦ in Korinth, Galatien und Rom gewonnen und von den Adressaten als Verstehenskoordinaten verwendet werden.

Die rhetorische Strategie im 1. Korintherbrief lässt sich mit Margaret M. Mitchell als „rhetoric of reconciliation"[50] beschreiben. I Kor 1,13.14.15.16 und 12,13[51] gehören in diesen paränetischen Zusammenhang der Einheitsermahnung. Der Rekurs auf die Taufe ist hier jeweils Bestandteil der Einheitsmahnung und hat kein eigenes thematisches Gewicht und damit auch keine besondere hermeneutische Qualität. Der ungewöhnliche Text I Kor 10,1ff. dagegen ist Bestandteil von „der Form nach an einen Midrasch…erinnernde(n) Ausführungen zur Interpretation biblischer Überlieferung"[52]. Das Ziel dieser Passage ist aber ebenfalls paränetisch (V. 11): es gibt keine Sicherheit aufgrund (bloßer) Teilhabe an Mose oder Christus, sondern gerade die Teilhabe an Taufe und Herrenmahl[53] muss zur ethischen Bewährung führen. Paulus stößt mit dieser

---

49   Yarbro Collins, „Baptism as Transformation", 6.
50   M. M. Mitchell, *Paul and the Rhetoric of Reconciliation*.
51   1,17 dagegen ist eine der vielen autobiographischen Sätze des Paulus, in denen er sich selbst in seinem spezifischen Apostolat darstellt.
52   Lindemann, *Der Erste Korintherbrief*, 217, vgl. die Analyse bei Ostmeyer, *Taufe und Typos*, 137–161.
53   Wieweit sich I Kor 10,4 auf die Taufe oder das Herrenmahl bezieht und ob überhaupt diese beiden Größen hier im Blick sind, kann an dieser Stelle nicht erörtert werden.

Argumentation zu einem Grundproblem der Taufdeutungen vor, das zu einem klassischen Problem werden sollte: der ethischen Wirksamkeit und Nachhaltigkeit des mit der Taufhandlung vollzogenen neuen Status. Er expliziert diese Dimension der Deutung der Taufe in Röm 6. Die Problematik wird, wie schon angedeutet, im Lauf der Geschichte der Taufe für alle Glieder des Dreiecks von Täufer-Taufe-Täufling relevant werden.

In Gal 3,26–29 verwendet Paulus die Taufe argumentativ im Zusammenhang des großen Nachweises der Abrahamkindschaft aller christusgläubigen – und getauften – Heiden[54]. Trotz der starken Deutungskraft dieses Textabschnittes gewinnt die Taufe keine eigene Deutungsqualität im argumentativen Großzusammenhang, sondern wird nur als ein wichtiges Argument neben anderen herangezogen, um die eschatologische Einheit der Gemeinde zu beweisen[55]. Zugleich tritt die kommunitäre Qualität der Taufe in Erscheinung. Erst in Röm 6 findet Paulus zu einer *thematisch* eigenen Taufdeutung, und zwar im literarischen Zusammenhang seiner christologisch-soteriologischen Ausführungen in Röm 5–8. Hier liegen die hermeneutisch entscheidenden Deutungspotentiale der paulinischen Taufinterpretation.

3. Taufe im Markusevangelium

Bei Paulus und in der nachpaulinischen Briefliteratur begegnet weder ein Hinweis auf Johannes den Täufer und die sog. Johannestaufe noch auf die Taufe Jesu durch Johannes und eine mögliche Tauftätigkeit Jesu und/oder seiner Jünger, es fehlen darüber hinaus alle Hinweise auf die Anfänge der Taufe als eines Ritus der christusgläubigen Gemeinden. Völlig anders ist das Bild im ältesten Evangelium. Der Beginn der Evangelienerzählung in 1,4 mit ἐγένετο führt sogleich auf Johannes, der nicht unter seinem Eponym βαπτιστής[56], sondern von seiner Tätigkeit her dargestellt wird: „Er war taufend in der Wüste". Bei den Rezipienten kann anscheinend die Kenntnis Johannes des Täufers vorausgesetzt werden. In den Versen 4–8 entwirft der Erzähler ein ebenso knappes wie prägnantes Bild von dem Ort der Predigt des Johannes, von der Taufhandlung und ihrem speziellen Platz, von der Person des Täufers und seiner eigenen Deutung seiner Taufe. In den Versen 9–11 folgt die noch kürzere Szene von der Taufe Jesu durch Johannes, an die sich sofort die Offenbarung der Gottessohnschaft in Gestalt einer Vision und einer Audition Jesu anschließt. Der Evangelist vermeidet jede Beziehung zwischen diesen beiden Grunderzählungen und der späteren Taufe in den christusgläubigen Gemeinden, wie sie dann im sekundären Markusschluss

---

54 Betz versteht den Passus als Paulus überkommene Formel: Betz, *Galatians*, 181–201.
55 Vgl. dazu O. Wischmeyer, „Wie kommt Abraham in den Galaterbrief".
56 So Mk 6,25 und 8,28 (in Fremdnennungen).

andeutungsweise hergestellt wird[57]. Das verbindet die Darstellung der Taufe Jesu im Markusevangelium mit der Darstellung seines Letzten Mahles, das auch ausschließlich in die Jesuserzählung eingebettet ist und keinen Wiederholungs- oder Erinnerungsbefehl enthält, der auf das Herrenmahl der christusgläubigen Gemeinden vorausweisen könnte[58].

3.1. Rituelle Handlung

Als rituelle Handlung haben wir im Markusevangelium nur die Taufe des Johannes, nämlich die Taufe an einem bestimmten *Ort*: im Jordan[59], mit einer bestimmten *Materie*: fließendem Wasser[60], zu einer bestimmten *Zeit*: der Endzeit, vollzogen von einer bestimmten historischen *Person*: „Johannes dem Täufer", gedacht für eine bestimmte *Gruppe*: die Juden, durchgeführt zu einem bestimmten religiösen *Zweck*: der Sündenvergebung. Dass es sich um einen einmaligen Taufvorgang handelte, wird im Markusevangelium nicht eigens gesagt, lässt sich aber aus der Semantik in 1,4 und aus der Erzählung der Taufe Jesu, die eine Wiederholung ausschließt, folgern. Ob die Täuflinge in einem eigenen Akt des Ritus ihre Sünden bekennen, – dies wäre dann neben Täufer, Taufhandlung und Täufling ein viertes Element des Ritus – wie man aus V. 5 schließen könnte, muss offen bleiben.

3.2. Semantik

Die Semantik unterscheidet sich nicht von der des Paulus. Wir finden dieselbe frühchristliche Sprache ohne semantische Hinweise auf eine eigene Taufterminologie des Täufers. Zwei Punkte verdienen im Rahmen der hermeneutischen Fragestellung Aufmerksamkeit. *Erstens* wird Johannes zweimal mit dem Epitheton „Täufer"[61] belegt, das zeigt, „dass man das Auftreten dieses Mannes als schlechthin neu und einzigartig empfand, und zwar auch deshalb, weil er nicht sich selbst[62], sondern gegen alles jüdische Herkommen andere taufte"[63]. An Jesus und seinen Jüngern haftet dies Epitheton dagegen nicht. *Zweitens* wird βάπτισμα in 10,38f. metaphorisch verwendet, und zwar in der Bedeutung von „Taufe, die den Tod bedeutet". Die dem Verbum inhärente Todeskonnotation, die wir schon

---

57 Mk 16,16. Hier kann eine Beeinflussung durch Mt 28 vorliegen. Allerdings steht die Bedeutung der Taufe gegenüber dem Glauben zurück. Der Akzent liegt auf dem Glauben.
58 Erst bei Paulus findet sich dieser Aspekt: I Kor 11,23–26.
59 Vgl. die reinigende Wirkung des Jordanflusses schon in IV Kön 5,14 (βαπτίζω).
60 Die späteren Johannesjünger haben sich von diesem Ort gelöst.
61 So auch bei Josephus, *Ant*, 18,5,2: Ἰωάννου τοῦ ἐπικαλουμένου βαπτιστοῦ.
62 So z.B. Bannus: Josephus, *De vita sua*, 11.
63 Art. „βάπτω κτλ.", in: *ThWNT* 1, 544.

bei Paulus fanden, ist hier auf das in den christusgläubigen Gemeinden neu gebildete Substantiv übertragen.

3.3. Deutungsmöglichkeiten

Die Deutung der Johannestaufe wird vom Evangelisten explizit in der Genitivverbindung „Taufe der Buße bzw. Umkehr (μετάνοια)" und der Zweckbestimmung „εἰς ἄφεσιν ἁμαρτιῶν" gegeben[64]. Der Tauritus des Johannes wird damit in direkte Beziehung zum Leben der Israeliten vor Gott gestellt und ist Ausdruck der Umkehr in der Endzeit, die der Evangelist in der Zitatkette zur Eröffnung seines Evangeliums aufruft. Wieweit der Ritus der Taufe des Johannes selbst schon diese Umkehr bewirkt oder ob er sie nur einleitet, bleibt im Markusevangelium offen, wie überhaupt das erzählerische Gewicht auf der Taufe Jesu liegt und Johannes (nur) die Vorläuferrolle bleibt. Aus hermeneutischer Sicht ist besonders wichtig, dass Jesus als derjenige in der Erzählung eingeführt wird, der in Kontinuität und Erfüllung bzw. Überbietung zur Verheißung Jesajas und zur Taufe des Johannes steht. Damit stellt der Verfasser des Markusevangeliums gleich zu Beginn einen Deutungsraum für das Auftreten Jesu her, der die Verheißung Jesajas und die Johannestaufe mit der Sohnschaft Jesu (Mk 1,1.9–11) verbindet. Auf der Sohnschaft liegt das eigentliche erzählerische und theologische Gewicht. Das vormarkinische Logion Mk 1,8[65] stellt in diesem Zusammenhang einen Fremdkörper dar. Hier wird die Taufe mit Wasser Johannes zugeschrieben, während Jesus ἐν πνεύματι ἁγίῳ taufen wird[66]. Bei dieser verbalen Metapher „mit Geist taufen" geht es nicht (nur) darum, dass Taufe und Geist zueinander in Beziehung gesetzt, sondern dass sie einander entgegengesetzt werden, so dass Jesus gar nicht mit Wasser taufen wird. Das Markusevangelium kommt nirgends auf diese Prophezeiung einer Geisttaufe zurück, die eine Diskontinuität nicht nur zwischen Johannes und Jesus, sondern auch zwischen Jesus und der Gemeindetaufe insinuiert. Die Geisttaufe spielt dagegen im lukanischen Werk eine wichtige Rolle. Im Markusevangelium dient das Logion lediglich der Vorbereitung der Taufe Jesu und liefert das Stichwort πνεῦμα.

Vor diesem Deutungshorizont wird die Taufe Jesu erzählt. Ob Jesu Umkehr und Sündenbekenntnis beim Taufvorgang vom Erzähler mitgedacht sind, lässt sich der aufs Äußerste verknappten Erzählnotiz in 1,9 nicht entnehmen. Der Deutungshorizont wird erzählerisch erst in den Versen 10 und 11 entworfen. Der Geist in Gestalt einer Taube, die Himmelsstimme und die Adoption Jesu

---

[64] Damit ist nichts über das Verständnis des Johannes selbst gesagt. Zu den exegetischen Problemen der Markusperikope vgl. Yarbro Collins, *Mark*, 138–155.

[65] Vgl. Q 3,16f.

[66] Die Q-Version, die Frage nach einer möglichen Rückführung einer älteren Version des Logions auf den Täufer sowie das Verhältnis von Q 3,16f. und Mk 1,8 können hier nicht berücksichtigt werden, vgl. Yarbro Collins, *Mark*, 146f.

zum geliebten Sohn Gottes[67] schließen sich direkt an den Taufvorgang an. Während sich die Geistbegabung als Deuteelement der Taufe ebenso aus der Gemeindetheologie[68] wie aus dem prophetischen Hintergrund von Mk 1 erklären lässt[69], ist die Sohnschaft im Sinne des geliebten bzw. einzigen Sohnes nicht nur als Folge der Taufe zu interpretieren, sondern dient eher der Absetzung Jesu von Johannes dem Täufer[70]. Die beiden anderen Sohnestexte in 9,1–8 und 15,39 zeigen deutlich, dass der Sohnestitel nicht an der Taufe hängt. Die Beziehung Jesu zu Johannes und seine Taufe steht für den Evangelisten historisch unbestritten am Anfang von Jesu öffentlicher Wirksamkeit, tritt aber in seiner Darstellung deutlich hinter der Geistbegabung und der Proklamation Jesu zum Sohn Gottes zurück.

Mk 1,8 enthält drei eigene hermeneutische Aspekte. Erstens hebt der Täufer auf die Materie der Taufe ab, ordnet diese seiner Person zu und spricht dabei der „Wassertaufe" eine mindere und nur vorläufige Bedeutung zu[71]. Wir finden also in Mk 1,8 jene Distanzierung von der Wassertaufe, die sich ansatzweise bei Paulus fand, sowie die Antithese von Wasser und Geist, die das Taufverständnis im Johannesevangelium prägt. Beide Motive werden aber auf Johannes und Jesus verteilt. Zweitens stellt Markus keine Rückbindung der christlichen Taufpraxis an Jesus her, diese schafft erst das Johannesevangelium. Drittens gibt Mk 1,8–11[72] den späteren Evangelien das Thema des πνεῦμα im Zusammenhang mit der Taufe auf, mit dem sich besonders das lukanische Doppelwerk beschäftigen wird.

Ergeben sich aus Mk 1,8.9–11 trotz der Abständigkeit von der Gemeindetaufe auch Deutungspotentiale für die Taufe der christusgläubigen Gemeinden? Adela Yarbro Collins hat auf die Leserschaft als deutunggebende Größe hingewiesen und kommentiert Mk 1,8 daher folgendermaßen: „In relation to at least part of the audience of Mark, the passage seems to have functioned as a cult legend. The reference to baptism in the Holy Spirit in v. 8 would have called to mind the ritual of initiation into the community of the followers of Jesus (1 Cor 6:11; Acts 2:38). In light of that ritual and communal context, the narrative of Jesus' baptism in vv. 9–11 would call to mind the baptism of his followers, their

---

67 „Gott" wird nicht genannt. Insoweit bleibt auch diese Eröffnungsepiphanie eine verborgene, zumal sie nur von Jesus wahrgenommen wird.

68 Siehe das oben zu Paulus Gesagte.

69 Vgl. dazu YARBRO COLLINS, Mark, 139.146–150. Collins weist außer auf Jes 40,3 auf Hes 36,25–28 hin.

70 Die Geistbegabung kann auch in diesem Zusammenhang verstanden werden: V.8. Vgl. dazu YARBRO COLLINS, Mark, 146f.

71 Ob hier tatsächlich Täufertradition in dem Sinn vorliegt, dass sich der Täufer selbst als Vorläufer der Endzeit verstand, kann hier nicht erörtert werden. Vgl. YARBRO COLLINS, Mark, 138–140, und C. K. ROTHSCHILD, Baptist Traditions and Q.

72 Basis ist wohl das Q-Logion.

reception of the Holy Spirit, and their being made sons and daughters of God"[73]. Beide Gesichtspunkte, die Abständigkeit von Mk 1 von der Gemeindetaufe und die gleichzeitige Durchsichtigkeit der Tauferzählung auf die Gemeindetaufe, müssen hermeneutisch zusammengedacht werden.

Schließlich findet sich in 10,38f. eine substantivische Taufmetapher[74]. Hier wird, wie schon gesagt, Jesu Tod in einem komplexen zweigliedrigen Bildwort als Deutehorizont aufgerufen. Zugleich scheinen beide Metaphern: Taufe und Kelch, auf die beiden Rituale von frühchristlicher Taufe und Herrenmahl anzuspielen[75], so dass hier unter Umständen der Evangelist eine – einmalige – Brücke zwischen Jesuserzählung und den beiden Gemeinderitualen schlägt und zeigt, dass er die Deutungen der paulinischen Theologie kennt, die diese Riten mit Jesu Tod verbinden.

3.4. Literarische Zusammenhänge

Hier kann ich mich kurz fassen, da ich in der Einführung zum Markusevangelium schon auf die literarischen Unterschiede zwischen den Paulusbriefen und dem Markusevangelium und ihre Folgen für die Deutungen der Taufe hingewiesen habe. Das Markusevangelium ist – trotz seiner starken Verpflichtung auf das Konzept des εὐαγγέλιον – das erste Jesusbuch im Sinne einer Erzählung seines Wirkens und Sterbens[76]. Dies ist der allgemeine Deutehorizont der gesamten Erzählung. Die gänzliche Konzentration auf die Person Jesu[77] stellt auch die dem Evangelisten aus der Tradition zugekommene Tauferzählung in den Zusammen-

---

73   Yarbro Collins, *Mark*, 147. Vgl. auch das klare Votum von Avemarie im Art. „Taufe", in: *RGG*[4] 8, 55: „Die Synopt. nehmen in ihrer Schilderung der T. Jesu durch Johannes (Mk 1,9–11 parr.) implizit auch auf die christl. Taufpraxis Bezug", sowie Hahn, *Theologie des Neuen Testaments*, Bd. 2, 509 zu Mk 1,9–11: „Dieser Text besitzt nicht nur christologische Relevanz, sondern ist zugleich Urbild der christlichen Taufe".

74   Vgl. Lk 12,50: Todestaufe. Zum Motiv der Todestaufe vgl. Hahn, *Theologie des Neuen Testaments*, Bd. 2, 513: „Das Motiv der Todestaufe ist seinem Ursprung nach vorpaulinisch, wie Lk 12,49f. und Mk 10,38f. ... zeigen .... Für den Getauften ist, solange er lebt, die *participatio* am Leiden Jesu kennzeichnend". In dem Logion Q 3,16 zeichnet sich auch das apokalyptisch kodierte Motiv der Feuertaufe ab (dazu Hahn, *Theologie des Neuen Testaments*, Bd. 2, 508). Geisttaufe, Feuertaufe und das spätere Motiv der Bluttaufe setzten alle bei der *reinigenden* Materie der Wassertaufe ein, die sie substituieren. Die „Todestaufe" setzt demgegenüber bei der *tödlichen* Wirkung der Materie ein: dem Ertrinken.

75   Damit ist keine Aussage über die Traditionsgeschichte des Logions gemacht. Vgl. dazu Yarbro Collins, *Mark*, 146.

76   Die komplizierte Debatte um die Frage nach der Gattung kann hier nicht behandelt werden. Vgl. dazu Becker, *Das Markus-Evangelium im Rahmen antiker Historiographie*, 76–100. Anders zuletzt G. Theissen, *Die Entstehung des Neuen Testaments als literaturgeschichtliches Problem*. Theissen plädiert für die literarische Form der Biographie.

77   Becker, *Das Markus-Evangelium im Rahmen antiker Historiographie*, 191–194, spricht von „personenzentrierter Geschichtsschreibung".

hang der Sohneschristologie, die thematisch das Buch eröffnet (1,1). Der Taufperikope sind in diesem Zusammenhang zwei eigene christologische Deutungselemente zu entnehmen: die Geistverleihung und damit der Geistbesitz Jesu und das Epitheton „geliebter Sohn".

4. Taufe im Matthäusevangelium

Es ist das Matthäusevangelium, in dem der Bogen zwischen der Johannestaufe, der Taufe Jesu durch Johannes und der Taufe in den christusgläubigen Gemeinden geschlagen wird, indem diese unterschiedlichen Aspekte in *einen* Erzählzusammenhang im Horizont der Jesusgeschichte gebracht werden. Im Taufbefehl in 28,19 wird die Taufe vom auferstandenen Jesus den Elf anbefohlen. 28,19 ist so etwas wie eine Einsetzungsparadosis der Gemeindetaufe[78], die ihren Ausgangspunkt allerdings nicht im Leben Jesu und seiner eigenen Taufe[79], sondern in der Zeit der Erscheinung des Auferstandenen vor den Jüngern hat. Auch Matthäus knüpft also in 28,19 nicht an die Johannestaufe und an die Taufe Jesu durch Johannes an, so dass der Erzählbogen zwar eine formale narrative Verbindung schafft, ohne dass aber Deutungselemente der Johannes- und Jesustaufe auf die Gemeindetaufe übertragen würden. In 28,19 spricht Jesus als der endzeitliche himmlische Kyrios und macht die Elf zu den Boten seiner Herrschaft in der Endzeit. Ihr Auftrag gilt im Gegensatz zur Johannestaufe den Völkern, d.h. allen Nichtjuden. Der Auftrag der Elf ist Taufe und Lehre. Die Taufe wird als Ritus verstanden und von dem dritten Aspekt der Taufhandlung, der Taufformel, her angesprochen, die hier prototrinitarisch angereichert ist[80]. Im Taufbefehl fungieren Taufe und Lehre Jesu als die beiden Identitätsmerkmale der christusgläubigen Gemeinden[81]. Eine Deutung der Taufe im Sinne des Paulus wird nicht gegeben, denn die „Völker", die getauft werden sollen, werden nicht partizipatorisch in das Todesschicksal Jesu einbezogen, sondern dem Gehorsam gegenüber dem

---

78 Man könnte religionsgeschichtlich durchaus von einem Gründungsmythos oder einer Kultlegende (so YARBRO COLLINS schon für Mk 1,8–11, s.o. Anm. 76) sprechen. Zum Text vgl. U. LUZ, *Das Evangelium nach Matthäus. 4. Teilband*, 427–459. Luz ordnet den Text den „Erscheinungs- und Beauftragungsgeschichten" zu (432). Für VV. 18b–20 spricht er von einem gattungsgeschichtlichen „Unikat" (433).

79 Diese ist für den Evangelisten eher wenig verständlich. Er macht ihre Bedeutung unter seinem hermeneutischen Schlüsselbegriff der Gerechtigkeit klar (3,13).

80 Vgl. dazu LUZ, *Das Evangelium nach Matthäus. 4. Teilband*, 452–454.

81 Bei diesem Text legt die textinterne Hermeneutik die Formulierung *identity marker* nahe.

himmlischen Christus zugeführt[82]. Die Taufe ist ebenso Ausdruck dieses Gehorsams wie das „Halten der Lehre Jesu"[83].

5. Taufe in der Apostelgeschichte

5.1. Rituelle Handlung

In der Apostelgeschichte[84] ist der Taufritus überall gegenwärtig[85]. Die große Erzählung vom Weg des Evangeliums von Jerusalem nach Rom (1,8) bietet einen Einblick in unterschiedliche Aspekte der rituellen Handlung der Gemeindetaufe. Der Maßstab wird in der Pfingsterzählung gesetzt: Taufpredigt-Buße-Taufe-Geistverleihung (2,37–41).

Täufer sind die Apostel, wobei der Begriff nicht eng gefasst wird[86]. Der *Taufvorgang* weist keine Besonderheiten auf. Getauft wird in Großstädten wie Jerusalem oder Damaskus, ohne dass etwas über die Art des Wassers und den Vollzug der Taufe gesagt wird, oder im Freien in „irgendeinem Wasser", in dem Täufer und Täufling stehen (8,36–38)[87]. Besondere Begleitriten werden nicht erwähnt, weder was Täufer und weitere Personen noch was den Wasserritus als solchen betrifft[88]. Die *Taufformel* ἐπὶ τῷ ὀνόματι Χριστοῦ begegnet nur (2,38)[89]. In 8,16 finden wir eine Formel mit εἰς, in 10,48 mit ἐν, in 19,3.5 wieder mit εἰς. Die formale Nähe zur Taufformel in Korinth ist offensichtlich[90]. Das εἰς in 19,3.5 bezeichnet beide Male deutlich eine Zugehörigkeit. Das Taufen „auf (εἰς)

---

82 Bei Paulus wäre dies die Rolle der πίστις Röm 1,5, die auf die Verkündigung des Evangeliums antwortet: Röm 10.

83 Der sekundäre Markusschluss verwendet demgegenüber die Interpretamente von Evangeliumsverkündigung und Rettung und nimmt damit paulinische Deutungselemente auf. Mk 16,16 behandelt aber ähnlich wie Mt 28,19 Glaube und Taufe auch als Identitätskriterien (vgl. Hebr 6,2).

84 Das Lukasevangelium erwähne ich in diesem Abschnitt im Zusammenhang mit der lukanischen Konzeption der „Geisttaufe".

85 1,22; 2,38.41; 8,12.14–25; 8,26–39; 9,18; 10,37; 10,48; 16,15; 16,33; 18,25; 19,1–7; 22,16. Vgl. allgemein AVEMARIE, *Die Tauferzählungen der Apostelgeschichte*.

86 Nach 1,22 kann nur derjenige Apostel sein, der von Jesu Taufe bis zu seiner Himmelfahrt Jesu Weg begleitet hat. Petrus ist der erste „Täufer" (vgl. I Kor 1). Später taufen Johannes, Philippus, der zu den „Sieben" gehört, Ananias und Paulus.

87 Ob der Autor meint, Lydia sei am Fluss, an dem sie ihre Gebetsstätte hatte, getauft worden, wie die heutige Lokalüberlieferung will, bleibt offen (16,11–15).

88 Das Fasten des Paulus in 9,9.19 bezieht sich eher auf seine Bekehrung als auf seine Taufe. Erst Did 7,1ff. spricht von einem vorangehenden Fasten. Hier begegnen auch Begleitpersonen. Bei Ignatius soll der Bischof bei der Taufe sein (IgnSm 8,2).

89 In Act kann die Wendung „Name Jesu Christi" für Jesus Christus stehen: 8,12.

90 Vgl. zur Namensformel AVEMARIE, *Die Tauferzählungen der Apostelgeschichte*, 26–43, und das oben zu I Kor Gesagte.

die Taufe des Johannes" ist aber nicht analog zu dem „Taufen auf (εἰς) den Namen des Herrn Jesus". Der Ausdruck „die Taufe des Johannes" wird ist *terminus technicus* für die Zugehörigkeit zu einer – aus der Sicht des Verfassers anderen, d.h. fremden – rituellen Handlung. Die „Taufe auf den Namen des Herrn Jesus" vermittelt dagegen jene personale und autoritative Beziehung des Täuflings zur Person Jesu, wie sie Paulus intendiert. Einen bestimmten festen Wortlaut für die Formel scheint der Verfasser nicht zu kennen. Eine zunehmende Ritualisierung des Taufvorgangs[91] lässt sich ebenso wenig erkennen wie ein von Paulus abweichender Sprachgebrauch mit einer eigenen Semantik. Deutlich wird dagegen die Funktion der Taufe als Eintritt in die christusgläubige Gemeinde, angefangen von der ersten Gemeinde in Jerusalem bis zu den zahlreichen Eintrittserzählungen *ad personam* – beginnend mit dem Äthiopier[92]. *Getauft werden* zunächst christusgläubige Juden, dann ein Proselyt, schließlich Heiden (10,44–48).

5.2. Deutungsmöglichkeiten

Die erste Deutung, die der Verfasser Petrus im Anschluss an seine Pfingstpredigt geben lässt, nimmt die Deutung der Johannestaufe bei Markus auf: εἰς ἄφεσιν ἁμαρτιῶν ὑμῶν (2,38) und bezieht sie auf die Gemeindetaufe. Die Johannestaufe begrenzt der Verfasser der Apostelgeschichte dementsprechend auf die „Bußtaufe" (19,4 βάπτισμα μετανοίας). Dem Interpretament der Sündenvergebung entspricht die Wendung ἀπολύσαι τὰς ἁμαρτίας σου in 22,16, mit der Paulus von seiner Taufe erzählt. Eine andere Deutung der Taufe findet sich in der Apostelgeschichte nicht. Vereinfacht gesagt hat der Verfasser der Apostelgeschichte die Johannestaufe und die Gemeindetaufe auf zwei Zwecke reduziert, die aneinander anschließen: die Johannestaufe ist auf den Zweck der Buße oder Umkehr zentriert und stellt die sachliche Voraussetzung für den Zweck der Gemeindetaufe dar: die Sündenvergebung. Sprachlich wird dieser Vorgang im Sinne eines Reinigungsbades mit dem metaphorisch gebrachten Verbum „abwaschen" dargestellt. Damit verwendet der Verfasser der Apostelgeschichte das originäre Deutungspotential des Wassers explizit für die Taufe. Paulus in I Kor 6,11 und die nachpaulinischen Briefautoren in Eph 5,26, Tit 3,5 und Hebr 10,22 beziehen dasselbe Deutungspotential der Wassermetapher auf das Leben der Christen, ohne aber die Taufe selbst zu erwähnen. Aus paulinischer Sicht liegt in der Apostelgeschichte eine Beschränkung der Deutungspotentiale der Taufe vor. Wo bleiben diese? Bleibt die Taufe einfach ein formaler Akt, ein *conversion ritual*, um auf den Ausdruck von Hans Dieter Betz zurückzugreifen?

---

91 Vgl. allerdings die Handauflegung: s.u.
92 Dazu E. DINKLER, „Philippus und der ΑΝΗΡ ΑΙΘΙΟΨ (Apg 8,26–40)".

Die Antwort liegt bei der Geistauffassung des Verfassers der Apostelgeschichte[93]. Er hat die Geistverleihung ebenso konsequent an die Gemeindetaufe gebunden wie von ihr getrennt und zugleich das eigentliche, zukunftweisende Bedeutungspotential der Gemeindetaufe in der anschließenden Geistverleihung gesehen. In der Schlüsselerzählung der Taufe in Jerusalem (Act 2,37–41) wird die Gabe des heiligen Geistes an den vorherigen Empfang der Taufe gebunden (V. 38)[94]. Mehrfach wird dafür der auf die Taufe folgende Ritus der Handauflegung erwähnt: 8,14–25[95] und 19,1–7. Dies Muster zieht sich durch die Tauferzählungen der Apostelgeschichte und unterscheidet zugleich die „Wassertaufe" des Johannes von der „Geisttaufe" der Gemeinde[96].

Hier könnte sich eine Schwierigkeit ergeben, denn es wird nicht wirklich deutlich, inwieweit sich die Johannes*taufe* und die Gemeinde*taufe* in ihrer Bedeutung unterscheiden[97], zumal die oben genannte Unterscheidung von Bußtaufe und Taufe zur Vergebung der Sünden im lukanischen Doppelwerk wenig aussagekräftig ist: in Lk 3,3 wird gerade die Taufe des Johannes als „Taufe der Umkehr zur Vergebung der Sünden" beschrieben[98]. In der Apostelgeschichte wird dies Problem dadurch gelöst, dass nur den Menschen, die die Gemeindetaufe empfangen haben, die Möglichkeit des Geistempfanges zugesagt wird. Dieser erfolgt durch den neuen Ritus der Handauflegung durch die Apostel, zu denen hier wieder Paulus gehört (19,1–7). Für die Taufe ergibt sich daraus in der Tat eine Bedeutungsverengung: sie ist eine erste rituelle (notwendige)[99] Handlung, der die zweite, wichtigere Handlung der Handauflegung folgt. Erst diese bringt die Geistbegabung und damit die wirkliche Sinndimension der Handlung mit sich.

Diese Bedeutungsverengung der Taufe steht in einem gewissen Gegensatz zur Taufinterpretation des Paulus und reduziert die Taufe auf das, was sie wahrscheinlich für die große Mehrzahl der Täuflinge war: auf eine notwendige Eintrittshandlung. Der Verfasser begnügt sich aber nicht mit dieser Reduktion der Bedeutung der Taufe, sondern verlagert die Deutungspotentiale der Taufe

---

93 Vgl. dazu AVEMARIE, *Die Tauferzählungen in der Apostelgeschichte*, 129–176.

94 AVEMARIE, *Die Tauferzählungen in der Apostelgeschichte*, 174, spricht von einem „kleine(n) tauftheologische(n) Kompendium".

95 Hier sind Taufe und Handauflegen zeitlich voneinander getrennt. In der Jerusalemer Tauferzählung fehlt die Handauflegung. Zur Handauflegung vgl. Art. „Handauflegung I (liturgisch)", in: *RAC* XIII, 482–493: „Die H. ist als wesentlicher, allein aber nicht ausreichender ... Bestandteil der meisten christl. Kulthandlungen seit dem Anfang des 3. Jh. sicher bezeugt" (Sp. 485f.). Weiter AVEMARIE, *Die Tauferzählungen in der Apostelgeschichte*, 164–167.

96 Damit knüpft das lukanische Werk an Mk 1,8 an.

97 Dies spiegelt auch die historische Situation.

98 Vgl. Mk 1,4.

99 Dabei kann in Ausnahmefällen die Reihenfolge von Geistverleihung und Taufe vertauscht werden. Stets aber muss Beides zusammenkommen. Vgl. HAHN, *Theologie des Neuen Testaments*, Band 2, 511f.

auf die folgende Handauflegung und die damit verbundene Geistverleihung – so die Reihenfolge in Kapitel 8 und 19. Diese neue Konstellation wird in vier Texten besonders deutlich. (1) In dem erzählenden Eröffnungstext der Apostelgeschichte in 1,4–5 verheißt der auferstandene Jesus den Elf die Geisttaufe, und zwar im Gegensatz zu der Wassertaufe des Johannes. Damit stellt der Evangelist die Verbindung zu Lk 3,16, dem Logion Q 3,16par her, mit dem Mk 1,8 verwandt ist[100], und schlägt so den Bogen von der Taufe des Johannes über die Taufe Jesu zur Taufverheißung[101] und zur Gemeindetaufe, besonders zur Taufe von Nichtjuden. In Act 11,16 zitiert Petrus dann den Satz aus 1,5 als ῥῆμα κυρίου und leitet aus der Geistbegabung der Heiden die Erlaubnis ab, sie zu taufen[102]. Durch die Wendung „ἐν πνεύματι ἁγίῳ" (Act 1,5), die analog zu (ἐν) ὕδατι gebildet ist, wird der Geist gleichsam materiell im Kontrast zum Wasser beschrieben. (2) Die Pfingsterzählung (2,1–4) setzt dies Konzept erzählerisch in Sturm und Feuerflammen um. Die Jünger werden sogleich mit dem Geist getauft[103]. Eine vorhergehende oder folgende Wassertaufe der Apostel findet gar nicht statt[104]. (3) Anders ist es in der umfangreichen Korneliuserzählung in Kapitel 10. Auch hier „fällt der Geist" gleich nach der Predigt des Petrus auf alle Anwesenden, unter denen auch Nichtjuden sind. Daraufhin lässt Petrus diese Heiden aber mit der Gemeindetaufe taufen. (4) In 11,1–18 wiederholt Petrus die Begebenheiten um die Taufe von Heiden vor den christusgläubigen Juden in Jerusalem. Sie sind von entscheidender Wichtigkeit für die Gesamtkonzeption der Geschichtsdeutung des Verfassers und für seine eigene Darstellung. Die Gemeindetaufe selbst tritt gerade in diesen vier Schlüsseltexten zugunsten der „Geisttaufe" zurück.

Im Zusammenhang meiner Themenstellung kann ich nicht auf das Syntagma der „Geisttaufe" eingehen. Der Begriff lässt sich nur als Metapher verstehen, die analog zur „Wassertaufe" gebildet worden ist und ein eigenes Deutungspotential kodiert, das der Wassertaufe einerseits Bedeutung nimmt, andererseits aber neue Bedeutung zuführt, da Wassertaufe und Geisttaufe in einem engen Verhältnis zueinander gedacht sind. Ich erwähne die Geisttaufe hier in ihrer deutenden Funktion als Kontrastiv zur Gemeindetaufe im lukanischen Doppel-

---

100 S. o. Anm. 68.
101 Diese steht in der Apostelgeschichte an der Stelle des Taufbefehls bei Matthäus.
102 Mt 28 begründet die Taufe der „Völker" mit einem Wort des Erhöhten.
103 Petrus erklärt diesen Vorgang in seiner Predigt als endzeitliches Geschehen: 2,17–21. Es handelt sich nach der Erzählung um „alle", d.h. nicht nur die Zwölf, sondern zusätzlich um die „hundertzwanzig Brüder" von Act 2,15.
104 Einzig die Jerusalemer Apostel brauchen nach der Apostelgeschichte keine Wassertaufe! Sie sind gleichsam diejenigen, für die das Logion Q 3,16 gilt. Vgl. dazu AVEMARIE, *Die Tauferzählungen in der Apostelgeschichte*, 141f. mit Anm. 67.

werk[105]. Die Vorstellung, die Taufe des Täufers sei an das Medium des Wassers gebunden, Jesus dagegen „taufe" mit dem Geist und mit Feuer, ist alt. Sie heftet sich, wie schon erwähnt, an Q 3,16b–17 und begegnet in einer anderen Version bei Mk 1,7b–8[106] sowie dann in veränderter Form in den ersten Kapiteln des Johannesevangeliums. Ob ein Zusammenhang mit der Geistbegabung Jesu bei seiner Taufe durch Johannes besteht, lässt sich hier nicht klären. Für meine Fragestellung ist interessant, dass – nur – im Lukasevangelium die Geisttaufe Jesu (Lk 3,22) ihre Fortsetzung in der Antrittspredigt in Nazareth findet (4,16–19). Dem entspricht die Geistverheißung des Auferstandenen an die Jünger in 24,49, die in Act 1,4 variierend aufgenommen wird. Weder in Lk 24 noch in Act 1 spricht Jesus von der Gemeindetaufe, wie sie sich in Mt 28,19 findet. Hier liegt ein eigenes pneumatologisches Konzept des Verfassers des lukanischen Doppelwerkes vor, das die Deutungspotentiale der Gemeindetaufe deutlich reduziert, so stabil der Ritus in den christusgläubigen Gemeinden auch ist.

5.3. Literarische Zusammenhänge

Das lukanische Doppelwerk kann in seinem ersten Teil, der Jesuserzählung, und in seinem zweiten Teil, der Erzählung vom Lauf der Zeugenschaft der Apostel von Jesus, alle Aspekte der frühchristlichen Taufüberlieferungen und -vorstellungen in einen narrativen Zusammenhang bringen. Es hat sich gezeigt, dass der Autor der Apostelgeschichte für die Geist- und Wassertaufe ein einheitliches Deutungskonzept hat, dass die Bedeutung der Gemeindetaufe begrenzt. Trotzdem spielt die Gemeindetaufe eine entscheidende Rolle in der Gesamterzählung der Apostelgeschichte. Kapitel 2 enthält die Einsetzungsgeschichte der Gemeindetaufe (2,37–41), 8,26–40 erzählt von der Taufe eines hochrangigen äthiopischen Proselyten, Kapitel 10 und 11 stellen in großer Breite die Berechtigung der Taufe von Heiden dar (besonders 10,47).

6. Taufe im Johannesevangelium

Entsprechend dem verbal geprägten Idiolekt des Johannesevangeliums begegnet im vierten Evangelium ausschließlich das Verbum βαπτίζειν[107]. Die bekannten narrativen und dialogischen Auseinandersetzungen um die Taufe des Johannes und seine Zurückstufung hinter Jesus in den Kapiteln 1–4 des Johannesevangeliums müssen hier nicht dargestellt werden. Auch die allgemeine Bedeutung, die

---

105 Texte: Act 8;10;19. Vgl. AVEMARIE, *Die Tauferzählungen der Apostelgeschichte*, zu den Einzeltexten.

106 Vgl.: die Spruchquelle Q, 35.

107 Semantische Besonderheiten finden sich in Joh 1–4 nicht. Das Verbum wird ausschließlich als term. techn. für den rituellen Vorgang verwendet.

das Thema der Taufe in den ersten Kapiteln des Evangeliums hat, darf vorausgesetzt werden. Für unsere Fragestellung ist *ein* Motiv entscheidend: nach 3,22–4,3 taufte Jesus selbst. Das gilt trotz der Einschränkung in 4,2[108]. Ich stelle hier nicht die Frage nach einer möglichen Historizität dieser Angaben, sondern nach ihrer Relevanz als Deutungselement. Erst hier, nicht im Matthäusevangelium, ist der Bogen von der Johannestaufe über die Taufe Jesu zur Gemeindetaufe wirklich überzeugend geschlagen. Denn schon *Jesus* beginnt mit dem Taufen, wenn auch seine Jünger dann die eigentlichen Träger der neuen Taufe werden (4,2)[109]. Und schon Jesus selbst, nicht erst der Auferstandene wie im Matthäusevangelium, lehrt über die Taufe, indem er Nikodemus über die „Geburt aus Wasser und Geist" belehrt (3,5). Erst jetzt entsteht eine Kontinuität der Taufe von Johannes bis zur Gemeindetaufe mit folgenden Stationen: die Johannestaufe als bloße Wassertaufe (1,26.31.33; 3,23) ohne eine eigene Bedeutung[110], das Zeugnis von der Geistbegabung und der Sohnschaft Jesu sowie die Vorhersage der Geisttaufe Jesu in 1,33[111], die vorgezogene Belehrung des Nikodemus durch Jesus über das wahre Wesen der Gemeindetaufe mit dem folgenden Bericht über das Taufen Jesu und seiner Jünger. Hier wird die Gemeindetaufe fest im Wirken Jesu selbst verankert.

Nun macht der Evangelist im Zuge der Zurückdrängung des Täufers und seiner Taufe aber überhaupt keine deutenden Aussagen über die Taufe. Er beschränkt sich gänzlich auf die Gegenüberstellung von Wassertaufe des Johannes und Geisttaufe Jesu und seiner Jünger (1,33), ohne dass in den Notizen von der Tauftätigkeit Jesu und seiner Jünger irgendeine Deutung gegeben würde. Damit steht er sachlich in der Linie des lukanischen Doppelwerkes. Zugleich leidet der Evangelist unter dem hermeneutischen Defizit der Gemeindetaufe[112] und lässt Jesus in Kapitel 3 unter dem Stichwort der „Wiedergeburt"[113] eine Taufdeutung im Fadenkreuz von Wasser und Geist geben. Hier wird ganz deutlich, welche hermeneutischen Folgen die Reduktion der Johannestaufe auf das Medium „Wasser" in der Kontrastierung mit dem „Geist" hat. Denn der Geist kann der Gemeindetaufe nicht eindeutig zugeordnet werden, weil der Evangelist die „Geisttaufe" in der Tradition der markinischen Erzählung von Jesu Taufe und parallel zur lukanischen Verbindung Jesu ganz auf Jesus konzentriert und anders als die Apostelgeschichte *nicht* auf die Gemeindetaufe überträgt. Hier unterscheiden sich das Johannesevangelium und das lukanische

---

108 Schon die Frage in 1,25 weist in diese Richtung.
109 Hier liegt eher eine theologische Erzählung vor als eine historische Reminiszenz.
110 Das Johannesevangelium vermeidet jegliche Deutung der Taufe des Johannes.
111 Analog zum Lukasevangelium.
112 Analog zum Problem des Herrenmahls.
113 Wieder findet sich kein Substantiv, etwa παλιγγενεσία oder ἀνακαίνωσις (z.B. Tit 3,5), sondern γεννηθῆναι mit δεύτερον oder ἄνωθεν.

Doppelwerk. Beide verstehen die Taufe des Täufers, die Taufe Jesu[114] und die Gemeindetaufe von der Materie oder dem Medium – Wasser und Geist – her. Aber während das lukanische Doppelwerk in diesem Deuterahmen eine zwar enge, aber kohärente Taufdeutung gelingt, bleibt das Johannesevangelium bei der blassen Formel: „(wieder)geboren aus Wasser und Geist" stehen (3,5), die über eine paradoxe Zusammenordnung jener Medien, die sonst immer gerade kontrastiv verwendet werden, nicht hinauskommt. Die Lehrrede Jesu über die Taufe geht nicht zufällig in eine Offenbarungsrede über. Die theologische Abständigkeit des vierten Evangelisten von den Gemeinderitualen von Taufe und Herrenmahl zeigt sich auch darin, dass in dem Nikodemusgespräch die Taufe selbst nicht erwähnt wird. Eine Deutung der Gemeindetaufe aus ihrem eigenen Bedeutungspotential heraus gelingt im vierten Evangelium nicht. Eine Deutung der Johannestaufe wird konsequent unterdrückt.

7. Späte neutestamentliche Texte

In den späteren Briefen begegnen Aussagen zur Taufe eher selten und wenig profiliert[115]. Eph 4,5[116] zählt die Taufe als eines der Verbindungsglieder der christusgläubigen Gemeinden auf und schließt sich damit der Textpragmatik des 1. Korintherbriefes an. Eine Deutung im eigentlichen Sinn wird nicht gegeben. Kol 2,12 berührt sich mit Röm 6,4. Hier könnte man fast übersetzen: „Ihr seid mit ihm gemeinsam im Todesgeschick (βάπτισμα nicht als term.techn. übersetzt) begraben". Die bedeutende Veränderung gegenüber Paulus liegt in dem Nachsatz: „Ihr seid mit Christus auferstanden durch den Glauben durch die Kraft Gottes …". Diese kühne Korrektur des Römerbriefes schafft gleichzeitig Probleme: die Spannung zwischen der Bindung des Getauften an Christus einerseits und seiner Lebensführung als ethischer Bewährung andererseits ist weggefallen. Wie soll nun die Vorläufigkeit und Offenheit der christlichen Existenz gedacht werden? Für die Taufe ist die Nähe zur πίστις wichtig, die der Verfasser hier herstellt. Wir befinden uns in der gedanklichen Nähe zum sekundären Markusschluss (Mk 16,16): Glaube und Taufe werden einander beigeordnet, ohne dass ihr Verhältnis näher reflektiert oder definiert würde. Immerhin wird deutlich, dass auch das dritte Glied in dem Dreieck von Täufer-Taufhandlung-Täufling problematisch werden kann. Im Kolosserbrief und im sekundären Markusschluss wird von den Täuflingen die eigene „Leistung" des Glaubens erwartet, der Glaube wird nicht einfach vorausgesetzt. In den Versen 13–15 zeigt der Kolosserbrief noch einmal

---

114 Im Johannesevangelium handelt es sich um die Taufe an Jesus und die Tauftätigkeit Jesu!

115 Im Hebräerbrief wird der Taufe und der Tauflehre in 6,2 geradezu die tiefere theologische Bedeutung abgesprochen.

116 G. SELLIN, *Der Brief an die Epheser*, 324f.

seine Nähe zu Paulus, wenn die Sündenvergebung ganz bei Christus liegt und an sein Todesschicksal gebunden ist.

Es bleibt mit I Petr 3,18–22 ein sehr eigenständiger Text zu besprechen[117]. In den Zusammenhang eines Christusbekenntnisses wird ein Rettungsparadigma gestellt, die acht geretteten Seelen in der Arche Noah[118]. Wir begegnen hier der gleichen Typologie wie in I Kor 10: die Arche Noah ist ein Paradigma der Taufe. Wieder ist die deutende Logik invers. Gerade nicht die Sintflut, die doch dieselbe Materie wie das Taufwasser hat, stellt eine Vorabbildung der Taufe (ἀντίτυπος) dar, sondern eben die Arche, die das Wasser abhält[119]. Denkt man die Metapher von V. 20.21 nach, so ergibt sich noch einmal eine Anspielung auf die Todeskonnotation von Taufe. Wie die Acht durch die Arche aus dem Tod in der Sintflut errettet wurden, werden die Adressaten des 1. Petrusbriefes durch die Taufe vor den todbringenden Sünden und Lastern des heidnischen Lebens gerettet, die in dem Lasterkatalog 4,3 dargestellt sind. Die Taufe hat in I Kor 10 und I Petr 3 deutlich rettende[120] Funktion – theologisch ist sie soteriologisch gedeutet. Gleichzeitig verwahrt sich der Verfasser des 1. Petrusbriefes gegen eine äußerliche Deutung der Taufe als körperlicher Reinigung und betont ihre ethische Dimension, indem er das gute Gewissen als Ergebnis der Taufe benennt (V. 21). 4,1 verbindet dann das Leidensschicksal Christi mit demjenigen der Getauften und wandelt damit die soteriologische Interpretation von Röm 6 noch deutlicher als Paulus in eine ethische um. Das Urteil: „Wer im Fleisch gelitten hat, hat mit der Sünde aufgehört", gilt für die Getauften analog zu Jesus.

8. Fazit

Ein Rückblick auf die Deutungsangebote der neutestamentlichen Schriften zur Taufe soll das Gesagte weder wiederholen noch vereinfachen. Ich möchte vielmehr abschließend auf zwei strukturelle Aspekte hinweisen.

(1) Während des Durchgangs durch die Texte hat sich eine strukturelle hermeneutische Konstante ergeben. Die Taufe wird von ihrer *Materie* oder ihrem Medium, dem Wasser, her gedeutet. Von hier aus führen Wege zu der Frage nach der notwendigen Beschaffenheit des Wassers[121] und zu den späteren umfangreichen Spekulationen über Texte des Alten Testaments, die vom Wasser handeln und sich weitgehend von der Taufe lösen[122]. Benachbart sind Deutun-

---

117 Vgl. dazu OSTMEYER, Taufe und Typos, 145–161. Vgl. jetzt auch F. W. HORN, „Der Beitrag des 1. Petrusbriefes zur frühchristlichen Tauftheologie", 409–425.
118 N. BROX, Der erste Petrusbrief, 164–182.
119 Dementsprechend werden die Israeliten vor, nicht in dem Wasser des Schilfmeeres gerettet.
120 Vgl. σῴζει in I Petr 3,21.
121 So schon Did 7.
122 Z.B. Barnabas 11 oder Tertullian.

gen, die die *reinigende* Funktion des Mediums „Wasser" in den Vordergrund stellen, den Taufvorgang als eine besondere Form der Waschung verstehen und die physische oder rituelle Reinheit auf die ethische Reinheitsvorstellung übertragen. Die Deutungen im Zusammenhang mit der Geisttaufe oder der Geistverleihung (sowie der Feuertaufe) arbeiten mit der Kontrastmaterie: Geist statt Wasser[123]. Hier knüpft sich die eschatologische Erneuerung der Täuflinge an den Geistempfang, auch an den Glauben. Die Bedeutung liegt in der Überbietung der Wassertaufe, da das Medium des Feuers und vor allem des Geistes dem Medium des Wassers an *Reinigungskraft* überlegen ist[124]. Damit kann gleichzeitig die *Bedeutung* der Wassertaufe geschwächt werden, ohne dass die Handlung als solche an Stellenwert einbüßt, wie die Apostelgeschichte zeigt. Im Zusammenhang mit dem Geist hat sich ein eigener Bereich von Taufallusionen entwickelt: die Vorstellung von einer Salbung, wie sie im 1. Johannesbrief[125] begegnet[126].

Zu diesem Deutungskreis gehört ein semantischer und metaphorischer Kranz von Allusionen, deren direkter Rückbezug auf die Taufhandlung sich im Einzelnen nicht sicher bestimmen lässt. Das zeigt bereits ein Text wie I Kor 6,11[127]. Die Zusammenstellung von Waschen-Heiligen-Gerechtmachen und Geist deuten auf Taufvorstellungen hin, ohne dass die Taufe hier erwähnt würde. Die Reinigungs- und Bademetaphorik lässt sich hier anschließen[128].

Anders ist die Deutung in Röm 6[129]. Hier knüpft Paulus an die *tödliche* Komponente des Mediums „Wasser" und an die Bedeutung „*Todesgeschehen*" von βάπτισμα an und verbindet das Schicksal der Getauften mit dem Todesschicksal Christi unter dem Stichwort ὁμοίωμα, das das „Wie" dieser Verbindung offen hält oder dem Geschehen im Taufritus überlässt. Von hier aus ergibt sich eine doppelte Öffnung zur Ethik und zur Eschatologie.

Auch hier lässt sich ein Kreis von Allusionen und Metaphern anschließen. An die Todesvorstellung kann sich die Vorstellung einer neuen Geburt anschließen, bei der entweder die Diskontinuität zwischen dem Zustand vor und

---

123 Zur Materialität des πνεῦμα vgl. T. ENGBERG-PEDERSEN, „The Material Spirit: Cosmology and Ethics in Paul".

124 Zu den Fragen der Materialität der Elemente vgl. Engberg-Pedersen (s.o. Anm. 123).

125 I Joh 2,20.27.

126 Vgl. HAHN, *Theologie des Neuen Testaments*, Band 2, 524f weist auf den Zusammenhang mit der Geistverleihung hin (Lk 4,18; vgl. Act 10,38). II Kor 1,21 zeigt, dass die Verbindung von Salbung, Versiegelung und Geist als Allusion auf die Taufe schon bei Paulus vorliegt.

127 Zum Text vgl. LINDEMANN, *Der Erste Korintherbrief*, 140f. (vorsichtige Zustimmung zur Taufallusion). Zum Zusammenhang vgl. HAHN, *Theologie des Neuen Testaments*, Band 2, 516f.

128 Eph 5,25–27; Tit 3,5; Hebr 10,22 und die Wasserhinweise in I Joh 5,6f. u.ö.

129 Vgl. Mk 10,38f. Vgl. HAHN, *Theologie des Neuen Testaments*, Band 2, 508: auch die Motive der Todestaufe in Mk 10; Lk 12,50 und der Feuertaufe in Q 3,16 haben einen gemeinsamen Bedeutungshorizont, denn auch die reinigende Geist- und Feuertaufe hat mit ihrer Gerichtsperspektive unter Umständen tödliche Qualität.

nach der Taufe betont werden soll oder aber einfach die Qualität eschatologischer Neuheit zum Ausdruck gebracht wird[130].

(2) Das Dreieck von Täufer, Taufvorgang und Täufling stellt eine feste sachliche und narrative Struktur dar, die den Gesamtkomplex der Taufe im Neuen Testament durchsichtig macht. Die Gestalt des *Taufenden* kann im Rahmen der Gemeindetaufe zu Problemen führen, wie Paulus sie in Korinth wahrnimmt. Immer problematisch ist die Gestalt *Johannes* des Täufers in allen Evangelien. Einerseits ist er in allen Evangelien der erste βαπτιστής und er hat Jesus getauft. Andererseits begrenzt schon das Markusevangelium[131] die Bedeutung seiner Person und seiner Taufe sowie der Taufe Jesu durch Johannes[132]. Aber auch *Jesus* als Taufender ist problematisch. Nur im Johannesevangelium werden Jesus und seine Jünger als „Täufer" dargestellt, ohne dass die Erzählung in Joh 3,22; 4,1–3 die Problematik Jesu als des Täufers überzeugend auflösen könnte.

Der *Taufvorgang* wird überall in den neutestamentlichen Texten auf die Wassertaufe beschränkt. Zugleich erhalten aber Handauflegung und Geistempfang in der Apostelgeschichte eine stärkere eigene Bedeutungsakzentuierung. Die Tendenz zu Zusatzhandlungen wie der anschließenden Handauflegung wird ebenfalls in der Apostelgeschichte deutlich.

Problematisch ist in allen vier Evangelien Jesus als *Täufling*. Die Problematik der Taufe von *Heiden* ist ein zentrales Thema der Erzählungen der Apostelgeschichte. Zwei Fragen müssen in der Erzählung geklärt werden. *Erstens*: können Nicht-Juden getauft werden? Der Verfasser der Apostelgeschichte beantwortet diese Frage mit den klimaktisch angeordneten Erzählungen von dem äthiopischen Beamten, von dem gottesfürchtigen Hauptmann Kornelius und von der Taufe der Heiden, auf die der Geist gefallen war. *Zweitens*: welche Voraussetzungen müssen Taufwillige mitbringen? Verkündigung und Glaube sind die Voraussetzung für die Taufe, wie der Verfasser in 8,12 exemplarisch darstellt. Die Simon-Magus-Erzählung in 8,14–25 stellt klar, dass die Taufe nicht automatisch das richtige Ethos nach sich zieht. Ihm wird aber (eine zweite) Buße ermöglicht (VV. 22–24)[133].

---

130 Tit 3,5f.: das „Bad der Wiedergeburt und der Erneuerung durch den heiligen Geist"; Joh 3,3–8; I Petr 1,23; 2,2; I Joh 2,29; 3,9; 4,7; 5,1.4.18.

131 U.U. schon die Quelle Q.

132 Die Entwicklung hin zum Johannesevangelium wurde oben dargestellt.

133 Anders Hebr 6,2–6, im lockeren Zusammenhang mit der Taufe. Vgl. H.-F. WEISS, *Der Brief an die Hebräer*, 347–351 (Exkurs: Zur Frage der Ablehnung einer zweiten μετάνοια im Hebr).

Bibliographie

Art. „βάπτω κτλ.", in: *ThWNT* 1 (1933) 527–544 (A. OEPKE).

Art. „Bedeutung", in: *Lexikon der Bibelhermeneutik*, Berlin-New York: de Gruyter 2009, 67–73 (CH. HARDMEIER, O. WISCHMEYER, D. KORSCH, M. BECKER, U. KUNDERT, I. H. WARNKE, H. INEICHEN).

Art. „Handauflegung I (liturgisch)", in: *RAC* XIII (1986) 482–493 (C. VOGEL).

Art. „Identität", in: *Lexikon der Bibelhermeneutik*, Berlin-New York: de Gruyter 2009, 275f. (N. BÖHM, D. FELDMANN).

Art. „Interpretation/Interpretieren/Interpret", in: *Lexikon der Bibelhermeneutik*, Berlin-New York: de Gruyter 2009, 289–296 (S. KREUZER, O. WISCHMEYER, M. HAILER, L. FLADERER, G. KURZ, J. GREISCH).

Art. „Rites de passage", in: *RGG*[4] 7 (2004) 534f. (H.-G. HEIMBROCK).

Art. „Ritus/Ritual I. Religionswissenschaftlich", in: *RGG*[4] 7 (2004) 547–549 (M. STAUSBERG).

Art. „Ritus/Ritual II. Religionsgeschichtlich. 4. Christentum a) Neues Testament", in: *RGG*[4] 7 (2004) 552f. (H. D. BETZ).

Art. „Sakramente", in: *RGG*[4] 7 (2004) 752–770 (U. KÖPF, F.-J. NOCKE, K. CH. FELMY, K.-H. KANDLER, E. BUSCH, ST. SYKES, D. SATTLER, K. RICHTER).

Art. „Sinn", in: *Lexikon der Bibelhermeneutik*, Berlin-New York: de Gruyter 2009, 548–555 (CH. HARDMEIER, O. WISCHMEYER, D. KORSCH, E.-M. BECKER, U. KUNDERT, K. EHLICH, E. ANGEHRN).

Art. „Taufe", in: *RGG*[4] 8 (2005) 50–96 (G. D. ALLES, F. AVEMARIE, M. WALLRAFF, CH. GRETHLEIN, G. KOCH, P. PLANK, J. A. STEIGER, M. BEINTKER, ST. R. HOLMES, P. AVIS, CH. GRETHLEIN, R. MESSNER, CH. THIELE, A. F. WALLS, D. APOSTOLOS-CAPPADONA).

Art. „Taufe", in: *TRE* 32 (2001) 659–741 (P. GERLITZ, U. SCHNELLE, E. J. YARNOLD, J. ULRICH, K.-H. ZUR MÜHLEN, B. D. SPINKS, U. KÜHN, P. CORNEHL).

AVEMARIE, FRIEDRICH, *Die Tauferzählungen der Apostelgeschichte. Theologie und Geschichte* (WUNT 139), Tübingen: Mohr Siebeck 2002.

BECKER, EVE-MARIE, *Das Markus-Evangelium im Rahmen antiker Historiographie* (WUNT 194), Tübingen: Mohr Siebeck 2006.

— „Text und Hermeneutik am Beispiel textinterner Hermeneutik", in: O. WISCHMEYER/S. SCHOLZ (Hgg.), *Die Bibel als Text. Beiträge zu einer textbezogenen Hermeneutik* (NET 14), Tübingen: Francke 2008, 193–215.

Betz, Hans Dieter, "Transferring a Ritual: Paul's interpretation of Baptism in Romans 6", in: ders., *Paulinische Studien. Gesammelte Aufsätze III*, Tübingen: Mohr 1994, 240–271.

— *Galatians. A Commentary to Paul's Churches in Galatia* (Hermeneia), Philadelphia, Pa.: Fortress Press 1979.

Brox, Norbert, *Der erste Petrusbrief* (EKK XXI), Zürich-Einsiedeln-Köln/Neukirchen Vluyn: Benziger/Neukirchener 1979.

Collins, Adela Yarbro, *Mark. A Commentary* (Hermeneia), Minneapolis, Minn.: Fortress Press 2007.

— "Baptism as Transformation", in: *FS B. Holmberg* (im Druck).

Delling, Gerhard, *Die Zueignung des Heils in der Taufe*, Berlin: Evangelische Verlags-Anstalt 1961.

Die Spruchquelle Q, hg. und eingeleitet von P. Hoffmann/Ch. Heil, Darmstadt-Leuven: Wissenschaftliche Buchgesellschaft 2002.

Dinkler, Erich, "Philippus und der ANHP AIΘIOΨ (Apg 8,26–40)", in: E. E. Ellis/E. Grässer (Hgg.), *Jesus und Paulus*, FS W. G. Kümmel, Göttingen: Vandenhoeck & Rupecht 1975, 85–95.

Engberg-Pedersen, Troels, "The Material Spirit: Cosmology and Ethics in Paul", in: *NTS* 55 (2009) 179–197.

Hahn, Ferdinand, *Theologie des Neuen Testaments*, 2 Bände, Tübingen: Mohr Siebeck 2002.

Hartman, Lars, *"Into the Name of the Lord Jesus". Baptism in the Early Church*, Edinburgh: T & T Clark 1997.

Heitmüller, Wilhelm, *Im Namen Jesu. Eine sprach- und religionsgeschichtliche Untersuchung zum Neuen Testament, speziell zur altchristlichen Taufe*, Göttingen: Vandenhoeck & Ruprecht 1903.

Horn, F. W., "Der Beitrag des 1. Petrusbriefes zur frühchristlichen Tauftheologie", in: W. Kraus (Hg.), *Beiträge zur urchristlichen Theologiegeschichte* (BZNW 163), Berlin – New York: de Gruyter 2009, 409–425.

Lindemann, Andreas, *Der Erste Korintherbrief* (HNT 9/1), Tübingen: Mohr Siebeck 2000.

Loader, James Alfred, "Intertextualität in geschichteten Texten des Alten Testaments", in: O. Wischmeyer/S. Scholz (Hgg.), *Die Bibel als Text. Beiträge zu einer textbezogenen Hermeneutik* (NET 14), Tübingen: Francke 2008, 99–119.

Luz, Ulrich, *Das Evangelium nach Matthäus. 4. Teilband. Mt 26–28* (EKK I/4), Düsseldorf-Zürich/Neukirchen-Vluyn: Benziger/Neukirchener 2002.

Mitchell, Margaret Mary, *Paul and the Rhetoric of Reconciliation: An Exegetical Investigation of the Language and Composition of 1 Corinthians*, Louisville, Ky.: Westminster/John Knox Press 1991.

Ostmeyer, Karl-Heinrich, *Taufe und Typos. Elemente der Tauftypologien in 1. Korinther 10 und 1. Petrus 3* (WUNT 2/118), Tübingen: Mohr Siebeck 2000.

Rajak, Tessa/Noy, David, „ARCHISYNAGOGOI: Office, Title and Social Status in the Graeco-Jewish Synagogue", in: *JRS* 83 (1993) 75–93.

Rothschild, Clare K., *Baptist Traditions and Q* (WUNT 190), Tübingen: Mohr Siebeck 2005.

Scornaienchi, Lorenzo, *Sarx und Soma bei Paulus. Der Mensch zwischen Destruktivität und Konstruktivität* (NTOA 67), Göttingen: Vandenhoeck & Ruprecht 2008.

Sellin, Gerhard, *Der Brief an die Epheser* (KEK 8), Göttingen: Vandenhoeck & Ruprecht 2008.

Strecker, Christian, *Die liminale Theologie des Paulus. Zugänge zur paulinischen Theologie aus kulturanthropologischer Perspektive* (FRLANT 185), Göttingen: Vandenhoeck & Ruprecht 1999.

Theissen, Gerd, *Die Entstehung des Neuen Testaments als literaturgeschichtliches Problem*, (Schriften der Philosophisch-historischen Klasse der Heidelberger Akademie der Wissenschaften 40), Heidelberg: Winter 2007.

— *Die Religion der ersten Christen*, Gütersloh: Kaiser 2000.

Weiss, Hans-Friedrich, *Der Brief an die Hebräer* (KEK 13), Göttingen: Vandenhoeck & Ruprecht 1991.

Wischmeyer, Oda, „Wie kommt Abraham in den Galaterbrief? Überlegungen zu Gal 3,6–29", in: *FS I. Broer*, hg. von B. Kollmann/M. Bachmann (im Druck).